Spurgeon's Sermons Volume 10: 1864
By Charles Haddon Spurgeon
Edited by Anthony Uyl

Devoted Publishing
Woodstock, Ontario, 2017

Spurgeon's Sermons Volume 10: 1864

By Charles Haddon Spurgeon (1834-1892)
Edited by Anthony Uyl

What kind of philosophies do you have?
Let us know!

Contact us at: devotedpub@hotmail.com
Visit our shop on Facebook: @DevotedPublishing

Published in Woodstock, Ontario, Canada 2017

For bulk educational rates, please contact us at the above email address.

ISBN: 978-1-77356-081-6

Table of Contents

Suffering And Reigning With Jesus

DELIVERED ON SUNDAY MORNING JANUARY 3, 1864,
BY THE REV. C. H. SPURGEON,
AT THE METROPOLITAN TABERNACLE, NEWINGTON.

"If we suffer, we shall also reign with Him: if we deny Him, He also will deny us." 2 Timothy 2:12.

MY venerable friend who has up to now sent me a text for the New Year, still ministers to his parish the Word of Life and has not forgotten to furnish the passage for our meditation today. Having preached from one of a very similar character a short time ago, I have felt somewhat embarrassed in preparation. But I will take courage and say with the Apostle, "To write the same things to you, to me, indeed, is not grievous, but for you it is safe." If I should bring forth old things on this occasion, be you not unmindful that even the wise householder does this at times. For oft-recurring sickness the same wine may be prescribed by the most skillful physician without blame. No one scolds the contractor for mending rough roads again and again with stones from the same quarry. The wind which has borne us once into the haven is not despised for blowing often from the same quarter, for it may do us good service yet again. And therefore I am assured that you will endure my repetitions of the same Truths of God, since they may assist you to suffer with patience the same trials.

You will observe that our text is a part of one of Paul's faithful sayings. If I remember rightly, Paul has four of these. The first occurs in 1 Timothy 1:15, that famous, that chief of all faithful sayings, "This is a faithful saying and worthy of all acceptation, that Christ Jesus came into the world to save sinners; of whom I am chief. "A golden saying, whose value Paul himself had most marvelously proved. What shall I say of this verse, but the same--the lamp of a lighthouse, it has darted its ray of comfort through leagues of darkness and guided millions of tempest-tossed spirits to the port of Peace.

The next faithful saying is in the same Epistle, at the fourth chapter and the ninth verse. "Godliness is profitable unto all things, having the promise of the life that now is and of that which is to come. This is a faithful saying and worthy of all acceptation." This, too, the Apostle knew to be true, since he had learned in whatsoever state he was in to be content. Our text is a portion of the third faithful saying. And the last of the four you will find in Titus 3:8, "This is a faithful saying and these things I will that you affirm constantly, that they which have believed in God might be careful to maintain good works. These things are good and profitable unto men." We may trace a connection between these faithful sayings.

The first one, which speaks of Jesus Christ coming into the world to save sinners, lays the foundation of our eternal salvation in the Free Grace of God, as shown to us in the mission of the great Redeemer. The next affirms the double blessedness which we obtain through this salvation--the blessings of the upper and nether springs--of time and of eternity. The third faithful saying shows one of the duties to which the chosen people are called. We are ordained to suffer for Christ with the promise that "if we suffer, we shall also reign with Him." The last faithful saying sets forth the active form of Christian service, bidding us diligently to maintain good works.

Thus you have the root of salvation in Free Grace. You have next the privileges of that salvation in the life which now is and in that which is to come. And you have also the two great branches of suffering with Christ and service of Christ loaded with the fruits of the Spirit of all Divine Grace. Treasure up, dear Friends, those faithful sayings, "Lay up these words in your heart; bind them for a sign upon your hand that they may be as frontlets between your eyes." Let these choice sayings be printed in letters of gold and set up as tablets upon the doorposts of our house and upon our gates. Let them be the guides of our life, our comfort and our instruction. The Apostle of the Gentiles proved them to be faithful. They are faithful still, not one word shall fall to the ground. They are worthy of all acceptation--let us accept them now and prove their faithfulness--each man for himself.

This morning's meditation is to be derived from a part of that faithful saying which deals with suffering. We will read the verse preceding our text. "It is a faithful saying: For if we are dead with Him, we shall also live with Him." All the elect were virtually dead with Christ when He died upon the tree--they were on the Cross--crucified with Him. In Him, as their representative, they rose from the tomb and live in newness of life. Because He lives, they shall live also. In due time the chosen are slain by the Spirit of God and so made dead with Christ to sin, to self-righteousness, to the world, the flesh and the powers of darkness.

Then it is that they live with Jesus! His life becomes their life and as He was, so are they also in this world. The Spirit of God breathes the quickening Grace into those who were once dead in sin and thus they live in union with Christ Jesus. When Believers die, though they may be sawn in sunder, or burnt at the stake, yet, since they sleep in Jesus, they are preserved from the destruction of death by Him and are made partakers of His immortality. May the Lord make us rooted and grounded in the mysterious but most consolatory doctrine of union with Christ Jesus.

We must at once advance to our text--"If we suffer, we shall also reign with Him: if we deny Him, He also will deny us." The words naturally divide themselves into two parts--suffering with Jesus and its reward--denying Jesus and its penalty.

I. SUFFERING WITH JESUS AND ITS REWARD. To suffer is the common lot of all men. It is not possible for us to escape from it. We come into this world through the gate of suffering and over death's door hangs the same escutcheon. We must suffer if we live, no matter in what style we spend our existence. The wicked man may cast off all respect for virtue and riot in excess of vice to the utmost degree, yet, let him not expect to avoid the well-directed shafts of sorrow. No, rather let him look for a tenfold share of pain of body and remorse of soul. "Many sorrows shall be to the wicked."

Even if a man could so completely degrade himself as to lose his intellectual powers and become a brute, yet even then he could not escape from suffering. For we know that the brute creation is the victim of pain as much as more lordly man. Only, as Dr. Chalmers well remarks, the brutes have the additional misery that they have no mind endowed with reason and cheered by hope to fortify them under their bodily affliction.

Understand, O Man, that however you may degrade yourself, you are still under the yoke of suffering--the loftiest bow beneath it nor the meanest can avoid it. Every acre of humanity must be furrowed with this plow. There may be a sea without a wave but never a man without sorrow. He who was God as well as Man had His full measure pressed down and running over! Let us be assured that if the Sinless One was not spared the rod, the sinful will not go free. "Man that is born of woman is of few days and full of trouble." "Man is born unto trouble as the sparks fly upward."

If then, a man has sorrow, it does not necessarily follow that he shall be rewarded for it since it is the common lot brought upon all by sin. You may smart under the lashes of sorrow in this life but this shall not deliver you from the wrath to come. Remember, you may live in poverty and drag along a wearisome existence of ill-requited toil. You may be stretched upon a bed of sickness and be made to experience an agony in every single member of your body. And your mind, too, may be depressed with fears, or plunged in the depths of despair. And yet, by all this you may gain nothing of any value to your immortal spirit, for, "Except a man be born again, he cannot see the kingdom of God."

And no amount of affliction upon earth can alter that unchanging rule so as to admit an unregenerate man into Heaven. To suffer is not peculiar to the Christian--neither does suffering necessarily bring with it any recompense of reward. The text implies most clearly that we must suffer with Christ in order to reign with Him. The structure of the preceding verse plainly requires such a reading. The words, "with Him," may be as accurately supplied at the close of the one clause as the other. The suffering which brings the reigning with Jesus must be a suffering with Jesus.

There is a very current error among those poor people who are ignorant of true religion that all poor and afflicted people will be rewarded for it in the next state. I have heard working men refer to the parable of the rich man and Lazarus with a cruel sort of satisfaction at the pains of Dives because they have imagined that, in the same manner, all rich people would be cast into the flames of Hell without a drop of water to cool their tongue--while all poor persons like Lazarus would be triumphantly carried into Abraham's bosom.

A more fearful mistake could not be made! It was not the suffering of Lazarus which entitled him to a place in Abraham's bosom. He might have been licked by all the dogs on earth and then have been dragged off by the dogs of Hell! Many a man goes to Hell from a dunghill. A drunkard's hovel is very wretched--is he to be rewarded for bringing himself to rags? Very much of the beggary we see abroad is the result of vice, extravagance, or folly--are these things so meritorious as to be passports to Heaven?

Let no man deceive himself so grossly! On the other hand the rich man was not cast into Hell because he was rich and fared sumptuously. Had he been rich in faith, holy in life and renewed in heart, his purple and fine linen would have done him no hurt. Lazarus was carried above by the angels because his heart was in Heaven--and the rich man lifted up his eyes in Hell, because he had never lifted them up towards God and heavenly things. It is a work of Free Grace in the heart and character which shall decide the future--not poverty or wealth. Let intelligent persons combat this notion whenever they meet with it.

Suffering here does not imply happiness hereafter. It is only a certain order of suffering to which a reward is promised--the suffering which comes to us from fellowship with the Lord Jesus and conformity to His image. A few words here, by way of aiding you in making the distinction. We must not imagine that we are suffering for Christ and with Christ if we are not in Christ. If a man is not a branch of the Living Vine, you may prune and cut until the sap flows and the branch bleeds but he will never bring forth heavenly fruit. Prune the bramble as long as ever you like. Use the knife until the edge is worn away--the brier will be as sharp and fruitless as ever!

You cannot by any process of pruning translate it into one of the vines of Eshcol. If a man remains in a state of nature, he is a member of the earthly Adam--he will not, therefore, escape suffering--but ensure it. He must not, however, dream that because he suffers he is suffering with Christ! He is plagued with the old Adam. He is receiving with all the other heirs of wrath the sure heritage of sin. Let him consider these sufferings of his to be only the first drops of the awful shower which will fall upon him forever--the first tingling cuts of that terrible whip which will lacerate his soul forever.

If a man is in Christ, he may then claim fellowship with the second Man, who is the Lord from Heaven and he may expect to bear the image of the heavenly in the Glory to be revealed. O my Hearers, are you in Christ by a living faith? Are you trusting in Jesus only? If not, whatever you may have to mourn over on earth, you have no hope of reigning with Jesus in Heaven. Supposing a man to be in Christ--it does not even follow, then, that all his sufferings are sufferings with Christ. If a good man were, out of mistaken views of mortification and self-denial, to mutilate his body, or to flog his flesh as many a sincere enthusiast has done, I might admire the man's fortitude, but I should not allow for an instant that he was suffering with Christ!

Who called men to such austerities? Certainly not the God of Love! If, therefore, they torture themselves at the command of their own fancies, fancy must reward them, for God will not. If I am rash and imprudent and run into positions for which neither Providence nor Grace has fitted me, I ought to question whether I am not rather sinning than communing with Christ. Peter drew his sword and cut off the ear of Malchus. If somebody had cut his ear off, what would you say? He took the sword and he feels the sword! He was never commanded to cut off the ear of Malchus and it was his Master's gentleness which saved him from the soldiers' rage.

If we let passion take the place of judgment, and let self-will reign instead of Scriptural authority, we shall fight the Lord's battles with the devil's weapons! And if we cut our own fingers we must not be surprised. On several occasions, excited Protestants have rushed into Romish cathedrals, have knocked down the priest and dashed the wafer upon the ground, trod upon it and in other ways exhibited their hatred of idolatry. Now when the Law has interposed to punish such outrages, the offenders are hardly to be considered as suffering with Christ! This I give as one instance of a class of actions to which overheated brains sometimes lead men under the supposition that they will join the noble army of martyrs.

The martyrs were all chosen to their honorable estate. And I may say of martyrdom as of priesthood, "No man takes that honor upon himself but he that is called thereunto as was Aaron." Let us mind we all make a distinction between things which differ and do not pull a house down on our heads and then pray the Lord to console us under the trying Providence.

Again, in troubles which come upon us as the result of sin, we must not think we are suffering with Christ. When Miriam spoke evil of Moses and the leprosy polluted her, she was not suffering for God. When Uzziah thrust himself into the temple and became a leper all his days, he could not say that he was afflicted for righteousness' sake. If you speculate and lose your property, do not say that you are losing all for Christ's sake! When you unite with bubble companies and are duped, do not whine about suffering for Christ--call it the fruit of your own folly. If you will put your hand into the fire and it gets burned, why, it is the nature of fire to burn you or anybody else! Be not so silly as to boast as though you were a martyr.

If you do wrong and suffer for it, what thanks have you? Go behind the door and weep for your sin, but come not forth in public to claim a reward. Many a hypocrite, when he has had his deserts and has been called by his proper name, has cried out, "Ah, I am persecuted!" It is not an infallible sign of excellence to be in bad repute among men. Who feels any esteem for a cold-blooded murderer? Does not every man reprobate the offender? Is he, therefore, a Christian because he is spoken against and his name cast out as evil? Assuredly not! He is a heartless villain and nothing more. Brethren, truthfulness and honesty should stop us from using expressions which involve a false claim. We must not talk as if we suffered nobly for Jesus when we are only troubled as the result of sin. O, to be kept from transgression! Then it matters not how rough the road of obedience may be--our journey shall be pleasant because Jesus walks with us.

Be it observed, moreover, that suffering such as God accepts and rewards for Christ's sake must have God's Glory as its end. If I suffer that, I may earn a name, or win applause among men. If I venture into trial merely that I may be respected for it, I shall get my reward--but it will be the reward of the Pharisee and not the crown of the sincere servant of the Lord Jesus. I must mind, too, that love to Christ and love to His elect is ever the mainspring of all my patience, remembering the Apostle's words, "Though I give my body to be burned and have not charity, it profits me nothing."

If I suffer in bravado, filled with proud defiance of my fellow men. If I love the dignity of singularity and out of dogged obstinacy hold to an opinion, not because it is right--but because I choose to think as I like, then I suffer not with Jesus. If there is no love to God in my soul. If I do not endure all things for the elect's sake, I may bear many a cuff and buffeting, but I miss the fellowship of the Spirit and have no recompense.

I must not forget, also, that I must manifest the Spirit of Christ or I do not suffer with Him. I have heard of a certain minister, who, having had a great disagreement with many members in his Church, preached from this text, "And Aaron held his peace." The sermon was intended to portray himself as an astonishing instance of meekness. But as his previous words and actions had been quite sufficiently violent, a witty hearer observed that the only likeness he could see between Aaron and the preacher, was this, "Aaron held his peace and the preacher did not."

It is easy enough to discover some parallel between our cases and those of departed saints, but not so easy to establish the parallel by holy patience and Christ-like forgiveness. If I have, in the way of virtue, brought down upon myself shame and rebuke. If I am hot to defend myself and punish the slanderer. If I am irritated, unforgiving and proud--I have lost a noble opportunity of fellowship with Jesus. I must have Christ's Spirit in me, or I do not suffer acceptably. If like a sheep before her shearers, I can be dumb. If I can bear insult and love the man who inflicts it. If I can pray with Christ, "Father, forgive them, for they know not what they do." If I submit all my case to Him who judges righteously and count it even my joy to suffer reproach for the cause of Christ--then and only then, have I truly suffered with Christ.

These remarks may seem very cutting and may take away much false but highly-prized comfort from some of you. It is not my intention to take away any true comfort from the most humble Believer who really suffers with my Lord. But God grant we may have honesty enough not to pluck flowers out of other men's gardens, or wear other men's honors. Truth will only be desired by true men.

I shall now very briefly show what are the forms of real suffering for Jesus in these days. We have not now to rot in prisons, to wander about in sheepskins and goatskins, to be stoned, or to be sawn in sunder--though we ought to be ready to bear all this if God wills it. The days of Nebuchadnezzar's furnace are past, but the fire is still upon earth. Some suffer in their estates. I believe that to many Christians it is rather a gain than a loss, so far as pecuniary matters go, to be Believers in Christ. But I meet with many cases--cases which I know to be genuine--where persons have had to suffer severely for conscience sake.

There are those present who were once in very comfortable circumstances, but they lived in a neighborhood where the majority of the business was done on a Sunday. When Divine Grace shut up their shop, trade left them. And I know some of them are working very hard for their bread, though once they earned abundance without any great toil. They do it cheerfully for Christ's sake, but the struggle is a hard one. I know other persons who were employed as servants in lucrative positions involving sin, but upon their becoming Christians they were obliged to resign their former post and are not at the present moment in anything like such apparent prosperity as they were.

I could point to several cases of persons who have really suffered to a very high degree in pecuniary matters for the Cross of Christ. Brethren, you may possess your souls in patience and expect as a reward of Grace that you shall reign with Jesus your Beloved! Those feather-bed soldiers who are broken-hearted if fools laugh at them should blush when they think of those who endure real hardship as good soldiers of Jesus Christ. Who can waste his pity over the small griefs of faint hearts when cold, hunger, and poverty are cheerfully endured by the true and brave?

Cases of persecution are by no means rare. In many a country village squires and priests rule with a high hand and smite the godly villagers with a rod of iron. "No blankets, no coals, no almshouse for you if you venture into the Meeting House. You cannot live in my cottage if you have a Prayer Meeting in it. I will have no religious people on my farm." We who live in more enlightened society little know the terrorism exercised in some of the rural districts over poor men and women who endeavor conscientiously to carry out their convictions and walk with Christ.

True Christians of all denominations love each other and hate persecution, but nominal Christians and ungodly men would make our land as hot as in the days of Mary if they dared. To all saints who are oppressed, this sweet sentence is directed--"If we suffer, we shall also reign with Him." More usually, however, the suffering takes the form of personal contempt. It is not pleasant to be pointed at in the streets and have opprobrious names shouted after you by vulgar tongues. Nor is it a small trial to be saluted in the workshop by opprobrious epithets, or to be looked upon as an idiot or a madman.

And yet this is the lot of many of the people of God every day of the week. Many of those who are of the humbler classes have to endure constant and open reproach. And those who are richer have to put up with the cold shoulder and neglect and sneers as soon as they become true disciples of Jesus Christ. There is more sting in this than some dream. And we have known strong men who could have borne the lash brought down by jeers and sarcasms, even just as the wasp may more thoroughly irritate and vex the lion than if the noblest beast of prey should attack him. Believers have also to suffer slander and falsehood. It is not expedient for me, doubtless, to glory, but I know a man who scarcely ever speaks a word which is not misrepresented and hardly performs an action which is not misconstrued.

The press at certain seasons, like a pack of hounds, will get upon his track and worry him with the most bases and undeserved abuse. Publicly and privately he is accustomed to be sneered at. The world whispers, "Ah, he pretends to be zealous for God, but he makes a fine thing of it!" Mark you, when the world shall learn what he does make of it, maybe it will have to eat its words! But I forbear such is the portion of every servant of God who has to bear public testimony for the Truth of God.

Every motive but the right one will be imputed to him. His good will be evil spoken of. His zeal will be called imprudence--his courage, impertinence--his modesty, cowardice. It is impossible for the true Believer in Christ who is called to any eminent service to do anything right. He had better at once learn to say with Luther, "The world hates me and there is no love lost between us, for as much as it hates me, so heartily do I hate it." He meant not the men in the world, for never was there a more loving heart than Luther's. But he meant the fame, the opinion, the honor of the world he trod beneath his feet. If in your measure you bear undeserved rebuke for Christ's sake, comfort yourselves with these words, "If we suffer, we shall also reign with Him: if we deny Him, He also will deny us."

Then again, if in your service for Christ you are enabled to sacrifice yourself--bearing upon yourself inconvenience and pain, labor and loss--then I think you are suffering with Christ. The Missionary who tempts the stormy deep--the herald of the Cross who penetrates into unknown regions among savage men--the tract distributor toiling up the mountainside--the teacher going wearily to the class--the village preacher walking many toilsome miles--the minister starving on a miserable pittance--the evangelist content to break down in health--all these and their like suffer with Christ.

We are all too much occupied with taking care of ourselves. We shun the difficulties of excessive labor. And frequently behind the entrenchments of taking care of our constitution we do not half as much as we ought. A minister of God is bound to spurn the suggestions of ignoble ease--it is his calling to labor! And if he destroys his constitution, I for one, thank God that He permits us the high privilege of so making ourselves living sacrifices. If earnest ministers should bring themselves to the grave, not by imprudence, for that we would not advocate--but by honest labor, such as their ministry and their consciences require of them--they will be better in their graves than out of their graves if they come there for the cause of Christ. What? Are we never to suffer? Are we to be carpet-knights? Are God's people to be put away in padding, perfumed with lavender and boxed up in quiet softness? No! Not unless they would lose the reward of true saints!

Let us not forget that contention with inbred lusts, denials of proud self, resistance of sin and agony against Satan are all forms of suffering with Christ. We may, in the holy war within us, earn as bright a crown as in the wider battlefield beyond us. O for Grace to be ever dressed in full armor, fighting with principalities and powers and spiritual wickedness of every sort! There is one more class of suffering which I shall mention and that is, when friends forsake, or become foes. Father and mother forsake sometimes. The husband persecutes the wife. We have known even the children turn against the parents. "A man's foes are they of his own household." This is one of the devil's best instruments for making Believers suffer. And those who have to drain this cup for the Lord's sake shall reign with Him.

Brethren, if you are thus called to suffer for Christ, will you quarrel with me if I say, in adding all up, what a very little it is compared with reigning with Jesus? "For our light affliction, which is but for a moment, works for us a far more exceeding and eternal weight of Glory." When I contrast our sufferings of today with those of the reign of Mary, or the persecutions of the Albigenses on the mountains, or the sufferings of Christians in Pagan Rome--why ours are scarcely a pin's prick--and yet what is the reward? We shall reign with Christ!

There is no comparison between the service and the reward. Therefore it is all of Grace. We do but little and suffer but little--and even that little, Grace gives us! And yet the Lord grants us, "A far more exceeding and eternal weight of Glory." We are not merely to sit with Christ, but we are to reign with Christ. All that the pomp imperial of His Kingship means. All that the treasure of His wide dominions can yield. All that the majesty of His everlasting power can bestow-- all this is to

belong to you--given to you of His rich, Free Grace, as the sweet reward of having suffered for a little time with Him!

Who would draw back, then? Who among you will flinch? Young man, have you thought of flying from the Cross? Young woman, has Satan whispered to you to shun the thorny pathway? Will you give up the crown? Will you miss the Throne? O Beloved, it is so blessed to be in the furnace with Christ, and such an honor to stand in the pillory with Him that if there were no reward, we might count ourselves happy! But when the reward is so rich, so super-abundant, so eternal, so infinitely more than we had any right to expect--will we not take up the Cross with songs and go on our way rejoicing in the Lord our God?

II. DENYING CHRIST, AND ITS PENALTY. "If we deny Him, He also will deny us." Dreadful "if," and yet an "if which is applicable to every one of us. If the Apostles, when they sat at the Lord's Supper, said, "Lord, is it I?" surely we may say as we sit here, "Lord, shall I ever deny You?" You who say most loudly, "Though all men shall deny You, yet I will not"--you are the most likely to do it!

In what way can we deny Christ? Some deny Him openly, as scoffers do, whose tongue walks through the earth and defies Heaven. Others do this willfully and wickedly in a doctrinal way, as the Arians and Socinians do who deny His deity--those who deny His Atonement, who rail against the inspiration of His Word--these come under the condemnation of those who deny Christ. There is a way of denying Christ without even speaking a word and this is the more common.

In the day of blasphemy and rebuke, many hide their heads. They are in company where they ought to speak up for Christ. But they put their hands upon their mouths. They come not forward to profess their faith in Jesus. They have a sort of faith, but it is one which yields no obedience. Jesus bids each Believer to be baptized. They neglect His ordinance. Neglecting that, they also despise the weightier matters of the Law. They will go up to the House of God because it is fashionable to go there. But if it were a matter of persecution, they would forsake the assembling of themselves together.

In the day of battle they are never on the Lord's side. If there is a parade, and the banners are flying and the trumpets are sounding, if there are decorations and medals to be given away, there they are. But if the shots are flying, if trenches have to be carried and forts to be stormed, where are they? They have gone back to their dens and there will they hide themselves till fair weather shall return.

Mind, mind, mind, for I am giving a description, I am afraid, of some here. Mind, I say, you silent ones, lest you stand speechless at the bar of Judgment. Some, after having been long silent and so practically denying Christ, go farther and apostatize altogether from the faith they once had. No man who has a genuine faith in Christ will lose it, for the faith which God gives will live forever. Hypocrites and formalists have a name to live while yet they are dead--and after a while they return like the dog to its vomit and the sow which was washed to her wallowing in the mire. Certain professors do not run this length, yet practically deny Christ by their lives, though they make a profession of faith in Him.

Are there not some here who hove been baptized and who come to the Lord's Table but what is their character? Follow them home. I would to God they never had made a profession because in their own houses they deny what in the House of God they have avowed. If I see a man drunk. If I know that a professor indulges in lasciviousness. If I know a man to be harsh and overbearing and tyrannical to his servants. If I know another who cheats in his traffic and another who adulterates his goods. And if I know that such men profess allegiance to Jesus--which am I to believe--their words or their deeds? I will believe that which speaks loudest! And as actions always speak louder than words, I will believe their actions--I believe that they are deceivers whom Jesus will deny at the last.

Should we not find many present this morning belonging to one or other of these grades? Does not this description suit at least some of you? If it should do so, do not be angry with me but stand still and hear the Word of the Lord. Know, O Man that you will not perish even if you have denied Christ, if now you fly to Him for refuge. Peter denied, but yet Peter is in Heaven. A transient forsaking of Jesus under temptation will not bring on everlasting ruin, if faith shall step in and the Grace of God shall intervene. But persevere in it--continue still in a denial of the Savior and my terrible text will come upon you--"He also will deny you."

In musing over the very dreadful sentence which closes my text, "He also will deny us," I was led to think of various ways in which Jesus will deny us. He does this sometimes on earth. You have read, I suppose, of the death of Francis Spira. If you have ever read it, you never can forget it to your dying day. Francis Spira knew the Truth of God. He was a reformer of no mean standing, but when brought to death, out of fear, he recanted. In a short time he fell into despair and suffered Hell upon earth. His shrieks and exclamations were so horrible that their record is almost too terrible for print. His doom was a warning to the age in which he lived.

Another instance is narrated by my predecessor, Benjamin Keach, of one whom, during Puritanical times, was very earnest for Puritanism but afterwards, when times of persecution arose, forsook his profession. The scenes at his deathbed were thrilling amid terrible. He declared that though he sought God, Heaven was shut against him. Gates of brass seemed to be in his way. He was given up to overwhelming despair. At intervals he cursed. At other intervals he prayed and so perished without hope.

If we deny Christ, we may be delivered to such a fate. If we have stood highest and foremost in God's Church and yet have not been brought to Christ--if we should become apostates--a high soar will bring a deep fall. High pretensions bring down sure destruction when they come to nothing. Even upon earth Christ will deny such. There are remarkable instances of persons who sought to save their lives and lost them. One Richard Denton, who had been a very zealous Lollard and was the means of the conversion of an eminent saint, when he came to the stake, was so afraid of the fire that he renounced everything he held and went into the Church of Rome.

A short time after, his own house took fire, and going into it to save some of his money, he perished miserably, being utterly consumed by that fire which he had denied Christ in order to escape. If I must be lost, let it be any way rather than as an apostate. If there is any distinction among the damned, those have it who are wandering stars, trees plucked up by the roots, twice dead, for whom Jude tells us, is "reserved the blackness of darkness forever." Reserved! As if nobody else were qualified to occupy that place but themselves. They are to inhabit the darkest, hottest place because they forsook the Lord.

Let us, my dear Friends, rather lose everything than lose Christ. Let us sooner suffer anything than lose our ease of conscience and our peace of mind. When Marcus Arethusus was commanded by Julian the apostate to subscribe towards the rebuilding of a heathen temple which his people had pulled down upon their conversion to Christianity, he refused to obey. And though he was an aged man, he was stripped naked and then pierced all over with lancets and knives. The old man still was firm.

If he would give but one halfpenny towards the building of the temple, he could be free--if he would cast in but one grain of incense into the censer devoted to the false gods, he might escape. He would not countenance idolatry in any degree. He was smeared with honey and while his innumerable wounds were yet bleeding, the bees and wasps came upon him and stung him to death. He could die, but he could not deny his Lord. Arethusus entered into the joy of his Lord, for he nobly suffered with Him!

In the olden time when the Gospel was preached in Persia, one Hamedatha, a courtier of the king, having embraced the faith, was stripped of all his offices, driven from the palace and compelled to feed camels. This he did with great content. The king, passing by one day, saw his former favorite at his ignoble work, cleaning out the camel's stables. Taking pity upon him he took him into his palace, clothed him with sumptuous apparel, restored him to all his former honors and made him sit at the royal table. In the midst of the dainty feast, he asked Hamedatha to renounce his faith.

The courtier, rising from the table, took off his garments with haste, left all the dainties behind him, and said, "Did you think that for such silly things as these I would deny my Lord and Master?" And away he went to the stable to his ignoble work. How honorable is all this! How shall I denounce the meanness of the apostate--his detestable cowardice to forsake the bleeding Savior of Calvary to return to the beggarly elements of the world which he once despised and to bow his neck again to the yoke of bondage? Will you do this, O followers of the Crucified?

You will not! You cannot! I know you cannot if the Spirit of the Lord dwells in you and it must dwell in you if you are the children of God. What must be the doom of those who deny Christ, when they reach another world? Perhaps they will appear with a sort of hope in their minds and they will come before the Judge, with, "Lord, Lord, open to us." Who are you? He says. "Lord, we once took the Lord's Supper--Lord, we were members of the Church, but there came very hard times. My mother bade me give up religion. Father was angry. Trade went bad. I was so mocked at, I could not stand it. Lord, I fell among evil acquaintances and they tempted me--I could not resist. I was Your servant--I did love You--I always had love towards You in my heart, but I could not help it--I denied You and went to the world again."

What will Jesus say? I know you not! "But, Lord, I want You to be my Advocate." I know you not! "But, Lord, I cannot get into Heaven unless You should open the gate--open it for me." I do not know you! I do not know you! "But, Lord, my name was in the Church Book." I know you not--I deny you. "But will You not hear my cries?" You did not hear Mine--you did deny Me and I deny you. "Lord, give me the lowest place in Heaven, if I may but enter and escape from wrath to come." No, you would not brook the lowest place on earth and you shall not enjoy the lowest place here. You had your choice and you did choose evil. Keep to your choice. You were filthy, be you filthy still. You were unholy, be you unholy still.

O, Sirs, if you would not see the angry face of Jesus! O, Sirs, if you would not behold the lightning flashing from His eyes and hear the thunder of His mouth in the day when He judges the fearful and the unbelieving and the hypocrite. If you would not have your portion in the lake which burns with fire and brimstone, cry this day mightily unto God, "Lord, hold me fast, keep me, keep me. Help me to suffer with You, that I may reign with You. But do not, do not let me deny You, lest You also should deny me."

Forward! Forward! Forward!

DELIVERED ON SUNDAY EVENING, OCTOBER 18, 1863,
BY THE REV. C. H. SPURGEON,
AT THE METROPOLITAN TABERNACLE, NEWINGTON.

"And the Lord said unto Moses, Why cry you unto Me? Speak unto the children of Israel, that they go forward." Exodus 14:15.

SPIRITUAL men, in their distresses, turn at once to prayer even as the stag when hunted takes to flight. Prayer is a never-failing resort. It is sure to bring a blessing with it. Even apart from the answer of our supplications, the very exercise of prayer is healthy to the man engaged in it. Far be it from me ever to say a word in disparagement of the holy, happy, heavenly exercise of prayer. But, Beloved, there are times when prayer is not enough--when prayer itself is out of season. You will think that a hard saying and say, "Who can bear it?" But my text is to the point. Moses prayed that God would deliver His people. But the Lord said to him, "Why cry you unto Me?" As much as to say this is not the time for prayer, it is the time for action. "Speak unto the children of Israel, that they go forward." When we have prayed over a matter to a certain degree, it then becomes sinful to tarry any longer. Our plain duty is to carry our desires into action, and having asked God's guidance and having received Divine power from on high, to go at once to our duty without any longer deliberation or delay.

Brethren, a vigorous faith will often shut its eyes to difficulties. When faith looks upon a difficulty as being exceedingly great, then she turns to prayer. But, on the other hand, after having sought God's help and having received it, she frequently laughs at the impossibility and cries, "It shall be done." and then, instead of betaking herself any longer to her knees, she boldly marches on, believing that the difficulty will vanish before her, that the crooked will be made straight and the rough places plain. We are not to be always praying over a difficulty. When we have fairly committed it to God, we are to act upon the assurance that He has heard us.

Nor will such an action be the fruit of rashness for it is a solid and substantial fact that prayer does avail with God. Beloved, it strikes me that the advice which the Lord gave to Moses was such as He has given to the preacher tonight-- and that the message which Moses delivered to the children of Israel is a very fit one for me to deliver to you. Short, prompt, soldier-like, here is the whole of it--"Forward! Forward!" If you have been sitting down or tempted to go back--"Forward!" We have long been praying, let us tonight, "go forward." The one subject we shall take up and try to deliver to different classes of characters, is, "Thus says the Lord, you children of Israel, Forward!"

I. First, we will contemplate THE CHILDREN OF ISRAEL AS A FLOCK OF FUGITIVES. And in this light they give encouragement to trembling sinners flying from the curse of the Law and from the power of their sins. I think I see those poor Israelites crowding together, all alarmed and afraid, whispering to one another some such trembling words as these--"I saw them. I saw my old master on horseback riding after me. I looked and I saw regiment upon regiment of warriors marching in long red lines." "I heard," says another, "the sound of their war music. I heard the clash of their spears. We cannot stand against them! We are only defenseless multitudes and they are the well-trained sons of Mizraim. Their swords will be drunk with our blood."

They huddled together as a company of doves seeking to escape the hawk. Alas! What can they do? They are crying to God and to Moses, thinking of this plan and devising another. And Moses himself, in some sort of alarm, is crying out to God for them--"Lord, help this people! They are in great straits. They are in frightful difficulties. The enemy says, 'I will pursue them. I will overtake them. I will divide the spoil. My lust shall be satisfied upon them.' Lord, what am I to do with this company?" Here comes the Divine answer, full of wisdom and love--"Speak unto them and bid them go forward."

Now such is my message to the company of fugitives who are here tonight. You have been awakened. Your conscience has been alarmed. You have begun to feel the terrors of the Law. You have heard the crack of the whip and felt it on your back. You are trying to escape from your sins. You are not as you used to be, a contented bondsman, but you pant to be delivered altogether from sin and its power and its guilt. You have been flying as best you could from sin. But the whole of your sins are after you and your conscience, with its quick ear, can hear the sound of threatening judgment. "Alas," your heart is saying, "unless God helps me, I shall be in Hell!" "Alas," says your judgment, "unless God is merciful, I shall soon perish!" Every power of your manhood is now upon the alarm. The different parts of your heart are talking to one another and they are all foreboding desperate mischief.

Now what shall I do for you? Shall I pray for you? Yes, that I will. Shall I bid you pray? Yes, that I may. And we may blend our prayers together--"God be merciful to us sinners! Lord save us, or we perish!" But I think while I am praying for you, I hear my Master saying, "Why cry you unto Me?

Tell them to go forward! Preach Christ to them instead of praying any longer or bidding them pray.

Deliver to them the message of the Gospel--"Forward, Sinner, forward to the Cross! Forward to the five wounds! Forward to the bloody sweat and to the crown of thorns! Go forward to the agonies of Gethsemane and to the death struggles of Golgotha. Forward! Forward to the place--

'Where the full Atonement's made, Where the utmost ransom's paid.'"

I know what you say. "Right before me rolls the great sea of God's wrath. I am surrounded with a dark, dark night and I see no light but the sheen of these terrible waves of fire. If I go forward, God's eternal wrath is in the way." Forward, Sinner, whatever may obstruct the way! Let not Hell itself block up the road! Do you not know that when Jesus is your Leader, He will at once divide the Red sea of Jehovah's wrath? He did divide it! He went through it Himself when He suffered the wrath of God instead of you!

As you go forward, you shall find Almighty Justice standing up as a protecting wall on either hand and no longer rolling as a devouring flood. Forward in the way of faith in the Savior's name! And when you have passed through the dry bed of a sea once deep and stormy, you shall look back and see the deep sea swallowing up your sins and shall sing, "The depths have covered them, there is not one of them left." Forward, Sinner, forward! "Well," says one, "I will pray about it." Beware of substituting prayer for faith--faith is your present duty--Believe on the Lord Jesus Christ and you shall be saved. "I will think about it a little longer." Do no such thing! Thinking is a very poor substitute for believing. Forward! Forward at once and on the spot! Believe on the Lord Jesus Christ and you shall be saved.

"But I am not fit to believe!" Forward, in God's name--forward! What have you to do with fitness? God commands you to believe in His Son Jesus Christ. Forward is my message--I come not here to tamper with you--to deal with your "ifs" and "buts," and excuses and perhapses. Hell is behind you--you are shut up on the right hand and on the left by God's Providence, your own fears, and Divine Justice. There is but one way of safety and that is the way of faith. Forward, Sinner! Believe on the Lord Jesus Christ and you shall be saved!

Why, some of you have been frittering away your time--weeks and months and years! You have been thinking about it, praying about it, reading about it, hoping about it, fearing about it--but never coming to Jesus just as you are. It is wrong--it is all wrong! God's command is neither work, nor feel, nor fear--it is simple and plain--BELIEVE! Forward! Trust a Savior's wounds. And in trusting there is life. In a look at Him you are saved! O, I wish I could get behind some of you and whisper a word in your ear, for I know what Satan says. He says, "Tarry, tarry, tarry!" Ah, he loves to have you in the place of breaking forth as children, that he may vex and torment you.

"Go back," he says, "go back!" Ah, I know he would like to have you at your cups again and in your old sins, but you cannot go back if God has once brought you out of Egypt! I know what he whispers. He says, "It is of no use going forward. If you believe in Jesus," says he, "you will perish after all." Back, you old Liar, back! God never did permit a man yet to walk in a path in which He commanded him to go and not to walk safely. Forward, Sinner, FORWARD! Christ is before you and Heaven in Him is before you. If you stay where you are, you shall die. If you go forward, you can but die. And, therefore, take the captain's word tonight, for it is the word of the captain's King--"Speak unto the children of Israel that they go forward."

II. Secondly, we may view the great company who came out of Egypt as AN ARMY UNDER COMMAND. Therefore they must obey. The command given to them is, "Forward! Forward! Forward!" Might the wise men have said in the host of Israel, "How can we go forward? That narrow beach leads down to the foaming billow. Forward? What do you mean? We are altogether as dead men if we go forward! Would you have us swim? Do you know where you are? There are miles and miles of deep water and who knows the bottom of the sea? Forward? Absurd!--We shall lose the camels and the sheep and the baggage and our wealth and our children and our little ones--yes, and our own lives also."

But thus says the Lord, "Forward!" You came out of Egypt under Moses' command, will you play the rebel's part? If the Lord is your Captain, you must do absolutely what He bids you at any loss and at any cost. If He says, "Forward," and it is into the Red Sea or into a gulf of fire, forward you must go. Now, Beloved, this presents us a picture of those who are savingly converted, who, on a sudden, meet with difficulties in following Christ and run to their minister or to their friend, and say, "What are we to do?"

The Lord's message by me tonight to your anxious inquiry is this--"Forward!" It is a simple one--"Forward!" "Sir, I have just begun to be a Christian, but if I continue in it, I shall lose my business. My calling is such that I cannot be honest in it and serve my God faithfully without sinking all my capital and bringing myself and family to beggary. What ought I to do? Ought I not to give up my religion?" Forward! Forward! No matter what is before you. Forward! You are not fit to be a soldier of Christ unless you can count all costs and still hold fast to the Cross of Christ.

"Ah," says one, "but what is to become of my children, my family, my household?" Friend, I cannot tell you, but God can. It is yours to trust them with Him, for the only command I have for you is, Forward! Forward! "But my husband says I shall never come into the house again! My father tells me he will turn me out of doors." Be it so, no one pities you more than I do. But I dare not alter my message to your soul. I am to bid you, Go forward! "Well," says one, "these are hard commands."

Yes, but the martyrs had harder still. Theirs was the stake, the gibbet, the rack. They must rot in prison. They must be dragged at the heels of the wild horse. But what is the command? "Forward.!" On went the goodly host through floods, through fires, through seas of blood. They never paused. And if you would be worthy followers of them, you must do the same. The Master's message to you is, "Forward!" At the famous charge of Balaclava, when the order was given to charge the batteries, what could that troop do but ride into the valley of death? There they go! On, on, up to the very cannons' mouths! The word of command must not be questioned but obeyed--

"Theirs not to make reply. Theirs not to reason why. Theirs but to do and die-- Into the valley of death Rode the six hundred."

And you, if you are fit to be God's soldiers--if you are really His and filled with His Holy Spirit--you must do the same. What would you think of our soldiers if, when they were bid to charge, they should say, "There is a ditch in the way." Jump in it! "But there are soldiers in the way." Cut them to pieces! "But they have very sharp fixed bayonets." Fix yours, too! Push them at the bayonet's point and drive them back. England expects every man to do his duty. What God commands must surely have a higher claim on men than what England commands them to do! Comrades in arms, all my message to you is, "Forward! Forward!" If God has called you to honor and glory and immortality and eternal life--if loss of business, comfort, honor, fame, friends. If relatives should threaten you, you must not be daunted--for He who loves any of these more than Christ is not worthy of Him.

There are cowards of another sort with whom I must have a word. They do not like going forward. They would not lose by it if they did, but they feel a quivering sensation of nervousness come over them. And though they know their Master's commands, yet they say, "Well, I must think the matter over." Now suppose one instance--and I take only one of the sort--suppose you know it (as it certainly is, whether you know it or not), to be your duty to be baptized? How often I have heard people say, "Well, yes, the Lord is my gracious Master and I am His servant and I believe it is the duty of Believers to be baptized. But if the Lord ever reveals it to me, then I will do it"?

There is a soldier for you! He is not content to get the same orders as his fellow soldiers! No, he cries, "When the regiment is on the march, if the captain will come round to my tent and talk to me by myself, I will not mind going." Why, he deserves to be flogged as a deserter! I will not wish anything hard to my Christian Brothers and Sisters, but I do venture to prophesy that they will be beaten with many stripes if they talk in that way. "Ah," says one, "but the Lord must apply it to me." What for? The thing is clear enough without its being applied. If there is anything in the Bible which is plain at all, it is that he who believes in Christ should he buried with Him in Baptism. Then, if it is your clear duty, you ought to do it at once.

"Well, I will pray about it." And do you believe God will hear such a wicked prayer as that? If I tell my child that there is something for him to do and he tells me, "Well, I will think about it." I shall let him know that I am not to be thus impudently trifled with. If I say to him, Now, my child, do so-and-so. "Father, I will pray about it." Believe me, I shall not put up with such hypocritical rebellion! It will not do in one's own house, much less in the House of God. Are you to be permitted to trifle with positive precepts and then to lay your sin upon God's back? I do not think so.

Dear Brothers and Sisters, if you have been sitting down timidly and saying, "Well, one of these days I will come out and own my Lord," instead of that, I am bid to command you on this point and on every other, if it is a plain duty, whether it is pleasant to the flesh or not, "Forward! Forward! Forward!" What are your marching orders? Does your Lord tell you to do it? Do it! Do the Scriptures bid you? Do it! It is not yours to reason why any more than it is the soldier's. But as the seed of Israel marched right on, even though the sea was in their way, so must you--though death itself should be the result. "Speak to the children of Israel, that they go forward."

III. We will change the topic once again and we will take a third view of it. Let us view these people as ON THE MARCH TOWARDS CANAAN. Many of you are on your way towards Heaven and the Lord's command to you is, "Forward! Forward!"

I would that I could sound that one word in the ears of many whom I believe to be the Lord's people but who have for a long time settled upon their lees. There are some persons who cannot be persuaded to make an advance in the Divine life. The moment you urge them to anything practical they call you legal. They seem to consider themselves as inanimate clay ordained to lie passively in the hands of the Holy Spirit. But they forget that the Holy Spirit works in us, not to be idle and powerless, but to will and to do of God's good pleasure. They neither will, nor do, but talk about the Spirit as though He were to will and to do everything for them.

To such who have been converted but have made no progress let me, in my Master's name, give clear utterance to that word, "Forward." Brothers and Sisters, you and I ought to go forward in knowledge. If I know no more of Scripture than I did ten years ago, what have I done with my time? If I am no better instructed myself as a scribe in my Master's kingdom, of what use shall I be to others? If you have been in this world these years and yet doctrine has not become more clear, nor experience more plain it is time you should look about you and follow on to know the Lord. We do not keep boys at school year after year if they make no progress. And yet how many there are of professing Christians who seem to have been stunted in their early profession so that they positively have not advanced in knowledge one iota beyond where they were ten or twenty years ago? In this point, however, they are not so much to blame as in others.

"Forward," should be the motto as to our faith. You were doubting and fearing twenty years ago. If I recollect, when I was but a lad ten years ago, I heard you lament--

"It is a point I long to know, Oft it causes anxious thought." Have you not a better time than that now? Can you not sing--

"A debtor to mercy alone, Of Covenant mercy I sing; Nor fear with Your righteousness on, My person and offerings to bring-- The terrors of Law and of God, With me can have nothing to do; My Savior's obedience and blood Hide all my transgressions from view."

I do not suppose you will altogether be rid of fears, but I do think your motto should be-- "Forward!"--that your faith should become more constant and your doubts less frequent. Surely the venerable saint who has proved his Master a hundred times ought to find his faith more strong than those of us who are but babes in the family! Ought we to be always limping, always hoping and trusting, doubting and fearing? Is it not time for us to use the strong muscles of the fully developed man--and, leaving all nursery carts--ought we not to stand upright with Abraham with a faith which staggers not because of unbelief? Forward, Christian, forward as to your faith!

May I not use the same word in reference to our fellowship with Christ? I am afraid most of us make no progress as to nearness to Christ. Some of us, I am afraid, go backwards. We said, years ago, "Nearer, my God, to You, nearer to You." Are we nearer? Have we come closer to the wounds of Jesus? Do we more frequently recline upon His bosom and sit at His feet? If not, I am commanded with Moses, "Speak unto the children of Israel, that they go forward."

Above all, have we made any progress as to work for our Master? Some, as they grow old, give up their work. I do not understand it! I must confess an inability of comprehending how any man who once preached the Gospel can ever leave his ministry while his strength lasts. If the Master has once allotted you a field of labor, unless it is sheer inability, I cannot understand how you can ever cease to till the ground, or reap the sheaves. No, you will, if God has called you, want to do more and more and more for Jesus!

You will feel a growing thirst after precious souls--at least you ought to. You will be moved with greater yearnings of your heart towards your fellow immortals and a higher zeal for the spread of your Master's kingdom. Christian men, when I think of some of you who have tasted that He is gracious, and are content with the taste. You who have been into the river of Jesus' love until you are up to the ankles, but are loath to wade into the deeper parts of the heavenly stream. When I think of some of you who are worshipping in the outer courts and have no ambition to enter into that which is within the veil. When I remember how some of you seem never to comprehend the resurrection life, nor what it is to be raised up together to sit in heavenly places in Christ Jesus--I do marvel at you that you thus stand back and in the name of God, whose servant I am, I give you this motto--"Forward! Forward!"

Press onward in the Divine life! Forget the road already trod and onward urge your way. Cry for the Spirit of God! Ask for more unction, more power, more consciousness of the Divine indwelling and then take for the motto on your banner--"Forward! Forward! Forward!"

IV. In the fourth place, but with very great brevity, TO CHRISTIANS IN TROUBLE our text is applicable. The children of Israel were in great straits. They were in a trial into which God had brought them. And it is an absolute certainty that if God brings you in, He will bring you out. He never did take a saint where he must of necessity perish. The rocks of daily life rise on the right and on the left. The raging enemy is behind. The equally raging sea is before. What is to be done now? God's word is--"Forward!"

God shall fight for you and you shall hold your peace. In this vast assembly there may be several Christians who said to themselves last Saturday night, "I will go up to the House of God and enquire at the hand of the man of God what the Lord will do for me." This is the answer to your enquiry. You cannot help yourself--that is clear. Your trouble is none of your own finding--that you know. And your escape will not be of your own working--that you know, also. You have nothing now to do but to cast yourselves upon your God and go forward!

Beloved, it is a blessed thing to be absolutely stripped of creature comforts that you may be wholly clothed upon with the Creator. It is not pleasing to flesh and blood to be brought down to abject nothingness. But faith never is more happy than when the strength of the mortal is altogether dead--because then the immortal God comes in and clothes our weakness with His Omnipotence. If I might have any choice between having abundant wealth, or being brought to absolute dependence upon daily supplies. If in the latter case I could have greater power to exhibit and to exert faith in Christ, I must confess that I should prefer the mode of living which would give me most room to enjoy the luxury of depending upon my God.

I believe it is more happy and more Divine a life to live from hand to mouth, dependent upon the Providence of God and having the confidence to trust Him, than it is to have all the abundance of this world but to have nothing about which faith may exercise itself. Often when our joys are thick about us and we have ten thousand creature comforts, we are then naked and poor and miserable in spirituals. But when the creature comforts fall as the leaves are falling from the trees in autumn, then it is that we have frequently the most joy and the most peace in God. "Give me back my sickbed," said a saint when he remembered what joy he had had upon it!

Theodoret, the martyr, said that his persecutors had done him an injury when they took him off the rack. "For," said he, "while I was on the rack, God sent His angels to comfort me. And now you have taken me off, I am afraid I shall lose their heavenly presence." Experimentally I have learned, dear Friends, that at the Red Sea of affliction we see most of the right arm of God. I am glad there was a Red Sea! I bless God that it had deep and foaming billows! I praise His name that there were fierce and cruel Egyptians--for if there had never been that Red Sea, never would the song of Moses and the shout of Miriam have been heard--"Sing unto the Lord, for He has triumphed gloriously: the horse and his rider has He thrown into the sea."

Your tribulations will yet yield you music. All you have to do now is to honor God by going forward! Hold your peace and God shall fight for you! "Be still and know that I am God." When the worst has come to the worst, that God--

"Who moves in a mysterious way His wonders to perform, Will plant His footsteps in the sea, And ride upon the storm. Forward! Christian, forward!"

V. Let me not weary you, but I must, again, use my text in another manner--for the exhortation of all of you who are followers of my Lord and Master. THE ISRAELITES WERE UPON A DIVINE MISSION. They were going up to slay the Canaanites, Hivites, Jebusites and Hittites. They must all be slain with the sharp sword of Israel. But a difficulty rolls between them and their prey! The message, however, of God's captain, is still, "Forward! Forward!"

My Brothers and Sisters, let me specially address you who are associated in Church fellowship here. Some of you will remember when I came up from the country. I remember better than you do, for I have hidden these things in my heart. A child, almost a babe, I came into your place of worship which was half empty, no, not one-sixth full. You may, some of you, remember that sermon when the youth preached of the faithfulness of God and tried to magnify Divine Immutability. I believe the note of the charge that morning, was, "Forward!"

Hope was kindled in the breasts of many. The few there who were faithful to the cause hoped and believed that God had better days for them and we took heart. You will remember, some of you, when the people began to throng the aisles. Within three or four Sundays, when the place was full, our cry was "Forward!" We had more Prayer Meetings, more earnestness every day! I recollect it was thought a strange thing to see such zeal! Then we wanted to enlarge the Chapel. And one Sunday evening, preaching from that text--"By faith the walls of Jericho fell down"--when certain ones had objected to any alteration because it was a mere spasm, a mere excitement--the young lad from the country would soon be forgotten--I said concerning that wall at the back, "By faith this wall will fall down," for our motto was "Forward!"

We held a little meeting, raised the money at once--down went the wall--the place was enlarged. The enlargement was of no use, our motto was, "Forward!" God opened the doors of Exeter Hall to us. We went there. The place was crowded, multitudes of souls were converted. The Church increased--did we stop? Our motto was "Forward!" The Surrey Hall was proposed to us, a larger structure. We went about it and we said, "This is too immense a place, too bold a venture."

I thought in my own mind, "The place will never be filled." You remember we still dared it, for our motto was "Forward!" Then came a crushing blow, a terrible disaster which seemed to shatter us all and, most of all, the man who was called to take the brunt of the battle. He was laid upon the ground all broken-hearted and wretched by the catastrophe, but God suffered him not to lose heart! He rose from the dust of despondency. The Spirit of the Lord was upon him. His cry was "Forward!" And once again he stood among you and again the thousands gathered and on, on, on, from that time, "Forward!" has been the cry.

"We will build a tabernacle," said we. Thirty thousand pounds! We stood back. Where would it come from? "The silver and the gold are Mine," was the promise of God. Some bold hearts went on, for our motto was "Forward!" And we prayed and worked and believed and lo--we entered this spacious house without a debt and we worship in it, remembering that of our own we gave unto God and that this goodly structure is a proof of the power of faith. Our motto was still "Forward!"

The pastor took one or two young men to educate. He soon had a dozen. He asked your help, you helped him. He had a score. Some said it was too many. He had forty--before long fifty--now seventy. And still the cry is, "Forward! Forward!" What I want to do tonight is just to stir your souls with a little of the old enthusiasm, to scatter among you some coals of that holy fire which once set you in a blaze. "Forward! Forward!" is what we want! Brethren, we want to be doing more for Christ!

Compared with our congregation I believe we are doing much, but still not what we might do--not what we ought to do. Here is this great city teeming with its multitudes and the proportion of evangelistic work which we take is far too small. "Forward! Forward!" At this time we have men ready to preach the Word. But we do not know where to find the room for them. There are rich men in this congregation and men in middling circumstances who might take a little room and pay the rent and let some young man come and preach in it and try to raise a Church in a destitute neighborhood. Some of you might cry, "Forward!" and do that.

Others of you in the Providence of God live in poor neighborhoods and you may have a room which holds twenty, perhaps. Could you not let some one preach in it? Preaching is the great weapon of God for pulling down strongholds. It will pull down the largest blocks of stone the enemy can pile together. Preach the Gospel, the gates of Hell shake! Preach the Gospel, prodigals return! Preach the Gospel to every creature--it is the Master's mandate and it is the Master's power--"the power of God unto salvation unto everyone that believes."

I would I could make every member of this Church feel in earnest about doing good. Do you not long to win souls? Do you not desire to spend and to be spent for your Master? I will venture to say that if you do not, you are not worthy of membership with such a Church as this! If no Divine zeal stirs you. If no heavenly fire has fallen on your soul, you might find a more congenial place of rest among some dull and sluggish people who care not for God. As for my own soul, God knows how I yearn over souls--I work and if there is any man living who can work more for God than I do, I envy him his strength and endurance!

It is not twelve, nor thirteen, nor fourteen, or fifteen hours a day which will satisfy me in the service of my Master. I wish I could be cut in pieces to preach His Gospel and that every drop of blood might tell it to my perishing fellow men. As I cannot do that, I do love to see my young men preaching the Word of God. They are so many new mouths for me, so many tongues for some of you who have no power of speech for your Master. They speak for you, if you have a share in their maintenance. But, oh, what I can do seems to be nothing but contributing a drop, but taking out a cupful from the great see of the world's sorrow and the world's sin!

Do help me! Do help me, I pray you! Brethren, pray for us! If you can do nothing else, pray that the Spirit of God may rest upon us in our preaching and in our efforts to extend His Kingdom--and may every one of you take a hand in this good work. I would sooner have half of you and have you all alive and earnest, than have the whole of you and have some of you a drag upon the wheels. If this Church does not serve God--mark these words, I speak, I think, prophetically--God will make this House a hissing and write "Ichabod" upon these walls!

Never was a Church more favored than you have been! For more than two hundred years God has given you a succession of faithful pastors. We have, each of us in our, lot strived to do our work. We have stood upon the walls of Zion and those who have gone before, at least, have not been found unfaithful. And as God helps me, neither will I be unfaithful either to God's Truth or to the souls of men.

But if with such appliances--with such preaching of the Gospel and helped so marvelously--

and so many of you great sinners saved from great sins, having had much forgiven. If you do not love much and serve much, O my God, let me not live to see the curse fall upon this Church! But at least in my day let the blessing continue! Yes, and when this head sleeps among the clods of the valley, find them better men than we are to preach the Word and let this Church still be a star in Your right hand to shine amidst the thick darkness of the world!

Dear Friends, if you are not in earnest about this, I am. Oh, we must not let this opportunity pass! There is much which you can do. I want you to help the heathen world, but I want you to begin with caring for this great heathen world of London. And if you can do nothing else, at least give us your prayers.

VI. I have done when I shall say that soon you and I will stand on the brink of Jordan's river. The deep sea of death will roll before us. Trusting in Jesus, washed in His blood, hoping in His mercy we shall not fear the last solemn hour. We shall hear the angel say, "Forward!" We shall touch the chilly stream with our feet, the flood shall fly, and we shall go through the stream dry-shod. If the flood gathers and the Jordan overflows its banks, still the Divine watchword, "Forward!" shall speed us on and we will enter Heaven's gates among the blood-washed throng and sing unto Him who has enabled us to triumph gloriously in obedience to that command, "Forward! Forward!" God help you to go forward and unto Him be praise forever and ever. Amen.

A Desperate Case--How to Meet It

A Sermon (No. 549)
Delivered on Sunday Morning, January 10th, 1864, by the
Rev. C. H. SPURGEON,
At the Metropolitan Tabernacle, Newington

"Then came the disciples to Jesus apart, and said, Why could not we cast him out? And Jesus said unto them, Because of your unbelief: for verily I say unto you, If ye have faith as a grain of mustard seed, ye shall say unto this mountain, Remove hence to yonder place; and it shall remove: and nothing shall be impossible unto you. Howbeit this kind goeth not out but by prayer and fasting."
-- Matthew 17:19-21.

THE NARRATIVE, of which our text forms a part, describes a scene which took place immediately after the transfiguration of our Lord. Not to divorce it therefore from its connection, let us glance at the antecedents of the case, that nothing may be lost by negligence, or that peradventure we may gain something by meditation.

How great the difference between Moses and Christ! When Moses had been forty days upon the mountaintop, he underwent a kind of transfiguration, so that his face shone with exceeding brightness when he came down among the people, and he was obliged to put a veil over his face; for they could not bear to look upon his glory. Not so our Saviour! He had been really transfigured with a greater glory than Moses could ever know, and yet, as he came down from the mount, whatever radiance shone upon his face, it is not written that the people could not look upon him, but rather they were amazed, and running to him, they saluted him. The glory of the law repelled; for the majesty of holiness and justice, drive the awed spirits away from God. But the greater glory of Jesus attracts; though he is holy, and just, and righteous too, yet blended with these there is so much of truth and grace that sinners run to Jesus, amazed at his goodness, attracted by the charming fascination of his love, and they salute him, become his disciples, and take him to be their Lord and Master. Some of you may be just now blinded by the dazzling brightness of the law of God. You feel its claims on your conscience, but you cannot keep it in your life. It is too high; you cannot attain to it. Not that you find fault with the law; on the contrary, it commands your profoundest esteem. Still you are in no wise drawn by it to God; you are rather hardened in your heart, and you may be verging towards the inference of desperation: "As it is impossible for me to earn salvation by the works of the law, I will continue in my sins." Ah, poor heart! Turn thine eye away from Moses, with all his repelling splendour, and look to Jesus, yonder, crucified for sinful men. Behold his flowing wounds, and thorn crowned head! He is the Son of God, and therein he is greater than Moses. He bear the wrath of God, and therein he shows more of God's justice than Moses' broken tablets could ever do. Look thou to him, and as thou feelest the attraction of his love, fly to his arms and thou shalt be saved.

How different the spirit of Moses and Jesus! When Moses comes down from the mountain, it is to purge the camp. He seems to grasp the fiery sword; he breaks the golden calf; he smites the idolaters; but when Jesus comes down from the mountain, he finds a strife in the camp, as Moses did; he finds his own apostles worsted and beaten, just as Aaron had been defeated by the clamours of the people; but he has not a word of cursing; there is a gentle rebuke--"O faithless and perverse generation, how long shall I be with you? how long shall I suffer you?" His actions are actions of mercy--no breaking in pieces, but healing; no cursing, but blessing: love sits smiling on his brow, as he touches the poor wretch who is almost dead with diabolical possession, and restores him to life and health. Go you then, to Jesus; leave the law and your own self-righteousness, for these can do nothing but curse you. Fly to Jesus, for be you whomsoever you may, there are pardons on his lips; there are blessings in his hands; there is love in his heart; and he will not disdain to receive even you.

How much of condescension there is in the manner of Christ! Our Lord, we have told you, had been very glorious on the mountain's top, with Moses and Elias, yet, when he comes down into the midst of the crowd, he doth not disdain the cry of the poor man, not refuse to touch him who was possessed with a devil. Observe my Masters condescension, for he deigns attention, and yet his manner softens into pity and presently it melts into a gracious sympathy, as if this was the only channel through which his peerless power could flow. Then remember, he is the same to-day as he was then.

"Now though he reigns exalted high,
His love is still as great:"--

He is willing now to receive sinners as when it was said of him, "This man receiveth sinners and eateth with them:" just as ready to receive you, poor sinners, as when he was called "The friend of publicans and sinners." Come to him. Bow at his feet. His love invites you still. Believe that the transfigured and glorified Jesus is still a loving Saviour, willing to pardon and forgive.

Once again what choice instruction there is in history! After Jesus had been absent for some time, he came back. You may ask for what purpose he had retired? Evidently he went up into the mountain to pray. It was while he was praying (and I make no doubt, fasting likewise) that the fashion of his countenance changed. By his own personal devotion, and by the Father's special revelation, he had thus come back, as it were, with great refreshment to carry on his ministry. Hence we become witnesses of a marvelous power which he immediately showed forth, and of no less remarkable counsel which he spoke to his disciples, when they felt their own weakness. Thus we have before us, on our text, a peculiar case--a patient, who utterly baffled the skill of all his disciples, healed at once by the great Master; and we have a reason given why the apostles themselves were not able to deliver him.

Let us look for a little time at this very sad case; not so singular either, methinks, but that we may find the round about us. Then let us notice the scene around the case--the father, the disciples, the scribes. Afterwards we shall joyfully observe the Saviour's coming into the midst and deciding all the difficulty; and, lastly, we shall attend to the reason he gives in private to his disciples, why they, before his coming, were utterly powerless to achieve the work.

I. First we have before us a VERY PECULIAR CASE.

It appears that the disciples had cast out devils of all sorts. Wherever they had gone, heretofore, this was their uniform testimony, "Lord, even the devils are subject unto us;" but now they are baffled. They seem to have encountered a devil of the worst kind. There are grades in devilry as there are in human sin. All men are evil, but all men are not alike evil. All devils are full of sin, but they are not all sinful to the same degree. Do we not read in Scripture, "Then goeth he and taketh unto him seven other spirits more wicked than himself?" It may be there is a gradation in the wickedness of devils, and perhaps, also, in their power to fulfil their wicked impulses. We can scarcely think that all devils are Satans. There seems to be one chief arch-spirit, one great Diabolus, who is an accuser of the brethren--one mighty Lucifer, who fell down from heaven and has become the prince of the powers of darkness. In all his hosts it is probable that there is not his like. He stands first and chief of those fallen morning stars; the rest of the spirits may stand in different grades of wickedness, a hierarchy of hell. This poor wretch seems to have been possessed of one of the worst, most potent, and violent, and virulent of these evil spirits. I believe, brethren, that here we have a picture of a certain class of individuals who are not only desperately sinful, but subject to extraordinary impulses which carry them to infernal lengths and depths of infamy; they are incapable of restraint, a terror to their kinfolk, and a misery to themselves. All men are sinful, as I have said before; but the power of depravity in some men is much stronger than in others; at least, if it be not intrinsically stronger, yet it certainly has manifestations in some which we have never perceived in common among men. Let us try and pick out the case according to the narrative. How frequently, dear friends, too frequently, alas! have we seen young people who have answered to the description here given. They have had a precocity of wickedness. When Jesus asked the father, "How long has he been in this way?" the answer was, "Of a child." I remember having once known such a child, over whom, paroxysms of passion came, in which his face would turn black. When he was able to run about, and was sent to a public school, a flint-stone, a club, a brick-bat, anything which might come next to hand, he would throw, without a moment's thought, at any one who vexed him. His knife would be drawn from his pocket and opened in an instant. The young assassin has often been prevented from stabbing others by a careful hand and watchful eye which guarded him. We have noticed this, I say, in the very young. They begin to lie early and to thieve soon, and the young lip even assays to swear, while the anxious mother cannot understand where the child could have learnt it. You have protected such a child from contamination, and seemed to shut him in and girdle him about with holy influences; and yet, in these desperate instances, as soon as ever the child could know the right from the wrong, he has deliberately chosen the wrong with a violence of self-will and recklessness of consequences altogether unusual. Some such cases we have seen. O, may God grant it never be your lot or mine, to be the parents of such children. Yet such there have been, and such men there are who have grown up now, and the youthful passions of their childhood have become developed; and you may find them with the low forehead and dark scowling eye, if you will, in our prison-houses. Or if you see them in the streets, you may hopefully wish that they may be in prison ere long, for they are unsafe abroad. Of a child they seem to have been possessed with the chief of devils, and to have been carried captive by him at his will.

This lad seems also to have been afflicted with what is here called lunacy, which was, indeed, only a form of epilepsy. He was constantly subjected, it seems, to epileptic fits; for I think we can hardly understand lunacy to mean anything short of occasional madness. Attacks of such outrageous violence would come upon him, that there would be no enduring him. He would then dash himself into the fire, or if water were near, he would attempt self destruction by plunging in to it. We have met with persons of this kind, perfectly outrageous and beyond all command, when fits of evil came upon them. I will instance cases which I have observed.

I know a man now, he may be here this morning; if he is , he will recognize his own portrait. At times he is as reasonable as anyone I could wish to associate with. He enjoys listening to the Word of God. He is, in some respects, an amiable, excellent, and respectable man. But occasionally fits of drunkenness come upon him, in which he is perfectly powerless under the influence of the demon; and while it lasts, it matters not, even when he knows he is wrong, a thousand angels could not drag him from it. He is thrown into the water of self-destruction, and he will continue in it. You may urge him and reason with him, and you may think--oh, how often some have thought who love him!--he will never do that again; he is too sensible a man; he has been too well-taught; the Word of God has had such an effect upon him, that he will never do it again; yet he does; he repeats the old paroxysms, and has done for twenty or thirty years; and, if he lives, unless sovereign grace prevent it, he will die a drunkard, as sure as he is a living man, and go from his drink to damnation.

Another case, from which I likewise draw from life. The man is kind, tender, and generous--generous to a fault. He has a home--he had one, I ought to say--he had a home, and he was the light of it. No one ever suspected him--that is, in his better times--of any grievous faults; but sometimes--and this has been concealed by many an indulgent friend--an attack of lasciviousness comes upon him, and at such seasons it matters not what the temptation may be, nor how foul the vice may be, the man runs into it. If you should meet him in the street, and talk with him, and argue with him, it would be all time and labour thrown away; nay, I have known him break up his home, and cross the sea to go to another land, that he might indulge his vile passions without rebuke, or the restraint of associating with former friends. He will come back again, broken-hearted, wondering that he ever could be such a fool; but he will go again. It is in him. The devil is in him, and, unless God casts it out, he will do the same again, deliberately choosing his own damnation. Though he knows it, yet so possessed of the love of sin is he, that when the fit comes upon him, this diabolical epilepsy, he falls into sin with his whole might and power.

I might go on describing cases of the kind, but you will not need that I should picture any more; it could only be to vary the different forms of sin. However, let me try once more. A lad had as good a father as a child could have. He was bound apprentice. It became whispered in a few weeks that little moneys were missing. The father was very grieved, so indeed was the master, and the matter was quietly hushed up. A little while after the same thing occurred. The indentures were cancelled, and nothing more was said of it; but the father was sorely perplexed. He looked out for some other situation for the boy where he might, perhaps, recover his character. After a time it was precisely the same again. Bad companions had got hold of him, or rather, he had become a ringleader among other bad companions. Well, something else must be tried. It was tried. He has had twenty situations, and they have all been thrown up from the very same cause. And now, what think you is his treatment of his parents? Instead of being grateful for the repeated kindness and longsuffering shown to him, he will break out sometimes into such dreadful passions, that even the lives of his parents are scarcely safe; and when he has been in his old haunts a little more than usual, he is really so terrible a being, that his mother who loves him and who weeps over him, would almost as soon see a fiend from hell as see him; for when he comes home, everything goes wrong; confusion, is in the house, and terror in every heart; he acts precisely as if he were a madman. They have said, "Send him to Australia, or send him to America"--where they do send many of that sort--but if he goes there he will turn up, sooner or later, at the foot of the gallows; he is desperately set on evil, and nothing turns him aside. He tears and foams at the mouth with passion; his whole heart goes forth outrageously after anything like vice, and there appears to be not one redeeming trait in his character; or, if there be, it only seems to be subjected tot he power his lusts. He devises means to be more mighty to do mischief in the world.

What dreadful cases these are! Wherefore am I talking of them? Dear friends , I have taken them because it has been laying upon my heart to encourage and comfort you who are constrained to carry a daily cross in having such relations and such children as these. It is one of the heaviest afflictions which can come upon you.

In the case before us, the child was both deaf and dumb--not, I suppose, through any organic effect, but through the epilepsy, and the Satanic possession. So often we have seen children--shall I look them in the face this morning, as I stand here?--they are no children now--who are positively deaf to all spiritual sounds. They have been pleaded with, but it is vain. They know the truth, they know the whole truth, but they do not know the power of it. They are never absent from family prayer, nor in any prayer are they ever forgotten by their parents. They come to this place; they attend our classes; they go to revival services. Now and then there is something like a little emotion, but it does not come to much; they are precisely similar to the deaf adder which cannot be charmed, charm we never so wisely. Others of the family have been converted. Nearly all the household has now been brought to Christ. Lydia has had her heart opened; God has been much pleased to call young Timothy; but this one remains, and after much anxiety, much effort, much labour, no good has been achieved. The adamant seems as soft as their heart, and the ear of the deaf as much alive to rebuke as their conscience. This again is a very sad case.

I meet sometimes, too, with cases of another kind--persons who are beset with very high doctrine, who have got the devil in them, puffing up their fleshly minds with a vain conceit of sound understanding, and degrading their carnal profession with a loathsome impurity of heart and life. You will talk with them; they will tell you they wish to be saved--would give their right arm to be saved; but it is not in their power. You bid them believe in Jesus. They have no sense, they tell you, of the need of a Saviour; they are not in a fit state to believe. When God's time comes, the thing will occur. They love high doctrine; they will hear nothing else but it; but then their Sunday, if there is a temptation which comes across their path, will be spent anywhere but in the worship of God; and during the week they give way to all sorts of sins. Whatever temptation comes, they go after it. The comfort they get from their religion, which they wrap about them like a cloak, is this--that no minister speaks the truth except one or two; that the truth is fatalism; that all they have to do is to be carried along like dead, inanimate logs down the stream, and that they are not at all responsible; or if they are responsible, it is merely to maintain with unflinching hardihood their own crude sentiments. I have seen some of these people--good people in their own way too--of whom I have thought that the conversation of drunkards was more hopeful than theirs; for that damnable fatalism, which by some is put instead of the predestination of the Scriptures, has locked them up--put them in an iron cage: and so they are beyond the reach of help, going on in their sin, rejecting the gospel of Christ, while assaying to be connoisseurs of its choicest mysteries.

Now, brothers and sisters, why are such cases as these permitted? Why doth the Lord allow the devil thus to fill the soul with sin?

I think it is, first, to show that there is a reality of sin. If we were all moral and outwardly respectable, we should begin to think sin was but a fancy. These daring sinners show the reality of it.

It is to manifest the reality of divine grace; for when these are saved, then it is we wonder, and we are compelled to say, "There is something in this. If such a hard, iron nature yet melts before the power of divine love, there must be a majesty in it."

It is to humble us too, to throw us on our back, and let us see how utterly powerless human agency is. When you cannot get in the thin end of the wedge, much less the whole wedge; when the ploughshare breaks on the edge of a hard rock; when the edge of the sword turns against the armour, then it is to draw yourself out of self to God. You see it is a deadly evil, where only omnipotence can help. Your soul says, "Lord, put out thine arm! Now do it, and the glory shall be thine." This is probably the chief reason; it is in order that God may get great glory to himself. He lets the devil have it all his own way. "There," he says, "pick your own ground, fight in your own territory, manoeuvre in your own way, and, with a word, I will crush your power." He gives Satan great advantage, lets him entrench himself firmly in the soul from youth up, so that the victory may be splendid to the greatest degree.

We have thus before us now, for our sorrowful contemplation, the case of one whose disease mocks the physician, laughs at all human endeavours, and defies the watchful care of mild and gentle treatment to mitigate its force, or ameliorate its fearful symptoms.

II. Turn we now with passing glance, to LOOK AT THE SCENE AROUND. The company is made up of five sorts of people.

There are the scribes--cynics, methinks, to a man--"We told you so! We told you so!" they say. "Your Master pretended to give you power to cast out devils. No such thing! you cannot cast out devils. Those whom you healed were not truly possessed. Little enough was ever the matter with them, and so they got better. They were fanciful, and they believed you through enthusiasm. The dupes of credulity, your incantations bewitched them, and so they got better. But you cannot cast out a devil--you cannot cast that devil out." "Now then," says one of the scribes to Andrew, "cast it out. Come, Phillip, try what you can do!" And inasmuch as after all trying, the devil would not go out--"Ah! just so!" they say, "they are impostors. There is nothing in it" Just recall it, friends, to your own memories, have not you seen men of that kind? "Ah yes," they say, " the gospel converts one sort of people, such as always go to places of worship, the more intelligent and respectable of the community, but, you see, it is no good in these tough cases. These hardened ones--it cannot touch them. They are beyond its power." "Aha!" they say, "where is the boasted might of this great physician? He can heal your finger-aches; he does not know how to make these foul diseases fly."

Then here is the poor father, all dejected. "I brought him to you--I knew you did cast out devils, and I thought you could cast my son's devil out, and he would be healed. I am disappointed in you all. Yet I do think your Master can do it, but I am not sure that even he can. If such excellent apostles, as you are, have tried so hard, and have failed, I do not think there can be any chance for me. I am full of unbelief. O, I wish I had never brought my child here at all, to make a public spectacle of him, that he might be a witness to your failures." That is the poor father. Perhaps that poor father is here this morning and he is saying, "Ah, I do believe, but still I am full of unbelief. I have brought my daughter; I have brought my child under the sound of the Word; I have prayed, and wrestled with God in prayer, and my child is not saved." "I have brought my husband," says one good woman, "but he is just as full of Satan as he ever was. I must give it up in despair."

And then, there are the disciples, and they look pitiable indeed. "Well," they say, "we do not know how to account for it. We cannot tell you how it is. We have said the same in this case that we were wont to say in others." "Why" says one of them, "when I went abroad and just said In the name of Jesus Christ I command thee to come out of him,' the unclean spirit always did come out in every other case. I cannot comprehend this. I must give it up." "We all must give it up," says the apostles. For some unknown cause, this seems to be quite out of the catalogue of cases which we are commissioned to cure. And so we sometimes hear dejected ministers, after preaching long at such hard shells as these--they say, "Well, we cannot understand it. The gospel is the power of God unto salvation to every one that believeth.' Oh, it must be that these are fore-ordained unto damnation; we must give it up." That is how unbelieving ministers talk--or at least the most part of ministers in their season of misgiving and chagrin.

But then there is the general crowd. They are neither this way nor that. They say they will see fair. "Come, clear the ring out. If Jesus Christ be not an impostor--if he be God--certainly he can heal this poor man." Now here is the test and the ordeal, "If that man be not healed, we," says the crowd, "will not believe; but, if he be, then we will believe that Jesus Christ is sent of God." O dear friends, how often we have thought of those very hard cases in this way. There are hundreds of undecided people looking on and saying, "Ah, if So-and-so were converted, then I should say there was something in it. If truly we could have a new heart and a right spirit, then I, too, would turn to God with full purpose of heart.

There was the fifth party there, and that was the devil himself. Oh, how triumphant was he! "Ah!" he seemed to say, "try your exorcism; go on with your words; preach at him; pray at me; weep over me; do what you will, you cannot get me out." There he seems to stand intrenched within the stronghold of the poor tortured heart. "Do your best, do your worst, I am not afraid of you. I have got this man, and I will keep him. I have so fixed myself in him that no power shall ever be able to heal him." So we seem to hear that vile shriek of hell over some men, "Yes," saith he, "I will trust him to go into Spurgeon's Tabernacle. I know the thousands there have felt the power of the Holy Ghost in making new men of them, this is a case I can trust. There is nothing that will ever touch him. The great hammer has knocked the chains off many, but it cannot touch his chains; they are harder than iron. I have no fear for him;" and perhaps he is gloating his thoughts now with the torments of the man in another world. Ah, thou foul fiend! if our Master should come here this morning, thou shouldst sing another tune. if he should say, "Come out of him thou foul spirit," thou wilt go back howling to thy vile den; for his voice can do what our voice never could have done. And may we not easily realize such a scene enacted in this congregation? You have the scoffers, you have the anxious parent, the ministry confessedly powerless in the matter; the crowd looking on, and the devil rejoicing that such cases are quite beyond human strength. What more can you want to vivify the picture before your imagination?

III. But look! THE MASTER COMES.

Ah! the master comes! Forthwith the scene changes. The lieutenants and the captains who began the battle did not understand the art of war; the were precipitant and hasty. The right wing was broken; the left began to reel; the centre almost fails. The trumpets of the adversary begin to sound a victory. Here they come--their dread artillery in front. What will become of the army now? Hold! Hold! What is that I see? A cloud of dust. Who comes galloping there? It is the commander-in-chief. "What are you at?" says he, "What are you at?" In a moment he sees this is not the way to fight. He comprehends the difficulties of the case in an instant. "Forward there! Forward There! Backward there!" The scale is turned. The mere presence of the commander-in-chief has changed the whole face of the field; and now, ye adversaries, ye may turn your backs and fly. It was so in Jesus' case exactly. His lieutenants and captains--the apostles--had lost the day. He comes into the field; comprehends the state of the case. "Bring him hither to me," says he, and the poor wretch, foaming and tormented, is brought to him, and he says, "Come out of him, thou unclean spirit." The thing is done; the victory achieved; the undecided receive Christ as a prophet; the scoffers' mouths are shut; the trembling father rejoices, and the poor demoniac is cured.

And yet when Jesus Christ came to cure this poor man, he was in as bad a state as he well could be. Nay, the very presence of the Saviour seemed to make it worse. As soon as ever the devil perceived that Christ was come he began to rend and tear his poor victim. As quaint old Fuller says--like a bad tenant whose lease is out, he hates the landlord, and so he does all the damage he can, because he has got notice to quit. Often just before men are converted, they are worse than ever; there is an unusual display of their desperate wickedness, for then the devil hath great wrath, now that his time is short.

The struggles of this child are appalling. The devil seemed as if he would kill him before he would be healed; and after great paroxysms of the most frightful kind, the poor youth laid upon the ground, pale, and still as a corpse, insomuch that many said, "He is dead." It is just the same with many conversions of these desperate sinners. Their convictions are so terrible; frequently the work of the devil within them keeping them from Christ is so furious that you would give up all hope. You say, "That man will be driven mad; those acute feelings, the intense agony of his spirit will rob him of all mental power, and then in abject persecution he will die in his sin." Ah! dear friends, this again is only a piece of Satan's infamy. He knew, and knew right well that Christ would set that poor young man free, and therefore he sets upon him with all his might, to torment him while he may. Have I any such desperate case among my hearers this morning--one who has been as a son of Belial among the children of men? Is the devil tormenting you to-day? Do you feel tempted to commit suicide? Are you urged to some freak of yet greater sin in order to drown your griefs and strangle your conscience? O poor soul, do no such thing, for my Master will soon stoop over you, and take you by the hand and lift you up, and your comfort shall begin, because the unclean spirit is cast out. "Ah! he means to destroy me," says the soul under conviction. Nay, soul, God does not destroy those whom he convinces of sin. Men do not plough fields which they have no intention to sow. If God ploughs you with conviction he will sow you with gospel comfort, and you shall bring forth a harvest of his glory. As a woman at her work first plies the needle with its sharp prick, and then draws the thread after it, so in your case the sharpness of sorrow for sin will be speedily followed by the silver thread of joy and peace in believing.

And oh, mark it! The vision just now, up there on the mountain of glory, resolved itself into "Jesus only." His peerless radiance eclipsed every other. So, too, it is "Jesus only," down there in the valley. His matchless grace can encounter no rival. Keep this forever in your mind's eye--it is the Master who did it all. His appearance on the scene removed all difficulties. In such extreme cases, there will be, and there must be, a most eminent display of God's power; and that power may be unassociated with means. Under any circumstances, it will be the Lord alone doing it, to the praise and glory of his grace.

IV. Now, we come to the last, and perhaps the most important part of the sermon. The riddle is perplexing. "WHY COULD NOT WE CAST HIM OUT?" Let the Master tell us the reasons why these cases thwart our power.

The Saviour said it was for want of faith--want of faith. No man may expect to be the means of the conversion of a sinner without having faith which leads him to believe that the sinner will be converted. Such things may occur, but it is not the rule. If I can preach in faith that my hearers will be saved, they will be saved. If I have no faith, God may honour his Word, but it will be in no great degree; certainly he will not honour me. Abandoned sinners, if converted by means, are usually brought under the power of divine grace through ministers of great faith. Have you observed--there were persons who heard all the small fry of the Whitefieldian age; they had listened to this preacher and to that. Under whom were they converted? Under Mr. Whitefield, because Mr. Whitefield was a man of masterly faith. He believed that the lost could be reclaimed--that the worst diseases could be healed, the most heinous, abandoned, profligate, blasphemous sinners could be saved. He preached to them as if he expected the deaf would be charmed by the gospel melody, and the dead would be quickened at the commanding call of the great Redeemer's name. At Surrey Chapel, over yonder, in Rowland Hill's day, some of the grossest blackguards and biggest scamps who ever infested London, were saved. Why? Because Rowland Hill preached the gospel to big sinners, and believed the fact of big sinners being converted. The respectable people of his day said, "Oh, yes! it is only tag, rag, and bob-tail who go to hear Mr. Hill." "Just so," said Mr. Hill, " and welcome tag, and welcome rag, and welcome bob-tail; they are the very people that I want" "What is the good of such people as they are, going to hear the gospel? Why does Mr. Hill try to preach to harlots and thieves?" they said. "They are just the very people," said Mr. Hill. "I believe that these people can be saved." It was want of faith in the others; for if a man have faith as a grain of mustard seed, let it be ever so little, yet, if it is true, it is mighty in proportion to its power. Mr. Hill had the power of

faith, and he was the means of the conversion of very great sinners. A few years ago it was utterly hopeless to try and reclaim fallen daughters of sin, but a few men had faith that it could be done, and it has been done; and I will now make bold to say that if there be a great sinner here, such as I tried to describe just now, some gross case of infernal possession, if that person be not saved, it is for the want of faith in our case. If we have brought that person before God, and have not been anxious about his salvation, and God has not heard that prayer, it is because we could not believe it possible such a case could be saved. If God gives you the power to believe that any soul will be saved, it will be saved; there is no doubt about that.

Still, our Saviour added, "Howbeit this kind goeth not out but by prayer and fasting." What does he mean by that? I believe he meant that in these very special cases ordinary preaching of the Word will not avail, and ordinary prayer will not suffice. There must be an unusual faith, and to get this there must be an unusual degree of prayer; and to get that prayer up to the right point, there must be, in many cases, fasting as well. No doubt there is something special about the admonition to prayer, from the association in which it stands. One sort of Christian will use formal supplications; and the petitions they ask are founded upon a sense of propriety, without any glow of feeling. Another sort will wait for the Spirit to move them; and when certain impulses stimulate their minds, they rejoice in a sense of liberty. Yet I show you a more excellent way There be those who watch unto prayer, wait before the Lord, seek his face, and exercise patience till they get an audience. Such disciples continue in their retirement until they have an experience of access for which they crave.

And what is fasting for? That seems to be the difficult point. It is evidently accessory to the peculiar continuance in prayer, practised oftentimes by our Lord, and advised by him to his disciples. Not a kind of religious observance, in itself meritorious, but a habit, when associated with the exercise of prayer, unquestionably helpful. I am not sure whether we have lost a very great blessing in the Christian Church by giving up fasting. It was said there was superstition in it; but, as an old divine says, we had better have a spoonful of superstition than a porringer full of gluttony. Martin Luther, whose body, like some others, was of a gross tendency, felt as some of us do, that in our flesh dwelleth no good thing, in another sense than the apostle meant it; and he used to fast frequently. He says his flesh was wont to grumble dreadfully at abstinence, but fast he would, for he found that when he was fasting, it quickened his praying. There is a treatise by an old Puritan, called, "The soul fattening institution of fasting," and he gives us his own experience that during a fast he has felt more intense eagerness of soul in prayer than he had ever done at any other time. Some of you, dear friends, may get to the boiling point in prayer, without fasting. I do think that others cannot, and probably if we sometimes set apart a whole day for prayer for a special object, we should at first feel ourselves dull, and lumpish, and heavy. Then let us resolve, "Well, I shall not go down to my dinner. I shall stop here. I feel anxious for a praying frame of mind, and I will keep alone; and if when the time for evening meal came on, we should say, "I feel a little craving of hunger, but I will satisfy them with some very slender nutriment--a piece of bread, or something of the kind--and I will continue in prayer," I think that very likely towards evening our prayers would become more forcible and vehement than at any other part of the day. We do not exactly recommend this for those who are weak. There are some men with little or no encumbrance of flesh about them; but others of us of a heavy make, with sluggishness for a temptation, have to cry out because we are rather like stones on the ground than birds in the air. To such, I think, we can venture to recommend it from the words of Christ. At any rate, I can suppose a father here setting apart a day of prayer, going on wrestling with God without any intermission; pleading with him till, as it was said of the famous martyr of Brussels, he would so pray that he forgot everything except his prayer; and when they came to call him to meat, he made no answer, for he had got out of all earthly things in his wrestling with the angel, that he could not think of anything besides. Such a man taking up the case of a gross sinner, I believe, would be the means of that sinner's conversion; and the reason why some are never brought to Christ, is, speaking after the manner of men, because we have not got the qualified to deal with them; for "this kind goeth not out save with prayer and fasting." When we have prayed, and have reached the point of true faith, then the sinner is saved by the mighty power of God, and Christ is glorified. Methinks I have some in this house who are ready to say, "Well, if such be the case, I will try it. I will take the Master at his word." Brother, brother, if half-a-dozen of us joined together, it might be better; nay, "If two agree as touching any one thin," it would be done. Let some of us put it to the test upon some big sinner, and see whether it does not come true. I think I may fairly ask you who are lovers of souls, who have eyes which do weep, and hearts which can feel, to try my Master's prescription, and see if the most unmanageable devil which ever took possession of a human heart, be not driven out, as the result of prayer and fasting, in the exercise of your faith. The Lord bless you in this thing, and may he bring us all to trust in Jesus by a saving faith. To him be glory, for ever and ever. Amen.

The Ship on Fire--A Voice of Warning

A Sermon (No. 550)
Delivered on Sunday Evening, November 8th, 1863, on the burning of the Ship "Amazon," by the Rev. C. H. SPURGEON,
At the Metropolitan Tabernacle, Newington

"Escape for thy life." -- Genesis 19:17.

"Thou hast magnified thy mercy, which thou hast shewed unto me in saving my life." -- Genesis 19:19.

HERE IS THE ALARM of mercy declaring the sinner's duty--"Escape for thy life." Here is the work of grace, and the gratitude of the sinner after he is saved. "Thou hast magnified thy mercy, which thou hast shewed unto me in saving my life."

The other day, there sailed down the Thames as stout a vessel as had ever ploughed the deep. The good ship "Amazon," had sailed the broad Pacific many a time, and what is there to hinder her from once more reaching America in safety? Who would refuse to underwrite her? Who among her crew or passengers has a fear for her safety? But in the book of providence, there was a black line against that ship, and never more could she reach her desired haven. The wind was exceedingly high: the vessel tarried awhile at Gravesend. There was a little improvement in the weather: she sailed a little further; but cast anchor again, and remained off Broadstairs. Matters went as usual in such weather. Night came on; the watch was changed as usual; the captain turned in, feeling that all was right and safe. The passengers were snug in their berths--a little the worse, perhaps, for the roll of the ship, but as assured of security as men could be. In a moment, what a change had taken place! A passenger perceives a smell of fire; the warning cry is raised. Everyone rushes upon deck. Attempts arc made to quench the fire; but when the hatches are lifted up, the wind rushes in, and the fire is fanned to a dreadful, all-devouring conflagration. Further effort is of no avail. Rockets are fired, as the signals of distress. The boats are let down, crowded with the passengers. A lugger puts off to her, and a steam-tug hastens to the rescue, and, thanks be unto the God of providence, all the passengers--the captain and chief officers last--are on board the vessels and carried to Margate, where they see the melancholy, and yet satisfactory spectacle of their vessel burning to the water's edge, and then disappearing from view.

Now, as the good brother who was captain to that vessel, constantly comes here when he is on shore, and as he is sitting in the midst of you to-night, I thought I might use the burning of this vessel as a picture of spiritual things, out of which I might make an illustrated sermon These things happen not without design, and should not escape without improvement.

Two things, then, to-night: they are both in the text and in the story of the ship on fire. First, an alarm--"Escape for thy life;" secondly, grateful acknowledgment--"Thou hast magnified thy mercy, which thou hast shewed unto me in saving my life."

I. First, AN ALARM.

We come here to-night, to raise an alarm. True ministers of God. are great alarmists. It is their duty to be like Barnabas, who was a son of consolation; but it is equally their duty to be like Boanerges--sons of thunder. Thunder does not rock men to sleep, and plays no pleasant tune for fools to dance to; with its crash and roar, it wakes a slumbering world, and its dread volleys, echoed peal on peal, afford no dulcet notes for dainty ears. God's servants should learn to thunder; for when God speaketh through them, the voice of the Lord is powerful and full of majesty; and in his temple doth everyone speak of his glory.

The alarm we have to give to-night, is that of the angel to Lot, with an emphasis of meaning--"Escape for thy life." It is an alarm suggested by tremendous danger. When the cry of "Fire! fire! fire!" ran along the decks, and the cabins, and the saloons of the "Amazon," everyone knew that there was no small danger to be encountered, for flame is a cruel tyrant and devours remorselessly. The very word "Fire!" has a razor-edge about it, cutting to the very quick. Terror has fire for her first-born. But the alarm we have to raise, is concerning a matter more terrific still--add to the word "Fire," that dreadful syllable "Hell," and then what shall more alarm than "Hell fire?" In that cry, we comprehend such weighty matters as eternity alone can reveal. The wrath to come! The judgment of the Eternal! The wrath of the Most High! Fire, when it is at its most furious pitch, is but a plaything compared with hell fire; yea, when it consumes a city; when it runs down the red lips of a volcano, and buries thousands; when it sets the sky and earth upon a blaze as in Egypt's plagues, it is but child's-play compared with the wrath of God, and that Tophet which is prepared of old, the pile whereof is wood and much smoke. Here is something at which the joints of a man's loins may well be loosed, for there is eternity in it, infinity in it, deity in it; and where these three are set against a man,. woe unto him. It is as when the fire is set in battle array against the stubble. Well may it be written by the prophet, "The sinners in Zion are afraid; fearfulness hath surprised the hypocrites. Who among us shall dwell with the devouring fire? Who among us shall dwell with everlasting burning?" Sinner, by the crushing terror of the woe which cometh, I beseech thee, "Escape for thy life."

It is a danger not to be overcome. The fire-engine was brought out upon the deck of the burning ship; attempts were made to extinguish the fire; but the mischief was far too much in power to be driven from its stronghold. The like may be boldly declared of the evil which cometh upon the ungodly. Sinner, your danger is such that you cannot contend with it by any power of your own. There is a fire of sin within you which you cannot quench; there is a fire of hell without you which no drops even of your own blood shall be able to extinguish. You are in a danger which you are unable to cope with. There is no possibility that if you remain in it, your utmost exertions or most strenuous efforts can avert the certain ruin which your state must bring upon you. If you neglect the only way of salvation, how can you escape? What awaits you but a fearful looking for of judgment and of fiery indignation? The pillars of heaven tremble and are astonished at the reproof of the Lord of hosts--how, then, canst thou endure the tempest of his anger, and the fury of his hot displeasure?

"O sinner, seek his face,
Whose wrath thou canst not bear;
Fly to the dying Savior's wounds,
And find salvation there."

It is a danger, too, a terrific danger which makes no exception to anyone. The captain is as much in danger as the poorest cabin-boy, if he cannot escape from the burning ship. The rich man, with ingots of gold in his cabin, will as certainly be burned alive as the poor traveler who could scarcely pay his passage. There is no distinction of persons in the judgments of God. Sinner, you may be great and mighty, but you shall go down to hell unless grace shall save you. Woman, thou mayst be amiable in thy temper and excellent in thy deportment, but thou shalt perish as surely as a harlot, unless Christ have pity upon thee. Man, thou mayst be upright, and shine before thy fellow-merchants as one of excellent repute, but the wrath of God abideth on thee except thou fleest to Jesus; for there is none other name given under heaven whereby ye must be' saved; and out of that name, and apart from that name, whoever thou mayst be, though thou wert monarch of seven empires, thou art still in danger. Rich and poor, high and low, learned and ignorant, my cry is to you all, "O earth, earth, earth, hear the Word of the Lord!"

Do not forget that we are in danger of a consuming fire--a danger which kills without remedy. It is not a fire which merely singes and scorches, but a fire which burns to ashes. As yonder ship must be burned up, and every passenger who cannot leave its burning deck must. be consumed, so you, O unconverted men, are in danger of utter destruction from the presence of the Lord. "For, behold, the day cometh, that shall burn as an oven; and all the proud, yea, and all that do wickedly, shall be stubble: and the day that cometh shall burn them up, saith the Lord of hosts, that it shall leave them neither root nor branch." I would I could speak upon this dreadful subject in a proper manner. Whitfield had tones and emotions which were fitting for such a subject. He would cry out, "Oh, the wrath to come! The wrath to come! The wrath to come!" He would cry, I say, until all his hearers responded. with, "What must we do to be saved?" And good Baxter, trembling lest be should he guilty of men's blood, while he delivered the message, as a dying man to dying men--knew the terrors of the law, and right earnestly he persuaded men to escape for their lives. O sirs, if I saw you. in a burning house, there were not half so much need of earnestness as when I see you in the midst of a mass of sin and corruption which must be consumed by God's anger, and you with it. Sinner, why wilt. thou die? What can ail thee? What besots thee that thou dost not perceive anything dreadful in the wrath of him who made thee? He can dash whole worlds to pieces--what can he not do with thee? Hast thou. learned to be callous when thou hearest of eternity? Hast thine ear grown cold to that dreadful word, "Condemnation?" Canst thou read the story of those to whom he said, "Depart, ye cursed," and not tremble? Canst thou know that thou art this day in danger of the judgment, and not be afraid? When the sword is sharp, and furbished, and taken out of its sheath, canst thou play about its edge? Canst thou yet make mirth? Then is there indeed, need for me to cry to thee, and for all God's faithful ministers to cry with louder voice than mine--"Escape! escape! escape for thy life."

The alarm of fire was needed because of the security of the persons in danger. Many on board the "Amazon" were sound asleep. Oh, how dreadful to be awakened out of sleep with the cry of "Fire! fire! fire! Some of them, when they awoke, seemed to have been so startled and so confused, that they had fairly to be dragged out of their berths that they might be rescued. There were none there, we have reason to believe, who would have been kept below through their own drunkenness or the carelessness of the crew. They were in a right state, with this exception, of course, that they were all alarmed--and men alarmed are not always ready to do the wisest thing, and as for the captain and his men they seem to have been as sensible as they were brave. My hearers, God's ministers have to deal with passengers much more difficult to handle. Are not men asleep? Till the voice of God awakens us, we are all asleep. How you and I walked for years, and years, and years, upon the brink of the grave, as utterly unconcerned as though we were to live for ever; and when sometimes we were a little impressed by the passing bell, or an open grave, or an earnest sermon, how soon we went back again to our old frivolity, and toyed with the flames of hell as though they were fancy's dream. It is not so now. God has awakened us; but we had never been awakened if the voice which awakes the dead had not cried in our ear, "Escape for thy life." Nay, worse, men are not only asleep, but when they do perceive their danger, they love their sins too well to leave them, even though hell stares them in the face. The best of them cry with Solomon's sluggard, "Yet a little sleep, a little slumber, a little folding of the hands to sleep." Sinner, how hard it is to bring thee to serious consideration of thy ways. We cannot touch thy wits, or make thee reason like a man of sound mind. Thou wilt sooner be damned by thoughtlessness thau give an hour's careful meditation to thy soul's affairs. We would fain drag thee out of thy sleeping berth, and even kick thee and strike thee, treating thee to rough usage, if we could by this means drag thee from the devouring flames; thou wouldst thank us well enough afterwards for these rough cuffs, if we could but wake thee. We hear complaints that the minister speaks too harshly and talks too much of judgment. Saved sinners never make that complaint. They know that nothing but these terrors will awaken some slumbering minds; and if they be awakened themselves, they are but too glad, however rough the means may have been. Are there not some in this house to-night who are hard, fearfully hard, to be brought to sober thinking, because they are drunken and besotted with sin? Some of you, with your Sunday trading, will rather gain your sixpences and your paltry pence on the Sunday, than find eternal felicity in faith in the Lord Jesus. Others of you, with your tap-room companions, with your theatres, your balls, and worse places still, where lust wears no mask, are cutting the throats of your poor miserable souls. You cannot give up your vices; you will sooner be damned than be Christians. Well, so it must be, sirs, if ye will have these things, and will pawn your souls for them, so it must be; you have chosen your own delusions, and you shall inherit them. But O, do listen once more, while we warn you in God's name, " Escape for thy life," and trifle no more with hell and heaven, with thine own soul and judgment, God and his dear bleeding Son. If every preacher in London should suddenly begin to preach nothing but alarms, it would all be needed, for what a secure and reckless city is this. If every corner in the street had a Jonah in it, and that Jonah's sermon were nothing but this--"Yet a few more days and thou shalt be destroyed!" it were not too much for a city so given to slumber. We have waxen rich; we have grown careless, till we have become like Nineveh of old, a people at ease, and dwelling carelessly Isaiah might well say concerning London--"Thou saidst, I shall be a lady for ever: so that thou didst not lay these things to thy heart, neither didst remember the latter end of it." Let us take heed unto ourselves lest in the world to come this carnal security of ours should be like faggots to the fire, and the remembrance of our sloth should pour oil upon the flames. O God, let the alarm be heard, to-night by those who crowd this house, for thou knowest that many of them are sound asleep.

Again, it is an alarm which requires instant attention. A man on board a vessel, when he hears the cry of "Fire!" must not stop to arrange his clothes; he must not be concerned to see that his face is washed, that he has bound together that little bundle of papers, or packed up the portmanteau, or counted over the little purse of gold, or even snatched his little property from the cabin. At once, at once, must he climb the stairs and reach the deck, or he will never have stairs to climb, nor feet to climb with. Now or never. Quick is the word. Waste a moment, and it is all over with you; the fire is upon you, for it tarries not in its march. So is it with you to-night who fear not God. "Escape for thy life," is a cry for the present moment. Now is the accepted time; behold, now is the day of salvation." Now, now, NOW. This is the only period God has allotted to you, take care that you use it, lest when your to-days are past, and you hope to see your to-morrow, you should have to spend your to-morrows in the pit of hell. Procrastination is not only the thief of time, but the thief of souls. Now is the day of salvation; I have never heard of any other day. I do not know, but I think this is one of the most difficult things in the gospel ministry, a matter worthy of the Holy Ghost's power--to make men seriously think about their souls at this present. I know, young man, you intend to

think of these things when you are ill; you expect to have a long time upon a sick-bed, and then you suppose all will be right before you die. Who told you you would ever lie upon a sick-bed at all? Yours may be a sudden death; and sudden death to such as you, are would be sudden damnation. As men stand upon the bank, and spring head-first into the water, so may you dash into hell. Death enters men's doors without knocking. The judgment may follow on the heels of your next sins. And what if you should lie upon a bed of sickness? You will have enough to do to bear the pain, to mourn over your weeping wife, and worry yourself about those little children who will be left fatherless: I tell you, sir, it is hard repenting upon a dying bed. Do not sew pillows to thine armholes, and make for thyself this fond hope, that thou shalt one day be saved. It is now or never, it is now or never with you. I speak as a prophet of God at this moment, I know I do; there are some of you to whom this now or never is a more applicable thing than you suppose. You will not see a new year. No Christmas festivities will be yours. You will be at home on Christmas-day, but it will be your long, lost home. "Set thine house in order; for thou shalt die, and not live." As the Lord my God liveth, before whom I stand, thus saith the Lord unto some of you--"There is but a step between you and death." Be warned, then, for as I will meet you on the other side the stream, at my Master's judgment-seat, I have bidden you give immediate, instantaneous attention to the Word of God. Consider your ways, O sinners, born to die. Believe in the Lord Jesus Christ, O trembler, and thou shalt be saved. Trust him, trust him. God help thee to trust Jesus to-night, for it is now or never with thy soul.

Again, this alarm demands of every one of us who are unsaved, an undivided attention. You have fifty things to think about. You tell me you have a thousand cares. O sirs, a man whose life is in danger, has no other care than to save his life. Did those who were rescued from the "Amazon," have time to save their money and their gold? We are told that they were utterly destitute when they landed at Margate, and what signifies it? Would not a flush of joy be on their cheeks because their lives were preserved! If one said to his fellow, "Where is thy purse?" "Oh," saith the other, "never mind my purse, I am in the lifeboat; my life is saved." What shall it profit you, if you gain the whole world, and lose your own soul? And what is the loss after all, if you lose the world, if you gain your soul? Nay, those on board the ship had not time to save their clothes. The instincts of self-preservation made them run, just as they were, half-naked, to the vessel's deck, and so must you. I know you will tell me you are not living to make money; if you could just make ends meet, keep your family, and supply the wants of your children--that is all--are you not to think of this? It is well and good; far be it from me to discourage prudent carefulness in all matters; it is your business to see to temporal matters, but still your paramount business must be your soul; even necessaries must not come between your soul and your most serious thoughts. You must see to this first and foremost, and remember there is a promise about it--"Seek ye first the kingdom of God, and his righteousness; and all these things shall be added unto you." Those persons who escaped from the blazing vessel had, some of them, even to suffer in body. We read of one who broke his arm in the medley of the escape, but what of that?* (*I hear since, from the friends of the second mate, that the man did not break his arm.) Better to escape with a broken arm, than fry in those horrible flames with every bone in its place. It would be very little comfort to the poor passenger to save his bones entire, and to have his body consumed. "It is better for thee to enter into life halt or maimed, rather than having two hands or two feet to be cast into everlasting fire." You are rightly considerate of your bodies, but still, if that poor body, which is to become worm's meat one day, is worthy of so much thought, how much more ought you to give to your immortal spirit, which is to live for ever with God in glory, or with fiends in torment? Think first, I pray you, think chiefly, think now to-night with undivided heart, with consecrated thought upon your soul. Let comforts go, let pelf go, let raiment go, let life itself go--but do see to that which is better than life--thy soul--thine everlasting destiny.

Now, the alarm which I have tried to give--"Escape for thy life!" seems to me to suggest a very solemn question. "How can I escape?" says cue. Dost thou sincerely ask that question--"What must I do to be saved?" Remember there is but one way of rescue--the lifeboat of faith must put thee into the vessel of salvation--Christ Jesus. Stop in thine own vessel, and thou art burned; leap into those floods of wrath, and thou art drowned; get into that boat of saving faith, let that boat bear thee into the vessel of Christ Jesus, and thou art safe. Sinner, the road of salvation is, out of self into Christ. There are only two steps to heaven--out of self, into Christ. That man who has left himself as a burning vessel behind, left sin and left self-righteousness as a thing to be destroyed--that man who has taken Christ to be his all in all, and takes the cross to be the only thing to which he clings, is safe. Escape, I pray thee, for thy life, awakened and seeking sinner, for Jesus is the only foundation, he only is thy rock and thy salvation; come to him for shelter, and you are saved.

To conclude this matter of alarm, our meditation arouses a very solemn enquiry--Will all be safe? Will all in the vessel escape? What joy must there have been in the captain's heart when he heard that not one had been left to burn in the vessel! Will all escape? Will every hearer in this huge house of prayer to-night be a singer in heaven? Dare we, in the judgment of charity, hope so? Well, well, let us try to hope, if so your charity wishes it, but I fear me, I fear me it will be hope without any grounds; for there are some here who love the drunkard's cup, others who vomit the swearer's oaths, and some who have the proud, self-righteous look which God hateth. O that we could hope that these would be transformed by grace through Jesus Christ, that so they might be saved! I am, I own it, very much afraid that all of you will not be saved, but that some of you will perish in your iniquities. It is not, however, our duty to pry into futurity, let us therefore, turn to that which far more concerns us, our own personal salvation. The enquiry changes--"Shall I be saved? If there be an alarm given, Escape for thy life!' Shall I be saved?" And what if it should be the preacher's lot to be lost for ever! What, if after talking to you this morning of being sick of love to Christ, he should have to hear those doleful words, "I never knew you, depart, ye cursed!" And what if this were to be the lot of the church-officers who sit around me, or of any one amongst you? Brother, you have passed the sacramental cup to others, what if the cup of devils be your portion for ever and ever! My brethren and sisters in Church fellowship, you may well put the question as did the apostles of old, "Lord is it I?"

"Shall I be banished for my life,
And yet forbid to die?
Shall I endure eternal death,
Yet death for ever fly?"

Shall it be so! My dear hearer, thou who makest no profession of religion, will you ask the question, Shall I, shall I perish in devouring flames, or shall I escape? The answer to that question, so far as you are concerned, at this moment, must depend upon whether there is now a work of grace in your heart. If thou believest that Jesus is the Christ, thou canst never perish. If thou dost not, and wilt not believe, thy destruction is most sure. O God Almighty, thou who alone canst impress the heart, lead everyone of us now to take such sure hold of Christ that we may never perish, neither may any pluck us out of his hand.

II. My time is fled, woe is me, when I had meant to have spoken with my whole heart upon another topic. It was GRATITUDE. Well, we will just run over the points, although most briefly. I will hope that you and I are saved; I will trust that we have been put into thy grace-vessel; I will believe that we have laid hold on Christ; may me belief be warranted by facts? Then this calls for gratitude. Gratitude of what kind? Gratitude that I was awakened. O my God, I bless thee that I was not permitted to sleep the sleep of death. I thank thee for that fever which made me fear, that loss which made me think, that dear dead babe which brought the parent to a Savior's feet. I bless thee, Lord, for the minister's earnest voice which shook me in my slumbers, for a mother's tears which fell like cold drops on my sleeping brow, and made me wake. I thank thee, O God, that though others slumber, yet, thou hast awakened me, and made me look to my soul's concerns. It is no slight mercy to be able to hear the trumpet of warning. It is a foundation mercy, but it is not the least of mercies to have an awakened conscience.

Secondly, I would thank God, and let every believer join with me, that when you and I were awakened, the ship was not out to sea. If the "Amazon" had been far out to sea when the cry of "Fire" was given, what must have been the result? How few could have escaped! But there she was, close to land. You and I, when we were awakened, were not in hell--not like the rich man, lifting up our eyes where hope could never come--we were still on praying ground, still on pleading terms with God, still off the Foreland, still where mercy could come to us, and grace could meet us. Sinner, if you have been awakened to-night, thank God for this, thank him that the trumpet which wakes you is not the trumpet of the archangel summoning you to judgment, but the silver trumpet of God's messenger of mercy, inviting you to mercy banquet.

Let us thank God it did not blow harder, for there might have been much trouble in reaching the boat. When you and I were awakened to a sense of sin, it might have been just when death was coming, or when the terrors of conscience would have been too much for us, and when the fears of death might have kept us from a Savior. But, blessed be God, when we were aroused there was wind enough, we were conscience-stricken and smitten, but still not too much, or else the fire had been too vehement, and we had not escaped. Thank God, then, that he awakened us while there was really time to avail ourselves of the covenant lifeboat.

Let us be thankful again, that we could use the signals. I told you that the vessel sent up its rockets--signals of distress. Ah! what a thousand mercies it was that we could pray. I remember well when this was the only comfort my bursting spirit had, I could pray. Oh, to be on pleading terms with God! Thank God for this, awakened sinner, bless God for this. If you have not got so far as being completely saved, yet do praise him that you are allowed to fire off the rockets of desires, sighs, groans, sobs, tears, longings, and pantings, and that you can send them up where God can see them. Your cries, and groans, and tears will yet bring comfort and peace from heaven through the Lamb's redeeming blood. Rejoice, my beloved brethren, that the Lord has not abolished a mercy-seat, nor forgotten to be gracious. He saith "not to the seed of Jacob, Seek ye me in vain." He waits to be gracious. He delighteth in mercy. Before you call he will answer, and while you are yet speaking he will hear.

Thank God that there were good officers on board to direct the passengers. Without firm authority, men become a mob, and then, with every appliance which might save, few are rescued. Awakened sinner, be grateful that you have gospel ministers. Oh! what a mercy to have a gospel ministry! What an awful thing to sit under a half-and-half milk-and-water, yea-and-nay ministry, as was my lot when under conviction. I attended different places of worship, but what I heard was not the gospel. And I venture to say it, that a few years ago, in nine places out of ten in London, and in the suburbs, and throughout England, such a thing as the gospel was not preached, except by accident. It is preached NOW. It is not preached now as it should be, but it is preached now. What I mean by the gospel, is the doctrine that Jesus Christ came to save sinners, and that the simple trusting upon him is saving faith. This is a doctrine which the revival has brought up more clearly, and which the revival keeps before the public mind; but before that great movement came, it was a doctrine ignored and cast behind; too much of the preaching was a dry morality, or else philosophy which might tickle the ears of men who claimed intellect, but could never move the heart. Oh, thank God, poor sinner, that you do hear it rung in your ears--Come as you are! Come as you are! You hear the gospel sung to you:--

"Just as I am, without one plea,
But that thy blood was shed for me,
And that thou bidd'st me come to thee,
O Lamb of God, I come! I come!
Just as I aim-thy love I own,
Has broken every barrier down:
Now, to be thine, yea, thine alone,
O Lamb of God, I come! I come!"

We hold up to you no ceremonies, no feelings, no works, no orthodoxies; we only hold up Christ, Christ crucified, a substitute for sinners, a substitute for you if you trust him; and we tell you again and again, till we half fear of tiring you, that, trusting Jesus, you are saved. Now we have reason, if saved, to be grateful to God for gospel officers.

Then how grateful ought you and I to be that the ship is come to the rescue. Jesus came all the way from heaven to earth to save us--"Who though he was rich, yet for our sakes became poor, that we through his poverty might be made rich." How shall we be grateful enough for this unspeakable gift?

"O, for this love let rocks and hills
Their lasting silence break,
And all harmonious human tongues
The Savior's praises speak."

Better still: how grateful we ought to be that we have got on board that ship. Oh! joy! joy! joy! that blessed step which set me upon Christ! that blessed act which made me one with him. My soul would repeat now that grace-wrought deed of faith.

"A wounded, weak, and helpless worm,
On Christ's kind arms I fall;
Be thou my strength and confidence,
My Jesus and my all."

Be grateful for this; and, sinner, if thou canst now step into Christ and trust him with thyself, make earth ring with thy joy, and make heaven resound with thy praise.

Our gratitude, methinks, will be greatest of all when we get safe on shore, and look on this old hulk, the burning world, without a fear; we, will see her blaze and cast her dreadful splendours over the infinite leagues of space, until beings in far-off worlds shall ask, "What is this? A world on fire, whose elements dissolve with fervent heat." But we, caught up together with the Lord, to dwell for ever with him, shall look on with complacency, having lost nothing because saved in him; having found in him our Savior, better than all we had before, and being, once for all on heaven's terra firma, never to put to sea again, never to fear tempest, rock, wreck, or fire; but saved! saved! saved eternally!

Escape, sinner, escape for thy life. Remember, though thus I talk to thee, if thou shalt escape, free grace must have all the praise; and in the language of good Lot, thou wilt have to say--"Thou hast magnified thy mercy in saving my life." May God send you away with a blessing, for Jesus' sake. Amen.

Faith and Life

A Sermon (No. 551)
Delivered on Sunday Morning, January 24th, 1864, by the
Rev. C. H. SPURGEON,
At the Metropolitan Tabernacle, Newington

"Simon Peter, a servant and an apostle of Jesus Christ, to them that have obtained like precious faith with us through the righteousness of God and our Saviour Jesus Christ; grace and peace be multiplied unto you through the knowledge of God, and of Jesus our Lord, according as his divine power hath given unto us all things that pertain unto life and godliness, through the knowledge of him that hath called us to glory and virtue: whereby are given unto us exceeding great and precious promises: that by these ye might be partakers of the divine nature, having escaped the corruption that is in the world through lust." -- 2 Peter 1:1-4.

THE two most important things in our holy religion are faith and life. He who shall rightly understand these two words is not far from being a master in experimental theology. Faith and life! these are vital points to a Christian. They possess so intimate a connection with each other that they are by no means to be severed; God hath so joined them together, let no man seek to put them asunder. You shall never find true faith unattended by true godliness; on the other hand, you shall never discover a truly holy life which has not for its root and foundation a living faith upon the righteousness of our Lord Jesus Christ. Woe unto those who seek after the one without the other! There be some who cultivate faith and forget holiness; these may be very high in orthodoxy, but they shall be very deep in damnation, in that day when God shall condemn those who hold the truth in unrighteousness, and make the doctrine of Christ to pander to their lusts. There are others who have strained after holiness of life, but have denied the faith; these are comparable unto the Pharisees of old, of whom the Master said, they were "whitewashed sepulchres;" they were fair to look upon externally, but inwardly, because the living faith was not there, they were full of dead men's bones and all manner of uncleanness. Ye must have faith, for this is the foundation; ye must have holiness of life, for this is the superstructure. Of what avail is the mere foundation of a building to a man in the day of tempest? Can he hide himself among sunken stones and concrete? He wants a house to cover him, as well as a foundation upon which that house might have been built; even so we need the superstructure of spiritual life if we would have comfort in the day of doubt. But seek not a holy life without faith, for that would be to erect a house which can afford no permanent shelter, because it has no foundation on a rock--a house which must come down with a tremendous crash in the day when the rain descends, and the floods come, and the winds blow, and beat upon it. Let faith and life be put together, and, like the two abutments of an arch, they shall make your piety strong. Like the horses of Pharaoh's chariot, they pull together gloriously. Like light and heat streaming from the same sun, they are alike full of blessing. Like the two pillars of the temple, they are for glory and for beauty. They are two streams from the fountain of grace; two lamps lit with holy fire; two olive-trees watered by heavenly care; two stars carried in Jesus' hand. The Lord grant that we may have both of these to perfection, that his name may be praised.

Now, it will be clear to all, that in the four verses before us, our apostle has most excellently set forth the necessity of these two things--twice over he insists upon the faith, and twice over upon holiness of life. We will take the first occasion first.

I. Observe, in the first place, what he says concerning the character and the origin of faith, and then concerning the character and origin of spiritual life.

"Simon Peter, a servant and an apostle of Jesus Christ, to them that have obtained like precious faith with us through the righteousness of God and our Saviour Jesus Christ." So far the faith. "Grace and peace be multiplied unto you through the knowledge of God, and of Jesus our Lord, according as his divine power hath given unto us all things that pertain unto life and godliness, through the knowledge of him that hath called us to glory and virtue." These two verses, you see, concern the spiritual life which comes with the faith.

Let us begin where Peter begins, with the FAITH. You have here a description of true saving faith.

First, you have a description of its source. He says, "to them that have obtained like precious faith." See, then, my brethren, faith does not grow in man's heart by nature; it is a thing which is obtained. It is not a matter which springs up by a process of education, or by the example and excellent instruction of our parents; it is a thing which has to be obtained. Not imitation, but regeneration; not development, but conversion. All our good things come from without us, only evil can be educed from within us. Now, that which is obtained by us must be given to us; and well are we taught in Scripture that "faith is not of ourselves, it is the gift of God." Although faith is the act of man, yet it is the work of God. "With the heart man believeth unto righteousness;" but that heart must, first of all, have been renewed by divine grace before it ever can be capable of the act of saving faith. Faith, we say, is man's act, for we are commanded to "believe on the Lord Jesus Christ," and we shall be saved. At the same time, faith is God's gift, and wherever we find it, we may know that it did not come there from the force of nature, but from a work of divine grace. How this magnifies the grace of God, my brethren, and how low this casts human nature! Faith. Is it not one of the simplest things? Merely to depend upon the blood and righteousness of the Lord Jesus Christ, does it not seem one of the easiest of virtues? To be nothing, and to let him be everything--to be still, and to let him work for me, does not this seem to be the most elementary of all the Christian graces? Indeed, so it is; and yet, even to this first principle and rudiment, poor human nature is so fallen and so utterly undone, that it cannot attain unto! Brethren, the Lord must not only open the gates of heaven to us at last, but he must open the gates of our heart to faith at the first. It is not enough for us to know that he must make us perfect in every good work to do his will, but we must be taught that he must even give us a desire after Christ; and when this is given, he must enable us to give the grip of the hand of faith whereby Jesus Christ becomes our Saviour and Lord. Now, the question comes (and we will try and make the text of today, a text of examination all the way through) have we obtained this faith? Are we conscious that we have been operated upon by the Holy Spirit? Is there a vital principle in us which was not there originally? Do we know today the folly of carnal confidence? Have we a hope that we have been enabled through divine grace to cast away all our own righteousness and every dependence, and are we now, whether we sink or swim, resting entirely upon the person, the righteousness, the blood, the intercession, the precious merit of our Lord Jesus Christ? If not, we have cause enough to tremble; but if we have, the while the apostle writes, "Unto them that have obtained like precious faith," he writes to us, and across the interval of centuries his benediction comes as full and fresh as ever, "Grace and peace be multiplied unto you."

Peter having described the origin of this faith, proceeds to describe its object. The word "through" in our translation, might, quite as correctly, have been rendered "in"--"faith in the righteousness of our God and our Saviour Jesus Christ." True faith, then, is a faith in Jesus Christ, but it is a faith in Jesus Christ as divine. That man who believes in Jesus Christ as simply a prophet, as only a great teacher, has not the faith which will save him. Charity would make us hope for many Unitarians, but honesty compels us to condemn them without exception, so far as vital godliness is concerned. It matters not how intelligent may be their conversation, nor how charitable may be their manners, nor how patriotic may be their spirit, if they reject Jesus Christ as very God of very God, we believe they shall without doubt perish everlastingly. Our Lord uttered no dubious words when he said, "He that believeth not shall be damned," and we must not attempt to be more liberal than the Lord himself. Little allowance can I make for one who receives Jesus the prophet, and rejects him as God. It is an atrocious outrage upon common sense for a man to profess to be a believer in Christ at all, if he does not receive his divinity. I would undertake, at any time, to prove to a demonstration, that if Christ were not God, he was the grossest impostor who ever lived. One of two things, he was either divine or a villain. There is no stopping between the two. I cannot imagine a character more evil than that which would be borne by a man who should lead his followers to adore him as God, without ever putting in a word by way of caveat, to stop their idolatry; nay, who should have spoken in terms so ambiguous, that two thousand years after his death, there should be found millions of persons resting upon him as God. I say, if he were not God, the atrocity of his having palmed himself upon us, his disciples, as God, puts aside altogether from consideration any of the apparent virtues of his life. He was the grossest of all deceivers, if he was not "very God of very God." O beloved, you and I have found no difficulties here; when we have beheld the record of his miracles, when we have listened to the testimony of his divine Father, when we have heard the word of the inspired apostles, when we have felt the majesty of his own divine influence in our own hearts, we have graciously accepted him as "the Wonderful, the Counsellor, the mighty God, the everlasting Father;" and, as John bear witness of him and said, "The Word was in the beginning with God, and the Word was God," even so have we received him; so that at this day, he that was born of the virgin Mary, Jesus of Nazareth, the king of the Jews, is to us "God over all, blessed for ever."

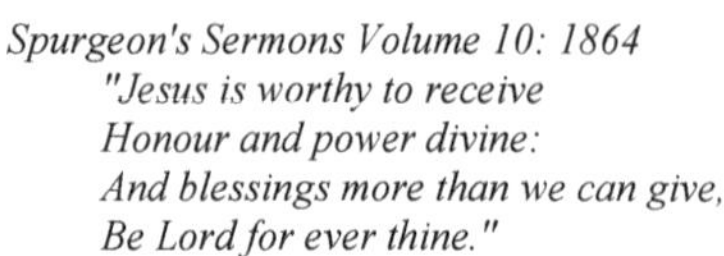

"Jesus is worthy to receive
Honour and power divine:
And blessings more than we can give,
Be Lord for ever thine."

Now, beloved friends, have we heartily and joyfully received Jesus Christ as God? My hearer, if thou hast not, I pray thee seek of God the faith that saves, for thou hast it not as yet, nor art thou in the way to it. Who but a God could bear the weight of sin? Who but a God shall be the "same yesterday, to-day, and for ever?" Concerning whom but a God could it be said, "I am the Lord, I change not; therefore ye sons of Jacob are not consumed." We have to do with Christ, and we should be consumed if he changed; inasmuch, then, as he does not change, and we are not consumed, he must be divine, and our soul rolls the entire burden of its care and guilt upon the mighty shoulders of the everlasting God, who--

"Bears the earth's huge pillars up,
And spreads the heavens abroad."

Remark in further dwelling upon the text, that the apostle has put in another word beside "God", and that is, "of God and our Saviour." As if the glory of the Godhead might be too bright for us, he has attempered it by gentler words "our Saviour." Now, to trust Jesus Christ as divine, will save no man, unless there be added to this a resting in him as the great propitiatory sacrifice. Jesus Christ is our Saviour because he became a substitute for guilty man. He having taken upon himself the form of manhood by union with our nature, stood in the room, place, and stead of sinners. When the whole tempest of divine wrath was about to spend itself on man, he endured it all for his elect; when the great whip of the law must fall, he bared his own shoulders to the lash; when the cry was heard, "Awake, O sword!" it was against Christ the Shepherd, against the man who was the fellow to the eternal God. And because he thus suffered in the place and stead of man, he received power from on high to become the Saviour of man, and to bring many sons into glory, because he had been made perfect through suffering. Now, have we received Jesus Christ as our Saviour? Happy art thou, if thou hast laid thy hand upon the head of him who was slain for sinners. Be glad, and rejoice in the Lord without ceasing, if today that blessed Redeemer who has ascended upon high has become thy Saviour, delivered thee from sin, passing by thy transgressions, and making thee to be accepted in the beloved. A Saviour is he to us when he delivers us from the curse, punishment, guilt and power of sin, "He shall save his people from their sins." O thou great God, be thou my Saviour, mighty to save.

But be pleased to notice the word "righteousness." It is a faith in the righteousness of our God and our Saviour. In these days, certain divines have tried to get rid of all idea of atonement; they have taught that faith in Jesus Christ would save men, apart from any faith in him as a sacrifice. Ah, brethren, it does not say, "faith in the teaching of God our Saviour;" I do not find here that it is written, "faith in the character of God our Saviour, as our exemplar." No, but "faith in the righteousness of God our Saviour." That righteousness, like a white robe, must be cast around us. I have not received Jesus Christ at all, but I am an adversary and an enemy to him, unless I have received him as Jehovah Tsidkenu, the Lord our righteousness. There is his perfect life; that life was a life for me; it contains all the virtues, in it there is no spot; it keeps the law of God, and makes it honourable; my faith takes that righteousness of Jesus Christ, and it is cast about me, and I am then so beauteously, nay, so perfectly arrayed, that even the eye of God can see neither spot nor blemish in me. Have we, then, today a faith in the righteousness of God our Saviour? For no faith but this can ever bring the soul into a condition of acceptance before the Most High. Why," saith one, "these are the very simplicities of the gospel." Beloved, I know they are, and, therefore, do we deal them out this morning, for, thanks be to God, it is the simplicities which lie at the foundation; and it is rather by simplicities than by mysteries that a Christian is to try himself and to see whether he be in the faith or no. Put the question, brethren, have we, then, this like precious faith in God and our Saviour Jesus Christ?

Our apostle has not finished the description, without saying that it is "like precious faith." All faith is the same sort of faith. Our faith may not be like that of Peter, in degree, but if it be genuine, it is like it as to its nature, its origin, its objects, and its results. Here is a blessed equality. Speak of "liberty, equality, and fraternity," you shall only find these things carried out within the Church of Christ. There is indeed a blessed equality here, for the poorest little-faith who ever crept into heaven on its hands and knees, has a like precious faith with the mighty apostle Peter. I say, brethren, if the one be gold, so is the other; if the one can move mountains, so can the other; for remember, that the privileges of mountain-moving, and of plucking up the trees, and casting them into the sea, are not given to great faith, but "if ye have faith as a grain of mustard seed," it shall be done. Little faith has a royal descent and is as truly of divine birth as is the greatest and fullest assurance which ever made glad the heart of man, hence it ensures the same inheritance at the last, and the same safety by the way. It is "like precious faith."

He tells us too, that faith is "precious;" and is it not precious? for it deals with precious things, with precious promises, with precious blood, with a precious redemption, with all the preciousness of the person of our Lord and Saviour Jesus Christ. Well may that be a precious faith which supplies our greatest want, delivers us from our greatest danger, and admits us to the greatest glory. Well may that be called "precious faith," which is the symbol of our election, the evidence of our calling, the root of all our graces, the channel of communion, the weapon of prevalence, the shield of safety, the substance of hope, the evidence of eternity, the guerdon of immortality, and the passport of glory. O for more of this inestimably precious faith. Precious faith, indeed it is.

When the apostle, Simon Peter, writes "to them that have obtained like precious faith with us, through the righteousness of God, and our Saviour Jesus Christ," does he write to you? does he write to me? If not, if we are not here addressed, remember that we can never expect to hear the voice which says, "Come ye blessed of my Father;" but we are today in such a condition, that dying as we now are, "Depart ye cursed" must be the thunder which shall roll in our ears, and drive us down to hell. So much, then, concerning faith.

Now we shall turn to notice with great brevity, the LIFE. "Grace and peace be multiplied unto you through the knowledge of God and of Jesus our Lord, according as his divine power hath given unto us all things that pertain unto life and godliness, through the knowledge of him that hath called us to glory and virtue." Here we have, then, brethren, the fountain and source of our spiritual life. Just as faith is a boon which is to be obtained, so you will perceive that our spiritual life is a principle which is given. A thing which is given to us, too, by divine power--"according as his divine power hath given unto us all things that pertain unto life and godliness." To give life at all is the essential attribute of God. This is an attribute which he will not alienate; to save and to destroy belong unto the Sovereign of heaven. "He can create, and he destroy," is one of the profoundest notes in the ascription of our praise. Suppose a corpse before us. How great a pretender would he be who should boast that it was in his power to restore it to life. Certainly, it would be even a greater pretence if anyone should say that he could give to himself or to another the divine life, the spiritual life by which a man is made a Christian. My brethren, you who are partakers of the divine nature, know that by nature you were dead in trespasses and sins, and would have continued so until this day if there had not been an interposition of divine energy on your behalf. There you lay in the grave of your sin, rotten, corrupt. The voice of the minister called to you, but you did not hear. You were often bidden to come forth, but ye did not and could not come. But when the Lord said, "Lazarus, come forth," then Lazarus came forth; and when he said to you, "Live," then you lived also, and the spiritual life beat within you, with joy and peace through believing. This we ought never to forget, because, let us never fail to remember, that if our religion is a thing which sprang from ourselves, it is of the flesh, and must die. That which is born of the flesh in its best and most favourable moments, is flesh, and only that which is born of the Spirit is spirit. "Ye must be born again." If a man's religious life be only a refinement of his ordinary life, if it be only a high attainment of the natural existence, then is it not the spiritual life, and does not prepare him for the eternal life before the throne of God. No, we must have a supernatural spark of heavenly flame kindled within us. Just as nothing but the soul can quicken the body and make it live, so the Spirit alone can quicken the soul and make the soul live. We must have the third master-principle infused, or else we shall be but natural men, made after the image of the first Adam. We must have, I say, the new spirit, or else we shall not be like the second Adam, who was made a quickening spirit. Only of the Christian can we say that he is spirit, soul, and body; the ungodly man has only soul and body, and as to spiritual existence, he is as dead as the body would be if there were no soul. Now the implantation of this new principle, called the spirit, is a work of divine power. Divine power! What stupendous issues are grasped in that term, divine power! It was this which digged the deep foundations of the earth and sea! Divine power, it is this which guides the marches of the stars of heaven! Divine power! it is this which holds up the pillars of the universe, and which one day shall shake them, and hurry all things back to their native nothingness. Yet the selfsame power which is required to create a world and to sustain it, is required to make man a Christian, and unless that power be put forth, the spiritual life is not in any one of us.

You will perceive, dear friends, that the apostle Peter wished to see this divine life in a healthy and vigorous state, and therefore he prays that grace and peace may be multiplied. Divine power is the foundation of this life; grace is the food it feeds upon, and peace is the element in which it lives most healthily. Give a Christian much grace, and his spiritual life will be like the life of a man who is well clothed and nurtured; keep the spiritual life without abundant grace, and it becomes lean, faint, and ready to die; and though die it cannot, yet will it seem as though it gave up the ghost, unless fresh grace be bestowed. Peace, I say, is the element in which it flourishes most.

Let a Christian be much disturbed in mind, let earthly cares get into his soul, let him have doubts and fears as to his eternal safety, let him lose a sense of reconciliation to God, let his adoption be but dimly before his eyes, and you will not see much of the divine life within him. But oh! if God shall smile upon the life within you, and you get much grace from God, and your soul dwells much in the balmy air of heavenly peace, then shall you be strong to exercise yourself unto godliness, and your whole life shall adorn the doctrine of God your Saviour.

Observe, again, that in describing this life, he speaks of it as one which was conferred upon us by our being called. He says, "We were called unto glory and virtue." I find translators differ here. Many of them think the word should be "By"--"We are called by the glory and virtue of God"--that is, there is a manifestation of all the glorious attributes of God, and of all the efficacious virtue and energy of his power in the calling of every Christian. Simon Peter himself was at his fishing and in his boat, but Jesus said to him, "Follow me;" and at once he followed Christ. He says there was in that calling, the divine glory and virtue; and, doubtless, when you and I shall get to heaven, and see things as they are, we shall discover in our effectual calling of God to grace, a glory as great as in the creation of worlds, and a virtue as great as in the healing of the sick, when virtue went from the garments of a Saviour. Now, can we say today, that we have a life within us which is the result of divine power, and have we, upon searching ourselves, reason to believe, dear friends, that there is that within us which distinguishes us from other men, because we have been called out by mankind by the glory and energy of the divine power? I am afraid some of us must say "Nay." Then the Lord in his mercy yet bring us into the number of his people. But if we can, however, tremblingly say, "Yes, I trust there is something of the life in me;" then as Peter did so, do I wish for you that benediction, "Grace and peace be multiplied unto you through the knowledge of our Lord and Saviour Jesus Christ." O brethren, whatever men may say against the faith of God, there is nothing in the world which creates virtue like true faith. Wherever true faith enters, though it be into the heart of a harlot or of a thief, what a change it makes! See her there; she has polluted herself many times; she has gone far into sin. Mary has been a sinner; she hears the preaching of the Saviour; standing in the crowd she listens to him one day as he preaches concerning the prodigal, and how the loving father pressed him to his bosom; she comes to Jesus and she finds forgiveness. Is she a harlot any longer? Nay, there she is, washing his feet with her tears, and wiping them with the hairs of her head. The woman who was a sinner, hates her evil ways and loves her gracious Lord. We may say of her, "But she is washed, but she is sanctified, but she is saved." Take Saul of Tarsus. Foaming with blood, breathing out threatenings, he is going to Damascus to drag the saints of God to prison. On the road he is struck down; by divine mercy he is led to put his trust in Jesus. Is he a persecutor any longer? See that earnest apostle beaten with rods--shipwrecked--in labours more abundant than all the rest of them--counting not his life dear unto him, that he may win Christ and be found in him. Saul of Tarsus becomes a majestic proof of what the grace of God can do. See Zaccheus, the grasping publican, distributing his wealth, the Ephesians burning their magical books, the jailer washing the apostle's stripes. Take the case of many now present. Let memory refresh itself this morning, with the recollection of the change which has been wrought in you. We have nothing to boast of; God forbid that we should glory, save in the cross of Christ, but yet some of us are wonderful instances of renewing grace. We were unclean, our mouths could utter blasphemy; our temper was hot and terrible; our hands were unrighteous; we were altogether as an unclean thing, but how changed now! Again, I say, we boast of nothing which we now are, for by the grace of God we are what we are, yet the change is something to be wondered at. Has divine grace wrought this change in you? Be not weary with my reiteration of this question. Let me put it again to you till I get an answer; nay, till I force you to an answer: Have you this precious faith? Can you not answer the question? Then, have you not that divine life, that life which is given by divine calling? If you have the one, you have the other; and if you have not both, you have neither; for where there is the one, the other must come, and where the one has come, the other has been there.

II. I have thus fully but feebly brought the subject before you, allow me to remind you that another verse remains which handles the same topics. In the fourth verse, he deals with the privileges of faith, and also with the privileges of the spiritual life.

Notice the PRIVILEGE OF FAITH first. "Whereby are given unto us exceeding great and precious promises"--here is the faith, "That by these ye might be partakers of the divine nature, having escaped the corruption that is in the world through lust." Here is the life resulting from the faith. Now, the privileges of faith first. The privileges of faith are, that we have given to us "Exceeding great and precious promises." "Great and precious"--two words which do not often come together. Many things are great which are not precious, such as great rocks, which are of little value; on the other hand, many things are precious which are not great--such as diamonds and other jewels, which cannot be very great if they be very precious. But here we have promises which are so great, that they are not less than infinite, and so precious, that they are not less than divine. I shall not attempt to speak about their greatness or their preciousness, but just give a catalogue of them, and leave you to guess at both. We have some of them which are like birds in the hands--we have them already; other promises are like birds in the bush, only that they are just as valuable and as sure as those which are in the hand.

Note here, then, we have received by precious faith the promise and pardon. Hark thee, my soul, all thy sins are forgiven thee. He who hath faith in Christ hath no sin to curse him, his sins are washed away, they have ceased to be; they have been carried on the scape-goat's head into the wilderness; they are drowned in the Red Sea; they are blotted out; they are thrown behind God's back; they are cast into the depths of the sea. Here is a promise of perfect pardon. Is not this great and precious?--as great as your sins are; and if your sins demanded a costly ransom, this precious promise is as great as the demand.

Then comes the righteousness of Christ: you are not only pardoned, that is, washed and made clean, but you are dressed, robed in garments such as no man could ever weave. The vesture is divine. Jehovah himself has wrought out your righteousness for you; the holy life of Jesus the Son of God, has become your beauteous dress, and you are covered with it. Christian, is not this an exceeding great and precious promise? The law was great--this righteousness is as great as the law. The law asked a precious revenue from man, more than humanity could pay--the righteousness of Christ has paid it all. Is it not great and precious?

Then next comes reconciliation. You were strangers, but you are brought nigh by the blood of Christ. Once aliens, but now fellow-citizens with the saints and of the household of God. Is not this great and precious?

Then comes your adoption. "Beloved, now are we the sons of God, and it doth not yet appear what we shall be: but we know that, when he shall appear, we shall be like him; for we shall see him as he is." "And if children, then heirs, heirs of God, joint heirs with Jesus Christ, if so be we suffer with him that we may be glorified together." Oh, how glorious is this great and precious promise of adoption!

Then we have the promise of providence: "all things work together for good to them that love God, to them that are called according to his purpose." "Thy place of defence shall be the munitions of rocks." "Thy bread shall be given thee and thy waters shall be sure." "As thy days thy strength shall be." "Fear not, I am with thee; be not dismayed, I am thy God." "When thou passest through the rivers, I will be with thee, the floods shall not overflow thee. When thou goest through the fire, thou shalt not be burned, neither shall the flames kindle upon thee." When I think of providence, the greatness of its daily gifts, and the preciousness of its hourly boons, I may well say, here is an exceeding great and precious promise.

Then you have the promise too, that you shall never taste of death but shall only sleep in Jesus. "Write, blessed are the dead which die in the Lord from henceforth. Yea, saith the Spirit, that they cease from their labours; and their works do follow them." Nor does the promise cease here, you have the promise of a resurrection. "For the trumpet shall sound, and the dead shall be raised incorruptible, and we shall be changed. For this corruptible must put on incorruption, and this mortal must put on immortality." Beloved, we know that if Christ rose from the dead, so also them who sleep in Jesus, will the Lord bring with him. Nor is this all, for we shall reign with Jesus; at his coming, we shall be glorified with him, we shall sit upon his throne, even as he has overcome and sits with his Father upon his throne. The harps of heaven, the streets of glory, the trees of paradise, the river of the water of life, the eternity of immaculate bliss--all these, God hath promised to them who love him. "Eye hath not seen, nor ear heard, the things which God hath prepared for them that love him, but he hath revealed them unto us by his Spirit;" and by our faith we have grasped them, and we have today "the substance of things hoped for, and the evidence of things not seen." Now, beloved, see how rich faith makes you!--what treasure!--what a costly regalia!--what gold mines!--what oceans of wealth!--what mountains of sparkling treasures has God conferred upon you by faith!

But we must not forget the life, and with that we close. The text says, he has given us this promise, "that"--"in order that." What then? What are all these treasures lavished for? For what these pearls? For what these jewels? For what, I say, these oceans of treasure? For what? Is the end worthy of the means? Surely God never giveth greater store than the thing which he would purchase will be worth. We may suppose, then, the end to be very great when such costly means have been given; and what is the end? Why, "that by these ye might be partakers of the divine nature, having escaped the corruption that is in the world through lust." O, my brethren, if you have these mercies today by faith, do see to it that the result is obtained. Be not content to be made rich in these great and precious promises, without answering God's design in your being thus enriched. That design, you perceive, is twofold; it is first that you may be partakers of the divine nature; and, secondly, that you may escape the corruption which is in the world.

To be a partaker of the divine nature is not, of course, to become God. That cannot be. The essence of Deity is not to be participated in by the creature. Between the creature and the Creator there must ever be a gulf fixed in respect of essence; but as the first man Adam was made in the image of God, so we, by the renewal of the Holy Spirit, are in a yet diviner sense made in the image of the Most High, and are partakers of the divine nature. We are, by grace, made like God. "God is love;" we become love--"He that loveth is born of God." God is truth; we become true, and we love that which is true, and we hate the darkness and the lie. God is good, it is his very name; he makes us good by his grace, so that we become the pure in heart who shall see God. Nay, I will say this, that we become partakers of the divine nature in even a higher sense than this--in fact, in any sense, anything short of our being absolutely divine. Do we not become members of the body of the divine person of Christ? And what sort of union is this--"members of his body, of his flesh, and of his bones?" The same blood which flows in the head flows in the hand, and the same life which quickens Christ, quickens his people; for, "Ye are dead, and your life is hid with Christ in God." Nay, as if this were not enough, we are married into Christ. He hath betrothed us unto himself in righteousness and in faithfulness; and as the spouse must, in the nature of things, be a partaker of the same nature as the husband, so Jesus Christ first became partaker of flesh and blood that they twain might be one flesh; and then he makes his Church partakers of the same spirit, that they twain may be one spirit; for he who is joined unto the Lord is one spirit. Oh, marvellous mystery! we look into it, but who shall understand it? One with Jesus, by eternal union one, married to him; so one with him that the branch is not more one with the vine than we are a part of the Lord, our Saviour, and our Redeemer. Rejoice in this, brethren, ye are made partakers of the divine nature, and all these promises are given to you in order that you may show this forth among the sons of men, that ye are like God, and not like ordinary men; that ye are different now from what flesh and blood would make you, having been made participators of the nature of God.

Then the other result which follows from it, was this, "Having escaped the corruption that is in the world through lust." Ah, beloved, it were ill that a man who is alive should dwell in corruption. "Why seek ye the living among the dead?" said the angel to Magdalene. Should the living dwell among the dead? Should divine life be found amongst the corruptions of worldly lusts? The bride of Christ drunken! Frequenting the ale-house! A member of Christ's body found intoxicated in the streets, or lying, or blaspheming, or dishonest! God forbid. Shall I take the members of Christ, and make them members of a harlot? How can I drink the cup of the Lord, and drink the cup of Belial? How can it be possible that I can have life, and yet dwell in the black, dark, foul, filthy, pestiferous tomb of the world's lusts? Surely, brethren, from these open lusts and sins ye have escaped: have ye also escaped from slothfulness? Have ye clean escaped from carnal security? Are we seeking day by day to live above worldliness, and love of the things of the world, and the ensnaring avarice which they nourish? Remember, it is for this that you have been enriched with the treasures of God. Do not, oh, I conjure you, do not, chosen of God and beloved by him, and so graciously enriched, do not suffer all this lavish treasure to be wasted upon you.

There is nothing which my heart desires more than to see you, the members of this Church, distinguished for holiness: it is the Christian's crown and glory. An unholy Church! it is of no use to the world, and of no esteem among men. Oh! it is an abomination, hell's laughter, heaven's abhorrence. And the larger the Church, the more influential, the worse nuisance does it become, when it becomes dead and unholy. The worst evils which have ever come upon the world, have been brought upon her by an unholy Church. Whence came the darkness of the dark ages? From the Church of Rome. And if we want to see the world again sitting in Egyptian darkness, bound with fetters of iron, we have only to give up the faith, and to renounce holiness of life, and we may drag the world down again to the limbo of superstition, and bind her fast in chains of ignorance and vice. O Christian, the vows of God are upon you. You are God's priest: act as such. You are God's king: reign over your lusts. You are God's chosen: do not associate with Belial. Heaven is your portion; live like a heavenly spirit, so shall you prove that you have the true faith; but except ye do this, your end shall be to lift up your eyes in hell, and find yourself mistaken when it will be too late to seek or find a remedy. The Lord give us the faith and the life, for Jesus' sake. Amen.

Do You Know Him?

A Sermon (No. 552)
Delivered on Sunday Morning, January 31st, 1864, by the
Rev. C. H. SPURGEON,
At the Metropolitan Tabernacle, Newington

"That I may know him." -- Philippians 3:10.

THE object of the apostle's life--that for which he sacrificed everything: country, kindred, honor, comfort, liberty, and life itself, was, that he might know Christ. Observe that this is not Paul's prayer as an unconverted man, that he may know Christ, and so be saved; for it follows upon the previous supplication that he might win Christ and be found in him. This is the desire of one who has been saved, who enjoys the full conviction that his sins are pardoned, and that he is in Christ. It is only the regenerated and saved man who can feel the desire, "That I may know him." Are you astonished that a saved man should have such a desire as this? A moment's reflection will remove your astonishment. Imagine for a moment that you are living in the age of the Roman emperors. You have been captured by Roman soldiers and dragged from your native country; you have been sold for a slave, stripped, whipped, branded, imprisoned, and treated with shameful cruelty. At last yon are appointed to die in the amphitheatre, to make holiday for a tyrant. The populace assemble with delight. There they are, tens of thousands of them, gazing down from the living sides of the capacious Colosseum. You stand alone, and naked, armed only with a single dagger--a poor defense against gigantic beasts. A ponderous door is drawn up by machinery, and forth there rushes the monarch of the forest--a huge lion; you must slay him or be torn to pieces. You are absolutely certain that the conflict is too stern for you, and that the sure result must and will be that those terrible teeth will grind your bones and drip with your blood. You tremble; your joints are loosed; you are paralyzed with fear, like the timid deer when the lion has dashed it to the ground. But what is this? O wonder of mercy!--a deliverer appears. A great unknown leaps from among the gazing multitude, and confronts the savage monster. He quails not at the roaring of the devourer, but dashes upon him with terrible fury, till, like a whipped cur, the lion slinks towards his den, dragging himself along in pain and fear. The hero lifts you up, smiles into your bloodless face, whispers comfort in your ear, and bids you be of good courage, for you are free. Do you not think that there would arise at once in your heart a desire to know your deliverer? As the guards conducted you into the open street, and you breathed the cool, fresh air, would not the first question be, "Who was my deliverer, that I may fall at his feet and bless him?" You are not, however, informed, but instead of it you are gently led away to a noble mansion house, where your many wounds are washed and healed with salve of rarest power. You are clothed in sumptuous apparel; you are made to sit down at a feast; you eat and are satisfied; you rest upon the softest down. The next morning you are attended by servants who guard you from evil and minister to your good. Day after day, week after week, your wants are supplied. You live like a courtier. There is nothing that you can ask which you do not receive. I am sure that your curiosity would grow more and more intense till it would ripen into an insatiable craving. You would scarcely neglect an opportunity of asking the servants, "Tell me, who does all this, who is my noble benefactor, for I must know him?" "Well, but" they would say, "is it not enough for you that you are delivered from the lion?" "Nay," say you, "it is for that very reason that I pant to know him." "Your wants are richly supplied--why are yon vexed by curiosity as to the hand which reaches you the boon? If your garment is worn out, there is another. Long before hunger oppresses you, the table is well loaded. What more do you want?" But your reply is, "It is because I have no wants, that, therefore, my soul longs and yearns even to hungering and to thirsting, that I may know my generous loving friend." Suppose that as you wake up one morning, you find lying up on your pillow a precious love-token from your unknown friend, a ring sparkling with jewels and engraved with a tender inscription, a bouquet of flowers bound about with a love-motto! Your curiosity now knows no bounds. But you are informed that this wondrous being has not only done for you what you have seen, but a thousand deeds of love which you did not see, which were higher and greater still as proofs of his affection. You are told that he was wounded, and imprisoned, and scourged for your sake, for he had a love to yon so great, that death itself could not overcome it: you are informed that he is every moment occupied in your interests, because he has sworn by himself that where he is there you shall be; his honors you shall share, and of his happiness you shall be the crown. Why, methinks you would say, "Tell me, men and women, any of you who know him, tell me who he is and what he is;" and if they said, "But it is enough for you to know that he loves you, and to have daily proofs of his goodness," you would say, "No, these love-tokens increase my thirst. If ye see him, tell him I am sick of love. The flagons which he sends me, and the love-tokens which he gives me, they stay me for awhile with the assurance of his affection but they only impel me onward with the more unconquerable desire that I may know him. I must know him; I cannot live without knowing him. His goodness makes me thirst, and pant, and faint, and even die, that I may know him."

Have I imagined emotions which would not be natural? I think not. The most cool and calculating would be warmed with desires like these. Methinks what I have now pictured before you will wake the echoes in your breasts, and you will say, "Ah, it is even so! It is because Christ loved me and gave himself for me that I want to know him; it is because he has shed his blood for me and has chosen me that I may be one with him for ever, that my soul desires a fuller acquaintance with him."

Now may God, the Holy Ghost, very graciously lead me onward that I may also quicken in you the desire to know HIM.

I. Beloved, let us PASS BY THAT CROWD OF OUTER-COURT WORSHIPPERS WHO ARE CONTENT TO LIVE WITHOUT KNOWING CHRIST. I do not mean the ungodly and profane; we will not consider them just now--they arc altogether strangers and foreigners to him--I mean children of God: the visible saints. How many there are of these whom I must call outer-court worshippers, for they are strangers to this panting to know him. They can say with Paul, "That I may win him and be found in him"--that they do want; but this higher wish, "That I may know him," has not stirred their hearts. How many brethren we know, who are content to know Christ's historic life! They read the evangelists and they are charmed with the perfect beauty of the Savior's history. "Never man spake like this man," say they; and they confess that never man acted with such love as lie did. They know all the incidents of his life, from his manger to his cross; but they do not know HIM. They are as men who have read " Caesar's Commentaries," but who have never seen Caesar. They know the battles which Caesar fought; they can even recognize the mantle which Caesar wore "that day he overcame the Nervii;" but they do not know Caesar himself. The person of the Lord Jesus is us much hidden from their eyes us the golden pot of manna when concealed in the ark. They know the life of Christ, hut not Christ the Life; they admire his way among men, hut they see not himself as the way.

Others there are who know Christ's doctrine, and prize it too, but they know not Him. All which he taught is dear to them; orthodoxy--for this they would burn at Smithfield, or lay down their necks at Tower Hill. Many of them are well-instructed and divinely-illuminated in the doctrine of Christ, and the wonder is, that they should stop there; because, beloved, it does seem to me when I begin to know a man's teaching, that the next thing is the desire to know his person. Addison, in one of the " Spectators," tells us that the reason why so many books are printed with the portraits of the authors is just this, that as a man reads a book, lie feels a desire to know what sort of appearance the author had. This, indeed, is very natural. If you have ever been refreshed under a minister's printed sermons, if you have at any time received any benefit from his words, I know you have said, "I would like to see that man; I would like to hear the truth flow hot and fresh from his living lips; I would like to know just how he said that sentence, and how that passage sounded as it came from his earnest heart." My beloved, surely if you know the doctrine of Jesus, if you have so been with Christ as to sit at his feet and hear what he has to say, you must, I hope, have had some longings to know him--to know his person; and if you have, you will have had to pass by multitudes of followers of Jesus who rest satisfied with his words, but forget that he is himself "THE WORD."

Beloved, there are others--and against them I bring no complaint; they go as far as they can--who are delighted with Christ's example. Christ's character is in their esteem the mirror of all perfection. They desire to walk in his footsteps; they listen to his sermon upon the Mount; they are enchanted with it--as well they may be; they pray to he obedient in all things to Christ, as their Master and their Lord. They do well. Mark, I am finding no fault with any of these who prize the history, or who value the doctrine, or who admire the precept; but I want more. I do want, beloved, that you and I should "know HIM." I love his precepts, but I love HIM better. Sweet is the water from Bethlehem's well; and well worth the struggle of the armed men to win but a bucket from it; but the well itself is better, and deserves all Israel's valor to defend it. As the source is ever more valuable than the stream, so is Christ ever better than the best words of his lips, or the best deeds of his hand. I want to know him. I do care for his actions; my soul would sit down and admire those masterly works of holy art--his miracles of humiliation, of suffering, of patience, and of holy charity; but better far I love the hands which wrought these master-works, the lips which spoke these goodly words, and the heart which heaved with that matchless love which was the cause of all. Yes, beloved, we must get farther than Immanuel's achievements, however glorious; we must come to "know him."

Most believers rest perfectly at ease with knowing Christ's sacrifice. They see Jesus as the great High Priest, laying a great sacrifice upon the altar for their sins, and with their whole heart they accept his atonement. By faith they know that all their sin is taken away by precious blood. This is a most blessed and hallowed attainment, I will grant you; but it is not every Christian who perceives that Christ was not only the offerer of a sacrifice, but was himself the sacrifice, and, therefore, loves him as such. Priest, altar, victim, everything Christ was. He gathers up all in himself, and when I see that he loved me, and gave himself for me, it is not enough to know this fact: I want to know him, the glorious person who does and is all this. I want to know the man who thus gave himself for me. I want to behold the Lamb once slain for me. I want to rest upon the bosom which covers the heart which was pierced with the spear; I pray him to kiss me with the kisses of that mouth which cried, "Eloi, Eloi, lama sabachthani?" I love Calvary, the scene of woe, but I love Christ better, the great object of that agony; and even his cross and all his sufferings, dear though these must ever be to the Christian mind, only occupying a second place; the first seat is for himself, his person, his deity, and humanity.

Thus, you see, we have to leave a great many believers behind; nor have we enumerated all, for I believe that even some of those saints who have received grace to look for the coming of Christ, yet in their vision of his coming too much forget him. Is it not possible for nine to pant for the second advent as to lose sight of him who is to make that advent? So to long for a millennium, that I may forget him who is to reign King of kings? So to pant after that glory of Israel that I may forget him who is Israel's glory? Anywhere short of knowing him, I would not have you stop, beloved; and even when you know him, I would urge you still to be impelled with the same desire, and to press forward, crying with the apostle, "That I may know him."

Beloved, how many there are who have heard of Christ and read about Christ, and that is enough for them! But it is not enough for me, and it should not be enough for you. The apostle Paul did not say "I have heard of him, on whom I have believed," but " I know whom I have believed." To hear about Christ may damn you, it may be a savor of death unto death to you. You have heard of him with the ear; hut it is essential that you know him in order that you may be partakers of eternal life. My dear hearers, be not content unless you have this as your soul's present portion.

Others there be who have been persuaded by the judgment and encouragement of others, that they know something about the great Redeemer. They do not know him, but still they are persuaded by others that they have an interest in him. Let me warn you of second-hand spirituality, it is a rotten, soul-deceiving deception. Beware of all esteeming yourself according to the thoughts of others, or you will be ruined. Another man's opinion of me may have great influence over me, I have heard of a man in perfectly good health killed by the opinion of others. Several of his friends had foolishly agreed to play him a practical trick; whereupon one of them met him and said, "How ill you look this morning." He did not feel so; he was very much surprised at the remark. When he met the next, who said to him, "Oh! dear, how bad you look," lie began to think there might be something in it; and us he turned smart round the corner, a third person said to him, "What a sight you are! How altered from what you used to be!" He went home ill, he took to his bed and died. So goes the story, and I should not marvel if it really did occur. Now, if such might be the effect of persuasion and supposed belief in the sickness of a man, how much more readily may men be persuaded into the idea of spiritual health! A believer meets you, and by his treatment seems to say, " I welcome you as a dear brother"--and means it too. You are baptized, and you are received into Church-fellowship, and so everybody thinks that von must be a follower of Christ; and yet you may not know him. Oh, I do pray you, do not be satisfied with being persuaded into something like an assurance that you are in him, but do know him--know him for yourself.

There are many who I hope will be saved ere long; but I am in great doubt of them, because they can only say they half think they know Christ; they do not quite believe in him, but they do not disbelieve in him; they halt between two opinions. Ah, dear hearer, that is a very dangerous place to stand in. The border-land is the devil's hunting ground. Undecided souls are fair game for the great fowler. God give you once for all the true decision by which through grace you shall know him. Do not be satisfied with thinking you know him; hoping you know him, but know him. Oh, it is nothing to have heard about him, to have talked about him, to have eaten and have drank with him, to have preached him, or even to have wrought miracles in his name, to have been charmed by his eloquence, to have been stirred with the story of his love, to have been moved to imitate him--this shall nothing avail you, unless you win him and are found in him. Seek with the apostle, to give up everything of your own righteousness, and all other objects and aims in life, and say, "This I seek after, that I may know him." Thus much, then, on the first point. Leaving those behind who do not

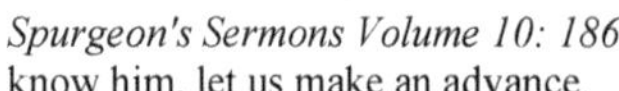

know him, let us make an advance.

II. Secondly, let us DRAW CURTAIN AFTER CURTAIN WHICH SHALL ADMIT US TO KNOW MORE OF CHRIST.

Did you ever visit the manufactory of splendid porcelain at Sevres? I have done so. If anybody should say to me, "Do you know the manufactory at Sevres?" I should say, " Yes, I do, and no, I do not. I know it, for I have seen the building; I have seen the rooms in which the articles are exhibited for sale, and I have seen the museum and model room; but I do not know the factory as I would like to know it, for I have not seen the process of manufacture, and have not been admitted into the workshops, as some are. "Suppose I had seen, however, the process of the moulding of the clay, and the laying on of the rich designs, if anybody should still say to me, "Do you know how they manufacture those wonderful articles?" I should very likely still be compelled to say, "No, I do not, because there are certain secrets, certain private rooms into which neither friend nor foe can be admitted, lest the process should be open to the world." So, you see, I might say I knew, and yet might not half know; and when I half knew, still there would be so much left, that I might be compelled to say, "I do not know." How many different ways there are of knowing a person--and even so there are all these different ways of knowing Christ; so that you may keep on all your lifetime, still wishing to get into another room, and another room, nearer and nearer to the great secret, still panting to "know him." Good Rutherford says, "I urge upon you a nearer communion with Christ, and a growing communion. There are curtains to be drawn by, in Christ, that we never shut, and new foldings in love with him. I despair that ever I shall shall win to the far end of that love; there are so many plies in it. Therefore, dig deep, and set by as much time in the day for him as you can, he will be won by labor."

To begin with. We know a person when we recognize him. You know the Queen. Well, I do. I recollect seeing her, and if I were to see any quantity of ladies, I think I should know which was the Queen and which was not. You may say honestly that you know her to that extent. Beloved, every Christian must in this sense know Christ. You must know him by a divine illumination so as to know who he is and what line is. When Jesus said to Simon Peter, "Whom sayest thou that I am," he said, "Thou art the Christ, the Son of the living God;" and the Lord replied, "Blessed art thou, Simon Barjonas, for flesh and blood hath not revealed this unto thee." It is an early step in this knowledge of Christ, to know and to believe that Jesus Christ is Lord; to know that Christ is God, divine to me; that Christ is man, brother to me--bone of my bone and flesh of my flesh--that as such line is a sin-subduing Savior; that line is for inc an intercessor, pleading before the throne; my prophet, priest, and king--in this sense I trust that most of you know him. If you do not, breathe the silent prayer now, "Lord, help me that I may know him." But this knowledge of recognition is comparatively a low attainment, one of the lowest rounds of the ladder of light.

In the second place, a believer knows Christ, to a higher degree when he knows him by practical experiment at acquaintance with what he does. For instance, I know Christ as a cleanser. They tell me he is a refiner, that he cleanses from spots; he has washed me in his precious blood, and to that extent I know him. They tell me that he clothes the naked; he hath covered me with a garment of righteousness, and to that extent I know him. They tell me that he is a breaker, and that he breaks fetters, he has set my soul at liberty, and therefore I know him. They tell me that he is a king and that he reigns over sin; he hath subdued my enemies beneath his feet, and I know him in that character. They tell me he is a shepherd: I know him for I am his sheep. They say he is a door: I have entered in through him, and I know him as a door. They say he is food: my spirit feeds on him as on the bread of heaven, and, therefore, I know him as such. You know if anyone says, "Do you know doctor So-and-so?" It is a very satisfactory answer, if you can reply, "Oh, yes, I know him, for he attended me the last time that I was ill." There is more knowledge in that, than if on could only say, " Oh, yes, I know him: he wears such-and-such a hat or "line is a man of such-and-such an appearance." So, Christian, thing is a second and higher step to know Christ, because you have experienced in your own soul that he is just what God has revealed him to be.

But we know a man in a better sense than this when we are on speaking terms with him. "Do you know So-and-so?" " Yes," you say, I not only know him by name, so as to recognize him; I not only know him as a tradesman having dealt with him, but I know him because when we pass each other in the morning, we exchange a word or two; and if I had anything to say upon matters--any request to make--I should feel no difficulty about asking him." Well, now. the Christian knows his Lord in this sense, line has every day official communication with Christ, line is on speaking terms with him. There may be persons here, perhaps, who know the Queen in a sense in which I do not know her--perhaps they speak to him. They have so done; I have never done that; they go beyond me there. But you see, dear friends, this is not a very great thing because you may be on speaking terms with a man, but you may not know much of him for all that. So you may be in the habit of daily prayer, and you may talk with Christ every morning and every evening, and you may know exceedingly little of him. You are on speaking terms with him; but there ins something beyond this, very far beyond this. As I might say that I know a man merely because I meet him every day, and ask him for what I want, and understand that he is kind and generous; but how shallow is such an acquaintance, for I do not know his private character nor his inward heart. Even so a believer may have constant dealings with Christ in his prayers and in his praises, and yet for all that, he may have only gone a certain distance, and may have need still to pray, "That I may know him."

But you are said to know a person better still when he invites you to his house. At Christmas time there is a family party and a romp, and he asks you there, and you are one of the children, and enter into all their sports around the fire-side, and you indulge as they do in the genialities of social life. You are asked again; you go there pretty often; in fact, if there is a happy evening in that house they generally expect to see friend So-and-so there. Well, now, that is better. We are getting now into something like knowing a man; and I do trust there are many of you, beloved, who have got as far as this with regard to your divine Lord. Christ has entertained you with some rare visits from his gracious presence. He brought you into the banquetting-house, and his banner over you was love. When he manifested himself, he did it unto you as he did not unto the world. He was pleased in the majesty of his condescension, to take you aside and show you his hands and his side. He called you "Friend;" he treated you as such, and permitted you to enjoy thine sweets of being one of the family.

Ah, but you may go into a man's house as a constant visitor, and yet you may not know him--that is to say, not in the highest sense. You speak to the man's wife and say, "Your husband is a marvellously charming man; what a cheerful, joyful, spirited man he is; he never seems to have any depressions of spirit, and experiences no changes whatever." She shakes her head. and she says, "Ah! you do not know him, you do not know him as I do;" because shine sees him at all times and at all hours; she can read the very heart of the man. That Christian has grown much in grace who has advanced not only to be the friend of Christ, having occasional fellowship with him, but who comes to recognize his marriage-union with the person of his Lord, and of whom it can be said, "The secret of the Lord is with them that fear him; and he will show them his covenant," Now we have the intimacy of love, with its perfect frankness, nearness, sweetness, joyousness, delight. The rending away of every separating veil makes the communion to be as near as it well can be this side the black river; but a Christian may get farther than this.

Even the spouse may not know her husband. The most loving wife who ever entered into the cares of her husband, must have discovered that there is a something which separates his experience from her powers of comprehension. Luther's wife. Catherine, was of all women the wife for Luther; but there were times in Luther's gigantic tribulations, when he must leave Kate behind. There were extraordinary times within him; times both of ecstatic joy, when like a great angel, he stretched his mighty wings, and flew right up to heaven, and of awful misery, when he seemed to sink down to the very depths of hell; and in either case, no other heart could keep pace with him. Then it was himself alone who had communion with himself. And a Christian may so grow in grace as to become identified with Christ, a member of his body; not so much married to him as a part of him, a member of the great body of Christ, so that he suffers with Christ, sympathizes with Jesus, his heart beating to the same dolorous tune, his veins swollen with the sumac floods of grief, or else his eyes sparkling with that same gleam of joy, according to the Master's Word, "That my joy might remain in you, and that your joy might be full."

Well, have not you waded out of your depth some of you? I have certainly got out of my own. I feel as if the Master might come on to this platform, look round on many of us, and say, "Have I been so long time with you, and yet hast thou not known me, Philip?" for truly even in the minor sense, though I trust we arc saved, though we have believed in Jesus, yet we have not reached the height of this great text--"That I may know him."

III. Having taken you so far, let us SIT DOWN A FEW MINUTES AND CONSIDER WHAT SORT OF KNOWLEDGE THIS KNOWLEDGE OF CHRIST IS--"That I may know him."

Then it is clear, if I know him I shall have a very vivid sense of his personality. "That I may know him." He will not be to me a myth, a vision, a spirit, bat a person, a real solid person, as much real as I am myself, or as my dearest friend can be to me. My soul, never be satisfied within a shadowy Christ. My heart, be thou never content until he hath embraced thy soul, and proved to thee that he is the lover of his people. This knowledge, then, must be a knowledge of him in his personality. Then, beloved, it must be a personal knowledge on our part. I cannot know Christ through another person's brains. I cannot love him with another man's heart, and I cannot see him with another man's eyes. Heaven's delight is, "Mine eyes shall see him and not another." These eyes shall behold the King in his beauty. Well, beloved, if this be heaven, we certainly cannot do without a personal sight of Christ here. I am so afraid of living in a second-hand religion. God forbid that I should get a biographical experience. Lord save us from having borrowed communion. No, I must know him myself. O God, let me not be deceived in this. I must know him without fancy or proxy; I must know him on mine own account.

Then these few thoughts upon what sort of knowledge we must have. It must be an intelligent knowledge--I must know him. I must know his natures, divine and human. I must know his offices--I must know his attributes--I must know his works--I must know his shame--I must know his glory; for I do not know him if it be merely a subject of passion and not of intellect. I must let my head consciously meditate upon him until I own something like an idea of him, that I may "Comprehend with all saints what is the breadth, and length and depth, and height; and to know the love of Christ, which passeth knowledge."

Then I must have an affectionate knowledge of him; and, indeed, if I do know him at all, I must love him. As it is said of some men, that there is such a charm about them, that if you once get into their company you cannot criticise any longer, but must admire; so you feel with Christ. It is said of Garibaldi, that if you are in his society he charms all, so that even malice and slander must be silent in his presence. Infinitely, supremely so is it with Christ. Being near him, his love warms our hearts, till we glow with intense love to him.

Then I shall find, if I know Christ, that this is a satisfying knowledge. When I know Christ my mind will he fill to the brim--I shall feel that I have found that which my spirit panted after. "This is that bread whereof if a man eat he shall never hunger."

At the same time it is an exciting knowledge; the more I know of Christ, the more I shall want to know. The deeper I plunge the greater the deeps which will be revealed. The higher I climb the loftier will be the summits which invite my eager footsteps. I shall want the more as I get the more. My spiritual thirst will increase, though in another sense it will be entirely quenched.

And this knowledge of Christ will be a most happy one, in fact, so happy, that sometimes it will completely bear me up above all trials, and doubts, and sorrows; and it will, while I enjoy it, make me something more than "Man that is born of a woman who is of few days, and full of trouble;" for it will fling about me the immortality of the ever-living Savior, and gird me with the golden girdle of his eternal happiness. To be near to Christ, is to be near to the pearly gates of the golden-streeted city. Say not, "Jerusalem, my happy home, my labors have an end in thee;" but say, "Jesus, thou art my rest, and when I have thee, my spirit is at peace." I might thus keep on speaking in praise of this knowledge, but I will not.

Only permit me to say, what a refreshing, what a sanctifying knowledge is this, to know him. When the Laodicean Church was neither hot nor cold, but lukewarm, how did Christ seek her revival? Did he send her precious doctrines? Did he send her excellent precepts? Mark you, he came himself, for thus it is said, "Behold, I stand at the door, and knock: if any man hear my voice, and open the door, I will come into him, and will sup with him, and he with me." That is a cure for it all, you see. No matter how lukewarm, though God may say, "I will spue thee out of my mouth," yet, if Christ comes, that is the cure. The presence of Christ with his Church puts away all her sicknesses. When the disciples of Christ were at sea in a storm, do you recollect how he comforted them? Did he send them an angel? No. "It is I, line not afraid;" and when they knew him, then they had no more fears. They were assembled one night, "the doors being shut for fear of the Jews:" how did he comfort them? Jesus himself stood in the midst of them, and said, "Peace be unto you." There was Thomas, full of doubts and fears. How did Jesus Christ take away his doubts? "Reach hither thy finger, and behold my hands; and reach hither thy hand, and thrust it into my side." Oh! it is Christ, it is Christ who cures all. The company of Christ is the only thing which a Christian wants. I will undertake that if his heart be like an iceberg, as soon as Jesus comes, it shall flame like Vesuvius. His spirit shall be dead and like a rotten corpse; but if Jesus comes he shall leap like a hart, and become strong as a young unicorn. Thy presence makes me like the chariots of Amminadib. Now, do not think I am talking what I do not know. Do not imagine that I am talking mere fanatical slip-slop which I cannot prove. I do assert (and God who searcheth all hearts, knows how true this is), I do assert that, from the depths of doubt, of dullness, of worldliness, I have leaped in one moment into love, and life, and holy enthusiasm, when Jesus Christ has manifested himself to nine. I cannot describe the difference between my spirit, water-logged, worm-eaten, ready to sink to the bottom without Christ, and that same spirit, like a strong stanch ship, with sails full, with favorable wind, speeding into harbor, with a golden freight. Like you poor little bird which some cruel boy has torn from the nest and almost killed--it is not fledged yet, and cannot fly, and it lies down to die, trampled in the mire in the streets--that is my heart without Christ. But see that other bird! The cage-door is opened, its wings vibrate, it sings within all its might. and flies up to talk with the sun--that is my heart when I have the conscious presence of my Lord Jesus Christ! I only bring in my own consciousness because I do not know yours; but I think I will now venture to say that every believer here will admit it is the same with him--

"Midst darkest shades if he appear
My dawning is begun;
He is my soul's bright morning star,
And he my rising sun.

IV. I shall close by urging you, dearly beloved, who know the Lord, to take this desire of the apostle, and by exhorting you, make it your own, "That I may know him." I wish I had time this morning--time will fly--I wish I had time to urge and press you, believers, onward to seek to know him. Paul, you see, gave up everything for this--you will be seeking what is worth having. There can be no mistake about this. If Paul will renounce all, there must be a reward which is worthy of the sacrifice. If you have any fears, if you seek Christ and find him, they will be removed. You complain that you do not feel the guilt of sin; that you cannot humble yourself enough. The sight of Christ is the very best means of setting sin in its true colors. There is no repenting like that which comics from a look of Christ's eye: the Lord turned and hooked upon Peter, and he went out and wept bitterly. So it is not a sight of the law, it is the sight of Christ looking upon us which will break our hearts.

There is nothing like this to fill you with courage. When Dr. Andrew Reed found some difficulties in the founding of one of his orphan asylums, he sat down and drew upon a little piece of paper the cross, and then he said to himself, "What, despair in the face of the cross?" and then he drew a ring round the cross, and wrote in it nil desperandum! and took it for his coat of arms. Oh, there cannot be any despair in the presence of the cross. Thou dying Lamb, didst thou endure the cross, despising the shame, and shall I talk of difficulties when thy glory is in the way? God forbid! O holy face, bedewed with bloody sweat, I pledge myself in thy solemn and awful presence, that though this face of mine should be bedewed with sweat of the like sort, to accomplish any labor upon which thou shalt put me; by thy will and in thy strength, I will not shrink from the task. A sight of Christ, brethren, will keep you from despondency, and doubts, and despair. A sight of Christ! How shall I stir you to it? It will fire you to duty; it will deliver you from temptation; it will, in fact, make you like him. A man is known by his company; and if you have become acquainted with Christ, and know him, you will be sure to reflect his light. It is because the moon hath converse within the sun, that she hath any light for this dark world's night; and if you talk with Christ, the Sun, he will shine on you so gloriously, that you. like the moon, shall reflect his light, and the dark night of this world shall be enlightened by your radiance. The Lord help us to know him.

But I do seem, this morning, to have been talking to you about him, and not to have brought him forward. O that I knew how to introduce you to him! You who do not love him, O that I could make you seek after him! But you who do love him and have trusted in him, O that I could make you hunger and thirst until you were filled with him! There he is, nailed to his cross, suffering--oh! how much!--for you; there he is, risen, ascended, pleading before the throne of God for you. Here he is: "Lo, I am with you alway, even unto the end of the world." Here he is, waiting to be comforted with your company, desiring communion with you, panting that his sister, his spouse, would be no longer a stranger to him. Here he is, waiting to be gracious, saying, "Come unto me all ye that labor and are heavy laden, and I will give you rest." Come, Christian, come, let this be thy desire, "That I may know him."

And you who do not know him, and have not loved him, I pray you, breathe this prayer with me, " Lord, be merciful to me a sinner." O sinner, he is a gentle Christ; line is a loving Savior, and they that seek him early shall find him. May you seek and find him, for his name's sake. Amen.

Election no Discouragement to Seeking Souls

A Sermon (No. 553)
Delivered on Sunday Morning, February 7th, 1864, by the
Rev. C. H. SPURGEON,
At the Metropolitan Tabernacle, Newington

"I will be gracious upon whom I will be gracious, and will show mercy upon whom I will show mercy." -- Exodus 33:19.

BECAUSE GOD IS THE MAKER, and creator, and sustainer of all things, he has a right to do as he wills with all his works. "Shall the thing formed say to him that formed it, Why hast thou made me thus? Hath not the potter power over the clay of the same lump to make one vessel unto honor, and another unto dishonor?" God's absolute supremacy and unlimited sovereignty naturally flow from his omnipotence, and if it were not so, the superlative excellence of the divine character would entitle him to absolute dominion. He should be chief who is best. He who cannot err, being perfect in wisdom; he who will not err, being as perfect in holiness; he who can do no wrong, being supremely just; he who must act in accordance with the principles of kindness, seeing he is essentially love, is the most fitting person to rule. Tell me not of the creatures ruling themselves: what a chaos were this! Talk not of a supposed republic of all created existences, controlling and guiding themselves. All the creatures put together, with their combined wisdom and goodness--if, indeed, it were not combined folly and wickedness--all these, I say, with all the excellencies of knowledge, judgment, and love, which the most fervid imagination can suppose them to possess, could not make the equal of that great God whose name is holiness, whose essence is love, to whom all power belongeth, and to whom alone wisdom is to be ascribed. Let him reign supreme, for he is infinitely superior to all other existences. Even if he did not actually reign, the suffrages of all wise men would choose the Lord Jehovah to be absolute monarch of the universe; and if he were not already King of kings and Lord of lords, doing as he wills among the armies of heaven and the inhabitants of this lower world, it were the path of wisdom to lift him up to that throne. Since men have sinned, there becomes a yet further reason, or, rather a wider scope for the display of sovereignty. The creature, as a creature, may be supposed to have some claim upon the Creator; at least, it may expect that he shall not make it intentionally and despotically to put it to pain; that he shall not arbitrarily and without cause or necessity, cause its existence to be one of misery. I will not venture to judge the Lord, but I do think it is altogether incompatible with his goodness that he should have made a creature, and, as a creature, have condemned it to misery. Justice seems to demand that there shall be no punishment where there is no sin. But man has lost all his rights as a creature. If he ever had any, he has sinned them away. Our first parents have sinned, and we, their children, have attainted ourselves, by high treason against our liege lord and sovereign. All that a just God owes to any one of us on the footing of our own claim, is wrath and displeasure. If he should give to us our due, we should not longer remain on praying ground, breathing the air of mercy. The creature, before its Creator, must now be silent as to any demands upon him; it cannot require anything of him as a matter of right. If the Lord willeth to show mercy, it shall be so; but, if he withholds it, who can call him to account? "Can I not do as I will with mine own?" is a fit reply to all such arrogant enquiries; for man has sinned himself out of court, and there remains no right of appeal from the sentence of the Most High. Man is now in the position of a condemned criminal, whose only right is to be taken to the place of execution, and justly to suffer the due reward of his sins. Whatever difference of opinion, then, there might have been about the sovereignty of God as exercised upon creatures in the pure mass, there should be none, and there will be none, except in rebellious spirits, concerning the sovereignty of God over rebels who have sinned themselves into eternal ruin, and have lost all claim even to the mercy, much more the love of their offended Creator.

However, whether we all of us agree to the doctrine that God is sovereign or not, is a very little matter to him, for he is so. De jure, by right, he should be so; de facto, as matter of fact, he is so. It is a fact, concerning which you have only to open your eyes and see that God acts as a sovereign in the dispensation of his grace. Our Saviour, when he wished to quote instances of this, spake on this wise: many widows there were in Israel in the time of Elias the prophet, but unto none of these was Elias sent, save unto Sarepta, a city of Sidon, unto a woman who was a widow. Here was election! Elias is not sent to nourish and to be nourished by an Israelitish widow, but to a poor idolatress across the border, the blessing of the prophet's company is graciously granted. Again our Saviour says, "Many lepers were in Israel in the time of Eliseus the prophet; and none of them were cleansed, save only Naaman the Syrian"--not an Israelite at all, but one who bowed in the house of Rimmon. See how distinguishing grace finds out strange objects! Although our Saviour only gave these two instances, and no more, because they sufficed for his purpose, there are thousands of such cases on record. Look at man and the fallen angels. How is it that fallen angels are condemned to endless fire, and reserved in chains of darkness unto the great day? There is no Saviour for angels; no precious blood was ever shed for Satan. Lucifer falls, and falls for ever, never to hope again. There is no dispensation of mercy to those nobler spirits; but man who was made lower than the angels, is selected to be the object of divine redemption. What a great deep is here! This is a most illustrious and indisputable instance of the exercise of the prerogatives of divine sovereignty. Look again at the nations of the earth. Why is the gospel preached today, to us Englishmen? We have committed as many offenses--I will even venture to say we have perpetrated as many political crimes as other nations. Our eye is always prejudiced toward everything which is English; but if we read our history fairly, we can discover in the past, and detect in the present, grave and serious faults which disgrace our national banner. To pass by as minor offenses the late barbarities in Japan, and our frequent wars of extermination in New Zealand, and at the Cape, let it crimson the cheek of every inhabitant of the British Isles when we do but hint at the opium traffic with China. Yet to us the gospel is graciously sent, so that few nations enjoy it so fully as we do. It is true that Prussia and Holland hear the Word, and that Sweden and Denmark are comforted by the truth, but their candle burns but dimly; it is a poor flickering lamp which cheers their darkness, while in our own dear land, partly from the fact of our religious liberty, and yet more graciously through the late revival, the sun of the gospel shines brightly, and men rejoice in the light of day. Why this? Why no grace for the Japanese? Why no gospel preached to the inhabitants of Central Africa? Why was not the truth of God displayed in the Cathedral of Santiago, instead of the mummeries and follies which disgraced both dupes and deceivers, and were the incidental cause of the horrible burnings of that modern Tophet? Why today is not Rome, instead of being the seat of the beast, become the throne of Jesus Christ? I cannot tell you. But assuredly, divine sovereignty passing by many races of men, has been pleased to pitch upon the Anglo-Saxon family, that they may be as the Jews were aforetime, the custodians of divine truth, and the favorites of mighty grace.

We need not further speak upon national elections, for the principle is plainly carried out in individuals. See ye anything, my brethren, in that rich publican whose coffers are gorged with the results of his extortion, when he climbs the sycamore-tree, that his short stature may not prevent his seeing the Saviour--see ye anything in him why the Lord of glory should halt beneath that sycamore-tree and say, "Zaccheus, make haste, and come down; for today I must abide at thy house?" Can you find me a reason why yonder adulterous woman, who has had five husbands, and who is now living with a man who is not her husband, should constrain the Saviour to journey through Samaria that he might tell her of the water of life? If you can see anything, I cannot. Look at that bloodthirsty Pharisee, hurrying to Damascus with authority to hail men and women to prison, and shed their blood. The heat of midday cannot stop him, for his heart is hotter with religious rage than the sun with noontide rays. But see, he is arrested in his career, a brightness shines round about him; Jesus speaks from heaven the words of tender rebuke; and Saul of Tarsus becomes Paul, the apostle of God. Why? Wherefore? What answer can we give but this? "Even so, Father, for so it seemed good in thy sight." Read the "Life of John Newton;" had he not ripened into the grossest of all villains? Turn to the history of John Bunyan, by his own confession the lowest of all blackguards, and tell me, can you find in either of these offenders any sort of reason why the Lord should have chosen them to be among the most distinguished heralds of the cross? No man in his senses will venture to assert that there was anything in Newton or Bunyan why they should engross the regard of the Most High. It was sovereignty, and nothing but sovereignty. Take your own case, dear friends, and that shall be the most convincing of all to you. If you know anything of your own heart, if you have formed a right estimate of your own character, if you have seriously considered your own position before the Most High, the reflection that God loveth you with an everlasting love, and that, therefore, with the bands of his kindness he has drawn you, will draw forth from you at once the exclamation, "Not unto us, O Lord, not unto us, but unto thy name give glory, for thy mercy and for truth's sake." Brethren! the whole world is full of instances of divine sovereignty, for in every conversion some beam of the absolute dominion of God shines forth upon mankind.

When a sinner is anxiously disturbed about his soul's affairs, his chief and main thought should not be upon this subject; when a man would escape from wrath and attain to heaven, his first, his last, his middle thought should be the cross of Christ. As an awakened sinner, I have vastly less to do with the secret purposes of God, than with his revealed commands. For a man to say, "Thou commandest all men to repent, yet will I not repent, because I do not know that I am chosen to eternal life," is not only unreasonable, but exceedingly wicked. That it is unreasonable you will clearly see on a moment's reflection. I know that bread does not of itself nourish my body, "For man shall not live by bread alone, but by every word which proceedeth out of the mouth of God." It depends, therefore, upon God's decree whether that bread shall nourish my body or not; for if he has not purposed that it shall, it may even choke me, and so become rather the cause of my death than the staff of my life. Do I therefore, when I am hungry, thrust my hands into my pockets and stand still, and refuse to help myself from the well-loaded table, because I do not know whether God has decreed that the bread shall nourish me or not? If I did, I should be an idiot or madman; or if in my senses, I should starve myself on such a pretence, I should richly deserve the burial of a suicide. I am not absolutely sure that there will be a harvest upon my field next year: unless God has ordained that the corn shall spring up and shall ripen, all my husbandry will be labor lost. There are worms in the earth, frosts in the air, birds in the sky, mildews in the winds--all of which may destroy my corn, and I may lose every single grain of the handsful which I throw into my furrows. Shall I, therefore, leave my farm to be one perpetual fallow, because I do not know whether God has decreed that there shall be a harvest or not next year? If I become a bankrupt--if I am unable to pay my rent--if the thorn and the thistle grow taller and higher, and if at last, my landlord thrusts me from my tenancy, all that men will say, will be, "It serves him right!"--because I was such a fool as to make the secret purposes of God a matter of paramount consideration, instead of performing my known duty. I am ill and sick: a physician comes to me with medicine. I am not clear that his medicine will heal me; it has healed a great many others, but if God has decreed that I shall die, I shall die, let me take any quantity of physic, or take none at all. My arm mortifies, but I will not have it cut off, because I do not know whether God has decreed that I shall die of mortification or not. Who but a crazed idiot, or raving maniac, would talk thus? When I put the case in that light, you all reply, "Nobody ever talks in that way; it is too absurd." Of course, nobody does. And the fact is, even in the things of God, nobody really does argue in that way. A man may say, "I will not believe in Christ, because I am afraid I am not elected;" but the thing is so stupid, so absurd, that I do not believe that any man, not absolutely demented, can be so grossly foolish as to believe in his own reasoning. I am far rather inclined to think that is a wicked and perverse method of endeavoring to stultify conscience, on the theory that a bad excuse is better than none, and that even a foolish argument is better than having one's mouth shut in speechless confusion.

But since men will everlastingly be getting to his point, and there are so many who are always giving this as a reason why they do not believe in the Lord Jesus Christ, because, "It is not of him that willeth, nor of him that runneth, but of God that showeth mercy," I shall try, this morning, to talk with these people on their own ground; and I shall endeavor, by the help of the Holy Spirit, to show that the doctrine of the sovereignty of God, so far from discouraging anybody, has not in it, if regarded aright, any sort of discouragement whatever, for any souls believing in Jesus Christ.

For one moment let me detain you from my object, while I reply to a very common method of misrepresenting the doctrine. It may be as well to start with a clear idea of what the doctrine really is. Our opponents put the case thus: suppose a father should condemn some of his children to extreme misery, and make others supremely happy, out of his own arbitrary will, would it be right and just? Would it not be brutal and detestable? My answer is, of course, it would; it would be execrable in the highest degree, and far, very far be it from us to impute such a course of action to the Judge of all the earth. But the case stated is not at all the one under consideration, but one as opposite from it as light from darkness. Sinful man is not now in the position of a well-deserving or innocent child, neither does God occupy the place of a complacent parent. We will suppose another case far nearer the mark, indeed, it is no supposition, but an exact description of the whole matter. A number of criminals, guilty of the most aggravated and detestable crimes, are righteously condemned to die, and die they must, unless the king shall exercise the prerogative vested in him, and give them a free pardon. If for good and sufficient reasons, known only to himself, the king chooses to forgive a certain number, and to leave the rest for execution, is there anything cruel or unrighteous here? If, by some wise means, the ends of justice can be even better answered by the sparing of the pardoned ones, than by their condemnation, while at the same time, the punishment of some tends to honor the justice of the lawgiver, who shall dare to find fault? None, I venture to say, but those who are the enemies of the state and of the king. And so may we well ask, "Is there unrighteousness with God? God forbid." "What if God, willing to shew his wrath, and to make his power known, endured with much longsuffering the vessels of wrath fitted to destruction: and that he might make known the riches of his glory on the vessels of mercy, which he had afore prepared unto glory, even us, whom he hath called, not of the Jews only, but also of the Gentiles?" Who is he that shall impugn the mingled mercy and severity of heaven, or make the eternal God an offender, because "he hath mercy on whom he will have mercy?" Let us now proceed to our proper subject, and endeavor to clear this truth from the terrors supposed to cluster around it.

I. Let us begin with this assertion, which we are absolutely sure is correct: THIS DOCTRINE DOES NOT OPPOSE ANY COMFORT DERIVED FROM OTHER SCRIPTURAL TRUTHS.

This doctrine, stern as it may seem to be, does not oppose the consolation which may be rightly derived from any other truth of revelation. Those who hold the free-will theory, say that our doctrine, that salvation is of the Lord alone, and that he will have mercy on whom he will have mercy, takes away from man the comfort derivable from God's goodness. God is good, infinitely good in his nature. God is love; he willeth not the death of any, but had rather that all should come to repentance. "As I live, saith the Lord, I have no pleasure in the death of him that dieth, but had rather that he should turn unto me and live." Our friends very properly insist upon it that God is good to all, and his tender mercies are over all his works; that the Lord is merciful and gracious, slow to anger, and plenteous in mercy; let me assure them that we shall never quarrel on these points, for we also rejoice in the same facts. Some of you have listened to my voice for these ten years: I ask you whether you have heard me utter a single sentence which at all contradicts the doctrine of God's great goodness? You may have so construed it by mistake, but no such teaching has passed my lip. Do I not, again and again, assert the universal benevolence of God--the infinite and overflowing goodness of the heart of the Most High? If any man can preach upon the great text, "God is love," though I may not be able to preach with the same eloquence, I will venture to view with him in the decision, heartiness, delight, earnestness, and plainness, with which he may expound his theme, be he who he may, or what he may. There is not the slightest shadow of a conflict between God's sovereignty and God's goodness. He may be a sovereign, and yet it may be absolutely certain that he will always act in the way of goodness and love. It is true that he will do as he wills; and yet it is quite certain that he always wills to do that which, in the widest view of it, is good and gracious. If the sons of sorrow fetch any comfort from the goodness of God, the doctrine of election will never stand in their way. Only mark, it does with a two-edged sword cut to pieces that false confidence in God's goodness which sends so many souls to hell. We have heard dying men singing themselves into the bottomless pit with this lullaby, "Yes, sir, I am a sinner, but God is merciful; God is good." Ah! dear friends, let such remember that God is just as well as good, and that he will by no means spare the guilty, except through the great atonement of his Son Jesus Christ. The doctrine of election, in a most blessedly honest manner does come in, and breaks the neck, once for all, of all this false and groundless confidence in the uncovenanted mercy of God. Sinner, you have no right to trust to the goodness of God out of Christ. There is no word in the whole Book of Inspiration, which gives the shadow of a hope to the man who will not believe in Jesus Christ. It says of him, "He that believeth not shall be damned." It declares of you, who are resting upon such a poor confidence as the unpromised favor of heaven, "Other foundation can no man lay than that which is laid, Jesus Christ the righteous." If this be an evil to rob you of a false refuge, the doctrine of election certainly does this; but from the comfort properly derivable from the largest view of God's bounteous goodness and unlimited love, election does not detract a single grain.

Much comfort, too, flows to a troubled conscience from the promise that God will hear prayer. "Ask, and it shall be given you; seek, and ye shall find; knock, and it shall be opened unto you, for every one that asketh receiveth; and he that seeketh findeth; and to him that knocketh it shall be opened." If you ask anything of God in the name of Jesus Christ, you shall receive it. Now, there are some who imagine that they must not pray because they do not know whether they are God's chosen people. If you refuse to pray on the ground of such bad reasoning as this, you must do so at your own expense; but do mark our solemn assurance, for which we have God's warrant, that there is nothing in the sovereignty of God which at all militates against the great truth, that every sincerely seeking soul, craving divine grace by humble prayer through Jesus Christ, shall be a finder. There may be an Arminian brother here who would like to get into this pulpit and preach the cheering truth, that God hath not said to the seed of Jacob, seek ye my face in vain. We not only accord him full liberty to preach this doctrine, but we will go as far as he can, and perhaps a little further, in the enunciation of that truth. We cannot perceive any discrepancy between personal election and the prevalence of prayer. Let those who can, vex their brains with the task of reconciling them; to us the wonder is how a man can believe the one without the other. Firmly must I believe that the Lord God will show mercy to whom he will show mercy, and have compassion on whom he will have compassion; but I know as assuredly that wherever there is a genuine prayer, God gave it; that wherever there is a seeker, God made him seek; consequently if God has made the man seek and made the man pray, there is evidence at once of divine election; and the fact stands true that none seek who shall not find.

Very much comfort also is supposed to be derived, and naturally so, from the free invitations of the gospel. "Ah," cries one, "what a sweet thing it is that the Saviour cried, Come unto me all ye that labor and are heavy laden, and I will give you rest.' How delightful to read such a word as this, Ho, every one that thirsteth, come ye to the waters, and he that hath no money; come ye, buy, and eat; yea, come, buy wine and milk without money and without price,' Sir, my heart is encouraged when I find it written, Whosoever will, let him take the water of life freely.' But, sir, I dare not come because of the doctrine of election." My dear hearer, I would not say anything harshly to you, but I must express my conviction that this is nothing but an idle excuse for not doing what you have no mind to do; because invitations of the most general character, nay, invitations which shall be universal in their scope, are perfectly consistent with the election of God. I have preached here, you know it, invitations as free as those which proceeded from the lips of Master John Wesley. Van Armin himself, the founder of the Arminian school, could not more honestly have pleaded with the very vilest of the vile to come to Jesus than I have done. Have I therefore felt in my mind that there was a contradiction here? No, nothing of the kind; because I know it to be my duty to sow beside all waters, and like the sower in the parable, to scatter the seed upon the stony ground, as well as upon the good land, knowing that election does not narrow the gospel call which is universal, but only affects the effectual call, which is and must be from the Spirit of God. My business is to give the general call, the Holy Spirit will see to its application to the chosen. O my dear hearers, God's invitations are honest invitations to every one of you. He invites you; in the words of the parable he addresses, "All things are ready; come ye to the supper, my oxen and my fatlings are killed." Nay, he saith to his ministers, "Go out into the highways and hedges, and compel them to come in." Though he foreknows who will come in, and has before all worlds ordained who shall taste of that supper, yet the invitation in its widest possible range, is a true and honest one; and if you accept it you shall find it so.

Furthermore, if we understand the gospel at all, the gospel lies in a nutshell. It is this:-- "Believe in the Lord Jesus Christ, and thou shalt be saved." Or, to use Christ's words, "He that believeth and is baptized shall be saved, and he that believeth not shall be damned." This promise is the gospel. Now, the gospel is true, whatever else may be false. Whatever doctrine may or may not be of God, the gospel certainly is. The doctrine of sovereign grace is not contrary to the gospel, but perfectly consonant therewith. God has a people whom no man shall number, whom he hath ordained unto eternal life. This is, by no means, in conflict with the great declaration, "He that believeth on him is not condemned." If any man who ever lived, or ever shall live, believes in Jesus Christ, he hath eternal life. Election or no election, if you are resting upon the rock of ages you are saved. If you, as a guilty sinner, take the righteousness of Christ--if all black, and foul, and filthy, you come to wash in the fountain filled with blood, sovereignty or no sovereignty, rest assured of this, that you are redeemed from the wrath to come. O my dear friends, when you say, "I will not believe in Christ because of election," I can only say as Job did to his wife, "Thou speakest as one of the foolish women speaketh." How dare you, because God reveals to you two things, which two things you cannot make square with one another--how dare you charge either the one or the other with being false? If I believe God, I am not only to believe what I can understand, but what I cannot understand; and if there were a revelation which I could comprehend and sum up as I may count five upon my fingers, I should be sure it did not come from God. But if it has some depths vastly too deep for me--some knots which I cannot untie--some mysteries which I cannot solve--I receive it with the greater confidence, because it now gives me swimming-room for my faith, and my soul bathes herself in the great sea of God's wisdom, praying, "Lord, I believe; help thou mine unbelief."

Let it be said over and over again, that there shall be no doubt about this matter, that if there be any comfort derivable from the gospel; if there be any sweet consolation flowing from the free invitations and the universal commands of divine truth, all those may be received and enjoyed by you, while you hold this doctrine of divine sovereignty as much as if you did not hold it, and received some wider scheme. Methinks I hear one voice say, "Sir, the only comfort I can ever have lies in the infinite value of the precious blood of Christ; O sir, it seems to me such a sweet thing that there is no sinner so black that Christ cannot wash away his sins, and no sinner so old that the meritorious virtue of that atonement cannot meet his case--not one in any rank or in any condition whom that blood cannot cleanse from all sin. Now, sir, if that be true, how can the doctrine of election be true?" My dear friend, you know in your own heart that the two things are not opposed to each other at all. For what does the doctrine of election say? It says that God has chosen and has saved some of the greatest sinners who ever lived, has cleansed some of the foulest sins ever committed, and that he is doing and will do the same to the world's end. So that the two things exactly tally. And I will venture to say that if in the fulness of a man's heart he shall say, "There is no sin except the one excepted sin, which cannot be forgiven," if he boldly announce that "All manner of sin shall be forgiven unto men," and if he shall plead with power and earnestness that souls would now come to Christ and lay hold upon eternal life, he may go back to his Bible, and he may read every text teaching the sovereignty of God, and every passage upholding divine election; nd he may feel that all these texts look him in the face, and say, "Well done, our spirit and your spirit are precisely the same; we have no conflict together; we are two great truths which came from the same God; we are alike the revelation of the Holy Ghost." But we leave that point. If there be any comfort, sinner, which you can truthfully and rightly get from any passage of Scripture, from any promise of God, from any invitation, from any open door of mercy, you may have it, for the doctrine of election does not rob you of one atom of the consolation which the truth of God can afford you.

II. But now will take another point for a moment. Our second head is, that THIS DOCTRINE HAS A MOST SALUTARY EFFECT UPON SINNERS. These may be divided into two classes: those who are awakened, and those who are hardened and incorrigible.

To the awakened sinner, next to the doctrine of the cross, the doctrine of distinguishing grace is perhaps the most fraught with blessings and comfort. In the first place, the doctrine of election, applied by the Holy Ghost, strikes dead for ever all the efforts of the flesh. It is the end of Arminian preaching to make men active, to excite them to do what they can; but the very end and object of gospel preaching is to make men feel that they have no power of their own, and to lay them as dead, at the foot of God's throne. We seek, under God, to make them feel that all their strength must lie in the Strong One who is mighty to save. If I can convince a man that, let him do what he may, he cannot save himself; if I can show him that his own prayers and tears can never save him apart from the Spirit of God; if I can convince him that he must be born again from above; if I lead him to see that all which is born of the flesh is flesh, and only that which is born of the spirit is spirit, brethren! three parts of the great battle are already won. "I kill and I make alive," saith God: "when a man is killed the work is half done." "I wound and I heal: when a man is wounded his salvation is commenced." What! am I to set a sinner industriously to labor after eternal life by his own works? Then, indeed, am I an ambassador of hell. Am I to teach him that there is a goodness in him which he is to evolve, to polish, and educate and perfect, and so to save himself? Then I am a teacher of the beggarly elements of the law and not the gospel of Christ. Are we to set forth man's prayers, repentings, and humblings as the way of salvation; if so, let us renounce the righteousness of Christ at once, for the two will never stand together! I am a mischief-maker if I excite the activities of the flesh instead of pointing to the arms of the Redeemer! But if the potent hammer of electing sovereignty dashes out the brains of all a man's works, merits, doings, and willings, while it pronounces over the dead carcass this sentence: "It is not of him that willeth, nor of him that runneth, but of God that showeth mercy;" then, the best thing is done for a sinner that can be done as a stepping-stone to the act of faith. When a man is weaned from self, and totally delivered from looking to the flesh for help, there is hope for him: and this the doctrine of divine sovereignty does through the Holy Spirit's power.

Again, this doctrine gives the greatest hope to the really awakened sinner. You know how the case stands. We are all prisoners condemned to die. God, as sovereign, has a right to pardon whom he pleases. Now, imagine a number of us shut up in a condemned cell, all guilty. One of the murderers says within himself: "I know that I have no reason to expect to be delivered. I am not rich: if I had some rich relations, like George Townley, I might be found insane, and delivered. But I am very poor; I am not educated. If I had the education of some men I might expect some consideration. I am not a man of rank and position; I am a man without merit or influence, therefore I cannot expect that I should be selected as one to be saved." No, I believe that if the present authorities of our land were the persons to be taken into consideration, a man who was poor might have a very poor chance of expecting any gratuitous deliverance. But when God is the great sovereign the case is different. For then, we argue thus: "Here am I; my salvation depends entirely upon the will of God: is there a chance for me? We take down a list of those whom he has saved, and we find that he saves the poor, the illiterate, the wicked, the godless, and the worst of the worst, the base things, and things that are despised. Well, what do we say? Then, why may he not choose me? Why not save me? If I am to look for some reason in myself why I should be saved, I shall never find any, and consequently never shall have a hope. But if I am to be saved for no reason at all but that God wills to save me, ah! then there is hope for me. I will to the gracious King approach, I will do as he bids me, I will trust in his dear Son, and I shall be saved." So that this doctrine opens the door of hope to the worst of the worst, and the only persons it discourages are the Pharisees, who say: "Lord, I thank thee that I am not as other men are"--those proud, haughty spirits who say: "No! if I am not to be saved for something good in myself, then I will be damned!" as damned they will be with a vengeance, too.

Moreover, do not you see, dear friends, how the doctrine of election comforts the sinner in the matter of power. His complaint is, "I find I have no power to believe; I have no spiritual power of any kind." Election stoops down and whispers in his ear--"But if God wills to save you, he gives the power, gives the life, and gives the grace; and therefore since he has given that power and might to others as weak as you, why not to you? Have courage, look to the cross of Christ and live." And oh! what emotions of gratitude, what throbbings of love does this doctrine cause in human hearts. "Why," saith the man, "I am saved simply because God would save me, not because I deserved it, but because his loving heart would save me; then, I will love him, I will live to him, I will spend and be spent for him." Such a man cannot be proud, I mean not consistently with the doctrine. He lies humbly at God's feet. Other men may boast of what they are, and how they have own eternal life by their own goodness, but I cannot. If God had left me, I had been in hell with others; and if I go to heaven, I must cast my crown at the feet of the grace which brought me there. Such a man will become kind to others. He will hold his opinions, but he will not hold them savagely, nor teach them bitterly, because he will say, "If I have light, and others have not, my light was given me from God, therefore, I have no cause to plume myself upon it. I will try to spread that light, but not by anger and abuse. For why should I blame those who cannot see, for could I have seen if God had not opened my blind eyes?" Every virtue this doctrine fosters, and every vice it kills, when the Holy Spirit so uses it. Pride it treads under foot, and humble, trustful confidence in the mercy of God in Christ, it cherishes as a darling child.

My time is gone; but I wanted to have said a word as to the effect of this gospel upon incorrigible sinners. I will just say this: I know what the effect of it ought to be. What do you say who have made up your minds not to repent, you who care not for God? Why, you believe that any day you like you can turn to God, since God is merciful, and will save you; and therefore, you walk about the world as comfortably as possible, thinking it all depends upon you, and that you will get into heaven just at the eleventh hour. Ah! man, that is not your case. See where you are. Do you see that moth fluttering in my hand! Imagine it to be there. With this finger of mine I can crush it--in a moment. Whether it shall live or not depends absolutely upon whether I choose to crush it or let it go. That is precisely your position at the present moment. God can damn you now. Nay, let us say to you, "Yours is a worse position than that." There are some seven persons now doomed for murder and piracy on the high seas. You can clearly say that their lives depend upon Her Majesty's pleasure. If Her Majesty chooses to pardon them she can. If not, when the fatal morning comes, the bolt will be drawn and they will be launched into eternity. That is your case, sinner. You are condemned already. This world is but one huge condemned cell in which you are kept, until the execution morning comes. If you are ever to be pardoned, God must do it. You cannot escape from him by flight; you cannot bribe him by actions of your own. You are absolutely in the hand of God, and if he leaves you where you are and as you are, your eternal ruin is as certain as your existence. Now, does not this make some sort of trembling come upon you? Perhaps not; it makes you angry. Well, if it does, that will not frighten me, because there are some of you who will never be good for anything until you are angry. I believe it is no ill sign when some persons are angry with the truth. It shows that the truth has pierced them. If an arrow penetrates my flesh, I do not like the arrow, and if you kick and struggle against this truth, it will not alarm me; I shall have some hope that a wound is made. If this truth should provoke you to think, it will have done for some of you one of the greatest things in the world. It is not your perverse thinking which frightens me; it is the utterly thoughtless way in which you go on. If you had sense enough to consider these things and fight against them, I should then have some faint hope of you. But alas! many of you have not sense enough, you say, "Yes, yes, it is all true," you accept it, but then it has no effect upon you. The gospel rolls over you, like oil adown a slab of marble, and produces no effect.

If you are at all right in heart, you will begin to see what your state is, and the next thing that will startle your mind will be the reflection: "Is it so? am I absolutely in God's hands? can he save me or damn me as he will? Then, I will cry to him, O God, save me from the wrath to come--from eternal torment--from banishment from thy presence. Save me, O God! What wouldst thou have me to do? Oh! what wouldst thou have me to do, that I may find thy favor and live?'" Then comes the answer to you:--"Believe in the Lord Jesus Christ and you shall be saved;" for "whosoever believeth in him shall never perish, but shall have eternal life."

O that God might bless this divine doctrine to you. I have never preached this doctrine without conversions, and I believe I never shall. At this moment God will cause his truth to attract your hearts to Jesus, or to affright you to him. May you be drawn as the bird is drawn by the lure, or may you be driven as a dove is hunted by the hawk into the clefts of the rock. Only may you be sweetly compelled to come. May my Lord fulfill this desire of my heart. O that God may grant me your souls for my hire; and to him shall be the glory, world without end. Amen.

Enduring to the End

A Sermon (No. 554)
Delivered on Sunday Morning, February 14th, 1864, by the
Rev. C. H. SPURGEON,
At the Metropolitan Tabernacle, Newington

"He that endureth to the end shall be saved." -- Matthew 10:22.

THIS PARTICULAR TEXT was originally addressed to the apostles when they were sent to teach and preach in the name of the Lord Jesus. Perhaps bright visions floated before their minds, of honor and esteem among men. It was no mean dignity to be among the twelve first heralds of salvation to the sons of Adam. Was a check needed to their high hopes? Perhaps so. Lest they should enter upon their work without having counted its cost, Christ gives them a very full description of the treatment which they might expect to receive, and reminds them that it was not the commencement of their ministry which would win them their reward, but "He that endureth to the end, the same shall be saved." It would be well if every youthful aspirant to the gospel ministry would remember this, if merely to put our hand to the plough proved us to be called of God, how many would he found so; but alas, too many look back and prove unworthy of the kingdom. The charge of Paul to Timothy, is a very necessary exhortation to every young minister: "Be thou faithful unto death." It is not to be faithful for a time, but to be "faithful unto death," which will enable a man to say, "I have fought a good fight." How many dangers surround the Christian minister! As the officers in an army are the chosen targets of the sharpshooters, so are the ministers of Christ. The king of Syria said to his servants, "Fight neither with small nor great, save only with the king of Israel;" even so the arch-fiend makes his main attack upon the ministers of God. From the first moment of his call to the work, the preacher of the Word will be familiar with temptation. While he is yet in his youth, there are multitudes of the softer temptations to turn the head and trip the feet of the youthful herald of the cross; and when the blandishments of early popularity have passed away, as soon they must, the harsh croak of slander, and the adder's tongue of ingratitude assail him, he finds himself stale and fiat where once he was flattered and admired; nay, the venom of malice succeeds to the honeyed morsels of adulation. Now, let him gird his loins and fight the good fight of faith. In his after days, to provide fresh matter Sabbath after Sabbath, to rule as in the sight of God, to watch over the souls of men, to weep with them who weep, to rejoice with those who do rejoice, to be a nursing father unto young converts, sternly to rebuke hypocrites, to deal faithfully with backsliders, to speak with solemn authority and paternal pathos to those who are in the first stages of spiritual decline, to carry about with him the care of the souls of hundreds, is enough to make him grow old while yet he is young, and to mar his visage with the lines of grief, till, like the Savior, at the age of thirty years, men shall count him nearly fifty. "Thou art not yet fifty years old, and hast thou seen Abraham?" said the adversaries of Christ to him when he was but thirty-two. If the minister should fall, my brethren; if, set upon a pinnacle, he should be cast down; if, standing in slippery places, he should falter; if the standard-bearer fall, as fall full well he may, what mischief is done to the Church, what shouts are heard among the adversaries, what dancings are seen among the daughters of Philistia! How hath God's banner been stained in the dust, and the name of Jesus cast into the mire! When the minister of Christ turns traitor, it is as if the pillars of the house did tremble; every stone in the structure feels the shock. If Satan can succeed in overturning the preachers of the Word, it is as if yon broad-spreading tree should suddenly fall beneath the axe; prone in the dust it lies to wither and to rot; but where are the birds of the air which made their nests among its boughs, and whither fly those beasts of the field which found a happy shadow beneath its branches? Dismay hath seized them, and they flee in affright. All who were comforted by the preacher's word, strengthened by his example, and edified by his teaching, are filled with humiliation and grief, crying, "Alas! my brother." By these our manifold dangers and weighty responsibilities, we may very justly appeal to you who feed under our ministry, and beseech you, "Brethren, pray for us." Well, we know that though our ministry be received of the Lord Jesus, if hitherto we have been kept faithful by the power of the Holy Ghost, yet it is only he who endureth to the end who shall be saved.

But, my brethren, how glorious is the sight of the man who does endure to the end as a minister of Christ. I have photographed upon my heart just now, the portrait of one very, very dear to me, and I think I may venture to produce a rough sketch of him, as no mean example of how honorable it is to endure to the end. This man began while yet a youth to preach the Word. Sprung of ancestors who had loved the Lord and served his Church, he felt the glow of holy enthusiasm. Having proved his capabilities, he entered college, and after the close of its course, settled in a spot where for more than fifty years he continued his labors. In his early days, his sober earnestness and sound doctrine were owned of God in many conversions both at home and abroad. Assailed by slander and abuse, it was his privilege to live it all down. He outlived his enemies, and though he had buried a generation of his friends, yet he found many warm hearts clustering round him to the last. Visiting his flock, preaching in his own pulpit, and making very many journeys to other Churches, years followed one another so rapidly, that he found himself the head of a large tribe of children and grandchildren, most of them walking in the truth. At the age of fourscore years, he preached on still, until laden with infirmities, but yet as joyful and as cheerful as in the heyday of his youth, his time had come to die. He was able to say truthfully, when last he spake to me, "I do not know that my testimony for God has ever altered, as to the fundamental doctrines; I have grown in experience, but from the first day until now, I have had no new doctrines to teach my hearers. I have had to make no confessions of error on vital points, but have been held fast to the doctrines of grace, and can now say that I love them better than ever." Such an one was he, as Paul, the aged, longing to preach so long as his tottering knees could bear him to the pulpit. I am thankful that I had such a grandsire. He fell asleep in Christ but a few hours ago, and on his dying bed talked as cheerfully as men can do in the full vigor of their health. Most sweetly he talked of the preciousness of Christ, and chiefly of the security of the believer; the truthfulness of the promise; the immutability of the covenant; the faithfulness of God, and the infallibility of the divine decree. Among other things which he said at the last was this, which is, we think, worth your treasuring in your memories. "Dr Watts sings--

'Firm as the earth thy gospel stands,
My Lord, my hope, my trust.'

What, Doctor, is it not firmer than that? Could you not find a better comparison? Why, the earth will give way beneath our feet one day or another, if we rest on it. The comparison will not do. The Doctor was much nearer the mark, when he said--

"Firm as his throne his promise stands,
And he can well secure
What I've committed to his hands.
'Till the decisive hour.'"

"Firm as his throne," said he, "he must cease to be king before he can break his promise, or lose his people. Divine sovereignty makes us all secure." He fell asleep right quietly, for his day was over, and the night was come, what could he do better than go to rest in Jesus? Would God it may be our lot to preach the Word, so long as we breathe, standing fast unto the end in the truth of God; and if we see not our sons and grandsons testifying to those doctrines which are so dear to us, yet may we see our children walking in the truth. I know of nothing, dear friends, which I would choose to have, as the subject of my ambition for life, than to be kept faithful to my God to death, still to be a soul-winner, still to be a true herald of the cross, and testify the name of Jesus to the last hour. It is only such who in the ministry shall be saved.

Our text, however, occurs again in the twenty-fourth chapter of Matthew, at the fourteenth verse, upon which occasion it was not addressed to the apostles, but to the disciples. The disciples, looking upon the huge stones which were used in the construction of the Temple, admired the edifice greatly, and expected their Lord to utter a few words of passing encomium; instead of which, he, who came not to be an admirer of architecture, but to hew living stones out of the quarry of nature, to build them up into a spiritual temple turned their remarks to practical account, by warning them of a time of affliction, in which there should be such trouble as had never been before, and he added, "No, nor ever shall be." He described false prophets as abounding, and the love of many as waxing cold, and warned them that "He that endureth to the end, the same shall be saved." So that this solemn truth applies to every one of you.

The Christian man, though not called to the post of danger in witnessing publicly of the grace of God, is destined in his measure to testify concerning Jesus, and in his proper sphere and place, to be a burning and a shining light. He may not have the cares of a Church, but he hath far more, the cares of business: he is mixed up with the world; he is compelled to associate with the ungodly. To a great degree, he must, at least six days in the week, walk in an atmosphere uncongenial with his nature: he is compelled to hear words which will never provoke him to love and good works, and to behold actions whose example is obnoxious. He is exposed to temptations of every sort and size, for this is the lot of the followers of the Lamb. Satan knows how useful is a consistent follower of the Savior, and how much damage to Christ's cause an inconsistent professor may bring, and therefore he emptieth out all his arrows from his quiver that he may wound, even unto death, the soldier of the cross. My brethren, many of you have had a far longer experience than myself; you know how stern is the battle of the religious life, how you must contend, even unto blood, striving against sin. Your life is one continued scene of warfare, both without and within; perhaps even now you are crying with the apostle, " wretched man that I am! who shall deliver me from the body of this death?" A Christian's career is always fighting, never ceasing; always ploughing the stormy sea, and never resting till he reaches the port of glory. If my God shall preserve you, as preserve you he must, or else you are not his; if he shall keep you, as keep you he will if you have committed your souls to his faithful guardianship, what an honor awaits you! I have in my mind's eye, just now, one who has been for about sixty years associated with this Church, and who this week, full of years, and ripe for heaven, was carried by angels into the Savior's bosom. Called by divine grace, while yet young, he was united with the Christian Church early in life. By divine grace, he was enabled to maintain a consistent and honorable character for many years; as an officer of this Church, he was acceptable among his brethren, and useful both by his godly example and sound judgment; while in various parts of the Church of Christ, he earned unto himself a good degree. He went last Sabbath day, twice to the house of God where he was accustomed of late years to worship, enjoying the Word, and feasting at the Communion-table with much delight. He went to his bed without having any very serious illness upon him, having spent his last evening upon earth in cheerful conversation with his daughters. Ere the morning light, with his head leaning upon his hand, he had fallen asleep in Christ, having been admitted to the rest which remaineth for the people of God. As I think of my brother, though of late years I have seen but little of him, I can but rejoice in the grace which illuminated his pathway. When I saw him, the week before his departure, although full of years, there was little or no failure in mind. He was just the picture of an aged saint waiting for his Master, and willing to work in his cause while life remained. I refer, as most of you know, to Mr. Samuel Gale. Let us thank God and take courage--thank God that he has preserved in this case, a Christian so many, many years, and take courage to hope that there will be found in this Church, many, at all periods, whose grey heads shall be crowns of glory. "He that endureth to the end," and only he "shall be saved."

But, dear friends, perseverance is not the lot of the few; it is not left to laborious preachers of the Word, or to consistent Church-officers, it is the common lot of every believer in the Church. It must be so, for only thus can they prove that they are believers. It must be so, for only by their perseverance can the promise be fulfilled, "He that believeth and is baptized, shall be saved." Without perseverance, they cannot be saved; and, as saved they must be, persevere they shall through divine grace.

I shall now, with brevity and earnestness, as God enables me, speak upon our text thus: perseverance is the badge of saints--the target of our foes--the glory of Christ--and the care of all believers.

I. First, then, PERSEVERANCE IS THE BADGE OF TRUE SAINTS. It is their Scriptural mark. How am I to know a Christian? By his words? Well, to some degree, words betray the man; but a man's speech is not always the copy of his heart, for with smooth language many are able to deceive. What doth our Lord say? "Ye shall know them by their fruits." But how am I to know a man's fruits? By watching him one day? I may, perhaps, form a guess of his character by being with him for a single hour, but I could not confidently pronounce upon a man's true state even by being with him for a week. George Whitfield was asked what he thought of a certain person's character. "I have never lived with him," was his very proper answer. If we take the run of a man's life, say for ten, twenty, or thirty years, and, if by carefully watching, we see that he brings forth the fruits of grace through the Holy Spirit, our conclusion may be drawn very safely. As the truly magnetized needle in the compass, with many deflections, yet does really and naturally point to the pole; so, if I can see that despite infirmities, my friend sincerely and constantly aims at holiness, then I may conclude with something like certainty, that he is a child of God. Although works do not justify a man before God, they do justify a luau's profession before his fellows. I cannot tell whether you are justified in calling yourself a Christian except by your works; by your works, therefore, as James saith, shall ye be justified. You cannot by your words convince me that you are a Christian, much less by your experience, which I cannot see but must take on trust from you; but your actions will, unless you be an unmitigated hypocrite, speak the truth, and speak the truth loudly too. If your course is as the shining light which shineth more unto the perfect day, I know that yours is the path of the just. All other conclusions are only the judgment of charity such as we are bound to exercise;

but this is as far as man can get it, the judgment of certainty when a man's life has been consistent through out.

Moreover, analogy shows us that it is perseverance which must mark the Christian. How do I know the winner at the foot-race? There are the spectators, and there are the runners. What strong men! what magnificent muscles! what thews and sinews! Yonder is the goal, and there it is that I must judge who is the winner, not here, at the starting-point, for "They which run in a race run all, but one receiveth the prize." I may select this one, or that other person, as likely to win, but I cannot be absolutely sure until the race is over. There they fly! see how they press forward with straining muscles; but one has tripped, another faints, a third is out of breath, and others are far behind. One only wins--and who is he? Why, he who continueth to the end, So I may gather from the analogy, which Paul constantly allows us, from the ancient games, that only he who continueth till he reaches the goal may be accounted a Christian at all. A ship starts on a voyage to Australia--if it stops at Madeira, or returns after reaching the Cape, would you consider that it ought to be called an emigrant ship for New South Wales? It must go the whole voyage, or it does not deserve the name. A man has begun to build a house, and has erected one side of it--do you consider him a builder if he stops there, and fails to cover it in or to finish the other walls? Do we give men praise for being warriors because they know how to make one desperate charge, but lose the campaign? Have we not, of late, smiled at the boasting despatches of commanders, in fights where both combatants fought with valor, and yet neither of them had the common sense to push on to reap the victory? What was the very strength of Wellington, but that when a triumph had been achieved, he knew how to reap the harvest which had been sown in blood? And he only is a true conqueror, and shall be crowned at the last, who continueth till war's trumpet is blown no more. It is with a Christian as it was with the great Napoleon: he said, "Conquest has made me what I am, and conquest must maintain me." So, under God, conquest has made you what you are, and conquest must sustain you. Your motto must be, "Excelsior;" or, if it be not, you know not the noble spirit of God's princes. But why do I multiply illustrations, when all the world rings with the praise of perseverance?

Moreover, the common-sense judgment of mankind tells us, that those who merely begin and do not hold out, will not be saved. Why, if every man would be saved who began to follow Christ, who would be damned? In such a country as this, the most of men have at least one religious spasm in their lives. I suppose that there is not a person before me, who at some time or other did not determine to be a pilgrim. You, Mr. Pliable, were induced by a Christian friend, who had some influence with you, to go with him some short way, till you came to the Slough of Despond, and you thought yourself very wise when you scrambled out on that side which was nearest to your own home. And even you, Mr. Obstinate, are not always dogged; you have fits of thoughtfulness and intervals of tenderness. My hearer, how impressed you were at the prayer meeting! how excited you were at that revival service! When you heard a zealous brother preach at the theater what an impression was produced! Ah! yes; the shop was shut up for a Sunday or two; you did not swear or get drunk for nearly a month, but you could not hold on any longer. Now, if those who were to begin were saved, why you would be secure, though you are at the present time as far from anything like religion, as the darkness at midnight is from the blazing light of midday. Besides, common sense shows us, I say, that a man must hold on, or else he cannot be saved, because the very worst of men are those who begin and then give up. If you would turn over all the black pages of villany, to find the name of the son of perdition, where would you find it? Why, among the apostles. The man who had wrought miracles and preached the gospel, sold his Master for thirty pieces of silver--Judas Iscariot, betrays the Son of Man with a kiss. Where is a worse name than that of Simon Magus? Simon "believed also," says the Scripture, and yet he offered the apostles money if they would sell to him the Holy Ghost. What an infamous notoriety Demas has obtained, who loved the present evil world! How much damage did Alexander the coppersmith do to Paul? "He did me much evil," said he, "the Lord reward him according to his works." And yet that Alexander was once foremost in danger, and even exposed his own person in the theater at Ephesus, that he might rescue the apostle. There are none so bad as those who once seemed to be good. "If the salt has lost its savor, wherewith shall it be seasoned?" That which is best when ripe, is worst when rotten; liquor which is sweetest in one stage, becomes sourest in another. Let not him that putteth on his armor boast as though he putteth it off; for even common sense teaches you, that it is not to begin, but to continue to the end which marks the time of the child of God.

But we need not look to analogy and to mere common sense. Scripture is plain enough. What says John? "They went out from us." Why? Were they ever saints? Oh! no--"They went out from us, because they were not of us, for if they had been of us, doubtless they would have continued with us, but they went out from us, that it might be manifest that they were not of us." They were no Christians, or else they had not thus apostatized. Peter saith, "It hath happened unto them according to the proverb, the dog hath returned to its vomit, and the sow that was washed to her wallowing in the mire," indicating at once most clearly that the dog, though it did vomit, always was a dog. When men disgorge their sins unwillingly, not giving them up because they dislike them, but because they cannot retain them; if a favorable time comes, they will return to swallow once more what they seemed to abandon. The sow that was washed--ay, bring it into the parlour, introduce it among society; it was washed, and well-washed too; whoever saw so respectable a member of the honorable confraternity of swine before? Bring it in! Yes, but will you keep it there? Wait and see. Because you have not transformed it into a man, on the first occasion it will be found wallowing in the mire. Why? Because it was not a man, but a sow. And so we think we may learn from multitudes of other passages, if we had time to quote them, that those who go back into perdition are not saints at all, for perseverance is the badge of the righteous. "The righteous shalt hold on his way, and he that hath clean hands shall wax stronger and stronger." We not only get life by faith, but faith sustains it; "the just shall live by faith;" "but if any man draw back, my soul shall have no pleasure in him."

What we have learned from Scripture, dear friends, has been abundantly confirmed by observation. Every day would I bless God that in so numerous a Church we have comparatively so few who have proved false; but I have seen enough, and the Lord knoweth, more than enough, to make me very jealous over you with a godly jealousy. I could tell of many an instance of men and women who did ran well. "What did hinder them that they should not obey the truth?" I remember a young man of whom I thought as favourably as of any of you, and I believe he did at that time deserve our favorable judgment. He walked among us, one of the most hopeful of our sons, and we hoped that God would make him serviceable to his cause. He fell into bad company. There was enough conscience left, after a long course of secret sin, to make him feel uncomfortable in his wickedness, though he did not give it up; and when at last his sin stared him in the face, and others knew it, so ashamed was he, that, though he bore the Christian name, he took poison that he might escape the shame which he had brought upon himself. He was rescued--rescued by skill and the good providence of God; but where he is, and what he is, God only knoweth, for he had taken another poison more deadly still which made him the slave of his own lusts.

Do not think it is the young alone, however. It is a very lamentable fact that there are, in proportion, more backslidings among the old than the young; and, if you want to find a great sinner in that respect, you will find him, surely, nine times out of ten, with grey hairs on his head. Have I not frequently mentioned that you do not find in Scripture, many cases of young people going astray. You do find believers sinning, but they were all getting old men. There is Noah--no youth. There is Lot, when drunken--no child. There is David with Bathsheba,--no young man in the heat of passion. There is Peter denying his Lord--no boy at the time. These were men of experience and knowledge and wisdom. "Let him that thinketh he standeth, take heed lest he fall."

With sorrow do we remember one whom, years ago, we heard pray among us, and sweetly too; esteemed and trusted by us all. I remember a dear brother saying very kindly, but not too wisely, "If he is not a child of God, I am not." But what did be, my brethren, to our shame and sorrow, but go aside to the very worst and foulest of sins, and where is he now? Perhaps the ale-house may tell or worse places still. So have we seen, that earth's sun may be eclipsed, earth's stars may go out, and all human glory melt into shame. No true child of God perishes--hold that fast; but this is the badge of a true child of God: that a man endures to the end; and if a man does not hold on, but slinks back to his old master, and once again fits on the old collar, and wears again the Satanic yoke, there is sure proof that he has never come out of the spiritual Egypt through Jesus Christ, his leader, and hath never obtained that eternal life which cannot die, because it is born of God. I have thus then, dear friends, said enough to prove, I think, beyond dispute, that the true badge of the Christian is perseverance, and that without it, no man has proved himself to be a child of God.

II. Secondly, PERSEVERANCE IS THEREFORE, THE TARGET OF ALL OUR SPIRITUAL ENEMIES.

We have many adversaries. Look at the world! The world does not object to our being Christians for a time; it will cheerfully overlook all misdemeanors in that way, if we will now shake hands and be as we used to be. Your old companions who used to call you such good fellows, when you were bad fellows, would they not very readily forgive you for having been Christians, if you would just go back and be as in days gone by? Oh! certainly, they would look upon your religion as a freak of folly, but they would very easily overlook it, if you would give it up for the future. "O!" saith the world, "come back; come back to my arms once more; be enamored of me, and though thou hast spoken some hard words against me, and done some cruel deeds against me, I will cheerfully forgive thee." The world is always stabbing at the believer's perseverance. Sometimes she will bully him back; she will persecute him with her tongue--cruel mockings shall be used; and at another time, she will cozen him, "Come thou back to me; O come thou back! Wherefore should we disagree? Thou art made for me, and I am made for thee!" And she beckons so gently and so sweetly, even as Solomon's harlot of old. This is the one thing with her, that thou shouldst cease to

be a pilgrim, and settle down to buy and sell with her in Vanity Fair.

Your second enemy, the flesh. What is its aim? "Oh! " cries the flesh, "we have had enough of this; it is weary work being a pilgrim, come, give it up." Sloth says, "Sit still where thou art. Enough is as good as a feast, at least, of this tedious thing." Then, lust crieth, "Am I always to be mortified? Am I never to be indulged? Give me at least, a furlough from this constant warfare?" The flesh cares not how soft the chain, so that it does but hold us fast, and prevent our pressing on to glory.

Then comes in the devil, and sometimes he beats the big drum, and cries with a thundering voice "There is no heaven; there is no God; you are a fool to persevere." Or, changing his tactics, he cries, "Come back! I will give thee a better treatment than thou hadst before. Thou thoughtest me a hard master, but that was misrepresentation; come and try me; I am a different devil from what I was ten years ago; I am respectable to what I was then. I do not want you to go back to the low theater or the casino; come with me, and be a respectable lover of pleasure. I tell thee, I can dress in broad cloth as well as in corderoy, and I can walk in the courts of kings, as well as in the courts and alleys of the beggar. O come back!" he saith, and make thyself one of mine." So that this hellish trinity, the world, tine flesh, and the devil, all stab at the Christian's perseverance.

His perseverance in service they will frequently attack: "What profit is there is in serving God? The devil will say to me sometimes, as he did to Jonah, "Flee thou unto Tarshish, and do not stop in this Nineveh; they will not believe thy word, though thou speak in God's name?" To you he will say, "Why, you are so busy all the six days of the week, what is the good of spending your Sunday with a parcel of noisy brats in a Sunday School? Why go about with those tracts in the streets? Much good you will get from it. Would not you be better with having a little rest?" Ah! that word rest--some of us are very fond of it; but we ought to recollect that we spoil it if we try to get it here, for rest is only beyond the grave. We shall have rest enough when once we come into the presence of our Lord. Perseverance in service, then, the devil would murder outright.

If he cannot stay us in service, he will try to prevent our perse verance in suffering. "Why be patient any longer?" says he; "why sit on that dunghill, scraping your sores with a potsherd?--curse God, and die. You have been always poor since you have been a Christian; your business does not prosper; you see, you cannot make money unless you do as others do. You must go with the times, or else you will not get on. Give it all up. Why be always suffering like this?" Thus the foul spirit tempts us. Or you may have espoused some good cause, and the moment you open your mouth, many laugh and try to put you down. "Well," says the devil, "be put down--what is the use of it? Why make yourself singularly eccentric, and expose yourself to perpetual martyrdom? It is all very nice," saith he, "if you will be a martyr, to be burnt at once, and have done with it; but to hang, like Lord Cobham, to be roasted over a slow fire for days, is not comfortable. Why," saith the tempter, "why be always suffering--give it up." You see, then, it is also perseverance in suffering which the devil shooteth at.

Or, perhaps, it is perseverance in steadfastness. The love of many has waxed cold, but you remain zealous. "Well," saith he, "what is the good of your being so zealous? Other people are good enough people, you could not censure them: why do you want to be more righteous than they are? Why should you be pushing the Church before you, and dragging the world behind you? What need is there for you to go two marches in one day? Is not one enough? Do as the rest do; loiter as they do. Sleep as do others, and let your lamp go out as other virgins do." Thus is our perseverance in steadfastness frequently assailed.

Or else, it will be our doctrinal sentiments. "Why," says Satan, "do you hold to these denominational creeds? Sensible men are getting more liberal, they are giving away what does not belong to them--God's truth; they are removing the old landmarks. Acts of uniformity are to be repealed, articles and creeds are to be laid aside as useless lumber, not necessary for this very enlightened age; fall in with this, and be an Anythingarian. Believe that black is white; hold that truth and a lie are very much akin to one another, and that it not does matter which we do believe, for we are all of us right, though we flatly contradict each other; that the Bible is a nose of wax to fit any face; that it does not teach anything material, but you may make it say anything you like. Do that," saith he, "and be no longer firm in your opinion."

I think I have proved--and need not waste more words about it--that perseverance is the target for all enemies. Wear your shield, Christian, therefore, close upon your armor, and cry mightily unto God, that by his Spirit you may endure to the end.

III. Thirdly, brethren, PERSEVERANCE IS THE GLORY OF CHRIST.

That he makes all his people persevere to the end, is greatly to his honor. If they should fall away and perish, every office, and work, and attribute of Christ would be stained in the mire. If any one child of God should perish, where were Christ's covenant engagements? What is he worth as a mediator of the covenant and the surety of it, if he hath not made the promises sure to all the seed? My brethren, Christ is made a leader and commander of the people, to bring many souls into glory;

but if he doth not bring them into glory, where is the captain's honor? Where is the efficacy of the precious blood, if it does not effectually redeem? If it only redeemeth for a time and then suffereth us to perish, where is its value? If it only blots out sin for a few weeks, and then perniits that sin to return and to remain upon us, where, I say, is the glory of Calvary, and where is the lustre of the wounds of Jesus? He lives, he lives to intercede, but how can I honor his intercession, if it be fruitless? Does he not pray, "Father, I will that they also, whom thou hast given me, be with me where I am;" and if they be not finally brought to be with him where he is, where is the honor of his intercession? Hath not the Pleader failed, and the great Mediator been dismissed without success? Is he not at this day in union with his people? But what is the value of union to Christ, if that union does not insure salvation? Is he not to-day at the right hand of God, preparing a place for his saints; and will he prepare a place for them, and then lose them on the road? Oh! can it be that he procures the harp and the crown, and will not save souls to use them? My brethren, the perishing of one true child of God, would be such dishonor to Jesus, that I cannot think of it without considering it as blasphemy. One true believer in hell! Oh! what laughter in the pit--what defiance, what unholy mirth! "Ah! Prince of life and glory," saith the prince of the pit, "I have defeated thee; I have snatched the prey from the mighty, and the lawful captive I have delivered; I have torn a jewel from thy crown. See, here it is! Thou didst redeem this soul with blood, and yet it is in hell." Hear what Satan cries--"Christ suffered for this soul, and yet God makes it suffer for itself. Where is the justice of God?" Christ came from heaven to earth to save this soul, and failed in the attempt, and I have him here;" and as he plunges that soul into deeper waves of woe, the shout of triumph goes up more and more blasphemously--"We have conquered heaven! We have rent the eternal covenant; we have foiled the purposes of God; we have defeated his decree; we have triumphed over the power of the Mediator, and cast his blood to the ground!" Shall it ever be? Atrocious question! It can never be. They who are in Christ are saved. They whom Jesus Christ hath really taken into union with himself, shall be with him where he is. But how are you to know whether you are in union with Christ? My brethren, you can only know it by obeying the apostle's words, "Give all diligence to make your calling and election sure."

IV. I close, therefore, with but a hint on the last point, PERSEVERANCE SHOULD BE THE GREAT CARE OF EVERY CHRISTIAN--his daily and his nightly care. O beloved! I conjure you by the love of God, and by the love of your own souls, be faithful unto death. Have you difficulties? You must conquer them. Hannibal crossed the Alps, for his heart was full of fury against Rome; and you must cross the Alps of difficulty, for I trust your heart is full of hatred of sin. When Mr. Smeaton had built the lighthouse upon the Eddystone, he looked out anxiously after a storm to see if the edifice was still there, and it was his great joy when he could see it still standing, for a former builder had constructed an edifice which he thought to be indestructible, and expressed a wish that he might be in it in the worst storm which ever blew, and he was so, and neither himself nor his lighthouse were ever seen afterwards. Now you have to be exposed to multitudes of storms; you must be in your lighthouse in the worst storm which ever blew; build firmly then on the Rock of Ages, and make sure work for eternity, for if you do these things, ye shall never fall. For this Church's sake, I pray you do it; for nothing can dishonor and weaken a Church so much as the falls of professors. A thousand rivers flow to the sea, and make rich the meadows, but no man heareth the sound thereof; but if there be one cataract, its roaring will be heard for miles, and every traveler will mark the fall. A thousand Christians can scarcely do such honor to their Master as one hypocrite can do dishonor to him. If you have ever tasted that the Lord is gracious, pray that your foot slip not. It would be infinitely better to bury you in the earth than see you buried in sin. If I must be lost, God grant it may not be as an apostate. If I must, after all, perish, were it not better never to have known the way of righteousness than after having known the theory of it, and something of the enjoyment of it, turn again to the beggarly elements of the world? Let your prayer be not against death, but against sin. For your own sake, for the Church's sake, for the name of Christ's sake, I pray you do this. But ye cannot persevere except by much watchfulness in the closet, much carefulness over every action, much dependance upon the strong hand of the Holy Spirit who alone can make you stand. Walk and live as in the sight of God, knowing where your great strength lieth, and depend upon it you shall yet sing that sweet doxology in Jude, "Now unto him that is able to keep you from falling, and to present you faultless before the presence of his glory with exceeding joy, to the only wise God our Savior, be glory and majesty, dominion and power, both now and ever. Amen." A simple faith brings the soul to Christ, Christ keeps the faith alive; that faith enables the believer to persevere, and so he enters heaven. May that be your lot and mine for Christ's sake. Amen.

Nothing But Leaves

A Sermon (No. 555)
Delivered on Sunday Morning, February 21st, 1864, by the
Rev. C. H. SPURGEON,
At the Metropolitan Tabernacle, Newington

"He found nothing but leaves." -- Mark 11:13.

MOST of the miracles of Moses were grand displays of divine justice. What were the first ten wonders but ten plagues? The same may be said of the prophets, especially of Elijah and Elisha. Was it not significant both of the character and mission of Elias when he called fire from heaven upon the captains of fifties; nor was he upon whom his mantle descended less terrible when the she-bears avenged him upon the mockers. It remained for our incarnate Lord to reveal the heart of God. The only begotten was full of grace and truth, and in his miracles pre-eminently God is set forth to us as LOVE. With the exception of the miracle before us, and perhaps, a part of another, all the miracles of Jesus were entirely benevolent in their character; indeed this one is no exception in reality, but only in appearance. The raising of the dead, the feeding of the multitude, the stilling of the tempest, the healing of diseases--what were all these but displays of the lovingkindness of God? What was this to teach us but that Jesus Christ came forth from his Father on an errand of pure grace?

"Thine hands, dear Jesus, were not arm'd
With an avenging rod,
No hard commission to perform
The vengeance of a God.
But all was mercy, all was mild,
And wrath forsook the throne,
When Christ on his kind errand came
And brought salvation down."

Let us rejoice that God commendeth his love towards us, because in "due time Christ died for the ungodly."

Yet, as if to show that Jesus the Savior is also Jesus the Judge, one gleam of justice must dart forth. Where shall mercy direct its fall? See, my brethren, it glances not upon a man, but lights upon an unconscious, unsuffering thing--a tree. The curse, if we may call it a curse at all, did not fall. on man or beast, or even the smallest insect; its bolt falls harmlessly upon a fig tree by the wayside. It bore upon itself the signs of barrenness, and perhaps was no one's property; little, therefore, was the loss which any man sustained by the withering of that verdant, mockery, while instruction more precious than a thousand acres of fig trees has been left for the benefit of all ages. The only other instance at which I hinted just now was the permission given to the devils to enter into the swine, and the whole herd ran violently down a steep place into the sea, and perished in the waters. In that case, again, what a mercy it was that the Savior did not permit a band of men to become the victims of the evil one. It was infinitely better that the whole herd of swine should perish than that one poor man should be rendered a maniac through their influence. The creatures choked in the abyss were nothing but swine--swine which their Jewish owners had no right to keep; and even then they did not perish through Jesus Christ's agency, but through the malice of the devils, for needs must even swine run when the devil drives.

Observe, then, with attention, this solitary instance of stern judgment wrought by the Savior's hand. Consider seriously that if only once in his whole life Christ works a miracle of pure judgment, the lesson so unique must be very full of meaning. If there be hut one curse, where does it fall? What is its symbolic teaching? I do not know that I ever felt more solemnly the need of true fruitfulness before God than when I was looking over this miracle--parable--for such it may justly be called. The curse, you at once perceive, falls in its metaphorical and spiritual meaning upon those high professors who are destitute of true holiness; upon those who manifest great show of leaves, but who bring forth no fruit unto God. Only one thunderbolt, and that for boasting pretenders; only one curse, and that for hypocrites. O blessed Spirit, write this heart-searching truth upon our hearts!

I. We will commence our exposition with the remark that THERE WERE MANY TREES WITH LEAVES ONLY UPON THEM, AND YET NONE OF THESE WERE CURSED BY THE SAVIOR, SAVE ONLY THIS FIG TREE. It is the nature of many trees to yield to man nothing but their shade. The hungering Savior did not resort to the oak or to the elm to look for food, nor could the fir tree, nor the pine, nor the box, offer him any hope of refreshment; nor did he breathe one hard word concerning them, for he knew what was in them, and that they neither were, nor pretended to be fruit-bearing trees. So, dear friends, there are many men whose lives bear leaves, but no fruit--and yet, thanks be unto God, almighty patience bears with them. They are allowed to live out their time, and then it is true they are cut down and cast into the fire; but while they are permitted to stand, no curse withers them: the longsuffering of God waiteth to be gracious to them. Here are some of the characters who have leaves but no fruit.

There are thousands who ignorantly follow the sign and know nothing of the substance. In England, we think ourselves far in advance of Popish countries; but how much of the essence of Popery peeps out in the worship of very many! They go to Church or chapel, and they think that the mere going into the place and sitting a certain time and coming out again is an acceptable act to God: mere formality, you see, is mistaken for spiritual worship! They are careful to have their infants sprinkled, but what the ceremony means they know not; and without looking into the Bible to see whether the Lord commands any such an ordinance, they offer him their ignorant will--worship either in obedience to custom, or in the superstition of ignorance. What the thing is, or why it is, they do not enquire, but go through a performance as certain parrots say their prayers. They know nothing about the inward and spiritual grace, which the Catechism talks about, if indeed, inward spiritual grace could ever be connected with an unscriptural outward and visible sign. When these poor souls come to the Lord's Supper, their thoughts go no farther than the bread and wine, or the hands which break the one and pour out the other; they know nothing whatever of communion with Jesus, of eating his flesh and drinking his blood; their souls have proceeded as far as the shell, but they have never broken into the kernel to taste the sweetness thereof. They have a name to lives and are dead; their religion is a mere show; a signboard without an inn a well-set table without meat; a pretty pageant where nothing is gold, but everything gilt nothing real, but all pasteboard, paint, plaster, and pretense. Nonconformists, your chapels swarm with such, and the houses of the Establishment are full of the same! Multitudes live and die satisfied with the outward trappings of religion, and are utter strangers to internal vital godliness. Yet such persons are not cursed in this life! No, they are to be pitied, to be prayed for, to be sought after, with words of love and honest truth; they are to be hoped for yet, for who knoweth but that God may call them to repentance, and they may yet receive the life of God into their souls?

Another very numerous class have opinion but not faith, creed but not credence. We meet them everywhere. How zealous they are for Protestantism! They would not only die for orthodoxy, but kill others as well. Perhaps it is the Calvinistic doctrine which they have received, and then the five points are as dear to them as their five senses. These men will contend, not to say earnestly, but savagely for the faith. They very vehemently denounce all those who differ from them in the smallest degree; and deal damnation round the land with amazing liberality to all who are not full weight according to the balance of their little Zoar, Rehoboth, or Jireh: while all the while the spirit of Christ, the love of the Spirit, bowels of compassion, and holiness of character are no more to be expected from them than grapes from thorns, or figs from thistles. Doctrine, my brethren, is to be prized above all price! Woe to the Church of God when error shall be thought a trifle, for truth be lightly esteemed; and when truth is gone, what is left? But, at the same time, we grossly mistake if we think that orthodoxy of creed will save us. I am sick of those cries of "the truth," "the truth," "the truth," from men of rotten lives and unholy tempers. There is an orthodox as well as a heterodox road to hell, and the devil knows how to handle Calvinists quite as well as Arminians. No pale of any Church can insure salvation, no form of doctrine can guarantee to us eternal life. "Ye must be born again." Ye must bring forth fruits meet for repentance. "Every tree which bringeth not forth fruit is hewn down, and cast into the fire." Stopping short of vital union to the Lord Jesus by real faith, we miss the great qualification for entering heaven. Yet the time is not come when these mere head-knowers are cursed. These trees have leaves only, but no fatal curse has withered them hopelessly. No; they are to be sought after; they may yet know the Lord in their hearts, and the Holy Spirit may yet make them humble followers of the Lamb. O that it may be so!

A third class have talk without feeling. Mr. Talkative, in "Pilgrim's Progress," is the representative of a very numerous host. They speak very glibly concerning divine things. Whether the topic be doctrinal, experimental, or practical, they talk fluently upon everything. But evidently, the whole thing comes from the throat and the lip; there is no welling up from the heart. If the thing came from the heart it would be boiling, but now it hangs like an icicle from their lips. You know them--you may learn something from them, but all time while you are yourself aware that if they bless others by their words, they themselves remain unblessed. Ah! let us be very anxious lest this should be our own case. Let the preacher feel the anxiety of the apostle Paul, lest, after having preached to others, he himself should be a castavay; and let my hearers feel the same concern, lest, after talking about the timings of God, they should prove to be mere lip-servers, and not accepted children of the Most High.

Another tribe springs up just now before my eye--those who have regrets without repentance. Many of you under a heart-searching sermon feel grieved on account of your sins, and yet never have the strength of mind to give them up. You say you are sorry, but yet go on in the same course. You do really feel, when death and judgment press upon you, a certain sort of regret that you could have been so foolish, but the next day the strength of temptation is such, that you fall a prey to the very same infatuation. It is easy to bring a man to the river of regret, but you cannot make him drink the water of repentance. If Agag would be killed with words, no Amalekite would live. If men's transient sorrows for sin were real repentance on account of it, there is not a man living who would not, sometime or other, have been a true penitent. Here, however, are leaves only, and no fruit.

We have yet again, another class of persons who have resolves without action. They will! Ah! that they will! but it is always in the future tense. They are hearers, and they are even feelers, but they are not doers of the Word: it never comes to that. They would be free, but they have not patience to file their fetters, nor grace to submit their manacles to the hammer. They see the right, but they permit the wrong to rule them. They are charmed with the beauties of holiness, and yet deluded with the wantonness of sin. They would ran in the ways of God's commandments, but the road is too rough, and running is weary work. They would fight for God, but victory is hardly won, and so they turn back almost as soon as they have set out; they put their hand to the plough, and then prove utterly unworthy of the kingdom.

The great majority of persons who have any sort of religion at all, bear heaves, but they produce no fruit. I know there are some such here, and I solemnly warn you, though no curse falls upon you, though we do not think that the miracle now under consideration has any relation to you whatever, yet remember, there is nothing to be done with trees which bring forth only leaves, but in due time to use the axe upon them, and to cast them into the fire: and this must be your doom. As sure as you live under the sound of the gospel, and yet are not converted by it, so surely will you be cast into outer darkness. As certainly as Jesus Christ invites you, and ye will not come, so certainly will he send his angels to gather the dead branches together, and you among them, to cast them into the fire. Beware! beware! thou fruitless tree! thou shalt not stand for ever! Mercy waters thee with her tears now; God's lovingkindness digs about thee still; still the husbandman comes, seeking fruit upon thee year after year. Beware! the edge of the axe is sharp, and the arm which wields it is nothing less than almighty. Beware! lest thou fall into the fire!

II. Secondly, THERE WERE OTHER TREES WITH NEITHER LEAVES NOR FRUIT, AND NONE OF THESE WERE CURSED!

The time of figs was not yet come. Now, as the fig tree either brings forth the fig before the leaf, or else produces figs and leaves at the same time, the major part of the trees, perhaps all of them, without exception of this one, were entirely without figs and without leaves, and yet Jesus did not curse any one of them, for the time of figs was not yet come.

What multitudes are destitute of anything like religion; they make no profession of it; they not only have no fruits of godliness, but they have no leaves even of outward respect to it; they do not frequent the court of the Lord's house; they use no form of prayer; they never attend upon ordinances. The great outlying mass of this huge city--how does religion affect it? It is a very sad thing to think that there are people living in total darkness next door to the light; that you may find in the very street where the gospel is preached, persons who have never heard a sermon. Are there not, throughout this city, tens and hundreds of thousands who know not their right hand from their left, in matters of godliness? Their children go to Sabbath schools, but they themselves spend the whole Sabbath day in anything except the worship of God! In our country parishes, very often neither the religion of the Establishment nor of Dissent, at all affects the population. Take, for instance, that village which will be disgracefully remembem'ed as long as Essex endures, the village of Hedingham. Theme are in that place not only parish Churches, but Dissenting meetinghouses, and yet the persons who foully murdered the poor wretch supposed to be a wizard, must have been as ignorant and indifferent to common sense, let alone religion, as even Hottentots or Kaffirs, to whom the light of religion has never come. Why was this? Is it not because there is not enough of missionary spirit among Christian people to seek out those who are in the lowest strata of society, so that multitudes escape without ever coming into contact with godliness at all? In London, the City Missionaries will bear witness that while they can sometimes get at the wives, yet there are thousands of husbands who are necessarily away at the time of the missionary's visit, who have not a word of rebuke, or exhortation, or invitation, or encouragement, ever sounding in their ears at all, from the day of their birth to the day of their death; and they might, for all practical purposes, as well have been born in the center of Africa as in the city of London, for they are without God, without hope, aliens from the commonwealth of Israel, far oft; not by wicked works only, but by dense ignorance of God.

These persons we may divide into two classes, upon neither of whom does the withering curse fall in this life. The first we look upon with hope. Although we see neither leaves nor fruit, we know that "the time of figs is not yet." They are God's elect, but they are not called. Their names are in the Lamb's Book of Life, and were there from before the foundations of the world; though they be dead in trespasses, they are the objects of divine love, and they must, in due time, be called by irresistible grace, and turned from darkness to light. "The Lord hath much people in this city," and this should be the encouragement of every one of you, to try to do good, that God has among the vilest of the vile, the most reprobate, the most debauched and drunken, an elect people who must be saved. When you take the Word to them, you do so because God has ordained you to be the messenger of life to their souls, and they must receive it, for so the decree of predestination runs; they must he called in the fullness of time to be the brethren of Christ and children of the Most High. They are redeemed, beloved friends, but not regenerated--as much redeemed with precious blood as the saints before the eternal throne. They are Christ's property, and yet perhaps, they are waiting around the ale-house at this very moment until the door shall open--bought with Jesus' precious blood, and yet spending their nights in a brothel, and their days in sin; but if Jesus Christ purchased them he will have them. If he counted down the precious drops, God is not unfaithful to forget the price which his Son has paid. He will not suffer his substitution to be in any case an ineffectual, dead thing. Tens of thousands of redeemed ones are not regenerated yet, but regenerated they must be; and this is your comfort and mine, when we go out with the quickening Word of God. Nay, more, these ungodly ones are prayed for by Christ before the throne. "Neither pray I for these alone," saith the great Intercessor, "but for them also which shall believe on me through their word." They do not pray for themselves; poor, ignorant souls, they do not know anything about prayer; but Jesus prays for them. Their names are on his breast, and ere long they must bow their stubborn knee, breathing the penitential sigh before the throne of grace. "The time of figs is not yet." The predestinated moment has not struck; but, when it comes, they shall, for God will have his own; they must, for the Spirit is not to be withstood when he cometh forth with power--they must become the willing servants of the living God. "My people shall be willing in the day of my power." "He shall justify many." "He shall see of the travail of his soul." "He shall divide a portion with the great, and he shall divide the spoil with the strong."

No curse falls upon these; they deserve it, but eternal love prevents it. Their sins write it, but the finished sacrifice blots it out. They may well perish because they seek not mercy, but Christ intercedes for them, and live they shall.

Alas! however, among those who have neither leaves nor fruit, there is another class which never bring forth either the one or the other; they live in sin and die in ignorance, perishing without hope. As these leave the world, can they upbraid us for neglecting them? Are we clear of their blood? May not the blood of many of them cry from the ground against us? As they arc condemned on account of sins, may they not accuse us because we did not take the gospel to them, but left them where they were? Dread thought! but let it not be shaken off, there are tens of thousands every day who pass into the world of spirits unsaved, and inherit the righteous wrath of God. Yet in this life, you see, no special curse falls upon them, and this miracle has no special bearing upon them; it bears upon a totally different class of people, of whom we will now speak.

III. WE HAVE BEFORE US A SPECAL CASE.

I have already said, that in a fig tree, the fruit takes the precedence of the leaves, or the leaves and the fruit come at the same time; so that it is laid down as a general rule, that if there be leaves upon a fig tree, you may rightly expect to find fruit upon it.

To begin then with the explanation of this special case, in a fig tree fruit comes before leaves. So in a true Christian, fruit always takes the precedence of profession. Find a man anywhere who is a true servant of God, and before he united himself with the Church, or attempted to engage in public prayer, or to identify himself with the people of God, he searched to see whether he had real repentance on account of sin--he desired to know whether he had a sincere and genuine faith in the Lord Jesus Christ, and he perhaps tarried some little time to try himself to see whether there were the fruits of holiness in his daily life. Indeed, I may say that there are some who wait too long; they are so afraid lest they should make a profession before they have grace in possession, that they will wait year after year--too long--become unwise, and make what was a virtue become a vice. Still this is the rule with Christians: they first give themselves to the Lord and afterwards to the Lord's people according to his will. You who are the servants of God--do you not scorn to vaunt yourselves beyond your line and measure? Would you not think it disgraceful on your part to profess anything which you have not felt? Do you not feel a holy jealousy when you are teaching others, lest you should teach more than God has taught you? and are you not afraid even in your prayers lest you should use expressions which are beyond your own depth of meaning? I am sure the true Christian is always afraid of anything like having the leaves before he has the fruit.

Another remark follows from this--where we see the leaves we have a right to expect the fruit. When I see a man a Church-member, when I hear him engage in prayer, I expect to see in him, holiness, the character and the image of Christ. I have a right to expect it, because the man has solemnly avowed that he is the partaker of divine grace. You cannot join a Church without taking upon yourselves very solemn responsibilities. What do you desire when you come to see us, and ask to be admitted into fellowship? You tell us that you have passed from death unto life, that you have been born again, that there has been a change in you, the hike of which you never knew before, one which only God could have wrought. You tell us you are in the habit of private prayer; that you have a desire for the conversion of others. If you did not so profess, we dare not receive you. Well now, having made these professions, it would be insincere on our part if we did not expect to see your characters holy, and your conversation correct; we have a right to expect it from your own professions. We have a right to expect it from the work of the Spirit which you claim to have received. Shall the Holy Spirit work in man's heart to produce a trifle? Do you think that the Spirit of God would have written us this Book, and that Jesus Christ would have shed his precious blood to produce a hypocrite? Is an inconsistent Christian the highest work of God? I suppose God's plan of salvation to be that which has more exercised his thoughts and wisdom than the making of all worlds and the sustenance of all providence; and shall this best, this highest, this darling work of God, produce no more than that poor, mean, talking, unacting, fruitless deceiver? Ye have no love for souls, no care for the spread of the Redeemer's kingdom, and yet think that the Spirit, has made you what you are! No zeal, no melting bowels of compassion, no cries of earnest entreaty, no wrestling with God, no holiness, no self-denial, and yet say that you are a vessel made by the Master and fitted for his use! How can this be? No; if you profess to be a Christian, from the necessity of the Spirit's work, we have a right to expect fruit from you. Besides, in genuine professors we do get the fruit, we see a faithful attachment to the Redeemer's cause, an endurance to the end, in poverty, in sickness, in shame, in persecution. We see other professors holding fast to the truth, they are not led aside by temptation, neither do they disgrace the cause they have espoused; and, if you profess to be one of the same order, we have a right to look for the same blessed fruits of the Spirit in you, and if we see them not you have belied us.

Observe further that our Lord hungers for fruit. A hungry person seeks for something which may satisfy him, for fruit, not leaves! Jesus hungers for your holiness. A strong expression, you will say, but I doubt not of its accuracy. For what were we elected? We were predestinated to be conformed unto the image of God's Son; we were chosen to good works, "which God hath before ordained that we should walk in them." What is the end of our redemption? Why did Jesus Christ die? " He gave himself for us that he might redeem us from all iniquity, and purify unto himself a peculiar people, zealous of good works." Why have we been called but that we should be called to be saints? To what end are any of the great operations of the covenant of grace? Do they not all point at our holiness? If you will think of any privilege which the Lord confers upon his people through Christ, you will perceive that they all aim at the sanctification of the chosen people--the making of them to bring forth fruit that God the Father may be glorified in them. O Christian, for this the tears of the Savior! for this the agony and bloody sweat! for this the five death-wounds! for this the burial and the resurrection, that he makes you holy, even perfectly holy like unto himself! And can it be, that when he hungers after fruit, you think nothing of fruit-bearing? O professor, how base art thou, to call thyself a blood-bought child of God, amid yet to live unto thyself! How darest thou, O barren tree, professing to be watered by the bloody sweat, and digged by the griefs and woes of the wounded Savior--how darest thou bring forth leaves and no fruit? Oh! sacrilegious mockery of a hungry Savior! oh! blasphemous tantalizing of a hungry Lord! that thou shouldst profess to have cost him all this, and yet yield him nothing! When I think that Jesus hungers after fruit in me, it stirs me tip to do more for him. Does it not have the same effect on you? He hungers for your good works; he hungers to see you useful. Jesus the King of kings, hungers after your prayers--hungers after your anxieties for the souls of others; and nothing ever will satisfy him for the travail of his soul but seeing you wholly devoted to his cause.

This brings us into the very midst and meaning of the miracle. There are some, then, who make unusual profession, and yet disappoint the Savior in his just expectations. The Jews did this. When Jesus Christ came it was not the time of figs. The time for great holiness was after the coming of Christ and the pouring out of the Spirit. All the other nations were without leaves. Greece, Rome, all these showed no signs of progress; but there was the Jewish nation covered with leaves. They professed already to have obtained the blessings which he came to bring. There stood the Pharisee with his long prayers; there were the lawyers and the Scribes with their deep knowledge of the things of the kingdom. They said they had the light. The time of figs was not come, but yet they had the leaves, though not a single fruit; and you know what a curse fell on Israel; how in the day of Jerusalem's destruction the tree was withered altogether from its root, because it had its leaves, but had no fruit.

The same will be true of any Church. There are times when all the Churches seem sunken alike in lethargy--such a time we had, say ten years ago--but one Church, perhaps, seems to be all alive. The congregations are large. Much, apparently, is proposed for the growth of the Savior's kingdom. A deal of noise is made about it; there is much talk, and the people are all expectation; and, if there be no fruit, no real consecration to Christ, if there be no genuine liberality, no earnest vital godliness, no hallowed consistency, other Churches may live on; but such a Church as this, making so high a profession, and being so precocious in the produce of leaves, shall have a curse from God. No man shall eat fruit of it for ever, and it shall wither away.

In the case of individuals the moral of our miracle runs thus. Some are looked upon as young believers, who early join the Church. "The time of figs is not yet;" it is not a very ordinary case to see children converted, but we do see some, and we are very grateful. We are jealous however lest we should see leaves but not fruit. These juveniles are extraordinary cases; and on that account we look for higher results. When we are disappointed what shall come upon such but a curse upon their precocity, which led them to the deception. Some of us were converted, or profess to have been, when young, and if we have lived hitherto, and all we have produced has been merely words, resolves, professions, but not fruit unto God, we must expect the curse.

Again, professsors eminent in station. There are necessarily but few ministers, but few Church officers; but when men so distinguish themselves by zeal, or by louder professions than others, as to gain the ear of the Christian public and are placed in responsible positions--if they bring forth no fruit, they are the persons upon whom the curse will light. It may be with other Christians that "the time of figs is not yet;" they have not made the advances which these profess to have made; but having been, upon their own profession, elected to an office which essentially requires fruit, since they yield it not, let them beware.

To those who make professions of much love to Christ, the same caution may be given. With the most of Christians, I am afraid, I must say that "the time of figs is not yet," for we are too much like the Laodicean Church. But you meet with some men--how much they are in love with Christ! How sweetly they can talk about him, but what do they do for him? Nothing! nothing! Their love lies just in the wind which comes out of their own mouths, and that is all. Now, when the Lord has a curse, he will deal it out on such They went beyond all others in an untimely declaration of a very fervent love, and now they yield him no fruit. "Yes," said one, "I love God so much, that I do not reckon that anything I have is my own. It is all the Lord's--all the Lord's, and I am his steward." Well, this dear good man, of course, joined the Church, and after a time, some mission work wanted a little help. What was his reply? "When I pay my seat rent, I have done all I intend to do." A man of wealth and means! After a little time, this same man found it inconvenient even to pay for his seat, and goes now to a place not quite so full, where he can get a seat and do nothing to support the ministry! If there is a special thunderbolt anywhere, it is these unctions hypocrites who whine about love to Christ, and bow down at the shrine of mammon.

Or, take another case. You meet with others whose profession is not of so much love, but it is of much experience. Oh! what experience they have had! What deep experience! Ah! they know the humblings of heart and the plague of human nature! They know the depths of corruption, and the heights of divine fellowship, and so on. Yes, and if you go into the shop you find the corruption is carried on behind the counter, and the deceit in the day-book; if they do not know the plague of their own hearts, at least they are a plague to their own household. Such people are abhorrent to all men, and much more to God.

Others you meet with who have a censorious tongue. What good people they must be; they can see the faults of other people so plainly! This Church is not right, and the other is not right, and yonder preacher--well some people think him a very good man, but they do not. They can see the deficiencies in the various denominations, and they observe that very few really carry out Scripture as it should be carried out. They complain of want of love, and are the very people who create that want. Now if you will watch these very censorious people, the very faults they indicate in others, they are indulging in themselves; and while they are seeking to find out the mote in their brother's eye, they have a beam in their own. These are the people who are indicated by this fig tree, for they ought, according to their own showing, taking t hem on their own ground, to be better than other people. If what they say be true, they are bright particular stars, and they ought to give special light to the world. They are such that even Jesus Christ himself might expect to receive fruit from them, but they are nothing but deceivers, with these high soarings and proud boastings; they are nothing after all but pretenders. Like Jezebel with her paint, which made her all the uglier, they would seem to be what they are not. As old Adam says, "They are candles with big wicks and no tallow, and when they go out they make a foul and nauseous smell." "They have summer sweating on their brow, and winter freezing in their hearts." You would think them the land of Goshen, but prove them the wilderness of sin. Let us search ourselves, lest such be the case with us.

IV. And now to close, SUCH A TREE MIGHT WELL BE WITHERED. Deception is abhorred of God. There was the Jewish temple, there were the priests standing in solemn pomp, there were the abundant sacrifices of God's altar. But was God pleased with his temple? No, because in the temple you had all the leaves, you had all the externals of worship, but there was no true prayer, no belief in the great Lamb of God's passover, no truth, no righteousness, no love of men, no care for the glory of God; and so the temple, which had been a house of prayer, had become a den of thieves. You do not marvel that the temple was destroyed. You and I may become just like that temple. We may go on with all the externals of religions, nobody may miss us out of our seat at Tabernacle, nay, we may never miss our Christian engagements; we may be in all external matters more precise than we used to be, and yet for all that, we may have become in our hearts a den of thieves; the heart may be given to the world while external ceremonies are still kept up and maintained. Let us beware of this, for such a place cannot be long without a curse. It is abhorrent to God.

Again, it is deceptive to man. Look at that temple! What do men go there for? To see holiness and virtue. Why tread they its hallowed courts? To get nearer to God. And what do they find there? Instead of holiness, covetousness; instead of getting nearer to God, they get into the midst of a mart where men are haggling about the price of doves, and bickering with one another about the changing of shekels. So men may watch to hear some seasonable word from our lips, and instead of that, may get evil; and as that temple was cursed for deluding men, so may we be, because we deceive and disappoint the wants of mankind.

More than this, this barren fig tree committed sacrilege upon Christ, did it not? Might it not have exposed him to ridicule? Some might have said, "How goest thou to a tree, thou prophet, whereon there is no fruit?" A false professor exposes Christ to ridicule. As the temple of old dishonored God, so does a Christian when his heart is not right; he does dishonor to God, and makes the holy cause to be trodden under foot of the adversary. Such men indeed have reason to beware.

Once more, this tree might well be cursed, because its bringing forth nothing but leaves was a plain evidence of its sterility. It had force and vitality, but it turned it to ill account, and would continue to do so. The curse of Christ was but a confirmation of what it already was. He did as good as say, "He that is unfruitful, let him be unfruitful still." And now, what if Christ should come into this Tabernacle this morning, and should look on you and on me, and see in any of us great profession and great pomp of leaves, and yet no fruit, what if he should pronounce the curse on us, what would be the effect? We should wither away as others have done. What mean we by this? Why, they have on a sudden turned to the world. We could not understand why such fair saints should, on a sudden, become such black devils; the fact was, Christ had pronounced the word, and they began to wither away. If he should pronounce the unmasking word on any mere professor here, and say, "Let no man eat fruit of thee for ever," you will go into gross outward sin and wither to your shame. This will take place probably on a sudden; and taking place, your case will be irretrievable; you never afterwards will be restored. The blast which shall fall upon you will be eternal; you will live as a lasting monument of the terrible justice of Christ, as the great head of the Church; you will be spared to let it be seen that a man outside the Church may escape with impunity in this life, but a man inside the Church shall have a present curse, and be made to stand as a tree blasted by the lightning of God for ever. Now, this is a heart-searching matter. It went through me yesterday when I thought, "Well, here am I, I have professed to be called of God to the ministry; I have forced myself into a leading place in God's Church; I have voluntarily put myself into a place where sevenfold damnation is my inevitable inheritance if I be not true and sincere." I could almost wish myself back out of the Church, or at least in the obscurest place in her ranks, to escape the perils and responsibilities of my position; and so may you, if you have not the witness of the Spirit in you that you are born of God--you may wish that you never thought of Christ, and never dreamed of taking his name upon you. If you have by diligence worked yourself into a high position among God's people; if you have mere leaves without the fruit, the more sure is the curse, because the greater the disappointment of the Savior. The more you profess, the more is expected of you; and if you do not yield it, the more just the condemnation when you shall be left to stand for ever withered by the curse of Christ. O men and brethren, let us tremble before the heart-searching eye of God; but let us still remember that grace can make us fruitful yet. The way of mercy is open still. Let us apply to the wounds of Christ this morning. If we have never begun, let us begin now.

Now let us throw our arms about the Savior, and take him to be ours; and, having done this, let us seek divine grace, that for the rest of our lives we may work for God. Oh! I do hope to do more for God, and I hope you will. O Holy Spirit, work in us mightily, for in thee is our fruit found! Amen.

The Sinner's Friend

A Sermon (No. 556)
By the Rev. C. H. SPURGEON,
At the Metropolitan Tabernacle, Newington

"A friend of publicans and sinners." -- Matthew 11:19.

MANY A TRUE WORD is spoken in jest, and many a tribute to virtue has been unwittingly paid by the sinister lips of malice. The enemies of our Lord Jesus Christ thought to brand him with infamy, hold him up to derision, and hand his name down to everlasting scorn, as "a friend of publicans and sinners." Short-sighted mortals! Their scandal published his reputation. To this day the Savior is adored by the title which was minted as a slur. It was designed to be a stigma, that every good man would shudder at and shrink from; it has proved to be a fascination which wins the heart, and enchants the soul of all the godly. Saints in heaven, and saints on earth delight to sing of him thus--

"Savior of sinners they proclaim,
Sinners of whom the chief I am."

What the invidious Jews said in bitter spleen, has been turned by the Holy Spirit to the most gracious account. Where they poured out vials of hate, odours of sacred incense arise. Troubled consciences have found a sweet balm in the very sound. Jesus, "the friend of publicans and sinners," has proved himself friendly to them, and they have become friends with him; so completely has he justified the very name which his enemies gave him in ribald affront.

We shall take this title of Jesus to-night as an order of distinction which sets forth his excellency, and as God helps us, we shall try to exalt his name and proclaim his fame, while we attempt to explain how he was the friend of sinners; and how he shows that he is still the same.

I. OUR LORD PROVED HIMSELF IN HIS OWN TIME TO BE THE FRIEND OF SINNERS.

What better proof could he give of it than coming from the majesty of his Father's house to the meanness of Bethlehem's manger? What better proof could he give than leaving the society of cherubim and seraphim, to lie in the manger where the horned oxen fed, and to become the associate of fallen men? The incarnation of the Savior in the very form of sinners, taking upon himself the flesh of sinners, being born of a sinner, having a sinner for his reputed father--his very being a man, which is tantamount to being in the same form with sinners--surely this were enough to prove that he is the sinner's friend.

When you take up the roll of his earthly lineage and begin to read it through, you will be struck with the fact that there are but few women mentioned in it; and yet three out of those mentioned were harlots, so that even in his lineage there was the taint of sin, and a sinner' s blood would have run in his veins if he had been the true son of Joseph; but inasmuch as he was begotten by the Holy Ghost, who overshadowed the Virgin, in him was no sin; yet his reputed pedigree ran through the veins of sinners. Tamar, and Rahab, and Bath-sheba are three names which bring to remembrance deeds of shame, and yet these stand in the records as the ancestors of the Son of Mary, the sinner's friend!

As soon as Jesus Christ, being born in the likeness of sinful flesh, has come to years of maturity, and has commenced his real life-work, he at once discloses his friendship for sinners by associating with them. You do not find him standing at a distance, issuing his mandates and his orders to sinners to make themselves better, but you find him coming among them like a good workman who stands over his work; he takes his place where the sin and the iniquity are, and he personally comes to deal with it. He does not write out a prescription and send by another hand his medicines with which to heal the sickness of sin, but he comes right into the lazar-house, touches the wounded, looks at the sick; and there is healing in the touch; there is life in the look. The great Physician took upon himself our sicknesses and bare our infirmities, and so proved himself to be really the sinner's friend. Some people appear to like to have a philanthropic love towards the fallen, but yet they would not touch them with a pair of tongs. They would lift them up if they could, but it must be by some machinery--some sort of contrivance by which they would not degrade themselves or contaminate their own hands. Not so the Savior. Up to the very elbow he seems to thrust that gracious arm of his into the mire, to pull up the lost one out of the horrible pit and out of the miry clay. He takes himself the mattock and the spade, and goes to work in the great quarry that he may get out the rough stones which afterwards he will himself polish with his own bitter tears and bloody sweat, that he may make them fit to shine for ever in the glorious temple of the Lord his God. He comes himself into direct, personal contact with sin, without being contaminated with it. He comes as close to it as a man can come. He eats and drinks with sinners. He sits at the Pharisee's table one day, and does not rise because there is a crowd of people no better than they should be coming near him. Another day he goes to the publican's house, and the publican had, no doubt, been a great extortioner in his time; but Jesus sits there, and that day does salvation come to that publican's house. Beloved, this is a sweet trait about Christ, and proves how real and how true was his love, that he made his associations with sinners, and did not shun even the chief of them.

Nay, he not only came among them, but he was always seeking their good by his ministry. If there was anywhere a sinner, a lost sheep of the house of Israel, Christ was after that sinner. Never such an indefatigable shepherd; he sought that which was lost till he found it. One of his earliest works of mercy we will tell you of in brief. He was once on a journey, and Samaria was a little out of his way; but there lived in a city of that country a woman--ah! the less said of her the better. She had had five husbands, and he whom she then had was not her husband, nor were any of the others either. She was a disgrace to that city of Samaria. But Jesus, who has a keen eye for sinners, and a heart which beats high for them, means to save that woman, and he must and he will have her. Being weary, he sits down on a well to rest. A special providence brings the woman to the well. The conventionalities of society forbid him to talk with her. But he breaks through the narrow bigotry of caste. A Samaritan by birth, he cares not for that; but will that most holy being condescend to have familiar conversation with her--a dishonor to her sex? He will. His disciples may marvel when they come back and find him talking with her, but he will do it. He begins to open up the Word of life to her understanding, and that woman becomes the first Christian missionary we ever hear of, for she ran back to the city, leaving her water-pot, and crying, "Come, see a man which told me all things that ever I did: is not this the Christ?" And they came and believed; and there was great joy in that city of Samaria. You know, too, that there was another sinner. He was a bad fellow--I fear him. He had been constantly grinding the faces of the poor, and getting more out of them by way of taxation than he should have done; but the little man had the bump of curiosity, and he must needs see the preacher, and the preacher must needs love him; for I say there was a wonderful attraction in Jesus to a sinner. That sinner's heart was like a piece of iron: Christ's heart was like a loadstone; and wherever there was a sinner the loadstone began to feel it, and soon the sinner began to feel the loadstone too. "Azccheus," said Christ, "make haste, and come down; for to-day I must abide at thy house;" and down comes the sinner, and salvation has come to his house at that hour, Oh! Christ never seemed to preach so sweetly as when he was preaching a sinner's sermon. I would have loved to have seen that dear face of his when he cried, "Come unto me all ye that labor and are heavy laden, and I will give you rest;" or, better still, to have seen his eyes running with whole showers of tears when he said, "O Jerusalem, Jerusalem . . . how often would I have gathered thy children together, as a hen gathereth her chickens under her wings, and ye would not even!" or to have heard him preach those three great sermons upon sinners when he described the woman as sweeping the house and taking away the dust, that she might find the lost piece of her money; and the shepherd going from hill to hill after the wandering sheep; and the father running to welcome that rag-clad prodigal; kissing him with the kisses of love, clothing him with the best robe, and inviting him into the feast, while they did dance and make merry because the lost was found, and he who was dead was alive again. Why, he was the mightiest of preachers for sinners, beyond a doubt, Oh! how he loved them! Never mind the Pharisees: he has thunderbolts for them. "Woe unto you, Scribes and Pharisees!" But when publicans and harlots come, he always has the gate of mercy ajar for them. For them he always has some tender word, some loving saying, such as this--"Him that cometh unto me, I will in no wise cast out." "All manner of sin and blasphemy shall be forgiven unto men;" or such like words of tender wooing. The very chief of sinners was thus drawn into the circle of his disciples.

And you know, dear friends, he did not prove his love merely by preaching to them, and living with them, and by his patience in enduring their contradiction against himself, and all their evil words and deeds, but he proved it by his prayers too. He used his mighty influence with the Father in their behalf. He took their polluted names on his holy lips; he was not ashamed to call them brethren. Their cause became his own, and in their interest his pulse throbbed. How many times on the cold mountains he kept his heart warm with love to them! How often the sweat rolled down his face when he was in an agony of spirit for them I cannot tell you. This much I do know, that on that self-same night when he sweat as it were great drops of blood falling down to the ground, he prayed this prayer--after having prayed for his saints, he went on to say--"Neither pray I for these alone, but for them also which shall believe on me through their word." Here, truly, the heart of the Savior was bubbling up and welling over towards sinners. And you never can forget that almost his last words were, "Father, forgive them; for they know not what they do." Though wilfully and wickedly they pierced his hands and his feet, yet were there no angry words, but only that short, loving, hearty prayer--"Father, forgive them; for they know not what they do." Ah! friends, if there ever was a man who was a friend to others, Jesus was a friend to sinners his whole life through.

This, however, is but little. As for the river of the Savior's love to sinners, I have only brought you to its banks. You have but stood on the bank and dipped your feet in the flood; but now prepare to swim. So fond was he of sinners that he made his grave with the wicked. He was numbered with the transgressors. God's fiery sword was drawn to smite a world of sinners down to hell. It must fall on those sinners. But Christ loves them. His prayers stay the arm of God a little while, but still the sword must fall in due time. What is to be done? By what means can they be rescued? Swifter than the lightning's flash I see that sword descending. But what is that in vision I behold? It falls--but where? Not on the neck of sinners; it is not their neck which is broken by its cruel edge; it is not their heart which bleeds beneath its awful force. No; the "friend of sinners" has put himself into the sinner's place! and then, as if he had been the sinner, though in him was no sin, he suffers, bleeds, and dies--no common suffering--no ordinary bleeding--no death such as mortals know. It was a death in which the second death was comprehended; a bleeding in which the very veins of God were emptied. The God-man divinely suffered. I know not how else to express the suffering. It was a more than mortal agony, for the divine strengthened the human, and the man was made vast and mighty to endure through his being a God. Being God and man he endured more than ten thousand millions of men all put together could have suffered. He endured, indeed, the hells of all for whom he died, the torments, or the equivalent for the torments, which all of them ought to have suffered--the eternal wrath of God condensed and put into a cup, too bitter for mortal tongue to know, and then drained to its utmost dregs by the loving lips of Jesus. Beloved, this was love. "Herein is love, that while we were yet sinners, in due time Christ died for the ungodly." "Greater love hath no man than this, that he lay down his life for his friends." This Christ has done, and he is, therefore demonstrated to be the friend of sinners.

But the trial is over; the struggle is passed; the Savior is dead and buried; he rises again, and after he has spent forty days on earth--in that forty days proving still his love for sinners--he rose again for their justification; I see him ascending up on high. Angels attend him as the clouds receive him.

"They bring his chariot from on high,
To bear him to his throne;
Clap their triumphant wings and cry,
'The glorious work is done.'"

What pomp! What a procession! What splendor! He will forget his poor friends the sinners now, will he not? Not he! I think I hear the song, "Lift up your heads, O ye gates; and be ye lifted up, ye everlasting doors, that the King of Glory may come in." The bars of massy light are all unloosed; the pearly gates are all wide open flung; and as he passes through, mark you, the highest joy which swells his soul is that he has opened those gates, not for himself, for they were never shut on him, but that he has opened them for sinners. It was for this, indeed, he died; and it is for this that he ascends on high, that he may "open the kingdom of heaven for all believers." See him as he rides through heaven's streets! "Thou hast ascended up on high; thou hast led captivity captive; thou hast received gifts of men." Ah! but hear the refrain, for this is the sweetest note of all the hymn, "Yea, for the rebellious also--yea, for the rebellious also, that the Lord God might dwell among them." The scattered gifts of his coronation, the lavish bounties of his ascension, are still for sinners. He is exalted on high--for what? To give repentance and remission of sins. He still wears upon his breastplate the names of sinners; upon his hands and upon his heart does he still bear the remembrance of those sinners; and every day for the sinner's sake he doth not hold his peace, and for the sinner's sake he doth not rest, but cries unto God until every sinner shall be brought safely home. Every sinner who believeth, every sinner who was given to him, every sinner whom he bought with blood--he will not rest, I say, till all such are gathered to be the jewels of his crown, world without end.

Methinks we cannot say more; and 1 think you will say we could not have said less concerning the way in which the Savior proved himself to be the sinner's friend. If there are any of you who dare to doubt him after this, I know not what further to advance. If there can be one who has proved himself your friend, surely Jesus did it, and he is willing to receive you now. What he has done he still continues to do. O that you might have grace to perceive that Jesus is the lover of your soul, that you might find the blessedness which all these tokens of friendship, of which we have been speaking, have brought for believing sinners.

II. While we change the subject a little, we shall still keep to the text, and notice WHAT CHRIST IS DOING NOW FOR SINNERS.

There is a deep principle involved here--a principle the Pharisee of old could not understand, and the cold heart of humanity is slow to embrace it to-day. I have two explanations to offer of the way in which Jesus personally discovers himself to be the friend of sinners, and I will just mention these before I come to the application of the subject I intend. Once upon a time a woman was brought to Jesus by the Scribes and Pharisees: she was an adulteress, she had been taken in the very act. They tell "the sinners friend" what sentence Moses would pronounce in such a case, and they ask him, how sayest thou? This they said tempting him. They were not much concerned about the unhappy creature; the accusation they were intent to lay was against the Man of Nazareth. You know how he disposed of the case, and put her accusers out of countenance. He did not bring the sinner up before the magistrate; nay, he would not act the judge's part, and pronounce sentence, rather would he act the neighbor's part; he acquitted himself as a friend. There is a proverb among a certain class of hard-dealing tradesmen, "We know no friendship in business;" and full well they carry it out, while they grind the faces of the poor without pity, and strive to over-reach one another without fairness. And there was in like manner no friendship, no mercy whatever, among those gentlemen of the long robe. Righteousness, to their idea, stood in exacting justice with rigid severity; and as for wickedness, it was only shameful when it was found out. She who was taken in the act must be stoned. They who had done it secretly must prosecute. The real friendship of Jesus appears in his singling out the object of pity; and where they accused him of winking at crime and harbouring the criminal, he was truly laying the axe at the root of the tree, and sheltering the victims while he upbraided the arrogant rulers, whose secret vices were the genuine cause of the wretchedness which had fallen upon the dregs of the nation. I commend this thought to your consideration. When it is said of him, he is a "friend of pubhicans and sinners," it was implied that he was not a friend of Scribes and Pharisees. Yet again, I want you to notice that the office which Christ came to fulfill towards sinners was that of pure, unmingled friendship. Let us give you an illustration. There is an awful story abroad: a murder has been committed; and the poor wretch who committed it has cut his own throat. The policeman and the surgeon are quickly on the spot. The one comes there in the interest of law, the other attends in the interest of humanity. Says the officer of police, "Man, you are my prisoner;" says the doctor, "My dear fellow, you are my patient." And now he lays a delicate hand upon the wound, he stanches the blood, applies soft liniments, binds it up with plasters, and, bending down his ear, listens to the man's breathing: taking hold of his hand, he feels his pulse: gently raising his head, he administers to him some wine or stimulant, takes him to the hospital, gives the nurse instructions to watch him, and orders that he shall be given nutritious diet as he is able to bear it. Day after day he still visits him, and uses all his skill and all his diligence to heal the man's Wounds. Is that the way to deal with criminals? Certainly it is not the manner in which the police deal. Their business is to find out all the traces and evidences of his guilt. But the medical attendant is not concerned with the man as an evil doer, but as a sufferer. So is it with the sinner. Moses is the officer of justice who comes to arrest him. Christ is the good Physician who comes to heal him; he says, "O Israel, thou hast destroyed thyself but in me is thy help." He deals with the disease, with the wounds, with the sufferings of sinners. He is therefore their friend. Of course the parallel will only go a little way. In the instance of the murderer, the surgeon would hand his patient over to the officers as soon as his wound was recovered; but in the conduct of our Savior he redeems the soul from under the law, and delivers it from the penalty of sin, as well as restores it from the self-inflicted injuries. But oh! if I could but show thee that Christ treats the sinner with pity, rather than with indignation; that the Son of man is not come to destroy men's lives, but to save them; that his visit to our world was mediatoral, not to condemn the world, but to give his life a ransom for many; surely, then, thou wouldst see reason enough why the sinner should look to him as a friend indeed.

Ah! then; I would go further. I would entreat thee to make the case thine own. Thou art a sinner; can I not convince thee that he is thy friend?

You were sick the other day. The physician looked very grave, and whispered something to your wife. She did not tell you what it was, but your own life trembled in the scale, and it is a wonder you are here to-night. Shall I tell you why you are here? Do you see that tree yonder? It has been standing in its place for many years, but it has never yielded any fruit, and several times the master of the garden has said, "Cut it down." The other day the woodman came with his axe; he felt its edge, it was sharp and keen enough, and he began to cut, and the chips were flying, and he made a deep gash. But the gardener came by, one who had watched over the tree, and had hope of it even yet, and he said, "Spare it--spare it yet a little longer; the wound thou hast made may heal; and I will dig about it, and dung it, and if it bring forth fruit well; spare it another year, and if not then cut it down." That tree is yourself. The woodman is Death. That chipping at the trunk of the tree was your sickness. Jesus is he who spared you. You had not been here to-night--you had been there in hell among damned spirits, howling in unutterable woe, if it had not been that the friend of sinners had spared your life.

And where are you to-night? Perhaps, my hearers, you are in an unusual place for you. Your Sunday evenings are not often spent in the house of God. There are other places which know you, but your seat there is empty to-night. There has been much persuasion to bring you here, and it may be that you have come against your will; but some friend has asked you to conduct him to the spot, and here you are. Do you know why you are here? It is a friendly providence, managed by the sinner's friend which has brought you here, that you may hear the sound of mercy, and have a loving invitation tendered to you. Be grateful to the Savior that he has brought you to the gospel-pool. May you--O, may you this night be made to step in and be washed from sin! But it is kind of him, and proves how true a friend he is of sinners, that he has brought you here. I will leave you now where you are, and I will tell you how he has dealt with other sinners, for mayhap this may lead you to ask him to deal the same with you.

I know a sinner--while I live I must know him. Full well do I remember him when he was hard of heart and an enemy to God by a multitude of wicked works. But this friend of sinners loved him; and passing by one day, he looked right into his soul with such a look, that his hard heart began to break. There were deep throes as though a birth of a divine sort were coming on. There was an agony, and there was a grief unutterable; and that poor soul did not think it kind of Jesus; but, indeed, it was kindness too intense ever fully to estimate, for there is no saving a soul except by making it feel its need of being saved. There must be in the work of grace an emptying and a pulling down before there can be a filling and a building up. That soul knew no peace for many a year, and the sole of its foot had no rest; but one day

"I heard the voice of Jesus say,
Come unto me and rest;
Lay down, thou weary one, lay down,
Thy head upon my breast.
I came to Jesus as I was,
Weary, and worn, and sad,
I found in him a resting-place,
And he has made me glad!
I heard the voice of Jesus say,
Behold, I freely give
The living water, thirsty one,
Stoop down, and drink, and live.
I came to Jesus and I drank
Of that life-giving stream;
My thirst was quench'd, my soul revived,
And now I live in him.
I heard the voice of Jesus say,
I am this dark world's light,
Look unto me, thy morn shall rise,
And all thy days be bright.
I look'd to Jesus and I found
In him my star, my sun
And in that light of light I'll walk,
Till travelling days are done."

Ay, said I, Christ is the friend of sinners! So say I, and so will I say while this poor lisping stammering tongue can articulate a sound. And methinks God had a design of abundant mercy when he saved my soul. I had not then believed it, though a mother's loving accents might have whispered it in my ears. But he seems to remind me of it over and over again, till love and terror mingle in my breast, saying, "Woe is me if I preach not the gospel." O my blessed Master, thou dost trust my lips when thou dost bear witness to my heart. Thou givest charge to my tongue when thou constrained my soul. "Am I a chosen vessel?" It is to bear his name to sinners. As a full bottle seeks vent, so must my testimony pant for utterance. O sinner, if thou trustest him, he will be such a friend to thee; and if thou hast now a broken heart and a contrite spirit, these are his work; and it is a proof of his great love to thee if he has made thee to hunger and thirst after him.

Let me impress upon you that Jesus is the friend of the friendless. She who had spent all her money on physicians without getting relief, obtained a cure gratis when she came to him. He who bath "nothing to pay" gets all his debts cancelled by this friend. And he who was ready to perish with hunger, finds not only a passing meal, but a constant supply at his hands.

We know of a place in England still existing, where there is a dole of bread served to every passer-by who chooses to ask for it. Whoever he may be he has but to knock at the door of St. Cross Hospital, and there is the dole of bread for him. Jesus Christ so loveth sinners that he has built a St. Cross Hospital, so that, whenever a sinner is hungry, he has but to knock and have his wants supplied. Nay, he has done better; he has attached to this hospital of the cross a bath; and whenever a soul is black and filthy it has but to go there and be washed. The fountain is always full, always efficacious. There is no sinner who ever went into it and found it, could not wash away his stains. Sins which were scarlet and crimson have all disappeared, and the sinner has been whiter than snow. As if this were not enough, there is attached to this hospital of the cross a wardrobe, and a sinner, making application simply as a sinner, with nothing in his hand, but being just empty and naked, he may come and be clothed from head to foot. And if he wishes to be a soldier, he may not merely have an under garment, but he may have armor which shall cover him from the sole of his foot to the crown of his head. Nay, if he wants a sword he shall have that given to him, and a shield too. There is nothing that his heart can desire that is good for him which he shall not receive. He shall have spending-money so long as he lives, and he shall have an eternal heritage of glorious treasure when he enters into the joy of his Lord.

Beloved, I cannot tell you all that Christ has done for sinners, but this I know, that if he meets with you to-night, and becomes your friend, he will stand by you to the last. He will go home with you to-night. No matter how many pairs of stairs you have to go up, Jesus will go with you. No matter if there be no chair to sit down on, he will not disdain you. You shall be hard at work to-morrow, but as you wipe the sweat from your brow he shall stand by you. You will, perhaps, be despised for his sake, but he will not forsake you. You will, perhaps, have days of sickness, but he will come and make your bed in your sickness for you. You will, perhaps, be poor, but your bread shal be given you, and your water shall be sure, for he will provide for you. You will vex him much and grieve his Spirit. You will often doubt him--you will go after other lovers. You will provoke him to jealousy, but he will never cease to love you. You will, perhaps, grow cold to him, and even forget his dear name for a time, but he will never forget you. You may, perhaps, dishononr his cross, and damage his fair fame among the sons of men, but he will never cease to love you; nay, he will never love you less--he cannot love you more. This night he doth espouse himself unto you. Faith shall be the wedding-ring which he will put upon your finger. He plights his troth to you,

"Though you should him ofttimes forget
His lovingkindness fast is set."

His heart shall be so true to you that he will never leave you nor forsake you. You will come to die soon, but the friend of sinners, who loved you as a sinner and would not cast you off when your sinnership kept breaking up, will still he with you when you come to the sinner's doom, which is to die. I see you going down the shelving banks of Jordan, but the sinner's friend goes with you. Ah! dear heart, he will put his arm beneath you, and bid you fear not; and when in the thick shades of that grim night you expect to see a fearful visage--the grim face of Death--you shall see instead thereof, you shall see his sweet and smiling face, bright as an evening star, by your soul, and you shall hear him say, "Fear not, I am with thee; be not dismayed; I am thy God." You will land in the world of spirits by-and-by; but will the sinner's friend forsake you then? No; he will be pleased to own you; he will meet you on the other side the Jordan, and he will say, "Come, my beloved, I have loved thee with an everlasting love, and have bought thee, though thou wast a sinner vile, and now I am not ashamed to confess thee before my holy angels; nay, come with me, and I will take thee to my Father's face, and will confess thee there." And when the day shall come in which the world shall be judged, he will be thy friend then. Thou shalt sit on the bench with him. At the right hand of the Judge shalt thou stand, accepted in him who was thine Advocate, and who is now thy Judge, to acquit thee. And when the splendours of the millennium shall come, thou shalt partake of them; and when the end shall be, and the world shall be rolled up like a worn-out vesture, and these arching skies shall have passed away like a forgotten dream; when eternity, with its deep-sounding waves shall break upon the mocks of time and sweep them away for ever--then, on that sea of glass mingled with fire, thou shalt stand with Christ, thy friend still, owning thee notwithstanding all thy misbehaviour in the world which has gone, and loving thee now, loving thee on as long as eternity shall last. Oh! what a friend is Christ to sinners, to sinners!

Now do recollect, that we have been talking about sinners; there is a notion abroad that Jesus

Christ came into the world to save respectable people, and that he will save decent sort of folks; that those of you who go regularly to a place of worship, and are good sort of people, will be saved. Now Jesus Christ came into the world to save sinners; and who does that mean? Well, it includes some of us who have not been permitted to go into outward sin; but it also includes within its deep, broad compass those who have gone to the utmost extent of iniquity.

Talk of sinners! Walk the streets by moonlight, if you dare, and you will see sinners then. Watch when the night is dark, and the wind is howling, and the picklock is grating in the door, and you will see sinners then. Go to you jail, and walk through the wards, and see the men with heavy, over-hanging brows, men whom you would not like to meet out at night, and there are sinners there. Go to the Reformatories, and see those who have betrayed an early and a juvenile depravity, and you will see sinners there. Go across the seas to the place where a man will gnaw a bone upon which is reeking human flesh, and there is a sinner there. Go you where you will, and ransack earth to find sinners, for they are common enough; you may find them in every lane and street, of every city and town, and village and hamlet. It is for such that Jesus died. If you will select me the grossest specimen of humanity, if he be but born of woman, I will have hope of him yet, because the gospel of Christ is come to sinners, and Jesus Christ is come to seek and to save sinners. Electing love has selected some of the worst to be made the best. Redeeming love has bought, specially bought, many of the worst to be the reward of the Savior's passion. Effectual grace calls out and compels to come in many of the vilest of the vile; and it is therefore that I have tried to-night to preach my Master's love to sinners.

Oh! by that love, looking out of those eyes in tears; oh! by that love, streaming from those wounds flowing with blood; by that faithful love, that strong love, that pure, disinterested, and abiding love; oh! by the heart and by the bowels of the Savior's compassion, I do conjure you turn not away as though it were nothing to you; but believe on him and you shall be saved. Trust your souls with him and he will bring you to his Father's right hand in glory everlasting.

May God give us a blessing for Jesus' sake. Amen.

Where to Find Fruit

A Sermon (No. 557)
Delivered on Sunday Morning, February 28th, 1864, by the
Rev. C. H. SPURGEON,
At the Metropolitan Tabernacle, Newington

"From me is thy fruit found." -- Hosea 14:8.

THE text has a double significance. It may indicate the fruit upon which we feed, or the fruit which we are enabled to produce. If it shall mean the first, there is mach of comfort in it. The Lord has compared himself, in his condescending mercy, to a green fir tree in the sentence which precedes the text. The fir tree in the East yields a most goodly shade. Neither the burning heat of the sun, nor the drops of pouring rain can.pass through the dense foliage, and therefore it affords a welcome shelter to the traveler. But shade is not enough for a man; he requires food, and the fir tree fails in that respect, for it yields no repast for the hungry. To complete the picture, therefore, when the Lord deigns to compare himself to a green fir tree, he adds, "From me is thy fruit found." Our gracious God is like a fir tree for shade, but like the apple tree among the trees of the wood for fruit. We sit under his shadow with great delight, and his fruit is sweet unto our taste. Living souls must have food to feed upon, or however well housed, they would be comparable to the king of Israel in the besieged city of Samaria. He sat in his palace of ivory, he wore his mantle of purple, and placed the crown of gold upon his head; but what availed his splendor, when neither barn-floor nor winepress could relieve his hunger? In vain all other blessings if the soul received no nourishment from on high; Jesus must not only be our life, but the bread of heaven by which that life is sustained. Glory be to his name! he is all in all to his people: we may gather fruit from him which shall satisfy the cravings of the soul.

According to Master Trapp, some read this passage, "In me is thy fruit ready." Certain it is that at all times, whenever we approach to God, we shall find in him a ready supply for every lack. The best of trees have fruit on them only at appointed seasons. Who is so unreasonable as to look for fruit upon the peach or the plum at this season of the year? No drooping boughs beckon us to partake of their ripening crops, for Winter's cold still nips the buds. But our God hath fruit at all times: the tree of life yieldeth its fruit every month; nay, every day and every hour, for he is "a very present help in time of trouble."

Another translator reads the passage, "In me thy fruit is enough." Whatever may be the accuracy of the translation, the sentiment itself is most correct. In God there is enough for all his people; and well there may be, since in him there is infinity. "I have enough, my brother," said Esau when he met Jacob: "I have all things," said Jacob in reply. None but the believer can say, "I have all things;" and therefore only he can be sure of having enough. Ishmael had his bottle of water, and went away into the wilderness; but it is written, that Isaac abode by the well: how happy is the soul which bath learned how to live by the well of his faithful God! for the water will be spent in the bottle, but the water will never be spent in the well. Christian, remember the all sufficiency of thy God! Let that ancient name, "El Shaddai"--God all-sufficient, sound like music in thine ear--as some translate it, "The many-breasted God," yielding from himself the sustenance of all his creatures.

As we find the text translated, we have it, "From me is thy fruit found;" but the particle from does not mean apart from, but out of me; and to prevent misunderstanding, I shall not err if I read it in, for this is the force of the word in this place. The text speaks of fruit being found, implying perhaps, that we must look for it--not because there is little, or here and there a cluster, like the grape-gleanings of Abi-ezer; but because the Lord will be enquired of by the house of Israel, and would exercise our faith by making us search for the needed benefit. It is of essential service to us to make us seek, and hence we have the promise of finding to excite our diligence. Christian, look up longingly! Is thy spirit hungering? Look up to thy God now with intense desire; come before him with earnest, vehement pleadings, and thou shalt find in thy God whatsoever thy heart desireth.

Mark that little word "thy." As if the Lord had said, "It is thine already; I have freely given it; it is thy fruit. I bear it, but I bear it for thee; every golden apple, every luscious cluster, I will bestow on thee. Thou canst not ask me for anything which I have not given thee. For behold, I have given thee my Son, and in him dwelleth all the fullness of the Godhead bodily.'" Believer, hast thou not learned the sweet logic of the beloved disciple, "He that spared not his own Son, but delivered him up for us all, how shall he not with him also freely give us all things?" In the eternal covenant, God has made over--not only all created things--but himself unto his people. "I will be their God, and they shall be my people." "God, even our God," saith the Psalmist. Is not that a delightful expression, "Even our own God?" And so, as God is your own, his fruit is your own. Every outgoing of power, every outflow of love is yours already. "In him is thy fruit found." Surely this word "thy" is as a little golden cup filled with a rare cordial; he who drinketh of it shall forget his misery, and remember his poverty no more. Let us not fail then, dearly beloved, to receive boldly that which is our own by covenant engagement and faithful promise. What dost thou want this morning? Surely out of the "twelve manner of fruits," there shall be something which will suit thy necessities; stand not back through shame or fear, but come boldly to the throne of the heavenly grace.

Thus much for the first sense of the text; but we do not intend to use the words in that signification this morning. We think that, understanding the text the other way--"From me is that fruit found which grace produces in thee," it will be a very fitting sequel to the sermon of last Sabbath morning. You will recollect we spoke upon the withering of the fig tree which mocked the Savior with its leaves, but yielded him no fruit. There may be some who were alarmed under that sermon, and even believers who were shaken by it; such anxieties will do none of us any hurt, especially if they lead us to pant after fruitfulness. Our text, following upon the other, will direct earnest seekers where to find fruit. There are three sorts of preachers, all useful in their way, the doctrinal, the experimental, and the practical; we will try to blend the three this morning, and so handle the words doctrinally, experimentally, and practically.

I. First. THE DOCTRINE OF THE TEXT. The doctrine of the text is twofold. First, that the believer's fruit is his own--it is called "thy fruit;" secondly, that though it is the believer's own, yet it proceeds entirely from his God.

1. The first doctrine is that true fruit is a believer's own. You will think this a very trite remark, but it is one which needs to be made in these days, for there are certain persons who talk of man as if he were not a thinking, intelligent, free agent. They forget his will, judgment, reason, and affections: they leave out of their consideration everything in fact which constitutes the man, and then speak of the operations of grace as though they were manual works upon wood or stone. For aught I can see, according to their way of talking, the grace of God might just as well have produced holiness in monkeys as in men, for men are generally represented as merely passive existences to be moved by them to gratitude, or repentance, or faith, as horses are groomed in a stable or led out to be exercised. Be it never forgotten that our God deals with men as intelligent beings, having will and reason and all the other powers which make man a responsible creature; he does not ignore our manhood when he converts us by his grace. He uses means fitted for our constitution as men, "I drew them with the cords of love, with the bands of a man."

Good works are a believer's own. It were an ill thing for him if they were not; to what could we compare him but to those dead sticks with fruits tied on them, which women sell to little children? a sorry picture for a branch of Christ's vine. The believer produces fruit from his own inner self when grace has renewed him; and if his holiness were not really the outgrowth of his new heart and his renewed nature, it would be no sign of spiritual life. It is not fruit tied on us, but fruit growing out of us which proveth us to be engrafted into Christ.

True fruit is the believer's own because he wills through divine grace to do good works. If I performed what looked like a good work against my will, I do not see how it could be truly a good work as far as the doer is concerned. If a man could be compelled to virtue while his heart staggered away to sin, would he not be really transgressing? There is a gracious willingness towards the right thing bestowed upon us by the Holy Spirit. Nay, there is not only a will to holiness, but a desire after it. The true Christian longs after holiness and usefulness; he hungers and thirsts to do the will of his Father who is in heaven. Like his Lord in some measure, it is to him his meat and his drink to do the will of him who sent him. He can say, "The zeal of thine house hath eaten me up." He is constrained, but mark, it is not a physical constraint, for "the love of Christ constraineth us." So you see, beloved, good works are a believer's own because he is willing to do them and desires to perform them.

They are his own, again, because he actually does them. The Holy Ghost does not repent, nor feed the hungry, nor clothe the naked, nor preach the gospel. He gives us grace to do all these, but we ourselves do them. If the poor be fed, it must be by these hands; if souls are edified, it must be by these lips; we do not fold our arms, and shut our mouths, and then bring forth fruit unto God. We do not find ourselves taken up by the hair of our head as the prophet Habakkuk was said to have been, according to the Apocrypha, and so carried away whether we will or no, to perform a deed of charity. All glory be to the Holy Spirit, but he is not glorified by making him appear to be a physical force instead of the great spiritual Worker. We do, my brethren, bring forth fruit which is properly our own when we consider ways of usefulness, meditate methods of working, plan designs of good, act out deeds of mercy, persevere in labor, and continue in service before God.

I will tell you why I am absolutely sure a believer's works are his own, namely, because he grieves over them. The best works he ever performs he feels are his own, because they are imperfect. If there is anything good in them, he ascribes it wholly to the fact that they proceeded from God; but, inasmuch as there is something imperfect in them, he is obliged to say, "Ah! yes, this is my fruit. If it had been God's fruit independent of me, it would have been perfect, but inasmuch as it is imperfect, I am compelled to see that I had a hand in it. The stream was clear enough as it came from the fountain, but flowing through the wooden spout of my nature, it is become in some measure defiled, and so far at least is mine."

Dear friends, the whole analogy of fruitbearing must show to you that the Christian does bring forth fruit unto God, real fruit from his inner self; and if any of you think that you are going to attain to holiness by simply being passive, you are wonderfully mistaken. If you imagine you will be a pilgrim by sitting down at the wicket-gate, or be carried in a sedan-chair to glory, you will find yourselves left behind. No, we must fight if we would win; we must travel if we would reach the Celestial City; we must wrestle, and fight, and pray. The Word of God does say "It is God that worketh in us to will and to do of his own good pleasure," but it does not stop there, it bids us for this very reason "Work out our own salvation with fear and trembling." The passive first, but then the active. We must lie as dead at Jehovah's feet to be quickened, but being quickened, what then? Why then we walk in holiness and in the fear of God. We are first of all made trees of the Lord's right-hand planting, and we receive grace from him, and then through his grace, we ourselves do really bring forth fruit. The truth is clear enough, prove by your energetic strivings that you under stand it.

2. The pith of the doctrine lieth here, that all a believer's fruit proceeds from his God, and that in several senses from the divine purpose. If you are holy, it is because he has called you to holiness. If you have good works they come to you, according to the word of the apostle concerning good works, "which God hath before ordained that we should walk in them." When you see a costly vase which is the admiration of all eyes, you know that whatever of beauty there is in that vessel was originally in the artist's plan. If you have examined his sketches, you have seen every elegant line, and every graceful figure. Even so, beloved, if you have been sanctified it is according to the eternal design, which was settled in grace and wisdom, before the skies were formed.

All our fruit springs from our God as to calling. You were dead in trespasses and sins. There were no good works in you by nature, and there never would have been, but he who commanded the light to shine out of darkness hath shined in your heart, to give you the knowledge of God, and then to turn you from dead works to serve the living and true God. You owe everything to your calling. The tree which is loaded with fruit, owes its fruit first of all, to its having been chosen to be in the garden, and next to its having been really planted there; for in our case, had we been left to grow in the wide wilderness, we should have brought forth no fruit unto God; but he took us up out of the place of barrenness, and put us in the rich soil which Jesus had watered with his own bloody sweat, and therefore we bring forth fruit.

Our fruit is found from God as to union. The fruit of the branch is really traceable to the root. Cut the connection and the branch dies, and no fruit is hereafter produced. By virtue of our union with Christ we bring forth fruit. Every branch of grapes has been first in the root, it has passed through the stem, and flowed through the sap vessels, and fashioned itself externally into fruit, but it was first internal in the stem; so also every good work was first in Christ, and then was brought forth in us. O Christian, prize this precious doctrine of union to Christ; hold it firmly, because it is the source of every atom of fruitfulness which thou canst ever hope to know. If thou wert not joined to Jesus Christ, no fruit could ever be in thee.

Our fruit comes from God, and from God alone, as to providence. When the dew-drops fall from heaven, each one may whisper to the tree and say, "From me is thy fruit found." When the cloud looks down from on high, and is about to distil its liquid treasure, it may thunder to the earth beneath, "From me is thy fruit found." And the bright sun above all others, as he paints the cheek of the apple, or swells the berries of the cluster, may well say to all the trees of the garden, "From me is your fruit found." The fruit owes much to the root--that is essential to fruitfulness--but it owes very much also to external care. Beloved, how much we owe to God's grace-providence! We are greatly debtors to his common providences, in that he maketh all things work together for good. But his grace-providence, in which he provides us constantly with quickening, teaching, correction, consolation, strength, or whatever else we want--to this we owe our all of usefulness or virtue.

Our fruit is found in God as to the matter of husbandry. The knife which the gardener taketh from his pocket, might talk to the tree and say, "Much of thy fruit is found in me. Thou wouldst not yield such an abundance if it were not for my sharp edge. I make thee bleed a little, as I take away thy superfluous shoots, but thou hadst not such goodly clusters if it were not of me." So is it, Christian, with that pruning which the Lord gives to thee. "My Father is the husbandman. Every branch in me that beareth not fruit he taketh away: and every branch that beareth fruit, he purgeth it, that it may bring forth more fruit."

Thus the text may be read in very many ways. They will all come to one--that we have nothing, except as we receive it from above. "What hast thou which thou hast not received?" I may say, to conclude this head, that all our fruit is found in God, because he will, having been the author of it, get all the glory of it. Of all our spiritual life he shall have the praise, for it is all due to him, and if he giveth us a crown at the last, we will cast it at his feet.

Brethren, you know this doctrine well enough without my enlarging upon it; you know how constantly Scripture teacheth us that we can do nothing without Christ. We can sin; we can ruin our own souls; we can bring forth the apples of Sodom and the grapes of Gomorrah, but anything which is lovely, and honest, and of good repute, must come from him who is glorious in working. You have no question or quibble about this. "You hath he quickened;" you trace your life to him You doth he quicken day by day; you owe the continuance of your life to him. You know as a matter of doctrine that "in him we live and move and have our being," and that "every good gift and every perfect gift is from above." I need not confirm this doctrine: no argument is required. You have never erred from the truth in this respect; you could not be Christians if you did, for I hold this to be fundamental truth, in all godliness, that salvation from first to last is of the Lord. Salvation is not of yourselves, it is the gift of God. Let us heartily praise him whose workmanship we are.

II. We come now to THE EXPERIENCE. Experimentally we have proof that all our fruit is in God. Let me remind you of your experience when you were the servants of the flesh. What fruit had ye then in those days? What repentance did your natural mind bring forth? What faith in Christ did your unrenewed soul ever beget or foster? What love to God ever stirred your carnal heart? What affection for the brotherhood possessed your alienated spirit? You must say that at that time you were without God and without hope, and certainly without fruit. "What fruit had ye then in those things whereof ye are now ashamed?" A painful remembrance of your former estate compels you to feel the truth of the Lord's Word, "In me is thy fruit found."

Again, when the law began to work in your heart, and you were in a state of bondage, having enough of light to see your darkness, and enough of life to mourn your death--what fruit had ye then when ye were under the law? The law told you what you should do; did it enable you to do anything? The ten commandments set before you a perfect rule: but was it not "weak through the flesh?" You had a very clear perception of the justice and righteousness of God: did the perception reconcile you to justice or to holiness? Let me ask you, did the law of God ever make you love him? Did the awakenings of your conscience, which proceeded from it ever lead you to trust in Jesus Christ? They may have been overruled to this purpose, but the law worketh wrath, and as long as you were under it, it rather produced sin in you than righteousness. Such was Paul's experience, "When the commandment came, sin revived, and I died," "for I had not known lust, except the law had said, Thou shalt not covet." As a child might never care to run into the street, but being told not to do it, he straightway doth it by reason of the perversity of his nature, just so it is with us by nature; the forbidden thing our flesh lusteth after. All the enmity of carnal nature is provoked to yet greater sin by the law. That which should have been a bit, becomes a spur. Cold water quencheth fire, and yet when poured on lime, produceth a vehement heat. So the law acts contrary to its own nature, by reason of the depravity of the human heart. Thus were you, my brethren, led by a very sorrowful experience, to feel that from Christ must come your fruit; for none could be produced by the efforts of the flesh, backed up by the most earnest resolution and most devout prayer, and driven onward by the whip of the law.

A sweeter experience has proved this to you. When did you begin to bear fruit? It was when you came to Christ and cast yourselves on the great atonement, and rested on the finished righteousness. Ab! what fruit you had then! Do you remember those early days? Did not your faith, and love, and zeal, form a garden of nuts, an orchard of pomegranates, with pleasant fruits? Then indeed the vine flourished, the tender grape appeared, the pomegranates budded forth, and the beds of spices gave forth their smell. Have you declined since then? Even if you have, I charge you to remember that time of love. Jesus remembers it, for he says, "I remember thee, the kindness of thy youth, the love of thine espousals, when thou wentest after me into the wilderness." He recollects that time of the singing of birds, when the voice of the turtle was heard in your land. Would God this were with you ever! He has not forgotten it, do you not forget it, but seek to enjoy it still. Your fruit began, you know it did, when you camne to Jesus Christ.

My brethren, when have you been the most fruitless? This is another part of experience. Has not it been when you have lived farthest from the Lord Jesus Christ, when you have slackened in prayer, when you have departed somewhat from the simplicity of your faith, when your graces engrossed your attention instead of your Lord, when you said, "My mountain standeth firm, I shall never be moved;" and forgot where your strength lieth--has not it been then that your fruit has ceased? Some of us know that we have nothing out of Christ by terrible soul-emptyings and humblings of heart before the Lord. Brethren, it is no pleasant thing to be clean emptied out; but such times have happened to some of us, when we have felt that if one prayer would save us, if the Holy Spirit did not aid us, we were damned; if one good thought would take us to heaven, we could not reach it; the vileness of our heart has been so clear before our eyes, that had not it been that there was a mighty God to trust to we should have given up in despair.

"How seldom do I rise to God,
Or taste the joys above!
Corruption presses down my faith,
And chills my flaming love.
When smiling mercy courts my soul
With all its heavenly charms,
This stubborn, this relentless thing,
Would thrust it from my arms."

In such seasons we do well to cry, "Quicken thou me, O Lord, according to thy word." Then you feel that to will is present with you, but how to perform that which is good, you find not. It is a very easy thing for me to exhort you, but sometimes I do not find it very easy to do myself what I exhort you to do. And there are times with us, dear friends, when, though we know our interest in Christ, we are wretched under a deep sense of the creature's fickleness, sinfulness, and death. Our moan is, " wretched man that I am! who shall deliver me from the body of this death?" When you have seen the utter emptiness of all creature confidence, then you have been able to say, "From him all my fruit must be found, for no fruit can ever come from me." We shall find from Scripture, I am sure--let our past experience confirm it--that the more we depend upon the grace of God in Christ Jesus, and wait upon the Holy Spirit, pleading that his influences may operate in our hearts, the more we shall bring forth fruit unto God. If I could bear fruit without my God, I would loathe the accursed thing, for it would be the fruit of pride--the fruit of an arrogant setting up of one's self in independence of the Creator No; the Lord deliver us from all faith, all hope, all love which do not spring from himself! May we have none of our own-manufactured graces about us. May we have nothing but that which is minted in heaven, and is therefore made of the pure metal. May we have no grace, pray no prayer, do no works, serve God in nothing except as we depend upon his strength and receive his Spirit. Any experience which comes short of a knowledge that we must get all from God, is a deceiving experience. But if you have been brought to find everything in him, beloved, this is a mark of a child of God. Cultivate a spirit of deep humiliation before the Most High; seek to know more your nothingness, and to prove more the omnipotence of the eternal God. There are two books I have tried to read, but I have not got through the first page yet. The first is the book of my own ignorance, and emptiness, and nothingness--what a great book is that! It will take us all our lives to read it, and I question whether Methuselah ever got to the last page. There is another book I must read, or else the first volume will drive me mad--it is the book of God's all-sufficiency. I have not got through the first word of that, much less the first page, but reading the two together, I would spend all my days. This is heaven's own literature, the wisdom which cometh from above. Less than nothing I can boast, and yet "I can do all things through Christ which strengtheneth me." Having nothing yet possessing all things." Black as the tents of Kedar, yet fair as the curtains of Solomon: dark as hell's profoundest night, and yet "Fair as the moon, clear as the sun, and terrible as an army with banners."

III. We now arrive at the PRACTICAL POINT.

1. First then, dear friends, let us look to Jesus Christ for fruit in the same way in which we first looked to him for shade. That sounds like something you have heard a great many times before. Very well, but have you really understood it? To give an illustration--you want to overcome an angry temper! You are given to ebullitions of passion--you try to overcome that. How do you go to work? It is very possible there are even believers here who have never tried the right way. How did I get salvation? I came to Jesus just as I was, and I trusted him to save me. Can I kill my angry temper in the same way? It is the only way in which I can ever kill it. I must go to Christ with it, and say to him, "Lord, I trust thee to deliver me from it." This is the only death-blow it will ever receive. Are you covetous? Do you feel the world entangle you? You may struggle against this evil as long as you like, but if it be your besetting sin, you will never be delivered from it in any way but the cross. Take it to Christ. Tell him, "Lord, I have trusted thee, and thy name is Jesus--Thou shalt call his name Jesus, for he shall save his people from their sins'--Lord, this is one of my sins; save me from it!" Do not take Jesus Christ with the blood only, and without the water--that is to have

only half-a-Christ. Pray to be forgiven, but ask also to be sanctified. Sing with Toplady--

> *"Let the water and the blood,*
> *From thy river side which flowed,*
> *Be of sin the double cure,*
> *Cleanse me from its guilt and power."*

I know what some of you do. You go to Christ for forgiveness, and then you go to the law for power to fight your sins. " foolish Galatians, who hath bewitched you, that ye should not obey the truth?" Tell me, did ye receive faith by the law, or by the operation of grace? "Are ye so foolish? having begun in the Spirit, are ye now made perfect by the flesh?" The only weapon to fight sin with is the spear which pierced Christ's side. Nothing can kill the viprous brood of hell but drops of Jesus' precious blood. Take your sins to Christ's cross, sir, for the old man can only be crucified there: we are crucified with him; we are buried with him. If I be dead to the world, I must be dead with him, and if I rise again to newness of life, I must rise in him. Ordinances are nothing without Christ as means of mortification. Baptism is nothing, except as we are buried with him in baptism unto death. The Lord's Supper is nothing, except as we eat his flesh and drink his blood, and have communion with him. And your prayers and your repentances, and your tears--the whole of them put together--are not worth a farthing apart from him. Every flower which grows in your garden will wither, and the sooner it is blasted and withered the better for you; only the rose of Sharon will bloom in heaven. "None but Jesus can do helpless sinners good;" or helpless saints either. You must overcome by the blood of the Lamb.

2. Another practical observation is this--let us cultivate those graces most which bring us most to Christ, for these will be the most fruitful. Let me look well to my faith; let me see that I keep it purely stayed on him, having no supplementary confidence, but resting wholly and absolutely upon the finished work of my Lord. Let me see to my love. Let my Lord be to me altogether lovely. Lord, help me to sing, "My beloved is mine, and I am his." Sometimes graciously enable me to sing, "He brought me to the banqueting-house, and his banner over me was love. His left hand is under my head, and his right hand doth embrace me." Faith and love are the great fruitbearers. A gardener says, "There is such and such a twig, I must not cut that off, because it is to the young wood that I am looking for my summer fruits." So he taketh care of it. There is that, believer, a growing faith and growing love to which you must look as the fruitbearing shoots, because they pre-eminently link your soul to Christ, and most evidently have intercourse with him. Cultivate those things which lead you most to him.

3. A third practical piece of advice. Be most in those engagements which you have experimentally proved to draw you nearest to Christ, because it is from him that all your fruits proceed. Any holy exercise which will bring you to him will help you to bear fruit Do you find prayer the channel of Jesus' manifestations? Do you find yourself profited in the public means of grace? Is it the breaking of bread which we love to celebrate every Sabbath day, which is most precious to you? If so, wherever Jesus Christ layeth bare his heart to you, there be you found; and if there be any one means of grace which has been more rich to you than another, use it with the greatest perseverance. Use them all, dear friends, do not neglect any, hut especially use those most which bring you nearest to your Lord.

4. Lastly, let none of us--whether we be the Lord's people or not--let none of us ever insult Christ by thinking that we are to bring fruit to him as a recommendation to his love. "From me is thy fruit found." Now there may be some saint here who has lost his evidences, and he dare not approach the throne of grace as he used to do, because he says "I have sinned--I must produce fresh fruit before I dare come." My dear friend! My dear friend! Bring fruit to Christ! How can you talk in so legal a fashion? All the fruit you ever will have you must first get from him! Come to him as you are and get your fruit out of him. Never suppose that you must bring Christ a present or else you must not come to him. He does not want your money. If he takes it he will give it back to you in your sack's mouth. He will receive your fruit as an offering, but never as a reconciliation. There are those here this morning who are not converted as yet. They are saying, "I dare not seek the Lord, I dare not trust Christ. I know the gospel is, trust Christ and you are saved. He that believeth on him is not condemned; but I must not trust him, I am a drunkard, I have been a swearer, I am a Sabbath-breaker, I will wait until I am better and then I will come to Christ." Why how can you talk thus? "From him is thy fruit found." If there be any fruit you must come to Jesus Christ for it. Am I, if I am poor and ragged, am I to buy a new coat before I may beg a garment? What a strange proposal that I should do for myself what Christ came to do. How can that be reasonable? If I saw a man standing outside the baths and wash-houses, and he should say, "Well really, I've just come home from my work and am as black as a sweep, but I dare not go into those baths until I have washed my face first." I should say, "How foolish! it is in the bath that your washing is to be

found." There is no fitness wanted for Christ but that which is in Christ: nothing wanted in you, everything is in him. To use the old proverb," Why carry coals to Newcastle?" Who would think it a profitable business for our London merchants, in the cold winter time, when the price of coals is very high, to charter all the ships they can, and send them laden with coals to Newcastle? If they did so, you would think them mad. And yet there are many sinners penniless, comfortless, with no good thing of their own, who want to bring good works to Jesus! This is carrying coals to Newcastle with a vengeance. Oh! folly! folly! folly! Go with your ship all black and empty, sail up the harbour, and the pit's mouth will soon yield to you an abundance of precious store. Go to Jesus as you are. Do you want faith to-day--repentance--grace? Go to Christ for it. Go to him, resting on him, dependent on him, believing that he is ready to save you, to begin, to carry on, and finish your salvation. He will be as good as you ever believe him to be, and infinitely better. If thou canst believe him princely enough to put all thy sins away, and to cover thee with his righteousness, he will do it, for never man thought too well of Christ. If thou canst get a big thought of Christ, thou big sinner--if thou canst believe on the eternal Son of the eternal Father, who once poured out his blood in streams on Calvary thou art secure. God help thee. Amen.

A Bundle of Myrrh

A Sermon (No. 558)
Delivered on Sunday Morning, February 28th, 1864, by the
Rev. C. H. SPURGEON,
At the Metropolitan Tabernacle, Newington

"A bundle of myrrh is my well-beloved unto me; he shall lie all night betwixt my breasts." -- Song of Solomon 1:13.

CERTAIN DIVINES have doubted the inspiration of Solomon's Song; others have conceived it to be nothing more than a specimen of ancient love-songs, and some have been afraid to preach from it because of its highly poetical character. The true reason for all this avoidance of one of the most heavenly portions of God's Word lies in the fact that the spirit of this Song is not easily attained. Its music belongs to the higher spiritual life, and has no charm in it for unspiritual ears. The Song occupies a sacred enclosure into which none may enter unprepared. "Put off thy shoes from off thy feet, for the place whereon thou standest is holy ground," is the warning voice from its secret tabernacles. The historical books I may compare to the outer courts of the Temple; the Gospels, the Epistles, and the Psalms, bring us into the holy place or the Court of the priests; but the Song of Solomon is the most holy place: the holy of holies, before which the veil still hangs to many an untaught believer. It is not all the saints who can enter here, for they have not yet attained unto the holy confidence of faith, and that exceeding familiarity of love which will permit them to commune in conjugal love with the great Bridegroom. We are told that the Jews d id not permit the young student to read the Canticles--that years of full maturity were thought necessary before the man could rightly profit by this mysterious Song of loves; possibly they were wise, at any rate the prohibition foreshadowed a great truth. The Song is, in truth, a book for full-grown Christians. Babes in grace may find their carnal and sensuous affections stirred up by it towards Jesus, whom they know, rather "after the flesh" than in the spirit; but it needs a man of fuller growth, who has leaned his head upon the bosom of his Master, and been baptized with his baptism, to ascend the lofty mountains of love on which the spouse standeth with her beloved. The Sung, from the first verse to the last, will be clear to those who have received an unction from the holy One, and know all things. (1 John 2:20.) You are aware, dear friends, that there are very few commentaries upon the Epistles of John. Where we find fifty commentaries upon any book of St. Paul, you will hardly find one upon John. Why is that? Is the book too difficult? The words are very simple; there is hardly a word of four syllables anywhere in John's Epistles. Ah! but they are so saturated through and through with the spirit of love, which also perfumes this Book of Solomon, that those who are not taught in the school of communion, cry out, "We cannot read it, for it is sealed." The Song is a golden casket, of which love is the key rather than learning. Those who have not attained unto heights of affection, those who have not been educated by familiar intercourse with Jesus, cannot come near to this mine of treasure, "seeing it is hid from the eyes of all living, and kept close from the fowls of heaven." O for the soaring eagle wing of John, and the far-seeing dove's eyes of Solomon; but the most of us are blind and cannot see afar off. May God be pleased to make us grow in grace, and give us so much of the Holy Spirit, that with feet like hind's feet we may stand upon the high places of Scripture, and this morning have some near and dear intercourse with Christ Jesus.

Concerning our text, let us talk very simply, remarking first, that Christ is very precious to believers; secondly, that there is good reason why he should be; thirdly, that mingled with this sense of preciousness, there is a joyous consciousness of possession of him; and that therefore, fourthly, there is an earnest desire for perpetual fellowship with him. If you look at the text again, you will see all these matters in it.

I. First, then, CHRIST JESUS IS UNUTTERABLY PRECIOUS TO BELIEVERS. The words manifestly imply this: "A bundle of myrrh is my well-beloved unto me." She calls him her "well-beloved," and so expresses her love most emphatically; it is not merely beloved, but well-beloved. Then she looks abroad about her, to find a substance which shall be at once valuable in itself and useful in its properties; and lighting upon myrrh, she saith, "A bundle of myrrh is my well-beloved unto me." Without looking into the figure just now, we keep to the statement that Christ is precious to the believer.

Observe first, that nothing gives the believer so much joy as fellowship with Christ. Ask yourselves, you who have eaten at his table and have been made to drink of his cup, where can such sweetness be found as you have tasted in communion with Jesus? The Christian has joy as other men have in the common mercies of life. For him there are charms in music, excellence in painting, and beauty in sculpture; for him the hills have sermons of majesty, the rocks hymns of sublimity, and the valleys lessons of love. He can look upon all things with an eye as clear and joyous as another man's; he can be glad both in God's gifts and God's works. He is not dead to the happiness of the household: around his hearth he finds happy associations, without which life were drear indeed. His children fill his home with glee, his wife is his solace and delight, his friends are his comfort and refreshment. He accepts the comforts which soul and body can yield him according as God seeth it wise to afford them unto him; but he will tell you that in all these separately, yea, and in all of them added together, he doth not find such substantial delight as he doth in the person of his Lord Jesus. Brethren, there is a wine which no vineyard on earth ever yielded; there is a bread which even the corn-fields of Egypt could never bring forth. You and I have said, when we have beheld others finding their god in earthly comforts, "You may boast in gold, and silver, and raiment, but I will rejoice in the God of my salvation." In our esteem, the joys of earth are little better than husks for swine compared with Jesus the heavenly manna. I would rather have one mouthful of Christ's love, and a sip of his fellowship, than a whole world full of carnal delights. What is the chaff to the wheat? What is the sparkling paste to the true diamond? What is a dream to the glorious reality? What is time's mirth in its best trim compared to our Lord Jesus in his most despised estate? If you know anything of the inner life, you will all of you confess that our highest, purest, and most enduring joys must be the fruit of the tree of life which is in the midst of the Paradise of God. No spring yields such sweet water as that well of God which was digged with the soldier's spear. As for the house of feasting, the joy of harvest, the mirth of marriage, the sports of youth, the recreations of maturer age, they are all as the small dust of the balance compared with the joy of Immanuel our best beloved. As the Preacher said, so say we, "I said of laughter, It is mad: and of mirth, What doeth it?" "Vanity of vanities; all is vanity." All earthly bliss is of the earth earthy, but the comforts of Christ's presence are like himself heavenly. We can review our communion with Jesus, and find no regrets of emptiness therein; there are no dregs in this wine; no dead flies in this ointment. The joy of the Lord is solid and enduring. Vanity hath not looked upon it, but discretion and prudence testify that it abideth the test of years, and is in time and in eternity worthy to be called "the only true delight."

"What is the world with all its store?
"Tis but a bitter sweet;
When I attempt to pluck the rose,
A pricking thorn I meet.
Here perfect bliss can ne'er be found,
The honey's mix'd with gall;
'Midst changing scenes and dying friends,
Be thou my All in All."

We may plainly see that Christ is very precious to the believer, because to him there is nothing good without Christ. Believer, have you not found in the midst of plenty a dire and sore famine if your Lord has been absent? The sun was shining, but Christ had hidden himself and all the world was black to you; or it was a night of tempest, and there were many stars, but since the bright and morning star was gone on that dreary main, where you were tossed with doubts and fears, no other star could shed so much as a ray of light. O, what a howling wilderness is this world without my Lord! If once he groweth angry, and doth, though it be for a moment, hide himself from me, withered are the flowers of my garden; my pleasant fruits decay; the birds suspend their songs, and black night lowers over all my hopes. Nothing can compensate for the company of the Savior: all earth's candles cannot make daylight if the Sun of Righteousness be gone.

On the other hand, when all earthly comforts have failed you, have you not found quite enough in your Lord? Your very-worst times have been your best times? You must almost cry to go back to your bed of sickness, for Jesus made it as a royal throne, whereon you reigned with him. Those dark nights--ah! they were not dark, your bright days since then have been darker far. Do you remember when you were poor? Oh! how near Christ was to you, and how rich he made you! You were despised and rejected of men, and no man gave you a good word! Ah! sweet was his fellowship then, and how delightful to hear him say, "Fear thou not; for I am with thee: be not dismayed; for I am thy God!" As afflictions abound, even so do consolations abound by Christ

Jesus. The devil, like Nebuchadnezzar, heated the furnace seven times hotter, but who would have it less furiously blazing? No wise believer; for the more terrible the heat the greater the glory in the fact that we were made to tread those glowing coals, and not a hair of our head was singed, nor so much as the smell of fire passed upon us, because the Son of God walked those glowing coals in our company. Yes, we can look with resignation upon penury, disease, and even death; for if all comforts be taken from us, we should still be blest, so long as we enjoy the presence of the Lord our Savior.

Nor should I be straining the truth if I say that the Christian would sooner give up anything than forsake his Master. I have known some who have been afraid to look that text in the face which saith, "He that loveth son or daughter more than me is not worthy of me," or that--"Except a man hate (or love less) his father and mother, and wife and children, he cannot be my disciple." Yet I have found that those have frequently proved to be the most sincere lovers of Jesus who have been most afraid that he had not the best place in their hearts. Perhaps the best way is not to sit down calmly to weigh our love, for it is not a thing to be measured with cool judgment, but put your love to some practical test. Now, if it came to this, that you must deny Christ, or give up the dearest thing you have, would you deliberate? The Lord knoweth I speak what I feel in my own soul--when it comes to that, I could not hesitate a second. If there were a stake and burning faggots, I might flinch from the fire, but so mighty is divine love that it would doubtless drive me to the flames sooner than let me leave Jesus. But if it comes to this, "Wilt thou lose thine eyes or give up Christ?" I would cheerfully be blind. Or if it were asked, "Wilt thou have thy right arm withered from its socket or give up Christ?" Ay; let both arms go; let them both drop from the shoulder blades. Or if it should be, "Wilt thou be from this day dumb and never speak before the multitude?" Oh! better to be dumb than lose him. Indeed, when I talk of this it seems to be an insult to my Master, to put hands, and eyes, and tongue, in comparison with him.

"Nor to my eyes is light so dear
Nor friendship half so sweet."

If you compare life itself with Jesus, it is not to be named in the same day. If it should be said, "Will you live without Christ or die with Christ?" you could not deliberate, for to die with Christ is to live with Christ for ever; but to live without Christ is to die the second death, the terrible death of the soul's eternal perdition. No, there is no choice there. I think we could go further, dear friends, and say, not only could we give up everything, but I think, when love is fervent, and the flesh is kept under, we could suffer anything with Christ. I met, in one of Samuel Rutherford's letters, an extraordinary expression, where he speaks of the coals of divine wrath all falling upon the head of Christ, so that not one might fall upon his people. "And yet," saith he, "if one of those coals should drop from his head upon mine and did utterly consume me, yet if I felt it was a part of the coals that fell on him, and I was bearing it for his sake, and in communion with him, I would choose it for my heaven." That is a strong thing to say, that to suffer with Christ would be his heaven, if he assuredly knew that it was for and with Christ, that he was suffering. Oh! there is indeed a heavenliness about suffering for Jesus. His cross hath such a majesty and mystery of delight in it, that the more heavy it becometh, the more lightly doth it sit upon the believer's shoulders.

One thing I know proveth, beloved, that you esteem Christ to be very precious, namely, that you want others to know him too. Do you not feel a pining in your souls till others hearts be filled with the love of Christ? My eyes could weep themselves out of their sockets for some of you who are ignorant of my Master's love. Poor souls! ye are sitting outside the feast when the door is wide open, and the king himself is within. Ye choose to be out in the highways and under the hedges sooner than come to this wedding-feast, where the oxen and fatlings are killed, and all things are ready--oh! did you know him, did you know him, you would never be able to live without him. If your eyes had ever seen him once, or if your heart had ever known the charm of his presence, you would think it to be a hell to be for a moment without Christ. O poor blind eyes which cannot see him, and deaf ears which cannot hear him, and hard stony hearts which cannot melt before him, and hell-besotted souls which cannot appreciate the majesty of his love, God help you! God help you! and bring you yet to know and rejoice in him. The more your love grows, beloved, the more insatiable will be your desire that others should love him, till it will come to this that you will be, like Paul, "in labors more abundant," spending and being spent that you may bring the rest of Christ's elect body into union with their glorious head.

II. But, secondly, THE SOUL CLINGETH TO CHRIST, AND SHE HATH GOOD REASON FOR SO DOING, for her own words are "A bundle of myrrh is my well-beloved unto me." We will take the myrrh first, and then consider the bundle next.

1. Jesus Christ is like myrrh. Myrrh may be well the type of Christ for its preciousness. It was an exceedingly expensive drug. We know that Jacob sent some of it down into Egypt as being one

of the choice products of the land. It is always spoken of in Scripture as being a rich, rare, and costly substance. But no myrrh could ever compare with him, for Jesus Christ is so precious, that if heaven and earth were put together they could not buy another Savior. When God gave to the world his Son, he gave the best that heaven had. Take Christ out of heaven, and there is nothing for God to give. Christ was God's all, for is it not written, "In him dwelleth all the fullness of the Godhead bodily?" Oh! precious gift of the whole of deity in the person of Christ! How inestimably precious is that body of his which he took of the substance of the virgin! Well might angels herald the coming of this immaculate Savior, well might they watch over his holy life, for he is precious in his birth, and precious in all his actions. How precious is he, dear friends, as myrrh in the offering of his great atonement! What a costly sacrifice was that! At what a price were ye redeemed! Not with silver and gold, but with the precious blood of Christ. How precious is he too, in his resurrection! He justifies all his people at one stroke--rising from the dead--that glorious sun scatters all the nights of all his people by one rising. How precious is he in his ascension, as he leads captivity captive, and scattereth gifts among men! And how precious to-day in those incessant pleadings of his through which the mercies of God come down like the angels upon Jacob's ladder to our needy souls! Yes, he is to the believer in every aspect like myrrh for rarity and excellence.

Myrrh, again, was pleasant. It was a pleasant thing to be in chamber perfumed with myrrh. Through the nostrils myrrh conveys delight to the human mind; but Christ gives delight to his people, not through one channel, but through every avenue. It is true that all his garments smell of myrrh, and aloes, and cassia, but he hath not spiritual smell alone, the taste shall be gratified too, for we eat his flesh and drink his blood. Nay, our feeling is ravished, when his left hand is under us and his right hand doth embrace us. As for his voice it is most sweet, and our soul's ear is charmed with its melody. Let God give him to our sight, and what can our eyes want more? Yea, he is altogether lovely. Thus every gate of the soul hath commerce with Christ Jesus in the richest and rarest commodities. There is no way by which a human spirit can have communion with Jesus which doth not yield unto that spirit fresh and varied delights. O beloved, we cannot compare him merely to myrrh. He is everything which is good to look upon, or to taste, or to handle, or to smell--all put together in one, the quintessence of all delights. As all the rivers run into the sea, so all delights center into Christ. The sea is not full, but Jesus is fall to the very brim.

Moreover, myrrh is perfuming. It is used to give a sweet smell to other things. It was mingled with the sacrifice, so that it was not only the smoke of the fat of kidneys of rams, and the flesh of fat beasts, but there was a sweet fragrance of myrrh, which went up with the sacrifice to heaven. And surely, beloved, Jesus Christ is very perfuming to his people. Does not he perfume their prayers, so that the Lord smelleth a sweet savor? Doth he not perfume their songs, so that they become like vials full of odour sweet? Doth he not perfume our ministry, for is it not written, "He causeth us to triumph in Christ, and maketh manifest the savor of his knowledge by us in every place. For we are unto God a sweet savor of Christ, in them that are saved, and in them that perish." Our persons are perfumed with Christ. Whence get we our spikenard but from him? Whither shall we go to gather camphire which shall make our persons and presence acceptable before God but to him? "For we are accepted in the beloved." "Ye are complete in him"--"perfect in Christ Jesus"--"for he hath made us kings and priests unto our God, and we shall reign for ever and ever."

Myrrh has preserving qualities. The Egyptians used it in embalming the dead: and we find Nicodemus and the holy women bringing myrrh and aloes in which to wrap the dead body of the Savior. It was used to prevent corruption. What is there which can preserve the soul but Christ Jesus? What is the myrrh which keeps our works, which in themselves are dead, and corrupt, and rotten--what, I say, keeps them from becoming a foul stench in the nostrils of God, but that Christ is in them? What we have done out of love to Christ, what we have offered through his mediation, what has been perfumed by faith in his person, becomes acceptable. God looketh upon anything we say, or anything we do, and if he seeth Christ in it, he accepteth it; but if there be no Christ, he putteth it away as a foul thing. See to it then, beloved, that you never pray a prayer which is not sweetened with Christ. I would never preach a sermon--the Lord forgive me if I do--which is not full to overflowing with my Master. I know one who said I was always on the old string, and he would come and hear me no more; but if I preached a sermon without Christ in it, he would come. Ah! he will never come while this tongue moves, for a sermon without Christ in it--a Christless sermon! A brook without water; a cloud without rain; a well which mocks the traveler; a tree twice dead, plucked up by the root; a sky without a sun; a night without a star. It were a realm of death--a place of mourning for angels and laughter for devils. O Christian, we must have Christ! Do see to it that every day when you wake you give a fresh savor of Christ upon you by contemplating his person Live all the day, trying as much as lieth in you, to season your hearts with him, and then at night, lie down with him upon your tongue. It is said of Samuel Rutherford, that he often did fall asleep talking about Christ, and was often heard in his dreams, saying sweet things about his Savior. There is nothing which can preserve us and keep us from sin, and make our works holy and pure, like this "bundle of myrrh."

Myrrh again, was used as a disinfectant. When the fever is abroad, we know people who wear little bags of camphor about their necks. They may be very good; I do not know. But the Orientals believed that in times of pest and plague, a little bag of myrrh worn between the breasts would be of essential service to whoever might carry it. And there doubtless is some power in myrrh to preserve from infectious disease. Well, brethren, certain I am it is so with Christ. You have to go into the world which is like a great lazar-house; but if you carry Christ with you, you will never catch the world's disease. A man may be worth never so much money, he will never get worldly if he keepeth Christ on his heart. A man may have to tug and toil for his livelihood, and be very poor, he will never be discontented and murmuring if he lives close to Christ. O you who have to handle the world, see to it that you handle the Master more than the world. Some of you have to work with drunken and swearing men; others are cast into the midst of frivolities--O take my Master with you! and sin's plagues can have no influence upon your moral nature.

But myrrh was believed by the ancient physicians to do more than this--it was a cure--it did not merely prevent, but it healed. I do not know how many diseases are said to be healed by the use of myrrh, nor do I altogether suppose that these Oriental physicians spoke from facts, for they were too much given to ascribe qualities to drugs, which those drugs did not possess; however even modern physicians believe myrrh to have many valuable medical properties. Certain is it that your Christ is the best medicine for the soul. His name is Jehovah Rophi--"I am the Lord that healeth them." When we see Luke called "the beloved physician," we almost grudge him the name. I will take it from him and give it to my Master, for he deserves it far more than Luke. The beloved physician! he touched the leper, and he was made whole. He did but look upon those who were lame. and they leaped as a hart. His voice startled the silence of Hades, and brought back the soul to the body. What cannot Christ do? He can heal anything. You who are sick this morning, sick with doubts and fears, you who are sick with temptation, you who struggle with an angry temper, or with the death-like sleep of sloth, get Christ, and you are healed. Here all things meet, and in all these things we may say, "A bundle of myrrh is my well-beloved unto me."

I have not done yet, for myrrh was used in the East as a beautifier. We read of Esther, that before she was introduced to Ahasuerus, she and the virgins were bidden to prepare themselves, and among other things, they used myrrh. The belief of Oriental women was, that it removed wrinkles and stains from the face, and they used it constantly for the perfecting of their charms. I do not know how that may be, but I know that nothing makes the believer so beautiful as being with Christ. He is beautiful in the eyes of God, of holy angels, and of his fellow-men. I know some Christians whom it is a great mercy to speak to: if they come into your cottage, they leave behind them tokens of remembrance, in the choice words they utter. To get them into the Church is a thousand mercies, and if they join the Sunday-school, of what value they are! Let me tell you that the best gauge of a Christian's usefulness will be found in the degree in which he has been with Jesus and learned of him. Do not tell me it is the scholar, do not say to me it is the man of eloquence, do not say it is the man of substance--well we would have all these consecrate what they have to Christ--but it is the man of God who is the strong man; it is the man who has been with Jesus who is the pillar of the Church; and a light to the world. O brethren, may the beauty of the Lord be upon us through being much with Christ.

And I must not close this point without saying that myrrh might well be used as an emblem of our Lord from its connection with sacrifice. It was one of the precious drugs used in making the holy oil with which the priests were anointed and the frankincense which burned perpetually before God. It is this, the sacrificial character of Christ, which is at the root and bottom of all that Christ is most precious to his people. O Lamb of God our sacrifice, we must remember thee.

2. Now there has been enough, surely, said about the myrrh. Have patience while we just notice that he is called a bundle of myrrh, or as some translate it, a bag of myrrh, or a box of myrrh.

There were three sorts of myrrh; there was the myrrh in sprigs, which being burnt made a sweet smell; then there was myrrh, a dried spice; and then thirdly, there was myrrh a flowing oil. We do not know to which there is reference here. But why is it said "a bundle of myrrh?" First, for the plenty of it. He is not a drop of it, he is a casket full. He is not a sprig or flower of it, but a whole bundle full. There is enough in Christ for my necessities. There is more in Christ than I shall ever know--perhaps more than I shall understand even in heaven.

A bundle again, for variety; for there is in Christ not only the one thing needful, but "ye are complete in him;" there is everything needful. Take Christ in his different characters, and you will see a marvellous variety--prophet, priest, king, husband, friend, shepherd. Take him in his life, death, resurrection, ascension, second advent, take him in his virtue, gentleness, courage, self-denial, love, faithfulness, truth, righteousness--everywhere it is a bundle. Some of God's judgments are manifold, but all God's mercies are manifold, and Christ being the sum of God's mercies, hath in fold upon fold of goodness. He is "a bundle of myrrh" for variety.

He is a bundle of myrrh again, for preservation--not loose myrrh to be dropped on the floor or trodden on, but myrrh tied up, as though God bound up all virtues and excellencies in his Son: not myrrh spilt on the ground, but myrrh in a box--myrrh kept in a casket. Such is Christ. The virtue and excellence which goeth out of Christ is quite as strong today as in the day when the woman touched the hem of his garment and was healed. "Able to save unto the uttermost them that come unto God through him," is he still unto this hour.

A bundle of myrrh again, to shew how diligently we should take care of it. We must bind him up, we must keep our thoughts of him and knowledge of him as under lock and key, lest the devil should steal anything from us. We must treasure up his words, prize his ordinances, obey his precepts, tie him up and keep him ever with us as a precious bundle of myrrh.

And yet again, a bundle of myrrh for speciality, as if he were not common myrrh for everybody. No, no, no; there is distinguishing, discriminating grace--a bundle tied up for his people and labelled with their names from before the foundation of the world. No doubt there is an allusion here to the scent bottle used in every land. Jesus Christ is a bottle of myrrh, and he doth not give forth his smell to everybody but to those who know how to draw forth the stopper, who understand how to get into communion with him, to have close dealings with him. He is not myrrh for all who are in the house but for those who know how to put the bottle to their nostrils and receive the sweet perfume. Oh! blessed people whom the Lord hath admitted into his secrets! Oh! choice and happy people who are thus made to say "A bottle of myrrh is my well-beloved unto me."

But I am afraid I tire you, especially those of you who do not know anything about my subject. There are some such here who know no more about what I am talking of than if they were Mahometans. They are listening to a new kind of religion now. The religion of Christ is as high above them as is the path of the eagle above that of the fish, and as much hidden from them as the way of the serpent on the rock from the eye of man. This is a path which the eagle's eye hath not seen, nor hath the lion's whelp trodden it; but I trust there are some here who know it.

III. Our third remark was to be--that with a sense of Christ's preciousness is combined A CONSCIOUSNESS OF POSSESSION. It is "my well-beloved." My dear hearer, is Christ your well-beloved? A Savior--that is well; but my Savior--that is the best of the best. What is the use of bread if it is not mine? I may die of hunger. Of what value is gold, if it be not mine? I may yet die in a workhouse. I want this preciousness to be mine. "My well-beloved." Have you ever laid hold on Christ by the hand of faith?

Will you take him again this morning, brethren, in Jesus? I know you will. Would that those who never did take him, would take him now and say, "My saviour." There stands his atonement, freely offered to you, may you have the grace to take it, and say, "My Savior, my Savior," this morning. Has your heart taken him? It is well for us to use both hands, not only the hand of faith, but the hand of love, for this is the true embrace when both arms meet around our beloved. Do you love him? O souls, do you LOVE Christ, with an emphasis upon the word. Do not talk to me about a religion which dwells in the head and never gets into the heart. Get rid of it as quickly as you can; it will never bring you to heaven. It is not "I believe this and that" merely, but "I love." Ah! some who have been great fools in doctrine have been very wise in love. We tell our children to learn things "by heart." I think you can, you love Jesus, and if you cannot you must confess as I do,

"A very wretch, Lord, I should prove,
Had I no love to thee;
Sooner than not my Savior love,
O may I cease to be."

But that is not the only word. "A bundle of myrrh is my well-beloved unto me." That is not a redundant expression, "unto me." He is not so to many. Ah! my Lord is a root out of a dry ground to multitudes. A three-volume novel suits them better than his Book. They would sooner go to a play or a dance than they would have any fellowship with him. They can see the beauties upon the cheeks of this Jezebel world, but they cannot see the perfections of my Lord and Master. Well! well! well! Let them say what they will, and let them think as they please, every creature hath its own joy, but "a bundle of myrrh is my well-beloved unto me"--unto me--unto me, and if there is not another who finds him so, yet "a bundle of myrrh is my well-beloved unto me." I would it were not with others as it is--I would that others did think so also of him; but let them say what they will, they shall not drive me out of my knowledge of this--"a bundle of myrrh is my well-beloved unto me." The infidel saith, "There is no God." The atheist would altogether laugh me to scorn. They shall say what they will, but "a bundle of myrrh is my well-beloved unto me." Even bishops have been found who will take away a part of his Book, and so rend his garments, and rob him; and there be some who say his religion is out of date, and grace has lost his power; and they go after philosophy and vain conceit, and I know not what, but "a bundle of myrrh is my well-beloved unto me." They may have no nostril for him, they may have no desire after him; so let it be, but "a bundle of myrrh is my well-beloved unto me." I know there are some who say they have tried him and not found him sweet, and who have turned away from him and gone back to the beggarly elements of the world because they see nothing in Christ that they should desire him; but "a bundle of myrrh is my well-beloved unto me." Ah! Christian, this is what you want, a personal experience, a positive experience; you want to know for yourself; for there is no religion which is worth a button which is not burnt into you by personal experience; and there is no religion worth a straw which does not spring from your soul, which does lay not hold upon the very vitals of your spirit. Yes, you must say--I hope you can say as you go down those steps this morning, and enter again to-morrow into that busy, giddy world--you must say, "Let the whole world go astray, a bundle of myrrh is my well-beloved unto me.'"

IV. Now the practical point closes it. A SENSE OF POSSESSION AND A SENSE OF ENJOYMENT WILL ALWAYS LEAD THE CHRISTIAN TO DESIRE CONSTANT FELLOWSHIP. "He" or rather "it shall lie all night betwixt my breasts." The Church does not say, "I will put this bundle of myrrh on my shoulders"--Christ is no burden to a Christian. She does not say, "I will put this bundle of myrrh on my back"--the Church does not want to have Christ concealed from her face. She desires to have him where she can see him, and near to her heart. The bundle of myrrh shall lie all night upon my heart. The words "All night" are not in the original; I do not know how they got into the translation. He is to be always there, not only all night but all day. It would be always night if he were not there, and it cannot be night when he is there, for

"Midst darkest shade, if he appear,
My dawning has begun."

He shall always be upon our heart. I think that expression just means these three things. It is an expression of desire--her desire that she may have the consciousness of Christ's love continually. Do not you feel the same desire. O Christian, if thou hast ever been made like the chariots of Amminadib, it will be ill for thee if thou canst be content to be otherwise. If thou hast but once tasted Christ, thou wilt wait to feed upon him all day and all night, and as long as thou livest. My desire is that Jesus may abide with me from morn till even, in the world and in the Church, when I awake, when I sleep, when I go abroad, and when I come home into the bosom of my family. Is not that your desire that he may be always with you?

But then, it is not only her desire, but it is also her confidence. She seems to say, "He will be with me thus." You may have a suspension of visible fellowship with Christ, but Christ never will go away from people really. He will be all night betwixt your breasts; he will at all times abide faithful to you. He may close his eyes and hide his face from you, but his heart never can depart from you. He has set you as a seal upon his heart, and increasingly will make you sensible of it. Recollect there is no suspension of Christ's union with his people, and no suspension of those saving influences which always make his people to stand complete in him.

To conclude, this is also a resolve. She desires, she believes, and she resolves it. Lord, thou shalt be with me, thou shalt be with me always. I appeal to you, brethren, will you not make this resolve in God's strength this morning to cling close to Christ. Do not go talking, as you go home, about all sorts of nonsense; do not spend this afternoon in communion with folly and vanity, but throughout this day let your soul keep to Christ, to nothing but Christ. This evening we shall come to his table, to eat bread and drink wine, in remembrance of him, let us try if we can, that nothing shall make us give up Christ all this day. Have you got him, hold him and do not let him go till you bring him to your mother's house, to the chamber of her who bare you. Then there will be the family prayer at night. O, seek to keep him till you put your head upon the pillow. And then, on Monday morning, some of you have to go to work, and as soon as you get into the workshop or the factory, you say, "Now I must lose my Master." No, do not lose him. Hold him fast when your hand plies the hammer, and when your fingers hold the needle, still cling to him, in the market or in the exchange, on board ship, or in the field, do not let him go. You may have him with you all day. The Mahometan usually wears a piece of the Koran round his neck, and one, when converted to Christianity, put his New Testament in a little silken bag, and always wore it there. We need not such outward signs, but let us always have the Savior there; let us hang him about our neck as a charm against all evil; seek his blessed company, place him as a star upon your breast to be your honor and joy.

Well, I have done, but I must have a word with the unconverted. There are some who can say, "I will have Christ always on my tongue." Away with tongue religion. You must have him on your heart. Ah! there are some who say, "I hope I shall have Christ on my heart in all eternity." You cannot have Christ in eternity if you do not have him in time. If you despise him to-day--in this life, he will reject you to-morrow in the world to come; and if he call and you refuse, one day you will call and he refuse. Do not put up with desires merely, dear friends--some of you have desires, and nothing more. Do not only desire Christ, but get him. Do not stop short with saying, "I should like to have him in my heart;" give no sleep to your eyes nor slumber to your eyelids, till by humble faith you have taken Christ to be your all in all. May the Lord bless these poor words, for Jesus' sake. Amen.

The Cripple at Lystra

A Sermon (No. 559)
by the Rev. C. H. SPURGEON,
At the Metropolitan Tabernacle, Newington

"The same heard Paul speak: who stedfastly beholding him, and perceiving that he had faith to be healed, said with a loud voice, Stand upright on thy feet. And he leaped and walked." -- Acts 14:9-10.

I HAVE READ in your hearing the story of the preaching of Paul and Barnabas in the town of Lystra. The name of Christ was there totally unknown. They were a sort of country people, partly pastoral and partly agricultural, who seem to have been deeply sunken in superstition. At the gates of their city there stood a great temple dedicated to Jupiter, and they appear to have been his zealous votaries. Coming down from the mountainside Paul and Barnabas enter the town, and when a fitting time has come, they stand up in the marketplace, or the street, and begin to talk concerning Jesus, the Son of God, who had come down from heaven, had suffered and died, and had again ascended up on high. The people gather round them. Among the rest a cripple listens with very marked attention. They preach again. The crowds are still greater, and on one occasion, while Paul is in the middle of a sermon, using his eyes to watch the audience as all preachers should do, and not looking up at the ceiling, or at the gallery-front as some preachers are wont to do, he marks this cripple, fixes his eyes upon him, and looks earnestly in his face. Either by the exercise of his judgment, or by the promptings of revelation, the apostle gathers that this man has faith--faith to be healed. In order to attract the attention of the people, to glorify the name of Christ, to publish more widely his glorious fame, and to make the miracle well known, Paul stops the sermon, and with a loud voice cries, "Stand upright on thy feet." The cripple leaps and praises God. The population are all amazed, and knowing that there was a tradition that Jupiter and Mercury had once appeared in that very town, a tradition preserved in the Metamorphoses of Ovid to the present day, they at once conclude that surely Jupiter and Mercury must be come again. They fix upon Barnabas, who was probably the elder and the nobler looking man, for Jupiter; and as Jupiter was always attended by Mercurins, as a messenger, and Mercury was the god of eloquence, they conclude that Paul must be Mercury. They rush to the temple, they tell the priests that the gods have come down. The priests, only too ready to foster popular credulity, and pander to it, bring forth the sacred bullocks and the garlands, and are about to offer sacrifice before Paul and Barnabas. Such homage these men of God indignantly refuse; they rend their clothes; they beseech them to do no such thing, for they are nothing but men; yet hardly with earnest words can they stay the people. But the next day certain Jews came thither and produced a counter irritation in the simple minds of the people. No very difficult task where a rude fanaticism rouses the wild passions of the mob. Such an assembly must rage, whether it he with redundant applause or with derisive jeers. Accordingly, Paul finds himself exposed to peril; he is stoned through the streets, dragged forth as dead, and left by the very men who worshipped him but yesterday as a god, left to die as a villain outside the city gates. But Paul's preaching had not been in vain. There were some few disciples who remained faithful. His ministry was rewarded and owned of God.

There are two or three points in this narrative to which I shall call your attention to-night, making, however, the lame man the center of the picture. We shall notice, first of all, what preceded this lame man's faith; secondly, wherein lay his faith to be healed; and thirdly, what is the teaching of the miracle itself, and the blessing which the lame man obtained through faith.

I. WHAT WAS IT WHICH PRECEDED HIS FAITH?

That "Faith cometh by hearing, and hearing by the word of God," is a great and universal rule; but the hearing of what? Doubtless the hearing of the gospel is intended. On turning to your Bibles you will find it is written--"And there they preached the gospel." What, Paul, dost thou not change thy voice? Thou hast preached the gospel in the cities of Iconium and Antioch, where there were enlightened and intelligent hearers; if the gospel suited them, surely it will not do for these wolfish boors! Why go and preach to these poor, ignorant, superstitious fanatics the very same truths which you spoke to your enlightened Jewish brethren? But he does do so, my friends. The very gospel which he preached at Damascus in the synagogue he preaches here at Lystra in the market-place. He makes no difference between the education of his hearers in different places; he has the same gospel to preach to them both. You recollect that Paul went to Ephesus, and Ephesus, as a city, was besotted with a belief in sorcery. The people had given themselves up to practice magical arts. What is the right way to begin to preach at Ephesus? Deliver a course of lectures upon the impossibility and absurdity of such superstition? No, sir, nothing of the kind. Preach Christ, preach the gospel; and as Jesus Christ is lifted up they bring their magical books and make a bonfire of them in the open forum. But here is a polished governor, Sergius Paulus, sitting upon the judgment-seat. What shall be preached to him? Would it not be well to begin with a dissertation on politics, and to show that the Christian religion does not interfere with proper government, that it does not stir up the people to anarchy? No, sir, nothing of the kind. There is nothing for Sergius Paulus any more than there is for Elymas the sorcerer, but the preaching of the gospel of Jesus Christ. Paul goes to Athens. Now the Athenians are the most learned and philosophical of the whole race of men. What will Paul preach there? The gospel, the whole gospel, and nothing but the gospel. He may change his tones, but never his matter. It is the same remedy for the same disease, he the men what they may. He comes to Corinth, and here you have not only polished manners, but the very refinement of vice. It is a city, an emporium of trade, and a sort of central depot of sin. What then? Will he now, to please the trader, assume a different dialect? Not he! The Christ for Athens is the Christ for Corinth too. And now see him. He has come to Lycaonia, and is preaching at Lystra. Here is an ignorant set of people who worship an image. Why does he not begin by preaching of the deity? Why does he not talk to them of the Trinity in unity? Why does he not try and confute their notions about their gods? No, my dear sir, he will do nothing of the kind; that may be done incidentally, but the first and the last thing that Paul will do at Lystra is, there he will preach the gospel. O glorious gospel of the blessed God! Wherever we take thee thou art suited to the wants of men. Take thee to Persia with all its gems and jewels, and thou dost suit the monarch on his throne; or take thee to the naked savage with all his poverty and squalid filth, and thou dost suit him too. Thou mayst he preached, thrice glorious wisdom of God, to the wisest of men; but thou are not too great a mystery to be understood and believed even by the fools and the babes; the things which are not can receive thee as well as the things which are. Never, I pray you brethren, lose heart in the power of the gospel. Do not believe that there exists any man, much less any race of men, for whom the gospel is not fitted. Wherever you go, do not cut, and trim, and shape, and alter; hut just bring out the whole truth as God has taught it to you, and rest assured that you will be unto God a sweet savor of Christ in every place, both in them who are saved and in them who perish.

What then, was this gospel which the apostle Paul did preach everywhere? Well, it was a gospel which had in it three things, certain facts, certain doctrines, and certain commands.

It was a gospel of facts. Every time Paul stood up to preach he told the following unvarnished tale: God, looking upon the race of men, beheld them lost and ruined. Out of love to them he sent his only begotten Son, the Lord Jesus Christ, who was born of the virgin Mary, lived some thirty-two or thirty-three years a life of spotless innocence and perfect obedience to God. He was God: he was man. In due time he was delivered up by the traitor Judas. He was crucified, and actually put to death. Though he was the Lord of life and glory, who only hath immortality, yet he bowed his head and gave up the ghost. After three days he rose again, and showed himself to many of his disciples, so that they were well assured he was the same person who had been put into the grave; and when the forty days were finished he ascended up to heaven in the sight of them all, where he sitteth at the right hand of God, and shall also come ere long a second time to judge both the quick and the dead. These were the facts which Paul would state. God was made flesh and dwelt amongst us, and we beheld his glory, the glory as of the only-begotten of the father, full of grace and truth. "This is a faithful saying, and worthy of all acceptation, that Christ Jesus came into the world to save sinners; of whom I am chief." Briefly, these were the facts which Paul would preach, and if any one of these facts he preached doubtfully, or he left out of any ministry, then the gospel is not preached; for the foundations upon which the gospel rests have been removed, and then what can the righteous do?

Following upon these facts, Paul preached certain doctrines, the doctrines flowing out of the facts. To wit, he preached that Jesus Christ had offered a full atonement to divine wrath for the sin of his people, so that whosoever would believe on him, and trust him, should be saved. The doctrine of the atonement would form the most prominent feature in the gospel of the apostle Paul, Christ also hath suffered for us, the just for the unjust, to bring us to God. "God commendeth his love towards us, in that, while we were yet sinners, Christ died for the ungodly." Then would come the doctrine of pardon. Paul with glowing tongue would tell how God could be just, and yet the justifier of him who believeth; how all manner of sin and iniquity shall be forgiven unto men, the simple condition being that the man believes in Christ, and this not so much the man's own work, as a gift of the Holy Ghost. Everywhere Paul would he unmistakable in this--"Ye chief of sinners, look to the wounds of Jesus, and your sins shall he forgiven you." Equally clear would he be upon the doctrine of justification. "Christ," he would say, "will wash you; nay, more, he will clothe you; the perfect holiness of his character shall he imputed unto you, and being justified, you shall have peace with God, and there shall be no condemnation, because you are in Christ Jesus." I think I see the flashing eye of the apostle; methinks I listen to his earnest voice, while he pleads with men to lay hold upon eternal life, to look to Jesus Christ, to forsake the deeds of the law, to put their trust in nothing which cometh from man, but to look to Jesus, and to Jesus only. These great truths, atonement, pardon, and justification, with all the other truths connected with them, of which we cannot now speak particularly, were just the gospel which the apostle Paul preached.

And out of these we said their sprung certain commands. The commands were these--"Believe in the Lord Jesus Christ and thou shalt be saved." Nor do I suppose that the apostle for a moment stammered to preach that other command--"Arise, and he baptized." He would not preach half the gospel, but the whole of it--"He that believeth and is baptized shall he saved; but he that believeth not shall he damned;" and often after his hearers had cried, "What must we do to he saved," and they had believed in Christ, they would say to him--"See, here is water, what doth hinder me to he baptized?"

The apostle then preached a gospel which was made up of certain authenticated facts, out of which there flowed certain most gracious evangelical doctrines, which were enforced and driven home with divine authority, by Christ's own commands. "Well," says one, "do you think the world will be turned upside down by this?" Sirs, it has been, and it will he again. In vain do those who seek after human learning, and who aim at dreamy sentiment or spurious science in preference to the standard teaching which is from above, attempt to find a nobler instrument. This is the great battering-ram which shall yet shake the bastions of error. This is the sword, the true Escalabar, which, if any man knoweth how to wield it, shall cut through joints and marrow, and make him more than a conqueror. He who getteth a hold of the gospel of Christ, and knoweth how to use it, hath that before which the devils tremble, and in the presence of which angels adore, which cherubs long to look into, and which God himself smiles upon as his noblest work. The truth we proclaim is not that which is discovered by us, but that which has been delivered to us. Do ye ask, then, where this man's faith came from? It came from Paul's preaching of the gospel.

II. Now WHEREIN LAY THIS MAN'S FAITH?

Paul looked at the man, we are told, and perceived "that he had faith to be healed." What meaneth this "faith to be healed?" In this man's case I think it was something like this. Poor fellow! As he listened to Paul's preaching, he thought perhaps--"Well, that looks like true; that seems to be the truth; it is the truth; I am sure it is true; and, if it is true that Jesus Christ is so great a Savior, perhaps I may be healed; these lame legs of mine, which never would carry me anywhere, may yet come straight; I--I--I think they may; I hope they may; I believe they may; I know it can be done if Christ wills it; I believe that, and from what Paul says of Christ's character, I think he must be willing to do it; I will ask the apostle; the first convenient season that I have I will lift up my cry, for I believe it can be done, and I think there is a perfect willingness, both in the mind of the apostle and of the Master that it should be done; I believe it will be done, and that I shall yet stand upright." Then Paul said to him, "Stand upright on thy feet," and he did so in a moment, for "he had faith to he healed."

Do you think I am overstraining the probabilities of the case? You will perhaps say, "It does not appear that Paul had any communication with the poor cripple before the miracle was performed." Now I venture to draw quite an opposite inference. I know from my own experience that it is no uncommon thing for some one individual to arrest the preacher's attention. The group of countenances which lay before him in a large assembly like the present, might to the first glance of a stranger look confused and inexplicable, as a Chinese grammar does to those who know not the language. But you need not doubt that a practiced eye can learn to read the one as well as the other. The languor and indifference of some; the curious enquiring look of others; the cold, critical attention of a considerable number, and the countenances of those who are rather absorbed in a train of thought just awakened in their own minds--these have all a peculiar impressiveness, and form a picture which often reacts upon us, and kindles a vehement desire in our breasts to reach the souls of those who, for a brief hour, hang upon our lips. But there will sometimes be one who has faith dazzling in his very eyes, as they are fixed with an intentness, of which it were vain for me to attempt a description, seeming to drink in every word and every syllable of a word, till the preacher becomes as absorbed in that man as the man had been in the preacher. And while he pursues the discourse, gaining liberty at every step, till he forgets the formality of the pulpit in the freedom of conversation with the people, he perceives that at last this man has heard the very truth which meets his case. There is no concealing it. His features have suddenly relaxed. He listens still, but it is no longer with painful anxiety; a calm satisfaction is palpable on his face now. That soul of communion which is in the eye has unravelled the secret. Preacher and hearer, unknown to all the rest of the audience, have secretly saluted ench other, and met on the common ground of a vital faith. The anxious one feels that it can be done. And I can readily conclude that the apostle perceived that feeling with greater certainty than he would have done had the man whispered it in his ears. So have I sometimes known that the exhortation to believe has become from these lips a positive command to the struggling conscience of some one, who has been brought to a point where the remedy is instantly applied, and the cure instantly effected.

Most unquestionably there is such a thing as faith to be saved. I do not know how many here may possess it; but, thank God, there are hundreds of you here who have faith that you are saved. That is better; that is the ripest faith, the faith which knows you are saved and rejoices in hope of the glory of God. Alas! there are others who have no faith at all. But it is with those who have faith, and that only faith to be saved, not faith that you are saved, I am more particularly concerned at this moment.

Shall I describe this "faith to he saved?" for I believe that there may be some here who may just now stand upright on their feet; some who may at this time leap for joy of heart because they are saved and did not know it. You have "faith," but you have not fully exercised it. Now, you believe that Jesus Christ is God's Son? "Yes." That he has made a full atonement for his people? "Yes." You believe that they are his people who trust him? "Yes." You believe he is worthy to be trusted? "Yes." You have nothing else to trust to? "No, sir." You depend on nothing which you have ever felt, or thought, or done? "No, sir, I depend on nothing but Christ." And you do, after a sort of fashion, trust Christ. You hope that one of these days he will save you, and you think, and sometimes you almost know, he will. You are ready to trust him. You do believe he is able, you do not think he is unwilling; you have got faith in his ability, and you have almost got faith in his willingness; sometimes you half think to yourself, "I am a child of God." But then, there is some ugly "but" comes in. Those lame legs again; those lame legs again. You are still afraid. You have "faith to he saved," but you have not the full assurance of faith which can utter forth this joyous psalm, "Behold, God is my salvation; I will trust, and not he afraid: for the Lord Jehovah is my strength and my song; he also is become my salvation."

Well now, I do not know whether I have picked you out, whether I have given a right description of you or not. I recollect the time when I was in that state. I can honestly say I did not doubt Christ. I then partly believed that he would save me. I knew he was worthy of my trust, and I did trust him as far as this, that I resolved, if I did perish, I would perish crying to him, and that if I was east away, it should be clinging to the cross. I believe I had "faith to be saved," and was for months in bondage, when there was no necessity that I should have been in bondage at all, for, when there is "faith to he saved," then the man only needs that gracious command--"Stand upright on thy feet," and forthwith he leaps out of his infirmity, and walks freely in the integrity of his heart.

III. I shall not enlarge further upon this, because I want to go to THE SPIRITUAL TEACHING OF THE MIRACLE, AND OF THE BLESSING CONFERRED.

Are there not many, who though they have "faith to be saved," are still entirely lame or painfully limping? The reasons may be different in different cases. Some have been so stunned by the grief which they have suffered on account of sin, and the frightful convictions through which they have passed, that while they do believe that Christ is able and willing to save, they cannot get a hold of the fact that they are saved; such is the faintness of spirit and the languishing of soul brought on by long despair. "Stand upright on thy feet," thou trembling sinner. If thou believest in Jesus, whatever thy fears may be, there is no cause for them. As for thy sins, they were laid on him, every one of them, and though thou hast been sore broken in the land of dragons, thus saith the Lord unto thee, "I have put away thy sin; thou shalt not die; I have blotted out like a cloud thy transgressions, and like a thick cloud thy sins." Rejoice, then, and he glad. If you do trust Christ, you are saved; though as yet it only looketh like faith which heralds the tidings of a salvation which has not yet arrived. Still, it is the grace of God which bringeth salvation which has enabled thcc to believe; and he who believeth on the Son bath everlasting life. O receive the welcome message; spring up at the sound of the words; stand upright on thy feet and rejoice.

Some are still lame, though they have faith, through ignorance. They do not know what being saved is. They entertain wrong expectations. They are trusting in Christ, but they do not feel any surprising emotions; they have not had any remarkable dreams, or visions, or striking ebullitions of excited joy, and therefore, though they have "faith to be saved," they have not the faith of a present salvation. They are waiting for something, they hardly know what, to embellish their faith, or to fortify it with signs and wonders. Now, poor soul, wherefore do you wait? These things are not necessary to salvation. In fact, the fewer you have of them, methinks, the better, especially of things which are visionary. I rather tremble for those who talk much about sensible evidences; they are too often the frivolities of unstable hearts. Beloved, though you may have never had any ecstatic joys, or suffered any deep depression of your spirits, if you are resting on Christ, it does not matter one whit what your feelings have been or have not been. Do you expect to have an electric shock, or to

go through some mysterious operation? The operation is mysterious, too mysterious for you to discern it; but all that you have to do with is this--"Do I believe in Jesus? Am I simply depending upon him for everything?" If you do you are saved, and I pray you to believe this. Stand upright on your feet, and leap for joy; for whether you believe it or not, if you are now depending upon Christ, your sins are forgiven you; you are a child of God; you are an heir of heaven.

How many, too, are kept lame because of a fear of self-deception. "I do trust Christ, but I am afraid lest I should deceive myself; suppose I were to get confidence, and it should he presumption! suppose I should think myself saved, and I am not!" Now, sir, if thou wert dealing with thyself there would be reason to be afraid of presumption, but thy faith hath to deal with God, who cannot deceive thee, and with Christ who will never tempt thee to be a deceiver. Doth not the Lord Jesus Christ himself tell thee that if thou believest in him thou art saved? Thou believest that, dost thou not? Then, soul, if thou believest on him, it is not presumption to say, "I am saved." Away with all that affectation of modesty, which some good people think to he so pretty--saying, "I hope;" "I trust;" but "I feel such doubts, such fears, and such gloomy misgivings." My dear sir, that is not humility: that is a vain unseemly questioning of God. The God and Father of our Lord Jesus Christ tells you, and he gives his own unequivocal word for it, that if you rest upon Christ you rest upon a rock; that if you believe in him you are not condemned. Is it an evidence of the lowliness of your heart that you suspect the veracity of God, or the faithfulness of his promise? Surely this were no fruit of the meekness of wisdom. No, beloved; it may seem too good to he true, but it is not too good for my God to give, though it is too good for you to receive. You have his word for it, that if you trust his Son to save you, and simply trust him, and him alone, even if the pillars of the heavens should shake, yet you would be saved. If the foundations of the earth should reel, and the whole earth should like a vision pass away, yet this eternal promise and oath of God must stand fast.

Others again, cannot stand upright on their feet, because they are afraid that if they did begin they would go back again, and so bring dishonor to Christ. This would be a very proper fear if you had anything to do with keeping yourselves. If you had to carry yourselves to heaven, it would he reasonable enough for you to despair of doing it. Of your own impotence it is impossible you can be too deeply convinced. You cannot do anything whatever, but Christ gives you his promise to preserve you even to the end. If you believe on him you shall be saved. He does not say you shall he saved for a year, or for twenty years, and then, perhaps, he lost at last. No; but "he that believeth and is baptized, shall he saved." If one man who believes in Christ is cast away, that promise of Christ is not true. Brethren, it is true, and it must he true, and let its glorious truth be sweetly familiar with you now--if you give your soul to Christ, putting simple faith in his person as the Son of God, and in his work as the Mediator between God and man, you shall as surely see his face within the pearly gates of heaven as your eyes see me to-night. There may he a question about your seeing me, but there can be no question about Christ fulfilling his promise and keeping his word. Now sit down in the dust no longer, thou doubting, mourning, trembling sinner. With a loud voice I say unto thee, as Paul did, "Stand upright on thy feet." Wherefore dost thou mourn? There is nothing to mourn about. Thy sin is forgiven; thine eternal salvation is secure; a crown in heaven is provided for thee, and a harp of gold awaits thee. If thou believest in Jesus none can lay anything to thy charge. Not even the principalities of darkness shall be able to prevail against thee. Eternal love secures thee against the malice of hell. Stand upright, then, on thy feet, for if thou believest thou art saved, completely saved, saved in time, and for eternal days, saved in the Lord with an everlasting salvation.

Then possibly there is one here who cannot stand upright because of his many sins. Ah! while I have been talking about Christ it may be something has been saying in your heart, "Ah! ah! what is it? Christ taking men's sins, suffering in their stead? That suits me. Is God doing this? Ah! then he must be able to save, and I am told that whosoever trusteth in him shall never perish; is it so? Why, here I am; I who have not been in a place of worship for months, for years, I have strayed in here to-night, and if what this man says be true, well then I will even venture my soul upon it; I have got nothing, I know, but he says there is nothing wanted; I am not prepared to trust Christ, but he says there is no preparation required, and if I trust Jesus Christ just as I am, Christ will save me; why, I will do it; by the grace of God I will do it; can he save me?" Then comes in the bitter reflection--"Look what a sinner I have been! why, I should be ashamed to say how foully I have sinned; he must shut me out; I have been too great a villain, too gross an offender; I have cursed and sworn at such a rate; he cannot mean that if I trust Christ I shall be saved; 1 believe he can save me; I see the fitness of the plan, and the excellency of it; I believe it, but see what a sinner I am!" Sinner, stand upright on thy feet, for "all manner of sin and blasphemy shall be forgiven unto men." Return, thou wanderer, return to thy Father's house! He comes to meet thee. On thy neck he will fall, and thou shalt be his child for ever. Only believe thou in his Son Jesus Christ, and though this he the first time thou hast ever heard his Word, I would settle mine eyes upon thee earnestly, and say, "Stand upright on thy feet."

Oh! how often I do wish that somebody had come to me when I was under depression of mind, and had told me about the simple gospel of Jesus Christ. I think I should have stood upright on my feet long before I did, but, alas! I kept hearing about what people felt before they believed in Christ--very proper preaching--and I was afraid I did not feel it, though now I know I did. I heard a great deal about what Christians ought to be, and a great deal more about God's elect, what they are in his esteem, but I did not know whether I was one of God's elect, and I knew I was not what I ought to be. O for the trumpet of the archangel, to sound the words, "Believe and live," as loud as the voice which shall wake the dead in their graves! and O for the quickening Spirit to go with voice, as it shall go with the ringing of the archangel's trump, when the graves shall open, and the dead shall arise! Go, you who know it, and tell it everywhere, for there are multitudes, I doubt not, who are really seeking Christ, and who have his Spirit in them, but it is like as the prophet hath it, "The children have come to the birth and there is no strength to bring forth." They have come to the very edge of light, and they only want one helping hand to bring them into noonday. They are slipping about in the Slough of Despond, and they are almost out of it, but they want just a helping hand to pull them out. This hand of help is stretched out by thus telling them, telling them plainly, it is in Jesus their help is found, and that trusting him, relying upon him, they shall never perish. neither shall any pluck them out of his hand.

I would to God that some of you, who have been long hearing me, might be found in this class. I have been bowed down in spirit at some sad things which have been brought to my hearing of late. I know that there are some here, and there always have been some few attending my ministry, who have a personal affection for me, and who listen to the Word with very great attention, and who, moreover, are very greatly moved by it, but who have some besetting sin which they either cannot or will not give up. They do renounce it for a time, but either bad associates, or else the strength of their passions, take them away again. O sirs! I would ye would take warning. There was one of whom we had some sort of hope, who listened to our ministry. There came a turning point with him; it was this, either that he must give up sin, or else give up coming to the Tabernacle; and what--oh! what became of him? I could indicate the place where he sat. He died of delirium tremens! And I do not wonder. When you have heard the gospel preached Sabbath after Sabbath, when your response to the solemn appeals you have earnestly listened to has only been that you reject Christ and refuse eternal life--is it any marvel that in making the choice of your own damnation reason should resign its seat as director of your actions, and cease to curb your headstrong will, leaving the maddened passions to dash on with reckless fury, and precipitate your destruction. Am I clear of their blood? I have asked myself the question. I may not be in some things, but I know I am as far as my ministry is concerned. I have not shunned to declare unto any of you the whole counsel of God. When I have known any vice, or any folly--which of you have I been afraid of, or before whom of you all have I trembled? God is my witness; him have I served in the spirit; and if these turn aside unto their crooked ways, they have not done it without well knowing the consequences; nay, they have not done it without being warned and entreated, and persuaded to look unto Jesus Christ. And I do conjure some of you--you know to whom I refer--I do conjure those of you who have a conscience which is not seared, but who, nevertheless, persevere in your sins--I conjure you by the love of God, do me this one favor at the last: if you choose your own ruin, bear witness for me that I have not hesitated to warn you of it. I had infinitely rather, however, that you would do yourselves this great favor, to love your own souls. If you have anything to throw into the fire, throw it in, but let it not be your soul. If you have anything to lose, go and lose it, but do not lose your soul. Sirs, if you must play the fool, indulge your sport at a cheaper rate than this. If sin be worth having, then I pray you pay a cheaper price than your own souls for it, for it does seem to me so pitiful, so sorrowful a thing, that you who have been so short a time among us and are passing away before my very eyes, should still prefer the fleeting joy of the moment to the eternal joy, and risk everlasting torment for temporary mirth. By the tears of Jesus when he wept over Jerusalem, by the blood of Jesus which he shed for guilty men, by the heart of the eternal Father who willeth not the death of a sinner but had rather that he should turn unto him and live, I pray you he wise and consider your ways. Choose ye this day whom ye will serve, and may the Lord guide your choice. May you fall into the arms of divine mercy and say, "If thou wilt help me, Jesus, here I am; I give myself to thee." May my Master teach me how to address you if I do not know how to gasp the words of simplicity, tenderness, of terrible apprehension, but of persuasive power. If there were any words in any language that would melt you, this tongue is at your service to utter them. If there is any form of speech, though it should make me to be called vulgar, and subject me to the shame and hissing which once I endured, if the furnace could be heated seven times hotter than that, I would but laugh at it if I might but win your souls. Tell me, sirs, how shall I put the case? Would you have argument? I wish that I could reason with you. Would you have tears? There, let them flow! Ye dry eyes, why do ye not weep more for these perishing souls? Would you have God's Word without my word? Sirs, I would read it, and let my tongue he dumb if that would teach you. Would my death save you? That God who seeth in secret knoweth that to-night it were a joy to me to enter into my rest, and so it were little for me to talk of being willing to give a life for you, and it were, indeed, but a trifle to me. Oh! why will ye perish? Why should I plead with you, and you not care for yourselves? What is it that besets you? Poor moths! Are ye dazzled with the flames? Are ye not content to have singed your wings? Must they also consume body and soul? How can ye make your bed in hell? How can ye abide with eternal burnings? In the name of Jesus of Nazareth, I command you--for I can do no less--I command you to turn unto him and live. Believe on him and you shall he saved. But remember, at your hazard you reject the message to-night. It may he the last message that shall ever come to your soul with power, if ye cast this away--

"What chains of vengeance must they feel,
Who slight the bonds of love?"

I would have you saved just now. I cannot talk about to-morrow. I would have you decide it at once. Oh! you have come as far as this twenty times, and have you gone back again? You have been aroused, you have made vows and you have broken them, resolutions and you have belied them. O sirs, for God's sake do not lie to the Almighty again. Now be true this time. May the Spirit of God make you speak the truth, even though you should he compelled to say, through your wickedness, "I will not submit myself unto the Son of God." Do speak the truth. Procrastinate not. As Elijah said, "How long halt ye between two opinions?" so say I. If God he God serve him, but if Baal he God serve him. But do not keep on coming here and then going to the pot-house. Do not come and take your seat here and then go to the brothel. Sirs, do not this foul scandal for God's sake, and for your own sake. If you will serve the devil serve him, and he a true servant to him. If you mean to go to hell, go there; but if you seek eternal life and joys to come, give up these things. Renounce them. Why drink poison and drink medicine too? Have done with one or the other and be honest. Be honest to your own souls. May the Lord grant that tonight some may have given to them, not only "faith to be saved," but the faith which saves, for his name's sake. Amen.

Christ is Glorious--Let Us Make Him Known

A Sermon (No. 560)
Delivered on Sunday Morning, March 20th, 1864, by the
Rev. C. H. SPURGEON,
At the Metropolitan Tabernacle, Newington

"And he shall stand and feed in the strength of the Lord, in the majesty of the name of the Lord his God; and they shall abide: for now shall he be great unto the ends of the earth." -- Micah 5:4.

YOU HAVE A VERY VIVID IDEA of the sufferings of Christ. Your faith has seen him sweating great drops of blood in the garden of Gethsemane. You have looked on with amazement while he gave his back to the smiters, and his cheeks to them who plucked off the hair, and hid not his face from shame and spitting. With sorrowful sympathy you have followed him through the streets of Jerusalem, weeping and bewailing him with the women. You have sat down to watch him when he was fastened to the tree; yon have wept at his hitter complaint--"My God, my God, why hast thou forsaken me?" and you have rejoiced in his shout of victory--"It is finished!" With Magdalene and Nicodemus, you have followed his dead body to the tomb, and seen it wrapped about with spices, and left to its lonely sleep. Are your perceptions quite as keen concerning the glory which did follow and is following? Can you see him quite as distinctly when on the third morn the Conqueror rises, bursting the bonds of death with which he could not be holden? Can yon as clearly view him ascending up on high, leading captivity captive? Can you hear the ring of angelic clarions, as with dyed garments from Bozrah the Yictor returns from the battle, dragging death and hell at his chariot wheels? Do you plainly perceive him as he takes his seat at the right hand of the Father, henceforth expecting until his enemies be made his footstool? And can you be as clear this morning about the reigning Christ as you have been about the suffering Christ? Lo! my brethren, "the Lion of the tribe of Juda, the Root of David, hath prevailed to open the book, and to loose the seven seals thereof!" At this hour he goeth forth, riding upon his white horse, conquering and to conquer. Lo! at his girdle swing the keys of heaven, and death, and hell, for "the government shall be upon his shoulder: and his name shall be called Wonderful, Counsellor, The mighty God, T he everlasting Father, The Prince of Peace." "God also hath highly exalted him, and given him a name which is above every name: that at the name of Jesus every knee should bow." Behold him, my brethren, in his present plenitude of glory, and endeavor to get as clear a perception of it as you have had of his shame. Not only weep at his burial, but rejoice at his resurrection; not only sorrow at his cross, but worship at his throne. Do not merely think of the nails and of the spear, but behold the imperial purple which hangs so nobly upon his royal shoulders, and of the divine crown which he wears upon his majestic brow.

I want to conduct you in such a frame of mind through the glories of my text. First, bidding you observe the perpetual reign of Christ: "He shall stand and feed in the strength of the Lord, in the majesty of the name of the Lord his God;" then I shall beg you to observe that flowing from this is the perpetual continuance of his church: "and they shall abide;" and then proceeding both from his continued reign and from the Church's consequent perpetual existence comes the greatness of our King: "for now shall he be great unto the ends of the earth."

I. At the outset, observe carefully THE PERPETUAL REIGN OF CHRIST. He lives, he reigns, he is king over his people.

Notice first, that his reign is shepherd-like in its nature. The kings of the Gentiles exercise lordship over them, but our Master washed his disciples' feet. Earthly monarchs are often tyrants; their yoke is heavy, and their language domineering; but it is not so with our King; his yoke is easy, and his burden is light, for he is meek and lowly of heart. He is a shepherd-king. He has supremacy, but it is the superiority of a wise and tender shepherd over his needy and loving flock; he commands and receives obedience, but it is the willing obedience of the well-cared-for sheep, rendered joyfully to their beloved Shepherd, whose voice they know so well. He rules by the force of love and the energy of goodness. His power lies not in imperious threatenings, but in imperial lovingkindness. Let the children of Zion he joyful in their King, for "men shall be blessed in him: all nations shall call him blessed." Never people had such a king before. His service is perfect freedom; to be his subject is to be a king; to serve him is to reign. Blessed are the people who are the sheep of his pasture; if they follow in his footsteps their road is safe; if they sleep at his feet no lion can disturb their peace; if they are fed from his hand they shall lie down in green pastures, and know no lack; if they abide close to his person they shall drink of rivers of delight. Righteousness and peace are the stability of his throne, joy and gladness are the ornaments of his reign. Oh! how happy are we who belong to such a prince. Thou King in Jeshurun, we pay thee homage with loyal hearts; we come into thy presence with thanksgiving, and into thy courts with praise, for thou art our God, and we are the people of thy pasture, and the sheep of thy hand.

Notice that the reign of Jesus is practical in its character. It is said "he shall stand and feed." The great Head of the Church is actively engaged in providing for his people. He does not sit down upon the throne in empty state, or hold a scepter without wielding it in government. No, he stands and feeds. The expression "feed," in the original is like an analogous one in the Greek, which means to shepherdize, to do everything expected of a shepherd: to guide, to watch, to preserve, to tend, as well as to feed. Our Lord Jesus Christ, the great Head of the Church, is always actively engaged for the Church's good. Through him the Spirit of God constantly descends upon the members of the Church; by him ministers are given in due season, and all Church-officers in their proper place. When he ascended up on high he received gifts for men; "And he gave some, apostles; and some, prophets; and some, evangelists; and some, pastors and teachers; for the perfecting of the saints, for the work of the ministry, for the edifying of the body of Christ." Our Lord does not close his eyes to the state of his Church. Beloved, he is not a listless spectator of our wants. He is this day standing and feeding his people. They are scattered, I know, wide as the poles asunder, but our mighty Shepherd can see every sheep and lamb of his flock, and he gives them all their portion of meat in due season. He it is that like a mighty Breaker, goes forth at the head of his flock, and they follow where he clears the way, "He shall stand and feed." Oh! blessed carefulness and divine activity of our gracious King! always fighting against our enemies, and at the same the shedding his benignant influences upon his friends.

Consider again, for it is in our text, that this active reign is continual in its duration. It is said, "He shall stand and feed;" not " he shall feed now and then, and then leave his position;" not, "he shall one day grant a revival, and then next day leave his Church to barrenness." Beloved, there is no such pastor as Christ. "I know my sheep," he can say, in a very high and peculiar sense. He knows them through and through; he feels with them; in all their afflictions he is afflicted; he is one with them eternally. There is no such wakeful watchman as the Lord Jesus. Is it not written, "I the Lord do keep it; I will water it every moment: lest any hurt it, I will keep it night and day." Those eyes never slumber, and those hands never rest; that heart never ceases to beat with love, and those shoulders are never weary of carrying his people's burdens. The Church may go through her dark ages, but Christ is with her in the midnight. She may pass through her fiery furnace, but Christ is in the midst of the flame with her. Her whole history through, wherever you find the Church, there shall you find the Church's Lord. The head is never severed from the body, nor is the watchful care of this gracious husband towards his spouse suspended for an instant.

I beseech you labor to realize the noble picture. Here are his sheep in these pastures this morning, and here is our great Shepherd with the crown upon his head, standing and feeding us all; nay, not us all alone, but dispensing his tender mercies to all the multitudes of his elect throughout the whole world. He is at this moment King in Zion, ruling, and overruling, present everywhere, and everywhere showing himself strong in the defense of his saints. I would that our Churches could be more influenced by a belief in the abiding power, presence, and pre-eminence of their living and reigning Lord. He is no dead King whose memory we are bidden to embalm, but a living Leader and Commander whose behests we must obey, whose honor we must defend.

Do not fail to discern that the empire of Christ in his Church is effectually powerful in its action; "He shall feed in the strength of Jehovah." Wherever Christ is, there is God; and whatever Christ does is the act of the Most High. Oh! it is a joyful truth to consider that he who redeemed us was none other than God himself, he who led oar captivity captive was Jehovah-Jesus; he who stands to-day representing the interests of his people is very God of very God, he who has sworn that every one of his people whom he hath redeemed by blood shall be brought safe to his Father's right hand, is himself essential Deity. O my brethren, we rest upon a sure foundation when we build upon the Incarnate God; and O ye saints of God, the interests of each one of you, and of the one great Church, must be safe, because our champion is God; Jehovah is our Judge, Jehovah is our Lawgiver, Jehovah is our King, he will save us. How can he fail or be discouraged? When he maketh bare his arm, who shall stand against him? Let us rehearse the mighty deeds of the Lord and tell of his wonders of old. Remember how he got him victory upon Pharaoh and the pride of Egypt! Pharaoh said, "Who is the Lord, that I should obey his voice to let Israel go?" Ten plagues of terrible majesty taught the boaster that the Lord was not to be despised, and the humbled tyrant bade the people go their way. With a high hand and an outstretched arm did the Lord bring forth his people from the house of bondage. When the proud high stomach of Egypt's king again rose against the Most High, the Lord knew how to lay his adversary lower than the dust. Methinks I see the hosts of Mizraim, with their horses and their chariots, hurrying after the Lord's fugitives. Their mouths are foaming with rage. "The enemy said, I will pursue, I will overtake, I will divide the spoil; my lust shall be satisfied upon them." See how they ride in all their pompous glory, swallowing the earth in their fury. O Israel, where shall be thy defense? How shalt thou escape from thy tyrannic master? Be still, O ye seed of Jacob; ye sons of Abraham, rest ye patiently, for these Egyptians whom ye see to-day, ye shall see no more for ever. With their horses and their chariots the fierce foemen descended into the depths of the sea, but the Lord looked upon them, and troubled them. "Thou didst blow with thy wind, the sea covered them: they sank as lead in the mighty waters." The depths have covered them; they sank into the bottom like a stone. "Let us sing unto the Lord, for he hath triumphed gloriously; the horse and his rider hath he thrown into the sea." Surely it shall be so at the last with Jesus our King, and all his saints; we also shall sing "the song of Moses, the servant of God, and of the Lamb," in that day when the arch-enemy shall be overthrown, and the hosts of evil shall be consumed, and they who hate the Lord shall become as the fat of rams, into smoke shall they consume, yea, into smoke shall they consume away.

One other word remains; our Lord's kingdom is most majestic in its aspect. You will observe it is written by the prophet--"He shall feed in the majesty of the name of the Lord his God." Jesus Christ is greatly to be reverenced; the familiarity with which we approach him is always to be tempered with the deepest and most reverent adoration. He is our brother, bone of our bone, and flesh of our flesh, but still he counteth it not robbery to be equal with God. I know he made himself of no reputation, and took upon him the form of a servant, and he calleth himself to-day our husband, and maketh us to be members of his body, of his flesh, and of his bones; but yet we must never forget that it is written, "Let all the angels of God worship him," and "At the name of Jesus every knee shall bow, of things in heaven, and things in earth, and things under the earth; and that every tongue should confess that Jesus Christ is Lord, to the glory of God the Father." Yes, Christ is majestic in his Church. I would, brethren, we always thought of this. There is a glory and a majesty about all the laws of Christ, and all his commands, so that whether we baptize at his command, or break bread in remembrance of him, or lift up his cross in ministry--in whatever we do, in his name, which is in fact, what he does through us, there is an attendant majesty which should make our minds feel perpetually reverent before him. O that the world could see the glory of Christ in the Church! O that the world did but know who it is that is in the midst of the few, the feeble, the weak, the foolish as they call them. O Philistia! if thou didst but know who is our champion, thy Goliath of Gath would soon hide his diminished head. O Assyria, if thou didst but know that the ancient might of him who smote Sennacherib, still abideth with us, thy hosts would turn their backs and yield us an easy victory. There is a true and mysterious presence of Christ with his people, according to the promise "Lo I am with you alway, even unto the end of the world;" it is because the world ignores this that she despises and sneers at the Church of God. Therein is our comfort and our glory. We have a majesty about us if we be the people of God, which is not to be gainsayed; angels see it and wonder--a majesty of indwelling Godhead, for the Lord is in the midst of us for a glory and around us for a defense.

II. We will now occupy one or two minutes with THE CONSEQUENT PERPETUITY OF THE CHURCH. Because of the unseen but most certain presence of Christ as King in the midst of his people, his Church ABIDES--so says the text. Here reflect first that a Church exists. What a wonder this! It is perhaps, the greatest miracle of all ages that God has a Church in the world. You who are conversant with human history will hear me out when I say that the whole history of the Church is a series of miracles, a long stream of wonders! A little spark kindled in the midst of oceans, and yet all her boisterous waves cannot quench it! Here is the great wonder which John saw in vision, and which history reveals in solemn, sober fact. A woman, "being with child, cried, travailing in birth, and pained to be delivered. And there appeared another wonder in heaven; and behold a great red dragon . . . stood before the woman which was ready to be delivered, for to devour her child as soon as it was born." The man-child who is to rule all nations with a rod of iron, was brought forth and caught up to God and to his throne. As for the woman, the Church, she fled as on eagles' wings to her wilderness-shelter prepared of God, until, in great wrath, the dragon pursued and persecuted her. Apt enough is that metaphor, "The serpent cast out of his mouth water as a flood after the woman that he might cause her to be carried away of the flood . . . And the dragon was wroth with the woman, and went to make war with the remnant of her seed, which keep the commandments of God, and have the testimony of Jesus Christ." Yet, my brethren, as surely as that glorious man-child, the Lord Jesus, lives and sits upon the throne, so surely shall the woman, the poor afflicted Church, live on until the dragon's time is over, and the King shall reign upon the

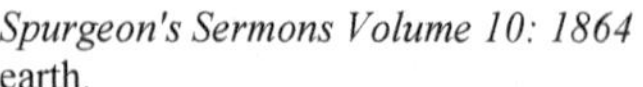

earth.

To what trials, my brethren, has not the Church of God been subjected? What new invention can Satan bring forth? The fire, the rack, imprisonment, banishment, confiscation, slander, all these have been tried, and in them all the Church has been more than conqueror through him who loved her. False doctrine without, heresy and schism with in, hypocrisy, formalism, fanaticism, pretences of high spirituality, worldliness, these have all (lone their worst. I marvel at the wondrous ingenuity of the great enemy of the Church, but methinks his devices must nearly have come to an end. Can he invent anything further? We have been astounded in these ages by the prodigy of an infidel bishop; we have been struck dumb with sorrow and amazement at a decree which declares that a Church professing to be a Church of Christ must permit men to be her ministers who deny the inspiration of Holy Scripture. This is a new thing under the sun. Popery and infidelity are to be both legalized and fostered in a Church professing to be Christian and Protestant. What next? and what next? Bat what of all this? The Church, I mean the company of the Lord's called and faithful and chosen still exists; the Lord has his elect people who still hold forth the Word of truth, and in the most reprobate Church still he may say, "I hay e a few names even in Sardis which have not defiled their garments; and they shall walk with me in white; for they are worthy."

Observe, the text says, "she abides," which means, not that she exists now and then by starts and spasms, but she exists always. This is wonderful! Always a Church! When the full force of the Pagan Emperors came like a thundering avalanche upon her, she shook off the stupendous load as a man shaketh the flakes of snow from his garment, and she lived on uninjured. When papal Rome vented its malice yet more furiously and ingeniously; when cruel murderers hunted the saints among the Alps, or worried them in the low country; when Albigenses and Waldenses poured out their blood in rivers, and dyed the snow with crimson, she lived still, and never was in a healthier state than when she was immersed in her own gore. When after a partial reformation in this country, the pretenders to religion determined that the truly spiritual should be harried out of the land, God's Church did not sleep or suspend her career of life or service. Let the covenant signed in blood witness to the vigor of the persecuted saints. Hearken to her psalm amidst the brown heath-clad hills of Scotland, and her prayer in the secret conventicles of England. Hear ye the voice of Cargil and Cameron thundering among the mountains against a false king and an apostate people; hear ye the testimony of Bunyan and his compeers who would sooner rot in dungeons than bow the knee to Baal. Ask me "Where is the Church?" and I can find her at any and every period from the day when first in the upper room the Holy Ghost came down even until now. In. one unbroken line our apostolic succession runs; not through the Church of Rome; not from the superstitious hands of priest-made popes, or king-created bishops, (what a varnished lie is the apostolic succession of those who boast so proudly of it!) but through the blood of good men and true, who never forsook the testimony of Jesus; through the loins of true pastors, laborious evangelists, faithful martyrs, and honorable men of God, we trace our pedigree up to the fishermen of Galilee and glory that we perpetuate by God's grace that true and faithful Church of the living God, in whom Christ did abide and will abide until the world's crash.

Observe, dear friends, that in the use of the term "Abide," we have not only existence, and continued existence, but the idea of quiet, calm, uninjured duration. It does not say she lingers, hunted, tempted, worried, but she abides. Ohm! the calmness of the Church of God under the attacks of her most malicious foes. Thou crue1 adversary, the virgin daughter of Zion hath shaken her head at thee and laughed thee to scorn! She abides in peace when the world rages against her. It is most noteworthy how in most instances the Church of God still keeps her foothold where she has been most savagely persecuted. In modern times we find in Madagascar, after years of exterminating persecution, the Church of God rises from her ashes, like the phoenix from the flames. The chief wonder is that she abides perfect. Not one of Cod's elect has gone back; not one of the blood-bought has denied the faith. Not one single soul which ever was effectually called call be made to dolly Christ, even though his flesh should be pulled from his bones by hot pincers, or his tormented body flung to the jaws of wild beasts. All that the enemy has done has been of no avail against the Church. The old rock has been washed, and washed, and washed again by stormy waves, and submerged a thousand times in the floods of tempest, hut even her angles and corners abide unaltered and unalterable. We may say of the Lord's tabernacle, not one of he stakes thereof has been removed, nor one of her cords boom broken. The house of he Lord from foundation to pinnacle is perfect still: "The rain descended, and the floods came, and the winds blew, and beat upon that house and it fell not;" nay, nor a single stone of it "for it was founded upon a rock."

But why all this, dear friends, why is it that we have seen the Church endure to this day? How is it that we are confident that even should worse times arrive, the Church would weather the storm and abide till moons shall cease to wax and wane? Why this security? Only because Christ is in the midst of her. You do not believe, I hope, in the preservation of orthodoxy by legal instruments and trust deeds. This is what too many Dissenters have relied upon. We certainly cannot depend upon creeds; they arc good enough in their way, as trust deeds are too, but they are as broken reeds if we rely upon them. We cannot depend upon parliament, nor kings, nor queens. We may draw up the most express and distinct form of doctrine, but we shall find that the next generation will depart from the truth unless God shall be pleased to give it renewed grace from on high. You cannot, by Presbytery, or Independency, or Episcopacy, secure the life of the Church--I find the Church of God has existed under an Episcopacy--a form of government not without its virtues and its faults. I find the Church of God flourish under a Presbytery, and decay under it too. I know it can be successful under an Independent form of Church government and can decline into Arianism quite as easily. The fact is that forms of government have very little to do with the vital principle of the Church. The reason why the Church of God exists is not her ecclesiastical regulations, 11cr organization, her formularies, her ministers, or her creeds, but the presence of the Lord in the midst of her; and while Christ lives, and Christ reigns, and stands and feeds his Church, she is safe; but if he were once gone, it would be with her as it is with you and with me when the Spirit of God has departed from us, we are weak as other men, and she would be quite as powerless.

III. But now, thirdly, flowing from both these, from the perpetual presence of Christ and from the continued existence of his Church, is THE GREATNESS OF OUR KING. "Now shall he be great unto the ends of the earth." Christ is great in his Church. Oh! how great in our hearts where he reigns supreme! My heart, it doth leap at the sound of his name--

"Jesus, the very thought of thee,
With rapture fills may breast."

O for crowns! for golden crowns! Let us crown him King in Zion! O for a well-tuned harp, and for David's feet, to dance before the ark at the very mention of Jesus' name! Now shall he be great indeed in our hearts! But he is to be great to the ends of the earth. That is a promise, of which we will say it is accomplished in a measure even now. Christ is made great ill the conversion of every sinner. When he suppliant penitent cries, "God be merciful to me a sinner," and the peace-speaking blood comes dropping upon the troubled conscience, and the soul bows meekly to accept he finished righteousness, then is Christ great. And he is great in the consecration of every one of his bloodbought saints; when they live for him; when in their prayers they make mention of him; when they give him their heart's music, their life's light, and their hips' testimony; when they feel that tribulation is joyous if endured for him, and the sternest toil a dear delight when undertaken for his sake--then Christ is great. Think, my brethren, this morning, how many ships are now furrowing the blue sea in which there are hearts which love the name of Jesus. Hark! across the waves of the Atlantic and the Pacific I hear the sound of prayer and praise from many a vessel bearing the British flag. From many an islet of the sea the song is borne upon the breeze. And there across the waters in the land of our American brethren, now so sadly chastened with war, multitudes of hearts beat as high as ours at the mention of the Savior's name. Here across you narrow Channel, in Holland, in Sweden, in Germany, in Switzerland, and even in France and Italy, how many own his name and praise him this day! We speak of our Queen's dominions and say that the sun never sets upon them. We may in truth say this of our Lord Jesus; men of all colors trust in his blood; they who look upward to the southern cross and they who follow the Polar star, alike worship his dear name; and when England ceases her strain of joy, in the hush of night, Australia takes up the song, and so from land to land, and from shore to shore, a sacrifice of a pure offering is brought to his shrine. It is accomplished, in some degree, but oh! how small the degree when we think of the thick darkness which covers the multitude of the people.

Again, it is a promise which is guaranteed as to its fulfillment in the fullest sense. Courage! brethren, courage! thc night is not for ever, the morning cometh! Watchman, what sayest thou? Are there not streaks reddening the east? Hath not the God of day, the Lord Jesus, began to shoot his divine arrows of light upwards into the thick darkness? It is even so. As I think of the signs of the times, I would fondly hope that we shall live to see brighter and better days. "Now," says the text, "shall he be great unto the ends of the earth." Prophet, I would that thy "now" were true this day. Now, even mow, let him reign! why doth he tarry? Why are his chariots so long in coming? Will it be, my brethren, that Christ will come before the world is converted? If so, welcome Jesus. Or will the world be converted first? If so, thrice welcome the mercy. But whether or no, this we do know, he shall have dominion from sea to sea, and from the river even unto the ends of the earth. They who dwell in the wilderness shall bow before him, and his enemies shall lick the dust. The day shall come when the fifth great monarchy shall be co-extensive with the world's bounds, and everywhere the Great Shepherd shall reign.

But remember, dear friends, that while this promise is thus guaranteed as to its fulfillment, it is to be prayed for as to its accomplishment. "I will yet for this be enquired of by the house of Israel, to do it for them." The mountain of the Lord shall be in the latter days, but mark you, though there be no sound of trowel or a hammer, there will be heard be sound of prayer and praise, as upward the mountain of Cod's house shall ascend. You know the picture. The prophet had seen the Lord's house standing, as it were, in a valley, and as he looked upon it, presently it became a little hill; the ground began to heave; by-and-by it had swollen from a little hill into a lofty mountain, and up it rose, and grew more great before his eyes, till Alps were dwarfed and Himalayas were stunted, and up it still went, not the house only, but the mountain too, till infinitely higher than the projected tower of Babel, which man meant to be the world's center, this house stood out clear and sharp above the clouds, having pinnacles high up in God's heaven, and yet deep foundations in man's earth, and all nations began to flow to it as to the great center. What a dream! What a vision! Yet such shall it be. The Church is as it were, in a plain just now, she begins to misc. Oh! stupendous movement! she begins to rise, her mountains swell and grow; she attracts observers; she cannot he held down. Who can attempt to restrain the swelling mass? Who shall prevent the gigantic birth? Up rises the mountain, as though swollen by some inward fire, anti up it swells, and swells, and swells, till earth touches heaven, and God communes with men. Then shah be heard the great hallelujah, "The tabernacle of God is with men, and he will dwell with them."

But then, and this is the conclusion, and I hope God may help me to press it on your hearts. All this is to be labored for as well as prayed after. My soul pants and pines to see Christ glorious in the eyes of men. Lives there a Christian here with soul so dead that he does not desire the extension of his Master's kingdom? Sirs, is there one among you who counts it little to see Jesus Christ lifted up in men's hearts? I know I speak to a people--and the Lord knoweth it to many of whom Christ is he dearest of all which is beloved, the fairest among ten thousand, and the altogether lovely. Now, if Christ is to be glorified, he must be glorified by you; if his kingdom is to come, it must come through you. God works, but God works by means. He worketh in you "to will and to do of his own good pleasure." Souls are to be saved, but they are not saved without instruments. The feast is to be furnished with guests, but you are to go into the highways and hedges, and compel them to come in. I know my Master is to have many crowns, but they are to be crowns for which you grace, and which you have fought, which you have won through his you place at his feet, that he may honor you by wearing them upon his brow. Now we, as a people, have been greatly blessed and helped of God, and I believe the Master has a very high claim upon us. We, above all the Churches in the world are indebted to the grace and mercy of God, and we ought to be doing something for the extension of the Savior's kingdom. We cannot boast of wealth; we cannot profess to build all over London a multitude of Churches as the Bishop hopes to do. Any scheme of raising three millions of money by us, must be looked upon as being entirely a dream; we cannot attempt such a. thing; if London is to be converted by money we must give up the task. We have no mitred bishops, no queens to subscribe, and no nobles and dukes, and the like to add their thousands and their tens of thousands of pounds. We are a feeble folk; what then can we do for Cod? Why, do as much as the strong! What call we do for God? Do as munch as the mighty! Nay, my brethren, our very weakness and want of power shah be our adaptation to Cod's work; and he who often putteth by the sword of Saul, and the armor of the son of Kish, will use David, and his sling and his stone, and smite Goliath's brow therewith.

I have been musing all this week upon that celebrated scene in ancient history, which seems to me to be so much like the state of our Church just now; the story of Gideon, the son of Joash, threshing wheat in the winepress, because he was afraid to be seen; the Midianites having spoiled the land. Now we, as Baptists, have generally been too much afraid to be seen; we have threshed our corn somewhere away in the winepress--up a back court--down a narrow street; any dirty hole would do to build a chapel in; so long as people could not find it tine site was thought advantageous; and if nobody could ever see it that was the place for our fathers, and for some who still linger among us. It was threshing wheat in the winepress, to hide it from the enemy. Well now, I think the time has come that we should not be afraid of these Midianites any longer. Long has he Church of God been oppressed and kept back; she has been content to let the world devour liner increase. There have been few additions to the Churches; they remain very much what they were twenty or thirty years ago; but, my brethren, some of us think that we have seen our fleece wet with dew, while all around was dry; and we believe the Lord has said to us, "The Lord is with thee, thou mighty man of valor." We think we have had the Lord's commission, "Go in this thy strength." We do not expect all of you to go with us, for the people are too many. We expect that there are many of the trembling and faint-hearted who will step back from the battle; men who are look ill for their families, mind must provide for them; men who are saving up money, and grudge their sovereigns, and so on--these of course will stand back, and let them; such men encumber our march. We fear that you are not all men who lap; but we have a few who care ery little for the ease and repose of life, but who snatch a hasty draught as they run, and with heat, and zeal, and passionate earnestness run to meet the adversary. Now, these we expect to go with us to the fray. In the name of the Lord, I proclaim a new crusade against the sin and vice of this huge city. What are we to do? The hosts of

Midian are to be counted by millions. Here in this great city we have three millions of people, and what if I were to say, two-and-half millions of them do not know their right hand from their left in matters of religion, I believe I should speak too charitably; for if I could believe there were half a million of true believers in London, I should have vastly greater hopes of it than I have now. But, alas! that is not the case. Millions, millions are gathered in he valley of indecision who are not upon the Lord's side. What can you and I do? We can do nothing of ourselves, but we can do everything by he help of our God. Where Christ is there is might and where God is there is strength; let us therefore in God's name determine to plant new Churches wherever openings occur. Like Gideon's men let us rally under our Church-officers, and follow where a warm heart leads the way. Gideon took his men, and bade them do two things; covering up a torch in an earthen pitcher, he bade them, at an appointed signal, break tine pitcher and let the light shine, and then sound with their trumpets, crying, "The sword of the Lord and of Gideon! the sword of he Lord and of Gideon!" This is just what all Christians must do. First, you must shine; break the pitcher which conceals you; throw aside the bushel which has been hiding your candle, and shine. Let your light shine before men; let your good works be such, that when they look upon you, they shall know that you have been with Jesus. There is much good done by the shining. Then there must be the sound, the blowing of the trumpet. O dear friends, the great mass of London will never hear r the gospel, unless you go and blow the trumpet in their ears. Many who are members of this Church never heard a gospel sermon, until they heard some of you preaching in the street. "Why," said one "I never went to a place of worship; but I went down a street, and there stood a young man at the corner; I listened to him, and God was pleased to send tine arrow to my conscience, and I came into the house of God afterwards." Take the gospel to them; carry it to their door; put it in their way; do not suffer them to escape it; blow the trumpet right against their ears. In the name of God, I pray you do this. Remember that the true war cry of the Church is Gideon's war-cry, "The sword of the Lord!" God must do it, it is God's work. But we are not to be idle; instrumentality is to be used--"The sword of the Lord and of Gideon!" Mark you, if we only cry, "The sword of the Lord!" we shall be guilty of an idle presumption, and shall be tempting God to depart from his fixed rule of procedure. This is the cry of every, lazy lie-n-bed. What good ever comes of saying, "The Lord will do his own work, let us sit still?" Nor must it be "The sword of Gideon" alone, for that were idolatrous reliance on an arm of flesh; we can do nothing of ourselves. Not "The sword of the Lord" only, that were idleness; but the two together, "The sword of the Lord and of Gideon." O my brethren, God help you to learn this lesson well, and then you will go forth shining and sounding, living and teaching, testifying and living out the truth? Ye shall most assuredly make the kingdom of Christ to come, and his name shall be honored if you will do this. It seems to me that now is a glorious opportunity. There is a spirit of hearing upon the people. Almost anyone may get a hearing who is willing to preach Christ. Now or never! Sons of Jacob! Ye are to be like a lion among the flock of sheep, and will ye lie down and slumber? Up and every man to the prey! Sons of Jacob! ye are to be as dew upon the grass, and will ye tarry for men and wait for the sons of men? No. In God's name, go forward, and let something be done for God, and for his Christ, for a perishing age, for a dark world, for heaven's glory, and for hell's defeat. Up! ye who know the Lord; ye swordsmen of our Israel, up and at them, and God give you a great victory and deliverance!

I want you to make some practical point of these things to-day. God has been pleased to put a sword into my hand, and to give me my lamp and my pitcher; my College of young men is now become in the Lord's hands a marvellous power for good. A blessing greater than I could have expected rests on this work. We are continually sending them out, and God owns them in the conversion of souls. I have never seen any agency more blessed to the conversion of souls, than the agency of our College. Without saying anything to depreciate other efforts, I do believe God has conferred on our Institution a crowning and special blessing, and will continue to do so yet more and more. I want you all, both hearers and readers of my sermons, to feel that this is your work, and to help me in it while I continue to cry, "The sword of the Lord and of Gideon! God works, and therefore we work; God is with us, and therefore we are with God, and stand on his side. Inasmuch as many of these men raise Churches, we want you to help to build the places where the new congregations can be accommodated afterwards; and to that end we have striven to raise a fund of five thousand pounds, to be lent out to these new Churches on loan to be repaid by installments without interest. It is but a small sum, but it is as much as I think we can do, and frugal care will turn it to good account. Some three thousand pounds have been promised by our seven shepherds and principal men; but there are many who have not promised anything yet, and we shall be glad if they will come forward, for otherwise this useful fund cannot be raised. When this is done with, once for all, we will go on and do something else for Jesus. Do break this pitcher; get this done, and let tine light of this thing shine. We must be doing something for God. I speak to you now upon the practical point, and come to it at once. If you are content to live without serving God, I am not; and if you are willing to let these hours roll by without doing something to extend the kingdom of Jesus, let me be gone from you; let me be gone from you to those of warmer spirits and of holier aspirations, for I must fight for God! there must be victories won for him! We must extend the range of the gospel; we must find places where souls can be brought to hear the Word. Hell shall not for ever laugh at our inactivity, and heaven shall not eternally weep at our sloth! Let us be up and doing, and let this thing be done by the mainly, the few have already done their parts. Promises reaching over five years are asked of you, you can all do something. And then, every one of you, when you have done your share in this, go out personally and serve with your flaming torch of holy example, and with your trumpet tones of earnest declaration and testimony serve your Lord, and God shall be with you, and Midian shall be put to confusion, and the Lord of hosts shall reign for ever and ever. "He that believeth and is baptized shall be saved; but he that believeth not shall be damned." Hear ye that note, O dead souls, and live.

Expiation

A Sermon (No. 561)
By the Rev. C. H. SPURGEON,
At the Metropolitan Tabernacle, Newington

"Thou shalt make his soul an offering for sin." -- Isaiah 53:10.

BOTH Jews and Gentiles knew pretty well what an offering for sin meant. The Gentiles had been in the habit of offering sacrifices. The Jews, however, had by far the clearer idea of it. And what was meant by a sin-offering? Undoubtedly, it was taken for granted by the offerer, that without shedding blood there was no remission of sin. Conscious of guilt, and anxious for pardon, therefore he brought a sacrifice, the blood of which should be poured out at the foot of the altar--feeling persuaded that without sacrifice there was no satisfaction, and without satisfaction there was no pardon. Then the victim to be offered was, on all occasions, a spotless one. The most scrupulous care was taken that it should be altogether without blemish; for this idea was always connected with a sin-offering, that it must be sinless in itself; and being without spot or wrinkle, or any such thing, it was held to be a competent victim to take the offender's place. That done, the victim being selected, the offerer put his hand upon the sin-offering--and this indeed was the essence of the whole transaction--putting his hand on the victim, he confessed his sin, and a transferrence took place, in type at least, from the offender to the victim. He did, as it were, put the sin from off his own shoulders on to those of the lamb, or the bullock, or the he-goat which was now about to be slaughtered. And, to complete the sin-offering, the priest draws his knife and kills the victim which must be utterly consumed with fire. I say this was always the idea of a sin-offering,--that of a perfect victim; without offense on its own account, taking the place of the offender; the transferrence of the offender's sin to that victim, and that expiation in the person of the victim for the sin done by another.

Now, Jesus Christ has been made by God an offering for sin; and oh that to-night we may be able to do in reality what the Jew did in metaphor! May we put our hand upon the head of Christ Jesus; as we see him offered up upon the cross for guilty men, may we know that our sins are transferred to him, and may we be able to cry, in the ecstasy of faith, "Great God, I am clean; through Jesus' blood I am clean."

I. In trying now to expound the doctrine of Christ's being an offering for sin, we will begin by laying down one great axiom; which is, that SIN DESERVES AND DEMANDS PUNISHMENT.

Certain divines have demurred to this. You are aware, I suppose, that there have been many theories of atonement; and every new or different theory of atonement involves a new or different theory of sin. There are some who say that there is no reason in sin itself why it should be punished, but that God punishes offenses for the sake of society at large. This is what is called the governmental theory,--that it is necessary for the maintenance of good order that an offender should be punished, but that there is nothing in sin itself which absolutely requires a penalty. Now, we begin by opposing all this, and asserting, and we believe we have God's warrant of it, that sin intrinsically and in itself demands and deserves the just anger of God, and that that anger should be displayed in the form of a punishment. To establish this, let me appeal to the conscience--I will not say to the conscience of a man who has, by years of sin, dwindled it down to the very lowest degree, but let me appeal to the conscience of an awakened sinner,--a sinner under the influence of the Holy Spirit. And are we ever in our right senses, brethren, till the Holy Spirit really brings us into them? May it not be said of each of us as it was of the prodigal, "He came to himself?" Are we not beside ourselves till the Holy Spirit begins to enlighten us? Well, ask this man, who is now really in the possession of his true senses, whether he believes that sin deserves punishment; and his answer will be quick, sharp, and decisive. "Deserve it," saith he, "ay, indeed; and the wonder is that I have not suffered it. Why, sir, it seems a marvel to me that I am out of hell, and Wesley's hymn is often on my lips,--

'Tell it unto sinners, tell,
I am, I am out of hell.'"

"Yes, sir," says such a sinner, "I feel that if God should smite me now, without hope or offer of mercy, to the lowest hell, I should only have what I justly deserve; and I feel that if I be not punished for my sins, or if there be not some plan found by which my sin can be punished in another, I cannot understand how God can be just at all: how shall he be Judge of all the earth, if he suffer offenses to go unpunished?" There has been a dispute whether men have any innate ideas, but surely this idea is in us as early as anything, that virtue deserves reward, and sin deserves punishment. I think I might venture to assert that if you go to the most degraded race of men, you would still find, at least, some traces of this--shall I call it tradition? or is it not a part of the natural light which never was altogether eclipsed in man? Man may put bitter for sweet, and sweet for bitter; darkness for light, and light for darkness; but this follows him as a dog at the heels of its master,--a sense that virtue should be rewarded, and that sin must be punished. You may stifle this voice, if you will, but sometimes you will hear it; and terribly and decisively will it speak in your ears to say to you, "Yes, man, God must punish you; the Judge of all the earth cannot suffer you to go scot free." Add to this another matter; namely, that God has absolutely declared his displeasure against sin itself. There is a passage in Jeremiah, the forty-fourth chapter and the fourth verse, where he calls it "That abominable thing which I hate." And then, in Deuteronomy, the twenty-fifth chapter, at the sixteenth verse, he speaks of it as the thing which is an abomination to him. It must be the character of God, that he has a desire to do towards his creatures that which is equitable. "Shall not the Judge of all the earth do right?" If there is anything in them which deserves reward, rest assured he will not rob them of it; and, on the other hand, he will do the right thing with those who have offended, and if they deserve punishment, it is according to the nature and character of a just and holy God that punishment should be inflicted. And we think there is nothing more clear in Scripture than the truth that sin is in itself so detestable to God that he must and will put forth all the vigor of his tremendous strength to crush it, and to make the offender feel that it is an evil and a bitter thing to offend against the Most High. Beware, ye who forget God in this matter, lest he tear you in pieces, and there be none to deliver you. Sin must be punished.

The other idea, that sin is only to be punished for the sake of the community, involves injustice. If I am to be damned for the sake of other people, I demur to it. No, sir: if I am to be punished, Justice says; at any rate, that it shall be for my own sins, but if I am to be eternally a castaway from God's presence merely as a sort of trick of government to maintain the dignity of his law, I cannot understand the justice of this. If I am to be cast into hell merely that I am to teach to others the tremendousness of the divine holiness, I shall say there is no justice in this; but if my sin intrinsically and of itself deserves the wrath of God, and I am sent to perdition as the result of this fact, I close my lips, and have nothing to say. I am speechless; conscience binds my tongue. But if I am told that I am only sent there as a part of a scheme of moral government, and that I am sent into torment to impress others with a sense of right, I ask that some one else should have the place of preacher to the people, and that I may be one of those whose felicity it shall be to be preached to; for I see no reason in justice why I should be selected as the victim. Really, when men run away from the simplicities of the gospel in order to make Jehovah more kind, it is strange how unjust and unkind they make him. Sinner, God will never destroy you merely to maintain his government, or for the good of others. If you be destroyed, it shall be because you would not come to him that you might have life; because you would rebel against him; because sin from stern necessity did, as it were, compel the attribute of divine justice to kindle into vengeance, and to drive you from his presence for ever. Sin must be punished.

The reverse of this doctrine, that sin demands punishment, may be used to prove it; for it is highly immoral, dangerous, and opens the floodgates of licentiousness to teach that sin can go unpunished. O sirs, it is contrary to fact. Look ye! Oh! if your eyes could see to-night the terrible justice of God which a being executed now,--if these ears could but hear it,--if ye could be appalled for a moment with

"The sullen groans and hollow moans
And shrieks of tortured ghosts,"

you would soon perceive that God is punishing sin! And if sin deserve not to be punished, what is Tophet but injustice on a monstrous scale? What is it but an infinite outrage against everything which is honest and right, if these creatures are punished for anything short of their own deserts. Go and preach this in hell, and you will have quenched the fire which is forever to burn, and the worm of conscience will die. Tell them in hell that they are not punished for sin, and you have taken away the very sting of their punishment. And then come to earth, and go, like Jonah went, though with another message than Jonah carried, through the highways and the broadways, the streets and thoroughfares of the exceeding great city, and proclaim that sin is not to be punished for its own intrinsic desert and baseness. But if you expect your prophecy to be believed, enlarge the number of your jails, and seek for fresh fields for transportation in the interests of society; for if any doctrine can breed villains, this will. Say that sin is not to be punished, and you have unhinged government; you have plucked up the very gate of our commonweal; you have been another Samson to another Gaza; and we shall soon have to rue the day. But, sirs, I need not stop to prove it; it is written clearly upon the consciousness of each man, and upon the conscience of every one of us, that sin must be punished. Here are you and I to-night brought into this dilemma. We have sinned; we all like sheep have gone astray; and we must be punished for it. It is impossible, absolutely, that sin can be forgiven without a sacrifice. God must be just, if heaven falls. If earth should pass away and every creature should be lost, the justice of God must stand, it cannot by any possibility be suffered to be impugned. Let this, then, be fully established in our minds.

You need not to be told, as for the first time, that God in his infinite mercy has devised a way by which justice can be satisfied, and yet mercy can be triumphant. Jesus Christ, the only begotten of the Father, took upon himself the form of man, and offered unto Divine Justice that which was accepted as an equivalent for the punishment due to all his people.

II. Now, the second matter that I wish to bring under your notice is this,--THAT THE PROVISION AND ACCEPTANCE OF A SUBSTITUTE FOR SINNERS IS AN ACT OF GRACE.

It is no act of grace for a person to accept a pecuniary debt on my behalf of another person. If I owe a man twenty pounds, it is no matter to him whatever who shall pay the twenty pounds so long as it is duly paid. You know that you could legally and at once demand a receipt and an acquittance from any one who is your creditor, so long as his debt is discharged, though it is discharged by another, and not by you. It is so in pecuniary matters, but it is not so in penal matters. If a man be condemned to be imprisoned, there is no law, there is no justice which can compel the lawgiver to accept a substitute for him. If the sovereign should permit another to suffer in his stead, it must be the sovereign's own act and deed. He must use his own discretion as to whether he will accept the substitute or not; and if he do so, it is an act of grace. In Gods case, if he had said in the infinite sovereignty of his absolute will, "I will have no substitute, but each man shall suffer for himself, he who sinneth shall die," none could have murmured. It was grace, and only grace which led the divine mind to say, "I will accept of a substitute. There shall be a vicarious suffering; and my vengeance shall be content, and my mercy shall be gratified."

Now, dear friends, this grace of God is yet further magnified not only in the allowance of the principle of substitution, but in the providing of such a substitute as Christ--on Christ's part that he should give up himself, the Prince of Life to die; the King of glory to be despised and rejected of men; the Lord of angels to be a servant of servants; and the Ancient of days to become an infant of a span long. Think of the distance

"From the highest throne in glory
To the cross of deepest woe,"

and consider the unexampled love which shines in Christ's gift of himself. But the Father gives the Son. "God so loved the world that he gave his only-begotten Son, that whosoever believeth in him should not perish, but have everlasting life." To give your wealth is something, if you make yourself poor; but to give your child is something more. When the patriot mother tears her son from her bosom, and cries, "Go, my first-born, to your country's wars; there, go and fight until your country's flag is safe, and the hearths and homes of your native land are secure," there is something in it; for she can look forward to the bloody spectacle of her son's mangled body, and yet love her country more than her own child. Here is heroism indeed; but God spared not his own Son, his only-begotten Son, but freely delivered him up for us all. "God commendeth his love toward us, in that, while we were yet sinners, Christ died for us." I do implore you, do not look upon the sacrifice of Christ as an act of mere vengeance on the Father's part. Never imagine, oh! never indulge the idea, that Jesus died to make the Father complacent towards us. Oh, no, dear friends: Jesus' death is the effect of overwhelming and infinite love on the Father's part; and every blow which wounds, every infliction which occasions sorrow, and every pang which rends his heart, speaks of the Father's love as much as the joy, the everlasting triumph, which now surrounds his head.

Let us add, however, to this, that, although Jesus Christ's dying as a substitute does give to him lawful right to all promised privileges, and does make him, as the covenant head of his people a claimant of the divine mercy, yet it does not render any of the gifts which we receive from God the less gifts from God. Christ has died; but still everything that we receive comes to us entirely as a gratuitous outflow of God's great heart of love. Never think you have any claim to anything because Christ purchased it. If you use the word claim at all, let it always be in so humble and modified a sense that you understand that you are still receiving, not of debt, but of grace. Look upon the whole transaction of a substitute, and of Christ becoming the second Adam, as being a matter of pure, rich, free, sovereign grace, and never indulge the atrocious thought, I pray you, that there was justice, and justice only here; but do magnify the love and pity of God in that he did devise and accomplish the great plan of salvation by an atoning sacrifice.

III. But now to go a step further, and with as much brevity as possible. The Lord having established the principle of substitution, having provided a substitute, and having through him bestowed upon us gratuitously innumerable mercies, let us observe THAT JESUS IS THE MOST FITTING PERSON TO BE A SUBSTITUTE, AND THAT HIS WORK IS THE MOST FITTING WORK TO BE A SATISFACTION.

Let every sinner here who desires something stable to fix his faith upon, listen to these simple truths, which I am trying to put as plainly as possible. You do understand me, I trust, that God must punish sin; that he must punish you for sin unless some one else will suffer in your stead; that Jesus Christ is the person who did suffer in the room and place of all those who ever have believed on him who do believe in him, or ever shall believe in him, --making for those who believe on him a complete atonement by his substitution in their place. Now we say that Christ was the best person to be a substitute; for just consider what sort of a mediator was needed. Most absolutely he must be one who had no debt of his own. If Christ had been at all under the law naturally, if it had been his duty to do what it is our duty to do, it is plain he could only have lived for himself; and if he had any sin of his own, he could only have died for himself, seeing his obligations to do and to suffer would have been his just due to the righteousness and the vengeance of God. But on Christ's part there was no natural necessity for obedience, much less for obedience unto death. Who shall venture to say that the Divine Lord, amidst the glories of heaven, owed to his father anything? "Who shall say it was due to the Divine Father that Christ should be nailed to the accursed tree, to suffer, bleed, and die, and then be cast into the grave? None can dare to say such a thing. He is himself perfectly free, and therefore can he undertake for others. One man who is drawn for the militia cannot be a substitute for another person so drawn, because he owes for himself his own personal service. I must, if I would escape, and would procure a substitute, find a man who is not drawn, and who is therefore exempt. Such is Jesus Christ. He is perfectly exempt from service, and therefore can volunteer to undertake it for our sake. He is the right person.

There was needed, also, one of the same nature with us. Such is Jesus Christ. For this purpose he became man, of the substance of his mother, very man, such a man as any of us. Handle him, and see if he be not flesh and bones. Look at him, and mark if he be not man in soul as well as in body. He hungers; he thirsts, he fears, he weeps, he rejoices, he loves, he dies. Made in all points and like unto us, being a man, and standing exactly in a man's place, becoming a real Adam,--as true an Adam as was the first Adam, standing quite in the first Adam's place,--he is a fit person to become a substitute for us.

But please to observe (see if you cannot throw your grappling-hooks upon this), the dignity of his sacred person made him the most proper person for a substitute. A mere man could at most only substitute for one other man. Crush him as you will, and make him feel in his life every pang which flesh is heir to, but he can only suffer what one man would have suffered. He could not, I will venture to say, even then have suffered an equivalent for that eternal misery which the ungodly deserve; and if he were a mere man, he must suffer precisely the same. A difference may be made in the penalty, when there is a difference in the person; but if the person be the same, the penalty must be precisely and exactly the same in degree and in quality. But the dignity of the Son of God, the dignity of his nature, changes the whole matter. A God bowing his head, and suffering and dying, in the person of manhood, puts such a singular efficacy into every groan and every pang that it needs not that his pangs should be eternal, or that he should die a second death. Remember that in pecuniary matters you must give a quid pro quo, but that in matters of penal justice no such thing is demanded. The dignity of the person adds a special force to the substitution; and thus one bleeding Saviour can make atonement for millions of sinful men, and the Captain of our salvation can bring multitudes unto glory.

It needs one other condition to be fulfilled. The person so free from personal service, and so truly in our nature, and yet so exalted in person, should also be accepted and ordained of God. Our text gives this a full solution, in that it says, "He shall make his soul an offering for sin." Christ did not make himself a sin-offering without a warrant from the Most High: God made him so. "The Lord hath laid on him the iniquity of us all." It was the sovereign degree of heaven which constituted Christ the great substitute for his people. No man taketh this office upon himself. Even the Son of God stoopeth not to this burden uncalled. He was chosen as the covenant-head in election; he was ordained in the divine decree to stand for his people. God the Father cannot refuse the sacrifice which he has himself appointed. "My son," said good old Abraham, "God shall provide himself a lamb for a burnt-offering." He has done so in the Saviour; and what God provides, God must and will accept.

I wish to-night that I had power to deal with this doctrine as I would. Poor trembling sinner, look up a moment. Dost thou see him there--him whom God hath set forth? Dost thou see him in proper flesh and blood fastened to that tree? See how the cruel iron drags through his tender hands! Mark how the rough nails are making the blood flow profusely from his feet! See how fever parches his tongue, and dries his whole body like a potsherd! Hearest thou the cry of his spirit, which is suffering more than his body suffers--"My God, my God, why hast thou forsaken me?" This is none other than God's only-begotten Son; this is he who made the worlds; this is the express image of his Father's person, the brightness of Jehovah's glory! What thinkest thou, man? Is there not enough there to satisfy God? Truly it has satisfied God: is there not enough there to satisfy thee? Cannot thy conscience rest on that? If God's appointed Christ could suffer in thy stead, is it not enough? What can Justice ask more? Wilt thou now trust Christ with thy soul? Come, now, sir, wilt thou now fall flat at the foot of the cross, and rest thy soul's eternal destiny in the pierced hands of Jesus of Nazareth? If thou wilt, then God has made him to be a sin-offering for thee; but if thou wilt not, beware, lest he whom thou wouldst not have to be thy Saviour should become thy Judge, and say, "Depart, thou cursed one, into everlasting fire in hell!"

IV. We come now to our fourth remark,--THAT CHRIST'S WORK, AND THE EFFECTS OF THAT WORK, ARE NOW COMPLETE.

Christ becomes a substitute for us. We have seen how fit and proper a person he was to be such. We hinted that from the dignity of his person the pains he suffered were a good and sufficient equivalent for our own suffering on account of sin. But now the joyous truths come up that Christ's work is finished. Christ has made an atonement so complete that he never need suffer again. No more drops of blood; no more pangs of heart; no more bitterness and darkness, with exceeding heaviness, even unto death, are needed.

"Tis done--the great transaction's done."

The death-knell of the penalty rings in the dying words of the Saviour,--"It is finished." Do you ask for a proof of this? Remember that Jesus Christ rose again from the dead. If he had not completed his work of penalty-suffering, he would have been left in the tomb till now; our preaching would have been in vain, and your faith would have been in vain; ye would have been yet in your sins. But Jesus rose. God's sheriff's officer let him out of "durance vile" because the account had been discharged, and God's great Court of King's Bench sent down the mittimus to let the captive go free. More than that: Christ has ascended upon high. Think you he would have returned thither with unexpiated sin red upon his garments? Do you suppose he would have ascended to the rest and to the reward of an accomplished work? What! sit at his Fathers right hand to be crowned for doing nothing, and rest until his adversaries are made his footstool, when he has not performed his Father's will! Absurd! Impossible! His ascension in stately pomp, amidst the acclamations of angels, to the enjoyment of his Father's continued smile, is the sure proof that the work is complete.

Complete it is, dear brethren, not only in itself, but, as I said, in its effects; that is to say, that there is now complete pardon for every soul which believeth in Christ. You need not do anything to make the atonement of Christ sufficient to pardon you. It wants no eking out. It is not as if Christ had put so much into the scale and it was quivering in the balance; but your sins, for all their gravity, utterly ceased their pressure through the tremendous weight of his atonement. He has outweighed the penalty, and given double for all your sins. Pardon, full and free, is now presented in the name of Jesus, proclaimed to every creature under heaven, for sins past, for sins present, and for sins to come; for blasphemies and murders; for drunkenness and whoredom; for all manner of sin under heaven. Jesus Christ hath ascended up on high, and exalted he is that he may give repentance and remission of sin. Ye have no need of shillings to pay the priests; nor is baptismal water wanted to erect the pardon: there is no willing, doing, being, or suffering of yours required to complete the task. The blood has filled the fountain full: thou hast but to wash and be clean, and thy sins shall be gone forever.

Justification, too, is finished. You know the difference. Pardon takes away our filth, but then it leaves us naked; justification puts a royal robe upon us. How no rags of yours are wanted; not a stitch of yours is needed to perfect what Christ has done. He whom God the Father hath accepted as a sin offering hath perfected forever thou who are set apart. Ye are complete in Christ. No tears of yours, no penance, no personal mortifications, nay, no good works of yours, are wanted to make yourself complete and perfect. Take it as it is. O sirs! may you have grace to take it as it is freely presented to you in the gospel. "He that believeth on him is not condemned;" "There is therefore now no condemnation to them that are in Christ Jesus." Trust Christ--implicitly trust Christ; and all that he did shall cover you, while all that he suffered shall cleanse you.

Remember, too, that acceptance is finished. There are the Father's arms, and here are you, a black sinner to-night. I do not know you, but it may be you have trodden the pavements, or you have gone further than that, and added drunkenness to shame; you have gone to the lowest vice, perhaps to robbery,--who knoweth what manner of person may step into this place?--but the great arms of the Eternal Father are ready to save you as you are, because the great work of Christ has effected all that is wanted before God for the acceptance of the vilest sinner. How is it that the Father can embrace the prodigal? Why! he is fresh from the swine-trough! Look at him: look at his rags; how foul they are! We would not touch them with a pair of tongs! Take him to the fire and burn the filth! Take him to the bath and wash him! That lip is not fit to kiss; those filthy lips cannot be permitted to touch that holy cheek of the glorious Father! Ah! but it is not so. While he was yet a great way off, his father saw him,--rags and poverty and sin and filth and all,--and he did not wait till he was clean, but ran and fell upon his neck and kissed him, just as he was. How could he do that? Why, the parable does not tell us; for it did not run on with the subject to introduce the atonement. But this explains it,--when God accepts a sinner, he is, in fact, only accepting Christ. He looks into the sinner's eyes, and he sees his own dear Son's image there, and he takes him in. As we have heard of a good woman, who, whenever a poor sailor came to her door, whoever he might be, would always make him welcome, because, she said, "I think I see my own dear son who has been these many years away, and I have never heard of him; but whenever I see a sailor, I think of him, and treat the stranger kindly for my son's sake." So my God, when he sees a sinner long for pardon and desirous of being accepted, thinks he sees his Son in him, and accepts him for his Son's sake. Do not imagine that we preach a gospel in this place for respectable, godly people. No: we preach a gospel here for sinners. I heard, the other day, from one who told me that he believed we were saved by being perfect, that when we committed sin we at once fell out of God's mercy. Well now, supposing that were true, it would not be worth making a large splutter about. It would not be worth angels singing "Glory to God in the highest" about it, I should think. Any fool might know that God would accept a perfect man. But this is the thing of marvel, for which heaven and earth shall ring with the praises of the Mediator, that Jesus Christ died for the ungodly,--that Jesus Christ gave himself for their sin; not for their righteousness, not for their good deeds. If he had looked to all eternity, he could not have seen anything in us worthy of so great a suffering as that which he endured; but he did it for charity's sake,--for love's sake.

And now, in his name,--oh that I could do it with his voice and with his love and with his fervor!--I do beseech you to lay hold upon him. No matter who you may be, I will not exclude you from the invitation. Hast thou piled thy sins together till they seem to provoke heaven? Do thy sins touch the clouds? Yet come, and welcome; for God has provided a sin-offering. Has man cast thee out? Say, poor woman, does the dreary river seem to invite thee to the fatal plunge? God has not cast thee out. O thou who feelest in thine own body the effect of thy sin, till thou art loathing thyself, and wishing thou hadst never been born--perhaps thou sayest, like John Bunyan, "Oh that I had been a frog, or a toad, or a snake, sooner than have been a man, to have fallen into such sin, and to have become so foul!" Have courage, sinner; have courage. "Let the wicked forsake his way, and the unrighteous man his thoughts; and let him return unto the Lord, and he will have mercy upon him; and to our God, for he will abundantly pardon." Do not doubt this message: God has sent it to you. Do not reject it: you will reject your own life if you do. Turn you at his rebuke! It is a loving voice which speaks to you, and that would speak, perhaps, better and more forcibly if it were not choked with love. I do implore thee, sinner, come to Jesus! If thou art damned it is not for want of invitation. If thou wilt perish, it is not for want of earnest pleading with thee. I tell thee, man, there is nothing of thine own wanted. All this is found in the sin-offering; for thou needest not find it. There is no merit of thine needed; there is merit enough in Christ. Is it not the old proverb that you are not to take coals to Newcastle? Do not take anything to Christ. Come as you are--just as you are. Nay, tarry not till you go out of this house. The Lord enable you to believe in Jesus now, to take him now as a complete and finished salvation for you, though you may be the most sunken and abandoned and hopeless of all characters. Why did God provide a sin-offering but for sinners? He could not have wanted to provide it if there was no necessity. You have a great necessity. You have, shall I say? compelled him to it. Your sins have nailed Christ's hands to the cross,--your sins have pierced his heart; and his heart is not pierced in vain, nor are those hands nailed there for naught. Christ will have you, sinner, Christ will have you. There are some of God's elect here, and he will have you. You shall not stand out against him. Almighty love will have you. He has determined that you shall not do what you have vowed. Your league with hell is broken to-night, and your covenant with death is disannulled. The prey shall not be taken from the mighty; the lawful captive shall be delivered. The Lord will yet fetch you up from the depths of the sea. Oh! what a debtor to grace you will be! Be a debtor to that grace to-night. Over head and ears in debt, plunge yourself by a simple act of trusting in Jesus, and you are saved.

Pray, ye who know how to pray, that this message may be made effective in the hand of God. And you who have never prayed before, God help you to pray now. May he now be found of them who sought not for him, and he shall have the glory, world without end. Amen.

"Alas For Us, If Thou Wert All, and Nought Beyond, O Earth"

A Sermon (No. 562)
Delivered on Sunday Morning, March 27th, 1864, by the
Rev. C. H. SPURGEON,
At the Metropolitan Tabernacle, Newington

"If in this life only we have hope in Christ, we are of all men most miserable." -- 1 Corinthians 15:19.

YOU WILL UNDERSTAND that the apostle is arguing with professedly Christian people, who were dubious about the resurrection of the dead. He is not saying that all men are now miserable if there be no hope of the world to come, for such an assertion would be untrue. There are very many who never think of another life, who are quite happy in their way, enjoy themselves, and are very comfortable after a fashion. But he speaks of Christian people--"If we, who have hope in Christ, are led to doubt the doctrine of a future state and of a resurrection, then we are of all men most miserable." The argument has nothing to do with some of you who are not Christians; it has nothing to do with you who have never been brought out of a state of nature into a state of grace; it only respects those who are real, living followers of the Savior, and who are known by this, that they have hope in Christ--hope in his blood for pardon, in his righteousness for justification, in his power for support, in his resurrection for eternal glory. "If we who have hope in Christ, have that hope for this life only, then we are of all men most miserable." You understand the argument; he is appealing to their consciousness; they, as Christians, had real enjoyments, "but," says he, "you could not have these enjoyments if it were not for the hope of another life; for once take that away, if you could still remain Christians and have the same feelings which you now have, and act as you now do, you would become of all men most miserable," therefore to justify your own happiness and make it all reasonable, you must admit a resurrection; there is no other method of accounting for the joyous peace which the Christian possesses. Our riches are beyond the sea; our city with firm foundations lies on the other side the river: gleams of glory from the spirit-world cheer our hearts, and urge us onward; but if it were not for these, our present joys would pine and die.

We will try and handle our text this morning in this way. First, we are not of all men most miserable; but secondly, without the hope of another life we should be--that we are prepared to confess--because thirdly, our chief joy lies in the hope of a life to come; and thus, fourthly, the future influences the present; and so, in the last place, we may to-day judge what our future is to be.

I. First then, WE ARE NOT OF ALL MEN MOST MISERABLE. Who ventures to say we are? He who will have the hardihood to say so knoweth nothing of us. He who shall affirm that Christianity makes men miserable, is himself an utter stranger to it, and has never partaken of its joyful influences. It were a very strange thing indeed, if it did make us wretched, for see to what a position it exalts us! It makes us sons of God. Suppose you that God will give all the happiness to his enemies, and reserve all the mourning for his sons? Shall his foes have mirth and joy, and shall his own home-born children inherit sorrow and wretchedness? Are the kisses for the wicked and the frowns for us? Are we condemned to hang our harps upon the willows, and sing nothing but doleful dirges, while the children of Satan are to laugh for joy of heart? We are heirs of God, and joint-heirs with Christ Jesus. Shall the sinner, who has no part nor lot in Christ, call himself happy, and shall we go mourning as if we were penniless beggars? No, we will rejoice in the Lord always, and glory in our inheritance, for we "have not received the spirit of bondage again to fear; but ye have received the Spirit of adoption, whereby we cry, Abba, Father." The rod of chastisement must rest upon us in our measure, but it worketh for us the comfortable fruits of righteousness; and therefore by the aid of the divine Comforter, we will rejoice in the Lord at all times. We are, my brethren, married unto Christ; and shall our great Bridegroom permit his spouse to linger in constant grief? Our hearts are knit unto him: we are members of his body, of his flesh, and of his bones, and though for awhile we may suffer as our Head once suffered, yet we are even now blessed with heavenly blessings in him. Shall our Head reign in heaven, and shall we have a hell upon earth?

God forbid: the joyful triumph of our exalted Head is in a measure shared by us, even in this vale of tears. We have the earnest of our inheritance in the comforts of the Spirit, which are neither few nor small. Think of a Christian! He is a king, and shall the king be the most melancholy of men? He is a priest unto God, and shall he offer no sweet incense of hallowed joy and grateful thanksgiving? We are fit companions for angels: he hath made us meet to be partakers of the inheritance of the saints in light; and shall we have no days of heaven upon earth? Is Canaan ours from Dan to Beersheba, and shall we eat no fruit from Eshcol's vine on this side of Jordan? Shall we have no taste of the figs, and of the pomegranates, and of the flowing milk and honey? Is there no manna in the wilderness? Are there no streams in the desert? Are there no streaks of light to herald our eternal sunrising? Heritors of joy for ever, have we no foretastes of our portion? I say again, it were the oddest thing in the world if Christians were more miserable than other men, or not more happy. Think again of what God has done for them! The Christian knows that his sins are forgiven; there is not against the believer a single sin recorded in God's book. "I have blotted out, as a thick cloud, thy transgressions, and, as a cloud, thy sins." More than that, the believer is accounted by God as if he had perfectly kept the law, for the righteousness of Christ is imputed to him, and he stands clothed in that fair white linen which is the righteousness of the saints, And shall the man whom God accepts be wretched? Shall the pardoned offender be less happy than the man upon whom the wrath of God abideth? Can you conceive such a thing? Moreover, my brethren, we are made temples of the Holy Ghost, and is the Holy Ghost's temple to be a dark, dolorous place, a place of shrieks, and moans, and cries, like the Druidic groves of old? Such is not like our God. Our God is a God of love, and it is his very nature to make his creatures happy; and we, who are his twice-made creatures, who are the partakers of the divine nature, having escaped the corruption which is in the world through lust, is it to be supposed that we are bound by a stern decree to go mourning all our days? Oh! if ye knew the Christian's privilege, if ye understood that the secret of the Lord is laid open to him, that the wounds of Christ are his shelter, that the flesh and blood of Christ are his food, that Christ himself is his sweet companion and his abiding friend, oh! if ye knew this, ye would never again foolishly dream that Christians are an unhappy race. "Happy art thou, O Israel: who is like unto thee, O people saved by the Lord?" Who can be compared with the man who is "satisfied with favor and full with the blessing of the Lord." Well might the evil prophet of Bethor exclaim, "Let me die the death of the righteous, and let my last end be like his."

We will go a step farther. We will not only say that from the nature of his position and privileges, a Christian should be happy, but we declare that he is so, and that among all men there are none who enjoy such a constant peace of mind as believers in Christ. Our joy may not be like that of the sinner, noisy and boisterous. You know what Solomon says--"The laughter of fools is as the crackling of thorns under a pot"--a great deal of blaze and much noise, and then a handful of ashes, and it is all over. "Who hath woe, who hath redness of the eyes? They that tarry long at the wine-men of strength to mingle strong drink." The Christian, in truth, does not know much of the excitement of the bowl, the viol and the dance, nor does he desire to know; he is content that he possesses a calm deep-seated repose of soul. "He is not afraid of evil tidings, his heart is fixed, trusting in the Lord." He is not disturbed with any sudden fear: he knows that "all things work together for good to them that love God, to them who are the called according to his purpose." He is in the habit in whatever society he may be, of still lifting up his heart to God; and therefore he can say with the Psalmist, "My heart is fixed, O God, my heart is fixed: I will sing and give praise."

"He waits in secret on his God;
His God in secret sees;
Let earth be all in arms abroad,
He dwells in heavenly peace.
His pleasures rise from things unseen,
Beyond this world and time,
Where neither eyes nor ears have been,
Nor thoughts of sinners climb.
He wants no pomp nor royal throne
To raise his figure here:
Content and pleased to live unknown,
Till Christ his life appear.

"There is a river the streams whereof make glad the city of God." Believers drink of that river and thirst not for carnal delights. They are made "to lie down in green pastures," and are led "beside the still waters." Now this solid, lasting joy and peace of mind sets the Christian so on high above all others, that I boldly testify that there are no people in the world to compare with him for happiness. But do not suppose that our joy never rises above this settled calm; for let me tell you, and I speak experimentally, we have our seasons of rapturous delight and overflowing bliss. There are times with us when no music could equal the melody of our heart's sweet hymn of joy. It would empty earth's coffers of every farthing of her joy to buy a single ounce of our delight. Do not fancy Paul was the only man who could say, "Whether in the body or out of the body, I cannot tell; God knoweth," for these ecstasies are usual with believers; and on their sunshiny days when their unbelief is shaken off and their faith is strong, they have all but walked the golden streets; and they can say, "If we have not entered within the pearly gate, we have been only just this side of it; and it we have not yet come to the general assembly and Church of the firstborn, whose names are written in heaven, if we have not joined the great congregation of the perfect in actual body, yet still--

"E'en now by faith we join our hands
With those that went before,
And greet the blood-besprinkled bands
On the eternal shore."

I would not change one five minutes of the excessive joy my soul has sometimes felt for a thousand years of the best mirth that the children of this world could give me. O friends, there is a happiness which can make the eye sparkle and the heart beat high, and the whole man as full of bounding speed of life as the chariots of Amminadib. There are raptures and high ecstasies, which on festival days such as the Lord allotteth to his people, the saints are permitted to enjoy. I must not fail to remind you that the Christian is the happiest of men for this reason, that his joy does not depend upon circumstances. We have seen the happiest men in the most sorrowful conditions. Mr. Renwick, who was the last of the Scotch martyrs, said a little before his death, "Enemies think themselves satisfied that we are put to wander in mosses and upon mountains, but even amidst the storm of these last two nights I cannot express what sweet times I have had when I have had no coverings but the dark curtains of night: yea, in the silent watch my mind was led out to admire the deep and inexpressible ocean of joy wherein the whole family of heaven do swim. Each star led me to wonder what He must be who is the star of Jacob, and from whom all stars borrow their shining." Here is a martyr of God driven from house and home and from all comforts, and yet having such sweet seasons beneath the curtains of the black night as kings do not often know beneath their curtains of silk. A minister of Christ going to visit a very, very poor man, gives this description. He says, "I found him alone, his wife having gone out to ask help of some neighbor. I was startled by the sight of the pale emaciated man, the living image of death, fastened upright in his chair by a rude mechanism of cords and belts hanging from the ceiling, totally unable to move hand or foot, having been for more than four years entirely deprived of the use of his limbs, and suffering extreme pain from swellings in all his joints. I approached him full of pity, and I said, "Are you left alone, my friend, in this deplorable situation?" He answered with a gentle voice--his lips were the only parts of his body which he appeared to have power to move--"No, sir, I am not alone, because the Father is with me." I began to talk with him, and I soon observed what was the source of his consolation, for just in front of him lay the Bible upon a pillow, his wife having left it open at some choice Psalm of David so that he might read while she was gone, as he had no power to turn over the leaves. I asked him what he had to live upon, and found that it was a miserable pittance, scarcely enough to keep body and soul together, "But," said he, "I never want anything, for the Lord has said, Your bread shall be given you, and your water shall be sure,' and I trust in him, and I shall never want while God is faithful to his promise." "I asked him," says this minister "whether he did not often repine on account of suffering so acutely for so many years. "Sir," said he, "I did repine at first, but not for the last three years, blessed be God for it, for I know whom I have believed, and though I feel my own weakness and unworthiness more and more, yet I am persuaded that he will never leave me nor forsake me; and so graciously does he comfort me that when my lips are closed with lock-jaw and I cannot speak a word for hours together, he enables me to sing his praises most sweetly in my heart." Now here was a man to whom the sun of all earthly comfort was set, and yet the sun of heaven shone full in his face, and he was more peaceful and happy in deep poverty and racking pain than all you or I have been in the health and strength of youth. John Howard spent his time in visiting the gaols and going from one haunt of fever to another, he was asked how he could find any ground of happiness when he was living in miserable Russian villages, or dwelling in discomfort in an hospital or a gaol. Mr. Howard's answer was very beautiful. "I hope," said he, "I have sources of enjoyment which depend not upon the particular spot I inhabit. A rightly cultivated mind, under the power of divine grace and the exercise of a benevolent disposition affords a ground of satisfaction that is not to be affected by heres and theres." Every Christian will bear you his witness that he has found his sad times to be his glad times, his losses to be his gains, his sicknesses means to promote his soul's health. Our summer does not depend upon the sun, nor our flood-tide upon the moon. We can rejoice even in death. We look forward to that happy hour when we shall close our eyes in the peaceful slumbers of death, believing that our last day will be our best day. Even the crossing of the river Jordan is but an easy task, for we shall hear him say, "Fear not; I am with thee: be not dismayed, I am thy God; when thou passest through the rivers I will be with thee, and the floods shall not overflow thee." We dare to say it, then, very boldly, we are not of all men most miserable: we would not change with unconverted men for all their riches, and their pomp, and their honor thrown into the scale.

"Go you that boast in all your stores,
And tell how bright they shine,
Your heaps of glittering dust are yours,
And my Redeemer's mine.

II. This brings us to the second point--WITHOUT THE HOPE OF ANOTHER LIFE, WE WILL ADMIT, THAT WE SHOULD BE OF ALL MEN MOST MISERABLE.

Especially was this true of the apostles. They were rejected by their countrymen; they lost all the comforts of home; their lives were spent in toil, and were daily exposed to violent death. They all of them suffered the martyr's doom, except John, who seems to have been preserved not from martyrdom, but in it. They were certainly the twelve most miserable of men apart from that hope of the world to come, which made them of all men the most happy. But this is true, dear friends, not merely of persecuted, and despised, and poverty-stricken Christians, but of all believers. We are prepared to grant it, that take away from us the hope of the world to come we should be more miserable than men without religion. The reason is very clear, if you think that the Christian has renounced those common and ordinary sources of joy from which other men drink. We must have some pleasure: it is impossible for men to live in this world without it, and I can say most truthfully I never urge any of you to do that which would make you unhappy. We must have some pleasure. Well then, there is a vessel filled with muddy filthy water which the camels' feet have stirred: shall I drink it? I see yonder a rippling stream of clear flowing water, pure as crystal and cooling as the snow of Lebanon, and I say, "No, I will not drink this foul, muddy stuff; leave that for beasts; I will drink of you clear stream." But if I be mistaken, if there be no stream yonder, if it be but the deceitful mirage, if I have been deluded, then I am worse off than those who were content with the muddy water, for they have at least some cooling draughts; but I have none at all. This is precisely the Christian's case. He passes by the pleasures of sin, and the amusements of carnal men, because he says, "I do not care for them, I find no pleasure in them: my happiness flows from the river which springs from the throne of God and flows to me through Jesus Christ--I will drink of that," but if there were no hereafter, if that were proved to be a deception, then were we more wretched than the profligate and licentious.

Again, the Christian man has learned the vanity of all earthly joys. We know when we look upon pomp that it is an empty thing. We walk through the world, not with the scorn of Diogenes, the cynical philosopher, but with something of his wisdom, and we look upon the common things in which men rejoice, and say with Solomon, "Vanity of vanities, all is vanity." And why do we say this? Why, because we have chosen eternal things in which there is no vanity, and which are satisfying to the soul. But, my brethren, it is the most unhappy piece of knowledge which a man can acquire, to know that this world is vain, if there be not another world abundantly to compensate for all our ills. There is a poor lunatic in Bedlam, plaiting straw into a crown which he puts upon his head, and calls himself a king, and mounts his mimic throne and thinks that he is monarch over all nations, and is perfectly happy in his dream. Do you think that I would undeceive him? Nay, verily, if I could, I would not. If the delusion makes the man happy, by all means let him indulge in it; but, dear friends, you and I have been undeceived; our dream of perfect bliss beneath the skies is gone for ever; what then if there be no world to come? Why then it is a most sorrowful thing for us that we have been awakened out of our sleep unless this better thing which we have chosen, this good part which shall not be taken from us, should prove to be real and true, as we do believe it is.

Moreover, the Christian man is a man who has had high, noble, and great expectations, and this is a very sad thing for us if our expectations be not fulfilled, for it makes us of all men most miserable. I have known poor men waiting and expecting a legacy. They had a right to expect it, and they have waited, and waited, and borne with poverty, and the relative has died and left them nothing; their poverty has ever afterwards seemed to be a heavier drag than before. It is an unhappy thing for a man to have large ideas and large desires, if he cannot gratify them. I believe that poverty is infinitely better endured by persons who were always poor, than by those who have been rich and have had to come down to penury, for they miss what the others never had, and what the originally poor would look upon as luxuries they consider to be necessary to their existence. The Christian has learned to think of eternity, of God, of Christ, of communion with Jesus, and if indeed it be all false, he certainly has dreamed the most magnificent of all mortal visions. Truly, if any man could prove it to be a vision, the best thing he could do would be to sit down and weep for ever to think it was not true, for the dream is so splendid, the picture of the world to come so gorgeous, that I can only say, if it be not true, it ought to be--if it be not true, then there is nothing here worth living for, my brethren, and we are disappointed wretches indeed--of all men most miserable.

The Christian, too, has learned to look upon everything here on earth as fleeting. I must confess every day this feeling grows with me. I scarce look upon my friends as living. I walk as in a land of shadows, and find nothing enduring around me. The broad arrow of the great skeleton king is, to my eye, visibly stamped everywhere. I go so often to the grave, and with those I least expected to take there, that it seems to be rather a world of dying than of living men. Well, this is a very unhappy thing--a very wretched state of mind for a man to be in, if there be no world to come. If there be no resurrection of the dead, then is the Christian indeed committed to a state of mind the most deplorable and pitiable. But, O my brethren, if there be a world to come, as faith assures us there is, how joyous it is to be weaned from the world, and to be ready to depart from it! To be with Christ is far better than to tarry in this vale of tears.

"The cords that bound my heart to earth
Are broken by his hand;
Before his cross I find myself,
A stranger in the land.
My heart is with him on his throne,
And ill can brook delay;
Each moment listening for the voice,
'Make haste, and come away.'"

May I not pant to be in my own sweet country with my own fair Lord, to see him face to face? Yet, if it be not so and there be no resurrection of the dead, "we are of all men most miserable."

III. OUR CHIEF JOY IN THE HOPE OF THE WORLD TO COME. Think of the world to come, my brethren, and let your joys begin to kindle into flames of delight, for heaven offers you all that you can desire. You are, many of you, weary of toil; so weary, perhaps, that you can scarcely enjoy the morning service because of the late hours at which you have had to work at night. Ah! there is a land of rest--of perfect rest, where the sweat of labor no more bedews the worker's brow, and fatigue is for ever banished. To those who are weary and spent, the word "rest" is full of heaven. Oh! happy truth, there remaineth a rest for the people of God. " They rest from their labors, and their works do follow them." Others of you are always in the field of battle; you are so tempted within, and so molested by foes without, that you have little or no peace. I know where your hope lies. It lies in the victory, when the banner shall be waved aloft, and the sword shall be sheathed, and you shall hear your Captain say, "Well done, good and faithful servant; thou hast fought a good fight; thou hast finished thy course: henceforth wear thou the crown of life which fadeth not away." Some of you are tossed about with many troubles; you go from care to care, from loss to loss: it seems to you as if all God's waves and billows had gone over you; but you shall soon arrive at the land of happiness, where you shall bathe your weary soul in seas of heavenly rest, You shall have no poverty soon; no mud-hovel, no rags, nor hunger. "In my Father's house are many mansions," and there shall you dwell, satisfied with favor, and full of every blessing. You have had bereavement after bereavement; the wife has been carried to the tomb, the children have followed, father and mother are gone, and you have few left to love you here; but you are going to the land where graves are unknown things, where they never see a shroud, and the sound of the mattock and the spade are never heard; you are going to your Father's house in the land of the immortal, in the country of the hereafter, in the home of the blessed, in the habitation of God Most High, in the Jerusalem which is above, the mother of us all. Is not this your best joy, that you are not to be here for ever, that you are not to dwell eternally in this wilderness, but shall soon inherit Canaan? With all God's people their worst grief is sin. I would not care for any sorrow, if I could live without sinning. Oh! if I were rid of the appetites of the flesh and the lusts thereof, and the desires which continually go astray, I would be satisfied to lie in a dungeon and rot there, so as to be delivered from the corruption of sin. Well but, brethren, we shall soon attain unto perfection. The body of this death will die with this body. There is no temptation in heaven, for the dog of hell can never cross the stream of death; there are no corruptions there, for they have washed their robes and made them white in the blood of the Lamb; there shall by no means enter into that kingdom anything which defileth. Methinks as I hear the joyous song of the glorified this morning, as I catch floating down from heaven the sound of that music which is like many waters and like the great thunder, and as I hear the harmony of those notes which are sweet as harpers harping with their harps, my soul desireth to stretch her wings, and fly straight to yonder worlds of joy. I know it is so with you, my brethren in the tribulation of Christ--as you wipe the sweat your brow, is not this the comfort: there is rest for the people of God? As you stand out against temptation and suffer for Christ's sake, is not this your comfort: " If we suffer with him, we shall also reign with him." When you are slandered and despised by men, is not this your hope: "He will remember me when he cometh into his kingdom. I shall sit upon his throne, even as he has overcome, and sitteth down upon his Father's throne?" Oh! yes, this is the music to which Christians dance; this is the wine which maketh glad their hearts; this is the banquet at which they feast. There is another and a better land, and we, though we sleep with the clods of the valley, shall in our flesh see God, when our Redeemer shall stand in the latter days upon the earth. I think you catch my drift--we are not of all men most miserable; apart from the future hope we should be, for our hope in Christ for the future is the mainstay of our joy.

IV. Now, dear friends, this brings me to a practical observation in the fourth place, which is, that THUS THE FUTURE OPERATES UPON THE PRESENT.

I had some time ago a conversation with a very eminent man whose fame is familiar to you all, but whose name I do not feel justified in mentioning, who was once a professed believer but is now full of scepticism. He said to me in the course of our argument, "Why, how foolish you are, and all the company of preachers. You tell people to think about the next world, when the best thing they could do would be to behave themselves as well as they can in this!" I granted the truth of the observation; it would be very unwise to make people neglect the present, for it is of exceeding great importance, but I went on to show him that the very best method to make people attend to the present was by impressing them with high and noble motives with regard to the future. The potent force of the world to come supplies us through the Holy Spirit with force for the proper accomplishment of the duties of this life. Here is a man who has a machine for the manufacture of hardware. He wants steam power to work this machine. An engineer puts up a steam engine in a shed at some considerable distance. "Well," saith the other, "I asked you to bring steam power here, to operate upon my machine." "That is precisely," says he, "what I have done. I put the steam engine there, you have but to connect it by a band and your machine works as fast as you like; it is not necessary that I should put the boiler, and the fire, and the engine close to the work, just under your nose: only connect the two, and the one will operate upon the other." So God has been pleased to make our hopes of the future a great engine wherewith the Christian man may work the ordinary machine of every-day life, for the band of faith connects the two, and makes all the wheels of ordinary life revolve with rapidity and regularity. To speak against preaching the future as though it would make people neglect the present is absurd. It is as though somebody should say, "There, take away the moon, and blot out the sun. What is the use of them--they are not in this world?" Precisely so, but take away the moon and you have removed the tides, and the sea becomes a stagnant, putrid pool. Then take away the sun--it is not in the world--take it away, and light, and heat, and life; everything is gone. What the sun and moon are to this natural world, the hope of the future is to the Christian in this world. It is his light--he looks upon all things in that light, and sees them truly. It is his heat; it gives him zeal and energy. It is his very life: his Christianity, his virtue would expire if it were not for the hope of the world to come. Do you believe, my brethren, that apostles and martyrs would ever have sacrificed their lives for truth's sake if they had not looked for a hereafter? In the heat of excitement, the soldier may die for honor, but to die in tortures and mockeries in cold blood needs a hope beyond the grave. Would you poor man go toiling on year after year, refusing to sacrifice his conscience for gain; would yon poor needle-girl refuse to become the slave of lust if she did not see something brighter than earth can picture to her as the reward of sin? O my brethren, the most practical thing in all the world is the hope of the world to come; and you see the text teaches this, for it is just this which keeps us from being miserable; and to keep a man from being miserable, let me say, is to do a great thing for him, for a miserable Christian--what is the use of him? Keep him in a cupboard, where nobody can see him; nurse him in the hospital, for he is of no use in the field of labor. Build a monastery, and put all miserable Christians in it, and there let them meditate on mercy till they learn to smile; for really there is no other use for them in the world, But the man who has a hope of the next world goes about his work strong, for the joy of the Lord is our strength. He goes against, temptation mighty, for the hope of the next world repels the fiery darts of the adversary. He can labor without present reward, for he looks for a reward in the world to come. He can suffer rebuke, and can afford to die a slandered man, because he knows that God will avenge his own elect who cry day and night unto him. Through the Spirit of God the hope of another world is the most potent force for the product of virtue; it is a fountain of joy; it is the very channel of usefulness. It is to the Christian what food is to the vital force in the animal frame. Let it be said of any of us, that we are dreaming about the future and forgetting the present, but let the future sanctify the present to highest uses. I fear our prophetical brethren err here. They are reading continually about the last vials, the seventy weeks of Daniel, and a number of other mysteries; I wish they would set to work instead of speculating so much, or speculate even more if they will, but turn their prophecies to present practical account. Prophetical speculations too often lead men away from present urgent duty, and especially from contending earnestly for the faith once delivered to the saints; but a hope of the world to come is, I think, the best practical power which a Christian can have.

V. And now, to conclude, this will let us see very clearly WHAT OUR FUTURE IS TO BE.

There are some persons here to whom my text has nothing whatever to say. Suppose there were no hereafter, would they be more miserable? Why, no; they would be more happy. If anybody could prove to them that death is an eternal sleep, it would be the greatest consolation that they could possibly receive, It it could be shown, to a demonstration, that as soon as people die they rot in the grave and there is an end of them--why some of you could go to bed at night comfortable, your conscience would never disturb you, you would be molested by none of those terrible fears which now haunt you. Do you see, then, this proves that you are not a Christian; this proves as plainly as twice two make tour, that you are no believer in Christ; for if you were, the taking away of a hereafter would make you miserable. Since it would not tend to make you happy to believe in a future state, this proves that you are no believer in Christ. Well, then, what have Ito say to you? Why just this--that in the world to come, you will be of all men most miserable. "What will become of you?" said an infidel once to a Christian man, "supposing there should be no heaven?" "Well," said he, "I like to have two strings to my bow. If there be no hereafter I am as well off as you are; if there be I am infinitely better off. But where are you? Where are you?" Why then we must read this text in the future--"If in this life there be indeed a hope of a life to come, then you shall be in the next life of all men most miserable." Do you see where you will be? Your soul goes before the great Judge, and receives its condemnation and begins its hell. The trumpet rings; heaven and earth are astonished; the grave heaves; yonder slab of marble is lifted up, and up you rise in that very flesh and blood in which you sinned, and there you stand in the midst of a terrified multitude, all gathered to their doom. The Judge has come. The great assize has commenced. There on the great white throne sits the Savior who once said, "Come unto me, ye weary, and I will give you rest;" but now he sits there as a Judge and opens with stern hand the terrible volume. Page after page he reads, and as he reads he gives the signal, "Depart, ye cursed, into everlasting fire," and the angels bind up the fares in bundles to burn them. There stand you, and you know your doom; you already begin to feel it. You cry to the lofty Alps to fall upon you and conceal you. "O ye mountains, can ye not find in your rocky bowels some friendly cavern where I may be hidden from the face of him who sits upon the throne?" In terrible silence the mountains refuse your petition and the rocks reject your cry. You would plunge into the sea, but it is licked up with tongues of fire; you would fain make your bed even in hell if you could escape from those dreadful eyes, but you cannot; for now your turn is come, that page is turned over which records your history; the Savior reads with a voice of thunder and with eyes of lightning. He reads, and as he waves his hand you are cast away from hope. You shall then know what it is to be of all men most miserable. Ye had your pleasure; ye had your giddy hour; ye had your mirthful moments; you despised Christ, and you would not turn at his rebuke; you would not have him to reign over you; you lived his adversary; you died unreconciled, and now where are you? Now, what will ye do, ye who forget God, in that day when he shall tear you in pieces, and there shall be none to deliver you? In the name of my Lord and Master I do conjure you, fly away to Christ for refuge. "He that believeth in him shall be saved." To believe is to trust; and whosoever this morning is enabled by faith to cast himself upon Christ, need not fear to live, nor fear to die, You shall not be miserable here; you shall be thrice blessed hereafter if you trust my Lord.

"Come, guilty souls, and flee away
To Christ, and heal your wounds;
This is the welcome gospel-day
Wherein free grace abounds."

O that ye would be wise and consider your latter end! O that ye would reflect that this life is but a span, and the life to come lasts on for ever! Do not, I pray you, fling away eternity; play not the fool with such solemn things as these, but in serious earnestness lay hold upon eternal life. Look to the bleeding Savior; see there his five wounds, and his face bedewed with bloody sweat! Trust him, trust him, and you are saved. The moment that you trust him your sins are gone. His righteousness is yours; you are saved on the spot, and you shall be saved when he cometh in his kingdom to raise the dead from their graves. O that the Lord might lead us all thus to rest on Jesus, now and ever. Amen.

The Barley Field on Fire

A Sermon (No. 563)
Delivered on Sunday Morning,, April 3rd, by the
Rev. C. H. SPURGEON,
At the Metropolitan Tabernacle, Newington

"Absalom sent for Joab, to have sent him to the king; but he would not come to him; and when he sent again, the second time, he would not come. Therefore he said unto his servants, See, Joab's field is near mine, and he hath barley there: Go and set it on fire. And Absalom's servants set the field on fire. Then Joab arose, and came to Absalom unto his house, and said unto him, Wherefore have thy servants set my field on fire?" -- 2 Samuel 14:29-31.

YOU REMEMBER the historical narrative. Absalom had fled from Jerusalem under fear of David's anger. He was after a time permitted to return; but he was not admitted into the presence of the king. Earnestly desiring to be restored to his former posts of honor and favor, he besought Joab to come to him, intending to request him to act as mediator. Joab, having lost much of his liking for the young prince, refused to come; and, though he was sent for repeatedly, he declined to attend at his desire. Absalom therefore thought of a most wicked, but most effective plan of bringing Joab into his company. He bade his servants set Joab's field of barley on fire. This brought Joab down in high wrath to ask the question, "Wherefore have thy servants set my field on fire?" This was all that Absalom wanted; he wished an interview, and he was not scrupulous as to the method by which he obtained it. The burning of the barley-field brought Joab into his presence, and Absalom's ends were accomplished.

Omitting the sin of the deed, we have here a picture of what is often done by our gracious God, with the wisest and best design. Often he sendeth for us, not for his profit, but for ours. He would have us come near to him and receive a blessing at his hands; but we are foolish and cold-hearted and wicked, and we will not come. He, knowing that we will not come by any other means, sendeth a serious trial: he sets our barley-field on fire; which he has a right to do, seeing our barley-fields are far more his than they are ours. In Absalom's case it was wrong; in God's case he has a right to do as he wills with his own. He takes away from us our most choice delight, upon which we have set our heart, and then we inquire at his hands, "Wherefore contendest thou with me? Why am I thus smitten with thy rod? What have I done to provoke thee to anger?" And thus we are brought into the presence of God, and we receive blessings of infinitely more value than those temporary mercies which the Lord had taken from us. You will see, then, how I intend to use my text this morning. As the pastor of so large a church as this, I am constantly brought into contact with all sorts of human sorrow. Frequently it is poverty,--poverty too which is not brought on by idleness or vice, but real poverty and most distressing and afflicting poverty too, because it visits those who have fought well the battle of life, and have struggled hard for years, and yet in their old age scarce know where bread shall come from, except that they rest upon the promise--"Thy bread shall be given thee, and thy water shall be sure." Messengers come to me sometimes as fast as they came to Job, bearing sad tidings concerning one and another of you. There comes one--"I entreat your prayers for me, sir: God has been pleased to take away my wife with a stroke; she now lies in the cold grave." Another cries, "O sir, my wife is sore sick, and the physician saith that there is but little hope: pray for her, that she may be strengthened in the hour of her departure; and for me, that I may be enabled to kiss the Master's rod." Then comes another--"My son is afflicted; he is to undergo a painful operation: pray that the surgeon's knife may not be his death, but that he may be enabled to bear up under it." And when I have sympathized with a company of sad complaints like these, another set of messengers will be waiting at the door. How few families are long without severe trials! hardly a person escapes for any long season without tribulation. With impartial hand sorrow knocks at the door of the palace and the cottage. Why all this? The Lord, we know, "Doth not afflict willingly, nor grieve the children of men" for naught; why can it be that he employs so many frowning servants, and sendeth out so often his usher of the black rod? Wherefore can it be? Perhaps I may be able to give the fitting answer to this very proper inquiry, and it may be that I may be as serviceable to the afflicted as the jailer was to Paul and Silas when he washed their stripes.

I shall use my text, first of all, in reference to believers; and then, with regard to the unconverted. Oh for help from above!

I. First of all, brethren, let us use the text WITH REFERENCE TO BELIEVERS IN CHRIST.

My beloved brethren and sisters in Jesus Christ, we cannot expect to avoid tribulation. If other men's barley-fields are not burned, ours will be. If the Father uses the rod nowhere else, he will surely make his true children smart. As Paul saith, and as our hymnster hath rhymed it--

"Bastards may escape the rod,
Sunk in earthly vain delight,
But the true-born child of God,
Must not--would not if he might."

Your Saviour hath left you a double legacy, "In the world ye shall have tribulation; but in me ye shall have peace." You enjoy peace; you must not expect that you shall escape without the privilege of the tribulation. All wheat must be threshed: and God's threshing-floor witnesses to the weight of the flail as much as any other. Gold must be tried in the fire; and truly the Lord hath a fire in Zion, and his furnace in Jerusalem.

But you, beloved, have four very special comforts in all your trouble. You have, first, this sweet reflection, that there is no curse in your cross. Christ was made a curse for us, and we call his cross the accursed tree; but, truly, since Jesus hung upon it, it is most blessed; and I may now say concerning the cross of affliction, "Blessed is every man who hangeth on this tree." The cross may be very heavy, especially while it is green, and our shoulders unused to carrying it; but remember, though there may be a ton-weight of sorrow in it, there is not a single ounce of the curse in it. God doth never punish his children in the sense of avenging justice: he chastens as a father does his child, but he doth never punish his redeemed as a judge doth a criminal. It were unjust to exact punishment in their place and stead. How shall the Lord punish twice for one offence? If Christ took my sins and stood as my substitute, then there is no wrath of God for me; and though my cup may be bitter, yet there cannot be a single drop of the wormwood of Almighty wrath in it. I may have to smart, but it will never be beneath the lictor's rods of justice, but under the Parent's rod of wisdom. O Christian! how sweet this ought to be to you! There was a time when you were under conviction of sin,--when you thought you would rot in a dungeon or burn at the stake most cheerfully, if you could but get rid of the sense of God's wrath; and will you now become impatient? The wrath of God is the thunderbolt which scathes the soul; and now that you are delivered from that tremendous peril, you must not be overwhelmed with the few showers and gales which Providence sends you. A God of love inflicts our sorrows: he is as good when he chastens as when he caresses: there is no more wrath in his afflicting providences than in his deeds of bounty. God may seem unkind to unbelief, but faith can always see love in his heart. Oh! what a mercy that Sinai has ceased to thunder! Lord, let Jesus say what he will, so long as Moses is quieted forever. Strike, Lord, if thou wilt, now that thou hast heard the Saviour's plea and justified our souls.

You have, secondly, another ground of comfort; namely, that your troubles are all apportioned to you by divine wisdom and love. As for their number, if He appoint them ten, they never can be eleven. As for their weight, He who weigheth the mountains in scales and the hills in a balance, takes care to measure your troubles, and you shall not have a grain more than his infinite wisdom sees fit. The devil may seem to be turned loose upon you, but remember he is always a chained enemy. There is a tether to every trouble, and beyond that tether it can never stray. Nebuchadnezzar may heat the furnace seven times hotter than usual, but God's thermometer measures the exact degree of heat; and beyond it the flame cannot rage, even though a thousand Nebuchadnezzars should swear themselves out of breath in their fury. Consider everything that you have to suffer as the appointment of wisdom, ruled by love, and you will rejoice in all your tribulation, knowing that it shall reveal to you the loving-kindness and wisdom of your God.

You have a third consolation; namely, that under your cross you have many special comforts. There are cordials which God giveth to sick saints which he never putteth to the lips of those who are in health. Dark caverns keep not back the miners, if they know that diamonds are to be found there: you need not fear suffering, when you remember what riches it yields to your soul. There is no hearing the nightingale without night, and there are some promises which only sing to us in trouble. It is in the cellar of affliction that the good old wine of the kingdom is stored. You shall never see Christ's face so well as when all others turn their backs upon you. When you have come into such confusion that human wisdom is at a nonplus, then shall you see God's wisdom manifest and clear. Oh the love-visits which Christ payeth to his people when they are in the prison of their trouble! Then he layeth bare his very heart to them, and comforts them as a mother doth her child. They sleep daintily who have Jesus to make their beds. Suffering saints are generally the most flourishing saints; and well they may be, for they are Jesus' special care. If you would find a man whose lips drop with pearls, look for one who has been in the deep waters. We seldom learn much except as it is beaten into us by the rod in Christ's schoolhouse, under Madam Trouble. God's vines owe more to the pruning-knife than to any other tool in the garden; superfluous shoots are sad spoilers of the vines. But even while we carry it, the cross brings present comfort: it is a dear, dear cross, all hung with roses, and dripping with sweet-smelling myrrh. Rutherford seemed at times in doubt which he loved best, Christ or his cross; but then, good man, he only loved the cross for his Lord's sake. Humble souls count it a high honor to be thought worthy to suffer for Christ's sake. If ever heaven be opened at all to the gaze of mortals, the vision is granted to those who dwell in the Patmos of want and trouble. Furnace-joys glow quite as warmly as furnace-flames. Sweet are the uses of adversity, and sweet are its accompaniments when the Lord is with his people.

"Mid the gloom the vivid lightnings
With increasing brightness play;
'Mid the thorn-brake beauteous flowrets
Look more beautiful and gay.
So, in darkest dispensations
Doth my faithful Lord appear,
With his richest consolations,
To reanimate and cheer."

But then,--and this is the point to which my text brings me, and all I have already said is going astray from it,--you have this comfort, that your trials work your lasting good by bringing you nearer and nearer to God. This point we will illustrate by the narrative before us. My dear friends in Christ Jesus, our heavenly Father often sends for us and we will not come. He sends for us to exercise a more simple faith in him. We have believed, and by faith we have passed from death unto life, but our faith sometimes staggers. We have not yet reached to Abraham's confidence in God; we do not leave our worldly cares with him, but, like Martha, we cumber ourselves with much serving. We have faith to lay hold upon little promises; but we are ofttimes afraid to open our mouths wide though God has promised to fill them. He therefore sendeth to us. "Come, my child," saith he; "come and trust me. The veil is rent: enter into my presence, and approach boldly to the throne of my grace. I am worthy of thy fullest confidence: cast thy cares on me. Come thou into the sunlight, and read thy title clear. Shake thyself from the dust of thy cares, and put on thy beautiful garment of faith. " But, alas! though called with tones of love to the blessed exercise of this comforting grace, we will not come. At another time he calls us to closer communion with himself. We have been sitting on the doorstep of God's house, and he bids us advance into the banqueting-hall and sup with him; but we decline the honor. He has admitted us into the inner chambers, but there are secret rooms not yet opened to us; he invites us to enter them, but we hold back. Jesus longs to have near communion with his people. This is that which gives him "to see of the travail of his soul, and to be satisfied." It must be a joy to a Christian to be with Christ; but it is also a joy to Jesus to be with his people, for it is written, "His delights were with the sons of men." Now, one would think that if Christ did but beckon with his finger and say to us, "Draw nigh, and commune with me," we should fly as though we had wings to our feet; but, instead thereof, we are cleaving to the dust: we have too much business; we have too many carking cares; and we forget to come, though it is our Beloved's voice which calls us to himself. Frequently the call is to more fervent prayer. Do you not feel in yourself, at certain seasons, an earnest longing for private prayer? You have felt as if you could not be at ease until you could draw near unto God and tell him your wants; and yet, may be, you have quenched the Spirit in that respect, and still have continued without nearness of access to God. Every day the Lord bids his people come to him and ask what they will, and it shall be done. He is a bounteous God, who sits upon the mercy-seat, and he delights to give to his people the largest desires of their hearts; and yet, shame upon us, we live without exercising this power of prayer, and we miss the plentitude of blessing which would come out of that cornucopia of grace,--prevailing prayer with God. Ah, brethren, we are verily guilty here, the most of us. The Master sendeth to us to pray, and we will not come. Often, too, he calls us to a higher state of piety. From this pulpit I have labored to stir you up to nobler attainments; I have besought you to rest no longer satisfied with your dwarfish attainments, but to press forward to things more sublime and heavenly. Have I not cried unto you, beloved, and bid you

"Forget the steps already trod,
And onward urge your way."

I am persuaded there are Christians as much in grace beyond ordinary Christians as ordinary Christians are beyond the profane. There are heights which common eyes have never seen, much less scaled. Oh! there are nests among the stars where God's own saints dwell, and yet how many of us are content to go creeping along like worms in the dust! Would that we had grace to cleave the clouds and mount into the pure blue sky of fellowship with Christ! We do not serve God as we should. We are cold as ice, when we should be like molten metal, burning our way through all opposition. We are like the barren Sahara, when we should be blooming like the garden of the Lord. We give to God pence, when he deserveth pounds; nay, deserveth our heart's blood to be coined in the service of his church and of his truth. Oh! we are but poor lovers of our sweet Lord Jesus; not fit to be his servants, much less to be his brides. If he had put us in the kitchen to be scullions, I fear we are scarce fit for the service; and yet he hath exalted us to be bone of his bone and flesh of his flesh, married to him by a glorious marriage covenant. O brethren! God often calleth us to higher degrees of piety, and yet we will not come.

Now, why is it that we permit the Lord to send for us so often, without going to him? Let your own heart give the reason, in a humble confession of your offenses. O my brethren, we never thought we should have been so bad as we are. If an angel had told us that we should be so indifferent towards Christ, we should have said, as Hazael did to Elisha, "Is thy servant a dog, that he should do this great thing?" If any of us could have seen our own history written out by a prophet's pen, we should have said, "No; it cannot be. If Christ forgives me, I must love him; if he be pleased to make me his own brother, I must serve him; if I am the recipient of such splendid mercies, I must do something commensurate with his bounty." And yet, hitherto, here we have been ungrateful, unbelieving, and even refusing to listen to his call, or come at his bidding. He has said, "Seek ye my face;" and our heart did not say, "Lord, thy face will I seek." Because of all this, because we will not listen to the gentle call of God, there cometh trouble, just as there came the burning of the barley-field of Joab because he would not visit the young prince. Trouble comes in all sorts of shapes. Little doth it matter what form it cometh in, if it doth answer the purpose of making us obey the divine calling.

Some Christians have their trial in the shape of sickness: they drag about with them a diseased body all their lives; or they are suddenly cast upon a bed of sickness, and they toss to and fro, by night and by day, in pain and weariness. This is God's medicine; and when God's children have it, let them not think it is sent to kill them, but to heal them. Much medicine which the physician gives makes the man ill for a time: he is worse with it than he would have been without it; but if he be a clever physician, he knows that this is the consequence of the medicine; and thus he is not at all alarmed by the pain of his patient, but he expects that all this will work for good, and hunt out, as it were, the original disease. When the Lord sends us sore sickness, it for a time perhaps makes our former spiritual infirmities grow worse; for sickness often provoketh impatience and murmurings against God, but in due time our proud spirits will be broken, and we shall cry for mercy. As a file takes off rust, so does sickness frequently remove our deadness of heart. The diamond hath much cutting, but its value is increased thereby; and so with the believer under the visitations of God. I have heard say of many ministers that they preach best after sickness, till their people have scarce regretted all the pains they have felt when they have found how savory and full of marrow have been their words. My brother, if you will not come to God without it, he will send you a sick-bed that you may be carried on it to him. If you will not come running, he will make you come limping. If you will not come while your eyes are bright and while your countenance is full of health, he will make you come when your eyes are dull and heavy, and your complexion is sallow and sad. But come you must; and if by no other means, sickness shall be the black chariot in which you shall ride.

Losses, too, are frequently the means God uses to fetch home his wandering sheep: like fierce dogs, they worry the wanderers back to the shepherd. There is no making lions tame if they are too well fed; they must be brought down from their great strength, and their stomachs must be lowered a bit, and then they will submit to the tamer's hand: and often have we seen the Christian rendered obedient to his Lord's will by straitness of bread and hard labor. When rich and increased in goods, many professors carry their heads much too loftily and speak much too boastfully. Like David, they boast, "My mountain standeth fast; it shall never be moved." When the Christian groweth wealthy, is in good repute, hath good health, and a happy family, he too often admits Mr. Carnal Security to feast at his table. If he be a true child of God, there is a rod preparing for him. Wait awhile, and it may be you will see his substance melt away as a dream. There goes a portion of his estate--how soon the acres change hands! There goes a part of his business--no profits will ever come to him again in that direction. That debt yonder, a dishonored bill over there--how fast his losses come! where will they end? Now, as these embarrassments come in one after another, he begins to be distressed about them, and betakes himself to his God. O blessed waves, that wash the man on the rock of salvation! O blessed cords, though they may cut the flesh, if they draw us to Jesus! Losses in business are often sanctified to our soul's enriching. If you will not come to the Lord full-handed, you shall come empty. If God in his grace findeth no other means of making you to honor him

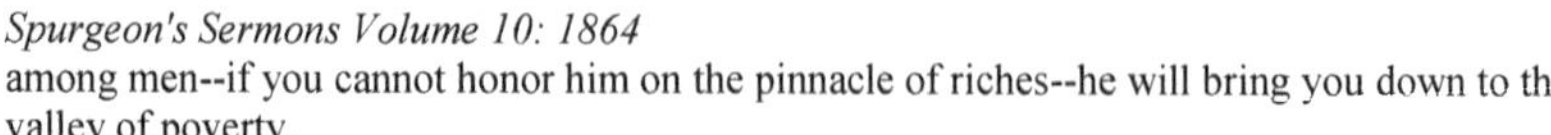

among men--if you cannot honor him on the pinnacle of riches--he will bring you down to the valley of poverty.

Bereavements, too,--ah! what sharp cuts of the rod we get with these, my brethren! We know how the Lord sanctifies these to the bringing of his people near to himself. How glad we should be to think that Christ himself once suffered bereavements as we have done. Tacitus tells us that an amber ring was thought to be of no value among the Romans till the emperor took to wearing one, and then straightway an amber ring was held in high esteem. Bereavements might be looked upon as very sad things; but when we recollect that Jesus wept over his friend Lazarus, henceforth they are choice jewels, and special favors from God. Christ wore this ring: then I must not blush to wear it. Many a mother has been stirred up to a holier life by the death of her infant,--many a husband has been led to give his heart more to Christ by the death of his wife. Do not departed spirits, like angels, beckon us up to heaven? "Come, come away," they say; "this is not your rest. I once could build upon the same tree, and sing upon the same bough; but now I am taken from you,--now I rest in heaven. Come hither, thou who wast once my fond mate--come hither, for all the trees where thou are building are marked for the axe; therefore come now, and dwell with me!" Yes, we must look upon our new-made graves in this light, and pray the Lord to dig our hearts with the funeral spade, and bury our sins as we bury our departed ones. Trials in your family, in your children, are another form of the burning barley-field. I do not know, brethren, but I think a living cross is much heavier to carry than a dead one. I know some among you who have not lost your children: I could have wished you had, for they have lived to be your grief and sorrow. Ah, young man! better that your mother should have seen you perish in the birth than that you should live to disgrace your father's name. Ah, man! it were better for you that the procession had gone winding through the streets, bearing your corpse down to the grave, than that you should live to blaspheme your mother's God, and laugh at the Book which is her treasure. It were better for you that you had never been born, and better for your parents too. Ah! but, dear friends, even these are meant to draw us nearer to Christ. We must not make idols of our children; and we dare not do it, when we see how manifestly God shows us that, like ourselves, they are by nature children of wrath. Sharper than an adder's tooth is an unthankful child; but the venom is turned to medicine in God's hand. God's birds would often keep down in the grass in their nests; but he fills their nests full of thorns, and then up they fly, and sing as a lark as they mount towards heaven. You must look upon these family trials as invitations from God--sweet compulsion to make you seek his face. Many are afflicted in another way, which is perhaps as bad as anything else,--by a deep depression of spirit. They are always melancholy; they know not why. There are no stars in the night for them, and the sun gives no light by day: melancholy has marked them for her own; but even this, I think, is often the means of keeping some of them nearer to God than they would be. You know there are some of our English plants which greatly affect damp, moist places under trees. If the sun were to shine in their faces they would die. Perhaps some minds are of the same order. Too many sweets make children sick, and bitters are a good tonic. A veil is needed for some delicate complexions, lest the sun look too fiercely on them: it may be, these mourners need the veil of sorrow. It is good that they have been afflicted, even with this heavy depression of spirit, because it keeps them near their God. Then there is that other affliction, the hiding of God's countenance--how hard to bear, but how beneficial! If we will not keep near to our Lord, he is sure to hide his face. You have seen a mother walking out with her little child, when it has just learned to walk; and as she goes through the street, the little one is for running sometimes to the right, and sometimes to the left, and so the mother hides herself a moment; then the child looketh round for the mother, and begins to cry, and then out comes the mother. What is the effect? Why, it will not run away from the mother any more: it is sure to keep hold of her hand afterwards. So, when we get wandering from God, he hides his face, and then, since we have a love for him, we begin crying after him; and when he shows his face once more, we cling to him the more lovingly ever afterwards. So the Lord is pleased to bless our troubles to us.

Now, Christian, what about all this? Why, just this. Are you under any sharp trouble now? Then I pray you go to God as Joab went to Absalom. "Wherefore have thy servants set my field on fire?" "Show me wherefore thou contendest with me." "Search me, O God, and know my heart; try me, and know my thoughts; and see if there be any wicked way in me, and lead me in the way everlasting." Make this a special season of humbling and heart-searching. Now let every besetting sin be driven out. When God sweeps, do you search. When you are under the rod, it is yours to make a full confession of past offenses, and pray to be delivered from their power in the future. Or, have you no trial to-day, my brother? Then see if there be not something which may provoke God to send one, and begin now to purge yourself from all filthiness of the flesh and of the spirit by the Holy Ghost. Prevention is better than a cure; and sometimes a timely heart-searching may save us many a heart-smarting. Let us see to that, then. Or have we been afflicted, and is the affliction over now? Then, let us say with David, "Before I was afflicted I went astray; but now have I kept thy word." Let us bless God for all that he has done, saying "It is good for me that I have been afflicted;" let us join together in one common hymn of praise for all the loving-kindness which God has been pleased to show us in the sharp cuts of his rod. I have said enough, I think, to the Christian, to work out the little picture before us. God has burned your barley-field, dear friends: now go to him, and the closer you can approach to him, and the more firmly you can cling to him, the better for your soul's health and comfort all your life. At the last, you and I shall sing to the praise of our afflicting God.

All I meet I find assists me
In my path to heavenly joy;
Where, though trials now attend me,
Trials never more annoy.
Blest there with a weight of glory,
Still the path I'll ne'er forget,
But, exulting, cry, It led me
To my blessed Saviour's seat.

II. A few words--God make them mighty--TO THE SINNER shall form the second part of our discourse. God also has sent for you. O unconverted man! God has often sent for you. Early in your childhood your mother's prayers sought to woo you to a Saviour's love, and your godly father's first instructions were as so many meshes of the net in which it was desired that you should be taken; but you have broken through all these, and lived to sin away early impressions and youthful promises. Since that you have often been called under the ministry. Our sermons have not been all shots wide of the mark, but sometimes a hot shot has burnt its way into your conscience and you have been made to tremble; but, alas! the trembling soon gave way before your old sins. Hitherto you have been called, but you refused. The hands of mercy have been stretched out, and you have not regarded them. You have had calls, too, from your Bible, from religious books, from Christian friends. Holy zeal is not altogether dead, and it shows itself by looking after your welfare. Young man, your shopmate has sometimes spoken to you; young woman, your companion has wept over you. There are some of you now present who have been called by the most loving of voices, in connection with our classes. Both in our Sunday-school and in the catechumenical classes there are men and women with deep love to the souls of those committed to them,--tender hearts, weeping eyes,--and you have been wept over that you might come to Christ; but still all the agency that has been employed has been up to this moment without effect; you are a stranger to the God who made you, and an enemy to Christ the Saviour.

Well, if these gentle means will not do, God will employ other agencies. Perhaps he has tried them already. If not,--if he intendeth in the divine decree your eternal salvation,--he will, as sure as you are a living man, use stronger ways with you; and if a word will not do, he will come with a blow, though he loveth to try the power of the word first. You, too, my hearer unconverted and unsaved, have had your trials. You weep as well as Christians. You may not weep for sin, but sin shall make you weep. You may abhor repentance because of its sorrow, but you shall not escape sorrow, even if you escape repentance. you have had your sickness. Do you remember it, when in the silent night you heard the watch ticking out, as you thought, your last few minutes, and foretelling your doom? Do you remember those weary days, when you tossed from side to side, and did but shift the place and keep the pain? Man, can you recollect your vows, which you have lived to break, and your promises with which you lied unto the eternal God? Then the Sabbath would be your delight, you said, if you were spared, and the house of God and the people of God should be dear to you, and you would seek his face. But you have not done so: you have broken your covenant, and have despised your promise made to God. Or, what is it, have you had losses in business? You began life well and hopefully, but nothing has prospered with you. I am not sorry for it; for I remember it is the wicked who spreadeth himself like a green bay tree, and it is concerning the reprobate that it is written, "There are no bands in their death; but their strength is firm. They are not in trouble as other men; neither are they plagued like other men." I am glad that you are plagued. I would sooner see you whipped to heaven than coached to hell. Doubtless many go, like Agag, delicately to their hewing in pieces, while others go sorrowing to eternal glory. You have had losses: what are these but God's rough messengers to tell you that there is nothing beneath the sky worth living for, to wean you from the breasts of earth and cause you to look for something more substantial than worldly riches can afford you? And you, too, have lost friends; may I recall those graves, whose turf is yet so newly laid? May I remind you of children fair and beautiful in your eyes, taken away from you despite your tears? Shall I remind you of the parent who sleeps in Jesus? of a sweet sister who withered like a lily by early consumption? Shall I bring these thoughts back to you? I would not wish to make your wounds bleed afresh, but it is for your good that I bid you

hearken to their solemn voice; for they say to you, "Come to your God. Be reconciled to him!" I do not think you ever will come to Jesus, unless the Holy Spirit shall employ trials to bring you. I find that the woman never found her piece of money till she swept the house. The prodigal never came back till he was hungry, and fain would have filled his belly with the husks which the swine did eat. I only hope that these troubles may be blessed to you. Besides this, you have had your depression of spirit. If I mistake not, I address some who are under such depressions now. You do not know how it is, but nothing is pleasant to you. You went to the theater last night. You wished you had not: it gave you no joy; and yet you have been as merry there as any, in former times. You go among your companions, and a day's pleasuring, as they call it, has become to you a very painful waste of time. You have lost the zest of life; and I am not sorry for it, if it should make you look for a better life, and trust in a world to come. My friends, again I say, this is the burning of your barley-fields. God has sent for you, and you would not come; and now he has sent messengers who are not so easily refused. He has sent these with sterner and rougher words, which speak to your flesh, if your spirit will not hear.

Well, now, what then? If God is sending these, are you listening to them? My hearer, if God has sent these, have you listened to them? There are some of you of whom I almost despair. God can save you, but I cannot tell you how he will do it. Certainly the Word does not seem likely to be blessed. You have been called and entreated; early and late we have entreated you. Our hearts have yearned with tenderness for you, but hitherto in vain. God knows I have been hammering away at the granite, and it has not yielded yet; I have smitten the flint, and it is not broken. Some of you all but break the plowshare: you are such rocks that it seems in vain to plow upon you. As for trouble, I do not see that that is likely to do you any good; for if you are smitten again, you will revolt more and more. The whole head is sick already, and the whole heart is faint. You have been beaten, till from the crown of the head to the sole of your foot there is nothing but wounds, bruises, and putrifying sores. You are poor--perhaps your drunkenness has made you so; you have lost your wife--perhaps your cruelty helped to kill her; you have lost your children, and you are left a penniless, friendless, helpless beggar, and yet you will not turn to God! What now is to be done unto you? O Ephraim! what shall I do unto thee? Shall I give thee up? How can I give thee up? "How shall I make thee as Admah? how shall I set thee as Zeboim?" The heart of mercy still yearns after thee. Return thou! return thou! God help thee to return, even now.

Others of you have not suffered all this in the past, but are just now enduring a part of it. Let me entreat you, by the mercies of God and by the blood of our Lord Jesus Christ, that you despise not him who speaketh unto you. God doth not continue to send his messengers forever. After he hath labored with you for a time, he will leave you to cursing. Long-suffering lasts not forever. Mercy hath its day. Behold, the King runs up the white flag of comfort to-day, and he invites you to come unto him. To-morrow he may run up the red flag of threatening; and if that answereth not, if that red flag will not make you turn, he will run up the black flag of execution, and then there will be no hope. Beware! The black flag is not run up yet: the red flag is there now in trials and troubles, which are God's threatenings to you, bidding you open wide your heart that grace may enter; but if it cometh to this that the red flag fail, the black flag must come. Perhaps it has come! God help you with broken heart to cry unto him that you may be saved, before the candle is blown out and the sun is set, and the night of the dead is come on without the hope of another sun rising on a blessed resurrection.

What is the drift of all this? My drift is this: If, now, a word of mine could make you come to the King this morning--I know it will not unless God the Holy Spirit compels you to do so by his irresistible power; but if he would bless it, I would rejoice as one who findeth great spoil. Wherefore do you stand out against God? If the Lord intendeth your eternal salvation, your resistance will be in vain; and how will you vex yourself in after years to think that you should have stood out so long! Wherefore dost thou resist? God's battering-ram is too mighty for the walls of your prejudice: he will make them fall yet. Why dost thou stand out against thy God, against him who loveth thee, who hath loved thee with an everlasting love, and redeemed thee by the blood of Christ? Why standest thou out against him who intends to lead thy captivity captive, and to make thee yet his rejoicing child? "Oh!" saith one, "if I thought there were such mercy as that, I would yield." If thou believest in the Lord Jesus Christ, this shall be an evidence that such mercy is ordained for thee. Oh that the Spirit of God would enable thee, sinner, to come just as thou art and put thy trust in Christ! If thou dost so, then it is certain that thy name is written in the Lamb's book of Life, that thou wast chosen of God and art precious to him, and that thy head is one on which the crown of immortality is to glitter forever. Oh that thou wouldst trust Christ! The joy and peace it works in the present is worth worlds; but oh the glory, the overwhelming glory which in worlds to come shall belong to those that trust in Jesus! God give you this morning to cast your souls upon the finished work of Jesus. His blood can cleanse; his righteousness can cover; his beauty can adorn; his prayer can preserve; his advent shall glorify; his heaven shall make you blessed. Trust him! God help you to trust him; and he shall have all the praise, both now and forever. Amen and amen.

A Promise For Us And For Our Children

DELIVERED ON SUNDAY MORNING, APRIL 10, 1864,
BY THE REV. C, H. SPURGEON,
AT THE METROPOLITAN TABERNACLE, NEWINGTON.

"Yet now hear, O Jacob, My servant. And Israel, whom Ihave chosen: thus says the Lord thatmadeyou and formed you from the womb, which will help you. Fear not, O Jacob, My servant. And you, Jesurun, whom Ihave chosen. For I will pour water upon him that is thirsty and floods upon the dry ground: I will pour My Spirit upon your seed and My blessing upon your offspring: and they shall spring up as among the grass, as willows by the water courses. One shall say, I am the Lord's, and another shall call himself by the name of Jacob. And another shall subscribe with his hand unto the Lord, and surname himself by the name of Israel." -- Isaiah 44:1-5.

WE ought not to overlook the first and immediate meaning of these words. There can be no doubt that we have here a promise made to God's ancient people, the Jews. Whatever their sins may have been, God has not forever cast them away. They have become like the dry and thirsty desert, but the day will yet dawn when God's sovereign love shall again visit them and His Spirit shall distil upon them until Israel shall be glorious among the nations and her children shall be multiplied and saved. O that the long-expected day would hasten! Break, hallowed morning, for earth's watchers are growing weary! The twelve tribes right longingly wait for the appearance of Messiah the Prince and we also who believe in Jesus, joyfully expect His advent and the gathering together of Israel.

How great will be the day of the Lord's gracious visitation! "For if the casting away of them is the reconciling of the world, what shall the receiving of them be, but life from the dead?" If the fall of them is the riches of the world and the diminishing of them the riches of the Gentiles, how much more their fullness? The vision tarries, but it will surely come! The Glory of the Lord shall be revealed and all flesh shall see it together, for the mouth of the Lord has spoken it. Be it ours to rejoice in that ancient promise, "There shall come out of Sion the Deliverer and shall turn away ungodliness from Jacob: for this is My Covenant unto them, when I shall take away their sins."

Leaving this interesting view of the text, we will meditate on it, for practical purposes of comfort to ourselves. Observe that the text begins with the word, "Yet." What an ominous word as to the past! What a cheering word as to the future! "Yet." "Yet." What black words are those which come before it? Surely all is not well. Look at the preceding verses and see. God's people were represented as being in a sadly backsliding state. They had lost their love to the service of God. They neglected His altar. They brought Him no thank offerings. No, they had fallen into a state of sin until they wearied God with their iniquity.

Consequently they fell into a condition of sorrow--God gave them up to the curse and the reproach. It may be that such is our case this morning, though we are God's people. Perhaps our soul lies cleaving in the dust. We have forgotten to run with diligence in the way of God's Commandments. We have fallen into a lukewarm state. We are following afar off. It may be that we have even fallen into sin and sitting in this House of Prayer we confess with Pharaoh's butler, "I do remember my faults this day."

It is very possible that we have been made too smart for our sins. God may have hidden His face from us. Our faith may be flagging--our graces may be withering. It will be so, it must be so when we forsake our God. If we leave the flowing Fountain to trust in broken cisterns, we shall soon know the bitterness of thirst. "Yet." "Yet," says the text--"yet," though you have fallen into this state, do not despair! Though you have transgressed very foully, do not think God has cast you away! "Yet now hear, O Jacob, My servant. And Israel, whom I have chosen." Yet--the word is a star of the morning, prophetic of brighter rays--yet I love you! Yet you are My chosen! Yet My loving heart is true to you! Yet will I return unto you in favor! Yet shall you rejoice in Me and be filled with My goodness!

Come then, Brothers and Sisters, if we have wandered ever so far, let this word sound like the shepherd's call to bring us back. You need not always be sad--there is no necessity that you should be always weak in righteousness and abundant in sin--yet the promise is yours! Yet God loves you!

Yet He invites you to come to Him! Return now and seek His face once more. You have lived in the feverish lowlands, yet climb the mountains! You have groveled in the dust, yet ascend as on eagles' wings! You have been covered with sackcloth, yet put on your beautiful array! Your neglect of the promises has not made them the less sure. The key of your faith may be rusted, but it will still open the door of mercy.

You may have been unbelieving, but God abides faithful. Up! Enjoy your sure inheritance. Let us feel comforted by the very first word of the text and let it encourage us to lay hold, despite our own unworthiness, upon the great promise of the Lord. The Lord, in order to comfort His people and bring them out of their present state, first, reminds them of what He has done for them. Secondly, He repeats His promise of what He will do. And thirdly, He adds to this a most gracious and full promise of what He will do for their offspring.

I. First, then, and O may the Lord refresh our memories by revealing to us the way by which He has led us--first of all HE COMFORTS HIS PEOPLE BY THE REMEMBRANCE OF WHAT HE HAS DONE FOR THEM. Come, my Brothers and Sisters, reach down for your biographies. Turn over your diaries. Go back with me a little while to that spot where first you knew the Savior. Then march on along the way by which the Lord has led you till you reach the day and hour which found you in the House of God, listening to His promise.

1. Taking the text as our guide, let us notice, first, the Grace we have experienced in its practical effect. The practical effect of Divine Grace in our case has been to make us God's servants--"Yet now hear, O Jacob, My servant." We may be unfaithful servants--we certainly are unprofitable ones--but blessed be His name, if not awfully deceived we are His true servants! We were once the servants of sin and the slaves of our own passions, but He who made us free has now taken us into His family and taught us obedience to His will. We can say with David, "I am Your servant. I am Your servant and the son of Your handmaid: You have loosed my bonds."

We do not serve our Master perfectly, but we would if we could. There are some of His Commandments which we forget, but there are none which we would despise. We do, through infirmity, turn aside unto crooked ways, but we find no comfort in them. Our meat and our drink is to do the will of Him who sent us and our prayer is--

"Make me to walk in Your commands, It is a delightful road. Nor let my head, nor heart, nor hands, Offend against my God."

Beloved, if God has made us His servants, let us be comforted. It is so great a change and so wonderful an effect of Irresistible Grace upon a man to transform him from an heir of wrath into a servant of the living God that we have herein ground for comfort.

2. Observe again, this Grace is peculiar, discriminating and distinguishing. He calls us, "My chosen." We have not chosen Him first, but He has chosen us. If we are God's servants, we were not always so--to Sovereign Grace the change must be ascribed. We might have been left, like other men, to continue in sin and to be rebels against the King of Heaven, but the eyes of Sovereignty singled us out from among others not more unworthy than we were and it was the voice of Love which said, "I have loved you with an everlasting love."

Long before those stars were kindled into flames--long before the sun begun his mighty course--long before the mountains lifted their hoary heads, or the deep clapped its hands in the tumultuous joy of tempest. Long before time began, or space was created, God had written upon His heart the names of His elect people. He had selected them, never to change His choice. He had united them unto the Person of His Son Jesus Christ by a Divine Decree never to be revoked. He had predestinated them to be conformed unto the image of His Son and had made them the heirs of all the fullness of His love, His Grace and His Glory.

Have you and I been chosen? Can we see the connection between the link of calling and the link of predestination? Have we made our calling sure? If so, we may infer most certainly that we must have been predestinated. What comfort is here! Would the Lord have loved us so long and will He cast us away? I know you are dead and barren and your soul feels heavy and your sins stare you in the face, but did not your God know all this beforehand? He made the choice, knowing all--why then, should He change His purpose? He knew how stiff-necked you would be! He understood that your heart was evil and that the imaginations of it would be only evil, and that continually, and yet He loved you!

Ah, my Savior is no fickle lover. He does not feel enchanted for awhile with some gleams of beauty from His Church's eye and then afterwards cast her off because of her unfaithfulness. No, my Brethren, He married her in old eternity and though, according to the words of the Prophet, she has played the harlot and done exceedingly evil, yet it is written of Jehovah, "He hates putting away." There is no divorce in the court of Heaven. Christ has espoused His people to Him in faithfulness and they shall know the Lord. Be this your comfort then--the activity of Grace has made you God's servant. The distinguishing character of Grace has made you His chosen.

3. Reflect again, in the light of the text, upon the ennobling influence of Grace. The people are first called Jacob, but only in the next line they are styled Israel. You and I were but of the common order. If we had boasted of anything we should have been called Jacobs, supplanters, boasting beyond our line. But as Jacob at the brook Jabbok wrestled with the angel and prevailed and gained the august title of prince--prevailing prince--"For as a prince have you power with God and with men and have prevailed," even so has Grace ennobled us!

It may be that we wear today the common well-worn garb of labor. Our names never glitter in the rolls of earth's mightiest--but we are allied unto the King of kings if the life of God is in our soul! We are of the royal family! We are princes of the blood imperial! We shall take our seats among those lordly spirits who forever dwell before the Majesty of the Most High. Priests and kings unto our God has Christ made us by virtue of His own position. Oh, to think that we, who were worse than dogs, should sit among the children! That we, who once stood at the swine trough and gladly would have filled our belly with the husks, now feed upon the fatted calf!

What love is this, that whereas we said, "I am not worthy that you should come under my roof," He has been pleased to make our bodies the temples of the Holy Spirit and God dwells in us and we in Him! My Brethren, what an honor to be one with Christ--to be united to the Person of Him who counts it not robbery to be equal with God--to be made at last to sit upon His Throne, even as He sits upon His Father's Throne! Why, when I look upon the dignity which belongs to the meanest Christian, the imperial pomp of all emperors and kings sinks into insignificance and like a shadow melts away. Think of this, my Brethren, and despite your low state of Grace this morning, take comfort. He would not have made you such mighty ones as you are in Him if He had not intended to bless you still.

4. Furthermore, the text conducts us onward to notice the creating and sustaining energy of that Grace. "Thus says the Lord that made you and formed you from the womb." How did you become Believers in Christ? By any internal energy of your own? Speak, Believer--was it your free will that brought you to the Savior's feet, or was it God's Free Grace? Men may hold free will doctrine as a matter of theory, but you never find a Believer hold it as a matter of experience. We can all say--

"Oh, to Grace how great a debtor Daily I'm constrained to be."

It was all of Your Grace I was brought to obey, while others were suffered to go the downward road! About this you can have no difficulty, for your own experience tells you that you were dead in trespasses and sins and it must have been something beyond any power of yours that quickened you into spiritual life. Men might as well claim the honors of creation or resurrection as boast of commencing their own spiritual life! The Lord alone shall have the Glory of that opening hour of love.

Since that happy day what has sustained you? Has your fire of piety been fed by internal, self-produced fuel? Have you kept yourselves from the power of Satan? My Brethren, have you kept yourselves in communion with God? You know that you have not. You are debtors for your soul's daily bread to your Father who is in Heaven. Every good thing which you have you have received from Him. The great Father of Lights, with whom is no variableness or shadow of turning, has given you every good and perfect gift which you have received. You have profited in nothing by the flesh, but in all things by the Spirit of the living God.

Taking you from your first conviction and tracking you to the present moment, it has been God's creating and forming. In the womb of conviction He fashioned you and He has nurtured you until now. Let this be your comfort--if God could quicken you when you were absolutely dead and if He has kept you until this moment, can He not revive you again? Can He not make that spark again become a flame? Have you fallen too low for Him? Is His arm shortened that He cannot save? Is His ear heavy that He cannot hear? No! He that has delivered you aforetime will deliver you yet again. Therefore be of good comfort.

5. We will leave this part of the subject when we notice once again that this Grace has the characteristic of intense affection in it. This is not very plain in our translation but I think we can make it clear. God gives to His people the title of Jesurun, which means the righteous people, according to some translators. But most interpreters are agreed that it is an affectionate title which God gives to His people. Perhaps it may be considered to be a diminutive of Israel. I do not know that we could pronounce it so as to make it plainly appear here, but very likely it is so--a diminutive of Israel.

Just as fathers and mothers, when they have great affection for their children, will frequently give them an endearing name--shorten their usual name--or call them by a familiar title only used in the family, so in calling Israel, Jesurun, the Lord sets forth His near and dear love. God's Grace to us is not merely the mercy of the good Samaritan towards a poor stranger whom he finds wounded by the way. It is the love of a mother to her sick child. The fondness of a husband towards a weeping wife. The tenderness of the head towards the wounded members.

Beloved, did you ever did try to grasp the thought that God loves you? Whenever I try it, it brings tears into my eyes and I can go no farther. That the Eternal God should pity me I can understand. That He should regard my misery and deliver me I can comprehend. That He should look upon me with eyes of benevolence seems reasonable enough. But that He should LOVE me? Love me, too, with a love infinitely stronger than any love I have to my own children, or to my own spouse! That He should so love me that His own darling Son, the Only-Begotten, was not better loved than I have been--this is a wonder of wonders!

I must not say that Jesus was not so well loved as poor sinful men, but I will say when the question came to this-- whether those poor sinful but beloved ones should die or Christ should die--He spared not His own Son, but freely delivered Him up for us all. Oh, what mysterious love! That Christ should suffer that we may go free! That the Father's Darling should hang upon the accursed Tree and bleed away His life that we might be received into the eternal bosom of Jehovah and might be forever accepted as the favored ones of His electing love! He loves you! Oh, there is nothing can melt the heart like this--God loves you!

And while it melts, it strengthens. While God loves me, whom shall I fear? If Jehovah has chosen me, if He has set His heart upon me, of whom shall I be afraid? Verily, with this I may walk through the valley of the shadow of death and fear no evil! With this in the midst of war I may have confidence! Upon this in famine I shall be fed. And in affliction I shall not be afraid. Oh, the joy which dwells in the thought that God loves His people! Jesus loved me and gave Himself for me! Can you say this, my Hearer? If you can, you can say more than Demosthenes or Cicero were ever able to say with all their eloquence.

It may be, as we have said before, that we have fallen into a low sad state this morning and are trying to get ourselves out of it by chastening ourselves with many dark and doleful fears. Now that is not the way to rise from the dust. It is not the Law but the Gospel which saves at first. And it is not a legal bondage but a Gospel liberty which can restore the fainting Believer. It is not slavish fear that brings back the backslider to God, but the sweet wooing of love allures him to Jesus' bosom.

As I sat the other night in my study, musing on my message for the coming Sunday, some little unbelief crossed my mind. Would the Lord sustain me in my ministry among such multitudes? Would He give fresh matter on the morrow? And there stood on my shelves nine volumes of my sermons, the records of nine years of gracious help. What witnesses did those volumes seem to be of the faithfulness of the Lord! Now you can look back, some of you, to ten, twenty, thirty, or forty years, which are like so many volumes of Grace received! Dare you distrust your God? David went forth to fight Goliath with past experience as his comfort, "Your servant slew both the lion and the bear: and this uncircumcised Philistine shall be as one of them."

Cannot you use the same argument? You have already slain your adversaries--what can stand against you? Be of good comfort and dash forward to the fray! Take as your war cry, "His mercy endures forever," and you need never quail, whatever difficulties assail you. So much for the first point. Now let us turn with great brevity to the second.

II. We are encouraged, in the second place, this morning, by THE PROMISE OF WHAT GOD WILL DO. He says "Fear not, I will help you." And then He adds, "I will pour water upon him that is thirsty and floods upon the dry ground." You feel thirsty this morning, that is, uncomfortable in heart. You have lost much of the joy of religion and your prayer is, "Restore unto me the joy of Your salvation."

You are conscious, also, that you are barren, like the dry ground. You are not bringing forth that fruit unto God which He has a right to expect of you. You are not so useful in the Church nor in the world as your heart desires to be. Well then, here is His promise of what He will do, "I will help you." You cannot pray this morning. You cannot wrestle as you desire--"I will help you." You feel unable to overcome sin--"I will help you." You are engaged in service too heavy for you--"I will help you."

Whether it is to suffer, to sacrifice, to labor, or to endure, take this comfort--"I will help you." I love this promise! It is a very short one, but it is all the longer in meaning because it is short in expression. You may avail yourself of it in all cases. The promise turns every way and blesses in every form. It is like a weapon which may be used for fifty purposes. It will be to you, if you will, a sword and you may beat it into a plowshare. Or it will prove a shield, a spear, a chariot, and I know not what besides. You cannot find any possible position into which the child of God can be brought in which this promise will fail to bless him!

Sit down no longer in lethargy! Lift up the hands which hang down and confirm the feeble knees, for if God says, "I will help you," how can you be afraid? Then comes a promise, fuller in words and as rich in Grace, "I will pour water on him that is thirsty." You shall have the Grace you want. Water refreshes the thirsty--you shall be refreshed--your desires shall be gratified. Water quickens sleeping vegetable life--your life shall be quickened by fresh Grace. Water swells the buds and makes the fruits ripe--you shall have fructifying Grace. You shall be made fruitful in the ways of God!

Whatever good quality there is in Divine Grace, you shall enjoy it to the full. All the riches of Divine Grace you shall receive in plenty. You shall be, as it were, drenched with it! And as sometimes the meadows become flooded by the bursting rivers and the fields turn into pools, so shall you! The thirsty land shall be springs of water. O my Brothers and Sisters, when the Holy Spirit visits a man, what a difference it makes in him!

I know a preacher, once as dull and dead a man as ever misused a pulpit. Under his slumbering ministrations there were few conversions and the congregation grew thinner and thinner. Good men sighed in secret and the enemy said, "Aha, so would we have it!" The revival came--the Holy Spirit worked gloriously! The preacher felt the Divine fire and suddenly woke up to energy and zeal. The man appeared to be transformed! His tongue seemed touched with fire! Elaborate and written discourses were laid aside and he began to talk out of his own glowing heart to the hearts of others. He preached as he had never done before. The place filled. The dry bones were stirred and quickening began! They who knew him once so elegant, correct, passionless, dignified, cold, lifeless and unprofitable, asked in amazement, "Is Saul also among the Prophets?"

The Spirit of God is a great wonder-worker! You will notice certain Church members. They have never been good for much. We have had their names on the roll and that is all--suddenly the Spirit of God has come upon them and they have been honored among us for their zeal and usefulness! We have seen them here and there and everywhere diligent in the service of God and foremost in all sorts of Christian labor, though before you could hardly get them to stir an inch! I would that the quickening Spirit would come down upon me and upon you--upon every one of us in abundance--to create us valiant men for Truth and mighty for the Lord!

O for some of the ancient valor of apostolic times, that, like good knights of the Cross we would dash forward against the foe and with irresistible courage deal heavy blows against the adversary of souls and his vast host! We may do this! We have only to plead the promise! God will be enquired of, but the promise stands true, "I will pour water upon him that is thirsty and floods upon the dry ground." Do not lose the blessing through remissness, but ask and you shall receive. Brethren, pray for me! For I need more Grace and in return I will plead the Lord's words on your behalf.

III. As a very great comfort to His mourning people, the Lord now promises A BLESSING UPON THEIR CHILDREN. You will observe, dear Friends, that they must get the blessing for themselves first, for the third verse has it--"I will pour water upon him that is thirsty and floods upon the dry ground"--that is first. And then afterwards--"I will pour My Spirit upon your seed."

We must not expect to see our children blessed unless we ourselves grow in Grace. It is often the inconsistency of parents which is the obstacle--the outward obstacle to the conversion of their children. No doubt there have been multitudes of children of professing parents who have been damned instrumentally by the ungodliness and inconsistency of their parents at home. The parents, let us hope, were Christians--but there has been so much of apparent inconsistency about them that the ruin of their children has been the consequence. It is a notorious fact that some of the worst of men have been the children of godly parents. I could give living instances but I forbear.

When good Mr. Williams was murdered at Eromanga--the fact should be well-known--the natives had first been exasperated by the most abominable conduct on the part of the son of a missionary, who, having gone there, had practiced all sorts of evil upon the natives. And then good Mr. Williams was sacrificed to their fury. You will find that among the most fearfully depraved there are a few of the very deepest dye who received an early Christian education and dashed down all its restraints that they might run greedily into iniquity.

I think the children of godly parents are like Jeremiah's figs--the good are very good, but the bad are very bad-- very naughty figs, such as cannot be eaten. Some of the children of God have been the parents of great offenders. Eli begets Hophni and Phinehas. David has an Absalom. Noah is father to Ham. Isaac begets profane Esau. The wise Solomon is followed by Rehoboam the fool. And pious Hezekiah is sire to persecuting Manasseh. Oh, how sad it is that it should be so, but so it is! We must, therefore, look to ourselves and our own careful walking before God, for we shall not get the promise for our offspring till we obtain its fulfillment in our own case.

But now, supposing that this is done. If we have had faith to receive much Grace from God, here comes a blessed promise for our children--"I will pour My Spirit upon your seed," in which, observe first of all, the need. Our children need the Spirit of God. They are not like children educated in the street, the tavern, or the low theater. They have not heard from our lips words of lust or profanity. They have been hushed to sleep by the name of Jesus as their lullaby. They breathe the air of religion. But for all that they need the Spirit of God!

We love to see the children of godly parents brought into Church membership, but we would avoid, above all things, anything like hereditary profession or inherited religion. It must be personal in each individual or it is not worth a gnat. I believe that the idea of birthright membership has tended materially to weaken the strength of that most respectable and once powerful denomination, the Society of Friends. Believing that their children have an inward Light which they ought to follow, I do fear they often teach their children to follow inward darkness rather than light. Forgetting the necessity of the Holy Spirit, which is infinitely superior to ordinary light of conscience, their children have grown up to attend meetings and to wear a particular garb without receiving the Spirit--certainly without that grand enthusiasm which honored their sires in bygone days.

We must not adulterate our membership by the reception of the children of godly parents unless we have clear proof that they, themselves, are converted to God. Your children need the Holy Spirit quite as much as the offspring of the Hottentot or the Kaffir. They are born in sin and shapen in iniquity--in sin do the best of mothers conceive their children, and, however well you may train them, you cannot take the stone out of the heart nor turn it into flesh. To give a new heart and a right spirit is the work of the Holy Spirit and of the Holy Spirit alone.

In the second place, the source of the mercy which God will give. "I will pour out My Spirit." It was the work of the Spirit which transformed their fathers--it is that which must transform them. The Word may come to them and not be blessed. We may be silly enough to take them to baby-Baptism and they would not be blessed. We may persuade them to come to the Lord's Table, but they would not be blessed. But when the Spirit of God comes upon them, then it is all done. Now comes the broken heart! Now comes the humble spirit! Now is breathed the earnest prayer! Now love to Christ flames forth and trust is built upon Him!

Do pray, dear Friends, for your children, that God will pour His Spirit upon them. And as to the rest, you may depend that all the fruits will come in due time. I do not know that the parent needs to say much to his child about Baptism or the Lord's Supper, except, sometimes, a gentle word as to the duty of the Believer, and a clear explanation of the meaning of the ordinances. But I do hold that the duty of the parent is to look first and foremost for the work of the Spirit and insist upon it that he must be born again or else no profession can be made. Tell the child that he his dead in trespasses and sins. Let there be no doubt about his natural condition and let this always be your prayer, "Almighty Grace, renew his heart! Turn him from darkness to Light and make him Yours!"

I think that in some Sunday school addresses there is not always the Gospel so clearly and decidedly proclaimed as it should be. It is not very easy, I know, to preach Christ to little children, but there is nothing else worth preaching. To stand up and say, "Be good boys and girls and you will get to Heaven," is preaching the old Covenant of Works, and it is no more right to preach salvation by works to little children than to those who are of mature age. We are all dead and as the Spirit of God can alone renew us, so He alone can renew them and there is no natural goodness, no amiability, no generosity of character which can supersede the work of the Holy Spirit. We must remember this and hold to it, that we pray to God to work by His Spirit in their hearts.

Then you have in the promise in the third place, the plenty of Grace which God gives. He says, "I will pour My Spirit upon your seed"--not a little of it--but they shall have abundance. It has charmed me, especially of late, when I have conversed with very many children--many of them children of godly parents and others we have brought into our school and instructed by good and loving teachers. I have been charmed, I say, in examining them for membership, at the profoundness of their knowledge and the abundance of their Grace. I have questioned them in a way I would not question some gray-headed men and women.

I have gone into points of intricate doctrine with many of them in a way which I would not use with many of middle age because I know I would take them out of their depth. But these children have been able to tell me from Scripture-- and generally their answers have been quotations of a text--the great plan of salvation and the doctrines connected with it as explicitly as the best Doctor of Divinity in any of our Universities. And I have been often pleased to notice that the very babes are those out of the mouths of whom God has ordained strength and He gives the perfect wisdom of the upright full often to those who are but as babes and sucklings. It is so good to notice this!

You are not to expect children merely to exhibit faint traces of Grace, but in the strength of this promise you may look for great things. In the deathbeds of your children--and very often children who are early saved are early caught up to Heaven--many very wonderful expressions have fallen from their lips. Mr. Janeway, in his, "Token for Children," has preserved many examples, showing that some dying children have been wondrously mature in piety and the expressions they have used have perfectly astounded the most experienced of the saints.

You ought not, in the case of children, to look merely for life--you will find vigorous life!

You may not expect a little surface-knowledge only, but you may expect to find in them a depth of knowledge in the things of God, for so God's promise has it, "I will pour My Spirit upon your seed." I must not leave the text without noticing the blessedness of all this. "And My blessing upon your offspring."

Oh, what a blessing it is to have our offspring saved! God give us each to see it! What a blessing to have our children enlisted in Christ's army! Beloved, we wish them well, we wish them the best of God's gifts. But if we were asked whether we would have them famous or wealthy, we should pause to ask whether it were good for them. But if it were put to us, "Shall they be saved?" we feel we would cheerfully give our life if that must be the price, to know that our children walked in the Truth of God. "I have no greater joy than this," said one in Holy Scripture and there can be no greater joy than this to the Christian parent. How happy the family becomes!

And when they grow up and go out from us, married in the Lord--for how else can they be gracious?--we should expect to see a gracious house built up. There is a very sad verse, I think you will find it in the second chapter of Judges, which runs thus--"And also all that generation were gathered unto their fathers: and there arose another generation after them, which knew not the Lord, nor yet the works which He had done for Israel." Oh, that is sad to see how soon religion dies out in a nation! But without household piety--without constant instruction both in the Sunday school and at home--the next generation in our case will be as ignorant of God as if Christ had not been known by their fathers!

Unless we are careful over the young, there may be none to bear the Lord's banner when we sleep among the clods. In matters of doctrine you will find orthodox congregations frequently change to heterodoxy in the course of thirty or forty years and that is because too often there has been no catechizing of the children in the essential doctrines of the Gospel. For my part I am more and more persuaded that the study of a good Scriptural Catechism is of infinite value to our children and I shall see that it is reprinted as cheaply as possible for your use. Even if the youngsters do not understand all the questions and answers in the "Westminster Assembly's Catechism," yet, abiding in their memories, it will be of infinite service when the time of understanding comes, to have known those very excellent, wise and judicious definitions of the things of God.

If we would maintain orthodoxy in our midst and see good old Calvinistic doctrines handed down from father to son, I think we must use the method of catechizing and endeavor with all our might to impregnate their minds with the things of God. It will be a blessing to them--the greatest of all blessings--a blessing in life and death, in time and eternity, the best of blessings God Himself can give. I will not prolong this, but there are still two points I must mention.

Carefully notice the vigor with which these children shall grow. "They shall spring up as among the grass, as willows by the water courses."

Close by the water's edge the grass grows very green and the willow is a well-known tree for speedily shooting forth its branches. Our farmers lop their willows often, but they very soon sprout again. As the old proverb has it, "A willow will buy a horse where an oak will not buy a saddle, because the willow being often lopped and then springing again, yields much to the grower." The willow grows fast and so do young Christians. If you want the eminent men in God's Church, look for them among those converted in youth. There are, of course, exceptions, but after all, our Samuels and Timothy's must come from those who knew the Scriptures from their youth.

O Lord! Send us many such whose growth and advance shall as much astonish us as the growth of the willows by the water courses. Why, since I have been among you these ten years and more, lads who used to come into the school and were the objects of our hope, where are they now? Why they are preaching the Gospel this very morning! And as I look at the happy parents here and remember the time when the now useful minister sat as a lad in the pew and remember that at this very moment they are preaching in the name of Jesus, they do seem to have grown quite as fast as the willows. They grow so fast and so well and serve the Lord so admirably! The promise has, indeed, been fulfilled to the very letter!

Then comes, last of all, the manifestation of this in public. It appears from the text that not only are our children to have the Spirit of God in their inward parts, but they are to make a profession of it. One shall say, "I am the Lord's"-- he shall come out boldly and avow himself on the Lord's side. And another shall so ally himself to God's Church that he "shall call himself by the name of Jacob." And then another who can hardly speak quite so positively, but who means it quite as sincerely--"shall subscribe with his hand unto the Lord," and a fourth shall, "surname himself by the name of Israel."

Oh, it is a joy, indeed, when those who know the Lord come forward and declare themselves to be on His side! May we, by God's Grace, be helped to train our children to an open avowal of that which is within them. A hint sometimes will do our sons and daughters good when we believe that they fear God. Indicate to them that religion is not meant to be kept under a bushel, that the

Grace of God is not to be covered and concealed--and before long, seeing their duty-- God will help them to walk in the way of it and it shall be your privilege and mine to rejoice at seeing them added to the Church. The promise upon which I have preached this morning needs to be pleaded before God, for God does not fulfill such promises as these without our bringing them before Him in earnest fervent prayer.

A banker gives me a check and it is a very good one, but I can never get the cash for it without going to the counter and presenting it for payment. And if God gives me a promise conditional upon my pleading it, I must never expect Him to fulfill it unless I enquire concerning it. I look upon some here who can remember the way by which God has led them--who look upon their children and their children's children walking in the Truth of God--you, my Brethren, can confirm the faith of the younger parents among us and make us feel that as God has dealt well with you, He will deal well with us!

Some of us, in looking back, can speak of a godly father and a godly grandfather. We can look for generations back, till as far as we can trace a line--Divine Grace has run in our family. O that the line may continue for years to come, till as long as generations are born there shall be one of our kith and kin to carry the standard and sound the trumpet and fight for the Lord of Israel! I invite you, therefore, to much earnest prayer, especially during the coming week, which is selected by the Evangelical Alliance as a prayer week for this special object. And I trust with regard to this promise none will be backward in pleading it.

As for you who are unconverted, you cannot pray for your children if you do not pray for yourselves. You never can expect a blessing, for you are under the Divine curse! Nevertheless I pray God to make you thirsty and if He makes you hunger and thirst after righteousness, then you can put your hand upon this promise, "I will pour water upon him that is thirsty and floods upon the dry ground." And afterwards the remainder of the blessing shall be yours. God bless the Word for Jesus' sake. Amen.--

"Wake, parents of Israel! O hasten to plead For the Spirit of Grace to descend. The Word has gone forth and the faithful have need Of your prayers the great cause to defend. From the youth of our country shall armies arise, The Gospel of peace to proclaim. Over the land and the seas, the glad message that flies, Shall re-echo Immanuel's name. Wake, parents in Israel! O, wrestle and pray That Grace to our youth may be given For the hands that in faith are uplifted today Shall prevail with our Father in Heaven."

The Great Liberator

DELIVERED ON SUNDAY MORNING, APRIL 17, 1864,
BY THE REV. C. H. SPURGEON,
AT THE METROPOLITAN TABERNACLE, NEWINGTON.

"If the Son therefore shall make you free, you shall be free, indeed." -- John 8:36.

BLESSED is that word "free," and blessed is he who spends himself to make men so. You did well to crowd your streets and to welcome with your joyous acclamations the man who has broken the yoke from off the neck of the oppressed. Many sons of Italy have done valiantly, but he excels them all and deserves the love of all the good and brave. Political slavery is an intolerable evil. To live, to think, to act, to speak at the permission of another! Better have no life at all! To depend for my existence upon a despot's will is death itself. Craven spirits may wear the dog collar which their master puts upon them and fawn at his feet for the bones of his table, but men who are worthy of the name had rather feed the vultures on the battlefield.

The burden of civil bondage is too heavy for bold spirits to bear with patience and therefore they fret and murmur beneath it. This murmuring the tyrant loves not and therefore he throws the sufferers into his dungeons and bids them wear out their days in captivity. Blessed is he who hurls down the despot, bursts the doors of his dungeons and gives true men their rights. We have never felt, and therefore we know not the bitterness of bondage. Our emancipators have gone to the world of spirits, bequeathing us an heirloom of liberty for which we should love their names and reverence their God.

If they could have lived on till now, how we should honor them! But as they are gone, we do well to applaud our illustrious guest as if we saw in him the spirit of all our glorious liberators worthily enshrined. Political liberty allows scope for so much of all that is good and ennobling and its opposite involves so much that is debasing, that the mightiest nation destitute of it is poor, indeed, and the poorest of all people, if they are but free, are truly rich. But, my Brethren, men may have political liberty to the very fullest extent and yet be slaves, for there is such a thing as religious bondage. He who cringes before a priest--he who dreads his anathema, or who creeps at his feet to receive his blessing--is an abject slave!

He may call himself a free man, but his soul is in vile bondage if superstition makes him wear the chain. To be afraid of the mutterings of a man like myself--to bow before a piece of wood or a yard of painted canvas--to reverence a morsel of bread or a rotten bone--this is mental slavery, indeed! They call the Negro a slave in the Southern Confederacy, but men who prostrate their reason before the throne of superstition are slaves through and through. To yield obedience to our Lord, to offer prayer to God Most High is perfect freedom! But to confess my heart out to a mortal with a shaven crown--to trust my family secrets and my wife's character to the commands of a man who may be all the while wallowing in debauchery is worse than the worst form of serfdom.

I would sooner serve the most cruel Sultan who ever crushed humanity beneath his iron heel than bow before the Pope or any other priest of man's making. The tyranny of priest-craft is the worst of ills. You may cut through the bonds of despots with a sword, but the sword of the Lord Himself is needed here. The Truth of God must file these fetters and the Holy Spirit must open these dungeons! You may escape from prison, but superstition hangs round a man and with its deadly influence keeps him ever in its dark and gloomy cell.

Skepticism, which proposes to snap the chains of superstition only supplants a blind belief with an unhallowed credulity and leaves the victim as oppressed as ever. Jesus the Son, alone, can make men truly free! Happy are they whom He has delivered from superstition. Blessed are our eyes that this day we see the light of Gospel liberty and are no longer immured in Popish darkness! Let us remember our privileges and bless God with a loud voice that the darkness is past and the true Light shines--since the name of Jesus, the preaching of His Word, and the power of His Truth have, in this respect, in a high degree--made our nation free!

Yet a man may be delivered from the bond of superstition and be still a serf, for he who is not ruled by a priest may still be controlled by the devil or by his own lusts which are much the same. Our carnal desires and inclinations are domineering lords enough, as those know who follow out their commands. A man may say, "I feel not supernatural terrors. I know no superstitious horrors," and then, folding his arms, he may boast that he is free. But he may all the while be a slave to his own evil heart. He may be grinding at the mill of avarice, rotting in the reeking dungeon of sensuality, dragged along by the chains of maddened anger, or borne down by the yoke of fashionable custom.

He is the free man who is master of himself through the Grace of God. He who serves his own passions is the slave of the worst of despots. Talk to me not of dark dungeons beneath the sea level! Speak not to me of pits in which men have been entombed and forgotten! Tell me not of heavy chains, nor even of racks and the consuming fire. The slave of sin and Satan, sooner or later, knows greater horrors than these--his doom is more terrible because it is eternal--and his slavery more hopeless because it is one into which he willingly commits himself.

Perhaps there are those present who claim liberty for themselves and say that they are able to control their passions and have never given away to impure desires. Yes, a man may get as far as that in a modified sense and yet not be free. Perhaps I address those who, knowing the right, have struggled for it against the wrong. You have reformed yourselves from follies into which you had fallen. You have, by diligence, brought the flesh somewhat under control in its outward manifestations of sin, and now your life is moral, your conduct is respectable, your reputation high. Still, for all that it may be that you are conscious that you are not free.

Your old sins haunt you, your former corruptions perplex you. You have not found peace for you have not obtained forgiveness. You have buried your sins beneath the earth for years, but conscience has given them a resurrection and the ghosts of your past transgressions haunt you. You can scarcely sleep at night because of the recollection of the wrath of God which you deserve. And by day there is a gall put into your sweetest draughts because you know that you have sinned against Heaven and that Heaven must visit with vengeance your transgression. You have not yet come to the full liberty of the children of God, as you will do if you cast yourselves into the hands of Jesus who looses the captives.

"If the Son therefore shall make you free, you shall be free, indeed"--free as the mere political liberator cannot make you--free as he cannot make you who merely delivers you from superstition! Free as reformation cannot make you. Free as God alone can make you by His free Spirit. "If the Son therefore shall make you free, you shall be free, indeed."

Now this morning may the Lord give His servant help from on high while I try to talk with you. To those who feel today their slavery, my message may be profitable. Our first point is that to those who are the bond slaves of Satan, liberty is possible. The text would not mock us with a dream--it says, "If the Son therefore shall make you free." All who are slaves shall not be set free, but there is the possibility of liberty implied in the text. Blessed "if." It is like the prison window through the stony wall--it lets in enough sunshine for us to read the word, "hope." "If the Son therefore shall make you free."

Secondly, there is a false freedom. You see that in the text--"You shall be free, indeed." There were some who professed to be free, but were not so. The Greek is, "You shall be free really," for there are some who are free only in the name and in the shadow of freedom, but who are not free as to the substance. Then thirdly, real freedom must come to us from the Son, that glorious Son of God, who, being free and giving Himself to us, gives us freedom. And then we shall close by putting a few personal questions as to whether the Son has made us free, or whether we still remain slaves.

I. First then, dear Friends, our text rings a sweet silver bell of hope in the ear of those who are imprisoned by their sin. FREEDOM IS POSSIBLE--the word "if implies it. The Son of God can make the prisoner free. No matter who you are, nor what you are, nor how many years you may have remained the slaves of Satan--the Son, the glorious Liberator--can make you free. "He is able also to save them to the uttermost, who come unto God by Him."

Perhaps that which weighs upon you most heavily is a sense of your past guilt. "I have offended God--I have offended often, willfully, atrociously, with many aggravations. On such-and-such a day I offended Him in the foulest manner and with deliberation. On other days I have run greedily in a course of vice. Nothing has restrained me from disobedience and nothing has impelled me to the service of God. All that His Word says against me I deserve. And every threat which His Book utters is justly due to me and may well be fulfilled. Is there a possibility that I can escape from guilt? Can so foul a sinner as I am be made clean? I know that the leopard cannot lose its spots, nor the Ethiopian change his skin by his own efforts. Is there a Divine power which can take away my spots and change my nature?"

Sinner, there is! No sin which you have committed need shut you out of Heaven. However damnable your iniquities may have been, there is forgiveness with God that He may be feared. You may have gone to the very verge of perdition, but the arm of God's Grace is long enough to reach you. You may sit today with your tongue padlocked with blasphemy, your hands fast bound by acts of atrocious violence, your heart fettered with corruption, your feet chained fast to the Satanic blocks of unbelief--your whole self locked up in the bondage of corruption--but there is One so mighty to save that He can set even you, free! "All manner of sin and blasphemy shall be forgiven unto men."

"The blood of Jesus Christ His Son cleanses us from all sin." In the matter of guilt, then, there is the possibility of freedom. "But can I be freed from the punishment of sin?" says another. "God is just: He must punish sin. It is not possible that the Judge of all the earth should allow such a rebel as I am to escape. Shall I go Scot free? Shall I have the same reward with the perfectly righteous? After years of unbelief am I still to be treated as though I had always been a willing and loving child? This is not just--I must be punished."

Sinner, there is no need that you should be cast into Hell. No, you shall not be, if your trust is placed in the blood shed on Calvary. There is an imperative need that sin should be punished, but there is no need that it should be punished in your person. The stern laws of Justice demand that sin should meet with satisfaction, but there is no Law which demands that it should receive satisfaction from you, for if you believe, Christ has given satisfaction for you. If you trust Jesus Christ to save you, be assured that Christ was punished in your place, and suffered the whole of Divine wrath, so that there is no fear of your being cast into Hell.

If you believe, you cannot be punished, for there is no charge against you--your sins having been laid on Christ. And there can be no punishment exacted from you, for Christ has already discharged the whole. God's justice cannot demand two executions for the same offense. O, let not the flames of Hell alarm you, Sinner! Let not Satan provoke you to despair by thoughts of the worm that never dies and of the fire that never can be quenched. You need not go there--there is a possibility of deliverance for you. And though your heart says, "Never, never, shall I escape," trust not your heart! God is greater than your heart and knows all things.

Believe His testimony and fly to the great Deliverer for liberty! Freedom, then, from punishment is possible through Christ. I think I hear one say, "Ah, but if I were saved from past sin and from all the punishment of it, yet still I should submit to the power of sin again. I have a wolf within my heart hungering after sin which will not be satisfied, though it is glutted with evil. The insatiable horseleech of my lust ever cries, 'Give, give!' Can I be delivered from it? I have been bound with many resolutions, but sin, like Samson, has snapped them as though they were but green twigs. I have been shut up in many professions, as though I was now, once and for all, a prisoner to morality. But I have taken up posts and bars and every other restraint which kept me in and I have gone back to my old uncleanness. Can /, can I be saved from all these propensities, and all this inbred corruption?"

My dear Friend, there is a hope for you that you may be. If you believe in the Lord Jesus Christ, that same blood by which sin is pardoned enables man to overcome sin. They in Heaven washed their robes and made them white in His blood. But they have another note in their song--they overcame through the blood of the Lamb. Not only were they delivered from guilt, but from the power of sin. I do not tell you that in this life Christ Himself will make you perfectly free from indwelling sin--there will always be some corruption left in you to struggle with--some Canaanite still in the land to exercise your faith and to teach you the value of a Savior. But the neck of sin shall be under your foot--God shall lead captive the great Adonibezek of your lust and you shall cut off his thumbs so that he cannot handle weapons of war.

If the enemy cannot be destroyed, at least his head shall be broken and he shall never have reigning power over you--you shall be free from sin, to live no longer in it. Oh, that blessed word "if"! How it sparkles! It may seem but a little star--may it herald the dawning of the Sun of Righteousness within you--"If the Son therefore shall make you free."

"Oh," says one, "that is a great 'if,' indeed. It cannot be! My guilt pardoned, my punishment remitted, and my nature changed? How can it be?" Dear Friend, it may be, and I trust it will be this morning, for this "if" comforts the preacher with a hope of success in delivering the Word. And may it give some hope to the hearers, that perhaps you may be made free yourselves. But I think I hear another exclaim, "Sir, I am in bondage through fear of death. Go where I may, enjoying no assurance of acceptance in Christ, I am afraid to die. I know that I must one of these days close these eyes in the slumbers of the grave, but oh, it is a dread thought to me that I must stand before my God and pass the solemn test. I cannot look into the sepulcher without feeling that it is a cold, damp place. I cannot think of eternity without remembering the terrors which cluster round it to a sinner, 'where their worm dies not and where their fire is not quenched.' "

Ah, but my dear Friend, if the Son makes you free, He will deliver you from the fear of death. When sin is pardoned then the Law is satisfied and when the Law is satisfied then death becomes a friend. The strength of sin is the Law--the Law is fulfilled--the strength of sin is broken. The sting of death is sin--sin is pardoned--death has a sting no longer. If you believe in Christ you shall never die in that sense in which you dread death. You shall fall asleep but you shall never die. That death of which you think is not the Christian's portion--it belongs to the ungodly. In it you shall have no share, if you trust the Savior. Borne on angels' wings to Heaven--up from calamity, imperfection, temptation and trial shall you mount--flitting with the wings of a dove far above the clouds of sorrow! Leaving this dusky globe behind you, you shall enter into the splendors of immortality. You shall not die, but wake out of this dying world into a life of Glory!

Come, Soul! If you trust in Christ, this "if shall be no if, but a certainty today--the Son shall make you free, indeed. I do not think I can bring out the full value of this liberty by merely speaking of the evils which we are delivered from. You know, Brethren, freedom consists not only in a negative but in a positive--we are not only free from, but we are free to. We hear of persons receiving the freedom of a city. This implies that certain privileges are bestowed. Now, "if the Son therefore shall make you free, you shall be free, indeed," in the sense of privilege--you shall be free to call yourself God's child. You shall be free to say, "Abba, Father," without rebuke. You shall be free to claim the protection of that Father's House and the provision of His bounty. You shall be free to come to His knees with all your trials and tell Him all your griefs.

You shall be free to plead His promises and to receive the fulfillment of them, too. You shall be free to sit at His table, not as a servant is permitted sometimes to sit down when the feast is over to eat the leftovers, but you shall sit there as a well-beloved son, to eat the fatted calf while your Father with you, eats, drinks and is merry. You shall be free to enter into the Church on earth, the mother of us all. Free to all her ordinances. Free to share in all those gifts which Christ has given to his spouse. And when you die, you shall be free to enter into the rest which remains for the people of God. Free to partake of the New Jerusalem which is above. Free to use her harps of gold and to her streets ofjoy. Free to feast in her great banquet which lasts forever. Free access to the heart of God, to the throne of Christ and to the blessedness of eternity!

Oh, how good it is to think that there is a possibility of a freedom to such privileges as these and a possibility of it to the vilest of the vile! For some who were grossly guilty, some who had gone far astray have nevertheless enjoyed the fullness of the blessing of the Gospel of Peace. Look at Paul! No man enters more into the mystery of the Gospel than he. He had freedom to do so--he could comprehend with all saints what are the heights and depths, and know the love of Christ which passes knowledge and yet it is he, it is he who once foamed out threats, who sucked the blood of the saints! It is he who dyed his hands up to the very elbows in murderous gore. It is he who hated Christ! It is he who was a persecutor and injurious and yet is he free from evil and he is free to all the privileges of the chosen of God!

And why not you? And why not you? Woman, tottering and trembling, why should not, why should not the Son make you free? Man, tossed about with many doubts, why should not the great Liberator appear to you? Can there be a reason why not? You have not read the rolls of predestination and discovered that your name has been left out. It has not been revealed that for you there is no Atonement, but it is revealed to you that whoever believes on Him is not condemned. And this is the testimony which comes to you--O that you would receive it!--"He that believes on the Lord Jesus Christ has everlasting life." O that you would be bold and trust Christ this morning and the "if which is in our text shall become a blessed certainty to you! So then there is a possibility for freedom. We will pause awhile and then warn you against false freedom.

II. BEWARE OF FALSE LIBERTY. Every good thing is imitated by Satan who is the master of counterfeits and therefore, liberty--a word fit to be used in Heaven and almost too good for fallen earth--has been used for the very basest of purposes and men have misnamed the devil's offspring by this angelic title. We have in spiritual matters things called liberty which are not liberty. There is Antinomian liberty--God deliver us from that! A man says, "I am not under the Law of God, therefore I will live as I like." A most blessed Truth of God followed by a most atrocious inference.

The Christian is not under the Law, but under Grace--that is a very precious fact--it is much better to serve God because we love Him, than because we are afraid of His wrath. To be under the Law is to give God the service of a slave who fears the lash. But to be under Grace is to serve God out of pure love to Him. Oh, to be a child and to give the obedience of a child and not the homage of a serf! But the Antinomian says, "I am not under the Law, therefore will I live and fulfill my own lusts and pleasures."

Paul says of those who argue thus, their damnation is just. We have had the pain of knowing some who have said, "I am God's elect--Christ shed His blood for me--I shall never perish!" And then they have gone to the ale-house, they have sung the drunkard's song and have even used the drunkard's oath. What is this, dear Friends, but a strong delusion to believe a lie? They who can do this must surely have been some time in Satan's oven, to be baked so hard. Why, these must have had their consciences taken out of them! Are they not turned to something worse than brutes? The dog does not say, "My master feeds me and he will not destroy me, but is fond of me, therefore will I snarl at him or rend him"?

Even the ass does not say, "My master gives me fodder, therefore will I dash my heels into his face." The ox knows its owner and the ass his master's crib, but these men only know God to provoke Him and they profess that His love to them gives them a liberty to rebel against His will! God deliver you from any such freedom as this! Be not legalists, but love the Law of God and in it make your delight. Abhor all idea of being saved by good works, but O, be as full of good works as if you were to be saved by them!

Walk in holiness as if your own walking would make you enter into Heaven and then rest on Christ, knowing that nothing of your own can ever open the gate of the Celestial City. Eschew and abhor anything like Antinomianism. Do not be afraid of high doctrine. Men sometimes mislabel good sound Calvinism as Antinomianism. Do not be afraid of that--do not be alarmed at the ugly word Antinomianism if it does not exist! But the thing itself--flee from it as from a serpent! Shake off the venomous beast into the fire as Paul did the viper which he found among the firewood. When you are gathering up the doctrines of Grace to cheer and comfort you, this deadly viper gets into the midst and when the fire begins to burn, he comes out of the heat and fastens upon you. Shake him off into the fire of Divine Love and there let the monster be consumed!

My Brethren, if we are loved of God with an everlasting love and are no more under the Law but free from its curse, let us serve God with all our heart's gratitude to Him. Let us say, "I am Your servant. I am Your servant and the son of Your handmaid--You have loosed my bonds." Let the loosing of our bonds be an argument for service. Then again, Beloved, there is another kind of freedom of which we must all be aware--it is a notional professional freedom. "Free? Yes, certainly we are. We are the people of God," say some. Not that they have ever passed from death unto life. Not that vital godliness is a matter they understand.

No. "We always went to Church, or Chapel. We have never stopped going in our lives. We are the most regular of religious people and we were baptized, and we go to the sacrament and what is there that we do not do? Who convicts us of any sin? If we are not going to the Celestial City, who can be? Surely, surely, we enjoy much of the things of God! We sit in God's House and we feel a pleasure when we listen to the Truth of God. Sacred song bears us on high as well as other men. We sit as God's people sit and we hear as God's people hear--surely we are free!"

Ah, but dear Friends, a man may think himself free and still be a slave. You know there are many in this world who dream themselves to be what they are not. And you have a faculty of dreaming in the same manner. Christ must have come to you and shown you your slavery and broken your heart on account of it, or else you are not free. And you must have looked to the wounds of Jesus as the only gates of your escape and have seen in His hands the only power which could snap your fetters or else, though you have professed and re-professed, you are as much slaves of Satan as though you were in the Pit itself!

Beware, I pray you, of hereditary religion! A man cannot hand down his godliness as he does his goods. And I cannot receive Grace as I may receive lands, or gold, or silver. "You must be born again." There must be the going up out of Egypt, the leaving the flesh pots and the brick kilns, and advancing through the Red Sea of Atonement into the wilderness and afterwards into the promised rest. Have you passed from death unto life? If not, beware of having a mere notional, professional liberty!

There are many, too, who have the liberty of natural self-righteousness and of the power of the flesh. They have fanciful, unfounded hopes of Heaven. They have never wronged anybody. They have never done any mischief in the world. They are amiable. They are generous to the poor. They are this, they are that, they are the other! Therefore they feel themselves to be free. They never feel their own inability. They can always pray alike and always sing alike. They have no changes. They are not emptied from vessel to vessel. Their confidence never wavers. They believe themselves all right and abide in their confidence.

They do not stop to examine--their delusion is too strong and their comfort is much too precious for them to wish to mar it by looking to its foundation--so they go on, on, on--sound asleep till one of these days, falling over the awful precipice of ruin, they will wake up where waking will be too late! We know there are some such. They are in God's House, but they are not God's sons! You remember the case of Ishmael. It is to that which our Lord seems to allude here. Ishmael was a son of Abraham according to the flesh, but he never was free. His mother being a bondwoman, he was a slave.

He might call himself Abraham's son if he could, but being only after the flesh he was still a slave, for it was not in the power of Abraham, in the power of the flesh, to beget anything but bondage. And Ishmael at his best was still the son of the bondwoman. Yet you see he sits at the table, he eats and drinks just as merrily as the child of the promise. No, in some things he is stronger than Isaac--he has the advantage of age and I dare say plumes himself on being heir. "Ah," says he, "I am the elder one of the family." At last he mocked Isaac--when the boys were at their sports he was violent towards his younger brother, even as many Pharisees are very cruel to true Believers.

What came of it? Why, "the servant abides not in the house forever, but the son abides forever," and so the day came in which Sarah said, "Cast out the bondwoman and her son," and away went Ishmael. He might cling to his father and say, "I am your son." "You must go, Sir, you are a slave. You were born after the flesh and therefore you take from your mother your state and condition and not from your father. Your mother was a bond slave and so are you and you must go. The privileges of the children's house are not for you. You must go into the wilderness. You cannot abide here." But Isaac, though feeble and tempted and tried and vexed, is never sent out of his father's house--never--he abides forever.

This is the position of many. They are very good people in their way. They do their best, but what is their best? It is the offspring of the flesh. And that which is born of the flesh is flesh, Consequently their best endeavors only make them slaves in the house, not sons. Only he who is born by faith according to the promise is the free Isaac and abides in the house. The day will come when God will ask every member of the Christian Church and all who profess religion, "Are you children by faith in the promise or not?" And if you are only children according to the flesh He will send you back again into the wilderness--to eternal ruin you must go unless the Spirit of God has given you the spirit of freedom.

There was a custom, observed among the Greeks and Romans that when a man died, if he left slaves, they went as a heritage to the elder son and if the elder son said, "Some of these are my own Brethren, though they are slaves, I therefore pronounced them free," they would be free. Emancipation was not always allowed in either Greek or Roman states--a man might not always set a slave free without giving a good reason. But it was always held to be a valid reason if the son, coming into a heritage of slaves, chose to set them free. No question was asked if the son made them free. The law did not step in.

So, dear Friends, if the Son shall make us free, we shall be free, indeed. If Jesus Christ, the great Heir according to the promise, the great Mediator whom God has created Heir of all things, by whom also He made the worlds--if He shall say to us who are as Ishmael, "I make you free," then are we free, indeed! And neither Law, Justice, Heaven or Hell can bring any argument against us why we should not be free. But do beware of all imaginary freedoms and shun them as you would poison! And God give you Divine Grace to enjoy the glorious liberty of the children of God!

III. TRUE FREEDOM COMES TO US THROUGH HIM WHO IS, IN THE HIGHEST SENSE, "THE SON." No man gets free except as he comes to Christ and takes Him to be his All in All. You may rivet on your fetters by going to the Law, to your own good works, to your willings and your praying and your doings, but you will never be free until you come to Christ. Mark you, Man, if you will come to Christ you shall be free this moment from every sort of bondage. But if you will go here and there, and try this and that and the other, you shall find all your trying will end in disappointment and you shall lie down in sorrow and in shame--for none but Jesus--none but Jesus--can make us free, indeed.

Real liberty comes from Him only. Let us think awhile of this real liberty. Remember it is a liberty righteously bestowed. Christ has a right to make men free. If I should set a slave free who belongs to his master, he might run for a time--but since I had not the power to give him a legal emancipation--he would be dragged back again. But the Son, who is heir of all things, has a right to make him free whom He wills to make free. The Law is on Christ's side. Christ has such power in Heaven and earth committed to Him that if He says to the sinner, "You are free," free he is before high Heaven.

Before God's great bar you can plead the word of Jesus and you shall be delivered! Think, too, how dearly this freedom was purchased. Christ speaks it by His power, but He still bought it by His blood. He makes you free, Sinner, but it is by His own bonds. You go free because He bore your burden for you. See Him bear His agony--"Crushed beneath the millstone of the Law till all His head, His hair, His garments were bloody." See Him yonder, dragged to Pilate's hall, bound, whipped like a common felon, scourged like a murderer and dragged away by hellhounds through the streets. Look at Him fastened by those cruel fetters which went through His flesh to the accursed wood. See Him yielding up His liberty to the dungeon of death.

There the Mighty One sleeps in Joseph of Arimathea's tomb. Dearly did He purchase with His own bondage the liberty which He so freely gives. But, though dearly purchased, let us take up that keynote--He freely gives it! Jesus asks nothing of us as a preparation for this liberty. He finds us sitting in sackcloth and ashes and bids us put on the beautiful array of freedom. He discovers us in a darkness which may be felt, sitting in the valley of the shadow of death and He brings the true Light in His hand and turns our midnight into blazing noon and all without our help, without our merit, and at first without our will.

Christ saves sinners just as they are! Christ died not for the righteous, but for the ungodly! His message is Grace, pure Grace, undiluted by a single condition or requisition which God might make of man. Just as you are, trust your soul with Christ and though there is in you no speck of anything that is good, He will save you and give you perfect liberty. Dearly has He bought it, but freely does He give it--even the faith by which we receive is the gift of God. It is a liberty which may be instantaneously received. The captive goes first through one door and then another and perhaps a hundred keys must grate in the wards of the lock before he feels the cool fresh air gladdening his brow.

But it is not so with the man who believes! The moment you believe, you are free! You may have been chained at a thousand points, but the instant you believe in Christ you are unfettered and free as the bird of the air. Not more free is the eagle which mounts to his rocky nest and afterwards outsoars the clouds--even he, the bird of God--is not more unfettered than the soul which Christ has delivered! Cut are the cords and in an instant you are clear of all and upward you mount to God! You may have come in here a slave and you may go out free!

God's Grace can, in a moment, give you the condition of freedom and the nature of it. He can make you say, "Abba, Father," with your whole heart, though up to this day you may have been of your father the devil, and his works you have done. In an instant is it worked! We are told in tropical lands that the sun seems to leap up from under the horizon and the dead of night is suddenly turned into the luster of day--so on a sudden does God's Grace often dawn upon the darkness of sinful hearts. You have seen, perhaps, at times after showers of rain have fallen upon the earth, how land which seemed all dry and barren was suddenly covered with green grass, with here and there a lily full in bloom. And so a heart which has been like a desert, when once the shower of Jesus' Grace falls on it, blossoms like the garden of the Lord and yields sweet perfume.

And that in a moment! You who have given yourselves up in despair--you who have written your own condemnation! You who have made a league with death and a covenant with Hell and said, "There is no hope, therefore will we go after our iniquities," I charge you, hear me, when I declare that my Lord and Master, who has broken my chains and set me free, can break yours, too--and that with one blow! Mark, that if this is done, it is done forever. When Christ sets free, no chains can bind again. Let the Master say to me, "Captive, I have delivered you," and it is done!

Come on, come on, you Fiends of the Pit! Mightier is He who is for us than all they who are against us. Come on, come on, temptations of the world--but if the Lord is on our side, whom shall we fear? If He is our defense, who shall be our destruction? Come on, come on, you foul corruptions, come on you machinations and temptations of my own deceitful heart--but He who has begun the good work in me will carry it on and perfect it to the end.

Gather, gather, gather all your hosts together, you who are the foes of God and the enemies of man, and come at once with concentrated fury and with hellish might against my spirit--but if God acquits--who is he that condemns? Who shall separate us from the love of God which is in Christ Jesus our Lord? The black stream of death shall never wash out the mark of Christian liberty! That skeleton monarch bears no yoke which he can put upon a Believer's neck. We will shout victory when we are breast-deep amidst the last billows and grapple with the king upon the pale horse--we will throw the rider and win the victory in the last struggle, according as it is written, "Thanks be unto God which gives us the victory through our Lord Jesus Christ."

Sparta and Greece refused to wear the yoke of Persia and broke the proud king's pomp. But we are free in a nobler sense! We refuse the yoke of Satan and will overcome his power as Christ overcame it in the days gone by. Let those who will, bend and crouch at the foot of the world's monarch! But as for those whom God has made free, they claim to think, to believe, to act, and to be as their Divine instinct commands them and the Spirit of God enables them--"Where the Spirit of the Lord is, there is liberty." "If the Son therefore shall make you free, you shall be free, indeed."

IV. And now we put round the QUESTION, are we free, then, this morning? Are we free? I will not answer it for you, nor need I just now answer for myself, but I would beseech you to make a searching enquiry into it. If you are free, then remember that you have changed your lodging place, for the slave and the son sleep not in the same room of the house. The things which satisfied you when a slave will not satisfy you NOW.

You wear a garment which a slave may never wear and you feel an instinct within which the slave can never feel. There is an Abba, Father, cry in you which was not there once. Is it so? Is it so? If you are free you lie not as you used to do. You go not to the slave's work--you have not now to toil and sweat to earn the wages of sin which is death. But now, as a son serves his father, you do a son's work and you expect to receive a son's reward--for the gift of God is eternal life through Jesus Christ our Lord!

One thing I know, if you are free then you are thinking about setting others free. And if you have no zeal for the emancipation of other men you are a slave yourself. If you are free you hate all sorts of chains, all sorts of sin and you will never willingly put on the fetters again. You live each day crying unto Him who made you free at first, to hold you up that you fall not into the snare. If you are free, this is not the world for you! This is the land of slaves. This is the world of bondage. If you are free, your heart has gone to Heaven, the land of the free. If you are free today, your spirit is longing for the time when you shall see the great Liberator face to face!

If you are free, you will bide your time until He calls you. But when He says, "Friend, come up here," you will fearlessly mount to the upper spheres--and death and sin shall be no hindrance to your advent to His Glory! I would we were all free! But if we are not, the next best thing I would is that those of us who are not free would fret under the fet-ter--for when the fetters are felt, they shall be broken! When the iron enters into the soul it shall be snapped. When you long for liberty you shall have it! When you seek for it as for hidden treasure and pant for it as the stag for the water brook, God will not deny you! "Seek and you shall find. Knock and it shall be opened. Ask and it shall be given you."

God lead you to seek and knock and ask now, for Christ's sake. Amen.

General And Yet Particular

DELIVERED ON SUNDAY MORNING, APRIL 24, 1864,
BY THE REV. C, H. SPURGEON,
AT THE METROPOLITAN TABERNACLE, NEWINGTON.

"You have given Him power o ver all flesh, that He should give eternal life to as many as You have given Him." -- John 17:2.

THIS was used by our Savior as an argument why the Father should glorify Him in His dread hour of conflict. Our Lord did as much as say, "You have already given Me what I now ask. Therefore, since You have virtually bestowed it upon me in the Covenant, give it Me now in very deed." So the Believer, when he prays, asks for what is already his own. And when we come before the Lord in prayer this should encourage us much, that our heavenly Father has already given us all things in giving us His Son, so that we ask for what is virtually our own.

The text itself we will try to open up briefly. It contains two statements--first, that Christ, as a Mediator, has received from God universal authority over all flesh. And secondly, that the object of this is special and peculiar, that He may give eternal life to as many as the Father has given to Him. You have universal power, but you have within it a special purpose. We know that our Lord Jesus Christ has all power given to Him in Heaven and in earth--"Angels and men before Him fall and devils fear and fly." All things, whether animate or inanimate, confess the majesty of Him who is King of kings and Lord of lords.

Our text, however, mentions the most stubborn thing in all the world--"flesh." Jesus has power over all flesh. That willful, wicked, disobedient thing called flesh Christ knows how to govern. He has power over all men as fallen men, for such the term, flesh, describes. I understand, then, that Christ has power over all men, to pardon all whom He wills. Christ has this day as Mediator, power to convict of sin every living soul by His Spirit, if so He wills. And power to bring all men to the footstool of His Grace and to give them pardon if so it seems good in His sight. We do not believe that there is any exception to this rule--Christ has power over every man born of Adam, to give to him the Grace of conviction and the Grace of pardon, if so it should please Him to do.

He has power also to make those who are not convicted of sin and who are not pardoned, subservient to His purpose. He has power to restrain their evil passions from running to an excess of riot. He can use them as His drudges to effect His purposes even when they proudly rebel against Him--so that though they boast themselves in their own free will--they shall really be working out His own eternal purpose. He has a bit often in the mouth of His fiercest enemy and a hook in the jaw of the bloodiest persecutor.

Over all flesh He has authority whether it is crowned with royalty or wrapped in rags! Whether it curses with profanity or bows down with reverent adoration. There is not a mortal man from the equator to the poles, of any rank or any language, or bearing any hue upon his skin who is not subject to this universal mediatorial power of the Lord Jesus Christ. If I understand my text and Scriptures parallel with it, it was ordained in order to the salvation of the chosen, that the whole world of man should be taken from under the immediate rule of God as absolute God and placed under a new form of government of which the Mediator should be King and Head.

As the result of this gracious arrangement a fallen race is permitted to exist--a sinful world coming into contact with an absolute God must have been instantaneously doomed to Hell. Man, while yet a rebel, lives on in virtue of the mediatorial power of Jesus! He has stepped in between avenging Justice and the sinner and so the sinner is spared. I trace to Christ's Atonement the continued life of the most obdurate. All the long-suffering mercy of God seems to me to flow through the channel of the Savior's authority over all flesh.

It is in virtue of this power that the Gospel is preached to all men--"All power is given unto Me in Heaven and in earth. Go you, therefore, and teach all nations." Hence the command to believe receives its Divine sanction and those are condemned who believe not in His name. On account of this universal dispensation of mediatorship, an honest, gracious, and sincere invitation is given to whomever will, to drink of the Water of Life freely. It is, I say, on account of this universal mediatorial power of Christ that I can stand upon this platform and say in the broadest possible terms, that whoever believes on the Lord Jesus shall never perish, but have eternal life! And I can preach a Gospel which, in its proclamation, is as wide as the ruin and as extensive as the Fall.

But why all this? The text tells us that the object and design of all this was not universal, but special--that the intention of God in thus putting all men under the power of Christ was not that all men might receive eternal life, but that He might give eternal life to as many as had been given to Him. So that in all this universal dealing there is the special and peculiar design that the chosen may receive life--that the elect may be filled with spiritual life on earth and afterwards enter into the Glory life above.

God might doubtless have acted upon another plan and have given Christ power only over His elect if He had willed, that He might give eternal life to them. But it has not so pleased God. It has, on the contrary, pleased Him to put the whole race under the mediatorial sway of Jesus in order that He might give eternal life to those who were chosen out of the world. God might have commissioned His servants to go into the world and preach the Gospel to the chosen only-- He might have told us to present Christ only to certain persons upon whom there should be a peculiar mark. It has not so pleased Him.

He bids us go "into all the world and preach the Gospel to every creature." His high decree and Divine intent being that those whom He has ordained unto eternal life shall, through believing, enter into the life which He has ordained for them. I do not know whether I have brought before you what I am certain is the full idea of the text--a general power given to the Mediator over all flesh--as the result of which a proclamation of mercy is universally published to men and a general declaration of salvation through faith presented to all creatures. But this always with a special, limited, definite design--that a chosen people--separated from before all worlds from the rest of mankind should obtain eternal life.

I have aimed in my ministry constantly to preach, as far as I can, the whole of the Gospel rather than a fragment of it. Therefore those Brethren who are sounder than the Bible abhor me as much as if I were an Arminian. And on the other side, the enemies of the Doctrines of Grace often represent me as an Ultra-Calvinist. I am rejoiced to receive the censure of both sides! I am not ambitious to be numbered in the roll of either party. I have never cultivated the acquaintance nor desired the approbation of those men who shut their eyes to Truths of God which they do not wish to see.

I never desired to be reputed so excessively Calvinistic as to neglect one part of Scripture in order to maintain another. If I am thought to be inconsistent with myself, I am very glad to be so, so long as I am not inconsistent with Holy Scripture. Sure I am that all the Truth of God is really consistent, but equally certain am I that it is not apparently so to our poor, finite minds. In nine cases out of ten he who is nervously anxious to be manifestly consistent with himself in his theological system, if he gains his end, is merely consistent with a fool!

He who is consistent with Scripture is consistent with perfect Wisdom. He who is consistent with himself is at best consistent with imperfection, folly and insignificance. To keep to Scripture, even though it should involve a charge of personal inconsistency, is to be faithful to God and men's souls. My text seems to me to present that double aspect which so many people either cannot or will not see.

Here is the great Atonement by which the Mediator has the whole world put under His dominion. But still here is a special object for this Atonement--the ingathering, or rather out-gathering--of a chosen and peculiar people unto eternal life.

I. Let us, this morning, meditate upon the principle of the text and our first remark shall be that THE DOCTRINE OF A GENERAL DISPLAY OF POWER FOR THE ACCOMPLISHMENT OF A SPECIAL OBJECT IS IN ACCORDANCE WITH THE ANALOGY OF NATURE. In the world around us we shall find the Creator accomplishing special purposes by a far wider display of power than the immediate object appears to require. Take, for instance, yonder plant. What is the main object for which a plant lives? Every botanist and every common observer will tell you that its object in living is that it may produce seed and perpetuate its like.

God's object, then, in yonder plant is to produce a seed from it that its species may be perpetuated. How will He do it? Will He send an angel to watch over the seed and the seed alone? No, my Brethren, there shall be a watchful care over root, stem, cells, tissues, leaves and flowers. Although when winter comes, every leaf will drop off and rot in the ground and never be heard of again, yet those leaves have been the object of a superintending care, most marvelous and wise. Though the real object of it all has been the seed alone, yet stem and leaf and cell have all been watched over.

Just so, I think, it is in God's dealings with His elect. He is looking to them as to the seed and substance of mankind, but those graceless ones who will perish forever like fading leaves have been the object of His tender care. If you tell me that the leaves were not absolutely necessary to the seed, I will give you another illustration still more clear. You are not to think that when God is about to accomplish a purpose He studies just how much will do it and then spends no more power than a pinching economy finds needful.

We are wanting rain. Our gardens and fields are crying out for showers. Well, our gracious God will send it to us very soon. But will He just allot a shower to that piece of ground which requires it--will He not rather send a wide range of rain? I have sometimes wondered at this, that when the shower falls it must be God's intention to bless the field and yet He scatters the liquid blessing upon the salt and briny sea where no plants can be nourished and where it seems to be a waste to pour the cooling drops. You shall find it rain quite as heavily upon the Atlantic as upon the thirsty earth which is opening its mouth for the moisture.

Why is this? Because it is the rule of God when He is accomplishing a purpose to deal after a general fashion though still the object is specific. Here is this air about us. Why is it made up of oxygen, hydrogen and nitrogen and so on? Is it not that plants and animals may live upon it? Surely this is the Creator's drift in making such a compound. But suppose you transfer yourself in imagination to the polar regions where life cannot exist, or to spots in the great desert of Sahara where even the vulture with swift wing has never flown. You will find the air composed of precisely the same particles!

Why is this? There is no animal to breathe it, no plant to bloom in it. Why then the same? Simply because God is not like finite man--He has not to stint Himself to such an expenditure as shall just accomplish His own purpose--He acts like a God and in the infinity of His Nature He gives more than is absolutely necessary for the accomplishment of His purpose. Think again, now, of nature in another aspect. We are proud enough to think that God made this world for the comfort of man and with an eye to human convenience. Suppose we grant that principle for a moment.

Here is a violet peeping out among the green leaves. Why has it that delicious perfume making glad the spring? Why, you tell me it is to gratify man. Very likely, very likely. But here are millions upon millions of violets which are never smelt by anybody which grow among the nettles at the back of the Church, or away in the woods where not even a child has wandered, or at a distance from the abodes of men where they are never seen or heard of, for--

"Full many a flower is doomed to blush unseen, And waste its fragrance on the desert air." Why is everything so painted by the sun? Why do crystals sparkle when the sunbeams fall upon them? How is it you see the many lines of a rainbow when the sun is shining on a crystal?

Why it must be to gratify the eye. God would have this world a place of beauty and a joy forever! But crystals sparkle in the polar regions where there is not even a bear to look upon them! In that inhospitable region where life goes out and where we believe no creature having life could possibly exist, the sun still shines and still the crystal flashes back to Him the colors of the iris. Why is this? Why is this? I cannot tell you, except that I perceive that God gives to the sun a power over all things that He may give pleasure to the eye.

What multitudes of landscapes were never gazed upon by the artist's eye, yet there they are, sleeping in their beauty beneath the eyes of God. How the birds are singing this morning, how they are pouring forth from their throats sweet melodious strains and yet they are singing quite as well in the deep forest glade where no man can ever hear them as in our gardens and walks. Why is this? Do we not think that the birds sing for our joy and that the landscape is spread out for man's mental delight?

It certainly is so, and yet there are landscapes and birds where there are no men to see and ears to hear. So I think I might continue all the morning giving you analogies from Nature in which God, in the accomplishment of a specific purpose adopts a general mode of action.

II. I will take another view of the question. THIS PRINCIPLE IS SEEN IN PROVIDENCE. All of you believe in a general Providence. You believe that God superintends all the affairs of the universe so that there is not a grain of dust blowing in the street today which has not its orbit ordained and fixed as much as the planets in the sky. You believe that God overrules the motions of the rush that waves by the river as much as he does the policy of kings and emperors. Do not you believe in a special Providence, too?

I do, and I believe you do. You believe that God is watching specially over His own people and that all things work together for good to them who love God, to them who are called according to His purpose. And did it ever strike you that there was any inconsistency in believing in a general and a special Providence? I do not suppose it ever did--I know it never did me. I know I feel quite easy in believing the two things and I should have been very uneasy in not being able to believe both. I do not see why the Christian may not transfer the idea and believe that there is a general influence for good flowing from the mediatorial sacrifice of Christ and yet its special design and definite object is the giving of eternal life to as many as the Father gave Him.

We will take one or two instances in Providence. There is Jonah going to Tarshish. He has betrayed his Master and has fled from Nineveh. The Lord will have him back. He intends to bring him back in a strange conveyance--He has prepared a great fish to swallow him! How is Jonah to be got out of the ship? The storm must come and when the storm comes what does it do? Does it shake Jonah? Does it expose Jonah's life to danger? It does, but it also shakes the whole ship and all who are in the ship are afraid that they shall suffer shipwreck. And what is more, if there were a thousand ships upon the sea that day they felt the storm and yet God's special object was to have Jonah thrown into the sea-- though all the ships upon the sea must be tossed with the tempest, still there is the special design.

Take another thing. It is ordained according to prophecy that Christ must be born at Bethlehem. Then Mary His mother, who is great with child, must be brought to Bethlehem. How shall it be done? Why, in order to fetch Joseph and Mary to Bethlehem, every man and woman in Judea must go to the place of their pedigree and still, though God's express design is to bring Mary there that Jesus may be born, He uses a general method in order to accomplish it and every other Jewish man and woman must go to the place of their pedigree!

Here, again, is a particular object accomplished by general means. I might continue with many, many other instances, but indeed, you have only to open your eyes and see. My Brethren, if you pray tomorrow for God to send a favorable wind to waft the missionary-ship to its haven, the same wind will waft a merchantman, or a pirate, too, if they are going the same way. It may be that you pray that rain may come to extinguish a fire, and perhaps a shower comes, but you do not expect it to fall just where the fire is, but also for miles around. If you know some poor man living in Lancashire and you pray for him, that God would deliver him from poverty--if your prayer is heard, it may very likely be by quickening the trade of the whole country and conferring a blessing on the people of the whole neighborhood!

In fact, you know yourselves if you are praying to God to bless your children, it is not possible that your children should be blessed without the blessing coming down upon others, because God's blessing any one man is the means indirectly of blessing other people. You cannot have a godly family down a court without the whole court being the better for it. You cannot have one Christian man favored by his God without his household having some portion of the favor. God sends the favor only to His servants--that is the special intention--but still there comes with that a wider blessing.

While thinking over this matter I could only compare it to the moon when surrounded with a halo. The interior ring was the moon's own self, but round about it was a halo of brightness. Such is God's dealing with His people. There is the central substance of eternal, immutable love--but round about it there is a Divine halo--it encompasses all the creatures of God and makes them, in some measure, to participate in the light of the great central love, which belongs peculiarly to His saints.

III. Let us for one moment show that this has been ILLUSTRATED BY MIRACLES. Joshua is fighting with the Ca-naanites. There has been a long battle, but he desires to see his enemy exterminated and boldly turning round he cries to the sun, "Stand still upon Gibeon. And you, moon, in the valley of Ajalon." What did the sun and moon stand still for? Why to help Joshua against the Canaanites! But do you not think all the people everywhere had a longer day as the result? Did not every man who looked up wonder how it was that the sun stood still? There was a poor man with a hard task and he was afraid he should not finish it before the sun went down. How glad was he to find an extra hour added to the day!

He knew nothing about the special purpose and yet there was a special purpose in it all. Every man and woman on that side of the hemisphere enjoyed a length of light unusual for that time and yet there was no design of blessing them in Joshua's prayer. They were blessed incidentally. The real object was that the children of Israel might fight the battle and complete it. Take another miracle--Sennacherib has come against Jerusalem--he is about to swallow up Hezekiah and all the little kingdom of Judah. Hezekiah takes Rabshakeh's letter and lays it before the Lord. As the result of this, the angel of the Lord went through the camp of Sennacherib and slew his mighty men and the power of Assyria was broken.

What was the effect of it? There was the little straggling kingdom of Babylon, then contending for existence with Assyria. That kingdom was spared and became afterwards the destroyer of Assyria. And you read that Berodachbaladan, the king, sent messengers to Hezekiah to thank him for what was done. You see Babylon gets good out of the destruction of Sennacherib, but was this the main design? Certainly not. The grand object of God in destroying Sennacherib was to deliver Hezekiah and His people and yet the whole earth rejoices and has rest when the great hammer of the Lord falls on Assyria and its empire is broken and destroyed. It was a blessing to all the East when the power of the despot was broken that night--but the object of it was for Israel and for Israel, alone.

Come to the days of Christ and observe another miracle--there is a ship tossed within the tempest. Her mast is ready to go over the side. Her timbers crack--she will be swamped and go down. No, she will not--for there sleeps with His head upon the helm, the Master of the tempest, the Lord High Admiral of the sea, King Jesus! And when He has been awakened He stands up and rebukes the winds and waves and instantly there is a great calm. Why did He make the calm? For the preservation of His disciples and His own ship. But did the calm end there and give no blessing to others? We are informed that there were with Him many other little ships and so they all enjoyed the calm, too. The direct and definite intention was to make His disciples at peace and in safety. But the effect of it did not end with the disciples, but every ship which was out upon the sea of Nazareth that night enjoyed the calm.

One more instance and I will not multiply them, lest I fatigue you. Paul and Silas are in prison--God's object is to terrify the jailer and to bring out of prison His two servants, Paul and Silas. What does it say?--"The foundations of the prison were shaken and Paul and Silas had their bands loosed"? No, Brethren. "And every man's bands were loosed." Was it God's object to bring every man out of prison? No one dreams of such a thing! This was merely a concurrent benefit which went with God's special object in dealing with His poor persecuted followers, Paul and Silas.

So I believe that as it was in these miracles, so it is in that grander miracle, the great work of Grace. Jesus Christ comes into the world as a Propitiation for our sins and not for ours only, but for the sins of the whole world. And yet it is true He loved His Church and gave Himself for it. He laid down His life for His sheep and for His people did He die and not for the world, in one sense, and yet in that other sense which I have tried to bring out, He was a Propitiation for the sins of the whole world.

IV. Let us now LOOK AT FACTS. How do we really find the Gospel operate? I think I see this island of Great Britain covered with forests with men living in them having their naked bodies painted, dwelling in caves, feeding upon herbs and acorns. I think I see a simple-minded man--some think it was Paul--landing upon the shore and coming forward, trying to teach these savages the way of salvation. Oh, what a prolific hour was that when first the Gospel was preached in Britain! What has been the effect of it?

Brethren, let us answer another question first--What was the immediate design of God in sending the Gospel to Great Britain? My answer is to save as many as He had ordained to eternal life. That was His great object. But what has been the effect of it? I trace the liberty, the happiness and the prosperity of our country throughout these many centuries, to the prevalence of the Gospel in it. And though I believe God's design in sending the Gospel--I mean the central design--was that He might separate unto Himself His own chosen people, yet in connection with the Gospel, innumerable and incalculable blessings have come to every Englishman.

And there does not live a man who claims the name of Briton who is not under solemn obligation to the preaching of the Gospel for ten thousand benefits. Christ has, indeed, in England, seemed to have power over all Englishmen, that He might give eternal life to as many as the Father gave Him. Look at the Reformation. What was God's object in raising up Luther and Calvin and Zwingle to work the Reformation? Why, for this grand purpose--that Christ might see of the travail of His soul and that His chosen might believe in Him. That was the purpose of the Reformation! But what did the Reformation accomplish?

Not only this, but a thousand things besides, for it was to the Reformation that arts and sciences owed their progress. The human mind was liberated and expanded. And millions of people who never obtained eternal life through Jesus Christ, nevertheless, through the glorious Reformation obtained their liberty and ten thousand other mercies beyond all price. This is a matter of fact. And if you take the Gospel to the South Seas, if you preach it to the benighted people there, you will find that it will subdue all flesh to its Divine power. But still the object is kept in view--that as many as God gave to Christ might have eternal life.

Let us observe one self-evident truth. It is a remarkable fact that where the Gospel is not preached in its general aspect, God does not seem to work out His special object to any large extent. I mean to say that if you will go into any Chapel in London and you find a minister there who preaches nothing whatever of the Word of God, except that one part of it which is most blessedly and sweetly true--God's electing love--if you will listen to that man and hear him preach from the first of January to the end of December upon that one topic--the specialty and peculiarity of Divine Grace--you need not go into the vestry to ask the deacons if they have many conversions.

I am certain you will find there are few, indeed, and those mostly among persons who were convicted of sin and aroused elsewhere, and who obtain liberty under the gracious doctrine. But the absolute conversion of many is not a thing to be expected, and certainly not a thing found where the preacher is so restrained by his sense of electing love as to be unable to boldly preach the rest of the Gospel and say, "Believe in the Lord Jesus Christ and you shall be saved." You have only to try it, dear Friends--put your feet into the Chinese shoes and prevent their growing to the proper size, in order to keep them in ecclesiastical comeliness--and you will soon find your walk of usefulness very much restricted.

Hold on to the point of being consistent! Make that the main thing--banish those texts which speak about anything general--never open your mouth with a universal invitation! Make it out that the Bible has not a word in it directed to men as men, but only to the chosen and I will undertake that unless there is an unprecedented act of God's Sovereignty, you shall preach from one end of the year to the other and you shall not be troubled at the number of the elect people. There will be very few who will ever come forward.

But I know also, (and he who will look candidly will see it), that the most effective ministry is that one which is not ashamed of the Doctrines of Grace! The ministry which does not stutter or stammer in talking about election! Does not trim or cut the Divine Sovereignty of God, but which is equally clear upon the other point that God has declared His own solemn oath, "I will not the death of a sinner, but had rather that he should turn unto Me and live." A ministry which holds Sovereignty but holds man's responsibility, too, which dares to talk about God's special object with bold voice and yet insists upon it that He has proclaimed to every creature under Heaven this gracious proclamation, "Believe in the Lord Jesus Christ and you shall be saved."

Well, now, these are facts and facts which are not to be disputed, either. We hear people sometimes sneer and say, "Ah, there are many conversions, but are they genuine?" Sir, they are genuine! For we will boast this much that if there are not genuine conversions found in this Church, for instance, there are no conversions genuine under Heaven. For when I see harlots made chaste and remaining honorable women year after year. When I know drunkards who forswear the cup and who labor with their might for the reclaiming of others. When I look upon those who were once singing the song of the lascivious on the ale-bench who now for years--mark you, not months--for years persevere in holiness, I make this my glory!

If any can find better conversions under Heaven let them find them! I am satisfied that they are such converts as Apostolic times added to the Church--such as honor God in their lives and glorify Christ daily by their walk and conversation. I believe you shall find most conversions where neither Truth of God is held back, but where, as in the text, the two are taught. "You have given Him power over all flesh, that He should give eternal life to as many as You have given Him."

V. OUR PRINCIPLE EXPLAINS MANY SCRIPTURES and this goes very much in its favor. I like to read my Bible so as never to have to blink when I approach a text. I like to have a theology which enables me to read it right through from beginning to end and to say, "I am as pleased with that text as I am with the other." You know, Brothers and Sisters, you must be conscious of it, that there are many texts of Scripture which look wonderfully like universal redemption. Wonderfully like it and if they do not intend some sort of generality, they certainly speak in a very singular manner.

Such a text as this, "He is the Propitiation for our sins: and not for ours only, but for the sins of the whole world." "Who gave Himself a ransom for all to be testified in due time." I might mention more of these--but if you get with an Arminian brother he will have them all at his fingertips, so you will spare me the trouble. These people are always dwell- ing upon these, and think they have quite upset the doctrine of particular redemption though that is as plain in Scripture as the nose upon a man's face! We know Scripture says, "He has laid down His life for the sheep." He has redeemed us from among men. "Christ loved the Church and gave Himself for it." And you know that passage--"Husbands love your wives even as Christ also loved the Church and gave Himself for it."

How did He love the Church? He loved the Church with a special love, far above that which He gives to others, or else according to that metaphor a husband ought to love his wife, and love every other woman just as much! That is the natural inference of that text. But you clearly see there must have been a special love intended in the husband towards the wife and so there must be a special love in Christ. He loved the Church and gave Himself for it.

Now do you not think, Brethren, as there are two sets of texts in the Bible, the one of which very clearly speaks about the infinite value of the Atonement and another which very evidently speaks about the intention of that Atonement being for the chosen and for the chosen only, that the best way is to believe them both and to say, "Yes, I see it--as the result of Christ's death all men are put under the system of mediatorial Grace, so that Christ has power over them. But the object of His doing this is not that He may save all of them, but that He may save out of these all which He now has in His own hands--those whom the Father has given Him"?

The shepherd trusts me with all his sheep in order that I may sever from them twenty which he has marked. A father tells me to go into the midst of his family, his whole family, in order that I may take out of it one of his sons to be educated. So God gives to Christ all flesh, says the text, but still always with this definite and distinct purpose--that He may give eternal life to those whom He has given to Him.

VI. Let us go on in the sixth place to say briefly that this seems quite CONSISTENT WITH

THE NATURE OF GOD. We too often measure God after a human standard and therefore make mistakes. Remember that God has such an abundance of mercy and Grace and power, that He never has to calculate how much will be necessary for the accomplishment of His purpose. He does largely and literally like one who cannot but act in an infinitely gracious manner. If you have some chickens and you wish to feed them, you will only throw down as much barley as the fowls will want, but you do not think of feeding all the sparrows of the neighborhood!

It would be a very good thing if you could for they all need food. But you throw down as much as will accomplish your purpose. Now our God never has to stint Himself in this way, but with large handfuls He feeds the special objects of His care and the ravens and kites besides. God, again, exhibits a kingly character in His great methods of general love. At the coronation of the old kings, the fountains in Cheapside ran with red wine. Now you will say, "What a waste!" The gutters ran down on both sides with wine. It was not necessary, was it? The king's object was that his subjects might have wine.

Well, if that were his only object that might have been accomplished by opening the bottles one by one and stopping when there was just enough to satisfy their thirst. Why did it run down the streets? Was it a waste? Not at all, it exhibited the royal glory. The king was glad to give the people wine to drink, but he wanted also to show himself a king and as nobody but a king could make gutters run with wine, therefore he did it to illustrate his own magnificence. And our God, when He is about to exhibit mercy, does not say, "So much will just accomplish My purpose and save My elect"-- that is His main object. But behold, He makes the rivers run with wine and the floods with milk, so there is enough and to spare and yet no waste, because His grander object is His own Glory, and He is glorified even by that love which does not effectually save.

When Napoleon was at war, his favorite tactics were, we are told, always to bring crushing battalions to bear upon some one point to carry everything before him. That, my dear Friends, is the mode of procedure in which you and I have to act. If we have to accomplish a purpose, we must concentrate the whole of our might upon that one point. But suppose one greater than Napoleon, or a Napoleon with ten times ten thousand times more troops than he had? He would not need to concentrate his battalions upon one point, but simply cry to all his hosts, "Advance!" and they would go crushing down his foes at every point of the line.

So our God cares for the salvation of His elect. But that is not the only thing He cares about-- His own Glory is higher than this. His Glory is the whole of the line and our God, while He effectually saves those whom He has chosen, has no need to bring all His power upon one point. He has abundance to spare after He has done all that we know of. He can, while He is blessing His people, also bless the entire universe according to His own will. And I doubt not that so He does and that Heaven and earth are full of the majesty of His Glory, because Heaven and earth, though they may not alike participate in the fullness of Divine complacency, are full of the beams of His love.

VII. I have to conclude by saying that this principle is a MODEL FOR OUR CONDUCT. I was talking the other day with a Brother. He said he did not think the conversion of the world was the legitimate object of missionary enterprise, because all that Christ intended by the Gospel was the gathering out of a people. Well now, it seems to me that my dear friend was quite right and quite wrong. As to God's purpose in the sending of the Gospel to the world he was quite right, it is the gathering out of a people.

But as to my work he was quite wrong, for the work of God's minister is not the gathering out of a people. Christ surely knows what His own disciple is to do. Just hear. "Go you and teach all nations, baptizing them in the name of the Father and of the Son and of the Holy Spirit." That is our work. He did not say, "Go you and sever out of all nations a people to be taught and to be baptized." No! Christ's marching orders to His people are in these words, "Preach the Gospel to every creature." What will be the result of this universal proclamation?

The chosen will be saved. Then, Lord, why not send me to Your chosen? Why send me to all nations? "What business have you to question your Master's will? Is not this the very way in which I have chosen, that My elect shall be brought, by the preaching of the Gospel to all nations?" I look as the result of missionary enterprise, not for the world's conversion--I do not expect it--I believe that God will gather out of all people His chosen, and that Christ will come and when He comes, then shall He reign from the river even to the ends of the earth. But all the missionary societies put together will never convert the world, nor do I believe they will do very much towards it unless they very soon alter their tactics.

We shall have to try something very different from all the societies which have ever been in operation before we see any great results. I am waiting for a good time to come. Till then we must use old vessels till we get better ones, but better ones will be found. My own impression is that the world will never be converted by missionary agencies, but that is not your business--I am not to make God's decrees the rule of my walk. I am to make God's revealed will my rule of action. Christ tells me to, "Preach the Gospel to every creature," and if I were absolutely certain there was not one elect man upon earth, I would obey and preach the Gospel for all that--because if there were not a single soul saved by it, we are unto God a sweet-smelling savor.

So then, I say to you individually, talk about Christ everywhere--preach Jesus Christ to every creature. Say to every man and woman you meet, "There is life in a look at the Crucified One." Tell men that, "Whoever comes unto Him, He will in no wise cast out," and let this be always your comfort, that all that the Father gives to Him shall come to Him! That Jesus shall see His seed. That of all that the Father has given Him He will lose none, but will present them all at His right hand at last. Fly back to God's electing love and the decrees of God as the pillow of your rest.

But take the general command and the universal power of Christ over all flesh as the sword with which you fight and the staff upon which you lean. It is for this end that I ask you, dear Friends, to contribute as you shall see fit, to the spreading of the Gospel in foreign lands by the Missionary Society. I do not believe it is a perfect organization--I believe it is full of faults. I believe, however, it is the only way in which we can send the Gospel to the heathen just now.

We will have a better plan by-and-by, I hope, but meanwhile--as this is the only one--let us use it with vigor, for, after all, it is not the instrumentality, but God. And if I have to look upon this as an ox-goad--an unfit tool to strike the Philistines, yet as I have not a better I will use it till a better shall be found! Meanwhile let us pray the Lord to speed His own cause and gather out His chosen by His Grace. Amen.

Labor In Vain

DELIVERED ON SUNDAY MORNING, MAY 1, 1864,
BY THE REV. C. H. SPURGEON,
AT THE METROPOLITAN TABERNACLE, NEWINGTON.

"Jonah said unto them, Take me up and cast me forth into the sea; so shall the sea be calm unto you: for I know that for my sake this great tempest is upon you. Nevertheless the men rowed hard to bring it to the land. But they could not: for the sea worked and was tempestuous against them." -- Jonah 1:12,13.

THESE mariners manifested most commendable humanity. They were not willing, even though it were to preserve their own lives, to cast overboard an innocent man. Therefore they first used their best endeavors. And when these failed they made a solemn appeal to God, entreating Him not to lay upon them innocent blood--and then, since necessity has no law, Jonah, as a last resource was given up to the boisterous element, but not till every effort had been made to save him. We should he very careful of human life, doing nothing which even indirectly may destroy or injure it.

And if we should be jealous over life, how much more anxious should we be concerning men's souls! And how watchful lest we should do anything by which the least of the human family may have his eternal interests endangered by our example or teaching! God give us Divine Grace, like these mariners, to row hard that if possible we may bring the ship to land laboring that none around us may be left to perish.

I shall not, however, dwell upon that aspect of the text. Our Savior selected Jonah as one of His peculiar types-- "There shall no sign be given," said He, "to the men of this generation but the sign of the Prophet Jonah." We believe, therefore, that we are not erring if we translate the details of the history of Jonah into spiritual illustrations of man's experience and action with regard to Christ and His Gospel.

We have before us a picture of what most men do before they will resort to God's remedy. That remedy is here most fairly imaged in the deliverance of the whole ship's company by the sacrifice of one on their behalf.

I. Our first observation is that SINNERS, WHEN THEY ARE TOSSED UPON THE SEA OF CONVICTION, MAKE DESPERATE EFFORTS TO SAVE THEMSELVES. The men rowed hard to bring the ship to land. The Hebrew is they "dug" hard, sending the oars deep into the water with much exertion and small success. The tempest so tossed the sea about that they could not row in a good and orderly manner. But they desperately tugged at the oars, which the towering waves rendered useless by too deep a digging.

Straining every sinew they labored by violence to get the ship in safety to the haven. Brethren, no word in any language can express the violence of earnest action with which awakened sinners strive and struggle to obtain eternal life. Truly, if the kingdom of God were in the power of him that wills and him that runs, they would possess it at once! Since they struggle, however, in an unlawful manner, the crown of victory will never be awarded them. They may kindle the fire and rejoice in the sparks, but thus says the Lord, "This shall you have of My hand: you shall lie down in sorrow."

Let us notice some forms of the fleshy energy of men straining after self-salvation. The most usual is moral reformation. We have seen the drunkard, when conscience has been awakened, renounce his cups altogether. He has gone further than temperance and has espoused total abstinence. And proceeding further still, it often happens that in the excess of zeal, he vomits forth furious words against all who go not the same length of abstinence as himself.

Yonder man was given up to blasphemy, but now an ill word never comes from his tongue--and he is therefore content with himself because he no longer curses God. Another has followed an ill trade, or has been in the habit of neglecting Sunday worship. Conscience has mercifully led him to give up his ill connections and attend a place of worship. Is not this well? It is, indeed, well. But it is not enough! It is marvelous how far men will push their reforms. And yet how little solid peace such purging can secure. For what is the sinner after his reformation but the blackamoor washed clean, a blackamoor still?

I would have the Ethiopian clean by all manner of means. But I would not let him fancy that the soap and the niter will make him white. I would have the leopard tamed and caged, but this will not remove his spots. Moral reforms are excellent in themselves, but they are dangerous if we rest in them. Let even a corpse be washed, but let no man dream that the most careful washing will restore it to life. "You must be born again" rings out the death knell of all salvation by human effort. Unless reforms are founded in regeneration, they are baseless things which fail in the end for want of foundation. They are deceptive things, affording a transient hope, which soon, alas, must melt away.

Ah, my Hearer, you may go on improving and reforming, but all your present and future amendments can never wipe out the old score of sin. There stands the black catalog of your sins, engraved as in eternal brass! The gloomy record remains unaltered and unalterable by any deeds of yours. Something more potent than your tears and change of life must take away the sins of your departed years. Beware, then, of thinking that you are getting the ship to land--no matter how hard you row with these oars of human resolution.

Others add to their reformation a superstitious regard to the outwards of religion. According to the sect with which they unite, they become excessively religious. They reverence every nail of the Church door and every panel of the pulpit. There is not a brick in the aisle which is not sacred to them, nor even tile on the roof! Every rubric, every "Amen," every vestment and candlestick has to them a world of sanctity about it. They are not content with the ordinary days of worship, but the Church bell rings every morning. And well it may, for if men are to earn salvation in God's House, they had need be there all day and all night, too!

Even in a Protestant Church, men row very hard with multitudinous observances and superstitious performances, but when you get into the Romish Church, the labor in vain comes to a climax! There are vows of poverty, celibacy, silence, passive obedience and a thousand other tortures! If the Moloch whom they worship is not satisfied he ought to be. We heard but the other day of a gentleman giving up all his goodly heritage, selling his broad acres and pouring all the purchase money into the coffers of the monks and priests in order that at last by rowing hard in this way he might get the ship to land.

It is remarked of the Hindus that they give vastly more to their idols than we bestow upon the cause of God and I suppose it is true--but then they also are rowing hard to get the ship to land. All they do is for themselves. Self is always a mighty power in the world. Do but teach men that they can gain their own salvation by their own doings and mortifications and offerings and I would expect to see the treasury filled! I would expect to hear the whip constantly going upon the shoulders. But I should despair of seeing anything like holiness surviving in the land. Superstition is hard rowing but the ship will not come to the land by it. Men invent ceremony after ceremony. There is this pomp and that show--this gaudy ornament and that procession. But the whole matter ends in outward display, no secret soul-blessing results flow from there. Priests and their votaries may go on piling up human inventions ad infinitum, but they will forever fail to ease the conscience, or give rest to a disturbed soul. Man's awful necessities crave something more than the husks of superstition!

You will find another form of the same thing among ourselves. Many persons row hard to get the ship to land by a notional belief in orthodox doctrine. This superstition is harder to deal with, but quite as dangerous as the belief in good works. It is quite as legal an idea for me to think to be accepted by believing good doctrine as to expect to be pardoned for doing good works. Yet we have scores of people who, if they can get hold of the Calvinistic creed at the right end--if they become masters of it and know how to argue against Arminianism--if they become not only sound Calvinists but a little sounder still, having not only the sixteen ounces to the pound but two or three ounces over and above, so as to make them ultra-Calvinistic--why then they fancy that all must be well!

"I never can hear a preacher," this man will say, "who is not sound. I can tell at once when there is a grain of free will in the sermon." This is all very well, but he who boasts thus may be no better than the devil! No, he may not be so good, for the devil believes and trembles--but these men believe and are too much hardened in their own conceit to think of trembling. Away with the idea that believing sound doctrine and chaining ourselves to a cast-iron creed is vital godliness and eternal life! Orthodox sinners will find that Hell is hot and that their knowledge of predestination will not yield a cooling drop to their parched tongues.

Condemning other people--cutting off the saints of God right and left--is but poor virtue and to have these blessed doctrines in the head while neglecting them in the heart is anything but a gracious sign. If you can "a hair divide between the west and north-west side," do not therefore fancy that your fine gifts and profound orthodoxy will ensure you an entrance into the kingdom of Heaven. Ah, you may row with those oars, but you will not get the ship to land--you must be saved by Sovereign Grace through the operation of the Holy Spirit upon the heart--or you will not be saved at all. As it is not by doing that we are saved, neither is it by subscribing to creeds. There is something more than this needed before the ship can reach the port.

Perhaps, in this congregation, we have other subtle methods of endeavoring to do the same thing. The pastor has noticed that many are resting upon their own incessant prayers. Ah, my poor Hearer, you know your need of something, you can hardly tell what. You have heard the subject of salvation explained to you a hundred times and now when it comes to the pinch you do not understand it after all. I thank God that you have learned how to pray--that your sighs and cries and groans come up before Him. But I sorrow because you trust in your prayers and rest in them. Remember that you will no more be saved for the sake of your prayers than for the sake of your good works.

If your knees become hard as the knees of St. James are said to have been--hard like the camel's through long kneeling--and if with the Psalmist you could say, 'My throat is dried, my eyes fail," yet all this, if you look to it and do not look to Christ, will never avail you. I knew what it was for months to cry out to God and to find the heavens above me as brass, because I had not understood clearly the soul-quickening words, "Believe and live," but dreamed that by praying I could get myself into a suitable state to receive mercy, or perhaps move the heart of God towards me!

Whereas that heart needed no moving towards me, it was full of love from before the foundation of the world. Pray, my dear Brethren. Let me never discourage you in that. But do let me beg you not to sit still, or recline upon your prayers, for if you get no further than your prayers, you will never get to Heaven. There is more wanted than crying to God! More wanted than earnest desires, however passionately they may be breathed. There must be faith in Jesus or else you will row hard with your prayers, and you will never bring the ship to land.

Then there are others who are toiling by--I scarcely know how to describe it--a sort of mental torture. Oh, the many who say, "If I could feel as I ought to feel. O, Sir, my heart is as hard as a nether millstone. And yet I do not feel that it is hard--I wish I did. I would give my eyes if I could repent. I would give my right arm if I could but weep for sin! I would be satisfied to be a beggar, or to lie rotting in a dungeon if I could but feel that I was fit to come to the Savior! But, alas, I feel nothing! If I did but feel my unfitness--did but know my own unworthiness--I should have hope. But I am made of such Hell-hardened steel that neither terrors or mercies can move me. O, that I could repent! O, that this rock could give forth streams like that Rock which Moses smote in the wilderness of old! O, that I could but bring my heart to melt into something like desires after God and Christ! Oh, I am everything but what I should be!"

Now, my dear Hearer, you will row very hard in this way before you will ever come to land, for self-righteousness lies at the bottom of all this. You want to save your heart from hardness and then come to Jesus, which is much as to say you wish to save yourself and then come to Him to put the finishing stroke upon you. You have a secret attachment to your own goodness or you would not be so eager to compass a fitness--you should at once do as you are bid and rest alone on Jesus. Your business is not with self, but with Jesus! With Jesus, just as you are. However hard your heart may be--however destitute of feeling you may have become--this, though it should be subject for lamentation, should never keep you from resting in Him who is able to save to the uttermost them that come unto God by Him.

I tell you, your trying to get your heart into a right state, your trying to repent, your trying to be humble is all labor in vain. It is all going the wrong way to work. Your business is with Christ! He can soften, cleanse and sanctify, but you can do none of these, try as you will. Come as you are to my Lord Jesus, hard-heart and all, and the sea shall soon be calm for you. While you row with your own oars, the sea will only work and be the more tempestuous.

Various are the shapes which this carnal energy assumes. I have met with many who are in this kind of case. They are constantly starting objections to their own salvation and trying to answer them. They have comfort for a moment and they say, "Yes, this is very sweet, but"--and then they will spend a week or two in trying to split up that but. When they are rid of this but, a mercy will come to them from another quarter and they are sure to meet it with, "Ah, blessed be God for that, but." They are always pulling away at these buts.

These big waves come sweeping up to the side of their vessel and they try to dig their oars into them. Friend, if you are never saved until you, an unpardoned sinner, have answered all objections, you will never be saved because there are a thousand objections to the salvation of any man which can only be met by one argument and that is the blood of Jesus. If you will go here and there seeking answers to the devil's suggestions of unbelief you may travel the whole world and end your fruitless task in despair.

But if you will come to Jesus, if you will see Him like another Jonah thrown out of the ship for your sake. If you will but see Him lost that you may be saved, then a peace which passes all understanding shall keep your heart and mind by Christ Jesus.

II. We will now take the second point. Like these mariners, THE FLESHY EFFORTS OF AWAKENED SINNERS MUST INEVITABLY FAIL. The text says, "The men rowed hard to bring it to the land. But they could not." With all man's rowing after mercy and salvation, he can never find it by his own efforts. For this good reason, first of all, that it is contrary to God's Law for a sinner to get comfort by anything he can do for and by himself. Here is the law--"By the works of the Law there shall no flesh living be justified."

That rule, then, fixed and fast as the laws of Nature, shuts out forever all hope of the attainment of joy and peace by anything that we can do, or be, or feel--for all these the Law already claims of us. How mad then will it be on our part if we run counter to a Divine Law! Success is impossible in so perverse a course. I do well, therefore, if I discourage all the efforts of awakened consciences to find peace anywhere except in the work of Christ. Let a man labor ever so earnestly, yet if he goes against the laws of Nature, you know his labor is lost.

Here is an oven to be warmed for hungry persons need bread. See the workers yonder, how they toil, bringing snow with all their might to heat the oven. "Well," you say, "do not discourage them. Do not discourage their earnest activity. It is a pity when you see people really determined to do anything, to discourage their efforts." Ah, it is a pity, indeed, except when these efforts are foolish. If I see them bringing snow to heat an oven I know they will never do it, work as hard as they may.

And when sinners bring their own works to yield them spiritual comfort, I know that they are spending their labor for that which profits not and I must and will discourage them! Some years ago certain persons engaged in a speculation to sink a coal mine in a part of England where coal was never found. Prospectuses were issued. Directors obtained. And shareholders duped! And the workmen began to sink their shaft. Now it was absolutely certain--any geologist could have told them so--that they would not find coal, let them dig to doomsday.

Suppose you and I had gone there and seen them digging and had laughed at them, or told them it was all of no avail? Wiseacres might have replied, "You ought not to discourage coal mining, you ought not to discourage men who are working so very hard." I would say, "I would not discourage coal mining in any place where there is coal to be had. But for these poor souls to throw away their sweat and their money for that which is not coal--I will discourage them in that insane enterprise and think I do them good service."

When we see men struggling after eternal life through their own efforts, we know eternal life is not to be had there. We are glad that they are awakened to anything like effort, for anything is better than spiritual sloth--but we are grieved to see them laboring in the very fire, toiling where success can never crown their endeavors. There is no salvation by the works of the Law--why then look for it there? If you dash your head against the law of Nature, the law of Nature will not change for you. And if you labor in opposition to the irreversible Law of God, you will pay the penalty of it in your utter failure.

The ancients fabled that it was one of the tortures of Hell to which the daughters of Danaus were condemned, that they should fill a tub without a bottom with buckets full of holes. Behold the picture of the self-righteous man's undertaking! He may labor, he may toil, but he is filling a bottomless tub with leaky buckets. And work as he may, though he drop down dead in the attempt, success is impossible. O that he knew it to be so and would trust in the Lord Jesus! Besides this, the man cannot succeed in obtaining salvation by his own efforts because in what he is doing he is insulting God! He is casting dirt in the face of Christ! He is denying the whole testimony of the Holy Spirit.

Ah, my Hearer, if you could save yourself, why was it necessary that Christ should die for you? If your prayers could avail, why did He sweat great drops of blood? Why, Man, if there were any merit in your mortification, or your reformation, what need that the Prince of Life and Glory should veil Himself in ignominy and suffer a death of shame? You do, in fact, say by your fleshly attempts, I want no Savior, I can save myself! You do, in fact, scoff at the great Atonement which God has made in the Person of Christ!

This insult will ruin your soul, except you turn from it. Repent of it, I pray you. Humble yourself and receive Jesus' finished work. If scorning the Jordan, Naaman had gone to Abana and Pharpar, he might have washed not only seven times but seventy times seven! He might have earnestly persevered in the constant immersion, but he would have remained a leper to his dying day. If you scorn the Atonement and neglect God's great command to believe and live. If you go about to try and feel, or be, or do, you will use these Abanas and Pharpars to your own damnation! And to your own salvation never.

I pray you, do not insult God by looking for balm in Gilead, or for a physician there. There is no balm in Gilead, there never was any. There is no physician there, or else the daughter of my people would long ago have been healed. Men would long ago have saved themselves. You must look higher than the Gilead of human energy. You must look higher than earth's physicians. You

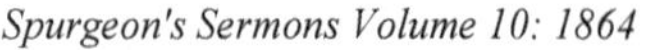

must look to the hills where comes our Help, the great mountains of a Savior's work and merit!

There are many other reasons why it is impossible that a man can ever get comfort in the way of works and feelings. The principal one I will mention is because that is the way of the curse. He who is under the Law is under the curse. So long as I stick to the Law, do what I may, I am under the curse of the Law and consequently under the curse. And how can I expect in the way of the curse to find the eternal blessing? Oh, folly, to choose the way of the curse as the way of blessing! But the best proof of it all is experience. Ask either saint or sinner and you shall find that peace was never obtained in the way of the flesh. Turn to the Christian and he will tell you, "Therefore being justified BY FAITH, we have peace with God."

He will tell you that when he turns away from faith and looks to himself his darkness begins at once. He will assure you that he never walks in perfect light and true comfort except when he keeps his eyes fast fixed upon the great Sacrifice of Calvary. I know, Brethren, whenever I am dull and drooping as to my eternal interests, it is always because I have thought more of my graces than of Christ's Grace, or more of the Spirit's work in me than of the finished work of Christ on my behalf. There is no living happily but by depending wholly upon Christ. A sinner resting upon his Savior as his only hope is blest.

Now, if this is the experience of all saints, and if no sinner living will dare to tell you that he can get his conscience quiet by his own works--why do any of you try? Heaven bears witness that salvation by faith is certain--Hell bears witness that works do but ruin us. O, hear the double testimony and lay hold upon eternal life through the Person of Christ Jesus! O my dear Friend, if you are really panting for salvation, go not round and round these dreary performances of your own doings! It must all end in misery, disappointment and despair. "They rowed hard to bring it to land. But they could not."

All human work which does not begin and end in the Lord Jesus must be a failure. All your works have been failures with you up to the present and so it will be to the end of the chapter. Give it up and God help you to try His method, for it is sure and efficacious.

III. Now, with very great brevity, I will bring you to the third point of the sermon which is that THE SOUL'S SORROW WILL CONTINUE TO INCREASE SO LONG AS IT RELIES UPON ITS OWN EFFORTS. What is the effect of all that the creature does before it believes in Christ? It may be overruled for good, but much of its effect is mischievous. The good effect which flows from it lies in this--the more a man strives to save himself, the more convinced will he become of his own impotence and powerlessness.

I thought that I could turn to God whenever I pleased till I tried to turn to Him. I thought repentance a very easy thing till I began to repent. I dreamed that faith in Christ must be mere child's play till I had to groan, "Lord, help my unbelief!" As for the Law, when we attempt to keep it, we groan under a heavy burden which we have no strength to bear--

"How long beneath the Law I lay in bondage and distress! I toiled, the precept to obey, But toiled without success."

Oh, it is hard serving the Law! He is a cruel taskmaster. The whip is always going and the flesh is always bleeding. It is hard service. Weary and faint, we fall down under it and feel it to be a load intolerable to be borne. Well is Haggi chosen as the type of the Law, for indeed it genders unto bondage.

And well was blazing Sinai chosen as its representative, for even Moses said, when standing upon that mountain, "I do exceedingly fear and quake." To be clean divorced from all legal hope is a blessed preparation for Gospel marriage with Christ. It was well that rowing hard made the mariners feel their inability to cope with the tempest--and it is best of all when creature efforts produce a clear discovery of creature weakness.

Another good result will sometimes follow. The man passionately striving to save himself by keeping the Law finds out the spirituality of that Law, a spirituality which he never saw before. He has given up outward acts of sin, but all of a sudden he is startled to find that even though he has given them all up in open fact, he is still condemned for allowing the thoughts of them in his heart! Even a look may be fornication, though no act of sin shall follow it. He remembers that even the wish of his heart may be theft. And that covetousness is not only straining after another man's goods, but envying him the enjoyment of them.

Now he finds the work is impossible, indeed, for he might sooner hold the winds in his fist than control his passions, or with his breath blow the sea into a calm sooner than he could restrain the impetuous propensities of his nature. O, Brethren, it is a good thing when we find that the Commandments of God are exceedingly broad--when we see the sharpness of this great axe of the Law and how it cuts at the very root of the tree and leaves us no green thing standing wherein we can boast!

So far so good. Fleshly effort, overruled by Divine Grace, has helped us to the discovery of the grandeur and dignity of the Divine Law. But I am afraid that much of this toil and labor is very mischievous because it makes unbelief take a firmer grip. It is easier to comfort a soul who has been a short time in darkness than it is to comfort one who has given way a long time to an unbelieving state of heart. I remember one, I believe she is in darkness now and if I remember right it is ten years ago since she first fell into these doubts and fears. I am sometimes afraid she will never see the Light because it has become chronic with her.

Giant Despair's prisoners do not all escape. He has a yard full of bones, remember. These are the relics of willing prisoners who would not be comforted and put out their own eyes to avoid the Light. I believe that some sinners make excuses for themselves out of their despair and that they let their doubts and fears grow till they cast a thick shadow, like Jonah's gourd. And then they sit down with a miserable sort of comfort beneath the leaves. "There is no hope, therefore will I go on in my sins. There is no hope for me, therefore let the worst come to me. I can but be damned. I will fold my arms and sit still."

Oh, this is a damnable temptation! It is one which ruins multitudes I am sure! This is Satan's man-trap! Beware of it! This is the devil's stocks in the inner prison--he is to be pitied who is laid by the heels in them. While you are rowing hard to get your vessel to land and standing out against the gracious plan which God has ordained, you are letting the nightmare of unbelief grow into a dread reality! You are letting this deadly incubus rest more terribly upon your hearts. O, Sinner, I pray God deliver you from this work-mongering, this horrible trying to save yourself by something homegrown and home-spun. If we could cut off the head of your self-righteousness, we would have hope of you! If you would give up all attempts to deliver yourselves and leave the case in Christ's hands, the thing would be done!

But while you are thus doubting and fearing, you are sinking deeper in the mire. And it is harder to get you out now than ever it was. Remember this one thing, that while the sinner is thus straining himself to get to Heaven by his own righteousness, his day of wrath is getting nearer. He is adding sin to sin. He is accumulating the fuel for his own burning, filling the sea of wrath in which he must be drowned forever. "What? When I am praying, groaning and crying to God and when I am trying to mend my ways and do my best, do you say I am only doing mischief?"

I do say it. I say these things are good in themselves, but if you are resting in them, you are so flying in the teeth of God's great Gospel, so insulting the dignity of the great Savior that you are adding sin to sin! And among the firewood for your burning there shall be none so dry which shall burn so terribly as your own good wicked works, your own rebellious virtues, your own proud detestable righteousness which you set up in opposition to the merit, blood and righteousness of God's appointed Mediator!

Gold is good enough, but if you bow down before the golden calf I will hate the gold because you worship it. Your morality is good enough, but if you trust to it I will hate your morality because it is your destruction. Sinner, I pray you remember that your life is being shortened all the while you tarry in the plains of self. Time flies and you fade like a leaf, while your righteousnesses, which are but filthy rags, are crying out against you! You are laboring without success. But more, you are losing time which might have been turned to better purpose. While you are spending your money for that which is not bread, you are getting nearer and nearer to the dread famine when there shall be no bread to buy.

While you are trying to get this fool's oil with which to keep your lamps burning, the Bridegroom is coming and the midnight is hastening when you shall have to say, "Give us of your oil, for our lamps are gone out." There shall be no time, then, for you to buy for the darkness shall have come upon you and the door shall be shut and the Bridegroom's supper shall have begun. O that I could have some power to induce you not to follow any longer these fine ways of yours, these proud deceptive plans! O that you would receive God's plan of redemption and enjoy the peace which it brings!

IV. We will try to explain God's plan and then we have done. That is our fourth point--THAT THE WAY OF SAFETY FOR SINNERS IS TO BE FOUND IN THE SACRIFICE OF ANOTHER ON THEIR BEHALF. Here is Jonah. Leave out the fact that he was sinful and he becomes an eminent type of Christ. "Take me up and cast me into the sea and the sea shall become calm under me." Substitution saves the mariners--Substitution saves sinners. This is the essential oil of Gospel Truth. Jesus Christ says to His people, "I am cast into the sea. There in that depth I sleep for a while, like Jonah, to rise again on the third day. But My being cast into the sea makes a deep calm for you." How very simple this process was. They take Jonah--he himself desires it--he is thrown overboard and the deeps swallow him up.

Ah, poor Jonah, what a fall! What a terrible descent! What a frightful end to his prophetical career! Down he goes. Did I not see huge jaws opening amid the billows? Was he not devoured by some terrible monster! Poor fellow, he must have our pity! But how strange it is! Why the wind has ceased--it has dropped dead! And the waves seem to be playing now where they were battling fiercely a moment ago! No, the sea is glassy! We need not the oars any longer! Up with the sails, we shall soon be safely in port!

An odd thing this, the drowning of one becomes the safety of all. Mariners, let us sacrifice to Jonah's God. Ah, it is a strange and marvelous thing! It is that which sets angels singing and makes the redeemed spirits wonder on forever, that Jesus came down into this ship of our common humanity to deliver it from tempest. The vessel had been tossed about on all sides by the waves of Divine wrath. Men had been tugging and toiling at the oar. Year after year philosopher and teacher had been seeking to establish peace with God. Victims had been offered and rivers of blood had flowed and even the first-born of man's body had been offered up.

But the deep was still tempestuous. Then Jesus came and they took Him and cast Him overboard. Out of the city they dragged Him. "Away with Him! Away with Him! It is not fit that He should live!" Out of all comfort they had cast Him long ago--now from society they cast Him, too. From pity they cast Him! From all sympathy they cast Him! And at last from life itself they hurled Him, while God stands there to help them to cast Him into a sea of woes. As He, Jesus, dies there is a calm. Deep was the peace which fell upon the earth that dreadful day. And joyous is that calm which yet shall come as the result of the casting out of that representative Man who suffered--the Just for the unjust to bring us to God!

Brethren, I wish I had better words with which I could fitly describe the peace which comes to a human heart when we learn to see Jesus cast into the sea of Divine wrath on our account. Conscience accuses no longer. Judgment now decides for the sinner instead of against him. Memory can look back upon past sins, with sorrow for the sin it is true, but yet with no dread of any penalty to come! It is a blessed thing for a man to know that he cannot be punished, that Heaven and earth may shake, but he cannot be punished for his sin!

If God is unjust I may be damned. But if God is just I never can be. That is how the saved sinner stands. Christ has paid the debt of His people to the last jot and tittle and received the Divine receipt. And unless God can be so unjust as to demand twice payment for one debt, no soul for whom Jesus died can ever be cast into Hell. It seems to be one of the very principles of our nature to believe that God is just. We feel it and that gives us our terror at first. But is it not marvelous that this very same first principle, the belief that God is just, becomes afterwards the pillar of our confidence and peace?

If God is just, I, a sinner, alone and without a substitute, must be punished. Christ stands in my place and is punished for me. And now, if God is just, I, a sinner, standing in Christ, can never be punished! God must change His Nature before one soul for whom Christ was a Substitute, can ever by any possibility suffer the lash of the Law. I must confess I do not understand the atonements which some preach. An atonement which does not atone--a redemption which does not redeem--a redemption which intends to redeem all men born of Adam and yet leaves the major part in slavery--an atonement which makes full atonement for all human sin and leaves men to be condemned afterwards--I cannot comprehend that!

But I do understand a Substitution--Christ taking the place of the Believer--Christ suffering the quid pro quo for the Believer's punishment--Christ rendering an equivalent to Divine wrath for all that His people ought to have suffered as the result of sin. I right well and right joyously understand that the Believer, knowing that Christ suffered in his place, can shout with glorious triumph, "Who shall lay anything to the charge of God's elect?" Not God, for He has justified! Not Christ, for He has died, "yes rather has risen again." My hope is not because I am not a sinner, but because I AM a sinner for whom Christ died. My trust is not that I am holy, but that being unholy Christ died for me!

My rest is here, not in what I am or shall be, or feel, or know, but in what Christ is and must be! In what Christ did and is still doing as He stands before yonder Throne of Glory. O Beloved, it is a blessed thing to get right out of self. But many Believers seem to have one foot on self and one on Christ. They are like the angel with one foot on the sea and the other on the land--only being angels--they cannot stand on such a footing. Put both feet on the Rock, Beloved! Stand altogether on Christ!

Arminianism is one foot on Christ and the other foot on self. "Christ has saved me," says the Arminian. There is His foot on the land. "But," he says, "I must hold on. It depends upon me whether I persevere to the end." There is his foot on the sea. If he does not look out, that foot will give way. But how blessed it is when the Christian can say, "I am saved." There is no if, no but about it. There is nothing for me to do to complete my salvation. It is all done. There is not one jot or tittle left to complete the Covenant of my salvation. The Covenant of effectual Grace is all written out in the fair handwriting of my Savior with a pen dipped in His own blood, and it guarantees all spiritual blessings to me forever! The edifice has been built and there is not wanted a beam or a brick, or even a nail or a tin tack to complete it!

From its foundation to its top stone it is all of Grace and all perfect. My garment of salvation has been woven from the top throughout--there is not a rag of thread or stitch of mine wanted to complete it. "It is finished," said the Savior, as He dipped it for the last time in the glorious carmine of His own blood and made a rich royal robe for His people to wear forever! O Brethren, if there were one stone to be put to the walls of our salvation--one single trowel full of mortar to make the stones set firmly--it would be all undone, all in ruin. But the whole of it has been completed! Stone and mortar, from basement to summit--all has been completed by Sovereign Grace!

And what shall you and I do? Since Jesus has been cast overboard for us, let us now rest in perfect quiet. Let us enjoy the peace "that passes all understanding, which shall keep our hearts and minds through Christ Jesus." And then, having been saved in such a way as this, let us now go to work for God--not to win life, not to win Heaven--life and Heaven are ours already! But loved by Him let us now love Him with a perfect heart!

The man who has not attained to rest in Jesus is incapable of virtue. A man who does anything for his own salvation acts from a selfish motive, does everything for himself. He has no virtue in him. But the man who is saved, who knows there is nothing for him to do, either to put himself into salvation or to keep himself in it--knowing that all is now finished, having no need to do anything for self--he does everything for God and is holy in heart and life. Now he can sing with Toplady--

"Loved of my God, for Him again, With love intense I'd burn. Chosen of Him before time began, I'd choose Him in return."

Let us show that this is the true root of virtue. Let us teach men who say this doctrine is licentious that it is the most heavenly soil in which the fruits of the Spirit can grow! Like a genial sunshine is this doctrine to our fruits to ripen them! Like a heavenly shower to bring them forth! God give you, Sinner, to rest in my Savior! God give you, Saint, to live to your Savior and He shall have the praise in both cases. Amen.

What God Cannot Do!

DELIVERED ON SUNDAY MORNING, MAY 8, 1864,
BY THE REV. C. H. SPURGEON,
AT THE METROPOLITAN TABERNACLE, NEWINGTON.

"God, that cannot lie." -- Titus 1:2.

TRUTH once reigned supreme upon our globe and then earth was Paradise. Man knew no sorrow while he was ignorant of falsehood. The Father of Lies invaded the garden of bliss and with one foul lie he blighted Eden into a wilderness and made man a traitor to his God. Cunningly he handled the glittering falsehood and made it dazzle in the woman's eyes--"God does know that in the day you eat thereof, then your eyes shall be opened and you shall be as gods, knowing good and evil."

Proud ambition rode upon that lie as a conqueror in his chariot and the city of Mansoul opened its gates to welcome the fascinating enemy. As it was a lie which first subjugated the world to Satan's influences, so it is by lies that he secures his throne. Among the heathen his kingdom is quiet and secure, because the minds of the people are deluded with a false mythology. The domains of Mahomet and the Pope are equally the kingdom of Satan and his reign is undisturbed, for human merit, priestly efficacy, and a thousand other deceptions buttress his throne. The darkness of ignorance, the dungeons of falsehood and the chains of superstition are the main reliance of that monster who oppresses all the nations with his infernal tyranny.

Since by the lie Satan now holds the world and maintains his power, he everywhere encourages lies and aids their propagation. Look about you and see what a prolific family falsehood has! The children of the untrue are as many as the frogs of Egypt, and like those plagues, they intrude into every chamber. The slime of falsehood may be seen upon most things, both in secular and religious life. You have lying news and garbled reports in print. And as for the flying gossip of the tongue, if it touches the characters of good men, beware of believing a word it utters. If you would not have complicity with those who make the lie, be not hasty to entertain it.

From the high places of the earth falsehood is not excluded. The untruth glides right royally from the kingly tongue, but is as much a lie as if the ragged mendicant had blurted it forth with low-lived oaths and curses. What is diplomacy for the most part? Is it not "the art of lying"? Was not he thought to be the best politician who used language to conceal his thoughts? In how many a conference have the plenipotentiaries labored which could overreach, dissimulate and intrigue to the greatest degree?

In the commerce of courts who knows not that flatteries and lies are the most abundant commodities? The art of king-craft, as practiced by the most high and mighty Prince James, whose name dishonors our English Bible, was only and simply the science of lying in the neatest possible manner. In these modern times, the difference between the promises of the politicians and the performances in the House of Commons proves that the lie is still commonly patronized. Falsehood is everywhere. It is entertained both by the lowest and the highest. It permeates all society. It has ruined the whole of our race and so defiled the entire world that upright men exclaim, "Woe is me, that I sojourn in Mesech, that I dwell in the tents of Kedar!"

In the so-called religious world, which should be as the Holy of Holies, here, too, the lie has insinuated itself. Of old there were prophets who prophesied lies and dreamers of false dreams. And there were others who spoke the Word of God with such bated breath and after such a fashion that it was no longer the Truth as it came from God, but truth alloyed with human falsehood. It is so today. There are those wearing the vestments of God's priests who do not hesitate to profess what they do not believe. Such men are the priests of Hell. To wear a bishop's miter and teach infidelity--how shall I stigmatize it? It is nothing less than detestable hypocrisy and robbery.

And what shall I say of men of all creeds, all subscribing to the same articles and catechism when all the world knows they cannot all honestly believe the same thing and yet differ as much from one another as light from darkness? What shall I say but that shame covers my face that there should be so many ministers of God who are untrue to their convictions and continue to do and say what they feel to be unscriptural? In other quarters philosophy is believed and Christianity professed--the traditions of men are put in the place of God's Truth. The prophets prophesy lies and the people love to have it so.

Brethren, we have everywhere to battle with falsehood and if we are to bless the world we must confront it with sturdy face and zealous spirit. God's purpose is to drive the lie out of the world and let this be your purpose and mine. His Holy Spirit has undertaken to drive falsehood out of our hearts--be this our determination, in His strength--that it shall be cut up root and branch and utterly consumed. Then let us walk in the Truth of God. "Buy the Truth and sell it not," hold fast the Truth, speak the Truth in love and act the Truth in all our deeds, for so shall we be known to be the children of that God of whom our text asserts that He is "God, that cannot lie."

After wandering over the sandy desert of deceit, how pleasant is it to reach our text and feel that one spot, at least, is verdant with eternal Truth! Blessed be You, O God, for You cannot lie!

We will use our text in the following manner this morning--first, while we do not attempt to prove it, we will remind you of a few things which may confirm your confidence that God cannot lie so that our opening remarks shall be upon the truth of the text. Then secondly, we will speak upon the breadth of the text, endeavoring to show that we must give no narrow interpretation to the words before us, but must receive them with an extent of meaning not usual to the expression. And then, thirdly, we will try to use the text for our own improvement, arguing from it that if God cannot lie He ought to receive our loving confidence.

I. First, then, let us commune together awhile concerning THE TRUTH OF THE TEXT, not, as we have said, to prove it, because we all believe it, but to confirm our confidence of it. I think we shall feel assured that God cannot lie when we remember that He is not subject to those infirmities which lead us into falsehood. Lord Bacon has said, "There are three parts in truth--first, the enquiry, which is the wooing of it. Secondly, the knowledge of it, which is the presence of it. And thirdly, the belief, which is the enjoyment of it."

In each of these three points, by reason of infirmity, men fail to be perfectly true. In the search after truth, our moral eye is not altogether clear and therefore we fail to see what we love not. We do not follow truth in a straight line, but are very liable to turn aside to the right hand or to the left, either to obey our prejudices or advance our profit. "Truth lies in a well," said the old philosopher. Many go down into that well to find Truth, but looking into the water they see their own faces and become so desperately enamored of their own beauty that they forget poor Truth, or dream that she is the counterpart of themselves.

Now the great God cannot be liable to this error, because there is no discovery of truth with Him. He needs not to search anything out, for "all things are naked and opened unto the eyes of Him with whom we have to do." When in Scripture that term is sometimes used--"Shall not God search this out?"--when we hear Him spoken of as "searching the heart and trying the reins of the children of men," it is not because He is not perfectly acquainted with all things, but only to set forth the certainty and accuracy of Divine knowledge.

God has no need to search, or if He had, having nothing in Him which should lead Him to make a dishonest search, He does not lie. When we have searched out the Truth of God there is the knowing of it. And here the falsehood gets a footing in the form of a sin of omission, for we often refuse to know all that we might know. It would be inconvenient, perhaps, for us to be too well acquainted with certain arguments, for then our prejudices must be given up and therefore we close our eyes to them for fear of knowing the truth.

Do not many men leave passages of Scripture altogether unread because they have no wish to receive the doctrines which are taught in them? Every time you refuse to give a hearing to God's Truth, you do in effect lie because you prefer not to know the Truth of God, which is really to prefer to hold error. Now nothing of this kind can ever happen with our only wise God. He knows all Truth, seeing it all at a glance and retaining it ever in His mind. In nothing is He ignorant, either willfully or otherwise.

He receives Truth as His own Beloved and when the world casts her out, she finds a happy shelter beneath His shield. We are quite clear that we frequently fall into the lie through a defect in our believing, for we sometimes know more than we care to believe. Truth is grasped by the understanding but thrust out by the affections. We know her as Peter knew his

Lord and yet deny it after the same fashion as that disciple did his Master. Moreover, through weakness, we are led to doubt what we know to be God's Truth and even to speak unadvisedly with our lips.

Now this can never occur with God, since God is One and is not to be divided into parts and passions and His tongue can never be diverse from His heart. God's tongue is His heart and God's heart is His hand. God is One. You and I are such that we can know in the heart, and yet with the tongue deny. But God is One and indivisible. God is Light, and in Him is no darkness at all. With Him is no variableness, neither shadow of turning.

Then again, the Scriptural idea of God forbids that He should lie. Just review your thoughts about God, if you can. What idea have you formed of Him? If you have read Holy Scripture and have gotten the slightest shadow of an idea of God, I think you will see that it is utterly inconsistent with the thrice Holy One, whose kingdom is over all, that He should lie. Admit the very possibility of His speaking an untruth and to the Christian there would be no God at all. The depraved mind of the heathen may imagine a monster to be a god who can live in adultery and in theft and in lying, for such the gods of the Hindus are described as being. But the enlightened mind of the Christian can conceive no such thing. The very word "God" comprehends everything which is good and great. Admit the lie and to us at once there would be nothing but the black darkness of Atheism. I could neither love, worship, nor obey a lying God.

Again, we all know that God is too wise to lie. Falsehood is the expedient of a fool. It is only a short-sighted man who lies. For some present advantage the poor creature who cannot see the end as well as the beginning states that which is not. But no wise man who can look far into the future ever thinks a lie to be profitable. He knows that Truth may suffer loss at first but that in the long run she is always successful. He endorses that worldly-wise proverb, that, "Honesty is the best policy" after all. And the man, I say, who has anything like foresight, or judgment, or wisdom, prefers always the straight line to the curve and goes directly to the mark, believing that this is in the end the best.

Do you suppose that God, who must know this, with an intensity of knowledge infinitely greater than ours, will choose the policy of the witless knave? Shall God, only wise, who sees the end from the beginning, act as only brainless fools will choose to behave themselves? Oh, it cannot be, my Brethren! God, the All-Wise, must also be All-True. And the lie, again, is the method of the little and the mean. You know that a great man does not lie. A good man can never be false. Put goodness and greatness together and a lie is altogether incongruous to the character.

Now God is too great to need the lie and too good to wish to do such a thing! Both His greatness and His goodness repel the thought. My dear Friends, what motive could God have for lying? When a man lies it is that he may gain something, but "the cattle on a thousand hills" are God's and all the beasts of the forest and all the flocks of the meadows. He says, "if I were hungry I would not tell you." Mines of inexhaustible riches are His and treasures of infinite power and wisdom. He cannot gain anything by untruth, for "the earth is the Lord's and the fullness thereof." Why, then, should He lie?

Men are false, oftentimes, to win applause. See how the sycophant cringes to the tyrant's foot and spawns his villainy. But God needs no honor and no fame, especially from the wicked. To Him it were the greatest disgust of His righteous soul to be loved by unholy creatures. His Glory is great enough even if there were no creatures! His own self-contained Glory is such that if there were no eyes to see it and no ears to hear it, He would be infinitely glorious. He asks nothing--no respect and no honor of man--and therefore has He no need to stoop to the lie to gain it. And of whom, again, could He be afraid? Men will sometimes, under the impulse of fear, keep back or even contradict the truth, but can fear ever enter into the heart of the eternal God?

He looks down upon all nations who are in rebellion against Him and He does not even care to rise to put them down. "He that sits in the heavens shall laugh: the Lord shall have them in derision!" Are not the chariots of the Lord twenty thousand, even thousands of angels? Even these are but as a drop in a bucket, when compared with the deep and infinite sea of His own power. Who, then, shall think that Jehovah needs to be afraid? "Fear," and "Jehovah," are two words which cannot meet together. Therefore, since there can be no motive whatever which should possibly lead God to lie, we feel well assured that the declaration of Paul is most certainly true--"God, that cannot lie."

Moreover, dear Friends, we may add to all this the experience of men with regard to God. It has been evident enough in all ages that God cannot lie. He did not lie when Adam fell. It seemed a strange thing, that after all the skill and labor which had been spent in making such a world as this, so fair and beautiful, God should resign it to the dominion of Satan and drive the man whom He had made in His own image, out of his home, his Eden, to labor in sweat and toil and suffer- ing until he came to his grave. But God did it and the fiery sword at the gate of Eden was proof that God could not and would not lie.

He might come to Adam and bemoan himself, crying, "Adam, where are you?" as if He pitied him and would, if it had been possible, have spared the stroke. But still it must be done and Eden is blasted and Adam becomes a wanderer upon the fruitless earth. Then afterwards, to quote a notable instance of God's faithfulness, when the flood swept away the race of men and Noah came forth the heritor of a new Covenant, we have clear proof that God cannot lie. No flood has ever destroyed the earth since then. Partial floods there have been and parts of provinces have been inundated, but no flood has ever come upon the earth of such a character as that which Noah saw--therefore the rainbow, every time it is painted upon the cloud--is an assurance to us that God cannot lie.

Then He made an oath with Abraham that he should have a son and that his seed should become possessors of all the land in which the Patriarch had sojourned. Did not that come true? They waited in Egypt two hundred years. They smarted under the tyrant's lash. They lay among the pots and yet, after all, with a high hand and with an outstretched arm He brought forth His people, led them through the wilderness and divided Canaan by lot to them, having driven out the inhabitants of the land before them. Since that time He made His Covenant with David and how fast has that stood! All the threats which He has uttered against the enemies of Israel--how surely have they been fulfilled!

Last of all and best of all, when the fullness of time was come, did not God send forth His own Son, born of a woman, made under the Law? Did He not, according to His ancient promise, lay upon Him the iniquity of us all? Were not the Incarnation and death of our Lord Jesus the grandest proof of the truthfulness of God which could be afforded? His own Son must leave Heaven emptied of His Glory, must be given up to be despised and rejected of men, must be nailed to the accursed wood and be forsaken in the hour of His bitterest grief--herein is Truth, indeed! I say if this must be according to the promise and if this was according to the fact, then we have the clearest and the surest evidence that God cannot by any possibility be false to His own Word. Rightly has He earned the title which His Nature claims--"God, that cannot lie."

May I not add as another argument that you have found Him true? You have been to Him, dear Friends, in many times of trial. You have taken His promise and laid it before His Mercy Seat. What do you say--has He ever broken His promise? You have been through the floods--did He leave you? You have passed through the fires--were you burned? You have cried to Him in trouble--did He fail to deliver you? O you poor and needy ones, you have been brought very low, but has He not been your Helper? You have passed hard by the gates of the grave and Hell has opened its horrid jaws to swallow you up, but are you not today the living monuments of the fidelity of God to His promise and the veracity of every Word of the Most High God? Let these things, then, refresh your memories that you may the more confidently know that He is "God, that cannot lie."

II. Let us pass on to look at THE BREADTH OF MEANING IN THE TEXT. When we are told in Scripture that God cannot lie there is usually associated with the idea the thought of immutability. As for instance--"He is not a man that He should lie, nor the son of man that He should repent." The word "lie," here includes beyond its ordinary meaning the thought of change, so that when we read that God cannot lie, we understand by it not only that He cannot say what is untrue, but that having said something which is true, He never changes from it and does not by any possibility alter His purpose or retract His Word.

This is very consolatory to the Christian, that whatever God has said in the Divine purpose is never changed. The Decrees of God were not written upon sand, but upon the eternal brass of His unchangeable Nature. We may truly say of the sealed Book of the Decrees, "Has He said and shall He not do it? Has He purposed and shall it not come to pass?" We read in Scripture of several instances where God apparently changed, but I think the observation of the old Puritan explains all these, He says, "God may will a change, but He cannot change His will." Those changes of operation which we sometimes read of in Scripture did not involve any change in the Divine purpose!

God, for instance, sent to warn Hezekiah that according to the common course of nature he must die, and yet afterwards fifteen years were added to his life--God's purpose having been all along that Hezekiah should live till the end of the fifteen years. But still His purpose equally included that Hezekiah should be brought so near to the gates of death that in the ordinary course of nature he must die. And then that the miracle should come in was still part of the purpose, that Hezekiah might be cured in a supernatural manner and be made to live nearer to his God in consequence. God wills a change, but He never changes His will.

And when the Last Great Day shall come, you and I shall see how everything happened according to that hidden roll wherein God had written with His own wise finger every thought which man should think, every word which he should utter and every deed which he should do. Just as it was in the Book of Decree, so shall it transpire in the roll of human history. God never changes, then, as to His purpose and here is our comfort. If He has determined to save us and we know He has, for all who believe in Him are His elect, then we shall be saved. Heaven shall never by any possibility be defeated by Hell. Hell and earth may combine together to destroy a soul which rests upon Christ, but while God's Decree stands fast and firm, that chosen soul is safe! And since that Decree never can be removed, let us take confidence and rejoice.

No promise has ever been altered and no threat, either. Still is His promise sure. "I have not said unto the seed of Jacob, seek you My face in vain." No new decrees have been passed repealing the past. We can never say of God's Book, as we can of old law books, that such-and-such an act is obsolete. There is no obsolete Statute in God's Book There stand promises, as fresh, as new, as vigorous and as forceful today as when they first dropped from the mouth of God. The words, then, "God, that cannot lie," include the very gracious and precious doctrine that He cannot by any possibility change.

But we must not, while talking in this manner, forget the primary meaning, that He cannot be false in His thoughts, Words, or actions. There is no shadow of a lie upon anything which God thinks, or speaks, or does. He cannot lie in His prophecies. How solemnly true have they been! Ask the wastes of Nineveh! Turn to the mounds of Babylon! Let the traveler speak concerning Idumea and Petra. Turn even to the rock of Sidon and to Your land, O Immanuel! We may boldly ask the traveler, "Has He said and has He not done it? Have His words fallen to the ground? Has God's curse been an idle Word?" No, not in one single case.

All the words of the Lord are sure. The prophecies will be as true as they have been and the Book of Revelation, though we may not comprehend it today, will doubtless be fulfilled in every stroke and in every line and we shall marvel how it was that we did not know its meaning. But at present it is enough for us to know its Truth--its meaning shall only be learned as the events explain the prophesy. As God is true in His prophecies, so is He faithful to His promises. Have you and I, dear Friends, a confidence in these? If so, let us try them this morning.

Sinner, weeping and bemoaning yourself, God will forgive you your sin if you believe in Jesus! If you will confess that He is faithful and just to forgive you, He has promised to do so and He cannot lie. Christian, if you have a promise today laid upon your heart, if you have been pleading it, perhaps for months and it has not been fulfilled, I pray you gather fresh courage this morning and again renew your wrestling. Go and say, "Lord, I know You cannot lie, therefore fulfill Your Word unto Your servant."

If the promises of God were not kept, God would lie. They must, therefore, be fulfilled. And let us believe that they will be and go to God, not with a wavering spirit which half hopes that the Words may be true, but with the full assurance that they cannot fail! As certainly as we know that day and night shall not cease and that summer will not fail, so surely let us be convinced that every Word of the Lord shall stand!

His threats are true, also. Ah, Sinner, you may go on in your ways for many a day, but your sin shall find you out at last. Seventy years God's long-suffering may wait over you, but when you shall come into another world you shall find every terrible Word of Scripture fulfilled. You shall then know that there is a place, "where their worm dies not and the fire is not quenched." You shall then experience the "wailing and gnashing of teeth" unless you repent. If you will believe in Jesus you shall find the promise true! But if you will not, equally sure shall be the threat.

This is a dreadful part of the subject to those who are out of Christ, who have never been partakers of the Holy Spirit. It will be in vain for you to cry to Him, then, and ask Him, then, to change His mind. No, though you should weep oceans of tears, Hell's flames cannot be quenched nor can your soul escape from the place to which it is finally doomed! Today, while mercy is preached to you, lay hold upon it! But remember, if you do not, as God cannot lie He cannot suffer you to escape--you must feel the weight and terror of His arm.

We might thus go through everything which concerns God, from prophesy to promises and threats and onwards and multiply observations but we choose to close this point by observing that every word of instruction from God is most certainly true. It is astounding how much sensation is caused in the Christian Church by the outbreak, every now and then, of fresh phases of infidelity. I do not think that these alarms are at all warranted. It is what we must expect to the very end of this dispensation.

If all carnal minds believed the Bible, I think the spiritual might almost begin to doubt it. But as there are always some who will attack it, I shall feel none the less confident in it. Really, the Book of God has stood so many attacks from such different quarters that to be at all alarmed about it shows a very childish fear. When a rock has been standing all our lifetime and has been known to stand firmly throughout all the ages of history, none but foolish people will think that the next wave will sweep it away.

Within our own short life--say some five-and-twenty years' recollection--have we not remembered, I was about to say almost as many as five-and-twenty shapes of infidelity? You know it must change about every twenty years at least, for no system of infidelity can live longer than that! There was the witty system of objection which Voltaire introduced. And how short-lived was that! Then came the bullying, low-lived, blackguard system of Tom Paine. And how short-lived was its race! Then, in more modern times, unbelief took the shape of Secularism--what particular shapes it takes now we scarcely know--perhaps Colensoism is the most fashionable--but that is dying out and something else will follow it.

These creations of an hour just live their little day and they are gone. But look at belief in Scripture and at Scripture itself. The Bible is better understood, more prized, and I believe, on the whole, more practiced than ever it was since the day when its Author sent it abroad into the world. It is still onward. And after all which has been done against it, no visible effect has been produced upon the granite wall of Scriptural Truth by all the pickaxes and boring rods which have been broken upon it.

Walking through our Museums nowadays, we smile at those who think that Scripture is not true. Every block of stone from Nineveh, every relic which has been brought from the Holy Land speaks with a tongue which must be heard even by the deaf adder of Secularism and which says, "Yes, the Bible is true and the Word of God is no fiction." Beloved, we may rest assured that we have not a Word in the Book of God which is untrue. There may be an interpolation or two of man's which ought to be revised and taken away, but the Book, as it comes from God, is Truth and nothing but Truth--not only containing God's Word, but being God's Word--being not like a lump of gold inside a mass of quartz, but all gold and nothing but gold!

And being Inspired to the highest degree--I will not say verbally inspired, but more than that--having a fullness more than that which the letter can convey! Having in it a profundity of meaning such as words never had when used by any other being, God having the power to speak a multitude of Truths at once. And when He means to teach us one thing according to our capability of receiving it, He often teaches us twenty other things which, for the time, we do not comprehend but which, by-and-by, as our senses are exercised, reveal themselves by the Holy Spirit. Every time I open my Bible I will read it as the Word of "God, that cannot lie." And when I get a promise or a threat, I will either rejoice or tremble because I know that these stand fast.

Dear Friends, this leads us, in closing this point, to say that when we read that passage--"God, that cannot lie"-- we understand that His very Nature cannot lie, for He hates lies! Wherever there is a lie God is its Enemy. It was to overcome the lie of sin that God sent His Son to bleed. And every day the thoughts of God are centered upon the extermination of evil and the extension of His own Truth. Nothing can set forth in words to us the hatred and detestation which God has in His heart of anything which is untrue. O that we knew and felt this and would glow with the same anger, seeking to exterminate the false, slaying it in our own hearts and giving it nothing to feed upon in our temper, our conversation, or our deeds!

III. But I shall now come to make a practical use of the text, in the third place, by observing HOW WE OUGHT TO ACT TOWARDS GOD IF IT IS TRUE THAT HE IS A "GOD THAT CANNOT LIE." Brethren, if it is so that God cannot lie, then it must be the natural duty of all His creatures to believe Him. I cannot resist that conclusion. It seems to me to be as clear as noonday that it is every man's duty to believe the Truth of God, and that if God must speak and act Truth and Truth only, it is the duty of all intelligent creatures to believe Him.

Here is "Duty-faith" again, which some are railing at, but how they can get away from it and yet believe that God cannot lie, I cannot understand. If it is not my duty to believe in God, then it is no sin for me to call God a liar. Will anyone subscribe to that--that God is a liar? I think not. And if to think God to be a liar would be a most atrocious piece of blasphemy, then it can only be so on the ground that it is the natural and incumbent duty of every creature understand- ing the truthfulness of God to believe in God! If God has set forth the Lord Jesus Christ as the Propitiation for sin and has told me to trust Christ, it is my duty to trust Christ, because God cannot lie.

And though my sinful heart will never believe in Christ as a matter of duty but only through the work of the Holy Spirit, yet faith does not cease to be a duty. And whenever I am unbelieving and have doubts concerning God, however moral my outward life may be, I am living in daily sin! I am perpetrating a sin against the first principles of morality. If I doubt God, as far as I am able I rob Him of His honor and stab Him in the vital point of His Glory. I am, in fact, living an open traitor and a sworn rebel against God upon whom I heap the daily insult of daring to doubt Him.

my Hearers, there are some of you who do not believe in Christ! I wish you would look at your character and position in this light. You are not trusting in Christ for your salvation. Remember, "He that believes not God, has made Him a liar." Those are John's own Inspired Words and you are, every day that you are not a Believer in Christ, virtually writing upon your doorpost and saying with your mouth, "God is a liar. Christ is not able to save me. I will not trust Him. I do not believe God's promise. I do not think He is sincere in His invitation to me to come to Christ. I do not believe what God says."

Remember that you are living in such a state as this and may God the Holy Spirit impress you with a sense of the sin of that state. And feeling this your sin and misery, I pray God to lead you to cry, "Lord, I believe, help You my unbelief!" This, then, is our first practical conclusion from the fact that God cannot lie. Other thoughts suggest themselves. If we were absolutely sure that there lived on earth a person who could not lie, how would you treat him? You know there cannot be such a man! There may be a man who will not lie, but there cannot be a man of whom it may be said that he cannot lie, for alas, we have all the power of evil in us and we can lie and to a certain degree it is quite true that "all men are liars."

But if you could be certain that there was a man out of whose heart the black drop had been wrung and that he could not lie--how would you act towards him? Well, I think you would cultivate his acquaintance. If you are true yourselves, you would desire his friendship. You would say, "He is the friend for me! I have trusted in such-and-such a man and he has played the Judas. I asked counsel of another, and he was an Ahithophel. But if this man cannot lie, he shall be my bosom companion if he will accept me. And he shall be my counselor if he will but have the goodness to direct me."

I should expect to see a levee of all the good in the world waiting at the man's door! You know how the world, with all its sinfulness, does reverence the man who is true! We had an instance in our streets the other day of the good man and the true, who received homage of all and yet that man could lie. But inasmuch as we never have seen that he did, but his life has been straightforward, therefore have we paid him honor and deservedly so. Well now, if such is the case, should not all Christians seek more and more the friendship of God. "O Lord, be You my familiar Friend, my Counselor, my Guide. If You cannot lie I will lay bare my heart to You. I will tell You all my secrets. I will trust You with all the desires of my heart. I know You can never betray me, or be unfaithful. Let there be a union established between my soul and Yours, and let it never be broken." Let communion with God be the desire of your hearts on the ground that He cannot lie.

If we knew a man who could not lie we should believe him, I think, without an oath. I cannot suppose that when he came into the court of justice they would pass him the Bible. No, his word would be better than the oath of ordinary men if he could not lie. You would not need any sign or evidence to prove what he said. You would take his word at once. So should it be with God. Ah, dear Friends, God has given us more than His Word, He has given us His Oath. And yet, strange is it that we who profess to be His children are vile enough to distrust our own Father. And sometimes, if He does not give us signs and evidences, we begin to distrust Him so that, after all, I am afraid we rather trust the signs than trust God and put more confidence in frames and evidences than we do in the naked promise, which is an atrocious sin, indeed!

Many Believers cannot be comfortable without signs and evidences. When they feel in a good frame of mind--ah, then God's promise is true! When they can pray heartily, when they can feel the love of God shed abroad in their hearts, then they say, "How God has kept His promise." Ah, but, my Brothers and Sisters, that is a seeing faith. "Blessed are they that have not seen and yet have believed." Faith is to believe in God when my heart is as hard as the nether millstone! When my frames are bad, when I cannot pray, when I cannot sing, when I can do nothing good. To say, "He has promised and will perform. He has said that whoever believes in Christ is not condemned. I do believe in Christ and therefore I am not condemned"--this is genuine faith.

Again, if we knew a man who could not lie we should believe him in the teeth of fifty witnesses the other way. Why, we should say, "they may say what they will, but they can lie." You might have good evidence that they were usually honest men, but you would say, "They can lie. They have the power of lying. But here is a man who stands alone and cannot lie. Then his word must be true!"

This shows us, Beloved, that we ought to believe God in the teeth of every contradiction. Even if outward Providence should come to you and say that God has forsaken you, that is only one. And even if another and another and another should come and fifty trials should all say that God has forsaken you, yet, as God says, "I will never leave you, nor forsake you," which will you take--the one promise of God who cannot lie, or the fifty outward Providences which you cannot interpret? I know what the devil has been whispering in your ear--

"The Lord has quite forsaken you, Your God will be gracious no more."

But then, remember who has said, "Fear you not, for I am with you: be not dismayed, for I am your God." Which will you believe--the devil's insinuation, or God's own testimony? My dear Sister, you have been praying for a certain thing for years? You pray, you pray, and you pray again, and now discouragement arises! Unbelief says, "God will not hear that prayer! That prayer of yours does not come up before the Throne of God and there will be no answer." But the Lord has said, "Ask and it shall be given you. Seek and you shall find. Knock and it shall be opened unto you." Which will you believe--your unbelief--the long months of weariness and the anxieties which prompted you to discouragement? Or will you believe in the naked promise?

Why, if God cannot lie, let us give Him what we would give to a man if he were of the same character--our full confidence even in the teeth of contradiction--for He is "God, that cannot lie." If a man were introduced to us and we were certain that he could not lie, we should believe everything he said, however incredible it might appear to us. I shall have an appeal to every soul here present. It does seem very incredible at first sight that God should take a sinner, full of sin and forgive all his iniquities in one moment simply and only upon the ground of the sinner believing in Christ! I remember the time when it seemed to me utterly impossible that I could ever have my sins forgiven.

I had a clear sense of the value of pardon and this thought would be always ringing in my ears--"It is too good to be true that you should be pardoned. That you, an enemy, should be made into a child! That you who have gone on sinning against light and against knowledge, should yet rejoice in union to Christ. The thing is too good to be true!" But, beloved Friends, supposing it should seem too good to be true, yet, since you have it upon the testimony of One who "cannot lie," I pray you believe it.

"But, Sir." No! None of your "buts"! He cannot lie. "Ah, but." Away with your "ahs" and your "buts," for Jehovah cannot lie! He has said it, "He that believes and is baptized shall be saved." To believe is to trust Christ. If therefore you are trusting Christ, you must be saved. And whatever you may be, or whatever you may have done, if you will now trust Jesus Christ you have God's Word for it--and He cannot lie--that you shall be saved! Come now, will you kick against the promise because of its greatness? Do not! Let your doubts and fears be hushed to sleep and now, with the promise of God as your pillow and God's faithfulness as your support, lie down in peace and behold in faith's open vision the ladder, the top of which leads to Heaven!

Trust the promise of God in Christ and depend upon it that He will be as good to you, even to you, as His own Word, and in Heaven you shall have to sing of the "God, that cannot lie." I would that these weak words of mine, for I am very conscious of their feebleness this morning, may nevertheless have comfort in them for any who have been doubting and fearing--that they may trust my Lord. And sure I am that if they begin a life of faith, they will begin a life of happiness and of security! "The just shall live by faith," and well may they do so, when they have trust in a "God, that cannot lie."

Adapted from The C.H. Spurgeon Collection, Version 1.0, Ages Software, 1.800.297.4307

The Arrows Of The Lord's Deliverance

DELIVERED ON TUESDAY EVENING, MARCH 22, 1864,
BY THE REV. C. H. SPURGEON,
AT THE OPENING OF UPTON CHAPEL, LAMBETH.

"You should have struck five or six times. Then had you struck Syria till you had consumed it: whereas now you shall strike Syria but thrice." -- 2 Kings 13:19.

THAT deathbed scene speaks volumes for the power of holiness. Elisha was the Prophet of God--a man of no honorable station except that he is always honorable whom God calls to serve Him. Joash the king of Israel--who has often rejected Elisha's admonitions and continued to worship in the groves of Baal though Elisha had denounced them and had proclaimed that Jehovah, alone, was their God. Now the Prophet is about to die at the good old age of ninety and Joash comes to weep at his bedside. It was something remarkable for the king to come there at all. Kings do not often visit deathbed scenes, especially the deathbeds of God's servants!

But it was something more remarkable for that king to stand and look upon the decaying form of the aged Prophet and to weep over his face. More notable still was the language in which the king expressed his sense of the value of the Prophet to the State--"O my Father, my Father, the chariot of Israel and the horsemen thereof." He felt as if now all his strength was cut off. The king had trusted in his cavalry, though he had but a slender force, and he compares the Prophet to that which he looked upon as being the strongest arm of his military service. Or he looks upon the State now as being a chariot with wild horses and no stately Prophet to stand erect and hold the reins. Now have the reins dropped and where will the chariot go? It will soon be overturned and the mad coursers will drag it here and there. So the king, out of a sort of selfish respect for the Prophet--for it was respect and yet it was selfishness--stands and weeps over Elisha's dying bed.

Dear Friends, let us seek to live so that even ungodly men may miss us when we are gone! It is possible for us in a quiet, unobtrusive manner to so adorn the doctrine of God our Savior in all things that when we die many shall say, "Let me die the death of the righteous and let my last end be like his." And men shall drop a tear and close the shutters and be silent and solemn for an hour or two when they hear that the servant of the Lord is dead. They laughed at him while he lived, but they weep for him when he dies. They could despise him while he was here, but now that he is gone they say, "We could have better missed a less-known man, for he and such as he, are the pillars of the commonweal. They bring down showers of blessing upon us all."

I would covet this earnestly as a gift, not for the honor and esteem of men, but for the honor and glory of God, that even the despisers of Christ may be compelled to see that there is a dignity, a respect about the walk of an upright man. Yet the scene at the deathbed of Elisha, fragrant as it is with the tribute of respect paid to the Prophet by an ungodly and unprincipled monarch, is memorable for the lessons then and there taught the king. And not less suggestive is it of profitable instructions to us. I propose, therefore, first of all to consider the significant sign. Then I want you to join with me in censuring the slack-handed king. After which we shall have no difficulty, I think, in unanimously justifying the righteous wrath of the Prophet.

I. VERY SIGNIFICANT WAS THE SIGN. Israel was at that time engaged in warfare against Syria. As a sign that God intended to give victory to His people, the king is bid to take the bow and arrows. Elisha, as God's representative, puts his hand upon the king's hands. The window is opened and the arrow is shot. As it flies through the air, the Prophet says that that arrow is the arrow of the Lord's deliverance of His people out of the hand of Syria. The interpretation of this symbolic act is simple enough. God will save.

Deliverance is of the Lord but it must be accomplished by human instrumentality. Joash must take the bow and arrows, but the hands of Joash cannot make the arrow speed unless Elisha, the representative of God, puts his hands there. So the man, Divinely strengthened by God, shoots the arrow and the deliverance comes. Such, from the beginning of time even until now, has been God's ordinary way of blessing His people and of gathering in His chosen. He works. The instrumentality is nothing without Him. He takes care to elect means which, from their very feebleness, convince the most skeptical that the power cannot be in the creature! While, at the same time He rarely effects any great thing for His people apart from human agency.

God, who created all things, is the Agent. But He uses the creatures as tools and weapons in the hand of the skillful and the mighty. He works in us to will and to do of His own good pleasure. It is His pleasure. It is He who works in us. But then it is for us to will and to do, because He works in us. Review the whole history of the Church as you find it in Scripture and you will see that this has ever been the fact. When God would save an elect company out of the mass of corruption grown, at last, too fetid for even His patience to endure, He saves the chosen eight--how? By a miracle?

Call it a miracle if you will, but it was mechanical enough when Noah begun to lay timber upon timber, fastened them with nails and constructed the ark. It was a simple act of faith and a very rational act, too, to build a ship! Yet in that ship God's chosen eight were preserved. You see the Grace of God and the obedience of Noah. You know that the Almighty devised the ark and human hands fashioned it according to the pattern He had given.

Go further on, to a yet more stupendous work of Divine power when God brought up His people out of Egypt with a high hand and with an outstretched arm. When He led them through the sea as through the wilderness and made the depths stand upright as a heap as though they were congealed in the heart of the sea. Here was God gloriously manifested so that the whole song was unto Jehovah and to Jehovah alone--"Sing unto the Lord for He has triumphed gloriously, the horse and his rider has He thrown into the sea"!

Still, still, see you not that calm, meek man, rod outstretched, the symbol of abiding human instrumentality in the midst of Jehovah's wonders? God divides the sea, not Moses. But God divides not the sea without Moses' rod. So, too, when the Rock gave water in the wilderness, Moses' voice, and afterwards Moses' rod, must fetch the water out of that Rock. And when Jordan was divided, the feet of the priests went first down to the river's edge and then--"What ailed you, O Jordan, that you were driven back?" Did the priests speak to it? Who dreams of such a thing? And yet God did it not without the priests.

So was it with the capture of the various cities under Joshua. In that first and memorable one, the taking of Jericho, they did but little when the walls fell flat to the ground on the seventh day. But you will remember that those walls did not fall until the people had compassed the city the seven days! Nor did they fall without the sound of the rams' horns and the shouts of the multitude. So again, turn to the time of the Judges and how did God deliver His people then? Why, my Friends, you find at one time it is the ox-goad of Shamgar, and at another time it is the jawbone in the hand of Samson! Sometimes it is Gideon's lamp and pitcher and then it is Jephthah's good and true sword.

Ever is it true that God has means, selecting for His purposes things of earth to execute the fiats of Heaven. But I might, perhaps, weary you with mentioning the history of the kings and running on through the Prophets. Therefore let us come at once to Apostolic times. Old Rome was to be subdued. The deep-seated idolatries of ages were to be rooted up and the fabulous deities were to be shaken from their pedestals. The Spirit of the Lord could do it in a moment--He might have convinced all men of the folly of idolatry--silently breathing upon human minds they might have been convicted of sin and turned to the great Father of Spirits.

A Revelation of Christ might have been given to every man without a single minister. But did He choose to do it? No, my Brethren, He did not. The twelve fishermen must first proclaim the Word and afterwards such men as Timothy and those who were the true "successors of the Apostles," must in every region preach the Words of Truth. Or, point me to a single period in the history of the Church where God has worked without instrumentality and I will tell you that I suspect whether God has worked at all if I do not see the instruments He has employed.

Take the Reformation. Can you think of it without thinking of God? At the same time can you mention it without the names of Luther, and Calvin, Zwingle and Melancthon? Then in the later Reformation in England, when our slumbering Churches were suddenly started from their sleep--who did it? The Holy Spirit Himself--but you cannot talk of the revival without mentioning the names of Whitfield and Wesley--for God worked by means then, and He works by means still.

I used to notice a remark which was made concerning the revival in the north of Ireland, that there seemed to be no prominent instrumentality. The moment I saw that, I mistrusted it. Had it been God's work more fully developed through instrumentality, I believe it had not so speedily come to a close. We grant you that God can work without means and even when He uses means He still takes the Glory to Himself, for it is all His own. Yet it has been the rule, and will be the rule till the day of means shall come to an end, that just as God saved man by taking upon Himself man's flesh, so everywhere in the world He calls men by speaking to them through men of their own flesh and blood.

God Incarnates Himself--if I may use so strong an expression in a restricted sense--in His Spirit Incarnates Himself in the chosen men, especially in His Church, in which He dwells as in a temple. And then through that Church He is pleased to bless the world. Now we must hold this forever. We are not to let the arrows lie still and say, "God will do His own work. Elisha will shoot the arrows." This is idleness. We have had enough of this! Look at those Churches which say, "God will do His own work." You will find that the more these people talk about God's doing His own work, the more they sink into a fatal apathy.

No Sunday school. No care for the conversion of souls. Just bigotry, bitterness of spirit, carping and backbiting against all those who are willing to labor in the Master's vineyard. And when they have entangled Brethren whose conversion was effected under other ministries than their own, they talk as if they had been re-converted and did not know the Truth of God till they heard the particular, excellent, superfine, hot pressed Gospel which they deliver! There is all that sort of thing among them. You see a spirit the reverse of amiable. A mind palpably contrary to that which was in Jesus Christ.

On the other hand, it is an equally dangerous error to suppose that we are to take the arrows and shoot without God. This is, in fact, the more dangerous of the two. Although, if I have to compare two devils together, I know not which is the worst of these evil spirits--the spirit that idly says--"Leave it to God"--or the spirit which goes about God's work without depending on Him. O Lord of Hosts, it is not by might, nor by power, but by Your Spirit! Nevertheless the love of Christ constrains us to spend and be spent in His cause.

II. And now, secondly, let us CENSURE THE SLACK-HANDED KING. The Prophet gave him the bow and the arrows and bade him shoot down upon the ground. It was left to him. God foreknew and had predestinated how many victories he should win. But still, at the same time, it is marvelous how our free actions tally exactly with God's predestination! He is bid to shoot and he shoots once. He draws his bow and shoots again. A third time he draws the bow and then throws it down slack upon the ground.

The Prophet is angry with him for he will only have three victories. If he had struck the ground six times he would have had six victories. But inasmuch as he only shot the three times, he is only to have three triumphs. The king is to be censured and censured severely. But as he is dead and gone and our censure cannot much affect him, let us censure those who now imitate him. And we think that we can find very many of the same sort!

How many Believers have but little faith and seem quite content to have but that little? They cannot grasp the promise of God and believingly expect to have it fulfilled. They scarcely know their own interest in Christ. They are safe enough, but they are generally wretched enough. They cannot take God at His Word and therefore their temporal troubles and their spiritual cares press very heavily upon them. Oh that they had Grace to strike the ground six times! Oh that they knew how to cast all their burdens on Him who cares for them! Oh that the Lord would give them new faith so that they would trust Him implicitly and leave their souls in the hands of Him who shed His heart's blood that He might redeem them from wrath!

Why, I do not know, dear Friends, that there is any necessity for us to be always doubting and fearing and trembling! Some think there is. But this is because they have not a high idea of the standing of the child of God and of the position which God would have him attain. They shoot the three arrows and they say--"I am saved, that is enough. I shall get to Heaven." Oh that they would go on shooting till they could get a Heaven below, till they could begin by strong faith to--

"Read their title clear, To mansions in the sky," and rejoice with joy unspeakable and full of glory!

Then you see another class of people who are just the same as to their knowledge. They do not understand the deep things of God. They are content to know that which saves the soul from ruin and the remedy which is provided in Christ, but they do not know, and perhaps do not care to know, the doctrine of God's electing love. They never dive into the doctrine of God's immutable faithfulness to His chosen people. They let the deep things of God lie still for strong men, but they, themselves, are content to be babes.

Oh, dear Friends, how much you miss who neglect to study God's Word. And what blessings do you cast away from yourselves who are willing to be ignorant of the most sublime Truths of Revelation! I would that instead of shooting three times, you would have Grace to shoot more and more and more till you comprehend with all saints what are the heights and depths and lengths and breadths of the love of Christ which passes knowledge. You will see, perhaps, these same people, or others like them, who are very content about their daily walk and conversation. They are not drunkards. They do not swear. They are scrupulously truthful. They commit no breach of Sunday--but when you have said this, you have said about as much as you can say of them.

Their religion seems to have made them moral, but it would be difficult to perceive that it has made them holy. There is very little family prayer--not much interest taken in the conversion of the children. There is an angry temper, perhaps, which is somewhat curbed but still the Brother thinks that it is impossible to curb it any more and so he tolerates himself in the occasional indulgence of it. There is much which is not inconsistent, perhaps, in the eye of the world, but which is most certainly not consistent in the mind of the Spirit of God. These Brethren have, in fact, shot three times and they have struck the ground once or twice, but they have not made a clean sweep of their besetting sins. They still tolerate some of them. They have not reached to a high point of holiness.

Now I am as far as anybody from believing that a man ever will be perfect in this life, but I will never be satisfied till I am! And if I cannot be perfect, I will seek, by God's Grace, to get as near to it as possible. And this should be the labor of every Christian. Not in order to save himself, but because he is saved he should labor after the very highest degrees of holiness and seek that God might shine through him as through a lamp and that men may take knowledge of him that he has been with Jesus and learned of Him. High faith, high knowledge, high living--oh what blessed Christians should we have if these three went together!

So, too, there are many Christians who do not shoot more than three times, inasmuch as they are content with very low enjoyments. Oh the many, the many professors who all their days are subject to bondage! Now Christ came to deliver such from the fear of death. And yet though Christ came to do it, it is not done in their case. They do not receive the Spirit of Adoption, but they seem to have received the spirit of bondage again to fear, and they think that this is the rule with God's people. When they read of some saints who have climbed the mountains and have had sweet fellowship with Christ, they say, "Ah, such men are uncommon and such experiences are like angels' visits, few and far between. We cannot get up to this."

I do believe, dear Friends, that this spirit creeps over us all. We read the biography of such a man as Brainerd and we shut up the book and sigh and say, "Oh I could never be so devoted as he was!" We have turned over the life of Whitfield and when we have read it, we have said, "Ah, a very extraordinary man--a very extraordinary man! It is not likely that I shall ever get his zeal." And when we turn to the Old Testament and read of Abraham, we say, "Yes, Abraham's faith was very wonderful. But we do not look upon him as a pattern which we are to imitate--we believe that his faith is something set up high in a niche--to which we can never get."

My Brethren, this is all wrong! I believe that the Christian man ought not to be content to be equal with Abraham, because Abraham lived in the dark, before the Sun had risen. It was, at least, but twilight in Abraham's day. And yet if he had so much faith when he could only see through the dim smoke of sacrificial rams and bulls, how much more faith and confidence in God ought you and I to have when we see Christ Himself, and when God speaks to us through His Son? Shame on us that we are content to be such dwarfs when we might grow into giants--that we are here frittering away our time when we might immortalize ourselves and glorify our Lord.

How is it that we are content to bring forth a lean ear, and then a scanty ear, when there should be seven ears upon one stalk, like the plenty of Egypt? How is it that we have here and there a cluster, when instead, if we did but shoot more, if we had more faith and more confidence in God, we might be like the grapes of Eshcol, whose clusters were too heavy for one man to carry? Yes, I am afraid there is in this Christian land very, very much of this stopping short of what we might be. We do not press on and reach to that which is before, but saying, "I am saved," we are content and sit down before we reach the goal, or have apprehended that for which we were apprehended of Christ Jesus.

Now I want your attention for just a moment while I try to show some of the reasons why the king did not shoot more. I cannot tell certainly, but I think some of the reasons which I am going to give you may be correct. Perhaps he felt rather tender towards the Syrians. It is just possible that he felt he did not want to hurt them too much. He would be victorious--he would get his enemy under his feet. But if he did more he would crush him outright and he hardly wanted to do that.

So I think that some professors do not want to be too hard with their sins--they have a sort of hidden tenderness towards their own corruptions. O, dear Friends, how very angry we get when somebody tells us a little too plainly about our faults! And how angry we are with anything which seeks to cut the throat of our favorite sin! Ah, we do not know how tender we are to our sins, any of us, whereas the viper's brood should be crushed in the nest! We are often saying as we wound them, "Yes, keep them under. But no--I could not give them all up--I could not--no, I must have just a little indulgence. There must be this and that."

The laying of the axe to the root of the tree is not pleasant work. Lop the big boughs off if you like, but laying the axe to the root--no, we do not quite like that. There is in us, after all, through our natural corruptions, a hankering attachment to our sins. The old man says, "Spare them," and it needs much Grace and triumphant Grace, too, to say, "No! Hew them to pieces before the Lord and let not even the best of the sheep or of the cattle be spared." Tenderness to sin will always check us in any great growth in Grace. We shall not use God's bow as much as we should if we once begin to pamper self-indulgence, to cultivate our own ease and make provision for the flesh.

Again, perhaps the king did not go on to shoot because he thought it was hardly his business to be employed as a bowman. "Why should I stay here forever," says he, "shooting arrows? I did not object when the Prophet's hand was upon me, to shoot. But to stand here and keep striking the ground is hardly the occupation for a king!" And then the thought, perhaps, that he should have three victories and that would be enough. "Why, it will be something wonderful! Three victories, one after another, will be quite enough to crown me with everlasting renown and I do not want more than that." And so he did shoot but three times.

And how many a Believer seems to say, "Can I always be keeping watch over my corruptions? Am I to be so precise and to live so near to God? What? Am I to be so much in prayer? Am I to be such a Bible student, and to be so much occupied? No, if I can overcome some of my sins and be a respectable Church member and do a little in the Sunday school, and get to Heaven--that is enough." You do not want, you see, to be made good. You do not want to be made Christlike. You do not want to be able to triumph over your sins. You mistake your high calling--you think you are called to be a slave, when you are called to reign! You fancy that you are called to wear sackcloth, when you are bid to put on scarlet and fine linen! You think that God has called you to a dunghill, whereas He has called you to a throne! You imagine that you are to be but here and there--the skirmishers in the battle--when He has called you to stand in the front rank and to fight constantly for His cause.

I think, also, that the king may have begun to doubt whether the victories would really come. He knew very well that he had not many soldiers and that Syria was very strong, so he thought, "Well, it takes some faith to think that I shall beat them three times, but it is not likely I shall do it the fourth." He doubted the Divine power and the Divine promise because of his own weakness. And many a Christian does that. I think, Brethren, that we who are in the ministry might do vastly more for God than we do, if, remembering our own weakness, we did not let that overshadow God's strength.

Why, what cannot a man do when he has faith in God? Without Christ we can do nothing. But remember the converse of that proposition--that with Him we can do all things. If He will be with me I can do all things, or can bear all sufferings. Let us not forget this. And never let a sense of human weakness mar our clear perception of the might and majesty of God. Let us shoot often, for as often as we shoot, God will answer our faith.

And do you not think, too, that it is very likely that the king despised the Prophet's plans? Why, he seemed to say, this was absurd, striking the ground in this way! If there were any men to be shot at, he would not spare the arrows. But to strike the ground in this way--absurd! Ridiculous! So, too often, we miss a blessing because we do not like God's plans. We have got some new scheme of our own. It is not preaching the Gospel--that is old-fashioned. We will try something else. It is better than going out into the highways and hedges and compelling them to come in. No, we want a shorter cut than that! We keep fancying that if we were to give up some ordinance--perhaps if we held our tongues about Baptism--or if we were to cut about this doctrine and that, we should get on better.

Ah, this is all wrong, dear Friends. Carnal policy may take its place in the cabinet and in the government of the land, but never in the House of God! If right is right, pursue it. If God commands it, do it and leave the consequences to Him! If He bids you shoot on the ground, you shoot on the ground. You may see no Assyrian there. But every time you shoot, that arrow finds the heart of your enemy and shall lay him low.

I would, dear Friends, that I could so speak tonight as to give the members of this Church a very high and noble ambition to do much and to get much for God--to get much Grace--to have much holiness--to do much work. In fact, I wish I could bring you into such a state of heart as the Prophet wished to see in Joash--that you would take the arrows and shoot them off.

III. THE RIGHTEOUS WRATH OF THE PROPHET is our third point. And we think WE CAN WELL JUSTIFY HIS ANGER. We do not like to see either an old man, or a dying man angry. But I think the Prophet here did well to be angry, even though at the hour of his death. Oh how he loved the people and how he wept to think that their king was standing in their light and was robbing them of precious privileges!

Now when I look, dear Friends, upon many Church members and see how utterly idle and careless they are about Christ's cause and how many professors seem to be as dead as the seats they sit upon and to have no more Grace than worldlings, I think if my soul were warmed with something like a holy passion against them, I might say, with more truth than Jonah, "I do well to be angry." How much Israel suffers from the slack-handedness of the king! Oh, Christians, you suffer yourselves! You miss a thousand comforts! What you might do for God you are unable to do! What you might sit down and feed upon yourselves you utterly miss because you will not go on farther and seek higher attainments!

And all your Brethren suffer, too. Your prayers at the Prayer Meeting have not that fervor and unction which they would have if you lived nearer to God. Your experience is not so profitable to them as it would be if you walked nearer to Christ. The whole Church treasury is robbed by you.

Church membership is a sort of joint-stock company. We, each one of us, take out of that stock and put into it. There is a prayer treasury--we all want to be prayed for. There is taking out of it. We must all put prayers into the treasury and those members who do not pray--and are there such? And those members who do not yearn over souls--and are there not such? Those members who have no zeal for God--and are there such?--rob the treasury of God! And I know not why I might not compare them to Ananias and Sapphira, for they keep back a part of the price. God have mercy upon them for this!

The Church has greatly suffered on this account. Why, if this king had shot more arrows, Syria would have been quite overcome and cut in pieces. But because he was slack in this, Syria waves her proud banner over captive maids and sorrowing widows whose husbands have been slain in battle and weep in the streets of Samaria. The devil rejoices when he sees slumbering Christians! The world laughs in its sleeve at professors nowadays because it says, "In the old Puritan times, when we saw a Christian we were afraid of him. Ah, when a man joined the Church in those days, he was a man who meant what he said. But ah, there are so many of them now who only join the Church to be respectable. And they only go to a place of worship because of custom that the people may trade with them and be cheated--that they may talk with them and hear such idle talk as they would not hear from men in the streets, who never profess anything! Ah, we have almost overcome and destroyed the Church when we see her members behaving so."

It is these people, who may be Christians, but who are only half Christians. These people who are not altogether cold, but who still are not hot. These people whom I would not shovel away with the dross, but who nevertheless are so adulterated with base metal that you can scarcely call them pure gold. It is these people who make the daughter of Philis-tia to rejoice and the sons of the adversary to triumph. How Jehovah's name was dishonored! In Assyria's streets they laughed at Jehovah. They said that their gods were greater than He. Oh what a shame it is that you and I should ever put Christ to more shame than He endured for our sakes!

My Brothers and Sisters, what do we think of ourselves if we have ever in any measure crucified the Lord afresh and put Him to open shame? It is not only inconsistent Christians who do this but those Christians who do not seek to come up to the standard--who are contented to be poor in Grace when they might be rich. I believe that such persons bring much dishonor to Christ by their doubting, by their hard thoughts of Christ, by their miserable countenances and often, too, by their want of zeal, their want of prayer and their shallowness in the ways of God.

Look abroad and see how busy men are in the world! When a man wants to make money, see how he rises early and sits up late and eats the bread of carefulness! It is wonderful what ingenuity men put forth to get a fortune, what desper- ate attempts they make! How they will go to India and sweat under the burning sky and brave the fever there. Why, there are thousands of England's sons who do this year by year. See how at the North Pole bold and brave men have sacrificed their lives to force a passage. Men have been willing, in scientific experiments, to sacrifice social comforts, risk their health and forfeit their lives!

It seems to me that everybody is enthusiastic except Christians, and that men can get their blood hot on any subject except religion! In these days the ice has been given to the Church of God and the fire has been cast upon the world. Look at the devil's advocates, how they compass sea and land to make one proselyte. If you are dead and dull, they will not be so here at your next-door neighbors--St. George's Cathedral! You may be careless about the poor, but they will not be! You may, perhaps, cease to be much in prayer and much in action, but you will find that they will not cease their incantations!

Why, when the devil comes to a man he will say to him, "Come with me! I want you to leave your wife and children tonight! Come with me," and away the man goes to some low pot-house. "I want you to go in here," says the devil, and the man goes in--perhaps a respectable man, as the world has it. "Now," says the devil, "I want you to drink ale and stout. It will make your brain reel. It will make your eyes red tomorrow morning and perhaps send you into delirium tremors." "I will do it," says the man and he drinks it pleasantly and sweetly as though he were drinking draughts of Heaven's own nectar.

It may be that he goes reeling home, or has to be carried there, but he is quite ready to go again and again, though he may beggar his children and see his weeping wife and his starving family. He does it all so cheerfully and thinks, in fact, that he is a very fine fellow and is only enjoying himself, though he brings untold miseries unto his family. You will sometimes see a man go into vice and bring his own body to the verge of the grave and make himself a mass of rottenness at the command of the devil and yet he never grumbles at his master, never thinks of running away from him!

And here is my Lord, whose service is perfect freedom, who gives us to eat and to drink of better food than angels ever tasted! Who the more we do for Him the more He rewards us and the more strength He gives us to work with. And yet we are cold and dull and dead! And if we are asked to do something, we say we have so many calls. Or if we are asked to go upon some enterprise which has a little dishonor or discomfort connected with it, we go back--would lie in bed and take our ease! Oh what a shame, what a shame this is!

Prophet, you did well to be angry! I would that some burning spirits would come among us and speak even bitterly to us, if they could but make us feel that--

"Life is real, life is earnest," and that the cause of Christ demands that spirit, soul and body should be at the highest tension, at the very sternest stretch, spending and being spent, even unto blood--resisting sin and contending for the mastery of Christ!

Well now, I took this text because it seemed to me--I do not know how it seems to you--as if it were a lesson to your minister and to you tonight. Here you are, come into this new Chapel and into a neighborhood new to you. We who are come here from other Churches, as the old Prayer Book version puts it, "Wish you good luck in the name of the Lord." We wish for you the highest and the best prosperity that we desire for ourselves. But we do want to impress upon you that while God will help you and stand by you, always remember that the Church must be active.

Every single individual must take his portion in this sacred fight, in this grand crusade against sin. I pray Brother Evans never to stay his hand from the shooting of the arrows. If God shall bless him in one effort, let him go on to another. If he sees seven souls converted, let him mourn that it is not eight. If he sees the place filled, let him, even then, not rest satisfied but let his cry still be for something beyond. And, as the eagle rests not, but flies upward, ever facing the sun, such may his course be--onward and upward and true to the line--until the Master shall take him into His Glory in the rest which remains for the people of God.

And you who are here, do you sit still? Do not say, "Well, if we get these seats comfortably filled we shall be content." I hope you may have them filled, but I hope you will not, then be content! No, let it be your aim, then, to pray that God will convert the seat-holders, that the congregation shall become the Church. And do not be content, then! Ask that the aisles may be filled, that God will convert the standers and that your Church may burst the walls of the house in which you meet. Do not think that your standard of a Prayer Meeting is to be a low one. Do not begin to say, "If we have twenty or thirty at a Prayer Meeting that will do."

Why, many of our Churches are below even that standard! Do not be content even with fifty, but go on shooting. Yes, Brother Evans, go on. And you members of this Church--go on shooting your arrows! Do not ask God for a little, but open your mouth wide and God will fill it! Take care that you open it as wide as ever you can. Ask Him for great things and when you ask do not ask as though you thought you were very venturesome. No, but ask because He is sure to give! Believe that God can and will give you a gracious justification for believing in Him. Ask, too, because He knows what your hearts cannot even conceive of, for He is able to do exceeding abundantly beyond what you can ask!

Do not be content, I pray you, at Upton Chapel, with being a nice, respectable, strong Church in the denomination! Do not be content with that! I say it very sorrowfully, but we have known some Churches which did run well. They have got a good place of worship, a very handsome building with little bits of colored glass and the people's faces on Sundays are all sorts of colors. And when they have got to this pitch they have said, "Well, we are very respectable people. We do not want the poor people. We do not want to go into the lanes and highways and hedges and fetch them in." In fact, they get sometimes to be like some of your old servants--you hardly know which is master and which is servant. And so the Lord may hardly know which is master in the Church--these people, or Himself--for they will not do what He tells them. They have got too big for that. They could do it once, but they cannot do it now.

Now that will not be the case here for years to come. I hope it may never be the case here. But may you ever be a faithful Church! May you ever be a working Church till the Lord Himself shall come. May God grant that you may keep on shooting your arrows, that you may expect great things and do great things. And now, you members of the Church and all of us who are here present, let us consecrate ourselves anew unto God. Let us ask ourselves tonight whether we have not been shooting too few arrows. Whether we have not thought too much of the little we have been doing. Whether we might not have done more. Whether we must not do more. Whether now, for the future, we will not believe God's promises more firmly. Preach His Word more boldly. Tell it to others more frequently. Give to God more liberally. Pray to God more earnestly, consecrate and devote ourselves to the Lord more perfectly.

I am sure there is room for great improvement in the best of us. O Lord, what a spark is my love to You! Oh that You would blow it into a flame, till it were as coals ofjuniper! To use the words of an old minister--"David said, 'The zeal of Your house has eaten me up,' but it will be a long time before some people are eaten up. It has not begun to nibble at them yet and there is no fear of their being eaten up."

Now I would like to see a man "eaten up" with his religion! I would that the Christian would give himself up so completely to the mighty whirlwind of Divine Grace that it might carry him away and make him but as a particle of straw in its tremendous course! The Lord grant you power and Grace thus to be given up to Him and thus to serve Him! May God now add His own blessing, for Christ Jesus' sake. Amen.

The First Five Disciples

DELIVERED ON SUNDAY MORNING, MAY 15, 1864,
BY THE REV. C. H. SPURGEON,
AT THE METROPOLITAN TABERNACLE, NEWINGTON.

"And the two disciples heard him speak and they followed Jesus. Then Jesus turned and saw them following and said unto them, What do you seek? They said unto Him, Rabbi, (which is to say, being interpreted, Master), where do You dwell? He said unto them, Come and see. They came and saw where He dwelt and abode with Him that day for it was about the tenth hour. One of the two which heard John speak and followed Him was Andrew, Simon Peter's brother. He first found his own brother, Simon, and said unto him, We have found the Messiah, (which is, being interpreted, the Christ). And he brought him to Jesus. And when Jesus beheld him, He said, You are Simon the son of Jona: you shall be called Cephas, (which is by interpretation, A Stone). The day following Jesus would go forth into Galilee and find Philip and say unto him, Follow Me. Now Philip was of Bethsaida, the city of Andrew and Peter. Philip found Nathanael and said unto him, We have found Him, of whom Moses in the Law and the Prophets, did write, Jesus of Nazareth, the son of Joseph. And Nathanael said unto him, Can there any good thing come out of Nazareth? Philip said unto him, Come and see. Jesus saw Nathanael coming to Him and said of him, Behold an Israelite, indeed, in whom is no guile. Nathanael said unto Him, Why do You know me? Jesus answered and said unto him, Before that Philip called you, when you were under the fig tree, Isaw you. Nathanael answered and said unto Him, Rabbi, You are the Son of God, You are the King of Israel. Jesus answered and said unto him, Because I said unto you, Isaw you under the fig tree, do you believe? You shall see greater things than these, And He said unto him, Verily, verily, I say unto you, Hereafter you shall see Hea ven open and the angels of God ascending and descending upon the Son of Man." -- John 1:37-51.

IF it is true that "Order is Heaven's first law," I think it must be equally true that variety is the second law of Heaven. The line of beauty is not a straight line but always the curve. The way of God's procedure is not uniform but diversified. You see this with a glance, when you look at the creation around us. God has not made all creatures of one species but He has created beasts, birds, fishes, insects, reptiles. All flesh truly is not the same flesh, neither are all bodies of the same order. The dull dead earth, itself, is full of variety. Gems sparkle not all with the same ray. The grosser and less precious rocks are marked and veined. Each one according to its own fashion. In the vegetable world what a variety of plants, shrubs, herbs, flowers and trees we have about us! In any one of the kingdoms of Nature, whether it is the animal, vegetable, or mineral, you shall find so many subdivisions that it would need a long schooling to classify them and a lifetime would not suffice to understand them all.

Consider the winged creatures which flit through the air--what a diversity there is between the tiny humming bird, which seems to be but a living mass of gems, and the eagle which, with soaring wings ascends to the sky and sports with the lighting! The whole world is full of marvels and no two marvels alike. You shall never be able to find God repeating Himself. This great Master may often paint two pictures which seem alike, but investigated with the microscope, what differences at once are revealed!

Even those stars which seem to shine with rays of the same brilliance are discovered by the aid of the telescope to be of different colors, forms and orbits. No, even the very clouds are piled in varied forms and the masses of nebulae which make up the Milky Way are distinguishable from each other. God, in no instance that we can ever find, has used the same mold a second time. He is so affluent of designs, so abundant in the wisdom that devises, so prolific in plans that even when He would accomplish the same end He chooses to take another road to it. And that new road is quite as direct as those by which He has formerly reached His purpose.

Certainly this observation holds good in Providence. What strange diversity there has been in the dealings of God with His Church! When He has chastened His people He has scarcely ever made use of the same rod twice. At one time Midianites shall come up and devour the land of Israel. Another day the Philistines with their giants shall invade the country. Then shall come the

Babylonians and the Assyrians. Later the Roman power shall tread Judea under foot. And as the rods of His chastisement have been always different on the great scale, so you have found it on the little scale.

God has seldom chastened you twice in the same way. You could trace diversities either in the manner of the blow or the instrument you were struck with, or in the part of your mind which seemed to be the most affected by His chastisements. In deliverers, again, how great a variety--you scarce find two alike! God raises up a Gideon, but Jephthah is not like Gideon and Samson is not like Jephthah, nor is David to be compared to Samson or Gideon. They are all diverse. And their weapons are varied, too. One man has to use an ass' jawbone, another must use a sling and a stone--one shall be content with the ox goad, while another must draw the dagger.

Different methods God ordains as well as different forms of man. And He delivers His people just according to His own will, but ever in a different form. Well may Providence be so diverse when you consider that men themselves whom God uses to be His principal instruments are so unlike each other. There are not merely the great differences of race and of nationality, nor even the differences of birth and education, but we are all different in constitution--no two minds being alike. There is an individuality about every one of us which will prevent our ever being mistaken for anyone else.

We might by accident be undistinguished, but let us be known and very soon important differences will be discovered. God is ever the God of variety and He will be so to the end of the chapter. He will do new things before He rolls up the book of history--we shall see new acts of the Lord--He will fight His battles after fresh methods, raise up deliverers different from any who have come before and will exalt and glorify His name upon new instruments of music. Let us expect it. He is the God of variety, both in Nature and in Providence.

My text is a very clear illustration that the same law applies in the work of Grace. There is ever the same kind of operation and yet ever a difference in the manner of operation. There is always the same Worker in the conversion of the soul and yet different methods for breaking the heart and binding it up again are continually employed. Every sinner must be quickened by the same life, made obedient to the same Gospel, washed in the same blood, clothed in the same righteousness, filled with the same Divine energy and eventually taken up to the same Heaven. And yet in the conversion of no two sinners will you find matters precisely the same.

From the first dawn of the Divine life to the day when it is consummated in the noontide of perfect sanctification in Heaven, you shall find that God works this way in that one, and that way in the other, and by another method in the third--for God still will be the God of variety. Let His order stand fast as it may, still will He ever be manifesting the variety, the many-sidedness of His thoughts and mind. If, then, you look at this narrative--somewhat long, but I think very full of instruction--you may notice four different methods of conversion. And these occur in the conversion of the first five who formed the nucleus of the college of Apostles--the first five who came to Christ and were numbered among His disciples!

It is very remarkable that there should be among five individuals four different ways of conversion! Were you, however, to examine any five persons, I suppose you would find similar disparity. Pick out five Christians indiscriminately and begin to question them how they were brought to know the Lord. You will find methods other than those you have here. And probably quite as many as four out of the five would be distinct from the rest.

I. The first case we have in the text is THE CONVERSION OF THE TWO DISCIPLES. One was probably John. We cannot speak with absolute certainty, but it was very probably John. We know it to have been the habit of this Evangelist to omit his own name whenever he could. Sometimes he speaks of "that other disciple," when he means himself. And now and then he puts it, "that disciple whom Jesus loved."

His love nurtured in him a kindly esteem of others, but an humble estimate of himself. While, therefore, he never omits to record the need of praise others obtained from the lips of Christ, as often as he can he omits his own name. It is supposed then--and I think rightly--that one was John. The other was Andrew, Simon Peter's brother. The first two disciples are the fruits ofpreaching.

May we not expect to find that the major part of our conversions are the result of the public ministry? "The two disciples heard him speak and they followed Jesus." Let us offer a few words concerning this first matter. We expect, Beloved, to see a great number of souls brought to God by the preaching of the Truth of God. The preaching of the Cross may be and it actually is to those who perish, foolishness. But unto us who are saved, it is the power of God and the wisdom of God. Wherever there is the most Gospel preaching, you will find the most conversions.

Many of our societies for carrying the Gospel to the heathen forget their main work. And while setting up colleges, translating Bibles and publishing tracts, they neglect to use this great hammer of God, this mighty battering ram which is to dash down strongholds. The preaching of the Cross, the crying of, "Behold the Lamb of God!"--this is God's appointed agency. Other labors are to be entered into, but this is the main and chief agency for the conversion of souls.

Observe in the case before us, the preacher. He was a man Divinely illuminated. Jesus Christ came to John's Baptism, but at first the Baptist did not know Him. After awhile, however, when the descending Spirit marked out the Messiah, John then knew to a certainty that this was He of whom Moses in the Law and the Prophets did write. Ever afterwards John's testimony was clear and bold. Though he ended his ministry with the loss of his head, he never lost the honesty of his purpose or the lucidness of his testimony. He continued faithfully to declare that the Messiah had come.

Brethren, it is of importance in the work of the ministry that the preacher be a God-illuminated man. Not that education is to be despised--on the contrary, we cannot expect the Spirit of God in these days to give to men the knowledge of languages if they can acquire that knowledge by a little perseverance. It is never the Divine rule to work a superfluous miracle. With the faculties and powers we possess, we must yield up our members unto God as instruments of righteousness. So far, then, as the education of the man is concerned, we believe God leaves that with us, for if we can do it there is no need that any miracle should be worked.

But let the man be educated ever so well, he is then but as the lump of clay--God must breathe into his nostrils the breath of spiritual life as a preacher, or else he will be of no service--just a dead weight upon the Church of God. What shall we say, then, of those men who enter into a pulpit because the family living is vacant, or because, indeed, being too great fools for either the army or the law, they must needs be put where their livelihood can be more easily obtained--in the Church? How crying is this sin in our times, that men should have Episcopal hands laid upon them, declaring that they are moved to the ministry by the Holy Spirit, when they know not whether there is a Holy Spirit, so far as any experimental knowledge of His power upon their own hearts is concerned!

The day, I hope, is passing away when men shall be more skilled at hunting the fox than at fishing for souls. And on the whole, God is raising up in this land a spirit of decision upon this point--that the Christian minister must be a man who knows experimentally in his own soul the Truths of God which he professes to preach. God may convert souls, it is true, by a bad preacher. Why, if the devil preached, I should not wonder at souls being converted--if only the devil preached the Truth. It is the Truth and not the preacher. Ravens, unclean birds though they are, brought Elijah his bread and his meat--and unclean ministers may sometimes bring God's servants their spiritual food. But for all that, unto the wicked, God says, "What have you to do to declare My statutes?" The minister must be a God-taught man whose eyes have been opened by the Holy Spirit. This, at least, is the standing rule--whatever exceptions may be pleaded.

Then, mark you, granted that this is the case we must not expect his ministry to be alike successful at all times, for in the present instance, on one occasion the Baptist gave a very clear testimony for Christ, but none of his disciples left him to follow Jesus. The next time he preached he was successful, for two of his disciples joined the Master, though on the former occasion we read not that one of his hearers was led to declare himself on the Lord's side.

My Brethren, God suffers His ministers to cast the net sometimes on the wrong side of the ship. Even a whole night they may toil and take nothing. They may sow upon the barren ground, upon the highway and among the thorns. They may cast their bread upon the waters, and as yet they may not find it, for the promise speaks of "many days." Still the minister must persevere. If souls are not saved today, they may be tomorrow. I was wondering, as I read this passage, whether there were some who heard last Sunday in vain, who perhaps would hear to profit today. I was lifting up my heart in prayer to God that these words, "the next day after," might come true to some here.

Whereas, the other day, I cried, "Behold the Lamb!" and you did not see Him or trust Him, I will repeat the cry, "Behold the Lamb!" again today. O that you may be led to follow Jesus! When you have well considered the preacher and his success, I would have you observe his Subject. How short the sermon!--a rebuke to our prolixity. How plain it was-- no difficult phrases--no high-flown elocutionary embellishments--no feats of oratory here! It is just, "Behold the Lamb!" But observe the Subject--John preaches of Jesus Christ, of nothing else but Christ. And of Christ, too, in that position and in that form in which He was most needed but least palatable.

The Jews accepted Christ the Lion. They looked for the mighty Hero of the Tribe of Judah who should break their bonds. Such Jesus was. But John did not preach Him as such. He preached Him as Christ the Lamb--the Lamb of God, the suffering, despised, meek, and patient Sacrifice. The Baptist held Him up to the sons of men on this occasion as the great Sin Bearer. He seems to have brought out most prominently in his own thoughts and before the minds of the people the picture of the paschal lamb and of the scapegoat. He dwelt upon this, that Jesus was the Lamb of God who takes away the sin of the world.

If there are to be many conversions worked in any place, the preacher must be a man taught of God and he must persevere, even though he has been unsuccessful. But he must see to it that this is the staple of all his sermons, the raw material out of which he makes every discourse--"Jesus and

Jesus the Lamb! Jesus the Sin Bearer." He must ever be crying, "You Sinners, see your sins laid on Him! You guilty, look to Him! Trust Him! There is life in a look at Him. He has taken your sins and carried your sorrows--look to Him!" Let the preacher stammer here and he is undone. Let him be unsound on the Atonement. Let him speak in feeble strains, as though he apologized for so old-fashioned a doctrine and you shall hear of no conversions from January to December.

But let him hold this to be the first and most important Truth--that Jesus Christ came into the world to be a Sin Bearer for sinners, even the chief, and there must be conversions! God were not true to His promise, the Truth were no longer the potent thing it has proved itself to be in the olden times if souls were not quickened and turned to God by such a ministry as this! O you who preach the Gospel, keep close to this, "Behold the Lamb of God!" You young men who stand up in the streets, make this your topic! And you who minister to the Church of God, give them all the doctrines of the Gospel, but still always come back to this as the needle comes to its pole--"Behold the Lamb of God which takes away the sin of the world!"

In these two conversions by public ministry it is interesting to observe the process. Carefully notice the narrative. A spirit of enquiry was stirred up in Andrew and his companion and they began to follow Christ, not exactly as disciples as yet, but as searchers. If I may say so, they followed Christ's back. They had not come to see His face yet, or to sit at His feet. They followed His back as some do who, being impressed under the Word, have a desire after Christ and intend to set about an honest investigation of His claims to their faith. While they are following behind Christ, He turns round and faces them.

Oh, what a blessed turning for them! It was a blessed turning for Peter when the Lord turned and looked upon him! And in this case while they are, as it were, following His back, He turns and He looks upon them. I cannot tell you how much love there was in His eyes. The love of a mother to her first child may perhaps picture the love of Jesus Christ to these, His first disciples. He was God, He was Man, He was God's own Son. But He had never been a Master of disciples till that moment. Now He springs to a rank which He had not obtained before. Now He has some who will call Him "Rabbi," and will be willing to be guided by His teaching. He looks round upon them. Even so, when enquiry is excited by the ministry, and men begin to search, Jesus Christ looks upon them. With an eye of earnest affection He regards them and assists them in their search.

Jesus put to them the question, "What do you seek?"--a very modest question. Notice it. It is the first word of Christ's ministry. It is the first word I find Christ speaking at all in public--"What do you seek?" And was not it a very comprehensive question? "What is that you seek?" If there are any honest enquirers here after salvation, He puts the same question to you this morning--"What do you seek?" Are you seeking pardon? You shall find it in Me. Are you seeking peace? I will give you rest. Are you seeking purity? I will take away your sin. A new heart will I give you and a right spirit will I put within you. What are you seeking? Some solid resting place for your soul upon earth and a glorious hope for yourself in Heaven? Whatever you seek, it is here.

What a text this might be for a missionary when first consulted by some of the awakened heathen, when he should say, "You are on the search after Truth. Now what is it you really want? What do you seek? What is it? Because whatever it is that the human heart in its right state can possibly seek after--all that is to be found in Christ." Christ meets the man who is in an enquiring frame of mind by suggesting to him further enquiry. He stirs up the heart. While the soul's fire is burning He puts fuel to the flame.

They say, "Master, where do you dwell?" And His answer to them is, "Come and see." This is just how the process of conversion is worked in men's hearts. They want to know more of Christ and He says to them, "Come and see." You would have peace--come and see whether I can give it to you. I tell you that if you trust Me, your peace shall be like a river and your righteousness like the waves of the sea. "Come and see." You say you want purity--just try now the effect of the obedience of faith. See if it does not change your heart and renew your spirit. "Come and see." O you who are seeking and asking questions about Christ and about His Gospel and His Person and His pedigree, "Come and see."

The best way to be convinced of the potency of our holy Gospel is to try it for yourselves. If you are honest seekers, if the Grace of God has made you so, then come and test and try! "Blessed is every man that trusts in Him." This is our witness and our testimony. But if you want to be sure of it for yourselves, "Come and see." They took Christ at His word. They came and they saw. We are not told what they saw, but we are told what was the result--they stopped with Him that night and they remained with Him all His days and became His faithful disciples.

My dear Friend, if you would but come and see Christ! If by humble earnest prayer you would give your heart up to Him and then trust in Him implicitly to be your Guide, you would never lament the decision! If Jesus proves a liar to you, then desert Him! If His promises are not true, then stand no longer numbered with His disciples. But give Him a trial--

" O make but trial of His love! Experience will decide how blest are they and only they, Who

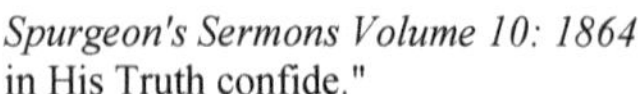

in His Truth confide."

You see, then, the way in which God's Grace works through the Word--it excites a spirit of enquiry, then a still further enquiry, then the test of experience--and afterwards leads to the giving up of the heart to Christ.

II. The next case is a very different one. The third of Christ's disciples, one Simon Peter, was brought in by PRIVATE INSTRUMENTALITY and not by the public preaching of the Word. Observe the forty-first verse, "Andrew first finds his own brother Simon, and says unto him, We have found the Messiah, which is, being interpreted, the Christ." This case is but the pattern of all cases where spiritual life is vigorous. As soon as ever a man is found by Christ, he begins to find others.

The word "first" implies that he did not give it up afterwards--he first found his own brother Simon! How many he found afterwards I cannot tell, but I will be bound to say that Andrew continued to be a fisher of men till he was taken up to the third Heaven. He found very many after he had found Peter. The first instinct of the new-born life is to desire the good of others. I will not believe that you have tasted of the honey of the Gospel if you can eat it all yourself. True Grace puts an end to all spiritual monopoly.

I know there are some who think there is no Grace beyond their own Chapel. They believe that God never works beyond the walls of their own tabernacle. Beyond the range of the voice of their minister everything is unsound, unorthodox, pretensions perhaps, but still fatally delusive. They hold that all others are out of the bond of the Covenant and, not unlike those ancient wranglers in the land of Uz, they say, "We are the men and wisdom will die with us." Surely God's people never talk in that fashion, or if they do, they are then speaking the language of Ashdod and not the speech of the child of Israel, for the Israelite's tongue drops with love and his speech is full of the anxious desire that others may be brought in!

Look at our Apostle Paul. You shall never find stronger predestinarianism than you read in the ninth chapter of Romans, and yet what does he say? His heart's desire and prayer to God for Israel is that they may be saved. He had heaviness of heart, he says, for his Brethren, his kinsmen according to the flesh. There was no man more anxious to convert souls than Paul, though there was no man more sound in the doctrine of the election of God. He knew it was not of him that wills, nor of him that runs, but yet he could say as Samuel did, "God forbid that I should sin against the Lord in ceasing to pray for you."

See, then, that the first desire of a Christian man is to endeavor to bring others to the Savior. Relationship has a very stern demand upon our first individual efforts. Andrew, you did well to begin with Simon. I do not know, my Brethren, whether there are not some Christians giving away tracts at other people's houses who would do well to give away a tract at their own. I wonder whether there are not some going out to the villages preaching who had better remain at home teaching their own children--or whether even in the Sunday school there may not be those who come before God to perform one duty, while their hands are stained blood-red with the murder of another duty. Your first business is at home. You may have a call to teach other people's children--that may be--but certainly you have an imperative call to teach your own. You may or you may not be called to look after the people of a neighboring town or village, but certainly you are called to see after your own servants, your own kinsfolk and acquaintances. Let your religion begin at home.

We have heard of some people who export their best commodities--many traders do--I do not think the Christian should imitate them in that. At least let the Christian have all his conversation everywhere of the best savor, but let him have a care to put forth the sweetest fruit of spiritual life and testimony at home and in the circle of his own kinsfolk and acquaintances. Andrew, you did well, first, to find your brother Simon. When he went to find him he may not have thought of what Simon would become. Why, Simon was worth ten Andrews, as far as we can gather from the Evangelists! Peter was a very prince among the Apostles! And with that ready tongue of his and that bold, dashing, daring spirit--with that confident, resolute soul--there were none of them a match for Peter!

John might excel in love, but still Peter was verily a leader among the Apostles, and Andrew would but little compare with him. You may be yourself but very deficient in talent and yet you may be the means of bringing a great man to Christ. Ah, dear Friend, you little know the possibilities which are in you! You may but speak a word to a child and in that child there may be slumbering now a great heart which shall stir the Christian Church in years to come. Andrew has only two talents, but then finds Peter. Andrew's testimony to Peter is worthy of remark. There was great modesty in it and that, I dare say, commended it to Peter.

He did not say, "I have found the Messiah"--he says, "We." Whoever was the other disciple, he gives him his share of the discovery. Our speech never loses force by losing pride but generally increases its power in proportion to its modesty, though that modesty must never interfere with boldness. His testimony was very plain and very positive. He did not beat around the bush or hesitate, but it is just this--"We have found the Messiah." Plain and unadorned was the statement, very positive. He did not say, "I think we have," or, "I trust we have," but, "we have." And this was just the thing for Simon Peter.

Peter wanted positive and plain dealing and he was a man who wanted it pushed home by a brother's friendly voice, or else it had little availed him to speak of Christ at all. When he was brought to Jesus, observe the process of conversion. Jesus describes to him his present state. He said, "You are Simon, son of Jona." Some interpret this, "You are Simon, the son of the timid dove." He explains to him what he was--shows that He knew him--that He understood both his boldness and his cowardice--both his rashness and his constancy. And then, when He had told him what he was, Jesus gave him a new name indicative of the nature which His Grace would give--"You shall be called Cephas, a stone."

Now this is the general plan of conversion. It is the plan in every case, really, though not apparently. Nature is discovered and Grace is imparted. The old name we are taught to read with sorrow and a new name is given to us and we rejoice in it. There may be some here who have not been converted to God under the ministry but under the words of a Sunday school teacher, or a sister, or a friend. Thank God and take courage. It does not matter how you are converted, so long as you are resting upon Jesus only!

If you have not been a searcher of the Word, if Christ has never seemed to say to you, "Come and see," yet if your nature has been changed and you have received a new name--if there is a radical change in the rest--you are a child of God. That you are brought into the fellowship of the saints is an illustration of the unity of God's purpose. That there should be distinctive marks in your conversion is quite in harmony with the diversity of His operations.

III. "The day following Jesus would go forth into Galilee and find Philip and say unto him, Follow Me." The fourth disciple is called without either the public Word or private instruction--he is called directly BY THE VOICE OF JESUS. Now in truth all men are so called, for the voice of John or the voice of Andrew is really the voice of Jesus Christ speaking through their instrumentality. But in some cases no apparent instrumentality is used. We have known some who on a sudden have felt impressions, from where they came or where they tended they did not know.

In the midst of business we have known the workman suddenly check his plane--a great thought has entered into his brain--where it came from he could not tell. We have known a man wake up at midnight--he could not tell why, but a holy calm was upon him and as the moon was shining through the window there seemed to be a holy light shining into his soul and he began to think. We have known such things to occur--surprising cases--when men have been planning deeds of vice.

Was it not so with Colonel Gardner--that very night about to perpetrate a crime and yet stopped by Sovereign Grace upon the very brink of it, without any apparent instrumentality? We can not tell, Brethren, when God may regenerate His elect, for though we are to use means and cry to God to send forth laborers into the vineyard, yet the Sovereign Lord of All will frequently work without them. The Word which has been heard in years gone by. The Scripture which was known in childhood may, by the direct power of the Holy Spirit, without any immediate apparent means, turn the man from darkness to Light. Jesus Christ spoke but two words, but those words were enough--"Follow Me"--and Philip at once obeyed. What preparation of heart there had been before, I cannot tell. What still small voice had been speaking before this in Philip's ear, we do not know. Certainly the only outward means was this voice of Christ, "Follow Me."

And there may be in this House some who will be converted this morning. You do not know why you are here. You cannot tell why you strayed in. But yet it may be--God knows--Christ would have you come here because He would come here Himself. Is not there something which invites a pause in that word, "would," as we read it in this verse?-- "The day following Jesus would go forth into Galilee." Is not there something of the Divine necessity which we have often noticed in another place?--"He must needs go through Samaria." Did not He feel instinctively that there was a soul there which He must meet with and He must go after it and speak the all-commanding, sin-subduing Word?

Perhaps this morning Jesus would come to the Tabernacle! Jesus would come here because He knows that Philip is come here, too. Philip, where are you? You may have lived in sin and despised Christ, but if He says, "Follow Me," I beseech you obey His word and follow Him! To follow Christ is the picture of Christian discipleship in every form. Follow Christ in your doctrines--believe what He teaches! Follow Christ in your faith--trust Him implicitly with your soul! Follow Him in your actions--let Him be your example and Guide! Follow Him in ordinances--in Baptism follow Him and at His Table follow Him!

To every deed of daring, to every place of spiritual communion, to the mountain of secret prayer, or to the crowd in open ministry, follow Him! According to your measure tread in the footsteps of your Lord and Master. And this, I say, may be directed to one who has had no other instrumentality used upon him, but just the mysterious voice of Christ-- "Follow Me." It was so with the third case. Perhaps of the three this experience is the highest. The first two were told, "Come and see," and they came to understand the value of Christ. But this one is made to follow--he carries out practically that which the others did but see.

The second conversion before us attains a higher degree than the first. But this is the highest of all when the change of nature, as in the case of Peter, now leads to a change of action, as in the case of Philip, who arises and follows Christ.

IV. I hope I have not wearied you, for there is yet the fourth case of the fifth disciple, which differs from them all-- Nathanael. What shall we say of Nathanael? Was he converted by ministry? It does not appear so. Was he converted by PRIVATE INSTRUMENTALITY? He was partly so. Philip finds Nathanael, but Philip's finding of Nathanael was not quite so effectual as Christ's finding of Philip. When Christ found Philip, Philip believed. But when Philip found Nathanael, Nathanael would not believe. He said, "Can there any good thing come out of Nazareth?"

Philip is partly the instrument, but there is something more. Jesus Christ Himself shows His own power BY TELLING TO NATHANAEL THE SECRETS OF HIS HEART. But still, Nathanael's conversion to Christ seems to me to be PARTLY OWING TO THE STATE IN WHICH HE THEN WAS. He was already in some sense a saved man--he was a devout Israelite. He was a true seeker of the Messiah beneath the fig tree. Well, then, there were these things put together--there was a preparation of heart which was doubtless worked of God.

But this preparation did not bring him to Christ, though it made him ready for Christ. It brought him to God in prayer, but it did not bring him yet to the Lamb of God who takes away the sins of the world. Then came Philip's instrumentality and then came Christ's Divine Word which convinced Nathanael and led him to put his trust in the Messiah. This is a sort of composite case and doubtless there are many in the Church of God, who, if you should ask them, "How were you converted?" would be somewhat puzzled to give the answer.

We find in our Church Meetings a very large proportion of people who say, "Well, I cannot trace my conversion to any one sermon--many sermons have impressed me--indeed, most do. I cannot say, Sir, that I was converted when I was a child, but I sometimes think I was, for even at that time I was the subject of many impressions and I certainly did offer prayer. Yet there was a time," they will tell you, "there was a time when I seemed to come out more distinctly into the Light. And when I could say of Christ, 'You are the Son of God! You are the King of Israel,' but I cannot say exactly when the sun rose."

Now this, I think, was Nathaniel's case. Perhaps trained and brought up by godly parents, he had been in the habit of prayer--that prayer was somewhat ignorant--but it was very sincere. He sought the solitude of his shady garden and under the fig tree poured out his heart unto the Lord. That man is not saved. No! But there is a great part of the work done. Do not tell me that that man in his prayer has nothing in him more than the blasphemer. I tell you that he needs as much as the blasphemer does to have an effectual Word from Christ, but still there is a preparatory work in this man which there is not even in Philip, or in Simon Peter. There is a something, not meritorious, but still preparatory to the reception of the Gospel of Christ.

And when you labor for the conversion of such a man as this--and I do hope there may be some in this crowd--then it does not matter whether it is the ministry, or whether it is private instrumentality--there is sure to be good result because there is good ground to begin with. God has already furrowed and plowed the soil and so when the seed is scattered, there may be a little objection at first, but ultimately it will take root. Be looking out then, dear Friends, you who know how to talk to others about their souls! And wherever you see anything like devotion, even if it is mistaken and ignorant, look at that case! Be especially hopeful about it and try, if you can, to inform that person, "We have found Him of whom Moses in the Law and the Prophets did write."

Introduce Christ, talk of Jesus, bring these Nathanaels to Jesus--these who are like the honest and good ground, these men without guile or cunning--bring them to Jesus! Still, mark you, their prayers and your instrumentality will not be enough unless Christ shall meet them with some startling, soul-discovering Word and shall say, "Before that Philip called you, when you were under the fig tree, I saw you." Ah, you seeking Soul, Christ sees you! Before you came here this morning Jesus saw you! Before you hear the challenge, "Look to Christ," Christ has looked upon you. If you are truly seeking in the loneliness of that upper room, or in that field behind the hedge, Jesus sees you!

When you are by the wayside and your heart is going up, "Lord, save me, or I perish," Jesus sees you! One of you has been writing to me this morning, and you say, "Pray for me that I may be saved, for I want to be saved." Ah, my Friend, if you want to be saved, Jesus wants to save you and so you are both agreed on that point! You, like Nathanael, are seeking Him. And I come this morning, like Philip and I long to bring you to Jesus, my Master. Oh, how I pray Him to speak to you and if so, He will tell you that He knew you when you were dead in sin and loved you, notwithstanding all!

And therefore He brought you to this House to hear His Word. Mark you, Nathanael's is the best case of the whole! He was favored above many. Who was the first man that ever had a promise from Christ? It was Nathanael! What was that? Why, that promise seems to me to be the sum of the Gospel--or rather the token-promise of the Gospel--which every Christian should carry in his hand. Jesus said, "Because I said unto you, I saw you under the fig tree, believe you? You shall see greater things than these." Nathanael was the first man who ever received a promise from the lips of the Lord Jesus when He was here on earth!

O you seeking Nathanaels, I think this is a promise for you--"You shall see greater things than these"--you shall see yourself pardoned! You shall see your prayers ascending Jacob's ladder and blessings coming down from God to rest upon your soul! I had hoped to have brought out many more points, but indeed, the chapter is too full for any to handle in so brief a time. You will observe, however, that I have given you just a glance at the surface of it which will suffice to show that the means of conversion and the general tenor of conversion will be found to differ in each case. Perhaps Nathanael's is the highest of all--he receives Christ in a fuller way than any of the others and he enjoys greater promises than they do.

But still they are all genuine, though they are not one of them like the other, except that John and Andrew may be put together. Judge not, therefore, your conversion by its means or by its particular form, but judge it by its fruit. Does it bring you to Jesus? Are you depending upon Him now? If so, go your way--your sins, which are many, are forgiven you! Eat the fat and drink the sweet, for God accepts you--therefore rejoice! But and if you have had a thousand conversions, if you are not resting on Jesus this morning, tremble, for your refuge is a refuge of lies! Your hope is a spider's web--God deliver you from it and bring you now to rest upon the finished work and the perfect Sacrifice of the Lord Jesus! And then, with Andrew and Peter and John, and Philip and Nathanael you shall meet before the Throne to praise Him who is the Son of God and the King of Israel! The Lord bless you, for Christ's sake. Amen.

Unbelievers Stumbling--Believers Rejoicing

DELIVERED ON SUNDAY MORNING, MAY 22, 1864,
BY THE REV. C, H. SPURGEON,
AT THE METROPOLITAN TABERNACLE, NEWINGTON.

"As it is written, Behold I lay in Zion a stumbling stone and rock of offense: and whoever believes on Him shall not be ashamed." -- Romans 9:33.

OUR Apostle was inspired of God and yet he was moved to quote passages out of the Old Testament. The Spirit of God might have dictated new words to him. He might have shown him how to confirm the Truth by other arguments, but He is not pleased to do so. He moves His servant to establish the present Truth by Truths formerly revealed and thus He sets us an example of searching the Scriptures and prizing the ancient Oracles of God. The passage before us appears to be composed of two Scriptures woven into one, a method not very infrequent with the Apostles. A part of the text before us is found in Isaiah 28:16.

The Apostle does not quote verbatim, but gives us rather the sense than the words--"Behold, I lay in Zion for a foundation a stone, a tried stone, a precious cornerstone, a sure foundation: he that believes shall not make haste." But the Apostle inlays this word of Prophecy with another, selecting this time from Isaiah 8:14--"And He shall be for a sanctuary. But for a stone of stumbling and for a rock of offense to both the houses of Israel." I cannot help making an observation or two upon these passages before I come to the text before us.

In Isaiah 8:14 you will perceive a striking proof of Christ's Divinity. Observe the thirteenth verse--"Sanctify the Lord of Hosts Himself. And let Him be your fear and let Him be your dread. And He," that is the Lord of Hosts, "shall be for a sanctuary" to Believers, "but a stone of stumbling and for a rock of offense to both the houses of Israel." Isaiah utters a prophecy of the Lord of hosts. Paul quotes it in reference to the Lord Jesus Christ, plainly intending us to infer that the Lord Jesus Christ is no other than Jehovah Himself!

We learn from the other passage another Truth of God which serves more closely to illustrate our text. In Isaiah 28:16, we read, "Behold, I lay in Zion for a foundation a stone." The Apostle has omitted the words "for a foundation," and has inserted the words of the other passage, "a stumbling stone, a rock of offense." But the original prophecy in Isaiah serves to show us that God's real object in laying Christ in Zion was not that men might stumble at Him, but that He might be a foundation for their hopes. The real object of God was that Christ might be the cornerstone of human confidence.

But the result has been that to one set of men, renewed by Almighty Grace, Christ has become a sanctuary of refuge and a stone of dependence. And to others left to their own depravity He has become a rock of offense and a stumbling stone--thus the remarks upon the primitive Scriptures which Paul quotes. And now let us come to the verse itself. Our text tells us that many persons stumble at Christ. And, then, secondly, it assures us that those who receive Christ and believe in Him, shall have no cause to be ashamed.

I. The first declaration needs no proof, for observation itself teaches us that MANY STUMBLE AT CHRIST. No sooner was God manifest in the flesh, than mortals began to stumble at Him. "Is not this the carpenter's son?" was the question of those who looked for worldly pomp and imperial grandeur. "His father and His mother we know, and His brothers and His sisters, are they not all with us?" was the whispered objection of His own townsmen. In His own country the greatest of all Prophets had no honor. Our Lord was rejected by all sorts of men. They looked at Him from different quarters, but all with the same scornful eye.

The Pharisee stumbled at Him because He was not superstitions and ostentatious. Indeed, He did not wash His hands before He ate! Nor did He pray at the corner of the streets! Why, He entered into the company of publicans and sinners! He did not make broad His phylactery. He healed the sick upon the Sunday! He had no respect for traditions and therefore every righteous Pharisee abhorred Him. The Sadducee, on the other hand, much as He hated Pharisaic superstition, despised Christ equally as much. His objections were shot from quite another quarter. To him Christ was too superstitious, for the Sadducee would not believe in angels or spirits, or the resurrection of the dead--all which beliefs the Prophet of Nazareth openly avowed.

Philosophical skepticism detested Jesus because His teaching had in it very much of the supernatural element. All His life long, in the high courts of Herod or of Pilate, or in the lowest rank of the mob of Judea, Christ was despised and rejected of men. They had long ago persecuted all the Prophets whom the Lord had sent and it was little marvel that they now assailed the Master Himself. "We have piped unto you and you have not danced. We have mourned unto you and you have not lamented," might all the Prophets of God say, for Israel received neither the lonely man, whose meat was locusts and wild honey, nor the more genial Spirit who came eating and drinking.

They put all God's Prophets away and would have none of their rebukes. And when the Son Himself had come, they said, "This is the Heir, let us kill Him, that the inheritance may be ours." The Jews, with one voice rejected Him, save only the remnant, according to the election of Grace. But the Jew is not alone in his offense at the Cross. We know that when the Gospel was carried afterwards to the Gentiles, Christ Crucified was a stumbling stone to them. The polished Greeks, with their various systems of philosophy, expected in the Messiah deep thinking and classic taste. But when they heard Paul preach the resurrection of the dead, they saw nothing flattering to their philosophy and therefore they openly mocked him.

While the Jew gathered up his broad-bordered garment and called Christ a stumbling block, the Greek marched off to his classic temple or to his scientific academe and cried, "Foolishness! The men who talk thus must be mad!" In every age, even to the present time, wherever Jesus Christ is preached, the human heart at once has been stirred with wrath against Him. God's ambassador has found men unwilling to receive the peace which he proclaims. God's dear Son, who came with no words but those of mercy and of tenderness, has been abhorred and rejected by the very men whom He came to bless. "He came unto His own and His own received Him not."

However, we have very little to do with these past ages--we have far more to do with the present and with ourselves. And it is a sad thing to know that among this assembly, though I suppose we all call ourselves Christians, there are many who still find Christ Jesus to be a stumbling stone to them and a rock of offense. It is a lamentable fact that there are hundreds of thousands in London to whom the Gospel of Christ is as little known as to Hindus or Tartars. Christ is not a stumbling block to these--they are unaware of Him and therefore they have not the guilt which some of you have--of having heard of Him and having rejected Him.

Among the present assembly there are some who stumble at Christ because of His holiness. He is too strict for them. They would be Christians but they cannot renounce their sensual pleasures. They would be washed in His blood, but they desire still to roll in the mire of sin. Willing enough, the mass of men would be to receive Christ, if, after receiving Him, they might continue in their drunkenness, their wantonness and self-indulgence. But Christ lays the axe at the root of the tree--He tells them that these things must be given up--"because of these things comes the wrath of God upon the children of disobedience," and, "without holiness no man can see the Lord."

Human nature kicks at this. "What? May I not enjoy one darling lust? May I not indulge myself at least now and then in these things? Must I altogether forsake my old habits and my old ways? Must I be made a new creature in Christ Jesus?" These are terms too hard, conditions too severe, and so the human heart goes back to the flesh pots of Egypt and clings to the garlic and the onions of the old estate of bondage and will not be set free even though a greater than Moses lifts up the rod to part the sea and promises to give to them a Canaan flowing with milk and honey. Christ offends men because His Gospel is intolerant of sin.

Others stumble at our blessed Lord because they do not like the plan of being saved altogether and alone through faith. Have I any such here? I suppose I have. They say, "What? Are our good works to go for nothing? Is there nothing that we can do to assist in our salvation? You tell us that it is trusting in Christ alone without anything else which justifies the soul. Then we do not understand it, or if we understand it we do not like it." This is too humbling, too simple, too easy. "Why," says the man who has always been to his parish Church or to his Meeting House, who owes nobody anything and is kind to the poor--"Why, then I am no better off than the harlot who walks the pavement at midnight! Or the thief who is spending his month at the treadmill."

You are no better off, my Hearer, as to your eternal salvation if you refuse to believe in Christ! The damnation of the openly ungodly is sure, but so is yours, if, after having heard the plan of salvation you turn upon your heels and despise it because you prefer your own righteousness to the righteousness of God! Ah, how many are shipwrecked upon this rock, swallowed up in this quicksand? They would be saved but they will not bow the knee. They are not content to take God's salvation by faith in Christ Jesus and so they perish through their willful pride.

I have known others who stumble at Christ because of the doctrine which He preaches, more especially the Doctrines of Grace. There will come into this House, some who, if we preach a sermon upon Christian virtue, will say, "I enjoyed that discourse." But if we preach Christ and begin to talk about the deep doctrines which lie underneath the Gospel, such as election, effectual calling, and eternal and immutable love, straightway they are angry almost to the gnashing of their teeth. They would have Christ, they say, but they cannot accept these doctrines. "What? God saves whom He wills and not so much as ask the creature's permission? Shall He do just as He pleases with us as a potter does with lumps of clay? Are we to be told to our face that it is not of him that wills, nor of him that runs, but of God that shows mercy? We cannot endure this--we will betake ourselves to some place where man is made more of and where God is not set so high above our heads!"

Ah, but my Friend, Jesus Christ will not shape His doctrine to please you, nor tone down the Truth of Scripture to suit your carnal taste. Mark you, it is in the ninth of Romans that my text is found, and in that ninth of Romans you have the most plain and bold declaration anywhere on record concerning the Sovereignty of Divine Grace and if you choose to make that Sovereignty a reason for not believing in Christ you will perish for your pains. And, perish deservedly, too, because you will quarrel with God's Word and damn your own soul to be avenged on God's Sovereignty.

But indeed, my dear Friends, when sinners are resolved to object to Christ, it is the easiest thing in the world to find something to object to. I have met with some who stumble at Christ's people. They will say, "Well, I would believe in Christ, but look at professors! See how inconsistent they are! See many Church members, in what an unholy way they walk and even some ministers," and then they will begin to quote various faults of some of God's eminent servants and they think this is an excuse for going to Hell themselves, because others do not walk straight in the way to Heaven!

O, will you send your soul to Hell because another man is not all he should be? What if David falls and David is restored, is this any reason why you should fall and never be restored? What if some pilgrims to Heaven do turn into Bypath Meadow and have to come limping back into the road--is this a reason why you should follow the road to the City of Destruction? I think, Man, that this should only make you the more diligent to make your calling and election sure! The shipwrecks of others should make you sail more carefully. The bankruptcies of other men should make you trade with greater diligence and humility. To quote the defects of others as a reason why you should continue in the error of your ways is a fool's method of reasoning! Take heed, lest you find out your folly in the flames of Hell!

The real objection of the natural man is not, however, to God's people, nor to the plan of salvation itself, so much as to Christ. The rock of offense is Christ--to the Person of Christ. You will not have this Man to reign over you! You are not willing that He should wear the crown and have all the honor of your salvation. You had rather perish in your sin than that Jesus Christ should be magnified in your salvation. This is a severe charge, you will tell me. If it is not true, I pray you prove it false by believing in Jesus! If you have no objection to Christ, accept Him! Sinner, I charge you, if you say you do not stumble at Christ, then lay hold upon Him! If He is not obnoxious to you, clasp Him in your arms now!

Why, Man, if you are in your senses, since Christ can save you with an eternal salvation, you will certainly grasp Him, unless there is some objection in the way. And because you do not lay hold of Him, I tell you there is some hindrance in your sinful heart--an offense at Christ which will be your ruin unless God delivers you from it. Now may God help me to reason a few minutes with those who are not believers in Christ, who have made Him a stumbling stone and a rock of offense.

Dear Friend, let me come close to you and take your hand and talk with you. Have you ever considered how much you insult God the Father by rejecting Christ? If you were invited to a man's feast and you should come to the table and dash down every dish and throw them on the ground and trample on them, would not this be an insult? If you were a poor beggar at the door and a rich man had bid you into his feast out of pure charity, what do you think you would deserve if you had treated his provisions in this way? And yet this is just your case. God owes you nothing. You are a poor sinner without any claim upon Him and yet He has been pleased to prepare a table for you. His oxen and His fatlings have been killed and now you will not come!

No! You do worse! You raise objections to the feast! You despise the pleasant land and the goodly provision of God! Just think at what an expense the provision of salvation has been made! The eternal Father gave His Son. Hark you--His Well-Beloved, the Darling of His heart, His only Son--He gave Him to DIE, and do you despise such a Gift as this? What do you think? Would it not bring the blood into your face if you should give your only son to fight for your country and they to whom he was given should despise you and your gift? If out of some superhuman patriotism for your country's good you should even slay your son, would it not cut you to the quick if men should laugh at you and scoff the deed?

And yet such you do to the eternal Father, who for the love of men has rent His Darling from His bosom, nailed Him to the tree and filled Him with unutterable pains. You despise the unspeakable gift, the richest deed of bounty which even the infinite heart of God could have imagined, or the infinite hand of God could have performed! You despise all this! You touch God, let me tell you, in the apple of His eye. You do now wound Him in the most tender part! You might better have run upon the edge of His sword or dashed yourself upon the bosses of His buckler than to despise and reject His Only-Begotten Son, slaughtered for human guilt!

Think again, what a proof is here of your sinfulness and how readily will you be condemned at the last when this sin is written on your forehead. Why, Man, there will be no reason to bring up any other sins against you! The book in which your faults have been recorded scarcely need be opened, for this, alone, will be enough! You have made Christ a stumbling block, you have objected to God's dear Son--why need we any other witness? Out of this one mouth you shall be condemned--"You did abhor the Prince of Glory. You did refuse Him your heart"--take him back to the place from where he came. What if he has never been an adulterer or a whoremonger, yet is not this enough? Does not this show the blackness of the traitor's heart and the vileness of his character? He would not have Christ! He made the foundation which God laid in Zion, "a stone of stumbling and a rock of offense." What do you think of this, my Hearer?

Moreover, as this will be a swift witness to condemn you, how will this increase your misery? Do you think God will be tender over you when you have not been tender with His Son? When He shall cast you into Hell, will He make the flames less hot? Do you think His vengeance will be cool towards the man who stumbled at His Son? No! But this shall whet the edge of His sword. "This traitor did do despite unto the blood of Christ." He will pour oil upon the flames. "This man made My Only-Begotten Son to be a stumbling stone. And now will I prove to him that whoever stumbles upon this stone shall be broken and upon whomever it shall fall, it shall grind him to powder."

Do you think that a king would be any the more inclined to be merciful towards a traitor if he knew that that traitor had despised his son? No. I think the sentence would be the more severe. Ah, Sinner! If all other sinners escape, you who have heard the Gospel shall not. If God's arrows miss other sinners, they shall strike you! You shall be the special object of almighty vengeance because you were disobedient, stumbling at this stumbling stone. Think again, Man, will not this seat the eternity of your woe? How can you escape if you neglect so great a salvation? You have broken down the only bridge which could have led you into safety! You have pulled down the only refuge which could have protected you from Divine wrath--"There remains no more sacrifice for sin."

How can there be? Do you think when you are in Hell that Christ will come a second time to die for you? Will He pour out His blood again to bring you from the place of torment? Man, do you have so vain an imagination as to dream that there will be a second ransom offered for those who have not escaped the wrath to come, and that God the Holy Spirit will again come and strive with sinners who aforetime willfully rejected Him? No, inasmuch as even your Savior is objected to and you put eternal life from you and the foundation itself is a stumbling stone, there can remain nothing for you but a fearful looking for of judgment and of fiery indignation.

And now one other word with you. Does not this view of the case make your heart tremble? Is it not enough to have broken God's Law? Why do you go the length of despising His Son? O my eyes! If you could weep forever you could never weep tears enough, because once you refused to look to Him who is now your daily joy. Is not this one of the worst sins we shall have to confess? And O Sinner, will not you confess it now? Will not this thought break your heart--that you have up to now despised the altogether lovely and loving One? May the Spirit of God drive that home as a nail in a sure place, and I think you will turn to the Redeemer and say, "My Lord and my God, forgive me that I have dealt so un- kindly with You. Accept me, receive me to Your bosom. Wash me in Your blood. Take me to be Your servant and save me with a great salvation."

Happy is the man who has been brought by Divine Grace thus to confess his fault and stumble no longer. After all, what is there to stumble at? O my Hearer, why should you reject Christ? He is not a hard taskmaster--"His yoke is easy and His burden is light." Why should you refuse your own mercy? To be saved--is that a misfortune? To be cleansed from sin--is this a calamity? To be made a child of God--is that a disadvantage? To escape from Hell and fly to Heaven--is not this the most desirable of all mercies? Why, then, despise Christ? It is unreasonable! God deliver you from this unreasonable sin and bring you now to accept Christ with a perfect heart and He shall be praised for it forever.

II. I shall now try, by the help of God's Spirit, to explain the second part--the more comforting part of the text, "WHOEVER BELIEVES ON HIM SHALL NOT BE ASHAMED." He shall be ashamed to think he did not believe be-fore--he shall be ashamed to think he does not believe more firmly now--he shall often feel shame and confusion of face on account of his ingratitude and his sinfulness and his wandering of heart. But the text means he shall not be ashamed of having trusted

Christ. He that believes on Christ shall never have any cause to be ashamed of so doing.

1. In handling this I shall first of all notice when those who trust Christ might be ashamed of having trusted Him. Well might they be ashamed if Christ should ever leave them. If it should ever come to this, that He who is the husband of my heart, should desert me and leave me a lone widow in the world. If, after having said, "I will never leave you nor forsake you," He should after all take Himself away and never indulge His servant with one smile from His face, I should then, indeed, have reason to be ashamed of having put my trust in such a fickle Savior.

The Arminian's christ is one whom they have good reason to be ashamed of because he redeems men with his precious blood and yet they go to Hell. The Arminian's christ loves today but hates tomorrow. He saves by grace, but that grace is dependent upon man's use of grace. He does bring men out of a state of condemnation and he does justify them--but, after all, he lets them go back into a state of condemnation and they still perish! But the Christian's Christ is a very different Person, whom once He loves He never leaves, but loves them to the end. Where He has begun a good work He carries it on and perfects it.

The Christian's Christ can say, "I give unto My sheep eternal life and they shall never perish, neither shall any pluck them out of My hands." Until the Christian finds that the Grace of God is clean gone, that Christ's love has ceased, he shall never have any cause to be ashamed. Again, the Christian would have cause to doubt if Christ were to fail him, either as to Providence or Grace, in his times of trial and temptation. When in the midst of the rivers, if the Lord does not sustain me, I shall have cause to blush for my hope. If, walking through the fires the flames do kindle upon me and I do not find the Lord to be my present help in the time of trouble, then I am put to shame.

O Beloved, when will this happen? In six troubles He has been with you and in seven no evil has touched you. You have been brought very low! You could not have been much lower unless you had been in your grave. You have been very poor, scarcely having bread to eat, or raiment to put on! Everything in which you trusted has been cut from under you. You are left orphans in the world, with the exception of your Father which is in Heaven. But still, for all that, has not your bread been given you? Have not your waters been sure? And today must not your testimony be concerning God that He has been a Friend who sticks closer than a brother? Well, then, you never need be ashamed, because there never shall come a time when He shall leave you to perish through stress of trials or suffer you to be destroyed by the force of temptations.

Again, a Christian would have cause to be ashamed if Christ's promises were not fulfilled. They are very rich and very full and there are very many of them--and if I take these promises and act upon God's Word and then, after all, find the promise to be mere waste paper--if the Lord breaks His own Oath, then I should be ashamed to have believed in an unfaithful God! But when will that be? Christian, has the time come with you yet? You have had promises applied with power to your heart and you have taken them to God in prayer. Let me appeal to your experience! Have they not been fulfilled beyond your expectation or your faith? Has not God done for you exceedingly abundantly above what you can ask or think?

And yet this morning, perhaps, you are afraid His promise will not be kept! You have come here in lowness of spirit, you have had so many troubles during the week that you really begin to be ashamed of having trusted in God. Be ashamed of yourself for being ashamed! And depend on it, your confidence is not a thing to blush over. But O my Broth- ers and Sisters, how ashamed would the Christian be if when he came to die he should find no support, no kind angels near his bed, no Savior to bear his head up amidst the billows! But have you ever heard of a Christian who was ashamed in his dying hour? Is it not rather the sure witness of all the departed that their last moments have been gilded with the sunlight of Heaven?

Have not they snug on their dying beds, with David, "Yes, though I pass through the valley of the shadow of death, I will fear no evil: for You are with me. Your rod and Your staff they comfort me"? If, indeed, we could wake up in the resurrection and find ourselves without a Savior. If we could stand at the judgment bar of God and find that Christ's blood had not made us clean. If, after all our faith in Him, we should hear Him say, "Depart, you cursed, into everlasting fire," then might we be ashamed! But our text assures us that we never shall have to suffer this. Let us then roll ourselves upon this sweet comfort--having believed in Christ we shall never in this life, nor in the life to come--need to be ashamed of our hope.

2. Having noticed when the Christian might be ashamed, let us notice why he might be ashamed if such things were to come. I have sometimes thought, dear Friends, that in some respects, if the Bible were proven to be false, I should never be ashamed of having believed it. If there should be no Savior, I think that when I stand before God's Throne I shall not be ashamed of having believed the Gospel because, I think, I could dare to say even to the eternal God, "Great God, I believed of You that which reflected the highest honor upon Your Character. I believed You capable of a great deed of kindness, the giving of Your own Son. I believed You to be so just that You would not forgive without a punishment and yet so gracious that You would sooner give Your

Son than not have mercy upon men.

"I believed of You higher things than either Jew, or Mahommedan, or Heathen--and my soul did love You for it. I did preach what I thought would honor Your name and now that it turns out to be a mistake, I am not ashamed of having believed it, for it was such a thing as should have been true--Your Nature and your Character made it likely to be true and I mourn to think it is not, but I am not ashamed! I wish it had been. It would make You, great God, even more glorious than You are."

Beloved, we are under no apprehension that it shall turn out to be so, for we know whom we have believed and we are persuaded that He is able to keep that which we have committed to Him. Why would a Christian be ashamed if the Gospel were untrue? We should be ashamed, first of all, because we have ventured our all upon its Truth. We have ventured our all upon Christ. The world says you should never put all your eggs in one basket. And when a man speculates in some one thing and it all comes down, wise people hold up their hands and say, "Ah, very imprudent, very imprudent! Better have three or four strings to your bow! You must not be depending on any one thing."

The world is quite right in human things. But here are we--we are depending everything upon one Man--my soul has not a shadow of a hope anywhere else but in Christ and I know that your spirits have not even the ghost of a shadow of dependence anywhere but in the blood and righteousness of that Divine Redeemer who has completed our salvation and ascended up on high. If He can fail us, then all our hopes are gone! We are, of all men, most miserable. If our hope should turn out to be a delusion, we should be foolish, indeed, and have reason to be ashamed of our hope.

We should be ashamed, again, because we have given up this life for the next--believing in the world to come, we have said, "This is not our rest, we have no abiding city here." The world's proverb is, "A bird in the hand is worth two in the bush." But we, on the other hand, have said that the bird in the hand is nothing at all--that the bird in the bush is everything. Our soul says, "Joy! We do not expect it here, it is there that joy is to be found." "Wealth? No man is rich on earth, riches are in Heaven, the true treasure is in Glory." "Love does not find a fit object here--our affection is set upon things above, where Christ dwells at the right hand of God."

Now if things should turn out wrong and we have believed in vain, then we shall be ashamed of our hope, but not till then! Not till then, Beloved! And that shall be never! We know whom we have believed and we are confident that in giving up this earth we have only given up a handful of ashes that we may enjoy riches and Glory forever. Again, if Christ should fail us, we should be ashamed because we began boasting before we had ended the battle. "My soul shall make her boast in the Lord."

I hope you can say, dear Friends, that though you have not entered Heaven and have not yet seen Christ face to face, yet you have learned to bask in the Cross of Christ and no man has been able to stop you in your glory. You have boasted in Christ! You have said that He is a sure Foundation, that He is a precious Husband, that He is All in All to you and worthy of your best love! But if He should fail you, why then, you would be in the position of a man who boasted before the time. But we shall never be ashamed! We do right to boast with a full mouth! Let us glory in the Lord. But oh, if He should fail us--which He never can--then were we ashamed, indeed!

Besides, we have done more than boast! You and I have actually divided the spoil! And oh, if the battle should be lost, then we should be ashamed! We are told that in one of the great battles on the continent in the olden times, the French, before the battle began, commenced selling the English captives to one another and calculated how much each man would have of the spoil. But then, fortunately, they never gained the victory. But you and I have already entered into our rest--we have had the earnest of our inheritance--we have begun, even on earth, to eat the clusters of Eshcol. And if it should be a delusion we should be ashamed, but not till then. Courage, dear Friends! We may go boldly on dividing the spoil! For while Christ is true and God is faithful, there shall be no reason for being ashamed.

I have known some ashamed when they have made a bad speculation because they have induced others to enter into it. They have been more ashamed to face their friends who have lost money than they have been to acknowledge that they lost themselves. You and I have been inducing others to embark in this great venture. We have taught others to believe in Christ. And some of us scarcely spend a day without winning some souls to confidence in Christ. Oh, sweet Assurance! We have not preached cunningly devised fables and shall never be ashamed!

3. I must crave your patience just a moment while I now pass on to notice who are they who shall never be ashamed? The answer is general and special. The text says, "Whoever believes"--that is, any man who ever lived, or ever shall live, who believes in Christ shall never be ashamed. Whether he has been a gross sinner or a moralist. Whether he is learned or illiterate. Whether he is a prince or a beggar, it matters not--"Whoever believes in Christ shall never be ashamed." You,

Man, over yonder, though you may very seldom come to the House of God, yet if you believe in Christ today you shall never be ashamed of Him. You who have sat in God's House for years and feel yourselves guilty of having rejected Christ, yet if now you trust Him you shall not be ashamed.

But there is a specialty, it is "Whoever believes." Others shall be ashamed. There must be a real and hearty believing. There must be a simple confidence in the Person and work of Jesus--wherever this is there shall be no shame. "Ah," says one, "but I have such a little faith. I am afraid I shall be confounded." No, you come in under the "Whoever"-- "Whoever believes," though his faith is ever so little, shall never be ashamed. "Ah," says another, "but I have so many doubts." Still, dear Heart, since you believe you shall not be ashamed. All your doubts and your fears shall never damn you, for your faith will prevail.

"Oh, but," says another, "my corruption is so strong! I have come this morning lamenting because of my imperfections. They have obtained the mastery of my faith and I have fallen during the week." Yes, Soul, all fallen as you are, yet if you believe you shall never be ashamed. Does sin stare you in the face? Do you feel very heavy under a sense of your own unworthiness? Dare to believe in Christ just as you are--sins and all--venture on Him without any other confidence. When frames are dark and graces dead, when evidences are black, when everything gives you a frown and a curse, yet dare to believe in Him!

Now take Him to be your Friend when you have no other! Now flee to this Refuge when every other door is shut! Now that winter has frozen every brook, now come and drink of this Brook which flows on forever! This Well of Bethlehem which is within the gate can never fail you! And you need not to put your life in jeopardy to get it, it is free to you this moment! Stoop and drink confidently! Stoop and drink and you shall thirst no more, for, "Whoever believes in Him shall never be ashamed."

4. To conclude, the text means more than it says, for whereas it says they shall not be ashamed, it means that they shall be glorified and full of honor! If you trust Christ today, it will bring you shame from men, it will ensure you trials and troubles--but it will also ensure you honor in the sight of God's holy angels and Glory at the last in the sight of the assembled universe! Where is the man who trusts Christ today? There he stands in the pillory and men say, "Aha! Aha! The fool! The fool! The fool! He trusts a God whom he cannot see! He believes in a Christ whom we have heard of but whom we never heard! He trusts in the blood of a crucified Galilean!

The worldling cries, "We are too wise for that! We will believe geological theories, spiritualism, or metaphysics! We will believe the devil himself sooner than we will believe in Christ!" So they scoff at the man who trusts Christ. The scene is changed, the generation of the living has passed away and the world has become one great burial field. There they lay.

Innumerable hillocks mark where the bodies of men are sleeping. The trumpet sounds, it rings clear through earth and Heaven and up from the graves rise bodies which have once been worm's meat and souls come back into those frames-- and now where is the man who trusted Christ?

The trumpet has startled them all from their tombs and they awake together--"Where is the man who trusted in Christ?" Who is it that inquires for him? The King Himself upon the Throne has asked the question! King Jesus, sitting on His judgment seat, searches for His friends--"Where is the man who trusted in Me? Bring him here." See the change, no hooting and yelling and laughter and slander now! A triumphant squadron of bright spirits carry up the Believer to the right hand of Jesus and there he sits enthroned like Christ, sitting with Him to judge men and angels, reigning upon Christ's Throne in all Christ's splendor!

"Thus shall it be done unto the man whom the King delights to honor," thus shall it be done to the man who puts his trust in Christ! Come, Christian, whatever may be your state today, however the world's mockery may ring in your ears, think of that unwilling honor which the crowd of sinners will have to give you at the Last Great Day! Think of how your fame and reputation shall rise with your bones! And as worms cannot devour your body to prevent your rising, so shall not slander and rebuke devour your character to prevent its rising, too! Glory shall be yours--everlasting Glory--while your enemies shall be clothed with shame and eternal contempt!

Well, what do you say, dear Hearers? On which side are you this morning? Is Christ a stumbling block to you? Will you go on stumbling at Him and objecting to Him? Do you say rather, "No, we will have Christ and trust Him." Oh, if the Lord has brought you to this, I will clap my hands for joy! And you, you Angels, strike your harps! You Seraphs! Tune your lyres anew, for there is joy in Heaven as there is joy on earth when a soul comes to put its trust in Christ! The Lord bring every one of us, for His name's sake. Amen. Amen.

Laus Deo

DELIVERED ON SUNDAY MORNING, MAY 29, 1864,
BY THE REV. C. H. SPURGEON,
AT THE METROPOLITAN TABERNACLE, NEWINGTON.

"For of Him and through Him and to Him, are all things: to whom be glory forever. Amen." --
Romans 11:36.

MY text consists almost entirely of monosyllables, but it contains the loftiest of sublimities. Such a tremendous weight of meaning is concentrated here that an archangel's eloquence would fail to convey its teaching in all its glory to any finite minds, even if seraphs were his hearers. I will affirm that there is no man living who can preach from my text a sermon worthy of it. No, among all the sacred orators and the eloquent pleaders for God, there never did live and never will live a man capable of reaching the height of the great argument contained in these few simple words. I utterly despair of success and will not, therefore, make an attempt to work out the infinite Glory of this sentence.

Our great God alone can expound this verse for He only knows Himself and He only can worthily set forth His own perfections. Yet I am comforted by this reflection that maybe, in answer to our prayers, God Himself may preach from this text this morning in our hearts. If not through the words of the speaker, yet by that still small voice to which the Believer's ear is so well accustomed. If thus He shall condescend to favor us, our hearts shall be lifted up in His ways.

There are two things before us, the one worthy of our observation and the second of our imitation. You have in the text, first of all, doctrine and then devotion, The doctrine is high doctrine--"Of Him and through Him and to Him, are all things." The devotion is lofty devotion--"To whom be glory forever. Amen."

I. Let us consider THE DOCTRINE. It is laid down by the Apostle Paul as a general principle that all things come of God--they are of Him as their source. They are through Him as their means. They are to Him as their end. They are of Him in the plan, through Him in the working and to Him in the Glory which they produce. Taking this general principle, you will find it applies to all things and it is ours to mark those in which it is most manifestly the case. May the Lord, by His Holy Spirit, open His treasures to us at this moment that we may be enriched in spiritual knowledge and understanding.

Meditate, dear Friends, upon the whole range of God's works in Creation and Providence. There was a period when God dwelt alone and creatures were not. In that time before all time, when there was no day but, "The Ancient of Days"--when matter and created mind were alike unborn and even space was not--God, the great I Am, was as perfect, glorious and blessed as He is now. There was no sun and yet Jehovah dwelt in light ineffable. There was no earth and yet His Throne stood fast and firm. There were no heavens and yet His Glory was unbounded.

God inhabited eternity in the infinite majesty and happiness of His self-contained greatness. If the Lord, thus abiding in awful solitude, should choose to create anything, the first thought and idea must come of Him, for there was no other to think or suggest. All things must be of Him in design. With whom can He take counsel? Who shall instruct Him? There existed not another to come into the council chamber, even if such an assistance could be supposed with the Most High.

In the beginning of His way before His works of old, eternal Wisdom brought forth from its own mind the perfect plan of future creations and every line and mark therein must clearly have been of the Lord alone. He ordained the pathway of every planet and the abode of every fixed star. He poured forth the sweet influences of the Pleiades and girt Orion with His hands. He appointed the bounds of the sea and settled the course of the winds. As to the earth, the Lord alone planned its foundations and stretched His line upon it. He formed in His own mind the mold of all His creatures and found for them a dwelling and a service.

He appointed the degree of strength with which He would endow each creature, settled its months of life, its hour of death, its coming and its going. Divine Wisdom mapped this earth--its flowing rivers and foaming seas--the towering mountains and the laughing valleys. The Divine Architect fixed the gates of the morning and the doors of the shadow of death. Nothing could have

been suggested by any other, for there was no other to suggest. It was in His power to have made a universe very different from this if He had so pleased. And that He has made it what it is must have been merely because, in His Wisdom and prudence, He saw fit to do so.

There cannot be any reason why He should not have created a world from which sin should have been forever excluded. And that He suffered sin to enter into His creation must again be ascribed to His own infinite Sovereignty. Had He not known that He would be master over sin and out of evil evolve the noblest display of His own Glory, He had not permitted it to enter into the world--but, in sketching the whole history of the universe which He was about to create, He permitted even that black spot to defile His work--because He foreknew what songs of everlasting triumph would rise to Himself when, in streams of His own blood, Incarnate Deity should wash out the stain. It cannot be doubted that whatever may be the whole drama of history in Creation and Providence, there is a high and mysterious sense in which it is all of God.

The sin is not God's, but the temporary permission of its existence formed part of the foreknown scheme and to our faith the intervention of moral evil and the purity of the Divine Character do neither of them diminish the force of our belief that the whole scope of history is of God in the fullest sense. When the plan was all laid down and the Almighty had ordered His purpose, this was not enough--mere arrangement would not create. "Through Him," as well as "of Him," must all things be. There was no raw material ready to the Creator's hand. He must create the universe out of nothing. He calls not for aid--He needs it not and besides, there is none to help Him. There is no rough matter which He may fashion between His palms and launch forth as stars.

He did not need a mine of unquarried matter which He might melt and purify in the furnace of His power and then hammer out upon the anvil of His skill--no, there was nothing to begin with in that day of Jehovah's work--from the womb of Omnipotence all things must be born. He speaks and the heavens leap into existence! He speaks again and worlds are begotten with all the varied forms of life so fraught with Divine Wisdom and matchless skill. "Let there be light and there was light," was not the only time when God had spoken and when things that were not, were, for aforetime had He spoken and this rolling earth and yon blue heavens had blossomed out of nothingness.

Through Him were all things--from the high archangel who sings His praises in celestial notes--down to the cricket chirping on the hearth. The same finger paints the rainbow and the wing of the butterfly. He who dyes the garments of evening in all the colors of Heaven has covered the kingcup with gold and lit up the glowworm's lamp. From yonder ponderous mountain piercing the clouds down to that minute grain of dust in the summer's threshing floor--all things are through Him. Let but God withdraw the emanations of His Divine power and everything would melt away as the foam upon the sea melts into the wave which bore it!

Nothing could stand an instant if the Divine foundation were removed. If He should shake the pillars of the world the whole temple of Creation falls to ruin and its very dust is blown away. A dreary waste, a silent emptiness, a voiceless wilderness is all which remains if God withdraws His power. No, even so much as this were not if His power should be withheld. That nature that is as it is, is through the energy of the present God. If the sun rises every morning and the moon walks in her brightness at night, it is through Him. Away with those men who think that God has wound up the world as though it were a clock and has gone away--leaving it to work for itself apart from His present hand!

God is present everywhere--not merely present when we tremble because His thunder shakes the solid earth and sets the heavens in a blaze with lightning--but just as much so in the calm summer's eve when the air so gently fans the flowers and gnats dance up and down in the last gleams of sunlight. Men try to forget the Divine Presence by calling its energy by strange names. They speak of the power of gravitation. But what is the power of gravitation? We know what it does, but what is it? Gravitation is God's own power!

They tell us of mysterious laws of electricity and I know not what. We know the laws, and let them wear the names they have. But laws cannot operate without power. What is the force of nature? It is a constant emanation from the great Fountain of power, the constant out-flowing of God Himself--the perpetual going forth of beams of light from Him who is "the great Father of Lights, with whom is no variableness, neither shadow." Tread softly, be reverent, for God is here, O Mortal, as truly as He is in Heaven! Wherever you are and whatever you look upon, you are in God's workshop where every wheel is turned by His hands. Everything is not God, but God is in everything and nothing works, or even exists, except by His present power and might. "Of Him and through Him are all things."

Beloved, the great glory of all is that in the work of Creation everything is to Him. Everything will praise the Lord--He so designed it. God must have the highest motive and there can be no higher motive conceivable than His own Glory. When there was no creature but Himself and no being but Himself, God could not have taken as a motive a creature which did not exist. His motive must be Himself. His own Glory is His highest aim. The good of His creatures He considers carefully. But even the good of His creatures is but a means to the main end--the promotion of His Glory. All things, then, are for His pleasure and for His Glory they daily work.

Tell me that the world is marred by sin and I lament it. Tell me that the slime of the serpent is upon everything beautiful here and I sorrow for it. But yet, even yet shall everything speak of the Glory of God. To Him are all things and the day shall come when with eyes spiritually illuminated you and I shall see that even the introduction of the Fall and the curse did not, after all, mar the splendor of the majesty of the Most High. To Him shall all things be. His enemies shall bow their necks unwillingly but abjectly, while His people, redeemed from death and Hell, shall cheerfully extol Him.

The new heavens and the new earth shall ring with His praise and we who shall sit down to read the record of His creating wonders, shall say of them all, "In His temple does everyone speak of His Glory and even until now to Him have all things been." Courage then, Beloved! When you think that matters go against the cause of God, throw yourselves back upon this as a soft couch. When the enemy hisses in your ears this note--"God is overcome! His plans are spoiled. His Gospel is thrust back. The honor of His Son is stained," tell the enemy, "No, it is not so! To Him are all things."

God's defeats are victories. God's weakness is stronger than man and even the foolishness of the Most High is wiser than man's wisdom and at the last we shall see most clearly that it is so. Hallelujah! We shall see, dear Friends, one day in the clear light of Heaven, that every page in human history, however stained by human sin, has nevertheless something of God's Glory in it. And that the calamities of nations, the falling of dynasties, the devastations of pestilence, plagues, famines, wars and earthquakes have all worked out the eternal purpose and glorified the Most High!

From the first human prayer to the last mortal sigh! From the first note of finite praise onward to the everlasting hallelujah all things have worked together for the Glory of God and have served His purposes. All things are of Him and through Him and to Him. This great principle is most manifest in the grand work of Divine Grace. Here everything is of God and through God and to God. The great plan of salvation was not drawn by human fingers. It is no concoction of priests, no elaboration of Divines. Grace first moved the heart of God and joined with Divine Sovereignty to ordain a plan of salvation.

This plan was the offspring of a Wisdom no less than Divine. None but God could have imagined a way of salvation such as that which the Gospel presents--a way so just to God--so safe to man. The thought of Divine Substitution and the Sacrifice of God on man's behalf could never have suggested itself to the most educated of all God's creatures. God Himself suggests it and the plan is "of Him." And as the great plan is of Him, so the fillings up of the details are of Him. God ordained the time when the first promise should be promulgated--who should receive that promise and who should deliver it. He ordained the hour when the great Promise-Keeper should come--when Jesus Christ should appear--of whom He should be born, by whom He should be betrayed, what death He should die, when He should rise and in what manner He should ascend.

What if I say more? He ordained those who should accept the Mediator, to whom the Gospel should be preached and who should be the favored individuals in whom effectual calling should make that preaching mighty for salvation! He settled in His own mind the name of every one of His chosen and the time when each elect vessel should be put upon the wheel to be fashioned according to His will. He ordained pangs of conviction should be felt when the time of faith should come! How much of holy light and enjoyment should be bestowed--all this was purposed from of old! He settled how long the chosen vessel should be glazing in the fire and when it should be taken up--made perfect by heavenly workmanship to adorn the palace of God Most High. Of the Lord's Wisdom every stitch in the noble tapestry of salvation most surely comes.

Nor must we stop here--through Him all these things come. Through His Spirit the promise came at last, for He moved the seers and holy men of old. Through Him the Son of God is born of the Virgin Mary by the power of the Holy Spirit. Through Him, sustained by that Spirit, the Son of God leads His thirty years of perfection. In the great redemption God alone is exalted. Jesus sweats in Gethsemane and bleeds on Calvary. None stood with our Savior there. He trod that winepress alone. His own arm worked salvation and His own arm upheld Him. Redemption work was through God alone! Not one soul was ever redeemed by human suffering! No spirit was emancipated by mortal penance. All is through Him.

And as through Him the Atonement, so through Him the application of the Atonement. By the power of the Spirit the Gospel is daily preached. Upheld by the Holy Spirit, pastors, teachers and elders still abide with the Church--still the energy of the Spirit goes forth with the Word to the hearts of the chosen. Still is "Christ crucified," the power of God and the wisdom of God because God is in the Word and through Him men are called, converted, saved. O my Brethren, beyond a doubt we must confess of this great plan of salvation that it is all to Him! We have not a note of praise to spare for another!

Silenced forever with everlasting confusion is the man who would retain a solitary word of praise for man or angel in the work of Grace. You fools! Who can be praised but God, for who but God determined to give His Son Jesus? You knaves! Will you rob Christ of His Glory? Will you steal the jewels out of His crown when He so dearly bought them with drops of His precious blood? O you who love darkness rather than light, will you glorify man's will above the energy of the Holy Spirit and sacrifice to your own dignity and freedom? God forgive you!

But as for His saints, they will always sing, "To God, to God alone be all the Glory! From the first to the last let Him who is the Alpha and the Omega have all the praise! Let His name be extolled, world without end." When the great plan of Grace shall be all developed and you and I shall stand upon the hilltops of Glory, what a wondrous scene will open up before us! We shall see more clearly then, than now, how all things sprang from the fountainhead of God's love. How they all flowed through the channel of the Savior's mediation and how they all worked together to the Glory of the same God from whom they came. The great plan of Grace, then, bears out this principle.

The word holds good, dear Friends, in the case of every individual Believer. Let this be a matter for personal enquiry. Why am I saved? Because of any goodness in me, or any superiority in my constitution? Of whom comes my salvation? My spirit cannot hesitate a single moment. How could a new heart come out of the old one? Who can bring a clean thing out of an unclean? Not one! How can the spirit come out of the flesh? That which is born of the flesh is flesh. If it is spirit it must be born of the Spirit. My Soul, you must be quite clear about this, that if there is in you any faith, hope, or spiritual life, it must have come of God!

Can any Christian here who possesses vital godliness differ from this statement? I am persuaded he cannot. And if any man should arrogate any honor to his own natural constitution, I must, with all charity, doubt whether he knows anything at all about the matter. But, my Soul, as your salvation must have come out of God--as He must have thought of it and planned it for you, and then bestowed it upon you--did it not also come to you through God? It came through faith, but where did that faith take its birth? Was it not of the operation of the Holy Spirit? And what did you believe in? Did you believe in your own strength, or in your own good resolution? No, but in Jesus, your Lord. Was not the first ray of light you ever had received in this way?

Did you not look entirely away from self to the Savior? And the Light which you now have, does it not always come to you in the same way, by having done once and for all with the creature, with the flesh, with human merit--and resting with childlike confidence upon the finished work and righteousness of the Lord Jesus Christ? Is not, dear Hearer, is not your salvation, if you are, indeed, saved, entirely "through" your God, as well as "of" your God? Who is it that enables you to pray every day? Who keeps you from temptation? By what Grace are you led onward in spiritual duty? Who upholds you when your foot would trip? Are you not conscious that there is a power other than your own?

For my part, Brethren, I am not taken to Heaven against my will, I know, but still so desperate is my nature and so prone to evil that I feel myself floated onward against the current of my nature. It seems as if all we could do were to kick and rebel against Sovereign Grace, while Sovereign Grace says, "I will save you. I will have you, whatever you may do. I will overcome your raging corruption. I will quicken you out of your lethargy and take you to Heaven in a fiery chariot of afflictions, if not by any other means. I will whip you to Paradise sooner than let you be lost."

Is not this your experience? Have you not found that if once the strong hand of God were taken from your soul, instead of going onward to Heaven you would go back again to Perdition? It is through God you are saved! And what do you say, Believer, to the last point? Is it not "to Him"? Will you take one single jewel out of His crown? Oh, there is not one of you who would wish to extol himself! There is no song we sing more sweetly in this House of Prayer than the song of Grace and there is no hymn which seems more in keeping with our own experience than this--

"Grace all the work shall crown, Through everlasting days. It lays in Hea ven the topmost stone, And well deserves the praise."

Let who will extol the dignity of the creature. Let who may boast in the power of free will--we cannot do it! We have found our nature to be a very depraved one and our will to be under bondage. We must, if other creatures do not, extol that unchangeable Omnipotent Grace which has made us what we are and will continue to keep us so till it brings us to the right hand of God in everlasting Glory! In each individual, then, this rule holds good.

Once more, in every work which the Christian is enabled to do, he should bear in mind the rule of the text. Some of you are privileged to work in the Sunday school and you have had many conversions in your class. Others of you are distributing tracts, going from house to house and trying to bring souls to Christ, not without success, by God's Grace. Some of us, too, have the honor of being sent to preach the Gospel in every place and we have sheaves of our harvest too many for our barns to hold. In the case of some of us, we seem to have received the promised blessing to its fullest extent. The Lord has spiritually made our children like the sand of the sea and the spiritual offspring of our heart like the gravel.

In all this it behooves us to remember that, "of Him and through Him and to Him," are all things. "Of Him." Who makes you to differ? What have you which you have not received? The burning heart, the tearful eye, the prayerful soul--all these qualifications for usefulness come of Him. The fluent mouth, the pleading tongue--these must have been educated and given by Him. From Him all the many gifts of the Spirit by which the Church is edified--from Him, I say, they all proceed. What is Paul? Who is Apollos, or Cephas--who are all these but the messengers of God in whom the Spirit works, dividing to every man according as He wills?

When the preacher has achieved his usefulness, he knows that all his success comes through God. If a man shall suppose himself capable of stirring up a revival, or encouraging even one saint, or leading one sinner to repentance, he is a fool! As well might we attempt to move the stars, or shake the world, or grasp the lightning flash in the hollow of our hand as think to save a soul, or even to quicken saints out of their lethargy! Spiritual work must be done by the Spirit. Through God every good thing comes to us. The preacher may be a very Samson when God is with him--he shall be like Samson when God is not with him only in Samson's degradation and shame!

Beloved, there never was a man brought to God except through God and there never will be! Our nation shall never be stirred up again into the celestial heat of piety except by the Presence of the Holy Spirit anew. Would God we had more of the abiding sense of the Spirit's work among us! That we looked more to Him! That we rested less in machinery and men and more upon that Divine but Invisible Agent who works all good things in the hearts of men! Beloved, it is through GOD that every good thing comes. And I am sure it is to Him. We cannot take the honor of a single convert. We do look with thankfulness upon this growing Church, but we can give the Glory alone to Him! Give glory to the creature and it is all over with it! Honor yourselves as a Church and God will soon dishonor you!

Let us lay every sheaf upon His altar, bring every lamb of the fold to the feet of the Good Shepherd feeling that it is His. When we go abroad to fish for souls, let us think that we only fill the net because He taught us how to throw it on the right side of the Church. And when we take them they are His, not ours. Oh, what poor little things we are and yet we think we do so much! The pen might say, "I wrote Milton's Paradise Lost." Ah, poor Pen! You could not have made a dot to an "i," or a cross to a "t," if Milton's hand had not moved you! The preacher could do nothing if God had not helped him. The axe might cry, "I have felled forests! I have made the cedar bow its head and laid the stalwart oak in the dust." No, you did not--for if it had not been for the arm which wielded you, even a bramble would have been too much for you to cut down!

Shall the sword say, "I won the victory! I shed the blood of the mighty! I caused the shield to be cast away?" No, it was the warrior, who with his courage and might made you of service in the battle, and apart from this you are less than nothing. In all that God does by us let us continue to give Him the praise--so shall He continue His Presence with our efforts. Otherwise He will take from us His smile and so we shall be left as weak men. I have, perhaps, at too great length for your patience, tried to bring out this very simple but very useful principle. And now, before I go to the second part, I wish to apply it by this very practical remark.

Beloved, if this is true, that all things are through Him and to Him, do you not think that those doctrines are most likely to be correct and most worthy to be held which are most in keeping with this Truth of God? Now, there are certain doctrines commonly called Calvinistic (but which ought never to have been called by such a name, for they are simply Christian doctrines), which I think commend themselves to the minds of all thoughtful persons. For this reason, mainly, that they do ascribe to God everything.

Here is the doctrine of election, for instance. Why is a man saved? Is it the result of his own will or God's will? Did he choose God, or did God choose him? The answer, "Man chose God," is manifestly untrue because it glorifies man. God's answer to it is, "You have not chosen Me, but I have chosen you." God has predestinated His people to salvation from before the foundation of the world. Ascribing the will, which is the hinge of the whole matter, and turns the balance--ascribing that to God--we feel we are speaking in keeping with the doctrine of our text.

Then take effectual calling. By what power is a man called? There are some who say that it is by the energy of his own will, or at least that while God gives him Grace, it depends upon him to make use of it. Some do not make use of the Grace and perish. Others make use of the Grace and are saved--saved by their own consenting to allow Grace to be effectual. We, on the other hand, say no--a man is not saved against his will--but he is made willing by the operation of the Holy Spirit. A mighty Grace which he does not wish to resist enters into the man, disarms him, makes a new creature of him and he is saved. We believe that the calling which saves the soul is a calling which owes nothing at all to man, but which comes from God. The creature being, then, passive, while God, like the potter, molds the man like a lump of clay. Clearly the calling, we think, must be through God--for so it coincides with this principle, "of Him and through Him and to Him are all things."

Then next, the question of particular redemption. Some insist upon it that men are redeemed not because Christ died, but because they are willing to give efficacy to the blood of Christ. He died for everybody according to their theory. Why, then, are not all men saved? Because all men will not believe? That is to say that believing is necessary in order to make the blood of Christ efficacious for redemption! Now we hold that to be a great lie! We believe the very contrary-- namely, that the blood of Christ has in itself the power to redeem and that it does redeem and that faith does not give efficacy to the blood but is only the proof that the blood has redeemed that man. Hence we hold that Christ did not redeem every man, but only redeemed those men who will ultimately attain unto eternal life.

We do not believe that He redeemed the damned! We do not believe that He poured out His life blood for souls already in Hell! We never can imagine that Christ suffered in the place of all men and that then, afterwards, these same men have to suffer for themselves--that in fact Christ pays their debts--and then God makes them pay their debts over again! We think that the doctrine that men, by their wills, give efficacy to the blood of Christ is derogatory to the Lord Jesus and we rather hold to this that He laid down His life for His sheep and that His laying down His life for His sheep involved and secured the salvation of every one of them. We believe this because we hold that, "of Him and through Him and to Him are all things."

So, again, take the total depravity of the race and its original corruption--a doctrine much abhorred of those who lift up poor human nature--but is, nevertheless, true. We hold that man must be entirely lost and ruined, because if there is some good thing in him, then it cannot be said that, "of God and through God and to God, are all things," for at least some things must be of man. If there are some relics of virtue and some remnants of power left in the race of man, then some things are of man and to man will some things be. But if of God are all things, then in man there must be nothing--man must be set down as ruined--hopelessly ruined--

"Bruised and mangled by the Fall," and his salvation must be described as being from the first to the last, in every jot and every tittle of that almighty Grace of God, which at first chose him, at length redeemed him, ultimately called him, constantly preserved him and perfectly shall present him before the Father's Throne.

I put these doctrines before you, more especially today, because last Friday many Believers both in Geneva and London met together to celebrate the centenary of the death of that mighty servant of God, John Calvin. I honor Calvin, not as teaching these doctrines himself, but as one through whom God spoke and one who, next to the Apostle Paul, propounded the Truth of God more clearly than any other man that ever breathed. He knew more of Scripture and explained it more clearly than most. Luther may have as much courage, but Luther knows little of theology. Luther, like a bull, when he sees one Truth, shuts his eyes and dashes against the enemy, breaking down gates, bolts and bars, to clear away for the Word!

But Calvin, following in the opened pathway with clear eyes, searching Scripture, ever acknowledging that of God and through God and to God are all things, maps out the whole plan with a delightful clearness which could only have come of the Spirit of God. That man of God expounds the doctrines in so excellent and admirable a manner that we cannot too much bless the Lord who sent him, or too much pray that others like him may be honest and sincere in the work of the Lord. Thus much then, of doctrine, but one or two minutes by way of devotion.

II. The Apostle puts his pen back into the ink bottle, falls on his knees--he cannot help it--he must have a doxol-ogy. "To whom be glory forever. Amen." Beloved, let us imitate this DEVOTION. I think that this sentence should be the prayer, the motto for every one of us--"To Him be glory forever. Amen." I will be but very brief, for I would not weary you. "To Him be glory forever." This should be the single desire of the Christian. I take it that he should not have twenty wishes, but only one. He may desire to see his family well brought up, but only that, "To God may be glory forever."

He may wish for prosperity in his business, but only so far as it may help him to promote this--"To Him be glory forever." He may desire to attain more gifts and more graces, but it should only be that, "To Him may be glory forever." This one thing I know, Christian--you are not acting as you ought to do when you are moved by any other motive than the one motive of your Lord's Glory. As a Christian you are "of God and through God." I pray you be "to God." Let nothing ever set your heart beating but love to Him. Let this ambition fire your soul! Be this the foundation of every enterprise upon which you enter, and this your sustaining motive whenever your zeal would grow chill--only, only make God your object! Depend upon it, where self begins, sorrow begins. But if God is my supreme delight and only object--

"To me 'tis equal whether love ordain My life or death appoint me ease or pain."

To me there shall be no choice, when my eyes singly look to God's Glory, whether I shall be torn in pieces by wild beasts or live in comfort--whether I shall be full of despondency or full of hope. If God is glorified in my mortal body, my soul shall rest content. Again, let it be our constant desire, "To Him be glory." When I wake up in the morning, O, let my soul salute her God with gratitude--

"Wake and lift up yourself, my Heart, And with the angels bear your part, Who all night long unwearied sing High praises to the eternal King." At my work behind the counter, or in the Exchange, let me be looking out to see how I may glorify Him. If I am walking in the fields, let my desire be that the trees may clap their hands in His praise. May the sun in his march shine out the Master's Glory and the stars at night reflect His praise.

It is yours, Brethren, to put a tongue into the mouth of this dumb world and make the silent beauties of creation praise their God. Never be silent when there are opportunities and you shall never be silent for want of opportunities. At night fall asleep praising your God! As you close your eyes let your last thought be, "How sweet to rest upon the Savior's bosom!" In afflictions praise Him--out of the fires let your song go up! On the sick-bed extol Him! Dying, let Him have your sweetest notes. Let your shouts of victory in the combat with the last great enemy be all for Him. And then, when you have burst the bondage of mortality and come into the freedom of immortal spirits--then, in a nobler, sweeter song--you shall sing unto His praise!

Be this, then, your constant thought--"To Him be glory forever." Let this be your earnest thought. Do not speak of God's Glory with cold words, nor think of it with a chilly heart, but feel, "I must praise Him. If I cannot praise Him where I am, I will break through these narrow bonds, and get where I can." Sometimes you will feel that you long to be disembodied--that you may praise Him as the immortal spirits do. I must praise Him! Bought by His precious blood, called by His Spirit I cannot hold my tongue! My Soul, can you be dumb and dead? I must praise Him! Stand back, O Flesh! Away, you Fiends! Away, you Troubles! I must sing, for should I refuse to sing, surely the very stones would speak!

I hope, dear Friends, while thus earnest, your praise will also be growing. Let there be growing desire to praise Him of whom and through whom are all things. You blessed Him in your youth, do not be content with such praises as you gave Him then. Has God prospered you in business? Give Him more as He has given you more. Has God given you experience? O, praise Him by better faith than you exercised at first. Does your knowledge grow? Oh, then you can sing more sweetly! Do you have happier times than you once had? Have you been restored from sickness and has your sorrow been turned into peace and joy? Then give Him more music! Put more coals in your censer, more sweet frankincense, more of the sweet cane bought with money. Oh, to serve Him every day, lifting up my heart from Sunday to Sunday, till I reach the ever-ending Sunday! Reaching from sanctification to sanctification, from love to love, from strength to strength, till I appear before my God!

In closing, let me urge you to make this desire practical. If you really glorify God, take care to do it not with lip-service which dies away in the wind, but with solid homage of daily life. Praise Him by your patience in pain, by your perseverance in duty, by your generosity in His cause, by your boldness in testimony, by your consecration to His work. Praise Him, my dear Friends, not only this morning in what you do for Him in your offerings, but praise Him every day by doing something for God in all sorts of ways, according to the manner in which He has been pleased to bless you. I wish I could have spoken worthily on such a topic as this, but a dull, heavy headache sits upon me and I feel that a thick gloom overshadows my words, out of which I look with longing, but cannot rise.

For this I may well grieve, but nevertheless God the Holy Spirit can work the better through our weakness and if you will try and preach the sermon to yourselves, my Brethren, you will do it vastly better than I can. If you will meditate upon this text this afternoon, "Of Him and through Him and to Him, are all things," I am sure you will be led to fall on your knees with the Apostle and say, "To Him be glory forever," and then you will rise up and practically, in your life, give Him honor, putting the "Amen" to this doxology by your own individual service of your great and gracious Lord. May He give a blessing now and accept your thank offering through Christ Jesus. Amen.

Baptismal Regeneration

A Sermon (No. 573)
Delivered on Sunday Morning, June 5th, 1864, by the
Rev. C. H. SPURGEON,
At the Metropolitan Tabernacle, Newington

"And he said unto them, Go ye into all the world, and preach the gospel to every creature. He that believeth and is baptized shall be saved; but he that believeth not shall be damned." -- Mark 16:15-16.

IN the preceding verse our Lord Jesus Christ gives us some little insight into the natural character of the apostles whom he selected to be the first ministers of the Word. They were evidently men of like passions with us, and needed to be rebuked even as we do. On the occasion when our Lord sent forth the eleven to preach the gospel to every creature, he "appeared unto them as they sat at meat, and upbraided them with their unbelief and hardness of heart, because they believed not them which had seen him after he was risen;" from which we may surely gather that to peach the Word, the Lord was pleased to choose imperfect men; men, too, who of themselves were very weak in the grace of faith in which it was most important that they should excel. Faith is the conquering grace, and is of all things the main requisite in the preacher of the Word; and yet the honoured men who were chosen to be the leaders of the divine crusade needed a rebuke concerning their unbelief. Why was this? Why, my brethren, because the Lord has ordained evermore that we should have this treasure in earthen vessels, that the excellency of the power may be of God and not of us. If you should find a perfect minister, then might the praise and honour of his usefulness accrue to man; but God is frequently pleased to select for eminent usefulness men evidently honest and sincere, but who have some manifest infirmity by which all the glory is cast off from them and laid upon Himself, and upon Himself alone. Let it never be supposed that we who are God's ministers either excuse our faults or pretend to perfection. We labour to walk in holiness, but we cannot claim to be all that we wish to be. We do not base the claims of God's truth upon the spotlessness of our characters, but upon the fact that it comes from him. You have believed in spite of our infirmities, and not because of our virtues; if, indeed, you had believed our word because of our supposed perfection, your faith would stand in the excellency of man and not in the power of God. We come unto you often with much trembling, sorrowing over our follies and weaknesses, but we deliver to you God's Word as God's Word, and we beseech you to receive it not as coming from us poor, sinful mortals, but as proceeding from the Eternal and Thrice Holy God; and if you so receive it, and by its own vital force are moved and stirred up towards God and his ways, then is the work of the Word sure work, which it could not and would not be if it rested in any way upon man.

Our Lord having thus given us an insight into the character of the persons whom he has chosen to proclaim his truth, then goes on to deliver to the chosen champions, their commission for the Holy War. I pray you mark the words with solemn care. He sums up in a few words the whole of their work, and at the same time foretells the result of it, telling them that some would doubtless believe and so be saved, and some on the other hand would not believe and would most certainly, therefore, be damned, that is, condemned for ever to the penalties of God's wrath. The lines containing the commission of our ascended Lord are certainly of the utmost importance, and demand devout attention and implicit obedience, not only from all who aspire to the work of the ministry, but also from all who hear the message of mercy. A clear understanding of these words is absolutely necessary to our success in our Master's work, for if we do not understand the commission it is not at all likely that we shall discharge it aright. To alter these words were more than impertinence, it would involve the crime of treason against the authority of Christ and the best interests of the souls of men. O for grace to be very jealous here.

Wherever the apostles went they met with obstacles to the preaching of the gospel, and the more open and effectual was the door of utterance the more numerous were the adversaries. These brave men who wielded the sword of the Spirit as to put to flight all their foes; and this they did not by craft and guile, but by making a direct cut at the error which impeded them. Never did they dream for a moment of adapting the gospel to the unhallowed tastes or prejudices of the people, but at once directly and boldly they brought down with both their hands the mighty sword of the Spirit upon the crown of the opposing error. This morning, in the name of the Lord of Hosts, my Helper and Defense, I shall attempt to do the same; and if I should provoke some hostility--if I should through speaking what I believe to be the truth lose the friendship of some and stir up the enmity of more, I cannot help it. The burden of the Lord is upon me, and I must deliver my soul. I have been loath enough to undertake the work, but I am forced to it by an awful and overwhelming sense of solemn duty. As I am soon to appear before my Master's bar, I will this day, if ever in my life, bear my testimony for truth, and run all risks. I am content to be cast out as evil if it must be so, but I cannot, I dare not, hold my peace. The Lord knoweth I have nothing in my heart but the purest love to the souls of those whom I feel imperatively called to rebuke sternly in the Lord's name. Among my hearers and readers, a considerable number will censure if not condemn me, but I cannot help it. If I forfeit your love for truth's sake I am grieved for you, but I cannot, I dare not, do otherwise. It is as much as my soul is worth to hold my peace any longer, and whether you approve or not I must speak out. Did I ever court your approbation? It is sweet to everyone to be applauded; but if for the sake of the comforts of respectability and the smiles of men any Christian minister shall keep back a part of his testimony, his Master at the last shall require it at his hands. This day, standing in the immediate presence of God, I shall speak honestly what I feel, as the Holy Spirit shall enable me; and I shall leave the matter with you to judge concerning it, as you will answer for that judgment at the last great day.

I find that the great error which w e have to contend with throughout England (and it is growing more and more), is one in direct opposition to my text, well known to you as the doctrine of baptismal regeneration. We will confront this dogma with the assertion, that BAPTISM WITHOUT FAITH SAVES NO ONE. The text says, "He that believeth and is baptized shall be saved;" but whether a man be baptized or no, it asserts that "he that believeth not shall be damned:" so that baptism does not save the unbeliever , nay, it does not in any degree exempt him from the common doom of all the ungodly. He may have baptism, or he may not have baptism, but if he believeth not, he shall be in any case most surely damned. Let him be baptized by immersion or sprinkling, in his infancy, or in his adult age, if he be not led to put his trust in Jesus Christ--if he remaineth an unbeliever, then this terrible doom is pronounced upon him--"He that believeth not shall be damned." I am not aware that any Protestant Church in England teaches the doctrine of baptismal regeneration except one, and that happens to be the corporation which with none too much humility calls itself the Church of England. This very powerful sect does not teach this doctrine merely through a section of its ministers, who might charitably be considered as evil branches of the vine, but it openly, boldly, and plainly declares this doctrine in her own appointed standard, the Book of Common Prayer, and that in words so express, that while language is the channel of conveying intelligible sense, no process short of violent wresting from their plain meaning can ever make them say anything else.

Here are the words: we quote them from the Catechism which is intended for the instruction of youth, and is naturally very plain and simple, since it would be foolish to trouble the young with metaphysical refinements. The child is asked its name, and then questioned, "Who gave you this name?" "My godfathers and godmothers in my baptism; wherein I was made a member of Christ, the child of God, and an inheritor of the kingdom of heaven." Is not this definite and plain enough? I prize the words for their candour; they could not speak more plainly. Three times over the thing is put, lest there should be any doubt in it. The word regeneration may, by some sort of juggling, be made to mean something else, but here there can be no misunderstanding. The child is not only made "a member of Christ"--union to Jesus is no mean spiritual gift--but he is made in baptism "the child of God" also; and, since the rule is, "if children then heirs," he is also made "an inheritor of the kingdom of heaven." Nothing can be more plain. I venture to say that while honesty remains on earth the meaning of these words will not admit of dispute. It is clear as noon day that, as the Rubric hath it, "Fathers, mothers, masters, and dames, are to cause their children, servants, and apprentices," no matter how idle, giddy, or wicked they may be, to learn the Catechism, and to say that in baptism they were made members of Christ and children of God. The form for the administration of this baptism is scarcely less plain and outspoken, seeing that thanks are expressly returned unto Almighty God, because the person baptized is regenerate. "Then shall the priest say, Seeing now, dearly beloved brethren, that this child is regenerate and grafted into the body of Christ's Church, let us give thanks unto Almighty God for these benefits; and with one accord make our prayers unto him, that this child may lead the rest of his life according to this beginning.'" Nor is this all, for to leave no mistake, we have the words of the thanksgiving prescribed, "Then shall the priest say, We yield thee hearty thanks, most merciful Father, that it hath pleased thee to regenerate this infant with thy Holy Spirit, to receive him for thine own child by adoption, and to incorporate him into thy holy Church.'"

This, then, is the clear and unmistakable teaching of a Church calling itself Protestant. I am not now dealing at all with the question of infant baptism: I have nothing to do with that this morning. I am now considering the question of baptismal regeneration, whether in adults or infants, or ascribed to sprinkling, pouring, or immersion. Here is a Church which teaches every Lord's day in the Sunday-school, and should, according to the Rubric, teach openly in the Church, all children that they were made members of Christ, children of God, and inheritors of the kingdom of heaven when they were baptized! Here is a professedly Protestant Church, which, every time its minister goes to the font, declares that every person there receiving baptism is there and then "regenerated and grafted into the body of Christ's Church."

"But," I hear many good people exclaim, "there are many good clergymen in the Church who do not believe in baptismal regeneration." To this my answer is prompt. Why then do they belong to a Church which teaches that doctrine in the plainest terms? I am told that many in the Church of England preach against her own teaching. I know they do, and herein I rejoice in their enlightenment, but I question, gravely question their morality. To take oath that I sincerely assent and consent to a doctrine which I do not believe, would to my conscience appear little short of perjury, if not absolute downright perjury; but those who do so must be judged by their own Lord. For me to take money for defending what I do not believe--for me to take the money of a Church, and then to preach against what are most evidently its doctrines--I say for me to do this (I judge others as I would that they should judge me) for me, or for any other simple, honest man to do so, were an atrocity so great, that if I had perpetrated the deed, I should consider myself out of the pale of truthfulness, honesty, and common morality. Sirs, when I accepted the office of minister of this congregation, I looked to see what were your articles of faith; if I had not believed them I should not have accepted your call, and when I change my opinions, rest assured that as an honest man I shall resign the office, for how could I profess one thing in your declaration of faith, and quite another thing in my own preaching? Would I accept your pay, and then stand up every Sabbath-day and talk against the doctrines of your standards? For clergymen to swear or say that they give their solemn assent and consent to what they do not believe is one of the grossest pieces of immorality perpetrated in England, and is most pestilential in its influence, since it directly teaches men to lie whenever it seems necessary to do so in order to get a living or increase their supposed usefulness: it is in fact an open testimony from priestly lips that at least in ecclesiastical matters falsehood may express truth, and truth itself is a mere unimportant nonentity. I know of nothing more calculated to debauch the public mind than a want of straightforwardness in ministers; and when worldly men hear ministers denouncing the very things which their own Prayer Book teaches, they imagine that words have no meaning among ecclesiastics, and that vital differences in religion are merely a matter of tweedle-dee and tweedle-dum, and that it does not much matter what a man does believe so long as he is charitable towards other people. If baptism does regenerate people, let the fact be preached with a trumpet tongue, and let no man be ashamed of his belief in it. If this be really their creed, by all means let them have full liberty for its propagation. My brethren, those are honest Churchmen in this matter who, subscribing to the Prayer Book, believe in baptismal regeneration, and preach it plainly. God forbid that we should censure those who believe that baptism saves the soul, because they adhere to a Church which teaches the same doctrine. So far they are honest men; and in England, where else, let them never lack a full toleration. Let us oppose their teaching by all Scriptural and intelligent means, but let us respect their courage in plainly giving us their views. I hate their doctrine, but I love their honesty; and as they speak but what they believe to be true, let them speak it out, and the more clearly the better. Out with it, sirs, be it what it may, but do let us know what you mean. For my part, I love to stand foot to foot with an honest foeman. To open warfare, bold and true hearts raise no objection but the ground of quarrel; it is covert enmity which we have most cause to fear, and best reason to loathe. That crafty kindness which inveigles me to sacrifice principle is the serpent in the grass--deadly to the incautious wayfarer. Where union and friendship are not cemented by truth, they are an unhallowed confederacy. It is time that there should be an end put to the flirtations of honest men with those who believe one way and swear another. If men believe baptism works regeneration, let them say so; but if they do not so believe it in their hearts , and yet subscribe, and yet more, get their livings by subscribing to words asserting it, let them find congenial associates among men who can equivocate and shuffle, for honest men will neither ask nor accept their friendship.

We ourselves are not dubious on this point, we protest that persons are not saved by being baptized. In such an audience as this, I am almost ashamed to go into the matter, because you surely know better than to be misled. Nevertheless, for the good of others we will drive at it. We hold that persons are not saved by baptism, for we think, first of all that it seems out of character with the spiritual religion which Christ came to teach, that he should make salvation depend upon mere ceremony. Judaism might possibly absorb the ceremony by way of type into her ordinances essential to eternal life; for it was religion of types and shadows. The false religions of the heathen might inculcate salvation by a physical process, but Jesus Christ claims for his faith that it is purely spiritual, and how could he connect regeneration with a peculiar application of aqueous fluid? I cannot see how it would be a spiritual gospel, but I can see how it would be mechanical, if I were sent forth to teach that the mere dropping of so many drops upon the brow, or even the plunging a person in water could save the soul. This seems to me to be the most mechanical religion now existing, and to be on a par with the praying windmills of Thibet, or the climbing up and down of Pilate's staircase to which Luther subjected himself in the days of his darkness. The operation of water-baptism does not appear even to my faith to touch the point involved in the regeneration of the soul. What is the necessary connection between water and the overcoming of sin? I cannot see any connection which can exist between sprinkling, or immersion, and regeneration, so that the one shall necessarily be tied to the other in the absence of faith. Used by faith, had God commanded it, miracles might be wrought; but without faith or even consciousness, as in the case of babes, how can spiritual benefits be connected necessarily with the sprinkling of water? If this be your teaching, that regeneration goes with baptism, I say it looks like the teaching of a spurious Church, which has craftily invented a mechanical salvation to deceive ignorant, sensual, and grovelling minds, rather than the teaching of the most profoundly spiritual of all teachers, who rebuked Scribes and Pharisees for regarding outward rites as more important than inward grace.

But it strikes me that a more forcible argument is that the dogma is not supported by facts. Are all persons who are baptized children of God? Well, let us look at the divine family. Let us mark their resemblance to their glorious Parent! Am I untruthful if I say that thousands of those who were baptized in their infancy are now in our goals? You can ascertain the fact if you please, by application to prison authorities. Do you believe that these men, many of whom have been living by plunder, felony, burglary, or forgery, are regenerate? If so, the Lord deliver us from such regeneration. Are these villains members of Christ? If so, Christ has sadly altered since the day when he was holy, harmless, undefiled, separate from sinners. Has he really taken baptized drunkards and harlots to be members of his body? Do you not revolt at the supposition? It is a well-known fact that baptized persons have been hanged. Surely it can hardly be right to hang the inheritors of the kingdom of heaven! Our sheriffs have much to answer for when they officiate at the execution of the children of God, and suspend the members of Christ on the gallows! What a detestable farce is that which is transacted at the open grave, when "a dear brother" who has died drunk is buried in a "sure and certain hope of the resurrection of eternal life," and the prayer that "when we shall depart this life we may rest in Christ, as our hope is that this our brother doth." Here is a regenerate brother, who having defiled the village by constant uncleanness and bestial drunkenness, died without a sign of repentance, and yet the professed minister of God solemnly accords him funeral rites which are denied to unbaptized innocents, and puts the reprobate into the earth in "sure and certain hope of the resurrection to eternal life." If old Rome in her worst days ever perpetrated a grosser piece of imposture than this, I do no read things aright; if it does not require a Luther to cry down this hypocrisy as much as Popery ever did, then I do not even know that twice two make four. Do we find--we who baptize on profession of faith, and baptize by immersion in a way which is confessed to be correct, though not allowed by some to be absolutely necessary to its validity--do we who baptize in the name of the sacred Trinity as others do, do we find that baptism regenerates? We do not. Neither in the righteous nor the wicked do we find regeneration wrought by baptism. We have never met with one believer, however instructed in divine things, who could trace his regeneration to his baptism; and on the other hand, we confess it with sorrow, but still with no surprise, that we have seen those whom we have ourselves baptized, according to apostolic precedent, go back into the world and wander into the foulest sin, and their baptism has scarcely been so much as a restraint to them, because they have not believed in the Lord Jesus Christ. Facts all show that whatever good there may be in baptism, it certainly does not make a man "a member of Christ, the child of God, and an inheritor of the kingdom of heaven," or else many thieves, whoremongers, drunkards, fornicators, and murderers, are members of Christ, the children of God, and inheritors of the kingdom of heaven. Facts, brethren, are against this Popish doctrine; and facts are stubborn things.

Yet further, I am persuaded that the performance styled baptism by the Prayer Book is not at all likely to regenerate and save. How is the thing done? One is very curious to know when one hears of an operation which makes men member s of Christ, children of God, and inheritors of the kingdom of heaven, how the thing is done. It must in itself be a holy thing truthful in all its details, and edifying in every portion. Now, we will suppose we have a company gathered round the water, be it more or less, and the process of regeneration is about to be performed. We will suppose them all to be godly people. The clergyman officiating is a profound believer in the Lord Jesus, and the father and mother are exemplary Christians, and the godfathers and godmothers are all gracious persons. We will suppose this--it is a supposition fraught with charity, but it may be correct. What are these godly people supposed to say? Let us look to the Prayer Book. The clergyman is suppose to tell these people, "Ye have heard also that our Lord Jesus Christ hath promised in his gospel to grant all these things that ye have prayed for: which promise he, for his part, will most surely keep and perform. Wherefore, after this promise made by Christ, this infant must also faithfully, for his part, promise by you that are his sureties (until he come of age to take it upon himself) that he will renounce the devil and all his works, and constantly believe God's holy Word, and obediently keep his commandments." This small child is to promise to do this, or more truly others are to take upon themselves to promise, and even vow that he shall do so. But we must not break the quotation, and therefore let us return to the Book. "I demand therefore, dost thou, in the name of this child, renounce the devil and all his works, the vain pomp and glory of the world, with all covetous desires of the same, and the carnal desires of the flesh, so that thou wilt not follow, nor be led by them?" Answers "I renounce them all." That is to say, on the name and behalf of this tender infant about to be baptized, these godly people, these enlightened Christian people, these who know better , who are not dupes, who know all the while that they are promising impossibilities--renounce on behalf of this child what they find it very hard to renounce for themselves--"all covetous desires of the world and the carnal desires of the flesh, so that they will not follow nor be led by them." How can they harden their faces to utter such a false promise, such a mockery of renunciation before the presence of the Father Almighty? Might not angels weep as they hear the awful promise uttered? Then in the presence of high heaven they profess on behalf of this child that he steadfastly believes the creed, when they know, or might pretty shrewdly judge that the little creature is not yet a steadfast believer in anything, much less in Christ's going down into hell. Mark, they do not say merely that the babe shall believe the creed, but they affirm that he does, for they answer in the child's name, "All this I steadfastly believe. Not we steadfastly believe," but I, the little baby there, unconscious of all their professions and confessions of faith. In answer to the question, "Wilt thou be baptized in this faith?" they reply for the infant, "That is my desire." Surely the infant has no desire in the matter, or at the least, no one has been authorized to declare any desires on his behalf. But this is not all, for then these godly, intelligent people next promise on the behalf of the infant, that "he shall obediently keep all God's holy will and commandments, and walk in the same all the days of his life." Now, I ask you, dear friends, you who know what true religion means, can you walk in all God's holy commandments yourselves? Dare you make this day a vow on your own part, that you would renounce the devil and all his works, the pomps and vanities of this wicked world, and all the sinful lusts of the flesh? Dare you, before God, make such a promise as that? You desire such holiness, you earnestly strive after it, but you look for it from God's promise, not from your own. If you dare make such vows I doubt your knowledge of your own hearts and of the spirituality of Gods's law. But even if you could do this for yourself, would you venture to make such a promise for any other person? For the best-born infant on earth? Come, brethren, what say you? Is not your reply ready and plain? There is not room for two opinions among men determined to observe truth in all their ways and words . I can understand a simple, ignorant rustic, who has never learned to read, doing all this at the command of a priest and under the eye of a squire. I can even understand persons doing this when the Reformation was in its dawn, and men had newly crept out of the darkness of Popery; but I cannot understand gracious, godly people, standing at the font to insult the all-gracious Father with vows and promises framed upon a fiction, and involving practical falsehood. How dare intelligent believer s in Christ to utter words which they know in their conscience to be wickedly aside from truth? When I shall be able to understand the process by which gracious men so accommodate their consciences, even then I shall have a confirmed belief that the God of truth never did and never will confirm a spiritual blessing of the highest order in connection with the utterance of such false promises and untruthful vows. My brethren, does it not strike you that declarations so fictitious are not likely to be connected with a new birth wrought by the Spirit of truth?

I have not done with this point, I must take another case, and suppose the sponsors and others to be ungodly, and that is no hard supposition, for in many cases we know that godfathers and parents have no more thought of religion than that idolatrous hollowed stone around which they gather. When these sinners have taken their places, what are they about to say? Why, they are about to make the solemn vows I have already recounted in your hearing! Totally irreligious they are, but yet they promise for the baby what they never did, and never thought of doing for themselves--they promise on behalf of this child, "that he will renounce the devil and all his works, and constantly believe God's holy Word, and obediently keep his commandments." My brethren, do not think I speak severely here. Really I think there is something here to make mockery for devils. Let every honest man lament, that ever God's Church should tolerate such a thing as this, and that there should be found gracious people who will feel grieved because I, in all kindness of heart, rebuke the atrocity. Unregenerate sinners promising for a poor babe that he shall keep all God's holy commandments which they themselves wantonly break every day! How can anything but the longsuffering of God endure this? What! not speak against it? The very stones in the street might cry out against the infamy of wicked men and women promising t hat another should renounce the devil and all his works, while they themselves serve the devil and do his works with greediness! As a climax to all this, I am asked to believe that God accepts that wicked promise, and as the result of it, regenerates that child. You cannot believe in regeneration by this operation, whether saints or sinners are the performers. Take them to be godly, then they are wrong for doing what their conscience must condemn; view them as ungodly, and they are wrong for promising what they know they cannot perform; and in neither case can God accept such worship, much less infallibly append regeneration to such a baptism as this.

But you will say "Why do you cry out against it?" I cry out against it because I believe that baptism does not save the soul, and that the preaching of it has a wrong and evil influence upon men. We meet with persons who, when we tell them that they must be born again, assure us that they were born again when they were baptized. The number of these persons is increasing, fearfully increasing, until all grades of society are misled by this belief. How can any man stand up in his pulpit and say Ye must be born again to his congregation, when he ha s already assured them, by his own "unfeigned assent and consent" to it, that they are themselves, every one of them, born again in baptism. What is he to do with them? Why, my dear friends, the gospel then has no voice; they have rammed this ceremony down its throat and it cannot speak to rebuke sin. The man who has been baptized or sprinkled says, "I am saved, I am a member of Christ, a child of God, and an inheritor of the kingdom of heaven. Who are you, that you should rebuke me? Call me to repentance? Call me to a new life? What better life can I have? for I am a member of Christ--a part of Christ's body. What! rebuke me? I am a child of God. Cannot you see it in my face? No matter what my walk and conversation is, I am a child of God. Moreover, I am an inheritor of the kingdom of heaven. It is true, I drink and swear, and all that, but you know I am an inheritor of the kingdom of heaven, for when I die , though I live in constant sin, you will put me in the grave, and tell everybody that I died in sure and certain hope of the resurrection to eternal life.'"

Now, what can be the influence of such preaching as this upon our beloved England? Upon my dear and blessed country? What but the worst of ills? If I loved her not, but loved myself most, I might be silent here, but, loving England, I cannot and dare not; and having soon to render an account before my God, whose servant I hope I am, I must free myself from this evil as well as from every other, or else on my head may be the doom of souls.

Here let me bring in another point. It is a most fearful fact, that in no age since the Reformation has Popery made such fearful strides in England as during the last few years. I had comfortably believed that Popery was only feeding itself upon foreign subscriptions, upon a few titled perverts, and imported monks and nuns. I dreamed that its progress was not real. In fact, I have often smiled at the alarm of many of my brethren at the progress of Popery. But, my dear friends, we have been mistaken, grievously mistaken. If you will read a valuable paper in the magazine called "Christian Work," those of you who are not acquainted with it will be perfectly startled at its revelations. This great city is now covered with a network of monks, and priests, and sisters of mercy, and the conversions made are not by ones or twos, but by scores, till England is being regarded as the most hopeful spot for Romish missionary enterprise in the whole world; and at the present moment there is not a mission which is succeeding to anything like the extent which the English mission is. I covet not their money, I despise their sophistries, but I marvel at the way in which they gain their funds for the erection of their ecclesiastical buildings. It really is an alarming matter to see so many of our countrymen going off to that superstition which as a nation we once rejected, and which it was supposed we should never again receive. Popery is making advances such as you would never believe, though a spectator should tell it to you. Close to your very doors, perhaps even in your own houses, you may have evidence ere long of what a march Romanism is making. And to what is it to be ascribed? I say, with every ground of probability, that there is no marvel that Popery should increase when you have two things to make it grow: first of all, the falsehood o f those who profess a faith which they do not believe, which is quite contrary to the honesty of the Romanist, who does through evil report and good report hold his faith; and then you have, secondly, this form of error known as baptismal regeneration, and commonly called Puseyism, which is not only Puseyism, but Church-of-Englandism, because it is in the Prayer Book, as plainly as words can express it--you have this baptismal regeneration preparing stepping-stones to make it easy for men to go to Rome. I have but to open my eyes a little to foresee Romanism rampant everywhere in the future, since its germs are spreading everywhere in the present. In one of our courts of legislature but last Tuesday, the Lord Chief Justice showed his superstition, by speaking of "the risk of the calamity of children dying unbaptized!" Among Dissenters you see a veneration for structures, a modified belief in the sacredness of places, which is idolatry; for to believe in the sacredness of anything but of God and of his own Word, is to idolize, whether it is to believe in the sacredness of the men, the priests, or in the sacredness of the bricks and mortar, or of the fine linen, or what not, which you may use in the worship of God. I see this coming up everywhere--a belief in ceremony, a resting in ceremony, a veneration for altars, fonts, and

Churches--a veneration so profound that we must not venture upon a remark, or straightway of sinners we are chief. Here is the essence and soul of Popery, peeping up under the garb of a decent respect for sacred things. It is impossible but that the Church of Rome must spread, when we who are the watch-dogs of the fold are silent, and others are gently and smoothly turfing the road, and making it as soft and smooth as possible, that converts may travel down to the nethermost hell of Popery. We want John Knox back again. Do not talk to me of mild and gentle men, of soft manners and squeamish words, we want the fiery Knox, and even though his vehemence should "ding our pulpits into blads," it were well if he did but rouse our hearts to action. We want Luther to tell men the truth unmistakably, in homely phrase. The velvet has got into our ministers' mouths o f late, but we must unrobe ourselves of soft raiment, and truth must be spoken, and nothing but truth; for of all lies which have dragged millions down to hell, I look upon this as being one of the most atrocious--that in a Protestant Church there should be found those who swear that baptism saves the soul. Call a man a Baptist, or a Presbyterian, or a Dissenter, or a Churchman, that is nothing to me--if he says that baptism saves the soul, out upon him, out upon him, he states what God n ever taught, what the Bible never laid down, and what ought never to be maintained by men who profess that the Bible, and the whole Bible, is the religion of Protestants.

I have spoken thus much, and there will be some who will say--spoken thus much bitterly. Very well, be it so. Physic is often bitter, but it shall work well, and the physician is not bitter because his medicine is so; or if he be accounted so, it will matter, so long as the patient is cured; at all events, it is no business of the patient whether the physician is bitter or not, his business is with his own soul's health. There is the truth, and I have told it to you; and if there should be one among you, or if there should be one among the readers of this sermon when it is printed, who is resting on baptism, or resting upon ceremonies of any sort, I do beseech you, shake off this venomous faith into the fire as Paul did the viper which fastened on his hand. I pray you do not rest on baptism.

"No outward forms can make you clean,
The leprosy lies deep within."

I do beseech you to remember that you must have a new heart and a right spirit, and baptism cannot give you these. You must turn from your sins and follow after Christ; you must have such a faith as shall make your life holy and your speech devout, or else you have not the faith of God's elect, and into God's kingdom you shall never come. I pray you never rest upon this wretched and rotten foundation, this deceitful invention of antichrist. O, may God save you from it, and bring you to seek the true rock of refuge for weary souls.

I come with much brevity, and I hope with much earnestness, in the second place, to say that FAITH IS THE INDISPENSABLE REQUISITE TO SALVATION. "He that believeth and is baptized shall be saved; he that believeth not shall be damned." Faith is the one indispensable requisite for salvation. This faith is the gift of God. It is the work of the Holy Spirit. Some men believe not on Jesus; they believe not because they are not of Christ's sheep, as he himself said unto them; but his sheep hear his voice: he knows them and they follow him: he gives to them eternal life, and they shall never perish, neither shall any pluck them out of his hand. What is this believing? Believing consists in two things; first there is an accrediting of the testimony of God concerning his Son. God tells you that his Son came into the world and was made flesh, that he lived upon earth for men's sake, that after having spent his life in holiness he was offered up a propitiation for sin, that upon the cross he there and then made expiation--so made expiation for the sins of the world that Whosoever believeth in him shall not perish, but have everlasting life. If you would be saved, you must accredit this testimony which God gives concerning his own Son. Having received this testimony, the next thing is to confide in it--indeed here lies, I think, the essence of saving faith, to rest yourself for eternal salvation upon the atonement and the righteousness of Jesus Christ, to have done once for all with all reliance upon feelings or upon doings, and to trust in Jesus Christ and in what he did for your salvation.

This is faith, receiving of the truth of Christ: first knowing it to be true, and then acting upon that belief. Such a faith as this--such real faith as this makes the man henceforth hate sin. How can he love the thing which made t he Saviour bleed? It makes him live in holiness. How can he but seek to honour that God who has loved him so much as to give his Son to die for him. This faith is spiritual in its nature and effects; it operates upon the entire man; it changes his heart, enlightens his judgment, and subdues his will; it subjects him to God's supremacy, and makes him receive God's Word as a little child, willing to receive the truth upon the ipse dixit of the divine One; it sanctifies his intellect, and makes him willing to be taught God's Word; it cleanses within; it makes clean the inside of the cup and platter, and it beautifies without; it makes clean the exterior conduct and the inner motive, so that the man, if his faith be true and real, becomes henceforth another man to what he ever was before.

Now that such a faith as this should save the soul, is, I believe, reasonable; yea, more, it is certain, for we have seen men saved by it in this very house of prayer. We have seen the harlot lifted out of the Stygian ditch of her sin, and made an honest woman; we have seen the thief reclaimed; we have known the drunkard in hundreds of instances to be sobered; we have observed faith to work such a change, that all the neighbours who have seen it have gazed and admired, even though they hated it; we have seen faith deliver men in the hour of temptation, and help them to consecrate themselves and their substance to God; we have seen, and hope still to see yet more widely, deeds of heroic consecration to God and displays of witness-bearing against the common current of the times, which have proved to us that faith does affect the man, does save the soul. My hearers, if you would be saved, you must believe in the Lord Jesus Christ. Let me urge you with all my heart to look nowhere but to Christ crucified for your salvation. Oh! if you rest upon any ceremony, though it be not baptism--if you rest upon any other than Jesus Christ, you must perish, as surely as this Book is true. I pray you believe not every spirit, but though I, or an angel from heaven, preach any other doctrine than this, let him be accursed, for this, and this alone, is the soul-saving truth which shall regenerate the world--"He that believeth and is baptized shall be saved." Away from all the tag-rags, wax candles, and millinery of Puseyism! away from all the gorgeous pomp of Popery! away from the fonts of Church-of-Englandism! we bid you turn your eyes to that naked cross, where hangs as a bleeding man the Son of God.

"None but Jesus, none but Jesus
Can do helpless sinners good."

There is life in a look at the crucified; there is life at this moment for you. Whoever among you can believe in the great love of God towards man in Christ Jesus, you shall be saved. If you can believe that our great Father desireth us to come to him--that he panteth for us--that he calleth us every day with the loud voice of his Son's wounds; if you can believe now that in Christ there is pardon for transgressions past, and cleansing for years to come; if you can trust him to save you, you have already the marks of regeneration. The work of salvation is commenced in you, so far as the Spirit's work is concerned: it is finished in you so far as Christ's work is concerned. O, I would plead with you--lay hold on Jesus Christ. This is the foundation: build on it. This is the rock of refuge: fly to it. I pray you fly to it now. Life is short: time speeds with eagle's-wing. Swift as the dove pursued by the hawk, fly, fly poor sinner, to God's dear Son; now touch the hem of his garment; now look into that dear face, once marred with sorrows for you; look into those eyes, once shedding tears for you. Trust him, and if you find him false, then you must perish; but false you never will find him while this word standeth true, "He that believeth and is baptized shall be saved; but he that believeth not shall be damned." God give us this vital, essential faith, without which there is no salvation. Baptized, re-baptized, circumcised, confirmed, fed upon sacraments, and buried in consecrated ground--ye shall all perish except ye believe in him. The word is express and plain--he that believeth not may plead his baptism, may plead anything he likes, "But he that believeth not shall be damned;" for him there is nothing but the wrath of God, the flames of hell, eternal perdition. So Christ declares, and so must it be.

But now to close, there are some who say, "Ah! but baptism is in the text; where do you put that?" That shall be another point, and then we shall have done.

THE BAPTISM IN THE TEXT IS ONE EVIDENTLY CONNECTED WITH FAITH. "He that believeth and is baptized shall be saved." It strikes me, there is no supposition here, that anybody would be baptized who did not believe; or, if there be such a supposition, it is very clearly laid down that his baptism will be of no use to him, for he will be damned, baptized or not, unless he believes. The baptism of the text seems to me--my brethren, if you differ from me I am sorry for it, but I must hold my opinion and out with it--it seems to me that baptism is connected with, nay, directly follows belief. I would not insist too much upon the order of the words, but for other reasons, I think that baptism should follow believing. At any rate it effectually avoids the error we have been combating. A man who knows that he is saved by believing in Christ does not, when he is baptized, lift his baptism into a saving ordinance. In fact, he is the very best protester against that mistake, because he holds that he has no right to be baptized until he is saved. He b ears a testimony against baptismal regeneration in his being baptized as professedly an already regenerate person. Brethren, the baptism here meant is a baptism connected with faith, and to this baptism I will admit there is very much ascribed in Scripture. Into that question I am not going; but I do find some very remarkable passages in which baptism is spoken of very strongly. I find this--"Arise, and be baptized, and wash away thy sins, calling on the name of the Lord." I find as much as this elsewhere; I know that believer's baptism itself does not wash away sin, yet it is so the outward sign and emblem of it to the believer, that the thing visible may be described as the thing signified. Just as our Saviour said--"This is my body," when it was not his body, but bread; yet, inasmuch as it represented his body, it was fair and right according to the usage of language to say, "Take, eat, this is my body." And so, inasmuch as baptism to the believer representeth the washing of sin--it may be called the washing of sin--not that it is so, but that it is to saved souls the outward symbol and representation of what is done by the power of the Holy Spirit, in the man who believes in Christ.

What connection has this baptism with faith? I think it has just this, baptism is the avowal of faith; the man was Christ's soldier, but now in baptism he puts on his regimentals. The man believed in Christ, but his faith remained between God an d his own soul. In baptism he says to the baptizer, "I believe in Jesus Christ;" he says to the Church, "I unite with you as a believer in the common truths of Christianity;" he saith to the onlooker, "Whatever you may do, as for me, I will serve the Lord." It is the avowal of his faith.

Next, we think baptism is also to the believer a testimony of his faith; he does in baptism tell the world what he believes. "I am about," saith he, "to be buried in water. I believe that the Son of God was metaphorically baptized in suffering: I believe he was literally dead and buried." To rise again out of the water sets forth to all men that he believes in the resurrection of Christ. There is a showing forth in the Lord's Supper of Christ's death, and there is a showing forth in baptism of Christ's burial and resurrection. It is a type, a sign, a symbol, a mirror to the world: a looking-glass in which religion is as it were reflected. We say to the onlooker, when he asks what is the meaning of this ordinance, "We mean to set forth our faith that Christ was buried, and that he rose again from the dead, and we avow this death and resurrection to be the ground of our trust."

Again, baptism is also Faith's taking her proper place. It is, or should be one of her first acts of obedience. Reason looks at baptism, and says, "Perhaps there is nothing in it; it cannot do me any good." "True," says Faith, "and therefore will I observe it. If it did me some good my selfishness would make me do it, but inasmuch as to my sense there is no good in it, since I am bidden by my Lord thus to fulfil all righteousness, it is my first public declaration that a thing which looks to be unreasonable and seems to be unprofitable, being commanded by God, is law, is law to me. If my Master had told me to pick up six stones and lay them in a row I would do it, without demanding of him, What good will it do?' Cui bono? is no fit question for soldiers of Jesus. The very simplicity and apparent uselessness of the ordinance should make the believer say, Therefore I do it because it becomes the better test to me of my obedience to my Master.'" When you tell your servant to do something, and he cannot comprehend it, if he turns round and says, "Please, sir, what for?" you are quite clear that he hardly understands the relation between master and servant. So when God tells me to do a thing, if I say, "What for?" I cannot have taken the place which Faith ought to occupy, which is that of simple obedience to whatever the Lord hath said. Baptism is commanded, and Faith obeys because it is commanded, and thus takes her proper place.

Once more, baptism is a refreshment to Faith. While we are made up of body and soul as we are, we shall need some means by which the body shall sometimes be stirred up to co-work with the soul. In the Lord's Supper my faith is assisted by the outward and visible sign. In the bread and in the wine I see no superstitious mystery, I see nothing but bread and wine, but in that bread and wine I do see to my faith an assistant. Through the sign my faith sees the thing signified. So in baptism there is no mysterious efficacy in the baptistry or in the water. We attach no reverence to the one or to the other, but we do see in the water and in the baptism such an assistance as brings home to our faith most manifestly our being buried with Christ, and our rising again in newness of life with him. Explain baptism thus, dear friends, and there is no fear of Popery rising out of it. Explain it thus, and we cannot suppose any soul will be led to trust to it; but it takes it s proper place among the ordinances of God's house. To lift it up in the other way, and say men are saved by it--ah! my friends, how much of mischief that one falsehood has done and may do, eternity alone will disclose. Would to God another George Fox would spring up in all his quaint simplicity and rude honesty to rebuke the idol-worship of this age; to rail at their holy bricks and mortar, holy lecterns, holy alters, holy surplices, right reverend fathers, and I know not what. These things are not holy. God is holy; his truth is holy; holiness belongs not to the carnal and the material, but to the spiritual. O that a trumpet-tongue would cry out against the superstition of the age. I cannot, as George Fox did, give up baptism and the Lord's Supper, but I would infinitely sooner do it, counting it the smaller mistake of the two than perpetrate and assist in perpetrating the uplifting of baptism and the Lord's Supper out of their proper place. O my beloved friends, the comrades of my struggles and witnessings, cling to the salvation of faith, and abhor the salvation of priests. If I am not mistaken, the day will come when we shall have to fight for a simple spiritual religion far more than we do now. We have been cultivating friendship with those who are either unscriptural in creed or else dishonest, who either believe baptismal regeneration, or profess that they do, and swear before God that they do when they do not. The time is come when there shall be no more truce or parley between God's servants and the time-servers. The time is come when those who follow God must follow God, and those who try to trim and dress themselves and find out a way which is pleasing to the flesh and gentle to carnal desires, must go their way. A great winnowing time is coming to

God's saints, and we shall be clearer one of these days than we now are from union with those who are upholding Popery, under the pretence of teaching Protestantism. We shall be clear, I say, of those who teach salvation by baptism, instead of salvation by the blood of our blessed Master, Jesus Christ. O may the Lord gird up your loins. Believe me, it is no trifle. It may be that on this ground Armageddon shall be fought. Here shall come the great battle between Christ and his saints on the one hand, and the world, and forms, and ceremonies, on the other. If we are overcome here, there may be years of blood and persecution, and tossing to and fro between darkness and light; but if we are brave and bold, and flinch not here, but stand to God's truth, the future of England may be bright and glorious. O for a truly reformed Church in England, and a godly race to maintain it! The world's future depends on it under God, for in proportion as truth is marred at home, truth is maimed abroad. Out of any system which teaches salvation by baptism must spring infidelity, an infidelity which the false Church already seems willing to nourish and foster beneath her wing. God save this favoured land from the brood of her own established religion. Brethren, stand fast in the liberty wherewith Christ has made you free, and be not afraid of any sudden fear nor calamity when it cometh, for he who trusteth to the Lord, mercy shall compass him about, and he who is faithful to God and Christ shall hear it said at the last, "Well done, good and faithful servant, enter thou into the joy of the Lord." May the Lord bless this word for Christ's sake.

[Note.--Having been informed that the whole of the burial service is not usually read at executions, I have, for the sake of fairness, altered the passage upon page 318, although it strikes me that I might justly have retained it, since the rubric of the Church and not the practice of some of its ministers is that with which we must deal. The rubric says, "The office ensuing is not to be used for any that die unbaptized, or excommunicate, or have laid violent hands upon themselves." The victim of our capital punishment is not by this rubric shut out from the privileges (?) of the Anglican burial service, unless his condemnation may be viewed as tantamount to excommunication, which I can hardly think be the case, since many condemned persons receive the sacrament. I have also altered an incorrect expression on page 316, which has been pointed out to me by both friends and foes. May God grant that the controversy which this sermon has commenced may lead to the advancement of his truth, and the enlightenment of many.]

The Superlative Excellence Of The Holy Spirit

DELIVERED ON SUNDAY MORNING, JUNE 12, 1864,
BY THE REV. C. H. SPURGEON,
AT THE METROPOLITAN TABERNACLE, NEWINGTON.

"Nevertheless I tell you the truth. It is expedient for you that I go away: for if I go not away, the Comforter will not come unto you; but if I depart, I will send Him unto you." -- John 16:7.

THE saints of God may very justly reckon their losses among their greatest gains. The adversities of Believers minister much to their prosperity. Although we know this, through the infirmity of the flesh we tremble at soul-enriching afflictions and dread to see those black ships which bring us such freights of golden treasure. When the Holy Spirit sanctifies the furnace, the flame refines our gold and consumes our dross, yet the dull ore of our nature likes not the glowing coals and had rather lie quiet in the dark mines of earth. As silly children cry because they are called to drink the medicine which will heal their sicknesses, even so do we.

Our gracious Savior, however, loves us too wisely to spare us the trouble because of our childish fears. He foresees the advantage which will spring from our griefs and therefore thrusts us into them out of wisdom and true affection. It was a very great trouble to these first Apostles to lose their Teacher and Friend. Sorrow had filled their hearts at the thought that He should depart, but yet His departure was to give them the greater blessing of the Holy Spirit. And therefore their entreaties and tears cannot avert the dreaded separation. Christ will not gratify their wishes at so vast an expense as the withholding of the Spirit. Mourn as they may under the severe trial, Jesus will not remain with them because His departure is in the highest degree expedient.

Beloved, let us expect to be subject to the same loving discipline. Let us reckon upon losing happy frames and choice enjoyments when Jesus knows that the loss will be better for us than the enjoyment. God has given two great gifts to His people--the first is His Son for us. The second is His Spirit to us. After He had given His Son for us, to become Incarnate, to work righteousness, and to offer an Atonement--after that gift had been fully bestowed there remained no more to be conferred in that respect. "It is finished!" proclaimed the completion of Atonement and His Resurrection showed the perfection of Justification. It was not, therefore, necessary that Christ should remain any longer upon earth since His work below is forever finished.

Now is the season for the second gift, the descent of the Holy Spirit. This could not be bestowed until Christ had ascended, because this choice favor was reserved to grace, with highest honor, the triumphant ascension of the great Redeemer. "When He ascended up on high, He led captivity captive and gave gifts unto men." This was, as Peter tells us, the great promise which Jesus received of His Father. "Therefore being by the right hand of God exalted and having received of the Father the promise of the Holy Spirit, He has shed forth this, which you now see and hear." That His triumphal entrance into Heaven might be stamped with signal Glory, the gifts of the Spirit of God could not be scattered among the sons of men until the Lord had gone up with a shout, even the Lord with the sound of trumpet.

The first gift being completed, it became necessary that He, whose Person and work make up that priceless gift, should withdraw Himself that He might have power to distribute the second benefit by which alone the first gift becomes of any service to us. Christ Crucified is of no practical value to us without the work of the Holy Spirit. And the Atonement which Jesus worked can never save a single soul unless the blessed Spirit of God shall apply it to the heart and conscience. Jesus is never seen until the Holy Spirit opens the eyes--the water from the Well of Life is never received until the Holy Spirit has drawn it from the depths.

As medicine unused for want of the physician's word. As sweets untasted because out of reach. As treasure unvalued because hidden in the earth--such is Jesus the Savior--until the Holy Spirit teaches us to know Him and applies His blood to our souls. It is to the honor of the Holy Spirit that I desire to speak this morning and O, may the same hallowed flame which of old sat upon the Apostles now rest upon the preacher and may the Word come with power to our hearts!

I. We shall commence our discourse by the remark that THE BODILY PRESENCE OF CHRIST MUST HAVE BEEN EXCEEDINGLY PRECIOUS. How precious those alone can tell who much love Christ. Love always desires to be in the company of the thing beloved and absence causes grief. What is fully meant by the expression, "Sorrow has filled your heart," those only can know who anticipate a like painful bereavement. Jesus had become the Joy of their eyes, the Sun of their days, the Star of their nights--like the spouse, as she came up from the wilderness--they leaned upon their Beloved. They were as little children and now that their Lord and Master was going, they felt they should be left orphans.

Well might they have great sorrow of heart! So much love, so much sorrow, when the object of love is withdrawn. Judge, my Brethren, the joy which the bodily Presence of Christ would give to us this morning, and then you can tell how precious it must be. Have we not, some of us, been looking for years for the personal advent of Christ? We have lifted up our eyes in the morning and we have said, "Perhaps He will come this day." And when the day has closed we have continued our watching in our sleepless hours and renewed our hopes with the rising of the sun. We longingly expect Him according to His promise. And like men who watch for their Lord, we stand with loins girt about waiting for His appearing.

We are looking for and hastening unto the Day of the Lord. This is the bright hope which cheers the Christian, the hope that the Savior shall descend to reign among His people gloriously. Suppose Him to appear suddenly on this platform now--how would you clap your hands! Why, the lame among you would, at the joy of His appearance, leap like a hart and even the dumb might sing for joy! The Presence of the Master! What rapture! Come quickly! Come quickly, Lord Jesus!

It must be, indeed, a precious thing to enjoy the corporeal Presence of Christ. Think of the advantage it would be in the instruction of His people. No mystery need puzzle us if we could refer all to Him. The disputes of the Christian Church would soon be ended for He would tell us what His Word meant beyond dispute. There would be no discouragement to the Church in her work of faith and labor of love, for the Presence of Christ would be the end of all difficulties and insure conquest over all enemies. We should not have to mourn as we now do over our forgetfulness of Jesus, for we should sometimes catch a look at Him. And a sight of Him would give us a store ofjoy so that like the Prophet of Horeb we could go forty days in the strength of that meat!

It were a delightful thing to know that Christ was somewhere upon earth, for then He would take the personal supervision of His universal Church. He could warn us of apostates. He could reject the hypocrites. He would comfort the feeble-minded and rebuke the erring. How delightful would it be to see Him walking among the golden candlesticks, holding the stars in His right hand! Churches need not, then, be subdivided and rent with evil passions. Christ would create unity. Schism would cease to be and heresy would be rooted out. The Presence of Jesus, whose countenance is as the sun shining in his strength, would ripen all the fruits of our garden, consume all the weeds, and quicken every plant!

The two-edged sword of His mouth would slay His foes and His eyes of fire would kindle the holy passions of His friends. But I shall not enlarge upon that point because it is one in which fancy exercises itself at the expense ofjudgment. I question whether the pleasure, which the thought of Christ's being here in the flesh has given us just now, may not have had a leaven of carnality in it. I question whether the Church is yet prepared to enjoy the corporeal Presence of her Savior without falling into the error of knowing Him after the flesh. It may be it shall need centuries of education before the Church is fit to see her Savior in the flesh on earth again, because I see in my own self--and I suppose it is so in you-- that much of the delight which I expect from the company of Christ is according to the sight of the eyes and the judgment of the mind. And sight is ever the mark and symbol of the flesh.

II. However, leaving that point, we come to the second, which is THAT THE PRESENCE OF THE COMFORTER,

AS WE HAVE IT UPON EARTH, IS VERY MUCH BETTER THAN THE BODILY PRESENCE OF CHRIST. We have fancied that the bodily Presence of Christ would make us blessed and confer innumerable benefits. But according to our text the Presence of the Holy Spirit working in the Church is more expedient for the Church. I think this will be clear to you, if you think for a moment, that the bodily Presence of Christ on earth, however good it might be for the Church, would in our present condition involve many inconveniences which are avoided by His Presence through the Holy Spirit.

Christ, being most truly Man, must as to His Manhood inhabit a certain place and in order to get to Christ, it would be necessary for us to travel to His place of residence. Conceive all men compelled to travel from the ends of the earth to visit the Lord Jesus Christ, dwelling upon Mount Zion, or in the city of Jerusalem. What a lengthened voyage would that be for those who live in the far-off ends of the world!

Doubtless they would joyfully undertake it and as pence would be universal and poverty be banished, men might not be restrained from taking such a journey, but might all be able to accomplish it? As they could not all live where they could every morning see Christ, they must be content with every now and then getting a glimpse of Him. But see, my Brethren, the Holy Spirit, the vicar of Christ, dwells everywhere! And if we wish to apply to the Holy Spirit, we have no need to move an inch. In the closet we can find Him, or in the streets we can talk with Him. Jesus Christ could not be present in this congregation after the flesh and yet present in a neighboring Church, much less present in America and in Australia and in Europe and in Africa, at the same time.

But the Holy Spirit is everywhere! And through that Holy Spirit Christ keeps His promise, "Where two or three are met together in My name, there am I in the midst of them." He could not keep that promise according to the flesh--at least we are quite unable to conceive of His so doing. But through the Holy Spirit we sweetly enjoy His Presence and hope to do so to the world's end. Think again--access to Christ--if He were here in His corporeal Personality, would not be very easy to all Believers. There are only twenty-four hours in the day and if our Lord never slept, if, as a Man, He could still live and, like the saints above, rest not day nor night, yet there are only the twenty-four hours. And what were twenty-four hours for the supervision of a Church which we trust will cover the whole earth?

How could a thousand millions of Believers all receive immediate personal comfort either from His lips or the smiles of His face? Even at the present moment there are some millions of true saints upon earth--what could one man do by his personal presence--even though that one man were Incarnate Deity? What could He do in one day for the comfort of all of these? Why, we could not possibly expect each one of us to see Him every day--no, we could scarcely expect to have our turn once in the year!

But, Beloved, we can now see Jesus every hour and every moment of every hour! So often as you bow the knee, His Spirit, who represents Him, can commune with you and bless you. No matter whether it is in the dead of night that your cry goes up, or under the blaze of burning noon--there is the Spirit waiting to be gracious and your sighs and cries climb up to Christ in Heaven and return with answers of peace. These difficulties did not occur to you, perhaps, in your first thoughts. But if you meditate awhile you will see that the Presence of the Spirit, avoiding that difficulty, makes Christ accessible to every saint at all times. Not to a few choice favorites, but to every believing man and woman the Holy Spirit is accessible and thus the whole body of the faithful can enjoy present and perpetual communion with Christ.

We ought to consider yet once more that Christ's Presence in the flesh upon earth, for any other purpose than that of ending the present dispensation, would involve another difficulty. Of course every Word which Christ had spoken from the time of the Apostles until now would have been Inspired. Being Inspired it would have been a thousand pities that it should fall to the ground. Busy scribes would therefore be always taking down Christ's Words. And, my Brethren, if in the short course of three years our Savior managed to do and to say so much that one of the Evangelists informs us that if all had been written the world itself could not have contained the books which would have been written--I ask you to imagine what a mass of literature the Christian Church would have acquired if she had preserved the Words of Christ throughout these one thousand eight hundred and sixty-four years!

Certainly we should not have had the Word of God in the simple compact form of a pocket Bible--it would have consisted of innumerable volumes of the sayings and deeds of the Lord Jesus Christ! Only the studious, no, not even the studious could have read all the Lord's teachings! And the poor and the illiterate must ever have been at a great disadvantage. But now we have a Book which is finished within a narrow compass with not another line to be added to it. The canon of Revelation is sealed up forever and the poorest man in England, believing in Christ, going with a humble soul to that Book and looking up to Jesus Christ who is present through His Spirit, though not after the flesh, may, in a short time comprehend the Doctrines of Grace and understand with all saints what are the heights and depths and know the love of Christ which passes knowledge.

So then, on the score of inconvenience, precious as the corporeal Presence of Christ might be, it is infinitely better for the Church's good that, until the day of her Millennial Glory, Christ should be present by His Spirit and not in the flesh. Yet more, my Brethren! If Jesus Christ were still present with His Church in the flesh, the life of faith would not have such room for its display as it now has. The more there is visible to the eyes, the less room for faith--the least faith, the most show. The Romish Church, which has little enough of true faith, provides everything to work upon the senses-- your nostrils are regaled with incense and your ears are delighted with sweet sounds. The more faith grows, the less it needs outward helps. And when faith shows her true character and is clean divorced from sense and sight, then she wants absolutely nothing to rest upon but the invisible power of God!

She then has learned to hang as the world hangs--upon no seen support! Just as the eternal arch of yon blue sky springs right up without props, so faith rests upon the invisible pillars of God's

Truth and faithfulness, needing nothing to shore or buttress her. The Presence of Christ Jesus here in bodily flesh and the knowing of Him according to the flesh, would be the bringing back of the saints to a life of sight and in a measure spoil the simplicity of naked trust. You remember the Apostle Paul says, "We now know no man after the flesh. Yes," says he, "though we have known Christ after the flesh, yet now after the flesh know we Him no more." To the skeptic, who should ask us, "Why do you believe in Christ?" if Jesus had remained upon the earth, we could always give an easy answer--"There He is--there is the Man. Behold Him as He continues still to work miracles."

There would be very little room for faith's holy adherence to the bare Word of God and no opportunity for her to glorify God, trusting where she cannot trace. But now, Beloved, the fact that we have nothing visible to point to which carnal minds can understand--this very fact makes the path of faith more truly congenial with its noble character--

"Faith, mighty faith, the promise sees, And looks to that alone," which she could hardly do, if she could look upon the visible Person of a present Savior. Happy day will it be for us when faith enjoys the full fruition of her hopes in the triumphant advent of her Lord! But His absence, alone, can train and educate her to the needed point of spiritual refinement.

Furthermore, the Presence of Jesus Christ on earth would materially affect the character of God's great battle against error and sin. Suppose that Christ were to destroy the preachers of error by miracle. Suppose that persecuting monarchs had their arms dried up, or that all men who would oppose Christ were suddenly devoured by fire. Why then it would be more a battle between physical greatness and moral evil, than a warfare in which only spiritual force is employed on the side of right. But now that Christ has gone, the fight is all between Spirit and spirit--between God the Holy Spirit and Satan--between Truth and error. It is between the earnestness of believing men and the infatuation of unbelieving men. Now the fight is fair.

We have no miracles on our side--we do not want them--the Holy Spirit is enough! We call no fire from Heaven-- no earthquake shakes the ground beneath our foemen's feet. Korah is not swallowed up. Dathan does not go down alive into the pit. Physical force is left to our enemies--we do not ask for it. Why? Because by the Divine working we can vanquish error without it. In the name of the Holy One of Israel, in whose cause we have been enlisted--by His might we are enough--no need for miracles and signs and wonders. If Christ were here still working miracles, the battle were not so spiritual as it now is. But the absence of the corporeal Savior makes it a spiritual conflict of Spirit of the noblest and most sublime order.

Again, dear Friends, the Holy Spirit is more valuable to the Church in her present militant state than the Presence of Christ could be conceived to be, because Christ must be here in one of two ways--either He must be here suffering, or not suffering. If Christ were here suffering, then how could we conclude that His Atonement was finished? Is it not much better for our faith that our blessed Lord, having once and for all made expiation for sin, should sit at the right hand of the Father? Is it not much better, I ask, than to see Him still struggling and suffering here below? "Oh, but," you say, "perhaps He would not suffer!" Then I pray you, do not wish to have Him here till our warfare is accomplished, for to see an unsuffering Christ in the midst of His suffering people--to see His face calm and clear when yours and mine are wrinkled with grief--to see Him smiling when we are weeping, this were intolerable! No, it could not be! Brethren, if He is a suffering Christ in our sight, then we should suspect that He had not finished His work.

And, on the other hand, if He is an unsuffering Christ, then it would look as if He were not a faithful High Priest made like unto His Brethren. These two difficulties throw us back into a state of thankfulness to God that we have not the dilemma to answer, but that the Spirit of God, who is Christ present on earth, relieves us from these difficulties and gives us all the advantage we could expect from Christ's Presence in a tenfold degree. Only this one further remark, that the personal Presence of Christ, much as we think of it, did not produce very great results in His disciples until the Spirit was poured forth from on high.

Christ was their Teacher--how much did they learn? Why, there is Philip--Christ has to say to him, "Have I been so long time with you and yet have you not known Me, Philip?" They were puzzled by questions which little children can now answer! You can see that at the end of their three years course of training with Christ, they had made but slender progress. Christ is not only their Teacher, but their Comforter--yet how frequently Christ failed to console them because of their unbelief. After He had uttered that delightful discourse which we have been reading, He found them sleeping for sorrow. In this very chapter, when He is trying to comfort them, He adds, "But because I have said these things unto you, sorrow has filled your heart."

Christ's object was to foster the Graces of His disciples--but where were their Graces? Here is Peter--he has not even the Grace of courage and consistency, but denies his Master while the rest of them forsake Him and flee. There was not even the Spirit of Christ infused into them! Their zeal was not tempered with love, for they wanted fire from Heaven to consume His adversaries and

Peter drew a sword to cut off the High Priest's servant's ear. They scarcely knew the Truths which their Master taught and they were far enough from imbibing His heavenly Spirit. Even their endowments were slender. It is true they once worked miracles and preached, but with what success?

Do you ever hear of Peter winning three thousand sinners under a sermon till the Holy Spirit came? Do you find any of them able to edify others and build up the Church of Christ? No, the ministry of our Lord Jesus Christ, considered only as to its immediate fruits, was not to be compared with ministries after the descent of the Spirit. "He came unto His own and His own received Him not." His great work as a Redeemer was a complete triumph from beginning to end. But as a Teacher, since the Spirit of God was only upon Him and not upon the people, His words were rejected, His entreaties were despised and His warnings unheeded by the great multitude of the people.

The mighty blessing came when the words of Joel were fulfilled, "And it shall come to pass afterward, that I will pour out My Spirit upon all flesh. And your sons and your daughters shall prophesy, your old men shall dream dreams, your young men shall see visions: and also upon the servants and upon the handmaids in those days will I pour out My Spirit." That was the blessing and a blessing which, we venture to say again, was so rich and so rare that it was, indeed, expedient that Jesus Christ should go, that the Holy Spirit might descend.

III. I now pass on to the third point of the subject with brevity. We have come thus far--the Presence of Christ admitted to be precious, but the Presence of the Holy Spirit most clearly shown to be of more practical value to the Church of God than the corporeal Presence of the Lord Jesus Christ. Advance, then, to the third point, THE PRESENCE OF

THE COMFORTER IS SUPERLATIVELY VALUABLE. We may gather this, first, from the effects which were seen upon the day of Pentecost. On the day of Pentecost the heavenly Wind sounded the alarm of war. The soldiers were ill prepared for it. They were a slender band, having only this virtue--they were content to wait until power was given to them.

They sat still in the upper room. That mighty sound was heard across Jerusalem. The forceful Whirlwind travels on until it reaches the chosen spot. It fills the place where they are sitting. Here was an omen of what the Spirit of God is to be to the Church! It is to come mysteriously upon the Church according to the Sovereign will of God. But when He comes like the Wind, it is to purge the moral atmosphere and to quicken the pulse of all who spiritually breathe. This is a blessing, indeed! A gift which the Church greatly wants--I would that this rushing mighty Wind would come upon this Church with an irresistible force which should carry everything before it--the force of Truth, but of more than Truth-- the force of God driving His Truth home upon the heart and conscience of men!

I would that you and I could breathe this Wind and receive its invigorating influence that we might be made champions of God and of His Truth. O that it would drive away our mists of doubt and clouds of error! Come, Sacred Wind, England needs You--the whole earth requires You! The foul gases which brood in this deadly calm would fly if Your Divine lightning enlightened the world and set the moral atmosphere in commotion. Come, Holy Spirit, come. We can do nothing without You! If we have Your Wind, we spread our sails and speed onward towards Glory!

Then the Spirit came as fire. A fire-shower accompanied the rushing mighty Wind. What a blessing is this to the Church! The Church wants fire to quicken her ministers, to give zeal and energy to all her members. Having this fire, she burns her way to success! The world meets her with the fire of firewood, but she confronts the world with the fire of kindling spirits and of souls aglow with the love of Jesus Christ. She trusts not to the wit and eloquence and wisdom of her preachers, but to the Divine Fire which clothes them with energy. She knows that men are irresistible when they are filled with hallowed enthusiasm sent from God. She trusts, therefore, in this and her cry is, "Come, Holy Fire, abide upon our pastors and teachers! Rest upon every one of us!" This Fire is a blessing Christ did not bring us in Person, but which He now gives through His Spirit to the Church.

Then there came from the fire-shower a descent of tongues. This, too, is the privilege of the Church. When the Lord gave the Apostles different tongues, He did, as it were, give them the keys of the various kingdoms. "Go," says He, "Judea is not My only dominion. Go and unlock the gates of every empire. Here are the keys, you can speak every language." Dear Friends, though we can no longer speak with every man in his own tongue, yet we have the keys of the whole world swinging at our girdle if we have the Spirit of God with us. You have the keys of human hearts if the Spirit of God speaks through you. I have this day the keys of the hearts of the multitudes here if the Holy Spirit wills to use them!

There is an efficacy about the Gospel, when the Spirit is with us, little dreamed of by those who call it the foolishness of men. I am persuaded that the results which have followed ministry in our lifetime are trivial and insignificant compared with what they would be if the Spirit of God were more mightily at work in our midst. There is no reason in the nature of the Gospel or the power of the Spirit why a whole congregation should not be converted under one sermon! There is no reason in God's Nature why a nation should not be born in a day and why, within a single twelve months, a dozen ministers preaching throughout the world might not be the means of converting every elect son and daughter of Adam to a knowledge of the Truth of God. The Spirit of God is perfectly Irresistible when He puts forth His full power!

His power is so Divinely Omnipotent that the moment He goes forth the work is achieved, The great prophetic event, we see, occurred on the day of Pentecost. The success given was only the first fruits--Pentecost is not the harvest. We have been accustomed to look on Pentecost as a great and wonderful display of Divine power not at all to be equaled in modern times. Brethren, it is to be exceeded! I stand not upon Pentecost as upon a towering mountain, wondering at my height, but I look at Pentecost as a little rising knoll from which I am to look up to mountains far loftier! I look not to Pentecost as the shouting of our harvest home and the bringing in of the sheaves into the garner. No! But as an offering of the first wave sheaf before the altar of God!

You must expect greater things, pray for greater things, long for greater things! Here is this England of ours, sunk in stolid ignorance of the Gospel. Weighing like a nightmare upon her bosom we have baptismal regeneration supported by a horde of priests who either believe that dogma, or hold their benefices by subscribing to a lie. How is this incubus to be shaken off from the living bosom of England? "Not by might, nor by power, but by My Spirit, says the Lord." There is France cursed with infidelity, fickle, gay, given up to pleasure--how is she to be made sober and sanctified unto God? "Not by might, but by My Spirit, says the Lord." Yonder is Germany, with her metaphysical skepticism, her half-Romanism, that is to say, Lutheranism--and her abounding Popery! How is she to arise? "Not by might, nor by power, but by My Spirit, says the Lord." Away there in Italy sits old Rome, the harlot of the seven hills, still reigning queen triumphant over the great part of the earth! How is she to die? Where is the sword which shall find out her heart? "Not by might, nor by power, but by My Spirit, says the Lord."

The one thing, then, which we need, is the Spirit of God! Do not say that we need money--we shall have it soon enough when the Spirit touches men's hearts. Do not say that we need buildings, Churches, edifices--all these may be very well in subservience--but the main need of the Church is the Spirit and men into whom the Spirit may be poured! If there were only one prayer which I might pray before I died, it should be this: "Lord, send to Your Church men filled with the Holy Spirit and with fire." Give to any denomination such men and its progress must be mighty--keep back such men, send them college gentlemen of great refinement and profound learning, but of little fire and Grace--dumb dogs which cannot bark--and straightway that denomination must decline. Let the Spirit come and the preacher may be rustic, simple, rough, unmannered--but the Holy Spirit being upon him--none of his adversaries shall stand against him! His word shall be with power to the shaking of the gates of Hell!

Beloved, did I not say well when I said that the Spirit of God is of superlative importance to the Church and that the day of Pentecost seems to tell us this? Remember, Brethren, and here is another thought which should make the Spirit very dear to you--without the Holy Spirit no good thing ever did or ever can come into any of your hearts--no sigh of penitence! No cry of faith! No glance of love! No tear of hallowed sorrow! Your heart can never palpitate with Divine life except through the Spirit! You are not capable of the smallest degree of spiritual emotion, much less spiritual action, apart from the Holy Spirit! Dead you lie, living only for evil, and absolutely dead for God until the Holy Spirit comes and raises you from the grave!

There is nothing good in you today, my Brothers and Sisters, which was not put there. The flowers of Christ are all exotics--"In me, that is, in my flesh, dwells no good thing." Who can bring a clean thing out of an unclean? No one! Everything must come from Christ and Christ gives nothing to men except through the Spirit of all Grace. Prize, then, the Spirit as the channel of all good which comes into you. And further, no good thing can come out of you apart from the Spirit. Let it be in you, yet it lies dormant except God works in you to will and to do of His own good pleasure. Do you desire to preach? How can you unless the Holy Spirit touches your tongue? Do you desire to pray? Alas, what dull work it is unless the Spirit makes intercession for you! Do you desire to subdue sin? Would you be holy? Would you imitate your Master? Do you desire to rise to superlative heights of spirituality? Are you wanting to be made like the angels of God, full of zeal and ardor for the Master's cause? You cannot without the Spirit--"Without Me you can do nothing."

O branch of the vine, you can have no fruit without the sap! O child of God, you have no life within you apart from the life which God gives you through His Spirit! Said I not well, then, that the Holy Spirit is superlatively precious, so that even the Presence of Christ after the flesh is not to be compared to His Presence for glory and for power?

IV. This brings us to the conclusion, which is a practical point. Brethren, if these things are so, let us, who are believers in Christ, view the mysterious Spirit with deep awe and reverence. Let us so reverence Him as not to grieve Him or provoke Him to anger by our sins. Let us not quench Him in one of His faintest motions in our soul. Let us foster every suggestion and be ready to obey every prompting. If the Holy Spirit is, indeed, so mighty, let us do nothing without Him. Let us begin no project and carry on no enterprise and conclude no transaction without imploring His blessing. Let us pay Him the due homage of feeling our entire weakness apart from Him, and then depending alone upon Him, having this for our prayer, "Open my heart and my whole being to Your incoming and uphold me with Your free Spirit when I shall have received that Spirit in my inward parts."

You who are unconverted, let me beseech you, whatever you do, never despise the Spirit of God. Remember, there is a special honor put upon Him in Scripture--"All manner of sin and of blasphemy shall be forgiven unto men, but the sin against the Holy Spirit shall never be forgiven, neither in this world nor in that which is to come." Remember, "If a man speaks a word against the Son of Man, it shall be forgiven him. But if he speaks a word against the Holy Spirit, it shall never be forgiven him." This is the sin which is unto death, of which even the loving John says--"I do not say that you shall pray for it." Tremble, therefore, in His Presence! Take your shoes off, for when His name is mentioned, the place where you stand is holy ground. Let the Spirit be treated with reverence.

In the next place, as a practical remark, let us, viewing the might of the Spirit, take courage today. We know, Brethren, that we, as a body of people seeking to adhere closely to Scripture and to practice the ordinances and hold the doctrines as we have received them from the Lord Himself, are but poor and despised. And when we look at the great ones of the earth, we see them on the side of the false and not of the true. Where are the kings and the nobles? Where are the princes, and where are the mighty men?

Are they not against the Lord of Hosts. Where is the gold? Where is the silver? Where is the architecture? Where is the wisdom? Where is the eloquence? Is it not banded against the Lord of Hosts? What? Shall we, then, be discouraged? Our fathers were not! They bore their testimony in the stocks and in the prison, but they feared not for the good old cause! As John Bunyan, they learned to rot in dungeons, but they learned not to play the coward. They suffered and they testified that they were not discouraged. Why? Because they knew (not that Truth is mighty and will prevail, for Truth is not mighty and will not prevail in this world until men are different from what they are), but they knew that the Spirit of God is mighty and will prevail!

Better to have a small Church of poor men and the Spirit of God with them, than to have a hierarchy of nobles, to have an army of titled princes and prelates without the Holy Spirit! For this is not merely the sinew of strength, but it is strength itself! Where the Spirit of God is--there is liberty and power! Courage then, Brethren! We have only to seek for that which God has promised to give and we can do wonders. He will give the Holy Spirit to them that ask Him. Wake up, members of this Church, to earnest prayer. And all Believers throughout the world, cry aloud unto God to let His bare arm be seen. Wake, children of God, for you know the power ofprayer!

Give the Covenant angel no rest till he speaks the word and the Spirit works mightily among the sons of men. Prayer is work adapted to each of you who are in Christ. You cannot preach, you cannot teach, but you can pray! And your private prayer, unknown by men, shall be registered in Heaven, Those silent but earnest cries of yours shall bring down a blessing. The other morning, when we were holding special prayer, there were some Brethren present who kept saying during the prayer to themselves, scarcely loud enough to be heard, "Do Lord! Do! Grant it! Hear it!" That is a kind of praying which I love in Prayer Meetings!

I would not care for the loud shouts of some of our Methodist Brethren, though if they like they are welcome to it. But I do like to hear friends praying with the groaning which cannot be uttered, "Lord, send the Spirit! Send the Spirit, Lord! Work! Work! Work!" During sermon time it is what numbers of Churches should be doing, crying out to God in their hearts. As you walk the streets when you see sin you should pray, "Lord, put it down by Your Spirit!" And when you mark a struggling Brother striving to do good, you should cry, "Lord, help him! Help him by Your Spirit." I am persuaded we only need more prayer and there is no limit to the blessing! You may evangelize England, you may evangelize Europe, you may Christianize the world--if you do but know how to pray.

Prayer can get anything of God, prayer can get everything--God denies nothing to the man who knows how to ask. The Lord never shuts His storehouse till you shut your mouth! God will never stop His arm till you stop your tongue. Cry aloud and spare not! Give Him no rest till He sends forth His Spirit once again to stir the waters and to brood over this dark world till light and life shall come! Cry day and night, O you elect of God, for He will avenge you speedily. The time of battle draws near! Rome sharpens her sword for the fight! The men of error gnash their teeth in rage! Now for the sword of the Lord and of Gideon! Now for the old might and majesty of the ancient days! Now for the shaking of the walls of Jericho, even though we have no better weapons than rams' horns! Now for the driving out of the heathen, and for the establishment of God's Israel in the land! Now for the coming of the Holy Spirit with such might and power that as Noah's flood covered the mountaintops, Jehovah's flood of Glory shall cover the highest summits of sin and iniquity and the whole world over, the Lord God Omnipotent shall reign!

You who have not the Spirit pray for it. May He prompt you to pray this morning! Unconverted Sinners, may the Spirit give you faith! Remember that the Holy Spirit tells you to trust Christ. If you honor the Holy Spirit, trust Christ. I know you must be regenerate, for the man who trusts Christ is regenerate. You must repent, you must be holy, but the man who trusts Christ shall repent and shall be made holy. The germs of repentance and holiness are in him already. Trust Christ, Sinner! It is the Holy Spirit's mandate to you this morning. May He constrain you to trust Him and He shall have the Glory, world without end. Amen.

The Pierced One Pierces The Heart

DELIVERED ON SUNDAY MORNING, JUNE 19, 1864,
BY THE REV. C. H. SPURGEON,
AT THE METROPOLITAN TABERNACLE, NEWINGTON.

"And I will pour upon the house of Da vid and upon the inhabitants of Jerusalem, the spirit of Grace and of supplications: and they shall look upon Me whom they have pierced and they shall mourn for Him, as one mourns for his only son and shall be in bitterness for Him, as one that is in bitterness for his first-born." -- Zechariah 12:10.

THIS prophecy, first of all, refers to the Jewish people. And I am happy that it confirms our hearts in the belief of the good which the Lord will do unto Israel. We know of a surety, because God has said it, that the Jews will be restored to their own land and that they shall inherit the goodly country which the Lord has given unto their fathers by a Covenant of salt forever. But, better still, they shall be converted to the faith of our Lord Jesus Christ and shall see in Him the house of David restored to the throne of Israel. The day is coming when they shall see in Jesus of Nazareth, that Messiah for whom their saints looked with joyful expectation, of whom the Prophets spoke with rapture, but who was despised and rejected of their blinded sires.

Happy day! Happy day! When our Jewish Brethren shall all be found worshipping before the Lord of Hosts through their great High Priest, who is a Priest forever, after the order of Melchizedek! We must remember the prophecy concerning this thing. We must enquire of the Lord concerning His promise. We must expect its fulfillment, labor for it and then beyond a doubt, when the due season shall have arrived, Israel shall own her king and upon the house of David and the inhabitants of Jerusalem the Spirit of Grace and supplication shall be poured out.

We intend to hear our text, upon the present occasion, as it speaks to ourselves. A great mistake is very common among all classes of men--it is currently believed that we are, first of all, to mourn for our sins and then to look by faith to our Lord Jesus Christ. Most persons who have any concern about their souls but are not as yet enlightened by the Spirit of God think that there is a degree of tenderness of conscience and of hatred of sin which they are to obtain, somehow or other, and then they will be permitted and authorized to look to Jesus Christ. Now you will perceive that this is not according to the Scripture, for, according to the text before us men first look upon Him whom they have pierced and then, but not till then, they mourn for their sin!

This is the common folly of men--they look for the effect in order to produce the cause. They forget the old proverb and put the cart before the horse. But our text plainly indicates what is the cause, and puts it first, assuring us that the effect will follow. Repentance is in no sense a title to faith in Christ. It is, on the other hand, a legitimate consequence of faith. In certain diseases the surgeon aims at producing an outward eruption which carries off the internal poison and so assists in the cure. But no man would be justified in refraining from medical advice until he could see the eruption in his skin--that being a healthy sign, a prognostic of cure--a result of medicine, and by no means a preparation for it.

So repentance is the bringing into our own sight the sin which lurks within. It is a result of the medicine of faith. But we should be foolish, indeed, if we refused to believe until we saw in ourselves that repentance which only faith can produce! That repentance which is unattended by faith in the Lord Jesus is an evil repentance which works wrath and only sets the soul at a greater distance from God than it was before. Sweet, heart-melting, reconciling repentance brings the soul to love the Lord and to hope in His mercy--this precious gem always glitters on the hand of faith and nowhere else.

Without faith it is impossible to please God. And consequently an unbelieving repentance has nothing in it acceptable to God. Unbelieving repentance may be so deep as to drive us to hang ourselves, like Judas, but its only result would be to secure for us Judas's doom. Without faith, if our hearts could break--if our eyes could become perpetual fountains of tears--our repentance would in no way whatever be regarded by God except as a continuance of our sin. We would really be rejecting the Lord Jesus and setting up our own bitterness of soul in competition with the finished work of our Lord Jesus Christ. Let us be quite clear on this point, then, to start with, that it is not mourning for sin which causes or prepares the way for our looking to Christ.

It is our looking to Jesus which makes us weep and mourn for Him and works in us the sweet bitterness of true repentance. We will consider three points--first, what there is in a sight of the Pierced One to make us mourn. Secondly, what is the character of true mourning for sin. And thirdly, what is that which connects Jesus and this true mourning. The text tells us that looking does it all--"They shall look upon Me whom they have pierced and they shall mourn for Him."

I. WHAT IS THERE IN A SIGHT OF JESUS TO MAKE US MOURN FOR SIN? Let us not answer this question merely in a doctrinal fashion. But as we proceed let us pray that the Holy Spirit may bring our minds to feel the melting force of the great Sacrifice on Calvary so that we may bedew His Cross with tears of holy penitence. Come with me, Brethren, to Golgotha's terrible mount of doom that we may sit down and watch the death-pangs of the great Lover of men's souls. There on that transverse wood bleeds the Incarnate Son of God. His head yields ruby drops where the crown of thorns has pierced it.

His hands and feet flow with rivulets of blood. His back is all one wound. His face is marred with bruises and filthy with the spittle of the mockers. His hair has been plucked from His cheeks. His eyes are bloodshot. His lips are parched with fever. His whole body is a mass of concentrated agony. He hangs yonder in physical pain impossible to be fully described, while the misery of His soul, crushed beneath the wheels of the chariot of Justice, constitutes a woe far more terrible. His soul is exceedingly sorrowful, even unto death, while His body is as a cup full to the brim with grief--what if I say a sponge saturated with infinite miseries?

While Jesus bleeds on yonder tree, our hearts bleed, too. If we have tears at any time, let us shed them now, for now or never must we weep. The first cause for deep sorrow lies in the excellency of the Sufferer's Person. He who hangs there is no other than that Son of God before whom angels veil their faces with their wings. He is Lord of Heaven and earth-- concerning Him the Father said of old, "Let all the angels of God worship Him." At His behests the cherubim and seraphim fly to the utmost verge of space, glad to be the messengers of His good pleasure. He is the Light and Brightness of Heaven, the express Image of his Father's Glory.

"Without Him was not anything made that was made," and by Him all things consist. And yet the King of Heaven lays aside His crown, strips Himself of His purple, takes off His golden rings, becomes an Infant of a span long and after a life of suffering yields Himself to a slave's death upon the wretched gibbet of the Cross! My Soul, do you not sorrow that so Divine a Person should sink so low? Think of the purity of His Character as Man! In Him was never any sin and yet He suffers! His whole life was spent in doing good. Unselfishly He spared not Himself.

And now men do not spare Him their worst cruelty! He gives food to the hungry, health to the sick, life to the dead. He has not time for Himself so much as to eat bread. He shuns no labor for the good of others. He seeks no ease for Himself. And yet the men whom He would bless conspire to curse Him! He lives a life of perfect holiness, in no way causing any to offend. His life is the pure light of the sun of love, it has no darkness whatever in it. His acts are as a river flowing with crystal streams of loving kindness, untainted by selfishness or ambition. And yet He bleeds! Heaven's brightest Jewel is cast into the mire--earth's purest Gold is trod in the streets. He who is of Heaven the Sun, suffers an eclipse! He who is of earth the brightest Star, is hidden beneath black clouds.

O You Immaculate Man, shall I see You bleed without compassion? O You Almighty God, shall I see You Incarnate in the flesh, suffering throes and pangs unworthy of Your Godhead, without feeling the commiseration of my soul stirred towards You? Can we, Brethren, think of the beauty of our Lord without being filled with bitterness of soul for Him? Shall those eyes which are as the eyes of doves by the rivers of waters, which once were washed with milk, now be drowned in tears of blood? His cheeks, which are as a bed of spices, as sweet flowers--shall these be given to them that pluck off the hair? Those hands which are set with jewels, shall they be pierced? Shall His legs, which are as pillars of marble set upon sockets of fine gold become all bespattered with the stream of His heart's gore?

Oh, here is sorrow if you will! That precious casket of His body, so rich that Heaven's treasures and earth's wealth together could not furnish such another! That dear case of jewels is cast out as an unclean thing and made a Victim without the camp! O, who will give me tears? I weep, I must weep for my sins!--

"My sins, my hateful, cruel sins, His chief tormentors were! Each of my crimes became a nail, And unbelief the spear. 'Twas you that pulled the vengeance down, Upon his guiltless head, Break, break my heart! O burst my eyes, And let my sorrows bleed."

All human eyes, if they were forever full of tears, could not express the woe that One so glorious, so pure, so loving, so condescending, should in His own world find no shelter, and among His own creatures find no friends! But contrariwise, in this world be racked upon the Cross and among His creatures meet His murderers! This should make us mourn bitterly for sin.

Look up again, my Soul, and perhaps another word may help to melt you, stubborn though you are. Let us remind ourselves of His sufferings. Remember Gethsemane? In that garden His soul is exceedingly sorrowful. Though He is not in labor, but simply in the exercise of prayer, a sweat comes streaming from every pore--not the common sweat of men who toil, but, O God, it is a sweat of blood! "He sweat, as it were, great drops of blood falling down to the ground." The pains of Hell alone can furnish a fit parallel for the awful misery of Christ that night. And perhaps even there such sufferings were never sustained as Christ endured in the garden! Betrayed by His chosen friend, He is hurried away to the Sanhedrim and there accused of blasphemy.

Oh, cruel charge against the Son of the Highest! Then He is dragged away to Pilate and then away to Herod, to be slandered before both tribunals. Meanwhile, they scourge His back with the scourge, the very thought of which is enough to make a man shudder--it is said to have been made of the sinews of oxen intertwisted with pieces of sharp and ragged bone--so that every blow tore through the flesh to the very bone. He is scourged thus and then beaten with rods. He is set upon a mimic throne and crowned with thorns. They spit in His face. They insult His Person. They bow the knee and say, "Hail, King of the Jews." They buffet Him with their hands. Shame never descended to a lower depth--mockery could devise nothing worse than that crown of thorns and that reed scepter.

Away they hound Him, tearing off the purple robe which must have glued itself to His bleeding flesh--they roughly tear it away. And then they put on His own garments and hasten Him to the malefactor's Tyburn. Rudely they strip Him. Cruelly they fling Him down. Savagely they pierce His hands and His feet. They lift up His Cross and dislocate His every bone with the jar given to it, as it is fastened in the earth. They sit down to look at Him in derision and gloat over His pains. The weight of the body tears the nails through His hands and when the weight falls upon His feet, the nails force themselves in long wounds through the nerves of His blessed feet!

Fever is brought on by His fearful wounds. He is faint with pain. His mouth is dried like an oven. In His extremity, He cries, "I thirst!" They thrust vinegar into His mouth--that is the only comfort they will render Him--vinegar mingled with gall! The hot sun scorches Him until He cries, "All My bones are out of joint: My heart is like wax. It is melted in the midst of My bowels. My strength is dried up like a potsherd. And My tongue cleaves to My jaws. And You have brought Me into the dust of death."

Even the light is denied Him. He hangs shivering in midday-midnight. The thick darkness did but express the darkness which might be felt which covered all His soul. His agonies had become so intense that they must not be beheld by any onlooker. The darkness, therefore, formed as it were, a secret chamber wherein Christ might do battle with His direst griefs. Griefs like Himself, immense, unknown. Godlike sorrows now hold fast the Son of God--only His Deity enabled Him to sustain the struggle. The storm passes and at last, shouting, "It is finished," with bowed head, He gives up the ghost.

Have we no tears for such sorrows as these? Shall we have no mourning for such griefs? How is it that if we read the story of a common man, suffering by his own folly, we freely weep? And over the silly story of a love-sick maid we will feel our pity stirred? But here on Calvary, where the King of Heaven is tortured with unutterable woe, tormented with sorrows so tremendous that they overtop all other griefs as a mountain exceeds the molehills, we are like flints or steel and scarcely feel compassion move? O God, pour out upon us the spirit of grief and commiseration, that we may mourn for Him--

"Strike, mighty Grace, my flinty soul, Till melting waters flow, And deep repentance drowns my eyes In agonizing woe."

Perhaps we have not come to the very center of heart-breaking thought. The wonder is that Jesus Christ should suffer thus as the result of sin--of our sin. A young man ran away from home and left his aged mother that he might plunge into sin--after a few shameful years he came back to his country and sought his home. When he knocked at the cottage door he asked for his mother, but she was not there. "What name did you say, Sir? She died years ago." "And how did she die?" Well, they say she had a son who treated her with cruelty and at last left her to indulge his own evil passions. She could not bear it, for she loved him much. She sickened and no one could comfort her. She died, they say, of a broken heart. And that is her grave over the hedge yonder in the Churchyard."

Well might the sinner turn away with reeling brain and wish himself under the turf at her side. "I slew my mother by my sins." If he weeps not at this he must be a devil, indeed. Jesus Christ, my Lord, hangs on that tree slain by my sins-- shall I not sorrow now? Had I never sinned, there had been no need of a Savior for me. Had we never rebelled against God, there would have been no sword of vengeance to plunge into His heart--

"Was it for crimes that I had done He groaned upon the tree?"

This is sad, indeed. Can you get the thought, my dear Friends, that you made Christ die--yes, you--if there were no other man. You could not, if there had been only you to save--you could not enter Heaven without the dying groans of that Savior. There must be an Atonement made no less than His great Sacrifice for you and you alone. Therefore take the whole of it to yourself, and now, will you not sorrow at the sight of the pierced Savior?

Let us remember, too, as we continue at the foot of the Cross, that Jesus Christ does not merely suffer for sin but He suffers FOR YOU. I do not know, but perhaps this may be the heart-breaker with some who never did repent of sin before. O you who look to Him believingly, Jesus Christ loves your poor guilty soul at such a rate that He suffers all this for you! I pray you as you look to Him dying upon the Cross, forget not that every drop yonder flows for you. How could you have despised Him who died for you! Determined to save you He went down to the very lowest depths to bring you up and yet you have heard the Gospel and neglected it! You have lived all these years in sin! You have been day after day a neglector of the Word of God, perhaps a Sunday-breaker! It may be a swearer, using this very name of Christ to curse by and yet He suffered this for you.

O believing Sinner, for you these wounds, for you that sweat of gore, for you that Cross, for you that spear, for you that mangled frame lying in the tomb motionless in the grasp of death! Will not this make you feel that you cannot any longer harbor the lusts which are the enemies of Christ, but that you must cast out, once and for all from your soul, these cruel foes which made the Savior bleed? While I am talking upon this theme, I feel more than at any other time in my own life my own insufficiency. I cry as Elijah did, "Woe is me! For I am undone, because I am a man of unclean lips and I dwell in the midst of a people of unclean lips!"

O, it needs an angel's tongue to tell out a Savior's grief! Yes, even a seraph might fail. It needs the Savior Himself to tell you in worthy words how He suffered and what was the love which led Him through the woe. Surely the Cross makes sin hateful when we see it by the light of the Spirit of all Truth. One more remark here upon this first point. It should make us mourn for sin when we think that this suffering of Christ for us can be attributed to nothing else than His own marvelous love towards us who were so undeserving. What could have brought Christ from on high except motives of pure affection? Can you conjecture any other cause? Did He want Glory?

My Brothers and Sisters, was not the Glory of Heaven enough for Him? Besides, if it could have been possible for Him to need Glory, is He not Omnipotent? Could He not, in a moment, have created ten thousand thousand worlds filled with inhabitants all too glad to be permitted to sing His praise? Could He gain anything, let me ask you, by coming here below? And was there anything in you or me to merit what He did? Far, far away be the accursed thought of my merit! But even if we could merit anything, could we merit this Sacrifice? Could we merit that bloody sweat? O Virtue, you could never merit this! No, heroism at its highest point and self-sacrifice sublime to its most exalted degree could never merit that the Son of God should die!

Sin accomplished what Virtue could not. Sin brings the Savior from on high--Virtue never could have procured this. Ah, Brethren, the love of Jesus must have been a strange love, indeed. We have heard of men who out of love to some poor countrywoman have left their kingdom and their throne to follow her poverty and lift her up ultimately to their wealth. But who ever heard of the equal of this? That God's own Son, "though He was rich, yet for our sakes He became poor, that through His poverty we might be made rich"? Worms were never raised so high above their meanest fellow worms and therefore they could never stoop as Christ did! If an angel could die for ants, that would look like condescension--but for Christ to die for men is more wondrous by far!

If the noblest cherubim before the Throne should shed his heart's blood for a poor insect, you would think it marvelous! But for God Himself to take a creature's form, to bleed for such insignificant, despicable, worthless things as men-- this is a wonder which has set Heaven ringing ever since it was known and will make eternity echo with shouts of praise. Surely, dear Friends, if nothing else can make us loathe sin and weep before God, this should do so. And yet, I confess, I spoil the theme. When Mark Anthony brings out the body of Julius Caesar, he excites the sympathies of the Roman people by the sight of the mantle of the murdered man.

He makes them weep and then he cries, "What? Do you weep when you but behold your Caesar's vesture wounded! Look you here--here is himself--marred, as you see, by traitors." Such speech puts tongues into the silent stones of Rome! Whereas, alas, I, poor worthless creature as I am, talk of my Master, stabbed by ourselves, bleeding out of love to us, at so poor a rate that I cannot stir your souls, nor scarce my own! Almighty Spirit, well is it written that You will come to give the spirit of supplication, for except You shall come, we shall neither look to Christ, nor weep, nor mourn because of Him!

II. Secondly WE ARE TO SPEAK UPON WHAT TRUE MOURNING FOR SIN IS. It is not necessarily feeling great terrors nor frightful tears. There is no need that you should doubt the mercy of God--all these things may come with repentance, as smoke attends fire, but they are not a part of it. They often spoil repentance--they cannot make it more acceptable.

1. True mourning for sin is the work of the Spirit of God. There is no mourning until first the Spirit is poured out. Then men look and then they mourn. Repentance is too choice a flower to grow in Nature's garden. If you have one sigh after Christ--if you have one particle of hatred of sin--God the Holy Spirit must have given it to you, for poor human nature with its utmost strain can never reach to a spiritual thing. "That which is born of the flesh is flesh. And that which is born of the Spirit is spirit." True repentance, then, must come from on high. Lord, send it to us now!

2. True repentance has a distinct and constant reference to the Lord Jesus Christ. If you repent of sin without looking to Christ, away with your repentance! If you are so lamenting your sin as to forget the Savior, you have need to begin all this work over again. Whenever we repent of sin we must have one eye upon sin and another upon the Cross. Or, better still, let us have both eyes upon Christ, seeing our sin punished in Him and by no means let us look at sin except as we look at Jesus. A man may hate sin just as a murderer hates the gallows--but this does not prove repentance. If I hate sin because of the punishment, I have not repented of sin--I merely regret that God is just.

But if I can see sin as an offense against Jesus Christ and loathe myself because I have wounded Him, then I have a true brokenness of heart. If I see the Savior and believe that those thorns upon His head were plaited by my sinful words. If I believe that those wounds in His heart were pierced by my heart sins. If I believe that those wounds in His feet were made by my wandering steps and that the wounds in His hands were made by my sinful deeds--then I repent of sin after a right fashion. Only under the Cross can you repent. Repentance elsewhere is remorse which clings to the sin and only dreads the punishment. Let us then seek, under God, to have a hatred of sin caused by a sight of Christ's love.

3. True repentance is real and often intense in its bitterness. The text tells us it is a sorrow like that of one who weeps for his only son. A son is a gift from God. A good son, especially, is a treasure to his father's heart. But here is a dead son before me--I think I hear the father's cries, "O my son Absalom, my son, my son Absalom! Would God I had died for you, O Absalom, my son, my son!" Here I see an only son, which was not David's case, for he had Solomon yet spared to him.

I think I see the woman at the gate of Nain with her only son carried out to be buried, making much lamentation, with grievous pomp of heartfelt woe. Yes, and it is not only that, it is the first-born son, the beginning of the father's strength. And the man who has watched him and seen himself in his first-born's growing form, will not be comforted because his son--his only son, his first-born son is dead. Such is true weeping for sin--it cuts to the heart--it pierces to the quick.

"Oh," says one, "I cannot believe in Christ, for I have no such bitterness." My dear Friend, you never will have it till you believe in Christ! You are to trust in Jesus Christ to get this! You are not to feel this and then trust in Christ. Come, you hard Heart, come to Christ to be softened. Come, you Hell-hardened Steel, come to Christ to be melted in the furnace of His Divine affection. Come as you are, Sinner, feeling or unfeeling and look up to Jesus! There is life in a look at Him and life for you now. And the first sign of life will be a real and intense sorrow for sin.

4. True sorrow for sin is eminently practical. No man may say he hates sin if he lives in it. It will make us see the evil of sin, not merely as a theory, but experimentally--as a burnt child dreads fire. We shall be as much afraid of it as a man who has lately been stopped and robbed is afraid of the thief upon the highway. And we shall shun it--shun it in every-thing--not in great things only, but in little things, too. True mourning for sin will make us very jealous over our tongue lest it should say a wrong word. We shall be very watchful over our daily actions lest in anything we should offend. And each night we shall close the day with painful confessions of shortcoming and each morning awaken with anxious prayers, that this next day God would hold us up that we might be saved.

5. Once again, true repentance is continual--a man does not repent for a few weeks and then have done with it. Rowland Hill said that repentance was one of the sweetest earthly companions. And the only regret he had in the thought of going to Heaven was that his dear friend, Repentance, could not go with him there. Repentance is the most heavenly thing out of Heaven. Well did our hymn say--

"Lord, let me weep for nothing but sin! And after none but You! And then I would-- O that I might-- A constant weeper be!"

True Believers repent to their dying day--they are always repenting. Their life is made up, it is said, of sinning and repenting--I will not say that--believing and repenting is their life--and sin is the disease which mars it. No time can wear away the bitterness of repentance. If a man loses his child, time happily softens his grief. Every other trouble yields to time, but this never does. It is so sweet a sorrow that we can only thank God we are permitted to enjoy and to suffer it until we enter into our eternal rest.

This, then, is true sorrow for sin. But let me say, whatever is or is not true sorrow for sin, I do entreat my hearers not to try and get sorrow for sin before they come to Christ. The Gospel is, "He that BELIEVES in Jesus is not condemned." Whether you have sorrowed enough for sin or not, if you trust Jesus Christ, you are not condemned. Your salvation is not procured by your tears, nor by your feelings, but by Him whom you have pierced! Look to Him, away from self. Look not even to your own faith, but look to the Object of your faith. Now fixedly behold Him and trust Him and your heart will break and be poured out like water before the Lord.

III. WHAT IS THAT WHICH CONNECTS JESUS CHRIST AND THE MOURNING? How am I to get at Christ?

This used to puzzle me. I thought if I could walk a thousand miles to see Him, I would set off joyously. Oh, if I could but fall at His feet and lay hold of Him! I thought this would be very easy--touching the hem of His garment--or crying, "God be merciful to me!" But this thought long puzzled me--"How can I get to Christ?" So many fleshly notions mix themselves with our thoughts before we are born again that we are very much like poor Nicodemus and say, "Can a man enter his mother's womb a second time, and be born again?"

We have gross and carnal thoughts concerning spiritual things. Now, our connection with Jesus is a look, not with these eyes, of course, but with the eyes of the heart. We all know what it is to look at a thing. We are told to look at a certain subject in politics or science--we are told to look into it. There is nothing to see with your eyes, but you see into it with your mind. And this is the kind of look which is intended here, "They shall look upon Me whom they have pierced."

You cannot, with all your looking, see Christ with these eyes! But thinking of Him and believing in Him is the look which is meant. In describing this look, let me say that it is very simple. Why, looking is not a hard thing! I never heard of a college for training people to look. I never in my life heard of anyone trying to teach another person to look! There may be a defect in people's eyes, but still if they have any eyes at all, they may look. They may happen to have cross eyes, but a crossed-eyed look at Christ will save the soul. They may have a waterfall in the eye, so that there is scarcely a corner left, but it is not looking with a full eye, it is not looking with a bold eye--it is the looking in any way--the simple act of looking which saves a soul.

A man may not be able to read a single letter in a book, but he can look to Jesus. A man may not be able to spell a word of one syllable, but he can look. A man may have no moral courage, but he can look. He may be destitute of all the virtues and yet he can look. A man may be a thief, a whoremonger, an adulterer, but he can look. A man may be cast out of society, transported, shut up between stone walls, but he can look. Looking is a thing so simple that neither moral nor physical preparations are required. Looking! Such is faith in Jesus Christ. As the sin-bitten ones looked to the brazen serpent so do we look away from self to Christ and we live!

Observe, secondly, as it is a simple look so it is a look which requires no merit in order to precede it. We have an old proverb, to wit, "a cat may look at a king," and certainly a poor man may. There is no hurt done by looking. If the queen were here, I should not ask her leave to let me look. And if there were a crossing sweeper, or a mud-lark, or even a pickpocket here, he certainly would commit no offense by looking. On the other hand, there would be no merit in looking. Where is the merit of looking at a thing? It is too simple either to need merit before it or to have merit in it.

So you who are the worst of the worst! You who feel nothing in yourself which is good! You who can not even say that you feel your own emptiness and vileness--nothing of your own is needed to precede that look by way of preparation. Look, look to Jesus as you are, and you shall be saved! The look which saves the soul, again, should be an attentive look. If you have looked to Christ and cannot see anything there to comfort you, look again! Look again! Perhaps each man is comforted in a different way by looking to Christ. One sees Christ to be God and he says, "Ah, then, He can save me." Another dwells mainly upon Christ's being Man and he says, "Ah, then, He can pity me and be willing to receive me."

One fixes his eyes upon God's having appointed Christ to save him--that comforts him. Another remembers the infinite value of Christ's sufferings and that cheers him. If one point in Christ does not comfort you, look to another. Keep your mental eyes fixed upon what Jesus Christ is. Ah, my dear Friends, I am telling you this, but how difficult it is to make you do it until the Holy Spirit brings you! Why the first thing I get from any of you when I talk to you about your souls is, "O Sir, I do not feel." I know then that you are looking to self. O my dear Hearers, you who have some concern about your souls, I would beseech my God to wean you from this which must damn your souls--this looking to SELF!

Come, I pray you, consider! You are too vile, too sinful ever to have anything good in you to look at! Why will you search for goodness where there is none? "Why do you spend money for that which is not bread? And labor for that which satisfies not? Hearken diligently unto Me and eat that which is good and let your soul delight itself in fatness." You can do so if you look at the Cross! I know you will raise your "buts," or cry, "But I cannot believe." There you are, looking to your faith instead of Christ. There He hangs! He bears upon His shoulders the sin of man and whoever trusts Him shall be saved. Can you not trust Him? Not trust your God? Can you not trust Him, your Brother born to bear your adversities? Not trust GOD? Why I protest before you all if I had all your sins upon my shoulders, I could trust Him!

When John Hyatt lay a-dying, someone said to him, "Can you trust Jesus with your soul now?" "Ah," said he, "I could trust Him if I had a million souls! I could trust Him with them all." Do not tell me, awakened Souls, you cannot trust your Master! When did He ever lie to you? Whom did He ever cast out? When did He break His promise? Who ever came to Him and was rejected? When did He say to the chief of sinners, "Your sins shall never be forgiven"? Thousands have been to Him and He has received them.

I sought the Lord and He heard me. I tried to save myself by feelings of repentance and praying, but it was all of no avail. At last, in sheer despair, I flew like a dove pursued by the hawk straight away to Jesus Christ, the Rock, and found shelter in His wounds. O that you would do so! Come, I pray you, have done with that self of yours--

"None but Jesus, none but Jesus Can do helpless sinners good."

This look is sometimes a wondering look--I know it was to me. When I saw Him hanging on the Cross for me, I could not understand such love, and I cannot fathom it now. I can understand some of the things which Christ has done for me. But I cannot make out why He should die for me--why He should love such a heap of filth, such a walking dunghill as man is! Why He should give His blood--every drop of which is more costly than rubies! Why He should give His tears, which are richer than diamonds! Why He should give His heart, which is better than a mine of gold! Why He should close those lips which are sweeter than harps of angels and shut those eyes, which are brighter than so many suns--and all for such a clod of earth, such a rebellious piece of rottenness as man! Oh, this is marvelous! How can we understand it? We can only fall down before His feet and while we trust Him add to our faith a holy adoring wonder!

This look must, in every case, be a personal one. You cannot be saved by another man's faith. I do beseech of all to whom this word shall come--detest, loathe, abominate the lie that any man can perform spiritual acts for another! No "sponsor" can promise to renounce the works of the flesh for another! No man can stand at the font and declare that he believes for another! No man can promise that an unconscious slumbering baby shall believe in God. No man can say in God's name what he knows is a lie--that the child does believe--when it cannot believe and probably is asleep at the time and not occupied with any mental operation, much less believing what it never heard and what it could not understand if it did hear!

O, I pray you, shun this blasphemy! The curse of England has been this dogma of baptismal regeneration, for it leads men to shake off their personal responsibility and obligations to God. Your godfathers and godmothers, your confirmation, your priests and rural deans and canons and I know not what of man's invention, can do no more for you than so many witches with their incantations. You must flee to Christ yourselves and by simple faith lay hold on Jesus! All this frippery and nonsense of man's invention must be pulled down! O for a rough hand to pull it down, to let the sinner see that he stands before God, naked and defenseless, except as he flees to Christ, and in the passion and life of Jesus, finds salvation!

A personal faith it must be and what if I urge you to let it be an immediate faith? It will be no easier to flee tomorrow than it is today. It is the same thing that you will have to believe tomorrow as it is today--that Jesus Christ gave Himself for your sins. This is God's testimony, that Christ is able to save. O that you would trust Him! My Soul, you have regretted a thousand things, but you have never regretted trusting Christ in your youth! Many have wept that they did not come to Christ before, but none ever lamented that they came too early. Why not this very day? O Holy Spirit, make it so! Behold, the fields are showing the green ears ready for the harvest! The season advances and the fields are prophesying the harvest. O that we might see some green ears today, some green ears prophetic of a blessed harvest of souls!

As to myself, I cross this day into another year of my own life and history and I bear witness that my Master is worth trusting! Oh, it is a blessed thing to be a Christian! It is a sweet thing to be a Believer in Christ and though I, of all men, perhaps, am the subject of the deepest depression of spirits at times, yet there lives not a soul who can say more truthfully than I, "My soul does magnify the Lord and my spirit has rejoiced in God my Savior." He who is mighty has looked upon me with eyes of love and made me His child and I trust Him this day as I have trusted Him before.

But now I would to God that this day some of you would begin to trust in Him! It is the Spirit's work only, but still, He works through means. I think He is working in your heart now. Young Man, those tears look hopeful--I thank God that those eyes feel burning now. I pray you do not go chatting on the road home and miss any good impression. Go to your chamber, fall upon your knees, cry out to God, entreat His favor! This day let it be! None of the devil's tomorrows--away with them! Away with them!

"Today if you will hear His voice, harden not your heart." May the Spirit of God constrain you to "Kiss the Son, lest He be angry and you perish from the Way, when His wrath is kindled but a little. Blessed are all they that put their trust in Him." Amen.

Quiet Musing!

A SERMON DELIVERED
BY THE REV. C. H. SPURGEON,
AT THE METROPOLITAN TABERNACLE, NEWINGTON.

"While I was musing the fire burned." -- Psalm 39:3.

OUR subject this evening will not stand in need of much preface. The Psalm may teach us that there are times when solitude is better than society and silence is wiser than speech. The company of sinners was a grief to David's soul and because their converse was profane he chose, rather, to fly away from their midst--or if they must still continue in his presence, he determined that he would resolutely seal his lips. Touchingly he says, "I was dumb with silence (that is, utterly dumb), I held my peace, even from good." This painful necessity soon proved to him a pleasing occasion. While he yielded himself up to the thoughts, the reveries and the pensive workings of his own heart, a sacred fire of devotion was kindled in his breast.

And, Brethren, whatever the circumstances of the Psalmist, you will all see that the exercise was profitable. And however peculiar the advantages of meditation at particular seasons, it may not be amiss for us to make it a common habit. Inverting a popular proverb, "What was one man's medicine may be food for others," there is much that is light and frothy in our ordinary communion. And our communications, one with another, soon grow frothy and insipid when we have no definite matter in hand. Whether, therefore, to free ourselves from the stress of business, or to escape from the temptations of idleness, let it be thought worthy of note that "musing" has sweet charms and calm reflection is capable of kindling a bright fire.

Our remarks will now run in two directions. First, we shall say something in praise of musing. And then, secondly, we shall supply you with some fuel to burn on the altar of your hearts.

I. First, then, LET US SAY SOMETHING IN PRAISE OF MUSING. We do not muse much in these days of ours. We are too busy. We are hurrying here and there, doing much and talking much, but thinking very little and spending but very little time, indeed, in the modesty of retirement--

"The calm retreat, the silent shade," are things which we know very little about. We would be better men if we were more alone. And I suppose that we should do more good, after all, if with even less of active effort we spent more time in waiting upon God and gathering spiritual strength for labor in His service. Where lives there upon earth, in these days, a man who spends hour after hour of the day in meditation upon God? There may be such and if there is I wish that I had their acquaintance.

Where will you find giants such as those who lived in the Puritanical times, whose lips dropped pearls because they themselves had dived down deep in the fathomless ocean of mercy by the sweet aid of meditation? There may be such and I wish that it were our lot to sit under their ministry. But I fear that the most of us are so little in retirement--so seldom in communion with God in private and even when there, the communion is for so short a time--that we are but tiny dwarfs, and can never, while we live thus, attain to the stature of a perfect man in Christ Jesus.

The world has put a little letter before the word "musing," and these are the days, not for musing, but for amusing. People will go anywhere for amusement. To muse is a strange thing to them and they think it dull and wearisome. Our good sires loved the quiet hour and loved it so well that they cherished those times which they could spend in musing as the most happy because they were the most peaceful seasons of their life. We drag such time off to execution in a moment and only ask men to tell us how we may kill it.

Now there is much virtue in musing, especially if we muse upon the best, the highest and the noblest of subjects. If we muse upon the things of which we hear and read in sacred Scripture, we shall do wisely. It is well to muse upon the things of God because we thus get the real nutriment out of them. A man who hears many sermons is not necessarily well-instructed in the faith. We may read so many religious books that we overload our brains and they may be unable to work under the weight of the great mass of paper and of printer's ink. The man who reads but one book and that book his Bible, and then muses much upon it, will be a better scholar in Christ's school than he who merely reads hundreds of books and muses not at all.

And he, too, who gets but one sermon in a day, though it is an ill habit to stay away from half our Sunday engagements and only go out once, yet, he who hears but one sermon in a day, if he meditates much upon it, will get far more out of it than he who hears two or three but meditates not! The Truth of God is something like the cluster of the vine--if you would have wine from it, you must bruise it--you must press and squeeze it many times. The bruisers' feet must come down joyfully upon the bunches or else the juice will not flow. And they must leap and leap and leap again, and well tread the grapes, or else much of the precious liquid will be wasted.

You must, by the feet of meditation, tread the clusters of Truth if you would get the wine of consolation from them. Our bodies are not supported by merely taking food into the mouth--the process which really supplies the muscle and the nerve and the sinew and the bone is the process of digestion. It is by digestion that the outward food becomes assimilated with inner life. And so is it with our souls. They are not nourished merely by what we hear by going here and there and listening awhile to this and then to that and then to the other.

Hearing, leading, marking and learning all require inward digesting. And the inward digesting of the Truth of God lies in the meditating upon it. Ruminating creatures chew the cud and these have always been considered clean animals. And so it is a mark of a true child of God that he understands how to chew the cud of meditation. Why is it that some people are always in a place of worship and yet they are not holy though they make some slight advances in the Divine life? It is because they neglect their closets. They love the wheat, but they do not grind it. They would have the corn, but they will not go forth into the fields to gather it.

The fruit hangs upon the tree, but they will not pluck it. The water flows at their feet, but they will not stoop to drink it. They are either too idle, or too busy--I will not say which--but often to be busy is to be idle. And when some men think us idle, we are then best at work. You who know anything of the Divine life know very well what I mean by that. Meditation is not idleness and retirement is not forsaking the good of the world. I suppose that Moses did as much for Israel on the mountain's summit with uplifted hands as ever Joshua did in the valley with his drawn sword. And Elijah upon the top of Carmel, yes, even by the brook Cherith, or in the house of the widow of Zarephath was as much serving Israel as when he smote the priests of Baal and hewed them in pieces before the Lord. I commend meditation to you, then, for fetching the nutriment out of the Truth of God.

Another note in the praise of this most blessed, but much-neglected duty is that it fixes the Truth upon the memory. You complain of short memories--you say that what you have heard you can scarcely remember to another day. If your paint is thin and you can not make your picture stand out in glowing colors, lay on many coats of your paint and so will you do what you want. If your memory will not retain the Truth the first time, then think it over and over and over again and so, by having these several coats of paint, as it were, the whole matter shall abide.

When the fly fisherman goes out to fish, it may be that in mid-stream he sees a great fish and having cast his fly, the hook is soon fairly in the fish's jaws. But what now? Why, he must let him run out the line and then he must drag him back again! And after all that he never thinks his fish safely his own till he gets him into the net. Well, now, hearing sermons is, as it were, getting the hook into the fish's mouth and meditation is the landing-net--it is this which gets the thing to shore!

And what if I say that after that the same meditation becomes a fire of coals upon which the fish is broiled and prepared for our spiritual food? If you cannot hold a thing well, try and get many hooks to hold it with and meditation will supply you, as it were, with a hundred hands--every one of which you may grasp the Truth of God. I am sure, dear Friends, that we give not earnest heed enough to these things, or else we should not let them slip. There are many photographers who can take a street view more rapidly than I can speak of it. They have but just to lift up the cover and put it down again and the whole thing is done.

But the same photographer, if he wishes for many things which are to endure and last, he likes, if he has time, to have the object long before the camera. And there it stands and fairly fixes itself upon the plate. And surely, there may be some few men who can just hear a sermon and retain the impression of it all their days. There are some who are quick of understanding in the things of God and as with a flash they get the Truth and never lose it. But the most of us need more than this. If we would have the Truth photographed upon our hearts we must keep it long before the spiritual lens or else it never will fix itself there.

Complain not, then, of your memory! Complain of yourself if you are not given to meditation. If your memory is frail let your closet rebuke you because you have not been there more often. Whereas another man may do with less meditation, if you say your memory is weak, the more reason why you should be a longer time and more often with your God in secret. All need this, but you need it more than others. See to it, then, that you neglect not this duty. For getting the nourishment out of Truth and moreover, for preserving, for salting down the Truth for future use, employ much meditation. Meditation clips the wings of thoughts which otherwise would fly away at the first clapping of the world's hands. You shall thus keep your prey, as it were, surrounded and entangled in a net or else it might escape you. Your meditation shall hold it fast until you need it.

Yet further, meditation is of great value in opening up the Truth of God and leading us into its secrets. There is some gold to be found on the surface of this land of Ophir, the Book of God. There are some precious jewels which may be discovered even by the wayfaring man--but the mass of the gold is hidden in the heart of the earth. And he who would be rich in these treasures must dig into Scripture as one who seeks for choice pearls. You must go down into its depths and you must rummage there until you get at last at the treasure.

Truth is sometimes like a flint, which, when it is struck the first time yields not, and you may even strike it yet again and still it yields not. But at last, one happy blow of the hammer shall make it fly to shivers. Meditation may be compared for its potency to the great battering ram which Sir Christopher Wren used when he built the present St. Paul's Cathedral. Old St. Paul's, you remember, had been destroyed by fire, but its walls were so extremely thick that it was found very difficult to take the old walls away.

And they were so lofty that there was also great danger to the workmen. Sir Christopher therefore invented a ram composed of a large piece of timber and intended to be used in the same way as the Romans used their rams of old. A number of men were set to work with this ram and of course, being a new instrument to them, they did not like it and they did not believe in it, either.

After hammering away some five or six hours and the wall showing no sign, whatever, of anything like an impression, they complained to Sir Christopher that he had given them a useless work to do. He set them at it again and the ram fell heavily but not a stone seemed to stir. One whole day they kept on thus, battering away at the walls. The architect knew full well that although it might not be palpable to the laborers, there must have been a degree of oscillation given to the whole structure. And so it proved, for the next morning when they began the work again, all of a sudden down tumbled the whole mass! Thus at length the men were convinced that the work of the day before had not been lost--it really had been telling when they could not chalk down the progress.

You will find it the same with Gospel doctrine that you want to understand but cannot. There is some difficulty you cannot surmount. Meditation comes and gives one stroke after another with all the weight of prayer and of thoughtful-ness, but it stirs not. But at last our diligence is rewarded and we see the whole mass of masonry which reason had piled together of fabulous traditions comes tumbling down. The foundation is discovered and the Truth of God made clear to our apprehension in a moment.

What? Do you think that the great thoughts of masterminds come in a minute? People say, "Oh, what a genius!" Nonsense! The man had been hard at work over that for years and years, and years--though perhaps the thing came at last to him suddenly. It was not a whit less a result of study--the success which crowns the patient brainwork of a meditative mind. Never despair, dear Friends, of understanding the Truth. If you will, in the name of Jesus, give your souls to the study and come resolved to sit at Christ's feet as Mary did--to believe just what He tells you, as He tells it to you though He may reveal dark things and speak of them to you in parables--you shall be able to comprehend with all saints what are the heights and depths, and you shall yet know the love of Christ which passes knowledge.

Be not weary of well-thinking! Use much diligence in musing! Yield up your heart to sacred meditation. Turn the matter over and over and over again in your minds. You remember the story of the great philosopher who had been attempting to discover how much alloy there was in the king's crown but who could find no way of doing it. By day and by night he pondered it. No, at night when he slept, his daydreams did but come to him again! But all of a sudden, when he was in bed, he sprang up and wrapped his garments about him and ran through the street, crying out, "Inveni, Inveni," I have found it! I have found it!"

And one of these days, Christian, when you are puzzling over some doctrine which you feel must be true but which you cannot grasp, you will spring upon your feet when God the Holy Spirit has revealed the Truth to you and you will cry, "I have found it! I have found it!" And great will be your joy at the discovery! Cultivate much, then, the habit of retirement and meditation because of the way in which it opens up the Truth of God. Here, almost unwittingly, I have touched upon another suggestion. This musing is a charmed exercise, for, mark you, the joy which it brings.

There is a text in Scripture which speaks of the sinner as rolling sin under his tongue as a sweet morsel, an allusion to the habit of the man, who, when he gets a dainty thing, swallows it not at once but rolls it under his tongue, trying to draw out more and more of its sweetness. Well, now, this is what the Christian should do with doctrinal Truth--he should roll it under his tongue! You will have far more enjoyment while it is in your mouth than you will afterwards, so keep it there! Meditate much upon it--roll it under your tongue again and again and again--until you get more to find its savor.

Scripture is often like a bone, but meditation is the hammer which cracks it and then the soul gets the marrow and the fatness. The beauties of Christ are not to be seen by the passerby who merely glances at Him. There is something to arrest attention at a glance, it is true, but he who would see the beauties of Jesus must look and look and look again until his whole soul is enamored of the Savior. And as he looks and is transformed into the Savior's image, he shall have such enjoyment that this side of Heaven there is none other like it! Communion comes after musing. "My meditation of Him shall be sweet," said the Psalmist, and so truly it is.

When I can walk with Him, as the old philosophers walked with Plato in the groves of the Academe, then am I indeed made wise unto salvation! And then, too, is my heart made glad. There is no riding in the chariots of Amminadib except by being much with Christ. The spouse does not say, "I stood under His shadow," no, but, "I sat under His shadow with great delight." Sitting down is the posture of waiting in which we ungird the loins of the mind and indulge the repose of meditation. Let us sit down, then, beneath His shadow and we shall have great delight in musing upon Christ.

But perhaps, after all, the best reason--at least the best to clench all the other reasons I have given, why we should spend much time in musing--is because musing, then, becomes easier to us. I never did light an oven fire in my life, but I have heard that sometimes when a baker goes to light a coal oven, if his fuel is a little damp, he gets no blaze. But when the fire is once up then he may throw in what he will and everything is speedily consumed by the vehement heat. So sometimes you and I feel our hearts to be like cold ovens. And we try to put some fresh Truth in but it will not burn. But, ah, when the heart gets hot and the fire is roaring, then even such damp material as I am able to give you on Sundays will burn right well and the feeble words of a poor servant of God will make your hearts hot within you!

We can meditate better after we have addicted ourselves to a meditative frame. When we have mused a little, then the fire begins to burn. And you will perceive that as the fire burns meditation gets easier and then the heart gets warm. And oh, what holy affections, what blessed excitements those have who are much alone with Christ! Such a man never has a cold heart or a slack hand who is much in meditation with his Lord Jesus. His heart comes to be like a mass of molten lard and before long he verifies the experience of the Psalmist and can make my text his own!

"Then spoke I with my tongue." He cannot help it, for this lava will soon be running over in burning hot words. And if this man should be a preacher, he will preach with holy power! His heart being hot, his words will burn their way into his hearers' hearts. Nor will it end there--this hot heart will soon make a hot hand and the man who once has his soul full of Christ will not have his hand empty for Christ. Now he will work! Now he will preach for Christ! Now he will pray! Now he will plead with sinners! Now he will be in earnest! Now he will weep! Now he will agonize! Now he will wrestle with the angel and now he will prevail!

As the fire burns his whole being gets into a glow. And the man, like a pillar of fire, warms those who are round about him--burns his way to the glory of success and gives his Master fresh renown! Commend me, then, for all these reasons which we have given this blessed art of holy musing.

II. And now we have to spend the few minutes which remain in PUTTING SOME FUEL ON THE FIRE OF MEDITATION. The man who says that he has nothing to think about can surely have no brains. And that professing Christian who says he has nothing to muse upon must be a laughingstock for devils. A Christian man without a subject for contemplation? Impossible! Only give us the time and the opportunity and there are a thousand topics which at once present themselves for our consideration.

Let me just suggest a few of these to the Christian. Your heart will surely burn like an oven, my Christian Brothers and Sisters, if you think, first, upon eternal love! What a topic to muse upon!--

"Sing we, then, eternal love, Such as did the Father move, When He saw the world undone, Loved the world and gave His SON."

Think of that love without beginning and which, blessed be God, shall never, never cease! Give the wings of your imagination full play and go back to the time before all time--when there was no day but the Ancient of Days--when ages had not begun to be, but God dwelt alone!

Remember, if you are one of His people, the Father loved you even then and He continues still to love you and will love you when, like a bubble, this earth has melted and like a gypsy's tent the universe has been rolled up and put away! Why, as you think of this, surely you will say with our songster--

"Loved of my God, for Him again With love intense I'd burn-- Chosen of God before time began, I'd choose Him in return."

If you want meditation, dear Friends, here is an ocean to swim in! That one doctrine of election, that precious Truth of predestinating love and all the consequences which flow from it--why, here is a well--an overflowing well which you can never drink dry. Take deep draughts of it, then, and while you are musing you shall find that your heart is warmed.

Then, next, there is dying love to think of. Oh, think of the Savior descending from the starry heights of Glory and coming down to the Virgin's womb, and then descending from that lowly manger of Bethlehem even to the Cross and to the grave for you! He counted it not robbery to be equal with God and yet for your sake He took upon Himself the form of a servant and made Himself of no reputation, but became obedient unto death, even the death of the Cross!

Many of the ancient saints were accustomed to spend hours in meditating upon the wounds of Christ, and many of the martyrs were for days engaged in solemn meditation upon those wounded hands and feet and that pierced side. Oh, of all the volumes which were ever written, this volume, printed in crimson upon the pure, lily-like flesh of Christ, is the best to read! Talk you of pictures? Was there ever such a picture as that which God drew with the pencil of eternal love, dipped into the color of Almighty wrath on Calvary's summit?

Angels desired to see it, but there was a veil before the picture until Jesus came and drew it up--then the spectacle was revealed--to be gazed upon throughout eternity by adoring spirits, with fresh wonder and admiration forevermore! You cannot exhaust this subject, but, O, let me beseech you to give it the first and chief place in your meditation. "I have set the Lord always before me," would be a good motto for the Believer and well would it be for him to have the Cross painted upon his very eyeballs so that everywhere he should be reminded of Christ Crucified and so should be led always to say, "For me to live is Christ." That topic never can be exhausted and there are kindred ones connected with it--your justification, the work of the Spirit--and so on.

Let me now hint at one or two other matters which I wish you should solemnly brood over. You will do well, Christian, to meditate much upon death. What? Man, did I see you turn away? A Christian afraid of death? No, verily, for death is our Lord's doorkeeper. Life keeps the key and says to us, "You shall not enter into your Father's mansions." But Death comes and with his bony hand snatches the key out of the grasp of the tyrant, Life, and puts it into the lock and opens the gate and lets us in! Why, we say sometimes, "the last enemy which shall be destroyed is death," but if he is "the last enemy," he is not altogether the less a friend, for he is a friend, too, now that Christ has transformed him.

It is to be greatly wise, Christian, to think sometimes of the grave, the mattock, and the shroud. The catacomb is no ill place for musing, and a little cemetery, with its green knolls and its white memorial stones will be a good place in which to study for the man who wishes to muse upon life and immortality in the midst of death. The old naturalists, who tell us a good many things which are not true, as well as some which are, say that the birds of Norway always fly more swiftly than any others because the summer days are so short and therefore they have so much to do in such a little time.

I do not know anything about the birds of Norway, but this I do know, that Christ's birds would surely fly more swiftly if they would only meditate upon the fact that the day is so short and that the night is so near at hand. Surely they would fly more swiftly and work more earnestly if they only thought more of the nearness of eternity! And then, Christian, if that does not make your heart burn, let me persuade you to think of Heaven! O, carry your thoughts from this poor dunghill world up to the golden streets and to the music-begetting harps! Up yonder, I say, let your souls soar and dwell where your treasure is--with Christ upon His Throne.

Listen how they sing tonight the eternal hallelujah louder than the voice of many waters and yet sweet as harpers harping with their harps! Listen how the music swells in a sea of Glory round about the Throne of the eternal God! And you and I shall soon be there--leaving behind the sweat of toil, the rags of poverty, the shame of persecution, the pangs of sickness and the groans of death--of the death of sin. We shall soon be immortal, celestial, immaculate, glorified with the Glory which Christ had with His Father before the world was. Oh, your hearts will surely glow if you can muse thus upon Heaven, if you can sing with me tonight--

"My soul amid this stormy world Is like some fluttered dove, And fain would be as swift of wing To flee to Him I love. My heart is with Him on His Throne, And ill can brook delay, Each moment listening for the voice, 'Rise up and come away! I would, my Lord and Savior, know That which no measure knows, Would search the mystery of Your love, The depth of all Your woes. I fain would strike my harp divine Before the Father's Throne, There cast my crown of righteousness, And sing what Grace has done. Ah, leave me not in this base world, A stranger still to roam, Come,

Lord and take me to Yourself, Come, Jesus, quickly come!"

Why is His chariot so long in coming? Why does He tarry? Come quickly, come, Lord Jesus, come! Lash the white horse and bid him come as soon as may be, that Death may meet me and that I may meet my God!

And if that stirs you not, Christians, there is one other subject necessary for you to muse upon. Sometimes, Christians, think of Hell. No, start not, I pray you, for you will never have to feel it and therefore you need not shrink from thinking of it. Think of that Hell from which you have escaped and it will surely fire you with gratitude. Think of that place of doom into which multitudes are going every day and if this brings not the tears to your eyes and makes not your heart palpitate with zeal, I know not what will!

Consider that now, while I have been speaking, a soul has passed into eternity and oh, since we have been here how many spirits have taken the last dreadful plunge into the lake which burns with fire and brimstone--lost, lost--lost beyond my call and beyond your prayers! No sermons can save them now! No tears can bring them to repentance now! They are gone, gone! Yes, and there are others who are going--who walk the streets of this great London! What multitudes do we meet who will forever have to magnify the awful justice of that God whom they have slighted, and of that Savior whom they have rejected!

And will not this make you bestir yourselves? O my Brethren, if we can think of Hell and yet be idle. If we can meditate upon the wrath to come and yet be prayerless, then surely feeling has been given to beasts and we are turned to stone. What? Believe in judgment and in eternal wrath and yet not weep for sinners? Believe in Hell and yet not weep for sinners? Surely, we may expect to be turned, like Lot's wife, into pillars of salt if we thus show signs of looking back with careless and wicked eyes on burning Sodom, instead of fleeing from it and urging others to escape from the wrath to come!

Christians, I have given you topics enough to meditate upon. May I fondly hope that some of you will try during the next week to scrape up some fragments of time to be alone? I should not have a cold-hearted congregation--I should not have need to stir you up to liberality in giving, or in earnestness, or in service, if you would but muse much--for well am I persuaded that while you are musing the fire will burn.

But I address myself now--stealing a minute of your time which might, perhaps, be worse spent than here--though I go beyond the allotted hour, I address myself to those who are not yet converted to God. I could have hope for you, my dear Hearer, I could have good hope for you if I knew that you were given to musing. And if you are so given, may I suggest a few topics which are most likely to be useful to you? Muse, I pray you, unregenerate man and woman, upon your present state. "Dead in trespasses and sins," as you now are, the wrath of God abides on you! Heirs of wrath even as others, afar off, without God, without hope and without Christ in the world, I pray you remind yourselves of the hole of the pit where you now are and out of which you have never yet been dug.

Perhaps I have thought more about your soul than you have ever thought about it in your life! I pray you now let your own thoughtfulness begin to exercise itself--examine yourself--see what your state is. And when you have thought that over, I pray you consider what your end must be if you continue what you are. If you are resolved to perish, at least look your doom in the face. If you mean to make your bed in Hell, I pray you look at it and see the dreadful coverlet of flame in which you shall be wrapped forever! If you have made a league with Hell, I pray you see where that league will take you!

Count the cost, I beseech you, for every wise man should do it. Can you dwell with the devouring flames? Can you? Can you dwell with everlasting burnings? I know you cannot--for while I do but even use the word--my bones seem to tremble and rottenness takes hold upon my heart. And how will you endure it when God comes forth to tear you in pieces and there shall be none to deliver? Oh, what will you do in that day of your visitation? What will you do when the sharp and furbished sword is drawn from its scabbard--when God comes forth dressed as a man of war--to take vengeance upon your iniquities?

I pray you, then, muse upon these things and perhaps the fire may burn, perhaps the heart may melt, perhaps tears of penitence may come streaming down from both your eyes in rivers. But if you will not think of this, at least let me give you a better and a sweeter topic to muse upon. Think of my Lord and Master Jesus Christ--

"Is it nothing to you, all you that pass by, Is it nothing to you that Jesus should die?" I pray you sit down at the foot of His Cross and answer these questions. Did He die for you, or not? Remember, my Hearers, Christ did not die for everyone. Some of you will have no lot and no part in His blood. If you die without faith in Him, that blood will never cleanse you--that precious blood is not an Atonement for your sins.

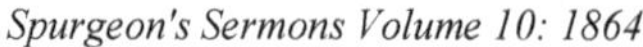

Do not suppose that Christ came into the world to save damned souls. No, those whom He came to save He will save and every vessel of mercy bought with His blood shall glitter upon the tables of Heaven--not one of His precious sheep shall be cast out. The question is--Is that blood shed for you? And you may know whether it is or not by this--Are you willing to trust Him? If you trust Him, this is the mark of redemption, this is the blood mark upon the purchased sheep. Can you, as you sit there, think upon this--that He died for sinners, the Just for the unjust--that He might bring them to God and that He died for those who hated Him?

I think I see Him now. There on the Cross He hangs and suffers for those who cursed Him. He bleeds for those who hounded Him through the streets. He bows His head upon His bosom in an extremity of anguish for the very men who put the vinegar and the gall into His mouth. "Of whom I am chief," says Paul, when he spoke of sinners for whom Jesus died. Sinner, you can not have sinned so foully as Paul did and if you rest on the blood of Christ you shall be saved! Some men tell me that they do not know how to get faith. Faith is the gift of God, but then faith usually comes by meditating much upon Christ. "Faith comes by hearing and hearing by the Word of God." As it comes in this way, hearing begets meditation. And while we are meditating upon the great and marvelous story of the condescension and the suffering of Jesus, something seems to say within us, "Yes, it is true, I will believe it," and faith is thus worked in us before we are aware of it and we cast ourselves upon Jesus Christ.

And then, Sinner, if this topic will not suit you, let me remind you that there shall come a day when you will have to muse without any hope. Abraham said to Dives, "Son, remember." Son, remember, you may forget today. You have, perhaps, forgotten until now and you will forget when you leave this Tabernacle what I have said to you, or what God has said--but you will never be able to forget when once you have come into Hell-fire. Then it will be, "Son, remember," and you will remember your mother's tears and your father's prayers! You will remember your privileges. The invitations and the wooings of love which you had will all rise up before you anew and you will see how guilty you have been.

"Son, remember," and then all your sins will rise again before you--the nights, the days, the words, the thoughts, the deeds--will all start up and people Hell with multitudes of worse than Fiends to plague and torment you forever. "Son, remember," and then you will remember the Christ who was preached to you, the stirrings of conscience which you once had and how you sinned against it all and choked the good seed. "Son, remember," and then you will be made to remember all that is yet to come! You will remember God's threats concerning the wrath which never can be appeased, the fire which never shall be quenched, and the worm which shall never die. O I pray you, instead of remembering then, remember now! O that I could plead with you!

I stand here so far away from you--would that I could come and take you by the hand and say, "Why will you perish? Men and women, why will you die?" O you who are strangers to my Lord and Master, do you find any pleasure in your sins? Are the ways of the world, after all, so fair and so pleasant as you once thought them to be? Is there not an emptiness? Do you not find "an aching void" in all your pleasures? Tell me now, will you be able to die quietly as you now are? Can you put your head down upon your death pillow softly and in peace? Can you think of meeting God and hearing the thunders of the last tremendous day and beholding the wonders of the resurrection--can you think of these things with anything like composure? You cannot! I know you cannot!

O, then--

"Come, trembling souls and flee away To Christ and heal your wounds! This is the glorious Gospel day In which free Grace abounds!"

May the Spirit of God now sweetly bring you to the Savior. Poor Dove, poor Dove, the hawk is after you and you can not fight him, nor can you escape him. Hearken to One who loves you! There is a cleft in yonder Rock to hide yourself in and then the hawk would lose his prey. Soul, the wounds of Jesus are the clefts in the Rock! Flee there and the fowler, Satan, shall seek, but shall never be able to reach you, for there is salvation in Him who died that we might live. Save us now, for His name's sake. Amen.

Let Us Go Forth

DELIVERED ON SUNDAY MORNING, JUNE 26, 1864,
BY THE REV. C. H. SPURGEON
AT THE METROPOLITAN TABERNACLE, NEWINGTON.

"Let us go forth therefore unto Him outside the camp, bearing His reproach." -- Hebrews 13:13.

MODERN professors have discovered a very easy way of religion. There is a method by which a man may attain to great reputation as a Christian and yet avoid all the trials of the Believer's estate. He may go through the world finding his path as smoothly turfed as the flesh could desire. Blessed with the smiles of friendly formalists and with the admiration of the ungodly, he may pass from his first entrance into the Church to his grave without experiencing so much as a single shower to dampen his happiness. The sun may smile sweetly upon him all the way, the birds may sing--not a raven may dare to croak, not a single owl may hoot--his road to glory and immortality shall be all that ease could wish!

Let him adopt the modern theory of universal love. Let him believe that a lie is a truth and that whether it is a lie or a truth is of no consequence at all. Let him be complacent towards every man, and with a smooth and oily tongue chime in with every other man's principles, having none of his own worth mentioning. Let him trim his sails whenever the wind changes. Let him in all things do in Rome as Rome does. Let him yield at all times to the current and float gently with the stream and he shall come to the haven--though I fear not the desired one--he shall come to some sort of haven at last, without any storm or tempest by the way.

But a daring thought comes across one's mind. Is this the kind of religion which we read of in the Bible? Is this the way in which Scriptural saints went to Heaven? It would be a very pleasant thing if we could please men and please God, too--if we could make the best of both worlds and have the sweets of this and of the next also! But a warning cry arises from the pages of Holy Scripture, for the Word of God talks very differently from this. It talks about a straight and narrow way and about few that find it. It speaks of persecution, suffering, reproach, contending even unto blood, and striving against sin! It talks about wrestling and fighting, struggling and witnessing. I hear the Savior say not, "I send you forth as sheep into the midst of green pastures," but, "as sheep in the midst of wolves."

I hear him prophesy that we should be hated of all men for His name's sake. Truly these things are enough to startle those good easy souls who go so delicately onward! Surely they may at once enquire, "Can it be that this smooth-faced godliness--this very delightful way of getting to Heaven--is the right one?" Is it not all a delusion? Are we not buoyed up with a false hope, if that hope is never assailed by trouble and persecution? All is not gold that glitters--may not the glittering religion of the many be, after all, only a pretense and a sham?

O you lovers of carnal ease, woe unto you! Inasmuch as you take not up the Cross, you shall never win the crown! The disciples of Christ must expect to follow their Master not merely in obedience to His doctrines, but also in the reproach which gathers about His Cross. I do not find Christ carried on flowery beds of ease to His Throne. I do not find Him applauded with universal acclamations! On the contrary, wherever He goes He is a protestor against things established by human wisdom. And in return, the things established vow His destruction and are not satisfied until at last they gloat their cruel eyes with His martyrdom upon the Cross.

Jesus Christ has no life of pleasure and of ease! He is despised and rejected of men--a Man of Sorrows and acquainted with grief! And let us rest assured that if we bear faithfully our testimony we shall discover that the servant is not above his Master, nor the disciple above his Lord--if they have called the Master of the house "Beelzebub," much more shall they call them of His household by titles as ignominious and shameful. We must expect, if the Christian soldier is really a soldier and not a mere pretender to the art of war, that he will have to fight until he joins the Host triumphant. If the Church is properly imaged by a ship, she must expect to have storms. And every man on board her must look to bear his share.

From the first day, when Cain and Abel divided the first family into two camps, even until now, the flesh lusts against the Spirit. The evil contends with the good and the good wrestles with the evil. Wherever the true and the good have pitched their tents, there the enemy have gathered to attack them. Righteousness courts no peace or truce with sin--our peaceful Savior came not to form an alliance so unhallowed. Hear His own words--"Think not that I am come to send peace on earth: I came not to send peace, but a sword. For I am come to set a man at variance against his father and the daughter against her mother and the daughter-in-law against her mother-in- law. And a man's foes shall be they of his own household."

Turning to Scripture, then, I find nothing about this pretty by-path meadow and its quiet, respectable walk to Heaven. I find nothing about riding in the gilded chariots of ease or walking in silver slippers. But I do find contention and strife, and rebuke and suffering, and cross-bearing and if need be, resistance unto blood striving against sin! Our text seems to convey that thought to us most powerfully. Let us take it up, and may the Holy Spirit lead us to its true meaning. We have before us, first of all, the Believer's path. Secondly his Leader. Thirdly, his burden. And fourthly, his reason for following that path.

I. We have, first of all, THE BELIEVER'S PATH. The Believer's path is, "Let us go forth outside the camp." The Divine Command is not, "Let us stop in the camp and try to reform it--things are not anywhere quite perfect--let us, therefore, stop and make matters right." No, the Christian's watch cry is, "Let us go forth." Luther caught this note. Many there were who said, "The Church of Rome has in it good and true men--let us try and reform her. Her cloisters are not without piety, her priests are not without sanctified lives--let us try and restore her purity." But Luther heard the voice of God, "Come you out from among her, lest you be partakers of her plagues," and therefore he led the van, taking for his watchword, "Let us go forth outside the camp."

To this day the Christian's place is not to tarry in the camp of worldly conformity, hoping, "Perhaps I may aid the movement for reform." It is not the Believer's duty to conform to the world and to the world's ways and say, "Perhaps by so doing I may gain a foothold and men's hearts may be the more ready to receive the Truth of God." No, from the first to the last day of the Church of God, the place of witness is not inside, but outside the camp. And the true position of the Christian is to go forth outside the camp bearing Christ's reproach.

In this respect Abraham becomes an example to us. The Lord's first word to Abraham is that he should leave his father, his kinsfolk and the idolatrous house in which he lived and go to a land which God would show him. Away he must go--Faith must be his guide--Providence his provision and the living God his only keeper! The separate life of Abraham, in the midst of the sons of Canaan, is a type of the separated walk of the Church of God.

Again, when Israel had gone down to Egypt they were not commanded to stay there and subdue their oppressors by force of arms, or petition the legislature that they might obtain gentler usage--no, but with a high hand and an outstretched arm, the Lord brought forth His people out of Egypt! Egypt was no place for the seed of Israel. And while they wandered in the wilderness and afterwards when they settled in isolation in the midst of the promised land, God's Word was fulfilled, "The people shall dwell alone: they shall not be numbered among the nations."

As if to keep up the type, the Jewish people at this very period, though mingled with all the nations of the world, are as distinct as men can be. And you cannot pass by a Jew without remarking at once in his face that he is distinct and separate from all mankind. This, I say, is but a type of the Church of God--the Church of God is to be distinct and separate from all other corporations or communities! Her laws come from no human legislator! Her officers claim no royal appointment! Her endowments are not from the coffers of the State! Her subjects are a peculiar people and her spirit is not of this world!

What is meant then, dear Friends, by this "going forth without the camp"? I understand it to mean, first of all, that every Christian is to go forth by an open profession of his faith. You that love the Lord are to say so. You must come out and avow yourselves on His side. You may be Christians and make no profession, but I cannot be sure that you are a Believer, nor can any other man. While you make no profession, we must, to a great extent, judge you by the non-profession. And since you do not acknowledge yourselves to be a part of Christ's Church we are compelled to adjudge you as not a part of that Church! We cannot suppose you to be better than you profess to be for the most of men are not half so good as their professions.

Usually, as a rule, no man is as good as his religion and certainly no man is ever better than his religion. If you do not profess to be on Christ's side--with all charity we are forced to accept your own confession of having no interest in Jesus. Come out, Christians! Your Master commands you and warns you that if you are ashamed of Him in this generation, He will be ashamed of you in the day of His Glory! He bids you acknowledge Him, for if you confess Him before men He will confess you when He comes in the Glory of His holy angels. I pray you, then, come out from among them by taking up the name of a Christian!

Why, what is there to shudder at? Are you a soldier and will you not wear your Captain's livery? What? Do you love Christ and blush to admit it? You ought to be glad to plead guilty to the blessed impeachment. Why do you stand back? Let not fear or shame restrain you. If you are Christians there is really nothing discreditable in it. Up! Stand shoulder to shoulder with the people of God and say, "I will go with you because the Lord is with you." This done, the Christian is to be separate from the world as to his company. He must buy and sell and trade like other men in the world, but he is not to find his bosom friends in it.

He is not to go out of society and shut himself up in a monastery--he is to be in the world, but not of it. And his choice company is not to be among the loose, the immoral, the profane! No, not even among the merely moral--his choice company is to be the saints of God. He is to select for his associates those who shall be his companions in the world to come. As birds of a feather flock together, so the birds of paradise are gregarious. Like the speckled birds they are peeked at by the common flock. As idle boys were wont to mock at foreigners in the streets, so do worldlings jeer at Christians. Therefore the Believer flies away to his own company when he wants good fellowship. The Christian must come out of the world as to his company.

I know that this rule will break many a fond connection, but be not unequally yoked with unbelievers. I know it will snap ties which are almost as dear as life, but it must be done. We must not be overruled even by our own brother when the things of God and conscience are concerned. You must follow Christ, whatever may be the enmity you excite-- remembering that unless you love Christ better than husband, or father, or mother, yes and your own life also--you cannot be His disciple. If these are hard terms, turn your backs and perish in your sins! Count the cost. And if you cannot bear such a cost as this, do not undertake to be a follower of Christ!

The follower of Jesus goes without the camp as to his pleasures. He is not without his joys nor his recreations. But he does not seek them where the wicked find them. The mirth which cheers the worldly makes the Christian sad--the carrion which delights the crow would disgust the dove. And so those things which are delightful and full of pleasure to un-renewed men shock and grieve the hearts of the regenerate. If you have no separation from the world as to your pleas-ures--since your heart is generally in your pleasures--your heart, therefore, is with the wicked and with them shall your doom be when God comes to judge mankind!

Furthermore, the true follower of Christ is divided from the world as to his maxims. He does not subscribe to the laws which rule most men in their families and their business. Men generally say, "Everyone for himself and God for us all." That is not the Christian's maxim. "Look not every man on his own things, but every man also on the things of others," is the Christian's rule. Some men will sail very near the wind. They would not absolutely cheat, but still they use very sharp practices. They would not lie, but their puffs and recommendations are not quite the truth. The Christian scorns all this questionable dealing and in all matters keeps to the rule of uprightness.

If the Believer is true to his Master and goes outside the camp to follow Him, his actions are as clear as the noonday. His word is his bond and in his trade he would as soon think of becoming absolutely a thief as to condescend to the common tricks of trade. From my soul I loathe those men, who, under the pretense and profession of religion, use the very respectability of their position to gain credit among others that they may defraud by obtaining credit which they do not deserve! Such persons are the greatest possible disgrace to the Christian Church.

The bankruptcy courts may whitewash them but the devil has blackened them beyond all power of bankruptcy to cleanse them. Their black deceitfulness shows through! Men may escape censure when standing at the easy bar of the commissioner and get a certificate, but they will find it very difficult to get a certificate when God comes to judge them in the Last Great Day. Our laws in England really seem to me to be made on purpose that men may thieve and rob with impunity, so long as they do it under color of commerce. Well, if man's law will not touch such men, God's Law shall! And the Church should see that she cleanses herself as much as possible from them. If we are followers of Christ, we must go forth without this camp of discrepancy and thieving! Ours must be a downright and honest religion that will not let us swerve a hair's breadth from the straight line of integrity and uprightness.

Once more, and here is a very difficult part of the Christian's course--the Christian is to come out not only from the world's pleasures and sins and irreligion--but there are times when the true followers of Christ must come out from the world's religion as well as irreligion. Every nation has a religion. In the days of Abraham the little nationalities round him all had their god. In the days of Christ there was am established religion in Judea--and I suppose that out of its synagogues our Lord Jesus Christ was thrust with fury. There was an established religion with its priests and its proud Pharisaic professors--but our Lord and Savior Jesus Christ boldly proclaimed His protest against its distortions of Scripture, its want of true spirituality, its worldliness, its pomp and pride.

In His day Jesus Christ was as true a Dissenter as any of us and separated Himself and His little company from the authorized and established ecclesiastical camp. Judaism was not the religion of Abraham, neither were the Pharisees the true exponents and successors of Moses.

Therefore Christ, with burning words, though full of charity and with a loving heart--but with a thundering tongue--bore an awful witness against the religion of His own age! He knew how the multitude respected it and how the great ones lived upon it, but for all this, though His life must be shed for His protest, Christ led His disciples away from the national religion to something better, nobler and more sublime. And you and I, too, Brethren, must see that we never fall in with the religion of the times because it happens to be fashionable and because the multitude follow it, or the law of the land patronizes it!

If there exists anywhere on earth a Church which teaches for doctrine the commandments of men, come out of her and bear your witness for the Truth of God. I see before me now a Church which tolerates evangelical truth in her communion, but at the same time lovingly embraces Puseyism and finds room for infidels and for men who deny the authenticity of Scripture. This is no time for us to talk about friendship with so corrupt a corporation. The godly in her midst are deceived if they think to mold her to a more gracious form. Her bishops will not touch the Burial Service, although four thousand clergymen petition for a little ease for their consciences.

Nor will they give up reading in God's own worship the filthy story of "Susannah and the Elders," nor the nursery tale of "Bell and the Dragon"--though one of their priests asserts that he would quite as soon read "Jack and the Beanstalk." We have waited long enough--her space for repentance has been already too long! Flee out of her, all of you who love your souls! Come out from among her! Be you separate--touch not the unclean thing lest you be partakers of her plagues, for her plagues are many. Often have I read works in which the Puseyites call the Church of Rome their sister Church! Well, if it is so let the two harlots make a league together, but let good and honest men come out of both apostate churches! And those who love the Lord Jesus, whether clergy or laity, must leave them to their doom.

I know it is hard work. It calls upon many to be poor and give up their livings, but they must do it. Scotland witnessed, a few years ago, one of the noblest spectacles the world ever beheld. My heart would break with joy for England if I should live to see such a day and such a deed of heroism--but there is not spirit enough left in us. There is not Divine Grace enough left in us. I fear we have fallen upon a degenerate age.

The "land of brown heath and shaggy wood, land of the mountain and the flood," has nurtured a noble race of brave, bold men and these could give up house and home and living for the Truth and for God's sake. But it is not so in England. No, they will sell their consciences. They will cower down and mutter a lie at the command of the State. They will bury adulterers and seducers in sure and certain hope of a blessed resurrection. They will teach a catechism which their conscience tells them is not true, for riches, for station! For the sake of the loaves and fishes, the men of God (and many of them we hope are such) will hold still to the false Church. Our protest is lifted up against her and our foot stands altogether without her camp. Come you out from among her! Be you separate! Touch her not! Have no communion with her false doctrines!

As for each of us who knows the Truth, our place is with Christ outside the camp, bearing His reproach. I am sure my text contains all this and more. And I would to God that His Church would take up her true position now and be separate in all things from anything that defiles and makes a lie.

II. But now, secondly, we have in the text, THE CHRISTIAN'S LEADER. It does not say, "Let us go forth outside the camp" merely, but, "Let us go forth therefore unto Him." Here is the heart of the text--"unto Him." Beloved, we might leave society--we might forsake all its conventionalities and become Nonconformists in the widest sense and yet not carry out the text--for the text is, "Let us go forth unto Him." O Beloved, it is this point that I would urge upon you! I am no politician! I care not one whit what Church has the State-pay, or what has not. I care not for political dissent--but I do care for religiously following my Master's Word and, by His Grace, I will.

And when I read this text, "Let us go forth therefore unto Him," I set myself to learn what the Word means. It means, first, let us have fellowship with Him. He was despised. He had no credit for charity. He was mocked in the streets. He was hissed at. He was hounded from among society. If I take a smooth part, I can have no fellowship with Him--fellowship requires a like experience. Come, then, my Soul, put on the Savior's garb--walk through the mire with Him! Off with your silver slippers--go barefoot within Christ! Be you, yourself, like the bush which burns but is not consumed. Be content that your shoulders should be raw with His rough Cross--He carried it--do not shirk the labor! Expect not to wear the crown where Christ carried the Cross, but, for fellowship's sake, follow Him.

Again, if I am to follow Him, I am to follow His example. What Christ did I am to do. I am to go forth unto Him. It is never to be a rule unto me that Mr. So-and-So did such-and-such a thing, or Mrs. So-and-So--what Christ did is to be my rule. Some men are for hanging on what Luther did, or what Calvin did--that is nothing to the Christian--he says, "I am to go forth unto Jesus." Follow

Jesus Christ and none but Jesus Christ and then you will be separate, indeed, from the rest of men. I am to go forth unto Him--that is, I am to go forth to His Truth. Wherever I see His Truth, I am to espouse it--wherever I see error I am to denounce it without hesitation.

I am to take His Word to be my only standard. And just where His Word leads me, there I am to go, no matter where. I may have been educated in one way but I am to bend my education to this Book. I may have conceived prejudices but they must give way before His Truth. I may know that such-and-such a belief is profitable to me but my profit shall go for nothing in comparison with the Word of God. And then I can to go forth to Christ's witness-bearing. The present age does not believe in witness-bearing but the whole Bible is full of it. The duty of every Christian is to bear witness for the Truth of God. Christ says, "For this purpose was I born and came into the world." He who knows the Truth but lays the finger of silence on his lips, saying, "Peace, peace, when there is no peace," is a sorry Christian!

If you have been washed in Jesus' blood and saved by His righteousness, I do implore you, take your position with Christ as witness-bearers for the Truth as it is in Jesus. My Master wants today a band of men and women who are prepared to be singular, so long as to be singular is to be right. He wants men and women of bold, unflinching, lion-like hearts who love Christ first and His Truth next--and Christ and His Truth beyond all the world! Men and women, too, whose holy lives and consistent conversation are not to be perverted by the bribes of this world and whose testimony is neither to be distorted nor silenced by frowns or by smiles.

Happy souls shall they be who dare to take their stand with Christ today! The struggles of the Covenanters of old need to be renewed at this moment. The strife of the Puritan age needs to return once more to the Church. And what if the stakes of Smithfield come again? And what if the times of persecution return to us? The good old vessel which outrode the blood-red storm, will outride it still and with all her passengers and crew safe on board, be received by the King and honored with His gracious smile!

We are to take care, however, that it is to Christ we go! Not to party, not to denomination--not to anything but Christ and His Truth! Out with denominationalism or anything else which savors not of Christ Jesus! Whether it is the Baptist Church, or the Episcopalian, or the Presbyterian Church which errs from Christ's way, it is nothing to any one of us which it may be. It is CHRIST we are to care for and Christ's Truth. And this we are to follow over all the hedges and ditches of men's making--straight away to Christ, clinging to Christ's mantle, fighting a way straight through where He Himself fought and opened the path to His Crown. Thus have we spoken of the Christian's Leader.

III. Now, in the third place, we have THE CHRISTIAN'S BURDEN. He is to bear the Lord's reproach. The reproach of Christ, in these days, takes this shape. "Oh," they say, "the man is too precise." "He is right. But still, Truth is not always to be spoken. The thing is wrong, no doubt, which he denounces, but still, the time has not come yet--we must be lenient towards these things. The man is right in what he says, but we must not be too precise nowadays. We must give and take a little--there must be charity." God's Word, in this age, is a small affair. Some do not even believe it to be Inspired. And those who profess to revere it set up other books in a sort of rivalry with it.

Why, there are great Church dignitaries nowadays who write against the Bible and yet find bishops to defend them! "Do not, for a moment, think of condemning their books or them. They are our dear Brethren and must not be fettered in thought." How many days ago is it since a bishop talked in this way in convocation? Some believe in Popery. But here, again, the plea will be, "They are our dear Brethren." Some believe in nothing at all--but they are still all safely housed in one Church, like the beasts, clean and unclean, in Noah's ark.

Those who come out with Christ, get this reproach--they are too precise--in fact, they are "bigots." That is how the world brings it out at last--"bigots"--a set of "bigots!" I have heard say that the word, "bigot," took its rise from this--that a certain Protestant nobleman being commanded, in order to gain his lands, to kneel down and in some way or other commit the act of idolatry towards the host, said, when he came at last to the point, "By God, I will not!" And they called him henceforth a "By-God." If this is the meaning of the word "bigot," we cheerfully adopt the title! And were it right to swear, we would declare, "By Him that lives! By Heaven! We cannot speak a lie and we cannot bend our knee to the shrine of Baal, bigots or no bigots." The Truth of God is first and our reputation next.

Then they say, "Ah, these people are behind their time. The world has made such advances. We are in the nineteenth century--you ought to know better! The discoveries of science put your narrow views out of court." Very well, Christian, be content to be behind the times for the times are getting nearer to judgment and the last plagues. "Ah, but," they say, "these people seem to us to be so self-righteous. They think themselves right and nobody else." Very well, Christian, if you are right, think yourself right! And if everybody else should call you self-righteous, that does not mistake you so. The Lord knows how we cling to the Cross and as poor sinners, look up to Christ

and Jesus Christ alone. Our conscience is void of offense in this matter.

"Ah," they say, "they are not worth noticing. They are all a pack of fools." It is very remarkable that in the judgment of their own age good men always have been fools. Fools have been they who have turned the world upside down. Luther and Calvin, Wesley and Whitfield were all fools. But somehow or other God managed, by these fools, to get to Himself a glorious victory. And then they turn round and say, "It is only the poor--only the lower orders. Have they any of the nobility and gentry with then?" Well, this reproach we can pretty well bear because it is the old standard of Christ that the poor have the Gospel preached unto them. And it has ever been a sweet reflection that many who have been poor in this world have been made rich in faith!

Brethren, you must expect, if you follow Christ, to endure reproach of some sort or another. Let me just remind you what reproach your Master had to bear. The world's Church said of Christ, "He is a deceiver! He deceives the people." Incarnate Truth of God and yet a deceiver! Then they said, "He stirs up the people! He promotes rebellion. He is no friend of good order. He incites anarchy! He is a mere demagogue." That was the world's cry against Christ and, as that was not enough, they went further and said, "He is a blasphemer!" They put Him to death on the charge that He was a blasphemer! They whispered to one another, "Did you hear? He said such-and-such last Sunday in His sermon. What a shocking thing he did in such a place! He is a blasphemer!"

Then came the climax. They all said He had a devil and was mad. Surely they could go no further than this! But they supplemented it by saying when He cast out devils that He did it through Beelzebub, the prince of the devils! A sorry life your Master had, you see. All the filth in earth's kennels was thrown at Him by sacrilegious hands. No epithet was thought coarse enough! No terms hard enough--He was the song of the drunkard and they that sat in the gate spoke against Him. This was the reproach of Christ. And we are not to marvel if we bear as much. "Well," says one, "I will not be a Christian if I am to bear that." Skulk back, then, you Coward, to your own damnation! But oh, men and women that love God and who seek after the eternal reward, I pray you do not shrink from this Cross! You must bear it!

I know you may live without it if you will fawn and cringe and keep back part of the price. But do not do this--it is unworthy of your manhood--much more is it unworthy of your Christianity! God and for Christ are so holy and so truthful that you compel the world to give its best acknowledgment of your goodness by railing at you--it can do no more, it will do no less. Be content to take this shame for there is no Heaven for you if you will not--no crown without the Cross--no jewels without the mire. You must stand in the pillory if you would sit in Glory! You must be spit upon and be treated with shame if you would receive eternal honor! And if you reject the one you reject the other.

IV. We close by noticing THE CHRISTIAN'S REASON FOR BEARING HIS REPROACH AND GOING WITHOUT THE CAMP. It is in the text, "Let us go forth therefore"--there is the reason. Why then? First, because Jesus did. Jesus Christ came into the world pure and holy. His life and His testimony were a witness against sin. Jesus Christ would not conform. If He would but have done so He might have been King of the Jews. But no, the most loving spirit that ever lived was also the most firm. Nobody shall say that Christ was either self-willed or harsh, or that He hated other men-- nothing of the kind! Never was there such pure generosity, such overflowing affection for men as you find in Christ.

But yield the truth, yield holiness? No, never! Not a grain of it! Be silent? No, He rebukes the Pharisees. And when the lawyer pulls His coat and says, "Master, in so doing, you rebuke us," then Jesus Christ begins, "Woe unto you lawyers!" All classes have their portion from His mouth. The Herodians come to Him. Does He for a moment yield to them? Or when the opposite party tempts does He side with them? Does He side with either the Sadducee or with the Pharisee? No, Christ's course was ever an independent one--He committed himself unto no man--for He knew what was in man. The whole of His life through you cannot mistake Him for a Pharisee, or a Sadducee, or any one of the other teachers. He stands out like a lone mount of light, separate and apart from the chain of dark mountains. And so must the Christian. Christ was separate. And so must you be! Christ was pure, holy, truthful. So must you be! I pray you either renounce your profession or else seek Grace to carry it out.

Moreover, the connection of the text tells us that Christ set apart His people by going outside the camp, that He might sanctify His people. He suffered outside the camp. Christ's separation was in order that His People might be separated. The Head is not of the world and shall the members be of it? The Head is despised and rejected--shall the members be honored? "If any man loves the world, the love of the Father is not in him." The world rejects Christ--shall the world receive us? No, if we are truly one with Him, we must expect to be rejected, too. Christ's separation is the type and symbol of the separateness of all the elect.

Again, Christ would have His people separate for their own sanctification. You cannot grow in Grace to any high degree while you are conformed to the world. The path of separation may be a path of sorrow, but it is the path of safety. And though it may cost you many pangs and make your life like a long martyrdom and every day a battle, yet it is a happy life after all. There is no such life as that which the soldier of Christ leads--for though men frown upon him-- Christ so sweetly smiles upon him that he cares for no man! Christ reveals Himself as a sweet refreshment to the warrior after the battle and so blessed is the vision that the warrior feels more calm and peace in the day of strife than in his hours of rest.

Believe me, the highway of holiness is the highway of communion! A blot on your conscience will certainly separate Christ from you as to communion. Be pure, be clear, be chaste as before the Lord and you may walk as on the mountaintops--having Christ for your Companion--enjoying with Him a Heaven on earth! The Covenanters and martyrs tell us in their diaries that they were never so happy as when they were in the dungeon alone with Christ for company! Their best days were often their days of burning--they called them their wedding days and went to Heaven singing and chanting the triumphal Psalm as they mounted in their chariots of fire!

Let us close with this last thought and reason. Thus we shall hope to win the crown if we are enabled, by Divine Grace, faithfully to follow Christ in all respects. Oh, the crown! The crown! The crown! Come, let me hold it up to you! Is not this a treasure? Eternal life! Likeness to Christ! Sitting at His right hand! Do you not hear them--the harps of angels--the songs of the redeemed? Do you not hear them, I say, as in one perpetual Psalm of joyfulness they salute the Lord their God with thanksgiving?

It is but a flea-bite here--and then an eternity of bliss! A moment's shame and then an eternal honor! A little while of witness-bearing, a little while of suffering, a little while to be rebuked and then "forever with the Lord"! This reward is so great that it transcends the light affliction which is but for a moment. I will not put so little shame in contrast with it all. Why, in this age we suffer nothing--a few hard words, a jeer, a sneer--now and then a friend who leaves us because we speak the Truth. But what is that? O Brethren, we are denied the honor of those favored saints who died for Jesus! Our weak spirits love these softer times! The real days of honor were the days of persecution. The times when saints won brightest crowns were when they suffered most.

I fear the Church of Christ is growing sleepy. Men of God have lost muscle and nerve. Our fathers died for half a Truth and we will not bear rebuke for a whole one. Two women were tied to the stake at Wigton and drowned in the rising tide--do you know what for? Simply because they would not say, "God save the king." You say, "What does that matter?" Well, it was comparatively a theological trifle. They held a certain theory concerning the bearing of the Headship of Christ upon the political position of the king. Because they thought the thing was wrong--though I, for my part, would say, "God save the king" a thousand times--yet they would not say it once and died in constancy to their belief.

The two women were actually tied to stakes by the seaside. The tide came up and when the elder woman of the two was drowned they asked the younger whether she would say it now. But no, she would not. She believed it to be a Truth concerning Christ and His kingdom. And though it only touched one of the smallest jewels of His crown, yet she would not do it and therefore the gurgling waters came up to her chin and at last rolled over one who had faithfully borne witness to a portion of Truth which seems very trifling to us nowadays, but which to her seemed to be worth dying for!

Nowadays, I say, we would not die for the whole Bible though in other ages saints would have died for the dot of an i, or the cross of a t. We turn tail and are frightened because somebody has said a hard thing to us for defending the Truth which concerns Jesus and has the salvation of man wrapped in it. I say we will not fight for the great and they would fight for the little. O may God restore to us, dear Friends, more Grace, more piety, more love for souls, more care for the kingdom of Christ--a sterner prizing of the Truth of God and a determination solemnly avowed before the Lord of hosts, that come what may, we will contend earnestly for the faith once delivered unto the saints!

We stand upon the Rock of Ages confident that God will defend the right and that right in the end shall come off victorious! God give you Grace--especially you members of my charge--to, from this day, more than ever you have done, take your place outside the camp and cheerfully and joyfully to bear Christ's reproach! Some of you cannot do this. You cannot bear His reproach. You cannot go outside the camp for you have no vital faith--you have not believed in Jesus. O Sinner, you are not to carry Christ's Cross first--but look to that Cross for salvation! And when He has saved you, as He will if you trust in Him, then take up your cross and carry it and praise the name of God from this time forth, even forever!

A Bad Excuse Is Worse Than None

DELIVERED ON SUNDAY MORNING, JULY 3, 1864,
BY THE REV. C. H. SPURGEON,
AT BAYSWATER.

"And they all with one consent began to make excuses." -- Luke 14:18.

THE provisions of the Gospel of Christ may well be compared to a supper, provided as they were, in the evening of the world--"in these last days." The description, "a great supper," is well borne out if we consider the greatness of the provision--how much love and mercy God has displayed towards the sons of men in the Person of Christ Jesus--how much power and gracious working He has shown by His Holy Spirit. A great supper it is if we think of the richness and sweetness of the provision--it is a feast worthy of the great King. The flesh of Jesus is our spiritual meat and His blood our choicest wine. Our souls are satisfied with Covenant mercies, most fitly set forth as "A feast of fat things, a feast of wines on the lees, of fat things full of marrow, of wines on the lees well refined."

A great supper it is, moreover, when we consider the number of guests invited. "Go you into all the world and preach the Gospel to every creature." The call of the Gospel comes to every man and woman within hearing of the ministers of God--

"None are excluded there, but those Who do themselves exclude! Welcome the learned and polite, The ignorant and rude."

No other king ever sent out an invitation so broad as this! Wisdom "cries at the gates, at the entry of the city, at the coming in at the doors. Unto you, O men, I call. And my voice is to the sons of man." Is it not strange that when the householder made so great a supper--when he offered it without money and without price--that all his neighbors should with one consent begin to make excuse?

He did not call them to prison or to misery! How, then, came they to be so unwilling to obey the summons? Why this unanimity in the rejection? We find good men differing as to how it is that evil men can hold together so well. What? Not one who has respect enough to his generous friend to sit at his table and receive his bounty? Not one. Truly, here, Brethren, we have a picture of the universal depravity of man! All men are thus vile and refuse the mercy of God. We never know how bad man is till the Gospel is preached to him. The Gospel acts as a white background to set forth the blackness of man's heart.

Here human nature reaches to the greatest height of sin's enormity! Spitting forth his venom against the Lord of Infinite Love, man proves himself truly to be of the serpent's brood. The Gospel is preached to thousands and do all make excuse? So the parable has it and truly so the fact proves it. What? Is there not one whose free will is inclined towards Christ? Is there not one of so good a natural disposition that he will come to Jesus? No, the text says, not one--"They all with one consent began to make excuses." How thoroughly has father Adam ruined our understandings! What fools, as well as rebels, we are to refuse to partake of the banquet of love! We are altogether become unprofitable. There is not one who seeks after God!

You will, perhaps, remind me that there were other men besides those who made excuses. Most true. But these were in the highways and hedges, or in the streets and lanes of the city. And so those who do not hear the Gospel and therefore are not guilty of rejecting it, yet nevertheless are far off from God by wicked works and strangers to the commonwealth of Israel. Thus, taking the two characters to represent all mankind, we find all to be enemies of God. Those in the highways need to be "compelled" to come in--they had a natural reluctance to feast at the good man's table. And so all sorts of men are averse to the Gospel. They are perfectly willing to sin--content even to perish in sin! But to come to Christ, to accept the great Atonement, to put their trust in Jesus--this is a thing they care not for and with one consent, when they hear the Gospel--they begin to make excuses.

We fear that there are many in this meeting house this morning who have been blessed with hearing the Gospel for years but up to now the only treatment they have given to the gracious message is to make excuses about it. I hope to deal with such very simply and very affectionately--earnestly desiring that they make their last excuse this morning and that it may meet with its death blow. O that they may come to the feast which they have long rejected and rejoice in the mercy of God in Christ Jesus!

Why did they make excuses? Let us, first, try to account for their conduct. Secondly, what excuses did they make?-- let us recount them. And thirdly, how foolish thus to make excuses!--here let us encounter them.

I. Let us try to ACCOUNT for the fact, the sad fact, that men are so ready to make excuses rather than to receive the Word of God. We account for it in the first place by the fact that they had no heart at all to accept the feast. Had they spoken the truth plainly, they would have said, "We do not wish to come, nor do we intend to do so." If man's heart were not so deceitful, it would not make excuses, but it would say outright, "'We will not have this Man to reign over us. We do not feel our sinfulness. We will not, therefore, accept pardon. We believe that we can work out our own salvation with our own doings.

"Or, if not, we are content to take our chance. If it shall go ill with us, it will go ill with a great many people. We will run all risks--we do not need salvation--we choose rather to have our full swing of carnal delights. Your religion involves too much self-sacrifice. It is altogether contrary to the lusting of our minds and therefore we decline it." This is at the bottom of it. Some of you, my Hearers, have often been impressed and partially convinced of sin but you have put off Christ with excuses. Will you bear with me while I solemnly assure you that at its core your heart is at enmity to God? Your excuse may look very pretty but it is as flimsy as it is fair. If you were honest with your own soul you would say at once, "I do not love Christ. I do not need His salvation."

Your put offs, your false promises, your excuses are worthless. Anyone with half an eye can see through them, they are so transparent. You are an enemy of God! You are unreconciled and you are content to be so. This truth may be unpalatable but it is nevertheless most certain. May God help you to feel this and may it humble you before His Presence. Still, if they would not come to the good man's feast, why did they not say so? If the real secret of it was that they hated him and despised his provisions, is it not melancholy that they were not honest enough to give him a "no" at once? Well, they certainly were not and one reason might be because they wished to be upon good terms with their conscience. They felt they ought to go. He was one who had a claim upon their courtesy, if not their gratitude, and therefore feeling that they ought to go and yet not intending to go, they sought to compromise by an excuse.

Conscience is a very unamiable neighbor to men who live in sin. It is said of David, "David's heart struck him," and it is a very hard blow which the heart is able to give. In order to parry the blow men hold up a shield of excuses. You cannot quite extinguish your conscience, which is the candle of the Lord and therefore you put it under the bushel of an excuse. The thief fears the watchdog and therefore throws him a bone to keep him quiet--that bone is made of excuses. John Bunyan tells us that Mr. Recorder Conscience, when the town of Mansoul was in the keeping of Diabolus, used sometimes to cry out at such a rate that he made all the inhabitants afraid and so they put him in a very dark place and tried to put a gag in his mouth to keep him quiet. But for all that, sometimes when his fits came on he made the town feel very uneasy.

I know what conscience tells some of you--it says to you, "How is it you can forget Divine things? How can you trifle with the world to come? How can you live as if you never meant to die? What will you do when you come to die without an interest in the Lord Jesus Christ?" And so that conscience may be quiet awhile, you make an excuse and persevere in refusing to come to the feast. It may be that you make this excuse to satisfy custom. It is not the custom of this present age to fly immediately in the face of Christ. There are not many men of your acquaintance or mine who ostensibly oppose religion.

Your father fears God. Your mother is a woman of great devotion. Your friends go to the House of God and speak experimentally of Divine things--you do not like, therefore, to say to them, "I will never be a Christian! I dislike the ways of God! I do not choose the plan of Sovereign Grace," and therefore to spare their feelings you make an excuse. You do not want to grieve dear friends--you are afraid if you spoke out honestly what your soul feels it might bring your mother with gray hairs to the grave, or make your father's heart break--and so you make an excuse. And you think that they may entertain a comfortable hope whereas, while you make excuses, there is no hope for you at all.

For my part I would rather you speak outright and say what you mean! I would that you would say, "I am an enemy of Christ. I do not believe His Gospel. I will not serve Him!" This might sound very badly but it would show, at least, that there was some sincerity in you and we would hope that before long you might be bowed to the will of Christ. Excuses are curses and when you have no excuses left there will be hope for you!

It may be you make these excuses because you have had convictions which so haunt you at times that you dare not oppose Christ to His face. You have gone home from the services to weep. That little chamber of yours is a witness that you cannot live altogether without prayer. The other day when you went to a funeral you came home with your mind very solemn and you thought, then, that certainly you would yield to the commands of Jesus. When you were sick and had that week or two upstairs alone--then you vowed and resolved--but your resolves melted into thin air.

The tear starts in your eyes--you are almost persuaded to be a Christian--you breathe a prayer! But ah, some ill companion tempts you the next morning and there your are, according to the old proverb, "The dog has returned to his vomit and the sow that was washed to her wallowing in the mire." Ah, how many times did I have convictions of sin and terrible ones, too, and yet I said, like Felix to Paul, "Go your way for this time. When I have a convenient season, I will call for you"?

But I could not quench these convictions by downright opposition to Christ. I knew too much and felt too much to do that, and so I tried to patch up a truce between my soul and my convictions. Satan is always ready to help men with excuses. This is a trade of which there is no end. It certainly commenced very early, for after our first parents had sinned one of the first occupations upon which they entered was to make themselves aprons of fig leaves to hide their nakedness! Read the Scriptures through and you will find that excuse-making has been a habit in all ages and among all classes of people.

And till the last sinner shall be saved by Sovereign Grace, I suppose men will still be setting up their vain excuses in the temple of God! If you will fire the gun, Satan will always keep you supplied with ammunition. When he thinks that a Truth is about to come home to you, if you cannot frame an excuse he will do it for you. He will run between you and the cannon shot of God's Word to prevent your being wounded by it. If the preacher's sword should be too sharp for you and make your conscience bleed, the Evil One has a Satanic plaster with which he very soon binds up the wound! The natural self-righteousness of man prompts him to frame apologies. We are all the best men in the world according to our own gauge and measure. If we could sit as judges upon ourselves, the verdict would always be "Not guilty."

Sin, which would be very shocking in another, is very venial in us. No, what would be abominable in other men becomes almost commendable in ourselves so partially do we judge our own case. The sinner cannot think it quite right for himself to be an unbeliever in Christ--and since his enlightened conscience will not let him say that he is quite safe while he refuses to fly to the wounds of Jesus--he runs to excuses in order that he may still say, "I am rich and increased in goods," and not be driven to the unhappy necessity of crying, "I am naked and poor and miserable."

Sinful self is hard to conquer, but righteous self is the worst enemy of the two. When we can make men plead guilty, then God pronounces absolution upon them. But while men will interpose their extenuations there is little or no hope for them. O great God our Master, tear away the excuses from every sinner here and make him stand guilty before Your bar in his own consciousness, that he may cry, "God be merciful to me, a sinner," and find pardon through the blood of Jesus Christ! Take heed, O you ungodly ones, lest you go on excusing and excusing and excusing, until you excuse yourselves down to the pit of Hell! Know this--you will never be able to excuse yourselves out again.

II. We come to RECOUNT these excuses. Many will not come to the great supper--will not Christians be on the same ground as those in the parable? They are too busy. They have a large family and it takes all their time to earn bread and cheese for those little mouths. They have a very large business--many servants in their employ--and from the first thing in the morning to the last thing at night, if they do not see after business, their affairs would go wrong. Or else, if they have no business, yet they have so many pleasures and these require so much time--their butterfly visits during the morning take up so many hours--the dropping of their small pieces of pasteboard at other people's doors occupy all their leisure and they really have no opportunity to think about matters so unpalatable as death and eternity.

This excuse scarcely needs a word from me to answer it because every man knows that it is grossly false. Nobody goes starving because he has not time to eat. Now, if God has given time for us to support our natural frame, much more has He given us time to feed the soul. I do not find my friends in the street half dressed. But I find some of them spend many a half-hour over that other pin and that other ribbon. Now surely if they have time to dress the body, they must have had time given them in which to put on the robe of righteousness and array the soul!

If you have not the time, God gave it to you and you must have misspent it. God gives you time as a steward and if you say to your Master, "I have it not," He will reply to you, "I entrusted it to you. You must have spent it on yourself. You have robbed God." A little earlier rising, a little less time at the table--either of these might give you time enough. You know you have the time and when you say you have it not, the lie is too thin--you can see through it. O Soul! O Soul! When holy men can find hours for prayer--when such a man as Martin Luther, when he was very busy, used to say--"I must have three hours prayer today at least, or else I cannot get through my business"--do not tell me that you have not time to seek the Lord!

Besides, it is not an affair of time. Salvation may be worked in an instant! There is life in a look at the Crucified One. There is life at this moment for you. And between now and the time when this service shall have gone, there is time enough for you to have laid hold upon eternal life and to have received Christ Jesus to your soul's salvation. That excuse will not do. But then they fly to another. They are too good. When I have preached Free Grace and a full Christ, I have heard some say, "That is a good sermon for the crowd in a theater--for ignorant, low-lived people. But we respectable people do not require such salvation. To offer a free salvation to men who are neither drunkards nor swearers--why the thing is ridiculous! The sermon was very good for Magdalenes, for thieves and such like--but not for us."

No, you are too good to be saved! You need not a physician because you are whole. Your own table has enough upon it. You do not need to come to this feast. But think, I pray you, whether this is not all a mistake! In what are you better than other men, after all? What if you do not indulge in open sins--does not your heart often go a-lusting towards evil? Does your tongue always speak that which is right and true? If you cannot remember sins of commission, what about the sins of omission? Have you fed the hungry? Have you clothed the naked? Have you taught the ignorant? Have you loved God with all your heart and soul and strength? Have you given Him all that He demands of you? Why you cannot say this!

Now the perfection, the holiness which God demands in order to salvation must be like a perfect alabaster vase--if there is a single crack or spot on it--all is spoiled. You may say, "Well, it is not much broken. We have not seriously damaged it." No, but God requires it to be perfect and no matter how slight the damage it may have sustained, you cannot enter Heaven upon the footing of your good works--you are cast out forever! Hear these words, "By the deeds of the Law there shall no flesh be justified in His sight." "Cursed is everyone that continues not in all things which are written in the Book of the Law to do them." And, "As many as are of the works of the Law are under the curse." God save you from that false excuse!

Another class says, "We are too bad to be saved. The Gospel cries, 'Believe in Jesus Christ and live,' but it cannot mean me. I have been too gross an offender. When I was but young I went into evil and since then I have gone from bad to worse. O Sir, I have cursed God to His face! I have sinned against light and knowledge, against a mother's prayers and tears. I have spoken evil of God's Word! I have laughed at the very name of His Son Jesus Christ! I am too evil to be saved." Here is another bad excuse. You know, Sinner, if you have been a hearer of the Gospel, that this is not true! For bad as you are, no man is excluded from Christ on account of his vileness. "All manner of sin and of blasphemy shall be forgiven unto men."

The invitations of the Gospel do not stop at a certain point of sin. On the contrary, they seem to select the worst sinners first. What did the Savior say? "Begin at Jerusalem." But, Lord, the men who crucified You live there! "Begin at Jerusalem." But, Lord, it was in Jerusalem that they shed Your blood and thrust out the tongue and laughed at You and made a mockery of Your prayers! "Begin at Jerusalem"--the worst first--just as the surgeon in a battle is apt to look to the worst cases first. Here is a man who has lost his finger. Ah, well, let him bide awhile, we will see to that. But here is another who has lost a limb and he is bleeding fast and if the blood is not stopped, his life will ooze out. The surgeon sees him first.

O you great sinners, you who feel yourselves to have been notorious offenders, I pray you are not so guilty as to make this an excuse for not coming to Christ! On the contrary, use it as a reason why you should fly to Him at once. The more filth, the more need of washing. The more sick, the more need of a physician. The more hungry, the more welcome to the table. Come to Jesus just as you are, with all your sins--"Though they are as scarlet, they shall be as white as snow. Though they are red like crimson, they shall be as wool." No form of sin imaginable or unimaginable can by any possibility be a bar to any man's salvation if he will but believe on the Lord Jesus Christ!

Then comes another excuse, "Sir, I would trust Christ with my soul this morning, but I do not feel in any state to trust Christ. I have not that sense of sin which I think to be a fit preparation for coming to Christ--

" 'If anything is felt, 'tis only pain To find I cannot feel.'"

Ah, my dear Hearer, this is an excuse which looks like a very good one, but it has no truth in it! There is no fitness needed before you may trust in Christ! Whatever may be your present condition, if you trust Jesus Christ with your soul you are saved on the spot! Your sins are forgiven you! You are made a child of God! You are accepted in the Beloved! Where do you read of fitness for Christ in the Scriptures? Do you think the dead whom Jesus restored were fit to be raised? Why, Martha said of her brother, "Lord, by this time he stinks, for he has been dead four days"! Was there any fitness in Lazarus for a resurrection? And yet Jesus said, "Lazarus, come forth!" Does the

Gospel say, "He who is in a certain state, and then believes, shall be saved"? No, but, "He that believes and is baptized, shall be saved."

How am I bid to preach to you? Am I to say, "Whoever feels this is to come"? No, but, "Whoever will, let him come and take the water of life freely." Are you willing to have Christ? Then you may have Him, for Christ is as free to every needy sinner as the drinking fountain in the street is free to every thirsty passer-by. Trust Jesus, even if your heart is hard as granite--He can soften it! Trust Him though conscience is asleep--though all the mental faculties are perverted! Trust Him! It is His business to make you holy, not your business--trust Him to do it all! He is called Jesus because He saves His people from their sins!

Trust Him to overcome your corruptions, to kill your evil temper, to subdue your will, to soften your heart, to enlighten your conscience, to inflame your love--trust Him to do it ALL! O, be not so foolish as to say, "I am too ill to send for a doctor--when I get better, when I feel better, then I will send for him." Do not say, "I am so dirty. If I felt more clean, I would wash." No--wash because you are dirty! Wash because you have nothing but filth about you! Send for the Great Physician because there is no health in you! There is nothing in you but wounds, bruises and putrefying sores. Therefore let your faith entrust your healing entirely to Him.

Here comes another: "O Sir, I would trust Christ with my soul, but it seems too good to be true that God should save me on the spot, this morning. You little know where I was last night, or what I did yesterday. You cannot tell who I am nor how bad I have been and you tell me that if I trust Jesus Christ, I shall be saved. Sir, it is too good to be true! I cannot imagine it." My dear Friend, do you measure God's corn with your bushel? Because the thing seems an amazing thing to you, should it therefore be amazing unto Him? What if His thoughts should be as high above your thoughts as the heavens are above the earth? Is not this just what He has said in Scripture? I know you find it hard to forgive your fellow man, but my Father, my God, can readily forgive you!--

"Crimes of such horror to forgive, Such guilty daring worms to spare-- This is Your grand prerogative And none shall in the honor share."

He creates like a God! He does not make a few insects, or here and there a star! This great world He fashioned and He scattered the starry orbs about with both His hands. So when the Lord comes to pardon, He does not pardon some small offenses and wink at trifles--but the whole mass of sin He cleans away in a moment and all manner of sin and blasphemy, in an instant He casts behind His back. Believe that God is God and not such a one as you are! Believe that He is capable of doing greater things than you can dream of! Trust Him! Trust Him NOW and however good the things are you shall find them true! However great, they shall be yours! I think I hear one say, "It is too soon for me to come. Let me have a little look at the world first. I am scarcely fifteen or sixteen. There is plenty of time for me."

Have you been to the graveyard" Are there not there the records of those who have found fifteen or sixteen none too soon, for lo, at that age they were taken away to their last account? Too soon? Is it ever too soon to be happy? If religion made you miserable I might advise you to put it off to the last, but inasmuch as to be in Christ is to be happy, you cannot be in Him too soon! I have sat by many deathbeds and heard many regrets, but never did I hear a Christian regret that he was converted too soon! I have received many young converts into Church fellowship, but I never heard any one of them say they were sorry to be called by Grace so early!

If I were condemned to die and anyone should bring me a pardon, I should not think I received it too soon! The wrath of God abides on you--can it be too soon to escape from it? You are the subject of daily temptations and you daily add to your sins--can it be too soon to have a new heart and a right spirit? Others will row in the opposite direction, pleading, "Alas, it is too late!" The devil first puts the clock back and tells you it is too soon--and when this does not serve his turn--he puts it on and says, "The hour is passed, the day of Grace is over! Mercy's gate is bolted, you can never enter it!"

Let us answer this at once. It is never too late for a man to believe in Jesus while he is out of his grave. While the lamp of life continues to burn, the vilest sinner who returns shall find Christ ready to receive him. There have been men converted at a hundred years of age--we have instances on record of persons who have even passed the century and become children of Christ Jesus! How old are you? Are you in the sere and yellow leaf of eighty? Ah, you have many sins, but what a triumph of Grace it will be when eighty years of sin shall all be washed away in a moment! I tell you that if you were as old as Methuselah and in every year of that long life you had as many sins as you have already committed in the whole eighty years, yet the Grace of Jesus Christ is sufficient to put all this away!

Your sins may mount up like mountains, but the love of Christ, like Noah's flood, can go twenty cubits upwards and the tops of the mountains shall be covered. It is not too soon! It is not too late! Neither of these reasons are of any value though they delude many. "Well," says another, "I would believe in Christ but I do not know whether I am one of God's elect or not. Sir, that doctrine of election troubles me and staggers me. If I knew I was one of the elect, I would trust Christ."

That is--if God will show you His secrets then you will do God's will. And so the Almighty is to bend to your conditions and then you will do as He bids you? You will come to feast at the man's table if he will take you into his secret closet and show you all his treasure! He will do nothing of the kind! How foolish this talk is about election! The doctrine of election is a great and precious Truth of God, but it never can be a valid reason for a man's not believing in Christ! You are ill today and the doctor comes, "There," says he, "there is the medicine, I will guarantee if you take it, it will heal you." You say, "Sir, I would take it at once, but I do not know whether I am predestinated to get over this fever. If I am predestinated to live, why then, Sir, I will take the medicine, but I must know first." "Ah," says the doctor, "I tell you what. If you do not take it you are predestinated to die."

And I will tell you this--if you will not believe in Jesus Christ you will be damned, be you who you may--but you will not be able to lay it at predestination's door! It will be at your own. A man has fallen overboard. A rope is thrown to him, but he says, "I should like to grasp that rope only I do not know whether I am predestinated to be drowned." Fool! He will go down to the bottom with a lie in his mouth! We do not say, "I would sit down to dinner today, but I will not eat because I do not know whether I am predestinated to have any dinner today." We do not talk so foolishly in common things! Why, then, do we so in religion? When men are hard up for an excuse they are glad to run to the mysteries of God to use them as a veil to cover their faces. O my dear Friends, you must know that though God has a chosen people--yet when He commands you to believe in Christ--His having a chosen people, or not having a chosen people cannot excuse you from obedience to the Divine Command--"Believe on the Lord Jesus Christ and you shall be saved."

I could not attempt to go through all the excuses and therefore after handling two more, I will have done. "Well," says one, "if I were to believe in Christ I should be as bad, after a short time, as I used to be. I might be a little better for a time, but I should go back again--so it is of no use trusting Christ." That is to say, dear Friend, Jesus Christ says if you trust Him, He will save you--but you say if you trust Him, He will not save you! That is what it comes to. Jesus Christ promises that if you trust Him, He will save you from your sins. You say, "No, I should go back to my sins and be as bad as before."

Which am I to believe--your excuse, or His promise? Why, Christ's promise, surely! "But I tried once before," says one. Very likely you did, but Christ never tried! If He had tried He would have succeeded. "Well, but, I did hold on a certain length of time." I dare say you did--you held on. But if Christ had hold of you, He would never have let you go.

When you get hold of Christ you may soon drop Him--but when Jesus gets hold ofyou, He says, "I give unto My sheep eternal life and they shall never perish, neither shall any man pluck them out of My hand." If you had greatly trusted Christ He would not have suffered you to become what you used to be. "Well," says one, "I cannot trust Christ, I cannot believe Him."

You talk Latin, Brother! You talk Latin. "No," you say, "I do not talk Latin." Yes, you do. I will translate that word into the English for you. It means, "I will not." When you say, "I cannot," it means, "I will not." And understand, whenever the minister says, "You cannot," he means, "you will not," for he does not mean that you have any natural inability, but that you have a moral inability caused by your love of sin--a willful inability. "I cannot," is the Latin, but "I will not," is the English of it. A man once sent his servant to a certain town to fetch some goods. And he came back without them. "Well, Sir, why did you not go there?" Well, when I got to a certain place, I came to a river, Sir, a very deep river--I cannot swim and I had no boat--so I could not get over."

A good excuse, was it not? It looked so. But it happened to be a very bad one, for the master said, "Is there not a ferry there?" "Yes, Sir." "Did you ask the man to take you over?" "No, Sir." Surely the excuse was a mere fiction! So there are many things with regard to our salvation which we cannot do. Granted, but there is a ferry there! There is the Holy Spirit who is able to do all things and you remember the text, "If you, then, being evil, know how to give good gifts unto your children, how much more shall your Father which is in Heaven give good things to them that ask Him?" It is true you cannot make yourself a new heart, but did you ask for a new heart with sincerity and truth? Did you seek Christ? If you say, "Yes, I did sincerely seek Christ and Christ would not save me," why then you are excused.

But there never was a soul who could, in truth, say that! There never was a sinner yet who perished seeking Christ and there never will be! And if your heart's sincere desire is after the salvation which is treasured in Christ Jesus, then Heaven and earth may pass away but Christ will never cast you out while His own Word stands, "Him that comes to Me I will in no wise cast out."

"Still," you say, "I cannot trust Christ." Now, I am at issue with you here--I am at issue with every awakened sinner. I agree with you if you will let me give my own translation of the word "cannot"--that you will not--but if it is to stand as the word is generally used, I am at issue with you.

Suppose that you believe me to be an honest man. Would it be fair after that, to say, "Sir, I cannot believe you"? Now, if you believe me to be a liar, I can very well understand that you cannot trust me. But if you take it for granted that I am incapable of telling a falsehood and yet do not believe what I tell you, you are a liar! Now, you believe that Christ is incapable of falsehood--you are not like those who are ignorant of the Character of Christ and therefore you know Him to be incapable of untruthfulness. And then you say you cannot believe Him? Seeing that Jesus Christ cannot but speak Truth, it cannot be a difficult thing for any man to believe what He speaks! If you have sufficient light given you by the Holy Spirit to know that Christ is the Truth, I believe you have sufficient power from the same source to believe what Christ says.

I trace this to God's gift, but I pray you to exercise the power which you certainly have. Tell Christ you cannot believe Him? Will you tell Him that to His face when He sits upon the Judgment Seat at last? Will you dare to say this when His eyes of fire shall look you through and through? "Most holy Christ, I could not trust You! Most truthful Savior, I could not believe You! I suspected You. I doubted You!" "Why did you doubt Me? What cause had I ever given you? Why did you think Me a liar? In what had I ever broken My promises, or when did I err from the Truth?" "He that believes not," says John, "has made God a liar, because he believes not the record that God gave of His Son." O, think of this and never make that excuse again! Instead of saying, "I cannot believe," say, "I cannot make God a liar, I must therefore believe, for I know God is no liar--I must therefore trust His Son Jesus Christ!

I have recounted a few of the excuses. Perhaps you will make another batch before the evening comes on--you who determine not to be saved. It is only the mighty Spirit of God who can sweetly constrain your will to yield to Christ and so I close with these two or three words, upon the third point.

III. HOW FOOLISH THUS TO MAKE EXCUSES! For first remember with Whom it is you are dealing. You are not making excuses before a man who may be duped by them--you make these excuses before the heart-searching God! My dear Hearers, let me speak very solemnly and push this point closely home. You know that God can see through all this--why, then, do you hang up such thin veils? Confess before Him now your folly--"Lord, I have been an enemy to You. Lord, I have been averse to Your Son, Jesus Christ, and therefore have I dreamed up these excuses--forgive me. I see how foolish I have been. Grant that I may do so no more."

Remember again, what it is you are trifling with. It is your own soul, the soul which can never die! You are trifling with a Heaven which you will never see if you keep on with these excuses. You are trifling, Sinner, with that Hell which must be your never-ending portion if you continue as you are. Can you play with Hell-fire? O, can you make sport of Heaven? Can you laugh at the blood of Jesus? You are really doing so while you are thus halting between two opinions. If you must play the fool, find something cheaper to play with than this! O Sirs, if you must have mirth, I pray you have it out of something else than this.

To be saved! Listen to Heaven's music! To be lost! Listen to Hell's groans! Neither of these things are matters for you to play with. Say, as now you are sitting here--I pray God help you to say it before you leave this building--"Lord, I have been trifling with eternity. I have been making frivolous excuses rather than I would accept Your love in Christ. I have trifled with Heaven and Hell--grant, Lord, that this may be brought to an end--that I may love and trust You this day."

Remember, again, that these excuses will look very different soon. How will you make excuses when you come to die, as die you must? When death gets the grip of you and the strong man fails. When they wipe the death sweat from your fevered brow. When the glaze of death's night is coming over your eyeballs--what will you think of these excuses then? It may be you will rave with very fury at yourselves that you could have played with your souls to such an extent. What will you do with your excuses when you stand at the bar of Judgment? The trumpet rings, you have awakened from your grave, you stand amidst the myriads to be judged. The books are opened and Christ proclaims your doom--"Depart, you cursed, into everlasting fire." Will excuses comfort you then? Will you be able to say, then, "Lord, it was too soon! Lord, it was too late! Lord, I was too great a sinner to believe in Jesus! Lord I did not need a Savior"?

No, when the trumpet peals and the heavens are in a blaze. When the sun is turned into sackcloth and the moon into blood and the stars fall like fig leaves from the tree, you will find other work to do than excuse-making! You will weep and wail because of sin and when you are cast into Hell what will you make, then, of your excuses? Written in letters of fire you shall see in one tremendous arch above your heads, "You knew your duty, but you did it not! You heard the Gospel, but you made excuses!" Thundering more tremendous than the trump of resurrection shall come these words to you, "Because I have called and you refused, I have stretched out My hand and no man regarded, I, also, will laugh at your calamity. I will mock when your fear comes. When your fear comes as desolation and your destruction comes as a whirlwind. When distress and anguish come upon you."

O, the Lord have mercy upon you, excuse-makers, and bring you to look to Jesus now! Now, I say, for the Scripture says, "Today is the accepted time, today is the day of salvation." The only way to end your excuses is not by praying nor resolving, but by looking to Christ. There hangs the bleeding Savior on the Cross. He dies--the Just for the unjust--to bring us to God! He suffers there that sin may be forgiven! Look to Him! Trust Him and you shall be saved! My Hearer, I give you now in God's name this invitation, this command--trust your soul to Jesus, the Son of God, who suffered for sin--and you shall be saved!

But mind you, I may never meet you all this side the grave but I will meet you all at God's Great Day and if you receive not Christ and trust in Him, I am clear of your blood. Upon my garments your doom cannot fall. You have heard the Gospel! You have been told to trust Jesus as you are! You have been assured that He is able to save to the uttermost them that come to Him! You have been bid to come and now on your own heads be your soul's ruin if you come not!

May the Spirit of God take these things and apply them to your souls. May He be as a fire and as a hammer in your souls--as a fire to melt, or as a hammer to break. And may you, today, with brokenness of heart take Christ to be your Savior, both now and forever. Amen.

God Pleading For Saints, And Saints Pleading For God

DELIVERED ON SUNDAY MORNING, JULY 10, 1864,
BY THE REV. C. H. SPURGEON,
AT THE METROPOLITAN TABERNACLE, NEWINGTON.

"O Lord, You ha ve pleaded the causes of my soul; You have redeemed my life." -- Lamentations 3:58.

THE Prophet speaks experimentally as of a matter which he had proved for himself. There is no true understanding of the Truths of God except by a personal experience of them. We have heard of men sitting in their drawing rooms and writing volumes on voyages and travels--but such books always bear the marks of fiction upon their title page--they can never vie in interest and freshness with the adventures of men who have actually traversed lands unknown. The botanist who shall never have seen a flower must necessarily be a mere pretender to the science. And the soldier who has never shouldered a gun is nothing but a raw recruit.

And so the man who knows the Truth of God only in the letter of it, by what he has heard with his ears, but does not know it by what, "he has tasted and his hands have handled and his eyes have looked upon of the Word of Life," knows, indeed, nothing to any purpose and it were well for him to confess his ignorance. Our Prophet puts it not, "Lord, You have pleaded the causes of another man's soul," but, "You have pleaded the causes of my soul." At the opening of this discourse I invite you to ask yourselves whether you have an interest in this pleading. Has the Lord pleaded the causes of your soul?

Such a suggestion may be of great service to you. That eminent Puritan preacher, Mr. Thomas Dolittle, was once teaching the catechism to the children of the congregation, as was the custom of the Puritans on Sunday. He came to the question, "What is effectual calling?" The answer was given, as it stands in our admirable catechism, "Effectual calling is the work of God's Spirit, whereby, convincing us of our sin and misery, enlightening our minds in the knowledge of Christ and renewing our wills, He does persuade and enable us to embrace Jesus Christ freely offered to us in the Gospel."

The good man stopped and said to the lads around him, "Let us use the personal pronoun in the singular--are there any among you who can say that all this is yours?" To his great joy there stood up one who with many tears and many sobs, said, "Effectual calling is the work of God's Spirit, whereby, convincing me of my sin and misery, enlightening my mind in the knowledge of Christ and renewing my will, He has persuaded and enabled me to embrace Jesus Christ freely offered to me in the Gospel."

Now this is the true way to understand any doctrine as set forth in the Word of God--by being able to feel that in your own personal case God has worked upon your soul--has brought you into reconciliation with Himself and enabled you to rejoice in His gracious promises! You are greatly blessed if, like the Prophet, you can speak experimentally. You must not fail to observe how positively he speaks. He does not say, "I hope, I trust, I sometimes think that God has pleaded the causes of my soul." He speaks of it as a matter of fact not to be disputed. "You have pleaded the causes of my soul."

Let us, Brethren, by the aid of the gracious Comforter, shake off those doubts and fears which so much mar our peace and comfort! Be this our prayer today that we may have done with the harsh croaking voice of surmise and suspicion and may be able to speak with the clear, melodious voice of full assurance, "I know whom I have believed and am persuaded that He is able to keep that which I have committed unto Him." I like to hear a Christian, when he tells his own experience, speak of these things as one who knows what he is talking about--not as though it were all guesswork with him-- but as one who with infallible certainty, the Spirit of God bearing witness with his spirit, knows that he is speaking the Truth of God.

"You have pleaded the causes of my soul." Here I must bid you observe how gratefully the Prophet speaks, ascribing all the glory to God alone. You perceive there is not a word concerning himself or his own pleadings. He does not ascribe his deliverance in any measure to any man, much less to his own merit. But it is "You"--"You, O Lord, have pleaded the causes of my soul; You have redeemed my life." A grateful spirit should ever be cultivated by the Christian. And especially after deliverances we should prepare a song for our God. O Believers, wake up your hearts and tune your tongues to compete with angels before the Throne! Earth should be a temple filled with the songs of grateful saints and every day should be a censer smoking with the sweet incense of thanksgiving! How joyful Jeremiah seems to be while he records the Lord's mercy! How triumphantly he lifts up the strain!

He has been in the low dungeon and is even now no other than the Weeping Prophet, poor Jeremiah. And yet in the very book which is called, "Lamentations"--clear as the voice of Miriam when she dashed her fingers against the timbrel and shrill as the note of Deborah when she met Barak with shouts of victory--we hear the voice of Jeremy going up to Heaven--"You have pleaded the causes of my soul; You have redeemed my life"! O children of God, seek after a vital experience of the Lord's loving kindness and when you have it, speak positively of it! Sing gratefully! Shout triumphantly! And let none of your enemies stop your glorying this side of Heaven, for on the other side of the river the free Grace of God shall be your glory forever and ever--and you shall sing eternally, "You have pleaded the causes of my soul; You have redeemed my life."

We shall occupy the time allotted to the sermon this morning, first, by considering Divine pleading as the Christian's joy. And then by talking about the Christian's pleading the causes of his God as his duty and delight. God pleads my cause--this is my joy. I must plead God's cause--this is at once my privilege and my reasonable service.

I. First, then, let us come with heartfelt joy to the consideration of DIVINE PLEADING.

1. The Lord pleads our cause in the Court of Providence. Jeremiah was confined in the low dungeon. He was cast into a wet, damp hole--a pit. And here he would have been left to rot for no one spoke a word for him except Ebed-melech, an Ethiopian eunuch, in the service of the king. He went to Zedekiah and pleaded on behalf of poor Jeremiah. The king gave Ebedmelech leave to fetch Jeremiah out of the pit. Now, you observe, Jeremiah was never ungrateful to Ebedmelech. Ebedmelech had a blessing in return for what he did, yet Jeremiah ascribes his deliverance not to the eunuch, but to God--"You have pleaded the causes of my soul."

The Christian may expect that in the course of Providence, when he meets with trouble, God will raise up for him at different times and in unexpected quarters persons who will take an interest in him and be the means of working out his deliverance. God sits at the helm of Providence and when the vessel is almost on the rock, He can pilot it into the deep waters again! And when His servants have been obliged by the tempest to reef their sails, He knows how, as the Master of the seas, to change the winds to a gale so favorable that with all sails spread they can fly before the gale to the desired haven.

Sometimes God pleads the cause of His people by silencing their enemies. What a remarkable instance you have of this in the case of Jacob! His sons had most cruelly and basely killed the Shechemites. Having betrayed them by false promises they then slew them in cold blood. Jacob said, "You have troubled me to make me to stink among the inhabitants of the land, among the Canaanites and Perizzites: and I being few in number, they shall gather themselves together against me and slay me. And I shall be destroyed, I and my house." How strange was it that he suffered no molestation! Surely the Lord had cast a solemn awe upon the hearts of the Canaanites round about. His all-commanding voice was heard in their hearts, "Touch not My anointed and do my Prophet no harm."

Even though Jacob's family was grossly in the wrong and his sons had committed a foul deed, yet nevertheless, the Lord pleaded the cause of His chosen servant and his enemies were as still as stones. It will often be so with the Lord's peculiar ones. When your foot has slipped--when you have spoken unadvisedly with your lips--if you have deeply repented of the sin you may leave the matter before God, and He will either silence every dog's tongue, or turn their barking to His glory.

At other times our God has pleaded the cause of His people by raising up friends for them. Take the instance of Joseph. Reuben pleads for him when his Brethren intend to kill him. When in Egypt he is put into the dungeon through a false charge brought by the wife of Potiphar. He is not treated as a common criminal, for even in the dungeon God finds him friends. He behaves himself so discreetly that the master of the prison makes him one of the keepers of the ward! The Lord gave him favor in the eyes of men.

Observe another case. Here comes a poor maiden from Moab with her mother-in-law. God will plead the cause of her soul. She goes, as many another maid had done, to the field to glean. Providence guides her to the estate of an unknown kinsman. Boaz looks upon her and before long she becomes the joy of his house and the mistress of his fields. Take a yet more remarkable case. Moses is put into the ark of bulrushes. What can the child say for itself? Among the crocodiles it lies exposed to imminent hazard. Pharaoh's daughter comes. What was that mysterious influence which softened her heart when she looked upon that comely child as it wept in that little cradle which might soon have been its coffin?

Why was it that she said, "This is one of the Hebrews' children...take it and nurse it for me"? Why, it could only have been because God has a way of touching human hearts and making them friendly to His own people! He pleads the cause of His servants. He does not violate the wills of their enemies, but He wisely turns those wills into the channel of friendship. It was very remarkable that David, when he so much needed a friend through Saul's hostility to him, should have found one near to the throne--the heir-apparent to the kingdom. Strange that Jonathan, who naturally would have taken his father's part and would have hated David as a supplanter, should, nevertheless, have his soul so knit to the heart of David that he gives up his crown cheerfully and makes a covenant with David!

Dear Friends, you thus see that either by silencing enemies, or else by raising up friends, God can, in Providence, plead the cause of your soul! Or if men should seem to have even less than this to do with it, He knows how, by special Providences, to bring you out of the depth of your difficulties. You see this again in the case of Joseph. He was put in prison. The butler promised to speak for him, but forgot him. Well, what shall happen? The king must dream a dream. Pharaoh cannot sleep while Joseph is in the dungeon. Seven years of plenty must come and seven years of famine, in order that Joseph, falsely accused, might have his "righteousness brought forth as brightness and the salvation thereof as a lamp that burns."

Such cases will commonly occur. No Christian man, I think, can look back through many years of his life without observing some strange and singular workings of the Divine hand by which, in an unexpected manner, God has worked his deliverance. Come then, if this is so--let us be of good cheer this morning! We need not fret and worry ourselves about worldly things for our heavenly Father pleads our cause! Tried Soul, He knows what you need this morning! You have not told anybody your distress and you need not, for He "knows that you have need of these things." He knows when it will be best for you to receive help. And if He keeps you a little time in poverty, He knows it is good for you to be left in the shade.

He understands Providence better than you do and He can make the great world a broad work to bless the little world of your heart. There is not a single wheel by which the machinery of Providence is affected which is not turned by His hand. You know His love to be as infinite as His wisdom and His power to be as great as His love--then go where your Master went when He was in the storm--to the rear of the ship and fall asleep upon the pillow of the Providence of God! You have done your best. You have worked hard. You have strived to provide things honestly in the sight of all men--and yet things do not prosper with you as you wish they would. You are content to be poor--you are willing to be in just such a place as God would put you and yet your straits and your difficulties seem just now to be too many for you!

Now is the time to exercise faith upon a living God! Your God is not worth having if He cannot help you when you want help. Surely your religion must be a lie if it cannot buoy you up under troubles which, after all, are not the heaviest which fall to the lot of men. Come, cast your burden on your God--He cares for you! Before many days are past you shall come up to this house, if not with these words upon your tongue, yet with this sentiment in your heart, "You have pleaded the causes of my soul; You have redeemed my life."

2. Our text may be read with great comfort if we think upon the Court of Divine Law. You and I may picture ourselves this morning, without exaggeration or untruth, as being led into the Court of the Law. The Law at once arraigns us upon the charge of having positively broken the Commands of God. "He has broken every one of them," says the Law, "either in deed, or word, or thought. There is not a single precept which this man has not most distinctly set at defiance."

The witnesses appear. The devil willingly bears witness and adds many falsehoods to the accusation. The Omniscience of God stands as a swift witness against us. And our own conscience is compelled to bear testimony that we have, indeed, sinned and that we have "gone astray from the womb, speaking lies." What is now to be done? We are asked if we have anything to say. Why sentence should not be pronounced upon us. We are silent. Well may we hold down our heads, for what reason is there why we should not be punished for the sins which we have committed? There was a time when we would have pleaded, "Not guilty," but we know better now. We know our guilt. It stares us in the face. We cannot plead the force of temptation, for we know that often we have tempted ourselves and have, without any incentive beyond our own hearts, run greedily after sin.

The Law sits upon its throne of judgment and since we cannot plead, it makes proclamation, "Is there anyone in court who will act as advocate for this rebel whose silence and shame witness to his guilt? If there is none to show cause to the contrary, I will open the Great Book and read his sentence. I will put on the black cap and he shall be taken to doom." Up stands the bleeding Savior, the great Advocate for sinners! What does Jesus plead? "O Justice," says He, "I plead not that these men have not sinned--I do confess on their behalf that they have grievously erred. But I plead for them that their sin has been punished--punished in Me. All the curse of their sin was laid on Me.

"I loved them from before the foundations of the world. And having loved them I took their sin upon Myself and therefore it is not on them. I suffered in their place and therefore, Justice, you cannot punish two for one offense-- having struck Me for them--you cannot now strike them. I plead My blood--these wounds of Mine, once opened by the cruel nails--this side of Mine, once rent with the spear--I plead these--My groans, My tears, My agony, My death-- for these I suffered on their account. Their sin was punished in Me. Let them go free!"

Thus He pleads right gloriously. Who shall answer Him? What more is wanted? But the Law brings another charge. It says, "Granted that sin is condoned by the Atonement. Allowed that through Your sacrifice, most glorious Redeemer, Your people are free from sin, yet I demand on the behalf of God that the Law should be kept! These men were bound not merely to be negatively without sin, but they were bound positively to serve God with all their heart and soul and strength. And inasmuch as they have not done it, they cannot enter Heaven. How shall they be rewarded for service never performed--how shall they win the crown without having kept the command?"

Here, too, we are silent, for what have we ever done? What righteousness have we? Are not our righteousnesses filthy rags, the very best of them? We dare not say, "Lord, my prayers entitle me to Heaven. My preaching, my doings, my almsgivings." No, we know better than this! We feel that we are vile and full of sin and therefore put our finger on our lips and confess that we deserve to be shut out of Heaven. Again the Savior rises and He pleads, "I was appointed of God to be their Substitute and being such I kept the Law on their behalf! The whole of the Ten Commandments I have carried out to the fullest extent both in the letter and in the spirit. I have served God with all My soul and strength.

"I have loved My neighbor as Myself. I have been obedient to death, even to the death of the Cross. Have I not magnified the Law and made it honorable?" The Law bows its awful head and confesses, "You have, O Jesus, rendered better obedience than these men could have rendered, for You are Divine. You have brought the righteousness of God instead of the righteousness of man. You have brought Your own perfection, glorified and exalted by the splendor of Your Nature and laid it down in the place of the perfection of man which he could not bring. You have, indeed, paid the debt. You have pleaded well and the culprit is free!"

Beloved, "Who shall lay anything to the charge of God's elect? It is God that justifies. Who is he that condemns? It is Christ that died, yes rather, that is risen again, who is even at the right hand of God, who also makes intercession for us." My Soul, triumph in your God! This day rejoice with all your might, for Christ has prevalently pleaded your cause and you are acquitted--no, you are brought in as meritorious and accepted in the sight of God through the plea of the Beloved! Let us rejoice that in the court of Heaven's justice we can say, "You have pleaded the causes of my soul." O, can we all say it? Has Christ pleaded for you? Has your faith put your soul into Christ's hands? If not, I pity you. And let every child of God pity and pray for you. But if Jesus pleads for you we will rejoice together and be glad this morning!

3. In the third place, Jesus pleads the cause of my soul in the Court of Conscience which is a minor imitation of the great Court of Heaven. Let me talk to your hearts now, Brothers and Sisters, as the Lord helps me. Sometimes you have doubts and fears springing up and conscience assists them, for it says, "You know what a guilty worm you are! What? You a saved soul? It was but the other day that you were murmuring at God, and doubting His faithfulness!

Look at your prayers--what cold things they are! See your daily life--what inconsistencies mingle with it! Mark your temper--how quick! How fierce! Look at yourself as to spiritual things--was there ever a more poverty-stricken soul than you are? Why, you are as black as the tents of Kedar and quite as filthy. Can you see any good thing in your- self? Why, are you not a very sink of corruption, a walking dunghill, a mass of abominations? And yet you say, 'I am a child of God'? How can it be?" And now, when these thoughts arise, you and I find it sometimes rather hard to answer them. And if we go upon the common logic of human reason and begin to argue, "But I do find in myself some humblings of soul. I have some melting desires towards the Lord God. I find this and that and therefore I have some evidence," it is ten to one that conscience and the devil together will beat us and we shall be ready to lie down in despair.

But, oh, how sweet it is when our soul tells of the finished work of the Lord Jesus Christ! Then--I hope that I am now talking what you all know and many of you know sweetly--then as you turn to Jesus Christ and see the precious Person of the perfect Savior pouring out streams of cleansing blood--there is a voice which speaks to you and pleads the cause of your soul! You feel, "Let conscience say what he may, this blood has answered him! Let the devil suggest what he will, this complete Atonement shall shut his mouth!" "I will," says Rutherford, in one of his sweet letters, "I will hold to Christ under water and if I must drown I will not let go my hold of Him."

And so the Believer can say he has got such a grip of Jesus--such a hand-hold of the Savior--that though ten thousand times ten thousand fears should roll over his head, he sings--

"I do believe, I will believe That Jesus died for me."

Sometimes after stern conflicts a sweet peace pervades your mind. I cannot describe it better than by the calm which succeeds the tempest and its heavy showers. The whole earth appears to put on a greener dress than before. The flowers pour out their fragrance. The birds sing and men rejoice in the clear shining after the rain. So is it with us. "The time of the singing of birds is come and the voice of the turtle is heard in our land," because Jesus Christ applies with Divine power His own merits and His own blood to our conscience and all is well!

I do not know whether you know what this means, but if any of you do not, you have lost a joy worth a thousand worlds! For out of Heaven I know of no peace like that which pervades the conscience when Jesus pleads within. Guilty we are in ourselves, but we are "complete in Him." Foul and vile I am and yet I am perfect in Christ Jesus--lost, ruined and undone in the first Adam--but saved and redeemed--made to sit in heavenly places in the Second Adam. Ah, doubts and fears--where are they now--when Jesus pleads for my soul? Memory may come and tell me all the past. Fear may haunt me with black visions of the future--my powers may be perverted to the service of despair--yet if my soul can keep her hold upon the finished work of my Redeemer I shall yet come off more than conqueror, singing, "You have pleaded the causes of my soul; You have redeemed my life."

4. We have thus been to three courts--the Court of Providence, the Court of Justice and the Court of Conscience. And now, pausing awhile, I would not have you forget how Jesus Christ pleads our cause in the Court of Heaven. To a true-hearted man who lives a life of prayer it is ever a rich consolation that his prayers do not go up to Heaven alone. Jesus, our great High Priest, never ceases to intercede for His saints!

A poor man once wished to have a favor of a great one. This great lord had a son--a very kind and condescending one, who spoke to the poor man and said--"If you will write a petition to my father, he is very gracious and he will be sure to grant it. And so that you may have no doubts about the success of your petition, give it to me and I will take it in my own hand up to my father's house for you and make your case my own. I will say to him, 'My father, hear this poor man's petition, not for his own sake, but consider it as mine. Do me the personal favor and kindness of hearing this man's prayer, as though it were my prayer--for, indeed, I make it mine!' "

The poor man wrote out his petition, but when he had finished it, "Alas !"he said to himself, "this will never do to present before the great one. It is so full of errors! I have blotted it with my tears and where I have tried to scratch out a word which I had spelt wrongly, I have made it worse and have so badly worded the whole petition that I am afraid the great one will throw it in the fire, or never notice it." "But," said his friend, "I will write it out in a fair clear hand for you so that there shall be no blots and no blunders. And when I have done so, I will do as I have said--I will take it in my own hand, put my own name at the bottom of it with your name and will offer it as our joint petition. And I will put it upon this footing, 'My father, do it for me. Not for him, but for me.' "

When the poor man saw his petition thus written out and knew it was in such hands, he went his way sure that the answer must come. And come it did. You know that story well. This is what Jesus Christ has done for you! He takes our poor unworthy prayers and amends them. He makes them perfect and sprinkles His own blood upon them and takes them up before His Father's Throne, and says, "Father, for My sake hear this sinner. For My sake give him pardon. Accept him and preserve him." And then the gracious Father, who can deny nothing to His beloved Son, gives His glad assent and the blessing comes to you! This is a great mercy, but I will tell you of something which is a greater mercy still. It is transcendently encouraging that when we pray, Jesus Christ prays! But what is better still, is, that when we do not pray Jesus Christ prays!

Oh, my soul was ravished a little while ago when thinking over that passage about Peter--"Simon, Simon, Satan has desired to have you that he may sift you as wheat. But"--what? "But go and pray for yourself"? Well, that were good advice, but it is not so put. Our Master does not say, "But I will keep you watchful and so you shall be preserved." That were a great blessing, but it is, "But I have prayed for you, that your faith fail not." Oh, you do not know when Jesus Christ prays for you! We pass through unseen dangers and we little know what are the dangers through which we pass!

We are something like Christian, when Bunyan pictures him as going through the valley of the shadow of death. He could hear the howling on the right hand and on the left, but he did not know--for it was very dark--how very bad the way was. But when the sun rose and he looked back and saw the pits and the traps and the quagmires and the fiends and evil spirits--then he could not but lift up his hands in astonishment that he had been brought through them all! When you and I get on the hilltops of Heaven and look back upon all the way whereby the Lord our God has led us, even the songs of Heaven will not be loud enough for the gratitude we shall feel towards Him who, before the Eternal Throne, undid the mischief which Satan was doing upon earth!

O, how shall we thank Him that He never held His peace--that day and night He pointed to the wounds upon His hands and carried our names upon His breastplate? How we shall adore our great High Priest! With what transport shall we kiss those dear feet of His when we remember that He did never cease to intercede, but that even before Satan had began to tempt He had forestalled him and entered a plea in Heaven! You know He does not say, "Satan has sifted you and therefore I will pray," but, "Satan has desired to have you." He catches Satan even in his very desire--nips his desire in the bud--kills the cockatrice while it is yet in the shell.

He does not say, "But I have desired to pray for you." No, it is, "I have prayed for you. I have done it already. I have gone to Court and entered a counterplea even before the charge is made. I have countermined even before the mine has been dug. "O Jesus, what a comfort it is that You have pleaded the causes of my soul when I have been asleep! When I might have gone sleeping on down to Hell You were awake pleading the causes of my soul!" Here, then, is a cause of great joy and great gratitude!

5. Once more, Jesus Christ will plead the cause of His people and our heavenly Father will do so, too, in the Last Great Day of judgment. It is not a very pleasant thing for a man honestly to serve God and then to find his character taken from him. And yet, Beloved, this has been the lot of all true men in every age. The world never does permit a man to rebuke her follies without replying with a volley of mud. It she cannot stop the man's mouth, she blackens the man's character.

If you will turn to the lives of any of the saints of God you will discover that they were the victims of slanders of the grossest kind. To this very day it is asserted by Romanists that Martin Luther was a drunkard. In his own day he was called the German beast--that for lust he had to marry Catharine! If you turn to the life of Whitfield--our great and mighty Whitfield--in more modern times what was his character? Why he was accused of every crime that even Sodom knew! And Perjury stood up and swore that all was true. As for Wesley--I have heard that on one occasion he said that he had been charged with every crime in the calendar except drunkenness. And when a woman stood up in the crowd and accused him of that, he then said, "Blessed God, I have now had all manner of evil spoken against me falsely for Christ's name sake!"

You remember in the life of John Bunyan that episode concerning Agnes Beaumont? The good man suffered this young woman to ride behind him on his horse to a meeting at Gamlingay and for this his character was implicated in two charges before a magistrate which might have involved him in the crime of poisoning and laid the foundation for villainous reports of uncleanness! Yet John Bunyan was the purest and most heavenly-minded man who ever put his hand to paper. And he did put his hand to paper as no other man ever did who was not Inspired!

Now, this is not pleasant, but if you are a true Christian and you are called to occupy a prominent post in the service of God, be resigned to this fact--expect to lose your character. Expect not to have the good opinion of any but your God and those faithful ones, who like you, are willing to bear contempt. But what joy it is for all these holy men to know that at the last God will plead the cause of their souls! There will be a resurrection of persons as they really were, not as they seemed to be and were misrepresented. At the Last Great Day there will be a resurrection of reputations--reputations which had been laid into the dark grave which Calumny had dug--which had been covered with the sod of Contempt and over which there had been raised an epitaph of Infamy.

These reputations will all rise up! They have washed their robes and made them white. They are black no longer! The men who were pointed at and hooted and despised shall now go streaming up the shining way of fame and glory amidst the loud shouts of praise which the great Avenger shall receive from assembled worlds! They shall awake to Glory while others rise to shame and everlasting contempt! Oh, what must it be to be in the last day plucked and stripped of your plumes? What will be the fate of the Pharisee? Of the hypocrite who will find all his fine feathers torn away and himself left to hide his contemptible head in the caverns of the earth--but denied even that consolation--set out before the full blaze of day as an acknowledged liar before God and man?

But how different the condition of the poor man who lived and died in undeserved contempt! He who wakes up to find himself a bright and shining spirit and all his adversaries compelled to admit that God has pleaded the causes of his soul and has avenged him of his accusers! Thus, you see, our text is not a small one--the words are few but full of meaning. And I have but very poorly set forth what our soul, I trust, feels to be the truth--"You have pleaded the causes of my soul; You have redeemed my life."

II. Now I want your solemn and earnest attention while for a few minutes I plead for what is our reasonable service, namely, THAT IF THE LORD HAS PLEADED THE CAUSES OF OUR SOUL, WE SHOULD PLEAD HIS CAUSE WHILE WE HAVE ANY BREATH TO PRAY OR A TONGUE WITH WHICH TO BEAR WITNESS FOR HIM.

Pleading the cause of Christ is the lifework of the Christian--it has to be done by some in the high places of the field. This age has given up all witness-bearing for Christ. We have grown so enamored of that gilded idol called charity that nowadays the Truth of God is fallen in the streets. It has come to be, by general consent, allowed by all men that religion is all very well in its way. That every man must keep his own religion and not meddle with other people's--that a lie may be a truth, or a truth may be a lie and that whether a doctrine is a truth or a lie does not matter a button--that, in fact, we are all of us to be agreed upon this one point--that God's Truth is not worthy our contending for.

That which is of man's invention and that which is of God's teaching are now put side by side in alliance and a compromise is effected in the name of brotherly love. I look upon Christendom at this present day as too much like a putrid swamp, a stagnant pool--the calm is deep, but deadly. O for some holy wind to stir the rotting mass! Modern charity would gag the mouth of every advocate of the Truth of God and send every faithful minister of God back to his bed to sleep his time out until the millennium shall dawn!

Brethren, I trust that an end shall come to this! And if bickering and strife and ill-will shall follow, though I shall lament these attendant evils, I shall rejoice that an earnest and healthy love of Truth and an earnest contention for it have been revived in the land. Rutherford, whose name must be dear to every Believer who knows his writings, says, "I thank God that I did never for a single moment put so much as a hoof, or a hair's breadth of Christ's Truth into compromise. That I did take Christ only and alone and did never leave room for the Roman harlot, but only for Christ--or Christ only!"

Here was a man shut up in Aberdeen, driven away from Anworth, weeping because, as he said, he envied the very sparrows which flew around the old Kirk where he was used to having such sweet visions of his Lord. And yet he said if the giving up of a jot of the Truth of God could have given him his liberty and enabled him to go back to minister to his faithful flock, he would not give it up! For to him Truth was dearer than liberty--no, dearer than even life itself! He says, "I am prepared for all consequences. And if even black-faced Death should knock at my door, I would bid him enter." Our spiritual forefathers, on both sides the Tweed, were not men to be worried about the caprice of every oarsman.

They knew the Truth of God and they knew Christ and they did not divide between Christ and Truth and say, "Love Christ and then believe what you like." No, they believed that Christ and Truth were identical. They believed Truth to be the Savior's crown jewels and they would as soon think of loving a king and trampling on his crown as of pretending to love Christ and then trampling on His Truth!

What? Shall I pluck the clothes from my neighbor's back and tell him that I love him? Will you pluck the Truth from Christ and throw it away as though it were but old rags and then say you love Christ? You cannot love Christ if you do not love Truth. And you cannot have Jesus unless you are willing to take up your cross daily and follow Him. For my part, God helping me, my soul is set on this--to court no more the good word of any man--to be no more a worshipper at the shrine of that false goddess, Charity! To have all the brotherly love I can, but to show it by an honest, outspoken declaration that the day is come when Rome is not to stand in England unchallenged.

Dressed in garments half Protestant and half Popish, the Church, as by law established, continues to make a mockery of honesty by using language in an unnatural sense! Juggling with men's souls! Pampering Puseyites, indulging infidels, and yet claiming to be evangelical. An end must come to the infamy of teaching Popish doctrine in the Prayer Book and then preaching evangelical doctrine in the pulpit. The day is come when we must shake our garments of such a Church and when the best of her sons, though we have fraternized with them, must come out from her or we can have no more communion with them! The day of Babylon's destruction comes! The cup is prepared and her sons and her daughters shall drink of it.

And only they shall be found clear in the day of account who shall come out and plead the cause of God's pure Truth and God's pure Truth alone. I think my Master deserves this of those of us who stand upon the high places of the field. And of you who are less known, but love your Master none the less, march with us shoulder to shoulder! Bear reproach with us! We have to bear it! Be as willing to be rejected as we are willing to be rejected! Be as willing to lose character and name and reputation and standing as we are! And if you cannot speak with a voice which can be heard as far--yet proclaim with a voice as clear and plain--that you love Truth and Christ and that for Truth and Christ you will give up everything--but that you cannot give up these!

Beloved, there is a way of bearing witness for Christ which you must adopt--that of witnessing by your consistency of conduct. Holiness is, after all, the mightiest weapon which a Christian can wield. Be you holy as Christ is holy. Let no man spatter mire upon your garments. Walk so that you never put us to grief. As a Church be so pure and heavenly that you may be called the Nazarites of God who were purer than snow and whiter than milk. And then, though we have no wealth and boast not gorgeous architecture and the swell of pealing music, yet we shall have this for our music--your holiness, your purity, your separation from all uncleanness. And this for our architecture--that you are built up as a temple for the Lord!

Lastly, we can all plead for God in a private way. Oh, there is a great power in pleading for God with individuals. A man went to preach for seven summers on the village green and good was done. Joseph sometimes listened to the preacher, but only to ridicule him. There were many souls converted but he remained as hard as ever. A certain John who had felt the power of Truth, worked with him in the barn and one day, between the strokes of the flail, John spoke a word for Truth and for God. But Joseph laughed at him and hinted at hypocrisy and many other things.

Now John was very sensitive and his whole soul was filled with grief at Joseph's banter and after he had spoken, feeling a flush of emotion, he turned to the corner of the barn and hid his face while a flood of tears came streaming from his eyes. He wiped them away with the corner of his sleeve and came back to his flail. Joseph had noticed the tears though John had tried to hide them. And what argument could not do and what preaching could not do, those tears, through God the Holy Spirit, did effectually, for Joseph thought to himself, "What? Does John care for my soul and weep for my soul? Then it is time I should care and weep for it, too."

Beloved, witness thus for Christ! Be it mine to weep for the sins of the times and prophecy against them! Be it yours in your own private walk and conversation to rebuke private sin and by your loving earnestness to make Jesus Christ dear to many souls! Tell them that Jesus Christ came to save sinners! Tell them that He is able to save to the uttermost all who come to Him! Tell them that, "whoever believes on Him shall not perish, but have everlasting life," and in this way you shall plead the cause of God, who has pleaded the causes of your soul.

Adapted from The C.H. Spurgeon Collection, Version 1.0, Ages Software, 1.800.297.4307

God Is With Us

DELIVERED ON SUNDAY MORNING, JULY 17, 1864,
BY THE REV. C. H. SPURGEON,
AT THE METROPOLITAN TABERNACLE, NEWINGTON.

"If God is for us, who can be against us?" -- Romans 8:31.

THE Truth of God here asserted is indisputable. Even heathens have taken this for their motto and emblazoned it upon their standards of war. "God is for us!" has been the war cry of many a warrior as he has dashed to the fight, however out of place it was in such association its force was clearly perceived. Our text, however, protects itself from ill usage, for you observe that the text is guarded with the little word, "If," as a sentinel. No man, therefore, has any right to the treasures of this text unless he can give the password and answer the question!

It is not every man who can say that God is on his side. On the contrary, the most of men are fighting against the Lord. By nature we are the friends of sin and then God is against us--with all the powers of Justice He is against us for our destruction unless we turn and repent. Is God for us? Remember He is so if we have been reconciled to Him by the death of His Son. But an absolute God must be in arms against us, for even our God is a consuming fire. It is only when we behold the Lord Jehovah in the Person of Jesus Christ that our hope and joy can begin! When we see Deity Incarnate, when we see God surrendering the glories of His Throne to become Man and then stooping to the shameful death of the Cross--it is then that we perceive Emmanuel, "God with us," and perceiving Him, we feel that He is on our side.

Question yourself then, Soul, whether you are in Christ. He who is not with Christ is not with God. If you are without Christ, you are without God and a stranger from the commonwealth of Israel. But if through the sprinkled blood you can say that you are reconciled unto God, then take the full meaning of this text and feast upon it and be blessed, for "If God is for us, who can be against us?" We shall handle the text thus and may the Holy Spirit make it profitable--how is God for us? Secondly, who are against us? And thirdly, who are not against us?

I. First, HOW IS GOD FOR US? Augustine, in his notes upon the verses preceding our text has very beautifully said that God is for us according to the preceding words of the chapter in four senses. Look back a verse or two and you will find it. He is for us, for He has predestinated us. He is for us for He has called us. He is for us for He has justified us. He is for us because He has virtually glorified us and will actually do so. To the people of God here are four very prolific subjects of thought.

1. God is for us, because, according to the words of the Apostle He has predestinated His people to be conformed to the image of His own dear Son. Now, if God has predestinated us to eternal life, who can be against us? Must not the predestinating decree of God take effect? If God has determined it, who shall disannul it? If God has said it shall be, who is he that shall stay His hand, or resist the Omnipotent fiat of the Most High? He said, "Let there be light: and there was light." He bade the world spring out of nothing and forth it came. All things obey Him. Heaven adores Him. Hell trembles at Him. No creature can resist Him.

As the potter molds the clay according to his own will while it revolves upon the wheel, even so the Infinite, the Omnipotent Jehovah does according to His good pleasure in the armies of Heaven and among the inhabitants of this lower world. "It is He that sits upon the circle of the earth and the inhabitants thereof are as grasshoppers." He takes up the isles as a very little thing. Who then, out of these little things, can stand against or resist Him?

See, my Brethren, the force of God's decree of old in the case of Israel. The Lord had promised to Abraham that his seed should inherit the whole land of Canaan, from the river of Egypt unto the great river, the river Euphrates. See, amid the smoke of the brick kilns Israel toils in Egypt. How was God's decree to be fulfilled? When God makes bare His arm, you shall see and wonder! Pharaoh and all his hosts cannot hold those captives whom God determines to set free!

There they go, led forth like sheep by the hands of Moses and Aaron. They cross the desert until they come to the sea, even to the Red Sea. See, the mighty stream rolls before them and their ferocious enemies are behind but the Lord has determined that they shall inherit the land and therefore neither can the sea refuse to divide, nor can Pharaoh save himself when he goes down into the depths thereof. They are in the wilderness--famine shall destroy them! No, the heavens drop with manna! Thirst shall scorch them! No, the Rock follows them with its living stream! The serpents shall surely bite them! Yes, but the brazen serpent is lifted up and whoever looks shall be healed! The Amalekites attack them, but while Moses holds up his hands Joshua puts the foe to the route.

They come to the banks of the Jordan--what ailed you, O Jordan, that you were driven back? The priests go through dry-shod and all the people of God march after them. Then the Canaanites, with their chariots of iron, came against them in battle. The kings of mighty cities anointed the shield and laid hold on sword and buckler. But which of them prevailed? Did not Jehovah destroy them all? As He had given them Og, king of Bashan, "because His mercy endured forever," and Sihon, king of the Amorites, "because His mercy endured forever," so not a man could stand against them until they possessed the land!

The right hand of the Lord fulfilled His own decree. His own right hand and His holy arm have gotten Him the victory. As with a rod of iron He dashes His enemies in pieces like a potter's vessel. None could withstand the hosts of Israel! The walled cities were cast down and the people of God dwelt in the fat of the land. See, Beloved, the result of God's decree! The sons of Jacob were feeble and weak but the Lord made them strong enough to drive out the Anakim who were men of gigantic stature--for His purpose shall stand--He will do all His pleasure. Let us beware of fighting against one who has God in league with him! It is in vain to fight against God!

It was a good remark of the soothsayers to Haman of old. They said, "If Mordecai is of the seed of the Jews, before whom you have begun to fall, you shall not prevail against him but shall surely fall before him." And so if any man is of the company of the elect--if he is one of those whose names are written in the Book of Life--his enemies may contend but they shall never prevail against him! He must stand whom the Lord ordains to hold. And if God determines his salvation, neither mortal nor infernal power shall prevail to destroy him.

On this account we may boldly say with the Apostle, "If God is for us, who can be against us?" You cannot believe in a disappointed God--you cannot imagine the imperial decree from the Throne of Heaven treated as waste paper. It would be far from us so to blaspheme God as to think that any power, known or unknown, can ever overcome Him! "Has He said and shall He not do it? Has He commanded and shall it not come to pass?" If your soul is written upon the palms of Jesus' hands and engraved on His heart, no weapon which is formed against you shall prosper and every tongue which rises against you in judgment, you shall condemn!

2. But in looking back you observe the second thing--God is on our side for He has called us. In the Word of God much stress is laid upon calling. When Abraham left the land of his forefathers and went forth, not knowing where he went, he was quite safe, though in the midst of implacable enemies, because God had called him. "Who raised up the righteous man from the east, called him to his feet, gave the nations before him and made him rule over kings?" Who but the God that called him?

On that memorable occasion, when Abraham returned from the slaughter of the kings, you remember Melchizedek met him. At that time Abraham was in great peril for there was every probability that the defeated kings would gather their troops, would form alliances with other kings and would certainly come up to cut down so insignificant a person as that wandering shepherd, Abraham. But what does God say to him--"Fear not, Abraham, I am your shield and your exceedingly great reward." This became his comfort--God had called him. He was a called man and where God calls, He will not desert His chosen.

"The gifts and calling of God are without repentance." He does not reverse the call which He has given, but having once called His children He remains faithful to the call He has given. To use the illustration we have used before, when God called His son out of Egypt, when He fetched Israel from the furnace who could stand against the called Israelites? Plague after plague ravaged the land. The cattle died. The crops were blasted. Frogs came up into the king's chamber! Lice covered all their borders--at last the first-born of Egypt died and they besought Israel to go forth--for when God called them out, who could hold them in? When He said to His prisoners, "Go forth," what bolts of iron, or what gates of brass could keep them captives? Let the Lord call by the effectual voice--who is he that shall stand against Him?

Many of us, I trust, have heard the sacred call--we have made our calling and election sure. You know how you were called from darkness to light--from sin to holiness--from self-righteousness to spiritual faith in Jesus. Now, He who has called you is faithful and He will not forsake the work of His own hands. He has not called you in order to put you to shame! He has not quickened you and preserved you and brought you thus far to deliver you over to the hands of your enemies! "Be of good courage and He shall strengthen your heart." Wait upon the Lord for His call will give you comfort. "If God is for us, who can be against us?"

3. But again--God proves that He is for us by having justified us. All the people of God are wrapped about with the righteousness of Christ. And wearing that glorious robe, the eyes of God see no fault in them--Jehovah sees no sin in Jacob, neither iniquity in Israel. Christ is seen and not the sinner! Christ being therefore perfection's own self, the Believer is seen as perfect in Him. God regards His people with the same affection as that wherewith He loves His only-begotten Son!

He has pronounced them clean and clean they are. He has proclaimed them just, covered with the righteousness of Christ and just they are. Come on you accusing devil--come on you who lay a thousand things to our charge--if our Jesus pronounces our acquittal, who is he that condemns? If He mounts the chariot of salvation, who is he that can be against us? Is it not a mysteriously blessed thing to wear upon one's soul the mark of complete justification? The heathen have a custom of marking themselves upon the forehead with the seal of their God. But, oh, what a seal is this to wear-- what a mark of the Lord Jesus--to go about this world a perfectly justified man!

God looks upon common men with anger--they are not reconciled unto Him. But towards His people He looks always with eyes of love--no anger is in His heart to them--not a jot of wrath. All this has been put away through the great Sacrifice. Towards them His whole heart goes out--"The eyes of the Lord are upon the righteous and His ears are open to their cry." Being justified, they have peace with God through Jesus Christ their Lord. O dear Friends, if God is at peace with you, it matters not who is at war with you!

If your Master acquits, it little matters who condemns. If Jehovah absolves, it mattes not if your name is cast out as evil! It matters not if you are ranked among the vilest of the vile--if your name is a byword and a proverb only fit to be worked up into the drunkard's song--for who is he that can be against you? What are all these things if put into the balance but lighter than vanity, if Jehovah Himself has justified you?

4. And yet again, another sweet reflection comes here--He has also glorified us! Remember the four golden links of the chain--"Whom He did predestinate, them He also called: and whom He called, them He also justified: and whom He justified, them He also glorified." Now, in one sense God's people are glorified even now for He "has raised us up together and made us sit together in heavenly places in Christ Jesus."

Mark, it does not say, "He has promised that we shall sit there," but He "has" made us sit there! We do sit there at this hour for Christ is the Representative of every soul for whom He shed His blood! And when Christ took His seat in Heaven every elect soul took his seat in Heaven representatively. Remember, Beloved, that the glorification of God's people is a certain fact. It is not a thing which may be, but it is a thing which must be. What does Jesus Christ say to His people when He gathers them at His right hand? "Come, you blessed of My Father, inherit the kingdom prepared for you from the foundation of the world."

Observe that. Do you think God has prepared a kingdom and that He will not bring His people there? Moreover it is said, "Prepared for you"--for you--the chosen people of God. And do you imagine that the Covenant wisdom of God would prepare a kingdom for men who would not ultimately get there? Would He plan and arrange how to make them eternally blessed and yet allow them to perish by the way? "Prepared for you," remember, "from the foundation of the world."

There is a crown in Heaven which no head can fit but mine. There is a harp there which no fingers must ever touch but mine! Child of God there is a mansion in Heaven which will never be rightly tenanted if you do not get there! And there is a place at God's right hand which must be empty--it will be said, "David's seat was empty," unless you shall arrive there! Will it be so? Will there be empty mansions in Heaven? Will there be crowns without heads to wear them? Will there be harps without hands to strike them?

No! The muster roll of the redeemed shall be read and not one shall be found absent! As many as were written upon the breastplate of the great High Priest shall be securely found there--

"Not death nor Hell shall ever divide His chosen from His breast. In the dear bosom of His lo ve They must forever rest." This gives a fourth reason why God is for us. But, O my Brethren, though this brings in the context, I cannot--it is impossible for any human speech to bring out the depth of the meaning of how God is for us! He was for us before the worlds were made--He was for us, or else He never would have given His Son. He was for us even when He struck the Only-Begotten and laid the whole weight of His wrath upon Him! He was for us though He was against Him! He was for us when we were ruined in the Fall--He loved us notwithstanding all. He was for us when we were against Him and with a high hand were bidding Him defiance! He was for us, or else He never would have brought us humbly to seek His face. He has been for us in many struggles. We have had to fight through multitudes of difficulties. We have had temptations from without and within--how could we have held on until now if He had not been with us? He is for us, let me say, with all the Infinity of His heart, with all the Omnipotence of His love! He is for us with all His boundless wisdom. Arrayed in all the attributes which make Him God He is for us--eternally and immutably for us! He is for us when yon blue skies shall be rolled up like a worn out vesture--

for us throughout eternity! Here, Child of God, is matter enough for thought even though you had ages to meditate upon it--God is for you! And if God is for you, who can be against you? II. In the second place, WHO ARE AGAINST US? The Apostle never meant to say that Christians have no enemies for he knew better than that! An old Latin writer observes upon this text that the succeeding context will show us the enemies we have who are against us. Very briefly let us notice that there are four main enemies who conspire against the life of the children of God--these are man, the world, the flesh and the devil. These always will be against us but who are they? 1. First, there is man. How man has struggled against man! Man is the wolf of mankind. Not the elements in all their fury nor the wild beasts of prey in all their cruelty have ever been such terrible enemies to man as man has been to his own fellow! When you read the story of the Marian persecution in England, you are astounded that ever creatures wearing a human form could be so bloodthirsty. Call these Catholics who thus persecuted the Protestants? Call them Catholics? Much better call them cannibals for they behaved more like savages than Christians in their bloody martyrdoms and murders of the saints of God! We do not in this age feel the cruelty of man to that extent but this is only because the custom of the land will not allow it. There are many who dare not strike with the hand who are very busy in laying on their tongue--and this not by exposing our errors which they have a perfect right to do--but in many cases the children of God are misrepresented, slandered, abused, persecuted, ridiculed for Truth's sake. We know many instances where other means are resorted to-- anything to drive the servants of God away from their integrity and from their simple following of their Master. Well did the Lord Jesus say, "Beware of men." "Behold I send you forth as sheep in the midst of wolves. Be you wise as serpents and harmless as doves." Do not expect men to be the friends of your piety, or if they are, suspect the reality of that piety of which ungodly man is a friend. You must expect to be sometimes bullied and sometimes coerced--to be sometimes flattered and threatened. You must expect at one time to meet with the oily tongue which has under it the drawn sword and at another time with the drawn sword itself. Look out and expect that men will be against you. But what are they all? Suppose every living man in the world were against you and that you had to stand in solitude like Athanasius? You might say, as Athana-sius did, "I, Athanasius, against the whole world! I know I have Truth on my side and therefore against the world I stand."

Of what use was the malice of men against Martin Luther? They thought to burn him, but he died in his bed despite them all. They thought to put an end to him, but his little tracts went everywhere and the words of Luther seemed to be carried on the wings of angels until in the most distant places the Pope found an enemy suddenly springing up where he thought the good seed had all been destroyed. I do not know that it is of any great service to have numbers with you. I question whether Truth has not generally to be with the minority and whether it is not quite as honorable to serve God with two or three as it would be with two or three millions.

If numbers could make a thing right, idolatry ought to be the right religion and if in countries across the sea numbers made the thing right, why, those who fear the Lord would be few, indeed, and idolatry and Romanism would be the right thing! Never judge according to numbers--say they are nothing but men after all. If they are good men fight on their side. But if they and the Truth of God fall out, fall out with Truth! Be a friend to the Truth--make your appeal to the Law and to the Testimony--and if they speak not according to this Word it is because there is no light in them. And if there is no light in them do not trust your soul with them--for if the blind leads the blind, they shall both fall into the ditch.

Who then, what then, are men? Only puppets moved by God's hand. He has the string to pull them all which way He wills and if they will not serve Him He can soon put them quietly into the grave. Therefore be not afraid of the son of man who is but a worm, a little heap of dust! Be not dismayed by him. And if he puts on a black and terrific face, look him in the face with your own truthfulness and put him to the blush. That was grand of Latimer when he preached before Henry VIII. He had greatly displeased His Majesty by his boldness in a sermon preached before the king and was ordered to preach again on the following Sunday and to make an apology for the offense he had given.

After reading his text, the bishop thus began his sermon--"Hugh Latimer, do you know before whom you are this day to speak? To the high and mighty monarch, the king's most excellent majesty, who can take away your life if you offend. Therefore, take heed that you speak not a word that may displease. But then consider well, Hugh, do you not know from where you I? Upon whose message you are sent? Even by the great and mighty God who is All-Present, and who beholds all your ways and who is able to cast your soul into Hell! Therefore, take care that you deliver your message faithfully."

He then proceeded with the same sermon he had preached the preceding Sunday, but with considerably more energy! Such courage should all God's children show when they have to do with man. You are yourself nothing but a worm! But if God puts His Truth into you, do not play the coward or stammer out His message, but stand up manfully for God and for His Truth!

Some people are forever crying up what they call a becoming modesty. Modesty is very becoming but an ambassador of God must recollect there are other virtues besides modesty. If Her Majesty sent an ambassador to a country with whom we were at war and the little man should step into the conference and say, "I humbly hope you will excuse my being here. I wish to be in all things complacent to your honors and lordships the ambassadors. I feel I am a young man and you are much older than I am and therefore I cheerfully submit my judgment to your superior wisdom and experience," and so on. Why I am sure Her Majesty would command him back again and then command him into a long retirement!

What business has he to humble himself when he is an ambassador for the Queen! He must remember he is clothed with the dignity of the power which sent him. And even so is God's minister and he counts it foul shame to stoop to any man! He takes for his motto, Cedo nulli, "I yield to none," and preaching God's Truth in love and honesty, he hopes to be able to render a fair account to his Master at last--for only unto his Master does he stand or fall!

2. The second adversary is the world. This world is like a great field covered with brambles and thorns and thistles and as the Christian goes through it he is continually in danger of tearing his garments or cutting his feet. Yet--

"The dear path to our abode, Lies through this barren land."

Every citizen of Heaven must be taught with thorns and briars, as were the men of Succoth. Every child of God must march through the enemies' land, for Christ says, "I pray not that You should take them out of the world, but that You should keep them from the Evil One."

When is a Christian out of danger? Never. If he is prosperous, then he is apt to grow purse-proud or carnally secure. If adversities press upon him, then he is apt to murmur and to grow unbelieving. There are temptations in the high places of the earth and the valleys are not without them. When the Christian is in honor he is in great peril. Ah, how many have found the high places to be slippery ones? When the Believer is in shame and disrepute, he is in danger, too, for many professors have found this cross too heavy for their shoulders. A Believer ought to walk through this world expecting to meet with an enemy behind every hedge, reckoning it a wonder if he shall escape for a single day without a bullet from the foe!

You are in an enemy's country and this enemy is on the alert continually. You may sleep, but the world never sleeps! Its customs are always seeking to bind you with their chains. Its spirit is creeping over you while you are in the Exchange, or in the market, or even in the family! You will find the very atmosphere of this world tends to make you sleep as do others. You will have much ado while you are in this state of temptation to stand your ground and unless you watch and pray the world will be too much for you.

O Brethren, I would that we knew the world to be more our enemy than we do, for many walk as if they were friends with this world! But such is not the Christian's position--he can say, "The world is crucified unto me and I unto the world." Luther used to say there was no love lost between him and the world, for the world hated him and he hated it no less. There is a memorable story told of a good old minister when some young minister went weeping to him because he had been slandered. "Ah," said he, "that is a trouble I shall never have again, for I lost my character the first year of my ministry and Slander herself can say no more than she has said."

God's servants must expect to lose their characters, to have every virtue denied them and every vice imputed to them. But under all this they can face the world and say to it, "You think badly of me, do you? Not so badly as I think of you! You throw this and that in my teeth--I throw worse things in yours. And whereas you say I am a noisy busybody and a meddler, I will tell you I purpose to be wilder still and to be noisier still against you and to meddle yet more with your vanities which ruin the souls of men."

The world is a terrible assailant if we are left alone in the conflict, but what is the world, after all, if God is for us? As for this present age, where will it be in forty years? I see a long line of turf mounds and many a, "Here he lies"! And this generation is all gone, it passes away in the fashion thereof. It is like a candle-snuff and he that cares for it is like a man worshipping a dying taper. Care little for this world, but think much of the world to come! This poor quicksand--get off of it lest it swallow you up! But yonder Rock of Ages--build on it and you shall never suffer loss!

3. I think we said there is a third enemy and that is the flesh. It is the worst of the three. We should never need to fear man nor the world if we had not this wicked flesh to carry about with us. Inbred corruption is the worst corruption. "Lord," said Augustine, "deliver me from my worst enemy, that wicked man myself." If a Christian could lay himself down and run away from himself and never see himself again he would be delighted beyond measure, for, "truly in me, that is in my flesh, dwells no good thing," is the experience not of the Apostle only, but of every child of God!

When you would do good, evil is present with you. You want to flee, but like the hawk which has a chain to her leg you can but stretch your wings and flutter--you cannot mount aloft. You long to feel your heart as hot as an oven, but there is a mountain of ice within you which chills your flaming desires. To will is present with you--oh, if you could be what you would be! But how to perform that which is good you find not by reason of the infirmity and weakness of your nature and the depravity you have inherited from your parents.

Some of you have an irritable temper. It will be your plague until you die. Others find that though you desire to be liberal to the cause of God, yet a covetous disposition has to be struggled with. Some have to fight against levity, others against pride. And, on the other hand there are some of us whose daily burden is to fight against despondency and low-ness of spirits--so that we have all some besetting sin. But if God is for us, what matters the flesh? Ah, poor Flesh! You may kick and struggle as you will, but when God holds His silver scepter over you, you shall surely yield! When Jehovah decrees that a man shall be sanctified, that man's flesh may cry and groan but the furnace shall refine him. The Holy Spirit shall purify him and experience shall teach him and the blood of Christ shall perfect him. Despite that wicked heart of ours, we shall on eagles' wings ascend and be found without fault before the Throne of God!

4. The last enemy is the devil. I do not know whether he is worse than the flesh or not, but I think I may put him down as being about on a par with it. For when the devil meets our flesh, the two shake hands and say, "How do you do, Brother?" Truly the two are brothers--for our flesh was originally in the family of wrath.

Ah, that arch-traitor Satan! Little do we know what temptations he is plotting and planning for us even now. He is so crafty that he understands human nature better than human nature understands itself. He has been playing the trade of a tempter for six thousand years! He ought to be a thorough master of the business. And certainly he is. He who made us knows more of us than Satan does--but, next to God--Satan is the best student of humanity.

He knows our weak points, too. He understands where to touch us so as to touch our bone and our flesh. He knows how to cover up the hook with the bait--for every soul he has his lure and for every sinner he has his trap. He knows how to take one this way and the other the opposite--some by straining after pretended spirituality and others by descending into the grossest sensuality. Depend on it, my Brothers and Sisters, you may think yourself to be safe against Satan but there is a joint in your harness and he will find it. And remember, as one leak may sink a ship, so one weak point may be and would be your ruin if God did not prevent it! But what matters the devil when we have this text--"If God is for us, who can be against us?"

The devil is mighty, but God is Almighty! Satan is strong, but all strength belongs to God! What is Satan, after all, but an enemy who has had his head broken? He is a broken-headed dragon. The Lord has a hook in his nose and a bridle in his jaws and He knows how to pull him back. Sometimes I wish He would take him up a link or two, that he might not be so busy among some of our Churches. But he is a chained enemy--the Lord lets him go just so far--but never any further. Oh, if the Fiend could get just a little further, what havoc he would work!

You know how it was with Job--Satan dared not touch his flesh at first--he could only touch his children and cattle. He had to get permission to touch his flesh and even then he dared not touch his life. He went as far as his tether and vexed poor Job with sore troubles--but he could not go any further--for God restrained him. Rejoice, Christian, whether it is man, or the world, or your flesh, or Satan--if God has predestinated you, called you, justified you and in the Person of Jesus Christ glorified you--you may put the whole together and then say, "Who can be against us?" As chaff is driven away, so, O Lord, have You driven them away."

III. We shall close our meditation this morning--God make it profitable to His own people--by observing WHO ARE THOSE WHO ARE NOT AGAINST US. There are some who cannot be our enemies. Here is a very pleasing part of the subject. God the Father cannot be against us. He is our Father! He cannot be against His own children! He has chosen us--He will not cast us away--He has adopted us into His family, He will never discard us. He has been pleased to ordain us unto eternal life, He will never reverse the decree.

He was for us in the Covenant of Grace when He planned the way to save rebellious man. He has been for us in the great ordering of Providence--all things have worked together for good for us until now. We wonder how we have arrived where we now are--but surely Providence, under God, has worked wondrously on our behalf! He is for us in all the decrees which are yet to be fulfilled. There is not a single line in the great Book which is against the Christian. You may rest assured that whether the earth shall rock and reel, or the moon is black as a sackcloth of hair, or the earth is licked up with tongues of fire, still Jehovah has not a single thought, nor wish, nor word, nor look against any one of the blood-bought ones. They are all safe in Him! God the Father cannot be against us.

Then God the Son is not against us. O Beloved, how sweetly He has been for us! I think I see

Him now, lifting up that face all covered with bloody sweat and saying to every Believer, "I am for you. These gouts of gore fall to the dust for you. I sweat great drops of blood that I might redeem you." He stands before Pilate. And when He is brought forth with the "Ecce homo," I think I hear Him say, "Poor Sinner, I am for you." I see Him carrying the Cross upon His bleeding shoulders and every step He takes is to this tune, "I am for you."

I behold Him bleeding upon the Cross with outstretched hands and all His wounds and all the drops of blood which flow from His side, all say, "Christ is for you." Today, as He pleads before the Eternal Throne, this is the tenor of His plea, "I am for you." When He shall come a second time without a sin offering, unto salvation, the sound of the mighty trumpet which shall herald His advent will ring out, "Christ is for you, O you blood-bought saints." When He shall sit upon the Throne of His Father and His kingdom shall come--of which there shall be no end--this shall be the tenor of that kingdom, "I am for My people. I will rule My people righteously and bless the nations upon earth."

Christ cannot be against you. You cannot look into that dear face of His and think that He will ever leave you. Your Husband is married to you and He has proved His love by such indisputable tokens that you must not, oh, you cannot doubt it! Child of God, I almost defy you to doubt the love of your Lord Jesus Christ. How can He put you away? Could He have bought you at such a price--could He have suffered so much for you and yet leave you--throw you away upon the dunghill? Impossible! Impossible! Those wounds forever seal your everlasting security!

Then the Holy Spirit cannot be against us. He must always, as the Comforter, comfort His own people. As the Illuminator He must lead us into the Truth of God. As the great Giver of Life He must always quicken us from our death of sin. Whatever power the Holy Spirit has it is all engaged for us! "I am with you always, even unto the end of the world." Then the holy angels--these cannot be against us. Before Elisha opened his servant's eyes, the servant had cried, "Alas,

Master, what shall we do?" when he saw the Syrians and their chariots. But now he sees horses of fire and chariots of fire round about Elisha. It is so with you! The angels are ministering spirits who minister unto the heirs of salvation. They bear you up in their hands lest you dash your foot against a stone.

Millions of spiritual creatures walk this earth both when we wake and when we sleep--and when the black angels come to attack us, the good angels contend against them and many a heavenly duel is fought where none but spirit eyes can see! Many a sacred fight goes on for the defense of the saints, even as Michael fought with the dragon for the body of Moses. The good angels are all for us and here we may rejoice. Then we know the Law of God cannot be against us. It was our enemy once through our sins, but it is now satisfied. Christ has made it honorable. It has not a word to say against any soul that is justified in Christ.

The Justice of God has not a word to say against the Christian! On the contrary, Justice is well content to confirm the saving decree, "For," says Justice, "that sinner owes me nothing--Christ has discharged his debts. I will not put that sinner in prison--I have no right to do so, for Christ was imprisoned instead of him. I will not lay my whip upon his shoulders for Christ suffered with His much-plowed shoulders in the place of that poor believing soul." So, Christian, whoever may be against you, here is a comfort--God the Father, God the Son and God the Holy Spirit never can be against you! Nor the angels of Heaven, the Law and Justice of God--they must always be for you. And if it is so, who can be against you?

Two remarks and then I have done. One is there is an opposite to all this, and it belongs to some who are present here this morning. If God is AGAINST you, who can be for you? If you are an enemy to God this morning, your very blessings are curses to you! Your pleasures are only the prelude to your pains. Remember, Sinner, that whether you have adversity or prosperity, so long as God is against you, you can never truly prosper. If you spread yourself like a green bay tree it is only that you may be ready for the axe! You may be fattened with wealth but you are only prepared as the bullock for the slaughter. Take these words home, I pray you, and let them ring in your ears--"If God is against me"--just that supposition! A supposition which is fact because you have not believed in Christ--you have not given your heart to God. "If God is against me!"

Will you just think this over on your road home? Take half-an-hour this afternoon to think it over. "If God is against me, what then? What will become of me in time and eternity? If God is against me, how shall I die--how shall I rise again? How shall I face Him in the Day of Judgment if God is against me?" It is not an impossible "if," but an "if which amounts to a certainty, I fear, in the case of many who are sitting in this house today.

Then, Christian, here is another thought and I have done. If God is for you, do you not see how you ought to be for God? If God has espoused your cause, ought you not to espouse His? I pleaded with you last Sunday since Christ has pleaded the causes of your soul to plead the cause of Christ. There is a great battle which has only just began! The trumpet which musters the warriors sounds loud and long and the fight will be stern and desperate between Christ's pure Truth and the ceremonials of the world's Church.

You must take your post, every one of you, on one side or the other. "If the Lord is God, follow Him--but if Baal, then follow him." One side or the other you must be on and I beg you, if God has been for you and defended you, stand up for Him! Never deny a jot of Christ's Truth. Not a hair of the head of Christ's Truth must ever be suffered to be touched with the smell of the fire of compromise. Be not as the harlots were who stood before Solomon. You remember one was quite content to have half the living child. But be your motto, "All or none--I will never take a particle of error. Death to it all!" No amalgamation, no compromise, no peace with error!

The men of this generation cry to me and say, "Is there peace?" and my answer is, "What peace can there be so long as the sins of Jezebel are so many?" Then they revile me and say, "Are you he that troubles Israel?" I have not troubled Israel, but you and your father's house, in that you have forsaken the Commandments of the Lord and you have followed Baal."

Stand up and bear witness against regeneration by Baptism and against those who use Popish words and would have us believe that it is right to attach another sense to them! Take your part with Christ and His despised people and when the day comes when He shall distribute His rewards, happy shall that man be who never flinched. And blessed shall he be and shall she be who stood fast in the evil day and stood still in the integrity of the Lord and in the firmness of His Truth, firm even to the end! The Lord bless you in this thing for Christ's sake. Amen.

Children Brought to Christ, and Not to the Font

A Sermon (No. 581)
Delivered on Sunday Morning, July 24th, 1864, by the
Rev. C. H. SPURGEON,
At the Metropolitan Tabernacle, Newington

"And they brought young children to him, that he should touch them: and his disciples rebuked those that brought them. But when Jesus saw it, he was much displeased, and said unto them, Suffer the little children to come unto me, and forbid them not: for of such is the kingdom of God. Verily I say unto you, whosoever shall not receive the kingdom of God as a little child, he shall not enter therein. And he took them up in his arms, put his hands upon them, and blessed them" -- Mark 10:13-16.

MY attention has been specially directed to this passage by the fact that it has been quoted against me by most of the authors of those sermons and letters which are, by a stretch of imagination, called "replies" to my sermon upon "Baptismal Regeneration." Replies they certainly are not, except to one another. I marvel that a Church so learned as the Anglican, cannot produce something a little more worthy of the point in hand. The various authors may possibly have read my discourse, but by reason of mental absorption in other meditations, or perhaps through the natural disturbance of mind caused by guilty consciences, they have talked with confusion of words, and have only been successful in refuting themselves, and answering one another. They must have been aiming at something far removed from my sermon, or else I must give them credit for being the worst shots that ever practiced with polemical artillery. They do not so much as touch the target in its extreme corners, much less in its centre. The whole question is, Do you believe that baptism regenerates? If so--prove that your belief is Scriptural! Do you believe that baptism does not regenerate? Then justify your swearing that it does? Who will reply to this? He shall merit and bear the palm.

The Scripture before us is by several of the champions on the other side exhibited to the people as a rebuke to me. Their reasoning is rather ingenious than forcible: forsooth, because the disciples incurred the displeasure of Jesus Christ by keeping back the little children from coming to Him, therefore Jesus Christ is greatly displeased with me, and with all others like me, for keeping children from the font, and the performance there enacted; and specially displeased with me for exposing the Anglican doctrine of Baptismal Regeneration! Observe the reasoning--because Jesus was much displeased with disciples for hindering parents from seeking a blessing upon their children, therefore he is much displeased with us who do not believe in godfathers and godmothers, or the signing of the cross on the infant brow. I must say at the outset that this is rather a leap of argument, and would not ordinarily be thought conclusive, but this we may readily overlook, since we have long ceased to hope for reasonable arguments from those who support a cause based upon absurdity. My brethren, I concluded that there must be something forcible in such a text as this, or my opponents would not be so eager to secure it; I have therefore carefully looked at it, and as I have viewed it, it has opened up to me with a sacred splendour of grace. In this incident the very heart of Christ is published to poor sinners, and we may clearly perceive the freeness and the fulness of the mighty grace of the Redeemer of men, who is willing to receive the youngest child as well as the oldest man; and is greatly displeased with any who would keep back seeking souls from coming to him, or loving hearts from bringing others to receive his blessing.

I. In handling this text in what I believe to be its true light, I shall commence, first of all, by observing that THIS TEXT HAS NOT THE SHADOW OF THE SHADE OF THE GHOST OF A CONNECTION WITH BAPTISM. There is no line of connection so substantial as a spider's web between this incident and baptism, or at least my imagination is not vivid enough to conceive one. This I will prove to you, if you will follow me for a moment.

It is very clear, Dear Friends, that these young children were not brought to Jesus Christ by their friends to be baptized. "They brought young children to him, that he should touch them," says

Mark. Matthew describes the children as being brought "that he would put his hands on them and pray," but there is not a hint about their being baptized; no godfathers or godmothers had been provided, and no sign of the cross was requested. Surely the parents themselves knew tolerably well what it was they desired, and they would not have expressed themselves so dubiously as to ask him to touch them, when they meant that he should baptize them. The parents evidently had no thought of regeneration by baptism, and brought the children for quite another end.

In the next place, if they brought the children to Jesus Christ to be baptized, they brought them to the wrong person; for the Evangelist, John, in the fourth chapter, and the second verse, expressly assures us that Jesus Christ baptized not, but his disciples: this settles the question once for all, and proves beyond all dispute that there is no connection between this incident and baptism.

But you will say, "Perhaps they brought the children to be baptized by the disciples?" Brethren, the disciples were not in the habit of baptizing infants, and this is clear from the case in hand. If they had been in the habit of baptizing infants, would they have rebuked the parents for bringing them? If it had been a customary thing for parents to bring children with such an object, would the disciples who had been in the constant habit of performing the ceremony, have rebuked them for attending to it? Would any Church clergyman rebuke parents for bringing their children to be baptized? If he did so, he would act absurdly contrary to his own views and practice; and we cannot therefore imagine that if infant baptism had been the accepted practice, the disciples could have acted so absurdly as to rebuke the parents for bringing their little ones. It is obvious that such could not have been the practice of the disciples who were rebuked.

Moreover, and here is an argument which seems to me to have great force in it, when Jesus Christ rebuked his disciples, then was the time if ever in his life, to have openly spoken concerning infant baptism, godfathers and godmothers, and the whole affair. If he wished to rebuke his disciples most effectually, how could he have done it better than by saying, "Wherefore keep ye these children back? I have ordained that they shall be baptized; I have expressly commanded that they shall be regenerated and made members of my body in baptism; how dare you then, in opposition to my will, keep them back?" But no, dear friends, our Saviour never said a word about "the laver of regeneration," or, "the quickening dew," when he rebuked them--not a single sentence. Had he done so, the season would have been most appropriate if it had been his intention to teach the practice; in the whole of his life, there is no period in which a discourse upon infant regeneration in baptism could have been more appropriate than on this occasion, and yet not a single sentence about it comes from the Saviour's lips.

To close all, Jesus Christ did not baptize the children. Our Evangelist does not inform us that he exclaimed, "Where are the godfathers and godmothers?" Is it not recorded that he called for a font, or a Prayer Book? No; but "He took them up in his arms, put his hands upon them, and blessed them," and dismissed them without a drop of the purifying element. Now, if this event had any connection with baptism whatever, it was the most appropriate occasion for infant baptism to have been practiced. Why, it would have ended for ever the controversy. There may be some men in the world who would have raised the question of engrafting infants into the body of Christ's Church by baptism after all this, but I am certain no honest man would have done so who reverently accepted Christ as his spiritual leader. I, my brethren, would sooner be dumb than speak a single word against an ordinance which Christ himself instituted and practiced; and if on this occasion he had but sprinkled one of these infants, given him a Christian name, signed him with a cross, accepted the vows of his godparents, and thanked God for his regeneration, then the question would have been settled for ever, and some of us would have been saved a world of abuse, besides escaping no end of mistakes, for which we are condemned, in the judgment of many good people, for whom we have some affection, though for their judgment we have no respect.

So you see the parents did not ask baptismal regeneration; Christ did not personally baptize; the disciples were not in the habit of baptizing infants, or else they would not have rebuked the parents; Christ did not speak about baptism on the occasion, and he did not baptize the little ones.

I will put a case to you which may exhibit the weakness of my opponents' position. Suppose a denomination should rise up which should teach that babes should be allowed to partake at the Lord's Table. Such teaching could plead precedents of great antiquity, for you are aware that at one period, infant communion was allowed, and logically too; for if an infant has a right to baptism, it has a right to come to the Lord's Table. For years children were brought to the Lord's Table, but rather inconvenient accidents occurred, and therefore the thing was dropped as being unseemly. But if someone should revive the error, and try to prove that infants are to come to the Lord's Supper, he might prove it from this passage quite as clearly as our friends can prove infant baptism from it. Moreover do not forget that even if infant baptism could be proved from this text, the ceremony prescribed in the Prayer Book is quite as far from being established. Whether the baptism of infants may or may not be proved from other Scriptures I cannot now stay to enquire, but even if it can be, what are we to say for godfathers or godmothers, or the assertion that in baptism children are made "members of Christ, children of God, and inheritors of the kingdom of heaven?" Truly I might as well prove vaccination from the text before me, as the performance which the Prayer Book calls "infant baptism." I do not hesitate to say that I could prove any earthly thing, if I might but have such reasoning granted to me as that which proved infant baptism from this passage. There is no possible connection between the two. The teaching of the passage is very plain and very clear, and baptism has been imported into it, and not found in it. As a quaint writer has well said, "These doctrines are raised from the text as our collectors raise a tax upon indigent, nonsolvent people, by coming armed with the law and a constable to distrain for that which is not to be had. Certainly never was text so strained and distrained to pay what it never owed; never man so racked to confess what he never thought; never was a pumice stone so squeezed for water which it never held." Still hundreds will catch at this straw, and cry, "Did not Jesus say, Suffer the little children to come unto me?'" To these we give this one word, see that ye read the Word as it is written, and you will find no water in it but Jesus only. Are the water and Christ the same thing? Is bringing a child to a font bringing the child to Christ? Nay, here is a wide difference, as wide as between Rome and Jerusalem, as wide as between Anti-christ and Christ, between false doctrine and the gospel of our Lord Jesus Christ.

II. Now, for our second and much more pleasing task, WHY THEN WAS JESUS CHRIST DISPLEASED?

Read the passage and at once the answer comes to you. He was displeased with his disciples for two reasons: first, because they discouraged those who would bring others to him; and secondly, because they discouraged those who themselves were anxious to come to him. They did not discourage those who were coming to a font, they discouraged those who were coming to Jesus. There is a mighty distinction ever to be held between the font and Christ, between the sprinkling of the priest and living faith in the Lord Jesus Christ.

First, his disciples discouraged those who would bring others to him. This is a great sin, and wherever it is committed Jesus Christ is greatly displeased, for a true desire to see others saved is wrought in the believer by God the Holy Spirit, who thus renders the called ones the means of bringing wandering sheep into the fold. In this case they discouraged those who would bring children to him to be blessed. How can we bring children to Jesus Christ to be blessed? We cannot do it in a corporeal sense, for Jesus is not here, "he is risen;" but we can bring our children in a true, real, and spiritual sense. We take them up in the arms of our prayer. I hope many of us, so soon as our children saw the light, if not before, presented them to God with this anxious prayer, that they might sooner die than live to disgrace their father's God. We only desired children that we might in them live over again another life of service to God; and when we looked into their young faces, we never asked wealth for them, nor fame, nor anything else, but that they might be dear unto God, and that their names might be written in the Lamb's Book of Life. We did then bring our children to Christ as far as we could do it, by presenting them before God, by earnest prayer on their behalf. And have we ceased to bring them to Christ? Nay, I hope we seldom bow the knee without praying for our children. Our daily cry is, "O, that they might live before thee!" God knows that nothing would give us more joy than to see evidence of their conversion; our souls would almost leap out of our bodies with joy, if we should but know that they were the children of the living God. Nor has this privilege been denied to us, for there are some here who can rejoice in a converted household. Truly we can say with the apostle Paul, "I have no greater joy than this, that my children walk in the truth." We continue, therefore, to bring them to Christ by daily, constant, earnest prayer on their behalf. So soon as they become of years capable of understanding the things of God, we endeavour to bring them to Christ by teaching them the truth. Hence our Sabbath-schools, hence the use of the Bible and family prayer, and catechizing at home. Any person who shall forbid us to pray for our children, will incur Christ's high displeasure; and any who shall say, "Do not teach your children; they will be converted in God's own time if it be his purpose, therefore leave them to run wild in the streets," will certainly both "sin against the child" and the Lord Jesus. We might as well say, "If that piece of ground is to grow a harvest, it will do so if it be God's good pleasure; therefore leave it, and let the weeds spring up and cover it; do not endeavour for a moment to kill the weeds, or to sow the good seed." Why, such reasoning as this would be not only cruel to our children, but grievously displeasing to Christ. Parents! I do hope you are all endeavouring to bring your children to Christ by teaching them the things of God. Let them not be strangers to the plan of salvation. Never let it be said that a child of yours reached years in which his conscience could act, and he could judge between good and evil, without knowing the doctrine of the atonement, without understanding the great substitutionary work of Christ. Set before your child life and death, hell and heaven, judgment and mercy, his own sin, and Christ's most precious blood; and as you set these before him, labour with him, persuade him, as the apostle did his congregation, with tears and weeping, to turn unto the Lord; and your prayers and supplications shall be heard so that the Spirit of God shall bring them to Jesus. How much more like the Scripture will such labours be than if you were to sing the following very pretty verse which disfigures Roundell Palmer's "Book of Praise!"--

"Though thy conception was in sin,
A sacred bathing thou hast had;
And though thy birth unclean has been,
A blameless babe thou now art made.
Sweet baby, then forbear to weep;
Be still, my dear, sweet baby, sleep."

I cannot tell you how much I owe to the solemn words of my good mother. It was the custom on Sunday evenings, while we were yet little children, for her to stay at home with us, and then we sat round the table and read verse by verse, and she explained the Scripture to us. After that was done, then came the time of pleading; there was a little piece of "Alleyn's Alarm," or of Baxter's "Call to the Unconverted," and this was read with pointed observations made to each of us as we sat round the table; and the question was asked how long it would be before we would think about our state, how long before we would seek the Lord. Then came a mother's prayer, and some of the words of a mother's prayer we shall never forget, even when our hair is grey. I remember on one occasion her praying thus: "Now, Lord, if my children go on in their sins, it will not be from ignorance that they perish, and my soul must bear a swift witness against them at the day of judgment if they lay not hold of Christ." That thought of a mother's bearing swift witness against me, pierced my conscience and stirred my heart. This pleading with them for God and with God for them is the true way to bring children to Christ. Sunday-school teachers! you have a high and noble work, press forward in it. In our schools you do not try to bring children to the baptistry for regeneration, you point them away from ceremonies; if I know the teachers of this school aright, I know you are trying to bring your classes to Christ. Let Christ be the sum and substance of your teaching in the school. Young men and young women, in your classes lift up Christ, lift him up on high; and if anybody shall say to you, "Why do you thus talk to the children?" you can say, "Because my soul yearns towards them, and I pant for their conversion;" and if any should afterwards object, you can remember that Jesus is greatly displeased with them, and not with you, for you only obey the injunction, "Feed my lambs."

The case in our text is that of children, but objectors rise up who disapprove of endeavours to bring any sort of people to Christ by faith and prayer. There are some who spend their nights in the streets seeking after the poor harlot, and I have heard many harsh observations made about their work; some will say it is ridiculous to expect that any of those who have spent their days in debauchery should be converted. We are told that the most of those who are taken into the refuges go back and become as depraved as ever; I believe that to be a very sad and solemn truth; but I believe, if I or anyone else shall urge that or anything else as a reason why my brethren should not seek the harlot, that Jesus would be greatly displeased; for any man who stands between a soul-seeker and the divine object of getting a blessing for the sinner's soul, excites the wrath of Christ. Some have hopes of our convicts and criminals; but every now and then there is an outcry against those who even believe it possible for a transport or a ticket-of-leave man to be converted. But Jesus is greatly displeased with any who shall say about the work, "It is too hard; it is impossible." My brethren in Christ, labour for souls of all sorts: for your children and for those who are past the threescore years and ten. Seek out the drunkard; go after the thief; despise not the poor down-trodden slave; let every race, let every colour, let every age, let every profession, let every nation, be the object of your soul's prayers. You live in this world, I hope, to bring souls to Jesus; you are Christ's magnets with which through his Holy Spirit he will attract hearts of steel; you are his heralds, you are to invite wanderers to come to the banquet; you are his messengers, you are to compel them to come in that his house may be filled; and if the devil tells you you will not succeed, and if the world tells you that you are too feeble and have not talent enough, never mind, Jesus would be greatly displeased with you if you should take any heed to them; and meanwhile he is greatly displeased with your adversaries for endeavouring to stop you. Beloved, this is why Jesus Christ was greatly displeased.

A second ground of displeasure must be noticed. These children, it strikes me, and I think there is good reason for the belief, themselves desired to come to Christ to obtain a blessing. They are called "little children," which term does not necessarily involve their being infants of six months or a year; indeed, it is clear, as I will show in a moment, that they were not such little children as to be unconscious babes. They were "infants," according to our version of Luke, but then you know the English word "infant" includes a considerable range of age, for every person in his minority is legally considered to be an infant, though he may be able to talk to any amount. We do not, however, desire to translate the text with so great a license. There is no necessity in the language used that these should have been anything but what they are said to be--"little children." It is evident they could walk, because in Luke it is said, "Jesus called them;" the gender of the Greek pronoun used there refers it to the children, not to the persons, nor to the disciples. Jesus called them, he called the children, which he would hardly have done if they could not comprehend his call: and he said, "Suffer the little children to come," which implies that they could come, and doubtless they did come, with cheerful faces, expecting to get the blessing. These perhaps may have been some of those very children, who, a short time after, pulled down branches from the trees and strewed them in the way, and cried, "Hosanna," when the Saviour said, "Out of the mouths of babes and sucklings hast thou ordained strength." Now Christ was greatly displeased with his disciples for pushing back these boys and girls. They did, as some old folks do now-a-days, who cry out--"Stand back, you boys and girls! we do not want you here; we do not want children to fill up the place; we only want grown-up people." They pushed them back; they thought that Christ would have too much to do, if he attended to the juveniles. Here comes out this principle, that we must expect Christ's displeasure, if we attempt to keep anybody back from coming to Christ, even though it be the youngest child. You ask how persons can come to Christ now? They cannot come corporeally, but they can come by simple prayer and humble faith. Faith is the way to Jesus, baptism is not. When Jesus says, "Come unto me all ye that labour and are heavy laden," he did not mean, "be baptized," did he? No; and so when he said, "Suffer the little children to come unto me," he did not mean, "Baptize them," did he? Coming to Jesus Christ is quite a different thing from coming to a font. Coming to Christ means laying hold upon Christ with the hand of faith; looking to him for my life, my pardon, my salvation, my everything. If there be a poor little child here who is saying in her little heart, or his little heart, "I would like to come to Christ, O that I might be pardoned while I am yet a little one"--come, little lamb; come, and welcome. Did I hear your cry? Was it this?

"Gentle Jesus, meek and mild,
Look upon a little child;
Pity my simplicity,
Suffer me to come to thee."

Dear little one, Jesus will not despise your lispings, nor will his servant keep you back. Jesus calls you, come and receive his blessing. If any of you say a word to keep the young heart back, Jesus will be displeased with you. Now I am afraid some do that; those, for instance, who think that the gospel is not for little children. Many of my brethren, I am sorry to say, preach in such a way that there is no hope of children ever getting any good by their preaching. I cannot glory in learning or eloquence, but in this one thing I may rejoice, that there is always a number of happy children here, who are quite as attentive as any of my audience. I do love to think that the gospel is suitable to little children. There are boys and girls in many of our Sabbath-school classes down below stairs who are as truly converted to God as any of us. Nay, and if you were to speak with them about the things of God, though you should get to the knotty points of election and predestination, you would find those boys and girls well taught in the things of the kingdom: they know free will from free grace, and you cannot puzzle them when you come to talk about the work of Jesus and the work of the Spirit, for they can discern between things which differ. But a minister who preaches as though he never wanted to bring children to Christ, and shoots right over the little one's heads, I do think Jesus is displeased with him.

Then there are others who doubt whether children ever will be converted. They do not look upon it as a thing likely to happen, and whenever they hear of a believing child, they hold up their hands at the prodigy, and say, "What a wonder of grace!" It ought to be, and in those Churches where the gospel is simply preached, it is as common a thing for children to be converted as for grown-up people to be brought to Christ. Others begin to doubt the truth of juvenile conversions. They say, "They are very young, can they understand the gospel? Is it not merely an infantile emotion, a mere profession?" My brethren, you have no more right to suspect the sincerity of the young, than to mistrust the grey-headed; you ought to receive them with the same open-breasted confidence with which you receive others when they profess to have found the Saviour. Do, I pray you, whenever you see the faintest desire in your children, go down on your knees, as your servant does, when the fire is almost out, and blow the spark with your own breath--seek by prayer to fan that spark to a flame. Do not despise any godly remark the child may make. Do not puff the child up on account of the goodness of the remark, lest you make him vain and so injure him, but do encourage him; let his first little prayers be noticed by you; though you may not like to teach him a form of prayer--I shall not care if you do not--yet teach him what prayer is; tell him to express his desires in his own words, and when he does so, join ye in it and plead with God on his behalf, that your little one may speedily find true peace in a Saviour's blood. You must not, unless you would displease my Master, keep back the smallest child that longs to come to Christ.

Here let us observe that the principle is of general application; you must not hinder any awakened soul from seeking the Saviour. O my brethren and sisters, I hope we have such a love for souls, such an instinct within us to desire to see the travail of Christ's soul, that instead of putting stumbling-blocks in the way, we would do the best we could to gather out the stones. On Sabbath days I have laboured to clear up the doubts and fears which afflict coming sinners; I have entreated God the Holy Spirit to enable me so to speak, that those things which hindered you from coming to the Saviour might be removed; but how sad must be the case of those who delight themselves in putting stumbling-blocks in men's way. The doctrine of election for instance, a great and glorious truth, full of comfort to God's people; how often is that made to frighten sinners from Jesus! There is a way of preaching that with a drawn sword, and say, "You must not come unless you know you are one of God's elect." That is not the way to preach the doctrine. The true way of preaching it is, "God has a chosen people, and I hope you are one of them; come, lay hold on Jesus, put your trust in him." Then there be others who preach up frames and feelings as a preparation for Christ. They do in effect say, "Unless you have felt so much depression of spirit, or experienced a certain quantity of brokenness of heart, you must not come to Christ," instead of declaring, that whosoever will is permitted to come, and that the true way of coming to Christ is not with a qualification of frames and feeling and mental depressions, but just as you are. Oh! it is my soul's delight to preach a gospel which has an open door to it, to preach a mercy-seat which has no veil before it; the veil is rent in twain, and now the biggest sinner out of hell who desires to come, is welcome. You who are eighty years of age, and have hated Christ all the time, if now the Spirit of God makes you willing to come, Christ seems to say, "Suffer the grey- headed to come unto me, and forbid them not:" while to you little children, he stretches out his arms in the same manner, "Suffer the little children to come unto me." O my beloved, see to it that your heart longs to come to Christ, and not to ceremonies! I stand here this day to cry, "Come ye to the cross, not to the font." When I forget to lift up the Lord Jesus, and to cast down the forms of man's devising, "let my right hand forget her cunning," and "let my tongue cleave to the roof of my mouth"--

"None but Jesus, none but Jesus,
Can do helpless sinners good;"

The font is a mockery and an imposition if it be put before Christ. If you have baptism after you have come to Christ, well and good, but to point you to it either as being Christ, or as being inevitably connected with Christ, or as being the place to find Christ, is nothing better than to go back to the beggarly elements of the old Romish harlot, instead of standing in the "liberty wherewith Christ hath made us free," and bidding the sinner to come as a sinner to Christ Jesus, and to Christ Jesus alone.

III. In the third and last place, let us also gather from our text, that WHEN WE DISCOURAGE ANY, WE ALWAYS GO UPON WRONG GROUNDS. Here was the case of children. I suppose that the grounds upon which the apostles kept back the children would be one of these--either that the children could not receive a blessing, or else that they could not receive it worthily.

Did they imagine that these little children could not receive the blessing? Perhaps so, for they thought them too young. Now, brethren, that was a wrong ground to go upon, for these children could receive the blessing and they did receive it, for Jesus took them in his arms and blessed them. If I keep back a child from coming to Christ on the ground that he is too young, I do it in the face of facts; because there have been children brought to Christ at an extremely early period. You who are acquainted with Janeway's "Tokens for Children," have noticed very many beautiful instances of early conversion. Our dear friend, Mrs. Rogers, in that book of hers, "The Folded Lamb," gave a very sweet picture of a little son of hers, soon folded in the Saviour's bosom above, who, as early as two or three years of age, rejoiced and knew the Saviour. I do not doubt at all, I cannot doubt it, because one has seen such cases, that children of two or three years of age may have precocity of knowledge, and of grace; a forwardness which in almost every case has betokened early death, but which has been perfectly marvellous to those who have talked with them. The fact is that we do not all at the same age arrive at that degree of mental stature which is necessary for understanding the things of God. Children have been reported as reading Latin, Greek, and other languages, at five or six years of age. I do not know that such early scholarship is any great blessing, it is better not to reach that point so soon; but some children are all that their minds ever will be at three or four, and then they go home to heaven; and so long as the mind has been brought up to such a condition that it is capable of understanding, it is also capable of faith, if the Holy Spirit shall implant it. To suppose that he ever did give faith to an unconscious babe is ridiculous; that there can be any faith in a child that knows nothing whatever I must always take ground to doubt, for "How shall they believe without a preacher?" And yet they are brought up to make a profession in their long-clothes, when they have never heard a sermon in their lives. But those dear children to whom I have before referred, have understood the preacher, have understood the truth, have rejoiced in the truth, and their first young lispings have been as full of grace as those glorious expressions of aged saints in their triumphant departures. Children are capable, then, of receiving the grace of God. Do mark by the way, that all those champions who have come out against me so valiantly, have made a mistake; they have said that we deny that little infants may be regenerated; we do not deny that God can regenerate them if he pleases; we do not know anything about what may or may not happen to unconscious babes; but we did say that little children were not regenerated by their godparents telling lies at a font--we did say that, and we say it again, that little children are not regenerated, nor made members of Christ, nor children of God, nor inheritors of the kingdom of heaven, by solemn mockery, in which godfathers and godmothers promise to do for them what they cannot do for themselves, much less for their children. That is the point; and if they will please to meet it, we will answer them again, but till such time as that, we shall probably let them talk on till God gives them grace to know better.

The other ground upon which the apostles put back the children would be, that although the children might receive the blessing, they might not be able to receive it worthily. The Lord Jesus in effect assures them that so far from the way in which a little child enters into the kingdom of heaven being exceptional, it is the rule; and the very way in which a child enters the kingdom, is the way in which everybody must enter it. How does a child enter the kingdom of heaven? Why, its faith is very simple; it does not understand mysteries and controversies, but it believes what it is told upon the authority of God's Word, and it comes to God's Word without previous prejudice. It has its natural sinfulness, but grace overcomes it, and the child receives the Word as it finds it. You will notice in boyish and girlish conversions, a peculiar simplicity of belief: they believe just what Christ says, exactly what he says. If they pray, they believe Christ will hear them: if they talk about Jesus, it is as of a person near at hand. They do not, as we do, get into the making of these things into mysteries and shadows, but little children have a realizing power. Then they have great rejoicing. The most cheerful Christians we have are young believers; and the most cheerful old Christians are those who were converted when they were young. Why, see the joy of a child that finds a Saviour! "Mother," he says, "I have sought Jesus Christ, and I have trusted him, and I am saved." He does not say, "I hope," and "I trust," but "I am;" and then he is ready to leap for joy because he is saved. Of the many boys and girls whom we have received into Church-fellowship, I can say of them all, they have all gladdened my heart, and I have never received any with greater confidence than I have these: this I have noticed about them, they have greater joy and rejoicing than any others; and I take it, it is because they do not ask so many questions as others do, but take Jesus Christ's word as they find it, and believe in it. Well now, just the very way in which a child receives Christ, is the way in which you must receive Christ if you would be saved. You who know so much that you know too much; you who have big brains; you who are always thinking, and have tendency to criticism, and perhaps to scepticism, you must come and receive the gospel as a little child. You will never get a hold of my Lord and Master while you are wearing that quizzing cap; no, you must take it off, and by the power of the Holy Spirit you must come trusting Jesus, simply trusting him, for this is the right way to receive the kingdom.

But here, let me say, the principle which holds good in little children holds good in all other cases as well. Take for instance the case of very great sinners, men who have been gross offenders against the laws of their country. Some would say they cannot be saved; they can be for some of them have been. Others would say they never receive the truth as it is in Jesus in the right manner; ay, but they do. How do great sinners receive Christ? There are some here who have been reclaimed from drunkenness, and I know not what. My brethren, how did you receive Christ? Why in this way. You said, "All unholy, all unclean, I am nothing else but sin; but if I am saved, it will be grace, grace, grace." Why, when you and I stood up, black, and foul, and filthy, and yet dared to believe in Christ, we said, "If we are saved, we shall be prodigies of divine mercy, and we will sing of his love for ever." Well but, my dear friends, you must all receive Jesus Christ in that very way. That which would raise an objection to the salvation of the big sinner is thrown back upon you, for Christ might well say, "Except ye receive these things as the chief of sinners, ye cannot enter the kingdom." I will prove my point by the instance of the apostle Paul. He has been held by some to be an exception to the rule, but Paul did not think so, for he says that God in him showed forth all longsuffering for a pattern to them that believe, and made him as it were a type of all conversions; so that instead of being an exception his was to be the rule. You see what I am driving at. The case of the children looks exceptional, but it is not; it has, on the contrary, all the features about it which must be found in every true conversion. It is of such that the kingdom of heaven is composed, and if we are not such we cannot enter it. Let this induce all of us who love the Lord, to pray for the conversion both of children and of all sorts of men. Let our compassion expand, let us shut out none from the plea of our heart; in prayer and in faith let us bring all who come under our range, hoping and believing that some of them will be found in the election of grace, that some of them will be washed in the Saviour's blood, and that some of them will shine as stars in the firmament of God for ever. Let us, on no consideration, believe that the salvation of any man or child is beyond the range of possibility, for the Lord saveth whom he wills. Let no difficulties which seem to surround the case hinder our efforts; let us, on the contrary, push with greater eagerness forward, believing that where there seems to be some special difficulty, there will be manifested, as in the children's case, some special privilege. O labour for souls, my dear friends! I beseech you live to win souls. This is the best rampart against error, a rampart built of living stones--converted men and women. This is the way to push back the advances of Popery, by imploring the Lord to work conversions. I do not think that mere controversial preaching will do much, though it must be used; it is grace-work we want; it is bringing you to Christ, it is getting you to lay hold of him--it is this which shall put the devil to a nonplus and expand the kingdom of Christ. O that my God would bring some of you to Jesus! If he is displeased with those who would keep you back, then see how willing he is to receive you. Is there in your soul any desire towards him? Come and welcome, sinner, come. Do you feel now that you must have Christ or die? Come and have him, he is to be had for the asking. Has the Lord taught you your need of Jesus? Ye thirsty ones, come and drink; ye hungry ones, come and eat. Yea, this is the proclamation of the gospel to-day, "The Spirit and the bride say, Come. And let him that heareth say, Come. And let him that is athirst come. And whosoever will, let him take the water of life freely." I do trust there may be encouragement in this to some of you. I pray my Master make you feel it. If he be angry with those who keep you back, then he must be willing to receive you, glad to receive you; and if you come to him he will in no wise cast you out. May the Lord add his blessing on these words for Jesus' sake. Amen.

The Restoration And Conversion Of The Jews

PREACHED ON THURSDAY EVENING, JUNE 16, 1864,
BY THE REV. C. H. SPURGEON,
AT THE METROPOLITAN TABERNACLE, NEWINGTON,
In aid of the Funds of the British Society for the Propagation of the Gospel Among the Jews.

"The hand of the Lord was upon me and carried me out in the Spirit of the Lord and set me down in the midst of the valley which was full of bones and caused me to pass by them round about: and, behold, there were very many in the open valley. And, lo, they were very dry. And He said unto me, Son of man, can these bones live? And I answered, O Lord God, You know. Again He said unto me, Prophesy upon these Bones and say unto them, O you dry bones, hear the word of the Lord. Thus says the Lord God unto these bones: Behold, I will cause breath to enter into you and you shall live: and I will lay sinews upon you and will bring up flesh upon you and cover you with skin and put breath in you and you shall live. And you shall know that I am the Lord. So I prophesied as I was commanded: and as I prophesied, there was a noise and behold a shaking and the bones came together, bone to his bone. And when I beheld, lo, the sinews and the flesh came up upon them and the skin covered them above: but there was no breath in them. Then said He unto me, Prophesy unto the wind, prophesy, Son of man and say to the wind, Thus says the Lord God: Come from the four winds, O Breath and breathe upon these slain, that they may live. So I prophesied as He commanded me and the breath came into them and they lived and stood up upon their feet, an exceeding great army." -- Ezekiel 37:1-10.

THIS vision has been used, from the time of Jerome onwards, as a description of the resurrection and certainly it may be so accommodated with much effect. What a vision of the great day the words picture before the mind's eye! The great army of the quick, who once were dead, seem to start up as we read. Here, too, we have a very fit and appropriate question to be asked in a tomb--"Son of man, can these bones live?" Looking down into the dark grave, or watching the sexton as he throws up the moldering relics, once infused with life, well may unbelief suggest the enquiry--"Can these bones live?"

Faith cannot at all times give a more satisfactory answer than this--"O Lord God, You know." But while this interpretation of the vision may be very proper as an accommodation, it must be quite evident to any thinking person that this is not the meaning of the passage. There is no allusion made by Ezekiel to the resurrection and such a topic would have been quite apart from the design of the Prophet's speech. I believe he was no more thinking of the resurrection of the dead than of the building of St. Peter's at Rome, or the emigration of the Pilgrim Fathers! That topic is altogether foreign to the subject at hand and could not by any possibility have crept into the Prophet's mind.

He was talking about the people of Israel and prophesying concerning them. And evidently the vision, according to God's own interpretation of it, was concerning them and them alone, for, "these bones are the whole house of Israel." It was not a vision concerning all men, nor, indeed, concerning any men as to the resurrection of the dead--it had a direct and special bearing upon the Jewish people. This passage, again, has been very frequently and I dare say very properly, used to describe the revival of a decayed Church. This vision may be looked upon as descriptive of a state of lukewarmness and spiritual lethargy in a Church when the question may be sorrowfully asked--"Can these bones live?"

Can that dull minister wake up to living power? Can these cold deacons glow with holy heat? Can those unspiritual members rise to something like holy, earnest self-sacrifice? Is it possible that the drowsy formal Church could start up to real earnestness? Such suggestions might well have occurred to many minds at the time of the Reformation. It did seem impossible, when Popery was in its power, that spiritual life should ever again return to the Church. Piety seemed to be dead and buried and the cloister, the clergy, superstition and deceit, like great graves, had swallowed up everything that was good.

But the Lord appeared for His people and brought up the buried Truth of God out of its grave, and once more in every part of the known world the name of Jesus Christ was lifted up and sound doctrine was preached! So was it in our own country. When both the Establishment and

Dissent had fallen into spiritual death we might well have said--"Can these bones live?" But Whitfield and Wesley were raised up by God and they prophesied to the dry bones, and up they stood--filled with the Spirit of God--"an exceeding great army." Let the crowds of Kingsdown and the multitudes on Kennington Common tell of the quickening power of Jesus' name! Decayed Churches can most certainly be revived by the preaching of the Word accompanied by the coming of the heavenly "breath" from the four winds.

O Lord, send us such revivals now, for many of your Churches need them--they are almost as dead as the corpses which sleep around them in the graveyard. But while we admit this to be a very fitting accommodation of our text, yet we are quite convinced that it is not to this that the passage refers. It would be altogether alien to the Prophet's strain of thought to be thinking about the restoration of fallen zeal and the rekindling of expiring love. He was not considering the Reformation either of Luther or of Whitfield, or about the revival of one Church or of another. No, he was talking of his own people, of his own race and of his own tribe. He surely ought to have known his own mind, and led by the Holy Spirit, he gives us as an explanation of the vision. Not--"Thus says the Lord, My dying Church shall be restored," but--"I will bring My people out of their graves and bring them into the land of Israel."

With very great propriety, too, this passage has been used for the comforting of Believers in their dark and cloudy days. When they have lost their comforts, when their spiritual joys have drooped like withering flowers, when they have been no longer able to--

"Read their titles clear To mansions in the skies," they have been reminded that God could return to them in Grace and mercy, that the dry bones could live and should live! Then they remember that the Spirit of God could again come upon His people--that even at the time when they were ready to give up all hope and lie down in despair, He could come and so quicken them, that the poor trembling cowards should be turned into soldiers of God and should stand upon their feet an exceeding great army!

No grave of grief can hold the immortal joy of a Believer--on the third day it shall rise again, for, like the Lord who gave it, it shall never see corruption! Bone to his bone shall your comforts come together and an army of joys shall live in your soul. The passage certainly may be so used without violent wresting and might thus yield much comfort to the people of God. But still we take the liberty of saying that this is not the drift of the Prophet and that we do not believe he was thinking of anything of the kind. We think that he was speaking only of his own people, his own "kinsmen according to the flesh."

Once more. There is no doubt that we have in this passage a most striking picture of the restoration of dead souls to spiritual life. Men by nature are just like these dry bones exposed in the open valley. The whole spiritual frame is dislocated. The sap and marrow of spiritual life has been dried out of manhood. Human nature is not only dead, but, like the bleaching bones which have long whitened in the sun, it has lost all trace of the Divine life. Will and power have both departed. Spiritual death reigns undisturbed. Yet the dry bones can live! Under the preaching of the Word the vilest sinners can be reclaimed, the most stubborn wills can be subdued, the most unholy lives can be sanctified! When the holy "breath" comes from the four winds, when the Divine Spirit descends to own the Word, then multitudes of sinners as on Pentecost's hallowed day, stand up upon their feet--an exceeding great army--to praise the Lord their God.

But, mark you, this is not the first and proper interpretation of the text. It is, indeed, nothing more than a very striking parallel case to the one before us. It is not the case itself. It is only a similar one for the way in which God restores a nation is, practically, the way in which He restores an individual. The way in which Israel shall be saved is the same by which any one individual sinner shall be saved. It is not, however, the one case which the Prophet is aiming at. He is looking at the vast mass of cases--the multitudes of instances to be found among the Jewish people of gracious quickening and holy resurrection.

His first and primary intention was to speak of them and though it is right and lawful to take a passage in its widest possible meaning since, "no Scripture is of private interpretation," yet I hold it to be treason to God's Word to neglect its primary meaning and constantly to say-- "Such-and-such is the primary meaning, but it is of no consequence and I shall use the words for another subject." The preacher of God's Truth should not give up the Holy Spirit's meaning! He should take care that he does not even put it in the background. The first meaning of a text, the Spirit's meaning, is that which should be brought out first and though the rest may fairly spring out of it, yet the first sense should have the chief place.

Let it have the uppermost place in the synagogue. Let it be looked upon as at least not inferior, either in interest or importance, to any other meaning which may come out of the text. The meaning of our text as opened up by the context is most evidently, if words mean anything, first, that there shall be a political restoration of the Jews to their own land and to their own nationality. And then, secondly, there is in the text and in the context a most plain declaration that there shall be a spiritual restoration-- in fact a conversion--of the tribes of Israel.

I. First, THERE IS TO BE A POLITICAL RESTORATION OF THE JEWS. Israel is now blotted out from the map of nations. Her sons are scattered far and wide. Her daughters mourn beside all the rivers of the earth. Her sacred song is hushed--no king reigns in Jerusalem! She brings forth no governors among her tribes. But she is to be restored! She is to be restored "as from the dead." When her own sons have given up all hope of her, then is God to appear for her. She is to be reorganized--her scattered bones are to be brought together. There will be a native government again. There will again be the form of a political body.

A State shall be incorporated and a king shall reign. Israel has now become alienated from her own land. Her sons, though they can never forget the sacred dust of Palestine, yet die at a hopeless distance from her consecrated shores. But it shall not be so forever, for her sons shall again rejoice in her--her land shall be called Beulah--for as a young man marries a virgin so shall her sons marry her. "I will place you in your own land," is God's promise to them. They shall again walk upon her mountains, shall once more sit under her vines and rejoice under her fig trees!

And they are also to be reunited. There shall not be two, nor ten, nor twelve, but one--one Israel praising one God--serving one king and that one King the Son of David, the descended Messiah! They are to have a national prosperity which shall make them famous. No, so glorious shall they be that Egypt and Tyre and Greece and Rome shall all forget their glory in the greater splendor of the throne of David! The day shall yet come when all the high hills shall leap with envy because this is the hill which God has chosen! The time shall come when Zion's shrine shall again be visited by the constant feet of the pilgrim--when her valleys shall echo with songs and her hilltops shall drop with wine and oil.

If there is meaning in words this must be the meaning of this chapter! I wish never to learn the art of tearing God's meaning out of His own Words. If there is anything clear and plain, the literal sense and meaning of this passage--a meaning not to be spirited or spiritualized away--it must be evident that both the two and the ten tribes of Israel are to be restored to their own land and that a king is to rule over them. "Thus says the Lord God: Behold, I will take the children of Israel from among the heathen where they are gone and will gather them on every side and bring them into their own land: and I will make them one nation in the land upon the mountains of Israel. And one king shall be king to them all. And they shall be no more two nations, neither shall they be divided into two kingdoms any more at all."

I am not now going into millennial theories, or into any speculation as to dates. I do not know anything at all about such things and I am not sure that I am called to spend my time in such research. I am called to minister the Gospel rather than to open prophecy. Those who are wise in such things doubtless prize their wisdom, but I have not the time to acquire it, nor any inclination to leave soul-winning pursuits for less arousing themes. I believe it is a great deal better to leave many of these promises and many of these gracious outlooks of Believers to exercise their full force upon our minds without depriving them of their simple glory by aiming to discover dates and figures. Let this be settled, however, that if there is meaning in words, Israel is yet to be restored--

"Yet not in vain--over Israel's land The glory yet will shine. And He, your once rejected King, Messiah, shall be yours. His chosen Bride, ordained with Him To reign over all the earth, Shall first be framed, and you shall know Your Savior's matchless worth. Then you, beneath the peaceful reign Of Jesus and His Bride, Shall sound His Grace and Glory forth, To all the earth beside. The nations to your glorious light, O Zion, yet shall throng, And all the listening islands wait To catch the joyful song."

But there is a second meaning here. ISRAEL IS TO HAVE A SPIRITUAL RESTORATION OR A CONVERSION. Both the text and the context teach this. The promise is that they shall renounce their idols and, behold, they have already done so! "Neither shall they defile themselves any more with their idols." Whatever faults the Jew may have, he certainly has not idolatry. "The Lord your God is one God," is a Truth far better conceived by the Jew than by any other man on earth except the Christian. Weaned forever from the worship of all images of any sort, the Jewish nation has now become infatuated with traditions or duped by philosophy.

She is to have, however, instead of these delusions, a spiritual religion--she is to love her God. "They shall be My people and I will be their God." The unseen but Omnipotent Jehovah is to be worshipped in spirit and in truth by His ancient people. They are to come before Him in His own appointed way, accepting the Mediator whom their sires rejected. They will come into Covenant relation with God, for so our text tells us-- "I will make a Covenant of peace with them," and Jesus is our peace--therefore we gather that Jehovah shall enter into the Covenant of Grace with them--

that Covenant of which Christ is the federal Head, the Substance and the Surety.

They are to walk in God's ordinances and statutes and so exhibit the practical effects of being united to Christ who has given them peace. All these promises certainly imply that the people of Israel are to be converted to God and that this conversion is to be permanent. The tabernacle of God is to be with them! The Most High is, in a special manner, to have His sanctuary in the midst of them forever more so that whatever nations may apostatize and turn from the Lord in these latter days, the nation of Israel never can, for she shall be effectually and permanently converted. The hearts of the fathers shall be turned with the hearts of the children unto the Lord their God and they shall be the people of God, world without end.

We look forward, then, for these two things. I am not going to theorize upon which of them will come first--whether they shall be restored first, and converted afterwards--or converted first and then restored. They are to be restored and they are to be converted, too. Let the Lord send these blessings in His own order and we shall be well content whichever way they shall come. We take this for our joy and our comfort that this thing shall be and that both in the spiritual and in the temporal throne, the King Messiah shall sit and reign among His people gloriously.

II. Now I come to the practical part of my sermon this evening--THE MEANS OF THAT RESTORATION. Looking at this matter we are very apt to say, "How can these things be? How can the Jews be converted to Christ? How can they be made into a nation? Truly the case is quite as hopeless as that of the bones in the valley! How shall they cease from worldliness or renounce their constant pursuit of riches? How shall they he weaned from their bigoted attachment to their Talmudic traditions? How shall they be lifted up out of that hardness of heart which makes them hate the Messiah of Nazareth, their Lord and King? How can these things be?"

The Prophet does not say it cannot be. His unbelief is not so great as that, but at the same time he scarcely ventures to think that it can ever be possible. He very wisely, however, puts back the question upon his God--"O Lord God, You know." Now some of you are very expectant about this tonight and you are expecting to see the Jews converted very soon, perhaps in a month or two. I wish you may see it as soon as your desires would date it. Others of us are not as optimistic and take a more gloomy view of a long future of woes.

Well, let us both together come before God tonight and say, "O Lord God, You know. And if You know it, Lord, we will be content to leave the secret with You! Only tell us what You would have us do. We ask not food for speculation, but we do ask for work. We ask for something by which we may practically show that we really do love the Jew and that we would bring him to Christ."

In answer to this, the Lord says to His servants, "Prophesy upon these bones," so that our duty tonight, as Christians, is to prophesy upon these bones and we shall then see God's purpose fulfilled--when we obey God's precept. I want you to observe that there are two kinds of prophesying spoken of here. First, the Prophet prophesies to the bones--here is preaching. And next, he prophesies to the four winds--here is praying. The preaching has its share in the work, but it is the praying which achieves the result--for after he had prophesied to the four winds and not before--the bones began to live.

All that the preaching did was to make a stir and to bring the bones together, but it was the praying which did the work, for then God the Holy Spirit came to give them life! Preaching and praying, then, are the two heads of this part of my sermon tonight and we will speak upon each briefly.

1. It is the duty and the privilege of the Christian Church to preach the Gospel to the Jew and to every creature. And in so doing she may safely take the vision before us as her guide. She may take it as her guide, first, as to matter. What are we to preach? The text says we are to prophesy and assuredly every missionary to the Jews should especially keep God's prophecies very prominently before the public eye. It seems to me that one way in which the Jewish mind might be laid hold of would be to remind the Jews right often of that splendid future which both the Old and the New Testaments predict for Israel.

Every man has a tender side and a warm heart towards his own nation and if you tell him that in your standard book there is a revelation made that that nation is to act a grand part in human history and is, indeed, to take the very highest place in the parliament of nations--then the man's prejudice is on your side and he listens to you with the greater attention. I would not commend, as some do, the everlasting preaching of prophesy in every congregation. But a greater prominence should be given to prophecies in teaching the Jews than among any other people.

But still, the main thing which we have to preach about is Christ. Depend upon it dear Brethren, the best sermons which we ever preach are those which are fullest of Christ Jesus, the Son of David and the Son of God! Jesus the suffering Savior by whose stripes we are healed! Jesus able to save unto the uttermost--here is the most suitable subject for Gentiles. God has fashioned all hearts alike and therefore this is also the noblest theme for Jews. Paul loved his countrymen! He was no simpleton--he knew what was the best weapon with which to assail and overcome their prejudices and yet he could say, "I determined not to know anything among you save Jesus Christ and Him crucified."

Lift up the Messiah, then, both before Jew and Gentile. Tell of Mary's Son, the eternal Son of God, the Man of Nazareth who is none other than the Incarnate Word, God made flesh and dwelling among us! Preach His hallowed life--the righteousness of His people. Declare His painful death--the putting away of all their sins. Vindicate His glorious Resurrection! The justification of His people. Tell of His ascent on high. His triumph over the world and sin! Declare His second advent, His glorious coming to make His people glorious in the Glory which He has won for them! And Christ Jesus, as He is thus preached, shall surely be the means of making these bones live!

Let this preaching resound with Sovereign mercy! Let it always have in it the clear and distinct ring of Free Grace. I was thinking as I read this chapter just now, that of all the sermons which were ever preached, this sermon to the dry bones is the most Calvinistic, the most full of Free Grace of any which were ever delivered. If you will notice it you will find that there is not an "if," or a "but," or a condition in it!

And as for free will, there is not even a mention of it. It is all in this fashion--"Thus says the Lord God unto these bones: Behold, I will cause breath to enter into you and you shall live: and I will lay sinews upon you and will bring up flesh upon you and cover you with skin and put breath in you and you shall live. And you shall know that I am the Lord." You see it is all "shalls," and "wills," and Covenant purposes. It is all God's decrees declared and declared, too, as if there were no possibility of man's resisting them.

He does not say, "You dry bones, you shall live if you like. You shall if you are willing." He does not say to them, "You shall stand upright and be an exceeding great army if it pleases you to consent to My power." No, but it is, "I will," and, "you shall." As for will, it is altogether put out of the question, for how shall the dead have a will in the matter? And so, dear Friends, I would have the Gospel preached both to the Jew and the Gentile with a very clear and distinct note of free, Sovereign, almighty Grace.

Man has a will and God never ignores that will--but by His almighty Grace He blessedly leads it in silken fetters. He never stops to ask that will's consent when He comes forth upon His errands of effectual Grace. He wins that consent by the sweet persuasions of His own Omnipotent love. He comes arrayed in the robes of His Omnipotent Grace and the most hardened of rebels see at once such an attractive force in the love of God in Christ that with full consent against their ancient wills they yield themselves captives to the Grace of God! I do not believe that the Jews, or anybody else, will ever be converted as a usual thing by keeping back any of the Doctrines of Grace.

We must have God's Truth and the whole of it. And more distinct utterances concerning evangelical doctrines and the Grace of God are required both for Jews and for Gentiles. Preach, preach, preach, then--but let it be the preaching of Christ and the proclamation of Free Grace. The Church, I say, has a model here as to the matter of preaching. And I am certain that she has also a model here as to her manner of preaching. How shall we preach the Gospel? Was Ezekiel to do what some of my hyper-Calvinistic Brethren say preachers ought to do--to warn the sinner, but never to invite him?

Was Ezekiel to go and talk to these bones, but never say a word to them by way of command? Was he to explain the way of salvation but never bid them walk in it? No! After he had declared Covenant purposes, he was then to say, "Thus says the Lord, you dry bones live." And so the message of the Gospel minister, when he has declared the purposes of Divine Grace, is to say to sinners, "Thus says the Lord, believe in the Lord

Jesus Christ! Trust Christ and you are saved!" Whoever you may be, Jew or Gentile. Whether your speech is that of the land of Canaan or of a Gentile tongue. Whether you spring of Shem, Ham, or Japheth--trust Christ and you are saved! Trust Him, then, you dry bones, and live! Withered arm be outstretched! Lame men, leap! Blind eyes, see! You dead, dry bones, live!

The manner of our preaching is to be by way of command as well as by way of teaching. Repent and be converted, every one of you. Lay hold on eternal life. "Seek and you shall find. Knock and it shall be opened unto you." "Believe in the Lord Jesus Christ and you shall be saved!" We have a model here, moreover, as to our audience. We are not to select our congregation, but we are to go where God sends us. And if He should send us into the open valley where the bones are very dry, we are to preach there. I trust that my Brethren of the Society for the Propagation of the Gospel Among the Jews will never confine their labors to the good Jew, the respectable Jew, the enlightened Jew--let them seek after him among the rest--but I hope they will also seek after the ignorant, the degraded, the poor and the fallen.

The Church's best harvests have generally been reaped among the poor. For every grain of wheat which has fructified upon the hillsides of wealth, thousands have sprung up to bring forth much fruit in the valleys of poverty and obscurity. "The poor have the Gospel preached to them"--

this is the Gospel's pride! The poor receive the Gospel--this is its success! Preach to the dry bones, then. Do not say, "Such-and-such a man is too bigoted." The case rests not with him, nor with his bigotry, but with God! These bones were very dry, but yet they lived.

There is very little to choose, after all, between one man and another when all are dead! A little difference in the dryness does not come to much account when all are dead in sin. That some men are drunk and some are sober, that some men are debauched and some are chaste makes a very great difference in the moral and civil world. But very little difference, indeed, in the spiritual world, for there the same things happen to them both. If they believe not they shall alike be lost. And if they trust Jesus Christ they shall alike be saved! Let not, therefore, the greater vi-ciousness of a people, or their greater hardness of heart, ever stand in our way--but let us say to them, dry as they are--"You dry bones, live."

And here, again, we have another lesson as to the preacher's authority. If you will observe you will see the Prophet says, "Hear the Word of the Lord." We are to go neither to Jew nor to Gentile upon our own errand, or bearing our own words. I have no right to command a man to believe this or that unless I am an ambassador of God. And then, with God's authority to direct and empower me, I speak no longer as a man following his own wit but as the mouth of God.

So let every one of us go, when we are trying to save souls, feeling the hand of God upon us, with a soul big with anxious thoughts and heaving high with earnest desires. Let us speak--

"As though we never might speak again, As dying men to dying men," taking hold upon God's arm and beseeching Him to work by us and through us for the good of men. Remember, Christian, however humble you may be--when you speak God's Word--that Word has an authority about it which will leave a man without excuse if he rejects it. Always put to your fellow man the Truth of God which you hold dear--not as a thing which he may play with or may do what he likes with--or which is at his option to choose or to neglect as he sees fit. But put it to him as it is in truth--the Word of God. And be not satisfied unless you warn him that it is at his own peril that he rejects the invitation and that on his own head must be his blood if he turns aside from the good Word of the command of God.

Thus, we have, I think, all the directions which are necessary for us to preach. And what this Society and every other Society which aims at the conversion of sinners has to do is to go and preach, preach, preach--not spending too much upon printing, nor upon schools, nor ecclesiastical buildings--but preaching the Word of God! For after all, this is the battering-ram which is to shake the gates of Hell and break its iron bars. God has chosen "the foolishness of preaching" that He might, by it, save those who believe! Preaching is the blast of the ram's horn ordained to level Jericho and the sound of the silver trumpet appointed to usher in the jubilee. It is God's chariot of fire for bearing souls to Heaven and His two-edged sword to strike the hosts of Hell. His ordained servants are at once warriors and builders, and the Word serves them both for spear and trowel. Preach, then, from morning till night--at every time and on all occasions, "the unsearchable riches of Christ," and Israel shall yet live!

I cannot leave this point without noticing how the Prophet describes the effect of his preaching--there was a voice and there was a noise. Was this the noise of God's voice going with man's voice? Or was this the noise of the bones themselves creeping over one another? Does this represent opposition on the part of those preached to? Truly opposition is always a good sign! When you can get a man to oppose you, you may have some hope of him. If he has enough religious thought to try and refute what you bring before him, you may be thankful. Is this stir, then, the stir of opposition, or is it the stir of enquiry?

Does not the creeping of the bones together represent the people coming together to hear, to talk with one another, to reason about Divine things? When the various muscles and the flesh come upon the bones, does this represent the appearance of certain converts, destined to be the leaders of others? Are these sinews and muscles the representatives of men who are to move the rest of the corporate body by-and-by? It may be so and we may expect to see, as Christ is preached among Jews or Gentiles, more and more stir and excitement--the people coming together in greater numbers and the whole mass fermenting by the force of the leaven. Anything is better than stagnation--of a persecutor I have quite as much hope as of a quiet despiser.

2. But now we come to speak of that in which you can all take a part. Perhaps you cannot take a part in preaching the Word, though I wish that you all could. And I covet for you all the best gifts. But in the second form of prophesying you can all take your share. After the Prophet had prophesied to the bones, he was to prophesy to the winds. He was to say to the blessed Spirit, the Life-Giver, the God of all Grace, "Come from the four winds, O Breath and breathe upon these slain, that they may live."

Preaching alone does little. It may make a stir. It may bring the people together. There is an attractiveness about the Gospel which will draw the people to hear it. And there is, moreover, a force about it which will excite them, for it is "quick and powerful and sharper than any two-edged sword." But there is no life-giving power in the Gospel of itself apart from the Holy Spirit! The "Breath" must first blow and then these bones shall live! Let us betake ourselves much to this form of prophesying.

Brothers and Sisters in Christ, you who care for Israel, go before the Lord now and from now on in earnest, importunate prayer! Strive to be more than ever conscious of the utter indispensability of this matter. Feel that without Christ you can do nothing! In vain your society, your machinery, your committees, your secretaries, your collectors, your contributors, your missionaries without the Holy Spirit! Blow your trumpet and proclaim loudly what you have done--you have sown much--but you shall reap little unless you are trusting in the Spirit of God! There is always this danger to which we are exposed, though some, I know, think that it is a danger which does not exist--I mean the peril of looking to the strength or the weakness of the instrumentality and being either puffed up by the one or dejected by the other.

You are enough for your work if God is with you! And if you are but a handful you are too many for your work if God is not with you. God never objects to human weakness--when He comes to work He prefers it--for it makes a platform for Divine power. What did He say to Gideon--"The people are too many for Me." He did not say that they were too few. You never find a case in Scripture of God's saying that the people were too few--it was, "The people are too many for Me." Man's strength is more in God's way than man's weakness. No, human weakness, inasmuch as it makes elbow room for God's strength, is God's chosen instrument! "Therefore will I glory in infirmities," said the Apostle, "that the power of God may rest upon me." Rest then, upon the Holy Spirit as indispensable and go to God with this for your cry, "Come from the four winds, O Breath and breathe upon these slain, that they may live."

Observe, Beloved, that this second prophesying of Ezekiel is just as bold and as full of faith as the first. He seems to have no doubt, but speaks as though he could command the wind. "Come," says he and the wind comes. We need more faith in God. When we are engaged in any spiritual work we shall always find our success proportioned to our faith. Little faith, slender harvests! Much faith, plenteous sheaves! Little fishes come in slender numbers to Little-Faith's net. But Strong-Confidence can hardly hold all the great fishes which load her boat. I will not ask for your society, or for you any further gift than greater faith, for, getting greater faith you have Divine strength and sure success.

The Spirit always works with faithful men. My dear Friends, the Spirit of God is poured out! He abides in His Church as the ever-present Comforter. We are not to look upon His influences as a gift which we cannot reach for He is here waiting to give us all we need. He dwells in the midst of His people and we have but to cry unto Him and He will manifest His mighty power and we shall have souls saved, both Jews and Gentiles! Let your prayer, then, be with a sense of how much you need it, but yet with a firm conviction that the Holy Spirit will most surely come in answer to your petitions.

And then let it be earnest prayer. That, "Come from the four winds, O breath," reads to me like the cry, not of one in despair, but of one who is full of a vehement desire gratified with what he sees, since the bones have come together and have been mysteriously clothed with flesh! And he is now crying passionately for the immediate completion of the miracle--"Come from the four winds, O Breath and breathe upon these slain, that they may live." There is continual vehemence and force here--here is just that which makes a prayer prevalent. O, let us cry mightily unto God! We cannot expect to see great things unless we cry to Him--but we are only limited by our prayers. We are not straitened in Him! We are only straitened in ourselves.

We might see greater things if we could but believe. All things are possible to him that believes, but as of old, the Lord Jesus cannot do many mighty things nowadays because of our unbelief. We hamper the arm of Grace! We do, as it were, restrain the Almighty energy. O for greater faith to believe that nations may be born in a day! That multitudes may be turned unto God at once--and we shall yet see it--see what our fathers never saw and what our imaginations have never dreamed! We shall leap from victory to victory, marching on from one triumph to another until we meet the all-glorious Savior! Charging enemy after enemy and routing army after army, we shall go on, conquering and to conquer until we salute Him who comes upon the white horse of triumph followed by all the armies of Heaven! Brethren, be of good courage in your work of faith and labor of love for it is not and shall not be in vain in the Lord.

I address some tonight, I know, who have no interest in what I have been saying for they are not subjects of Messiah, themselves. Remember, faith is a sign of your allegiance to Him. Trust Christ and you are saved! Trust Jesus Christ and you are delivered from Divine wrath and from the power of your natural passions. The Lord grant you a resurrection tonight, O you who are dead in sin, and His name shall have all the praise!

Our friends here have for some little time been in a small way assisting this Society by their contributions. They, therefore, are well acquainted with it. I have not time this evening to enter into details about it, but I may just say that this Society has for a long time done a good work among the Jewish people. And I ask you to contribute to this among other good works as you feel moved to do whenever opportunity occurs.

The Lamb--The Light

DELIVERED ON SUNDAY MORNING, JULY 31, 1864,
BY THE REV. C. H. SPURGEON,
AT THE METROPOLITAN TABERNACLE, NEWINGTON.

"And the city had no need of the sun, neither of the moon, to shine in it: for the Gory of God did lighten it and the Lamb is its light." -- Revelation 21:23.

To the lover of Jesus it is very pleasant to observe how the Lord Jesus Christ has always stood foremost in Glory from before the foundation of the world and will do so as long as eternity shall last. If we look back by faith to the time of the creation, we find our Lord with His Father as one brought up with Him. "When there were no depths, I was brought forth, when there were no fountains abounding with water. While as yet He had not made the earth, nor the fields, nor the highest part of the dust of the world. When He prepared the heavens, I was there: when He set a compass upon the face of the depth: when He established the clouds above: when He strengthened the fountains of the deep."

He was that Wisdom who was never absent from the Father's counsels in the great work of creation, whether it was the birth of angels or the making of worlds of men. One of the first events ever recorded in Scripture history is, "When He brings in the First-Begotten into the world, He says, let all the angels of God worship Him." Such words were never spoken of any creature, but only of Him who is co-equal and co-eternal with the Father. He is glorious forever--the First-Born of every creature, the Head of the household of God--the express Image of His Person and the fullness of His Glory.

In the earliest periods of which we possess any knowledge, Jesus Christ stood exalted far above all principalities and powers and every name that is named. When human history dawns and the history of God's Church commences, you still find Christ preeminent. All the types of the early Church are only to be opened up by Him as the key. It would have been nothing to be of the seed of Israel if it had not been for the promise of the Shiloh that was to come! It would have been in vain that the sacrifices were offered in the wilderness, that the ark abode between the curtains, or that the golden pot which had the manna was covered with the Mercy Seat if there had not been a real signification of Christ in all these. The religion of the Jew would have been very emptiness if it had not been for Christ who is the Substance of the former shadows.

Run on to the period of the Prophets and in all their prophesying do you not see additional glimpses of the Glory of Christ? When they mount to the greatest heights of eloquence do they not speak of Him? Whenever their soul is carried up, as in a chariot of fire, is not the mantle left behind them a word telling of the Glory of Jesus? They could never glow with fervent heat except concerning Him. Even when they denounced the judgments of God, they paused between the crashes of God's thunder to let some drops of mercy fall on man in words of promise concerning Him who was to come. It is always Christ from the opening leaf of Genesis to the closing note of Malachi--Christ, Christ, Christ--and nothing but Christ!

It is very delightful, Brethren, when we come to such a text as this, to observe that what was in the beginning is now and ever shall be, world without end, Amen. In that millennial state of which the text speaks, Jesus Christ is to be the light and all its Glory is to proceed from Him. And if the text speaks concerning Heaven and the blessedness hereafter, all its light and blessings and Glory stream from Him--"The Lamb is its light." If we read the text and think of its connection with us today we must confess that all our joy and peace flow from the same fountain! Jesus Christ is the Sun of Righteousness to us as well as to the saints above.

I shall try, then--though I am conscious of my feebleness to handle so great a matter--I shall try as best I can to extol the Lord Jesus, first of all, in the excellence of His Glory in the millennial state. Next, in Heaven. And then, thirdly, in the condition of every heavenly-minded man who is on his way to Paradise--in all these cases, "the Lamb is its light."

I. First, then, a few words concerning THE MILLENNIAL PERIOD. We are not given to prophesying in this place. There are some of our Brethren who delight much in that. Perhaps it is well that there should be some who should devote their time and thoughts to that portion of God's

Word which abounds in mysteries. But for our part we have been so engaged in seeking to win souls and in endeavoring to contend with the common errors of the day that we have scarcely ventured to land upon the rock of Patmos, or to peer into the dark recesses of Daniel and Ezekiel.

Yet this much we have ever learned most clearly--that on this earth, where sin and Satan gained victory over God through the fall of man--Christ is to achieve a complete triumph over all His foes! Not on another battlefield, but on this. The fight is not over. It commenced by Satan's attack upon our mother Eve and Christ has never left the field from that day until now. The fight has lasted thousands of years. It grows sterner every day. It is not over. And it never shall be over until the serpent's head is effectually bruised and Christ Jesus shall have gotten unto Himself a perfect victory.

Do not think the Lord will allow Satan to have even so much as one battle to call his own. In the great campaign, when the history shall be written, it shall be said, "The Lord reigns." All along the line He has gotten the victory. There shall be victory in every place and spot. And the conquest of Jesus shall be complete and perfect. We believe, then, that in this very earth where superstition has set up its idols, Jesus Christ shall be adored! Here, where blasphemy has defiled human lips, songs of praise shall rise from islands of the sea and from the dwellers among the rocks!

In this very country, among those very men who became the tools of Satan and whose dwelling places were dens of mischief--there shall be found instruments of righteousness--and lips to praise God and occasions of eternal Glory unto the Most High. O Satan, you may boast of what you have done and you may think your scepter still secure, but He comes, even He who rides upon the white horse of victory! And when He comes you shall not stand against Him, for the two-edged sword which goes out of His mouth shall drive you and your hosts back to the place from where you came. Let us rejoice that Scripture is so clear and so explicit upon this great doctrine of the future triumph of Christ over the whole world!

We are not bound to enter into any particulars concerning what form that triumph shall assume. We believe that the Jews will be converted and that they will be restored to their own land. We believe that Jerusalem will be the central metropolis of Christ's kingdom. We also believe that all the nations shall walk in the light of the glorious city which shall be built at Jerusalem. We expect that the Glory which shall have its center there shall spread over the whole world-- covering it as with a sea of holiness, happiness and delight! For this we look with joyful expectation.

During that period the Lord Himself, by His glorious Presence, shall set aside the outward rites of His sanctuary. "The city has no need of the sun, neither of the moon, to shine in it." Perhaps sun and moon here are intended those ordinary means of enlightenment which the Church now needs. We need the Lords' Supper to remind us of the body and blood of Christ. But when Christ comes there will be no Lord's Suppers, for it is written, "Do this until He comes." But when He comes, then will be the final period of the remembrance-token because the Person of Christ will be in our midst.

Neither will you need ministers any longer any more than men need candles when the sun rises. They shall not say one to another, "Know the Lord: for all shall know Him, from the least to the greatest." There may be even in that period certain solemn assemblies and Sundays but they will not be of the same kind as we have now--for the whole earth will be a temple and every day will be a Sunday! The avocations of men will all be priestly--they shall be a nation of priests--distinctly so and they shall, day without night, serve God in His temple. Everything to which they set their hand shall be a part of the song which shall go up to the Most High.

Oh, blessed day! Would God it had dawned, when these temples should be left, because the whole world should be a temple for God. But whatever may be the splendors of that day--and truly here is a temptation to let our imagination revel--however bright may be the walls set with chalcedony and amethyst, however splendid the gates which are of one pearl--whatever may be the magnificence set forth by the "streets of gold," this we know--that the sum and substance, the light and Glory of the whole will be the Person of our Lord Jesus Christ, "for the Glory of God did lighten it, and the Lamb is its light."

Now I want the Christian to meditate over this. In the highest, holiest and happiest era that shall ever dawn upon this poor earth, Christ is to be her light! When she puts on her wedding garment and adorns herself as a bride is adorned with jewels, Christ is to be her Glory and her beauty! There shall be no earrings in her ears made with other gold than that which comes from His mine of love. There shall be no crown set upon her brow fashioned by any other hand than His hands of wisdom and of Grace. She sits to reign, but it shall be upon His Throne. She feeds, but it shall be upon His bread. She triumphs, but it shall be because of the might which ever belongs to Him who is the Rock of Ages! Come then, Christian, contemplate for a moment your beloved Lord!

Jesus, in a millennial age, shall be the light and the Glory of the city of the new Jerusalem. Observe then, that Jesus makes the light of the millennium because His Presence will be that which distinguishes that age from the present. That age is to be akin to Paradise. Paradise God first made upon earth and Paradise God will last make. Satan destroyed it. And God will never have defeated His enemy until He has reestablished Paradise--until once again a new Eden shall bless the eyes of God's creatures! Now the very Glory and privilege of Eden I take to be not the river which flowed through it with its four branches, nor that it came from the land of Havilah which has dust of gold. I do not think the Glory of Eden lay in its grassy walks, or in the boughs bending with luscious fruit.

I think its glory lay in this--that the "Lord God walked in the garden in the cool of the day." Here was Adam's highest privilege--that he had companionship with the Most High! In those days angels sweetly sang that the tabernacle of God was with man and that He did dwell among them. Brethren, the Paradise which is to be regained for us will have this for its essential and distinguishing mark--that the Lord shall dwell among us! This is the name by which the city is to be called--Jehovah Shammah--the Lord is there. It is true we have the Presence of Christ in the Church now--"Lo, I am with you always, even unto the end of the world." We have the promise of His constant indwelling--"Where two or three are gathered together in My name, there am I in the midst of them."

But still that is vicariously by His Spirit. Soon He is to be personally with us. That very Man who once died upon Calvary is to live here! He--that same Jesus--who was taken up from us shall come in like manner as He was taken up from the gazers of Galilee. Rejoice, rejoice, Beloved, that He comes, actually and really comes! And this shall be the joy of that age--that He is among His saints and dwells in them, with them, and talks and walks in their midst. The Presence of Christ it is which will be the means of the peace of the age. In that sense Christ will be the light of it, for He is our peace. It will be through His Presence that the lion shall eat straw like an ox, that the leopard shall lie down with the kid.

It will not be because men have had more enlightenment and have learned better through advancing civilization, that they shall beat their swords into plowshares. It is notorious that the more civilized nations become, the more terrible are their instruments of destruction. And when they do go to war, the more bloody and protracted their wars become. I venture to say that if in a thousand years' time Christ shall not come, if war were to break out, where we now fight for ten or twenty years we shall have the venomous hatred of one another and the means of carrying on a war for a century!

Instead of advancing in peacefulness, I do fear the world has gone back. We certainly cannot boast now of living in calm days of peace. But Christ's Presence shall change the hearts of men. Then spontaneously, at sight of the great Prince of Peace, they shall cast away their armor and their weapons of war and shall learn war no more. In that sense, then, because His Presence will be the cause of that happy period, He is the light of it.

Again, Christ's Presence is to that period its special instruction. They shall need no candle, neither light of the sun, nor of the moon. Why? Because Christ's Presence will be sufficiently instructive to the sons of men. When the Lord Jesus Christ comes, superstition will not need an earnest testimony to confute it--it will hide its head. Idolatry will not need the missionary to preach against it--the idols He shall utterly abolish and shall cast them to the moles and to the bats. Men and women, at the sight of Christ, and at the knowledge that He is reigning gloriously upon earth, will give up their unbelief.

The Jew will recognize the Son of David and the Gentile will rejoice to worship Him who was once slain as the King of the Jews. The Presence of Christ shall do more for the enlightenment of His Church than the teaching of all her officers and ministers in all ages. She shall then, in the sight of her Lord, come to a fullness of knowledge and have a perfect understanding of God's Word. Once again, Christ will be the light of that period in the sense of being its Glory. Oh, it is the glory of the Christian now to think that Christ reigns in Heaven! In this we boost in every season of depression and when we are downcast--that He is exalted and sits at the right hand of the Father!

But the glory of that age shall be that Christ is come, that He sits upon the throne of David as well as upon the Throne of God--that His enemies bow before Him and lick the dust. Think, my Brethren, of the splendor of that time when from every nation and land they shall bring Him tribute! When praises shall ascend from every land! When the streets of that city shall be thronged every day with adoring worshippers! When He shall ride forth conquering and to conquer and His saints shall follow Him upon white horses!

We sometimes have high days and holidays when kings and princes go abroad and the streets are full and people crowd even to the chimney pots to see them as they ride along. But what shall it be to see King Jesus crowned with the crown which His mother crowned Him in the day of His espousals? What a contrast between the cavalcade winding its way along the streets of Jerusalem, along the Via Dolorosa up to the mount of execution--what a contrast, I say! Then women followed Him and wept, but now men will follow Him and shout for joy! Then He carried His Cross, but now He shall ride in state! Then His enemies mocked Him and gloated their eyes with His sufferings--now His enemies shall be put to confusion and covered with shame! And upon Himself shall His crown flourish! Then it was the hour of darkness and the time of the Prince of the Pit, but now it shall be the day of light and the victory of Emmanuel and the sounding of His praise both on earth and in Heaven!

Contemplate this thought. And though I speak of it so feebly, yet it may ravish your hearts with transport that Christ is the Sun of that long-expected, that blessed day! Christ shall be the highest mountain of all the hills of joy, the widest river of all the streams of delight! Whatever there may be of magnificence and of triumph, Christ shall be the center and soul of it all! Oh, to be present and to see Him in His own light--the King of kings and Lord of lords!

II. And now we will turn our thoughts another way from the millennial period to THE STATE OF THE GLORIFIED IN HEAVEN ITSELF. "The city has no need of the sun, neither of the moon, to shine in it." The inhabitants of the better world are independent of creature comforts. Let us think that over for a minute. We have no reason to believe that they daily pray, "Give us this day our daily bread." Their bodies shall dwell in perpetual youth. They shall have no need of raiment. Their white robes shall never wear out, neither shall they ever be defiled.

Having food and raiment on earth we are content, but in Heaven, "they toil not, neither do they spin: and yet I say unto you, That even Solomon in all his glory was not arrayed like one of these." Yet the fields yield them neither flax nor any other material for clothing, neither do the acres of Heaven yield them bread. They are satisfied by leaning upon God, needing not the creature for support. They need no medicine to heal their disease, "for the inhabitant shall not say, I am sick."

They need no sleep to recruit their fatigue and although sleep is sweet and balmy--God's own medicine--yet they rest not day nor night, but unweariedly praise Him in His temple. They need no social ties in Heaven. We need here the associations of friendship and of family love, but they are neither married nor are given in marriage there. Whatever comfort they may derive from association with their fellows is something extra and beyond--they do not need any-- their God is enough. They shall need no teachers there. They shall doubtless commune with one another concerning the things of God and tell one another the strange things which the Lord has worked for them, but they shall not need this by way of instruction. They shall all be taught of the Lord, for in Heaven "the Glory of God does lighten it and the Lamb is its light."

There is an utter independence in Heaven, then, of all the creatures. No sun and no moon are wanted--no, no creatures whatever! Here we lean upon the friendly arm, but there they lean upon their Beloved and upon Him alone. Here we must have the help of our companions, but there they find all they want in Christ alone. Here we look to the meat which perishes and to the raiment which decays before the moth, but there they find everything in God. We have to use a bucket to get water from the well, but there they drink from the wellhead and put their lips down to the Living Water. Here the angels bring us blessings, but we shall want no messengers from Heaven then.

They need no Gabriels there to bring their love-notes from God, for there they see Him face to face. Oh, what a blessed time shall that be, when we shall have mounted above every second cause and shall hang upon the bare arm of God! What a glorious hour when God and not His creatures, God and not His works, but God Himself, Christ Himself shall be our daily joy!--

"Plunged in the Godhead's deepest sea, And lost in His immensity."

Our souls shall then have attained the perfection of bliss. While in Heaven it is clear that the glorified are quite independent of creature aid--do not forget that they are entirely dependent for their joy upon Jesus Christ. He is their sole spiritual light. They have nothing else in Heaven to give them perfect satisfaction but Himself.

The language here used, "the Lamb is its light," may be read in two or three ways. By your patience, let us so read it. In Heaven Jesus is the light in the sense of joy, for light is ever in Scripture the emblem of joy. Darkness betokens sorrow but the rising of the sun indicates the return of holy joy. Christ is the Joy of Heaven. Do they rejoice in golden harps, in palm branches and white robes? They may do so, but they only rejoice in these things as love-gifts from Him. Their joy is compounded by this--"Jesus chose us, Jesus loved us, Jesus bought us, Jesus washed us, Jesus robed us, Jesus kept us, Jesus glorified us: here we are entirely through the Lord Jesus, through Him alone."

Each one of these thoughts shall be to them like a cluster from the vines of Eshcol. Why I think there is an eternal source of joy in that one thought, "Jesus bought me with His blood." Oh, to sit on the mountains of Heaven and look across to the lowly hill of Calvary and see the Savior bleed! What emotions of joy shall stir the depths of our soul when we reflect that there upon the bloody tree He counted not His life dear unto Him that He might redeem us unto God!--

"Calvary's summit shall I trace, View the heights and depths of Grace, Count the purple drops and say, 'Thus my sins were washed away.'"

In Glory they think of the Character and Person of Jesus and these are wells of delight to them. Thus they muse-- Jesus is eternal. God. His enemies reviled Him but still He is God. Jesus became the virgin's Child. Jesus lived a life of holiness and Jesus died. But see what triumph springs from His condescension and His shame--He rises, He ascends and leads captivity captive--He scatters gifts among men! He reigns over earth and Hell and Heaven--King of kings and Lord of lords. "The government shall be upon His shoulder: and His name shall be called Wonderful, The Counselor, The Mighty God, The Everlasting Father, The Prince of Peace."

When I have listened to Handel's music in "The Messiah," where that great musician wakes every instrument to praise the name of Jesus, I have felt ready to die with excess of delight that such music should ever have been composed by mortal man to the honor of our great Messiah. But what will be the music of celestial choirs? How would such hearts as ours burst and such souls as ours leap out of their bodies if they could but know, while here, such joys as celestials know above!

But, Beloved, our faculties shall be strengthened, our capacities shall be enlarged, our whole being shall be expanded and thus we shall be able to bear the full swell of seraphic music and join in it without fainting from delight, while they sing of the Glory of the Son of Man--the Son of God! Christ is the Light of Heaven, then, because He is the Substance of its joy. Light may be viewed in another sense. Light is the cause of beauty. That is obvious to you all. Take the light away and there is no beauty anywhere. The fairest woman charms the eye no more than a heap of ashes when the sun has departed. Your garden may he bright with many colored flowers, but when the sun goes down you cannot know them from the grass which borders them.

You look upon the trees, all fair with the verdure of summer--but when the sun goes down they are all hung in black. Without light no radiance flashes from the sapphire, no peaceful ray proceeds from the pearl. There is nothing of beauty left when light is gone. Light is the mother of beauty. In such sense the Lord God Almighty and the Lamb are the Light of Heaven--that is to say, all the beauty of the saints above comes from God Incarnate. Their excellence, their joy, their triumph, their glory, their ecstatic bliss all spring from Him. As planets, they reflect the light of the Sun of Righteousness. They live as beams proceeding from the central orb, as streams leaping from the eternal fountain.

If He withdrew, they must die. If His Glory were veiled, their glory must expire. Think of this, Christian, and I am sure you will be reminded how true this is beneath the sky, as well as above, that if light is the mother of beauty, Christ is the Light! There is nothing good, nor lovely, nor gracious about any one of us except as we get it from Christ and from Christ Jesus alone. "The Lamb is its light." Another meaning of light in Scripture is knowledge. Ignorance is darkness. Now in Heaven they need no candle, nor light of the sun because they receive light enough from Christ--Christ being the fountain of all they know.

I think it is Dr. Dick who speaks about the enjoyments of Heaven consisting very likely in going from star to star and viewing the works of God in different portions of His universe, admiring the anatomy of living creatures, studying geology, ferrying across the waves of ether and voyaging from world to world. I do not believe in such a Heaven for a moment! I do not conceive it a worthy employment for immortal spirits, and, if there were nothing else to make me think so, the text would be enough. "And the city had no need of the sun, neither of the moon, to shine in it." There is no need of the works of God to give instruction to its inhabitants, "for the Glory of God did lighten it. "The Glory, not of God's works, but of God's Son, is their glorious Light--

"The spacious earth and spreading flood Proclaim the wise and powerful God. And Your rich glories from afar Sparkle in every rolling star But in His looks a glory stands, The noblest labor of Your hands. The pleasing luster of His eyes Outshines the wonders of the skies."

They need no light of the sun and moon where Jesus is. However well the sun and moon may tell of God, we shall not need them from day to day to send forth their light throughout all the earth and their word unto the end of the world, for the Glory of Christ will teach us all we wish to learn. And beholding the unveiled Glory of God will be far better than prying into the works of Nature even though we had an angel's power of discovery. We shall know more of Christ in five minutes, when we get to Heaven, than we shall know in all our years on earth. Dr. Owen was a master of theology, but the smallest child who goes to Heaven from a Sunday school knows more of Christ after being in Heaven five minutes, than Dr. Owen did.

John Calvin searched very deep and Augustine seemed to come to the very door of the great secret. But Augustine and Calvin would be but children on the first form there--I mean if they knew no more than on earth. Oh, what manifestations of God there will be! Dark dealings of Providence which you never understood before will then be seen without the light of a candle or of the sun. Many doctrines puzzled you and you could not find the clue to the labyrinth of mystery. But there all will be simple and plain so that the wayfaring man may run and understand it. You have had many experiences and tossing to and fro and you have felt your ignorance, your corruption and weakness. But there you shall see to the very bottom of human nature--you shall understand the virulence of man's depravity and the heights of God's Sovereignty--the marvels of His electing love and the magnificence of His Divine power by which He has made us to be partakers of the Divine Nature--

"There you shall see and hear and know All you desired or wished below, And every power find sweet employ In that eternal world of joy."

And this knowledge, I say, shall not come from any inferior agent but from the Lord God who shall be your Glory and from Jesus Christ Himself who shall teach you all Truth. I must not dwell longer on this point except to say this one thing, that light also means manifestation. "Everyone that does evil hates the light, neither comes to the light, lest his deeds should be reproved. But he that does truth comes to the light, that his deeds may be made manifest, that they are worked in God." Light manifests. In this world it does not yet appear how great we must be made. God's people are a hidden people--their life is hid with Christ in God. They possess God's secret and that secret other men cannot discover.

Christ in Heaven is the great revealer of God's mind. And when He gets His people there, He will touch them with the wand of His own love and change them into the image of His manifested Glory. They were poor and wretched but what a transformation! Their rags drop off and they are acknowledged as princes. They were stained with sin and infirmity, but one touch of His finger and they are bright as the sun and clear as crystal--transformed even as He was upon Mount Tabor--whiter than any fuller can make them.

They were ignorant and weak on earth but when He shall teach them, they shall know even as they are known. They were buried in dishonor but they are raised in glory. They were sown in the grave in weakness but they are raised in power. They were carried away by the hands of remorseless Death but they arise to immortality and life. Oh, what a manifestation! Light is sown for the righteous and Christ is the sacred rain that brings the harvest above ground. The righteous are always pearls but they are hidden, as it were, in the oyster and Christ brings them forth. They were always diamonds, they were far away in the Golconda of sin. But Christ has fetched them up from the deep mines. They were always stars but they were hidden behind the clouds. Christ, like a swift wind, has blown the clouds away and now they shine like stars in the firmament forever and ever.

In this sense Christ is the Light of Heaven, because it is through Him that the true and real character of all the saints has been manifested. Come, my Soul, take wing a moment--it is not far for you to fly--mount and walk the golden streets and as you walk you shall see nothing but Jesus glorified! Come up to the Throne and you shall see Christ on it. Sit down and listen to the song--Christ is the theme! Go to the banquet--Christ is the meat! Mingle with the dancers-- Christ is their joy! Make you one in their great assemblies and Christ is the God they worship--"Worthy the Lamb that died," they cry--

"To be exalted thus-- 'Worthy the Lamb,' our lips reply, For He was slain for us."

III. Let us turn to our last thought. And here I hope we can speak experimentally, whereas on the other two points we could only speak by faith in the promise of God. THE HEAVENLY MAN'S STATE MAY BE SET FORTH IN THESE WORDS. First, then, even on earth the heavenly man's joy does not depend upon the creature. Brethren, in a certain sense we can say today that, "the city has no need of the sun, neither of the moon, to shine in it." We love and prize the happy brightness which the sun scatters upon us. As for the moon, who does not admire the fair moonlight when the waves are silvered and silent Nature wears the plumage of the dove?

But we do not need the sun or the moon! We can do without them for the Sun of Righteousness has risen with healing beneath His wings. There are Brothers and Sisters here this morning who are very happy and yet it is long since they saw the sun. Shut up in perpetual night, through blindness, they need not the light of the sun nor of the moon, for the Lord God is their Glory--Christ is their Light. If our eyes should be put out, we could say, "Farewell, sweet light, farewell, bright sun and moon--we prize you well, but we can do without you--Christ Jesus is to us as the light of seven days."

As we can do without these two most eminent creatures, so we can be happy without other earthly blessings. Our dear friends are very precious to us--we love our wife and children, our parents and our friends--but we do not need them. May God spare them for us! But if they were taken it does not come to a matter of absolute need, for you know, Beloved, there is many a Christian who has been bereft of all and he thought, as the props were taken away one after another, that he should die of very grief. But he did not die--his faith surmounted every wave and he still rejoices in his God!

I know that at the thought of those dear ones who are taken from you the sluices of your grief are drawn up, but still I hope you will not be so false to Christ as to deny what I now say--that His Presence can make amends for all losses-- that the smile of His face will make a paradise so sweet that no sorrow or sighing shall be heard in it--

"You, at all times will I bless. Having You, I all possess! How can I bereaved, Since I cannot part with You?"

It is a very happy thing to be placed in circumstances where one knows no lack of bread--to have a house, a comfortable home and sufficient monies for our family is very pleasant--but O dear Friends, if it comes to actual need, the Christian does not want this! He needs no sun nor moon even here! Look at the chosen sons of poverty--they toil from morning to night and never get a single inch beyond. Living from hand to mouth they are happy! Ah, some of them infinitely happier than the rich man with all his sumptuous fares and the fine linen with which he wraps himself. Why there have been men reduced to all but beggary who have rejoiced far more in their poverty than others in their wealth--we have seen some of God's saints in the workhouse--or lingering in a dark ill-furnished alms room and we have heard them speak as joyously about God and their state as if they were dwelling in mansions or palaces! Yes, many a poor child of God has learned to sing--

"I would not change my blessed estate For all the world calls good or great. And while my faith can keep her hold, I envy not the sinner's gold."

For "this city has no need of the sun, nor of the moon, to shine in it, for the Glory of God does lighten it and the Lamb is its light." Health, too--who can prize it enough? When stretched upon the bed of sickness--then we begin to know how priceless a gift was a sound body! But ah, the Christian, though he loves health can do without it. I have heard of Christians who have been blind and who have been bedridden and have not stirred from their bed for many years. They could scarcely lift their hands through paralysis and never had stood upon their feet for many years through some stroke of God's hand. Yet they have delighted themselves in the Lord!

They have laid there ill-nursed, ill-cared for--simply living to illustrate to what degree a mortal man may become a mass of suffering and a prodigy of grief! And yet, as I have sometimes stood by such bedsides, I have heard more rapturous expressions concerning present joy and future prospects than from God's strongest saints in their healthiest hours! The dying girl, when consumption has paled her cheek and taken the flesh from off her poor aching bones, has nevertheless appeared in a sacred majesty of might which showed me that she needed no moon nor sun to lighten her, no health nor strength to give her spirits--for the Presence of Christ made her conqueror in the extremity of weakness and victorious in the grim presence of Death itself!

The Christian, then, dear Friends, leans upon the arm of God--he has pressed through the crowd of creatures--he has bid them all retire that he might live nearer to his All-Sufficient Lord! And if, when he has reached his Lord, the creatures turn their backs and go away, he says, "There, you may all go! I have Him now! I embrace Him now! He has kissed me with the kisses of His lips. You may spit on me and you will--now He has spoken softly to me--you may curse me if you please. Now that He has told me I am His and He is mine, even my father and mother may forsake me, for the Lord has taken me up." Yes, the heavenly man, even before he gets to Heaven has no need of the sun nor of the moon, for the Glory of God does lighten him.

We finish by observing that such a man, however, has great need of Christ--he cannot get on without Christ. O Beloved, if the sun were struck from the spheres what a poor, dark, dreary world this would be! We should go groping about, longing for the grave. But that would be nothing compared with our misery if Christ were taken away! O Christian, what would you do without a Savior? We should be of all men the most miserable--we who have once known Him!

Ah, you who do not know Christ--you can get on pretty well without Him--like a poor slave who has never known liberty and rests content in bondage. The bird in its cage which never did fly over the fields--which has been born in the cage--can be pretty easy. But after we have once stretched our wings and once know what liberty means we cannot be shut out from our Lord. As the dove mourns itself to death when its mate is taken away, so should we if Christ were gone. We can do without light, without friendship, without life--but we cannot live without our Savior! Oh, to be without Christ? My Soul, what would you do in the world without Him in the midst of its temptations and its cares? What would you do in the morning without Him when you wake up and look forward to the day's battle?

What would you do if He did not put His hand upon you and say, "Fear not, I am with you"? And what would you do at night, when you come home jaded and weary, if there were no prayer, no door of access between you and Christ? What should we do without Christ in our trials, our sicknesses? What should we do when we come to die with no one to make our dying bed feel soft as downy pillows? Oh, if the infidel's laugh has truth in it, it may well ring bitterly in our ears, for it were a bitter truth to us. No Christ? Then to die is dreadful, indeed!

To have such high hopes and to have them all blasted! High, loud boasting and to have our mouths stopped forever! But, Beloved, we need not suppose such a thing for we know that our Redeemer lives and we know that He never forsakes the work of own hand. Married as He is to our souls, He will never sue for divorce against any one of His dear people, but He will hold and bless us till we die. And we on our part will confess of our spiritual life that the Lamb is its light. Of every day and every night--of every joy and every sorrow--the Lamb has been until now our light and shall be till we die.

If this is so, how dark is the case of those who do not know the Lamb? In what misery and ignorance do you grope who do not know the Savior? Would you know Christ, would you have the happiness of resting upon His bosom? Trust Him, then--for whoever trusts Him is saved. To trust Christ is that saving faith which brings the soul out of condemnation. "He that believes on Him is not condemned." Trust, guilty as you are--trust to His Atonement and it shall wash you! Trust to His power--it shall prevail for you! Trust to His wisdom--it shall protect you! Trust to His heart--it shall love you, world without end. Amen.

A Hearer In Disguise

DELIVERED ON SUNDAY EVENING, JULY 31, 1864,
BY THE REV. C. H. SPURGEON,
AT THE METROPOLITAN TABERNACLE, NEWINGTON.

"Audit was so, when Ahijah heard the sound of her feet, as she came in at the door, thathe said, Come in, you wife of Jeroboam; why do you pretend to be another? For I am sent to you with heavy tidings." -- 1 Kings 14:6.

AHIJAH the Prophet was blind. Did I not tell you this morning that God's servants could be happy without the light of the sun? If God should be pleased to deprive their natural eyes of the pleasures of light their souls would not be without joy, for as in the New Jerusalem, so in the renewed heart--"the glory of God does lighten it and the Lamb is its Light. " Doubtless this was the case with that venerable Prophet. He was not like Moses, whose eyes did not wax dim and whose natural strength did not abate. But his eyes were set with age. The organs of vision had so decayed through the multitude of his years that he could not see so much as a ray of light.

Yet doubtless when he could not look out of the windows, God looked in. And when there was no beam coming in from the sun, much light was darted in from Heaven. What man of modern times saw more than blind Milton? It were well for us to feel the influence of that "drop serene," and close our eyes forever if we could but see such visions of God as Milton has penned in his Paradise Lost and Paradise Regained. Here is a fine picture for you. Behold the venerable Prophet sitting alone in his humble cottage. And yet not alone, because his God is with him. Blind, but yet in the highest sense a Seer, looking into the invisible and by faith beholding things which we blind men who have our sight can never see!

Ahijah beheld what eye has not seen and heard what ear has never heard. This, then, may furnish a word of comfort at the outset to any who are suffering under infirmity--Jesus can mend you. You are not the only persons who have been called to suffer. Full many of your humble guild--the company of the blind--have been gifted with spiritual sight. If you have lost hearing, or the use of any of the members of your body, remember that no strange thing has happened to you but such as is common to man. There is a way by which, in proportion as your tribulations abound, so your consolations may abound through Jesus Christ!

No, these very privations which you feel so sadly, which so loudly demand our sympathy, may by God's love be transmuted into mercies by a holy alchemy which really turns iron into gold! He can turn your losses into gains and your curses into blessings. Mark well this venerable Prophet--a man so old as to have survived the senses which give life its charm--is it not time for him to die? Has he not outlived his usefulness when he is made entirely dependent upon his fellow creatures and a burden to himself? Why does not the Prophet's Master send a convoy of angels to take the good man Home?

There he sits without any apparent perception of the scenes transpiring around him. Surely, surely it is time for the Master to call him away! But no, He does not. Ahijah must not die! He has another message to deliver and he is immortal till his work is done. I have no doubt he sweetly slept after he had delivered his last message, but not till then. Brothers and Sisters, you and I have no right to want to go to Heaven till our work is done! There is a desire to be with Christ which is not only natural but spiritual. There is a sighing to behold His face which if a man is without I shall question if he is a Christian at all! But to wish to be away from the battle before we win the victory and to desire to leave the field before the day is over is but lazy and listless! Therefore let us pray God to save us from it.

Whitfield and a company of ministers were talking together and expressing their desire to go to Heaven. Good Mr. Tennant was the only man who differed from them. He said he did not wish to die. And he thought that if his Brother Whitfield would but consider for a time, he would not wish to be gone, either. He said, if you hire a man to do a day's work and he is saying all the day, "I wish it were evening, I wish it were time to go home," you would think," what a lazy fellow he is," and you would wish you had never engaged him. "So," he said, "I am afraid it is nothing but our idleness that often prompts us to desire to be away from our work."

If there is a soul to win, let me not stop until I have won it. Truly some of us might summon up courage enough to say, "I would gladly barter Heaven for the Glory of Christ and not only wait twenty years out of Heaven if I may have twenty years of glorifying Him the better, but wait out altogether if I may outside Heaven sing to Him sweeter songs and honor Him more than I can inside its walls. For outside Heaven shall be Heaven to me if it shall help me to glorify my Lord and Master the better."

You have heard, I dare say, that anecdote of good Mr. Whitfield? In his early ministry, lying down, as he thought, to die in a high fever, a poor Negro woman was sitting by his side and tending him. In his sad moments Whitfield thought of dying, but the black woman said, "No, master Whitfield, you are not to die yet. There are thousands of souls to bring to Christ! So keep up your spirits, for you must live and not die--your Master has yet work for you to do."

All this comes to my mind as I think of that venerable old Prophet, sitting in his chair, waiting until he shall have spoken to Jeroboam's wife. And then after that ascending to his Father and his God--but not until his work was done. We have introduced to you Ahijah, the venerable Prophet. We must now address you upon an incident connected with his closing ministry. In our text we have before us an occasional hearer. Secondly we observe a useless disguise. And thirdly we listen to heavy tidings.

I. We have before us, first of all, THE OCCASIONAL HEARER. Jeroboam and his wife did not often go to hear Ahijah. They were not people who went to worship Jehovah. They neither feared God nor regarded His Prophet. There may be some such here tonight. You do not often come to a place of worship. I am glad you are here now. It may be my Master has sent me with tidings for you. Give earnest heed, I pray, that the tidings may be received and blessed. I am sometimes tired of preaching to those who hear me every Sunday for I fear some of them never will be saved.

They get hardened by the Gospel. All the blows of the hammer have only tended to weld their hearts to their sins and make them harder instead of melting them. May God grant, however, that my fears may be removed and that some who have long resisted the wooings of the Gospel may yet yield. I have more hope of you occasional hearers--I know that when my Master has helped me to cast the net on the right side of the ship I have taken some of you. There are among those numbered with us some of the best in the Church and the most useful men in our society who were brought in by dropping into the place just as stray hearers--passing by, perhaps, or coming out of curiosity. But God knew who they were, knew how to adapt the sermon to the case and affect the heart with the Word!

Now, here was an occasional hearer. And we make the observation that this occasional hearer was totally destitute of all true piety. Most occasional hearers are. Those who have true religion are not occasional hearers. You will find that truly gracious persons are diligent in the use of the means. Instead of thinking it a toil to come up to the place of worship, I know there are some of you who wish there were two Sundays in the week. And the happiest times you ever have are when you are sitting in these seats and joining in our sacred songs--

"Your earthly Sabbaths, Lord, we love." There is no verse which gives you a better idea of Heaven as a place than that--

"Where congregations never break up, And Sabbaths have no end."

Gracious souls love the place where God's honor dwells and the assembling of themselves together is always a blessed thing to them. But occasional hearers are generally graceless persons. I know how you spend your Sunday. There is the morning--you are not up very early. It takes a long time to dress on a Sunday morning. Then follows the Sunday paper, with the news of the week that must be gone through. The wife has been toiling hard all the morning with the dinner-- what do you care? Then there is the afternoon, when there is a little more lolling about. Then in the evening there is the walk. But the day, after all, is not very happy and comfortable--and sometimes you have wished there were no Sundays except that they give your body a little rest.

You do not fear God, nor do you care for His service. Nevertheless I am glad you have come here tonight for who can tell?--my Lord, who found out Jeroboam's wife, can find you out. And though it is many a day since you darkened the walls of God's sanctuary, this shall be the beginning of many such days to you. And who can tell?--this may be your new-birth night when you shall turn over a new leaf! No, not turn over a new leaf, but get a new look altogether and find your name written in the Lamb's Book of Life.

The second remark about these occasional hearers is that when they do come, they very generally come because they are in trouble. When Jeroboam's wife came and spoke to the Prophet it was because the dear child was ill at home. I know some occasional hearers who go to a place of worship as people go to a pharmacy--that is when they want something because they do not feel quite right. Yes, your child is very sick. You have been watching all day and you have thought, "I cannot stand it any longer. I will just walk out and go to a place of worship tonight. I want something to cheer me."

You have had such trials lately that your wife said to you, "John, we must not keep on in this way any longer. It is clear all we do ends without any prosperity. We put our money into a bag which is full of holes. We spend it for that which is not bread. We labor for that which does not profit." So you have come here to see if the Lord may have a word of comfort through His servant who speaks to you. I can only say you are very welcome to come in, you wife of Jeroboam! We are as glad to see you as though you always came and we do hope that this sorrowful affliction may be overruled by God for your lasting good.

There are persons who profess to be atheists, but their atheism is not very deep. Addison tells us of a man who, on board ship in a storm, knelt down to pray and expressed his firm belief in a God. When he got ashore someone laughed at him for it and he challenged the man to a duel. They fought together and the atheist fell wounded. When the blood was flowing he believed there was a God and he began to cry to God with all his might to save him. The physician bound up the wound. The man put the question to him--"Is it mortal?" "No," the doctor said, "it is only a flesh wound." "Then," said the man, "there is no God. I am a thorough atheist."

He believed in God when he thought he was going to die--the moment he felt himself better he returned to his unbelief. A pretty religion, that, to live in and a pretty religion to die with! Your absence from God's House will do very well when things go well with you--you can go out with a young wife to dissipate in frivolity hours which should be sacred to worship. But when sickness comes and when affliction falls heavily upon you--when you have trial after trial and you, yourself, begin to get gray with many cares, and feeble and helpless with many years. And when death comes near and casts his pale shadow across your cheek. And strange thoughts, oblivious of all around, come over you by day, and singular dreams which throw you into the company of the long since dead, surprise you by night.

When fears and frights and signs and calls and bodings of imagination prove the wanderings and weakness of your brain--then, but possibly not till then--you will think of going to the house of God. I am glad, therefore, if this trouble has visited you early, or ever "the grinders cease because they are few and those that look out of the windows are darkened." And I am very glad that you have come to the House of God. Come in, you wife of Jeroboam, for I bear you tidings from the God of Heaven tonight!

There is a third point--this woman would not have come but that her husband sent her on the ground that he had heard Ahijah preach before. It was this Prophet who took Jeroboam's mantle and rent it in pieces and told him he was to be king over the ten tribes. That message proved true--therefore Jeroboam had confidence in Ahijah. There are some of you who at times used to hear the Gospel. You have not been of late. But there were seasons when you did come up to God's House--yes, and times when you used to tremble under God's Word. If I am not mistaken, there are men and women here tonight who once were conscience-stricken. The Word of God used to come home to you with exceeding great power and make you tremble.

Did you not even profess faith in Christ? Why, some of you were very busy at revival meetings trying to bring others to the Savior. But your religion was like smoke out of the chimney--it has all blown away. Like early mist it was soon scattered when the sun had risen. Yet the remembrance of these things sticks by you now. You cannot help it--you feel there must be something in religion. The old stings which were in your conscience have not been quite extracted. Therefore at the present moment you are quite willing to listen to the Word--perhaps even hoping that it may come with true power now and that you may, after all, be saved!

I wish I could wake the echoes of the slumbering consciences of some of you! O that I could recall the days of your youth--the times of your boyhood and girlhood--when you went up to the assembly of the saints to keep holy day! Those things you cannot quite forget. I pray that such remembrances may often turn your feet towards the place of wor- ship. We have brought out three points of character--they were persons of no piety. In trouble they sought the Prophet. And they had confidence in him because they had heard him preach before.

But there is one more point--they had one godly member of their family and that brought them to see the Prophet. Their child was sick and ill and it was that which led them to enquire at the hands of the Lord. I hope there is no family here which has the misfortune to be without a Believer in it. You, Man, have no fear of God. But strange to say, the Lord has taken one out of your family to be a witness for Him. That daughter of yours, you sometimes jeer at her, but you know you value her! You used to send her to the Sunday school just to get rid of her, but the Lord met with her. And what a comfort she has been to you! How glad she has made your heart, though you do not tell her so!

Perhaps the godly one in the family is like this young Ahijah in the text, he is sick and near death. You can remember, though you do not fear God, how the darling boy was sick! How you sat by his little bed and took his hand in yours when it was scarcely anything but skin and bone! How he prayed for you at night, that God would save father and mother and take them to Heaven! And how, just as he died, he looked out on you with those bright eyes so soon to be filmed in death and said, "Father, will you not follow me?"

Since that time you have often felt that something is beckoning you up yonder. And though you have gone on forsaking God and despising holy things, yet still there is a little link between you and Heaven which is not snapped yet and you sometimes feel it tugging at your heart. I pray God it may tug so hard tonight that your heart may go up to God and lay hold of Jesus, the Savior of sinners! What joy it causes me to think that God does call one out of a godless household because where there is one there is sure to be another before long! It is like putting a light into the midst of stubble-- there will soon be a blaze.

I have hope of a family when one child is converted, for Grace is like precious ointment--it spreads a perfume all around. When a box of fragrant spice is put into a room the perfume soon fills the entire chamber, then creeps silently up the stairs into the upper rooms and ceases not its work until it has filled the whole house. So when there is true Grace in a house, the Holy Spirit blesses its hallowed power, till even the lodgers and family acquaintances begin to feel the influence of it! Is it your one praying child that has brought you here tonight? May God grant that he may be the means of bringing you to Heaven as well!

But there is one sad reflection which should alarm the occasional hearer. Through Jeroboam's wife did come to the Prophet that once and heard tidings, yet she and her husband perished after all. Oh, if there were the register kept of the many thousands who come inside the Tabernacle gates and listen to our voice, I am afraid--I am sadly afraid it would be found that there were many who did hear the tidings and did tremble at them, too--who nevertheless despised the counsels of the Most High! They have turned not at His rebuke, went on in their sin and perished without hope. Shall it be so with any of you?

Are you to be firewood in Hell? Will you make your bed among the flames? My Hearers, will you die without God and without hope? Will you leap into the black unknown with no bright promise of the Savior to cheer you in the thick darkness? May God prevent it! May He be pleased to bring you to Christ, the Rock of your salvation, that you may depend upon Him with your whole heart! While thus speaking about the occasional hearer, an idea haunts my mind that I have been drawing somebody's portrait. I think there are some here who have had their character and conduct sketched out quite accurately enough for them to know who is meant. Do remember that if the description fits you, it is meant for you. And if you, yourself, have been described, do not look about among your neighbors and say, "I think this is like somebody else." If it is like you, take it home to yourself and God send it into the center of your conscience so that you cannot get rid of it.

II. Our second consideration is the USELESS DISGUISE. Jeroboam's wife thought to herself, "If I go to see Ahijah, as he knows me to be the wife of Jeroboam, he is sure to speak angrily and give me very bad news." Strange to tell, though the poor old gentleman was blind, she thought it necessary to put on a disguise! So she removed her best garment and put on a countrywoman's russet gown and away she went. She left the scepter and crown behind and took a basket, as though she had just come from market.

In this basket she did not put gold, jewels and silver, but a present such as a farmer's wife might bring. There were loaves and biscuits and a jar of honey. And as she went along, she thought, "The old gentleman will not know me." She traveled through her own dominions and nobody knew her. She went into the neighboring dominions of Judah as far as Shiloh. And she pleased her imagination with the thought, "How I shall deceive him! I will ask him a question, as if I were a farmer's wife and he will not know who I am. He will be pleased with my present and prophesy soft things concerning my child."

How great was her surprise! No sooner did the blind Prophet hear her footsteps, than he said, "Come in, you wife of Jeroboam. Why do you pretend to be another? For I am sent to you with heavy tidings." How she started back with astonishment! She had deceived hundreds who were blessed with eyes, but here was a man who not only could not be deceived, but found her out before she had opened her lips and recognized her before she had time to test her sorry lies or tell her subtle tale! "Come in, you wife of Jeroboam." I do not suppose there is anybody come here disguised as to dress tonight, though such things may happen. The working man who is afraid he shall be laughed at if he is known may come here in disguise.

Now and then a clergyman may come in who would not be very comfortable in his conscience if it were known he did such a thing and so he does not show himself exactly in his regular garb. Notwithstanding whoever you may be, disguised or not, it is of no use where God's Gospel is preached! It is a quick discerner and will find out the thoughts and intents of the heart. It will search you out and unmask your true character, disguise yourself as you may. Many who come to God's House not disguised in dress, are still disguised in manner and appearance. How good you all look! When we sing and you take your books, how heavenly-minded! And when we pray, how reverent you are! How your heads are all bowed-- your eyes covered with your hands!

I do not know what you all say in your hats when you come in and I should not like to know. I do not know how much praying there is when you sit in a devout posture, though you assume the attitude and compose your countenance as those who draw near to supplicate the Lord. I am afraid there are many of you who do not pray a word or present a petition, though you assume the posture of suppliants. When the singing is going on there are many who never sing a word with spirit and understanding. In the house of God I am afraid there are many who wear a mask--they stand as God's people stand, sit as they sit, pray as they pray, and sing as they sing--and all the while what are you doing?

Some of you have been attending to your children while we have been singing tonight. Some of you have been casting up your ledger, attending to your farms, scheming about your carpentering and bricklaying! Yet all the while if we had looked into your faces we might have thought you were reverently worshipping God. Oh, those solemn faces and those reverent looks! They do not deceive the Most High God! He knows who and what you are. As you are in His House, He sees you as clearly as men see through glass.

As for hiding from the Almighty, how can you hide yourself from Him? As well attempt to hide in a glass cage, for all the world is a glass cage before God. When you look into a glass beehive, you can see the bees and everything they do--such is this world--a sort of glass beehive in which God can see everything. The eyes of God are on you continually. No veil of hypocrisy can screen you from Him. There may be some among you who occasionally sit here, some members of this Church who, after all, may pretend to be other than you are. It is a melancholy and a most solemn reflection that there are many who profess to be Christians who are not Christians.

There was a Judas among the twelve. There was a Demas among the early disciples. And we must always expect to find chaff on God's floor mingled with the wheat. I have tried, the Lord knows, to preach as plainly and as much home to the mark as I could to sift and try you. But for all that the hypocrite will come in. After the most searching ministry there are still some who will wrap themselves about with a mantle of deception. Though we cry aloud and spare not and bid you lay hold on eternal life, yet, alas, how many are content with a mere name to live but are dead? Many come here and even hold office in the Church, yes, the minister himself may even preach the Word and, after all, be hollow and empty.

How many who dress and look fair outside are, as John Bunyan said, only fit to be tinder for the devil's tinder box-- for they are all dry and sere within! God save us from a profession if it is not real! I pray that we may know the worst of our case. If I must be damned, I would sooner go to Hell unholy than as a hypocrite. That backdoor to the pit is the thing I dread most of all! Oh, to sit at the Lord's Table and to drink of the cup of devils! To be recognized among God's own here and then to find one's own name left out when He reads the muster roll of His servants! Oh, what a portion for eternity!

I bid you tear off this mask, and if the Grace of God is not in you, I pray you go into the world which will be your fitting place! Abstain from joining the Church if you are not really a member of the body of Christ. You see why I urge this--because no dressing up, however neatly it may be done--can conceal us from God. Oh, how some who have been fair on earth have been startled when they thought they were going into Heaven! They had their foot almost on the doorstep, but the angel came and said, "Get out of here, wife of Jeroboam. I know you! You could deceive the minister! You could deceive the deacons! You could get baptized and join the Church. But you can not enter here! Get out! Your portion is with the filthy in the pit of Hell."

O, may Jesus never say this to you and me! But may we all be so real here that He may say, "Come, you blessed of My Father, inherit the kingdom prepared for you from the foundation of the world." "O God, see me!" Write that on the palm of your hand and look at it. Wake up in the morning with it. Sleep with it before you on your curtains. "O, God, see me!"--

"O may this thought possess my breast, Wherever I rove, wherever I rest Nor let my weaker passions dare Consent to sin, for God is there!"

III. Now we come to a close with a few words upon the HEAVY TIDINGS. The woman stood amazed as the Prophet proceeded to expose the iniquity of her husband's house, the certain judgment which God would execute, and the terrible disgrace with which the name of Jeroboam should be execrated because they had revolted from God and set up for themselves the calves of Baal. As for the child, respecting whom she had come to enquire, he should die. That death was the quenching of a bright spark in the heart of the parents but none the less a mercy for the youth.

"All Israel shall mourn for him and bury him: for he only of Jeroboam shall come to the grave, because in him there is found some good thing toward the Lord God of Israel in the house of

Jeroboam." Let me linger on this part of the narrative a moment. In that wicked house there was one bright gem upon which the Lord put a high value. The lad was taken from the evil to come. The kindness of the Lord appeared in his death--while all the judgments were reserved for his father's family.

Do I not speak to some of you ungodly persons who have lost your little children and while you wept bitter tears as you carried them to the grave, you said, "Well, he is better off," or, "she sleeps in Jesus"? Did you ever think, that as for you, you are worse off? You have no hope and are living without God in the world. Let us picture Jeroboam and his wife at the tent of their son. There was everything to cheer the heart as to him who had departed. But everything to fill the soul with gloom concerning those who remained. The like has been the case at the funerals of your gracious little ones. We need shed no tears over the bier. Let us keep our lamentations for the mourners who attend the funeral.

Ah, but you may make the reflections all your own. You, too, have been outside the gates of the city to carry your offspring to the spot in God's acre where they now slumber. Did you think in that mournful hour that the first fruits of your household was holy unto the Lord? We never cease to wonder that the young should die. Yet it has ever been so. And well, indeed, can I believe that mercy of a sweet-smelling savor is to be found in those dispensations of God's Providence which so often darken the windows of our heart and wither the fairest buds in our garden.

Where of old did Death strike its first dart? Did it pierce the heart of Adam, the sinner, or strike down the relentless Cain? No, but righteous Abel was the first of men who departed from earth to be absent from the body and present with the Lord! Even so have you, full many of you, committed your children to the dust in an assured hope for them, according to the Word of the Lord. A hope which you cannot cherish for yourselves! O Sinners, be cautious of your tears, your sighs and your groans--pour them not out with such profuseness as an offering at the graves of those who sleep in Jesus and are blest. You will need them all for your own souls presently! Take up a lamentation for your own doom! Unless you repent, your funerals, O ungodly ones, will call for shrill notes of endless despair!

Let me pause. I have glad tidings to preach to some of you before I yet again deliver these heavy tidings to those who despise the Word. Is there one soul here that desires to be saved? Sinner, I have glad tidings for you! Here are the words, "Whoever will, let him come and take of the Water of Life freely." Though you have been a drunkard or a swearer-- though you have been a whoremonger or a thief--yet there is salvation for any man who comes to Jesus Christ for it. And if the Spirit of God moves you to come now--

"Let not conscience make you linger. Nor of fitness fondly dream. All the fitness He requires, Is to feel your need of Him. This He gives you! It is His Spirit's rising beam."

You say, "How can I go to Christ?" It is no great effort. It is, in fact, the absence of all effort. You have not to climb to Heaven to reach Him, nor to travel to the ends of the earth to find Him. Never doubt, if the Holy Spirit is with you, you may find Him tonight. The way to be saved is simply to trust Christ. Jesus Christ took the guilt of His people and carried it Himself. If you trust Him, you shall have peace, for Jesus took your sin. An old woman servant was once carrying a large bough of a tree to have it cut into pieces to make a fire. A little boy, one of the family, seeing the end of it dragging along the ground and making it very heavy, came and took hold of the end, and the burden grew light. Then said the servant, "Ah, master Frank, I wish you could take hold of one end of the greater burden that I have to carry--I have a burden of sin. The more I drag it about, the heavier it becomes. I wish Jesus Christ would take hold of one end of it."

The little boy said, "My mother told me yesterday that Jesus Christ carries all our sins, therefore, you do not need Jesus Christ to carry one end of it, He will take the whole of it." The poor woman, who had been long seeking rest, found it by that remark of the child. Yes, Jesus does take your sins! If you trust Christ, this is the evidence that all your sins are laid on Him--

"Sinner, do nothing, Either great or small. Jesus did it, did it all, Long, long ago."

Your salvation is finished by Christ if you believe. Not only the first strokes, but the finishing touch Christ has given. The bath you shall wash in, He has filled it. The robe you shall wear, He has woven it. The crown you shall wear, He has bought it. The Heaven you shall inhabit, He has prepared it. "It is finished!" All you have to do is to wear it. Take it and wear it! Accept it as a gift of His Free Grace.

May God bring you into such a mind that you may be willing to receive it. And if you are willing to receive it, take it, take it and go your way rejoicing. Thus you see, I bring good tidings to seekers. But I have a heavy message for some of you. Let me deliver it as in the sight of God, with deep solemnity of purpose. Sinner, unrepentant Sinner, I have heavy tidings for you. You are now under God's wrath. The wrath of God abides on you. It is not as though a tempest hovered in the sky--it has gathered round your devoted head! "God is angry with the wicked every day." Sinner, God has bent His bow and made it ready and fitted His arrow to the string and He has pointed it at you.

He has furbished His sword and made it sharp and it is sharp for you! O barren fig tree, the axe is laid at your root! God even now looks upon you with anger as you do offend Him and sin against Him with a high hand. Turn! Turn! For it is either turn or burn! And God give you to turn lest you burn forever! I have worse tidings still, worse than you think. There is speedy death for you. I know not how long you may live. But out of this vast assembly there is every probability that one or two of us will be in eternity before next Sunday. You can calculate that as well as I can. There is a certain number of deaths in the population every week.

Here are several of you gathered here--some six or seven thousand immortal souls. And we may die--but there are some of us who must die. It is rarely a week passes without a death of someone in this Church, much more in the congregation. I suppose I never did address the same assembly twice and never shall. And though you were all willing to come next Sunday, yet there would be some of you who could not come because you will have appeared at the bar of God. Prepare to meet your God! There is no cholera abroad, but death has other weapons. The fever sleeps, but the gates to the grave are many and you may pass through one of them before ever you are aware of it. Prepare! Prepare! Because He says, "Prepare to meet your God, O Israel!"

I have heavy tidings for some of you. I give you warning to set your house in order, for you must die and not live. I speak now prophetically of some here present! Let them take heed unto their ways lest the day of Grace pass and they die are they have thought of Christ. I have heavier tidings still. After death the judgment. First comes the skeleton king. And then Hell follows him. Oh, is it true that some of us may be in Hell before another week? True! Alas! Too true! I do evoke you, then--since there is this possibility, no, since there is an absolute certainty that before long, except we repent, we shall all likewise perish--I do plead with you to think upon your eternal state!

By the wrath of God and by the love of God--by your own soul and by the value of it--by Heaven and its joys, which you will lose! By Hell and its torments, which you must endure! By the blood of Jesus! By the groans and sweat of that Redeemer who delights to receive sinners and who declares that any who come to Him He will in nowise cast out, I beseech you, as your Brother and your friend, fly, fly, fly to Jesus!

May the Lord help you to trust Him now. There, just as you are, flat before the Cross, Sinner--no stopping, no waiting, no preparing--come to Jesus in all your sin--all black and filthy, just as you are! "Mercy's gate is never shut, Jesus' heart is never hard." His blood shall never lose its power. Do you trust Him? Trust Him! Trust Him and we will meet in Heaven to praise His name, world without end. Amen.

A Mystery! Saints Sorrowing and Jesus Glad!

A Sermon (No. 585)
Delivered on Sunday Morning, August 7th, 1864, by the
Rev. C. H. SPURGEON,
At the Metropolitan Tabernacle, Newington

"Then said Jesus unto them plainly, Lazarus is dead. And I am glad for your sakes that I was not there, to the intent ye may believe; nevertheless let us go unto him" -- John 11:14-15.

There lived in the little village of Bethany a very happy family. There was neither father nor mother in it: the household consisted of the unmarried brother Eleazar, or Lazarus, and his sisters, Martha and Mary, who dwelt together in unity so good and pleasant that there the Lord commanded the blessing, even life for evermore. This affectionate trio were all lovers of the Lord Jesus Christ, and were frequently favoured with His company. They kept open house whenever the Great Teacher came that way. Both for the Master and for the disciples there was always a table, a bed, and a candlestick in the prophet's chamber, and sometimes sumptuous feasts were prepared for the whole company. They were very happy, and rejoiced much to think that they could be serviceable to the necessities of one so poor, and yet so honoured as the Lord Jesus. But, alas! affliction cometh everywhere; virtue may sentinel the door, but grief is not to be excluded from the homestead. "Man is born unto trouble, as the sparks fly upward;" if the fuel be a log of sweet-smelling sandal wood, yet the sparks must rise, and even so the best of families must feel affliction. Lazarus sickens. It is a mortal sickness beyond the power of physicians. What is the first thought of the sisters but to send for their friend Jesus? They know that one word from His lips will restore their brother: there is no absolute need that He should even risk His safety by a journey to Bethany; He has but to speak the word and their brother shall be made whole. With glowing hopes and moderated anxieties, they send a tender message to Jesus--"Lord, behold, he whom Thou lovest is sick." Jesus hears it, and sends back the answer which had much comfort in it, but could hardly compensate for His own absence: "This sickness is not unto death, but for the glory of God, that the Son of God might be glorified thereby." There lies poor Lazarus after the message is come; he does not recover; he is a little more cheerful, because he hears that his sickness is not unto death, but his pains do not abate; the clammy death-sweat gathers on his brow; his tongue is dry; he is full of pains and racked with anguish, at last he passes through the iron gate of death, and there lies his corpse before the weeping sisters' eyes. Why was not Jesus there? Why did He not come? Tender hearted as He always was, what could have made Him thus unkind? Why tarrieth He so? Why is He so long in coming? How can His words be true? He said, "This sickness is not unto death"; and there lies the good man cold in death, and the mourners are gathering for the funeral. Look at Martha! She has been sitting up every night watching her poor brother; no care could have been more constant, no tenderness more excessive. There is no potion in the range of her housewifery which she has not compounded; this herb and the other she has gathered, and she has administered all sorts of medicinal drinks and nourishing foods; and anxiously has she watched until her eyes are red for want of sleep. Jesus might have spared her all this. Why did He not? He had only to will it, and the flush of health would have returned to the cheek of Lazarus, and there would have been no more need of this weary nursing, and this killing watchfulness. What is Jesus doing? Martha was willing to serve Him, will He not serve her? She has even cumbered herself about much-serving for His sake, giving Him not only necessaries but dainties, and will He not give her what is so desirable to her heart, so essential to her happiness--her brother's life? How is it He can send her a promise which He doth not seem to keep, and tantalize her with hope, and cast down her faith? As for Mary, she has been sitting still at her brother's side, listening to his dying words, repeating in his ear the gracious words of Jesus which she had been wont to hear when she sat at His feet, catching the last accents of her expiring brother, thinking less about the medicine and about the diet than Martha did, but thinking more about his spiritual health and about his soul's enjoyment. She has endeavoured to stay the sinking spirits of her beloved brother with words like these, "He will come; He may wait, but I know Him, His heart is very kind, He will come at the last; and even if He let thee sleep in death it will be but for a little; He raised the widow's son at the gates of Nain, He will surely raise thee whom He loves far more. Have ye not heard how He wakened the daughter of Jairus? Brother, He will come and quicken thee, and we shall have many happy hours yet, and we shall have this as a special love-token from our Master and our Lord, that He raised thee from the dead." But why, why was she not spared those bitter tears which ran scalding down her cheeks when she saw that her brother was really dead? She could not believe it. She kissed his forehead, and oh! how cold was that marble brow! She lifted up his hand--"He cannot be dead," said she, "for Jesus said this sickness was not unto death;" but the hand fell nerveless by her side: her brother was really a corpse, and putrefaction soon set in, and then she knew that the beloved clay was not exempt from all the dishonour which decay brings to the human body. Poor Mary! Jesus loved thee, it is said, but this is a strange way of showing His love. Where is He? Miles away He lingers. He knows thy brother is sick; yea, He knows that he is dead, and yet He abides still where He is. Oh! sorrowful mystery that the pity of such a tender Saviour should sink so far below their plumb-line to gauge, or His mercy should range so high beyond their power to reach.

Jesus is talking of the death of His friend, let us listen to His words; perhaps we may find the key to His actions in the words of His lips. How surprising! He does not say, "I regret that I have tarried so long." He does not say, "I ought to have hastened, but even now it is not too late." Hear, and marvel! Wonder of wonders, He says, "I am glad that I was not there." Glad! the word is out of place? Lazarus, by this time, stinketh in his tomb, and here is the Saviour glad! Martha and Mary are weeping their eyes out for sorrow, and yet their friend Jesus is glad! It is strange, it is passing strange! However, we may rest assured that Jesus knoweth better than we do, and our faith may therefore sit still and try to spell out His meaning, where our reason cannot find it at the first glance. "I am glad," saith He, "for your sakes that I was not there, to the intent ye may believe." Ah! we see it now: Christ is not glad because of sorrow, but only on account of the result of it. He knew that this temporary trial would help His disciples to a greater faith, and He so prizes their growth in faith that He is even glad of the sorrow which occasions it. He does as good as say, "I am glad for your sakes that I was not there to prevent the trouble, for now that it is come, it will teach you to believe in me, and this shall be much better for you than to have been spared the affliction."

We have thus plainly before us the principle, that our Lord in His infinite wisdom and superabundant love, sets so high a value upon His people's faith, that He will not screen them from those trials by which faith is strengthened. Let us try to press the wine of consolation from the cluster of the text. In three cups we will preserve the goodly juice as it flows forth from the winepress of meditation. First of all, brethren, Jesus Christ was glad that the trial had come, for the strengthening of the faith of the apostles; secondly, for strengthening the faith of the family; and thirdly, for giving faith to others; for you find by the forty-fifth verse that the goblet passed round to sympathizing friends--"Many of the Jews which came to Mary, and had seen the things which Jesus did, believed on Him."

I. Jesus Christ designed the death of Lazarus and his after-resurrection FOR THE STRENGTHENING OF THE FAITH OF THE APOSTLES. This acted two ways: not only would the trial itself tend to strengthen their faith; but the remarkable deliverance which Christ gave to them out of it would certainly minister to the growth of their confidence in Him.

1. Let us at once observe that the trial itself would certainly tend to increase the apostle's faith. Faith untried may be true faith, but it is sure to be little faith. I believe in the existence of faith in men who have no trials, but that is as far as I can go. I am persuaded, brethren, that where there is no trial faith just draws breath enough to live, but that is all; for faith, like the fabled salamander, has fire for its native element. Faith never prospers so well as when all things are against her: tempests are trainers, and the lightnings are her illuminators. When a calm reigns on the sea, spread the sails as you will, the ship moves not to its harbour; for on a slumbering ocean the keel sleeps too. Let the winds come howling forth, and let the waters lift up themselves, then, though the vessel may rock, and her deck may be washed with waves, and her mast may creak under the pressure of the full and swelling sail, yet it is then that she makes headway towards her desired haven. No flowers wear so lovely a blue as those which grow at the foot of the frozen glacier; no stars so bright as those which glisten in the polar sky; no water so sweet as that which springs amid the desert sand; and no faith so precious as that which lives and triumphs in adversity. Thus saith the Lord, by the mouth of the prophet, "I will leave in the midst of thee an afflicted and poor people, and they shall trust in the name of the Lord." Now, why afflicted and poor? Because there is an adaptation in the afflicted and poor among the Lord's people, to trust in the Lord. He does not say, "I will leave in the midst of thee a prosperous and rich people, and they shall trust." No! these scarcely seem to have such capacity for faith as the afflicted ones have. Rather I will leave in the midst of thee an afflicted and poor people, and they, by reason of their very affliction and poverty, shall be the more graciously disposed to repose their faith in the Lord. Untried faith is always small

in stature; and it is likely to remain dwarfish so long as it is without trials. There is no room in the placid pools of ease for faith to gain leviathan proportions, she must dwell in the stormy sea if she would be one of the chief of the ways of God. Tried faith brings experience; and every one of you who are men and women of experience, must know that experience makes religion become more real to you. You never know either the bitterness of sin or the sweetness of pardon, till you have felt both. You never know your own weakness till you have been compelled to go through the rivers, and you would never have known God's strength had you not been supported amid the water-floods. All the talk about religion which is not based upon an experience of it, is mere talk. If we have little experience, we cannot speak so positively as those can whose experience has been more deep and profound. Once when I was preaching upon the faithfulness of God in time of trial in the earlier days of my ministry, my venerable grandfather was sitting in the pulpit behind me; he suddenly rose up and took my place, and coming to the front of the pulpit, said, "My grandson can preach this as a matter of theory, but I can tell you it as a matter of experience, for I have done business upon the great waters, and have seen the works of the Lord for myself." There is an accumulation of force in the testimony of one who has personally passed through the things whereof others can only speak as though they had seen them in a map or in a picture. Travellers who write from their easy chairs what they have seen from their bedchambers, may indite books to beguile the idle hours of those who stay at home; but he who is about to traverse regions full of danger, seeks a guide who has really trodden the road, The writer may excel in florid words, the veritable traveller has real and valuable wisdom. Faith increases in solidity, assurance, and intensity, the more she is exercised with tribulation, and the more she hath been cast down, and lifted up again. Let not this, however, discourage those who are young in faith. You will have trials enough without your seeking for them; the full portion will be measured out to you in due season. Meanwhile, if you cannot yet claim the result of long experience, thank God for what grace you have. Praise Him for that whereunto you have attained; walk according to that rule, and you shall yet have more and more of the blessing of God, till your faith shall remove mountains, and conquer impossibilities.

It may be asked, what is the method by which trial strengthens faith? We might answer in various ways. Trial takes away many of the impediments of faith. Carnal security is the worst foe to confidence in God. If I sit down and say, "Soul, take thine ease, thou hast much goods laid up for many years;" faith's road is barricaded, but adversity sets the barn on a blaze, and "the much goods laid up for many years," cease to block up the path of faith. Oh, blessed axe of sorrow, which clears a pathway for me to my God by cutting down the thick trees of my earthly comforts! When I say, "My mountain standeth firm, I shall never be moved," the visible fortification, rather than the invisible protector, engages my attention; but when the great earthquake shakes the rocks, and the mountain is swallowed up, I fly to the immovable Rock of Ages to build my confidence on high. Worldly ease is a great foe to faith; it loosens the joints of holy valour, and snaps the sinews of scared courage. The balloon never rises until the cords are cut: affliction doth this sharp service for believing souls. While the wheat sleeps comfortable in the husk it is useless to man, it must be threshed out of its resting-place before its value can be known. Trial plucks the arrow of faith from the repose of the quiver, and shoots it against the foe.

Nor is affliction of small service to faith, when it exposes the weakness of the creature. This trial would show the apostles that they must not depend upon the bounty of any one man, for though Lazarus may have entertained them and filled their little bag with food, yet Lazarus dies, and Mary may die, and Martha may die, and all friends must die, and this would teach them not to look to broken cisterns, but to fly to the ever-flowing fountain. Oh, dear friends, we are in much danger of making idols of our mercies! God gives us his temporal favours as refreshments by the way, and then straightway we kneel down and cry, "These by thy gods, O Israel." It is of the Lord's mercy that these idol-gods be broken in pieces. He blasts the gourds under which we sat in ample shade, in order that we may lift up our cry to Him, and trust in Him alone. The emptiness of the creature is a lesson we are so slow to learn, and we must have it whipped into us by the rod of affliction; but learned it must be, or else faith can never attain to eminence.

Furthermore, trial is of special service to faith when it drives her to her God. I make a sad confession, over which I mourn, that when my soul is happy and things prosper, I do not as a rule live so near to God as I do in the midst of shame and contempt, and casting down of spirit. O my God, how dear Thou art to my soul in the night; when the sun goeth down, Thou Bright and Morning Star, how sweetly dost Thou shine. When the world's bread is sugared and buttered, then we devour it till we grow sick; but when the world changes our diet, fills our mouth with vinegar, and makes our drink gall and wormwood, then we cry for the breasts of our dear God again. When the world's wells are full of sweet but poisonous water, we pitch our tents at the well's mouth, and drink again and again and forget the well of Bethlehem which is within the gate; but when earth's water becomes bitter like the stream of Marah, then we turn away all sick and faint, and cry after the water of life, "Spring up, O well!" Thus afflictions fetch us to our God, as the barking dog drives the wandering sheep to the shepherd's hand.

And then trial has a hardening effect upon faith. As the Spartan lads were prepared for fighting by the sharp discipline of their boyish days, so are God's servants trained for war by the afflictions which He sends upon them in the early days of their spiritual life. We must run with footmen, or we shall never be able to contend with horses; we must be thrown into the water, or we shall never learn to swim; we must hear the whizzing of the bullets, or we shall never become veteran soldiers. The gardener knows that if his flowers were kept always under glass and fostered in a great temperature, when he might put them out, should there come a cold night they would quickly die; so he does not give them too much heat, but exposes them by degrees and gets them used to the cold, that they may stand in the open air; and thus the only wise God does not put His servants in hothouses and rear them delicately, but He exposes them to trial that they may know how to bear it when it comes. If you want to ruin your son, never let him know a hardship. When he is a child carry him in your arms, when he becomes a youth still dandle him, and when he becomes a man still dry-nurse him, and you will succeed in producing an arrant fool. If you want to prevent his being made useful in the world, guard him from every kind of toil. Do not suffer him to struggle. Wipe the sweat from his dainty brow and say, "Dear child, thou shalt never have another task so arduous." Pity him when he ought to be punished; supply all his wishes, avert all disappointments, prevent all troubles, and you will surely tutor him to be a reprobate and to break your heart. But put him where he must work, expose him to difficulties, purposely throw him into peril, and in this way you shall make him a man, and when he comes to do man's work and to bear man's trial, he shall be fit for either. My Master does not daintily cradle His children when they ought to run alone; and when they begin to run He is not always putting out His finger for them to lean upon, but He lets them tumble down to the cutting of their knees, because then they will walk more carefully by-and-by, and learn to stand upright by the strength which faith confers upon them.

You see, dear friends, that Jesus Christ was glad--glad that His disciples were blessed by trouble. Will you think of this, you who are so troubled this morning, Jesus Christ does sympathize with you, but still He does it wisely, and He says, "I am glad for your sakes that I was not there." He is glad that your business does not prosper; He is glad that you have those pains and aches, and that you have so weak a body, to the intent that you may believe. You would never have possessed the precious faith which now supports you if the trial of your faith had not been like unto fire. You are a tree that never would have rooted so well if the wind had not rocked you to and fro, and made you to take firm hold upon the precious truths of the covenant of grace.

2. But not to tarry here, let us notice that the deliverance which Christ wrought by the resurrection of Lazarus, was calculated also to strengthen the faith of the apostles. At the worst Christ can work. Why, what a plight were they now in! Here was a case which had come to the very worst. Lazarus is not merely dead--he has been buried; the stone has been rolled to the mouth of the sepulchre--worse than that, he had become putrid. Here are miracles so many, that I must describe the resurrection of Lazarus not as one miracle, but as a mass of wonders. We will not go into detail, but suffice it to say, we cannot suppose anything to be a more prodigious exhibition of the divine strength, than the restoration of health and life to a body through which the worms did creep and crawl; and yet in the very worst case Christ is not brought to a nonplus. Here was a case where human power evidently could do nothing. Now bring the viol and the harp, and let music try its charms. Bring here, physician, thy most potent draught, now, for the true aqua vitoe! Now see what thou canst do. What! does the elixir fail? The physician turns away disgusted, for the stench may sooner destroy the physician's life, than he restore the corpse. Now, seek ye round the world and ask all men that are--Herod and his men-at-arms, and Caesar on the imperial throne--"Can you do anything here?" Nay, death sits with ghastly smile laughing at them all. "I have Lazarus," says he, "beyond your reach." Yet Jesus Christ wins the day.

Here divine sympathy became most manifest. Jesus wept when He thought of Lazarus and his weeping sisters. We do not find it often said that He wept. He was "a man of sorrows and acquainted with grief," but those were precious and rare drops which He shed over that dead body. He could do no more when He thought of Jerusalem: He doth no less now that He thinks of Lazarus.

What an exhibition these disciples had of the divine power as well as the divine sympathy, for Christ does but say, "Lazarus, come forth," and death can hold his captive no longer. Forth from the charnel house he comes, restored to perfect health.

Do you not think that all this must tend to confirm the apostles' faith? It seems to me to be a part of the best education they could possibly receive for their future ministry. I think I see the apostles in after-time shut up in prison: they are condemned to die, but Peter comforts John by saying, "He can bring us out of prison: do you not remember how He brought Lazarus out of his grave? He can certainly appear for us and set us free." When they went forth to preach to sinners, how would they be strengthened by remembering these cases! Their hearers were debauched, depraved, immoral--the apostles went into the midst of the worst conditions of human nature, and yet they feared not for the result, for they knew that putrid Lazarus revived at Christ's word. Peter would argue, "Did not Christ restore Lazarus when his body was stinking and decayed? He can certainly bring the most reprobate hearts to the obedience of the truth, and raise the vilest of the vile to new life."

Many of the apostolic Churches were far gone; they had in them unworthy members; but this would not too much buffet the faith of the apostles, for they would say, "That same Christ Who raised up Lazarus, can make Sardis, and Pergamos, and Thyatira, yet to be a praise in the earth, and Churches which seem to be corrupt and foul in the nostrils of the Most High, may yet be made a brightness and glory, and a sweet-smelling savour unto him." I am persuaded that very often such a miracle as this would recur to them, and strengthen them in the times of their suffering and labour and make them able to bear afflictions, and even martyrdom itself, in confidence in Christ.

I will not, however, say more, because the thing seems obvious enough; only you must not forget the principle we are trying to bring out, that in the case of the apostles, Christ considered that for them to have strong faith was worth any cost. No matter what pangs it cost Mary and Martha, or in what grief it might involve Himself or His apostles, they must bear it, because the result was so exceedingly beneficial. The surgeon handles the knife without tears, sharp is the cut, but he knows it will cure. The mother puts the draught to the child's mouth, and the child cries, and heaves, and loathes the bitterness, but the mother says, "Drink it all up, my child," because she knows there is life in every drop. So Christ is glad for the apostles' sake that He is not there, to the intent that they may believe.

II. Jesus Christ had an eye also to THE GOOD OF THE FAMILY. Mary and Martha had faith, but it was not very strong, for they suspected Christ's love when they said, "Lord, if Thou hadst been here, my brother had not died." There was a sort of under whisper--"Why wast Thou not here? Dost Thou love us? Wherefore then didst Thou tarry?" They certainly doubted His power. Martha, when she could believe in the resurrection, but could not believe in the present resurrection for her brother; and when again she said, "He has been dead four days," had faith, but it was very weak. Christ therefore sent the trial to Mary and Martha for their sakes, and was glad to send it, to the intent that they might believe.

Observe, dear friends, that these were choice favourites of the Lord Jesus Christ. He loves all the elect. They were three special favourites upon whom very distinguishing regard was set, and therefore it was that He sent them a special trial. The lapidary, if he takes up a stone and finds that it is not very precious, will not spend much care in cutting it; but when he gets a rare diamond of the first water, then he will be sure to cut, and cut, and cut again. When the Lord finds a saint whom He loves--loves much--He may spare other men trials and troubles, but He certainly will not this well-beloved one. It is an awful thing to be a favourite of heaven. It is a thing to be sought after and to be rejoiced in; but remember, to be of the King's council-chamber is a thing involving such work for faith that flesh and blood might shrink from the painful blessing. The gardener gets a tree, and if it is but of a poor sort he will let it grow as it wills, and take what fruit comes from it naturally; but if it be of a very rare sort, he likes to have every bough in its proper place, so that it may bear well; and he often takes out his knife an cuts here and there, because, says he, "That is a favourite tree, and it is one which bears such fruit that I would have much from it, and would leave nothing whatever that would cause it detriment." You who are God's favourites must not marvel at trials, but rather keep your door wide open for them, and when they come in, say, "Hail, messenger of the King! the sound of thy Master's feet is behind thee; thou art welcome here, for thy Master sent thee."

Special trial was attended with a special visit. It may be that Christ would not have come to Bethany if Lazarus had not been dead; but as soon as there is a corpse in the house, there is Christ in the house too. O Christian, it shall be much for your comfort, and for the strengthening of your faith, if Christ comes to you in your troubles. I tell you, if you see no smiles in His face in your prosperity, you shall not be without them in your adversity. The Lord Jesus will go out of His way to see you. You know when a mother is most kind to her child: she lets it run about, and scarcely notices it when it is well; but when it cries. "My head, my head!" and when they take it to the mother and tell her it is ill, how tender she is over it! How all the blandishments of love and the caresses of affection are lavished upon the little sick one! It shall be so with you, and in receiving these special visits, you shall know yourself to be highly favoured above the rest.

This special visit was attended with special fellowship. Jesus wept--wept with them that wept. Ah! you shall have Jesus sitting by the bedside, and weeping with you when you are sick. You may be well, and strong, and have but little fellowship with Christ, but He shall make all your bed in your sickness. Though you might walk along the green sward without the Saviour, when you come into the midst of the fire, like Shadrach, Meshach, and Abed-nego, you shall not be without Him then. I witness that there is no fellowship with Christ so near and sweet, as that which comes to us when we are in deep trials. Then the Master unbosoms Himself, and takes His child, not upon His knee, but to His very heart, and bids him lay his head upon His beating bosom. Christ will reveal His secrets to you when the world is against you, and trials surround you. "The secret of the Lord is with them that fear Him; and He will shew them His covenant;" but they shall never have such discoveries of that secret and that covenant, as when they most need it, in the darkest and most trying times. There are special loves, special trials, special visits, and special fellowship.

And soon you shall have special deliverance. In days to come you will talk about these trials. You will say, I fretted myself, and worried over it, but oh, if I could have seen the end as well as the beginning, I should have said--

"Sweet affliction! sweet affliction!
Thus to bring my Saviour near."

I tell you, you will sit yet under your own vine, and under your own fig-tree, and talk to the poor tried saints, and say, "Do not be cast down, for I cried unto the Lord and He heard me, and delivered me from all my fears." Perhaps in heaven this will help to make a part of your happiness, to remember God's love to you in your tribulations--

"There on a green and flowery mount
Our weary souls shall sit,
And with transporting joys recount,
The labours of our feet."

Shall we not tell to angels, and principalities, and powers, the faithfulness of Christ? We will tell all heaven that "His love was strong as death, and His jealousy as cruel as the grave" "many waters could not quench His love, neither could the floods drown it." What sayest thou, my friend, thou who are under the smarting rod? Wilt thou murmur any more? Wilt thou repine against it any more? I beseech you, rather take my text, and read it the other way say--God help thee to say it--"I am glad that my God did not deliver me, because the trial has strengthened my faith. I thank His name that He has done me the great favour to permit me to carry the heavy end of His cross. I thank my Father that He hath not left me unchastised, for Before I was afflicted I went astray: but now have I kept Thy word.' It is good for me that I have been afflicted.' " I tell you, this is the shortest way out of your troubles, as well as the most profitable spirit while you are in them. The Lord generally stays the rod when He finds His child receiving it as a favour. When thou art agreed with God's rod, then that rod will have no further quarrel with thee. When thou canst look into the Father's eyes, and say, "Thy will be done," then His afflicting hand has done its work.

III. Now I come to the third point, and here may God the Holy Spirit bless the word. This trouble was permitted for GIVING FAITH TO OTHERS.

I shall address myself chiefly to those who cannot say they are God's people, but who have some desire towards Christ. It is very likely you have had some great trouble in your life, and looking back, you wish you had never had it; but my Lord, who knows better than you do, says "I am glad for your sakes that I did not spare you that trouble, to the intent that you may be led to believe." Know assuredly that afflictions often lead men to faith in Christ because they give space for thought. The man was strong and hale and hearty, and went on working from day to day, and never had a thought about God. "The ox knoweth his owner, and the ass his master's crib;" but he did not know, he did not care. He left all thoughts of eternity to those who were silly enough to be religious, but for him--what did it matter to him? Death was a long way off, and besides, if it were not, he had not the time to think about it. An accident occurred; he had to lie upon his bed, and at first he fretted and fumed, but it could not be altered, and there in the ward of the hospital he groaned through many a weary hour at night. What could he think of? Why then the man began to think of himself, of his condition before God, of what would be his lot if he should die. When his life trembled like the even balance, and not one could tell which way it would turn, the man was forced to consider. Many a soul has been ploughed in the hospital, and then has been sown in the sanctuary. Many a man has been first brought to God by the loss of a limb, or by long sickness, or by deep poverty.

Afflictions lead men to faith full often by preventing sin. A young man had resolved to climb a mountain: he had determined against good advice to reach the summit, though one far older than himself had warned him of the danger. He had not proceeded far up the mountainside before a thick mist surrounded him. He was alarmed. The mist was so thick he could scarcely see his own hand. He retraced his steps following the way by which he came, and returned sorrowfully to his father's house, telling him that he had been in great peril. His father said he was glad of it; for if he had not met with that peril, he might have advanced a little farther, and fallen, never to rise again. Often trouble puts men out of temptation. They would have gone into bad company, to drunkenness, or lust, but they could not. The appointment was made--ah! the very night was set apart, but the black hand of God's kind angel came--I said a black hand, for so it seemed, and the man could not do what he had wished to do, and so his course was checked, and this in the hand of God was the means of bringing him to faith.

Troubles, again, often bring men to believe in Jesus because they compel them to stand face to face with stern realities. Did you ever lie upon the edge of death for a week? Did you ever lie with your body racked with pains, listening for the physician's whispers, and knowing that they amounted to this, that there were ninety-nine chances to one that you could not possibly recover? Did you ever feel that death was near? Did you ever peer into eternity with anxious eyes? Did you ever picture hell and think yourself there? Did you ever lie awake, and think of heaven and yourself shut out of it? Ah! it is in such times as these that God's Holy Spirit works great things for the sons of men. Hence Christ is glad when they are brought very low, when their soul abhorreth all manner of meat, and they cry unto God in their trouble. He is glad because this is the stepping-stone to real and genuine trust in Him, and so to eternal life. It is much better to lose an eye or a hand than to lose your soul--better to go to heaven poor and ragged, than to go to hell rich--better to melt into heaven by the process of consumption than it were to go down to hell with bones filled with marrow, and sinews full of strength. Glory be to God for the trials and troubles some of us have had, if they have been the means of bringing us to Christ.

Trials tend to make men believe in Christ when they are followed by deliverances. Perhaps some of you have been raised from a sick bed, or you have been helped over a time of temporal distress. Well, have you no gratitude? Do you not love God for His goodness? Does not your heart melt towards the Lord, for the kind deeds He has done to you? Have you no song of praise for His name? I have known many who have said, "Now that God has been pleased to raise me up and help me in this way, I will give Him my heart; what can I do for Him who has done so much for me?" Gratitude, I doubt not, has led many to put their trust in Christ. Besides, if you sought God and asked for help in time of trouble, and He did help you, this will tend to encourage you to pray again. If He helped you then, He will help you now; if He spared your life, why will He not spare your soul? If God has been pleased to lift you up from the grave, why may He not also deliver you from the pit of hell? I bless God there are many in this Church who were led to seek the Lord through answers to prayer. God was gracious to them in their distress; His mercy listened to their prayer; the blessing came, and the result is, that they cry unto Him, and will cry as long as they live.

If once we have prevailed with God, and believing in God we have had some deliverance, this I hope will be overruled to make us trust God for everything in the future. Remember that the one thing needful for eternal life is trusting in the Lord Jesus Christ. I know you will tell me you cannot be perfect. No, I know you cannot. You will say, "I have many sins; I have done much that is wrong." It is true, most true, but he who believeth in the Lord Jesus Christ has his sins forgiven. You know the story--Christ came down from heaven and took His people's sins upon His own shoulders. When God came forth to smite the sinner, Justice said, "Where is he?" and Christ came and stood in the sinner's place, and God's sword went through the Saviour's heart. Why? That it might never cut nor wound the heart of those for whom Jesus died. Did He die for you? He did, if you believe in Him; your faith will be to you the evidence that Christ was substitute for you, and oh! if Christ suffered for you, you cannot suffer. If God punished Christ He will never punish you. If Jesus Christ paid your debts, you are free. Before God's throne today, if thou believest, thou art as clear as the angels in heaven. Thou are a saved soul if thou art resting upon the atonement of Christ, and thou mayst go thy way and sing--

"Now, freed from sin, I walk at large,
The Saviour's blood's my full discharge;
At His dear feet my soul I lay,
A sinner saved, and homage pay."

If this be the result of your affliction, Christ may well say, "I am glad for your sakes that I was not there to stop the trouble, to the intent that ye may believe." May God bring you to faith for Jesus' sake. Amen.

The Child Samuel's Prayer

A SERMON DELIVERED
BY THE REV. C. H. SPURGEON,
AT THE METROPOLITAN TABERNACLE, NEWINGTON.

"Speak, Lord; for Your servant hears." -- 1 Samuel 3:9.

IN the days of Eli the Word of the Lord was precious and there was no open vision. It was well, when the Word did come, that one chosen individual had the hearing ear to receive it and the obedient heart to perform it. Eli failed to tutor his sons to be the willing servants and the attentive hearers of the Lord's Word. In this he was without the excuse of inability since he successfully trained the child Samuel in reverent attention to the Divine will. O that those who are diligent about the souls of others would look well to their own households!

Alas, poor Eli, like many in our day, you are made the keeper of the vineyards, but your own vineyard you have not kept! As often as he looked upon the gracious child, Samuel, he must have felt the heartache. When he remembered his own neglected and unchastened sons and how they had made themselves vile before all Israel, Samuel was the living witness of what Grace can work where children are trained up in God's fear. Hophni and Phinehas were sad specimens of what parental indulgence will produce in the children of the best of men. Ah, Eli, if you had been as careful with your own sons as with the son of Hannah they had not been such men of Belial, nor would Israel have abhorred the offering of the Lord because of the fornication which those priestly reprobates committed at the very door of the tabernacle!

O for Grace to so nurse our little ones for the Lord that they may hear the Lord when He shall be pleased to speak to them! Let us proceed at once to consider our short but very suggestive text in four aspects and I pray that the Holy Spirit may speak to us through His Word. We shall meditate upon this Scripture, first, as the prayer of a little child. Secondly, as the cry of an anxious soul. Thirdly, as the prayer of an earnest Believer. And fourthly as the spirit of a dying saint.

I. First of all we shall take our text AS THE PRAYER OF A LITTLE CHILD. Samuel was blessed with a gracious father and what is of even more importance, he was the child of an eminently holy mother. Hannah was a woman of great poetic talent, as appears from her memorable song--"My heart rejoices in the Lord, my horn is exalted in the Lord; my mouth is enlarged over my enemies, because I rejoiced in Your salvation." The soul of poetry lives in every line--a brave but chastened spirit breathes in every sentence! Even the Virgin Mary, the most blessed among women, could do no other than use expressions of a similar import.

Better still, Hannah was a woman of great prayer. She had been a woman of a sorrowful spirit, but her prayers at last returned to her in blessing and she had this son given her of the Lord. He was very dear to his mother's heart and she, therefore, to show her gratitude and in fulfillment of the vow which in her anguish she had vowed unto the Lord, would consecrate the best thing she had and presented her son before the Lord in Shiloh--a lesson to all godly parents to see to it that they dedicate their children unto God. How highly favored shall we be if our children shall all be like Isaac-- children of the promise! What blessed parents should we be if we saw our children all rise up to call the Redeemer blessed!

It has been the lot of some of you to see all your children numbered with the people of God--all your jewels are now in Jehovah's casket. In their early childhood you gave them up to God and dedicated them to Him in earnest prayer and now the Lord has given you your petition which you asked of Him. I like our friends to hold little services in their own houses when their family is increased. It seems good and profitable for friends to assemble and prayer to be offered that the child may be an inheritor of the promises--that he may be early called by mighty Grace and received into the Divine family.

You will perceive, dear Friends, that as Samuel was put under the care and tuition of Eli, Eli had instructed him in some degree in the spirit of religion. But he does not appear to have explained to him the peculiar form and nature of those special and particular manifestations of God which were given to His Prophets. Little dreaming, I dare say, that Samuel would ever be, himself, the subject of them. On that memorable night, when towards morning the lamp of God was about to go out, the Lord cried, "Samuel, Samuel." The young child was not able to discern--for he had not been taught--that it was the voice of God and not the voice of man.

That he had learned the spirit of true religion is indicated by his instantaneous obedience and the habit of obedience became a valuable guide to him in the perplexities of that eventful hour. He runs to Eli and says, "Here am I, for you did call me." And though this is three times repeated, yet he seems not at all loath to leave his warm bed and run to his foster-father to see if he could get him any comfort that his old age might require during the night, or otherwise do his bidding. This was a sure sign that the child had acquired the healthy principle of obedience though he did not understand the mystery of the prophetic call.

Better far to have the young heart trained to bear the yoke than to fill the childish head with knowledge, however valuable. An ounce of obedience is better than a ton of learning. When Eli perceived that God had called the child, he taught him his first little prayer. It is a very short one, but it is a very full one--"Speak, Lord; for Your servant hears." Many questions have been raised as to whether children ought to be taught a form of prayer. As far as I can judge I think not, for I do not think that forms of prayer, although they may be allowed and God may accept them, are ever of very great advantage to those who use them.

Forms of prayer are something like the stilts of a cripple. If a man begins with them, it is very probable that he will never be able to do without them. They resemble the copious notes and manuscripts of certain ministers who began with them and are quite unable, now, to preach without them. Children who are taught a form of prayer may, perhaps, by Divine Grace be enabled to use the form in all sincerity of heart--I hope they may. But I think they are more likely to understand the things of God if, instead of teaching them the form, you explain to them the meaning and the value of prayer.

I take this to be the best plan. Let the Christian parent explain to the child what prayer is--tell him that God answers prayer. Direct him to the Savior and then urge him to express his desires in his own language, both when he rises and when he goes to rest. Gather the little ones around your knee and listen to their words, suggesting to them their needs and reminding them of God's gracious promises. You will be amazed and, I may add, sometimes amused, too. But you will be frequently surprised at the expressions they will use, the confessions they will make, the desires they will utter. And I am certain that any Christian person standing within earshot and listening to the simple prayer of a little child earnestly asking God for what it thinks it wants, would never afterwards wish to teach a child a form, but would say that as a matter of education to the heart the extemporaneous utterance was infinitely superior to the best form and that the form should be given up forever.

However, do not let me speak too sweepingly. If you must teach your child to say a form of prayer, at least take care that you do not teach him to say anything which is not true. If you teach your children a catechism, mind that it is thoroughly scriptural, or you may train them up to tell falsehoods. Do not call the child up and command him to say, "in my Baptism, wherein I was made a member of Christ, a child of God and an inheritor of Heaven." If you want to educate him for the gallows, teach him to utter untruths about sacred things! If you would make him an habitual deceiver, teach him the Church Catechism and make him say, "God the Holy Spirit, who sanctifies me and all the elect people of God"-- when he is altogether unsanctified and has no evidence of being elected.

I pray you, if you would have honest children, do not teach them to say that he thanks his heavenly Father, "who has brought him into this state of salvation," when he knows--and you know--that he is not saved at all. Teach him nothing but the Truth as it is in Jesus so far as he can learn it, and pray the Holy Spirit to write that Truth of God upon his heart. Better to supply no signposts to the young traveler than to mislead him with false ones. The light of a wrecker's beacon is worse than darkness. Teach our youth to make untruthful statements in religions matters and Atheism can scarcely do more to corrupt their minds!

Formal religion is a deadly foe to vital godliness. If you teach a catechism, or if you teach a form of prayer to your little ones, let it all be true. And, as far as possible never put into a child's mouth a word which the child cannot truly say from his heart. Dear Friends, we must be more careful about truthfulness and correctness in speech. If a child looked out of a window at anything going on in the street and then told you that he saw it from the door, you ought to make him tell the tale over again so as to impress upon him the necessity of being truthful in every respect. Especially in things connected with religion keep your child back from any form until he has a right to be a partaker of it. Never encourage him to come to the Lord's Table unless you really believe that there is a work of Grace in his heart--for why should you lead him to eat and drink his own damnation?

Insist with all your heart that religion is a solemn reality not to be mimicked or pretended to and seek to bring the child to understand that there is no vice more abhorrent before God than hypocrisy. Do not make your young Samuel a young hypocrite, but train up your darling to speak before the Lord with a deep solemnity and a conscientious truthfulness! And let him never dare to say, either in answer to a catechism question, or as a form of prayer, anything which is not positively true. If you must have a form of prayer, let it not express such desires as a child never had, but let it be adapted to his young capacity.

At the same time, I would again say that it would be infinitely better to leave the child alone as to the words, having earnestly inculcated upon him the spirit of prayer. Beloved, when we see any trace of good in our youth, then, like Eli, we should be the more earnest to have them trained up in the faith. Let the child learn the Assembly's Catechism, even though he does not understand all that is in it--and as soon as the young heart can comprehend the things of Jesus, labor in power of the Holy Spirit to bring it to a simple dependence upon the great Sacrifice.

It is said of the Rev. John Angell James, "Like most men who have been eminent and honored in the Church of Christ, he had a godly mother who would take her children to her chamber and with each, separately, pray for the salvation of their souls. This exercise, which fulfilled her own responsibility, was molding the character of her children, and most, if not all of them, rose up to call her blessed. When did such means ever fail?"

I beseech you, the teachers of the Sunday school--though I scarcely need to do so, for I know how zealous you are in this matter--as soon as ever you see the first peep of day in your children, encourage their young desires. Believe in the conversion of children, as children! Believe that the Lord can call them by His Grace, can renew their hearts, can give them a part and a lot among His people long before they reach the prime of life. Oh, that the Lord may give us to see many Samuels added to this Church, as we have seen them in days gone by!

You that are little ones, when the Lord speaks to you, cry to Him, "Speak, Lord; for Your servant hears." And when in the class, or here in the Tabernacle, the Word of God is preached to sinners, remember it is preached to you quite as much as to the men who are six feet high. And do lift up your little hearts to God with the desire that while we are preaching, God would speak to you. Do, dear children, expect the Lord to meet with you. Boys and girls have been saved--

"Many dear children are gathering there, For of such is the kingdom of Hea ven." We have baptized many like you, at twelve, thirteen and fourteen years of age who have made a very clear profession of their faith. And rejoiced, indeed, shall we be if we see you boys and girls coming forward and saying, "God has called us, has brought us to put our trust in Jesus. And here we are."

Young Samuel, the Lord calls you! And you are a privileged one to be called so soon, for early Grace frequently becomes eminent Grace! And those who begin early with God are often preserved in this world to be of distinguished service in the courts of the Lord's House. May that be your lot and mine!

II. We have perhaps spoken enough upon this point. Let us now consider the words as THE CRY OF AN ANXIOUS SOUL. What an overwhelming sight is this vast crowd of immortal souls! What a joy would it be to me if I could hope that you were all anxious to find the Savior! Many of you who assemble constantly within these walls, though you have had serious impressions, are not yet saved. As you came in tonight this thought may have been uppermost--"Oh, that God would meet with my soul tonight."

Some of you young woman have been in my Sister's, Mrs. Bartlett's class, this afternoon and it is very hard to be in that class long without receiving solemn impressions. God has been visiting your class just lately. He has removed a heavenly-minded and well-beloved Sister. He has carried her aloft to the upper and better world. She could die singing and rejoicing in her Savior, for her usual frame of mind was set forth in these words, "Speak, Lord; for Your servant hears."

Well, dear Friends, this bereaving Providence has had a loud voice to your class! God has worked a solemn impression upon your minds by it and you prayed as you entered the Tabernacle, "O God, save my soul this night!" Let me recommend to you the use of this simple prayer now while you are sitting in the pew, "Speak, Lord; for Your servant hears." "Speak, Lord!" Pray that first. "Speak, Lord! While the minister is speaking, Lord, speak! I have heard the min- ister's voice and sometimes it awakens me, but I am not saved and I never shall be, Lord, if the minister speaks alone. Speak, Lord! My mother has talked with me. My earnest teacher has sought to lead me to the Savior. But I know that the words of blessed men and women will fall to the ground if they come alone. Speak, Lord!

"Your voice said, 'Let there be light,' and there was light. Speak, Lord! And make light in my darkened mind! Your voice called Lazarus from the grave though he had been dead four days. Speak, Lord! And make me live! Oh, let it be tonight a real work of Grace in my soul! Let Divine power come and operate upon me." My dear Friend, cannot you follow me in such petitions as these? You know my soul is going up for you and I am crying to God, "Speak, Lord!" And there are others here that you know of and who are dear to you who are even now wrestling in earnest with the angel of mercy and they are saying, "Speak, Lord!" Oh, what would your father give if he should hear that God had spoken to your soul? How would your mother leap for joy if she did but know that God had come to deal with you in a way of saving Grace! "Speak, Lord!" Let that be your prayer!

Then put it next, "Speak, Lord, to me! For if the Lord speaks in a sermon, it may be to another and then woe is me that I should be denied the priceless gift. I may be lying by Bethesda's pool, but another man may step in before me and I may miss the mercy. Speak, Lord, to me, even to me. Say unto my soul, 'I am your salvation.' May there be an unmistakable message to my heart. You have taken away one that I knew. It is a marvel, then, that You have not taken me away. It is a wonder that I am spared--such a rebel as I have been!

"O how great is Your patience that You have not dashed me in pieces and cast me into Hell! Lord, You have dealt graciously with me in sparing my life. Speak to me, Lord. If there are other souls in a like case with me, deal graciously with them, but oh, do chiefly so with me, for if there is one heart that wants You more than another I am that one! If there is one less likely than another to be saved--one who would give You more praise than another if saved--I am that one! Lord, speak to me!"

Dear young friend, you need not go home to pray that prayer. While you are sitting there, I pray God the Holy Spirit to lead you to offer it in silence--"Lord, speak to me." Personal possession of an interest in Christ Jesus is a blessing to be sought for with strong crying and tears--be not silent till the God of Heaven shall grant it to you. I will add another word to the prayer which I commend to you--it shall be the word of time. "Lord, speak to me now." How old are you? Perhaps you are young. Oh, but how well it is to let the Savior have the bud of our being--to consecrate to Him the early morning of life!

Blessed is the day of life when it begins with clear shining and opens with a morning without clouds. "Lord, I am young, but not too young to die. Speak to me now!" But are there not some of you who are past your one-and-twenty and are beginning to run into the ways of sin? It may be your feet have slipped. Have you wandered into evil? Are you living in the daily practice of outward vice? You know you have left the right path, some of you, and the pangs of conscience are upon you just now. Pray--"Lord, let me have had the last of my sins! Let me have done with them now. Sever, once and for all, the bonds between me and Satan and bind me fast to Your altar tonight!"

Perhaps you have passed even the prime of life. It may be that your hairs are turning gray. An old sinner is an old fool. He who is out of Christ at sixty or seventy is devoid of understanding. The young may die, but the old must. To be careless in youth is to sleep in a siege. But to be worldly in old age is to sleep in an attack, when already the scaling ladders are at the walls! Take heed, you who wear gray hairs, for if they are not crowns of Glory to you, they will prove to be fools' caps! Woe unto you who have spent your threescore years and ten and are yet the enemies of God! What will you do when He comes to require of you that which is past?

O, what will you do in the day when He shall deal out to you who have followed the flesh, the corruption thereof? O, what will you do when the heavens are in a blaze and the trumpet rings and the dead awaken and you are judged? I put this question to you in deep solemnity this night. And do, I pray you, before you leave these walls, send up the cry, "Speak, Lord to me and speak to me NOW!"

But can you say, like Samuel, "Your servant hears"? Truly, I am afraid many of you cannot for you do not hear God's word with your hearts. My eye runs down with grief when I think of some of you who listen to my voice year after year and yet do not hear. You hear me, but you do not hear my Master! Alas, how many have been the arrows out of God's bow which I have shot at you? Have they not been wasted? They have rattled upon your armor, but they have not pierced your hearts! I have run in vain! I have labored in vain for you! I have beaten the air so far as you are concerned.

You would not hear. I can say solemnly I have sometimes stood in this pulpit and have labored with your souls to the best of my power and I have felt that I would have cheerfully resigned all I had on earth if I might but have brought you to Christ!

If you, my Hearers who sit here constantly, might but be partakers of eternal life, I will leave my Master to do what He wills with me. Shame, contempt, disgrace--these shall be our joy and our crown for our faithfulness to God and your souls. But, oh, I must have you saved! I must have you lay hold on eternal life! I must see you look to Jesus! And my prayer is that you may this night look to a Savior Crucified! Can you say, "Your servant hears"? "Yes," says one, "I can. If now the Lord would say a word in mercy to me I would gladly hear it." Then He will speak to you, poor Soul, before long. If you will hear it, He will say it, for He never did give a hearing ear to any heart without intending to speak to it.

I know how you want Him to speak--you want Him to speak with conviction. You want the broken and the contrite heart such as He will not despise. Well, ask for it--say, "Speak, Lord, with

Your convicting voice, for I am ready to hear." And you want Him to speak with a converting voice--you desire to be turned from your evil ways and to follow the Lord. Cry to Him, then, "Speak, Lord, with the voice that turns men and turn me now from darkness to Light."

Or it may be that you want a comforting word. Well, then, pray for it--"Speak, Lord, with Your voice of comfort! Bind up my bleeding wounds and let my soul rejoice in You." Yet, truly, I do not know that He will speak anything more to you than this--"Look to Christ and live." He will speak with power, but that is the substance of it. Jesus is the sum of Mercy's message. He is the Word of God. Do not expect to have any other Gospel from God's lips than that which is revealed in God's Word. The Gospel of God's Word is, "Believe, and live." There is life in a look at the Crucified One! There is life at this moment for YOU! If you will not hear the voice of God when He says to you, "Trust Christ," remember He has no other glad tidings.

Effectual calling may speak this same thing more effectually, but the Holy Spirit never reveals any other Gospel. There is no other way to Heaven but just this--"Trust your soul to Christ--your sins are forgiven you and you are saved!" I am loath to leave this point because my heart is panting to know and to feel some inward emotion which might make me feel confident that some of you had breathed this prayer. O may the good Master who alone can drive these nails home use the Gospel hammer now! I do entreat you, by the shortness of life, by the certainty of death, by the glories of Heaven, by the terrors of Hell--seek the Lord and let this be, now, the voice of your seeking, "Speak, Lord! Speak to ME! Speak NOW! For Your servant hears."

III. We will turn to the third view of the text as the PRAYER OF AN EARNEST BELIEVER. I was led to select this text by finding it in the letter of one who has just been taken away from our classes and from our Church. She was about to change her position in life in some degree and the one prayer that seemed to be ever upon her mind was a prayer for guidance. She often prayed, "Speak, Lord; for Your servant hears." She said she felt that God was about to do something for her, but she did not know what it was. She little dreamed that she was so near the kingdom and the Glory, but yet that was the prayer, "Speak, Lord; for Your servant hears."

This is a very appropriate prayer for the Christian when he is in providential difficulty. You may not know what you ought to do tomorrow. Of two courses open to you, there may appear certain advantages connected with each and some friends have urged you to one plan and other friends have urged you to the other. Now if you have used your best judgment and have endeavored to direct your steps according to the Word of God, you may expect, in answer to prayer, to have a distinct directive from God. Not, perhaps, from the month of man, though that sometimes happens, for even from this pulpit cases which we never heard of have been unraveled and dilemmas with which the preacher was never acquainted have notwithstanding been solved by what seemed but a stray word, meant by God to be a finger, pointing out to His children--"This is the way, walk you in it."

Take your difficulty to the God of Wisdom. Spread it out before Him, and having divested yourself of your own will in the matter--having solemnly desired to know the will of God and not your own wish--you may then expect by some means or other--and God has different ways of doing it--to have an answer from the Most High. Take this as your prayer, "Speak, Lord; for Your servant hears." We want in our daily life more fully to acknowledge God in all our ways. We are, I am afraid, in this age, in great danger of forgetting God. We ought to acknowledge Him in the common transactions of the day, or else like the Israelites with the Gibeonites, we may be betrayed in the simplest transaction and deceived to our lasting injury.

Take your matters before the God of Abraham and the Urim and Thummim shall yet speak to you. Domino dirige nos, "Lord direct us," is a good motto, not only for the City of London, but for the citizens of Heaven! In points of doctrine this desire humbly uttered may bring us much light. God's Word is not all of it alike plain! Sometimes when you have heard conflicting views--this preacher earnestly declaring a doctrine and another denouncing it--you may be somewhat nonplussed. My advice to you is take your difficulty before God in prayer and say, "Speak, Lord; for Your servant hears."

Do not ask God to confirm your opinion, but ask Him to make your opinion conformable with His Truth. Do not go to God's Word to find texts to support your tenets, but go to Scripture for texts and tenets, too. Remember that to a true Christian no doctrine has any force upon the conscience, except as it comes with, "thus says the Lord." Follow the simple Word of God as you find it and rest assured you shall have the Light of the Holy Spirit streaming upon the sacred page. And as you read it you shall hear the Master say, "This is My Word." He shall make it come to your soul with such power that you shall have no doubt about it if your heart cries, "Speak, Lord; for Your servant hears."

The same course should be adopted by every Christian in matters of practice. I am afraid there are many Christians who have stopped their ears up. They may not hear the teaching of portions of the Word. There are certain Scriptures which they can never abide. I have heard of one who never would read the eighth or ninth chapter of Romans at family prayer. I have heard of another who invariably omitted that chapter in Acts about the Ethiopian eunuch--a very awkward chapter, I confess, for anyone to read who has not accepted Believer's Baptism.

You will find many professed Christians in these day's who do not like to meddle with certain questions because they are more than half afraid that a little examination would prove them to be in the wrong. They cannot bear us to put a finger upon their Prayer Book, their creed, or their Church for they know that they will not bear a close inspection. They will say, "Well, there are faults everywhere, let well enough alone." But the fact is that they do not care what the Truth of God is so long as they can be comfortable and go with the fashion of the day.

Some whom we gladly hope to be true Christians think Truth unimportant and are not prepared to "search the Scriptures whether these things are so or not." Brethren, I would be afraid of my own doctrine if I dared not test it both by Scripture and sound argument. If my foundation would not stand a good shaking, I would be afraid that it was not made of very solid material. Some people cry out if we say a word about their Church. It is a sign that their Church is hardly strong enough to endure an honest encounter. Pasteboard and tinsel always pray for peace and charity, but solid metal fears not the day of battle!

Be it ours to court the sunlight and above all let us beseech the Lord our God to be our light, for in His Light we shall see light. Sitting at the feet of Jesus is our position! To receive of His Words is our sweet employ! As melted wax is fitted to receive the impression of the seal, so let us be ready to accept the Master's teaching. Let His faintest Word bind us as with bonds of steel. And let his minutest Precept be precious as the gold of Ophir. "To obey is better than sacrifice and to hearken than the fat of rams." Let it be our chosen privilege to be taught of the Lord and to maintain His Truth. Here, in this House of Prayer, let us offer the petition, "Speak, Lord; for Your servant hears."

As for matters of duty--again, be ever ready to follow the Master and Him alone. Not Luther, nor Calvin, neither Wesley, nor Whitfield is to be your Rabbi. Jesus alone is Master in the kingdom of Heaven! Whatever he says to you, do it! But where you have not His warrant, let no traditions or ancient customs make you stir so much as a single inch.

IV. We will close by observing that our text seems to us rightly to express THE SPIRIT OF A DEPARTING CHRISTIAN, There he lies upon the bed--his pulse grows fainter. The many pains of death afflict him. His eyes are beginning to glaze, but a brighter light than that of earth has dawned upon him! And while the outward man decays, the inward man begins to renew his youth. I think I see him when his pains are worst. He desires to go, but he is willing to remain as long as his Master wills. He says sometimes, "I ill can brook delay," but the next moment he checks himself and he says, "Not my will, but Yours be done."

He sits patiently upon the river's bank, expecting that his Master shall open the passage for him to pass over dry shod. He is praying, "Speak, Lord and the sooner You will speak the more shall I rejoice. Say unto me, 'Come up here.' Speak, Lord; for Your servant hears"--hears now better and more distinctly than he ever did hear before! He is now nearer to You. The ear is almost closed to the din and bustle of the world, while in secret silence of the mind it waits the still small voice of Your lips. Speak, Lord and say, "Plunge into the river," and I will cheerfully do so if You will but come and meet me. "Speak, Lord; for Your servant hears."

I think I hear that Divine and mysterious voice, which, in fact, none can hear but those whose day of Glory is dawning. The messenger has come and whispered in the ear of the dying saint and I pray you, mark his joy for you may see it! Its light illuminates the countenance. The eye sparkles with supernatural Glory. "Now," says the man of God, "my journey is over and I am almost Home." "Now," says the expiring Sister, "it is victory, glory, triumph! The white horse is at the door--my Master bids me mount and ride in triumph, following my Lord Jesus and all the conquering ones. The Master is come in His garments of salvation and calls for me!"

The physician says he could see the death-change and the nurse bears the same witness, but the well-instructed Believer calls it the life-change and reads the true meaning of the mysterious transformation. He sees a something which is a prediction of the coming Glory! He marks those beaming eyes and that celestial smile. Now strange words drop from the lips--sometimes words that are scarcely lawful for a man to utter, by reason of the high and awful Glory of their meaning. Now come the shouts of victory over death--now the note of defiance of the grave! The soul has left all care, all doubt, all fear behind! Its foot is not only on the Rock of Ages, but on that part of the rock which is on the other side of Jordan. And the soul cries with transport, "I am with Him! Another moment I shall be in His arms! I see Him! The angelic chariots wait for me--I step into them and I ride to the kingdom! Victory, victory, victory, through the blood of the Lamb!"

Something like this was the departing scene of our beloved Sister who has gone Home this week and something like this, I trust, will be your departure and mine. But it will not, it cannot be thus with us unless we are resting upon Christ--

Spurgeon's Sermons Volume 10: 1864

"None but Jesus--none but Jesus Can do helpless sinners good."

Lo! These fifteen years have I been preaching Jesus' name and preaching nothing but His name and it has a savor about it sweeter than ever! And if I had but one word more to speak, I think this should be it--none but Jesus, none but Jesus!

Oh, fly to Him if you would have a blessed death and a glorious resurrection! Look out of yourselves away from your frames and your feelings! Look away from ceremonies, from priests and from all men! Look only to the bleeding wounds of my Master! Trust Jesus expiring on the Cross and trust in Him alone! You shall find eternal happiness in Him! The Lord bless you with His richest blessing, for Jesus' sake. Amen.

God's Strange Choice

DELIVERED ON SUNDAY MORNING, AUGUST 28, 1864,
BY THE REV. C. H. SPURGEON,
AT THE METROPOLITAN TABERNACLE, NEWINGTON.

"For you see your calling, Brethren, how that not many wise men after the flesh, not many mighty, not many noble, are called. But God has chosen the foolish things of the world to confuse the wise, and God has chosen the weak things of the world to confuse the things which are mighty. And base things of the world and things which are despised has God chosen, yes, and things which are not, to bring to nothing things that are: that no flesh should glory in His Presence." -- 1 Corinthians 1:26-29.

THE Apostle Paul had been led to make the confession that Christ Jesus was despised both by Jew and Gentile. He confessed that this was no cause of stumbling to him, for what others counted foolishness he believed to be wisdom and rejoiced that the foolishness of God was wiser than men, and the weakness of God stronger than men! Lest, however, any of the Corinthian Church should be confused by the fact that Christ was despised, the Apostle goes on to show that it was the general way of God's proceeding to select means which men despised in order that by accomplishing His purpose through them, He might have all the Glory.

And he reminds them, for the proof of this, to the one instance of their own election and calling--"You see your calling, Brethren," says he, "how that not many wise men after the flesh, not many mighty, not many noble, are called." But you, the poor, illiterate, the despised, you have been called--still for the same reason--that God may be All in All and that no flesh may glory in His Presence. It is clear to everyone who will observe either Scripture or fact that God never did intend to make His Gospel fashionable! The very last thing that was ever in His thoughts was to select the elite of mankind and gather dignity for His Truth from the gaudy trappings of rank and station.

On the contrary, God has thrown down the gauntlet against all the pride of manhood. He has dashed mire into the face of all human excellency. And with the battle-ax of His strength He has dashed the escutcheon of man's glory in two. "Overturn! Overturn! I overturn!" seems to be the very motto of the Lord of Hosts and shall be so "until He shall come whose right it is to reign and He will give it Him," for His is the kingdom and the power and the glory, forever and ever. There is no doctrine more truly humbling than the doctrine of election. And it was for this reason that the Apostle Paul refers to it--that the disciples at Corinth might be quite content to follow the humble and despised Cross-bearing Savior because the election of Grace consists of the humble and despised, who, therefore, cannot be ashamed to follow One, who, like themselves, was despised and rejected of men.

Coming then, at once to our text, we observe in it very clearly, first, the Elector. Secondly, a strange election. Then the elected. And when we have considered all these a little, we shall pause over the reasons which God has given for His election--that "no flesh should glory in His Presence."

I. First, then, let us this morning soar aloft upon the wings of thought to consider for awhile, the ELECTOR. Some men are saved and some men are not saved. It remains as a fact never to be questioned that some enter into eternal life and some pursue the evil way and perish. How is this difference caused? How is it that some mount to Heaven? The reason why any sink to Hell is their sin and only their sin. They will not repent, they will not believe in Christ, they will not turn to God--and therefore they perish willfully by their own act and deed.

But how is it that others are saved? Whose will is it that has made them to differ? The text three times most peremptorily answers the question. It says not "man has chosen," but it says three times, "God has chosen, God has chosen, God has chosen." The Grace which is found in any man, and the glory and eternal life to which any attain are all the gifts of God's election and are not bestowed according to the will of man. This will be clear to any thoughtful person if we first of all turn to facts. Wherever we find a case of election in the Old Testament, it is manifestly God who makes it. Go back, if you will, to the very earliest time. Angels fell--a multitude of bright spirits who surrounded the Throne of God and sang His praises were deceived by Satan and fell into sin.

The great serpent drew with him the third part of the stars of Heaven--they fell from their obedience--they were condemned to chains and to eternal fire forever. Man also sinned. Adam and Eve broke the covenant with God and ate of the forbidden fruit--were they condemned to eternal fire? No, but God, in the plenitude of His Grace, whispered this promise in the woman's ear--"The seed of the woman shall bruise the serpent's head." Some men are saved, but no devils are saved. Why? Did man make the difference?

Silence, you vain boaster who dreams of such a thing! It is God Himself who testifies, "I will have mercy on whom I will have mercy and I will have compassion on whom I will have compassion." It was from such sovereignty as this that the Lord virtually declared, "I purpose and decree that of the race of man I will save a multitude that no man can number. They shall be the vessels of My mercy, while yonder angels, once My servants but now traitors to their liege Lord, shall, without hope forever, experience the terror of My righteousness, the majesty of My justice." Here no one ever raises a question. I have never heard the most ultra-Pelagian enter a plea for the devil!

I have heard of Origen who did seem to plead that Satan should be included in the general law of mercy, but very few persons nowadays talk so. Here is an instance of election--some of the human race saved and the angelic race left forever to perish. Who could have made this distinction but Jehovah Himself? And we must say there of our favored race, "God has chosen." We are not at a loss to see the same discriminating Sovereignty at work among the individuals of our own race. All men were in the Patriarchal age sunk in heathenism with but a few exceptions. There were a few Patriarchs who still, chosen of God, held fast to the pure worship of the Most High.

The Lord determined to adopt a special people who should read the Oracles of God--preserve and maintain His Truth. He selected Abram as the progenitor of the chosen race. Did Abram choose God, or did God call and choose Abram? Was there anything naturally in Abram to entitle him to be the servant of the Most High? We have very plain proof in Scripture that there was not. He was, on the contrary, described as a Syrian ready to perish and his race was like the rest, tainted, to say the least, with idolatry. Nevertheless he was called out of the east and made the father of the faithful by God's own special will.

What was there, let me ask you, in the Jews? Why should they be blessed with Prophets and the sacrifices and the rites and ordinances of true worship, while all the nations were left to bow down before gods of wood and stone? We can only say God has done it--His will lights upon the race of Israel and leaves the rest in sin. Take any particular case of Divine Grace mentioned in the Old Testament, as, for instance, that of David. Do we find that David chose the throne and set himself apart to be the chosen messenger of God to Israel? Was there some manifest fitness in the youngest son of Jesse? No, on the contrary, men had chosen his Brethren! Even Samuel said, "Surely the Lord's Anointed is before me," as he saw Abinadab go forth.

But God sees not as man sees and He had chosen the ruddy David that he might be king in Jesurun. So might we multiply cases but your own thoughts will spare my words. All the facts of the Old Testament go to show that God does as He wills in the armies of Heaven and among the inhabitants of this lower world. He pulls down and He raises up! He lifts the beggar from the dunghill that He may set him among the princes of His people. God has chosen, God has chosen and not man! "It is not of him that wills, nor of him that runs, but of God that shows mercy."

Let us look at the matter in another light. Clearly the Lord's will must determine the matter if we consider His office and position towards men. God's office. God is a King. Shall not the king have his own will? Men may set up a constitutional monarchy and they are right in so doing. But if you could find a being who was perfection itself, an absolute form of government would be undeniably the best. At any rate, God's government is absolute and though He never violates righteousness, for He is Holiness and Truth itself, yet He regards this jewel of His crown as being the dearest that He has. "I Am and there is none beside Me."

He gives no account of His matters. Unto all questions He gives this answer, "No but, O man, who are you that replies against God? Shall the thing formed say to him that formed it, Why have you made me thus? Has not the potter power over the clay, of the same lump to make one vessel unto honor and another unto dishonor?" The absolute position of God as King demands that, especially in the work of salvation, His will should be the great determining force.

Let us state the case and you will see this. A number of criminals are shut up in prison, all deserving to die. Their guilt is the same. If they are all taken out to execution tomorrow morning, no one can say a word against justice. Now if some of these persons are spared, to whose discretion should the sparing be left? To their own? True, it will be most gracious to send a messenger and bid them all come forth and receive sparing mercy if they will come. But suppose they all, with one consent, refuse to be saved? Suppose that having been invited to be saved, every one of them refuses to accept pardon? If in such a case superior mercy determines to override their wicked wills and sets itself to secure that some of them shall effectually be saved, with whom shall the choice be left?

If it were left with them they would all of them still choose death rather than life. Therefore it were useless to leave it with them. Besides, to leave the attribute of mercy in the hand of the criminal would be an exceedingly strange mode of procedure. No, let it be the king! Let it be the king who shall say who it is that shall be spared in mercy and who shall die according to the rule of justice. The position of God as King and the position of men as criminals demands that salvation shall depend upon the will of God. And truly we may better leave it with His will than with our own, for He is kinder to us than we are to ourselves! He is more full of love to man than man is of love to himself. He is Justice, he is Love! Justice in full-orbed splendor--love in unbounded might. Mercy and Truth have met together in Him and kissed each other! And it is well, it is well! It is best of all that the rule and management of salvation should be left with Him.

We will now introduce to you a few figures made use of in Scripture in connection with the work of salvation and I think you will then see that the will must be left with God. Salvation consists in part of an adoption. God adopts sinners who were heirs of wrath, even as others, into His family. Who is to have authority in the matter of gracious adoption? The children of wrath? Surely not. And yet all men are such! No. It stands to nature, to reason, to common sense that none but the parent can have the discretion to adopt.

As a father I have a right, if any desire to enter my family, to adopt or to refuse to adopt the persons in question. Certainly no person can have a right to force himself upon me and say that I shall be considered as his reputed parent. The right must, I say, according to reason and common sense, lie with the parent. And in adoption it must be God who chooses His own children. The Church, again, is called a building. With whom does the architecture of the building rest? With the building? With the stones? Do the stones select themselves? Did that stone over yonder in the corner choose its place? Or that which is buried there in the foundation, did it select its proper position? No. The architect alone disposes of his chosen materials according to his own will. And thus, in building the Church which is the great House of God, the great Master Builder reserves to Himself the choice of the stones and the places which they shall occupy.

Take a yet more apparent case. The Church is called Christ's Bride. Would any man here agree to have any person forced upon him as his bride? There is not a man among us who would, for a single moment, so demean himself as to give up his rights to choose his own spouse! And shall Christ leave to human will who His Bride shall be? No. But my Lord Jesus, the Husband of the Church, exercises the Sovereignty which His position permits Him and selects His own Bride.

Again, we are said to be members of Christ's Body. We are told by David that in God's Book, "all our members were written, which in continuance were fashioned when as yet there was none of them"--thus every man's body had its members written in God's Book. Is Christ's Body to be an exception to this rule? Is that great Body of Divine manhood, Christ Jesus, the mystical Savior--is that to be fashioned according to the whims and wishes of free will--while other bodies, vastly inferior, have their members written in the Book of God? Let us not dream thus--it were to talk idly and not to know the meaning of the metaphors of Scripture! It seems clear to me, according to the figures and illustrations of Scripture, that the final choice of the men to be saved must be left with God.

Is not this, dear Friends, most agreeable to your own experience? I am sure it is to mine. There may be some who hate this doctrine--there may be some whose very mouths foam while they hear us talk of the Sovereignty of God! But I confess it touches a secret spring in my nature which can compel me to weep when nothing else can. There is a something in my consciousness which seems to say, "He must have chosen me, for I never could have chosen Him." Determined to live in sin was I! Prone to wander! Fond of iniquity! Drinking down evil as the ox drinks his fill of water! And now saved by Grace! Dare I for a moment impute that salvation to my own choice?

I do choose God most freely, most fully, but it must be because of some previous work upon my heart changing that heart--for my unrenewed heart never could have chosen Him. Beloved, do you not feel at this very time that the natural bent of your thoughts is away from God? If the Grace of God were taken from you, what would you be? Are you not just like the bow which is bent when the string keeps it so--but cut that string and it flies back to its old place? Would it not be so with you? Would you not at once return to your former ways if the mighty Grace of God were withdrawn from you? Well then, you clearly see that if even now you are regenerate, your corrupt nature does not choose God, much less could it have chosen Him when there was no new nature to keep it in check and to control it. My Master looks into your faces, O you His people, and He says, "You have not chosen Me, but I have chosen you." And we each feel that He wakes the echo of our hearts, for we reply, "Yes, Lord, we have not chosen You in our natural estate, but You have chosen us and unto Your free and Sovereign choice be honor forever and ever."

II. May we feel the present influences of the Holy Spirit while we dwell upon the ELECTION ITSELF. The Lord is about to choose a people who shall give honor to the Cross of Christ. They are to be redeemed by precious blood and they are to be in some sense a worthy reward for the great sufferings of Jesus. Now observe how strange is the choice He makes. I read with astonishment, "He has not chosen many wise men after the flesh, not many mighty, not many noble."

If man had received the power of choosing, these are just the persons who would have been selected! "But God has chosen the foolish things of the world to confuse the wise, and God has chosen the weak things of the world to confuse the things which are mighty. And base things of the world and things which are despised." If man had governed the selection, these are the very persons who would have been left out! The choice is very strange, very strange! I believe even in Heaven it will be the subject of eternal wonder, and except for the reasons given in our text, we should have been at a loss to know why it was that with Divine scorn He passed by the palaces of haughty kings and looked after the base-born and the lowly to make them the subjects of His choice.

Observe that while it is strange, it has this peculiarity about it--it is directly contrary to human choice! Man chooses those who would be most helpful to him--God chooses those to whom He can be the most helpful. We select those who may give us the best return--God frequently selects those who most need His aid. If I choose a friend, the tendency is to him because of a certain serviceableness that there may be in him to myself--this is the selfishness of man. But God chooses His friends according to the serviceableness which He Himself may render to the chosen one! It is the very opposite way of choosing.

We select those who are best because they are most deserving. God selects those who are worst because they are least deserving so that His choice may be more clearly seen to be an act of Grace and not of merit. I say it is clearly contrary to man's way of choosing. Man selects the most beautiful, the most lovely. God, on the contrary, seeing the blackness and filthiness of everything which is called lovely, will not select that which is called so, but takes that which even men discover to be unlovely. God then makes it lovely with the loveliness which He puts upon it. Strange choice! Is this the manner of men, O Lord?

You will observe that the choice is very gracious--oh, how gracious in your case and in mine! It is gracious even in its exclusion. It does not say, "Not any wise men," it only says, "Not many," so that the great ones are not altogether shut out. Grace is proclaimed to the prince and in Heaven there are those who on earth wore coronets and prayed. How blessed is the condescending Grace of the choice--it takes the weak things, the foolish things. One would have thought that when God said, "No," to the prince, He must have said it in order that He might be excused from giving mercy to anybody--for we are in the habit of saying, "Well, we have refused Mr. So-and-So and he is a much more important person than you are, therefore I cannot give the favor to you. Why, the king asked me such a favor and I would not do it for him! Do you think I would do it for you?"

But God reasons another way. He passes by the king on purpose that He may meet with the beggar. He leaves the noble that He may lay hold upon the base. He passes over the philosopher that He may receive the fool. Oh this is strange! It is unbelievably strange! It is marvelous! Let us praise Him for this wondrous Grace! Oh, how encouraging is this for us this morning. Some of us cannot boast of any pedigree. We have no great learning. We have no wealth. Our names are all unknown to fame. But oh, what a mercy! He has been pleased to choose just such foolish things as we are! Such despised creatures as ourselves! Such things that are not--to bring to nothing the things that are!

Not to spend all the time this morning in simply pointing out this strange choice and wondering at it, let it suffice us to observe that every Christian who finds himself chosen will think his own election to be the strangest choice that could have been made--

"What was there in you that could merit esteem, Or give the Creator delight? 'It was even so, Father!' you ever must sing, 'Because it seemed good in Your sight.'"

III. We will now turn to THE ELECTED. The chosen ones are described negatively and positively. They are described negatively. "Not many wise men after the flesh." Observe, it does not say, "Not many wise men merely," but, "not many wise men after the flesh," because God has chosen truly wise men, since all His people are made truly wise, but it is the "wise after the flesh" that God has not chosen. The "sophoi," as the Greek calls them. The philosophers, the men who pretend to have wisdom or to love wisdom. The cunning, the metaphysical, the great students, the keen observers, the rabbis, the doctors, the infallibles--the men who look down with profound scorn upon the illiterate and call them idiots--and treat them as if they were the dust beneath their feet. These are not chosen in any great number.

Strange, is it not? And yet a good reason is given. If they were chosen, why then they would say, "Ah, how much the Gospel owes to us! How our wisdom helps it!" If the first twelve Apostles had all been twelve doctors or sages, everybody would have said, "Why, of course the Gospel was mighty! There were the twelve picked wise men of Judea, or of Greece, to support it." But instead of that, God looks round the creeks and bays after twelve poor fishermen who are as ignorant as any He can find! He takes them and they become the Apostles. They spread the Gospel and the Gospel has the glory and not the Apostles. The wise are passed by in the wisdom of God.

Observe next, He says, "Not many mighty." The wise might have forced their way to Heaven by their wit, one would think, but there they are with their blind learning, fumbling for the latch of Heaven's door--while the illiterate and simple-minded have already entered in! Blind wisdom gropes in the dark and like the wise men, it goes to Jerusalem in vain, while poor, humble shepherds go to Bethlehem and find Christ at once! Here comes another order of great men! The mighty men, the valiant champions, the princes, his Imperial Highness, the conquerors, the Alexanders, the Napoleons-- are not these chosen? Surely when the king becomes a Christian, he can, with his sword, compel others to receive Christ--why not choose him?

"No," says the text, "not many mighty." And you see why--because if the mighty had been chosen, we should all say, "Oh, yes, we see why Christianity spreads so--it is the good temper of the sword and the strength of the arm that wields it." We can all understand the progress of Mohammedanism during its first three centuries. Men like Ali and Khaled were ready to strike whole nations! They leaped upon their steeds, waved their scimitars over their heads and dashed against hundreds, fearless of the fight! And it was only when they met such men as our Richard Coeur de Lion that Mohammedanism was put back for awhile. When the sword met sword, then they that took it perished with it!

Christ chose no warriors--one of his disciples used a sword but it was to very poor effect--for he only cut off a man's ear and Christ touched that and healed it! And that was the end of poor Peter's fighting. So the glory of the Lord's conquests does not depend upon the mighty! God has not chosen them. Then he says, "Not many noble," by which he means those with a long pedigree, descended through a line of princes, from the loins of kings, with blue blood in their veins. "Not many noble," for nobility might have been thought to stamp the Gospel with its prestige. "Oh, yes, there is no wonder that the Gospel spreads when My Lord This and the Duke of That bends to it."

Yes, but you see there were few such in the early Church. The saints in the catacombs were poor, humble men and women. And it is a very memorable fact that out of all the inscriptions in the catacombs of Rome written by the early Christians, there is scarcely one which is properly spelled. But nearly all of them are as bad in grammar as they are in spelling--a clear proof that they were scratched there by poor, illiterate, ignorant men who were then the defenders of the faith and the true conservators of the Grace of God. We have thus the negative side--not the wise, not the mighty, not the noble.

But now the positive side and I want your careful attention to the expression used by the Apostle. "God has chosen the foolish men"?--no, it does not say so! "The foolish things," as if the Lord's chosen were not by nature good enough to be called men, but were only "things." As if the world looked down on them with such scorn that they did not say, "Who are these men?" but, "Who are these things?" Once or twice in Luke you will observe Christ called a "fellow," but the word "fellow" is put in italics, not being in the original--for the Greek runs, "as for this, we know not where He is." They did not say what He was, did not even call Him a "fellow," though the translation is very good, as giving a correct idea to the ordinary reader.

They seem to say of Christ, "as for this--well, call Him a beast if you like--a thing if you like." And so Paul has put it here--"the foolish things"--not simply foolish men whom the world should consider to be unlearned, ignorant, stupid dolts led by the nose and easily deceived into believing this or that, but--"foolish things," which are nothing but stupidity has God chosen.

Next, God has chosen, "The weak things." Do observe the word "things" with care. They were not merely weak men, but the world thought them weak things. "Ah," said Caesar in the hall, if he said anything at all about it--"Who is King Jesus? A poor wretch who was hanged upon a tree! Who are these men that are setting Him up? Twelve poor fishermen who could hardly muster one single talent of gold between them! Who is this Paul who raves so lustily about Christ? A tentmaker! Who are his followers? A few despised women who meet him at the waterside! Is Paul a philosopher? No, he was publicly laughed at upon Mars' Hill--they counted what he said to be mere babbling." No doubt Caesar thought they were altogether too inconsiderable to be worthy of his notice. But the "weak things" God has chosen.

Observe the next description, "The base things." The word there signifies things without pedigree, things without a father, things which cannot trace their descent--no Sir Harry, no Right Honorable is akin to them. Their father was a nobody and their mother was a nothing. Such were the Apostles of old--they were the base things of this world and yet God chose them! As if this were not enough, it is written, "Things that are despised," sneered at, persecuted, hunted about, or treated with what is worse--with indifference--which is worse than scorn. They are not worth notice-- inconsiderable fools--pass them by and let them alone." And yet these had God chosen!

Once more, as if to outdo all and sum it up in one word, "Things that are not" has God chosen. Nothings, nonentities. "Oh," says the man of the world, "yes, I did just hear that there were a parcel of fanatics of that kind." "Oh," says another, "I never even heard of them! I never mix myself up in any way with such a low-bred, vulgar set. Did they ever have a bishop among them? A Right Reverend Father in God?" "No, nothing of the kind, Sir, they are foolish, base, mean, despised. The world, therefore, rejects them." "Yet," says God, "/choose them." They are the very people that He chooses.

Now observe that what was true in Paul's day is true now. The Bible does not change as years revolve. And in 1864 God chooses the things which are despised just as much as in the year 64. And He will yet let the world know that those who are ridiculed, styled fanatics, thought to be mad and wicked, are yet, after all, His chosen ones destined for God and for His Truth to rally the sacramental host of the elect and win for God the battle of the last day! In this we are not ashamed to glory, that God chooses the things which are despised. And we can take our place with the despised people of God, hopeful to partake in the election of His Sovereign Grace.

IV. To conclude, you have THE REASONS WHY GOD HAS CHOSEN THESE PEOPLE. There are two reasons given--the first is the immediate reason. The second is the ultimate reason. The first, or immediate reason, is contained in these words, "God has chosen the foolish things of the world to confuse the wise. And God has chosen the weak things of the world to confuse the things which are mighty. And base things of the world and things which are despised has God chosen, yes, and things which are not, to bring to nothing things that are."

Observe, then, the immediate reason is, first, to confuse the wise. For one wise man to confuse another wise man is remarkable. For a wise man to confuse a foolish man is very easy. But for a foolish man to confuse a wise man--ah, this is the finger of God! You know how it was with the first Apostles. A philosopher listened to Paul and when he had heard him, he said, "There is nothing in it! Perfect foolishness! Pack of stuff from beginning to end! No need for us to take the trouble to answer it." Years rolled on and when the philosopher was getting very gray, that pestilent heresy of Christianity was spreading everywhere--his own daughter was converted--even his wife used to steal out at night to the secret assembly!

The philosopher could not understand it. "There," he said, "I proved without a doubt that it was all stupidity and yet these people stick to it! I answered all their arguments, did I not? I not only answered and confuted, but I clinched my arguments in such a way that I thought I had put an end to the folly altogether. But here I see it, in my own household!" Sometimes the philosopher had to stand with tears in his eyes and say, "I feel it in my own heart, it has beaten me. It has confused me--I could reason and rationalize and beat poor Paul--but Paul has beaten me! What I thought was folly has confused my wisdom."

Within a few centuries after the death of Christ the Christian religion had spread over the civilized world, while Paganism which had all the philosophy of the east and of the west to back it up, had fallen into disrepute and was laughed to scorn. Again, God has chosen the weak things to confuse the mighty. "Oh," said Caesar, "we will soon root up this Christianity--off with their heads." The different governors hastened one after another of the disciples to death, but the more they persecuted them the more they multiplied. The proconsuls had orders to destroy Christians. The more they hunted them, the more Christians there were, until at last men pressed to the judgment seat and asked to be permitted to die for Christ!

The State invented torments. They dragged the saints at the heels of wild horses. They laid them upon red-hot gridirons. They pulled off the skin from their flesh piece by piece. Thy were sawn in two. They were wrapped in skins and daubed with pitch--and set in Nero's gardens at night to burn. They were left to rot in dungeons. They were made a spectacle to all men in the amphitheatre. The bears hugged them to death. The lions tore them to pieces--wild bulls tossed them upon their horns--and yet Christianity spread! All the swords of the legionaries which had put to rout the armies of all nations and had overcome the invincible Gaul and the savage Briton could not withstand the feebleness of Christianity--for the weakness of God is mightier than men.

If God had chosen the mighty men they would have turned round and said, "God is beholden to us." If He had chosen the wise they would have said, "Our wisdom has done it." But when He chooses the foolish and weak, where are you now, philosopher? Has not God laughed you to scorn? Where are you now, O sword and spear? O mighty man who wields them, where are you? God's weakness has routed you! It is said that He chose the things that are not to bring to nothing the things that are. This is even more than confusing them to bring them to nothing--"the things that are."

What were they in the Apostle's days? Jupiter seated upon his lofty throne holds the thunderbolt in his hand. Saturn reclined as the father of the gods. Venus delighted her votaries with her lustful pleasures. The chaste Diana sounded her horn. Here comes Paul with, "there is no God but God and Jesus Christ whom He has sent." He represents "the things that are not." So contemptible is the heresy of Christianity that if a list were made out of the religions of different countries, Christianity would have been left out of the catalog!

But see the result! Where is Jupiter now? Where Saturn? Where Venus and Diana? Except as classical names in the dictionaries of the learned, where are they? Who bows before the shrine of Ceres in the day of harvest, or who lifts up his prayers to Neptune in the hour of storm? Ah, they have gone. "The things that are" have been brought to nothing by the "things that are not." Let us reflect that what is true in Paul's day is true today. This year 1864 shall see repeated the miracles of the olden times--the things that are shall be brought to nothing by the things that are not.

See in Wickliffe's time. The things that are were the holy crucifixes in every Church. St. Winifred, St. Thomas of Canterbury are worshipped by all the multitudes of Englishmen. There comes My Lord Archbishop through the street! Yonder is the pope worshipped by thousands and there is the Virgin adored of all! What do I see? A solitary monk at Lutterworth begins to preach against the begging friars. And in preaching against them he finds out the Truth of God and begins to preach that Christ is the only ground of salvation and that they who trust in Him are saved!

Well, it was such a contemptible thing that at first they did not care to persecute him. It is true at last he was brought up before His Grace at St. Paul's, but there was a strong man, one John O'Gaunt, who came up with him and said a word or two in his rough way and Wickliffe was allowed to sit down. And though condemned, he returns to his parish of Lutterworth. "The thing that was not!" It was not worthy to be put down by blood, it would die out of itself. Did it die out? Where are your holy crucifixes today? Where is St. Thomas of Canterbury, where are St. Agnes and St. Winifred?

Ask our Puseyite friends, for they, alone, can tell you. True consorts of the moles and of the bats--they know where the idols have been cast--they seek to restore the superstitions of the past. But by God's Grace their task shall be no easy one. The present system of English superstition, with its water regeneration, its baptismal grace, its confirmations and its giving of grace through bread and wine--though it is attacked by those who are things that are not--shall yet cease to be! And the Truth as it is in Jesus--the pure simple faith that no man is a priest distinctively above his fellows--that every Christian is a priest unto God. The pure Truth, I say, that no water can necessarily bring the Spirit of God with it, and that no outward forms and rites have any virtue in them--apart from the faith of those who receive them--these, backed by the Spirit of God, shall bring to nothing the things that are.

Here we fall back upon the strength of God. I would not have God's champions stronger. Brethren, were they stronger they would take glory to themselves. Let them be weak and let them be few and let them be despised. Their fewness, their poverty, their weakness shall make the shout of praise unto the eternal Conqueror yet more loud and the music shall be undivided! There shall only be this refrain, "Not unto us, not unto us, but unto Your name give glory for Your Truth's sake." This, then, is God's immediate object in choosing foolish things, weak things, things that are not--to confuse the mighty.

But His ultimate reason is "that no flesh may glory in His Presence." I want you to notice that last sentence and I have done. He does not say, "that no man." No, the text is in no humor to please anybody. It says, "that no flesh." What a word! What a word, I say! Here are Solon and Socrates, the wise men. God points at them with His finger and calls them, "flesh." Flesh is sold in the shambles, is it not? Dogs tear it. Worms eat it--nothing but flesh. There is Caesar with his imperial purple cast about him and as he stands erect, the mighty Imperator, how the Praetorian guards unsheathe their swords and shout, "Great is the Emperor! Long may he live!" "Flesh," says God's Word, "flesh."

Here they come tramping on, hundreds in a line, the strong legionaries of Rome! Who can stand against their swords and shields? "Flesh," says the Word, "flesh." Here are men whose sires were of royal lineage and grandsires of imperial rank and they can trace back the long line of honor. "Flesh," says God, "flesh, nothing but flesh." Dogs' meat. Worms' meat when God wills it. "That no flesh may glory in His Presence." Do you see, then? God puts this stamp upon us all-- that we are nothing but flesh--and He chooses the poorest flesh and the most foolish flesh and the weakest flesh--that all the other flesh that is only flesh and only grass may see that God pours contempt on it and will have no flesh glory in His Presence!

Now what is your spirit this morning towards this subject? Do you kick at it? Do you say you cannot bear it? I am afraid you want to glory in God's Presence. Your views of things and God's views of things differ, and therefore you need to have a new heart and a right spirit. But, on the contrary, do you say this morning, "I have nothing to boast of. I would not glory in Your Presence, but I would lie in the very dust and say, 'Do with me as You will' "? Sinner, do you feel that you are nothing but flesh and sinful flesh? Are you so broken before God that you feel let Him do as He will with you? Do you know that He will be just and you can only appeal to His Sovereign Mercy?

Then God and you are one, you are reconciled! I can see that you are reconciled. When God and you are agreed that God should reign, then God is agreed that you should live! Sinner, touch the scepter of His Grace! Jesus Crucified stands before you now and bids you look to Him and live! That you are bid to look is an instance of mighty Grace--and that you are enabled to look this morning will be a wonder of Divine love for which you will have to bless Him in time and eternity! And now may that God whose name we have sought to honor this morning bless these stammering of ours, for Jesus' sake. Amen.

The Prodigal's Reception

DELIVERED ON SUNDAY MORNING, SEPTEMBER 4, 1864,
BY C. H. SPURGEON,
AT THE METROPOLITAN TABERNACLE, NEWINGTON.

"And he arose and came to his father. But when he was yet a great way off, his father saw him and had compassion, and ran and fell on his neck and kissed him." -- Luke 15:20.

THERE he is! He is as wretched as misery itself--as filthy as his brute associates who could satisfy themselves with husks--while he could not. His clothes hang about him in rags and what he is on the outside, that he is within. He is disgraced in the eyes of the good and the virtuous remember him with indignation. He has some desires to go back to his father's house but these desires are not sufficient to alter his condition. Mere desires have not scraped the filth from him, nor have they so much as patched his rags. Whatever he may or may not desire, he is still filthy, still disgraced, still an alien from his father's house--and he knows it--for, by God's Grace, he has come to himself.

He would have been angry if we had said as much as this before, but now we cannot describe him in words too black. With many tears and sighs he assures us that he is even worse than he appears to be and that no man can know all the depth of the vileness of his conduct--he has spent his living with harlots--he has despised a generous parent's love and broken loose from his wise control. He has done evil with both his hands to the utmost of his strength and opportunity. There he stands, notwithstanding this confession, just what I have described him to be--for even though he has said within himself, "I have sinned"--yet that confession has not removed his griefs.

He acknowledges that he is not worthy to be called a son--and it is true he is not. But his unworthiness is not removed by his consciousness of it nor by his confession of it. He has no claims to a father's love. If that father shuts the door in his face, he acts with justice. If he shall refuse so much as to speak a single word, except words of rebuke, no one can blame the father, for the son has so sadly erred. To this the son utters no denial. He confesses that if he is cast away forever, he well deserves it.

This picture, I know, is the photograph of some who are now present. You feel your vileness and sinfulness but you cannot look upon that sense of vileness as in any way extenuating or altering your condition. You feel, but you cannot plead, your feelings. You confess this morning that you have desires towards God but that you have no rights to Him-- you cannot demand anything at His hands. If your soul were sent to Hell, His righteous Law approves it and so does your own conscience! You can see your rags. You can mark your filthiness. You can long for something better but you are no better. You have no more claims than you used to have upon God's mercy. You stand here today a self-convicted offender against the loving kindness and holiness of God.

I pray that to such of you as are in this shape I may be the bearer of a message from God to your soul this morning. O you who know the Lord, put up earnest and silent prayers just now that my message may come home with power to troubled consciences! And I beseech you, for your own profit, look back to the hole of the pit where you were dug and to the miry clay where you were drawn and remember how God received you! And while we talk of what He is willing and able to do to the far-off sinners, let your souls leap with joyous gratitude at the recollection of how He received you into His love and made you partakers of His Grace in days gone by.

There are two things in the text--the first is the condition of many a seeker--he is yet a great way off. And then, secondly, the matchless kindness of the Father towards him.

I. First, dear Friends, THE CONDITION OF SUCH A SEEKER--HE IS YET A GREAT WAY OFF. He is a great way off if you consider one or two things. Remember his need of strength. This poor young man had, for some time, been without food--brought so very low that the husks upon which the swine fed would have seemed a dainty to him if he could have eaten them. He is so hungry that he has become emaciated and to him every mile has the weariness of leagues within it.

It costs him many pains and sore griefs to drag himself along, even though it is but an inch. So the sinner is a long way off from God when you consider his utter need of strength to come to God. Even such strength as God has given him is very painfully used. God has given him strength enough to desire salvation but those desires are always accompanied with deep and sincere grief for sin. The point which he has already reached has exhausted all his power and all he can do is fall down before Jesus and say--

"Oh, for this no strength have I, My strength is at Your feet to lie."

He is a great way off, again, if you consider his need of courage. He longs to see his father but yet the probabilities are that if his father should come he would run away--the very sound of his father's footsteps would act upon him as they did on Adam in the garden--he would hide himself among the trees. So instead of crying after his father, the great father would have to cry after him--"Where are you, poor fallen creature? Where are you?" His need of courage, therefore, makes the distance long--for every step up to now has been taken as though into the jaws of death. "Ah," says the sinner, "it must be a long time before I can dare to hope--for my inequities have gone over my head so that I cannot look up."

Are you, then, in alarm and dread this morning? Do your prayers seem to have been no prayers at all? When you think of God, does terror come over your mind and you feel that you are a long, long way from Him? Do you imagine that it is not likely that He will hear your cries nor give heed to your words? You are yet a great way off. You are a great way off when we consider the difficulty of the way of repentance. John Bunyan tells us that Christian found, when he went back to the arbor after his lost roll, that it was very hard work going back. Every backslider finds it so and every penitent sinner knows that there is a bitterness in mourning for sin comparable to the loss of one's only son.

A drowning man feels no great pain--the sensations of drowning are even said to be pleasant. It is only when the man is being restored to life--when the blood begins to make the veins tingle because life leaps there, when once again the nerves are sensitive--then, we are told, the whole body is full of many agonies! But then they are the agonies of life! And so the poor penitent feels the goal must be a great way off, for if he had to feel as he now feels, even for a month, it were too long a time. And if he had to journey many miles as he now journeys, so painfully, with such bleeding feet, it would, indeed, be a great way!

Let us look into this matter and show that while the road seems long on this account, it really is long if we view it in a certain light. There are many seeking sinners who are a great way off in their life. I think I see the man now and hear him thus bewail himself--"I have left off my drunkenness. I could not sit where I used to sit by the hour. I thank God I shall never be seen reeling through the streets again, for that groveling lust I detest. I have given up Sabbath-breaking and I am found in God's House. And I have endeavored, as much as I can, to renounce the habit of swearing, but still I am a great way off--I do not feel as if I could yet lay hold of Christ for I cannot master my own passions yet.

"An old companion stopped me this week and he had not long been talking before I found the old man was in me and the old lusting came up into my face again. Why, Sir, the other day an oath came rapping out. I thought 1 had got over it, but I had not--I am a great way off. When I read of what saints are and observe what true Christians are, I do feel that my conduct is so inconsistent and so widely apart from what it ought to be that I know that I am a great way off."

"Ah, dear Friend, you are. And if you had to come to God by the way of your own righteousness you would never reach Him for He is not thus to be found. Christ Jesus is the way! He is the safe, sure, and perfect road to God. He who sees Jesus has seen the Father. But he who looks to himself will only see despair. The road to Heaven by Mount Sinai is impassable by mortal man, but Calvary leads to Glory! The secret places of the stairs are in the wounds of Jesus.

Again, you feel yourself a great way off as to knowledge. "Why," you say, "before I felt thus I considered myself a master of all theology. I could twist the doctrines round my fingers. When I listened to a sermon I felt quite able to criticize it and to give my judgment. Now I see that my judgment was about as valuable as the criticism of a blind man upon a picture, for I was without spiritual' sight. Now I feel myself to be a fool! I do know what sin means, but only to a degree. Even here I feel that I am not conscious of the heinousness of human guilt. I have heard the doctrine of the Atonement of Christ and I thank God I know it to some degree, but the excellence and glory of the Substitutionary Sacrifice which Christ offered--I confess I do not fully comprehend."

The sinner's confession now is that instead of understanding Scripture he finds he needs to go, like a child, to school to learn the A B C of it. "O Sir," he says, "I am a great way off from God for I am so ignorant, so foolish. I seem to be but as a beast when I think of the deep things of God." Ah, poor Soul! Poor young wandering Brother! I wonder not that it seems so to you for the ignorance of the carnal man is, indeed, fearful, and only God can give you light. But He can give it to you in a moment and the distance between you and Him upon the score of ignorance can be bridged at once and you may comprehend even today, with all saints, what are the heights and depths and know the love of Christ which passes knowledge.

In another point many an earnest seeker is a great way off, I mean in his repentance. "Alas," says he, "I cannot repent as I ought. If only I could feel the brokenness of heart which I have heard and seen in some! Oh, what would I give for penitential sighs! How thankful would I be if my head were waters and my eyes fountains of tears. If I could even feel that I was as humble as the poor publican and could stand with downcast eyes and beat upon my breast and say, 'God be merciful to me a sinner.' But, alas, I have been a hearer of the Word for years and all the progress I have made is so little that while I know the Gospel is true, I do not feel it. I know myself to be a sinner, and sometimes I mourn over it, but my mourning is so superficial, my repentance is a repentance that needs to be repented' of O Sir, if God would use the heaviest hammer that He had--if He would but break my heart--every broken fragment should bless His name!"

"I wish I had a genuine repentance. Oh, how I pant to be brought to feel that I am lost and to desire Christ with that vehement desire which will not take a denial. But in this point my heart seems hard as Hell-hardened steel. Cold as a rock of ice. It will not, cannot yield though wooed by Divine love. Adamant itself may run in liquid torrents, but my soul yields to nothing. Lord, break it! Lord, break it!"

Ah, poor Heart. I see you are a great way off, but do you know if my Lord should appear to you this morning and say to you, "I have loved you with an everlasting love," your heart would break in a moment?--

"Law and terrors do but harden, All the while they work alone. But a sense of blood-bought pardon, Can dissolve a heart of stone."

Great way off as you are, if the Lord pardons you while yet callous and consciously hard of heart, will you not then fall at His feet and commend that great love with which He loved you--even when you were dead in trespasses and sins?

Yes, but I think I hear one say, "There is another point in which I feel a great way off, for I have little or no faith. I have heard faith preached every Sunday. I know what it is--I think I do--but I cannot reach it. I know that if I cast myself wholly upon Christ I shall be saved. I quite comprehend that He does not ask anything of me, any willings, or doings, or feelings--I know that Christ is willing to receive the greatest sinner out of Hell if that sinner will but come and simply trust Him. I have tried to do it! Sometimes I have thought I had faith, but then, again, when I have looked at my sins I have doubted so dreadfully that I perceive I have no faith at all! There are bright moments with me when I think I can say--

'My faith is built on nothing less, Than Jesus' blood and righteousness,' but oh, when I feel my corruptions within rising upon me, I hear a voice saying, 'The Philistines are upon you, Samson,' and straightway I discover my own weakness. I have not the faith that I want! I am a great way off from it and I fear that I shall never possess it."

Yes, my Brethren, I perceive your difficulty, for I have felt the sorrow of it myself. But oh, my Lord, who is the Giver of faith--who is exalted on high to give repentance and remission of sins--can give you the faith you so much desire and can cause you, this morning, to rest with perfect confidence upon the work which He has finished for you! To gather up all things in one word, the truly penitent sinner feels that he is yet a great way off in everything. There is no point upon which you can talk with him but it will be sure to lead to a confession of his deficiency. Begin to put him in the scales of the sanctuary and he cries, "Alas, before you put in the weights I can tell you I shall be found wanting." Bring him to the touchstone and he shrinks from it! "No," he says, "but I cannot endure any sort of trial--

'All unholy and unclean, I am nothing else but sin.'"

Look, look how well my Master has pictured your case in this parable--"Yet a great way off"--yet covered with rags! Yet polluted with filth! Yet in disgrace! Yet a stranger to your Father's house! There is only this one point about you--you have your face towards your Father--you have a desire towards God and you would, oh, you would if you could, lay hold upon eternal life! But you feel too far off for anything like comfortable hope.

Now I must confess I feel many fears about you who are in this state. I am afraid lest you should come so far and yet go back--for there are many whom we thought had come as far as this and yet they have gone back, after all. Oh, remember that desires after God will not change you so as to save you! You must find Christ! Remember that to say, "I will arise," is not enough, nor even to arise--you must never rest till your Father has given you the kiss--till He has put the best robe on you.

I am afraid lest you should rest satisfied and say, "I am in a good state. The minister tells us that many are brought to such a state before they are saved. I will stop here." My dear Friend, it is a good state to pass through, but it is a bad state to rest in. I pray you never are content with a sense of sin, never be satisfied with merely knowing that you are not what you ought to be. It never cures the fever for a man to know he has it. His knowledge is in some degree a good sign, for it proves that the fever has not yet driven him to delirium. But it never gives a man perfect health to know that he is sick. It is a good thing for him to know it, for he will not otherwise send for the physician--but unless it leads to that he will die whether he feels himself to be sick or not.

A mere consciousness that you are hungry while your father's hired servants have bread enough to spare will not lessen your hunger--you need more than this. You are a great way off and I beseech you remember what the danger is lest you should stop here or should lose what sensibility you already have. Perhaps despair may come upon you. Some have committed suicide while under a sense of the greatness of their distance from God because they dared not look to the Savior. Our prayers shall go up to God that the second part of our text may come true to you and that backsliding and despair alike may be prevented by the speedy coming of God dressed in the robes of Grace to meet your guilty soul and give you joy and peace through believing!

II. Secondly--and O, may the Master give us His help--we have to consider THE MATCHLESS KINDNESS OF THE HEAVENLY FATHER. We must take each word and dwell upon it. First of all we have here Divine observation. "When he was yet a great way off his father saw him." It is true He has always seen him. God sees the sinner in every state and in every position. Yes, and sees him with an eye of love, too--such a chosen sinner as is described in this text--not with complacency, but with affection God looks upon His wandering chosen ones.

I say that Father saw His son when he spent his living with harlots. He saw him with deep sorrow when he gladly would have filled his belly with the husks which the swine ate. But now, if there can be such a thing as for Divine Omniscience to become more exact, the Father sees him with an eye full of a more tender love, a greater care. "His father saw him." Oh, what a sight it was for a father to see! His son, it is true, but his reprobate son, who had dishonored his father's name--brought down the name of an honorable house to be mentioned among the dregs and scum of the earth!

There he is! What a sight for a father's eye! He is filthy, as though he had been rolling in the mire. And his fine clothing has long ago lost its fine colors and hangs about him in wretched rags. The father does not turn away and try to forget him--he fixes his full gaze upon him. Sinner, you know that God sees you this morning! Sitting in this house you are observed by the God of Heaven. There is not a desire in your heart unread by Him, nor a tear in your eye which He does not observe! I tell you He has seen your midnight sins. He has heard your cursing and your blasphemies and yet He has loved you notwithstanding all that you have done!

You could hardly have been a worse rebel against Him and yet He has noted you in His book of love and determined to save you! The eye of His love has followed you wherever you have gone. Is there not some comfort here? Why could not he see his father? Was it the effect of the tears in his eyes that he could not see? Or was it that his father was of quicker sight than he? Sinner, you can not see God for you are unbelieving and carnal and blind, but He can see you! Your tears of penitence block up your sight, but your Father is quick of eye and He beholds you and loves you now. In every glance there is love.

"His father saw him." Observe this was a loving observation, for it is written, "His father saw him." He did not see him as a mere casual observer. He did not note him as a man might note his friend's child with some pity and benevolence, but he marked him as a father, alone, can do. What a quick eye a parent has! Why, I have known a young man come home, perhaps for a short holiday--the mother has heard nothing, not even a whisper, as to her son's conduct and yet she cannot help observing to her husband, "There is a something about John which makes me suspect that he is not going on as he should do. I do not know, my Husband," she says, "what it is. But yet I am sure he is getting among bad companions." She will read his character at once. And the father notes something, too. He cannot precisely say what, but he knows it to be cause for anxiety.

But here we have a Father who can see everything and who has as much of the quickness of love as He has of the certainty of knowledge. He can, therefore, see every spot and bruise and note every putrefying sore. He sees His poor son right through as though he were a vase of crystal--He reads his heart--not merely the telltale garments. Not merely the sorrowful tale of the unwashed face and those clouted shoes, but He can read his soul! He understands the whole of his miserable plight. O poor Sinner, there is no need for you to give information to your God for He knows it already! You need not pick your words in prayer in order to make your case plain and easy to understand! God can see it! All you have to do is to uncover your wounds, your bruises and your putrefying sores and say, "My Father, You see it all, the black tale you read in a moment. My Father, have pity upon me."

The next thought to be well considered is Divine compassion. "When he saw him he had compassion on him." Does not the word "compassion" mean suffering with, or, fellow-suffering? What is compassion, then, but putting yourself into the place of the sufferer and feeling his grief? If I may say so, the father put himself into the son's rags and then felt as much pity for him as that poor ragged prodigal could have felt for himself. I do not know how to bring up your compassion this morning unless it is by supposing that it is your own case.

I saw, not many hours ago, a young man who brought to my mind the prodigal in this case--his face marked with innumerable lines of sin and wretchedness. His body lean and emaciated, his clothes close-buttoned--his whole appearance the very mirror of woe. He knocked at my door. I knew his situation--I cannot hurt him by telling it. He had disgraced his family--not once or twice--but many times. At last he drew out what money he had in the business of a respectable family, came up to London with four hundred pounds and in about five weeks spent it all!

And, without a single farthing to help himself, he often begs for bread. And I fear that he has often crept at night into the parks to sleep and thus has brought aches and pains into his bones which will be with him till he dies. He wanders the streets by day a vagabond and a reprobate. I have written to his friends--the case has been put before them. They will not have anything to do with him. And considering his shameful conduct, I do not wonder. He has no father and no mother left. If he were helped beyond mere food and lodging, as far as we can judge, it would be money thrown away.

If he were helped, he seems so desperately set on wickedness that he would do the same again. Yet, as I think, I can but desire to see him have one more chance, at least, and he would have it, I doubt not, if his father yet lived. But others feel the fountains of their love are stayed. As I think of him, I cannot but feel that if he were a son of mine and I were his father and I saw him in such a case come to my door, whatever the crime was that he had committed, I must fall upon his neck and kiss him. The biggest sin could not put out forever the sparks of paternal love. I might condemn the sin in sharpest terms and most severely. I might regret that he had ever been born and cry with David, "O my son Absalom, my son, my son Absalom! Would God I had died for you!" but I could not shut him out of my house, nor refuse to call him my child. My child he is and my child he shall be till he dies.

You feel just now that if it were your child you would do the same. That is how God feels towards you, His chosen, His repentant child. You are His child--I hope so, I trust so--those desires which you have in your soul towards Him make me feel that you are one of His children. And as God looks out of Heaven He knows what you mean. What is it? What shall I say? No, I need not describe, but, "Like as a father pities his children, so the Lord pities them that fear Him." He will have compassion upon you. He will receive you to His bosom--be of good courage, for the text says, "He had compassion on him."

Notice and observe carefully the swiftness of this Divine love. "He ran." Probably he was walking on the top of his house and looking out for his son, when one morning he just caught a glimpse of a poor sorry figure in the distance. If he had been anything but the father he would not have known it to be his son. But he looked and looked again, till at last he said, "It is he! Oh, what marks of famine are upon him and of suffering, too!" And down comes the old gentleman--I think I see him running downstairs and the servants come to the windows and the doors, and say, "Where is Master going? I have not seen him run at that rate for many a day."

See, there he goes! He does not take the road for that is a little round about. But there is a gap through the hedge and he is jumping over it! The straightest way that he can find he chooses. And before the son has had time to notice who it is, he is on him and has his arms about him, falling upon his neck and kissing him! I remember a young prodigal who was received in the same way. Here he stands. It is I, myself. I sat in a little Chapel, little dreaming that my Father saw me. Certainly I was a great way off.

I felt something of my need of Christ, but I did not know what I must do to be saved. Though taught the letter of the Word, I was spiritually ignorant of the plan of salvation. Though taught it from my youth up, I knew it not. I felt, but I did not feel what I wished to feel. If ever there was a soul that knew itself to be far off from God, I was that soul. And yet in a moment, in one single moment--no sooner had I heard the words--"Look unto Me and be you saved, all the ends of the earth"--no sooner had I turned my eyes to Jesus Crucified than I felt my perfect reconciliation with God! I knew my sins were then forgiven!

There was no time for getting out of my heavenly Father's way--it was done and done in an instant! And in my case, at least, He ran and fell upon my neck to kiss me. I hope that will be the case this morning--before you can get out of this place--before you can get back to your old doubts and fears and sighs and cries--I hope here the Lord of Love will run and meet you and fall upon your neck and kiss you!

After noticing thus--observation, compassion and swiftness, do not forget the nearness--"He fell upon his neck and kissed him." This I can understand by experience, but it is too wonderful for me to explain. "He fell upon his neck." He did not stand at a distance and say, "John, I would be very glad to kiss you but you are too filthy. I do not know what may be under those filthy rags. I do not feel inclined to fall upon your neck just yet--you are too far gone for me. I love you, but there is a limit to the display of love. When I have got you into a proper state, then I may manifest my affection to you but I cannot just now, while you are so very foul."

Oh, no! But beforehe is washed He falls on his neck--thereis the wonder of it! I can understand how God manifests His love to a soul that is washed in Jesus' blood and knows it. But how He could fall upon the neck of a foul, filthy sinner as such! There it is--not as sanctified, not as having anything good in himself--but as nothing but a filthy, foul, desperate rebel, God falls upon his neck and kisses him! Oh, strange miracle of love! The riddle is solved when you remember that God never had looked upon that sinner as he was in himself--He had always looked upon him as he was in Christ!

And when He fell upon that prodigal's neck, He did, in effect, only fall upon the neck of His once-suffering Son, Jesus Christ, and He kissed the sinner because He saw him in Christ! He did not see the sinner's loathsomeness, but saw only Christ's loveliness and therefore kissed him as He would have kissed his Substitute. Observe how near God comes to the sinner! It was said of that eminent saint and martyr, Bishop Hooper, that on one occasion a man in deep distress was allowed to go into his prison to tell his tale of conscience. But Bishop Hooper looked so sternly upon him and addressed him so severely, at first, that the poor soul ran away and could not get comfort until he had sought out another minister of a gentler aspect.

Now Hooper really was a gracious and loving soul, but the sternness of his manner kept the penitent off. There is no such stern manner in our heavenly Father! He loves to receive His prodigals. When He comes there is no, "Hold off!" No "Keep off!" to the sinner. No, He falls upon his neck and He kisses him! There is yet another thought to be brought out of the metaphor of kissing. We are not to pass that over without dipping our cup in the honey. In kissing his son the father recognizes relationship. He said, with emphasis, "You are my son," and the prodigal was--

"To his Father's bosom pressed, Once for all a child confessed."

Again, that kiss was the seal of forgiveness. He would not have kissed him if he had been angry with him. He forgave him, forgave him all. There was, moreover, something more than forgiveness--there was acceptance--"I receive you back into my heart as though you were worthy of all that I give to your elder brother and therefore I kiss you." Surely this was also a kiss of delight--as if he took pleasure in him, delighting in him, feasting his eyes with the sight of him and feeling more happy to see him than to see all his fields and the fatted calves and all the treasures that he possessed! His delight was in seeing this poor restored child. Surely this is all summed up in a kiss.

And if this morning my Father and your Father should come out to meet mourning penitents, in a moment He will show you that you are His children! You shall say, "Abba, Father," on your road to your own house! You shall feel that your sins are all forgiven, that every particle has been cast behind Jehovah's back! You shall feel today that you are accepted--as your faith looks to Christ you shall see that God accepts you--because Christ your Substitute is worthy of God's love and God's delight! I trust you shall, this very morning, delight yourself in God, because God delights Himself in you and you shall hear Him whisper in your ear, "You shall be called Hephzibah . . . for the Lord delights in you."

I wish I could picture such a text as this as it ought to be. It needs some tender, sympathetic heart--some man who is the very soul of pathos--to work out the tender touches of such a verse as this! But, oh, though I cannot describe it, I hope you will feel it and that is better than description. I come not here to paint the scene, except to be the brush in God's hand to paint it on your hearts. There are some of you who can say, "I do not want descriptions, for I have felt it. I went to Christ and told Him my case and prayed Him to meet me. Now I believe on Him and I have gone my way rejoicing in Him."

We will just say these words and have done. In summing up, one may notice that this sinner, though he was a great way off, was not received to full pardon and adoption and acceptance by a gradual process, but he was received at once! He was not allowed to enter into the outhouse first and to sleep in a barn at night. And then afterwards allowed to come, sometimes, and have his meals with the servants in the kitchen. And then afterwards allowed to sit at the end of the table and by degrees brought near. No. The father fell on his neck and kissed him the first moment! He gets as near to God, as he ever will, the very first moment! So a saved soul may not enjoy and know so much, but he is as near and dear to God the first moment he believes as he ever will be--a true heir of all things in Christ and as truly so as even when he shall mount to Heaven to be glorified and to be like his Lord.

Oh, what a wonder is this! Fresh from his pigsty, was he not? Yet in a father's bosom! Fresh from the swine with their grunts in his ears and now he hears a father's loving words! A few days ago he was putting husks to his mouth and now it is a father' s lips that are on his lips. What a change and all at once! I say there is no gradual process in this, but the thing is done at once--in a moment he comes to his father--his father comes to him and he is in his father' s arms!

Observe again, as there was not a gradual reception, there was not a partial reception. He was not forgiven on conditions. He was not received to his father's heart if he would do so-and-so. No. There were no "ifs," no "buts." He was kissed and clothed and feasted without a single condition of any kind whatever. No questions asked--his father had cast his offenses behind his back in a moment and he was received without even a censure or a rebuke. It was not a partial reception. He was not received to some things and refused others. He was not, for instance, allowed to call himself a child, but to think of himself an inferior. No! He wears the best robe. He has the ring on his finger. He has the shoes on his feet. And he joins in eating the fatted calf.

And so the sinner is not received to a second-class place, but he is taken to the full position of a child of God. It is not a gradual nor yet a partial reception. And once more, it is not a temporary reception. His father did not kiss him and then turn him out at the back door. He did not receive him for a time, and then afterwards say to him, "Go your way. I have had pity upon you. You have now a new start--go into the far country and mend your ways." No, the father would say to him what he had already said to the elder brother, "Son, you are ever with me and all that I have is yours."

In the parable, the son could not have the goods restored for he had spent his part. But in truth itself and matter of fact, God makes the man who comes in at the eleventh hour equal with the one who came in at the first hour of the day--He gives every man the penny. And He gives to the child who has been the most wandering the same privileges and ultimately the same heritage which He gives to His own who have been these many years with Him and have not transgressed His Commandments.

That is a remarkable passage in one of the Prophets, where he says, "Ekron as a Jebusite," meaning that the Philistine, when converted, should be treated just the same as the original inhabitants of Jerusalem--that the branches of the olive which were grafted in have the same privileges as the original branches! When God takes men from being heirs of wrath and makes them heirs of Grace they have just as much privilege at the first as though they had been heirs of Grace twenty years! In God's sight they always were heirs of Grace and from all eternity He viewed His most wandering sons--

"Not as they stood inn Adam's fall, When sin and ruin covered all. But as they'll stand another day, Fairer than the sun's meridian ray."

O, I would to God that He would in His infinite mercy bring some of His own dear children home this day and He shall have the praise, world without end. Amen.

Jesus Meeting His Warriors

DELIVERED ON LORD'S DAY MORNING, SEPTEMBER 11, 1864,
BY C. H. SPURGEON,
AT THE METROPOLITAN TABERNACLE, NEWINGTON.

"And Melchizedek king of Salem brought forth bread and wine: and he was the priest of the Most High God. And he blessed him and said, Blessed be Abram of the Most High God, possessor of Heaven and earth: and blessed be the Most High God, which has delivered your enemies into your hand. And he gave him tithes of all." -- Genesis 14:18-20.

What a splendid type is Abram, in the narrative before us, of our Lord Jesus Christ! Let us read this story of Abram in connection with our Savior and see how full of meaning it is. Our Lord Jesus Christ, in the abundance of His love, had taken us to be His brothers. But we, through our sin, had gone into the land of Sodom and Jesus Christ dwelt alone in His safety and His happiness, enjoying the Presence of God. The hosts of our enemies, with terrible force and cruel fury, carried us away captives. We were violently borne away, with all the goods which we possessed, into a land of forgetful-ness and captivity forever.

Christ, who had lost nothing by this, nevertheless being a "brother born for adversity," pursued our haughty foes. He overtook them. He struck them with His mighty hand--He took their spoil and returned with crimsoned vesture, leading captivity captive. He restored that which He took not away. I think, as I see Abram returning from the slaughter of the four kings, I see in him a picture of a greater than Abram, returning "from Edom, with dyed garments from Boz-rah, traveling in the greatness of His strength" who answers to my inquiry of who is he? "I that speak in righteousness, mighty to save." Abram was that righteous man raised in the East, to whom God gave his enemies as driven stubble to his bow.

And so the Lord Jesus has driven our enemies like chaff over to the wind, for they fled at the Presence of Jehovah Jesus, and by the valor of the atoning Lamb they have been utterly broken in pieces forever. Let that thought dwell with you--it may furnish you with matter for meditation at your leisure. We shall this morning rather consider Abram as the type and picture of all the faithful. He was the father of the faithful. And in his history you have condensed--as I think-- history of all faithful men. You will scarcely find a trial which will befall you which has not in some respect happened to Abraham.

I will not say that he was tempted in all points like as we are, but he was tempted in so many points that he well deserves to be called the father of the faithful--being partaker of flesh and blood even as all the children are who belong to his faithful family. Observe then, in handling our subject in this manner, that Believers are frequently engaged in warfare. Notice, secondly, that when they are thus engaged they may expect to be met by their Lord, the great Melchizedek! And remember, thirdly, that when they are favored with an interview with Him and are refreshed by Him as with bread and wine, then, like Abram, they consecrate themselves anew and as Abram gave tithes of all, even so do they.

I. We mention, then, what you must all know right well by experience--you who are God's people--that the Believer is often engaged in warfare. This warfare will be both within and without--within with the innumerable natural corruptions which remain--with the temptations of Satan, with the suggestions of his own wicked heart. And without he will frequently be engaged in warfare, wrestling "not against flesh and blood, but against principalities, against powers, against the rulers of the darkness of this world, against spiritual wickedness in high places."

The peculiar case of Abram leads me to remark that sometimes the Believer will be engaged in warfare, not so much on his own account as on the account of erring Brethren who, having gone into ill company, are by-and-by carried away captive. It was no quarrel of Abram's--it was Lot's matter. Lot had gone to Sodom. Instead of standing in the separated path of the true Believer he had joined himself to the world. And when evil days came Lot was carried away captive with the rest.

Abram cared little enough for the king of Sodom--I do not suppose he would have taken his sword from the sheath for all the men who dwelt in Admah or Zeboim. But for Lot's sake, seeing him in ill company and in danger, he draws the sword. And sometimes, Brethren, when we see those who are God's servants putting themselves into alliance with evil systems, we find them carried away captive and taken where we believe their hearts would never go. And so we feel compelled to come out and draw the sword against the common enemy of Christ and of all His people. And though they may heartily wish that we would let them alone in their sin and let them be quiet in their evil union, we see into what spiritual capacity it leads them and we cannot be silent. We must draw the sword when conscience and when God demand it and never sheath it until God's work is done.

However, this rarely occurs. For the most part the Christian spends his sword's edge upon his own spiritual foes-- and truly we have enough of these. What with pride, sloth, lust--what with the arch enemy of souls and his insinuations and blasphemies--the lust of the eyes, the pleasures of this world and the pride of life--what with enemies who come upon us even from Providence in the shape of temptations arising out of our trials and our vocations, we ought to carry our sword always drawn! And, above all, we should ever carry the shield of faith and take the weapon of all-prayer.

The Christian is never to feel himself at ease so long as he is on this side of Jordan. This is an enemy's land. Expect a foe behind every bush. Look to hear the shot come whistling by and each night adore almighty Grace that you have not fallen prey to your cruel and remorseless foes. The Christian is engaged throughout his whole life as a soldier--he is so called in Scripture--"A good soldier of Jesus Christ." And if any of you take the trouble to write out the passages of Scripture in which the Christian is described as a soldier and provision is made for his being armed and directions given for his warfare, you will be surprised to find there are more of this character than concerning any other metaphor by which the Christian is described in the Word of God!

His chief and main business seems to be, like his Master, to bear witness for the Truth of God. "For this purpose was I born and sent into the world." And though in himself a man of peace, yet he can say with his Master, "I came not to send peace but a sword." Wherever he goes he finds that his presence is the signal for war--war within him and war outside him--he is a man of peace and yet a man of war because a man of peace. The Christian is engaged in warfare with sin, Satan, error and falsehood and sometimes he is called to fight for erring friends.

Observe that this war is one against powerful odds. The four kings mentioned in this chapter were all great sovereigns. From what little we can glean from profane history, they appear to have been very mighty monarchs and they must have been assisted by very valiant armies to have struck the giants whose names are mentioned in the opening verses. They appear to have carried away the five kings of the plain with the greatest possible ease. Yet here is Abram, who has little more than three hundred of his own armed servants at his call--and yet he ventures against the embattled thousands of the kings of nations!

Such is the warfare of the Christian--he has to contend against foes far too many for him--he is like the worm that is to arise and thrash the mountain. He is little and despised and if he measures his own strength he will find it to be perfect weakness. And yet, for all this, he anticipates a victory and like Abram hastens to the holy war. Carefully notice that as it is a battle of fearful odds, it is one which is carried on in faith. Abram did not venture to this fight with confidence in his own strength, or reliance upon his own bow. He went in the name of the Lord of Hosts. Faith was Abram's continual comfort. Sometimes his faith failed, as it will in the best, but still, the spirit of the man's life was a simple confidence upon God--whom he had not seen--but whose voice he cheerfully obeyed.

The Christian is to carry on his warfare in faith. You will be vanquished, indeed, if you attempt it by any other method! Brethren, there is not a sin in your heart which will not master you if you seek to fight it by resolutions of your own. Faith in the precious blood of Christ must win you the victory and the world will laugh you to scorn if you assail it with any other weapons than such as Calvary will furnish you. "This is the victory which overcomes the world, even our faith." And if you ask Faith what weapon she uses, her reply is, "They overcame through the blood of the Lamb." Live near to Jesus Christ. Rest upon the power of His Atonement and the prevalence of His plea--and then go forward against every enemy without and every foe within--and you shall be more than a conqueror!

In this great battle, carried on by faith, Abram had a right given him from God and the promise of God's Presence virtually in that right. What business had Chedorlaomer to come to Canaan? Had not Jehovah said to Abram, "All this land will I give unto you"? Therefore he and his confederate monarchs were neither more nor less than intruders. For thirteen years they might have exercised sovereignty over the cities of the plain, but those cities and everything around them belonged virtually to Abram. It is true they would have laughed at the very idea of Abram's claiming the whole land of Canaan, but that claim was nevertheless valid in the court of Heaven and the Patriarch, by Divine right, was heir of all the land.

Christian, you are, by virtue of a Covenant made with you to drive out every sin as an intruder. "Sin shall not have dominion over you: for you are not under the Law, but under Grace."

You are to drive out every error, for you are a servant of the Truth of God and the Truth alone has a right to live and a right to exist. And in fighting this lawful warfare you may expect that the right arm of the Most High God--the Possessor of Heaven and earth--will be bared that He may show Himself strong on behalf of all those who are valiant for His Truth and for His name. Fear not! The battle is not yours, but God's. You go not to a warfare at your own charges. And though Hell may roar, as it will, and earth be all in arms--and your own heart may fail you and your flesh, when you take counsel with it, makes you feel a coward-- yet say, "In the name of God will I destroy them," and go forward and conquer! "They compass me about like bees," said David, "yes, like bees they compass me about: but in the name of God will I destroy them." And what David did you shall do through David's God!

Yet more--the Christian is engaged in a conflict in which he walks by faith and leans upon God. But yet it is a conflict in which he uses all means, calls in all lawful assistance and exerts himself with all vigor and speed. Abram did not sit still and say, "Well, God will deliver Lot. He has promised to keep His servants as the apple of His eye." Oh, no, that is not faith--that is foolish presumption! Abram did not take his time about it and go marching leisurely after the foe, nor did he go without the assistance of his friends, Aner and Eshcol and Mamre. So the Christian, if he sees any method by which he may be assisted in overcoming sin or promoting the Truth of God, uses it with wisdom and discretion. He trusts in God as though he did nothing himself and yet he does everything as if all depended upon himself. He knows that good works cannot save him and he equally knows that he is not saved unless there are some fruits of good works.

He understands that the means of Grace cannot of themselves convey Grace to him and yet at the same time he never despises them but looks to find a blessing in the use of them. He understands that the ministry and private prayer and the searching of the Scriptures cannot save him--but he also understands that thus using them helps which God has given him and diligently pressing forward and setting a bold face before the foe--he is in the path of God's ordinances and may expect to have God's help. And do observe, dear Friends, yet again, that Abram marching on thus with activity and using discretion--by attacking his enemies at night rather than by day--did not cease until he had gained a complete victory over them.

It was not enough to strike them at one corner of their host, nor merely to deliver Lot. Now that he is come out against them he will win a sure and decisive victory. O Beloved, you and I are never to sit still and say, "It is enough." Have I struck my drunkenness? Have I overcome by blaspheming habits? Am I delivered from Sabbath-breaking? Have I become honest and chaste? Yet this is not where I should stop. Have I sought to bring down my self-conceit, my pride, my sloth? It is well and good but let me never be satisfied with any attainment short of absolute perfection. We do not believe we shall be perfect in this life, but we will never be satisfied until we are. "Onward," is the Christian's motto! As long as there is one sin which is not removed we will fight and cry and groan and go to the Cross concerning it.

As long as there is one soul in this world unsaved, we will wrestle with the Mighty One of Jacob to stretch out His hand to save it! So long as there remains one error upon earth--so long as we have a tongue to speak and God gives us Grace--we will bear our witness against it. In this battle there is no keeping back our hand till the victory is wholly won. We must bring back the goods and the men and the women and Lot and the whole company--the victory must be complete. More than conquerors must we be through Him who has loved us. Let us anticipate the time when it shall be so.

O Brethren, I think I see the victors ascending the starry steeps in triumphal state! Christ at their head rides gloriously! He who loved them leads the van. The gates open to Him as the great Conqueror who has led their captivity captive. I think I see the glad faces of all those soldiers of the Cross as they enter the portals of eternal peace--

"I ask them where their victory came. They with united breath, Ascribe their conquest to the Lamb, Their triumph to His death."

See, then, Beloved, you are this morning soldiers! You are to fight by faith in God. However tremendous the power of your adversaries, you are not to fear since God is with you. You are to fight using discretion as your armor-bearer, but you are also to couple this with perseverance, continuing faithful to the end, for only those who overcome shall sit upon the Throne of God forever!

We have thus, perhaps, said enough concerning this first point and now may the Holy Spirit bedew with His holy influences while we talk of the second, for otherwise it will be only talk.

II. While engaged in such earnest spiritual contention the Believer may expect to see his Lord. When Shadrach, Me-shach and Abednego were fighting Christ's battles in the fiery furnace, then the Son of Man appeared to them. As in the building of Jerusalem in troublous times they had the sword in one hand and the trowel in the other, so our Lord Jesus Christ, while He teaches us to use the sword, takes care to edify and build us up in the faith at the same time! He understands that warriors require strengthening meat and that especially when they are under stern conflict they need extraordinary comforts that their souls may be stayed and refreshed.

Why does Jesus Christ, as set forth here under the type of Melchizedek, appear unto His children in times of conflict? Answer--He comes to them, first, because they are weary. In every conflict which the child of God has to wage, it is not the private person who goes to the warfare--it virtually is Christ fighting--Christ contending. It is a member of Christ's body laboring against Christ's enemy for the glory of the Head. Christ the Head has an intense feeling of sympathy with every member, no matter how humble. Since there is a vital union between Christ and every member, there is also an undying sympathy. And whenever, Brothers and Sisters, you contend for the faith till you grow weary, Jesus Christ will be sure to give you some proof of His close communion with you.

The martyrs proclaim that they never had such communion with God anywhere as among the caverns of the hills, or the swamps of the woods to which they were exiled for Christ. And even on the rack, in extremity of torture, or even upon the gridiron in the heat of the fire--even there the sweet Presence of Christ has been overpoweringly delightful to them so that they almost lost the sense of pain! You, Lord, do send a plenteous rain whereby You refresh Your heritage when it is weary! Spend your strength for God, Brothers and Sisters, for when fainting seems inevitable, then shall come such a sweet renewing of your strength that, like an eagle, you shall stretch your wings and mount aloft to commune with God in solitary joys! Christ, your Melchizedek, will meet you in your conflicts if He never did before!

The King of Peace met the returning warrior for another reason. Abram was probably flushed with victory and this is a very dangerous feeling for any child of God. When the seventy disciples returned to Christ they said, with evident exultation, "Lord, even the devils are subject unto us." But Jesus Christ sweetly and gently rebuked them by saying, "Nevertheless, rejoice not in this, but rather rejoice because your names are written in Heaven." The true secret of a Christian's joy is not to be his conquest over sin or over error, but the Person of his Lord Jesus Christ! The Lord knows that His people, if they are successful even in spiritual warfare--when they have used the best of means and felt the best of motives--are, nevertheless, very liable to the intoxication of pride. And therefore He either sends "a thorn in the flesh," or else, what is better still, He comes Himself!

I am persuaded, Beloved, that the best cure for pride is a sight of Christ. Oh, when your eyes see Him, then your own loathsomeness, blackness and deformity are clearly revealed. I am fair until I see the sun--then--then am I black, indeed! I think myself pure until I see Him whiter than any fuller could make Him and then I fall down and cry, "Unclean, unclean, unclean!" "Now my eye sees You," said Job, "why I abhor myself, and repent in dust and ashes." Down go your flaunting banners and your lofty plumes when you have a sight of Christ! No humbler man than George Herbert--no humbler man than Samuel Rutherford--and these were men who lived close to Christ. Christ's Presence is a cure-all.

When Melchizedek comes every spiritual disease flies before Him. The Church at Laodicean was very far gone and how did the Master propose to cure it? Here it is--"Behold, I stand at the door and knock: if any man hears My voice and opens the door, I will come into him and will sup with him." What? Lord, is this Your delightful treatment of Your sick Church? "Yes, My communion with you, poor lukewarm Laodicean, will revive you." Truly that is a most suggestive figure by which John describes the countenance of Christ--he says, "His countenance was as the sun shining in his strength." So, Lord, it does not matter how dark I am, the moment You show Your face, all must be light! This, I think, was the reason why the King of Righteousness met Abram--to turn away his thoughts from the tempting joys of victory to his sure portion in the Most High God, possessor of Heaven and earth.

Yet again, was not this visit bestowed because Abram was about to be tried in a yet more subtle manner than he had been before? It is easier to fight Chedorlaomer than to resist the King of Sodom. Joshua down in the plain never grew weary when he was fighting the Amalekites, but Moses on the mountain felt his hands grow heavy. Why? Because the more spiritual the exercise, the more apt are we to grow weary in it. And so the more spiritual the temptation the more likelihood of our becoming a prey to it and the more strength do we need to overcome it. That was a very subtle temptation to Lot, by the King of Sodom. Why it looked so right--perfectly right. Abram has brought back these captives-- he has a right to the spoil--he ought, therefore, to take it. If he had done so, no one would blame him on ordinary rules. But there is a higher rule for Believers than for other men!

Brethren, I contend that the common rules of morality are binding upon all--but that a supernaturally high rule of morality should regulate the Christian! The Christian is not allowed to wink at an evil because he has educated his conscience not to think it so--but he shall so act that there shall not be any wrong in the action upon the common judgment of any unbiased spectator. He who is of the King's Council must walk very daintily lest he offend his Master. I tell you, from experience, that the nearer you come to Christ and the more you have of communion with Him, the more jealous you must be of yourself, or else, if other men escape the rod you will not--you will have to smart for it behind the door where another may not see nor understand your grief.

Beloved, it is well to have communion with Christ to prepare us against subtle temptations, for to feed us upon Mel-chizedek's bread and wine is to make us more than a match for the King of Sodom. O Jesus! When I have seen Your face, my soul beholds not the dazzling beauties of earthly excellence. Brothers and Sisters, if ever you have seen Christ's face, that painted harlot, the world, will never win your love again! Did you ever eat the pure white bread of Heaven? Then the brown gritty bread of earth will never suit you but will break your teeth with gravel stones. You will never care to drink earth's sour and watery wine if you have once been made to drink of the wines on the lees well refined--the spiced wine of Christ's pomegranate. If you want to be strengthened against the most subtle worldly temptations, cry, "Let Him kiss me with the kisses of His mouth: for Your love is better than wine." And you may go forth to conflicts of every kind more than a conqueror, through Him that has loved you!

Thus we have spoken upon the fact that Melchizedek met Abram and the reasons. Now, let us look a little more closely at what he did. In what character did he meet Abram? The reply is easy--he met him as one possessed of a royal priesthood. Christ meets us, Brethren, as a Priest and a King in all our battles. What a mercy it is that Christ visits us as a Priest, for we never fight against sin without being in some measure partakers of it. I do not believe there ever was a controversy for the Truth of God upon which any gracious man, though engaged upon the right side, could look back without some regrets and some tears.

I much believe that even Martin Luther or John Knox, when upon their dying beds, though never regretting that they contended earnestly for the faith yet felt that while they were in the flesh something of flesh mingled with all that they did. Thus it will be to the end and even when contending against our own sins and lusts. Yet, Beloved, our very repentance has something in it to be repented of and our very flying to the Cross has something in it of a lingering from the Cross and therefore something of evil. Jesus, all hail! How much I need to meet You as a priest! And you, Beloved, do you not feel that you need Him, too? Do you not, as you look upon Calvary and the flowing blood, confess that you need, in all spiritual conflicts, to meet Christ?

But Melchizedek was also a king and truly thus we want to view our Lord whenever we are fighting His battles. "The Lord reigns," is perhaps one of the most comforting texts in the compass of God's Word to the contending Christian. "Ah," says the poor soul, "I am trod under foot of Satan, but rejoice not over me, O my enemy--though I fall, yet shall I rise again, for the Lord reigns!" Oh, that is our consolation when at any time we think we are routed! When we see our Church dismayed and our banner trailed in the mire--we then remember Jesus, for Him has God the Father exalted, "and given Him a name which is above every name: that at the name of Jesus every knee should bow, of things in Heaven and things in earth and things under the earth."

Hail, King of Righteousness and Peace, much do we need to meet You! Come, mount Your glorious chariot, ride forth conquering and to conquer drawn by Your three white horses, Meekness, Truth and Righteousness! Heaven adores

You, earth obeys You, Hell trembles at Your Presence! Gates of brass must burst at Your touch and bars of iron snap at Your Word! O King Immortal, ride gloriously and let Your people behold You and rejoice in You. But we must see Christ, see Him, by close communion with Him. You cannot see Him by my description. Melchizedek met Abram and Jesus Christ must meet you. He must stop you all of a sudden, when you least expect it, and reveal Himself to you as He does not unto the world.

Jacob, before wrestling, was met by hosts of angels at Mahanaim--but what are these when compared with the Lord Himself? There is a high blessing in being met by angels--do not mistake me there--but oh, to be met by the Angel of the Covenant, the Michael the Archangel, to be met by Him! Ah, what comfort is here! And will He meet me? Will He meet you? Yes, we can answer, He will--for we have met with Him. "My eyes have seen the King in His beauty." Many of us can say that and our souls are exceedingly comforted and full of holy joy because we have beheld Him as Priest and King.

The next inquiry is what did he do for him? He brought him bread and wine, precisely setting forth what Jesus does, who brings us His flesh and His blood. Carnal people say in order to understand Christ's words, that when you eat bread and drink wine at the Lord's Table, there is His flesh in the bread, or that the bread is transubstantiated into flesh and the same with the wine. But the spiritual mind understands that these emblems awaken the spiritual powers and that the spiritual powers--not the lips and the stomach, but the spiritual powers--do really and spiritually feed upon the flesh and blood of Jesus Christ and so the Word is fulfilled--"Except you eat My flesh and drink

My blood, there is no life in you."

I do not know that Christian people feed altogether on doctrine. I know that the Truth of God is food, but Believers get richer nourishment than even this affords. When I am very gloomy I like to take down some work upon the high doctrines--God's Sovereignty, election, perseverance--and I get comforted. But there are other times when I am brought very low and that kind of food will not suit me. I am obliged then to turn to my Lord Himself. There is, I believe, in times of conflict, no food which can be the stay of an immortal soul except the Master Himself--communion with Him--a putting of the fingers into the print of the nails and a thrusting of the hand into the side. This is the sovereign remedy for unbelief and the best food for faith. His manifest Presence is our noblest nutriment.

When Christ reveals Himself, all grows calm and peaceful. But until we can get Him we still abide in darkness and we see no light. The worshiper who came up to the temple could not live upon the brazen laver, nor the golden snuffers, nor even upon the cherubic emblems--he must partake with the priests of the lamb offered in sacrifice! And so the true food of the child of God is Jesus Christ Himself--not so much ordinances and doctrines, which are only the utensils and the vestments--but Christ Himself! The very Christ, made flesh for us, received with joy into our soul and fed upon, until, like Abram, we go on our way rejoicing. That is what the royal priest did for the Patriarch.

Bear with me patiently while I remark what Melchizedek said to him. First he blessed him and then he blessed God and that is just what we need our Lord to do for us. We want our Lord Jesus Christ first to bless us. "Blessed be Abram of the Most High God, possessor of Heaven and earth." We need a blessing upon our own persons and especially upon our own works. What are our works when we have done them all but futile vanity until God comes to strengthen us? Beloved, you and I may contend for Christ until we are dumb but not a soul will see the light or know the Truth of God by our witness of itself! We may go with tender hearts and seek to bring sinners to the Cross of Christ, but we shall never bring a sinner unless God's own arm is revealed.

We shall come back like the Prophet, saying, "Who has believed our report?" And feeling that the arm of God has not been revealed unto men. But when, on the other hand, the Possessor of Heaven and earth has blessed us, then our earthly substance is blessed and our earthly words are blessed and then we get a heavenly blessing! Heaven's rest and peace--Heaven's Omnipotence rest upon us and in the glory of a Heaven-given strength we go forth confident of victory. We want a blessing from Christ. Ask for it now, Beloved! Ask for it now, you who are weary with last week's fighting, you who can scarcely endure any longer by reason of your trials and troubles! Say to Him now, "Melchizedek, bless me! O Jesus, bless me now!"

Possessor of Heaven and earth, forget not one of us, Your beloved ones, but give us a blessing! Beloved Brethren, Melchizedek did not stop there, but he fulfilled another part of his priestly office--he blessed God. Whenever we are singing here, when I am in right order, my soul takes wing and wants to fly to Heaven! When we all sing with power and force there is a sweetness and grandeur about the song which we do not often meet. Yet I am always conscious that we cannot praise God as He deserves to be and herein I bless the great Melchizedek that though we cannot bless God as He should be blessed, yet He can! Jesus Christ presents the praises of His saints before God as well as their prayers. He is the Intercessor and while He has the vials full of odors sweet to present, He also presents the music of our harps. Both our offerings come up accepted in the Beloved.

Now what do you say, Brethren? Have you done anything this week that is of good repute? Has God given you any success? Dear Sister, have you won any souls for Christ? I know you have! Dear Brother, has God blessed you in any witness-bearing? Have you felt that God has been with you? Well now, come and lay your honors down at His feet, whatever they may be! Put them there and pray the great Melchizedek to take out of your heart every particle of self-glory and every atom of self-exaltation and ask Him to say for you in a higher sense than ever you can say it, "Blessed be the Most High God, possessor of Heaven and earth who has delivered my enemies into my hand." Thus you shall be glad that the great Melchizedek has met you!

I have talked thus, but truly one word from the lips of Christ will be worth ten thousand of mine! And if you ever have seen Him, you will think me a very dauber when I try to paint Him. If you get this day so much as ten minutes real fellowship with Jesus, you will wonder how it is, that I, if I know anything about Him, could talk in this cold way! Go your way, Brethren, and pray Melchizedek will meet you!

III. Lastly, and very briefly, indeed, since our time is gone--when a wrestling Believer is favored with a sight of the great Melchizedek--voluntarily and yet necessarily he makes a new dedication of himself to God. You see Abram does not appear to delay a moment but he gives to Melchizedek a tithe of all, by which he seemed to say, "I own the authority of my superior liege lord, to all that I am and all that I have." There is one of our hymns which says--

"Hail, Melchizedek Divine! You, great High Priest, shall be mine. All my powers before You fall Take not tithe, but take them all." And truly our holy faith deserves that we should give all to Christ!

I would that some Christians, however, practiced the rule of giving a tenth of their substance to the Lord's cause. The Lord's Church need never lack if you had a bag in which you stored up for Christ--when you gave anything, you would not feel it was giving of your own--your left hand would not know what your right hand did, for you would be taking out of the Lord's stock which you had already consecrated to the Lord's cause. Not less than one-tenth should be the Lord's portion, especially with those who have.

And more than this, I think, should be expected of those who have wealth. But there is no rule binding with iron force upon you for we are not under Law in Christ's Church, but under Grace and Grace will prompt you to do more than Law might suggest. But certainly the Christian should reckon himself to be not his own and that he has nothing to retain for his own private account. I pray God if I have a drop of blood in my body which is not His, to let it bleed away! And if there is one hair in my head which is not consecrated to Him, I would have it plucked out--for it must be the devil's drop of blood and the devil's hair. It belongs to either one or the other--if not to God, then to Satan. No, we must, Brethren, have no division of ourselves--no living unto this world and unto God, too.

Mark Anthony yoked two lions together and drove them through the streets of Rome--they do strange things at Rome and there are many people who can yoke two lions together and drive towards Rome. But you will never be able to yoke the lion of the tribe of Judah and the lion of Hell together--they are at deadly antagonism and Christ will not have you for His servants if you seek to serve two masters. I know that any talk of mine here will be in vain, but if, Beloved, you should see Christ and have communion with Him, your consecration to Him will be a matter of course. I will suppose that this afternoon one of you should sit down in your arm chair and, as you are sitting there, you will be thinking, "How little I have been giving of late to the cause of Christ! How seldom I have opened my mouth for Him!"

Perhaps you will think, "I have got on in the world, too, but I really cannot afford it! My expenses are so great!" Suppose the Lord Jesus Christ should come into the room with those pierced hands and bleeding feet--suppose He were to remind you of what He has done for you--how He visited you in your low estate when your heart was breaking under a sense of sin? You would not tell Him you could not afford to give to His cause! Suppose our Lord Jesus Christ should look you in the face and say to you, "I have done all this for you. What will you do for Me?" What would be your answer? Why, you would say, "Take it all, my Master, take it all, all that I am and all that I have shall be forever Yours."

Or, if you felt niggardly--supposing He should say to you, "If you will never ask anything of Me, I will never take anything from you." Would you agree to that? No! Because you still will have immense demands to make upon His liberality cease not to give your whole spirit, soul and body as a whole burnt-offering unto God. As Abram did before Mel-chizedek so you do in the Presence of Christ. Admit that you are His and give yourself to Him. My dear Brethren, I pray God that this may stir you up to seek a high grade of piety and to live in daily communion with a living Savior and He will bless and keep you.

But there are some of you who are not like Abram. You need not hope, yet, to see Melchizedek. There are some of you strangers, far off. Ah, I may rather compare you to the men of Sodom! Christ has done something for you as Abram did for Sodom. You know it was only for the sake of Lot that He brought them back, but He did bring them all back and for the sake of Lot gave a respite to them all--although a few years after they had grown so wicked that they were all destroyed. My Master has given a respite to free you all. While His great work was the salvation of His own chosen, yet He has spared you all in the land of the living. Take heed lest you do as did the men of Sodom, for then a hail more fiery, a destruction more terrible must come upon you, seeing that you turn not aside from your evil ways, nor seek His face.

Trust Christ and you are saved! Believe in Him and your sins are forgiven. But if you refuse, beware lest that come upon you which is written in the Prophets, "Behold, you despisers and wonder and perish!" The Master now send us away with His benediction. Amen.

The Backslider's Way Hedged Up

DELIVERED ON SUNDAY MORNING, SEPTEMBER 18, 1864,
BY C. H. SPURGEON,
AT THE METROPOLITAN TABERNACLE, NEWINGTON.

"She said, I will go after my lovers, who give me my bread and my water, my wool and my flax, my oil and my drink. Therefore, behold, I will hedge up your way with thorns and make a wall, that she shall not find her paths. And she shall follow after her lovers, but she shall not overtake them. And she shall seek them, but shall not find them: then shall she say, I will go and return to my first husband; for then was it better with me than now." -- Hosea 2:5-7.

GREAT and grievous was the apostasy of the seed of Abraham from the Lord their God. They had been chosen by special Grace from among all people and had the high honor to receive the oracles of God--yet they were bent on backsliding from God and were unfaithful to the Most High. The gods of the surrounding heathen were constantly a snare to them and they forsook the only living and true God to prostrate themselves before blocks of wood and stone. Though chastened a thousand times they learned nothing by the rod. And though as frequently forgiven and visited with mercy, the holy bonds of gratitude did not bind them to their God. As an abandoned woman leaves a kind and tender husband for the base love of the vilest of the vile, even so both Israel and Judah played the harlot towards the Lord who had espoused them in infinite love.

Yet God has not even now written a bill of divorcement, or cast away the people whom He did foreknow. Through eighteen hundred years the sons of Israel have had to wander to and fro without a settled dwelling place, yet God has not utterly given them up or broken His Covenant with them. For the day shall come when Israel shall return, when again she shall be called Hephzibah, and her land Beulah. Come, long expected day! Appear, glorious King of the Jews! And you, O Judah, return from your captivity! Shake yourself from the dust--put on your beautiful garments and salute the Lord, your Ishi, your tender loving Husband!

Beloved Brothers and Sisters, the apostasy of the children of Israel has been recorded for our learning. As they were prone to wander, so are we--and the methods by which God brought them back of old are precisely those which He uses with His erring children at the present day. Instead of wondering at Israel's wickedness, let us examine ourselves and repent for our sins! And while we see the hand of God upon them, let us learn to admire those methods of unerring wisdom by which Divine love preserves the ransomed ones from going down into the pit.

In considering our text, my aim will be to be used as the Holy Spirit's instrument to arouse, instruct and restore backsliders. Such wanderers may be present now. Their first love they have lost and their zeal is quenched. There may be some here who have gone further still and have forsaken the Church of God altogether, having given up their profession and all attendance upon Divine worship. O that the voice of Israel's God may be heard in their hearts this morning, crying, "If a man puts away his wife and she goes from him and becomes another man's, shall he return unto her again? Shall not that land be greatly polluted? But you have played the harlot with many lovers, yet return again to Me, says the Lord."

I. We commence the consideration of the passage before us with the remark that WHILE SINFUL MEN ARE IN PROSPERITY THEY PERVERT THE MERCIES OF GOD TO THEIR OWN INJURY, making them instruments of sin and weapons of warfare against God. While the children of Israel enjoyed an abundance of temporal comforts they ascribed all these blessings to their false gods. Hear the wicked and treacherous words--"I will go after my lovers who give me my bread and my water, my wool and my flax, my oil and my drink." Oh, base ingratitude to their bounteous Jehovah! Infamous ascription of His Glory to graven images!

Prosperous sinners make three great mistakes. At the outset they give their temporal mercies the first place in their hearts. Because their business prospers they do not consider that their soul is perishing! Because there is enough on the table for themselves and for their children they forget that their soul is famished for lack of Heaven's bread! They put the shadows of time before the realities of eternity. They say, "We must live." But they forget that they must also die. So long as the current glides smoothly and the gentle flow of the river of their joy is undisturbed they forget the waterfall, red with the blood of souls, down whose tremendous steeps those treacherous waters will soon hurry them!

Is it not a gross mistake to attach so much importance to this poor body of clay and forget the priceless jewel of the immortal soul? Why do you think so much of a world in which we only tarry for a few evil years and neglect the world where we must dwell forever? Such folly is most shameful in one who was once a professed Christian, because he knew, or professed to know, somewhat of the superiority of the eternal over the temporal. He supposedly knew of the vanity of things earthly and the glory of things heavenly.

Yet because things go well with him--because his wife is in health, his children blooming, his house well furnished, his property increasing, he says, "Soul, take your ease," and disturbs not himself though Heaven is black with lowering tempest and the light of God's countenance is hidden from him. The loss of God's Presence, the man thinks to be a trifle because he is succeeding in the world--as though a man should count it nothing to lose his life if he may but keep his raiment whole to be buried in!

O Fools, why do you put the last things first and the first things last? One error leads to another and therefore such people hold their temporal things upon a wrong tenure. Do observe how many times the word "my" is found in the text. "Give me my bread and my water and my wool and my flax, my oil and my drink." Why, they were not hers but God's, for the Lord expressly claims them all in the ninth verse and threatens to take them all away! Backslider, there was a time when you did confess yourself to be God's steward--when you said, "I am not my own, but bought with a price." Yet now you have so set your heart upon worldly things that all your talk runs in this fashion--my horses, my houses, my lands, my profits, my children and an endless list of things which you think to be altogether yours.

Why, Man, they are not yours! They are only lent you for a season! You are but God's under-bailiff. You have possession only as tenant-at-will, or as a borrower holding a loan. The Lord claims even now the prior right to all you have and the day shall come when He shall show you this! For if He has mercy upon you--and I pray He may--He may take these from you one by one and make you cry out in abject wretchedness of soul, "O God, forgive me that I made these my gods and claimed them as my own!"

Then further, backsliders are apt to ascribe their prosperity and their mercies to their sins. I have even heard one say, "Ever since I gave up a profession of religion I have made more headway in business than I did before." Some apostates have boasted, "Since I broke through Puritanical restraint and went out into worldly company, I have been better in spirits and better in purse than ever I was before." Thus they ascribe the mercies which God has given them to their sins and wickedly bow down before their lusts, as Israel did before the golden calf and cry, "These are your gods, O Israel, which brought us up out of the land of Egypt!"

Sinner, if you did but know it, a long-suffering God has given you these things! Even to you who will perish He has given many mercies as your portion in this life, seeing that you have no heritage hereafter. O take heed, lest you be fattened upon them as beasts for the slaughter. Unto you, Backsliders, He has given these things to try you, to see how far you will go--to what extravagances of ingratitude you will descend and how far you will despise His tender means. O Backslider, is it not marvelous that God has not long ago stretched you upon a bed of sickness, when you consider how much you have brought dishonor upon Christ's name--how you have vexed God's people--how you have made the wicked open their mouths against God?

Is it not a wonder that He did not take you away with a stroke when you first forsook Him? And yet, see--instead of this, He multiplies your mercies! Does He not as good as say, "Return unto your rest for I have dealt bountifully with you. I am married unto you and therefore I treat you as a husband treats his spouse. Although I might well proclaim a divorce against you, yet since I have betrothed you unto Me forever, My goodness and mercy shall not leave you even in your sins." Herein lies the gross mistake of the backslider--that he will attribute his present happiness and comfort to his sins rather than to the forbearance of God.

Here are three great errors and oh, I fear they are so deadly that unless God interposes in Providence and in Grace, they will be as fatal as the three darts which Joab thrust through the heart of Absalom as he was dangling by his proud hair in the wood of Ephraim! I fear that the goodly Babylonian garment and the talents of silver and the wedge of gold will ruin you as they did Achan of old. These three falsehoods, like the three daughters of the horseleech, will never be satisfied until they have utterly destroyed your soul! You will be wrapped in fine linen and fare sumptuously and all this shall but ensure you the torments of the damned.

Go now, weep and howl for the miseries which shall come upon you--your riches are corrupted! Your garments are moth-eaten! Your gold and silver are cankered and the rust of them shall be a witness against you and shall eat your flesh as it were fire. You have forsaken the right way and are gone astray--following the way of Balaam who loved the wages of unrighteousness.

Hear the Word of the Lord by the mouth of His servant Peter! Tremble at it and be afraid--"If after they have escaped the pollutions of the world through the knowledge of the Lord and Savior Jesus Christ, they are again entangled therein and overcome, the latter end is worse with them than the beginning. For it had been better for them not to have known the way of righteousness, than, after they have known it, to turn from the holy commandment delivered unto them. But it is happened unto them according to the proverb, The dog is turned to his own vomit again. And the sow that was washed, to her wallowing in the mire."

II. Let us turn from this gloomy side of our subject and observe with gratitude that THE LORD INTERPOSES ADVERSITY IN ORDER TO BRING BACK HIS WANDERING CHILDREN. Let us consider for a moment the hindrances which a God of Love frequently puts in the way of His elect when they backslide from Him. Here we have the matter opened up to our attention. "Therefore, behold, I will hedge up your way with thorns and make a wall, that she shall not find her paths."

Here you see that it is an unexpected hindrance, for it is placed right in the woman's way--"I will hedge up your way"--it was her way, her habit--she had fallen into it and she meant to keep on. But suddenly she met with an unlooked-for obstacle. Just as farmers, when a public path runs through their field and persons begin to wander too much into the grass or corn, will put up bushes to keep the public to the path. Or just as ranchers, to keep their cattle in their fields, make thick thorn hedges which the beasts cannot break through, so God puts a thorn hedge of troubles right in the way of His chosen to stop them in their sins.

This hedge may be placed in your way in different shapes--perhaps you will meet with it this day. I see the hand of God as it touches the elect but erring man! Suddenly business grows slack--customers fall off one by one--bad debts multiply. Bankruptcy stares him in the face. Where he had enough to lavish on his pleasures he now has not enough to supply his needs. A mighty famine has arisen in the land of sin and he begins to be in need. He little expected this. If anybody had told him when he was so proudly driving that fast-trotting horse along the streets that he would come to hard work, he would have laughed him to scorn!

He thought he should live like a millionaire, but now he seems far more likely to die a pauper. Or it may be that sudden sickness has fallen upon his once strong and healthy person. He could drink with the most drunken and no voice could ring so loud as his in the midnight revelry. But now he is paralyzed--he has lost the use of half his limbs! Or perhaps some internal complaint has weakened him and made him totter along the road in constant jeopardy of sudden death. Now the smooth road is rough, indeed, and the world has lost its many charms.

Ah, Sinner, the sound of music is hushed for you and the joys of the flowing bowl are yours no more. Your foaming tankards, your wantonness and chambering are gone--Mercy has torn them from you in love to your soul! Possibly the hedge is made of other thorns--perhaps the man's children sickened. There are many funerals in the house in quick succession. That first-born son, the expected heir, the joy of his father's heart falls like a withered flower. His wife is cut off as a lily snapped from its stalk and he stands weeping--a widowed husband--a childless man. Any of these ways, and thousands more which I need not here recount, are God's methods of building walls across the way of those whom He ordains to bless.

When the man breaks through one hedge, the Lord of Mercy will build another and maintains His hedges at such a degree of strength that the bullock which is most accustomed to the yoke shall not be able to push through. O Backslider, the Divine finger can touch you in the most tender part and though up to this moment you have boasted, "Nobody can make me wretched! Nothing shall ever make me fret," yet He can shut you up in such despair that none can remove the heavy bar! Think of what your brain may yet become--it is cool and calculating now and you can clearly see that your fellows are left behind in the race of competition--but remember how soon an unseen cause may soften that brain into imbecility, or excite it into incipient insanity! How soon may that boasted brain become like a burning sea throbbing with waves of fire!

Beware lest such a visitation become the prelude of the wrath eternal! My prayer for you is that more gentle means may bring you to repentance. But to that you will never come unless the Lord hedges up your way with thorns. Observe that it was a very disappointing impediment. While the prosperous sinner was securely pursuing his way he was stopped. "Why," says the man, "if it had not been for that, I should have made a fortune. Why did death come just when my fair girl looked so lovely in the bloom of opening womanhood and when my dear boy had grown so engaging that his company was my delight? Ah, this is trouble, indeed! To meet with misfortune just when I had built that new house and held my head so high, and expected to see my daughters so respectably married--why, this is very disappointing."

And the man kicks. And though once he professed to be a child of God, yet it is painfully possible that he is ready to curse God and die. But if he knew--oh, if he knew the Divine motive--he would thank God for his troubles on bended knees! You remember that story of the painter in St.

Paul's when on high he painted his picture upon the ceiling? As he went backward upon the stage to look at it and was so engrossed with his occupation he was just on the edge of the stage and in great danger of being dashed to pieces by a fall from that dizzy height. A friend saw him and knowing that if he called out to him he would be startled and thus his fall might be hastened, he took up a brush full of paint and threw it at the picture. The desired effect was produced, for the painter in great anger rushed forward to upbraid him and thus his life was spared!

God seeing you painting a fair scene of life and happiness on earth suddenly spoils it all--you rush forward, crying out against Him. But oh, what reason have you to thank Him for that disappointment which has robbed Satan of his prey and saved your soul! Moreover, what painful hindrances our heavenly Father often uses. He hedges the sinner's path not with rhododendrons and azaleas, not with roses and laurels, but with thorns. Prickly thorns which curse the soil and tear the flesh are God's instrument of restraint. Nothing but a thorn hedge would have stopped the man--he was so madly set upon his present course that he would dash through anything else.

But God, whose eternal mercy has marked that man out as a special object of love, uses the most effectual remedies and plants a fence of thorns. Are you smarting this morning--so smarting that you wish you had never been born? Do you feel so much the cuts and lashes of evil fortune that you would sooner end your existence than continue any longer as you are? I bless God for this, if you are one of His children, for it is this and this only, that will change your ways!

Furthermore, the fence is effectual if the thorn hedge will not suffice--it is written, "I will make a wall." There are some so desperate in sin that they will break through ordinary restraints. Then a wall shall be tried through which there is no breaking, over which there is no climbing. Ah, Backslider! Backslider! Perhaps you have already broken through the thorn hedge--your trials have not been sanctified. I have known some who have had enough trials, one would think, to have melted a heart of adamant and yet they have set their faces like a flint against God and gone on worse than ever. "Who is Jehovah, that I should obey Him?" said Pharaoh, when he was vexed with many plagues. And so have you said!

God, I trust, will not destroy you as He did Pharaoh, but He will break, one way or another, the iron sinew of your proud neck. For when it comes to a wrestle between God and you, you may be sure of a fall! The Lord never was defeated, even by the stoutest adversary and He will not, in your case, be frustrated in His design. If you are really one of His chosen, you shall meet with an affliction such as perhaps you never heard of in any other man. And if nothing but this will stop you, He will invent some new form of disease, some fresh method of pain in order to get at your soul. If you cannot be saved by the gentle wind, He will send the storm.

If this suffices not, He will try the hurricane and if you will not run into port even then, tornado shall follow tornado till you are broken to pieces like a wreck and compelled to swim to the Rock of Ages for rescue. These are but parts of His ways and even His hard things are full of mercy. The tender mercies of the wicked are cruel, but the cruel things of God are full of tender mercy! He only uses these methods because nothing else will do and He would sooner that you should enter into Heaven with every bone broken, than that you should descend into Hell with the full use of your powers.

III. In the third place, you would think that the sinner would now stop, but instead of it, according to the text, EVEN THOUGH GOD WALLS UP THE WAY OF SIN, MEN WILL TRY TO FOLLOW IT, BUT IN THE CHOSEN THIS RESOLVE WILL BE IN VAIN. "She shall follow after her lovers, but she shall not overtake them. And she shall seek them, but shall not find them." Do you see the man? He has suffered such loss that he cannot find the means to sin as he used to do! Where he had money to spend to indulge himself he now finds an empty purse but yet he tries to do his worst.

He goes up and down that wall to see if there is not a hole in it somewhere. He tries to scramble over it where there is a projecting stone--he climbs half-way up, and falling, cuts his hands--but he will try again and again. He runs all along that thorn hedge and looks and looks again for a gap and oh, if he could find but one! If he could but escape from God's boundaries! If he could but scrape enough money together to have another debauch. If he could find just enough to play the gentleman again. But he cannot--he has no means whatever to indulge his sin.

Perhaps the case runs another way--God has taken away from the man all the pleasure of sin. He cannot be so satisfied as he used to be with his money. As he puts it into the till he despises it--and when he sees it accumulating at his banker's it only brings him care and no content as once it did. His children turn out, one by one, a curse to him. In business everything seems determined to plague him. Whereas at the theater he could gaze and listen with ecstasy, the whole affair is now tame and dull. Those wines, so full of flavor, have now, through his satiety lost their usual charm. Let him do what he will, the world is all a blank and wretchedness for him!

Like Tiberius he would give a mint of gold to anyone who would invent him a new pleasure or restore the vigor of the old. But no, the thorn hedge is too well made--the Great Farmer has planted it too well. The sinner would become a spiritual suicide but he cannot, let him desire it as he may. He is desperately set on destruction as though it were to be desired. O Sinner, how is this--how has the fall spoilt us that we should be so enamored of our own destruction? O my God, what a creature is man! Though he knows that sin will be his ruin, yet he hugs it as though it were his chief mercy! He heaps to himself destruction as though it were gold and digs for his own ruin as for hid treasure!

Oh, if the righteous were half as intent in seeking after goodness as the wicked are in hunting after sin, how much more active would they be! If we were half as strongly set upon the things of God as sinners are set upon their own ways and their own pleasures, we should have no waverers, no timid, cowardly spirits! Truly this love of sin is so strange that if we did not see it in ourselves we should wonder at it! But Christian, this is in you as much as in the worst of men! You, too, if it had not been for Divine mercy, would have plunged on from bad to worse. If Omnipotence itself had not seized the reins and turned us into the way of Truth, we should at this moment have been dashing on in the road of sin!

I say if Omnipotence itself had not interposed--it was not the minister, it was not conscience, it was not merely Providence. It was more than this--Jehovah's own right arm threw back the horse on its haunches and cast the rider to the ground as He did Saul at Damascus, or else we should have hastened on to our destruction and perished through the hardness of our hearts. Let us sing unto Him whose mighty mercy has rescued us and let us pity those whom the restraints of Providence cannot bind--those who will, if they can--leap through stone walls to have their way and their sin.

Thus, dear Friends, we have presented to you the deplorable picture of the infatuated sinner, perfectly infatuated and drunken with the love of sin and enmity to God! And Mercy itself, so far as we have gone, foiled of its purpose. The thorn hedge not enough--the stone wall not enough. What shall come now?

IV. Our next business is to consider THAT THE BACKSLIDER'S FAILURE IS FOLLOWED BY A BLESSED RESULT. The hunt was very arduous but the greedy hunter has missed his prey and there he sits weary with the chase and ashamed of himself. What comes of it? Do observe it, for the result is one which I hope you and I know already. "Then shall she say, I will go and return to my first husband; for then it was better with me than now." O Lord, teach some who are here this morning to pray this prayer!

Observe here is repentance attended with sorrow. The poor creature in this case feels, deeply feels to the very soul, the wretchedness of her condition. She is in so bad a plight that though she had despised her former state she now confesses it to be better. Observe that it is an active repentance. It is not merely "I will return," but, "I will go and return." When the Grace of God sets a backslider upon returning, he will stir up all the powers of his soul to seek after God. He cries, "My soul waits for the Lord more than they that watch for the morning." I say more than they that watch for the morning.

There is much earnestness in a sinner seeking Christ, but, if possible, there is more in a backslider returning from the error of his ways--for he has not only the guilt of sin to mourn over--but the double guilt of having despised the Sav- ior, of having known the way of righteousness and having turned from it. Here are two spurs to make him speed on in his course. Observe, dear Friends, that the confession which this poor soul makes of folly is one which is sustained by the best of reasons. She says, "Then was it better with me than now." Let us see whether this is not true with you.

Well, Backslider, what have you gained by it, after all? Have you gained anything more comfortable than the light of your Father's face. You once could say, "Abba, Father!" You rejoiced to know that God was at peace with you. You were reconciled to Him by the death of His Son. Now God is angry with you! Your fears tell you that He has forgotten to be gracious. What can make up for this loss? When God lights a candle, what brightness is in the room! But when God's candle is gone, where is the sun and where the moon? They give no light to you.

Before, when you were in your right senses, you had the privilege of going to the Throne of Grace. You could tell your needs before God and spread your sorrows there. But you have no Throne of Grace to go to now. Why, you scarcely dare pray! As for your friends, you would not like to tell them your troubles. Poor Prodigal, what sorry friends are those who waited on you in your days of wealth! They sat with their legs under your mahogany and drank your wine while you had any--but you know that you would be a fool to expect any help from them now that you need it.

Your lovers have forsaken you and those who once were so kind--where is their love now? Do I see one among you who has been cast off by her companion in sin and shame! Ah, Woman! Poor wretched Woman! Have you been made to feel that smart so common to those who sin as you have done--cast into the street by him who first decoyed you by his fair promises of love? Your case is but one of many and there are thousands who find that the world knows not what faithfulness means.

First sin deludes, deceives, and pretends to love and then afterwards it casts off its victims. Ah, you had a father's house to go to and a father's mercy to plead. But you do not have it now--it was better with you then than now. And then, you had God's promises to fall back upon. If you had any trouble, you opened your Bible and there was a passage to cheer you. When you had losses, the cheering words exactly met your case. But now that Book is full of fire--it flashes lightning upon you as you read it--there is not a promise there which smiles on you!

Your fears whisper that the treasury of God is shut against you. Once you had communion with Christ Jesus--ah, now I touch a tender string--you did sit at the banqueting table of Christ! Unless you were awfully deceived and a gross hypocrite, you could say, "He has kissed me with the kisses of His mouth." After this, how could you go to the door of that deceiver Madame Wanton! How is this? O Soul, if you have ever known the love of Christ I am sure you will say, "It was better with me then than now."

What can the world afford you comparable to fellowship with Jesus? One hour upon His bosom is worth ten thousand years in the palaces and courts of the world's wealth and royalty and you know that it is so. There is no room to entertain a comparison for a moment--

"What peaceful hours you once enjoyed, How sweet their memory still But they have left an aching void The world can never fill."

O that your repentance, fixed upon such reasons as these, may be deep! May you make a confession of your extreme folly and now fall down before God and find mercy!

To close this point, this repentance was acceptable. It is not often that a husband is willing to take back his wife when she has so grossly sinned, as the metaphor here implies. And yet observe that God is willing to receive the sinner, though his sin is even more aggravated. By the mouth of Jeremiah He speaks these words--"Return unto Me, for I am married unto you." I do not know anything which should make the backslider's heart break like the doctrine of God's immutable love to His people! Some say that if we preach that "whom once He loves He never leaves, but loves them to the end," it will be an inducement to man to sin.

Well I know man is very vile and he can turn even love itself into a reason for sinning, but where there is as much as even one spark of Grace, a man cannot do that. A child does not say, "I will offend my father because he loves me." It is not even in fallen human nature, generally, unless inspired by the devil, to find motives for sin in God's love and certainly no backsliding child of God can say, "I will continue in sin that Grace may abound." They who do so show that they are reprobates and their damnation is just.

But the backslider who is a child of God at the bottom, will, I think, feel no cord so strong to hold him back from sin as this. Backslider, I hope it will also be a golden chain to draw you to Christ. Jesus meets you, meets you this morning. You were excommunicated. You were driven out from among God's people with shame but Jesus meets you, and pointing to the wounds which He received in the house of His friends at your hands, He nevertheless says, "Return unto Me, for I am married unto you." It is a relationship which you have broken and it might legally be broken forever if He willed it--but He does not will it--for He hates divorce.

You are married to Jesus. Come back to your first Husband, for He is your Husband still! The Fountain which washed you once can wash you again. "Though your sins are as scarlet, they shall be as white as snow. Though they are red like crimson, they shall be as wool." The robe of righteousness which covered you once can cover you again! Though you have cast it from you with scorn, yet it is yours and the Father bids His servants bring forth the best robe and put it on you. He says, "Come to Me!" You have forgotten the Lord, but He has not forgotten youl You love sin, but He will change your will and set your heart upon Himself, for He is determined that you shall be His forever!

Is not this a soul-melting doctrine? If there is so much as a spark of spiritual life in you, I think you will say, "Against such love as this I cannot sin! Against such tender mercy I will not rebel--I will return unto my first husband, for then it was better with me than now." I do not know, but I may be speaking very pointedly and personally to some here--I hope I am. I know that the most of you are not in this condition and for this I thank my God. I pray you, however, lift up your hearts in prayer for those who are and ask my Master that as this bow is drawn at a venture He may direct the arrow.

There are some such here--I know there are. There are some here who have come this very morning with no idea that God would meet with them. You have put the reins upon your neck and you have given yourselves up. The restraints of morality can scarcely bind you and yet once you prayed at the Prayer Meeting and sat at the sacramental table and you put on the Lord Jesus Christ by profession in Baptism. But oh, what are you now? Your life would not bear to be talked of. Your conduct has become so gross and vile you might have expected to have heard this morning some word that should have cut you off forever from hope! But, by God's Grace, instead of it the silver trumpet sounds today with notes of love and pity. Return! Return !--Your Husband woos you over again--return! For then it was better with you than now.

V. Not to be longer on the point, let us observe in the fifth place that THERE IS AN AWFUL CONTRAST TO ALL THIS. There are some who prosper in this world until, like a wide-spread tree, they are cut down and cast into the fire. There are backsliders, who, never having had the root of the matter in them, go back unto their own ways to the land from which they came out and continue there forever. I beseech you never trifle with backsliding. I have put God's Free Grace in the boldest manner that I could just now, but oh, let me warn any man who would pervert that Free Grace into an excuse for sin!

Let me warn him against playing with backsliding! One man may roll down a precipice and may scarcely be injured, but I would not try it, for I might break my neck. One man took poison and he was hurried off to the hospital and by the use of proper antidotes was spared, but I would not advise you to try it--no I would beg you to put it away from you. Chosen vessels of mercy, notwithstanding their backslidings, are brought back. But ah, remember that nine out of ten of those who backslide never were God's people! They go out from us because they were not of us and this is the history of their lives and may be the history of your life--ah, and may be the history of mine yet!

They joined the Church. They had been greatly impressed under a sermon. They were young, they knew little as yet of the trials of life--being in the Church they walked consistently for years. They kept the faith. But the Church was cold and they grew cold, too. They neglected weekday services. The closet was forsaken. Family prayer was hardly attended to. Then they forsook the sanctuary altogether, but they were still moral and upright. They began soon to associate with those whom once they avoided--their business went on well.

They had risen from the lowest grade of society to occupy a middle position. They still prospered--gold accumulated. They were the successful people. There was a worm at the root of it all, it is true, but nevertheless it looked so fair and seemed so well. The man did not like to remember that he ever had gone to that little Meeting House--he felt ashamed that ever he had associated with those whom once he knew to be the people of God. He went on still accumulating wealth, but one day he was found dead! Shall I pursue his history? In Hell he lifts up his eyes in torments forever!

With this as the special worm that never could die to gnaw his conscience--that he did know in his head the way of right-eousness--but had turned away from it in his heart!

In letters of fire he sees written across that burning sky: "YOU KNEW YOUR DUTY BUT YOU DID IT NOT. You have come from the cup of the Lord to the cup of devils--you turned aside from the people of God to the children of Satan! You deliberately chose the evil and you forsook the good--you perished not as the ignorant perish, not as they perished who were careless from their birth--not as those who were unvisited by pangs of conscience, or who knew not the Word! You perished in the light of the Gospel, with the sun of mercy shining upon your eyeballs! You perished, though you stood, as it were, on the very doorstep of Heaven! You drifted back to Hell in the teeth of a tide of mercy."

"This, I say, may be your case and mine, if we are not really rooted and grounded in Christ--we may fall by little and little. We may even continue till we die to be Church members and yet backslide in heart by slow degrees until we become rotten through and through and God casts us on the dunghill. I say by the special and miraculous mercy of God His elect will be ingathered, but take heed, Sirs, that you build not on your profession, for profession is no proof of election. You must be born again and only the man who continues to the end shall be saved. May we have such perseverance given us, for His name's sake.

VI. With this last we conclude--IS NOT THIS SUBJECT A VERY SOLEMN WARNING TO THE PEOPLE OF GOD? What some do others may do. If one man falls, another may. If one professor turned out to be a hypocrite, so may another. If one minister reels from the pinnacle of honor and is dashed upon the rocks beneath, so may another. I want to make a personal application of this to myself and I pray my Brothers in office behind me, venerable though some of them are in years, to remember that this may be their case.

And you, my associates and fellow members, many of you united to the Church before I was born, remember that age and habit are no security against apostasy! There must be the continual keeping and anointing of the Holy Spirit. I beseech you, and here I do beseech myself also, let us watch against the beginnings of backsliding. Let us take care of the little sins. O let us watch against the little coolnesses of heart. Brethren, no man backslides all at once. Few men who profess to be saints become outward sinners in one step. It is usually by little and by little. I pray you do not forsake the assembling of yourselves together!

Wake up from your coldness in private prayer if this has come over you. If your love to Christ has grown cold stay not in this state of danger but pray to the Master to inflame your heart again! If any of you have in any respect whatever fallen from your first love--if that old enthusiasm which was in us as a Church has departed from any of you--pray God to give it back to you. If any of you are not bringing forth such fruit unto God as you used to do, O be suspicious of yourselves! Carnal security may be the Heaven of fools, but it is the ruin of Believers--

"Be watchful, be vigilant, dangers may be, In an hour when all seems secure to you"

Especially at this time when the eyes of the world are fixed upon you as a Church and upon me as a witness for God, let us walk carefully. If ever I might ask your prayers, no, claim them as my right, it is now! I beseech you who love God, ask for me my Lord's upholding Grace that His servant may not flinch nor turn his back in the day of battle. Ask for yourselves the same, that when the fight shall grow less hot and there shall come an hour of calm and quiet thought, I, your pastor and yourselves, my fellow soldiers in Christ, may look down the ranks and say, "Not one comrade has fallen. The arrows flew thick about them but their armor was complete! The enemy was fierce, but the Master gave them strength equal to their day. He has kept those whom He gave to us and not one of them is lost."

May it be yours and mine on Heaven's starry steeps to look back upon the superlatively glorious Grace which shall have kept us to the end and brought us to the land where there shall be no more sin! Let us trust the Savior. There is the sinner's hope--there is the saint's strength! Let us cling to the Cross again and may Almighty Grace keep us there and so glorify itself forever. Amen.

"Thus Saith The Lord:" Or, The Book of Common Prayer Weighed in the Balances of the Sanctuary

A Sermon (No. 591)
Delivered on Sunday Morning, September 25th, 1864, by the
Rev. C. H. SPURGEON,
At the Metropolitan Tabernacle, Newington

"Thus saith the Lord." -- Ezekiel 11:15.

THE WISE MAN saith, "Where the word of a king is, there is power." What power must there be where there is the word of the King of kings, who ruleth over all! We are not left to conjecture as to the power of the divine word, for we know that "By the word of the Lord were the heavens made; and all the host of them by the breath of his mouth." Out of nothingness the glorious creation leaped at the bidding of the Most High, and when the earth was without form, and void, and darkness was upon the face of the deep, there was nothing wanted but that solemn voice, "Light be," and straightway light was. God's word was sufficient in itself to build the temple of the universe and to finish it from its foundations to its pinnacles. That same word upholdeth by its power, and ruleth all things by its might. The pillars of heaven stand because the divine word hath fixed them upon their bases, nor shall they be shaken until that same almighty word shall bid them remove; then as a moment's foam dissolves into the wave which bears it and is gone forever, so shall the whole creation melt away. His word, which created, shall also destroy; but until that word be spoken every atom of this world is imperishable. Consider, my brethren, what power is concentrated in him who is clothed with a vesture dipped in blood, and whose name is "THE WORD OF GOD." With what glorious power our Lord Jesus Christ uplifted the burden of our sins, carried the load up to the tree, and cast it forever into the Red Sea of his own atoning blood! Ye know how he burst the bars of death, tore away the gates of the grave, overthrew all the hosts of hell, and dragged the mightiest principalities of darkness as captives at his chariot wheels. At this day the government is upon his shoulders, and his name is the Mighty God, the Everlasting Father. Heaven and earth salute him as the Omnipotent Word. He sustains the spiritual life of all his people by feeding them upon himself; and he shall in due time perfect his saints, and present them without spot before his Father's throne. We ought, therefore, to bow with reverence to that which is truly the word of God, since it contains within itself the highest degree of power, and is ever the way in which divine omnipotence manifests itself.

It is in the word that we must find wisdom and power, "because the foolishness of God is wiser than men; and the weakness of God is stronger than men." The faintest whisper of Jehovah's voice should fill us with a solemn awe, and command the deepest obedience of our souls. Brethren, how careful should we be that we do not set up in God's temple anything in opposition to his word, that we do not permit the teachings of a creature to usurp the honor due to the Lord alone! "Thus saith antiquity," "thus saith authority," "thus saith learning," "thus saith experience,"--these be but idol-gods, which defile the temple of God; be it yours and mine, as bold iconoclasts, to dash them in pieces without mercy, seeing that they usurp the place of the word of God.

"Thus saith the Lord "--this is the motto of our standard, the war-cry of our spiritual conflict,--the sword with which we hope yet to smite through the loins of the mighty who rise up against God's truth. Nothing shall stand before this weapon in the day when God cometh out of his hiding-place; for even at this hour, when "Thus saith the Lord" sounds from the trumpet of the Lord's ministers, the hosts of Midian begin to tremble; for well they know the might of that terrible watchword in days of yore.

This morning, I shall first endeavor to show, briefly, the value of a "Thus saith the Lord;" and then, secondly, I shall, with as much calmness of spirit as I can command, request a "Thus faith the Lord" for certain things which are received and practiced in the State Establishment of our land, and close with a word of personal application, beseeching you to seek a "Thus saith the Lord" for any hopes which you may entertain of being partakers of the inheritance of the saints in light.

I. LET US CONSIDER THE VALUE OF A "THUS SAITH THE LORD."

1. Our first observation is that it is the minister's message. If he be God's minister, he does not found his teaching upon his own authority, for then his message would be only that of himself, and not to be esteemed; but he shows the authority of his Master, and none can gainsay him. He claims men's attention on the ground that he utters a "Thus saith the Lord." No matter how aged he may be, he does not proclaim the truth as merely the result of his long investigations or his extraordinary experience, but he grounds it upon "Thus saith the Lord." So spake the hoary-headed Joshua when for many a year he had known the faithfulness of God, and was about to die. He was singing his swan-song, preaching his last sermon; but he did not commence it, "Thus saith my age," "Thus say I upon mine own authority," but "Thus saith the Lord God of Israel." A God-sent minister is the ambassador of the Most High, but he has no right to go beyond his commission; and when he does so, his office cannot yield him support. The prophets of God did not say, "Thus I speak as a prophet," but, "Thus saith the Lord." When the prophet came in Gideon's days and spoke to erring Israel, he opened his mouth with, "Thus saith the Lord God of Israel." Turn to the pages of Isaiah, and mark how frequent he quotes the divine authority; study the plaintive words of Jeremiah, and observe how solemnly his prophetic woes are prefaced with, "Thus saith the Lord;" and the soaring Ezekiel, to whom was given, as it were, six wings, that he might take more lofty flights than the eagle knoweth--even he relied not upon the sublimity of his language or the glory of his imagery, but found the sinews of his strength in "Thus saith the Lord God." This is the trowel and this the hammer of God's builders,--this the trumpet of his watchmen and the sword of his warriors. Woe to the man who comes in any other name! If we, or an angel from heaven, shall preach unto you anything but a "Thus saith the Lord," no matter what our character or standing, give no heed to us, but cleave unto the truth as it is in Jesus. To the law and to the testimony, if we speak not according to this word, it is because there is no light in us. That test which we demand to be exercised upon others we cheerfully consent to be exercised upon ourselves, praying that we may have grace to forsake our errors as we would have other men forsake theirs.

2. "Thus saith the Lord" is the only authority in God church. When the tabernacle was pitched in the wilderness, what was the authority for its length and breadth? Why was the altar of incense to be placed here, and the brazen laver there? Why so many lambs or bullocks to be offered on a certain day? Why must the Passover be roasted whole and not sodden? Simply and only because God had shown all these things to Moses in the holy mount; and thus had Jehovah spoken, "Look that thou make them after their pattern, which was showed thee in the mount." It is even so in the church at the present day; true servants of God demand to see for all church ordinances and doctrines the express authority of the church's only Teacher and Lord. They remember that the Lord Jesus bade the apostles to teach believers to observe all things whatsoever he had commanded them; but he neither gave to them nor to any man power to alter his own commands. The Holy Ghost revealed much of precious truth and holy precept by the apostles, and to his teaching we would give earnest heed; but when men cite the authority of fathers and councils and bishops, we give place for subjection? no, not for an hour. They may quote Irenaeus or Cyprian, Augustine or Chrysostom; they may remind us of the dogmas of Luther or Calvin; they may find authority in Simeon, Wesley, or Gill--we will listen to the opinions of those great men with the respect which they deserve as men; but having so done, we deny that we have anything to do with these men as authorities in the church of God: for there nothing has any authority but "Thus saith the Lord of Hosts." Yea, if you shall bring us the concurrent consent of all tradition--if you shall quote precedents venerable with fifteen, sixteen, or seventeen centuries of antiquity--we burn the whole as so much worthless lumber, unless you put your finger upon the passage of Holy Writ which warrants the matter to be of God. You may further plead, in addition to all this venerable authority, the beauty of the ceremony, and its usefulness to those who partake therein, but this is all foreign to the point; for to the true church of God the only question is this: Is there a "Thus saith the Lord" for it? And if divine authority be not forthcoming, faithful men thrust forth the intruder as the cunning craftiness of men.

3. "Thus saith the Lord" is the most fitting word of rebuke for erring saints. God's people when they err, if they be rebuked, even though it should be in the gentlest manner, are too apt to resent the rebuff; but when we can come to them with "Thus saith the Lord," if there be a spark of spiritual life left, it is sure to catch at this flame. When the man of God came to Eli, how Eli's heart trembled when he began, "Thus saith the Lord," and described to him the doom of his house, because his sons had made themselves vile, and he had not restrained them. David the king might have been moved to anger against Nathan for that personal parable and pungent application; but his anger was stayed, nay, better still, his heart was broken, because the prophet could say, "Thus saith the Lord." My dear brethren in Christ, you and I have often risen in anger at the intrusive proofs of ignorant men; but I hope we have far more often felt the melting power of a "Thus saith the Lord."

When the heart is right, the word of God sweetly melts us, as the breath of the south wind melts the frozen rivers.

4. "Thus saith the Lord" is the only solid ground of comfort to God's people. Where can a child of God find true solace apart from that which cometh out of the mouth of the Most High! Truly, "Man doth not live by bread alone; but by every word that proceedeth out of the mouth of God doth man live;" "Thy words were found, and I did eat them;" "How sweet are thy words unto my taste! yea, sweeter than honey to my mouth!" When Nathan came to tell David of the covenant which the Lord would make with him and his house, David would scarcely have believed so great a mercy to be really his if the prophet had not began with "Thus saith the Lord." It was not "Thus saith Nathan," or "Thus do the ancients say," but "Thus saith the Lord;" and David's heart was full of holy joy when he saw the covenant to be ordered in all things and sure. When Hezekiah lay sick unto death, he turned his face to the wall and prayed; but there was no comfort to the royal suppliant until the prophet came with "Thus saith the Lord;" and when Sennacherib was about to besiege Jerusalem, and Lachish had fallen, Hezekiah prayed, and the people with him; but oh! they could not think it possible that there should be a hook put into the jaw of the mighty Assyrian, and that he should be turned back by the way in which he came, till the prophet reassured their hearts with a "Thus saith the Lord." Zion's sons and daughters feast upon the sure word of their faithful God. Brethren, I need not enlarge here, for I hope most of you know the preciousness of a divine promise. There is nothing wanted to stay your soul in your worst troubles but the Word of God applied with power. God may not seed you a friend; he may not raise up a deliverer; but if he shall only give you to believe his Word, that shall be enough for you. Martin Luther said: "I have covenanted with my Lord that he should not send me visions, or dreams, or even angels. I am content with this one gift of the Scriptures, which abundantly teaches and supplies all that is necessary, both for this life and that which is to come." O Lord, only feed me on thy Word, and I will not envy kings their delicacies, nor even the angels around thy throne the bread of heaven on which they live.

5. Yet again: "Thus saith the Lord" is that with which we must confront the Lords enemies. When Moses went in before Pharaoh, the words which he used were not, "The elders of Israel have consulted, and thus have they bidden me say," not "Our Father Abraham once said, and his words have been handed to us by long tradition "--such talk would have been readily resisted; but he confronted the haughty monarch with "Thus saith the Lord, Let my people go;" and it was the power of this divine word which rained plagues upon the fields of Zoan, and brought forth the captives, with silver and gold. Pharaoh might boast, "Who is the Lord, that I should obey his voice?" but ere long he knew that Jehovah's word was mightier than all the horsemen and chariots of Mizraim, and was not to be resisted without terrible defeat. To this day, if we would break sinners' hearts, our hammer must be "Thus saith the Lord;" and if we would woo them to obedience to King Jesus, our reasons must come from his own Word. I have often noticed in conversion, that, though sometimes a particular passage of the sermon may be quoted by the converted person as the means of enlightenment, yet in the majority of cases it is the text, or some passage of Scripture, quoted during the sermon, which is blessed to do the work. McCheyne says, "Depend upon it, it is God's Word, not our comment upon God's Word, that saves souls;" and so it is. Let us use much of Scripture, much of the pure silver of sacred revelation, and no human alloy. "What is the chaff to the wheat, saith the Lord?"

6. To close this point. Such an authority has a "Thus saith the Lord," that it is not to be despised without entailing upon the offender the severest penalty. Samuel came to Saul with "Thus saith the Lord," and bade him destroy the Amalekites. He was utterly to cut them off, and not to spare so much as one of them. But Saul saved the best of the cattle and the sheep, and brought home Agag; and what was the result? His kingdom was taken from him and given to a neighbor of his that was better than he; and because he exalted himself beyond measure to do otherwise than according to the letter of God's command, he was put away forever from having dominion over Israel. And mark this word: if any church in Christendom shall continue, after light is given and after plain rebuke is uttered, to walk contrary to the word of God, and to teach that which is inconsistent with Holy Scripture, as Saul was put away from the kingdom, so shall that church be put away from before the Lord of Hosts; and if any man, be he who he may, after receiving light from on high, continues willfully to shut his eyes, he shall not, if an heir of heaven, be rejected from eternal salvation, but he shall be cast off from much of the usefulness and comfort which he might otherwise have enjoyed. He knew his Master's will, and did it not: he shall be beaten with many stripes. He has been as the horse or the mule which have no understanding, and his mouth shall be held in with bit and bridle. Many sorrows shall be to those who dare to dash themselves against the thick bosses of Jehovah's buckler by opposing his "Thus saith the Lord." Upon whomsoever this stone shall fall, it shall grind him to powder; and whosoever shall fall upon it shall be broken, to his own lasting damage. O my brethren! I would that we trembled and stood more in

awe of God's word. I fear me that many treat the things of God as though they were merely matters of opinion, but remember that opinion cannot govern in God's house. God's word, not man's opinion, claims your allegiance. Remember that although our ignorant conscience may not accuse us of error, yet if we walk contrary to God's word, our conscientiousness does not screen us from sin; for conscience is not the sovereign arbiter of right and wrong, but the plain word of God is the rule of equity. I do not sin so foully as if I sinned against my conscience, but I still sin, if, having an unenlightened conscience, I ignorantly transgress. But if I wilfully keep my conscience in darkness, and continue in errors which I might easily know to be such by a little thought and searching of God's word, then my conscience can offer me no excuse, for I am guilty of blindfolding the guide which I have chosen, and then, knowing him to be blindfolded, I am guilty of the folly of letting him lead me into rebellion against God. O church of God! hear thou the voice of thy great Founder and Lord: "Whosoever, therefore shall one of these least commandments, and shall teach men so, he shall be called the least in the kingdom of heaven." "He that hath my commandments, and keepeth them, he it is that loveth me: and he that loveth me shall be loved of my Father, and I will love him, and will manifest myself to him." Oh for a stern integrity, that will hold the word, and will never depart from it, come what may. This much concerning the value of a "Thus saith the Lord."

II. Dear friends, the second part of our subject may be very displeasing to some who have strayed in here, but that I cannot help. I do not remember ever asking any one to come and hear me, and therefore, as you come of your own wills, when I have any truth to speak, I shall not conceal it because you choose to be present. At the present crisis, I feel that it is woe unto me if I do not lift up my voice like a trumpet, and urge with all my might the necessity of reformation in our State Church. I have, moreover, an excellent excuse for the inquiry I am about to make; for as I am publicly charged with ignorance, it is at once my duty and my privilege to seek instruction of those who claim authority to teach. When one is known to be profoundly ignorant, and there are certain fathers in the faith who have the power to instruct, the least thing that can be allowed us is to ask questions, and the smallest boon we can expect is to have them answered by men expressly ordained to instruct the ignorant.

The Rev. W. Goode, the Dean of Ripon, appears to be much better acquainted with the extent of my reading and mental acquirements than I am myself. He speaks with all the positiveness of a personal acquaintance concerning my reputed ignorance, and for my own part I am not at all anxious to question so very reverend an authority. He writes: "As to that young minister who is now raving against the Evangelical clergy on this point, it is to be regretted that so much notice has been taken of his railings. He is to be pitied, because his entire want of acquaintance with theological literature leaves him utterly unfit for the determination of such a question; which is a question, not of more doctrine, but of what may be called historical theology; and his charges are just a parallel to those which the Romanists would bring against himself as well as others for the interpretation of the words, This is my body.' But were he a wiser man than he is, he would know better what his qualifications are for passing Judgment on such a point, and be willing to learn from such facts, among others, as the Gorham Judgment and the cases of Mr. Maskell and Mr. Mozley, what ground there is for his charges against the Evangelical clergy. Let him hold and enforce his own view of doctrine as he pleases; but when he undertakes to determine what is the exclusive meaning of the Book of Common Prayer, and brings a charge of dishonesty against those who take a different view of that meaning from what he does, he only shows the presumptuous self-confidence with which he is prepared to pronounce judgment upon matters of which he is profoundly ignorant. To hold a controversy with him upon the subject would be to as little purpose as to attempt to hold a logically-constructed argument with a child unacquainted with logical terms."

When this paragraph caught my eye, my heart leaped with joy, for I knew that the sinners in Zion were afraid; and I thought I heard a voice crying from the Word, "Not many wise men after the flesh, not many mighty, not many noble, are called; but God hath chosen the foolish things of the world to confound the wise; and God hath chosen the weak things of the world to confound the things which are mighty; and base things of the world, and things which are despised, hath God chosen, yea, and things which are not, to bring to naught things that are: that no flesh should glory in his presence." My mind flew back to the valley of Elah, and I remembered the words of the old record: "And when the Philistine looked about, and saw David, he disdained him; for he was but a youth, and ruddy, and of a fair countenance. And the Philistine said unto David, Am I a dog that thou comest to me with staves? And the Philistine cursed David by his gods. And the Philistine said to David, Come to me, and I will give thy flesh unto the fowls of the air, and to the beasts of the field." My spirit kindled at these words of the boastful champion of yore, and at their modern reproduction by the vainglorious divine of Ripon, and the answer of David was in my heart as it is even now upon my tongue: "Thou comest to me with a sword and with a spear and with a shield;

but I come to thee in the name of the Lord of Hosts, the God of the armies of Israel, whom thou hast defied. This day will the Lord deliver thee into mine hand that all the earth may know that there is a God in Israel. And all this assembly shall know that the Lord saveth not with sword and spear; for the battle is the Lord's, and he will give you into our hands." Admitting the witness of the venerable dean to be correct, and that "the young minister" is inexpert in logic, I am not therefore ashamed; far otherwise, I will the rather glory in mine infirmities that the power of Christ may rest upon me; "for when I am weak, then am I strong." Take, O ye great ones of the earth, every profit that can be made out of your belief in my utter total ignorance, and your own profound and extensive learning, and then go your ways, and learn what this meaneth: "Thy wisdom and thy knowledge, it hath perverted thee; and thou hast said in thine heart, I am, and none else beside me. Therefore shall evil come upon thee: thou shalt not know from whence it riseth.. And now at this hour, having been condemned as intolerably ignorant, I feel I have the liberty to ask just a few explanations of those reverend divines who do know or ought to know the grounds of their faith and practice.

1. I open this little book,--the Prayer-Book, of whose occasional services the more I know the less I approve,--and I find in the Baptismal Service, that when little children are brought to be sprinkled, certain godfathers and godmothers promise for them that they shall renounce the devil and all his works, the vain pomp and glory of the world, with all covetous desires of the same, etc., and that they shall obediently keep all God's holy will and commandments, and walk in the same all the days of their life. To me it seems that they might as well promise that the infants should grow up with Roman noses, auburn hair, and blue eyes; for they are just as able to make them do the one as the other. I shall not however intrude my opinion further, but simply ask whether there is a "Thus saith the Lord" for any man's standing proxy for a babe, and making such promises in its name?--in other words, I ask for apostolical, prophetic, or any other form of scriptural precept, or precedent, for the use of proxies in baptism. True religion is a personal matter--is its first manifestation in regeneration to be connected with the impossible promises of others? Plain proof-texts are requested for godfathers and godmothers; and such important persons deserve to be defended by the clergy, if texts of Scripture can be discovered. As I cannot imagine where the texts will be found, I must pause till the learned shall produce them. Further, I find that these children enter into a covenant by proxy, of which we are assured that the promise our Lord Jesus will for his part most surely keep and perform; but the children are bound to do their part--that part being something more than the gigantic task of keeping all the commandments of God. Now I ask for a "Thus saith the Lord" for such a covenant as this. I find two covenants in the Word of God: one is the covenant of works, "This do, and thou shalt live;" I find another, the covenant of grace, which runs only in this wise, "I will be their God, and they shall be my people." I find it expressly declared that there cannot be a mixture of works and grace; for, says Paul, "If by grace, then it is no more of works: otherwise grace is no more grace; but if it be of works, then is it no more grace: otherwise work is no more work;" and I ask a "Thus saith the Lord" for this baptismal covenant, which is nominally of grace, but really of works, or at best an unnatural conglomerate of grace and works. I ask those who have searched Scripture through, to find me the form or the command for any baptismal covenant whatever. It is idle to say that such a covenant was allowed among the early Christians; their witness is not earlier enough for us: we want a "Thus saith the Lord," and nothing but this will justify this pretended covenant.

We then find that after this covenant has been made, and the water has been applied in a manner which we think needs also a "Thus saith the Lord" to justify it, it is publicly declared that the babe is regenerated,--"Seeing now, dearly beloved brethren that this child is regenerated and grafted into the body of Christ's church, let us give thanks unto Almighty God for these benefits, and with one accord make our prayers unto him, that this child may lead the rest of his life according to this beginning." And, again, "We yield thee hearty thanks, most merciful Father, that it hath pleased thee to regenerate this infant with thy Holy Spirit, to receive him for thine own child by adoption, and to incorporate him into thy holy church," etc. We are told we do not understand the meaning of "regeneration" as it is used in the services of the Anglican Church. The meaning of this passage is historical, hypothetical, ecclesiastical, and we know not what. The words "to be born again" did not formerly seem to us to be so very difficult to understand, nor do they appear so now as they stand in Scripture; for we find in them the one regeneration which has renewed us in the spirit of our mind, and we cannot consent to use those words in any other sense. Well, whether regeneration be or be not a very equivocal word, we simply ask, Is there a "Thus saith the Lord" for the assertion that a sprinkled infant is therefore regenerate in any sense in the world? Will any person find us a text of Scripture?--he shall have large rewards from clergymen with uneasy consciences! We put our inquiry again in plain terms, Will some one oblige us with a plain "Thus saith the Lord" proving that water baptism in any one instance makes an unconscious babe a member of Christ and a child of God, in any sense which any sane person chooses to attach to those words? Where is the passage--where? Echo answers "where?" But this subject you have been considering for some time, and are well convinced that the process of regenerating babies by occult influences conveyed by water is a pure--no, an impure--invention of priest-craft. There is therefore no necessity that I enlarge upon a point so well understood.

2. I have a second question to ask. There is prescribed in the Book of Common Prayer a peculiar ceremony called confirmation. I do not remember to have read of that in Scripture. I would like to have a "Thus saith the Lord" for that rite. As I am ready to yield as far as possible, suppose we take it for granted that this ceremony is defensible from Holy Writ, I would like to know whether there is any "Thus saith the Lord" allowing a person called a bishop to give to the assembled youths an assurance of divine favor by laying his hands on their heads? The bishop having laid his hands on every head presented to him, whether it be gracious or graceless, talks thus in the Collect, "Almighty and everliving God, who makest us both to will and to do those things that be good and acceptable unto thy divine majesty, we make our humble supplications unto thee for these thy servants upon whom (after the example of thy holy apostles) we have now laid our hands, to certify them (by this sign) of thy favor and gracious goodness towards them." Does this mean that the bishop's hand certifies the person touched thereby of special divine favor? So it seems to teach, as far as I can see. We want, then, a "Thus saith the Lord," authorizing this individual in lawn to exercise the office of an apostle! We then desire scriptural warrant permitting him to certify these kneeling youths of the enjoyment or possession of any particular divine favor by putting his hands on their heads. If this means the common goodness of God, the bishop's hands are not needed to certify them of that; but as he has already declared in prayer that they were regenerated by water and the Spirit, and had been forgiven all their sins, it is clear that special favor is intended; we inquire, therefore, for his authority for giving these young people a further certificate of special divine favor by the imposition of his hands. Why his hands? Who is he that he can certify these persons of God's favor more than any other man? Where is his scriptural warrant to confer by his hands a certificate of grace upon young people who in innumerable cases are thoughtless and unconverted, if not profane? We want a "Thus saith the Lord" for the whole thing, and then for each item in detail. Endless is the task thus proposed to the honest Churchman.

3. Another matter needs a little clearing up; and, as this Book was set forth by learned divines and bishops, I would like a lucid explanation. The priest visits a sick man, sits down by his bed-side, reads certain prayers, bids the patient remember his baptism, questions him as to his creed, gives him good advice about forgiving his enemies and making his will, moves him to make a special confession of his sin if he feels his conscience troubled with any weighty matter, after which confession the Rubric says "the priest shall absolve him" (if he humbly and heartily desire it), after this sort. Here is the absolution, and I humbly and heartily desire a "Thus saith the Lord" for it: "Our Lord Jesus Christ, who hath left power to his church to absolve all sinners who truly repent and believe in him, of his great mercy forgive thee thine offences; and by his authority committed to me, I absolve thee from all thy sins, in the name of the Father, and of the Son, and of the Holy Ghost." Sir Priest, I want you to give me a plain warrant from God's Word for your absolving my dying neighbor at this rate. Who are you that you should use such words? The season is solemn: it is the hour of death, and the matter is weighty, for it concerns the eternal interests of the dying man, and may--nay, will, if you be found to be acting presumptuously in this matter--involve your own soul in eternal ruin. Whence did you derive your right to forgive that sick man? Might he not raise his withered hands and return the compliment by absolving you? Are you quite sure as to the committal of divine authority to you? Then show me the deed of gift, and let it be clearly of divine origin. The apostles were empowered to do many things; but who are you? Do you claim to be their successors? Then work miracles similar to theirs; take up serpents, and drink deadly things without being harmed thereby; prove to us that you have seen the Lord, or even that cloven tongues of fire have sat upon each of you. You evangelical clergy, dare you claim to be successors of the apostles, and to have power to forgive sins? Your Puseyite brethren go the whole length of superstitious pretension; but you have too much light to be so superstitious; and yet you do what is quite as wicked,--you solemnly subscribe that this absolution is not contrary to the Word of God when you know it is? Gorham case, say you. I care nothing for your Gorham case: I want a "Thus saith the Lord" warranting you to swear to what you know to be false and dangerous. Mr. Mozley and Mr. Maskell may give you all the comfort which they can afford; but one word of Peter or of Paul would be of more weight in this matter than a thousand words from either of them.

You are aware, perhaps, that it is not every man who is permitted by the Established religion to pronounce this absolution. A person called a "deacon" is, I am informed, allowed to preach and do a great many things, but when he reads the Book of Common Prayer in the daily service he must not grant absolution; there is a supernatural something which the man has not yet received, for he has only once felt the episcopal imposition of hands. We shall see, by-and-by, where absolving power comes from. The deacon has attained to one grade of priestcraft, but the full vigor of mystic influence rests not upon him. Another touch, another subscription, and the keys of St. Peter will swing at his girdle; but his time is not yet. I ask him, whether he calls himself a deacon or a priest, where he gets a "Thus saith the Lord" for this absolution? which, if it be not of God, is a piece of impertinence, superstition, blasphemy, and falsehood.

4. I turn on and find that when the sick dies he is buried in consecrated ground; and though he may have cut his throat while under delirium tremens, if the jury do not return a verdict of suicide, the priest shall say, as he casts earth upon the body, "Forasmuch as it hath pleased Almighty God of his great mercy to take unto himself the soul of our dear brother here departed, we therefore commit his body to the ground,--earth to earth, ashes to ashes, dust to dust,--in sure and certain hope of the resurrection to eternal life." And again, "We give thee hearty thanks for that it hath pleased thee to deliver this our brother out of the miseries of this sinful world." And yet again, "We meekly beseech thee, O Father, to raise us from he death of sin unto the life of righteousness; that when we shall depart this life, we may rest in him, as our hope is this our brother doth." We beg a "Thus saith the Lord" for burying every baptized thief, harlot, rogue, drunkard, and liar who may die in the parish--"in sure and certain hope of the blessed resurrection." "Oh! it is commanded by authority." What authority? We challenge it, and permit none to pass muster but a "Thus saith the Lord." Until clergymen will bring us scriptural warrant for uttering falsehoods over a grave, we dare not cease our testimony against them. How long will the many godly laymen in that Church remain quiet? Why do they not bestir themselves, and demand revision or disruption?

5. Turning a little further on, into a part of the Prayer-Book not much frequented by ordinary readers, we come to the "Ordering of Priests," or the way in which priests are made. Why priests? Is one believer more a priest than another, when all are styled a royal priesthood? Let that pass. Of course, brethren, the priests are made by the bishops, as the bishops are made by Lord Palmerston, or Lord Derby, or any other political leader who may be in office. The Prime Minister of England is the true fountain from whom all bishops flow, and the priests are minor emanations branching off from the mitre rather than the crown. Here is the way of ordering priests. Let heaven and earth hear this and be astonished: "When this prayer is done, the bishop with the priests present shall lay their hands severally upon the head of every one that receiveth the order of priesthood; the receivers humbly kneeling upon their knees, and the bishop saying, Receive the Holy Ghost.'" Listen to it, now! Think you behold the scene: a man of God, a bishop whom you have been in the habit of considering a most gracious, godly man, and such no doubt he may be, in a sort,--think you see him putting his hands upon the head of some evangelical man whom you will go and hear, or, if you like, upon some young rake fresh from Oxford,--and think you hear him say, "Receive the Holy Ghost for the office and work of a priest in the church of God, now committed unto thee by the imposition of our hands. Whose sins thou dost forgive, they are forgiven, and whose sins thou dost retain, they are retained." We want a "Thus saith the Lord" for that; for that is putting it rather strongly in the popish line, one would think. Is the way of ordering priests in the Church of Rome much worse than this? That the apostles did confer the Holy Ghost, we never thought of denying; but that Oxford, Exeter, or any other occupants of the bench can give the Holy Spirit, needs some proof other than their silk aprons or lawn sleeves can afford us. We ask, moreover, for one instance in which an apostle conferred upon any minister the power to forgive sins, and where it can be found in Scripture that any man other than an apostle ever received authority to absolve sinners. Sirs, let us say the truth; however much yonder priest may pretend at his parishioner's bedside to forgive sin, the man's sins are not forgiven; and the troubled conscience of the sinner often bears witness to the fact, as the day of judgment and the fearful hell of sinners must also bear witness. And what think you, sirs, must be the curse that fills the mouth of damned souls, when in another world they meet the priest who absolved them with this sham absolution! With what reproaches will such deceived ones meet the priest who sent them down to perdition with a lie in their right hands! Will they not say to him, "Thou didst forgive me all my sins by an authority committed unto thee, and yet here am I cast into the pit of hell?" Oh! if I do not clear my Soul upon this infamous business, and if the whole Christian church does not cleanse herself of it, what guilt will lay upon us! This is become a crying evil, and a sin that is not to be spoken of behind the door, nor to be handled in gentle language. I have been severe, it is said, and spoken harshly. I do not believe it possible to be too severe in this matter; but, sirs, if I have been so, let that be set down as my sin if you will; but is there any comparison between my fault and that of men who know this to be contrary to the Word of God, and yet give it their unfeigned assent and consent? or the sin of those who can lie unto the Holy Ghost, by pretending to confer Him who bloweth where he listeth upon men who as likely as not are as graceless as the very heathen? Fresh from the dissipations of college-life, the sinner bows before the man in lawn, and rises a full-blown priest, fully able to remit or retain sins. After this, how can the priests of the Church of England denounce the Roman Catholics? It is so very easy to fume and bluster against Puseyites and Papists; but the moment our charity begins at home, and we give our Evangelical brethren the same benefit which they confer

upon the open Romanists, they are incensed beyond measure. Yet will we tell them to their faces, that they, despite their fair speeches, are as guilty as those whom they denounce; for there is as much Popery in this priest-making as in any passage in the mass-book. Protestant England! wilt thou long tolerate this blasphemy? Land of Wiclif, birthplace of the martyrs of Smithfield, is this long to be borne with? I am clear of this matter before the Most High, or hope to be, ere I sleep in the grave; and having once sounded the trumpet, it hall ring till my lips are dumb. Do you tell me it is no business of mine? Is it not the National Church?--does not its sin rest, therefore, upon every man and woman in the nation, Dissenter and Churchman, who does not shake himself from it by open disavowal? I am not meddling with anybody else's church; but the church that claims me as a parishioner would compel me, if it could, to pay its church rates, and that does take from me my share of tithe every year. I ask the sturdy Protestants of England, and especially the laity of the Church of England, whether they intend forever to foster such abominations? Arise, Britannia! nation of the free, and shake thy garments from the dust of this hoary superstition; and as for thee, O Church of England! may God bless thee with ministers who will sooner come forth to poverty and shame than pervert or assist in perverting the Word of God.

6. I have not quite done: I have another question to ask. Look at the thanksgiving which is offered on the twentieth day of June, on account of Her Majesty's accession: in this thanksgiving we very heartily join, although we decline to pray by book on the twentieth of June or any other day; look at the close that thanksgiving, and you see the name of Lord John Russell as a sort of official authority for the prayer! Is Earl Russell also among the prophets? And on the other side of the page, in order that the Tories may edify the church as well as the Whigs, I see the hand of S. H. Walpole. Is he also a governor in Christ's church? Hath the Lord given these men power to legislate for his church, or sign mandates for her to obey? But what is it all about? "Victoria Regina, our will and pleasure is that these four forms of prayer," etc. Do you see? here is royal supremacy! Further on, in the next page: "Now, therefore, our will and pleasure is," etc. See the Preface to the Articles, "Being by God's Ordinance, according to our just Title, Defender of the Faith, and Supreme Governor of the Church, within these our Dominions;" and again, "We are Supreme Governor of the Church of England." This is the way in which your Church bows herself before the kingdoms of this world. I demand, earnestly demand, a "Thus saith the Lord" for this royal supremacy. If any king, or queen, or emperor shall say, in any Christian church, "Our will and pleasure is," we reply, "We have another King,--one Jesus." As to the Queen, honored and beloved as she is, she is by her sex incapacitated for ruling in the church. Paul decides that point by his plain precept, "I suffer not a woman to teach, nor to usurp authority over the man, but to be in silence;" and if a king were in the case, we should say, "We render unto Caesar the things which are Caesar's, and unto God the things which are God's." In civil matters, we cheerfully obey princes and magistrates; but if any king, queen, emperor, or what not, usurps power in the church of God, we reply, "One is our Master, even Christ, and all we are brethren. The crown-rights belong to King Jesus: he alone is King in Zion." But I am met at once with the reply, "Well, but Christ is the Head of the Established Church, as well as the Queen." I remember reading about a three-headed dog which kept the gates of hell, but I never dreamed of a two-headed church till I heard of the Anglican Establishment. A two-headed church is a monster! The Queen the Head of the Church, and King Jesus the Head of the Church, too! Never. Where is a "Thus saith the Lord" for this? No man living who calls himself an Englishman has a word to say of Her Majesty except that which is full of honor and esteem and loyal affection; but the moment we come to talk about the church of Christ, whoever shall say, or think, or believe, that there is any headship to the church of Christ except the person of Christ himself, he knoweth not what he saith nor whereof he affirmeth. Our Lord Jesus Christ is the Head over all things to his church, which is his body: the fulness of him filleth all in all. Here stand the two letters "V. R." at the top of certain mandates, and they mean just this: "Our royal authority commands that you shall not believe this, and you shall believe that; you shall not pray this, and you shall pray that; and you shall pray on such a day," and so on. The church which thus bows to authority commits fornication with the kings of the earth, and virtually renounces her allegiance to Christ to gain the filthy lucre of state endowments. He is the freeman whom the truth makes free, and who wears no gilded collar, with a chain hanging therefrom held in a royal hand. Remember how the Chancellor laughed to scorn the whole bench of bishops, and rightly so; for he who voluntarily makes himself a bondman deserves to feel the lash. May the little finger of our state grow heavier than the loins of James or Elizabeth, until all good men flee from the house of bondage. Servants of God, will ye be servants of man? Ye who profess to follow King Jesus and see him crowned with the crown wherewith his mother crowned him in the day of his espousals, do you take off his diadem to put it upon the head of another? No, it shall never be. Scotland has repelled the royal intrusion right bravely by her sons of the Free Church, who have left all to follow King Jesus. Her bush burned in the olden times, but was not consumed; the covenant was stained with blood, but it was never slain. Let us revive that covenant, and, if need be, seal it with our

blood. Let the Church of England have what king she pleases, or what prince she pleases for her head; but this I know, that there is no "Thus saith the Lord" concerning the ecclesiastical supremacy of Victoria Regina, nor the authority of Lord John Russell, or S. H. Walpole, or any of that company, honorable though they be.

7. Now once more: one other question. I am profoundly ignorant, and have not the power to judge of these things (so am I informed), and therefore I would like to ask for a "Thus saith the Lord" for a few of the canons;--no, perhaps I had better not read them; they are too bad,--they are full of all malice and uncharitableness, and everything that cometh of the foul fiend. I will ask whether there can be found any "Thus saith the Lord" for this: Canon 10. "Maintainers of Schismatics in the Church of England to be censured. Whoever shall hereafter affirm that such ministers as refuse to subscribe to the form and manner of God's worship in the Church of England, prescribed in the Communion-Book, and their adherents, may truly take unto them the name of another church not established by law, and dare presume to publish it, that this their pretended church hath of long time groaned under the burden of certain grievances imposed upon it, and upon the members thereof before mentioned, by the Church of England, and the orders and constitutions therein by law established, let them be excommunicated, and not restored until they repent and publicly revoke such their wicked errors." What Scripture warrants one church to excommunicate another merely for being a church, and complaining of undoubted grievances?

Canon 11. "Maintainers of Conventicles censured. Whosoever shall hereafter affirm or maintain that there are within this realm other meetings, assemblies, or congregations of the king's born subjects, than such as by the laws of this land are held and allowed, which may rightly challenge to themselves the name of true and lawful churches, let him be excommunicated, and not restored but by the Archbishop, after his repentance and public revocation of such his wicked errors." Where doth Holy Scripture authorize the excommunication of every good man who is charitable enough to believe that there are other churches beside his own? Search ye out of to book of the Lord, and read!

For very much in this Book of Canons I beg to be informed of a "Thus saith the Lord." For matters which do not concern religion and have only to do with the mere arrangement of service, we neither ask nor expect a divine precept; but upon vital points of doctrine, ceremony, or precept, we cannot do without it. Scarcely can any document be more inconsistent with Scripture than the Book of Canons, and hence it is ever kept in the back ground, because those who know anything about it must be ashamed of it. And yet these are Canons of the Church of England,--canons which are inconsistent, many of them, with even the common rules of our own present enlightened law, let alone the Word of God. We ask a "Thus saith the Lord" for them, and we wait until a "Thus saith the Lord" shall be found to defend them.

Now some will say, why do I thus take this matter up and look into it? I have already told you the reason, dear friends. There is an opportunity for pushing another Reformation given to us just now, of which if we do not avail ourselves we shall be very guilty. Some have said, "Why not go on preaching the gospel to sinners?" I do preach the gospel to sinners, as earnestly as ever I did in my life; and there are as many conversions to God as at any former period. This is God's work: and beware lest any of you lift a finger against it. The hand of the Lord is in this thing, and he that lives shall see it. Let us have our prayers, that good may come of this controversy, even though you may deplore it. As for anything else that you can do, it shall not turn us a hair's-breadth from this testimony to which we feel God has called us, though it bringeth upon us every evil that flesh would shrink from. The words of Dr. Guthrie are well worth quoting here: "The servant is no better than his master; and I do believe, were we more true to God, more faithful and honest in opposing the world for its good, we should get less smoothly along the path of life, and have less reason to read with apprehension these words of Jesus: Woe unto you when all men shall speak well of you.' Not less true than shrewd was the remark of a Scotch woman respecting one who, just settled in the ministry, had been borne to his pulpit amid the plaudits of all the people: If he is a faithful servant of the Lord Jesus Christ, he will have all the blackguards in the parish on his head before a month is gone.'"

III. Now, to close, let me say to you, my hearers, have any of you a hope of heaven which will not stand the test of "Thus saith the Lord?" What are you resting upon? Are you resting upon something which you felt when excited at a prayer-meeting or under a sermon? Remember you will not have that excitement to bear you up in death, and the religion of excitement will not suffice in the day of judgment. Are you building upon your own works? Are you depending upon your own feelings? Do you rely upon sacraments? Are you placing your trust upon the word of man? If so, remember that when God shakes all things he will shake these false foundations; but oh! build upon the Word of my Lord and Master; trust your soul with Jesus. Hating sin, and clinging to the great sinbearer, you shall find in him a rock of refuge which can never, never fail you; but I do conjure you, as the Lord liveth, search and try yourselves by the Word of God. No doubt there are many among us who are not built upon the Rock of Ages, and we may any of us be deceived by a mere name to live. Do, then, since the test-day must come,--since you must be weighed in the balances,--weigh yourselves now, my hearers; and let none of us go down to the chambers of destruction believing ourselves to be heirs of heaven, being all the while enemies to the Most High God. May the Lord exalt his own Word, and give us a sure inheritance in the blessings which it brings. Amen.

The True Position Of Assurance

DELIVERED ON SUNDAY MORNING, OCTOBER 2ND, 1864,
BY C, H. SPURGEON,
AT THE METROPOLITAN TABERNACLE, NEWINGTON.

"In whom you also trusted, after that you heard the Word of Truth, the Gospel of your salvation: in whom also after that you believed, you were sealed with the Holy Spirit of promise." -- Ephesians 1:13.

MANY sincerely seeking souls are in great trouble because they have not yet attained to an assurance of their interest in Christ Jesus--they dare not take any comfort from their faith because they suppose that it has not attained to a sufficient strength. They have believed in the Lord Jesus and they have His promise that they shall be saved, but they are not content with this--they want to get assurance and then they suppose they shall have a better evidence of their salvation than the bare word of the Savior.

Such persons are greatly mistaken. But as that mistake is a very painful one, and exercises the most injurious influence upon them, we will spend this morning in trying, as God shall help us, to clear up their difficulty. We want them to see that if they believe in the Lord Jesus Christ, even though they should not have attained to the precious Grace of full assurance of faith, yet nevertheless they are saved! And being justified by faith, they may rightfully enjoy peace with God through Jesus Christ our Lord!

Their mistake seems to me to be this--they look for ripe fruit upon a tree in spring and because that season yields nothing but blossoms, they conclude the tree to be barren. They go to the head of a river--they find it a little rippling brook, and because it will not float a "Great Eastern," they conclude that it will never reach the sea, and that, in fact, it is not a true part of the river at all. They look upon themselves as being little children and such they are--but because they cannot speak plainly on account of having been so newly born, they therefore conclude that they are not the children of God at all!

They see strong men in Christ Jesus performing great exploits. And because they, as yet, are but young and feeble, they conclude that they are not in the family of Grace. They compare themselves with giants in the Church of God and then, because they rightly perceive the difference between themselves and these mighty ones, they imagine that they are not saved--that they cannot be numbered among the faithful and have no part nor lot in this matter. They put the last things first. They make comforts essentials. They consider that which is the fruit of Grace to be the root of Grace. And herein they pierce themselves through with many sorrows.

Perhaps they will not fall into this error again if they get a right understanding of the text before us. The Apostle Paul here explains the process by which sealing--the sealing of assurance--is obtained. There are three steps by which the hallowed elevation is reached. The first is hearing--they heard first the preaching of the Word. The second is believing. And then, thirdly, "after that you believed, you were sealed with the Holy Spirit of promise."

I. To begin then, faith comes by HEARING. The preaching of the Gospel is God's soul-saving ordinance. It has pleased God by the "foolishness of preaching" to save them that believe. In every age God raises up men who faithfully proclaim His Word and, as he departs, another arrives. Elijah ascends to Glory, but his mantle falls upon Elisha. Paul dies not until Timothy is in the field. This true Apostolic succession is continued evermore, for when we know not where to find ministers, we may rest assured that in nooks and corners the Lord is preparing men for His work.

The true preacher has a claim upon men's attention. If God has sent him, men should receive him. If he comes as an ambassador from the King of kings, let his commission be proved and he has a right to receive the careful and prayerful attention of all who come in his way. No, more--God's true ambassador not only claims a hearing, but he wins it--for there is an attractiveness in his theme which holds men by the ears! "I, if I am lifted up," said Christ, "will draw all men unto Me," and among the other drawings there is this peculiar fact that men are drawn to hear where Christ is preached!

He who preaches Christ has golden chains coming from his mouth with which he binds men's ears, if not their hearts. They are not all bound to salvation, but bound somehow they shall be--the savor shall go forth even though it should be a savor of death unto death and not of life unto life. The preacher claims a hearing and he wins it! What is that message which we are to hear in order to the attaining of faith, and, through faith, of full assurance?

Our text is very expressive, for it tells us, "You heard the Word of Truth, the Gospel of your salvation." It is of little use to hear that which is not the Word of Truth--no, it is worse than useless--for by error we shall soon be misled. And if the preaching is not concerning the Word of Truth, even though it should be a word of truth, yet it can be of no value to the getting of faith--it must be the Word--the Word peculiarly above all others having the Truth of God and substance in it. There is no doubt that the expression here is a Hebraism for, "the true Word," you heard the true Word.

O Brothers and Sisters, how joyous it is for us to know God's Word to be true! We have proved it in our own souls and thus can bear our witness to you concerning it. If we speak not according to the true Word of God, reject us, for that which will bless you must have a, "Thus says the Lord," to support it and must be based upon the Revelation of the Most High--otherwise it cannot be of saving service, seeing it is not the Word which is infallibly true!

No doubt that the expression signifies the highest truth, truth as much the truth among other truths, as the Bible is the book above all other books. What I must hear for my salvation is not an important doctrine which may or may not be believed, but the Word without which men must perish in their sins. We may also remind you that the "Word of Truth" is a phrase peculiar to the contradistinction to the Law. Compare the Revelation of Christ with that of Moses--Moses revealed much Gospel Truth, but it was in shadows, not by a plain word of teaching--and therefore we now declare that the Law was given by Moses--but Grace and Truth came by Jesus Christ.

Christ is the Substance of all those shadows which Moses had to bring before the people's minds. And therefore there is an emphasis about the Gospel as being not metaphorical Truth, but solid Truth--the essential Truth of God. As the mountain towers high above the surrounding plain, so the great Truth that, "God was made flesh and dwelt among us"--the faithful saying that, "Jesus Christ came into the world to seek and to save sinners"--towers above all other Truths of God and demands our first and our best thoughts. And as the sun outshines all other lights, even so the manifestation of Truth in the Gospel of Christ excels all other Revelations. It is the Word of Truth.

But the text also adds, "the Gospel"--"the Gospel of your salvation." You are to listen to the Gospel--to that which is good news--to a something totally new to the world's natural religion--a something which came fresh from God--God's great novelty--something good--good in the deepest sense--infinitely good--good for your soul's best interests--good in answering the craving appetite of your poor hungry spirit. It must be good news--it must be evangelical doctrine to which you must listen if you would get faith!

Faith does not come by seeing. Men do not get faith by looking at a priest manipulating bread and wine, or sprinkling drops of baptismal water. The symbols of the Church of Rome do not beget faith. They may beget attention. They may please the fancy and delight the taste, but they do not beget the faith of God's elect. It is the Gospel--the Gospel preached and heard which does this through the power of the Holy Spirit! We do not get faith through ordinances--no matter if God Himself prescribed them. They are not the channel through which faith comes. The Apostle expressly declares that, "faith comes by hearing and hearing by the Word of God."

It is not through eye-gate, but through ear-gate, that salvation comes to us. God may, and doubtless does, infuse Grace into us by channels other than the sense of hearing. But, at any rate, the usual way in which Grace comes streaming into the soul is by hearing--and that is the hearing of the Gospel--not the hearing of tradition! Not the hearing of supposition! Not the hearing of poetic imaginations, but the hearing of that old evangel, which was first proclaimed by Jesus on the Mount and afterwards by His Apostles and to this day is still proclaimed with trumpet-tongue by those who know its quickening power!

You must hear the Gospel--and observe it is called "the Gospel of your salvation." You will never get faith, dear Friends, unless you look upon the Gospel as the great means of salvation and come earnestly enquiring and desiring that it may be made to you the Gospel of your salvation! Not of another man's, but of your salvation. I cannot say to every unconverted man, "This Gospel will save you," but I can say this--if you receive this Gospel, it certainly will--and that the moment it is accepted by the heart it is the Gospel of your salvation.

Reject it--it will be a savor of death unto death to you! But if the Holy Spirit shall come with it and command your will and win your assent and consent, then it is, indeed, the Gospel of your salvation. Are you a sinner? "Christ Jesus came into the world to save sinners." Inasmuch as this is worthy of all acceptance, it is worthy of your acceptance and is, in a sense, even now the Gospel of your salvation! We know that Christ came to "seek and to save that which was lost." Are you lost? Then in a sense it is the Gospel of your salvation, seeing that you are lost. If you can grasp that cheering Word with the hand of faith, you will say, "Yes, lost as I am, I believe Christ came to save the lost and I trust Him alone to save me." Then it is the Gospel of your salvation in a very high and special sense, seeing that now you have been saved by it!

The great end, it seems to me, of the preaching of the Gospel is just this--the preacher should always be aiming so to preach it that he may find out those souls to whom this is the Gospel of their salvation--so laboring to bring it home, both by persuading by the terrors of the Law and by the love of Jesus! Then men shall--through the Spirit of God accompanying the Word--be led, through hearing, to lay hold upon Christ and so to be saved! Thus I have set forth what you have to hear.

May I beg you carefully to judge every preacher, not by his gifts, not by his elocutionary powers, not by his status in society, not by the respectability of his congregation, not by the prettiness of his Church, the grandeur of the ceremonies, or the peculiar beauty of his vestments, but by this--does he preach the Word of Truth, the Gospel of your salvation? If he does, your sitting under his ministry may prove to you the means of getting faith. But if he does not, you cannot expect God's blessing, for you are not using God's ordinance but the ordinance of man.

The hearing of the Gospel involves the hearer in responsibility. It is a great privilege to hear the Gospel. You may smile and think there is nothing very great in it. The damned in Hell know! Oh, what would they give if they could hear the Gospel now--if they could come back and entertain but a shadow of a hope that they might yet escape from the wrath to come? The saved in Heaven estimate this privilege at a high rate, for, having obtained salvation and eternal life through the preaching of this Gospel, they can never cease to bless their God for calling them by His Word of Truth.

That you knew it! On your dying beds the listening to a Gospel sermon will seem another thing than it seems now. Now you may come out of curiosity, and go away and forget it. But when grim Death and you shall stand face to face, you will find it quite another thing to have had God's Word spoken to you and you will hear such a word as this, "You stumbled at the Word because you were disobedient and therefore woe has come upon you to the uttermost." I must also add that if hearing is really so gracious an ordinance, it becomes Christian men and women to pray the Lord to send forth laborers into His vineyard--to entreat Him to bless all efforts used to train our young ministers for future conflict.

I beg you not to forget to aid our Pastor's College both with your gifts and your prayers! It should bring afresh to the thoughts of all of you the duty of praying for those who are engaged in preaching the Word, for their preaching is nothing, except as the Spirit goes with it. And though, when the Spirit goes with it the shout of the King is heard in our camps, let Him withdraw and there is nothing but disappointment and dismay in the hosts of God. Pray for us, Brethren!

We trust we have a good conscience and endeavor to free ourselves of the blood of souls. We want our hearers to pray for us and hold up our hands as Aaron and Hur held up the hands of Moses on the mount. Be diligent in hearing the Word. If you are saved, still listen to it for your soul's health. If you are not saved, neglect no opportunities of listening. Lie at this pool of Bethesda--who can tell but you may yet step in when the angel does move the waters--or Jesus Himself may come and walk through those five porches and bid you take up your bed and walk?

Waste no Sunday in going where you cannot hear the Gospel! And when you hear the Gospel, hear it with all your ears--give your whole soul to it--as the thirsty earth drinks in the descending showers, so drink in the Word of God! As new-born babes receive the unadulterated milk of the Word, so receive that which is able to save your souls! And through hearing may faith come and through faith may you gain the assurance which you so earnestly desire.

II. After hearing came BELIEF. We know that believing does not always immediately follow hearing. There is a case told of Mr. Flavel having preached a sermon which was blessed to a man, I think eighty-five years afterwards, so that the seed may lay long buried in dust! Yet, had not that man heard that sermon, speaking after the manner of men, he had not received the quickening Word of God!

You may have heard the Gospel long in vain and it should be to you a source of very serious enquiry if you have done so--it should set you trembling lest the Word should never be the savor of life unto you. But at the same time do not renounce the hearing because up to now you have had no blessing, for faith comes by hearing. Continue to listen! Continue to search the Word. And if your soul desires faith, God denies not faith to any in whom He has really implanted a desire after it. Faith will yet, we trust, come while you are hearing. This belief, you observe, is called trusting. Kindly look at the verse--"In whom you also trusted."

The translators have borrowed that word, "trusted," very properly, from the twelfth verse. Do not, because you see it in italics, think that it is not properly there. It is not in the original, but being in the twelfth verse it is very rightly understood here. Believing, then, is trusting. If you want it summed up in the shortest word, it is just this--trusting Christ. A message comes to me upon good authority--I believe it. Believing it, I necessarily trust it. My receiving of the message is so far good, but the essential act, the act essential to salvation is the trusting--the trusting Christ.

The process of faith may be thus illustrated. You know a friend of yours to be perfectly reliable--you are in debt. He tells you that if you will trust him to pay the debt, he will give you, on the spot, a receipt for it. Now you look at him. You consider his ability to pay it. You consider the probability that he means what he is saying. Having once made up your mind that he is truthful, you could not then say, "I cannot believe you." If you once know that person to be truthful, I utterly deny that you can hold any argument about your power to believe him!

So, if Jesus Christ declares that He came into the world to save sinners, and, if He tells me, as He does tell me, that "whosever believes in Him shall not perish, but have eternal life"--if I am already enabled by God's Spirit to believe in the perfect truthfulness of Christ, I should be lying unto my own soul if I said I had not power to believe in Him. Understand, power to believe in Christ is the gift of the Holy Spirit. But the Holy Spirit has given that power to all men who know the perfect truthfulness of Christ.

It must be so, if you just look at it for a moment--it must be so. If I know the perfect truthfulness of a man, I lie if I say to him, "I cannot believe you." Why, it follows, as a matter of course that I must believe if I am convinced that he is worthy of credit. Just so, when I am assured of Christ that His Testimony is worthy of my belief--I have no right, then, to plead that I cannot believe Him. Mark, I am only speaking to those who have got as far as that and there are hundreds of you who have! When you tell me you cannot believe, I reply, "My dear Friend, you can believe. In the Holy Spirit's giving you enough enlightenment to know that Christ is faithful and true, that enlightenment is your power to believe!"

And this is according to the rules of common sense as well as according to the rules of experience. Do not stand, therefore, and say, "I cannot believe what Christ says." Do you believe Him to be true? "Yes," you say, "I dare not say otherwise." Then you can believe what He says. But do you really believe that Christ is true? I fear you do not. I believe that John discovered the secret of your unbelief when he said, "He that believes not has made God a liar, because he has not believed on His Son." That is the bottom line.

You really think God is a liar! Do you shrink from that charge? Ah, but I must bring it against you again, for if you know God to be true, I insist upon it and your own reason tells you it is so--that you cannot help believing in a person you know to be true! I fear that you are making God a liar. And if you deny that charge, then I arrest you at the other point at once and demand of you that you do now exercise faith and trust in the Lord Jesus Christ! It is trusting Christ that saves the soul!

Now a few remarks about believing. Faith in Christ is the work of God's Holy Spirit. In proof of this we have many Scriptures. No man ever did yet believe in Christ until the Holy Spirit had quickened him and illuminated his understanding so that he perceived the truthfulness of Christ's Character and was then led to trust Him. But in the next place, although faith is the work of the Spirit, it is the act of man. The Holy Spirit does not believe for me--there is nothing for Him to believe! Repentance is the work of the Holy Spirit, but the Holy Spirit does not repent--He has nothing to repent of. He works in me to will and to do, but I will and I do--He does not will nor do what I ought to will and do.

If I have a person here who is ignorant and I teach him--when he acquires knowledge, that knowledge is my gift to him and my work in him. At the same time he acquires that knowledge himself, and it would never have been his if he had not yielded up his faculties to be taught. Man believes. And whenever persons say to you, "Well, if it is the work of the Holy Spirit, how can it be the duty of man?" remind them that while it is the work of the Holy Spirit, it is not the act of the Holy Spirit, The Holy Spirit does not believe--it is the man who believes.

The Spirit moves upon us and by His mysterious agency takes away the natural unbelief of the soul and then we believe. But man is not passive in the act of believing. A dead man does not believe--the man is quickened and then his quickened spirit lays hold of the revealed Truth of God. Observe this, further, that faith is due to Christ. The faithful and true witness demands of me that I should believe what He says. Sinner, this is the unkindest cut you can give to Christ-- to doubt Him. I tell you that all His sufferings on the tree did not insult Him so much as when you say, "I cannot trust You."

What? Not trust the eternal arm on which the earth hangs? Not trust the bleeding hands which have opened the gates of Heaven for the very chief of sinners? Not trust the streaming side out of which there gushes blood and water to cleanse the guilt and the power of sin? Not trust God's own Son, the Mighty God, the Redeemer of Men? It is due to Him that you should, with your whole heart, lean upon Him and give Him all your confidence. This faith is essential to salvation. Assurance is not essential, but no man can be saved unless he trusts in the Lord Jesus Christ. You may get to Heaven with a thousand doubts and fears--you may get to Heaven without some of those Graces of the Spirit which are the ornaments of the Believer's neck! But you cannot get there without the life-giving Grace offaith.

You must have that and so long as you continue to say, "I will not trust Christ. I want dreams, visions, experiences, revelations. I want terrors of conviction. I want this, I want the other"--so long you shut yourself out of peace. Till you set your seal to God's Word, God will never set His seal to your faith. Remark, again, this faith is not required in any particular degree. In order to salvation, it is not declared in Scripture that you are to believe to a certain strength--if you have faith as small as a grain of mustard seed--if that is a mountain-moving faith, surely it shall be a soul-saving faith!

Faith is not to be estimated by its quantity but by its quality. If you have no more faith than a smoking flax has of fire, yet He will not quench you--if you have no more power of faith than a bruised reed has of strength, yet He will not break you! If you are not a man, but an infant in Grace--no, if you are scarcely a healthy infant, if there is but faith in you, though you are cast out as unswaddled and unwashed--yet He passes by and looks upon you! Can you but trust Him? THAT is the thing. If you do but trust Him as a drowning man clutches a rope. If you look to Jesus, as it were, out of the corner of your eye, though there are so many tears in your eyes that you cannot see Him so completely as you desire--though you cannot see Him at all to your comfort--yet you see Him to salvation! If you have received Him, desire great faith, but remember that little faith will carry you to Heaven through Jesus Christ.

Observe, further, that this faith is very variable, but it is not perishable. Faith may go to an ebb, as the tide does, but it will come to a flood again. When faith is at its flood, the man is not, therefore, more saved! And when faith is at its ebb, the man is not, therefore, less saved! For, after all, salvation does not lie in faith, but in Christ. And faith is but the connecting link between the soul and Christ. Faith may take Christ up in its arms, like Simeon, and it is true faith. But, on the other hand, faith may only venture to touch the hem of Jesus' garment and that faith makes men whole.

Some of us can look the Savior in the face and even kiss Him with the kisses of our mouth and others may only venture to come behind Him in the throng, all timid and afraid--but faith, if it is faith, let it change as it may--still saves. Faith--if it is faith--let it sink as it may, never can drown--it may live in the flames, but it shall never be burned. He who once gets this incorruptible seed, shall find it lives and abides in him forever. This faith is worked in us by the Spirit of God, according to the laws of the mind.

When God works upon matter, He works according to the laws of matter. I do not find, apart from miracles, that God violates gravitation--that He breaks any of the great laws with which He has stamped matter. And when the Spirit of God comes to work on man, He does not break the laws with which He regulates the mind. Now, it seems to be one of the laws of the mind that a man should believe a thing not by trying to believe it, but by force of evidence. If you now sit down, for instance, and try to believe in the explosion of the powder magazines yesterday--if you have any doubt about it, you may try, as long as you like, to believe it--you cannot do it by trying. You must go through another process. You cannot pump faith up from your own mind.

How do I get to believe in the explosion of the powder mills? There are certain newspapers--I have confidence in those newspapers and as I read the account--I believe it. Or I meet with certain persons who either heard the explosion, or saw some of the effects produced thereby and now I believe without any effort at all--I cannot help believing! Belief comes necessarily from my having confidence in those who tell me so. Now, the Spirit of God, when about to produce faith, frequently leads men to think about Christ. Christ is set forth before them crucified. They perceive that, "Here is a great wonder--God clothed in human flesh to suffer for human sin!"

The mind thinks, "There is something here which meets my conscious needs. I can see how God can be just, for He punishes His Son--and how He can be gracious, for He forgives sin. I find it stated that if I trust myself in this Son of God, who suffered as Man and now pleads His infinite merits before the Throne of God--if I trust in Him I shall be saved. I cannot trust in Him by simply saying I will try to do it, but I look at the Bible--is that true? I look at the thing itself--does it look like truth?" I ask friends who have tried and proved it and they tell me that they have tasted that He is gracious. Upon this evidence and specially upon perceiving the power of this Truth of God in my own soul, I believe the Word of God. The Spirit of God, working thus, leads me from the evidence given, to believe the testimony borne and I believe it.

Dear Friends, if you want to get faith, it must come through the Spirit of God! But it usually comes in this way--if the Word is not blessed to you in hearing it and meditating upon it at home--thinking much of Christ and His great work--what you have been doing is this--you have been thinking of your sins only. What would you think of a judge who sat upon a bench and who would listen to all the complaints against a criminal, but as soon as the advocate arose to plead his cause, would say, "No, I do not intend to listen to that"? You have been doing that. Your poor soul stands on trial and you have been listening to the accusations of Satan and your own sins!

And the moment Christ gets up to show you His great Atonement--the moment the promise is quoted--you say, "It is presumption for me to hope." My dear Friends, it is never presumption to listen to the Truth of God. If it is true that in due time Christ died for the ungodly. If it is true that he who comes to Him He will in no wise cast out. If it is true that He has said, "Though your sins are as scarlet, they shall be as white as snow. Though they are red like crimson, they shall be as wool." If it is true that He has said, "I have blotted out, as a thick cloud, your transgressions and, as a cloud, your sins," why not listen to that as well as the other?

Surely you must look at the fair side as well as the foul. And while your ear is hearing of the work of Christ and the promise of God, you will be able to cry--

"I do believe, I must believe, That Jesus died for me. "I could not have thought it! Oh, it melts me! I have been trying to get a soft heart and could not get it, but I have it now all through this. Here have I been hurrying to and fro, looking after faith and assurance instead of looking to the Cross for it! But now I see it all and I am saved, for I trust in Jesus Christ alone!"

I have said as much as may be needed this morning upon faith. I have tried to be brief upon each point and packed as many things as I could into the time. Now we are to have a few words about assurance.

III. The text says, "You were sealed with the Holy Spirit of promise." I cannot take the fourteenth verse, except to hint at it--we will try and preach on that this evening. Sealing, which is another name for assurance, for the witness of the Holy Spirit with our spirit--that we are born of God, is evidently distinct from faith. Please observe that--for the text says, "After that you believed, you were sealed with the Holy Spirit of promise." Believing, then, is not this sealing.

And assurance, although it is akin to believing, is not believing. There is a distinction between the two things. I want you to notice the distinction. In faith the mind is active. The text uses verbs which imply action--"you trusted," "you believed." But when it comes to sealing it uses quite another verb--"you were sealed." I am active in believing--I am passive when the Holy Spirit seals me. The witness of the Spirit is a something which I receive, but faith is a something which I exercise as well as receive. In faith my mind does something--in being sealed my faith receives something. If I may say so, faith writes out the document--there she labors--but the Holy Spirit stamps the seal Himself and there is no hand wanted there except His own. He stamps His own impression to make the document valid. Notice the difference between the activeness and the passiveness.

Then, again, man is commanded to believe in Scripture in many places--but he never was commanded to be sealed. Faith is a duty as well as a privilege, but assurance a privilege only. I never find any man exhorted to get the sealing of the Spirit. I believe that every Christian should pray for it and seek it, but I know of no command. It is a gift, a priceless gift and, unlike faith, it does not constitute a subject or command. Again, we read in Scripture that men are saved by faith and live by faith, but neither salvation nor living are ever imputed to sealing or to assurance. We are not saved by assurance--we do not even live by assurance. The vital principle is couched in faith. That is the shell which holds the kernel of the inner spiritual life.

I may be saved though I never had assurance. But even if I fancied I had assurance, I could not be saved if I had not faith. To faith we say salvation is promised, but to assurance such a promise is not given. It is clear from the context that assurance follows faith--"after that you believed." The Apostle does not say how soon. I believe that many souls get full assurance with faith. I have known converts who have been as certified of their interest in Christ as though they had been seventy years experimentally walking with Him. But, mark you, this is not the case always--perhaps not often.

Brookes gives the case of a Mr. Frogmorton who was one of the most valuable ministers of his day, but was thirty-seven years without any assurance of his interest with Christ. He trusted Christ, but his ministry was always a gloomy one, for he could not read his title clear to mansions in the skies. He went to the house of a dear friend, Mr. Dodd, to die. Just before he died, the light of Heaven streamed in--he not only expressed his full assurance of faith, but triumphed so gloriously, that he was the wonder of all round about him!

He also tells us of one Mr. Glover, who had been for years without assurance of his interest in Christ. But when he came to the fire to be burnt, just as he saw the stake, he cried, "He is come! He is come!" And instead of being heavy of heart as he had been in prison, he went to the stake with a light step! Three martyrs were once chained to the stake, two of them rejoicing. But one was observed to slip from under the chains for a moment and prostrate himself upon the firewood and wrestle with God and then coming back to the stake, he said, "The Lord has manifested himself to me at the last and now I shall burn bravely." And so, indeed, he did, bearing his witness for his Lord and Master.

So it seems there are some of God's saints who do not get assured till even the last moment and I will not say that there are not some of them who even, like some children, are put to bed in the dark. Christ went up to Heaven in a cloud--Gideon saw the angel ascending in the smoke of the incense and many a good man ascends with clouds of darkness round about him--but still he goes to Heaven! I hope these cases are very few--still we bring them forward to show you that assurance is not to be looked for before faith. You might as well look for the pinnacle before the foundation, for the cream before the milk, for the apples before you plant the tree--for the harvest before you sow the seed. Assurance follows faith.

Observe in the next place--and it is worthy of your notice--that assurance is to be found where faith was found. Do observe those two words, "in whom"--"in whom you also trusted"--"in whom you were sealed." So that as I get my faith out of Christ, so I must get my assurance out of Christ. The virtual means of my faith is Christ Himself and the virtual means of my assurance must be the same. As I think of what He did for me, I believe in Him. As I continue to meditate upon that same thing, I have assurance of interest in Him. You must feed upon the flesh and blood of Christ if you would grow into strong men in Christ Jesus. A touch of Christ will heal you from all disease--but you must hold Him fast if you would enjoy spiritual health perpetually.

To believe in Christ will save you from Hell. To be assured of your interest in Christ will give you a Heaven upon earth! Do not be content with faith--be thankful for it, rejoice in it--but ask to have more. And when you want to have more, go to Christ for it--the same fountain which first quenched your thirst must be that which shall quench it till you are taken up to drink of the River of Life which flows through the midst of Paradise--which is no other than the Presence of Christ as a refreshment to His people.

This assurance, like faith, is the work of the Spirit of God. "You were sealed with the Holy Spirit of promise." He does this in various ways. Sometimes we get the seal of the Spirit through experience. We know that God is true because we have proved Him. Sometimes this comes through the hearing of the Word--as we listen our faith is confirmed. But there is doubtless, besides this, a special and supernatural work of the Holy Spirit whereby men are assured that they are born of God. You will observe in one place the Apostle says, "The Spirit also bears witness with our spirit, that we are born of God," so that there are two witnesses--first, our spirit bears witness, that is, by evidences. I look at my faith and see myself depending upon Christ and then I know, because I love the Brethren and for other reasons, that I am born of God.

Then there comes over and above the witness of evidence, faith and feeling--the Spirit Himself bearing witness with our spirit. Have you not felt it? I cannot describe this to you, but you who have felt it know it. Did you not the other day feel a heavenly calm as you meditated upon your state and condition in Christ? You wondered where it came from. It was not the result of protracted devotion but it stole over you--you knew not how it was--you were bathed in it as in sunlight and you rejoiced exceedingly. You rejoiced in Christ--that was your basis of confidence, and that confidence came through the Spirit bearing witness with your spirit.

This has occurred sometimes in the midst of sharp conflicts just when dark despair seemed ready to overwhelm you. You may have enjoyed this comfort under peculiar trials and losses of friends and you may expect to have it when you come to die. Then, if ever in your life, you should be able to say, "I will fear no evil, for You are with me (in a special sense) You are with me." The Holy Spirit, then, must give it to us, and we must wait upon Him to set His seal. And so to conclude, this is desirable to the highest degree, for it is the earnest of the inheritance. It is a part of Heaven on earth to get an assurance worked by the Spirit!

It is not merely a pledge, for a pledge is given back when you get the thing itself, but it is an earnest. It is one cluster from the vines of Eshcol--one shekel of the eternal wage--money of the Free Grace reward. What if I say it is a stray note from the harps of angels? It is a drop of the spray from the fountains of life. It is one ingot of gold from the pavement of Heaven. It is one ray of heavenly light from the eternal Sun of Righteousness. O Christian, if you have ever known assurance, you will pant till you have it again! You can never, after seeing the sunlight, put up with the candlelight of your doubts and fears in the dungeon of despondency.

But if assurance is gone, still hang onto Jesus--

"When your eye of faith is dim, Still hold onto Jesus, sink or swim. Still at His footstool bow the knee, And Israel's God your peace shall be." If you cannot feel His love in your heart, still trust Him! Oh, it was grand of Job--"Though He slay me, yet will I trust Him." Truly, the vitality of faith is such that if He should spurn me from His Presence--if He never gave me another look of love this side of Heaven--if He gave me up to the lowest depths and bade all His waves and billows go over me, yet is He such a faithful God and so true that I dare not even, then, doubt Him. Blind unbelief would do so, but victorious faith says, "Never! He cannot lie. Let God be true and every man a liar."

When faith is at her very worst, she is glorious and sparkles like a jewel in the dark mine and God will come and take her up out of all the depths and set her in His own crown as a precious jewel. "Your faith has saved you," says Jesus. No, Lord, it is not faith that has done it, it is Yourself. He takes the crown royal of salvation's glory, lifts it right off from His own head and puts it on the head of the poor feeble woman's faith. "Your faith has saved you: go in peace." And so will God do with your tempest-tossed and exercised faith! He will put the crown upon it and that faith of yours shall sing in Heaven!

Do not tell me that we shall have no faith in Heaven--nonsense! "Now abides faith, hope, charity, these three. But the greatest of these is charity." We shall find faith to be our sweet companion there. Shall I not believe God when I get to Heaven? Shall I give up trusting my God when I get there? No, I shall trust Him for my resurrection body! I shall trust Him for the millennial splendor! I shall trust Him for the gathering of the elect! Trust Him for an eternity of bliss! Trust Him for my safe standing where He has brought me. And so, happy faith, imperishable faith, shall live and reign when sense and sight are gone past recall. The Lord give you to hear the Word, to believe in it and afterwards to be sealed with the Holy Spirit of promise.

Inward Conflicts

DELIVERED ON SUNDAY MORNING, OCTOBER 9, 1864,
BY C. H. SPURGEON,
AT THE METROPOLITAN TABERNACLE, NEWINGTON.

"Return, return, O Shulamite; return, return, that we may look upon you. What will you see in the Shulamite? As it were the company of two armies." -- Song of Solomon 6:13.

THIS verse is not addressed to the Church in her doubting state, nor while seeking her absent Lord, but it refers to her in her very best condition--when she has lately come from the enjoyment of fellowship with her Divine spouse and when her soul, in consequence is like the chariots of Amminadib. Read the context and you will perceive that Believers who are rejoicing in the Lord may look upon this text as their own. Observe the title of the person addressed--it is a marriage name. She has been espoused to Solomon and she has taken his name and become Solyma, for such is the best rendering of the word rendered Shulamite. This name is appropriate to souls who are united to Christ, to those whom Christ has betrothed unto Himself in righteousness, who live in union with their Lord.

You who abide in the Lord Jesus are, by a mysterious bond, made one with Christ. And He has conferred upon you His own name--He is Solomon and you are Solyma. That is a remarkable expression in the book of Jeremiah--"This is her name whereby she shall be called, the Lord our Righteousness." One would have thought that such a title was incommunicable. But yet so close is the union between Christ and His people that the Holy Spirit actually transfers that dignified expression, "Lord our Righteousness," to His Israel--His Beloved.

The title Solyma also signifies both perfection and peace. There is perfection in every child of God, but not a perfection in the flesh. We are perfect in Christ Jesus! We are complete in Him--spotless, by being washed in His blood-- glorious, by being robed in His righteousness. Every child of God is right sumptuously arrayed in the wedding dress of the Savior's righteousness. We may truly say that, "Solomon in all his glory was not arrayed like one of these." Every Believer stands in Christ perfectly accepted!

The sweet name, Solyma, also signifies peace--"Therefore being justified by faith, we have peace with God through Jesus Christ our Lord." The true heir of Heaven is not at enmity with God, nor at war with his own conscience. The silver trumpet has proclaimed an everlasting peace. God's sword has been sheathed in the Savior's heart and Divine Justice is on the side of the chosen people. The request of the text next demands a moment's consideration. It is repeated four times. "Return, return, O Solyma. Return, return, that we may look upon you." Does not this request proceed from the daughters of Jerusalem who desire to behold her beauty?

Souls that are anxious about their own state may well desire to understand the experience of the true child of God. You want to know whether you, also, are a Christian, therefore you want to know how Christians feel, how they think of Christ, how they are moved by His Spirit--what is their appearance when His love is shed abroad in their hearts. You anxiously desire to see the true Christian that you may measure yourselves and see whether there is the life of God in you. These daughters of Jerusalem also desire to look upon her for their own delight. For as to gaze upon beauty is exceedingly pleasant--so is it specially delightful to the pure in heart to have fellowship with the pure in heart--to see the fruits which the Spirit has brought forth. To behold the cleanness of the Believer's walk and to know the savor of the Believer's conversation.

No beauty equals the beauty of holiness! Nothing is so lovely as uprightness. And therefore we wonder not that four times the request is made. Perhaps, too, these daughters wanted to look at her as an example to themselves. Saints look upon the beauty of others that they may be enabled to emulate their excellencies. Let us read with affectionate attention the biographies of holy men that they may be a stimulus to ourselves, exciting us to exert ourselves in the Redeemer's cause and may afford us some hope that the highest Christian attainments are not altogether beyond our reach. I think this is the reason why the daughters of Jerusalem said, "Return, return, O Solyma"--they would comfort themselves by seeing whether they are like she is.

They would delight themselves by beholding her perfections. They would also stir up their own souls by seeing her example. The rest of the text, you will observe, may be considered two ways--either the spouse asks the question, which is the most probable. She says, "What shall you see in Solyma?" She thinks that there is no beauty in her, nothing in her that anyone should delight, or fix his eyes upon her, or derive any profit from regarding her. "Why," she says, "all that You will see in me is a company of two armies--a conflict between good and evil. If You look upon me You see nothing but good and evil fighting together, darkness and light contending. I am not worth Your looking at."

And so she would gladly veil her face and go away if it were not for the earnest request which seems to hold her fast--or as some think, this question is asked by bystanders and is answered by the daughters of Jerusalem--"What shall you see in the Shulamite?" the giddy crowd enquires. And instructed Believers cry, "We shall see in her the concurrence of two triumphant armies returning as choristers with music and with dancing, from the field of battle! We shall see in her the King immortal, invisible, with all His hosts of Grace! We shall see in her the purified soul co-working with the glorious Savior! We shall see in the Christian Church the activity of sanctified manhood, combined with the majestic power of Deity residing within."

This is what she might not say of herself. But what they would see in her. Observe, then, the two meanings and let us dismiss the second until another occasion. There is in every Christian a sweet composition of Christ's power and of the activity of his own soul. There is the power of God and there is the creature himself made willing in the day of God's power. There is in the Christian, God working in him to will and to do of His own good pleasure and the man himself working out his own salvation with fear and trembling. In the Christian Church there is man working for God and God working in man--and all this in such a joyful manner as to be rather resembling the triumph of returning conquerors than the going forth to fight of those who make war. What shall we see in Solyma? We shall see the blessed confluence of the two great armies of sanctified humanity and of God made flesh!

But we are now coming to take the text in the first sense--the Church blushingly declares that there is nothing to be seen in her except conflict, turmoil, the wrestling of two great powers--two mighty armies contending for the mastery. Upon this point may God give us light for the comfort of many who are passing through this stage of Christian experience.

I. We shall, at the outset, this morning, first call upon you who know the Lord to OBSERVE THE FACT OF THE TWO ARMIES IN EVERY CHRISTIAN. This is very evident, but to aid your reflections let me remind you throughout this very book you see traces of it. This Canticle is a marriage song--it therefore speaks less of the battlefield than some other portions of Scripture, for at the marriage feast allusions to trial and to warfare ought to be few.

Yet, that the Church is not altogether sanctified is clear if you note such passages as the fifth verse of the first chapter. "I am black," she says, "but lovely, O you daughters of Jerusalem, as the tents of Kedar, as the curtains of Solomon." She is black--here is her natural state--here we have the manifestation of her continued depravity of heart. "I am black, but lovely"--here is her spiritual condition--the Spirit of God has clothed her with beauteous graces--Christ has washed her and made her fair in His sight. "I am like the tents of Kedar," she says, "the smoke-dried curtains of those Arab wanderers who dwelt in this country set forth my sinfulness."

And yet in Christ she compares herself to those embroidered curtains, heavy with gold and silver threads which hang about the throne of Solomon. In the third chapter she plainly proves that she is not always enjoying fellowship, but is in a mixed condition. "By night on my bed"--here is her slothfulness--"I sought Him whom my soul loves"--here is her activity. "I sought Him"--here is her desire--"but I found Him not"--here is her sad experience of His absence. Then in the fifth chapter, the second verse, there is a singular commixture. "I sleep"--I am sluggish, cold, dead, lethargic-- "but my heart wakes"--the inward principle is still vital, still panting after something better.

We find her in the third verse making vain excuses for not opening to her Lord. But before long you come to the fifth verse and you find her opening to her Beloved, though her Beloved has withdrawn--refusing but soon complying. The two natures battling. The one fast closing the door and the other opening it and seeking the Beloved with tearful complaint. Throughout the Song there is always this mixture. But, as I have said, we cannot expect to find much of this in a nuptial ode.

Turn, therefore, to the great Book of battle songs, the book of Psalms, and here you have in almost every Psalm indications of the complexity of the Christian character. So strange are some of the Psalms that it has been well said they might have been written rather by two persons than by one. David will begin out of the very depths calling unto God and then he will end with all the jubilant notes of a conqueror leading captivity captive. I shall not have time to refer to many passages, but the forty-second Psalm will strike you where the one David seems to be reasoning with another David.

"Why are you cast down, O my Soul? And why are you disquieted within me? Hope you in

God: for I shall yet praise Him." And the next Psalm is much to the same effect. Perhaps, however, the most eminent and striking paradox of the whole is the seventy-third Psalm, the twenty-second verse, There he says of himself, "So foolish was I and ignorant: I was as a beast before You." He could not go further than that, surely, in a description of himself. "Nevertheless, I am continually with You: You have held me by my right hand. You shall guide me with Your counsel and afterward receive me to Glory. Whom have I in Heaven but You? And there is none upon earth that I desire beside You."

Heavy as a stone he lies embedded in the mire and yet all of a sudden he takes wings to himself and outstrips the eagle's flight as he loses himself in the splendor of the Sun of Righteousness, mounting so high as to be entirely lost to all but God! David's experience, as we find it pictured to us in the Psalms, is but our own, written out in large capital letters! And here we see what strange incongruities, what marvelous paradoxes are found in men. If we need still further instruction upon this matter, let me refer you to the Epistles of our Apostle Paul.

I read in your hearing just now that extraordinary passage in the seventh of Romans. How could there have been more graphically described than we have there, the war and the contention which is always going on between the old nature and the Divine life which God has implanted within us? To the like effect is the seventeenth verse of the fifth chapter of the Galatians, where he says, "For the flesh lusts against the Spirit and the Spirit against the flesh: and these are contrary the one to the other: so that you cannot do the things that you would."

We are carnal and yet spiritual--lost in self yet saved in Christ. We are all imperfections and yet perfect-- incomplete in all things and yet complete in everything! Strange contradictions, but yet most strangely true! Another evidence of this matter is the concurrent experience of saved souls. I thought of just taking down at random biographies from my library shelves and writing out passages, but I had scarcely time for that. In truth you have but to read the truthful life of any Christian man and you soon find that he is not all Spirit but also flesh--not all renewed nature but still compassed with infirmity.

We have whole volumes upon this subject. There is "Bunyan's Holy War," describing God's conquest of the town of Mansoul and its subsequent attacks by sins lurking within and foes storming without. Sable's book, "The Soul's Conflict," contains a mass of experimental knowledge. But you will perhaps feel more pleased if I give you, instead of word prose, one or two expressions in the form of rhyme which will show you that our hymn-writers--they that should be among the more joyous of the Christian Church--have been compelled, sometimes, to sing paradoxes concerning themselves.

Ralph Erskine has left us that strange work, "The Believer's Riddle," the greatest riddle that was ever written, a perfect maze to all but those who have the clue within. He says--

"My heart's a mirror, dim and bright, A compound strange of day and night, Of dung and diamonds, dross and gold, Of summer's heat and winter's cold." Hart, whose hymns come, indeed, from the heart--rightly named was he--in his hymn called "The Paradox," says--

"How strange is the course that a Christian must steer, How perplexed is the path he must tread. The hope of his happiness rises from fear, And his life he receives from the dead. His fairest pretensions must wholly be waved, And his best resolutions be crossed. Nor can he expect to be perfectly saved Till he finds himself utterly lost. When all this is done and his heart is assured, Of the total remission of sins When his pardon is signed and his peace is procured, From that moment his conflict begins."

We have that hymn of Newton's, which you will find in your Rippon's Selection--

"I would, but cannot sing, I would, but cannot pray," and so on. Still more remarkable is that hymn-- "I asked the Lord that I might grow In faith and love and every Grace. Might more of His salvation know, And seek more earnestly His face."

But I need not repeat it, because you have it in your books.

You will there find that instead of God's working in the way in which he expected, the singer was made to feel the hidden evils of his heart and so he was humbled and brought in true penitence nearer to God. Cowper thus sings of himself in a hymn which is also in your book--

"The Lord will happiness Divine On contrite hearts bestow. Then tell me, gracious God, is mine A contrite heart or no? I sometimes think myself inclined To love You, if I could. But often feel another mind, Averse to all that's good. My best desires are faint and few, I gladly would strive for more! But, when I cry, 'My strength renew,'

Seem weaker than before.
O make this heart rejoice or ache!
Decide this doubt for me;
And, if it is not broken, break,
And heal it, if it be."

Thus, if time did not fail us, we might go through all those men who have at any time served the Church of God and say of them all that they have experienced, felt and confessed a struggle and a conflict between what God has implanted and what nature has left in them. Nor do I think, dear Friends, that we ought at all to wonder at this. It sounds strange in the carnal ear, but we ought not to marvel, for this is only according to the analogy of nature. If you look abroad, you will discern everywhere contending forces--and out of these contending forces the rule of nature comes.

See yonder orbs--moved by a mysterious impulse they seek to fly off into space--but the sun holds them by invisible bands. The bands of the sun's attraction would draw them at once into his heat, but on the other hand the centrifugal force would drive them far away into distant space! Between these two they keep the circular orbit which God has at present appointed. So we have a corrupt nature within us which would drive us to sin and on the other hand the Divine power within would draw us into perfect conformity and union with Christ! Between those two forces the Christian life becomes much what it is.

Observe how in this word death and life are contending together. Death crowds his graves, but Life wins the victory. Death may toll the knell and this is his note of triumph. But every cry of every new-born infant is another shout of the battle of life in which Life still claims to be victorious! Look at your own persons and in your own bodies you see this duplex action. You breathe, but the same lungs which receive the fresh, pure air, give forth the noxious vapor. There is scarcely an organ of the body which is without an apparatus for the secretion of an injurious substance and its expulsion.

The brightest eye that ever swam in light casts forth some defilement. The skin, if it is healthful, has a part of its functions to throw off from us that which would certainly breed disease. There is going on in every human body a strange conflict between life and death. And every moment our life stands, as it were, in the center of two great armies who are contending whether we should be the prey of the worm, or should still continue to breathe!

Do you wonder, therefore, if the whole world of nature is, or has fallen into this state that man, the little world, should be the same? Wonder or not, certain it is that it is so. And let those who have been staggered because they have felt a battle within, from this time forth rather rejoice because this is the path which all the people of God have trod before!

II. Now concerning THE ORIGIN OF THIS CONFLICT. There is but a slight battle in an unrenewed man. There is a sort of conflict of a minor kind between conscience and his grosser passions. Even Ovid could speak of this and several heathen writers confess a war within. But there is no conflict to any high degree in the ungodly man because, while the armed strong man keeps his house, his goods are at peace.

While there is one master, a man may cheerfully serve him. But in the moment of regeneration, a new master comes into the house--a stronger than he has come and He will bind the strong man! And after many conflicts, He will cast him out forever and get that house to be in his own possession. The new nature which God implants in His people is directly the opposite of the old one. As the old nature comes of Satan, being defiled and depraved by the Fall, so the new nature comes direct from Heaven, pure and without spot.

As the old nature is sin, is essentially sin, so the new nature is essentially Divine Grace--it is a living and incorruptible seed which lives and abides forever--a seed which cannot sin because it is born of God. When these two, therefore, come into conflict, it is as when fire and water meet--either the one or the other must die. There can be no truce, no parley. The two are deadly foes. The life of the one is the death of the other. The strength of the one the weakness of the other.

Now the old nature has been there beforehand. It is like a tree well rooted--it has been there twenty, thirty, forty, fifty, or sixty years according to the date of conversion--and it is not easily torn up by its roots. Even when Grace comes into the heart and makes sin fall, as Dagon did before the ark of God, yet is it true of sin as it was of Dagon--the stump is left and there is still enough vitality in that old stump to breed pain and confusion without limit. The reigning power of sin falls dead the moment a man is converted, but the struggling power of sin does not die until the man dies.

Bunyan said that unbelief had as many lives as a cat and sin has the same vitality. Until we are wrapped in our winding-sheets, we shall never have that black thread of depravity drawn out from us. It will, it must continue to be there till God shall sanctify us--spirit, soul and body--and take us Home. Remember how pure the new life is which God has given you! It is from God

Himself--an emanation from His Spirit as pure as Deity! And think how sinful, on the other hand, is your corrupt nature! Can it be possible that these two should be at peace? Can two walk together except they are agreed?

Can these two principles, which are entirely opposed to one another, by any chance live at peace? It cannot be! And even if it could be, there are allies without who will never be quiet! There is Satan, who will never rest from stirring up our corruptions. And on the other hand there is the Holy Spirit, who will never pause in the putting forth of His Divine power till all evil is cast out, root and branch. Since these two must fight--the Spirit of God and the spirit of evil--so the two principles within which are their children must continue in conflict till our dying day.

Here, then, is the source of this conflict. O my dear Hearers, some of you do not know anything about this! Remember, you are in the gall of bitterness if you do not. If you are all one way, then you are all the wrong way. If there is in you no conflict, it is because there is no Divine power there to drive the Evil One out. The more of these wars and fights you feel, the more have you cause to thank God and take courage! The battle is not yours, but God's. You are not alone in this warfare--you shall overcome, as thousands have done before you--through the blood of the Lamb!

III. This brings us to a third reflection. Let us for a moment consider THE REALITY OF THIS CONFLICT. The warfare in the Christian mind is not a thing of imagination, it is most true and real. If you want proof of it you must pass through it. Did you ever kneel down in an agony of spirit, resisting some furious temptation from within? Some of us know what it is to feel the cold sweat running down our brows when we have to fight against ourselves in fearful struggles against black thoughts of unbelief.

Perhaps it may be that the base heart within has even doubted the existence of God and dared to prompt us to defy the Deity. And we have loathed that thought and hated it so much that our whole spirit was put to the utmost stretch of tension in order to win a victory over ourselves. You must, if you are at all subject to strong emotions, have felt that this struggle was a terrible fact. To you there could be no doubt about it, for your whole soul felt it--your heart was like a field which is torn up and soaked with blood by the fury of battle. There is a frightful reality in this conflict when we remember how some Christians fall during it and sin gets the mastery.

Remember, sin may win a battle, but it cannot win the campaign. What? Were there no corruptions in David? What do you think made him sin with Bathsheba? Was there no corrupt heart left in Noah when he was naked to his shame? Was there no corruption in Lot when he sinned in the cave? Why, those black things which have stained the character of these holy men throughout all time prove to us how dreadful must be the power of sin and how mighty must be the power which keeps sin down!

Remember what the joy of a Christian is when he feels that he has triumphed over sin. Ah, there is something real here! If the daughters of Jerusalem praised David when he came back with Goliath's head, so do all our powers bless and praise God when he gives us the neck of our spiritual enemies. Like the songsters of old, we sing, "O my Soul, you have trod down strength." These are no fictions or imaginations of a poetic and fevered brain--he that has once been along the road to Heaven knows that above all things the traveler has need to be on the watch against himself.

IV. In the fourth place, let us notice THE CHANGES WHICH TAKE PLACE IN THIS WARFARE. The conflict in a Christian is not always carried on with the same fury. There is always war, but there is not always battle. The flesh always hates the Spirit and the Spirit is always the opponent of the flesh. But they are not always fighting, and when they fight it is not always with the same fury. You ask why? Well, sometimes the flesh is not so powerful as at other times. There are moments when, if sin were in the Christian's way, the flesh would not choose it.

I may not be able to tell you exactly why, but certain it is that partly from changes of body and also from certain phenomena of mind, there are seasons when the propensities to evil, though still as evil, are not so vigorous as they were--their strength is awful, but it sleeps. The young lion is ever a lion. But its claws are concealed and it plays like a lamb. The raging sea is not always in tempest, yet tempests sleep in its waves. Perhaps there is more to be dreaded in the quietness of our depravity than in the raging of it--for sometimes it is the treacherous calm which the Christian ought to fear more than the storm.

Again, it is quite certain that the Spirit's work within us is not always equally active. The Spirit of God is always in a Christian--He dwells in the Believer as in a temple. "My Spirit will I not utterly take from him," is true of every saint. But yet you must know that your faith is often weak--that your love is not always like a flame of fire. You cannot pray at all times as you wished, Ah, Brethren, we can sometimes dash along in service like the chariots of Amminadib, but at other times the wheels are taken off and we drag the chariots heavily like Pharaoh in the midst of the Red Sea! A change, then, in the flesh, or a change in the spirit, may produce a diversity in the present form of the conflict.

It is always there, but not always the same. I suppose that when it is most furious the reason of its fury may be sought for in the strength of both sides. I do not think that when the flesh is strong and the spirit is weak that there is much conflict--then, there is rather a speedy defeat. But when the Spirit of God is gloriously at work in our souls--when faith is vigorous, when hope is bright, when love is flaming, and when, at the same time the corrupt powers put forth all their might--then it is that the conflict is stern.

Some Christians do not enter into this state of strong conflict for two reasons--they are men of weak passions and Divine Grace in them is at a low ebb. But when a man is endowed with a strong mental nature and the Spirit is also vigorous within him, then there will be a contest something like the combat of two Samsons fighting and struggling together as to who shall get the victory. Ah, Brethren, these things may change, as I have said, but the war is never over! Do not any of you say, "I shall never be tempted again."

Gray-headed Brethren, do not think that the old man in you is dead! If professors fall into grave sin and dishonor the Church, they are as often old men as young men. No, I think I may say that they are more often elder men than younger ones. It is sad it should be so, but it is so. And there is many a professor who has stood well for forty years, but makes a fool of himself at the last. And though he has been honored in God's Church, yet he leaves a blot upon his name and the godly say in a whisper, "No doubt he was a child of God, but it is best that he should be dead, for in his old age he fell into sin."

No, we shall never be out of gunshot of the devil till we have crossed the river of death. Our carnal minds are like a powder magazine--there only needs the spark. And ah, what an explosion there would be with any of us! May the Lord keep the sparks away. Let us be very vigilant and very careful. There is an enemy behind every hedge. There is a foe waiting for us at every step. And before this Sunday's hallowed hours may be over, you and I may have slipped and have fallen into sin to our own perpetual hurt and hindrance, unless almighty Grace shall intervene.

V. A few words now upon THE EFFECTS OF THIS CONFLICT. Some will say, "But why does not God remove out of the Christian the old nature?" Some uninstructed Christians even think that in conversion the Lord turns the old nature into a new one, which is very far from the fact. The old nature remains in the Christian. It has received a blow which will ultimately be its death, but it still lives and the new nature in the Christian comes to struggle with it for the mastery.

But why is this? Well, we cannot tell you. Such a question reminds us of the Negro's enquiry to the minister--"You say that God is Omnipotent and therefore He is greater than Satan?" "Yes." Then why does not God kill the devil and have done with him?" We believe God to be as morally Omnipotent as He is physically Omnipotent. And if He willed it, we do not doubt but that evil of every form and shape might disappear out of the universe. Why, then, does He permit it? Ah, why? But there we leave it. Be amazed at the mystery if you will, but do not question God nor cast the blame of sin upon His holy Character.

There it is, He suffers sin to remain in the universe and after all we can say, we observe the fact--but the reason we cannot tell. Still I think we may in some respects see how sin is overruled in the Christian. Sin remaining in the Believer drives him humbly to confess his own nothingness, excludes all boasting from his tongue, compels him to trust in his God, takes away from him his propensity to trust in himself, leads him to value the precious blood which cleanses him, to prize the Holy Spirit who sanctifies him, to rejoice in the faithfulness and patience and long-suffering of God who still continues to be gracious to him! And oh, what songs will the man of God sing when he gets to Heaven!

How much sweeter will be the music because of the conflict! How much more glorious the victory because of the warfare! If I could be totally delivered from sin, root and branch, I certainly would. But yet am I conscious that no Christian would glorify God so much in Heaven as he now does if there were not sin to be contended with. A creature that could not sin could scarcely show forth much of the praise of God by its holiness. But that the creature can sin, no, that there is a strong drawing towards sin and yet the Divine Grace keeps a man from it and sanctifies him even to perfection--why this will make the song come swelling up of, "Hallelujah! Hallelujah! Hallelujah!"

If no adversaries had been tolerated, then no victories could have been won. If there were no temptations for us to struggle with, then there would have been no elbow room for our faith, no power for the display of the bare arm of God. Doubtless it is best as it is and when the winding up of the chapter comes, perhaps we shall see that our committed sins have been made the means of saving us from other sins which would have been our ruin. Many Believers would have grown too proud to be borne with if some infirmity had not plucked the plume from their helmets and made them mourn with brokenness of heart before God.

God can bring good out of evil by His overruling Grace, while on the other hand our good works have often been the greatest curse we have ever had. Good works have puffed us up and so have led us into pride--while our sins, though pulling us down, have, through almighty Grace, led us to make men work for eternity.

VI. I want your attention to the last point, which is, THE CONCLUSION OF IT ALL. This contest--is it forever to continue? Shall we forever tremble in the balances? Will there be no valley of decision where our souls may take their rest? Yes, Brethren, the fight will soon be over and the victory is guaranteed and glorious! Yes, even at the present day, the Christian is making progress.

I do not admire the term "progressive sanctification," for it is unwarranted by Scripture. But it is certain that the Christian does grow in Grace. And though his conflict may be as severe on the last day of his life as in the first moment of conversion, yet he does advance in Grace and all his imperfections and his conflicts within cannot prove that he has not made progress. Let me show you this. You know that at certain periods in your children's history they pass through diseases incidental to childhood. Here is your babe of a month old and there is your child of three or four years.

This child of three or four years of age is suffering from some of those complaints incidental to infancy. It is not in such good health as your child of a month old. It is far weaker and its life seems far more in danger. Yet you will not say that there is no progress, for this child of three years old has passed through three years of its difficulties and hazards, which this little one, newly-born, has yet to encounter. We all know that there are certain growing pains which the lad feels when he is verging out into his manhood, but these pains do not prove a want of strength, but the very reverse--the muscles are being braced and the sinews are being strengthened.

Stand by the seashore when the tide is coming up. There rolled up a big wave. Just mark the place in the sand. For the next few minutes there is no wave that comes up so high as that--no, some waves that suck back the rest and you might even think the sea was retiring! Is there, therefore, no progress made? Why, Friend, you will see in a moment, if you will but wait! Another great wave will come sweeping up, far outstripping the one that we marked just now. And when you shall come back in an hour's time and the sea has come to the fullness of its strength, you will see that the receding of any one individual wave is no mark of its retrogression. You have but to mark the whole sea and take time in which to examine it and then you discover there has been progress and that progress has been effected by alternate advance and retreat.

Along the coast of Essex the sea is greatly encroaching upon the land and every time we go to some of the watering places, we perceive that the cliff has fallen, hundreds or thousands of tons have been carried away. And yet if you are there at a tide which has gone far out, you will often think, "Why, surely the land is gaining on the sea! I never walked out so far as this before. I never saw these rocks exposed and dry before." Well, it is a strangely low tide. But at the same time ask the old fisherman who has lived there all his days and he will tell you that his mother was married out in a Church which stood where that ship is floating, far out to sea and that all the intervening soil has been washed away!

He recollects when this place, which is now a footpath on the cliffs brink, was a quarter of a mile inland--and then you understand that though on any one occasion the land may apparently have gained, yet, on the whole, there has been a progress in the sea. And so it is with spiritual life. There are times when it seems as if sin had gained upon you and you were going back in spiritual things. There is cause for alarm, but not despair! There is a cause for watchfulness, but not for terror--go to the Lord and pray to Him to send a mightier wave of His Irresistible Grace--that your soul may be filled with all the fullness of God.

The day is often gloomy at eleven o'clock, but that is no proof that you are not getting towards noon. Many a cold wind howls over the days of March and April, colder than there might have been at Christmas--but that is no proof that you are not getting on to summer. There may come a frosty night in May, nipping the flowers, but that is no proof that the frost is all coming back again. So you may feel within yourself such things as cause you to bow your head in sorrow and to cry out to God in grief! But even these things shall but speed you on your way towards your desired haven. The battle will certainly end right.

Just anticipate for a moment the glory of the victory! You shall be free from sin one day! You shall be perfect, even as your Father who is in Heaven is perfect! You shall wave the palm branch, and wave it the more joyously because you had to contend with flesh and blood and with spiritual wickedness! You shall join the eternal song and it shall roll up to the Throne of God all the more gloriously because you have--

"To wrestle hard as we do now, With sins and doubts and fears." Come, anticipate that triumph and pluck up courage! Go forth, all you servants of God, as Barak went against Sisera, and the day shall come when your foes shall be swept away! That river of death shall do for your enemies what the Kishon did for Jabin--it shall sweep them away forever! Standing by the Red Sea of the atoning sacrifice, you shall sing unto the Lord who has triumphed gloriously and cast the horse and the rider into the depths of the sea.

I have preached, this morning, especially for the comfort of those who are thus exercised and who are saying, "If it is so, why am I thus?" You will now see that instead of having cause for distress in all these conflicts, you have only a reason to come to Christ again. Come to Jesus again! Look up to Him once more and take Him today to be your Savior and your All. Put your case into His hands! Trust Him and you shall be more than conquerors through Him who loved you. Trust Him! Trust Him now and we will meet in Heaven at last to sing His praises forever! Amen.

An Awful Premonition

A SERMON DELIVERED
BY C. H. SPURGEON,
AT THE METROPOLITAN TABERNACLE, NEWINGTON.

"Assuredly I say unto you, there are some standing here who shall not taste of death till they see the Son of Man coming in His kingdom." Matthew 16:28.

I must confess that I have frequently read this verse with but a vague sense of its profound impressiveness and I have passed it over rapidly because I did not understand it clearly. Though well acquainted with the usual interpretations, none of them had ever satisfied my mind. It seemed to me as if the text had awakened surprise without suggesting a simple obvious meaning, and therefore the good commentators had invented explanations and offered suggestions widely different one from another, but all equally obscure and improbable. Lately, however, in reading a volume of sermons by Bishop Horseley, I have met with a view altogether new of the passage which I firmly believe to be the correct one.

Though I do not suppose I shall carry the judgment of all of you with me, yet I shall do my best to bring out of it that terrible denunciation which I believe the Savior has here left on record. With His own Cross and passion in view, He was admonishing His disciples to steadfastness, appealing to them at any sacrifice to take up their cross and follow Him. Then portraying the inestimable value of the soul and reflecting on the horror of the soul being lost--a doom, the full force of which would be impossible to comprehend until He should come in the Glory of His Father, with all His holy angels-- He stopped short, looked upon some of the company and said in words like these, "There are certain persons standing here who shall never taste of death till they see the Son of Man coming in His kingdom."

Now what did He mean by this? Obviously it is either a marvelous promise to some who were His disciples, indeed, or else it is a portent of woe to others who should die in their sins. How do the popular interpretations of our learned expositors look at it? Some say it refers to the Transfiguration and it certainly is remarkable that the account of the Transfiguration immediately follows this verse both in Mark and in Luke, as well as in this record of Matthew. But can you, for a moment, bring your minds to believe that Christ was describing His Transfiguration when He spoke of "the Son of Man coming in His kingdom"?

Can you see any connection between the Transfiguration and the preceding verse, which says, "For the Son of Man shall come in the Glory of His Father with His angels. And then He shall reward every man according to His works"? We grant you that Christ was in His Glory upon Mount Tabor, but He did not there "reward every man according to his works," nor is it fair to call that a "coming" of the Son of Man at all! He did not "come" on Mount Tabor, for He was on the earth already. And it is a misuse of language to construe that into an advent. Besides, where would be the occasion for such a solemn prefix--"Assuredly I say unto you"?

Does it not raise expectation merely to cause disappointment if He intended no more than this--"There are some standing here who shall see Me transfigured"? That scene took place six days afterwards. The next verse tells you so, "And after six days Jesus takes Peter, James and John, his brother, and brings them up into an high mountain apart." Why, the majesty of the prediction which carries our thoughts forward to "the last things" in the world's history makes us shrink from accepting an immediate fulfillment of it all! I cannot imagine, therefore, that the Transfiguration is in the slightest degree referred to here--and I do not think that anyone would have thought of such a thing unless he had been perplexed and utterly nonplussed for an explanation.

And again--though it seems almost incredible--Dr. Gill endorses this view, and moreover says that it also refers to the descent of the Holy Spirit. At this I am staggered! How any man can find an analogy with Pentecost in the connection here I cannot understand! Pentecost took place six months after this event and why Jesus Christ should say, "Assuredly I say unto you there are some standing here who will live six months," I really cannot comprehend! It seems to me that my Master did not waste people's time by talking such platitudes. Who, that reads this passage, can think it has any reference to the descent of the Holy Spirit?--"For the Son of Man shall come in the Glory of His Father with His angels. And then shall He reward every man according to his works."

Did Christ come at Pentecost in the Glory of His Father? Was there any company of angels at Pentecost? Did He then reward every man according to his works? Scarcely can the descent of the Holy Spirit, or the appearance of cloven tongues, like as of fire, be called the "coming of the Son of Man in the Glory of His Father with His angels, to give every man according to his works" without a gross misuse of our mother tongue, or a strange violation of symbolic imagery. Both these constructions, however, which I now mention, have now been given up as unsatisfactory by those modern students who have thought most carefully upon the subject.

The third still holds its ground and is currently received, though I believe it to be quite as far from the Truth of God as the others. Will you carefully read the chapter through at your leisure and see if you can find anything about the siege of Jerusalem in it? Yet this is the interpretation that finds favor at the present time! Some persons were standing there who would be alive when Jerusalem should be destroyed by the Romans!! Nothing, surely, could be more foreign to the entire scope of our Lord's discourse, or the narrative of the Evangelists. There is not the slightest shadow of a reference to the siege of Jerusalem!

It is the coming of the Son of Man which is here spoken of, "in the glory of His Father with His angels, to reward men according to their works." Whenever Jesus spoke of the siege of Jerusalem and of its coming, he was known to say, "Assuredly I say unto you, this generation shall not pass till all these things are fulfilled," but He never singled out some few persons and said to them, "Assuredly I say unto you, there are some standing here which shall not taste of death till the city of Jerusalem is besieged and destroyed."

If a child were to read this passage I know what he would think it meant--he would suppose Jesus Christ was to come and there were some standing there who should not taste of death until really and literally He did come. This, I believe, is the plain meaning. "Well," says one, "I am surprised! Do you think, then, that this refers to the Apostle John?" No--by no means. The fable passed current, you know, that John was to live till Christ came again. But John himself repudiated it. For at the end of his Gospel, he says, "Then went this saying abroad among the Brethren, that that disciple should not die: yet Jesus said not unto him, He shall not die, but, If I will that he tarry till I come, what is that to you?"

This, you see, was putting a suppositions case and in no sense the language of prediction. Now, dear Brethren, if you are so far convinced of the unreasonableness of each of these efforts to solve the difficulty by feigning a sense, I shall hope to have your minds in readiness for that explanation which appears to me to harmonize with every requirement. I believe the "coming" here spoken of, is the coming of the Son of God to judgment at the last great and terrible assize, when He shall judge the righteous and separate the wicked from among them. The next question is--"Of whom were the words spoken?"

Are we warranted in supposing that our Lord intended this sentence as a gracious promise, or a kindly expectation that He would kindle in the breast of His disciples? I suppose not. To me it appears to have no reference whatever to any man who ever had Grace in his soul--such language is far more applicable to the ungodly than the wicked. It may well have been aimed directly at those followers who should apostatize from the faith, grasp at the world, shrink at the Cross, endeavor to save their lives but really lose them and barter their souls. At the glorious appearing of Christ there are some who will taste death, but will they be the righteous? Surely, my dear Friends, when Christ comes, the righteous will not die!

They will be caught up with the Lord in the air. His coming will be the signal for the resurrection of all His saints. But mark you, at the time of His coming, the men who have been without God and without Christ, will begin, for the first time, to "taste of death." They passed the first stage of dissolution when the soul quitted the body, but they have never known the "taste of death." Till then, they will not have known its tremendous bitterness and its awful horror. They will never drink of the wormwood and the gall, so as really to "taste of death," till the Lord shall come.

This tasting of death here may be explained and I believe it is to be explained by a reference to the second death, which men will not taste of till the Lord comes. And what a dreadful sentence that was, when the Savior said--perhaps singling out Judas as He spoke--"Assuredly I say unto you, there are some standing here who shall never know what that dreadful word 'death' means, till the Lord shall come. You think that if you save your lives, you escape from death.

Ah, you do not know what death means! The demise of the body is but a prelude to the perdition of the soul. The grave is but the porch of death--you will never understand the meaning of that terrible word till the Lord comes."

This can have no reference to the saints, because in the eighth chapter of John and the fifty-first verse, you find this passage--"Verily, verily, I say unto you, If a man keeps My sayings, he shall never see death. Then said the Jews unto Him, Now we know that you have a devil. Abraham is dead and the Prophets. And you say, If a man keeps My sayings, he shall never taste of death." No righteous man, therefore, can ever "taste of death."

He will fall into that deep oblivious sleep in which the body sees corruption. But that is another and a very different thing from the bitter cup referred to as tasting of death. When the Holy Spirit wanted an expression to set forth what was the equivalent for the Divine wrath, what expression was used? "Christ, by the Grace of God, tasted death for every man." The expression, "to taste of death," means the reception of that true and essential death, which kills both the body and the soul in Hell forever. The Savior said then, as He might say, I fear, if He stood in this pulpit tonight--"Assuredly I say unto you, there are some standing here which shall not taste of death till they see the Son of Man coming in His kingdom."

If this is the meaning and I hold that it is in keeping with the context, it explains the verse, sets forth the reason why Christ bespoke breathless attention with the word "assuredly," answers both the grammar and the rhetoric and is not by any argument that I have ever heard of to be repudiated. If this is so, what thrilling denunciations are contained in my text! O, may the Holy Spirit deeply affect our hearts and cause our souls to thrill with its solemnity! What thoughts it stirs up! Compared with the doom which will be inflicted upon the ungodly at the coming of Christ, the death of nature is nothing.

We go farther--compared with the doom of the wicked at the coming of Christ, even the torments of souls in a separate state are scarcely anything. The startling question then comes up--"Are there any sitting or standing here who will have to taste of death when the Lord comes?"

I. THE SINNER'S DEATH IS BUT A FAINT PRESAGE OF THE SINNER'S DOOM AT THE COMING OF THE SON OF MAN IN HIS GLORY. Let me endeavor to show the contrast. We can make but little comparison between the two in point of time. Many men meet with their death so suddenly that it can scarcely involve any pain to them. They are crushed, perhaps, by machinery. A shot sends them to find a grave upon the battlefield, or they may be speedily poisoned.

If they are for hours, or days, or weeks, or months, upon the bed of sickness, yet the real work of dying is but short. It is more a weary sort of living than an actual sense of dying while hope lingers though even in fitful dreams. Dying is but the work of a moment--if it shall be said to last for hours, yet the hours are brief. Misery may count them long, but oh, with what swift wings do they fly! To die, to fall asleep, to suffer--it may be but a pin's prick--and then to have passed away from the land of the living to the realm of shades!

But oh, the doom which is to be brought upon the wicked when Christ comes! This is a death which never dies. Here is a heart palpitating with eternal misery. Here is an eye never filmed by the kind finger of generous forgetfulness. Here will be a body never to be stiffened in apathy--never to be laid quietly in the grave--never rid of keen pangs, wearing disease and lingering wretchedness! To die, I say, is nature's kind release--it brings ease. It comes to a man, for this world, at least, a farewell to his woes and griefs.

But there shall be no ease, no rest, no pause in the destination of impenitent souls. "Depart, you cursed," shall ever ring along the endless aisles of eternity. The thunderbolt of that tremendous word shall follow the sinner in his perpetual flight from the Presence of God--from its baleful influence he shall never be able to escape--no, never! A million years shall make not so much difference to the duration of his agony as a cup of water taken from the sea would to the volume of the ocean. No, when millions of years told a million times shall have rolled their fiery orbits over his poor tormented head, he shall be no nearer to the end than he was at first.

Talk of Death! I might even paint him as an angel when once I think of the terrors of the wrath to come. Soon come, soon gone, is Death. That sharp scythe gives but one cut and down falls the flower and withers in the heat of the sun. But eternity, eternity, eternity! Who shall measure its wounds? Who shall fathom the depths of the gashes? When eternity wields the whip, how dreadfully will it fall! When eternity grasps the sword, how deep shall be the wounds, how terrible its killing!--

"To linger in eternal pain, Yet death forever fly."

You are afraid of death, Sinner? You are afraid of death? Were you wise, you would be ten thousand times ten thousand times more afraid of the coming and the judgment of the Son of Man! In point of loss there is no comparison. When the sinner dies it is not tasting of death in its true sense, for what does he lose? He loses wife and children and friends. He loses all his dainty bits and his sweet draughts. Where now are his violin and his lute? Where now the merry dance and the joyful company? For him no more pleasant landscape nor gliding stream. For him no more light of the sun by day, nor light of moon and stars by night. He has lost, at one stroke, every comfort and every hope.

But then the loss, as far as death is concerned, is but a loss of earthly things--the loss of temporal and temporary comforts--and he might put up with that. It is wretched enough to lose these, but let your imagination follow me, faint as is my power to describe the everlasting and infinite loss of the man who is found impenitent at the last great Judgment Day. What does he lose then? The harps of Heaven and the songs. The joys of God's Presence and the light. The jasper sea and the gates of pearl. He has lost peace and immortality and the crown of life.

No, he has lost all hope--and when a man has lost that, what remains for him? His spirit sinks with a terrible depression, more frightful than a maniac ever knew in his wildest moods of grief. His soul sinks never to recover itself into the depths of dark despair, where not a ray of hope can ever reach him. Lost to God! Lost to Heaven! Lost to time! Lost to the preaching of the Gospel! Lost to the invitation of mercy! Lost to the prayers of the gracious! Lost to the Mercy Seat! Lost to the blood of sprinkling! Lost to all hope of every sort--lost, lost, forever! Compared with this loss the losses of death are nothing, and well might the Savior say that lost spirits shall not even "taste of death" until He shall come and they shall receive their sentence.

Neither does death bear any comparison with the last judgment in point of terror. I do not like to paint the terrors of the deathbed of unrepentant men. Some, you know, glide gently into their graves. It is, in fact, the mark of the wicked that they have no bands in their death--their strength is firm. They are not troubled like other men are. Like the sheep they are laid in the grave. A peaceful death is no sign of Grace. Some of the worst of men have died with a smile upon their countenance to have it changed for one eternal weeping. But there are more men of other exquisite sensibility, instructed men, who cannot die like brutes--and they have alarms and fears and terrors when they are on their deathbeds.

Many an atheist has cried to God under dying pangs and many an Infidel who up to then could brag and speak high things against God, has found his cheek turn pale and his throat grow hoarse when he has come there. Like the mariner, the boldest man in that great storm reels to and fro and staggers like a drunken man and is at his wits' ends--for he finds that it is no child's play to die. I try sometimes to picture that hour when we shall perhaps be propped up in bed, or lying down with pillows round about us, and diligently watched. And as they hush their footfalls and gaze anxiously on, there is a whisper that the solemn time has come and then there is a grappling of the strong man with the stronger than he.

Oh, what must it be to die without a Savior! To die in the dark without a light except the lurid glare of the wrath to come! Horrors there are, indeed, around the deathbed of the wicked! But these are hardly anything compared with the terrors of the Day of Judgment! When the sinner wakes from his bed of dust, the first object he will see will be the Great White Throne and the Judge seated upon it--the first sound that will greet his ears will be the trumpet sounding--

"Come to judgment, come to judgment, Come to judgment, Sinner, come."

He will look up and there will be the Son of Man on His judgment throne--the King's officers arranged on either side--the saints on His right hand and angels round about. Then the books will be opened. What creeping horror will come upon the flesh of the wicked man! He knows his turn will arrive in a moment. He stands expecting it. Fear takes hold upon him while the eyes of the Judge look him through and through and he cries to the rocks to hide him and the mountains to fall upon him! Happy would he be now to find a friendly shelter in the grave, but the grave has burst its doors and can never be closed upon him again. He would even be glad to rush back to his former state in Hell, but he cannot!

The judgment has come, the assize is set--again the trumpet rings--

"Come to judgment, come to judgment, Come to judgment, come away." And then the book is opened and the dread sentence is pronounced. And, to use the words of Scripture, "Death and Hell are cast into the lake of fire. This is the second death. And whoever was not found written in the Book of Life was cast into the lake of fire." The man never knew what death was before. The first death was but a flea-bite! This is death, indeed. The first death he might have looked back upon as a dream, compared with this tasting of death now that the Lord has come!

From what we can gleam darkly from hints of Scripture, the pains of death are not at all comparable to the pains of the judgment at the second advent. Who will speak in a depreciating manner of the pains of death? If we should attempt to do so, we know that our hearts would contradict us. In the shades of night, when deep sleep falls upon men, you sometimes suddenly awake. You are alarmed. The terror by night has come upon you. You expect--you hardly know what it is--but you are half afraid that you are about to die. You know how the cold sweat comes upon the brow. You may have a good hope through Grace, but the very thought of death brings a peculiar pang.

Or when death has really come in view, some of us have marked with terrible grief the sufferings of our dearest friends. We have heard the eye-strings break. We have seen the face all pallid and the cheek all hollow and sunken. We have sometimes seen how every nerve has become a road for the hot feet of pain to travel on and how every vein has been a canal of grief. We have marked the pains, and moans, and groans, and dying strife that frightens the soul away. These, however, are common to man. Not so the pangs which are to be inflicted both on body and soul at the coming of the Son of God!

They are such that I cast a veil over them, fearful of the very thought! Let the Master's words suffice--"Fear Him who is able to cast both body and soul into Hell; yes, I say unto you, fear Him." Then the body in all the parts shall suffer. The members which were once instruments of unrighteousness shall now be instruments of suffering. And the mind, the major sinner, shall be also the greater sufferer. The memory, the judgment, the understanding, the will, the imagination and every power and passion of the soul will become a deep lake of anguish. But I spare you these things! Oh, spare yourselves! God alone knows with what pain I have talking about these horrors!

Were it not that they must be spoken of, or else I must give my account at the Day of Judgment as a faithless servant. Were it not that I speak of them in mercy to your souls, poor Sinners, I would gladly forget them altogether, seeing that my own soul has a hope in Him who saves from the wrath to come. But as long as you will not have mercy upon yourselves, we must lay this axe at your root--so long as you will make a mockery of sin and set at nothing the terrors of the world to come--we must warn you of Hell.

If it is hard to talk of these things, what must it be to endure them? If a dream makes you quiver from head to foot, what must it be to endure really and in person, the wrath to come? O Souls, were I to speak as I ought, my knees would knock together with trembling! Were you to feel as you should, there would not be an unconverted man among you who would not cry, "Sir, what must I do to be saved?" I do beseech you to remember that death, with all its pangs, is but a drop in a bucket compared with the deep, mysterious, fathomless, shoreless sea of grief you must endure forever at the coming of the Lord Jesus unless you repent!

Death makes great discoveries. The man thought himself wise, but Death draws the curtain and he sees written up in large letters--"You fool!" He said he was prudent, for he hoarded up his gold and silver and kept the wages of the laborer. But now he finds that he has made a bad bargain while the question is propounded to him--"What does it profit you, to have gained the world and to have lost your soul?" Death is a great revealer of secrets. Many men are not believers at all until they die. But Death comes and makes short work with their skepticism. It gives but one blow upon the head of doubt and all is done. The man believes then, only he believes too late!

Death gives to the sinner the discovery that there is a God--an angry God--and punishment is wrapped up in the wrath to come. But how much greater the discoveries that await the Day of Judgment! What will the sinner see then? He will see the Man who was crucified sitting upon His Throne. He will hear how Satan has been defeated in all his craftiest undertakings. Read from those mysterious books, the secrets of all hearts shall then be revealed. Then men shall understand how the Lord reigned supremely even when Satan roared most loudly--how the mischief and the folly of man did but, after all, bring forth the great purposes of God.

All this shall be in the books and the sinner shall stand there defeated, terribly defeated, beaten at every point-- baffled, foiled, stultified in every act and every purpose by which he thought to do well for himself. Yes, and utterly confused in all the hostility and all the negligence of his heart towards the living and true God who would, and who did rule over him. Too late he will discover the preciousness of the blood he despised--the value of the Savior he rejected--the glory of the Heaven which he lost and the terror of the Hell to which he is sentenced! How wise, how dreadfully wise will he be when fully aware of his terrible and eternal destruction! Thus sinners shall not taste of death in the real meaning of the term until the Lord shall come.

II. Still further--IN THE STATE OF SEPARATE SPIRITS THEY HAVE NOT FULLY TASTED OF DEATH, NOR WILL THEY DO SO UNTIL CHRIST COMES. The moment that a man dies, his spirit goes before God. If without Christ, that spirit then begins to feel the anger and the wrath of God. It is as when a man is taken before a magistrate. He is known to be guilty and therefore he is remanded and put in prison till his trial shall come. Such is the state of souls apart from the body--they are spirits in prison--waiting for the time of their trial.

There is not, in the sense in which the Romanist teaches it, any purgatory! Yet there is a place of waiting for lost spirits which is in Scripture called, "Hell," because it is one room in that awful prison, in which must dwell forever spirits that die finally impenitent and without faith in Christ. But those of our departed countrymen and fellow citizens of earth who die without Christ have not yet fully tasted of death, nor can they until the advent of the Lord. Just consider why not. Their bodies do not suffer. The bodies of the wicked are still the prey of the worm--still the atoms are the sport of the winds and are traversing their boundless cycles and must do so until they are gathered up into the body again, at the trump of the archangel--at the voice of God.

The ungodly know that their present state is to have an end at the Judgment, but after the Judgment their state will have no end. It is then to go on and on and on, forever and forever, unchanged and unchangeable. Now there may be half a hope, an anticipation of some change, for change brings some relief. But to the finally damned--upon whom the sentence has been pronounced--there is no hope even of a change. Forever and forever shall there be the same ceaseless wheel of misery!

The ungodly, too, in their present state, have not as yet been put to the shame of a public sentence. They have, as it were, merely been cast into prison, the facts being too clear to admit of any doubt as to the sentence. And they are their own tormentors, vexing and paining themselves with the fear of what is yet to come. They have never yet heard that dreadful sentence--"Depart, you cursed, into everlasting fire, prepared for the devil and his angels." I was struck, while studying this subject, to find how little is said about the pains of the lost while they are merely souls and how much is said concerning them when the Lord comes.

You have that one parable of the rich man and Lazarus and there it speaks of the soul being already tormented in the flame. But if you turn to the thirteenth chapter of Matthew and read the parable of the tares, you will find it is at the end of the world that the tares are to be cast into the fire. Then comes the parable of the dragnet. It is when the dispensation comes to an end that the net is to be dragged to shore and then the good are to be put in vessels and the bad cast away. And then the Lord says, "The Son of Man shall send forth His angels and they shall gather out of His kingdom all things that offend, and them which do iniquity. And shall cast them into a furnace of fire: there shall be wailing and gnashing of teeth."

That memorable description in Matthew of those of whom He said, "I was hungry and you gave me no meat. I was thirsty and you gave me no drink," is described as happening when, the "Son of Man shall come in His glory and all His holy angels with Him." The Apostle Paul, too, tells us plainly in the Epistle to the Thessalonians that the wicked are to be destroyed at His coming by the brightness of His power. The recompense of the ungodly, like the reward of the righteous, is anticipated now--but the full reward of the righteous is to be at His coming. They are to reign with Christ. Their fullness of bliss is to be given them when the King Himself in His glory shall sit upon His Throne. So, too, the wicked have the beginning of their heritage at death, but the dread fullness of it is to be hereafter.

At the present moment, death and Hell are not yet cast into the lake of fire. Death is still abroad in the world slaying men. Hell is yet loose. The devil is not yet chained, but still does he go about the "dry places, seeking rest and finding none." At the last day, at the coming of Christ, "death and Hell shall be cast into the lake of fire." We do not understand the symbol. But if it means anything, one would think it must mean this--that at that day the scattered powers of evil, which are to be the tormentors of the wicked, but which have up to now been wandering up and down throughout the world, shall all be collected together--and then, indeed, shall it be that the wicked shall begin to "taste of death" as they have never tasted of it before!

My soul is bowed down with terror while I speak these words to you! I scarcely know how to find suitable words to express the weight of thought which is upon me. My dear Hearers, instead of speculating upon these matters, let us try to shun the wrath to come. And what can help us to do that better than to weigh the warning words of a dear and loving Savior when He tells us that at His coming such a gloom shall pass upon impenitent souls, that compared with it, even death itself shall be as nothing?

Christians, by the faith of their risen Lord, swallow death in victory. But if you die impenitent, you swallow death in ignorance. You do not feel its bitterness now. But, oh, that bitter pill has yet to work its way and that fierce draught has yet to be drained even to the dregs, unless you repent! And now, does not the meditation of these terrors prompt A QUESTION. Jesus said--"Assuredly I say unto you, there are some standing here which shall not taste of death till they see the Son of Man coming in His kingdom." Are there any standing or sitting here who shall not taste of death till then?

In that little group addressed by the Savior stood Judas. He had been trusted by His Master and he was an Apostle. But after all he was a thief and a hypocrite. He, the son of perdition, would not taste of death till Christ should come in His kingdom. Is there a Judas here? I look into your faces and many of you are members of this Church and others of you, I doubt not, are members of other Christian Churches--but are you sure that you have made sound work of it? Is your religion genuine? Do you wear a mask, or are you an honest man?

O Sirs, try your own hearts and since you may fail in the trial, ask the Lord to search you! For as the Lord my God lives, unless you thus search yourselves and find that you are in the right, you may come presumptuously to sit at the Lord's Table. Though with a name to live, you may be among His people here, but you will have to taste of death when the Lord comes. You may deceive us, but you cannot deceive Him! The preacher reflects that he himself may be mistaken. That he himself may be self-deceived. If it is so, may the Lord open my eyes to know the worst of my own state! Will you put up this prayer for yourselves, professors? Do not be too bold, you who say you are Christ's--never be satisfied till you are quite sure of it. And the best way to be sure is to go again just as you went at first and lay hold on eternal life through the power of the blessed Spirit and not by any strength of your own.

No doubt, however, there stood in that little throng around the Savior some who were careless sinners. He knew that they had been so during the whole of His teaching and that they would be so still, and therefore they would taste of death at His coming. Are there not some careless persons come in here tonight? I mean you who never think about religion, who generally look upon Sunday as a day of pleasure, or who loll about in your shirtsleeves nearly all the day. You who look upon the very name of religion as a bugbear to frighten children with--who mock God's servants and despise the very thought of earnestly seeking after the Most High.

Oh, will you, will you be among the number of those who taste of death when the Son of Man shall come in His kingdom? Oh, must I ring your death knell tonight? Must my warning voice be lost upon you? I beseech you to recollect that you must either turn or burn! I beseech you to remember this--"Let the wicked forsake his ways and the unrighteous man his thoughts. And let him turn unto the Lord and He will have mercy upon him. And to our God, for He will abundantly pardon." By the wounds of Jesus, Sinner, stop and think! If God's dear Son was slain for human sin, how terrible must that sin be! And if Jesus died, how base are you if you are disobedient to the doctrine of faith! I pray you, if you think of your body, give some thought to your soul! "Why do you spend money for that which is not bread? And labor for that which satisfies not?" Hearken diligently unto Jehovah's Word and eat of that which is good, real, and substantial food. Come to Jesus and your soul shall live!

And there are some here of another class--Bethsaida sinners, Capernaum sinners! I mean some of you who constantly occupy these pews and stand in yonder area and sit in yonder gallery Sunday after Sunday. The same eyes look down on me week after week. The same faces salute me often with a smile when Sunday comes and I pass you journeying to this, the Tabernacle of your worship. And yet how many of you are still without God and without Christ? Have I been unfaithful to you? If I have, forgive me and pray to God both for me and for yourselves that we may mend our ways.

But if I have warned you of the wrath to come, why will you choose to walk in the path which leads to it? If I have preached to you Christ Jesus, how is it that His charms move you not and that the story of His great love does not bring you to repentance? O that the Spirit of God would come and deal with you, for I cannot! My hammer breaks not your flinty hearts, but God's arm can do it and O, may He turn you yet! Of all sinners over whom a minister ought to weep, you are the worst--for while the careless perish you perish doubly!

You know your Master's will and yet you do it not. You see Heaven's gate set open and yet you will not enter. Your vicious free will ruins you! Your base and wicked love of self and sin destroys you! "You will not come unto Me that you might have life," said Christ. You are so vile that you will not turn even though Jesus should woo you. I pray you let the menace of judgment to come contained in my text stir you now if you have never been stirred before! May God have pity on you even if you will have no pity upon yourselves.

Perhaps among that company there were some who held the Truth of God, but who held it in licentiousness--and there may be such here present. You believe in the doctrine of election. So do I. But then you make it a cloak for your sin! You hold the doctrine of the perseverance of the saints, but you still persevere in your iniquity. Oh, there is no way of perishing that I know of worse than perishing by making the Doctrines of Grace an excuse for one's sins! The Apostle has well said of such that their damnation is just--it is just to any man, but to a seven-fold degree is it just to such as you are! I would not have you forget the doctrine, nor neglect it, nor despise it--but I do beseech you do not prostitute it--do not turn it to the vile purposes of making it pander to your own carnal ease.

Remember, you have no evidence of election except you are holy and you have no right to expect you will be saved at the last unless you are saved now. A present faith in a present Savior is the test. O that my Master would bring some of you to trust Him tonight! The plan of salvation is simple--trust Christ and you are saved! Rely upon Him and you shall live! This faith is the gift of God, but remember that though God gives it, He works in you to will and to do of His own good pleasure. God does not believe for you. The Holy Spirit does not believe for you--you must believe, or else you will be lost!

And it is quite consistent with the fact that it is the gift of God, to say that it is also the act of man. You must, poor Soul, be led to trust the Savior, or into Heaven you can never enter. Is there one here who says, "I desire to find the Savior tonight"? Go not to your bed until you have sought Him and seek Him with sighs and with tears. I think this is a night of Divine Grace. I have preached the Law and the terrors of the Lord to you, but it will be a night of Grace to the souls of some of you! My Master does but kill you that He may make you alive! He does but wound you that He may make you whole!

I feel a sort of inward whisper in my heart that there are some of you who even now have begun your flight from the wrath to come. Where do you flee? Fly to Jesus! Hurry, Sinner, hurry! I trust you will find Him before you retire to your beds, or if you lie tossing there in doubt and fear, then may He manifest Himself to you before the morning light. I think I would freely give my eyes if you might but see Christ! And I would willingly give my hands if you might but lay hold on Him! Do, I beseech you, put not from you this warning, but let it have its proper work upon you and lead you to repentance!

May God save you and may the prayer we have already offered this evening be answered, that the company of you may be found among His elect at His right hand. To that end let us pray. Our Father, save us with Your great salvation. We will say unto God, do not condemn us! Deliver us from going down to the pit, for You have found the ransom. May we not be among the company that shall taste of death when the Son of Man shall come. Hear us, Jesus, through Your blood. God be merciful to us sinners. Amen.

Barabbas Preferred To Jesus

DELIVERED ON SUNDAY MORNING, OCTOBER 16, 1864,
BY C. H. SPURGEON,
AT THE METROPOLITAN TABERNACLE, NEWINGTON.

"Then cried they all again, saying, Not this man, but Barabbas. Now Barabbas was a robber." -- John 18:40.

THE custom of delivering a prisoner upon the day of the Passover was intended, no doubt, as an act of grace on the part of the Roman authorities towards the Jews. And by the Jews it may have been accepted as a significant compliment to their Passover. Since on that day they, themselves, were delivered out of the land of Egypt, they may have thought it to be most fitting that some imprisoned person should obtain his liberty. There was no warrant, however, in Scripture for this--it was never commanded by God--and it must have had a very injurious effect upon public justice. The ruling authority would discharge a criminal, quite irrespective of his crimes or of his repentance--letting him loose upon soci-ety--simply and only because a certain day must be celebrated in a peculiar manner.

Since some one prisoner must be delivered on the paschal day, Pilate thinks that he has now an opportunity of allowing the Savior to escape without at all compromising his character with the authorities of Rome. He asks the people which of the two they will prefer, a notorious thief then in custody, or the Savior. It is probable that Barabbas had been up, till that moment, obnoxious to the crowd. And yet, notwithstanding his former unpopularity, the multitude, instigated by the priests, forget all his faults and prefer him to the Savior!

Who Barabbas was, we cannot exactly tell. His name, as you, in a moment will understand, even if you have not the slightest acquaintance with Hebrew, signifies "his father's son." "Bar" signifying "son," as when Peter is called Simon Barjona, son of Jonah. The other part of his name, "Abbas," signifying "father"--"Abba" being the word which we use in our filial aspirations, "Abba Father." Barabbas, then, is the "son of his father," and some mystics think that there is an imputation here, that he was particularly and specially a son of Satan. Others conjecture that it was an endearing name and was given him because he was his father's darling, an indulged child. His father's boy, as we say.

And these writers add that indulged children often turn out to be imitators of Barabbas and are the most likely persons to become injurious to their country, griefs to their parents and curses to all about them. If it is so, taken in connection with the case of Absalom and especially of Eli's sons, it is a warning to parents that they err not in excessive indulgence of their children.

Barabbas appears to have committed at least three crimes--he was imprisoned for murder, for sedition and for felony--a sorry combination of offenses, certainly. We may well pity the sire of such a son. This wretch is brought out and set in competition with Christ! The multitude are appealed to. Pilate thinks that from the sense of shame they really cannot possibly prefer Barabbas. But they are so bloodthirsty against the Savior and are so moved by the priests, that with one consent--there does not appear to have been a single objecting voice, nor one hand held up to the contrary--with a marvelous unanimity of vice, they cry, "Not this man, but Barabbas!"

Though they must have known, since he was a notable well-known offender, that Barabbas was a murderer, a felon and a traitor, they still preferred him. This fact is very significant. There is more teaching in it than at first sight we might imagine. Have we not here, first of all, in this act of the deliverance of the sinner and the binding of the innocent, a sort of type of that great work which is accomplished by the death of our Savior? You and I may fairly take our stand by the side of Barabbas. We have robbed God of His Glory! We have been seditious traitors against the government of Heaven--if he who hates his brother is a murderer, we also have been guilty of that sin.

Here we stand before the Judgment Seat. The Prince of Life is bound for us and we are allowed to go free. The Lord delivers us and acquits us, while the Savior, without spot or blemish, or shadow of a fault, is led forth to Crucifixion. Two birds were taken in the rite of the cleansing of a leper. The one bird was killed and its blood was poured into a basin. The other bird was dipped in

this blood and then, with its wings all crimson, it was set free to fly into the open field.

The bird slain well pictures the Savior and every soul that has, by faith, been dipped in His blood flies upward towards Heaven singing sweetly in joyous liberty--owing its life and its liberty entirely to Him who was slain!

It comes to this--Barabbas must die or Christ must die--you, the sinner must perish, or Christ Immanuel, the Immaculate, must die. He dies that we may be delivered! Oh, have we all a participation in such a deliverance today? And though we have been robbers, traitors, and murderers, can we rejoice that Christ has delivered us from the curse of the Law, having been made a curse for us?

The transaction has yet another voice. This episode in the Savior's history shows that in the judgment of the people, Jesus Christ was a greater offender than Barabbas. And, for once, I may venture to say that vox populi, (the voice of the people), which in itself was a most infamous injustice--if it is read in the light of the imputation of our sins to Christ-- was vox Dei, (the voice of God)! Christ, as He stood covered with His people's sins, had more sin laid upon Him than that which rested upon Barabbas. In Him was no sin--He was altogether incapable of becoming a sinner--holy, harmless and undefiled is Christ Jesus! But He takes the whole load of His people's guilt upon Himself by imputation and as Jehovah looks upon Him, He sees more guilt lying upon the Savior than even upon this atrocious sinner, Barabbas.

Barabbas goes free--innocent--in comparison with the tremendous weight which rests upon the Savior. Think, Beloved, then, how low your Lord and Master stooped to be thus numbered with the transgressors. Watts has put it strongly, but, I think, none too strongly--

"His honor and His breath Were taken both away, Joined with the wicked in His death, And made as vile as they."

He was so, in the estimation of the people and before the bar of justice--for the sins of the whole company of the faithful were made to meet upon Him. "The Lord has laid upon Him the iniquity of us all." What that iniquity must have been no heart can conceive, much less can any tongue tell! Measure it by the griefs He bore and then, if you can guess what these were, you can form some idea of what must have been the guilt which sunk Him lower before the bar ofjustice than even Barabbas himself.

Oh, what condescension is here! The Just One dies for the unjust! He bears the sin of many and makes intercession for the transgressors. Yet, again, there seems to me to be a third lesson before I come to that which I want to enforce from the text. Our Savior knew that His disciples would in all ages be hated by the world far more than outward sinners. Full often the world has been more willing to put up with murderers, thieves, and drunkards, than with Christians. And it has fallen to the lot of some of the best and most holy of men to be so slandered and abused that their names have been cast out as evil, scarcely worthy to be written in the same list with criminals.

Now Christ has sanctified these sufferings of His people from the slander of their enemies by bearing just such sufferings Himself, so that, my Brethren, if you or I should find ourselves charged with crimes which we abhor--if our heart should be ready to burst under the accumulation of slanderous venom--let us lift up our head and feel that in all this we have a Comrade who has true fellowship with us, even the Lord Jesus Christ who was rejected when Barabbas was selected! Expect no better treatment than your Master! Remember that the disciple is not above his Lord. If they have called the Master of the house Beelzebub, much more will they call them of His household. And if they prefer the murderer to Christ, the day may not be distant when they will prefer even a murderer to you.

These things seem to me to lie upon the surface--I now come to our more immediate subject. First, we shall consider the sin as it stands in evangelical history. Secondly, we shall observe that this is the sin of the whole world. Thirdly, that this sin we ourselves were guilty of before conversion. And fourthly, that this is, we fear, the sin of very many persons who are here this morning--we shall talk with them and expostulate, praying that the Spirit of God may change their hearts and lead them to accept the Savior.

I. A few minutes may be profitably spent in CONSIDERING, THEN, THE SIN AS WE FIND IT IN THIS HISTORY. They preferred Barabbas to Christ. The sin will be more clearly seen if we remember that the Savior had done no ill. No law, either of God or man, had He broken. He might truly have used the words of Samuel--"Behold, here I am: witness against me before the Lord and before His anointed: whose ox have I taken? Or whose ass have I taken? Or whom have I defrauded? Whom have I oppressed? Or of whose hand have I received any bribe to blind my eyes? And I will restore it to you."

Out of that whole assembled crowd there was not one who would have had the presumption to accuse the Savior of having done him damage. So far from this they could but acknowledge that He had only conferred great temporal blessings upon them! O ravening multitude, has He not fed you when you were hungry? Did He not multiply the loaves and fishes for you? Did He not heal your lepers with His touch? Did He not cast out devils from your sons and daughters? Raise up you paralytics? Give sight to your blind and open the ears of your deaf? For which of these good works do you conspire to kill Him?

Among that assembled multitude there were, doubtless, some who owed to Him priceless gifts and yet, though all of them His debtors if they had known it, they clamor against Him as though He were the worst trouble of their lives--a pest and a pestilence to the place where He dwelt. Was it His teaching that they complained of? Where did His teaching offend against morality? Where against the best interests of man? If you observe the teaching of Christ there was never any like it, even judged of by how far it would subserve human welfare. Here was the sum and substance of His doctrine, "You shall love the Lord your God with all your heart and your neighbor as yourself."

His precepts were of the mildest form. Did He bid them draw the sword and expel the Roman, or ride on in a ruthless career of carnage and rapine? Did He stimulate them to let loose their unbridled passions? Did He tell them to seek, first of all, their own advantage and not to care for their neighbor's needs? No! Every righteous State must own Him to be its best pillar, and the commonwealth of manhood must acknowledge Him to be its conservator. And yet, for all this, there they are, hounded on by their priests, seeking His blood and crying, "Let Him be crucified! Let Him be crucified!"

His whole intent, evidently, was their good. What did He preach for? No selfish motive could have been urged. Foxes had holes and the birds of the air had nests, but He had not where to lay His head. The charity of a few of His disciples kept Him from absolute starvation! Cold mountains and the midnight air witnessed the fervor of His lonely prayers for the multitudes who now are hating Him. He lived for others--they could see this. They could not have observed Him during the three years of His ministry without saying, "Never lived there such an unselfish soul as this." They must have known, the most of them--and the rest might have known, had they enquired ever so little--that He had no object whatever in being here on earth except that of seeking the good of men.

For which of these things do they clamor that He may be crucified? For which of His good works, for which of His generous words, for which of His holy deeds will they fasten His hands to the wood and His feet to the tree? With unreasonable hatred, with senseless cruelty they only answer to the question of Pilate--"Why, what evil has He done?"-- with, "Let Him be crucified! Let Him be crucified!"

The true reason of their hate, no doubt, lay in the natural hatred of all men to perfect goodness. Man feels that the presence of goodness is a silent witness against his own sin and therefore he longs to get rid of it. To be too holy in the judgment of men is a great crime, for it rebukes their sin. If the holy man has not the power of words, his very life is one loud witness-bearing for God against the sins of His creatures. This inconvenient protesting led the wicked to desire the death of the Holy and Just One.

Besides, the priests were at their backs. It is a sad and lamentable thing, but it is often the case that the people are better than their religious teachers. At the present moment the laity of the Church of England, as a whole, have honest consciences and would have their Prayer Book revised tomorrow if their voices could be heard. But their clerics care far too little about the Truth of God and are not very particular how they swear, or with whom they associate. So long as their Church can be kept together, Father Ignatius shall be heard in their assemblies, although Christ's call to the Church to purify herself, awakens only resentment and ill-will.

No matter that the throats of certain clergymen were exercised in hissing for a moment at the apparition of the bold Anglican monk--he is one of themselves, a brother of their own order--and their Church is responsible for all that he does. Let them come out and separate themselves and then we shall know that they abhor this modern popery. But so long as they sit in the same assembly and are members of the same Church, the sin is theirs, and we shall not cease to denounce both it and them!

If Evangelical clergymen remain in communion with Papists, now that they come out in their full colors, I will cease to say that they violate their consciences, but I shall doubt whether they have any consciences at all! Brethren, it is still the case that the people are better than their teachers. This people would not have crucified Christ had not the clergy of the day, the priests, the endowed ministers, cried out, "Let Him be crucified!" He was the Dissenter, the heretic, schis- matic, the troubler in Israel. He it was who cried aloud against the faults of their establishment! He it was who could not be put down--the ignorant man from Galilee who would continue to clamor against them! The mischief-maker and therefore, "Let Him be crucified! Let Him be crucified!" Anything is good enough for the man who talks about reform and advocates changes in established rules.

No doubt bribery also was used in this case. Had not Rabbi Simon paid the multitude? Was there not a hope of some feast, after the Passover was over, to those who would use their throats against the Savior? Beside, there was the multitude going that way. And so if any had compassion they held their tongue. Often they say that, "Discretion is the better part of valor," and truly there must be many valorous men, for they have much of valor's better part, discretion. If they did not join in the shout, yet at least they would not disturb the others and so there was but one cry, "Away with Him! Away with Him! It is not fit that He should live."

What concentrated scorn there is in this fortieth verse! It is not, "this Jesus." They would not foul their mouths with His name, but this fellow--"this devil," if you will. To Barabbas they give the respect of mentioning his name! But "this"--whom they hate so much--they will not even stoop to mention. We have looked, then, at this great sin as it stands in history.

II. But now let us look, in the second place, AT THIS INCIDENT AS SETTING FORTH THE SIN WHICH HAS BEEN THE GUILT OF THE WORLD IN ALL AGES, AND WHICH IS THE WORLD'S GUILT NOW. When the Apostles went forth to preach the Gospel and the Truth of God had spread through many countries, there were severe edicts passed by the Roman Emperors. Against whom were these edicts framed? Against the foul offenders of that day?

It is well known that the whole Roman Empire was infested with vices such as the cheek of modesty would blush to hear named. The first chapter of the Epistle to the Romans is a most graphic picture of the state of society throughout the entire Roman dominions. When severe laws were framed, why were they not proclaimed against these atrocious vices? It is scarcely fit that men should go unpunished who are guilty of crimes such as the Apostle Paul has mentioned, but I find no edicts against these things--I find that they were borne with and scarcely mentioned with censure.

But burning, dragging at the heels of wild horses, the sword, imprisonment, tortures of every kind were used against whom, do you think? Against the innocent, humble followers of Christ, who, so far from defending themselves, were willing to suffer all these things and presented themselves like sheep at the shambles, willing to endure the butcher's knife! The cry of the world, under the persecutions of Imperial Rome, was, "Not Christ, but Sodomites and murderers and thieves--we will bear with any of these--but not with Christ! Away with His followers from the earth!"

Then the world changed its tactics. It became nominally Christian and Antichrist came forth in all its blasphemous glory. The Pope of Rome put on the triple crown and called himself the Vicar of Christ. Then came in the abomination of the worship of saints, angels, images and pictures. Then came the mass and I know not what, of detestable error. And what did the world say? "Popery forever!" Down went every knee and every head bowed before the sovereign representative of Peter at Rome! The Church of Rome was equal in sin to Barabbas.

No! I do but compliment Barabbas when I mention him in the same breath with many of the popes, for their character was foul and black through and through, till even those who superstitiously looked upon them as infallible in their office could not defend their personal characters. The world chose the harlot of Rome and she who was drunk with the wine of her abominations had every eye to gaze upon her with admiration! And Christ's Gospel was forgotten--buried in a few old books and almost extinguished in darkness.

Since that day the world has changed its tactics yet again. In many parts of the earth Protestantism is openly acknowledged and the Gospel is preached, but what then? Then comes in Satan and another Barabbas, the Barabbas of mere ceremonialism and mere attendance at a place of worship is set up. "Yes, we are orthodox, so orthodox, so sound! Yes, we are religious, strictly religious! We attend our meeting house, or go to our Church. We are never absent. We attend every form." But you have no vital godliness--you have not been born again--you have not passed from death unto life! "That is all right! This will do! So long as we are as good as our neighbors and keep the outward rite, the inward does not matter."

This which is a foul robbery of God's Glory, this which murders men's souls, is the Barabbas of the present age! An outward name to live is set up and is received by those who are dead and many of you now present are quite easy and content though you have never felt the quickening Spirit of God--though you have never been washed in the atoning blood--yet you are satisfied because you take a seat in some place of worship! You give your guinea, your donation to an hospital, or your subscription to a good object, forgetting and not caring to remember that all the making clean of the outside of the cup and the platter will never avail, unless the inward nature is renewed by the Spirit of the living God!

This is the great Barabbas of the present age and men prefer it before the Savior! That this is true--that the world really loves sin better than Christ--I think I could prove clearly enough by one simple fact. You have observed sometimes Christian men are inconsistent, have you not? The inconsistency was nothing very great if you had judged them according to ordinary rules of conduct. But you are well aware that a worldly man might commit any sin he likes without much censure. But if the Christian man commits ever so little, then hands are held up and the whole world cries, "Shame!"

I do NOT want to have that altered! But I do want just to say this--"There is Mr. So-and-So, who is known to live a fast, wicked, evil life. Well, I do not see that he is universally avoided and reprobated, but on the contrary he is tolerated by most and admired by some. But suppose a Christian man, a well-known professor, to have committed some fault which, compared with this, were not worth mentioning--then what is done? "Oh, publish it! Publish it! Have you heard what Mr. So-and-So did? Have you heard of this hypocrite's transgression?" Well, what was it? You look at it. It is wrong, it is very wrong--but compared with what you say about it, it is nothing at all.

The world, therefore shows by the difference between the way in which it judges the professedly religious man and that with which it judges its own, that it really can tolerate the most abandoned, but cannot tolerate the Christian. Of course, the Christian never will be altogether free from imperfections. The world's enmity is not against the Christian's imperfections evidently, because they will tolerate greater imperfections in others! The objection must therefore be against the man--against the profession which he has taken up and the course which he desires to follow! Watch carefully, Beloved, that you give them no opportunity! When you see that the slightest mistake is laid hold of and exaggerated, in this you see a clear evidence that the world prefers Barabbas to the followers of the Lord Jesus Christ.

Now the world will change its various modes of dealing, but it will never love the Church better than it does now. We do not expect to see the world lifted up to become more and more absorbed into the Church, The union of the world with the Church was never the object of our religion. The object of Christ is to gather to Himself a people from among men. It is not the lifting up of all, but the calling out of some--the making of men to differ, the manifestation of His special and discriminating Grace--the gathering together of a people whom He has formed for Himself.

In this process morality is promoted and men are civilized and improved. But this is only indirectly God's object and not His immediate end. The immediate end of the Gospel is the salvation of the people whom He has ordained unto eternal life and who, therefore, in due season are led to believe in Him. The world, to the end of the chapter, will be as much at enmity with true Believers as ever it was. "You are not of the world, therefore the world hates you." This will be as true when Christ shall come as at the present moment. Let us expect it! And when we meet with scorn and persecution, let us not be surprised as though some strange thing had happened to us.

III. I come in the third place, and O for some assistance from on high, to observe that THE SIN OF PREFERRING BARABBAS TO CHRIST WAS THE SIN OF EVERY ONE OF US BEFORE OUR CONVERSION. Will you turn over the leaves of your diary, now, dear Friends, or fly upon the wings of memory to the hole of the pit where you were lifted? Did you not, O you who live close to Christ, did you not once despise Him? What company did you like best? Was it not that of the frivolous, if not that of the profane?

When you sat with God's people, their talk was very tedious. If they spoke of Divine realities and of experimental subjects, you did not understand them, you felt them to be troublesome. I can look back upon some whom I know now to be most venerable Believers, whom I thought to be a gross nuisance when I heard them talk of the things of God! What were our thoughts about? When we had time for thinking, what were our favorite themes? Not much did we meditate upon eternity. Not much upon Him who came to deliver us from the misery of Hell's torments. Brothers and Sisters, His great love with which He loved us was never laid to heart by us as it should have been.

No, if we read the story of the Crucifixion, it had no more effect upon our mind than a common tale. We knew not the beauties of Christ! We thought of any trifle sooner than of Him. And what were our pleasures? When we had what we called a day's enjoyment, where did we seek it? At the foot of the Cross? In the service of the Savior? In communion with Him? Far from it! The further we could remove from godly associations the better pleased we were. Some of us have to confess with shame that we were never more in our element than when we were without a conscience--when conscience ceased to accuse us and we could plunge into sin with riot.

What was our reading then? Any book sooner than the Bible--and if there had lain in our way anything that would have exalted Christ and extolled Him in our understandings--we would have put the book away as much too dry to please us. Any three-volume heap of nonsense, any light literature--no, perhaps, even worse--would have delighted our eyes and our heart. But thoughts of His eternal delight towards us--thoughts of His matchless passion and His Glory now in Heaven never came across our minds, nor would we endure those who would have led us to such meditations!

What were our aspirations then? We were looking after business, aiming at growing rich, famous for learning or admired for ability. SELF was what we lived for! If we had some regard for others and some desire to benefit our race, self was at the bottom of it all. We did not live for God--we could not honestly say, as we woke in the morning, "I hope to live for God today." At night we could not look back upon the day and say, "We have this day served God." He was not in our thoughts! Where did we spend our best praise? Did we praise Christ? No! We praised cleverness and when it was in association with sin, we praised it none the less.

We admired those who could most fully minister to our own fleshly delights and felt the greatest love to those who did us the worst injury. Is not this our confession as we review the past? Have I not read the very history of your life? I know I have of my own. Alas, for those dark days in which our besotted soul went after any evil, but would not follow after Christ! It would have been the same today with us if almighty Grace had not made the difference. We may as well expect the river to cease to run to the sea as expect the natural man to turn from the current of his sins! As well might we expect fire to become water, or water to become fire as for the unrenewed heart ever to love Christ!

It was mighty Grace which made us seek the Savior. And as we look back upon our past lives, it must be with mingled feelings of gratitude for the change and of sorrow that we should have been so grossly foolish as to have chosen Barabbas and have said of the Savior, "Let Him be crucified!"

IV. And now I shall come to the closing part of the sermon which is THAT THERE ARE DOUBTLESS MANY HERE WHO THIS DAY PREFER BARABBAS TO OUR LORD JESUS CHRIST. Let me first state your case, dear Friends. I would describe it honestly, but at the same time so describe it that you will see your sin in it. And while I am doing so, my object will be to reason with you, and pray the Lord may change your will.

There are many here, I fear, who prefer sin to Christ. I may say, without making a guess I know that there are those here who would long ago have been followers of Christ, but that they preferred drunkenness. It is not often, it is not every day, it is not even every week--but there are occasions when they feel as if they must go into company--and as a sure result they return home intoxicated. They are ashamed of themselves--they have expressed as much as that. They have even gone so far as to pray to God for Divine Grace to overcome their habit. But after being the subject of convictions for years, they have up to now made no advance.

It did seem once as if they had conquered it. For a long time there was an abstinence from the fault, but they have gone back to their folly. They have preferred the bestial degrading vice--did I say bestial? I insult the beasts!--for beasts are not guilty of such a vice as this! The drunk prefers this degrading vice to Christ Jesus. There stands drunkenness, I see it mirrored before me with all its folly, its witlessness, its greed and filth. But the man chooses all that, and though he has known by head knowledge something concerning the beauty and excellency of Christ, he virtually says of Jesus, "Not this man, but drunkenness!"

Then there are other cases where a favorite lust reigns supreme in their hearts. The men know the evil of the sin and they have good cause to know it. They know also something of the sweetness of religion, for they are never happier than when they come up with God's people. And they go home sometimes from a solemn sermon, especially if it touches their vice, and they feel, "God has spoken to my soul today and I am brought to a standstill." But for all that, the temptation comes again and they fall as they have fallen before. I am afraid there are some of you whom no arguments will ever move. You have become so set on this mischief that it will be your eternal ruin.

But oh, think! How will this look when you are in Hell--"I preferred that foul Barabbas of lust to the beauties and perfections of the Savior who came into the world to seek and to save that which was lost!" And yet this is the case, not of some, but of a great multitude who listen to the Gospel and yet prefer sin to its saving power. There may be some here, too, of another class, who prefer gain. It has come to this--if they become truly the Lord's people, they cannot do in trade what they now think their trade requires them to do. If they become really and genuinely Believers, they must, of course, become honest! But their trade would not pay, they say, if it were conducted upon honest principles! Or it is such a trade and there are some few such, as ought not to be conducted at all, much less by Christians.

Here comes the turning point--shall I take the gold, or shall I take Christ? True, it is cankered gold, and gold on which a curse must come. It is the fool's pence--it may be it is gain that is extorted from the miseries of the poor-- money that would not ever stand the light because it is not fairly come by. Perhaps it is money that will burn its way right through your souls when you get upon your deathbeds. But yet men who love the world, say, "No, not Christ, give me a full purse and away with Christ."

Others, less base or less honest, cry, "We know His excellence! We wish we could have Him, but we cannot have Him on terms which involve the renunciation of our dearly-beloved gain." "Not this Man, but Barabbas." Others say, "I would gladly be a Christian, but then I should lose so many of my acquaintances and friends. For the matter of what it comes to, my friends are not much good to me--they are such friends as are fondest when I have most money to spend with them. They are friends who praise me most when I am often at the ale-house--when I am seen plunging deepest into their vices. I know they do me mischief, but," says the man, "I could not venture to oppose them. One of them has such a glib tongue and he can make such telling jokes! I could not bear to have him down upon me. And there is another, I have heard him give Christians such stinging names and point at their faults in such a sarcastic manner--I could not run the gauntlet of his tongue! And therefore, though I gladly would be a Christian, yet I will not."

That is the way you prefer to be a serf, a slave, to the tongue of the scorner sooner than be a free man and take up the Cross and follow Christ! You prefer, I say, not merely by way of allegory, but as matter offact--you prefer Barabbas to the Lord Jesus Christ! I might thus multiply instances but the same principle runs through them all. If anything whatever keeps you back from giving your heart to the Lord Jesus Christ, you are guilty of setting up an opposition candidate to Christ in your soul and you are choosing, "not this Man, but Barabbas."

Let me occupy a few minutes with pleading Christ's cause with you. Why is it that you reject Christ? Are you not conscious of the many good things which you receive from Him? You would have been dead if it had not been for Him! No, worse than that, you would have been in Hell! God has sharpened the great axe. Justice, like a stern woodman, stood with the axe uplifted, ready to cut you down as a cumberer of the ground. A hand was seen stopping the arm of the Avenger and a voice was heard saying, "Let it alone, till I dig about it and feed it."

Who was it that appeared just then in your moment of extremity? It was no other than that Christ, of whom you think so little, that you prefer drunkenness or vice to Him! You are this day in the House of God listening to a discourse which I hope is sent from Him. You might have been in Hell--think one moment of that--shut out from hope, enduring in body and soul unutterable pangs. That you are not there should make you love and bless Him who has said, "Deliver him from going down into the pit." Why will you prefer your own gain and self-indulgence to that blessed One to whom you owe so much?

Common gratitude should make you deny yourself something for Him who denied Himself so much that He might bless you. Do I hear you say that you cannot follow Christ because His precepts are too severe? In what respect are they too severe? If you, yourself, were set to judge them, what is the point with which you would find fault? They deny you your sins? They deny you your miseries! They do not permit you, in fact, to ruin yourself. There is no precept of Christ which is not for your good and there is nothing which He forbids you which He does not forbid on the principle that it would harm you to indulge in it.

But suppose Christ's precepts to be ever so stern--is it not better that you should put up with them than be ruined? The soldier submits implicitly to the captain's command because he knows that without discipline there can be no victory and the whole army may be cut in pieces if there is a want of order. When the sailor has risked his life to penetrate through the thick ice of the north, we find him consenting to all the orders and regulations of authority and bearing all the hardships of the adventure because he is prompted by the desire of assisting in a great discovery, or stimulated by a large reward.

And surely the little self-denials which Christ calls us to will be abundantly recompensed by the reward He offers! And when the soul and its eternal interests are at stake, we may well put up with these temporary inconveniences if we may inherit eternal life! I think I hear you say that you would be a Christian, but there is no happiness in it. I would not tell you a falsehood on this point. I would speak the truth if it were so, but I do solemnly declare that there is more joy in the Christian life than there is in any other form of life! If I had to die like a dog and there were no hereafter, I would prefer to be a Christian! You shall appeal to the very poorest among us--to those who are most sick and most despised and they will tell you the same.

There is not an old country woman shivering in her old ragged red cloak over a handful of fire, full of rheumatism, with an empty cupboard and an aged body who would change with the very highest and greatest of you if she had to give up her religion! No, she would tell you that her Redeemer was a greater comfort to her than all the luxuries which could be heaped upon the table of Dives. You make a mistake when you dream that my Master does not make His disciples blessed. They are a blessed people who put their trust in Christ!

Still, I think I hear you say, "Yes, this is all very well, but still I prefer present pleasure." Do you not, in this, talk like a child? No! Like a fool! For what is present pleasure? How long does that word "present" last? If you could have ten thousand years of merriment I might agree with you in a measure, but even there I should have but short patience with you, for what would be ten thousand years of sin's merriment compared with millions upon millions of years of sin's penalty? Why, at the longest, your life will be but very short. Are you not conscious that time flies more hurriedly every day? As you grow older, do you not seem as if you had lived a shorter time instead of longer? Perhaps if you could live to be as old as Jacob, you would say, "Few and evil have my days been, for they appear fewer as they grow more numerous."

You know that this life is but a span and is soon over. Look at the graveyards! See how they are crowded with green mounds. Remember your own companions--how one by one they have passed away. They were as firm and strong as you, but they have gone like a shadow that declines.

Is it worthwhile to have this little space of pleasure and then to lie down in eternal pain? I pray you answer this question! Is it worth while to choose Barabbas for the sake of the temporary gain he may give you and give up Christ and so renounce the eternal treasures ofjoy and happiness which are at His right hand forevermore?

I wish that I could put these questions before you as they ought to be put. It needs the earnest seraphic voice of Whitfield, or the pleading tongue of Richard Baxter to plead with you! But yet I think I talk to rational men. And if it is a matter of arithmetic, it shall need no words of mine. I will not ask you to take your life at the longest that you expect it to be--at eighty, say--crowd it full of all the pleasures you can imagine. Suppose yourself in good health! Dream yourself to be without business cares, with all that heart can wish! Go and sit upon the throne of Solomon if you will, and yet what will you have to say when it is all over? Looking back upon it, can you make more of it than Solomon did, when he said, "Vanity of vanities, all is vanity. All is vanity and vexation of spirit"?

When you have cast up that sum, may I ask you to calculate how much you will have gained, if, in order to possess this vanity, you have renounced eternal happiness and have incurred everlasting woe? Do you believe the Bible? You say, "Yes." Well, then, it must be so. Many men profess to be Believers in Scripture and yet, when you come to the point as to whether they believe in eternal woe and eternal joy, there is a kind of something inside which whispers, "That is in the Book--but still it is not real, it is not true to us." Make it true to yourselves and when you have done it and have clearly proved that you must be in happiness or woe--and that you must here either have Barabbas for your master, or have Christ for your Lord--then, I say, like sane men, judge which is the better choice and may God's mighty Grace give you spiritual sanity to make the right choice!

But this I know, you will never make the right choice unless that mighty Spirit who alone leads us to choose the right and reject the wrong, shall come upon you and lead you to fly to a Savior's wounds! I need not, I think, prolong the service now, but I hope you will prolong it at your own houses by thinking of the matter. And may I put the question personally to all of you separate--whose are you? On whose side are you? There are no neuters. There are no betweenites--you either serve Christ or Belial! You are either with the Lord or with His enemies! Who is on the Lord's side this day? Who? Who is for Christ and for His Cross? For His blood and for His Throne?

Who, on the other hand, are His foes? As many as are not for Christ are numbered with His enemies. Be not so numbered any longer, for the Gospel comes to you with an inviting voice--"Believe in the Lord Jesus Christ and you shall be saved." God help you to believe and cast yourself upon Him now. And if you trust Him, you are saved now and you shall be saved forever! Amen.

Praying And Waiting

DELIVERED ON SUNDAY MORNING, OCTOBER 23, 1864
BY C. H. SPURGEON,
AT THE METROPOLITAN TABERNACLE, NEWINGTON.

"These things have I written unto you that believe on the name of the Son of God; that you may know that you have eternal life and that you may believe on the name of the Son of God. And this is the confidence that we have in Him, that, if we ask anything according to His will, He hears us: and if we know that He hears us, whatever we ask, we know that we have the petitions that we desired of Him." -- 1 John 5:13-15.

THE beloved Apostle John here addresses himself to those who have believed on the Son of God. And having himself ascended the high hill of fellowship with Jesus, he labors to conduct his fellow Believers up three glorious ascents of the mount of God. I think I see before me now three shining ladders and with the Glory of God reflected from his brow, I see John, like an angel of God, conducting the Lord's Jacobs up the glittering rounds. The first ascent he would have them take is from faith to the full assurance of faith.

He writes to them as Believers and he says, "These things have I written unto you that believe on the name of the Son of God; that you may know that you have eternal life." As Believers, they had eternal life, for, "He that believes on the Son of God has everlasting life," and shall never come into condemnation. Yes, "He that lives and believes in Christ, though he were dead, yet should he live." But it is one thing to have eternal life and another thing to know that we have eternal life.

In the third verse of the second chapter of this very Epistle, this Apostle draws a distinction between knowing Christ and knowing that we know Him, for he writes, "Hereby we do know that we know Him, if we keep His Commandments." A man may know Christ in his heart and yet at certain seasons, through weakness ofjudgment or stress of temptations, he may be cast into doubts as to whether he has any saving knowledge of the Lord Jesus at all. But he alone is happy, who, building upon the sure foundation of God's promise, gives all diligence to make his calling and election sure and enjoys an assured confidence of his interest in Christ.

I know there are some who do not like us to draw any distinction between faith and assurance. But the more I think upon the subject the more I am compelled to do it--not for the encouragement of unbelief--but for the consolation of those weaklings of the flock who, upon another ground must be rejected altogether since their trembling faith has never, as yet, ripened into assurance. Believers who have observed their own experience must have noticed that even when they can cast themselves in all simplicity upon Christ Jesus and consequently have a right to be confident of their own safety-- yet even then they cannot at all times enjoy the comfortable persuasion of security because their minds are distracted and Satan has gained an advantage over them.

They trust their God, but it is with something of the spirit of Job when he said, "Though He slay me, yet will I trust in Him." The shadow of the dark thought that perhaps you may prove an apostate darkens your path and you cling to the Lord, not with a joyful assurance which can say, "He is mine," but with that desperate faith which cries, "I must believe, for otherwise there is nothing before me but destruction!" "To whom shall I go but unto You, for You have the words of eternal life!"

Even the strongest of saints must be led, I think, in their experience to observe that while always believing they are not always assured. This must certainly be the case with the weaker ones and the beginners. I know faith is a sureness concerning the Truth of God. I cheerfully accept the definition. But I must bid you observe that there is a difference between being sure of the Truth of God and being sure that I am a partaker of Divine Life. I come to Christ not knowing whether He died especially for me, or not. But I trust in Him as the Savior of sinners--this is faith. And having trusted in Him I discover that I have a particular and special interest in the merit of His blood and in the love of His heart--this is rather assurance than faith.

Although assurance will grow out of faith and that is scarcely faith which does not lead to assurance, yet the two are not identical. You may believe in Christ and have eternal life and still be in doubt about it. You ought not to be, but still you may fall into such a state. The Apostle desires that if you believe, you may come to a still higher state and may infallibly and joyfully know that you have eternal life. O Brethren, do not fear to mount this ladder! The steps are very easy-- just continue to believe as you have believed! Receive the Word of God as it stands--you need no other ground of assurance but that which is written there--and the Spirit shall enable you to see your own title, sealed and sure. Continue to rest in Jesus and you shall find that in Him, as you have attained faith, so in Him you shall also obtain an assurance of faith. Here is the first heavenly staircase.

The Apostle desires to lead the disciples up a second ascent. Observe it. "And this is the confidence that we have in Him, that if we ask anything according to His will, He hears us." From the assurance of our interest in Christ the next step is to a firm belief in the power of prayer, in the fact that God does regard your prayer. And this you can hardly get unless you have attained to an assurance of your own interest in Him. Belief in the prevalence of my prayer, to a great extent, must depend upon my conviction of my interest in Christ. For instance, here is Paul's argument-- "He that spared not His own Son, but delivered Him up for us all, how shall He not with Him also freely give us all things?"

I must therefore be sure that God has given me Christ. And if He has given Christ to me, then I know that He will give me all things. But if I have any doubt about Christ's being mine and about my being the receiver of God's unspeakable gift in Christ, I cannot reason as the Apostle did and I cannot, therefore, have that confidence that my prayer is heard. Again, God's fatherhood is another ground of our confidence in prayer. "If you, then, being evil, know how to give good gifts unto your children, how much more shall your heavenly Father give the Holy Spirit to them that ask Him?"

But if I am not clear that God is my Father. If I have not the spirit of Adoption, then I cannot come to God with this confidence that He will give me my desire. My sonship being assured, I am confident that my Father knows what I have need of and will hear me. But my sonship being in dispute, my power in prayer vanishes--I cannot hope to prevail. Besides, the man who has faith in Christ and knows himself to be saved has already received answers to prayer! And answers to prayer are some of the best supports to our faith as to the future success of our petitions. "Because He has inclined His ear unto me, therefore will I call upon Him as long as I live." But if I have no reason to conclude that God has heard my prayer for forgiveness--if I am in doubt as to whether my first cries have ever reached His ear and obtained an answer-- how can I come with confidence?

No, Brothers and Sisters, seek in the first place, since you have believed in Jesus, to get the witness within you that you are born of God. Then go from this gracious ascent to the next-- knowing and being assured that He hears us always because we do the things which are pleasing in His sight and plead the name of our Lord Jesus Christ who is All in All to us. If you have climbed this second ascent, and I hope there are many here who have, the third is not difficult. It is to go from your belief that God hears prayer to a conviction that when you have prayed you have the petitions that you have desired of Him.

In other words, to ascend from a solemn conviction of the usefulness of prayer to a particular and special belief that in your own case, when you have desired anything of God in prayer through Jesus Christ, you have obtained the answer! Not that you have had the particular mercy at once given into your hands--for there is much that is really ours which, nevertheless, is not at present in our sensible possession--and yet is truly ours. We have Heaven, but we have it not in enjoyment as of yet. And so we may have answers to our prayers and yet, as far as our sense is concerned, we may not have received anything. We have it, but we see it not. It is ours, but our God sees fit to reserve it for a season for a further trial of our faith.

If a man had nothing more than he could see--there are many of you here who have possessions across the sea, or ships far off upon the water--and if you had only what you can see just now, your estates would be sorely diminished! So we may have the answers to many of our prayers--really have the answers--and yet for the present those answers, like a ship upon a long voyage, may not yet have returned. Yet we have the answer as the merchant has the ship which is as much his upon the Atlantic as when it shall lie alongside his wharf. May we, dear Friends, obtain the gracious position of knowing that having sought the Lord in prayer through Jesus Christ, we have the petitions which we desired of Him!

I want, this morning, as God may help me, to strengthen our dear Brethren to look for answers to prayer. Seeing that you have the promise of an answer to prayer and that the answer must come to you, look for it! Unless you believe that you have the answer in reality, you are not likely to watch for its appearance. But if you have come so far as to believe that you have the answer, I do now earnestly urge you to look for it and rejoice.

First, let me explain explanation. Secondly, let us say something in the praise of this believing in our answer to prayer, commendation. Thirdly, let us rebuke some who do not like to have their prayers answered--here we have rebuke. And then, fourthly, let us stir you up to exercise this gracious privilege which is your undoubted right as the children of God--this is exhortation.

I. EXPLANATION--and let the explanation be taken from instances in Holy Writ. Elijah bowed his knee on the top of Carmel and prayed to God for rain. For three years there had not been a single drop descending upon Israel. He pleads, and having finished his intercession, he says to his servant, "Go and look from the top of Carmel towards the sea." He did not think it sufficient to have prayed--he believed that he had the petition which he desired of God and therefore he sent his servant to see. The answer which was brought back was not encouraging. But he said to his servant, "Go again seven times," and seven times that servant went.

Elijah does not appear to have staggered in his faith--he believed he had the petition and therefore expected soon to see it--since seeing is often a blessed reward of believing. He sent his servant till at last he brought back the news, "There is a little cloud the size of a man's hand." Quite enough for Elijah's faith. He acts upon the belief that he has the petition, though not a drop of rain has fallen. He goes down to tell Ahab to make ready his chariot that the rain not stop him--in the full and firm conviction that as certainly as he had asked--so surely would the rain descend!

David is another case in point. Let me quote but this one expression, "In the morning will I direct my prayer unto You and will look up." As men take an arrow from the quiver, so David takes his prayer. He fits it to the string and bends the bow by vehemence of desire and then he takes aim--he directs his prayer to God. He is not shooting to the right hand or to the left, but upwards to his God he points his polished shaft. Not to those who will afterwards read the Psalm. Not to those who are listening to his voice--he directs it to Heaven. And having done so, draws the bow with all his strength and away flies the arrow.

Anxious to know how it speeds, he looks up to see whether the Lord accepts his desires and continues to look up to see whether a gracious answer is returned. This is what I mean by the Christian's knowing he has an answer to his petition and waiting and watching till it comes. Take the case of Samson, poor, strong, yet weak Samson--as strong in faith as he was in body. After his hair had grown again he is brought forth to make sport for the Philistines and he prays to God to strengthen him but this once.

Mark how he believed he had the petition--for he said to the man who conducted him blindfolded into the Philistine's temple, "Put me near the two pillars whereon the house does lean." And why does he seek to stand there? Because he believes he has his petition. Having taken up his position, he grasps the two pillars and bows himself with all his might. Why? Why does he strain himself so? Is it possible that he hopes to move those mighty columns from their bases? Yes, it is not only possible, but certain that he will work wonders, for he believes that he has his petition from his God!

See how in the strength of his belief he pulls down the temple of Dagon about the heads of the worshippers and proves the power of believing supplication! Something of that kind of spirit I want Believers to experience--to know that their prayer is heard and then to act upon the conviction that it is so. Take again, the case of Hannah, a woman of a sorrowful spirit. She prayed without an audible voice, only her lips moved. As soon as Eli told her that God had heard the prayer, observe the change which was worked in her, "Then was her countenance no more sad."

Why, Hannah, why do you smile? You have not yet seen your husband. You have no signs that God has visited you and granted the desire of your heart! No, but the Man of God has said it and that is enough for her! The wrinkles disappear from her brow and the tears from her eyes--you ask her why and she says, "I have the petition that I desired of God: I asked in faith and the Lord has been pleased to hear my prayer."

A yet more wonderful instance is that of Jacob, who not only believes in the utility of prayer but he will not let the Angel depart till he wins His blessing. This was going farther--not only believing that there was a blessing and that prayer could get it, but a determination not to cease prayer till he had some visible token that he had obtained it! Here was strong faith! The case may be exceptional and especially when we pray for temporal mercies I do not think we have any right to give the Lord such a time and to say we will not rise from our knees till the favor is bestowed. That might be presumption rather than faith.

But there are times when mercies are so necessary and when we are so clear that our prayer is according to God's will--when the prayer is so evidently indicted upon our heart by the Holy Spirit that we may even say unto the Covenant Angel, "I will not leave this closet till You give me Your answer. I will never cease to pray till You deign to smile--I will not let You go unless You bless me." I have to complain of myself and I suppose you have to complain in the same manner that so much of our prayer is lacking here. We do not send the servant to look to the sea. We do not let our countenance grow glad when we have poured out our hearts before God--

"At His feet we groan, yet bring our wants away."

This is base and wicked of us! O that we had true faith--the real faith which would honor God and comfort ourselves by believing that we have the petition which we have desired of Him. So much by way of explanation.

II. We come now to COMMENDATION. Let me commend the habit of expecting an answer to prayer and looking for it for many reasons. I will but give you an outline of them. By this means you put an honor upon God's ordinance of prayer. He who prays without expecting to receive a return mocks at the Mercy Seat of God. That Mercy Seat was made of gold, of pure gold, as if to show its preciousness to all true Believers. And, by not expecting to receive anything of God, you in effect despise the Throne of Grace.

Let me ask you, of what use can the Mercy Seat be if God has said, "Seek you My face" in vain? If no answers come to supplication, then supplication is a vain waste of time! You play with prayer when you do not expect an answer! You are not treating it in an earnest, solemn and devout manner. You are trifling with it. Little children get their bows and shoot their arrows--they care not where, up into the air, to the east, or to the west--it is nothing to them. But men in sober fight take their aim and watch their arrows. You are but playing with God's ordinances of prayer, if, when you pray you are careless about results.

The truly prayerful man is resolved in his own soul that he must have the answer. He feels his need of it! He sees God's promise. His heart is stirred to earnestness and he cannot be satisfied to go away without some token for good. You would not treat the Mercy Seat as though it were a place for boys to play at! You would honor it, would you not? You would not be among those of whom the Prophet said, "You have snuffed at it," and said, "What a weariness it is." No, but you would make the place where God meets with His people glorious. You would take your shoes off because it is holy ground. But you cannot do this except you believe that prayer has power in it and know that you have the petitions which you ask of Him.

Such a spirit, in the next place, having honored prayer, also honors God's attributes. To believe that the Lord will hear my prayer is honor to His truthfulness. He has said that He will and I believe that He will keep His Word. It is honorable to His power. I believe that He can make the Word of His mouth stand fast and steadfast. It is honorable to His love. The larger things I ask, the more do I honor the liberality, Grace and love of God in asking such great things. It is honorable to His wisdom, for if I ask what He has told me to ask and expect Him to answer me, I believe that His Word is wise and may safely be kept. If you would dishonor every attribute of God, pray with unbelief. But if, on the contrary, you would put a crown on the head of Him who has saved you and who is the God of your salvation, believe that if you ask He will give and if you knock He will open unto you!

Again, to believe that God hears prayer and to look for an answer is truly to reverence God Himself. If I stand side by side with a friend and I ask him a favor and when he is about to reply to me I turn away and open the door and go to my business, why what an insult is this! It is not always considered courteous if you do not answer a person. But it is always discourteous if, after having asked a question, you do not wait for the answer. If I send a petition to a man's door and then having earnestly asked, or pretended to ask earnestly, I am utterly careless about the answer, I have not treated the man respectfully. If that person should send me a letter in return to my request and I should not even take the trouble to open it, how could I provoke him worse?

So you first ask God to grant you a favor and then you do not stop to get it. And when He sends it, you receive it as a matter of course and do not praise it as a gracious answer to your supplication. Christian Brother, let me commend to you the gracious art of believing in the success of your prayers--because in this way you will help to insure your own success. A beggar knocks at your door. He wants charity. He has a firm belief that you will give it to him. The door does not open to him the first time--he knows you have seen him and that you understand his wants--he therefore knocks again. He is so confident of your generosity that he continues waiting at your doorstep.

You, at first, take little notice of him--you are busy with other matters. You come again to the window and you say, "What, is he still there?" Perhaps even then you are called away by urgent business and you attend to it rather than to him. But coming once more to the door, there he stands! "Why, then," you say to him, "you shall have your desire." And your hand is in your pocket to give him the relief he wants. It is even so with our God. When He sees us wait upon Him He will not permit us to wait without receiving the reward.

"He will strengthen your heart. Wait, I say, on the Lord." Merely to knock at Mercy's door without waiting for a reply is but like the runaway knocks of idle boys in the street--you cannot expect an answer to such prayers! Stand upon your watchtower and--

"Hear what God the Lord will speak-- For He will speak peace unto His people, And to His saints-- But let them not turn again to folly."

Furthermore, thus to believe in the result of prayer tries and manifests faith. Perhaps nine prayers out of ten which we offer might have been as well not offered for any good which they have done to us. Am I too severe? I mean our hurried morning prayers when business is calling us away. I mean our sleepy evening prayers when we are scarcely half awake. I mean those formal petitions, (I am not speaking of those who use a book, for you can be quite as formal without a book as with)--those formal petitions in which you have only expressed godly opinions without feeling godly emotions, passed over holy words without their really coming from your hearts.

But, Brethren, when we pray and expect the answer, this is a sure token that our prayer has not been a mere formality. Then Faith lays hold upon God and she waits. Patience stands by her side, knowing that the windows of Heaven, however fast they may be closed, will open soon and God's right hand will scatter His liberality upon waiting souls. So Faith waits and watches and waits and watches again. This is the reason why the glorious doctrine of the Second Advent has such a blessed effect on some of God's people. It exercises their faith and brings hope into the field.

And so answers to faith exercises our watching faith and trains our hope to look up. The devil says, "Surely God will never hear your prayer." You answer, "I have the petition and am waiting till He puts it into my hand--it is up there, labeled for me and set aside in the treasury for me and I shall have it. I am waiting till the time comes when I may safely receive that which is mine even now." So the flesh whispers, "It is in vain," but Faith says, "No, prayer is blessed, prayer is God's Spirit returning where it came and it will never fail."

"But how can such a sinner as you are hope to succeed with God," whispers Unbelief? But Faith, like Abraham, considers not its own body, though dead, neither the deadness of Sarah's womb, but staggers not at the promise through unbelief--it keeps on waiting till it gets its reward! Such a habit, moreover, helps to bring out our gratitude to God. None sing so sweetly as those who get answers to prayer! Oh, some of you would give my Master sweet songs if you did but notice when He hears you!

But perhaps the Lord may drop an answer to your prayer and you merely cry, "It is a fortunate circumstance," and God gets no praise for it. But if, instead, you had been watching for it and seen it come, you would fall on your knees in holy gratitude and say--

"I love the Lord--He heard my cries, And pitied every groan-- Long as I live, when troubles rise, I'll hasten to His Throne."

Let me add this would make your faith grow, would make your love burn, and every Grace would be put in active exercise if, believing in the power of prayer, you watched for the answer and when the answer came went with a song of praise to the Savior's feet!

I will not say more, lest by multiplying commendations I rather weaken the force of what I say. I could not praise this habit too much. The man whom God has taught to pray believingly has all God's treasures at his command. You have the privy key of Jehovah's secret cabinet. You are rich to all the extents of bliss. You have about you the Omnipotence of God for you have power to move the arm that moves the world! He who lacks this mercy is but weak and poverty-stricken, but he who has gained it is one of the mightiest in God's Israel and will do great exploits.

III. Having thus spoken by way of commendation, we pause awhile and turn to speak by way of REBUKE. But it shall be such a gentle rebuke as shall not break the head. I am not just now speaking to those who never pray at all--let me, however, solemnly remind them that prayerless souls are Christ-less souls and will be lost souls before long. Nor am I speaking to those of you who merely prattle through a form of prayer--I give you but this one word: remember that God will not forever be mocked by you and that your prayers are numbered with your sins--you do but insult the Majesty of Heaven while you pretend to worship Him.

I am communing this morning with those persons to whom John wrote--you who believe on the name of the Son of God. You who believe in the efficacy of prayer. How is it that you do not expect an answer? I think I hear you say, "One reason is my own unworthiness. How can I think that God will hear such prayers as mine? I am fickle as the wind that blows and full of infirmities. I am one of the meanest of His sheep. If I were one of His ministers I would believe that my prayer was heard. But I am the least in Israel and my father's house is all unknown. I do serve God sometimes a little, but oh, how little! And even that little is marred with selfishness! I am the very worst in the whole family. How can I think that my prayer will be heard?"

Brothers and Sisters, let me remind you that it is not the person who prays that commends the prayer to God, but the fervency of the prayer in the virtue of the Great Intercessor. Why do you think the Apostle wrote these words--"Elijah was a man of like passions with us"? Why was that statement made? Why, precisely to meet the case of those who say, "My prayer is not heard because I have such-and-such faults." Here is a case in point with yours--"Elijah was a man of like passions with us," and yet he prays earnestly that it might not rain and it rained not--so that the effectual fervent prayer of a righteous man is not prevented in its acceptance before high Heaven by the infirmity of the person who offers it.

"Yes," you say, "but, Sir, you do not know the particular state of mind I have been in when I have prayed. I am so fluttered and worried and vexed and troubled that I cannot expect my prayer, offered in such a state of mind, to prevail with God." Did you ever read the thirty-fourth Psalm and carefully consider where David was when his prayer had such good speed with God? He says, "O magnify the Lord with me and let us exalt His name together. I sought the Lord and He heard me and delivered me from all my fears." This poor man cried and the Lord heard him and saved him out of all his troubles.

Now where do you think David prayed that prayer which God thus heard? Read the heading of the Psalm--"A Psalm of David, when he changed his behavior before Abimelech, who drove him away and he departed." You remember what he did? He played the madman and let his spit run down his beard. He acted the fool and was never more a fool, except once, than he was then! And yet even then, in his fool's play, God heard his prayer! There is something very teaching here. Child of God, though you may have gone ever so far astray and played the fool, let not this keep you back from the Mercy Seat! It was built on purpose for unworthy sinners to come to. You are such. If God only heard you in your good times, why then, you would perish!

The gates of His Grace are open at night as well as at day and black-handed saints may come and find mercy as well as those who have kept their garments white. Do not, I pray you, get into the ill habit of judging that your prayers are not heard because of your failings in spirit. "But," says a third, "it is not merely that I do not so much doubt the efficacy of prayer on account of myself, but my prayers themselves are such poor things! I cannot! I cannot get the groan out of my heart before God. I would not ask to pray a happy prayer. If I could but pray an utterly wretched prayer. If my heart would but ache I would be content, but I cannot get to God. I do not know how to lay hold upon Him and wrestle with Him, and therefore I cannot expect to prevail."

Dear Brothers and Sisters, this is your sin as well as your infirmity! Be humbled and pray God to make you like the importunate widow, for only so will you prevail. But at the same time let me remind you that if your prayers are sincere it shall often happen that even their weakness shall not destroy them. When Christ was asleep in the ship His disciples came to Him and said, "Master, care you not that we perish?" And He rebuked them--"O you of little faith, why do you doubt?" But He did not refuse to hear their cry for all that! For He rebuked the winds and the waves and there was a great calm. He may rebuke the unbelief of your prayer and yet in infinite mercy He may exceed His promise!

There is no promise that He will hear unbelieving prayers. And he who wavers must not expect to receive anything-- but the Lord may go beyond His Word and give us mercies notwithstanding that fault. And all other failings He graciously overlooks and receives our prayers through Jesus Christ. Let your sense of the poverty of your prayers lead you to abhor your faults--but not to abhor praying. Let it make you long to pray better--but never cause you to doubt that if you can, with true fervency, come to God through Jesus Christ your Lord, your prevailing is not a matter of hope but a matter of certainty--your success is as absolutely sure as the laws of Nature.

Further, I have no doubt many of God's people cannot think their prayers will be heard because they have had, as yet, such very few manifest replies. I saw the other day a greyhound chasing a hare. The moment the hare ran through the hedge out of the greyhound's sight, the race was over, for he could not follow where he could not see. The true hound hunts by scent--but the greyhound only by sight. Now there are some Christians too much like the greyhound. They only follow the Lord as far as they can see His manifest mercy. But the true child of God hunts by faith and when he cannot see the mercy, he scents it and still pursues it till at last he lays hold upon it!

Why, Man, you say you have had no answers! How do you know that? God may have answered you though you have not seen the answer. "I am heard," says good Ralph Erskine--

"I'm heard when answered soon or late, Yes, heard when I no answer get! Yes, kindly answered when refused, And treated well when harshly used."

This is a riddle, but it is a fact. God has not promised to give you the particular mercy in kind, but He will give it to you somehow or other. If I pay my debts in gold no man can blame me because I do not pay them in silver. And if God gives you spiritual mercies in abundance, instead of temporal, He has heard your prayer. You may pray, like Paul, thrice, that the thorn in the flesh may be taken away from you--God's answer is given, and it is, "My Grace is sufficient for you." Christ prayed that God might hear Him, He was heard in that He feared, but He had not the cup taken from Him.

No, but He had an angel to comfort and strengthen Him. And this was, in Truth, an answer though not such as the prayer seemed to require. You have had an answer and if God has heard you but once, pluck up courage and go again! Many do not pray expecting an answer because they pray in such a sluggish spirit. Begging is a hard trade--a man that succeeds in it must throw his heart into it--and so is praying. If you want to win, you must pray hard. They called some of the early Christians on the Continent, "Beg-hards," because they did pray hard to God. And none can prevail but those who pray hard. Slothful souls may not expect an answer.

Then there are so many, again, who pray in a legal spirit. Why do you pray? Because it is my duty? Children of God know it is their duty to pray, but they pray because they believe in the efficacy of prayer! I should not expect God to hear me because the clock struck such and I began to pray from a sense of duty. No, I must go, not because the clock strikes, but because my heart wants to pray. A child does not cry because the time to cry has come, nor does a sick man groan because it is the hour of groaning--they cry and groan because they cannot help it. When the new-born nature says, "Let us draw near unto God," then is the time and the place.

A legal spirit would prevent our expecting answers to prayer. Inconsistencies after prayer and a failure to press our suit will bring us to doubt the power of prayer. If we do not plead with God again and again, and again, we shall not keep up our faith that God hears us. "Oh," says one, "we have no time to pray at that rate." What do you do with your time? It caused Domitian to be greatly despised when it was reported that he spent hours in killing flies. It was told, to the discredit of Artaxerxes, that he spent whole days in making handles for knives!

What shall be thought of us, when we confess that we have no time to pray--but there is time for trifles! Princes of the blood royal and yet no time to be at court? Kings of a Divine race and yet no time to put on your crowns and wear your robes of State? Time to play with toys and roll in the dust with the beggars of earth, but no time to sit upon the Throne of Glory and to offer the sacrifice of praise unto the Most High? Shame on such Christians! May God give us true shame for this and from this day forward may we be much in prayer and expect gracious answers.

IV. Alas, this morning time rebukes me, but eternity commends, and therefore I shall go on just a few minutes longer and that by way of EXHORTATION. Dear Friends, let us believe in God's answering prayer! I mean those of us who have believed in Jesus. And because we have God's promise for it. Hear what He says, "You shall make your prayer unto Him and He shall hear you." Know that the Lord has set apart him that is godly for Himself--the Lord will hear when I call upon Him. "He shall call upon Me, and I will answer him."

"Call upon Me in the day of trouble and I will deliver you and you shall glorify Me." "It shall come to pass that before they call I will answer. And while they are yet speaking, I will hear." "All things whatever you shall ask in prayer, believing, you shall receive." "Everyone that asks receives. And he that seeks finds. And to him that knocks it shall be opened." "Whatever you shall ask in My name, that will I do, that the Father may be glorified in the Son." "If you shall ask anything in My name, I will do it." "And whatever we ask we receive of Him because we keep His Commandments and do those things that are pleasing in His sight."

How is it possible after this that God should refuse to hear us? Is He a God and can He lie? Have we promise upon promise and will He break them all? God forbid, Brethren! If there is a God and if this Book is His Word, if God is true, prayer must be answered. And let us, on our knees, go to the sacred engagement as to a work of real efficacy. Again, prayer must be answered because of the Character of God our Father. Will He let His children cry and not hear them? He hears the young ravens and will He not hear His own people? He is a God of Love. Would you let your sick child lie and pine and not go in to answer its groanings?

Will a God of Love close His ears against His people's cries? Do you think He will let the tears stream down your cheeks when you are petitioning and not put them into His bottle? Oh, remember His loving kindness and you cannot, I think, doubt that He hears prayer! A God that hears prayer--this is His memorial throughout all generations. Do not rob Him of His Character by distrusting Him! Then think of the efficacy of the blood of Jesus. When you pray, it is the blood that speaks. Every drop of Jesus' blood cries, "Father, hear him! Father, hear him! Hear the sinner's cry!" That blood was sprinkled on the Mercy Seat that the Mercy Seat might be an efficacious Mercy Seat for you! Do not doubt the blood of Christ!

What? Can He die and yet that blood have no more efficacy in it than the blood of bulls or of goats? You will not think this. Then do not doubt that prayer prevails! Think, again, that Jesus pleads. He points to the wound upon His breast and spreads His pierced hands. Shall the Father deny the Son? Shall prayers offered by Christ be cast out from Heaven's register? Oh, these things must not--cannot be! Besides, the Holy Spirit Himself is the Author of your prayers. Will God incite the desire and then not hear it? Shall there be a schism between the Father and the Holy Spirit? You will not dream of such a thing!

Oh, believe me when I review my own personal experience during the fifteen years that I have known something of the Savior! It leads me to feel that it is as certain that God hears prayer as that twice two make four! As certain as that the rock, falling by the law of gravitation, seeks the earth.

We have not the time to give instances in proof but I hope your own experience furnishes them. May I beseech you by the love you bear to Jesus, do Him the honor of believing in the prevalence of His plea! By the light and life you have received of the Holy Spirit, do not discredit Him by thinking He can teach you to pray a prayer that will not be accepted before God!

Let us as a Church pray more. O that the Spirit of prayer would come down upon us! Let us expect greater blessings! I was led forth in prayer this morning beyond the usual limits. I do not know how the time fled, but I do know that we have the petitions. Let us stand on our watchtower and look. Let us meet again and again at special meetings and let us cry mightily unto the Most High, pouring out our hearts like water before Him and He will open the windows of Heaven and give us greater blessings than we have ever had before--great as those already received have been!

This very afternoon let the season of prayer begin and let it be well sustained. It is to Believers that these words are spoken. May God lead you who are not Believers to trust in Jesus. Amen.

Preparation for Revival

A Sermon (No. 597)
Delivered on Sunday October 30th, 1864 by
C. H. SPURGEON,
At the Metropolitan Tabernacle, Newington

"Can two walk together, except they be agreed?" -- Amos 3:3.

THE BELIEVER IS AGREED with God. The war between the most holy God and his offending creatures is over in the case of blood washed sinners; not suspended by a truce, but ended for ever by a peace which passeth all understanding. The believer is fully agreed with God concerning the divine law: he confesses that "the law is holy, and just, and good": he would not have it altered if he could. He rejoices in the way of God's testimonies more than in all riches; yea, in his precepts doth he take delight, praying evermore, "O let me not wander from thy commandments." He joyfully acknowledges that the Judge of all the earth rules mankind by a law in which there is no injustice, by statutes which subserve the best interests of the governed, while they secure the glory of the great Governor. The Christian "consents unto the law that it is good." He is agreed with God, moreover, that a breach of the law should be visited with penalty: he would be unwilling that sin should go unpunished. He feels that the sanctions of law, however terrible, are absolutely necessary, and required to be severe. Above all, he is agreed with God in that great atonement for sin which God himself has ordained and provided in the person of Jesus Christ. Gazing upon the matchless sacrifice of Calvary, while the Lord is content, the believer is satisfied; where God finds satisfaction for his injured honour, the believer finds the noblest object of admiration and adoration. Thou lovest Golgotha, O thou Judge of the earth; and thy people are perfectly agreed with thee in this. Henceforth the Christian is at one with God in his love of holiness: he delights in the law of God after the inward man. Sin, which is abhorrent to the Most High, is obnoxious to the Christian in that measure in which he is enlightened and conformed unto the image of Christ. Great God, thou hast unsheathed thy sword, and bathed it in heaven, for the destruction of all evil, and thy redeemed are on thy side, abhorring that which is evil, and resolving to fight under thy command till the last sin shall be cut off. Thou hast uplifted thy banner because of the truth, and around thy standard the soldiers of the cross are rallying; for thy battle, O Most High, is the battle of the Church; thy foes are our foes, and thy friends are the excellent of the earth, in whom is all our delight.

I trust that most of us who are here met in the name of Jesus, feel a deep, sincere, and constant agreement with God. We have been guilty of murmuring at his will; but yet our newborn nature evermore at its core and center knoweth that the will of the Lord is wise and good; and we therefore bow our heads with reverent agreement, and say, "Not as I will, but as thou wilt." "The will of the Lord be done." Our soul, when through infirmity she is tempted to rebellion, nevertheless struggles after complete resignation of her wishes and desires to the will of the Most High. We do not covet the life of self-will, but we sigh after the spirit of self-denial; yea, of self-annihilation, that Christ may live in us, and that the old Ego, the carnal I, may be altogether slain. I would be as obedient to my God as are those firstborn sons of light, his messengers of flaming fire. As the mercury feels the mysterious changes of the air, and sensitively moves in accordance with the atmosphere, so would I being surrounded by my God, evermore perceive his wish and will, and move at once in obedience thereto. Our strength shall be perfect when we have no independent will, but move and act only as we are moved and acted on by our gracious God. I hope that at this hour we can truly say, that notwithstanding our many sins, we do love the Lord our God; and if we could have our will this morning, we would follow his commands without the slightest departure from the narrow path. We are in heart agreed with God.

The text reminds us that this agreement gives us power to walk with God. May we be enabled to claim this privilege which divine grace has bestowed on us: power to walk with God in daily, habitual, friendly, intimate, joyous communion. Believer, you can walk with God this very day. He is as near to thee as he was to Abraham beneath the oak at Mamre, or Moses at the back of the desert. He is as willing to show thee his love as he was to reveal himself to Daniel on the banks of

Ulai, or to Ezekiel by the streams of Chebar. Thou hast no greater distance this day between thee and thy God, than Jacob had when he laid hold upon the angel and prevailed. He is thy father, as truly as he was the father of the people whom he covered by day with a cloud, and cheered by night with a pillar of fire; and though no Shekinah lights up a golden mercy-seat, yet the throne of grace is quite as glorious and even more accessible than in the days of old. He shall hide thee in his pavilion, as he did his servant David; yea, in the secret of the tabernacle shall be thy hiding-place. Enoch's privilege was not peculiar to him; it is thy birthright: claim it. Noah's high honour of walking with God was not reserved for him alone; it belongs to thee also, shut in as thou art in the ark of the covenant, and saved from the deluge of divine wrath. It should be the Christian's delight to be always with his God; walking with him in unbroken fellowship. Enoch did not take a turn or two with God, as Matthew Henry observes, but he walked with him four hundred years. O that we might cease to be with our God as wayfaring men who tarry but for a night: may we dwell in God, and may he dwell in us. Walking implies action; and our actions should always be in the Lord. The Christian, whatsoever he eateth, or drinketh, or doeth, should do all in the name of the Lord Jesus, giving thanks unto God and the Father by him. Walking has in it the thought of progress; but all our progress should be with God. As we are rooted and grounded in Christ, so we must ask to grow up in him; ever abiding in our highest moments with God, and never imagining or conceiving any progress which shall remove us from humble confidence in him. Beloved brother in the Lord, it may be that thy heart is agreed with God, and yet thou hast lost for a time thy walking with him; be not at ease in thy soul till thou hast regained it. Search thine own heart by the light of the Word and of the Holy Spirit; and when thou knowest thyself to be agreed with God, through Him who is our peace, hesitate not to draw near with holy confidence to thy Father and thy God, notwithstanding all thy past wanderings; for he welcomes thee to walk with him, seeing that thou art agreed.

At this season we, as a Church, have had our hearts set upon a revival of religion in our midst. Many of us will be greatly and grievously disappointed if such a revival shall not take place. We have felt moved to cry for it; I think I may say we have been almost unanimously thus moved. Already there are signs that God is visiting us in a very remarkable manner, but our souls are set upon a greater work than we have ever seen. Now, dear friends, we need as the first and most essential thing in this matter, that God should walk with us. In vain we shall struggle after revival unless we have his presence. If, then, we desire to have his presence with us, we must see to it that we are perfectly agreed with him both in the design of the work, and in the method of it; and I desire this morning to stir up your pure minds to heart-searching and vigilant self-examination, that every false way may be purged from us, since God will not walk with us as a Church, unless we be agreed with him.

The first remark, then, of this morning, is simply this,--we desire in this matter to walk together with God; but, in the second place, if we would have him with us we must be agreed with him; and therefore, thirdly, we desire to purge ourselves of everything which would mar our perfect agreement with God, and so prevent his coming to our aid. I do ask the prayers of God's people that he may enable me to speak to profit this morning, for if ever I felt my own unfitness to edify the saints, I do so just now: I will even confess that if I could have had my own choice, I should have left it to some one else to address you this morning. My harp is out of tune, and the strings are all loosened, but the chief musician understands his instruments, and knows how to get music out of us, and in answer to prayer he will doubtless sustain us and give you a blessing.

I. Let us, first, AVOW OUR DESIRE THAT IN OUR PRESENT EFFORT WE MAY WALK WITH GOD; otherwise our strivings after revival will be very wearisome.

I know of nothing more saddening than to attend a prayer-meeting where the devotion is forced, and the fervour laborious; where brethren puff and strain like engines with a load behind them too heavy for them to drag. It is painful to detect an evident design to get up an excitement, and wind up the people to the proper pitch; when the addresses are adapted to foster hotheadedness, and the prayers to beget superstition. God's true saints cannot but feel that to gain the graces of the Spirit by fleshly vehemence is sad work. They retire from such a meeting, and they say, "How different is this from occasions when God's Spirit has been really at work with us!" Then, like a ship with her sails filled with a fair wind, floating majestically along without tugging and straining, the Church, borne onward with the breath of the divine Spirit, with a full tide of heaven's grace, speeds on her glorious way. "If thy presence go not with me, carry us not up hence," was the request of Moses; and I think we may rather deprecate than desire a revival if God's presence be not in it. Lord, let us stay as we are, crying and groaning to see better days, rather than permit us to be puffed up with the notion of revival without thine own power in it; let us have no special prayer-meetings merely for the sake of them; but let us, O let us receive special blessings as the result of prayer: if thou dost not intend to help us now let us weep in secret, but let us not rejoice in a mere name if the substance be lacking. During a course of meetings by which we desire to excite the hearts of believers to a deeper interest in spiritual things; if there be not a gracious power in them, you will soon perceive a dulness, a flagging, a heaviness, a weariness stealing over the assembly; the numbers will decline, the prayers will become less fervent, and the whole thing will degenerate into a hollow sham or a mournful monotony. To come up from the wilderness is hard climbing unless we lean on our beloved. O thou who art our beloved and adorable Lord, lest our souls grow weary in well-doing, and faint for heaviness, be pleased to let us enjoy communion with thyself.

Not only is there weariness in our own attempts, but they always end in disappointment, unless God walketh with us. Ye may pray, and pray, and pray, but there shall be no conversions, no sense of quickening, until the Spirit's working be distinctly recognized. The minister shall be just as much a preacher of the mere letter as ever he was; the Church officers shall be as formal and official as ever they were; the Church members shall be as inconsistent and as indifferent as they were wont to be; the congregation shall be as uninterested and as unmoved as they were in the worst times, except the Spirit of God work with us. In this thing we may quote the words of the psalmist, "Except the Lord build the house, they labour in vain that build it: except the Lord keep the city, the watchman waketh but in vain. It is vain for you to rise up early, to sit up late, to eat the bread of sorrows: for so he giveth his beloved sleep." O friends, it is well to have a holy industry and a devout perseverance; it is well to strain every nerve, and put forth every effort; but all this must end in the most sorry, heart-sickening failure, unless the Lord rend the heavens and come down. I am telling you what you all do know, and what I trust you feel, but it is what we are constantly forgetting; for many are they that go a warfare at their own charges, and so become both bankrupt and defeated; and many be they who would build God's house simply by stress of human effort, but they fail, because God is not there to give them success.

Yet more; supposing that in this our attempt at revival, we should not be favoured with the presence of God; then prayer will be greatly dishonoured. I take it, that when a Church draws near to God in special prayer, asking any mercy, if she does not receive that mercy on account of some disagreement with God, then her belief in prayer is, for the future, greatly weakened; and this is a most serious evil, for it loosens the girdle of the loins of God's saints. Anything which makes men doubt the efficacy of prayer, is an injury to their spirituality; and thus upon the largest scale God's Church will suffer loss if her prayers shall remain unanswered. We must go on; it would be ruin to forbear or to turn our backs. As a Church, we must now conquer or die. How can I again stir you up to supplication, if on this occasion your prayers should be in vain? I shall come into this pulpit with but a faint heart to speak of my Master's faithfulness if he does not give you evidences of it. Ah! my brethren, when you are lifting up your voices in intercession, I cannot expect to mark your earnestness nor to behold your faith, unless that faith shall be confirmed just now by a shower of divine mercy. To the world at large the non-hearing of prayer would be a ready argument, either against the existence of God, or else against the reality of his promise. I hope such a thing as this will not occur. "Aha! aha!" saith the enemy, "see what has come of it all! The people cried, but they cried in vain. They met in large numbers; they approached the mercy-seat with tears and groans, but no result has come of it; there have been no more conversions than before, and God's strength has not been put forth." Would you desire that such a calamity as this should occur. The true soldiers of the cross in our Israel would almost as soon lay down their necks, as that God's honour should thus be attainted in the presence of his foes.

Moreover, every attempt at revival of religion which proves a failure,--and fail it must without the presence of God,--leaves the Church in a worse condition than it was before; because, if it should prove a failure, from the want of any stir at all; then God's people fall back into their former lethargy, with an excuse for continuing in it; or if a false stir be made, a reaction follows of a most injurious character. I suppose the worst time in the Christian Church is generally that which follows the excitement of a revival; and if that revival has had no reality in it, the mischief which is done is awful and incalulable. If no excitement shall come at all, the mischief is still as great; God's people, being disappointed, have little heart to listen to further exhortations to future zealous action, become contented with their Laodicean lukewarmness, and it becomes impossible to bestir them again. If a revival should apparently have success and yet God be not in it, perhaps this is even worse. The wild-fire and madness of some revivals have been a perfect disgrace to the common sense of the age, let alone the spirituality of the Church. I know, and speak not without book, when I declare that some churches have been seriously deteriorated and permanently injured by large admissions of excited but unconverted persons; so that the only thing a fresh pastor could do was to begin afresh, and purge the church book throughout, sweeping off scores of carnal persons; the beginning anew being almost hopeless, because, after the paroxysm of passion about religion has passed, there follows a season in which religion is treated with indifference, if not with disdain. I had rather see a Church asleep, than see it awake into the fever of fanaticism: better that she should lie still than do mischief. O dear friends, we have felt in our souls, not that we may have revival, but that we must have it; and when we think of the incalculable damage that shall be done to us all if the Lord does not visit us, I am sure we must again draw near to the angel and wrestle afresh, with this determination, that we will not let him go unless he bless us.

We may be confirmed in our anxious desire to have the Lord walking with us in this thing, when we consider the blessings which are sure to flow from his presence. Ah! what holy quickening shall come upon every one of us. The preacher will not have to lament that he has so little power in prayer; both alone and in your presence he shall be strengthened to intercede as an angel of God. You shall not have to mourn that the service lacks its former sweetness. You will feel the blessedness you knew when first you saw the Lord. You will not have to mourn that you are cold and dead, that your songs languish, and that your prayers expire; instead thereof, every action shall be fraught with vigour, every thought shall glow with earnestness, every word shall be clothed with divine power. Let God arise; and doubts and fears shall betake themselves to their hiding-places, as the bats conceal themselves at the rising of the dawn. Let the Lord visit you; and difficulties which frown like Alps, will sink to plains. Let him arise; and all your enemies shall flee before you, as the smoke before the wind; the heavens shall drop with showers of mercy; and even your sins and all the guilt thereof, shall shake as Sinai shook at the presence of the God of Israel. A Church with God's presence in it is holy, happy, united, earnest, laborious, successful; fair as the moon before the Lord, and clear as the sun in the eyes of men, she is terrible as an army with banners to her enemies.

If God shall be pleased to be with his Church, then direct good shall visit our congregation. We used to say at Park Street, that there were not many seat-holders unconverted. The like is to a great extent true here. The immense increase of our Church gives us the hope that the day will come when there will not be a single seat unoccupied by a believer: but it is not the case yet. I suppose the Church is about half the congregation now. There are some, however, that from the very first have listened; but so far as salvation is concerned, they have listened in vain: they have been moved to tears, they have made good resolutions; but after ten or eleven years of ministry, they are just where they were, except that they have accumulated fresh guilt. Some desire to be Christians, but they harbour some darling lust. We know some who used to feel under the Word, but do not feel now. The voice which once was like a trumpet, now lulls them to sleep. Some have made a compromise; and one day they will serve God and another day they will serve their sins; like the Samaritans who feared the Lord and served other gods. Now let our cries be heard for the Master's presence, and we shall soon see these brought in; hearts of stone shall be turned to flesh; the iron of the Word shall break the northern iron and steel; Jehovah Jesus shall ride victoriously through those gates which have been barred against him, and there shall be shouting in heaven because the Lord hath gotten him the victory.

Wider blessings will follow. A Church is never blessed alone. If any one Church shall stand in the vigour of piety, other Churches shall take example therefrom, and make an advance towards a better state. Here we have around us many Churches, hills which God has blessed; but they, like ourselves, have a tendency to slumber. Let God pour out his Spirit here, and the shower will not be confined to these fields, but will drop upon other pastures, and they shall rejoice on every side. Our testimony for God rings through this land; from one end of it to the other. Our ministry is not hidden under a bushel nor confined to a few. Tens of thousands listen every week to our word; and if the Lord shall be pleased to bless it, then shall it be as ointment poured forth, to load the moral atmosphere with a savour of Christ crucified. One nation cannot feel the power of God without communicating some of its blessing to another. The Atlantic cannot divide: no tongue or language can separate us. If God bless France or Switzerland, the influence shall be felt upon the Continent; if he should bless our island, all the whole earth must feel the power thereof. Therefore do we feel encouraged mightily to pray. O, my brethren, the world grows old; man's faith is getting weary of long waiting; the false prophets begin again to appear, and cry lo here, and lo there; but the Lord must come; of this are we confident: in such an hour as we think not, he may appear. How would we have him find us at his coming? Would we have him find his servants sleeping? his stewards wasting his goods? his vinedressers with neglected vines? his soldiers with swords rusted into their scabbards? No, we would have him find us watching, standing upon the watch-tower, feeding his sheep, tending his lambs, succouring the needy, comforting the weary, helping the oppressed. Gird up your loins then, I pray you, as men that watch for their Lord. If my words could have the power in them which I feel they lack, I would stir you up, dear brethren and sisters, to seek unto the mighty God of Jacob, that when the Son of Man cometh, if he find no faith upon the earth elsewhere, at least he may find it in you: if zeal shall be extinct in every other place, at least may he find one live coal yet glowing in your bosom. For this we want his presence, for without it we can do nothing.

II. This brings me, in the second place, to observe, that IF WE WOULD HAVE THE PRESENCE OF GOD, IT IS NECESSARY THAT WE SHOULD BE AGREED WITH HIM.

We must be agreed with God as to the end of our Christian existence. God hath formed us for himself, that we may show forth his praise. The main end of a Christian man is, that having been bought with precious blood, he may live unto Christ, and not unto himself. O brethren! I am afraid we are not agreed with God in this. I must say it, painful though it be, there are many professors, and there are some in this Church, who at least appear to believe that the main end of their Christian existence is to get to heaven, to get as much money as they can on earth, and to leave as much as they can to their children when they die; I say, "to get to heaven," for they selfishly include that as one of the designs of divine grace; but I question, if it were not for their happiness to go to heaven, whether they would care much about going, if it were only for God's glory; for their way of living upon earth is always thus: "What shall I eat? what shall I drink? wherewithal shall I be clothed?" Religion never calls out their thoughtfulness. They can judge, and weigh, and plot, and plan to get money, but they have no plans as to how they can serve God. The cause of God is scarcely in their thoughts. They will pinch and screw to see how little they can contribute in any way to the maintenance of the cause of truth, or to the spread of the Redeemer's kingdom; they will so far condescend to consider religion, as to think how they can profess it in the most economical manner, but nothing more. You will not hear me speak so foolishly and madly, as if I thought that it were not just and laudable in a man to seek to make money to supply the wants of his family, or even to provide for them on his own decease; such a thing is just and right: but whenever this gets to be the main thought; and I am persuaded it is the leading thought of too many professors, such men forget whose they are, and whom they serve; they are living to themselves; they have forgotten who it is that has said, "Ye were not redeemed with corruptible things, as with silver and gold." Oh! I pray God that I may feel that I am God's man, that I have not a hair on my head which is not consecrated, nor a drop of my blood which is not dedicated to his cause; and I pray, brethren and sisters, that you may feel the same; that selfishness may clean die out of you; that you may be able to say without any straining of the truth, "I have nothing to care for, nor to live for in this world, but that I may glorify God, and spread forth the savour of my Saviour's name." We cannot expect the Master's blessing till we are agreed about this. This is God's will: is it our will to-day? I know I have around me many faithful hearts, who will say, "My desire is, that whether I live or die, Christ may be glorified in me": if we be all of that mind, God will walk with us; but every one who is of another mind, and of a divided heart, is a hindrance and an injury to us in our progress. It would be no loss to lose such persons, but a spiritual benefit to the entire cause, if this dead lumber were cast out. When the body gets a piece of rotten bone into it, it never rests, till, with pain, it casts out the dead thing: and so with the Church; the Church may be increased by dead members, but when she begins to get vigorous and full of life, her first effort is with much pain, perhaps with much marring of her present beauty, to cause the dead substance to come forth; and if this should be the case, though we shall pity those who are cast forth, yet for our own health's sake, we may thank God and take courage.

If we would have God with us we must be agreed as to the real desirableness and necessity of the conversion of souls. God thinks souls to be very precious, and his own words are, "As I live, saith the Lord, I have no pleasure in the death of him that dieth, but had rather that he should turn unto me and live." Are we agreed with God in that? Our God thinks souls to be so precious, that if a man could gain the whole world and lose his soul, he would be a loser. Are we agreed with him there? In the person of Christ, our God wept over Jerusalem; watered with tears that city which must be given up to the flames. Have we tears, too? have we compassion, too? When God thinks of sinners it is in this wise: "How shall I give thee up, Ephraim? how shall I deliver thee, Israel? how shall I make thee as Admah? how shall I set thee as Zeboim?" Can we bemoan sinners in that way? Do we stir our souls to an agony of grief because men will turn from God and will wilfully perish in their sin? If, on the contrary, you and I selfishly say, "We are safe, it does not matter to us whether others are brought to know Christ," we are not agreed, God will not work with us; and such of you as feel this indifferentism, this cursed lethargy, are our bane, our burden, our hindrance. God forgive you, and stir you up to feel that your heart will not rest unless poor sinners are plucked as brands from the burning. Are we agreed here?

If we would have the Lord with us, in the next place, we must be agreed as to the means to be used in revival. We are agreed that the first means is the preaching of Christ. We do not want any other doctrine than that we have received-- Christ lifted up upon his cross, as the serpent was lifted up upon the pole. This is the remedy which we, in this house of prayer, believe in. Let others choose sweet music, or pictures, or vestments, or baptismal water, or confirmation, or human rites; we abhor them, and pour contempt upon them; as for us, our only hope lies in the doctrine of a substitute for sinners, the great fact of the atonement, the glorious truth that Christ Jesus came into the world to seek and to save sinners. I think we are agreed with God in this, that the preaching of

Christ is the way by which believers shall be saved. God's great agency is the Holy Spirit. We are agreed, brethren, that we do not want sinners to be converted by our persuasion, we do not want them brought into the Church by excitement; we want the Spirit's work, and the Spirit's work alone. I would not bend my knee once in prayer, much less day by day, to win a mere excitement; we have done without it, and we shall do without it by the grace of God; but I would give mine eyes, if I might but know that the Holy Spirit himself would come forth, and show what divinity can do in turning hearts of stone to flesh. In this thing, I think , that we are agreed with God. But God's way of blessing the Church is by the instrumentality of all her members. The multitude must be fed, but it must not be by Christ's hand alone, "He gave the bread to the disciples, and the disciples, to the multitude." Are you all agreed here? I am afraid not. Many of you are engaged in works of usefulness, and I will make this my boast this day, that I had never thought that I should meet with a people so apostolic in their zeal as the most of you have been. I have marvelled, and my heart has rejoiced when I have seen what self-sacrifice some of the poorest among you have made for Christ; what zeal, what enthusiasm you have manifested in the spreading abroad of the Saviour's name. But still there are some of you who are doing nothing whatever, you have a name to live, but I fear that you are dead; you are very seldom at a prayer-meeting--even some Church members and persons whom I know are not kept at home by business, but by sheer indifference to the cause of God. Some of you are never provoked to zeal and to good works. That you come and listen to us, is something; and for what you do we are grateful; but for what you do not do, over this we mourn, because we fear that we are restrained in our efforts for the spread of the Saviour's kingdom, because as a Church we are not agreed in God's plan; and we shall be restrained until every man in the Church can say, "I will consecrate myself this day unto the Lord of hosts; if there is anything to be done, be it to be a door-keeper in the house of God, here am I.

"There's not a lamb among his flock,
I would disdain to feed;
There's not a foe before whose face
I'd fear his cause to plead."

Yet again, dear friends, are we agreed this day as to our utter helplessness in this work? I caught a good sentence the other day. Speaking with a Wesleyan minister, I said to him, "Your denomination during the past year did not increase: you have usually had a large increase to your numbers. You were never so rich as now; your ministers were never so well educated; you never had such good chapels as now, and yet you never had so little success. What are you doing?--knowing this to be the fact, what are you doing? How are the minds of your brethren exercised with regard to this?" He comforted me much by the reply. He said, "It has driven us to our knees: we thank God that we know our state and are not content with it. We have had a day of humiliation, and I hope," he said, "some of us have gone low enough to be blessed." There is a great truth in that last sentence, "low enough to be blessed," I do fear me that some of us never do go low enough to be blessed. When a man says, "Oh! yes, we are getting on very well, we do not want any revival that I know of," I fear me he is not low enough to be blessed; and when you and I pray to God with pride in us, with self-exaltation, with a confidence in our own zeal, or even in the prevalence of our own prayers of themselves, we have not come low enough to be blessed. An humble Church will be a blessed Church; a Church that is willing to confess its own errors and failures, and to lie at the foot of Christ's cross, is in a position to be favoured of the Lord. I hope we are agreed, then, with God, as to our utter unworthiness and helplessness, so that we look to him alone.

I charge you all to be agreed with God in this thing, that if any good shall be done, any conversions shall occur, all the glory must be given to him. Revivals have often been spoiled, either by persons boasting that such-and-such a minister was the means of them, or else, as in the case of the North of Ireland, by boasting that the work was done without ministers. That revival, mark you, was stopped in its very midst and seriously damaged by being made a kind of curiosity, and a thing to be gazed at and to be wondered at by persons both at home and abroad. God does not care to work for the honour of men, either of ministers or of laymen, or of Churches either; and if we should say, "Ah! well, I should like to see the presence of God with us that we may have many conversions, and put it in the Magazine, and say, that is how things are done at the Tabernacle," why we should not have a blessing that way. Crowns! crowns! crowns! but all for thy head Jesu! laurels and wreaths! but none for man, all for him whose own right hand and whose holy arm hath gotten him the victory. We must all be agreed on this point, and I hope we are.

3. And now to conclude. LET US PUT AWAY ALL THOSE THINGS WHICH OFFEND OUR GOD.

Before God appeared upon Mount Sinai, the children of Israel had to cleanse themselves for three days. Before Israel could take possession of the promised rest of Canaan, Joshua had to see to it that they were purified by the rite of circumcision. Whenever God would visit his people, he always demands of them some preparatory purging, that they may be fit to behold his presence; for two cannot walk together, unless that which would make them disagree be purged out. A few suggestions then, as to whether there is anything in us with which God cannot agree. Here I cannot preach to you indiscriminately, but put the task into the hand of each man to preach to himself. In the days of the great weeping, we read that every man wept apart and his wife apart, the son apart, and the daughter apart, all the families apart. So it must be here. Is there pride in me? Am I puffed up with my talent, my substance, my character, my success? Lord purge this out of me, or else thou canst not walk with me, for none shall ever say that God and the proud soul are friends: he giveth grace to the humble; as for the proud, he knoweth them afar off, and will not let them come near to him. Am I slothful? do I waste hours which I might usefully employ? Have I the levity of the butterfly, which flits from flower to flower, but drinks no honey from any of them? or have I the industry of the bee, which, wherever it lights, would find some sweet store for the hive? Lord, thou knowest my soul, thou understandest me. Am I doing little where I might do much? Hast thou had but little reaping for much sowing? Have I hid my talent in a napkin? Have I spent that talent for myself, instead of spending it for thee? Slothful souls cannot walk with God. "My Father worketh," saith Jesus, "and I work"; and you who stand in the market-place idle, may stand there with the devil, but you cannot stand there with God. Let every brother who is guilty of this, purge away his sloth.

Or am I guilty of worldliness. This is the crying sin of many in the Christian Church. Do I put myself into association with men who cannot by any possibility profit me? Am I seen where my Master would not go? Do I love amusements which cannot afford me comfort when I reflect upon them; and which I would never indulge in, if I thought that Christ would come while I was at them? Am I worldly in spirit as to fashion? Am I as showy, as volatile, as frivolous as men and women of the world? If so, if I love the world, the love of the Father is not in me; consequently he cannot walk with me, for we are not agreed.

Again, am I covetous? do I scrape and grind? is my first thought, not how I can honour God, but how I can accumulate wealth? When I gain wealth, do I forget to make use of it as a steward? If so, then God is not agreed with me; I am a thief with his substance; I have set myself up for a master instead of being a servant, and God will not walk with me till I begin to feel that this is not my own, but his; and that I must use it in his fear.

Again, am I of an angry spirit? Am I harsh towards my brethren? Do I cherish envy towards those who are better than myself, or contempt towards those who are worse off? If so, God cannot walk with me, for he hates envy, and all contempt of the poor is abhorrent to him. Is there any lust in me? Do I indulge the flesh? Am I fond of carnal indulgences by which my soul suffers? If so, God will not walk with me; for chambering, and wantonness, and gluttony, and drunkenness, separate between a believer and his God: these things are not convenient to a Christian. Before the great feast of unleavened bread, a Jewish parent would sweep out every piece of leaven from his house; and so anxious would he be, and so anxious is the Jew at the present day, that he take a candle and sweeps out every cupboard, no matter though there may have been no food put in there at any time, he is afraid lest by accident a crumb may be somewhere concealed in the house; and so, from the garret to the cellar, he clears the whole house through, to purge out the old leaven. Let us do so. I cannot think you will do so as the effect of such poor words as mine; but if my soul could speak to you, and God blessed the utterance, you would. For my own part, I cry unto my Master, that if there be anything that can make me more fit to be the messenger of God to you and to the sons of men, however painful might be the preparatory process, he would graciously be pleased not to spare me of it. If by sickness, if by serious calamities, if by slander and rebuke, more honour can be brought to him, then hail! and welcome! all these things; they shall be my joy; and to receive them shall be delight. I pray you, utter the same desire: "Lord, make me fit to be the means of glorifying thee."

"The dearest idol I have known,
Whate'er that idol be;
Help me to tear it from its throne,
And worship only thee."

What! do you demur? Do you want for ever to go on in the old dead-and-alive way in which the Churches are just now? Do you feel no sacred passion stirring your breast to anguish for the present, and to hope for the future? O ye cravens, who dread the battle, slink to your beds; but ye who have your Master's spirit in you, and would long to see brighter and better days, lift up your heads with confidence in him who will walk with us if we be agreed.

My text has a main bearing upon the unconverted: I think of preaching from it this evening to those who are not agreed with God, and who cannot walk with him. I pray that they may be reconciled unto God by the death of his Son; and the most likely means to accomplish this, will be by your earnest and fervent prayers. O Lord, hear and answer for Jesus' sake. Amen.

[Mr. Spurgeon's Sermon on "Baptismal Regeneration" has now reached the 180th thousand; it is felt to be important that it should be still more widely circulated, and friends are urged to make an earnest effort to scatter it far and wide.]

Two Visions

DELIVERED ON SUNDAY MORNING, NOVEMBER 6, 1864,
BY C. H. SPURGEON,
AT THE METROPOLITAN TABERNACLE, NEWINGTON.

"I saw by night and behold a Man riding upon a red horse and He stood among the myrtle trees that were in the bottom and behind Him were there red horses, speckled and white. Then said I, O my Lord, what are these? And the angel that talked with me said unto me, I will show you what these are, And the Man that stood among the myrtle trees answered and said, These are they whom the Lord has sent to walk to and fro through the earth. And they answered the Angel of the Lord that stood among the myrtle trees and said, We have walked to and fro through the earth and behold, all the earth sits still and is at rest. Then the Angel of the Lord answered and said, O Lord of Hosts, how long will You not have mercy on Jerusalem and on the cities of Judah, against which You have had indignation these threescore and ten years? And the Lord answered the angel that talked with me with good words and comfortable words. So the angel that communed with me said unto me, Cry you, saying, Thus says the Lord of Hosts; Iam jealous for Jerusalem and for Zion with a great jealousy. And I am very sorely displeased with the heathen that are at ease: for I was but a little displeased and they helped forward the affliction.

Therefore thus says the Lord; I am returned to Jerusalem with mercies: My house shall be built in it, says the Lord of Hosts and a line shall be stretched forth upon Jerusalem. Cry yet, saying, Thus says the Lord of hosts: My cities through prosperity shall yet be spread abroad. And the Lord shall yet comfort Zion and shall yet choose Jerusalem. Then lifted I up my eyes and sa w and behold four horns. And I said unto the angel that talked with me, What are these? And he answered me, These are the horns which have scattered Judah, Israel and Jerusalem. And the Lord showed me four carpenters. Then said I, What come these to do? And He spoke, saying, These are the horns which have scattered Judah, so that no man did lift up his head: but these are come to scatter them, to cast out the horns of the Gentiles, which lifted up their horn over the land of Judah to scatter it." -- Zechariah 1:8-21.

THIS is a somewhat dark and mysterious passage. And if we should ask many a reader, "Do you understand what you are reading?" he would be compelled to reply as did the Ethiopian eunuch, "How can I, except some man should guide me?" Although there are some portions of the Word of God which are hard to be understood--by far the greater portion of Scriptures which are at first perplexing--will open up if we will carefully peruse them and prayerfully ask the illumination of God's Holy Spirit.

We should seek to know all of God's Word which can be known. You will perceive that the Prophet Zechariah himself was not content with beholding the two visions described in this passage, but had to ask, in the ninth verse, "O my Lord, what are these?" And then, again, in the nineteenth verse, "What are these?" Nor did he cease his enquiries! In the twenty-first verse he says, "What come these to do?" If the seer of the vision asked for an interpretation, much more may you and I.

He was not idly curious, but reverently teachable--let us imitate his holy diligence in desiring to learn. Be it remembered that God's Word is never out of date. It is not like an almanac which is useful this year, but which will be mere waste paper the next. It always stands good. And the promise of God, when once fulfilled, are still valid for another fulfillment. Unlike a check, which being once paid, ceases to be of any force, the promises of God have a perpetual value in them! And if we can lay hold upon them by faith, having once drawn upon the great bank of Divine Mercy, we may go again with the same word and get as much from the liberal hand of God as we did before.

Let us come, then, with reverent attention to this passage hoping that God will instruct us in its meaning and help us to grasp its promises and win a new fulfillment. The two visions before us describe the condition of Israel in Zechariah's day. But being interpreted in their aspect towards us, they describe the Church of God as we find it just now in the world. You notice that the first vision opens with a view of the Church of God. It is described as a myrtle grove flourishing in a valley.

The Church of God is hidden, unobserved, secreted as in a valley. The careless gazer doesn't see her. She courts no honor--she comes not with observation. The Church has endured neglect and shame from the time of the Cross until now--her day of glory is to come at the manifestation of the Lord from Heaven, but at present--

"It is no surprising thing That we should be unknown. The Jewish world knew not their King, God's everlasting Son."

When Christ came, despised and rejected of men, His Glory had not broken forth--He was like the sun in a mist. The Church is like her Head--she has a glory, but it is hidden from carnal eyes--persecutions, sins, infirmities and reproaches surround her. The time of her breaking forth in all her glory is not yet come.

She lies in the valley where none but a keen observer can discover her. You must see the towering mountains, but only a careful eye can discover this myrtle grove. Historians write the records of empires, but they take slight notice of the true Church of God. An historian who should pen the tale of English history might, now and then, come across the Church--but it would usually be the political establishment which arrogates that title and not the spiritual and separated host of the faithful in Christ Jesus--for they are not of the world, even as their Lord was not of the world.

"My kingdom is not of this world," is still most solemnly true. Perhaps the position of these myrtles in the valley may indicate the gloom which at seasons falls upon the Church--when she is in spiritual darkness, when no present favor is shown her by her God in Providence--when her pastors weep that their flocks are scattered by persecution and her ministers lament that their testimony is neglected. They cry, "Who has believed our report and to whom is the arm of the Lord revealed?" Then Zion is under a cloud--the myrtle grove is overshadowed and darkened.

But I think there is here the idea of tranquil security--the myrtle grove in the valley is still and calm, while the storm sweeps over the mountain summits. Tempests spend their force upon the craggy peaks of the Alps, but down there, where the stream flows which makes glad the city of God, the myrtles flourish by the still waters, all unshaken by the impetuous wind. How great is the inward tranquility of God's Church! She may be hunted upon the mountains, but in peace her martyrs possess their souls. She may hide herself in the catacombs of Rome, but the memorials upon the old slabs assure us that in the catacombs men lived in hallowed peace, and died in joy!

God's Church in the valley has a peace which the world gives not and which, therefore, it cannot take away. It is the peace of God which passes all understanding. It keeps the hearts and minds of God's people. Is there not also in the metaphor a peaceful, perpetual growth? The myrtle sheds not her leaves, she is always green. And the Church, in her worst time, still has a blessed verdure of Grace about her! No, she has sometimes exhibited most verdure when her winter has been sharpest. God's Church has prospered most when her adversities have been most severe.

The myrtle was the emblem of peace and a significant token of victory. Were not the brows of conquerors bound with myrtle and with laurel? Is not the Church of God, despite the neglect which she suffers from men and the occasional gloom which she endures through God's Providence, still a victor? May not her saints, as they die, be laid in the grave with the myrtle wreath upon them? Is not every Christian more than a conqueror through Him that loved him? Living in peace, do not the saints fall asleep in triumph?

You can readily picture to yourselves that quiet, calm, yet somewhat somber grove of myrtles. And forget not that in the midst of these myrtles, the Glory of the myrtle grove stands--the Son of Man! Oh, it is ever the Church's Glory that the Savior is present with her. "Where two or three are met together in My name, there am I in the midst of them." Here is the Church's strength! Here is her assurance of victory, the terror of her enemies, the confidence of her friends! If the Church is likened to golden candlesticks, John saw one like unto the Son of Man walking in the midst of them. And if she is a myrtle grove, then the Man upon the red horse is never absent from her, but stands in the midst!

He is the wall of fire round about the Church and the Glory in the midst of her evermore. For the comfort of God's people, let us closely view this vision. You say, O son of man, feeble and full of unbelief, that God's Church will become extinct, that Popery will devour her and infidelity will eat her as does a canker. You fear that the banner of the Truth of God will be dashed to the ground and that the enemies of the Lord will win the victory. Cast away your fear! Your God appears unto you this day and in the visions of His servant Zechariah, He reassures you and speaks "good words and comfortable words unto you."

I. Observe THE LORD JESUS ENGAGED AS THE GREAT DEFENDER OF HIS CHURCH. Behold a Man riding upon a red horse. This same Man is called an Angel of the Lord. Christ shows Himself among His people as a Man, since He is the Head of the new race of men. As Adam was the man, the representative man to the whole of fallen humanity, so Jesus stands forth the second Adam, the representative Man of twice-born and blood-bought humanity. Out of love to His people He became one flesh with them and is now most truly called, "The Man Christ Jesus." He is not ashamed to call them Brethren.

Once professors forgot the Godhead of Jesus--we are more likely to overlook His true and real Manhood. Bone of our bone is He--flesh of our flesh. In no respects different from the rest of men, save only that no sin has ever tainted His Nature. He feels as we feel. He thinks as we think--He once suffered and died, even as other men. O Church of God, rejoice! The glorious Man who is "God over all," is ever in your midst! He never forgets you! He never forsakes you! He abides with His people after a spiritual sort, forever! And never is this Covenant Head separated from His body the Church.

Inasmuch as He is also called an angel, this may suggest to us the doctrine that Christ is in a sense the Head of angels, as well as men. What if I were to surmise--and it were no new thought of mine, but one which many have indulged-- what if I were to suggest, not as a matter of doctrine, but only as a subject for thought--that the same great work which redeemed us who were fallen creatures, may have established the elect angels, so that they can never fall? I know not how it is that the angels have become consolidated in perfection so that they cannot now sin, unless it is through the virtue of the Savior.

Could they have been so created? A moral agent must necessarily have the power to sin--if it had no power to sin, it would need no Law. But for God to create a creature beyond all Law, to say the least, would be unsafe--it were, in fact, to set up other gods--for a creature that knew no Law would be a rival to the Godhead! But so long as a creature is under Law, it may offend and so fall. How, then, came the angels in such a condition that they cannot sin? Is it not that they are now removed by a special act of Grace from under the Law and put into a condition of gracious permanence such as Law could never give them? And was this act of Grace the result of that great transaction upon Calvary?

Is this one part of the Apostle's meaning when he says, "By Him all things consist"? Was there in the Atonement a virtue which has established the elect angels forever in perfect holiness so that they should never sin? Why is it that other creatures beside men join in the song? (Rev. 5:9, 10). "You are worthy to take the Book and to open the seals thereof: for You were slain and have redeemed US to God by Your blood, out of every kindred and tongue and people and nation. And have made us unto our God kings and priests: and we shall reign on the earth."

Why did the cherubic emblems stand upon the Mercy Seat and why were they made part and parcel of it, if not to show that while man bends as a sinner before that Mercy Seat and receives pardon, angels stand as sinless beings, looking down upon that Mercy Seat which is the groundwork of their eternal safety? It seems to me to magnify the greatness of the Atonement that it affected Heaven as well as earth and that throughout all the principalities and powers there would be a reason why they should bow with holy gratitude before Jesus the Lord, seeing that He has redeemed them from future falling by His precious blood.

Whether this is so or not, certainly Jesus is the true Archangel--He is the Head of principalities and powers, as well as the Head of redeemed men. He is called "the Angel of the Covenant," as God's messenger sent forth to fulfill God's will in Covenant purposes to His children. Oh, this is the joy of the Church, that Jesus the Man, Jesus the Angel, is ever in her midst! He is represented as riding upon a horse. This is to show His swiftness. He flies upon the wings of the wind to defend His people.

An ordinary commander cannot be in two places at once--and while the right wing has victory under his leadership, the left may be broken. But our Savior rides swiftly as the flashes of thought along the whole ranks, cheers them all on, and secures to every warrior the ultimate victory! Riding on the horse is a symbol of His zeal. He comes with all His power and might, flying with all speed so that none of His people should perish. He shows Himself strong on behalf of them that serve Him and is jealous for them with a fervent jealousy.

But why a red horse? Does this describe His Atonement? Does this picture His sufferings? Is it His own blood with which the horse is covered? Or is he bespattered with the blood of his foes slain in battle? "The Lord is a man of war: the Lord is His name." He comes from Edom, with dyed garments from Bozrah, glorious in His apparel, traveling in the greatness of His strength because He has trod the winepress of wrath and trod His foes in His fury. Does this manifest the terror, the strength, the majesty of Him whose name is "the Lion of the tribe of Judah"?

The day is coming when He will ride on His white horse and go forth conquering and to conquer. But today it is the red horse--for His Church still suffers--still is she stained with the blood of persecution. John says that when he saw the Son of Man, "His feet were like unto fine brass, as if they burned in a furnace," and so is it still with our Lord--His head is glorious in Heaven, but His feet, we that have fallen upon these evil days, glow still in the furnace! As far as earth is concerned, then, the fitting picture of Christ is the Man upon the red horse in the midst of the myrtle trees.

Rejoice, O you people of God, that Jesus is in the midst of His saints with His sword girt upon His thigh!

II. I take you a step farther. For the comfort of God's people we have not only Christ engaged, but we see THE WHOLE ANGELIC HOST READY TO DO US SERVICE. Observe that behind the Man on the red horse was a company of horses--of course these were not horses without riders, for they are represented as speaking. The Church of God has the angels of Heaven to be her protectors. These angels are described as mounted, to represent their swiftness--"He makes His angels spirits, His ministers a flame of fire."

You perceive also the strength of the horse mingled with its swiftness--what God bids His messengers perform, they do. Who can stay their hand! He gives them a charge and girds them with His own power. Zeal quickens every step of these burning ones. Standing with wings outstretched, they wait upon the Divine will. And when the command is given, no eagle cleaves the air so swiftly as the holy ones. They appear to be of different sorts. There are those who are commissioned for vengeance--these ride upon the red horses of God's tremendous wrath. Who knows how often and how terribly angels may have struck through the loins of kings! An angel slew Sennacherib's host. Was it not an angel that struck Herod? Has not God still upon His red horses, angels that shall speedily make an end of the Church's proudest persecutors?

Then there are those on the white horses that come to bless God's saints. Was it not such a spirit that delivered Peter from prison and cheered the heart of Paul in the stormy night? Who knows how often they strengthen the faint and comfort the broken-hearted? They are ever ascending and descending upon that ladder which Jacob saw. Some come to curse the wicked, but as many come to bless the righteous. As for the speckled or bay horses--these are the mingled circumstances in which you see both the mercy and judgment of God--angels are not strangers to these, for God employs them upon many occasions.

What part do angels take in the protection of the Church? I suppose it would be very difficult to describe precisely how they act. But that they do work for us is most certainly a Scriptural doctrine. They are represented as guarding the Lord's people. "He shall give His angels charge over you, to keep you in all your ways. They shall bear you up in their hands, lest you dash your foot against a stone." "The angel of the Lord encamps round about them that fear Him." Have we not some reason to believe that angels inject comforting thoughts into our minds? When Christ was in the garden, there appeared unto Him an angel strengthening Him. May it not be that those warm thoughts which come welling up in our minds, as we think, spontaneously, have been suggested by angels?

We are prone to ascribe our temptations to the devil--how is it we do not ascribe some of our excellent comforts to the work of angels? Are those bad spirits to have the monopoly of dealing with us? Are they to be the only spiritual agents? God forbid! Doubtless, as bad ones would cast us down from the pinnacle where we stand, so these good ones would bear us up! May there not be going on in the air strange battles between the demons and the spirits of light? Is the case mentioned in Jude the only one in which an angel has contended with the devil? Are there no combats such as that described by Daniel in his tenth chapter, where Gabriel and Michael seem to be both engaged against a prince of the power of the air?

May it not be that bright angelic squadrons are holding strange fights with hosts of demons while the Word is preached, contending for and against that glorious Truth which is the power of God unto salvation? We know not what spiritual agencies are continually at work. But that they are at work is clear enough in the Word of God. Spenser was no dreamer when he sang--

"How oft do they their silver bowers leave To come to succor us that succor need! How oft do they with golden pinions clea ve The flitting skies, like flying squadrons Against foul fiends to aid us militant! They for us fight, they watch and duly ward, And their bright squadrons round about us plant. And all for love and nothing for reward-- O why should heavenly God to men have such regard?"

Brethren, may not angels also operate upon the wicked? Is it not possible that the strong restraints which sometimes come upon ungodly men and the singular thoughts which make them, like Balaam, speak what they do not mean and say a good word where they would curse--is it not possible that these may be caused by the suggestions of angels? At any rate these bright spirits rejoice to minister to the heirs of salvation.

Courage! Courage! Warriors of the Cross! March on to victory, for I hear the wings of angels flying at your side! Strike, for angelic swords are drawn! Sound your clarions, for the trumpeters of God are near. Behold the mountain is full of horses of fire and chariots of fire round about the Church of God--more are they that are for us than all they that are against us! We are come unto an innumerable company of angels, all of whom salute us as fellow soldiers in the host of God. Here let us pause and bless the Grace which makes ten thousand times ten thousand angels the allies of the warriors of the Cross.

III. As you read on, you will perceive another ground of comfort to those of you who are alarmed for the Church of God. WE HAVE THE WHOLE OF PROVIDENCE ENGAGED UPON OUR SIDE. Thus it is written, "These are they whom the Lord has sent to walk to and fro through the earth." They gave the result of their reconnoiter--they said, "We have walked to and fro through the earth and behold, all the earth sits still and is at rest." According to the first chapter of the book of Ezekiel, the four living creatures, whom I take to represent angels, always co-worked with the wheels.

The mysterious agency of angels is at work together and in unison with the great work of Providence. Whatever may be occurring, great or small, is certainly happening for the good of God's Church and for the propagation of God's Truth. How singularly does God, in political events, prepare men's minds for the particular phase which His Church assumes! There was perfect peace over the whole world at the time when Christ was put to death. The whole world was subject to one dominion, so that the Apostle Paul and his coadjutors could preach everywhere the unsearchable riches of Christ.

I cannot go into the question this morning. But every Christian student of history knows that the circumstances of the outward world have ever been arranged by God so as to prepare the way for the advance of His great cause. How strangely Providence works to spread the Truth of God. They said of Martin Luther's writings, that they were scattered by angels. No such distributors were employed. But still they were scattered so widely that it was a perfect mystery how it was done. There was scarcely a little peddler who went about with jewels who did not somewhere in his stock keep a copy of the Word of God or Luther's Psalms.

It was said that in England, out of every three persons you met with in the road, though they might be but peasants breaking stones, there would be one of the three a Wickliffe--for Wickliffe's translation of the New Testament spread marvelously--though it was continually hunted after and burnt when discovered. You will find, if I am not mistaken, that soon God will scatter broadcast over all lands those testimonies which are most clear and most full of Christ! He will do it in such a way that our societies will have to hold up their hands in amazement and say, "We cannot tell how this was done."

God finds a market for his wares--he needs not to advertise them. God Himself, who revealed His Truth, will incline men's minds to procure the Truth. Then how singularly does God work in Providence to prepare individuals for His Truth! How many a man has come into this Tabernacle with a heart as much prepared for the particular sermon to be delivered as it possibly could be so that he has said that the preacher must have been told what his feelings were for the Word had come so pointedly home! It was nothing but God in Providence plowing the field for the seed!

How often can we see God opening the doors of nations to missionaries! It was marvelous that China should become accessible after being shut up so many years. And whatever may be said concerning our treatment of the Japanese, (and we are not among those who would vindicate or defend any tyranny on the part of the strong), yet Japan must be opened and the Gospel of God must be preached there!

For every nation that shuts her gates against the Truth of God shall find God's battering ram shake the nation to its foundations sooner than His Word shall be shut out. Courage, warriors of the Cross! Christ is with you as your Captain! Sound your trumpets and advance to battle! If Christ and His angels and the Providence of God all work with you, who can be against you?--

"When He makes bare His arm, What shall His work withstand? When He His people's cause defends, Who, who shall stay His hand?"

IV. I come now to point out to you something equally interesting and even more comfortable in this vision. We have here AN INTERCEDING SAVIOR. The twelfth verse--"Then the Angel of the Lord answered and said, O Lord of Hosts, how long will You not have mercy on Jerusalem and on the cities of Judah, against which You have had indignation these threescore and ten years?" That same Christ, who is on earth in spirit, on the red horse, is in Heaven in Person, pleading before the Throne of God.

Let me not talk coldly upon this, but carry up your hearts to Heaven. I think I see Him, the Angel of the Covenant-- He pleads--He pleads for mercy. Mercy that sent Him to earth--mercy is His petition now. He pleads for present mercy. His cry is, "How long? Eighteen hundred years is it since My blood was offered and yet My kingdom has not come! Lo, nearly two thousand years have rolled away and yet Antichrist is not slain, but Satan's seat is still upon the seven hills! How long? How long? How long?"

Observe the objects of His intercession. He pleads for Jerusalem and Judah. "I pray for them: I pray not for the world, but for them which You have given Me." With what pleading power He points to His wounds and declares Himself to be no other than that mighty One who discharged the

Father's will and bore the whole of Divine wrath! And must He not prevail? Church of God, if you can be rejected, yet He cannot be! Shall the Darling of the Father receive no answer to His cry? Does He plead for us and shall we be afraid? No! In the name of Him who lives and loves and pleads before the Eternal Throne, let us set up our banner! For God has given the victory into our hands in answer to the pleadings of His Son.

V. Nor is this all--observe that WE HAVE IN THIS VISION A GRACIOUS God--for as soon as the plea was put up, the Lord answered the Angel that talked with Him, "with good words and comfortable words." O Zion, there are good things in store for you! Church of God, your time of travail shall soon be over and your children shall be brought forth! Your captivity shall end and the day of manifestation shall appear. Bear patiently the rod for a season and under the darkness still trust in God, for He has not forgotten you. "Can a woman forget her sucking child, that she should not have compassion on the son of her womb? Yes, they may forget, yet will I not forget you. Behold, I have engraved you upon the palms of My hands. Your walls are continually before Me."

God loves the Church with a love too deep for human imagination to understand--He loves her with all His infinite heart. Therefore be of good courage, she cannot need anything, to whom God speaks "good words and comfortable words." What these comfortable words are the Prophet goes on to tell us--"I am jealous for Jerusalem and for Zion with a great jealousy." You perceive He loves her so much that He cannot bear she should go astray to others. And when she has done so, He cannot endure that she should suffer too much or too heavily. He will not have His enemies afflict her-- He is displeased with them because they increase her affliction.

When God seems most to leave His Church, yet His heart is very warm towards her. It is remarkable that whenever God uses a rod to chasten His servants, He always breaks it--as if He loathed the rod which gave His children pain. As soon as ever God struck Israel, whether by Moabite, or Midianite, Babylonian, Persian, Assyrian, Greek, or Roman--in every case He broke the rod in pieces as soon as He had used it, for He is loath to vex His people. He feels the smart far more than His people. "As a father pities his children, so the Lord pities them that fear Him," and the rod cuts Him more than it cuts His Church.

Let us be of good courage! God has not forgotten us. You may belong to a part of the Church which is in great obscurity, but He has not forgotten it. You may think that the Lord has passed you by, but He has not--He that counts the stars and calls them all by name has no limit to His understanding and no measure to His knowledge! He binds up the broken in heart and heals their wounds. And He knows your case and state as much and as perfectly as if you were the only creature He had ever made, or the only saint He had ever loved!

VI. We must now consider the second vision of Zechariah, prophetic of SUITABLE INSTRUMENTALITY. It was dark and as the Prophet looked into the air with wonder, the Rider on the red horse melted away and the myrtle grove disappeared. The horses, too--whether bay, or red, or white--with their angelic riders, were gone. Instead of these, he saw in the sky four terrible horns. They were pushing this way and that way, dashing down the strongest and the mightiest.

And the Prophet naturally asked, "What are these?" The answer was, "These are the horns which have scattered Israel." He saw before him a representation of those powers which had oppressed the Church of God. There were four of them, for the Church is attacked on all sides. Well might the Prophet have felt dismayed. But all of a sudden there appeared before him four carpenters. He asked, "What shall these do?" The original may as well be translated four blacksmiths. Perhaps the better way would be to make it four workmen. If they were carpenters, they were doubtless armed with their saws--or if blacksmiths they came with their heavy hammers. "What shall these do?"

Why, these are the men whom God has found to break those horns to pieces and scattered or frightened the powers which wield them. Brethren, God will always find men for His work. If He requires carpenters, He has only to call for them and there they are. If blacksmiths shall be better, "He creates the smith that blows the coals in the fire." You look upon the scarcity of ministers--it is true there is a great lack of faithful servants of God. But remember, you have but to pray that He would thrust forth more laborers into His vineyard and the thing is done!

God always knows where to find men for His work. And He finds men at the right time. The Prophet did not see the carpenters first, when there was nothing to do, but first the horns and then the carpenters. Of late, there has been a great increase of infidelity--infidelity of the worst kind--that lying infidelity which swears that it believes the Articles of the Christian faith and wears a miter, or a priest's frock, and believes nothing of the kind. Well, I suppose, any lie may find fitting refuge beneath the wings of the Anglican Establishment!

What solemn criminality must belong to those who utter falsehood in the name of the Holy Spirit, and, acting in the office of priests, justify the wicked for a reward! To say in God's name what I know to be untrue is a crime which transcends in infamy all other crimes of mankind--I will not even exclude murder--if it is upon provocation. For to murder souls deliberately by teaching a lie is as great a crime as to slay a man in haste. Let me give an instance of how our State Church sins against morality and Scripture--it is taken from last week's paper:

"One of the most shocking scenes that ever occurred in connection with the prize ring, took place in Sheffield yesterday (Sunday). A number of young men and youths, frequenters of some of the lowest brothels and beerhouses in the town, agreed to meet in the Old Park Wood and fight for a sum of money. One pair of boxers set to and fought for an hour. And then the arena was cleared for another couple, two young men named Dawes and Home. They fought for twenty minutes and Dawes received a heavy blow on the jugular. He was placed on his second's knee. Time was called, amidst much shouting and yelling. He got up and advanced to meet his antagonist but had not gone a yard before he reeled, fell and died instantly."

A few graphic lines from The Sheffield Daily Telegraph will describe the burial of this unhappy youth--"The remains of Dawes (who was killed in a prize fight on Sunday morning), were interred yesterday afternoon at the general cemetery. A heterogeneous multitude--old and young of both sexes from the squalling cherub in arms, to the decrepit hag--thronged the sacred edifice. Still more numerous, ill-mannered and ill-conditioned was the throng who clustered around the grave--pig-headed and bull-necked young fellows, mostly under twenty years of age who must have been the representatives of the 'P.R.' in Sheffield. The Service for the Dead was performed by the Rev. G. Sandford and at its conclusion the rabble departed."

Did this clergyman give God hearty thanks that it had pleased Him to deliver this brother out of the miseries of this sinful world? Did he pray the Father to raise the bystanders from their death in sin unto the life of righteousness, that when they shall depart this life, they may rest in Him, "as our hope is this, our Brother, does"? I am called uncharitable for denouncing this infamy. I beg to offer apologies. I have said I cannot understand how Evangelical clergymen can bring their conscience to perform such enormities. I apologize--I apologize altogether. I will not say again, "I wonder how they can bring their consciences to it"--for when men act thus, I believe they have no consciences at all!

Thus far I apologize, but no further. Conscience must be seared utterly, if not extinct, when the man can stand there, dressed in the habit of a priest of God and say over a sinner who has died in the very act of sin, that he buries him in sure and certain hope of the resurrection to eternal life! Let these men find a trade where truthfulness is not essential to success. But for them to stand as teachers and claim to be successors of the Apostles is an evil which might stir the very stones of the street to cry out against them!

But for the putting down of these giant evils, God will find men at the right time and as this evil seems to have mounted to the very highest pitch, He will find somewhere a hand to scatter this horn. Observe, again, He finds enough men. He did not find three carpenters, but four. There were four horns and there must be four smiths and each smith must take his proper place. And then He finds the right men--not four gentlemen with pens to write--not four architects to draw plans, but four mechanics to do rough work! He who wants to open an oyster, must not use a razor--there needs less of daintiness and more of force. For some works Providence does not find gentlemen to cut off the horns, but carpenters.

The work needs a man who, when he has his work to do, puts his whole strength into it and beats away with his hammer, or cuts through the wood that lays before him with might and main. Rest assured, you who tremble for the ark of God, that when the horns grow troublesome, the carpenters will be found. You need not fret concerning the weakness of the Church of God at any moment! There may be growing up in the chimney corner the man who will shake the nations! Chrysostoms may come forth from our Ragged Schools and Augustines from the thickest darkness of London's poverty!

The Lord knows where to find His servants--they may be in the Universities of Cambridge or Oxford, or possibly in the peasant's hut. He has but to hold up His finger and as Luther and Melanethon and Calvin and Zwingle and Bucer and Farrell and multitudes of the same kind were found--and as in modern times on the continent, Haldane was the means of calling forth Malan and Gaussen and Vinet and D'Aubigne and the whole company of the Monods and multitudes of faithful servants to bring back the Helvetian and Gallic Churches to their allegiance--so, let God but find one man at first to bear the brunt and they come! They come, an exceeding great army!

Be it ours to deliver the Word and leave the results with God. And His army, though it may now be hidden, shall stand forth ready for the battle. God has in ambush a multitude of mighty men and at His word they shall be ready for the battle--for the battle is the Lord's--and He shall deliver the enemy into our hands. These two visions seem to me to be full of comfort to the true Church of God. Let us abide then, dear Friends, faithful to Christ, faithful to His Word and who knows what may come?

But if we are God's enemies, let us fear and tremble, for the angels on the black horses shall be our destruction. And as God is strong to defend His people, so is He strong and swift to slay His enemies. Beware, you who forget God, lest He tear you in pieces and there be none to deliver you. Fly to Jesus, trust Him and live!

The Certainty And Freeness Of Divine Grace

DELIVERED ON SUNDAY MORNING, NOVEMBER 13, 1864,
BY C. H. SPURGEON,
AT THE METROPOLITAN TABERNACLE, NEWINGTON.

"All that the Father gives Me shall come to Me; and him that comes to Me I will in no wise cast out." -- John 6:37.

LET it be forevermore remembered that the words of Jesus Christ are full of Truth and Grace. And that in each of these two sentences, whether we perceive the fact or not, there is the surest Truth and the freest Grace. There will be some who from the peculiarity of their minds, will prize most the first sentence. They will say, as they read these words, "All that the Father gives Me shall come to Me"--why, here is high doctrine! Here is the security of the Covenant, the purpose of God effectually carried out! Here is the Truth of God which we love and the Grace in which we glory."

Other Brethren, overlooking the first sentence lest it should raise questions too hard to be answered, will rather grasp at the second sentence, "Him that comes to Me I will in no wise cast out." "Why," they say, "here is universality of description! Here is a freeness of invitation! Here is a gracious overflow of liberality--this is good free Gospel, indeed!" And they will therefore fall to proclaiming the second sentence to the neglect of the first.

But, Brothers and Sisters, let us not sin by setting one Scripture against another, or attempting to divide the living child of Revelation. It is one and it is alike glorious in all its parts. You who love to hear the Gospel preached to sinners do not be afraid of the doctrines of Sovereign Grace! And you who love Sovereign Grace but cannot well hear doctrine too high for your taste, do not be afraid of the free invitations of the Gospel and the wide door which Jesus opens for needy sinners in many passages of Scripture!

Let us receive all Truth and let us be willing to learn every lesson which the Lord has written, remembering that if we cannot as yet reconcile Truths of God, there is the promise--"What I do you know not now; but you shall know hereafter." If we could know everything, we would be gods! Being mortals, some things must be unknown to us. Let us know our ignorance and despair of becoming infallible and thus we shall be in the path to true wisdom! But, if we boast of our wisdom, we shall be on the high road to great folly.

Let us consider the text carefully. And as it divides into two branches, let us view them one by one. Here we have Grace and Truth triumphant in specialty. And, secondly, we have Grace and Truth triumphant in liberality. May God help us to handle these so that much instruction may flow from them.

I. In the first sentence, we have GRACE TRIUMPHANT IN SPECIALTY--

"All that the Father gives Me shall come to Me." I would bring out the meaning of this passage by a few observations.

1. You perceive here that the Lord Jesus leads us up to the original position of all things--for since a people were given to Him by the Father, it is clear that they must first have been in the Father's hands. All men, then, are naturally, from the beginning, in the hands of the Father. And so it should be, for He has fashioned them all and made them for His pleasure. God, absolutely considered, created all things and His kingdom rules over all. Having a right to make laws, to issue rewards, or to threaten with punishments at His own pleasure, Jehovah sits upon His Throne, judging rightly. The elect were specially in the hands of the Father for He had chosen them.

The choice is ever described as being with the Father--"I thank You, O Father, Lord of Heaven and earth, because You have hid these things from the wise and prudent and have revealed them unto babes. Even so, Father: for so it seemed good in Your sight." They belong to the Father, then, as Creator, as Governor and as the source and fountain of election. How often do Believers forget the part which the Father has in their salvation. And yet He is the basis and prompter of it all. Remember, Beloved, that He who first of all chose you was no other than our Father who is in Heaven. And though our Lord Jesus Christ undertook your cause, yet it was because the Father, first of all, out of His great love, gave you to His Son. Forget not the Father's Grace and cease not to sing of His love--

"'Twas with an everlasting love That God His o wn elect embraced Before He made the worlds above, Or earth on her huge columns placed. Long before the sun's refulgent ray Primeval shades of darkness drove, They on His sacred bosom lay, Loved with an everlasting love."

2. The Savior then proceeds to inform us of a great transaction. He says that the Father gave His people to the Son and put them into the hands of Christ--the God-man Mediator. As Jesus is God, these people always were His own. But as Mediator, He received them from the hands of the Father. Here was the Father's condescension in noticing us at all and in bestowing us upon the Son--here was the Son's infinite mercy and compassion, in accepting such poor souls as we are at the Father's hands and counting us to be His precious jewels, His peculiar portion. The persons referred to as being given by the Father are not all men, although, it is true that the Father has delivered all things into Jesus' hands and He has power over all flesh.

We must always interpret one passage of Scripture by another. And the thirty-ninth verse of this chapter very clearly interprets the thirty-seventh--"And this is the Father's will which has sent Me, that of all which He has given me I should lose nothing, but should raise it up again at the last day." The given ones, it is clear, are by appointment delivered from being lost and appointed to a glorious resurrection which is not true of any but the chosen. In the tenth chapter we find the same explained thus in the twenty-seventh verse--"My sheep hear My voice and I know them, and they follow Me: and I give unto them eternal life. And they shall never perish, neither shall any man pluck them out of My hands. My Father, which gave them to Me, is greater than all. And no man is able to pluck them out of my Father's hands."

And if this should not explain the matter sufficiently, we have it again in our Lord's prayer in the seventeenth chapter, sixth verse--"I have manifested Your name unto the men which You gave me out of the world: Yours they were and You gave them to Me, and they have kept Your word." So you see that the persons given were His own sheep. They are brought to know the voice of the Good Shepherd and to follow Him. They are in His hands and there they are safely kept beyond all fear of harm. Jesus manifests the Father's name unto them and they learn to keep the Father's word.

This does not respect any gift of all men which the Father has made to the Son--though in a certain sense all men have been given to Christ in order that they may be the unconscious instruments of His Glory, though not saved by His redemption. They are, even as His enemies, compelled to do His pleasure, though they shall never be lifted up to the adoption of children, nor to the dignity of being Brethren of the Lord.

We see, then, that there was a certain period when the eternal God gave into the hands of the Mediator a multitude which no man can number, whom He had chosen from among men to be His choice and peculiar treasure. The text speaks in the present tense. But then the thirty-eighth verse speaks in the past tense. And the passages we have been reading to you all have it in the past--therefore understand that the gift of the elect to Christ was performed in the past--before the skies were stretched abroad or the mountains lifted their heads to the clouds God had given a people to Christ.

But the deed may well be said to be performed in the present, since with God there is no time and what He did yesterday, He does today, and will do forever. Moreover, in a certain sense Christ does receive from His Father's hand His people in time as well as in eternity--the Father giving by effectual calling in time, the very people whom once He gave in secret Covenant in eternity. We are, by the words of our text, admitted into one of the secrets of the Divine council chamber and rejoice as we perceive that the chosen ones belonging to the Father were transferred by Him into the hands of the Mediator.

3. Further proceeding, Jesus assures us that this transaction in eternity involves a certain change in time. "All that the Father gives Me shall come to Me." They may be living in sin and they may continue so to do twenty, thirty, forty, fifty, sixty, seventy years--but before their time shall come to die, they shall be brought to Christ! To come to Christ signifies to turn from sin and to trust Christ. Coming to Christ is a leaving of all false confidences, a renouncing of all love of sin and a looking to Jesus as the solitary pillar of our confidence and hope.

Now every soul whom God the Father gave to Jesus must do this and this is the token by which the secretly chosen are known--they openly choose Christ because the Father has secretly chosen them. You can never know your election by any other means. That you are not one of His sheep will be proved by your continuance in unbelief. But if humbly and hopefully you come to Jesus and make Him all your salvation and your desire, let no doctrine of election alarm or keep you back--you are one of His, for this is the seal which He sets upon His sheep. In due time they hear His voice, are led by Him into the green pastures of Grace, follow Him through life and are brought by Him at last to the hilltops of Glory!--

"There is a period known to God, When all His sheep, redeemed by blood, Shall leave the hateful ways of sin, Turn to the fold and enter in. At peace with Hell, with God at war, In sin's dark maze they wander far, Indulge their lusts and still go on As far from God as sheep can run. But see how Heaven's indulgent care Attends their wanderings here and there Still hard at heel wherever they stray, With pricking thorns to hedge their way. Glory to God, they never shall rove Beyond the limits of His love. Fenced with Jehovah's halls and wills, Firm as the everlasting hills The appointed time rolls on apace, Not to propose, but call by Grace, To change the heart, renew the will, And turn the feet to Zion's hill."

4. Observe, yet further, that in the words of our text, Jesus hints at a power possessed by Him to constrain the wanderers to return. He says, "All that the Father gives Me shall come to Me." Oh, the power and majesty which rest in the words "shall come." He does not say they have power to come. He does not say they may come if they will, but they "shall come." There is no, "if," no "but," no "perhaps," no condition whatsoever! It is put down as an unconditional and absolute purpose of God and will of Christ that all whom the Father gave to Him shall come. "Well," says one, "but does Christ force any man to be saved?" I answer "No," in the sense in which the question is asked. No man was ever taken to Heaven by the ears or dragged there by the hair of his head! But, at the same time, the Lord Jesus does, by His messengers, His Word, and His Spirit, sweetly and graciously compel men to come in that they may eat of His marriage-supper.

And this He does, mark you, not by any violation of the free will or free agency of man! God never treats man as though he were a brute. He does not drag him with cart ropes--He treats men as men. And when He binds them with cords, they are the cords of love and the bands of a man. I may exercise power over another's will and yet that other man's will may be perfectly free because the constraint is exercised in a manner accordant with the laws of the human mind. If I show a man that a certain line of action is much for his advantage, he feels bound to follow it, but he is perfectly free in so doing. If man's will were subdued or chained by some physical process--if man's heart should, for instance, be taken from him and be turned round by a manual operation--that would be altogether inconsistent with human freedom, or indeed, with human nature.

And yet I think some few people imagine that we mean this when we talk of constraining influence and Divine Grace! We mean nothing of the kind! We mean that Jehovah Jesus knows how, by irresistible arguments addressed to the understanding--by mighty reasons appealing to the affections and by the mysterious influence of His Holy Spirit operating upon all the powers and passions of the soul--to subdue the whole man, that whereas it was once rebellious it becomes obedient! Whereas it stood stoutly against the Most High, it throws down the weapons of its rebellion and cries, "I yield! I yield! Subdued by Sovereign love and by the enlightenment which You have bestowed upon me, I yield myself to Your will!"

The weapons are not carnal, but mighty, through God, to the pulling down of strongholds. They are the invincible artillery of the love of Christ and the sword of the Spirit which is the Word of God! Of this teaching no Arminian should complain when he remembers the strong expressions used in Wesley's hymns! Let me quote an instance--

"O my God, what must I do? You alone the way can show. You can save me in this hour, I have neither will nor power! God, if over all You are Greater than my sinful heart, All Your power on me be shown, Take away the heart of stone. Take away my darling sin, Make me willing to be clean. Make me willing to receive All Your goodness waits to give! Force me, Lord, with all to part, Tear these idols from my heart! Now Your love almighty show, Make even me a creature new. Jesus, mighty to renew, Work in me to will and do. Turn my nature's rapid tide, Stem the torrent of my pride! Stop the whirlwind of my will, Speak and bid the sun standstill. Now Your love almighty show, Make even me a creature new. Arm of God, Your strength put on, Bow the heavens and come down! All my unbelief overthrow, Lay the aspiring mountain low! Conquer Your worst foe in me, Get Yourself the victory! Save the vilest of the race, Force me to be saved by Grace."

There is an influence put forth by the Holy Spirit which makes men willing in the day of God's power. And every soul that is numbered in the Covenant of Grace shall. Let the devil do his worst and let the human will do its utmost and let temptations strain themselves to the last degree of intensity--they shall, I say, in obedience to Divine decree, be brought to the foot of the Cross, to cry, "What must I do to be saved?"

5. And to conclude our remarks upon this first sentence, the Savior declares that there is no exception to this rule of Grace. He says, "All that the Father gives Me shall come to Me." Not some of them, but all! Not all but one or two, but every one! Each one in particular and the whole

collectively. It will be found when the archangel's trumpet shall ring through earth and Heaven, that every soul whom God ordained to eternal life has attained that eternal life to God's praise and honor! And when the census shall be read of all the children of the living God, not one of the blood-bought and blood-washed shall be absent--they shall all come to Christ in Heaven as they all come to Christ on earth.

Now, albeit that some stumble at this doctrine, here is the greatest possible comfort to the preacher of the Word. Day after day we proclaim our Master's Truth and yet to a great extent we have to cry--"Who has believed our report? And to whom is the arm of the Lord revealed?" So many are stony-hearted. So many resist the invitations of the Gospel. So many turn a deaf ear to the warnings of almighty mercy--what then? Have we sown in vain? Have we labored for nothing? No, verily, in no way! The purpose of God is certainly fulfilled in every jot and tittle and the Master's will is definitely and in every point accomplished!

Therefore we labor with no broken heart and we preach with no coward spirit in this matter. You, O proud and haughty sinners, may resist Him. But if you will not come, others shall--you are bid to come to the wedding. And if you will not come, the highways and the hedges shall find Him guests. His table shall not be empty. Think not that the blood of Christ shall be shed in vain! You may count it an unholy thing, but there are myriads who shall be washed in it and who shall rejoice in its power to cleanse. You may put from you the kingdom of Heaven and count yourselves unworthy of it--if it is a "savor of death unto death" to you--yet it shall be a "savor of life unto life" to others!

The great plans of Sovereign mercy shall not be thwarted by the enmity of man! Jehovah shall yet in the end get the victory. All ages shall crown His head with fresh honors when they see how, despite all the enmity of the human heart-- its treachery and its hardness--that His purpose did stand and He did all His pleasure and displayed the bounty of His Grace as He would, according to the good pleasure of His own will.

You will see, then, that this first sentence, if we understand it at all, involves, first, the doctrine of election--there are some whom the Father gave to Christ. It involves, next, the doctrine of effectual calling--those who are given must and shall come--however stoutly they may set themselves against it, they shall be brought out of darkness into God's marvelous light, And it also teaches us, and here I leave the first sentence, the indispensable necessity of faith--for even those who are given to Christ are not saved except they come to Jesus. Even they must come, for there is no other way to Heaven but by the Door, Christ Jesus.

I must not expect, whoever I may be, that I shall be saved by my morality! I must not reckon to enter Heaven by my integrity or my generosity! All that the Father gives to our Redeemer must come to Him. Therefore none can come to Heaven except they come to Christ. And it becomes indispensably requisite for princes and for peasants, for sages and for savages, for the polite and for the uneducated, for the most virtuous and the most vile to come just as they are and accept the mercy of God which is freely presented to them in the Person of Christ Jesus. And, mark, by this shall those be known whom God has chosen--that they do willingly and joyfully accept Christ Jesus and come to Him with simple and unfeigned faith, resting upon Him as all their salvation and all their desire!

Some of you do not like this doctrine. Well, I cannot help that. I find it in the Scriptures and I preach it. There is the text--to me it means nothing if it does not mean what I have now stated. It is as plain and expressive as the Saxon language employed in it could possibly make it. Do not kick at the doctrine because you do not like it! If it is taught in Scripture, like it or not like it, receive it. Perhaps however, it does some people good to grow angry over a doctrine for they would never think of it at all if they did not! And while this doctrine, like an arrow in a wound, rankles and frets them, it nevertheless is the means of making them consider spiritual things and so they are brought to Jesus.

I believe this is one of the virtues of this doctrine--that it excites people's prejudices and they grow vexed. But since they cannot get rid of it, it follows them--they dream of it, they argue about it--and at last there is a joint in the harness through which the good Word of the Gospel cuts its way and they come to receive Christ in the fullness and plenitude of His mercy.

II. In the second sentence we have GRACE TRIUMPHANT IN ITS LIBERALITY--"Him that comes to Me I will in no wise cast out."

1. Please observe the liberality of the character--it is "him that comes"--there is no description given whatever, except, "him that comes." It means the rich man, the poor man, the great man, the obscure man, the moral man, the debauchee, those who have sunken into the worst of crimes and those who have mounted to the best of virtues. Those who are next akin to devils and those who seem, by the correctness of their lives to be somewhat like angels are all included-- "him, him"! "Him that comes!" "What him?" says John Bunyan. "Why," says he, answering his own question, "any him in all the world that comes to Christ shall be in no wise cast out."

"Him that comes." To come, as I have explained before, is to leave something and to go to something. There is motion. We leave all other grounds of trust and we take Christ to be our solitary hope. We come to His blood to be washed, to His righteousness to be cleansed, to His wounds to be healed, to His life for life eternal and to His death for the death of our sins. We come to Jesus for everything! And the promise is that any man who comes, whoever he may be, shall find that he is not cast out. "But suppose," says one, "that the poor condemned wretch should come who has committed a foul and cruel murder?" Well, if he comes, he shall not be cast out!

If in addition to murder, or without murder, he should have been guilty of uncleanness impossible to describe-- suppose he to have wallowed in it year after year and to have brought himself to such a state that he is scarcely fit to be touched with a pair of tongs! Suppose he to be such an outcast that he is only fit to be swept into some back corner in Hell. Well, what then? If he comes to Christ, he shall not be cast out! I like to put it in such a light that he who deems himself to have gone furthest into sin may yet see that this text sets a door wide open whereby he may come for mercy!

It says, "him that comes," and this shuts out no comer. John Newton was a blasphemer of so gross a kind that even the sailors in the vessel in a storm said that they should never get to port with such a sinner as John Newton on board! But he came to Christ and was not cast out! He lived to preach the Word of God! John Bunyan was so foul a blasphemer that even a woman of the street, who passed him by and heard him swear, said that he was enough to corrupt the whole parish. And he was astonished that a woman of so bad a character should so rebuke him!

John Bunyan came to Jesus and he was not cast out! He lived to have the honor of suffering for his Master and to be the winner of multitudes of souls. Saul of Tarsus had stained himself with the blood of saints! He was a very wolf after Christ's sheep! He was not satisfied with worrying them in his own land, so he obtained power to persecute them in Damascus. But when he fell upon his face and cried for mercy he was not cast out! Manasseh was blood-red with the murder of God's Prophets. It is said that he cut the Prophet Isaiah in two with a saw. And yet, when out of the low dungeon he cried for mercy, he was not cast out!

So that any kind of "him," though he may have been a persecutor even unto blood--though he may have been exceedingly mad against God till he could not speak without blasphemies against the name of Christ--though he hated everything which is good and despised everything held precious by believing men and women--yet if he comes to Christ, he shall not be cast out! Every man, woman and child in this Tabernacle this morning is included in such a word as this, if he comes to Christ! That is the point--if you come to Christ, no matter what your past character may have been, nor yet what your present feelings may be, "him that comes to Me I will in no wise cast out." I thank God for so generous a liberality as that!

2. Then the next point of liberality is in the coming. Please notice it. "Him that comes to Me." Here is no adjective to qualify it--here is no adverb to set out the manner. It is, "him that comes to Me." That is the point, "to Me." We must come to Jesus as crucified and bearing our sin. We must come to Christ as pleading before the Throne of God and see the acceptance of our prayers there. It is not coming to Baptism! It is not coming to the Lord's Supper! It is not coming to the Church. It is not coming to worship--it is coming to Christ! "Him that comes to Me."

Take heed that you do not come elsewhere--for if you rest short of anything but Christ--you rest short of the promise. But, O Soul, if you build on nothing less than Jesus' blood and righteousness. If you touch the hem of His garment. If you look out of self entirely to Him--then rest assured of this--there is no other qualification to your coming but that you come to HIM!

Some come to Christ at once. The very first time they hear the Gospel, they lay hold of it and are saved. They are not cast out. Some are months in coming--they go from strength to strength in this matter and their faith is a thing of long growth. Well, they shall not be cast out! Some come running! Some come walking! Some come creeping on all fours! Some have to get others to carry them, as that man did who was borne of four! But so long as they do but come, He does not cast them out! Some feel as if all their bones were broken and they can only writhe into His Presence, as it were, wriggle themselves to the Mercy Seat all full of aches, pains, woes, doubts, fears, whispers, distrusts, bad habits and sins. But if they do but come, they shall not be cast out!

One man comes with a long prayer. Another comes with nothing but two words. One comes with many tears. Another could not shed a tear if it would save his soul, but he groans. Another can scarcely groan, but his heart feels as if it would burst. One has intense conviction, another has very little of it. One is shaken over Hell's mouth, another is attracted by the beauties of the Savior. One has to be thundered at as from the top of Sinai, another is but beckoned and His willing heart runs to Calvary. But, however you come, Sinner, He will not cast you out if you come to Him--that is the point!

Do not waste time questioning what your experience is, or raising the point of how you came or when you came-- for here it stands, "him that comes to Me"--not him that comes in this way, or that way, but, "him that comes to Me"!

Oh, the liberality of this precious verse! It shuts me in, it does not shut you out poor Sinner--"him that comes to Me I will in no wise cast out."

3. Observe the liberality of the time. "Him that comes." It does not say when. He may be seventy--if he comes he is not cast out! He may be but seven--and, thank God there have been many boys and girls who have come even at that age--but He will not cast them out! Your candle may be little more than a snuff, but He will not quench it. Or it may be but newly lit--He will accept either. The full-blown rose or the flower in the bud shall alike be received by His gracious hand!

Some came to Jesus when He was on earth--He did not cast them out. A long file of sinners saved by Grace has been streaming up from the Cross to the Throne ever since then and not one of them has ever been rejected! We have fallen upon 1864, and the year is almost spent, yet, think not that we have come to the dregs of Christ's mercy! Do not imagine that, because time grows old, Christ's love grows decrepit! Ah, no! He will not cast us out in 1864 any more than He did the thief who looked to Him upon the Cross and found mercy that day! What a blessed thing it is that there is no limit as to time!

I was remarking to myself the other day that the most of the conversions which occur in our place of worship are among new people--persons who come in once or twice and perhaps before they have heard a dozen sermons God blesses them. While those who have been hearing us for seven or eight years are not converted in anything like the same proportion. It is a very sad reflection, but still I couple with it this thought--"Well, if they have not come yet, still it is not too late. If they have been invited to come for seven, eight, nine, ten, twenty years--and oh, there are some of you who have heard the Gospel ever since you were children--yet it does not say that you shall be shut out because you come so late, but, "him that comes"!

You may have turned a deaf ear until you are now growing gray. You may have despised Christ times without number--He waited to be gracious--with outstretched arms He bade His minister woo you to come to Him, but you would not come! But still, if now, by Grace, you are led to come, He will not cast you out! At the last moment of life, if you come, He will not cast you out. And now this morning--God make it an auspicious hour to you--come and try Him this hour, it is just twenty minutes past noon, but you will find if you come that He will not cast you out, for the gates of the City of Mercy are never shut!

4. Further, notice that there is no limit as to the duration of the promise. I mean, He does not merely say, "I will not cast you out when you have come," but, "I will NEVER cast you out." The original reads, "I will not, not cast you out," or, "I will never, never cast you out." The text means that Christ will not at first reject a Believer. And that as He will not do it at first, so He will not to the last. If I come to Christ today, He will accept me. And He accepts me in that act forever--He will never cast me out!

Suppose the Believer sins after coming? "If any man sin we have an Advocate with the Father, Jesus Christ the righteous." Suppose that Believers backslide? "I will heal their backsliding, I will love them freely: for My anger is turned away from him." But Believers may fall under temptation. "God is faithful, who will not suffer you to be tempted above that you are able. But will, with the temptation, also make a way to escape, that you may be able to bear it." But the Believer may fall into sin as David did! Yes, but He will "Purge them with hyssop and they shall be clean. He will wash them and they shall be whiter than snow,"

From all their iniquities will He cleanse them--

"Once in Christ, in Christ forever, Nothing from His love can sever," and that doctrine this text teaches most expressly--"him that comes to Me I will never, never cast out." He will never suffer one who has once been grasped in His hands to be wrested from them! No member of Christ's body can ever be cut off, or else Christ would be mutilated. No sheep of His flock shall ever be torn by the lion--He will rend the lion and, as David did, He will take the lamb out of the jaws of the lion and out of the paws of the bear. "I give unto My sheep," says He, "eternal life. And they shall never perish, neither shall any man pluck them out of My hands."

What do you say to this, Sinner? Is not this a precious mercy--that if you come to Christ you do not come to One who will treat you well a month or two and then send you packing about your business, but will receive you and make you His child and you shall abide forever, no longer receiving the spirit of bondage again to fear, but the spirit of adoption whereby you shall cry, Abba, Father? Oh, the Grace of this passage! Would I had an angel's tongue to set it forth!

5. Still we have not exhausted it. Something of the liberality of this passage is to be found in its certainty. "Him that comes to me I will in no wise cast out." It is not a hope as to whether Christ will accept you--it is a CERTAINITY! Oh, if there were only half a shadow of a hope that the Lord Jesus would have mercy upon such a poor worm as I am, would I not go into His Presence hoping against hope? If it were a case of sink or swim, yet, since I could lose nothing by trusting Him, I would gladly do it, as the hymn puts it--

"I can but perish if I go! I am resolved to try! For if I stay away, I know I must forever die."

But, dear Friends, we must not put it in that way, or at least, only for the sake of bringing out a thought--for there is no "but" about it--you cannot perish if you go! O, try at once and you will find that him that comes in no wise can be cast out! We sometimes sing--

"Venture on Him, venture wholly, Let no other trust intrude," but there is no venture in the case--it is an absolute certainty. Merchants will often speculate at a high figure. But there is no speculation here. We drink the medicine which the physician gives us in the hope that it may cure--but this will cure--here is water that will quench your thirst! Here is a balm that will heal your wounds--"him that comes" He will receive--"He will in no wise cast out."

What a hammer that word "no wise" is with which to smash your fears to pieces. "Perhaps," says one, "He will reject me because I do not repent enough"--"in no wise." "Perhaps He will reject me because I have been so long coming"--"in no wise." "But He will reject me because I do not pray aright"--"in no wise." You cannot mention any shape or form of a fear which this does not slay upon the spot--"I will in no wise cast out." I say again, I wish I had an angel's tongue to put the liberality of this before you. The devil, I know, will be suggesting twenty reasons why you should not come--let this one reason why you should come be enough to answer all of his--that Jesus says, "I will in no wise cast out him that comes."

6. I must conclude by observing that there is great liberality in the text, if you notice its personality. Reading over this verse carefully I observed that in the first sentence, where everything was special, Jesus used a large word and He said, "All that the Father gives Me shall come." But in the second sentence, which is general, He uses a little word, a word which can mean only one and He says "him." There is a personality here--"him that comes." It does not say they that come, but "him that comes." Why? Why, because sinners want personal comfort! They need something that will suit their case. Do you see, Sinner, He does not take men in the lump, but He picks you out as if you were the only sinner in the world! He says to you, "him that comes to Me I will in no wise cast out"!

Had he put it in the plural, you might say, "Ah, but He did not think of me." But now He has put it so that it just fits your case. This is no medicine in the bottle of which many may drink, but here is a glass set for you! It is not a cordial which may be passed round the table, but it is put at your place! Drink and be satisfied--"him that comes." Lord, does "him" mean me?" Yes, it means you, if you will come. Come now! Put your trust in Jesus. What do you say? I hope the Spirit is speaking to you in these words of mine! And if He speaks to you as I speak to you, then shall it be well with you. Sinner, come!

There is a dying Savior! He died in the place of sinners. In the place of what sinners? Why, of all sinners who trust Him. Will you trust Him? Is it a hard thing to trust God to save you? To trust God who became man and so proved His love to you? To trust Him? "Why," says one, "that is simple enough," but that is all the plan of salvation. When I am preaching from such a text as this I feel as if I have no scope for metaphors and figures and illustrations--I do not need any--because this saving Truth of God must always he proclaimed as plainly as possible! And then if souls are saved by it, it is not the excellency of words, but the Truth itself which shall get the honor.

Now, do you see it, Soul? If you do, I am content--if you trust Christ to save you, you shall not be cast out! You have come to Him! Your coming to Him proves that the Father gave you to Him! You are saved! You are one of His chosen! You shall never be cast out! Your Heaven is secure! You shall sit at the right hand of God and sing the new song, as surely as they do now, who, white-robed, are hymning the Redeemer's praise! This is not an affair of months and weeks, is it? It does not need a moment--to look, is the work of an instant. But the moment that faith is exercised, perfect pardon is given! There is no sin in God's book against a soul that trusts Christ and there never can be--

"There's pardon for transgressions past, It matters not how black their cast! And, O my Soul, with wonder view, For sins to come, here's pardon too."

What? Are there none who will accept this? Are there none here who say, "I will trust my soul in Jesus' hands"? What? Will you build on your own righteousness? Ah, Fools! To pile up the sand which the next tide must sweep away! What? Do you despise the mercy of my God? Will you turn away from the bleeding wounds of His own dear Son? What? Is forgiveness not worth your having? Is God's free mercy a thing to be scoffed at? O Heavens, hear and be astonished! O Earth, hear and be amazed! God sends the Gospel unto men, but they refuse it! That Gospel says unto them, "Come now and let us reason together, says the Lord: though your sins are as scarlet, they shall be as white as snow; though they are red like crimson, they shall be as wool."

But though God calls, they refuse and will have none of His Words! May His mighty Spirit come and make a difference in some of you and bring you now to the foot of the Savior's Cross to look up! Do nothing else but look up! And looking there you shall never perish, but have eternal life! May the Master bless these words, feeble of themselves and only mighty because of the Truth they convey, for Jesus' sake. Amen.

The Centurion--Or An Exhortation To The Virtuous

A SERMON DELIVERED
BY C. H. SPURGEON,
AT THE METROPOLITAN TABERNACLE, NEWINGTON.

"And when they came to Jesus, they besought Him instantly, saying, That he was worthy for whom He should do this: for he loves our nation and he has built us a synagogue. Then Jesus went with them. And when He was now not far from the house, the centurion sent friends to Him, saying unto Him, Lord, trouble not Yourself: for I am not worthy that You should enter under my roof: why neither thought I myself worthy to come unto You: but say in a word and my servant shall be healed. For I also am a man set under authority, having under me soldiers and I say unto one, Go and he goes. And to another, Come and he comes. And to my servant, Do this and he does it. When Jesus heard these things, He marveled at him and turned Him about and said unto the people that followed Him, I say unto you, I have not found so great faith, no, not in Israel." -- Luke 7:4-9.

THIS Centurion certainly had a high reputation. Two features of character blend in him which do not often meet in such graceful harmony. He won the high opinion of others and yet he held a low estimation of himself. There are some who think little of themselves. And they are quite correct in their feelings as all the world would endorse the estimate of their littleness. Others there are who think great things of themselves--but the more they are known the less they are praised--and the higher they carry their heads the more the world laughs them to scorn!

Nor is it unusual for men to think great things of themselves because the world commends or flatters them. They robe themselves with pride and cloak themselves with vanity because they have by some means, either rightly or wrongly, won the good opinion of others. There are very few who have the happy combination of the text. The elders say of the centurion that he is worthy. But he says of himself, "Lord, I am not worthy!" They commend him for building God a house. But he thinks that he is not worthy that Christ should come under the roof of his house. They plead his merit. But he pleads his demerit.

Thus he appeals to the power of Christ apart from anything that he felt in himself or thought of himself. O that you and I might have this blessed combination in ourselves! To win the high opinion of others, so far as it can be gained by integrity, by uprightness and by decision of character and yet at the same time to walk humbly with our God! Now there are three things I shall speak about tonight and may God make them profitable. First, here is a high character. Secondly, here is deep humility. And, thirdly, here is, notwithstanding that deep humility, a very mighty faith.

I. To begin, then, dear Friends, here is A HIGH CHARACTER. Let us thoroughly appreciate it and give it a full measure of commendation. When preaching Jesus Christ to the chief of sinners, we have sometimes half dreamed that some who are moral and upright might think themselves excluded--they ought not to think so, nor is it fair for them to draw such an inference. We have heard the whisper of some who have said they could almost wish that they had been more abandoned and dissolute in the days of their unregeneracy so they might have a deeper repentance and be witnesses of a more palpable and thorough change and that they might never have cause to doubt of the triumph of Grace in their experience!

We have even heard some say, "I could have wished that I had groveled in the very mire of sin--not that I love it-- on the contrary, I loathe it. But because had I then to be rescued from such a course of life, the change would be so manifest and apparent that I should never dare to ask myself whether I was a changed man or not. I should feel it and see it in my daily course and conversation." Dear Friends, if anything we have ever said should have led you into this mistake we are sorry for it--it was never our intention. While we would open the gates of mercy so wide that the greatest blasphemer, the most unchaste and the most debauched may not be without hope--yet we never want to shut those gates in the face of such as have been brought up in a godly manner--those who through the Providence of God and the checks of education have been kept from the grosser vices.

On the contrary, we thought that when we opened it for the worst there would be room for the best! And if Noah's ark took in the unclean, certainly the clean would not be afraid to enter. If Jesus Christ was able to cure those who were far gone in sickness, you might infer that He would certainly be able to heal those who, though they were sick, might not be so far advanced in disease! Besides, a little reflection may suggest to you that the penitence of contrite Believers is not regulated by the extent of their crimes against what you call the moral code. It is one thing to estimate sin by its apparent turpitude and another and an infinitely better thing to have the eyes of the understanding enlightened--to see sin in its infinite malignity as it appears in the light of heavenly purity and perfection which proceeds from the Throne of God, or as it is reflected from Mount Calvary where the amazing Sacrifice of Christ was offered.

What? Do you think the whitewashed sepulcher of a Pharisee's heart is less loathsome to the Almighty than the open pollution of a Magdalene's life? Or, in the matter of experience, could the recollection of a thousand debaucheries give such a melting sense of contrition as a sight of the Crucified One? O Friends, let me remind you of the words of Jesus, "When He"--the Spirit of Truth--"is come, He will reprove the world of sin and of righteousness and of judgment: of sin, because they believe not on Me."

That one sin of unbelief is such a concentration of all wickedness that it could outweigh the crimes of Sodom and Gomorrah and make them more excusable in the Day of Judgment than the men of Capernaum who saw the mighty works of Christ and did not repent! That one sin of unbelief is so heinous that the groans of the whole creation were but pitiful sighs to deplore it! And rivers of tears were but a weak tribute to lament it. However, as mistakes do arise and misapprehensions will take place, let us have a few words concerning a high character in the sight of men. Such a character among your fellow creatures may be gained in any situation.

The centurion was a soldier--a profession of life not altogether the most favorable for moral excellence--though there have been in the army some of the brightest saints that ever lived. He was a soldier, moreover, in a foreign country--not the place where he was likely to win esteem. He was there as one of the representatives of a power which had conquered Judea and had treated it with great cruelty. Yet, notwithstanding the prejudices of race and nationality, this man's kindness of disposition and goodness of conduct had won for him the esteem of others.

Moreover, being a commander of soldiers, he, naturally, would be blamed for every act of violence committed by his soldiers. Whatever might be done by his hundred men would be laid to the captain, so that his was a condition of peculiar difficulty and yet, notwithstanding this, the elders said, "He is worthy." Let none of you despair! Wherever you may be placed, a noble character may be earned. You may serve God in the most menial capacity but you may compel your very foes to admit your excellence! You may stand without blame before men and you may walk so uprightly before God that those who watch for your stumbling may bite their lips with disappointment--while they shall not have a single word to say against you except it is about the religion of your God and King.

Let no man, wherever he may be thrown--though he is surrounded by those who tempt him--despair, especially if the Grace of God is in him. Let him pray like Joab that he may have favor in the eyes of his Master and expect to win it. This centurion must have been a man of sterling worth. He was not merely quiet and inoffensive like some men who are as dull as they are harmless. Though a high character may be won, it cannot be won without being earned. Men do not get character among their fellows by indolence and listlessness, or by pretensions and talk. Action! Action!--this is what the world wants!

And there is more truth than we have dreamed of in Nelson's opinion--"England expects every man to do his duty." Certainly men will not speak well of you unless you do well. This centurion did so, for you will observe that they said he was worthy--which must have signified that he was just in his dealings and generous in his habits--or they would not have thought him worthy. It would appear, too, that his private temperament as well as his public spirit contributed to the estimation in which he was held. You will notice in the circumstances which bring him before us, how his tender feelings and his intense anxiety were drawn out on behalf, not of a child, but of a servant--perhaps of a slave!

And then we might have thought it had been enough to have said that the man was highly valued by his master--but the expression is one of fondness--he was, "dear unto him." The fidelity of the servant may be implied, but it is the amiability of the master which is most prominent and chiefly arrests our attention. Nor need we overlook the fact that Matthew lays an emphasis upon the servant being, "at home," under his master's roof. We know that the Romans were not remarkable for the kindness they showed to their dependants--often they were merely looked upon as slaves.

Why, in our own days and in the midst of our boasted civilization, when Christianity has exerted a salutary influence upon all our social relations, I suppose it is not uncommon for a domestic servant to go home to her parents' house in the case of sickness. It is not every good man among us, I fear, whose gentleness would equal that of the centurion in the love which he bears to his servant and the comfort he provided for him in his own house!

Next to this you will observe his generosity. It is not, my dear Friends, by occasional deeds of showy luster but by the habitual practice of lovely virtues that a worthy character is built up. A thousand kindnesses may be nestling beneath the soil like the many-fibred root of a gigantic tree, when it is said, "He loves our nation," and then the conspicuous fruit appears in its season--"He has built us a synagogue." This example of liberality is spoken of as a mere supplement. The Jewish elders do not say, "He loves our nation" for--but they say, "he loves our nation and he has built us a synagogue." This last was a visible token of innumerable good offices which had already won their secret esteem before it bloomed in an open reputation.

I have heard all sorts of men praised and I have noted the qualities which win the plaudits of the crowd. Even the high and haughty have some to praise them. But I think I never heard a niggardly man praised, or one who was perpetually guilty of meanness. Let him have whatever virtues he may, if he lack liberality, few, if any, will speak well of him. Let me commend liberality to the Christian--in all his actions and benevolence--in all his thoughts. This may sound commonplace, but I am persuaded that the little tricks in trade--those little savings of the pence, those sharp dealings--are just the things which bring religion into disrepute. It were infinitely better that the Christian should pay too much than too little. He had better be blamed for an excess of generosity than take credit to himself for a rigid stinginess.

Rather let him become, now and then, the dupe of an imposter than shut up the heart of his compassion against his fellow man. I would seek, Christian man, to win a noble character. I cannot see how you can do so except you should put generosity into the scale and enroll it in the list of your virtues. A high character, when earned, is very useful. I am saying this because some might imagine that in the preaching of the Gospel we put the base and the wicked before those who have walked uprightly. A good character, a good reputation in the esteem of men, when earned, may win for us as it did for this centurion, kind thoughts, kind words, kind acts, kind prayers.

There is many a man who will pray for you if he sees you walk uprightly. Yes, and your very adversary who would otherwise have cursed you, will find the curse trembling on his tongue. Though he would gladly scorn, yet does he bate his breath, abashed at your excellencies. Let the Christian labor so to live that he shall not lack a friend. "Make to yourselves friends of the mammon of unrighteousness," is one of Christ's own precepts. If to stoop, to cringe, to lie, wins you friends, do not do it! But if with uprightness before God you can still mingle such affection and such generosity towards men that you shall win their support, do it, I pray you. The time may come when their sympathy shall befriend you.

But remember, and here I close this point, however good your character or however excellent your reputation, not one word of this is ever to be mentioned before the Throne of the Most High. Job could say when he was talking with his adversaries, "I am not wicked." He could boast in his excellencies, as he did. But in the Presence of God how he changed his note--"Now my eyes see You: why I abhor myself and repent in dust and ashes." Coming before the Lord, we must all come as sinners. When on your knees you have nothing to boast of more than the worst rogue or the man who has sinned against his country's laws. There, at the foot of the Cross, one needs the cleansing blood as much as the other. At mercy's gate we must alike knock and we must be fed by the same generous hand. There are no degrees here--we enter by the same door. We come to the same Savior.

And we shall ultimately--Glory be to His name!--sit together in the same Heaven whether we have earned a good reputation or not! Whether we have crept into Heaven, as the thief did at the eleventh hour, or through forty and five years of public service earned the applause of men, as did Caleb the son of Jephunneh--

"Nothing in my hand I bring, Simply to Your Cross I cling," must be the common footing and the like confession of both before the God of Mercy. Thus much by way of tribute to the high character of the centurion and the high motives to emulate it.

II. Secondly, in the centurion we see coupled with this high and noble repute, DEEP HUMILIATION OF SOUL. "I am not worthy that You should enter under my roof." Humility, then, it appears, may exist in any condition. There are some men who are too mean to be humble. Do you understand me? They are too crouching, crawling, sneaky and abject to be humble. When they use humble words, they disgrace the words they use! You perceive at once that it is rather a rise than a stoop for them to be humble.

How could it be otherwise? It certainly is not for the least vermin that creep the earth to talk about humility. They must be low--it is their proper place. Such the creatures who cringe and fawn--"Whatever you please, Sir," "Yes," "No," in the same breath. They have not a soul within them that would be worth the notice of a sparrow hawk. They are too little to be worthy of observation yet they say they are humble! A man, to be humble, needs to have a soul--to stoop, you must have some elevation to stoop from. You must have some real excellence within you before you can really understand what it is to renounce merit.

Had the centurion been unworthy, had he been ungenerous and an oppressor, he would have spoken the truth when he said, "I am not worthy that You should enter under my roof." But there would have been no true humility in what he said. It was because of his excellence, as acknowledged by others, that he could be humble in the modesty of his opinion of himself. We have heard of a certain monk who, professing to be humble, said he had broken all God's Commandments. He said he was the greatest sinner in the world--he was as bad as Judas. Somebody said, "Why tell us that? We have all of us thought that a long time!" Straightway the holy man grew red in the face and struck the accuser and asked him what he had ever done to deserve such an accusation!

We know some of that kind--they will use the words of humility, appear very contrite and perhaps even at Prayer Meetings you would think them the meekest and most broken-hearted of men--but if you were to take them at their word, straightway they would tell you they use the language as some ecclesiastical personages do, in a non-natural sense! They do not quite mean what they were supposed to mean, but something very different. That is not humility--it is a kind of mock-modesty which hankers after applause and holds out specious words as a bait for the trap of approbation.

Our centurion was truly humble. This a man may be, though possessing the highest excellence and standing in the most eminent position. I believe, in my soul, that no man had truer humility in him than John Knox and yet John Knox never cringed and never bowed. When Luther dared the thunders of the Vatican, no doubt many said how self-conceited, egotistical and proud he was. But for all that, God knew how humbly Martin Luther walked with Him. When Athana-sius stood up and said, "I, Athanasius, against the world," it had the ring of pride about it--but there was true and sound humility before God in it--because he seemed to say, "What am I? Not worthy of taking care of. And therefore I do not use the deceptions of cowardice for my own personal safety. Let the world do what it will to me, God's Truth is infinitely more precious than I am and so I give myself up as an offering upon its altar."

True humility will agree with the highest chivalry in maintaining Divine Truth and with the boldest assertion of what one knows in his own conscience to be true. Though it may be the lot of Christians to be thought proud, let it never be true or capable of being substantiated concerning them. The centurion, though worthy, was still humble. His friends and neighbors gauged him by what he said and what he did. He asked them to go for him, seeing he was not worthy. Then, finding that they asked too great a gift, he comes to stop them--"I am not worthy that You should enter under my roof."

You need not tell people that you are humble. You have no occasion to advertise that you have genuine humility-- let it discover itself as spice does, by its perfume--or as fire, by its burning. If you live near to God and if your humility is of the right kind it will tell its own tale before long. But the place where humility does speak out is at the Throne of Grace. Beloved, there are some things we would confess of ourselves before God which we would not confess before men. There is an attitude of prostration at the Throne of the Most High which will never be so gracefully or graciously taken as by that man who would spurn to prostrate himself before his fellows.

That is not true humility which bends the knee at the tyrant's throne--that is true humility which, having bearded the tyrant to his face, goes down on its knees before the God of Heaven--bold as a lion before men, but meek as a lamb before Jehovah! The true man, whom God approves, will not--dares not--turn aside the love he bears his sovereign Lord when he faces men. But when he is alone with his Maker he veils his face with something better than the wings of angels!

Wrapped all over with the blood and righteousness of Jesus Christ, he rejoices with fear and trembling that he is justified from all things. Yet, conscious of the total defilement of his nature, with deep prostration of soul he uses the leper's cry, "Unclean! Unclean! Unclean!" Thus does he fix all his hope upon that cleansing blood and depends alone on that meritorious obedience of Jesus upon which every sanctified Believer exclusively relies. Seek, then, as much as lies in you, that high character which the Christian should maintain among men. But with it always blend that true humility which comes of the Spirit of God and ever behooves us in the Presence of the Lord.

III. The main thing I am aiming at, because, after all, the most practical, lies in my third point. However deep our humility, however conscious we may be of our own undeservedness, WE SHOULD NEVER DIMINISH OUR FAITH IN GOD. Observe the confession--"I am not worthy that You should enter under my roof." What then will be the inference? "I fear, therefore, my servant will not be healed"? No, no! But--"Say in a Word and my servant shall be healed"!

It is all a mistake that great faith implies pride. Beloved, the greater the faith, the deeper the humility. These are brothers, not foes. The more the Glories of God strike your eyes, the humbler you will lie in conscious abasement but the higher you will rise in importunate prayer! Let us take this principle and endeavor to apply it to a few cases. I say that a deep sense of our own nothingness is not to prevent our having strong faith. We will take a few instances. There is a minister here who has been preaching the Word of God--he has so proclaimed it that God has been pleased to own it in some degree.

But, it may be, he has stirred up strife. He has caused, I know not what amount of turmoil and of noise, as the faithful servant of God will in his measure. And now, coming before God, he is asking that a greater blessing than ever may rest upon his labors. But something checks his tongue. He remembers his many infirmities. He remembers, perhaps, how slack he is in his private devotions and how cold he is in his pleading with the sons of men. He has before Him the promise, "My Word shall not return unto Me void." But for all that, he is so conscious that he does not deserve the honor of being useful that he is half afraid to pray as he should pray and to believe as he should believe.

Dear Brother, may I press upon you the case of the centurion? It is right for you--it is right for me, to say, "Lord, I am not worthy to be made the spiritual parent of one immortal soul." It is right for me to feel that it is too great an honor to be permitted to preach the Truth of God at all and almost too high a thing for such a sinner to have any jewels to present to the Redeemer to fix in His crown! But, oh, we must not from this infer that He will not fulfill His promise to us and hear our prayers! "Lord, speak in a Word and, feeble though the instrument may be, the congregation shall be blessed! Say but the Word and the marvelous testimony, though marred with a thousand imperfections, shall yet be 'quick and powerful and sharper than any two-edged sword.' "

Let this comfort and cheer any desponding pastor--let him take heart from this and learn that it is not himself to whom he is look to, but that he is to look to God. And that it is not his own arm upon which he is to depend, but the promise of God and the strong arm of the Most High. Or, am I addressing some Brother or Sister in a somewhat similar perplexity of mind? In your private life, dear Friend, you have laid upon your heart some of your relatives and neighbors who are very dear to you.

Or perhaps, you teach a class in the Sunday school, or possibly you have a larger class of adults and sometimes Satan will be very busy with you. The more useful you are, the more busy he will be. And he will say to you, "What are you, that you should ever hope to see conversions? Other men and women have had them, but they were better than you are-- they had more talent. They had more ability. They served God better. And God gave them a greater reward. You must not hope to see your children saved! You cannot expect it. How should such teaching as yours ever be useful?"

Friend, you are right in saying, "Lord, I am not worthy that you should enter under my roof." The more you can feel that, the more hopeful shall I be of your success! You are right in feeling that David is not fit to meet the giant and that the stones out of the brook are scarcely fit weapons for such a warfare. But, oh, do not push the right into a wrong! Do not, therefore, mistrust your God! No matter what a fool you may be--God has confused wise things by the foolish long before now. No matter how weak you are--God has brought down the mighty by weak instrumentalities often enough before this time!

Have hope in Him and tonight in your prayers, when you have made your confessions, do not let your faith fail you, but say, "Lord, say in a Word and my class shall be blessed! Say in a Word and those stubborn boys and girls, those to whom I have talked so often, who seem to be none the better--shall be saved." Have faith in God, beloved fellow work- ers! The result of all, under God, must rest with your faith! If you believe for little success, you shall have little success. But if you can believe for great things and expect great things, you shall certainly find your Master's Words fulfilling your desire!

Do I now also address parents here who have been praying for their children? Or a husband who has been pleading for his wife? Or a wife who has been making intercession for her husband? God only knows what heart-rending prayers are often heard in families where only a part is saved! Ah, what grief is it to a truly godly father to see his sons and daughters still heirs of wrath! And what a pang to know that the partner of your bosom must be separated from you forever by the stroke of death! I marvel not that you pray for your friends! Should I not marvel at you if you did not? And now, when you have been praying lately, a sense of your unworthiness has almost stopped you. And though, perhaps, there has been no public sin about you--before others you could have defended yourself--you have said in private, "Lord, I am not worthy of this blessing."

You have said, "Lord, my children are not saved because my example is not as good as it should be. My conversation is not as upright as it should be." You have felt, as I have sometimes, that there was no creature in the whole world so little and no man loved of God in all the world that was so great a wonder of ingratitude as you are. I say it is right that you should feel this--but do not let this stop your prayers! Offer your request! Depend upon the blood of Christ for its plea and upon the intercession of Christ for its prevalence! Do not be afraid!

An evil hand drops a letter into the post office, but the blackness of that hand will not hinder the dispatch of it. There is a stamp upon it and it will go. And your black hand drops a prayer before Christ's feet, but that black hand will not stop its being heard, for there is a stamp upon it--Jehovah Jesus' blood! It may be blotted and misspelled and there may be many blurs all over it, but do not be afraid, for God knows His Son's signature and that will give a worth to your prayers. It is the bloody signature of Him whose hand was nailed to the Cross that will carry the day with God. Therefore do not, I pray you, give place to fear--your prayers shall return into your bosom with an answer of peace.

"Well, but," says one, "I have prayed so long." Ah, Brother, do not, "limit the Holy One of Israel." Sister, do not let your doubts prevail. Renew your appeal to Jesus, "Say in a Word--only say one Word." It is all done if He shall speak! Darkness fled before Him in the primeval chaos and order followed confusion. Do you think, if He shall say, "Let there be light" in a dark heart, that there shall not be light there? Angels fly at His bidding--at His Presence the rocks melt and the hills dissolve--Sinai is altogether on a smoke. And when He comes forth, dressed in the robes of salvation, there are no impossibilities with Him. He can win and conquer to your heart's best desire. Therefore be humble, but be not unbelieving.

By your leave, I shall now turn the principle of my text to an account in another way. Concerning yourselves, Friends, what are the mercies which you want? If every man could write down his own peculiar prayer, what a variety we should have upon the paper as it just went round the front row of that gallery. If it went round to all, it would not be like Jeremiah's roll, written within and without with lamentations, but it would be filled within and without with many petitions! But now just imagine what your own case is and the case of others and let us apply this principle to it--we are utterly unworthy to obtain the temporal or spiritual mercy which, it may be, we are now seeking--we may feel this, but in asking anything for ourselves we must still ask in faith in God--in His promise and in His Grace--and we shall prevail.

This blessed principle may be turned to all sorts of uses. Whatever your desire may be, only believe and it shall be granted unto you if it is a desire in accordance with His will and in accordance with the promises of His Word--or else God's Word is not true. Be humble about it, but do not be doubtful about it. The case I have in my mind's eye is this-- there is an unsaved soul here tonight. It happens to be one whose character has been morally admirable. Nobody finds any fault with you, and, as I said before, you almost wish they could! You cannot feel, as some do, the terrors of the Lord. Your heart is not broken with conviction as the hearts of some are, but there is this desire in it, "Lord, save me, or I perish!"

Now, dear Friend, it is well that you should feel that there is nothing in you to commend you to Christ. I am glad that you feel this. Though before the eyes of men and even of your own parents there is nothing which can cause you a blush, I am glad that you feel that before God you have nothing whatever to boast of. I think I see you now--you are saying, "My Church goings, my Chapel goings, I do not trust in them--I would not give up attendance at the means of

Grace, but, Sir, I have no reliance upon all this. As for my Baptism, or my confirmation, or my taking the sacrament, I know that all this has nothing whatever in it which can save my soul. And though I love God's ordinances, yet I cannot trust in them. Sir, I have fed the poor. I have taught the ignorant. In my measure I would do anything to assist those who need my aid. But I do solemnly renounce all this as a ground of trust. I have nothing of which to glory."

Well now, dear Friend, there remains only one thing to give you perfect peace tonight! And may the Master give you that one thing! Lift up this prayer to Him, "Say in a Word and I shall be made whole." Christ can do it! The offering is made. The precious blood is spilt. There is an almighty efficacy in it--He can put away your sin. Christ lives to intercede before the Throne and "is able also to save them to the uttermost that come unto God by Him." Doubt not, then, but now, trusting yourself with Jesus Christ, remember you are saved!

I am not now looking for the vilest of the vile. How many times have we said from this place that none are excluded? None but those who exclude themselves. No mountains of sin nor height of vileness can shut a man out of Heaven if he believes in Jesus--but just now we are after you. I know you are a numerous class. You are, in some respects, our dear Friends. And though not of us, you hover round us. If there is anything to be done for the cause of God, you are, perhaps, first in it. And yet you, yourselves, are not saved! I cannot bear the thought of your being cast away--to be so near the gates of Heaven and yet to be shut out after all! Why should it be? The voice speaks to you now--the Spirit of the living God speaks through that voice.

There is life in a look for you as well as for the chief of sinners! Without the strong convictions, without the terrors of conscience, without a sense of any aggravated crimes--if you rest on Jesus, you are saved! There is no amount of sin specified there. You are lost in the Fall--wholly lost--even if you had no sin of your own. But your own actual sin has irretrievably ruined you apart from the Grace of Christ. You know this and to an extent you feel it. You will feel it all the more when you have believed in Jesus. But now the one message of mercy is, "Believe and you shall live." I feel as if I cannot get at you. My soul will not go out as I desire and yet you know that I am talking about you and about your case.

When we are firing our shots at sin we hardly ever strike you. You have become so used to our appeals that there seems no likelihood of our getting at you. Oh, there are some of you whom I would not find fault with if I could. You make your mother glad with your industry. You make your sister's heart rejoice at your many virtues. But yet there is one thing which you lack! Remember that when the strength of a chain is to be measured, it is measured at its one weakest link. If you have that one weak link, the vital union is snapped.

You may have anything and everything else, but you will be only a child of nature and not a living son! I am only telling you over and over Truths of God which you have known for many years. You will not dispute these things. And sometimes you feel an earnestness about your eternal portion, though, like so many others, you are putting off and putting off. But death will not put off! The Judgment Day will not be postponed for you. O may you be brought in now! What a happy Church we should be if such as you should be brought in. We rejoice over the chief of sinners--we make the place ring when the prodigals come in. But elder Brother, why will you not come in?

You who have not been standing all the day in the market idle, but only the first hour--say not, no man has hired you. O come in, that the house of mercy may be filled! God grant the desire of our hearts and to His name shall be the praise. Amen and Amen.

A Solemn Enquiry Concerning Our Families

DELIVERED ON SUNDAY MORNING, NOVEMBER 20, 1864,
BY C. H. SPURGEON,
AT THE METROPOLITAN TABERNACLE NEWINGTON.

"And the men said unto Lot, have you here any besides? Son-in-law and your sons, and your daughters and whatever you ha ve in the city, bring them out of this place." -- Genesis 19:12.

THE angelic messengers of mercy were not only earnest to bring Lot out of the city, but in their great kindness they reminded him of an important matter which, in the alarm of the tumult without and in the surprise of their fearful tidings, he might possibly have forgotten. They suggested to his distracted heart a loving care for his relatives and friends. His wife and his two daughters were already with him in the house, but he had two sons-in-law to whom his daughters were espoused, if not married. And the angels suggest to him to make an effort to rescue these, also, from the destruction which awaited the filthy city.

In the perturbation of mind which is so usual in the renewed heart at first, it is no marvel if a man should be so taken up with thoughts of his own safety as to forget the welfare of others. Therefore I see a wisdom in the saying of the Apostle Paul to the trembling jailer, "Believe in the Lord Jesus Christ and you shall be saved, and your house." The jailer's question was personal and confined to himself--"Sirs, what must I do to be saved?" In this we judge him not--for his own conversion must be the object of the deepest and most earnest thoughts of a convicted sinner. But Paul's answer was large and liberal--"You shall be saved, and your house."

There may be some here who have but lately passed from darkness to light. In the fear lest you should be mistaken, or in the joy of your new-found comfort, it may be you have scarcely begun to think of your wife, your children, or your relatives--is it not time to begin at once? Let this text come, this morning, fresh out of Holy Scripture as though it dropped anew from the angel's tongue--"Have you here any besides?" You are yourself privileged by Sovereign Mercy and singled out for safety--have you here in the land of sin any besides? Have you not some unconverted kinsfolk, some unsaved relative, some who are written in your family register but who are not written in the Lamb's Book of Life?

Come, Friend, think about this and give heed to the question, "Have you here any besides?" My heart is in a blaze with love to souls this morning and if there are no others who care for the salvation of their fellow men, I can truly say I agonize for conversions! Forgive me--in my excitement my thoughts should seem tame and feeble, for I have passed out of the realm of thoughts and am under the absolute dominion of my feelings. Come, Holy Spirit, come and aid my tongue which is all too feeble to express the language of my inmost heart!

I. We would observe, first, that such a question as this APPEALS TO OUR NATURAL AFFECTIONS. Surely, unless we have lost manhood, we love our kindred and desire their good! We have not yet become like the ostriches in the wilderness which care not for their young. Our flesh has not congealed into marble, nor are our hearts become like millstones. We have a very tender concern for those united to us by ties of nature and esteem them as parts of ourselves. What parent is not glad to see his children in good health? We will watch with them all through the weary night when they are ill and can we not pray for them when they are sick with sin?

It is a singular mercy when our children are born to us without deformity and in full possession of every sense. And it is a great blessing when a man can look round upon a numerous household and see them all full of cheerfulness and hope. Do we care for their bodily welfare and shall we neglect to pray that their souls may prosper? Can we see the deformity of sin without tears? Can we remark the blindness of our children towards Divine things? Can we observe how deaf they are to the admonitions of mercy? Can we discover clearly the depravity of their nature without deep grief and regret? We hasten to the best physicians when we see anything amiss and we spare no cost for their recovery.

Shall we ever be at peace, or know what rest means concerning them until we see their eyes open and the light of Jesus streaming into their souls--until we know that their tongues are loosed to tell of God's mercy towards them--until there is formed in them a new heart and a right spirit? We are anxious to see in our children a due share of intelligence. We are very quick to notice any signs of it. And perhaps we are over anxious to remark upon their shrewdness and good sense--it is an overwhelming sorrow to a parent to discover weakness or imbecility of mind in his offspring.

But what shall we say if we cannot perceive any knowledge of Christ in our children? Shall the folly of their hearts cause us no anxiety? Does it give us no concern if they put bitter for sweet and sweet for bitter, darkness for light and light for darkness? Do we seek to have them educated in the various arts and sciences and not desire that they should comprehend with all saints the love of Christ which passes all knowledge? One thing is necessary--all the rest may have a temporary necessity, but the one thing--acceptance in Christ and faith in Jesus is absolutely necessary! Can we be content when we see them neatly dressed, strongly framed and progressing in their learning, while their souls are not clothed with Christ's righteousness and they are ignorant of the power of Divine love?

Can we rest content while their souls are not trained for God, not tutored for Heaven, not educated for eternity? Why, common sense teaches our natural affection that the first thought should be the training of the soul and the highest desire of our spirits should be that they may live before God, whatever may become of them in their education as to the things of time and sense. It is only natural that we should care for the prosperity of our friends and children. We are grieved if we hear that they meet with any accident. If losses and calamities befall them, I trust we know how to weep with them that weep. We would sooner bear pain ourselves than that they should suffer. We have often felt our own cross to be very light, if we have thereby lifted a cross from the shoulders of those dear to us.

But can we think of their sinning against God and abiding under the anger of the Most High without any emotion? Above all, can we contemplate for an instant their death and their appearance before God unpardoned--their condemnation and their eternal doom--without a horror taking hold upon us? My friend, my sister, my wife, my child in Hell! How can I bear the dreadful thought? Mother, if your child were running in the streets and there were a fear that yonder wheel would go over it and crush it, your heart would be in your mouth! Can you see your child in danger of eternal destruction without your bosom heaving high with fond maternal anxiety?

If I saw my friend upon the edge of a precipice I would rush to his rescue. And can I be silent when I see so many whom I love walking upon the verge of eternal ruin, utterly unconcerned about their souls? Natural affection, which makes us care for our children and friends that they may prosper, will, if it is rightly trained, make us far more earnest for their salvation from the wrath to come. If there are any who are professedly Christians who nevertheless have no sort of interest in the welfare of their children, I only utter what I believe to be the solemn truth when I say that their profession is a mistake, if not an hypocrisy--they had better give it up! If you care not for the souls of others, you do not know the value of your own!

God's people are a tender-hearted people. Like their Savior, they cannot look upon Jerusalem without weeping over it--they cannot view with complacency the destruction of any, much less can they be careless concerning the condition of those who spring from their own loins--who are united to them by ties of blood! Like Doddridge, we dare say in the sight of God, that we love the souls of men--

"My God, I feel the mournful scene. My heart yearns over dying men! And gladly my pity would reclaim, And snatch the firebrands from the flame."

I set you down as nearer akin to a devil than to a saint if you can go your way and look into the face of your friend or child and know him to be on the downward road and yet never pray for him nor use any means for his conversion. May God grant that no doctrinal belief may ever dry up the milk of human kindness in our souls!

Certainly the doctrines of Divine Grace, such as election and effectual redemption, will not do so. Error may petrify, but the Truth of God melts. May we feel that no dogma can be Scriptural which is not consistent with a sincere love to men. Truth must be consistent with its Author's Character. And He who has revealed saving Truth is the God of Love-- no, He is Love itself! And that cannot be true which naturally and legitimately would lead men to be unloving! May we be such parents, such brothers, such sisters, such children that it shall be the first anxiety of our spirits that our children, our parents, our husband, our wife, our friends, our brothers and sisters should be brought to partake with us of the things of God!

I do think that the query which is suggested this morning, "Have you in Sodom any besides?" is one which forcibly appeals to the natural affections while it does no violence to the judgment. I shall hope, therefore, that in such a congregation as the present, where there are so many loving hearts, my question will drop like a spark upon dry tinder to set the soul on fire or melt into the soul as a snowflake into the sea, to increase the flood of holy earnestness. My own heart is stirred in its inmost depths by the enquiry and I cannot but hope that yours will be also. You who are friends, I now pray you show yourselves friendly. Parents, be parents, indeed. Brothers, act a true fraternal part. Sisters, let your tender love find a fitting channel. Husbands and wives, let your conjugal union awaken you to most tender emotions. Let every fond relationship stir us to care for others while the enquiry is made, "Have you here any besides?"

II. In the second place, the question is one which AROUSES HOLY SOLICITUDE. Shall I stop a moment while you think over the roll of your friends and kinsfolk? "Have you here any besides?" Are they all saved? Are you quite sure that all of them are rejoicing in Christ Jesus and are washed in His blood? Mother, it was such a comfort to you when your first-born was added to the Church. And what a joy when your fair daughters subscribed with their hand to the name of Jesus! Are there not others who are strangers to the commonwealth of Israel?

Brother, it has been a great delight to you to see your brother saved. Your heart has swollen high with holy joy to know that a sister has passed from death unto life. But there are others of the family--are they all converted? Are there not some still in the gall of bitterness and in the bonds of iniquity--concerning whom even in the judgment of charity you are compelled to say, "Lord, have mercy upon them, for they have no mercy upon themselves"? Have you no tears for the unsaved ones? No prayers for those who abide under the wrath of God? In your house you have seen your servants saved. And next to the salvation of one's children, there is no greater mercy than to see one's servants walking in the faith--but are all of your servants saved?

Is there not one in the house with you who still has not given her heart to Christ? You are happy, my Brother, thrice happy, if while I suggest this question you can read down the whole list with sparkling eyes and say, "Yes, I can say, like Noah, they are all with me in the ark--my wife and my sons and my sons' wives with them, they are all secure--and though the deluge sweep over the whole world, in that Covenant Ark of salvation, with my whole household, I hope to float in safety."

But it is not so, I am afraid, with the most of us. We have an Esau as well as a Jacob, an Ishmael as well as an Isaac. To provoke you to earnest solicitude this morning, let me remind you of times when we should be anxious about our friends and children. When first we ourselves look to Christ, we should care for others. Oh, what a joy it is to feel the burden rolling from our shoulders--to be able to say with holy delight--"Great God, I'm saved! The chief of sinners is at last at peace with You! Your enemy is reconciled, my sin is covered, my iniquity is cast into the depths of the sea." What should be the next thought? If this is so sweet to me, there are my sin-burdened relatives--O God, bring them to know this blessedness!

If I leap at the sound of Jesus' name and find it blessed to know that sin is forgiven, O my God, let others whom I love be set free and be enabled to triumph in justification through the blood of Jesus Christ! We would not eat our morsel alone lest it grow stale through our selfishness. The woods drops with honey--we cannot eat it all--let us call others to taste its sweetness. I think, dear Friends, there can be no better season than the first blush of your newborn piety in which to cry unto the Most High with strong crying and tears, that He would be pleased to pluck others, as He has done yourselves, like firebrands from the flame. "In the morning sow your seed."

Then there are times of Christian enjoyment. When we have been sitting round the table of our dying Lord, we have been made to feast at the banquet of wine with King Jesus--the banner over us has been love and His fruit has been sweet unto our taste. But while we were downstairs at the table, did we not think of those upstairs among the spectators? Will not our hearts wing their flight with anxious desires towards loved ones who cannot unite with us? Do we not hope that before long they will sit side by side with us? Let us remember those at home this morning--at home, did I say? Alas, some are worse than at home for they are now where we were once, spending the Sunday in sin--finding their pleasures anywhere but in the things of God!

A warm fire and a happy family gathering may well make us think of those shivering in the cold outside--I charge you, Believer, forget not your poor unconverted children. Let your highest and most rapt moments of communion with Christ be just the times when your soul shall speak to God as Abraham talked to his Father and his Friend and pleaded for the sinners of Sodom. I think when we are downcast, when our soul is filled with bitter trouble, then also is an appropriate season to pray for others. God turned the captivity of Job, when he prayed for his friends, and he may turn our captivity when we do the same. Why, if I who have an interest in Christ, yet feel so desponding, what must be the wretchedness of those who have no Christ to go to?

If we who live on the bread of Heaven, yet complain that our spirit oftentimes sinks within us, what must be the failings of heart--the horror of great darkness--which those must experience who feed upon the wind and would gladly fill their bellies with the husks which the swine eat? Let your own grief help you to arrive at some knowledge of the griefs of unconverted souls and go to the

Throne of Grace on their account. It may also help to stimulate this holy solicitude to think of how we shall feel in regard to our children and friends when they come to lie sick. They will be sick as well as others. And when they are in jeopardy of their lives and the physician tells us that their existence trembles in the scale, how shall we feel, then?

Can we gaze upon their pallid countenances without bitter reproaches for our past indifference? I am afraid I cannot say I have had a sick friend concerning whom I could feel that I had done all I ought to have done. I do not know whether you have--happy are you if you feel quite guiltless. When we have seen our friends on their beds of languishing, have we not thought, "Ah, would to God we had over again the occasions and opportunities of talking to them on Divine things, for now they are so racked with pain, so distracted with many thoughts that there is scarcely room to sow the good seed, because of the many thorns." O that the harvest may not be past and the summer ended before we begin our sowing!

Fools lose the spring and then lament in the time of harvest. May Heaven save us from the fool's lament. And what will you think if your children should die unconverted--your wife, your husband, your friend? To lose our loved ones is one of the sore, though common troubles of life. But oh, it can be little trouble to send on those who are ripe for Glory! Go where Glory waits you--we would not detain you here! To think that while we are weeping here they are singing around the eternal Throne wipes the tears from our eyes! But what must it be to bury them without "a sure and certain hope of a glorious resurrection"?

To put the body under the sod with this dread thought upon us, that, "we sorrow as those that have no hope"? It is the death of death to fear that our friends have not escaped the second death. Must you not confess, this morning, that if some of your kinsfolk were to die as they are, you could not, unless you were to stultify your own conscience, entertain anything like a sure hope of their entering into eternal life? Now, as you would wish you had prayed for them, as you would wish you had labored with them, when they are dead, so do now! While there is an opportunity, avail yourself of it for fear you should have to mourn with briny tears that the soul has gone, and that you have never rendered it any help. Before the sun goes down forever, use its light. It is vain to warn after the ship is wrecked. Hell will never give up its prey--nor will your tears mitigate the fury of its fires. It is now or never. Lord, make it now!

Think again, how you would care for your friends if you were, yourself, this morning very near death. O my Hearers, I sometimes think of the time when I shall lie a-dying--when all alone my spirit must cross the black brook of Kedron and leave the city of our solemnities for the other side of Jordan. Then such thoughts as these will surely steal over me-- "O that I might preach to this people again! O that I had the opportunity of addressing those thousands once more that I might preach in real earnest and not talk away the time! O that I might deal with their souls, as if they really were immortal and there were a judgment to come! O that I might set before them life and death, Hell and Heaven and plead with them, knowing the terrors of the Lord."

I can scarcely tell you what must be the sorrow of a dying man at the end of an unfaithful ministry. Then shall every wasted opportunity stuff his pillow with thorns. There shall be no sleep for that aching head, no rest for those weary eyes--he has damned the souls of men by his carelessness and sloth and now he must give his account. He is haunted by grim forebodings of wrath to come and knows not where to turn for comfort. He has insulted Heaven and played into the hands of Hell. What will be your thought, my Hearers, if in your narrower sphere you shall have been unfaithful?

There on the sick bed, though the comforts of complete forgiveness may take away from you the sting of death, which is sin, yet even the blood of Christ will not be able to remove those solemn heart-moving regrets which shall be suggested by a lively remembrance that you had opportunities of doing good and wasted them! And now that you are dying, but leaving unconverted children behind you--dying and the wife is still unsaved--dying, and your father still lives to whom you might have spoken of the way of God, but who now has no loving child to care about his soul!

As you must die, Believers, seek to live like dying men and labor for your sons and daughters and kinsfolk as those who must soon leave them and have no other opportunities of doing them good. You cannot come back from Heaven! If you have neglected a duty, you cannot leave Heaven to perform it. If there is one thing that can make an angel in Heaven envy a man on earth, it is his power to intercede for sinners, to preach, to woo and to win souls. If there is one thing which a glorified saint before the Throne of God might wish to come to earth for, it is surely this--that he might speak to impenitent brothers, that he might weep over unconverted friends and perhaps bring them to repentance. "Work while it is called today, for the night comes wherein no man can work."

III. And now we turn, seeking the same earnest object, to the third point of our discourse. Such a question as this is calculated to EXCITE US TO ANXIOUS EFFORT for mere solicitude without effort is not genuine. A man must not pretend that he cares for the souls of others so long as he leaves one stone unturned which might be the means of blessing them. It seems to me, then, that if we are in a right state of heart this morning, one of the first things we shall do will be to tell those dear to us of their danger.

I think I see Lot going out that night. No very safe place, the streets of Sodom, especially after that wretched scene which had been enacted at his own door--a miracle had rescued him. But yet with his life in his hand, the good old man goes to the door of his sons-in-law. Affection is not always so strong towards sons-in-law as towards those who are of our own blood. Still he goes with all solemnity of feeling, knowing that he, himself, should be rescued, but trembling lest these sons-in-law should refuse the invitation to escape with him.

The good old man finds his way through the winding streets of Sodom and begins to knock at the door with a resolute hand. They look down from the top of the house. "That is the voice of old Lot," says one, "what is he doing, disturbing our comfortable slumber?" They have but little love for him. They have put on some pretense of affection that they might win his daughters, but Sodomites cannot have much love for righteous men. And consequently they have no care for Lot. "What does the old fellow want at this time of night?" they say. "Why cannot he keep seasonable hours? Besides, what a disturbance there was at his own door just now! Does he not know better than to knock at our door, when he so resolutely shut his own to protect two tramping strangers? What does he want?"

He cries to them, "My sons, this city is to be burned with fire in the morning! Come, get up and flee with me, for the two men who came to me were angels sent from God to rescue me and they have bid me seek you. Come with me!" "Ah," they say. "What next? Old Lob--that is your name, Lob, instead of Lot--go your way and talk about your silly dreams to men of softer brains and not to us." "No," says he, "it is even so, by the love you bear my daughters, bear with me. If it is not so it will not matter, you can return. But if it is so, think what it will be to be destroyed with fire and brimstone out of Heaven! I pray you, come."

But they scoff at him--they tell him he is only mocking them--that he has some motive for wishing to get them into the street and they bid him go. And with an aching heart the poor old man goes back, feeling something more than Isaiah's grief--"Who has believed our report? And to whom is the arm of the Lord revealed?" Yet as he fled out of Sodom, if the sight of his daughters reminded him of their husbands, he would think, "I am clear of their blood. I did plead with them. I did exhort them to escape. And if they would not, why, they would not--and the sin lies at their own door."

It will be some comfort to the Christian, if the worst should come to worst, that he has warned the ungodly. Let us tell them of their danger and never cease to warn until they cease to sin. Having so done, it is the duty of every Christian to tell his friend the remedy. Plain speaking about Christ is the ordinary means of bringing sinners to repentance. Those ministers most useful in soul-seeking are those who put the doctrine of simple faith in the Atonement in the clearest light. Let not your friend perish through ignorance. Tell him that whoever comes unto Christ He will in no wise cast out-- that there is life in a look at the Crucified Savior! Tell him that whoever believes that Jesus is the Christ is born of God. Preach no salvation by works--but preach faith and works only as the fruit of faith.

And let the doctrine that Christ came to seek and to save that which was lost be clearly set before your friend's eyes. Remember, it is not enough coldly to warn them of danger and doctrinally to teach the remedy. There are many who will go so far. But I hold, my Brothers and Sisters, that we are bound to use a constraint with our friends. Do not misunderstand me--only a loving and a tender constraint, such as these angels used with Lot. Press them, plead with them, take them by the hand. Some are afraid to do this. They fear that they should be doing the Spirit's work. My dear Brother, that is the reason why I do it, for I know the Spirit of God works by means and I am in hopes that He will use me to do His own work.

"Well, but we cannot bring them to Christ," says one. That is true and that is false. That is true--you cannot, unless God is with you. But instrumentality is the ordinary method by which God accomplishes His purpose and therefore you may be enabled to bring sinners to Jesus. I do not, when I plead with sinners, plead as though I pleaded, or as though there were anything in my pleading which could do them good! I plead, as Paul says, "As though God did beseech you by us." This is the position the Christian parent should take up, the position of God pleading with men, "As though God did beseech you by us." Not man seeking to win a soul, but the Son of Man coming to seek and to save that which was lost.

Do not be afraid, dear Friends, that you will ever violate the doctrine of election or predestination by the most solemn determination you can make in the sight of God that you will wrestle and weep and agonize to bring your children to Himself. Rightly understood, this doctrine is an incentive to duty and never an opiate for sloth. "Compel them to come in," is the Savior's own command. I remember an old man who was a nursing father to all the young men in the parish where he lived. This one thing he used to do--there was scarcely a lad whom he would not know and speak to and there was a time with most of the lads when he specially sought to see them decided.

Suppose one of them was going away to London? He would be sure to ask him to have a cup of tea with him. "You are going away, John," he would say, "I should not like you to go without spending an evening with me." If it was a fine sunshiny evening, he would say, "You know I have often talked to you about the things of God and I am afraid that as yet there has been no impression produced. You are going to London and will meet with many temptations and I fear you may fall into them. I should like to pray with you once before you go. Let us walk down the field together."

There was a tree, an old oak tree in a solitary place, where he would say, "To help you to remember my words better, we will pray under this tree." The young and the old knelt together and the old man poured out his soul before God. And when he had wrestled with God and talked with his young friend, he would say, "Now, when I am dead and gone and you will perhaps come back to the place where you lived when a youth--let that tree be a witness between God and your soul that here I wrestled with you. And if you forget God and do not give your heart to Christ, let that tree stand to accuse your conscience till it yields to the entreaties of Divine love."

Now here was a using of what I have styled constraint. But it is not a constraint, you see, such as the Papist would use. And as for physical force, of course that is never to be used--but the constraint of spiritual force, Divine love and earnestness. May I ask whether we have all done our duty in this matter? Here stands one who has not. And if every Christian here who has something to repent of in this matter were to stand up, I question, Brothers and Sisters, whether many of us dare keep our seats.

Ah, if they perish, we cannot say that we wept after them! Whitfield could say to his congregations often, "Ah, if you are lost, it is not for want of weeping after, not for want of my groans and tears." But I am afraid if our children were lost, or our brothers and sisters were lost, we could not say so much as that. May God forgive the past and may He help us in the future. And from this time forth may we resolve as in the presence of the flowing wounds of Christ and as He enables us we will--

"Tell to sinners round, What a dear Savior we have found, Point them to the redeeming blood, And say, 'Behold the way to God.'"

IV. And now I shall not weary you, I trust, if I continue a little longer. It seems to me that our text FOSTERS A VERY CHEERING HOPE. It says, "Have you here any besides?," as much as if it would say, "Hope for them all. Why should they not all be brought out of Sodom? Why should one be left behind?" That was a grand saying of Moses when Pharaoh said, "Go, serve the Lord. Only let your flocks and your herds be stayed: let your little ones also go with you. And Moses said, You must give us also sacrifices and burnt offerings, that we may sacrifice unto the Lord our God. Our cattle also shall go with us. There shall not an hoof be left behind"--the smallest lamb, or the meanest goat--they shall all come out.

So it is glorious when in strength of faith the father of the family can feel that he will give the Master no rest till they are all saved. Not leaving William out, nor omitting Mary. Not saying, "Well, thank God, I am blessed above the aver- age--the most of my children are converted and if one shall perish, I must bear with it as a cross." No! But saying in your soul with humble boldness--

"Lord, I will not let You go, Till a blessing You bestow upon every child of my loins, upon every brother and every sister and every relative." I say the text fosters a hope that you may yet see them all brought to Jesus!

I stayed some few months ago with a Brother in Christ in a certain town in the midland counties. I might mention his name if I could, He is the banker of the town. I was delighted when staying there, to hear a story from his own lips which is also printed and worthy of your careful perusal. His wife, a godly woman, had been exercised with many thoughts for her husband and children. She did not live to see her prayers answered. She fell asleep, but with a good hope that yet her husband and her children would join her in the skies.

She said that her husband would experience a bad trial, but that it would be greatly blessed to him and so it turned out. Our esteemed friend, that excellent man of God, Mr. Denham Smith, went to preach in the town and the gentleman went to hear him. He did not go with any desire for conversion--he knew not its value--he merely went to hear Mr. Smith as a person well known as an evangelist. The Word, through Divine Grace, pierced his heart and about the same time it also reached the heart of one of his daughters. He was under deep distress of mind but through the simple teaching of our friend, Mr. Smith, he was led to rest upon Jesus and cast his anchor in the blessed anchorage of the Atonement.

His daughter, about the same time, through the united prayers of her newly-converted father and Mr. Smith, was brought into perfect peace. He thought, "This is a happy season--two of my sons are out on business, but I will send for them to come home." They were brought home--they were asked to go and hear Mr. Smith. One of them found the Savior. The other remained indifferent. The three converted ones began to pray for the others and, to make the story--a blessed story--very short, there were six in the household, sons and daughters, they were all saved, father included!

They had but three domestic servants--Mr. Smith visited them a second time. It had been a subject of prayer that the three servants might be saved and they were so and are now a whole family walking in the Truth of God! Such an instance as this in a somewhat large family should excite the desire of all Christian parents, that they may have the same blessing! Of course we cannot expect it where there are very little children. But we can expect, we ought to expect family conversions. And in answer to prayer we may have it where the children are come to an age in which they are capable of understanding the things of God and knowing the Truth as it is in Christ Jesus. I know that many of you feel your eyes watering at the thought of being able to say, "Here am I, and the children You have given me, for I have no greater joy than this--to see my children walking in the Truth."

Do not think that the conversion of children is a thing unusual or suspicious--look for it and believe in it. You cannot change their hearts, or give them Divine life --it is beyond your power. But it is not beyond the power of your God. And God will refuse His children nothing if they do but know how to plead His promise and ask in faith, doubting nothing. Only let us feel more about this and I am persuaded we shall see better times with regard to our young people. I am resolved, in connection with this Church, as soon as I can get over my many present engagements in the country, in Scotland and so on, that we will devote ourselves to looking more directly and personally after our young people.

We must have special meetings with them. The pastor must commune with them. The elders and deacons must meet them. We must be seeking to bring in more souls. God has dealt very graciously with this Church and for eleven years there has been one long revival. But I want to see greater things than these. I believe that the prayers of the last three weeks are being heard. Last Friday I met with many of my Brethren, the ministers of London, in this place, to pray. We did pray. Our hearts were knit together in holy love and we prayed for our Churches and congregations and pleaded with God that He would make us better ministers and help us to be free from the blood of our hearers.

And I expect in answer to the prayers of my Brethren that we shall get a blessing. Moreover we have all been pleading--may I not say all? We have been crying, "Will You not revive us again that Your people may rejoice in You?" But we must use the means. I must ask my dear Friends who love the Lord who are scattered about the Tabernacle to begin from this time forward to look after those who sit near them, to look after those who sit in the pews with them. Put questions to them and endeavor gently to lead them to the Savior. Instead of one address from this pulpit, make it a thousand addresses from Christians round about!

Let me give you the nail and the hammer by preaching the sermon--but YOU--as agents in the hands of the Holy Spirit, labor to drive home the Word. And if I can get all of you who love the Lord into a thoroughly warm and earnest state, I am persuaded the great things we have seen are only the beginning of greater things to come! We are on the threshold of an era of mercy! We have journeyed to the edge of a long stretch of glorious sunlight, emerging out of the shadows into the serene clear shining of Jehovah's face. We shall see these galleries and these aisles and this vast area full of Believers yet! We shall see the Word of God running, having free course, and being glorified! But we must, dear Friends, be stirred up to holy action for it.

V. Alas, I must conclude! Conclude, too, with a very dark and gloomy thought. The text SUGGESTS A VERY SOLEMN FEAR, namely, that there may be some in our households who will not be saved. Ah, young men and women! Ah, you who are fathers of Christian children, but not converted yourselves! You who are godless daughters and unregenerate sons of Christian people--you are lost now and you may be lost forever! Lot's sons-in-law were consumed and why not you? Saved shall the Patriarch be, but not saved the Patriarch's son, except he shall flee out of Sodom!

Beware! No kinship can save you! You may be allied to a race of saints, but, being yourself a sinner, your pedigree cannot save you. Unconverted souls, flee away, I pray you! And may God's Grace direct you to the Rock of Ages split for you. Hide yourself in the cracks there and let your soul find peace through Jesus the Savior. May God bless these feeble words of mine to every soul here, for Jesus' sake. Amen.

The Smoke Of Their Torments

DELIVERED ON SUNDAY EVENING, NOVEMBER 20, 1864,
BY C. H. SPURGEON,
AT THE METROPOLITAN TABERNACLE, NEWINGTON.

"And Abraham went early in the morning to the place where he had stood before the Lord. Then he looked toward Sodom and Gomorrah and to ward all the land of the plain; and he saw, and behold, the smoke of the country went up as the smoke of a furnace." -- Genesis 19:27,28.

EARLY in the morning Abraham sought that favored spot where but yesterday God had been pleased to manifest Himself and where he had been favored with a season of extraordinary communion. Where should the Believer go, but to that choice place, dear to his heart, where he has communed with the Lord?--

"Who that knows the worth of prayer, But wishes to be often there?"

It is a high privilege, the highest which mortals can enjoy, to talk with God, to plead with Him, to use arguments and to prevail. Such Divine Grace had Abraham found. No marvel that he goes back to the place where God had thus drawn near to him. Doubtless one reason why he rose early and went to the place and looked towards Sodom was an anxious desire to know how his prayers had speeded.

You remember he put a last "perhaps" to the Lord--"Perhaps ten shall be found there, And He said, I will not destroy it for ten's sake." He hopes, perhaps, that he need not go any further. He stops, for he feels sure in his heart that there must be ten righteous there! He turns his eyes to the quarter of the horizon where Sodom and Gomorrah should stand. So, when you have prayed, look out for answers. Elijah said to his servant, "Go and look towards the sea"--so say to your hopes--"Go and look towards the sea." If you have asked for rain, expect a cloud. If you have sought mercy, expect that God will stretch out His hand and bestow it upon you.

But God does not always answer His children's prayers just as they would desire. Besides, His children are sometimes slack in asking and therefore they do not get what they desire. So Abraham, as he looked towards Sodom--instead of seeing the verdant well-watered plain and the roofs and spires of the city, saw nothing but black smoke and a lurid glare going up to Heaven like the smoke of a furnace.

It is remarkable that he does not appear to have observed the storm as it came down from Heaven! From this fact we may infer how rapid the destruction of the cities must have been! God rained fire out of Heaven upon Sodom--it seems to have been done in a moment. The whole plain was destroyed. And all that Abraham saw after he rose up, which was probably just at sunrise, was merely the smoke that followed the conflagration.

So does God drive His enemies away. As wax is melted before the fire, as the smoke is driven before the wind, so does the enemy perish before the breath of God when He comes forth out of His hiding place to punish sin. Can you now picture to yourselves the reverent Patriarch, as he leans upon his staff and looks with wondering gaze towards the smoking furnace? What must have been his thoughts? What a spectacle for him to gaze upon--from the very spot where he had held communion with God!

Perhaps he could not have looked upon it from any other spot. He would have been too much afraid, too full of trembling. But there he felt safe. Standing where the Lord had talked with him he felt secure. And he could look even into that gruesome glare and that terrible blackness without dismay.

And now I want to summon you, my dear Christian Friends, to the scene of your own most hallowed privileges--to the spot, as it were, on which Divine Grace has been shown most clearly to your souls and intercessions have been poured out most freely from your hearts. From there I would have you lift up your eyes. To what, do you ask, would I draw your attention? Ah, then I want you to look upon the smoke of the torments of lost spirits. I want believing eyes to gaze upon that place, "where their worm dies not, and the fire is not quenched."

Only mind that you stand in the place where God has communed with you, beneath the Cross, where the blood shall drop upon you and you shall feel the sense of pardoned sin! From no other place can we view the wrath of God with proper and profitable emotions. But standing there our spirits shall be chastened, our souls comforted and with tears standing in our eyes--tears of gratitude and contrition--we shall venture to look upon that dark and terrible gulf where the wicked lie and shall derive some profit from the sight, even as Abraham doubtless did.

First, then, tonight, let me suggest the emotions which should be awakened in the Christian's spirit when he takes a view of the wrath to come. Secondly, let me gather up some lessons which God teaches to His people and to the world from the doom of the wicked. And then, in closing, let me turn your eyes another way to a yet more awful display of Divine vengeance--even more awful, I say--than that which is to be perceived in Tophet, where lost souls are shut up.

I. WITH WHAT EMOTIONS OUGHT WE TO GAZE UPON THE TORMENTS OF UNGODLY AND IMPENITENT SOULS? Certainly it should always be with an humble submission to the Divine will. The assurance that God is just, even in the midst of His hot displeasure, must ever be cherished. The Judge of all the earth cannot but do right. Though He is terrible and dreadful in His anger, as a consuming fire, yet is He still our God forever and ever, full of goodness and full of Truth.

There is a deep-seated unbelief among Christians just now, about the eternity of future punishment. It is not outspoken--in many cases it is whispered--and it frequently assumes the shape of a spirit of benevolent desire that the doctrine may be disproved. I fear that at the bottom of all this there is a rebellion against the dread Sovereignty of God. There is a suspicion that sin is not, after all, so bad a thing as we have dreamed. There is an apology, or a lurking wish to apologize for sinners who are looked upon rather as objects of pity than as objects of indignation and really deserving the punishment which they have willfully brought upon themselves.

I am afraid it is the old nature in us putting on the specious garb of charity which thus leads us to discredit a fact which is as certain as the happiness of Believers. Shake the foundations upon which the eternity of Hell rests and you have shaken Heaven's eternity, too. "These shall go away into everlasting punishment: but the righteous into life eternal." There is precisely the same word in the original. We have it translated a little more strongly in our version, but the word stands the same. And if the one is not eternal, the other is not!

Brethren, this is a fearful thing. Who can meditate upon the place appointed for the wicked without a shudder? Ungodly men seem to think we like to preach upon these topics. Far, far is it from being the case. I have had to censure myself of late for scarcely having preached at all upon them. They fancy that Christian men can look with complacency upon the torment of the lost, imagining themselves to be safe! They know not what they say. The very reverse of such a spirit is common among us.

We shudder so much at the thought of men being cast away forever and horror takes so strong a hold upon us that if we could doubt it, we would. And if we could disprove it altogether, we feel we should be glad. But we dare not attempt the task because we know that it were to impugn the sentence of the Almighty and provoke a quarrel against the Most High. Great Judge of all! You shall trample upon Your enemies in the day of Your wrath! Yet shall You be as glorious in that act as when You pardon sin and pass by transgression. Christian, look there and, as you look, rebel not, but say, "True and righteous are You, O God. Let Your name be honored evermore!"

Surely, too, another emotion, which a glance towards the dreary doom of the ungodly can never fail to prompt, is that of gratitude. "And why am I not there? They gnaw their fire-tormented tongues in vain--and why am I not there? Did they sin? I have sinned. Did they curse God and die? I, too, have cursed God. And it was a marvel that I did not die."--

"Oh, were it not for Grace Divine, That late so dreadful had been mine."

Some of you who were accustomed to frequent the ale house, whose voices were loud in the lascivious song, who polluted eventide with sin and spoiled the day with your ungodliness--thank God that you have been washed in the precious blood of Jesus--for as you read the list of the lascivious and so on, you are compelled to say, "Such were some of us. But we are washed, but we are sanctified, but we are justified in the name of the Lord Jesus and by the Spirit of our God."

Let the depths of Hell constrain you to heights of gratitude. And let the wailing and the gnashing of teeth which come up from there appeal to your lips, your heart, your very bowels and all that is within you--for the music of thank- fulness that you have escaped. Should there not also here be deep feelings of humility? Look to the hole of the pit where you were lifted and the rock where God has hewn you! What those sinners were, such were you!

There was nothing in you that would carry you to Heaven, but everything that would have carried you down to Hell. You are a brand plucked from the burning--you would have burned in that fire as well as others! And can you lift up your head, man, and boast of yourself and say, "O God, I thank You that I am not as other men"? No, not if you are in your senses. But humbled and yet thankful, you will go your way with a subdued heart, looking upon others with pity and with love and anxiously desiring to pluck them, also, from the flames and guide their feet into the way of peace.

And there is another sensation which must go through every nerve--and the thought will sometimes blanch our cheeks with terror--lest we also should go there. I think a glance of the eye towards the smoke of Gehenna would always prompt a holy jealousy over one's own heart and a diligent watchfulness of one's own walk. What do you say to this, professor? You see the smoke going up forever--what if you should go there after all? Remember, it is one thing to profess to be a Christian and quite another thing to be truly converted. You may go to the gates of Heaven by profession--but there is a back door to Hell.

High professor, take care. If your wings are made of wax they will melt. And the higher they soar, the greater your fall will be. It will be a dreary day for any of us if we have to go from the pulpit to perdition, from the Lord's Table to communion with devils and from drinking the cup in which we commemorate the sacrifice of Christ to the drinking of the cup of trembling--in which the dregs of God's wrath are to be found. If I must perish, I would rather perish as an openly-avowed sinner than as a hypocrite--for the doom of a man who has made a fair show in the flesh and a fine pretense of godliness must be increased by the loss which he suffers--the hopes which are disappointed--the professions which have turned out to be lies.

Members of this Church, I speak to you hoping that you will put the question among yourselves, "Is it I, Lord? Is it I?" My fellow laborers in this Church, deacons and elders, let us search ourselves! Let not your gray heads exempt you from the duty of self-examination. Let not your office screen you from the suspicion that, after all, you may be deceived. Come, let us go together as if we never went before to the Cross of Jesus! Let us look up to Him as He hangs bleeding there and if up to this moment we never have been saved, let us say, "Jesus, accept us now."--

"A guilty, weak and helpless worm, On Your kind arm I fall-- Be You my strength and righteousness, My Jesus and my All."

These at least are some of the feelings with which we, like Abraham, standing in the place where God has communed with us, may look towards Sodom and see the smoke going up as the smoke of a furnace. We shall pause awhile and then notice the teaching which seems to come from the dreadful doctrine of the wrath to come.

II. Look, Christian, if you can look and see there THE EVIL OF SIN. Are you startled? That is the true harvest of the sowing of iniquity. Come, Sinner, I charge you look at it. This is what sin brings forth--this is the full-grown child. You have dandled it on your knee. You have kissed and fondled it--see what it comes to. Hell is but sin full-grown, that is all. You played with that young lion--see how it ravishes and how it tears in pieces now that it has come to its strength. Did you not smile at the azure scales of the serpent? See its poison! See to what its stings have brought those who have never looked to the brazen serpent for healing!

Next time the enemy says to you, "Is it not a little one?" answer him, "Behold how great a matter a little fire kindles." Remind him that the mustard is the smallest among seeds but yet it grows to a great tree. Is it so? Do you account for sin as a peccadillo, a flaw scarcely to be noticed, a mere joke, a piece of fun? But see the tree which springs from it! There is no joke there--no fun in Hell. Fools make a mockery of sin, which is but an egg. But when the egg is hatched and the bird full-fledged, they will find that they must laugh on the other side of their mouths, if they laugh at all.

My God, from this day forward help me to see through the thin curtain which covers up sin and whenever Satan tells me that such-and-such a thing is for my pleasure, let me remember the pain of that penalty wrapped up in it! When he tells me that such a thing is for my profit, let me know that it can never profit me to gain the whole world and lose my own soul! Let me feel it is no sport to sin, for only a madman would scatter firebrands and death and say it is sport.

You did not know that sin was so evil. Some of you will never know how evil it is till the sweetness of honey has passed from your mouth and the bitterness of death preys at your organs! You will count it harmless till you are hopelessly stricken with its sting. What? Is there no way to teach you the evil of sin but to cast you into Hell to learn the lesson? There you cannot profit but only perish by the knowledge acquired too late! O that you were wise, you thoughtless ones, and looking at the smoke of the ruin of others would learn how dreadful is that sin which will before long ruin you, as it has already ruined them!

Do you think that God struck Sodom and that He will not strike you? Drunkard, swearer, shall

Gomorrah perish and shall you escape? No! He is the same God today to punish sin as He was then. I say see the blackness of your sin by the light of Hell's fire and as the smoke goes up forever, ask yourself will you sin when such is the inevitable result? Will you dwell with sin if this involves dwelling with tormenting fire? This doctrine I would to God we could learn in our hearts! It is hard for me to preach it! It is harder, still, for you to learn it! But none ever know the love of Christ till they know something of the evil of sin.

As the Christian, with downcast and blushing face looks to the place where their worm dies not and their fire is not quenched, he is awe-struck with the justice of God. What? Is God so just as this? He swears, "As I live, says the Lord, I have no pleasure in the death of him that dies, but had rather that he should turn unto Me and live." He is a God so good that He delights in mercy and never is His soul more glad than when He passes by transgression, iniquity and sin and receives His Ephraims to His bosom.

But is this God so severely just? Shall men, made in His own image, be broken by Him as with a rod of iron? Will He consign them to that Tophet, the pile where there is fire and much wood? Shall the ire of the Almighty be the flame that kindles it? Can He be a God of love and yet treat sinners thus? Then how awfully just must God be! How stern this attribute of unimpeachable justice! Some talk of God as though mercy were the sole quality of the Divine Character and He had no other attribute. But the God of Scripture is to be adored in every attribute by which He is revealed.

"God is Love." But know, too, that His justice shall beam forth with ineffable splendor when He whets His glittering sword and says, "Ah, I will ease Me of My adversaries and avenge Me of My enemies." My God, when He came on Sinai, touched the mountains and they smoked! Coals of fire went before Him. He did ride upon the wings of the wind! Thick darkness was round about Him. His voice was thunder and He spoke in lightning. Even Moses did exceedingly fear and quake. What will He be when He comes to punish for offenses if He is thus dreadful when He comes merely to give the Law?

May you never know the weight of the eternal arm when it shall come down upon a guilty conscience. May we never feel in body and in soul how strict, how severe, how unflinching is that mighty God who has unsheathed His sword forever and bathed it in Heaven and made this as His solemn oath that He will by no means spare the guilty, but will cut them off root and branch and destroy them forever! Admire the justice of God. Muse upon it much. Think with what solemn pomp it shall be vindicated.

Oh, what a holocaust of victims shall burn forever in attestation of His majesty! Let your soul be humbled! Boast no more! Bow at His feet! Submit yourself to Him! "Kiss the Son, lest He be angry, and you perish from the way, when His wrath is kindled but a little."

Another lesson now comes to us and one which I hope will be more pleasing and affect some minds that may not be moved by what we have, up to now, said. Looking at the destruction of the wicked, this reflection crosses our minds. We, His people, have been redeemed from destruction! What a price must that have been which redeemed us from such woe and rescued us from such a place of torment! You have learned from this pulpit the doctrine of Substitution, how the Lord Jesus Christ took the sins of His people and stood to suffer in their place. We do not say that Christ endured the Hell of His people--the precise torment which His people ought to have suffered--but we do say upon Scriptural warrant that Christ endured a pain and agony which was tantamount and accepted by God as the proper substitution for all the griefs which were due to the sins of His people.

Who can form an idea of what the torment of one soul must be that is cast away forever? Not, remember, the torment of an hour, a day, a month, a year, a century, a thousand years, but forever--FOREVER! You cannot measure that. But you will have to multiply that by ten thousand times ten thousand when you remember that Jesus laid down His life for many and gave Himself a ransom for His sheep. Nor are these a few, but a great multitude which no man can number. Well did the Psalmist say, as he typified the Messiah, "All Your waves and Your billows are gone over Me." One soul that is lost cannot feel all the waves and billows, but Jehovah Jesus did!

None but a God could bear what He endured. Beneath that ocean of tremendous fire the mighty Substitute bowed His majestic head--that very head which Heaven worshipped and which is crowned with everlasting splendor--bowed himself in the great Baptism of almighty wrath that the waves of swelling grief might roll over it. Yes, every wave and every drop of every wave of Divine wrath that was due to His people! Think, think, Christian, as you hear that solemn trampling, as you hear the wailing of the lost, as your eyes seek to penetrate that land of death, as your whole soul is alarmed with gloomy forebodings of that wrath--think what must have been in the tremendous cup--the Hells of all His people, not actually, but virtually condensed into the pangs of an hour!

He did but drink it and all His veins were flushed with hot blood. Every nerve became a high road for the hot chariots of pain to drive along. He cried, "If it is possible, let this cup pass from

Me." It was not possible! He set it to His lips. He drank, He drank right on. His back was scourged, but still He drank. His head was pierced with the crown of thorns, but He took not away His lips.

The spittle flowed down His cheeks. They were black with the bruising of mailed fists. Reproach had broken His heart and shame had covered His face--but on, still on He drank. They pierced His hands and His feet. They offered Him vinegar. They tore away His clothes. They stripped Him naked! They left Him without a comforter. Devils surrounded Him with mockery and men with scorn. But on, still on, He drank! O blessed Savior! Till at last He had swallowed every bitter drop--and turning the chalice upside down, not so much as one black drop trembled on its brim, for--

"At one tremendous draught of love, He drained destruction dry."

For every one of His people He exhausted the cup and there was not a pang, nor a grief, nor a penal groan left for any one of His elect. He suffered, the Just for the unjust, that He might bring them to God!

Here is a plummet to fathom the depths of the Savior's griefs. But who can throw the lead and who can tell when it strikes the bottom! God only knows the griefs of His dear Son. Even lost spirits can scarcely guess it. And oh, as you look into that smoke, ascending forever and ever, say, "Hallelujah, Jesus! For You have redeemed us unto God by Your blood and we shall reign with You forever and ever."

That fearful vision which beclouds my eyes and makes them feel heavy at the same time presses upon me with a tremendous weight while I mention another Truth of God. Behold here the solemnity of the Gospel ministry, the responsibility of those who listen to it and the need there is for earnestness in handling Divine things! Have I to deal with immortal souls? Then let me not trifle. Have I to talk with men who must spend eternity in Heaven or in Hell? Then wake up, sluggish flesh and bear not down my spirit! And you, my Soul, be stirred up to the highest degree of intensity of love, and of earnest devotedness that men may be, by some means, or by any means, brought to escape from the wrath to come!

I would to God I could preach as Baxter did! That man, the victim of many diseases, but sane and healthy in his mind, said he never came to his pulpit without tears and his knees knocking together, for he had to speak for God with men who must soon appear before His bar and he, himself, must appear there, too, to give an account of his preaching to them. O Sirs, it is perhaps but a matter of amusement for some of you to come on a Sunday evening into this place, or any other. But believe us, it is no matter of amusement for us who have to preach to you!

We would not have accepted our office if it had not been thrust upon us! Woe is unto us if we preach not the Gospel! But if we do preach the Gospel, still terrors seize hold upon us, for our heart is ready to break when we think how the multitude reject that Gospel and go their way to their farms and their merchandise and will not come to the Gospel-supper to be fed. Preaching will seem dreadful work to the preacher when he comes to die if he has not been faithful. And it will not seem slight work to you when you come to die, if you have heard in vain! What would you give for another Sunday, for another invitation to hear those faithful sermons once more--to be moved by Divine love once more?

What would you give when inexorable death shall tell you that your hour-glass is empty, that your candle is burnt out and that your soul must speed its way to stand before God? My Brothers in the faith, with what earnestness should this alarm you! You are dealing, remember again, with souls that must sink to Hell unless they find mercy in Christ Jesus. It is said that when Michelangelo painted his celebrated picture of the resurrection, he went by permission to the graveyard and took out the newly-buried dead and piled up the corpses by his bedside. He then slept in the midst of them that he might get his mind into something like a proper frame for picturing the horrors of that tremendous day.

I would not have you do such a thing as that. But living as you do in the midst of lost souls, I pray and beseech you to realize the prospect of their speedy perdition as a vivid fact. As you go to your bed, remember the despair and the dismay of those who dared to live in sin and have already died without hope. I think you will, then, be in a proper frame to paint that life-picture which I hope each and all of us have set our hearts upon--of the conversion of the souls of many by our means. Oh, we are not alive, we are half dead!

Whitfield could say, "When I think of these things, I wish I could stand upon the top of every hackney coach in London and preach to the passersby." We do not preach as if we meant it! I am afraid that we make Infidels by our lethargy and that you Christian people help to prevent the usefulness of the Word of God by the apparent indifference with which you treat eternal things. If Hell is a fiction, say so, and honestly play the Infidel. But if it is real and you believe it, wake up, you that so believe, and leave no stone unturned, no means untried by which through the power of the Holy Spirit sinners may be saved!

Pledge yourselves this night, as with your hands upon the horns of the altar! Pledge yourselves as you sit in the place where God has often met with you that from this hour you will seek, God helping you, to love your neighbor as yourself and prove your love by pitying earnestness in seeking his salvation. That Truth seems to be written clearly enough in letters of fire in the midst of the smoke that comes up from the desolation of lost souls. And yet it is not merely preaching, important as that is. It is not merely warning our friends and our neighbors, though we should never lose an opportunity of telling them of their danger with more feeling than mere fidelity can inspire--yes, with that repeated earnestness which deep convictions from the very Word of the Lord and strong affection for the souls of men alone can prompt.

Let me entreat you--consider the use that Abraham made of that extraordinary Revelation, "Shall I hide from Abraham," said the Lord, "the things which I do?" "And shall I cease to use the precious opportunity of pleading for my neighbors?" appears to have been the old Patriarch's spontaneous thought. My poor brother! Ah, poor Lot! His wife! His daughters! The city with its inhabitants! A thousand thoughts of melting pity come rushing up at once. He does not stand mute with astonishment. He immediately opens his heart with intercessions and fills his mouth with arguments!

Oh Brothers and Sisters! That is just such a response to the secret of the Lord which He shows to His servants, as you should have always ready at hand. You need not wait for an opportunity! You have it now! Pray, pray, pray--pray without ceasing! Let the breath of prayer be fervent with heat. Let the prayer be so eager that it repeats itself, as Abraham's did, each time waxing hotter, drawing nearer, growing more bold--till you verily tremble at the venture! "Who can tell?" This we know, we are in no danger of offending God by crying for mercy, even when we see the two-edged sword flaming from His mouth! You have no cause to lay limits upon your importunity or to check the rising passion of your vehement desire. Prayer is a fire that needs stirring. And intercession is a holy wrestling in which practice alone can make you adept.

Christians! Some of you may look at a doomed Sodom with other eyes than Abraham did. Lot is called a righteous man. And he was vexed with the filthy conversation of the wicked. He frowned at the men of Sodom and expostulated with them and wished that sinners would restrain their follies and not go to quite such lengths in sin. That is the sort of man Lot was. Have I not many a Lot before me now? The father of the faithful went a great deal beyond this. He lived far away from the scenes of vice and the haunts of impiety. I suppose he did not think it necessary to sleep a night in that cage of uncleanness, that he might familiarize himself with the profane customs of the people.

He stood on hallowed ground, and prayed with a tender heart. He interceded with God! He multiplied his intercessions. Every time he prayed and with each fresh note of prayer his spirit grew more ardent. Impressed with God's severity, he takes courage from His goodness. Here is a fitting example for us! It is an example which I know will not be lost on some of you. The courage that can rebuke man must come from the strength that takes hold upon God. When your face shines like an angel with the radiance that the Mercy Seat reflects upon it, then it shall come to pass that the scorner will not be able to resist the wisdom or the spirit by which you speak!

Oh how dreadful the jeopardy of the souls of unconverted men and women! Jonathan Edwards was once called upon to preach a sermon quite unexpectedly. I believe he had the habit of holding his manuscript close to his eyes, a most ungainly and apparently most inappropriate mode of uttering a discourse. He read it word for word. But as he read it, terror took hold upon his congregation! Weeping and sobbing were heard on every side, for the Holy Spirit was with him and each word came with power upon their souls.

I cannot speak such language as he used. But if I could, I might be the means of making some feel in what a state of jeopardy they now are. You stand over the mouth of Hell upon a single plank and that plank is rotten! You hang over the jaws of perdition by a solitary rope and the strands of that rope are snapping, one by one. Frailer than the spider's web is your life and yet that is the only thing which divides you from a world of despair! The slightest insect commissioned by

God's Providence may end your unhappy life. You know not where, or when, or how disease may overtake you. Death often floats in the atmosphere of the House of God. He may be looking through those stony eye sockets now!

The skeleton monarch may be looking at and marking you as his prey. Could Xerxes stand here tonight, could he have a little Christianity mingled with his philosophy, then doubtless the tears he wept as he saw his army and remembered that in fifty years all would be dead, were nothing to those he would weep as he remembered that thousands this day found within the walls of Churches and Chapels and tens of thousands who are not found in any sanctuary, within less time than that will not only be dead but damned!

Here is, indeed, subject for mourning, lamentation and woe. You stand upon the brink of that precipice and yet you play! You have heard the story of the monarch tyrant who invited one to a feast. When he came, the table was loaded with dainties and there was his chair on which he must sit, but just above him hung a sword suspended by a single hair. "Why do you not eat, Man? Is not the wine rich and rare? Fill your bowl and quaff it merrily." But he looks up. "Why do you not help yourself to all those dainty cakes which make the table groan. Why, Man, what ails you?" He looks up. And right wise is he in looking up, for on that hair his life depends.

Would that you were as wise as he, for you will go your way and eat the fat and drink the sweet, but you forget that hair, that sword. The sword of Damocles could only kill the body, but this sword will kill both soul and body and kill them both forever--and but a hair keeps it from you now.

III. I am weary with my picture. I am weary with looking into that thick darkness. Let me turn your eyes another way. Would you be saved? See yonder little hill outside Jerusalem's streets? God has become Man. He is bearing sin upon His shoulders. Here He comes all faint and weary with a ponderous beam upon His back. He struggles on. They remove the load a moment. But they force Him on with spears and goads and He, all willingly, leads the van. They come outside the city and while the sobbing daughters of Jerusalem stand looking on, they fling Him back upon the transverse piece of wood.

I see the rough executioners, each man taking hold of a hand or of a foot, holding the nail in his mouth a moment till he gets that blessed palm all ready and then with his hammer driving in the nails through the hands and feet of the Son of God! He is fastened to the wood. They roughly lift up the Cross. A place has been dug for it. They dash it down. That jar has dislocated all His bones. What pain He endures in that moment when He is lifted up between earth and Heaven! And now He has a long season of suffering before Him. They sit down. They mock Him. They point to His wounds, scoff at His prayers, gloat their eyes upon His miseries.

It is the Son of God suffering there. He shrieks "I thirst!" and they give Him vinegar to drink. He cries, "My God, My God, why have You forsaken Me?" Heaven is black above His head. Fever comes on--His tongue cleaves to the roof of His mouth--that mouth becomes hot as an oven. Blood comes streaming down from all His pores. Why do I picture this? Why, here is your salvation! You must have an interest in the sufferings of that Man, or you must suffer for yourself forever. Would you not desire to have Him as your Substitute? Then remember, whoever believes in Him is not condemned!

Can you believe in Him now? To believe on Him is to trust Him. Will you trust yourself with Jesus? Now, if you do trust, your sins are forgiven! Your soul is accepted! Your eternal state is blessed and you are delivered from the wrath to come! Go your way at peace with God and at rest in your conscience and rejoice forevermore! May the Master bless even my feebleness tonight to your profit and may we meet in Heaven to His praise. Amen.

Delivered On Sunday Morning, December 4, 1864,

BY C, H. SPURGEON,
AT THE METROPOLITAN TABERNACLE, NEWINGTON.

"For He says, I have heard You in a time accepted and in the day of salvation have I succored You: behold, now is the accepted time; behold, now is the day of salvation." -- 2 Corinthians 6:2.

WE frequently hear the question discussed as to which are the best times. Some are perpetually singing the praises of the "good old times," though, if one reads the pages of history it does not appear that the old times deserve any very special praise--unless oppression, ignorance, persecution and abundant suffering deserve to be the theme of song! It is the common habit of the fathers, with tears in their eyes, to say, "The former days were better than these." But we have the wisdom of Solomon on our side when we tell them they do not enquire wisely concerning this. "Do not say, Why were the former days better than these? For you do not enquire wisely concerning this" (Eccl. 7:10).

There are others who are always boasting of the present eventful period. There was none like it--this is the era of invention and of progress, the age of liberty and of light--when slavery must cast away her fetters and superstition must hide herself among her congenial associates--the moles and bats. But I cannot perceive that this century is so much the age of gold as to need very enthusiastic praises. Its greatest virtues are counterbalanced by greater sins. And the progress which has been made towards liberty has scarcely kept pace with its advance towards licentiousness--the barriers have been broken down, it is true--but in some places the bulwarks have fallen, too.

Many there are with bright eyes looking forward to the future and their declaration is that the "good time is coming," if we but "wait a little longer"--if we will but look ahead, till this beast shall have been slain, that vial shall have been poured out and the other seal shall have been broken--then it is that we shall arrive at halcyon times! We agree with these watchful waiters--the age of gold is yet to come. The Advent is the world's best and brightest hope, insomuch that every lover of his kind may importunately cry out, "Come quickly! Yes, come quickly, Lord Jesus!"

But there is one thought which should not leave us when talking about times and seasons, namely, that now, now, just now, this present flying moment--that second which is being recorded by the ticking of yonder clock--is the only time which we have to work with! I can do nothing with the days that are past. I can do nothing with the days future-- though I reach out towards them--I cannot improve them. The past and present are fields far beyond the reach of my culture. I can neither plow nor sow the future, nor can I prune and correct the past. For practical purposes, the only time I have is that which is just now passing.

Did I say I had it? While I said I had it, it is gone like the meteor which dashes adown the sky, or the eagle which flies afar, or the swift ships which disappear beyond the horizon! Time present is the only time I may ever have. Before any future shall have become present, I may be merged in eternity. As far as I know, this day may be the end of my life's career and when yonder sun sinks to his rest, I may sink to my rest also, so far as time is concerned. If there is more time allotted to me, yet it will never come to me in any other guise and form than as time present. I call it future now, but when I get, say, to 1866, or 1880, it will be just like these moments--it will be to me present then--and consequently, for practical purposes, however much we may speculate upon the past or the future, the present moment is the only time we have, may have, or ever can have!

And it becomes important that all our thoughts should be centered upon it if we would make our calling and election sure. Our text directs us to that solemn employment and it does so by a very telling argument. You perceive that our text is a quotation. How ought we to value the Old Testament! If inspired men of God, who spoke by the Holy Spirit quoted the Old Testament, how valuable must its bejeweled sentences be! The Apostle here quotes from the forty-ninth chapter of Isaiah, the eighth verse. In that passage the Lord God is speaking to the Messiah, speaking to our Lord Jesus Christ and He says to Him, "In an acceptable time have I heard You and in a day of salvation have I helped You."

The first part, then, of this verse is a quotation from Isaiah. The second part of the verse is Paul's commentary upon the passage--"Behold, now is the accepted time." He takes his text from the Old Testament, but he gives us a New Testament sermon upon it. Let us try, if we can, to catch the Apostle's meaning. When Paul was reading in Isaiah, he perceived that the Lord Jehovah had expressly said to him, "Whom man despises, to Him whom the nation abhors (and who is this but the Lord Jesus?) in an acceptable time have I heard You."

Jesus' sighs and tears and bloody sweat in the garden of Gethsemane did not fall unheeded. Like the blood of Abel, they cried from the ground and were heard acceptably above. An answer was given--this was plainly proved by the descent of the angel to strengthen the Savior. So the prophetic words add, "In a time accepted and in the day of salvation have I succored You." The Apostle infers from this that inasmuch as God has accepted Christ, the representative of His people, He has thereby ushered in an era of acceptance. Acceptance given to the Savior is, in the Apostle's view, acceptance given to sinners.

Inasmuch as Christ is heard--He prayed not for Himself, but for us--there is, therefore, an accepted time for us begun and commenced from the day when Christ went up to the tree, stretched His hands to the nails, bowed His head to death and said, "It is finished." Paraphrase the text thus--"I have heard Jesus, the Surety, in an acceptable time. In the day of salvation have I succored Him, the mighty Savior. And therefore to you, My people, to you, poor lost and wandering sinners, to you, now is the accepted time. Now is the day of salvation."

If Christ had not died, there had never been a day of salvation. If Christ had not been heard and accepted, an accepted time could never have come to us! But since He, man's representative, has obtained favor in the eyes of God and through His complete work has forever settled that favor upon Himself, there is favor in the heart of God to those whom Christ represented--even to those transgressors for whom He makes intercession!

We shall now take the text, as God may help us, using it, first, to look at the now of Believers. Then, at the now of sinners. And after this taking wing from the text, we shall offer a few reflections upon now in Heaven. And close with a few solemn thoughts upon now in Hell.

I. First, then, NOW, WITH THE BELIEVER. With him, "Now is the accepted time; behold, now is the day of salvation." As a Believer, it is well for the Christian to live in the present. I say, as a Believer, for, alas, there is a temptation to make our faith a thing of the past. It is nearly sixteen years since I first looked to the Crucified Redeemer and was lightened and my face was not ashamed. Is there a temptation in me to say the faith which I exercised in Christ in my youthful days has saved me, and therefore I am now in a different position from what I was then and need not feel now as I did at first?

If there is such a temptation, let me shake it off as a man would shake off the deadly sleep of frozen climates. Let me, this morning, feel myself to be still just what I was--a loathsome sinner, undeserving, ill-deserving, Hell-deserving. And what then? Why, let me, then, this morning stand where I stood in the first moment of my salvation--at the foot of the Savior's Cross and look up and view the flowing of His soul-redeeming blood, with Divine assurance, knowing He has made my peace with God. At this moment, my dear Brothers and Sisters, your proper standing is as a sinner saved by blood, looking up to those dear wounds from which your pardon streamed.

Have you had many virtues since then? Has the Grace of God led you on to add to your faith, courage? And to your courage, experience? And to your experience, brotherly kindness? And to brotherly kindness, charity? Yet, for all this, your safest, happiest, holiest, best position is at the foot of the Cross--with none of these things in your hand as the price of your salvation, but looking to your Redeemer--who alone has found a ransom for you. Since the day of your espousals you have committed many sins--dare you look at them without trembling? How often have we grieved our Lord? Our love to Him? Shall we dare call it love? Our faith in Him, how mixed with unbelief! Our zeal, how dashed with selfishness! Our humility, how stained with pride! Our patience, how spoiled with murmuring!

Our every good thing is marred and rendered worthless! What a crop of weeds the soil of our heart has produced! When we look within we see, "The spirit that dwells in us lusts to envy," and every unclean bird seeks a lodging place in our hearts as in a grove of vanities--what shall we do? Why, come just now with all these sins and wash once more in that fountain which has lost none of its fullness! And feel the power of that precious blood which has not diminished one whit in its efficacy! I know the temptation is to climb to some higher room, but let us be warned by the nonsuccess of the boasting Pharisee and taught by the justification of the humble publican, still to cry, "God be merciful to me a sinner."

Beware of trying to live before God as a minister. Brother minister, this is poor living--to live officially, to go to the closet or come into God's House merely as holding a certain profession! Oh, this is starving work! If your tendency is to live as Church members, if not altogether as worldly men, rouse yourselves from it, I pray you, and confess with Paul, "And the life which I now live in the flesh I live by the faith of the Son of God, who loved me and gave Himself for me."

The proper place of a Christian is never to get one inch beyond this--a monument of Grace--a sinner saved by blood. I live in Jesus, on Jesus, for Jesus, with Jesus and hope soon to be perfectly conformed to His likeness. Let me remember that if there could be a moment in which my soul might stand out of Christ--no longer leaning upon Him and no longer covered with His righteousness--that very moment I must be condemned! For there is no condemnation only to them that are in Christ Jesus. But there is a terrible condemnation against every soul that is out of Him.

Have you climbed so high that you have towered above the place of the poor thief? Come back again, Brother, for you have climbed to a dangerous altitude and maybe you shall find it a gallows where Haman was hanged and you shall hang with him. Or have you dived so deep in a sense of your own depravity, that you have forgotten to rest on Jesus Christ as able, still, to save you? My Brother, look up from the hole of the pit, for in it there is no water and you will perish there with a grievous famine.

O, then, away with all but Jesus! None but Jesus--this must be our watchword at the gates of death and we must enter Heaven with it! As we have received Christ Jesus the Lord, so must we walk in Him--He must be Alpha and Omega, Beginning and End, Author and Finisher, First and Last. As Believers, let us by God the Holy Spirit's Grace keep our trust just where it was at first--in Him whom God has set forth to be a Propitiation for our sins!

Take the word "now," again, and look at the Christian as a professor. Now you are in the House of God, my dear Friends and you remember that you profess to be followers of Christ. Now, therefore, you sing in holy hymns of praise and join in solemn prayers to God as Christians should do in the worship of God. Tomorrow morning, some of you, perhaps, will be at Copenhagen Fields' Market, some of you at Newgate Market, others of you will be lighting the fire in your master's house, others seeing to your numerous families, others taking down the shop shutters--will you then remember, dear Friends, that now, where you are then --you are a Christian?

You are not to say, "I was a Christian yesterday," but "now, now I am not a Christian." A customer will come in. The temptation will be, perhaps, to take more than you ought to do. Will you please remember, "Now I am a child of God"? not, "yesterday, when I was listening to Mr. Spurgeon at the Tabernacle," but now! When you are in the market, there will be much to plague and vex you and perhaps you will think, "I cannot enjoy the Presence of God here." Oh, but my dear Brothers and Sisters, "now is the accepted time." Buying sheep, selling bullocks, using the hammer, snipping with the scissors, working at the plow, tending your sheep--now, now, NOW is the day of salvation--you are still a Christian--therefore act as a Christian!

But you are much plagued and vexed. Somebody teases you, things go wrong--what could be a better stop to that little rising passion, what could keep the naughty spirit under control better than to remember--"Now, now I am a Christian--even now." A true Christian cannot shake off his character. He is really what he is--he always must be a Christian. I heard the other day of a certain Scotch moderate minister, who being much provoked by a person in his parish, said, "If I were not a minister, I would give you a sound thrashing, Sir." And when he was further irritated, he took off his coat and said, "There is the minister--there he lies." He was then in his shirt sleeves--"There is the minister and I am only So-and-So and will give you your due." And he proceeded at once to give the man a sound thrashing.

It is just possible the man may have deserved it. That is not my point. But if a man can say, "There lies the minister," or, when you take off your coat tonight, if you can say, "There lies the member of the Church." If you, good women, when you take off your gowns, can say, as you hang up your best attire in the wardrobe, "There goes the Christian," then you have no religion at all, you have none whatever worth having! You have the faith of devils that will damn you, but not the faith of Christians that will save you!

It is not a religious coat, but a renewed heart--I pray you keep this at all times on your mind--"Now I am accepted. Now I am saved--how can such a man as I do such a thing? How, then, can I do this great wickedness and sin against God?" Mordecai once wore the king's robe, but he soon took it off because he was not really a king. And thus do many act who wear the garb of religion in the House of God, but cast it off when they go home. When Lord Burleigh, Queen Elizabeth's counselor, reached his home he was so little pleased with the cares of State, that taking off his robe, he threw it down, saying, "Lay there, Lord Chancellor." Ah, how irksome must some men's religion be to them and how cheerfully would they lay aside its restraints! But you who are really the Lord's, will, I trust, feel your faith to be your constant help and your profession your perpetual honor. You will not, you cannot sin, because you are born of God.

Suppose a Brother has his pen in his hand and is going to write what we sometimes call a nasty letter--now suppose an angel should whisper in his ear as he is writing, "Now, now, you are one of God's chosen. You have been washed in the precious blood of Christ and now you profess to be a member of His body, a king and a priest unto God." Why, I think he would throw the pen away and tear the paper up. Or, just when you are about to proceed to extremities with some poor soul who asks your mercy, if you could remember that you are now, even now, an heir of Heaven, I think you would say, "Lord, give me Grace to act according to my profession and not to stain the character I have assumed." Let "now" stay upon your mind with regard to your profession and the duty which it brings.

Dear Friends, let me comfort your hearts by the remembrance that now, as a child of God, you are a possessor of present privileges. I do not know what your frame of mind may be this morning. You may have been very much tempted, you may feel, through some sickness of body, anything but cheerful. But if you believe in Christ, remember now you are a son of God and though it does not yet appear what you shall be, yet when He shall appear, you shall be like He, for you shall see Him as He is.

At this very moment, I, a Believer in Christ, am completely pardoned--no spot of sin remains on me if I believe in Jesus. White as the newly-fallen snow is every soul that has been washed in the precious blood. Think of this delightful Truth of God, desponding Christian, and let your countenance be sad no more! Your eye of faith is dim, your evidences are very slender, your graces are at a low ebb, but you are completely forgiven, absolved and acquitted at this moment, if your soul rests upon the Rock of Ages! You are completely justified at this moment, despite your sins. Wearing your Savior's righteousness, you stand all beauteous in the eyes of God at this very moment--the words of Solomon to the spouse are the words of Christ to you though you are vexed with a thousand cares--"You are all fair My love: there is no spot in you."

Covered with His righteousness and washed in His blood, even the pure and holy eyes of God can find no fault in you, and, as a consequence of this, you are this moment accepted! "He has not beheld iniquity in Jacob, neither has He seen perverseness in Israel." "Who shall lay anything to the charge of God's elect?" God does not look upon you with any anger. Though your heart may be struggling and tormented with sin, yet if you are resting upon God's Son, the love of God is flowing out to you in a stream which never can be stopped. Think of this sweet thought and let your soul be filled with the perfume of it! Loved of God now, the object of the almighty affection of the Blessed One are you NOW.

No, more than this, you are not only accepted--you are in union with Christ now. Beloved Believer, can you realize it? You are a member of His body, of His flesh and of His bones! There is a vital union at this instant between you and the Lord of Glory! The life-blood flows from Him, the Head, to you. And at this moment, whether in your worst state of feeling or your best, you are now one with Jesus, by eternal union--ONE! I would to God we realized our present privileges! We are thinking about the Heaven that is to come and forgetting the Heaven below. The first we should do--but the second we should not leave undone. The men of Divine Grace find that the fruits of Paradise hang over the wall and they begin to pluck and eat them before they pass the gates of pearl. Come, Christian, "Now is the accepted time; behold, now is the day of salvation." Since Jesus is accepted, so you are even now. Live upon your present privileges and be glad!

Remember that wherever there is present privilege there is also a present duty to be performed and so I touch a string which I made to sound just now. Since "now is the accepted time" with sinners, now is the accepted time for you to work, O Christian. I know what you intend to do--you have vast plans and machinery. My Brother, I do not care what you mean to do tomorrow, but I do care about what you intend to do today. Oh, those daydreams of ours! We are always intending in a year or two's time to be such valorous defenders of the faith, such good soldiers of Christ, such good winners of souls!

My dear Brothers and Sisters, what are you doing now? There flies that moment! What does it bear upon its wings? Another drop of the stream of time is passed away--what action of yours is reflected on its crystal surface? Are you doing anything now? "I do not know," says one, "I do not know that I can do anything just now. When the service is bro- ken up, I may get home and then try to do something." I would pray you remember that, "now is the accepted time," and therefore seek now to get your heart warm. And when the service is over, think you hear the now, and begin to speak to those in the pew, or on the way home talk to any person you may meet with. And then, tomorrow, do not say, "Sunday is over and I cannot do any good on the week-day," but think you hear the clarion sound of this word now!

You have a sister unsaved, pray for her now. You have a brother unconverted, write to him if you cannot speak to him and do it now. There is a court, a blind alley, which needs visiting. A dying man who needs instruction--do it now. Do you feel you have a talent? Use it now. You think you will have a better sphere in ten years' time? I pray you get a sphere now, for now is the day of salvation! I say again, I do not care what you do with your tomorrow. If you will but give God your now, your tomorrows will be all right. For duty, then, let the Christian prize the "now."

One more thought. The Christian remembers that now he may die. What is his prospect now? Let him take courage. If his Lord should come now, he has his loins girt about and his lamp well trimmed and he is ready to enter into the supper. He will not be overtaken as by a thief, but his Lord, when He comes, shall find him watching--and should death come before the Advent, then he can say, "Now shall I enter into my rest. Now shall I see the face of my Lord Jesus without a veil to hide Him and I shall be with Him supremely blest."

The glorious Advent or the bliss of Heaven is your prospect now! Not that you will go to Heaven if you die in twenty years' time--but if you die now--if the hand of death should take you in the street, or you should feel its numbing influence while you are in the pew! Now the celestial band shall bear you to the sublimities of Glory and introduce you to the Presence of Him whom you love! Now, Christian, rejoice, now labor, now live at the foot of the Savior's Cross!

II. May the Master give us power on the second point to deal with "NOW" AS IT RESPECTS THE SINNER. The great mischief of most men is that they procrastinate. It is not that they resolve to be damned, but that they resolve to be saved tomorrow. It is not that they reject Christ forever, but that they reject Christ today. And truly they might as well reject Him forever, as continue perpetually to reject Him "now."

Sinner, let me put your "now" before you as a man. You must soon pass away and be forgotten, like the flowers that withered in autumn and the insects which flitted through the summer hours. Now, then, is your time to think about eternity and to prepare yourself to meet your God. "See to your business first, James," said a careful father--"get a good trade and after that, look to your religion." There spoke a FOOL who knew not that infinite Wisdom has commanded, "Seek you first the kingdom of God and His righteousness. And all these things shall be added unto you." Would you give God the tail end of your life? Take care lest you have no old age at all! For many candles are blown out as soon as lit.

Would you, as a lamb, be Satan's? And when you are withered and worn out, shall the lean skeleton of tottering weakness be brought and laid upon the altar? Be it not so! Let your flower be plucked in the bud and put into the hand of Jesus. God grant you Grace to seek Him in the days of your youth, for the promise is, "They that seek Me early shall find Me." As a man, I charge you, since there is only a "day of salvation" before the sun goes down and the black night of eternal ruin shall come upon you, lay hold upon the hope that is set before you!

As a sinner, I also address you concerning this "now." Now is the day of salvation--you need it now. God is angry with you now. You are condemned already! It is not only the torment of Hell you have to dread, but if you have your senses, you would tremble at your present state. Now without God. Now without hope. Now an alien from the commonwealth of Israel! Now dead in trespasses and sins. Now in danger of the wrath to come! You need a Savior this morning, young man! Young woman, I do not charge you to store up medicine against the maladies of twenty years from now--it is the sickness of today of which I would gladly have you cured this very morning! It is not to look after a danger which shall press upon you when you grow old that I exhort you, but now you are on the brink of the precipice!

Now, therefore, you need to be saved! And here comes the beauty of my text--as a sinner under the Gospel, I pray you to remember--"Now is the accepted time"! The most of my unconverted hearers do not believe this. I know what you are saying. You say, "I have had a great many thoughts about religion." But why do you not believe in Christ now? "Well," you say, "I will endeavor to think seriously of it." But what will be the result of your thinking? After you have thought ever so much, do you imagine you will think yourself into salvation? If the Gospel command were, "Think and be saved," I would cheerfully allow you a month's thinking. But the command is, "Believe in the Lord Jesus Christ," and, "Now is the accepted time."

"But, Sir, I do not think such things should be done in a hurry." A hurry? What does David say? "I made haste and delayed not to keep Your commandments." A hurry? When a man is on the edge of damnation and on the borders of the grave? Do not talk of hurry, Sir--when it is a case of life and death. Let us fly swift as a flash of lightning. "Well, but I do not feel prepared." Do you think that disobeying God will make you more prepared? If you have lived a month without believing, you have lived a month in sin! Do you think when you have sinned more, you will be better prepared to obey the command which comes to you, "Believe now in the Lord Jesus Christ"? "Yes, but my heart feels so hard."

Dear Friend, do you think you will be able to soften it between this and next week, or next month, or next year? Is there anything in the Word of God which leads you to believe that you can, in any way, soften your own heart? Is not this a mighty work of Grace? And when the text says, "Now is the accepted time," does not this suppose that even if you have a hard heart, still it is true that NOW is the accepted time? "Well, but," says one, "I do not feel convicted enough." That is to say, dear Friend, you do not think that "now is the accepted time." You think that another time when you get more convicted will be the accepted time.

Here is a quarrel between God and you. He says "Now," you say, "No, no, it cannot be true! When I am more convicted, then will be the time." My dear Friend, are you not altogether mistaken? The likelihoods are that you never will be more convicted than now, if you are brought now to think upon these things. Your heart will certainly grow harder in the course of time--softer, never! I never heard the case of a man whose heart was made softer by delay. "Yes, but I should like to get home and pray." My text does not say it will be the accepted time when you get home and pray. It says, "Now!" And as I find you are "now" in this pew, "now" is the accepted time. If you trust Christ now, you will be accepted--if now you are enabled to throw yourself simply into the hands of Christ--now is the accepted time between God and you.

"Well," says another, "it does seem strange to think that I shall be saved this morning--there must be a little time occupied in it, surely?" The text says, "Now is the accepted time," it does not say, "There is an accepted time lasting through a period of weeks or months in which we pump ourselves up into a state of Grace." No! "Now," in a moment, acceptance is given. "But do you really mean it" says one, "that I, as I am, trusting Christ this morning, without any previous preparation whatever, shall be accepted?" My dear Friend, it is not what I mean--it is what the Scripture means. "Now is the accepted time; behold, now is the day of salvation." The moment a sinner trusts in Christ, he is saved and if you trust Him now, it is the day of salvation to you!

Will you kindly look at that text--just open your Bibles now and look at it--you especially who are unconverted-- whether my hearers or readers! It has two fingerposts to point to it--two beholds. "Behold, now is the accepted time." Now, stop and look at that. Do you believe it? Say, "Yes," or "No." There is another "Behold." "Behold, now is the day of salvation." Do you believe that? I have asked you to look at the text, because I want you to look in its face and, if you dare, say, "That is a lie"--no, you do not dare say that! Then if you do not dare to say so, away must go, in a single moment, all those excuses which you make about a hard heart, not being convicted enough, praying, reading, preparing, and so on.

Now, just as the clock ticks, not as an event to take place during a quarter of an hour, but in a moment the whole thing is done--"Now is the day of salvation." And what do you say to this? Does God the Holy Spirit now lead your soul to say, "Gracious Lord, I trust my soul with You now"? Oh, it is all done! Fly up to Heaven, angels! Bear the tidings! Tell the spirits who look down, anxiously watching for the spreading kingdom of the Savior, that another heir of Glory is born, another prodigal has returned to his Father's house! Now! Now! Now! O God, let conquering Grace get the victory!

How my soul has longed over this text! And now when I get at it, I cannot handle it as I would. But, if I might, I would gladly take some of you by the hand--think that I have your hand now--and I would put this to you! I may never have another opportunity of preaching this text in your ears, for you may be gone before there is another season to hear. "Will you be made whole?" "Can you believe?" "If you can believe, all things are possible to him that believes." Old Na-bal said to David, "There are many servants nowadays that break away every man from his master." A bad old fellow, but he spoke a good sentence there without knowing it. Are there not some here who will break away from their old master?

Are there not some who would gladly be servants of Christ and no longer servants of Satan? O Souls, if God has made you willing to break with Satan, to lay hold on Christ, this is not a day in which Christ will deny you, for He has expressly said He will accept you now, for, "Now is the accepted time." But, Sir, I am a harlot steeped up to the throat in vice." Still, "Now is the accepted time." Ah, but I have grown gray, Sir. I am seventy or eighty and have lived in sin all these years." Yes, but. "Now is the accepted time." Do you believe it or not? "Oh, I have refused the invitation a thousand times over." Yes, but still, still the abundant Grace of God says, "Now, is the accepted time." I would to God some of you would decide this very morning, this very morning in your pew where you are now sitting. Now, O Spirit of the living God, waken those whom You have chosen and set apart unto eternal life.

I have not time now to dwell on the other two points. We will merely, therefore, hint at them.

III. Now IN HEAVEN! Can you think of it? NOW in Heaven! They now delight in the society of Christ. They are now blest with communion with all the glorified spirits. They are now resting from their labors, their toils, their sufferings. They are now full of joys, while with their golden harps they sing. They are just now satisfied with the favor and full of the goodness of the Lord. They are now knowing what they knew not here, knowing even as they are known.

They are now more than conquerors, waving their palm branches. They are now safely shut in from all fear of danger. They are now perfect, without taint of sin or remnant of corruption. They are now supremely blest. I merely point the finger where my wing cannot carry me and where my eyes cannot see. Such are your friends who have departed. Your wife is there now. Your little infant children are there. Your brother is there, your grandsire is there and we, if we should now die, blessed be the name of God, many of us should know what they know and taste what they enjoy in an instant!

IV. But this is a dreary thought--Now IN HELL! Some of my hearers who listened to me last year and in the years that are past, are now--NOW--in Hell! Now, where no hope can come! Now, where no Gospel shall ever be preached! Now, where they bitterly regret their wasted Sabbaths and despised opportunities! Now, where memory holds a dreadful reign, reminding them of all their sins! Now, "Where their worm dies not, and the fire is not quenched"--where they gnaw their fire-tormented tongues in vain! Now, where God's fury is manifested to the full in Tophet's hideous fire!

Now, where devils, once their tempters, become their tormentors! Now, where sinners who kept jovial company, help to increase the doleful misery of sighs and groans and weeping and gnashing of teeth! Now, accursed of God, accursed forever and ever! And within a moment, that may be the lot of every sinner here! Within the twinkling of an eye, there is not a man or woman among us out of Christ who may not know this. One drop of blood goes wrong--a thousand chances, as we say--may cause it and Hell is your portion.

Every anatomist knows that hundreds of times in an hour, through the internal economy of the human frame, our life is in danger. No, there is not a second in which it is not so. "Great God! On what a feeble thread hang everlasting things!"--

"Our life contains a thousand springs, And dies if one is gone. Strange that a harp of a thousand strings Should keep in tune so long."

While we are in this danger, we are passing on to our doom--

"We nightly pitch our moving tent A day's march nearer home." But where is that home to be with you unconverted ones?

When the express trains first began to run to Scotland there was seen at the station, one evening, a gentleman tall and thin, whose cheek had the consumptive mark upon it. The porters asked him several questions about his luggage, of which there was a good deal. And when he had been asked several times by different persons, another came up and said, "Where are you going, Sir?" Being of short temper and in great haste, he said, "To Hell!" A servant of Christ passed by that moment and heard the answer. He sought to get in the same carriage and did so, but at the other end of it.

Now this gentleman was talking very freely to different persons upon common topics and the man thought, "I will get a word in if I can." So he joined in the general tenor of the conversation till they alighted at a refreshment station, when, taking the opportunity, he said to the gentleman, "When do you expect to get to the end of your journey?" "Oh," said he, "I am going to cross at such-and-such a town by the boat tonight and hope to get to my journey's end about twelve o'clock tomorrow morning."

The man said, "I think you misunderstand my question. You said when the porter asked you just now where you were going, that you were going to a very different place." "Ah, yes, I remember I did," said the gentleman, "but I am sometimes very hasty." The other said to him, "Was it true? Are you going to Hell? If so, when do you expect to get there?" And he began to talk to him about that sickness which he could see so certainly in his cheeks and warned him that unless he sought another road and fled to Christ, the only Refuge, he would certainly reach that dreadful end.

There are some in this place, who if they were labeled this morning as to where they are going, would have to be directed "to Hell." You know that this is the case! And when will you get to your journey's end? Some here may live another fifty years. I pray God that that question of mine may haunt you and if it is never blessed to you before, may it be then--"When will you yet to your journey's end? When will you arrive in Hell?"

This morning some of you may, in your hearts, say, "I am journeying there, but, by the Grace of God, I have come to a dead halt and not another inch will I go! Lord, make me ready to go to Heaven! Give me Grace now to trust the Savior that I may live." May God bless these feeble words of mine to His glory and your profit. Amen.

The Man With The Measuring Line

DELIVERED ON SUNDAY MORNING, DECEMBER 11, 1864,
BY C. H. SPURGEON,
AT THE METROPOLITAN TABERNACLE, NEWINGTON.

"I lifted up my eyes again and looked and behold a man with a measuring line in his hand. So I said, Where are you going? And he said to me, To measure Jerusalem, to see what is its width and what is the length. And there was the angel who talked with me, going out; and another angel was coming out to meet him, who said to him, "Run, speak to this young man, saying, 'Jerusalem shall be inhabited as towns without walls because of the multitude of men and livestock in it. For I,' says the Lord, 'will be a wall of fire around her and I will be the glory in her midst.'" -- Zechariah 2:1-5.

IT is evident that this vision and prophecy graciously reveal the future history of Jerusalem. You may spiritualize, if you will, and say that Jerusalem signifies the Church--but I pray you not forget the literal meaning of such words as these in the twelfth verse--"The Lord shall take possession of Judah as His inheritance in the holy land and will again choose Jerusalem." Jerusalem is spoken of and Jerusalem is meant. A man with a measuring line is about to measure the length and breadth of the city. He appears to be interrupted in his work by another angel who foretells that so greatly shall Jerusalem extend that she will be as a town without walls, for the number of men and livestock that shall be in it.

This prophecy has not as yet been fulfilled--it may have had some partial fulfillment in those times of peace before the coming of the Savior, but even then Jerusalem was surrounded by a triple wall. And though it is true that there was a large suburban population, yet the city was not then, "as towns without walls," nor was the Glory of God in the midst of her in any eminent degree. I believe this passage refers to a happy and glorious future yet to come when the city of Jerusalem shall have no walls, except the protection of the Lord, but shall be extended far and wide.

The Jewish people and their royal city shall remain the center of the manifestations of Divine Glory, just as the city of London still remains the center of the metropolis. But the nations of the earth shall be joined unto the Lord so that while Jerusalem remains the city of the Great King, the faithful among the people of all nations shall be, as it were, a suburban population to the chosen city and the kingdom of Messiah shall extend far and wide. Jerusalem will be rebuilt in more than her former splendor. The Jews will be restored to their own land. And Messiah will reign as a prince of the house of David.

We cannot understand many portions of Scripture except upon this belief. If it is so, it appears according to this prophecy that God shall be the protection of this great city and the glory in the midst of her. All her sons shall be gathered from their distant wandering places. And where they have associated themselves with Antichrist, they shall hear the voice which says, "Deliver yourself, O Zion, that dwell with the daughter of Babylon." Christ Himself shall fulfill His promise, "Lo, I come." The nations shall be judged. God shall shake His hands over all lands and give them as a spoil to His people. Zion shall sing and rejoice--her Lord and King shall dwell in the midst of her--many nations shall join themselves to Jehovah and He, from shore to shore, shall reign while all flesh is silent before Him because He is raised up out of His holy habitation.

I am not given to prophesying and I fear that the fixing of dates and periods has been exceedingly injurious to the whole system of pre-millennial teaching. But I think I clearly see in Scripture that the Lord Jesus Christ will come--so far I go and take my stand--that He will come personally to reign upon this earth. At His coming it appears clear to me that He will gather together the Jewish people. Jerusalem shall become the metropolis of the new empire which shall then extend from pole to pole, from the river even to the ends of the earth. If this is a correct interpretation of prophecy, you may read the whole of this chapter through and understand it--you have the key to every sentence! Without such a belief I see not how to interpret the Prophet's meaning.

Dear Friends, we may sometimes refresh our minds with a prospect of the kingdom which is soon to cover all lands and make the sun and moon ashamed by its superior glory! We are not to indulge in prophesies as some do, making them their spiritual food, their meat and drink. But still we may take them as choice morsels and special delicacies set upon the table. They are condiments which may often give a sweeter taste, or, if you will, a greater pungency and savor to other doctrines. Prophetic views light up the crown of Jesus with a superior splendor.

They make His Manhood appear illustrious as we see Him still in connection with the earth--to have a kingdom here as well as there--to sit upon a throne here as well as in yonder skies! To subdue His adversaries even upon this Aceldama, as in the realm of spirits! To make even this poor earth upon which the trail of the serpent is so manifest a place where the Glory of the Lord shall be revealed and all flesh shall see it together. If our view of prophecy is the correct one, it seems to be in perfect harmony with all the doctrines of the Gospel.

God certainly did elect His people the Jews. He made a Covenant with His servant Abraham and although you will remind us that this was only a temporal covenant, I would remind you that it was the type of the spiritual one and it would be an unhappy reflection for us if the typical Covenant should prove to be only temporary as well as temporal! If that came to an end and if God cast away, in any sense, the people whom He did foreknow, it might foretell to us the ill foreboding that perhaps He might cast away His spiritual seed also--and that those who were chosen as the spiritual seed of Abraham might yet be cut off from the olive into which they had been grafted. If the natural branches are cast away forever, why not the grafted branches, too?

But here is our joy--the God who swore unto His servant Abraham that to him and to his seed would He give the land forever has not gone back from His word--they shall possess the land. Their feet shall joyously tread its fruitful acres yet again. They shall sit, every man, under his own vine and under his own fig tree and none shall make them afraid. And so the spiritual seed to whom the spiritual heritage is given as by a Covenant of Salt shall also possess their heritage forever and of their rightful portion no robber shall despoil them.

Now, I think it cannot be said that I have avoided the immediate meaning of the passage before us and that I have selected the vision as a text merely to accommodate it to my own purpose. You have now before you the intention and mind of the Spirit of God, so far as I am able to perceive it. And having spoken thus far upon it, I now feel at liberty to interpret the vision in what is commonly called a more spiritual sense, begging you, however, not to think that I make the spiritual sense override the sense I have already given, for the mind of the Spirit in the passage is ever to be respected far beyond any human accommodation.

And though the accommodation may seem to be less historical and more suitable for Sunday food to the people of God, yet remember God's sense stands first and our sense is only to be regarded and respected as it stands in harmony with other portions of Holy Writ. My heart is so taken up with the present state of my Church and congregation that I feel moved to use my text in its application to us and I think it may well bear such an application. May God teach it and bless it to us!

First, dear Friends, I want you to lift up your eyes with Zechariah and see the man with the measuring line. Secondly open your ears with Zechariah and hear the voice of the prophesying angel. And then, thirdly, I want you to go your ways and publish abroad the commands of this angel.

I. First, then, LET US SEE THE MAN WITH THE MEASURING LINE IN HIS HAND. All Zechariah's visions are remarkably simple. They are not like Isaiah's when he saw the Lord sitting upon a throne, high and lifted up. Nor or they like Ezekiel's when he beheld living creatures with four faces and wheels full of eyes. Zechariah had not imagination enough to be capable of beholding with due appreciation visions so complicated and mysterious. He was not the proper instrument of God for the Revelation of these more mysterious matters. But the Lord had a place for him and a vision for him, too.

How sweet to be a servant of God in any position! He sees simply a man, an ordinary architect, going forth with a measuring line to measure the city of Jerusalem--a very simple sight--and without any stretch of the imagination you can all picture the man with his line. If this man in the text is to be viewed as an angel, commissioned by God to take measurements of that city, he would be sure to do it accurately and his measurements would be instructive, could he re- veal them to us. Since they are hidden from our eyes, let it be enough for us to perceive that the city has measurements-- has a settled length and breadth--and that the measurements can be taken and that we have Divine authority for asserting that they have been taken.

This leads us to contemplate the doctrine of predestinating love, with its line of Divine Grace, and its plans of wisdom. God's city of Jerusalem is not to be built haphazardly. The line marks out and measures how long the wall shall be and where the corner shall be placed. And how far the other wall shall be carried and where it shall come to an end. The towers are counted, the bulwarks are considered. Every single item and particular of the sacred architecture of the Church of God is written down in the decree of the Most High. Every man has his plan and shall not the Most High God?

He is esteemed to be a simpleton who begins to erect a building with no sort of idea how it will look at the end! Who, but a fool waits till the topstone is brought out before he conceives in his mind any sort of idea of what the building will be like? You would never employ a person without foresight as an architect. And if a man were foolish enough to do this with his own building, all who heard of it would make it the theme of laughter.

It cannot be supposed, therefore, to be so with God! Your belief in His wisdom supposes that He has a plan, no, necessitates that there should be a design in the Divine mind! Moreover, you cannot separate the thought of Omniscience from God. If God is Omniscient, He knows the end from the beginning. He sees in its appointed place not merely the cornerstone which He has laid in fair colors--in the blood of His dear Son--but He beholds in their ordained position each of the chosen stones taken out of the quarry of nature and polished by His Grace! He sees the whole from corner to cornice, from base to roof, from foundation to pinnacle.

He has in His mind a clear knowledge of every stone which shall be laid in its prepared space and how vast the edifice shall be and when the topstone shall be brought forth with shouts of, "Grace! Grace unto it!" Deny the decree of election and what do you see? You see the work of Grace without God's superintendence in it. What would creation be if God had not been absolutely present there? Can we conceive of a single creature formed without the creating purpose of God? Is there a fish in the sea, or a fowl in the air which was left to chance for its creation? No! In every bone, joint and muscle, sinew, gland and blood vessel you mark the Presence of God working everything according to the design of infinite Wisdom.

Shall God be present in creation, ruling over all and not in Grace? Shall Grace be left in a state of chaos while creation is ordered by the Most High? Look at Providence! Who knows not that not a sparrow falls to the ground without your Father? Even the hairs of your head are all numbered. Every dark and bending line meets in the center of your love. It is our joy to believe that the measuring line is used in our trials and our troubles. If He ordained the number ten, who can make it eleven? If He filled the cup but half-full, even Satanic agency cannot fill it to the brim. God weighs the mountains of our griefs in scales and the hills of our tribulation in balances.

And shall there be a God in Providence and not in Grace? What? Shall He ride in the chariot of the clouds and put a bit into the mouth of the tempest and rein in the wild steeds of the storm and yet shall He leave the greater work of His Grace--His third dominion, the grandest and the best--to the will of man, to the fickle choice of the creature? Shall He make the glorious salvation of Jesus an unsettled thing to be kicked about as a football by the free agency of man? Shall Divinity stand as lacquer to the creature's changeful choice? Never! He will have mercy on whom He will have mercy! He will have compassion on whom He will have compassion!

And at the last it shall be seen that in every chosen vessel of mercy Jehovah did as He willed with His own. And in every separate instance of salvation and in every part and portion of the work of Grace the Lord reigned as King forever and did as He willed and glorified His own name. I see a man with a measuring line and I rejoice to see him and thank God that it is written, "The foundation of God stands sure, having this seal, The Lord knows them that are His." It is just possible that the man in the text was nothing but a man. At any rate, we may often see apparitions of men with measuring lines. And while I have an intense reverence to the angel with the measuring line, I must confess an entire dislike to the man with the measuring line.

How often, Brethren, have we seen men with the measuring line endeavoring to estimate the length and breadth of God's true Church? Some of them take a very long line and they begin to calculate how many Protestants, Roman Catholics, and members of the Greek Church there may be throughout the world. Then they write down all these millions as being Christians! Now, we beg to differ from the estimate--how we wish we could agree with it!

Glad enough should we be to hope that these were all true members of the Church of God! But when we remember the errors with which one section of the Church is polluted almost beyond hope. When we remark the absence of all spirituality in others. When we see how the mass of nominal Christians are living without God and without Christ. When we reflect upon the many criminals, harlots and open sinners who would, according to this rule, be called Christians, we beg to remind the man with the measuring line, "They are not all Israel which are of Israel"! And although they may all lie upon the threshing floor, "What is the chaff to the wheat? says the Lord." The field is the world, but among the wheat many tares are growing--multitudes are gathered here, not in the valley of decision, but in the plains of outward profession--and a separating day must come!

If we were to measure in this way, we should certainly be deluded--we should find Christians whom we could not trust! Christians who did not know their creed! Christians who did not rejoice in the name of Christ--Christians without faith, without hope and strangers to the commonwealth of Israel! Christians merely in name cannot be Christians, for, "Except a man is born again, he cannot see the kingdom of God." "He that believes on Him is not condemned: but he that believes not is condemned already, because he has not believed in the name of the only begotten Son of God."

Again, I very frequently see another man with a measuring line. He is of a very sad countenance and looks out upon the universe through blue spectacles. He will never fall into the error of the first man but delights in the opposite extreme. "Oh," he says, as he wrings his hands in a kind of delicious misery, "the people of God are a handful, a remnant, a child might write them." He likes right well that hymn--

"Dear Shepherd, of Your chosen few, Your former mercies here renew." He wishes his minister to preach from, "Fear not, little flock." Or this one, "Strait is the gate and narrow is the way, which leads unto life and few there are that find it." Sometimes Despondency takes the shape of a man's fearing that he himself shall not enter--now there is something humble about that and therefore it is bearable--but in frequent instances, Despondency is married to Pride and then it is not despondency about themselves, but about all the rest of the human family. They are doubtless the men and "wisdom will die with them."

They hear of backsliders and they conclude that all professors will backslide. They have read a story of some famous minister who stained his character and they believe that all ministers are mere pretenders. They hear of Mr. Liberal, who was noted for his generosity and for his zeal in the cause of Christ and yet he turned out to be generous with other men's money and to be thought little better than a thief. And Despondency shakes her head and says, "I told you so--all men are liars." "Lord! Are there few who shall be saved?" is the constant question of Despondency.

And every day she lives, she keeps making the measuring line a little shorter till perhaps the day will come when Despondency shall prophesy the destruction of the Christian faith, the return of the Papacy and the outpouring of the vials and say, "The faithful fail from among men, Zion is under a cloud." A day of clouds and of thick darkness, is the only description of the present age which this spirit allows to be correct. Perhaps Despondency herself may die in the dark, believing that she is not included in the line of the Covenant of Grace.

Well, now, I must confess I am thankful that God has not set our desponding brother to measure His Zion! I am grateful that He is pleased to keep that in His own hands, or it might be woe forever to many of the brightest of the Lord's people. Certain men occasionally come across my path who carry a measuring line which was originally made either by one called Mr. False Experience or Mr. Proud Experience. These Brethren will not believe any to be Christians who have not experienced precisely the same emotions, doubts, fears, trembling, horrors, terrors, ecstasies, delights or raptures which they themselves have felt!

They get hold of every Christian professor and they do with him as Procrustes did with men in his day--they take him into their bedchamber and there is their bed of experience--the exact length that it should be. If the Brother to be judged is not long enough to reach from head to foot, then they have a rack ready for him and they will pull his limbs a little. Or, if he should happen to be rather longer than themselves, then their pride is more aggrieved, still, and it is likely enough that a sharp two-edged sword of censure will take off his head so as to accommodate him to the length of the couch.

Perhaps you know certain professors of this kind and if you live in their midst the only path of wisdom will be to hold your peace. They are supposed to have received information by special revelation from on high that their particular rut and that rut alone, leads to the land where sorrow is unknown. See them put on their spectacles and sit as a sort of jury to investigate a candidate for Church membership. This poor young man only professes to have been converted some three months. If they entertain his case at all it is with the decided determination ultimately to reject him. Thus they begin with him, "Have you ever experienced such-and-such law-work in your soul? Were you ever led to curse God and to feel the awful corruptions of your nature, tempting you to blaspheme the Holy Spirit?"

The poor young man can only say he knows himself to be a sinner lost by nature and saved by Grace through faith in Christ. They shake their heads and tell him it is a mere natural, notional faith. As he has not known the law-work which they have known, he is of no good whatever. They pretend to hope for him but they mean all the while that they do not believe in him an atom.

Another class of emotional religionists steer by another star. They question the enquirer from another catechism, "Have you been carried up to the third Heaven, like Paul? Can you say, 'Whether in the body, or out of the body, I cannot tell, God knows' "? Such Brethren sometimes will put such questions as this--"Do you feel any pleasure whatever when you are with your friends? Can you take a walk in the fields and find enjoyment in the singing of birds and in the foliage of the trees?" And if you answer, "Yes, thank God, I can," ah, they are sickened at you! You are not spiritually-minded, if you can look at works of art and admire them. If you can view the works of God in creation and feel any pleasure they are astonished at you and think you carnal!

As for themselves, they have attained to such a superfine degree of spirituality that they have purified all the common sins out of themselves as well as the "sense." Dr. Watts says--

"May purge ourselves from sense and sin, As Christ the Lord is pure."

He meant by "sense" feeling, mere carnal feeling. But I am afraid that some have really purged themselves from sense in the ordinary acceptance of the term and might very well claim that their spirituality was not at all akin to worldly wisdom, for it is remarkably akin to absurdity and cant. Now, I thank God that the measuring line is not in the hands of the experimentalists and bless my Master that it is written, "Whoever believes that Jesus is the Christ is born of God." And, "We know that we have passed from death unto life because we love the Brethren."

I have also seen the measuring line in the hands of others--Doctrinalists. Yes. And their line has five marks which were originally made by John Calvin. And if your opinions do not square exactly to the standard, you are cut off from all part and lot in the blessings of vital godliness. Zion is certainly built according to the arrangement of the five points and therefore if any Brother or Sister does not comprehend and receive them all, he is not a weak Believer, but according to the measuring line of our rigid friends, he is not a Believer at all!

You know, Brethren, that there is no soul living who holds more firmly to the Doctrines of Grace than I do and if any man asks me whether I am ashamed to be called a Calvinist, I answer, I wish to be called nothing but a Christian. But if you ask me do I hold the doctrinal views which were held by John Calvin, I reply, I do in the main hold them and rejoice to avow it. But, my dear Friends, far be it from me even to imagine that Zion contains none within her walls but Calvinistic Christians--or that there are none saved who do not hold our views. Most atrocious things have been spoken about the character and spiritual condition of John Wesley, the modern prince of Arminians. I can only say concerning him, that while I detest many of the doctrines which he preached, yet for the man himself I have a reverence second to no Wesleyan.

And if there were wanted two Apostles to be added to the number of the twelve, I do not believe that there could be found two men more fit to be so added than George Whitfield and John Wesley. The character of John Wesley stands beyond all imputation for self-sacrifice, zeal, holiness and communion with God. He lived far above the ordinary level of common Christians and was one of whom the world was not worthy. I believe there are multitudes of men who cannot see these Truths of God, or, at least cannot see them in the way in which we put them, who nevertheless have received Christ into their hearts and are as dear to the heart of the God of Grace as the soundest Calvinist out of Heaven.

I thank God we do not believe in the measuring line of any form of bigotry. I remember meeting with one who knew, yes, he knew how many children of God there were in the parish where he lived--there were exactly five. I was curious to know their names, and much to my amusement he began by saying, "There is myself." I stopped him at this point, with the query whether he was quite sure about the first one. Since then, his character has gone I know not where, but cer- tainly he will get on better without it than with it! Yet he was the first on his own list and a few others of his own black sort made up the five.

There were in the other places of worship to which he did not go, men whose characters for integrity and uprightness, yes, and for spirituality and prayerfulness, would have been degraded by being put into comparison with him. And yet he, he was set as judge in Israel and was to know exactly how many people of God were in the village! Oh, I bless God that we have learned to have very little respect for the vision of the man with the measuring line! When we see an angel with it, if such is the intention of the vision, we are glad enough. "The Lord knows them that are His." But when we see a man with it, we tell him that he must give us a warrant from God and show us how he is to know the elect by any other method than that laid down in Scripture--"By their fruits you shall know them"!

Notice that this vision soon departed. The Prophet does not seem to have dwelt long upon it. Almost as soon as it appeared it disappeared. Perhaps it is not a good thing for the people of God at any time to be much engaged in numbering the people. It is a question what was the particular sin of David in numbering the people. I will not enter into it just now, but I do fear that it is hard for us to number the people at any time without committing a sin--either the greatness of their number may lift us up and inflate us with pride or the littleness of their number may make us despond and doubt the strength of God.

The vision of the man with the measuring line is only to be looked upon for a moment and then it may depart. We therefore ask you to close your eyes to that and open your ears to the voice of that Covenant angel, who, interrupting the man, began to tell Zechariah good things concerning times to come.

II. From my text it appears, dear Friends, THAT WE ARE TO LOOK FOR A GREAT EXTENSION OF THE KINGDOM OF CHRIST. I hope we are to look for it now. Jerusalem shall be inhabited "as towns without walls." There are those in this place who remember when, if you crossed Blackfriars Bridge, you scarcely saw a house--as soon as you had crossed the bridge from London you were in the country at once. They still survive among us to see how this great city has not only swollen to this district, but has gone right on for miles and threatens to absorb mile after mile of the country.

Such an extension we are to expect in Christ's Church. It began with twelve Apostles. It was soon swollen to some four hundred Brethren. It was increased by three thousand more at the day of Pentecost. There were added afterwards to the Church daily of such as should be saved. The Gospel was preached throughout all regions. The children of God were found in Athens and Corinth, in Derbe and Lystra--from all parts of the earth the elect were gathered in. The kingdom extended. The Gospel was preached in Spain as well as Italy. It passed on to Gaul, it came to Great Britain. In these after days it still continues to spread.

A new world has been discovered, the religion of Jesus has been carried there. The emigrants who are peopling great islands of the southern seas bear with them the religion of Jesus Christ. Everywhere the kingdom grows. There is, as it were, a little core and center of Believers from among the Jewish people--but all around these there spreads a vast multitude of whom I might almost say that no man can number them. In our portion of Christ's Church it has been upon a small scale the same. Beginning with but a handful of men, God has been pleased to add hundred after hundred till He has extended our number to a great host.

But I do trust that what it is now is only the nucleus around which there is to be built a yet mightier Church. I would to God that now He might open the windows of Heaven and pour us out a blessing and so multiply us that the present thousands of this Church might be altogether lost in the numbers yet added. Truly, I would not ask it for this Church alone, but that other Churches all around may derive health from our prosperity--that God may raise up out of our loins Churches which shall be our sons and daughters--which shall again beget spiritual children, so that the kingdom of Christ may come and His name be exalted in the land! We are to look for an extension.

I want to encourage our elders and deacons and all our Brothers and Sisters to be looking for it. We have prayed for God's blessing--if ever a people prayed, we have. There has been an earnestness, I am sure, about the most of the Brethren here which cannot be without its reward. We have pleaded the name of Jesus even unto tears and God does not answer prayer if He does not send us a blessing! We have used His Son's name. We have pleaded His own promise. We have asked in faith, nothing doubting--and the blessing must come! Let us look for it and as sure as ever effect follows cause, so surely must we receive an extension of this Church!

It appears from the vision that the supply for all the number shall be as great as is required. "Jerusalem shall be inhabited as towns without walls for the multitude of men and livestock in it." The livestock are the provisions for the population. What is to be done with so large a Church? How are the converts to be seen after? How are the members to be fed with spiritual food? "As your day, so shall your strength be." Whatever provision the Church shall want, God will give it. Jehovah-Jireh is His name! This city of London has not overgrown its supplies--while we may be astonished at the population, we may be equally astonished at the provision.

It shall be so in the kingdom of Grace. God will raise up in the midst of any growing Church the proper men to look after the converts and see to their spiritual health. We have no need to be under any alarm in this respect--"All needful Grace will God bestow." Other friends are afraid that if there is so large an extension of the Church there will be many added to it who are not Believers and that consequently the Church may be increased, but not really strengthened. That too, is supplied in the text. "I, says the Lord, will be a wall of fire round her," both to keep out her enemies and to protect her from the incoming of false friends.

It is the Church's duty to see to it that she admits not unworthy persons knowingly, but her best guard is the Presence of God. It is written, "Of the rest no man dared join himself unto them." You remember the death of Ananias and Sapphira? It came in opportunely, just at the time when the Church was rapidly increased. That solemn judgment set a wall of fire round about the Church so that ungodly persons dared not hypocritically come to be united with them. And so will God do to His Church now.

The traveler, when he wishes to keep out the wild beasts, makes a ring of fire and then the lion is shut out. And God makes a ring of fire round His Church and the enemy is kept at a distance. China is said to be protected by a wall of stone. Old England is shielded by her wooden walls. But the Church of God has a better wall, still, for she has the Divine wall of fire! Her enemies cannot break through this to destroy the meanest of her citizens and her false friends shall say to themselves, "Who among us can dwell with the eternal burnings?" And so they shall keep back from a Church which is visibly sheltered and protected by the Presence of the Most High.

Observe, dear Friends, while the Church is thus supplied and thus protected, she does not lack for glory. Her glory, however, does not lie in her numbers, nor in the provision made for them, but in the Presence of God. "I will be the glory in her midst." Let us never cease to pray for this. Let the Church distinctly recognize that the Holy Spirit is in the midst of the Church now. When we sing--"Come, Holy Spirit, heavenly Dove," we mean rightly enough. But the words must not be understood to mean that the Spirit of God is not here--for He is in the midst of His Church always and He dwells among His people as the Shekinah in the temple! And your bodies are the temples of the Holy Spirit--God dwells in you!

Our prayer must be, "You that dwell between the cherubim, shine forth! Stir up Your strength and come and save us." The glory of a Church does not lie in the architecture of the place where she meets, nor in the eloquence of her minister, nor in the greatness of her number, nor the abundance of her wealth, nor the profundity of her learning. It lies in her God. "Let God arise, let His enemies be scattered." O God, when You went forth before Your people, when You marched through the wilderness, the earth shook! The heavens also dropped at the Presence of God--even Sinai itself was moved at the Presence of God, the God of Israel. Here, then, lies the Church's best hope! Let her make this the grand object of her prayer--that the Lord may be the glory in her midst!

To close up this point let us observe that doubtless at such seasons, Divine love shall be very sweetly enjoyed among all the members. For the eighth verse says--though I do not intend to push our investigations further than the text-- "He that touches you, touches the apple of My eye." We never know so much of our nearness and dearness to God as when we, in common with the rest of God's people, are visited with the joy of His Presence. How differently things look in the sunshine from the way in which they appear without it! Ride along this land of ours when the rain is pouring down, or the mists have gathered and what a dull, dreary wilderness it seems.

And these London streets! What a settlement for convicts they appear in the midst of our thick fogs! But let the sun shine forth as it did this morning! Let the mists be scattered, and then even the leafless trees have a golden light upon them and all nature rejoices and the meanest and poorest landscape becomes, after its sort, sublime! So when our hearts are dull and heavy and the Church of God is in the same state, how poor everything appears! But when the Lord shines forth and the Sun of Righteousness arises with healing in His wings, then the Doctrines of Grace, how precious! Then the ministry of the Gospel, how effectual! Then the means of Grace, how dear! The people of God, how estimable! The things of God, how delightful!

O that we may have this! We have a right to expect it! We do not deserve it, but God has promised it! Let us give Him no rest till we have it! Stop your measuring, O Despondency! Stop your measuring, O Bigotry! Stop your censures, you who cut off the people of God and hearken while the angel prophesies that the kingdom of Christ shall grow and increase, till, like a city without walls, Jerusalem shall have for her glory the Presence of the Lord--and for her boundary nothing but the will of the Most High!

III. I close with a few words on the third point and but a few. Where is this increase to come from, this great increase? It is to come from two sources indicated in the sixth and seventh verses. MULTITUDES ARE TO COME OUT OF THE WORLD. "Up, up! Flee from the land of the north, says the Lord, for I have spread you abroad as the four winds of the Heaven, says the Lord." God's chosen people are scattered here and there. There are many of them in this assembly of whom we know nothing--but God knows them. The preaching of the Gospel is a message to you to come forth!

That message is this: "Believe in the Lord Jesus Christ and you shall be saved." It comes to every soul among you with this commanding, but most consoling word, "He that believes and is baptized shall be saved." My Hearers, you know what believing means. It is simply trusting upon what Christ has done for sinners. "Now is the accepted time, now is the day of salvation." If you now trust Him, your many sins shall be forgiven you! You are a child of God and an heir of Heaven if you but trust Him!

Like prodigals you may have spent all your substance--spiritual hunger may have seized upon you--you would gladly fill your belly with the vain pleasures of the world, but you cannot. The Holy Spirit whispers in your heart, "Arise and go to your Father." Obey that heavenly whisper and though you are as yet a great way off, yet your Father sees you! He runs to meet you as you are! He falls upon your neck and kisses you, just as you are, undeserving and sinful. He cries to His servants, "Bring forth the best robe and put it on him." Will you trust that Father's love? Will you confide in it as it is set forth in the bleeding sacrifice of the Lord Jesus?

It is from you, O unconverted men and women, that we expect the greatest increase through the Spirit's power. We are looking for it and praying for it. I hope that the people of God this morning will be looking after you and when this sermon is done I hope they will speak with you, or if they cannot do so, at least pray for you. "Up, up, come forth"-- twice the shout is given--as if you were slumberers and needed to be awakened. "Up, everyone that thirsts, come to the waters." Here there are two "ups," as if you should be called with vehemence, with earnestness, with pleading--"Come forth!" The year is almost over--I pray God that a new year may not be begun by you in sin, but may God begin with you at the fall of the year and bring you now to know His power to save.

There is another class from which the Church is to get this increase, indicated in the next verse, "Deliver yourself O Zion, that dwell with the daughter of Babylon." There is a large number of this second class in this congregation. There are a number of you who believe in Christ but you dwell with the daughter of Babylon. If a census were taken of Christians according to the Church roll--and I do not know that it could be taken better by mortal man--then you must be put down as being of the world. When the Lord's Supper is spread and the Savior says, "Do this in remembrance of Me," you go away, or stay in the galleries.

You practically say to the Lord Jesus, "Lord, I will not do this in remembrance of You. I feel myself justified in disobeying Your command. I believe I have a valid reason for not doing what Your loving lips request me to do." I do not know if I put it in that shape that you will quite agree with your own assertion, because how can a man really have a justifiable reason for not doing what the Lord Jesus Christ expressly tells him to do? That word "separation" needs to ring in the ears of Christians, "Come out from among them and be you separate, says the Lord and touch not the unclean thing."

Though this is to be done practically by your actions, yet first and foremost it should be done by a distinct avowal of your Lord Jesus Christ and that avowal should be by Baptism and union with the Church. May God bless these remarks both to saints and sinners, for Jesus' sake. Amen.

Good Works In Good Company

DELIVERED ON SUNDAY MORNING, DECEMBER 18, 1864,
BY C, H. SPURGEON,
AT THE METROPOLITAN TABERNACLE, NEWINGTON.

"Come, my Beloved, let us go forth to the field. Let us lodge in the villages. Let us get up early to the vineyards. Let us see if the vine has budded, whether the grape blossoms are open and the pomegranates are in bloom. There will I give You my love. The mandrakes give off a fragrance, and at our gates are pleasant fruits, all manner new and old, which I have laid up for You, O my Beloved." Song of Solomon 7:11-13.

THE daughters of Jerusalem had been praising the Church as the fairest among women. They spoke of her with admiring appreciation, extolling her from head to foot. She wisely perceived that it was not easy to bear praise, and therefore she turned aside from the virgins to her Lord, making her boast not of her own loveliness, but of her being affianced to her beloved--"I am my Beloved's and His desire is toward me."

Solomon has said, in his Book of Proverbs, "As the fining pot for silver and the furnace for gold so is a man to his praise," meaning to teach us that praise is a serious ordeal. Very many men can bear censure and abuse, for their spirit rises so superior to it all that they are even profited thereby. But to be flattered, or even duly honored, is not so easy a thing to endure. The sun's warm beams made the traveler unbind his coat when the wind made him wrap it the more closely about him--the warmth of praise may make us relax our integrity--unless we are very watchful.

How many have been foolish enough, when standing upon a pinnacle, to look down and admire their own elevation and then their brain has reeled and they have fallen to their own shameful ruin? If we must at any time listen to the praises of our virtues. If we have served God so that the Church recognizes and rewards our usefulness, it is well for us to listen just as long as we are obliged to do, but no longer. And then let us turn aside at once to something more practical and more healthful to our own spirits.

The spouse seems abruptly to break off from listening to the song of the virgins and turns to her own husband-Lord, communion with whom is ever blessed and ever profitable. She says to Him, "Come, my Beloved, let us go forth into the field." To lodge in communion with Christ is a certain cure for every ill. Whether it is the bitterness of woe, or the overindulgence of earthly delight, close fellowship with the Lord Jesus will take the gall from the one and the satiety from the other. Live near to Jesus, Christian, and it is matter of secondary importance whether you live on the mountain of honor or in the valley of humiliation.

Live near to Jesus and the glowing coals of the furnace cannot consume you, nor the chill blasts of wintry affliction destroy you. Living near to Jesus you are covered with the wings of God and underneath you are the everlasting arms. If you read the three verses before us with attention, you will see that the Church all through anxiously desires fellowship with her Lord. It is, "Come with me," "let us." She will do nothing except as she is near to her beloved and in the enjoyment of His company.

I think she desires three things in her words. First, she desires to practice self-examination--she would go and see whether the vine flourishes and whether the tender grape blossoms appear. But it is self-examination with Him. She desires next to go into active service--it is to this end that she would lodge in the villages and go among the tender plants, that she may labor there, but it is with Him--"Let us go!" "Come with me!" In the third place, she has a store of fruits laid up for Him. Some things done and some things doing--things old and new--but they are all for Him and she will not mention them except for Him, much less bring them out for them to be enjoyed by a rival. "They are laid up for You, O my Beloved."

Let us try to make a personal matter of the text, this morning, and may God hear the desire of our hearts that we may have true fellowship with His own dear Son.

I. First, then, IS THE MATTER OF SELF-EXAMINATION. This is a most desirable and important business, but every Believer should desire to have communion with Christ while he is attending to it. Self-examination is of the utmost importance. No trader who would wish to succeed would neglect to keep his books. No farmer who wishes to prosper would be careless as to the state of his fields. No flock-master who would see his herds abundantly increase would leave his servants to care for them and fail to tend them with a watchful eye. If you would have your business prosper, see to it carefully yourself.

In soul-business it is of no use taking anything for granted where there are so many temptations to self-deception in our own hearts--where so many around us are deceived and are willing to help us to be deceived, too. And where Satan sedulously and craftily seeks to cry to us, "Peace, peace," where there is no peace--it is of the first and last importance that we should search ourselves whether we are in the faith and whether, being in the faith, our graces are growing, our faith increasing, and our love deepening.

Well does the spouse suggest that she should see whether the vine flourishes, whether the tender grape blossoms have appeared and the pomegranates budded forth--our spiritual vineyard needs perpetual watchfulness. While you are attending to this important business, see to it at the same time that you keep up your communion with Christ, for you will never know so well the importance of self-examination as when you see Him! Mark Him there--fastened to the accursed tree--wearing the crown of thorns all set with ruby drops of His own blood! Look at His griefs--if repenting tears do not blind you! Behold His awful agonies! Gaze into that visage more marred than that of any man and stay awhile and listen to the heart-rending shriek, "Eloi! Eloi! Lama sabachthani?" And did Christ suffer all this that souls might be saved?

Then surely, my Soul, it should be your chief business to see that you have an interest in Him. What? Shall I miss that which is purchased with such a price? When such a crimson stream from Christ's own heart flows to cleanse away sin, shall I think it a matter of no account whether I am cleansed or not? When that head which once was reverenced by angels, is now crowned with the thorns of mockery and cruelty, shall I not use all the thoughts of my head and brain to find out whether I am one with Christ, and a partaker of His passion? That cannot be a little heritage which Christ has purchased with such agonies--let me fear lest I should lose it!

That cannot be a slight evil which cost my Savior such griefs--let me search myself to see whether I am delivered from it. I am sure, Beloved, you cannot have a better candle to look into the secret recesses of your soul than a candle lit at the fire of Jesus' love. Know His love for you and all His griefs on your behalf and you will charge your own heart after this fashion--"See to it that you make sure work as to your interest in Jesus--that you are really one with Him. Be sure that your faith in Him is genuine and that you shall be found in Him in peace at the day of His appearing."

Self-examination, however, is very laborious work--the text hints at it. It does not say, "Let us go," but "Let us get up." Self-examination is ever up-hill work. It is by no means a pleasant task. It is one from which flesh recoils, for the flesh cries, "Let well enough alone! You are easy and comfortable! You have a hope which affords you much solace--do not dig too deep--the house stands well enough just as it is! Be not too anxious about the foundation--rest assured that it is all right--you would not have all these joys and present comforts if you had built upon sand."

We need to school ourselves to perform a duty so irksome. But, Beloved, if we attempt to examine this, feeling that Christ is with us and that we are having communion with Him, we shall forget all the labor of the deed. There I see Him in the garden, sweating great drops of blood in prayer! Can I view Him prostrate on that cold winter's night (when the ground was hard with frost), so burning with His soul's travail that huge clots of blood-red gore are falling upon the frozen earth? And shall I think any toil too great to make sure of my interest in Him?

Does He, when the cup is put to Him, say, "Not as I will, but as You will," and drink it up with resignation? And shall the far less bitter cup of self-examination, which is so much for my good, be refused by me? No, Savior of the world, I have not yet resisted unto blood striving against sin. But if it must be, if all my powers and members must be made to bleed, if my poor heart must be crushed as in a mortar, then let it be so that I may but be found one with You, washed in Your blood and covered with Your righteousness! Keep close to the Savior and the difficulties of self-examination will vanish and the labor will become light.

Self-examination should always be very earnest work. The text says, "Let us get up early." It has been well observed that all men in Scripture who have done earnest work rose up early to do it. The dew of the morning, before the smoke and dust of the world's business have tainted the atmosphere, is a choice and special season for all holy work. In this passage getting up early signifies that the Church felt she must give her best hour to this necessary work. And as the work might be long, she gets up early that she may have a long day before her--that before the sun goes down she may have examined every vine and looked to every pomegranate and examined all the mandrakes of the garden.

So must we set to work earnestly about self-examination. This is not child's play. If you would find out the trickery of your deceitful heart you must be very careful and watchful. If you would know on what foundation your hope is built, it is a laborer's work to dig out the rubbish and to find out where the foundation is laid. He who has to prove the title-deeds of his estate does not always find it an easy business--there are many manuscripts through which he must wade and numerous title-deeds to be read, verified and collated before the case will be clear.

And so it must be with you. The great matter, "Do I believe in Jesus," needs no hours of deliberation, for if I do not, I will now begin again. But to know the growing state of one's graces is not so easy. After all, you may be deceived. Therefore come to it with a soul all glowing with zeal, saying, in earnest prayer, "Search me, O God and know my heart: try me and know my thoughts: and see if there are any wicked ways in me and lead me in the way everlasting." Now I think there is nothing which can make you do this earnest work so well as to say to your Master and your Lord, "Lord, come with me." "While we examine ourselves, abide with us to help us in the work."

I cannot be careless when I hear Christ say, "My meat and My drink is to do the will of Him that sent Me." I cannot be careless in my own Christian career when I see Him straining every nerve that He may run the race and win the crown for me! When I see Him sitting yonder, above all principalities and powers, pleading for my soul with never-ceasing intercession, I cannot be dull and sluggish! Wake up, you drowsy powers! Be stirred up, you sleeping passions, to examine yourselves anxiously and carefully, since Christ, for Zion's sake does not hold His peace and for Jerusalem's sake does not rest!

And yet again, self-examination, it seems to me (I may be wrong), is not the simple work that some people think, but is beset with difficulties. I do believe that the most of self-examinations go on a wrong principle. You take Moses with you when you examine yourself and consequently you fall into despair. He who looks at his own character and position from a legal point of view will not only despair when he comes to the end of his reckoning, but he will be a wise man if he despairs not at the beginning! If we are to be judged on the footing of the Law, there shall no flesh living be justified. The very brightest members of Christ's family--those who wear the most of the Savior's image and honor Him best among men--may well shrink from the place where even Moses did "exceedingly fear and quake."

O Brothers and Sisters, remember to take Jesus with you and not Moses, lest you dishonor the Grace of God and harbor suspicion against the faithfulness of God when you ought rather to have suspected yourself If I take Jesus with me, see on what different principles the examination is carried on! I do not ask, "Am I perfect?" That question Moses would suggest--"Am I perfect in myself?" But I ask, "Am I perfect in Christ Jesus?" That is a very different matter. I do not put it thus, "Am I without sin, naturally?" but thus--"Have I been washed in the fountain opened for sin and for uncleanness?"

It is not, "Am I in myself well-pleasing to God?" but it is, "Am I accepted in the Beloved?" The Christian man sometimes looks at his evidences and grows ashamed of them and alarmed concerning his own salvation. "Why," says he, "my faith has unbelief in it! It is not able to save me!" Suppose he had looked at the Object of his faith instead of his faith? Then he would have said, "There is no failure in Him and therefore I am safe!" He looks at his hope--"Why," he says, "my very hope is marred and dimmed by an anxious carefulness about present things! How can I be accepted?" Yes, but if he had looked at the ground of his hope he would have seen that the promises of God stand sure and that whatever our hope may be, that promise never fails!

Then he looks at his love--"Oh," he says, "surely I am condemned, for my love is so cold!" But if he had looked at Christ's love, he would have said "No, I shall never be condemned--for many waters cannot quench His love--neither can the floods drown it and, loving me as He does, He will never condemn me, nor cast me away." I do not want you to look at Christ so as to think less of your sin, but to think more of it! You can never see sin to be so black as when you see the suffering which Christ endured on its behalf--and I do desire, dear Friends, that you never look at sin apart from the Savior. If you gaze at the disease and forget the remedy, you will be driven to despair. If you look at the gathering gangrene and forget the all-gracious Surgeon who is able to remove it, you may well lie down and die!

If you see your own emptiness and poverty and forget His fullness, you will never glorify His name. If you are lost in a sense of your own corruptions and forget the eternal glory which belongs to you in Christ, so that you are even now raised up together and made to sit together in heavenly places in Him--I say, if you forget this Grace-given brightness and only remember your native blackness--your spirit will turn aside from the path of faith and you will hang your harp upon the willows and fail to glorify your God.

Examine yourselves, but let it be in the light of Calvary--not by the blazing fires of Sinai's lightning, but by the milder radiance of the Savior's griefs. Am I resting upon You, Son of God? Are Your wounds my hiding place? Have Your nails nailed me to Your Cross? Has Your spear pierced my heart and broken it with grief for sin? And am I now crucified with You to the world, buried with You to the power of sin, risen with You to newness of life and, like Yourself, waiting for the day of manifestation when sin, death and Hell shall be trod under foot and You shall be All in All? Come, let us look to the vines and pomegranates, but let us make sure that our Crucified Lord accompanies us! Otherwise we shall do the work amiss.

It appears, from the words of the spouse, that the work of self-examination should be carried on in detail, if it is to be of real service. It is written, "Let us see if the vine has budded, whether the grape blossoms are opened and the pomegranates are in bloom." We must not take a general view of the garden, but particularize and give special attention to each point. If a candle is guarded on all sides, if there is but one place left open, the wind will find it out and blow out the light. So in self-examination, if we find ourselves right in many points, it is not enough--we must seek to be right in all points.

The main thing is your faith. Is that faith simple? Does it depend upon Jesus only? Is it real? Is it an active, living faith? Does it work by love? Does it purify the soul? When you have examined faith, you may possibly make a mistake. Therefore go on to see what your love is. Do you love the Savior? Can you truly say, "The very thought of You fills my breast with rapture"? Can you hear the music of His name without feeling your blood leap in your veins? Oh, if you can, I think, dear Friend, you have reason for grave questioning. Try your active graces--go from one to the other and search them all. The worm may be at the root just in that part of the soil where you have not upturned the sod.

One leak may sink a ship, therefore search well the vessel before you launch her upon the stormy deep. It is little by little that backsliders fall--even Judas does not betray his Master with a kiss at first. Men are schooled in the downward road. Let us be particularly anxious, therefore, that we do not fall little by little. And let us watch that we do not suffer small sins to get force and head, till, like little sparks, they have kindled a great fire!

If you wish to be exact in prying into every part and corner you cannot do better than take Jesus with you. Tempted in all points like we are, He will know all the points in which we are tempted. And, while we are earnestly examining, His gracious finger will point out the spots where our weakness may lie and we shall thus fulfill the prayer we have often prayed--"Search me, O God, and know my heart: try me and know my thoughts: and see if there are any wicked ways in me and lead me in the way everlasting."

When boys are at school and have to learn to write, every schoolmaster knows that at the first line they keep their eye upon the copy at the top. The next line they look at their own writing and their penmanship is not quite so good. And the next line they probably look at the last they have written and so they write worse and worse as they reach the bottom of the page because they have been imitating themselves and copying their own writing! It is well for the Christian if he does not fall into this mistake. He must keep his eyes upon his great Exemplar, not upon himself! He will be far more likely to see his own faults by looking to Christ than by looking at any of his own attainments.

What a delightfully white thing this snow is! When it has newly fallen, take the whitest linen you may have ever seen and put it down--you will find it looks positively yellow by the side of it. Take the fairest sheet of paper that ever came from the mill and compare it. It does not look white at all. There is no whiteness, that I know of, which can at all emulate the heavenly whiteness of snow. So, if I put my character side by side with another man's, I may say of it, "It will bear comparison," but if I put it by the side of Christ's perfections--since His whole life is like the pure and spotless snow--I discover at once my own failures and spots.

Oh, to have our great Pattern ever before our eyes! Jesus should not be a Friend who calls upon us now and then, but one with whom we walk forevermore. You have a difficult road to travel--see, O traveler to Heaven, that you go not without your Guide. You have to pass through the fiery furnace--enter it not, unless like Shadrach, Meshach and Abed-nego, there is a fourth with you like unto the Son of Man! You have to storm the Jericho of your own deceptions-- attempt not the scaling until, like Joshua, you have seen the Captain of the Lord's host with his sword drawn in his hand.

You have to meet the Esau of your many temptations--meet him not until at Jabbok's brook you have laid hold of the angel and wrestled with him and prevailed. In every case, in every condition, you need Jesus! But most of all, when you come to deal with your own heart's eternal interests, O, keep close to Him! Lean your head upon His bosom! Ask to be refreshed with the spiced wine of His pomegranates and then there shall be no fear but that you shall be found of Him at the last, without spot, wrinkle, or any such thing. Seeing you have lived with Him and lived in Him here, you shall live with Him forever.

II. THE CHURCH WAS ABOUT TO ENGAGE IN EARNEST LABOR and desires her Lord's company. It is the business of God's people to be trimmers of God's vines. Like our first parents, we are put into the garden of the Lord for usefulness. Observe that the Church, when she is in her right mind, in all her many labors desires to retain and cheerfully to enjoy communion with Christ. Some persons imagine that one cannot serve Christ actively and yet have fellowship with Him. I think they are very much mistaken.

I confess it is very easy to get into Martha's position and to be cumbered with much serving. You may have to preach here and there so many times a week--to attend committees, to visit sick people and to do so many other things that you may really, unless you are careful--fritter away your own inward life in outward exercises. You may have to complain with the spouse, "They made me keeper of the vineyards, but my own vineyard have I not kept." I do not think, however, that there is any reason why this should be the case except through our own folly. Certain is it that a person may do nothing at all and yet grow quite as lifeless in spiritual things as those who are most busy.

Mary was not praised for sitting still. No, but for sitting still at Jesus' feet! And so Christians are not to be praised if they neglect duties merely because they live in retirement and keep much at home--it is not sitting, I say, but sitting at Jesus' feet. Had Martha been sitting still, or had Mary been sitting anywhere else, I doubt not that the Master would have given a word of rebuke! He would never have said that mere sitting still was choosing the good part. Indeed, I know some of you who are none the better for doing nothing, but a great deal the worse! Those who do nothing grow sour and are always willing to find fault with the way in which others serve Christ.

Do not think, therefore, that mere activity is, in itself, an evil--I believe it is a blessing. Taking a survey of Christ's Church you will find that those who have most fellowship with Christ are not the persons who are recluses or hermits-- who have much time to spend with themselves--but they are the useful indefatigable laborers who are toiling for Jesus and who in their toil have Him side by side with them. They are workers together with God. Let me, then, try to press this lesson upon you--that when we as a Church and each of us as individuals have anything to do for Christ--we must do it in communion with Him.

We come up to His House and why do we come? It is said that among Church people the prayers are the main thing and among Dissenters the sermon. I believe that in both cases this would be a fault. Praying should not eclipse preaching! To preach or to listen to preaching is as true an act of worship as to pray. We never worship God better than when we hear His Word, reverently receive it and are moved thereby to love and gratitude. To hear preaching is, in a sense, praying, since the true effect of all preaching that is worth listening to draws us into a spirit of devotion and makes us ready for prayer and every other form of worship.

But why do we come here? I am afraid there are some who come merely because it is the time to come--because the hour of worship has come round. And others come only because a certain preacher happens to stand upon the platform. Ah, this is not how God's own beloved ones come up to His House! They desire to meet with Him. Their prayer, as they tread the hallowed courts of God's House will be, "My heart and my flesh cries out for the living God." There is no hymn sung so well as when we really do praise Jesus in it. No prayer is so true as that prayer which really comes to the Mercy Seat and spreads itself before the All-Seeing God. There is no preaching like that which is full of Christ, which gives forth a savor of His good ointments.

Worship is not to be commended because of the glorious swell of a Gregorian chant, or because of the equally majestic volume of sound which this great assembly may send forth from that sweet instrument, the human voice. A service is not to be commended because of the eloquence of the preacher or because of the display of learning which he is able to make in expounding his discourse. No, to the Christian it is, "Was the Master there?" The question on Sunday morning is, "What do you think, will He come up to the feast?" Coming to the Lord's Table, the child of God's business is not so much with the bread and the wine, as with His blood and with His flesh. May I feed on Him? May I see Him? And if I get to Him, then it is well with me.

If I have then to serve God in the public engagements of His House, let me say, "Come, my Beloved, let us get up to the vineyards." You have other service to do, dear Friends. This afternoon many of you will be occupied with your Sunday school classes. There will be a knot of lads or girls around you. You will, perhaps, be conducting classes of hundreds of young men and young women. This evening, again, many will be occupied in preaching, or you will be engaged at home with your own children. Oh, how blessed it is to go to the classes, or into the pulpit, having the Master with you! It sometimes happens to the preacher that he is like the butcher at the block--he has a cleaver in his hand and cuts off large pieces of meat as food for those present--but he himself gets none.

But it is otherwise with him when he has his Master with him! Then, whether the rest of the assembly are fed or not, certainly he himself is satisfied as with marrow and with fatness. After what a blessed sort the teacher can teach when the love of God is shed abroad in his heart! You will bear with the rudeness of those boys--you will put up with the inattention of those girls! You will not be angry at the folly of that youth--you will not forget to be in earnest with that poor wanderer--when Jesus Christ stands by your side!

A vision of the Crucified, my Brethren, is that which we want! When we are toiling in His harvest field and sit down to wipe the sweat from our brow, we grow very weary. The harvest is plenteous, but the laborers are few--we feel that the edge of our sickle is growing very, very blunt and we wish we could lie down under the spreading tree from the heat of the sun and toil no longer. But just then we see the Crucified One coming forward with His mighty sickle and we mark the drops of blood streaming from His brow and see the nail prints in the hands with which He grasps the sickle.

We see how He toils and how He labors! With what an awful love He sacrifices Himself--He has stripped off His very garments--and in all the nakedness of self-denial He gives Himself up that He may save others while Himself He cannot save. Then we pluck up our hearts again and take our sickle in the hands which once did hang down, saying, "Jesus, I will never be weary, for You were not weary. And when I shall be faint awhile, I will see You, whose meat and drink it was to do Your Father's will and I will make it my meat and my drink to serve You." Surely you cannot do God's work so well as when you have Jesus Christ with you!

But it is possible, dear Friends, that some of you may be engaged in the service of winning for God some one soul. I know those who have one soul laid upon their heart. Perhaps it is the most solemn work under Heaven to have to pray for one soul. I have so many to look after that I cannot but feel I may rightly excuse myself from any very sedulous attention to one. But there are some of you who have only one person to look after--one child, one friend, one soul. You tried to talk to that one person the other day--you burst into tears when you heard the answer you received. You have been praying for months, but instead of seeing any answer to your prayer the person prayed for is growing worse! You are sure that he is never more vile than when you are most earnest.

Friend, I should not wonder if Satan should whisper to you, "Give it up!" But let me, I pray you, urge you never to do so. And if you want something that will make you never to give up praying for that soul, see yonder, the eternal Son of God! He came into this world to save such a sinner as you yourself are! And you can never think you are doing anything too hard when trying to save your fellow man from destruction. O for a vision of the Savior's face covered with the spittle! See Him marred and bruised by the rough Roman soldiers! Behold Him as His back smarts beneath the thongs of the cruel whips! See Him as Pilate brings Him forth and cries, "Ecce homo."

Mark Him as He treads the Via Dolorosa! See Him while they lift Him up on high and dislocate His bones! Why, what is all that you can endure compared with this? When your soul swells with fearful grief you do not feel such grief as this! You do but sip at the cup which the Savior drained to the dregs! You do but feel a scratch from those nails which went right through His hands! You do not have but for a moment a flesh wound from that spear which pierced His heart!

Courage, solitary laborer--let Christ's griefs solace you. Come with me, my Beloved! Come with me, my Lord! And my toil shall be easy.

There are some Christians engaged in works of heroism, works of peculiar daring for Christ. I should not like to be misunderstood, but I really think that amid the gross darkness of the Popish Church there have been some who have caught the true idea of Christian life far better than the most of us. Let me tell you what I mean. There have been some who have denied themselves all the comforts of life and have lived in suffering and poverty out of love to Jesus and from a sincere desire to benefit their fellow men.

There have been produced in that Church men whose passionate love no labor or persecution could extinguish. They have fed the poor and nourished the sick. And women who have gone into the hospitals among diseases the most contagious and have risked life and lost life for the sake of nursing the sick. There are those living at this present moment upon the tops of such mountain passes as St. Bernard and the Simplon, spending the prime of their life in seclusion in inhospitable frost--where somebody must live--but where nobody ever would live if it were not for the sake of religion. They are there simply that they may serve the poor weary traveler when he comes wading through the snow, or is likely to be lost in a snow storm.

No man shall take precedence of me in my abhorrence of the thrice accursed doctrines of the harlot of Rome! But from our enemies it is right to learn--and I do learn and would teach this--that self-denial and consecration are among the highest of the Christian virtues. I would to God that our people had the spirit of self-consecration in proportion to the light which they enjoy. I would to God we had true Sisters of Mercy who devoted themselves to going from house to house among the sick. We have some--but we need more--more who would be hospital nurses and who would count it but a small sacrifice even if they gave up themselves for the good of others.

Missionaries we need who will face the malaria and deadly fever--our societies cry out for such--but very few are coming forward. We need men of substance who would take their substance and go out with it to a foreign land to evangelize. We need men who having prospered in business who would now count it an honor to spend the rest of their days in some new and special work of charity or piety. Oh, when I see the Savior in all His agonies doing so much for us I cannot but think that we as a Christian people do next to nothing for Him!

There are no stakes of Smithfield now, thank God. There are no dungeons of the Lollard's Tower. No crowns of martyrdom for suffering brows--but there are still special spheres of labor where we could make the name of Christ illustrious. Let me hold up for your imitation some in modern times, who by works of faith and labors of love, have made us feel that the old spirit of Christianity is not dead. Our beloved friend, Mr. George Muller, of Bristol, for instance. There burns a holy devotedness, an intensity of faith, a fervor of perseverance which I would to God we all possessed! May we have more of this and so by keeping close to Jesus we shall produce better fruits, richer clusters and more luscious grapes than are commonly produced upon those vines which are in a less happy part of the vineyard.

III. And now let me close by remaking that according to the text, THE CHURCH DESIRES TO GIVE TO CHRIST ALL THAT SHE PRODUCES. She has "all manner of pleasant fruits," both, "new and old," and they are laid up for her Beloved. We have some new fruits. This morning I hope we feel new life, new joy, new gratitude--we wish to make new resolves and carry them out by new labors. Our heart goes up in new prayers and our soul is pledging herself to new efforts.

But we have some old things, too. There is our first love--a choice fruit that is! And Christ delights in it. There is our first faith--that simple faith by which, having nothing, we became possessors of all things! There is our joy when first we knew the Lord--let us revive it. How happy we were then, when the candle of the Lord shone round about us! Old things? Why we have the old remembrance of the promises. How faithful has God been! In that sickness of ours, how softly did He make our bed! In those deep waters, how placidly did He buoy us up! In that flaming furnace, how graciously did He deliver us so that not even the smell of fire passed upon us. Old fruits, indeed! We have many of them, for His mercies have been more than the hairs of our head.

Old sins we must regret, but then we have had repentances, which He has given us, by which we have wept our way to the Cross and learned the merit of His blood. We have fruits, this morning, both new and old. But here is the point-- they are all to be for Christ. Do you not, after doing good service, detect yourself whispering, "I have done that well"? You intended that nobody should know it. You tried to do it as a secret act of devotion. You were half inclined to tell somebody when it was done, and though it came out, you say it was by accident. But you had a finger in that accident and you did not altogether regret that you had some of the honor of it.

Do you not find when you are really serving your Master that if somebody does not pat you on the back, you grow cold? I know some Sunday school teachers, who, if they are looked after and encouraged, can do well, but who, if they have no encouragement, could not keep on in their work. Oh, it is so easy for us to preach when there are many souls being fed under us and the Master honors us in the eyes of men! Would it be quite as easy to serve Him without honor? I have known Brethren who have met with a little bad feeling among their people. Perhaps they have not always been able to keep their temper--and they have run away from their charge--left the sheep in the wilderness because in their inmost heart they were serving themselves, at least to a degree.

Truly, Beloved, those are the best and most acceptable services in which Christ is the solitary aim of the soul--and His Glory without any mixture whatever is the end of all our efforts. Let your many fruits be laid up only for your Beloved--bring them forth when He is with you--bless His name for them. Put jewels into His crown, but never say, "Unto me be honor and unto my name be praise," but, "Sing unto Jesus, and to Jesus only be Glory while Heaven endures." O that strangers to Jesus would believe our testimony concerning Him!

We are asked, sometimes for proofs of our religion. There is one proof which we defy anyone to contradict and this is the intense joy which the love of Christ gives to us. We are not fools, and I may add we are not dishonest--our witness is that there is a joy in love to Christ and in the enjoyment of His Presence! A joy which could not possibly have come to us from any but a Divine source!

We do not speak because we have not tried other joys--some of us have had our fill of them. We can say of some that their sweet is soon lost in bitterness. Of others that they stale upon our taste. But communion with Christ has no aftertaste in it. It never grows stale. It is a sun without spots! It is a moon which never wanes! It is an ocean which never ebbs--it is a river which flows on forever--it is all Heaven and all bliss! Oh, if you did but know it you would never doubt again--your soul would rest implicitly upon Christ, whom God has set forth to be the Propitiation for sin! And, remember, if you rest upon Him and trust Him, you are saved and shall be with Him, where He is, to behold His Glory forevermore! May God bless these words for Jesus' sake. Amen.

Mary's Song

DELIVERED ON SUNDAY MORNING, DECEMBER 25, 1864,
BY C. H. SPURGEON,
AT THE METROPOLITAN TABERNACLE, NEWINGTON.

"And Mary said, My soul does magnify the Lord, and my spirit has rejoiced in God my Savior.'" -- Luke 1:46, 47.

MARY was on a visit when she expressed her joy in the language of this noble song. It were well if all our social communion were as useful to our hearts as this visit was to Mary. "Iron sharpens iron, so a man sharpens the countenance of his friend." Mary, full of faith, goes to see Elizabeth, who is also full of holy confidence and the two are not long together before their faith mounts to full assurance and their full assurance bursts forth in a torrent of sacred praise!

This praise aroused their slumbering powers and instead of two ordinary village women, we see before us two prophetesses and poetesses upon whom the Spirit of God abundantly rested. When we meet with our kinsfolk and acquaintance, let it be our prayer to God that our communion may be not only pleasant, but profitable. Let us pray that we may not merely pass away time and spend a pleasant hour, but may advance a day's march nearer Heaven and acquire greater fitness for our eternal rest!

Observe, this morning, the sacred joy of Mary that you may imitate it. This is a season when all men expect us to be joyous. We compliment each other with the desire that we may have a "Merry Christmas." Some Christians who are a little squeamish do not like the word "merry." It is a right good old Saxon word, having the joy of childhood and the mirth of manhood in it. It brings before one's mind the old song of the midnight peal of bells, the holly and the blazing log.

I love it for its place in that most tender of all parables, where it is written, that, when the long-lost prodigal returned to his father safe and sound, "They began to be merry." This is the season when we are expected to be happy. And my heart's desire is that in the highest and best sense, you who are Believers may be "merry."

Mary's heart was merry within her--but here was the mark of her joy--it was all holy merriment, it was every drop of it sacred mirth. It was not such merriment as worldlings will revel in today and tomorrow, but such merriment as the angels have around the Throne of God, where they sing, "Glory to God in the highest," while we sing, "On earth peace, goodwill towards men." Such merry hearts have a continual feast.

I want you, you children of the bride-chamber, to possess today and tomorrow, yes, all your days, the high and consecrated bliss of Mary that you may not only read her words but use them for yourselves, ever experiencing their meaning--"My soul does magnify the Lord and my spirit has rejoiced in God my Savior." Observe, first, that she sings. Secondly, she sings sweetly. Thirdly, shall she sing alone?

I. First observe that MARY SINGS. Her subject is a Savior. She hails the Incarnate God. The long expected Messiah is about to appear. He for whom Prophets and princes waited long is now about to come--to be born of the virgin of Nazareth. Truly there was never a subject of sweeter song than this--the stooping down of Godhead to the feebleness of manhood! When God manifested His power in the works of His hands the morning stars sang together and the sons of God shouted for joy. But when God manifests Himself, what music shall suffice for the grand Psalm of adoring wonder?

When wisdom and power are seen, these are but attributes. But in the Incarnation it is the Divine Person which is revealed wrapped in a veil of our inferior clay--well might Mary sing when earth and Heaven even now are wondering at the condescending Grace! Worthy of peerless music is the fact that "the Word was made flesh and dwelt among us." There is no longer a great gulf fixed between God and His people. The humanity of Christ has bridged it over. We can no more think that God sits on high indifferent to the wants and woes of men--for God has visited us and come down to the lowliness of our estate.

We no longer need bemoan that we can never participate in the moral glory and purity of God, for if God in Glory can come down to His sinful creature, it is certainly less difficult to bear that creature, blood-washed and purified, up that starry way that the redeemed one may sit down forever on His Throne. Let us dream no longer in somber sadness that we cannot draw near to God so that He will really hear our prayer and pity our necessities seeing that Jesus has become bone of our bone and flesh of our flesh! He was born a babe as we are born, living a man as we must live, bearing the same infirmities and sorrows and bowing His head to the same death.

O, can we not come with boldness by this new and living way and have access to the Throne of the heavenly Grace, when Jesus meets us as Immanuel, God with us? Angels sung, they scarcely knew why. Could they understand why God had become Man? They must have known that here was a mystery of condescension. But all the loving consequences which the Incarnation involved, even their acute minds could scarcely have guessed!

But we see the whole and comprehend the grand design most fully. The manger of Bethlehem was big with Glory-- in the Incarnation was wrapped up all the blessedness by which a soul, snatched from the depths of sin, is lifted up to the heights of Glory. Shall not our clearer knowledge lead us to heights of song which angelic guesses could not reach? Shall the lips of cherubs move to flaming sonnets and shall we, who are redeemed by the blood of the Incarnate God, be treacherously and ungratefully silent?--

"Did archangels sing Your coming? Did the shepherds learn their ways? Shame would cover me ungrateful, Should my tongues refuse to praise."

This, however, was not the full subject of her holy hymn. Her peculiar delight was not that there was a Savior to be born, but that He was to be born of her! Blessed among women was she and highly favored of the Lord. But we can enjoy the same favor--no, we must enjoy it--or the coming of a Savior will be of no benefit to us. Christ on Calvary, I know, takes away the sin of His people. But none would have ever known the virtue of Christ upon the Cross unless they have the Lord Jesus formed in them as the hope of Glory!

The stress of the virgin's canticle is laid upon God's special Grace to her. Those little words, the personal pronouns, tell us that it was truly a personal affair with her. "My soul does magnify the Lord and my spirit has rejoiced in God my Savior." The Savior was peculiarly and in a special sense, hers. She sung no "Christ for all," but "Christ for me," as her glad subject! Beloved, is Christ Jesus in your heart? Once you looked at Him from a distance and that look cured you of all spiritual diseases, but are you now living upon Him, receiving Him into your very vitals as your spiritual meat and drink?

In holy fellowship you have oftentimes fed upon His flesh and been made to drink of His blood. You have been buried with Him in Baptism unto death. You have yielded yourselves a sacrifice to Him and you have taken Him to be a sacrifice for you. You can sing of Him as the spouse did, "His left hand is under my head and His right hand does embrace me. . . My beloved is mine and I am His: He feeds among the lilies."

This is a happy style of living and anything short of this poor slavish work, oh, you can never know the joy of Mary unless Christ becomes truly and really yours! But oh, when He is yours, yours within, reigning in your heart! Yours controlling all your passions! Yours changing your nature, subduing your corruptions, inspiring you with hallowed emotions! When He is yours within, a joy unspeakable and full of Glory--oh, then you can sing, you must sing--who can restrain your tongue? If all the scoffers and mockers upon earth should bid you hold your peace, you must sing--your spirit must rejoice in God your Savior!

We should miss much instruction if we overlooked the fact that the choice poem before us is a hymn of faith. As yet there was no Savior born, nor, as far as we can judge had the virgin any evidence such as carnal sense required to make her believe that a Savior would be born of her. How can this thing be, was a question which might very naturally have suspended her song until it received an answer convincing to flesh and blood. But no such answer had been given. She knew that with God all things are possible. She had His promise delivered by an angel and this was enough for her--on the strength of the Word which came forth from God her heart leaped with pleasure and her tongue glorified His name! When I consider what it is which she believed and how unhesitatingly she received the Word, I am ready to give her, as a woman, a place almost as high as that which Abraham occupied as a man!

And if I dare not call her the mother of the faithful, at least let her have due honor as one of the most excellent of the mothers in Israel. The benediction of Elizabeth, Mary right well deserved, "Blessed is she that believes." To her the "sub- stance of things hoped for" was her faith and that was also her "evidence of things not seen." She knew, by the Revelation of God, that she was to bear the promised Seed who should bruise the serpent's head. But other proof she had none.

This day there are those among us who have little or no conscious enjoyment of the Savior's Presence. They walk in darkness and see no light. They are groaning over inbred sin and mourning because corruptions prevail. Let them now trust in the Lord and remember that if they believe on the Son of God, Christ Jesus is within them. And by faith they may right gloriously chant the hallelujah of adoring love. Though the sun gleam not forth today, the clouds and mists have not quenched his light.

And though the Sun of Righteousness shines not on you at this instant, yet He keeps His place in yonder skies and knows no variableness, neither shadow of a turning. If with all your digging the well springs not up, yet there abides a constant fullness in that deep which crouches beneath in the heart and purpose of a God of Love. What, if like David, you are much cast down, yet like he can you say unto your soul, "Hope in God, for I shall yet praise Him for the help of His countenance."

Be glad then with Mary's joy--it is the joy of a Savior completely hers--but evidenced to be so, not by sense, but by faith. Faith has its music as well as sense, but it is of a more Divine sort--if the food on the table make men sing and dance, feastings of a more refined and ethereal nature can fill Believers with a hallowed plenitude of delight! Still listening to the favored virgin's canticle, let me observe that her lowliness does not make her stay her song. No, it imports a sweeter note into it--"For He has regarded the low estate of His handmaiden."

Beloved Friend, you are feeling more intensely than ever the depth of your natural depravity. You are humbled under a sense of your many failings. You are so dead and earth-bound even in this House of Prayer that you cannot rise to God. You are heavy and sad, even while our Christmas carols have been ringing in your ears. You feel yourself to be today so useless to the Church of God, so insignificant, so utterly unworthy, that your unbelief whispers, "Surely, surely, you have nothing to sing for."

Come, my Brother, come my Sister, imitate this blessed virgin of Nazareth and turn that very lowliness and meanness which you so painfully feel into another reason for unceasing praise! Daughters of Zion, sweetly say in your hymns of love, "He has regarded the low estate of His handmaiden." The less worthy I am of His favors, the more sweetly will I sing of His Grace! What if I am the most insignificant of all His chosen? Then will I praise Him who with eyes of love has sought me out and set His love upon me. "I thank You, O Father, Lord of Heaven and earth, that while You have hid these things from the wise and prudent, You have revealed them unto babes: even so, Father, for so it seemed good in Your sight."

I am sure, dear Friends, the remembrance that there is a Savior and that this Savior is yours, must make you sing. And if you set side by side with it the thought that you were once sinful, unclean, vile, hateful and an enemy to God-- then your notes will take yet a loftier flight and mount to the third heavens to teach the golden harps the praise of God!

It is right well worthy of notice that the greatness of the promised blessing did not give the sweet songster an argument for suspending her thankful strain. When I meditate upon the great goodness of God in loving His people before the earth was, in laying down His life for us, in pleading our cause before the Eternal Throne, in providing a paradise of rest for us forever--the black thought has troubled me--"Surely this is too high a privilege for such an insect of a day as this poor creature, man."

Mary did not look at this matter unbelievingly--although she appreciated the greatness of the favor--she did but rejoice the more heartily on that account. "For He that is mighty has done to me great things." Come, Soul, it is a great thing to be a child of God, and your God does great wonders--therefore be not staggered through unbelief--but triumph in your adoption, great mercy though it is. Oh, it is a mighty mercy, higher than the mountains, to be chosen of God from all eternity, but it is true that even so are His redeemed chosen and therefore sing of it!

It is a deep and unspeakable blessing to be redeemed with the precious blood of Christ, but you are so redeemed beyond all question. Therefore doubt not, but shout aloud for gladness of heart! It is a rapturous thought that you shall dwell above and wear the crown and wave the palm branch forever. Let no mistrust interrupt the melody of your Psalm of expectation, but--

"Loud to the praise of love Divine, Bid every string awake.'

What a fullness of the Truth of God is there in these few words--"He that is mighty has done to me great things." It is a text from which a glorified spirit in Heaven might preach an endless sermon!

I pray you, lay hold upon the thoughts which I have in this poor way suggested to you and try to reach where Mary stood in holy exultation. The Grace is great, but so is its Giver. The love is infinite, but so is the heart from which it wells up. The blessedness is unspeakable, but so is the Divine Wisdom which planned it from of old. Let our hearts take up the Virgin's Magnificat and praise the Lord right joyously at this hour.

Still further, for we have not exhausted the strain, the holiness of God has sometimes dampened the ardor of the Believer's joy. But not so in Mary's case. She exults in it--"And holy is

His name." She weaves even that bright attribute into her song. Holy Lord! When I forget my Savior, the thought of Your purity makes me shudder! Standing where Moses stood upon the holy mountain of Your law, I do exceedingly fear and quake. To me, conscious of my guilt, no thunder could be more dreadful than the seraph's hymn of, "Holy! Holy! Holy! Lord God of Sabaoth." What is Your holiness but a consuming fire which must utterly destroy me--a sinner?

If the heavens are not pure in Your sight and You charged your angels with folly, how much less, then, can You bear with vain, rebellious man that is born of woman? How can man be pure and how can Your eyes look upon him without consuming him quickly in Your anger? But, O Holy One of Israel, when my spirit can stand on Calvary and see Your holiness vindicate itself in the wounds of the Man who was born at Bethlehem, then my spirit rejoices in that glorious holiness which was once her terror!

Did the thrice holy God stoop down to man and take man's flesh? Then there is hope, indeed! Did a holy God bear the sentence which His own Law pronounced on man? Does that holy God Incarnate now spread His wounded hands and plead for me? Then, my Soul, the holiness of God shall be a consolation to you. Living waters from this sacred well I draw. And I will add to all my notes of joy this one, "and holy is His name." He has sworn by His holiness and He will not lie. He will keep His Covenant with His Anointed and His seed forever.

When we take to ourselves the wings of eagles and mount towards Heaven in holy praise, the prospect widens beneath us--even so as Mary poises herself upon the poetic wings, she looks down the long aisles of the past and beholds the mighty acts of Jehovah in the ages long back. Mark how her strain gathers majesty. It is rather the sustained flight of the eagle-winged Ezekiel, than the flutter of the timid dove of Nazareth.

She sings, "His mercy is on them that fear Him from generation to generation." She looks beyond the captivity to the days of the kings--to Solomon, to David--along through the Judges into the wilderness, across the Red Sea to Jacob, to Isaac, to Abraham and onward, till, pausing at the gate of Eden, she hears the sound of the promise, "The Seed of the woman shall bruise the serpent's head." How magnificently she sums up the book of the wars of the Lord and rehearses the triumphs of Jehovah, "He has showed strength with His arm. He has scattered the proud in the imagination of their hearts."

How delightfully is mercy intermingled with judgment in the next canto of her Psalm--"He has put down the mighty from their seats and exalted them of low degree. He has filled the hungry with good things, and the rich He has sent empty away." My Brothers and Sisters, let us, too, sing of the past, glorious in faithfulness, fearful in judgment, teeming with wonders! Our own lives shall furnish us with a hymn of adoration. Let us speak of the things which we have made touching the King.

We were hungry and He filled us with good things. We crouched upon the dunghill with the beggar and He has enthroned us among princes. We have been tossed with tempest, but with the Eternal Pilot at the helm, we have known no fear of shipwreck. We have been cast into the burning fiery furnace, but the Presence of the Son of Man has quenched the violence of the flames. Proclaim to all, O you daughters of music, the long tale of the mercy of the Lord to His people in the generations long departed!

Many waters could not quench His love, neither could the floods drown it! Persecution, famine, nakedness, peril, sword--none of these have separated the saints from the love of God which is in Christ our Lord. The saints beneath the wings of the Most High have been ever safe! When most molested by the enemy they have dwelt in perfect peace--"God is their refuge and strength, a very present help in trouble."

Plowing at times the blood red wave, the ship of the Church has never swerved from her predestined path of progress. Every tempest has favored her--the hurricane which sought her ruin has been made to bear her the more swiftly onward. Her flag has braved, these 1800 years, the battle and the breeze and she fears not what may yet be before her. But, lo, she nears the haven! The day is dawning when she shall bid farewell to storms. The waves already grow calm beneath her. The long-promised rest is near at hand--her Jesus Himself meets her--walking upon the waters!

She shall enter into her eternal haven and all who are on board shall, with their Captain, sing of joy and triumph and victory through Him who has loved her and been her Deliverer! When Mary thus tuned her heart to glory in her God for His wonders in the past, she particularly dwelt upon the note of election. The highest note in the scale of my praise is reached when my soul sings, "I love Him because He first loved me." Well does Kent put it--

"A monument of Grace, A sinner saved by blood. The streams of love I trace, Up to the fountain, God. And in His mighty breast I see, Eternal thoughts of love to me." We can scarcely fly higher than the source of love in the mount of God. Mary has the doctrine of election in her song--"He has put down the mighty from their seats and exalted them of low degree. He has filled the hungry with good things. And the rich He has sent empty away." Here is distinguishing Grace, discriminating regard! Here are some suffered to perish! Here are others, the least deserving and the most obscure, made the special objects of Divine affection! Do not be afraid to dwell upon this high doctrine, Beloved in the Lord. Let me assure you that when your mind is most heavy and depressed you will find this to be a bottle of richest cordial.

Those who doubt these doctrines, or who cast them into the cold shade, miss the richest clusters of Eshcol. They lose the wines on the lees well refined, the fat things full of marrow. But you who by reason of years have had your senses exercised to discern between good and evil--you know that there is no honey like this--no sweetness comparable to it! If the honey in Jonathan's woods when but touched, enlightened the eyes to see, this is honey that will enlighten your heart to love and learn the mysteries of the kingdom of God!

Eat and fear not overindulgence! Live upon this choice dainty and fear not that you shall grow weary of it for the more you know, the more you will want to know. The more your soul is filled, the more you will desire to have your mind enlarged that you may comprehend more and more the eternal, everlasting, discriminating love of God!

But one more remark upon this point. You perceive she does not finish her song till she has reached the Covenant. When you mount as high as election, tarry on its sister mount, the Covenant of Grace. In the last verse of her song, she sings, "As He spoke to our fathers, to Abraham and to his seed forever." To her, that was the Covenant. To us who have clearer light, the ancient Covenant made in the council chamber of eternity is the subject of the greatest delight. The Covenant with Abraham was in its best sense only a minor copy of that gracious Covenant made with Jesus, the Everlasting Father of the faithful, before the blue heavens were stretched abroad.

Covenant engagements are the softest pillows for an aching head. Covenant engagements with the Surety, Christ Jesus, are the best props for a trembling spirit!--

"His oath, His Covenant, His blood, Support me in the raging flood. When every earthly prop gives way, This still is all my strength and stay." If Christ did swear to bring me to Glory and if the Father swore that He would give me to the Son to be a part of the infinite reward for the travail of His soul, then, my Soul, till God Himself shall be unfaithful, till Christ shall cease to be the Truth, till God's eternal council shall become a lie and the red roll of His election shall be consumed with fire, you are safe! Rest, then, in perfect peace, come what will! Take your harp from the willows and never let your fingers cease to sweep it to strains of richest harmony. O for Grace from first to last to join the Virgin in her song!

II. Secondly, SHE SINGS SWEETLY. She praises her God right heartily. Observe how she plunges into the midst of the subject. There is no preface, but "My soul does magnify the Lord and my spirit has rejoiced in God my Savior." When some people sing, they appear to be afraid of being heard. Our poet puts it--

"With all my powers of heart and tongue I'll praise my Maker in my song. Angels shall hear the notes I raise, Approve the song and join the praise."

I am afraid angels frequently do not hear those poor, feeble, dying whispers which often drop from our lips merely by force of custom.

Mary is all heart! Evidently her soul is on fire! While she muses, the fire burns. Then she speaks with her tongue. May we, too, call home our wandering thoughts and wake up our slumbering powers to praise redeeming love. It is a noble word that she uses here--"My soul does magnify the Lord." I suppose it means, "My soul does endeavor to make God great by praising Him." He is as great as He can be in His Being--my goodness cannot extend to Him. But yet my soul would make God greater in the thoughts of others and greater in my own heart.

I would give the train of His Glory a wider sweep. The light which He has given me I would reflect. I would make His enemies His friends. I would turn hard thoughts of God into thoughts of love. "My soul would magnify the Lord." Old Trapp says, "My soul would make greater room for Him." It is as if she wanted to get more of God into her, like Rutherford, when he says, "Oh, that my heart were as big as Heaven, that I might hold Christ in it," and then he stops himself--"But Heaven and earth cannot contain Him. Oh, that I had a heart as big as seven heavens, that I might hold the whole of Christ within it."

Truly this is a larger desire than we can ever hope to have gratified! Yet still our lips shall sing, "My soul does magnify the Lord." Oh, if I could crown Him! If I could lift Him higher! If my burning at the stake would but add a spark more light to His Glory, happy would I be to suffer! If my being crushed would lift Jesus an inch higher, happy were the destruction which should add to His Glory! Such is the hearty spirit of Mary's song!

Again, her praise is very joyful--"My spirit has rejoiced in God my Savior." The word in the Greek is a remarkable one. I believe it is the same word which is used in the passage, "Rejoice you in that day and leap for joy." We used to have an old word in English which described a certain exulting dance, "a galliard." That word is supposed to have come from the Greek word used here. It was a sort of leaping dance. The old commentators call it a "levalto." Mary, in effect, declares, "My spirit shall dance like David before the ark, shall leap, shall spring, shall hound, shall rejoice in God my Savior."

When we praise God it ought not to be with dolorous and doleful notes. Some of my Brethren praise God always on the minor key, or in the deep, deep bass--they cannot feel holy till they have the horrors. Why cannot some men worship God except with a long face? I know them by their very walk as they come to worship--what a dreary pace it is! How solemnly proper and funereal, indeed! They do not understand David's Psalm--

"Up to her courts with joys unknown, The sacred tribes repair."

No, they come up to their Father's house as if they were going to jail and worship God on Sunday as if it were the most doleful day in the week!

It is said of a certain Highlander, when the Highlanders were very pious, that he once went to Edinburgh and when he came back again he said he had seen a dreadful sight on Sunday--he had seen people at Edinburgh going to Church with happy faces! He thought it wicked to look happy on Sunday--and that same notion exists in the minds of certain good people hereabouts. They fancy that when the saints get together they should sit down and have a little comfortable misery but little delight.

In truth, moaning and pining is not the appointed way for worshipping God. We should take Mary as a pattern. All the year round I recommend her as an example to fainthearted and troubled ones. "My spirit has rejoiced in God my Savior." Cease from rejoicing in sensual things and with sinful pleasures have no fellowship--for all such rejoicing is evil-- but you cannot rejoice too much in the Lord! I believe that the fault with our public worship is that we are too sober, too cold, too formal. I do not exactly admire the ravings of our Primitive-Methodist friends when they grow wild. But I should have no objection to hear a hearty, "Hallelujah! "now and then.

An enthusiastic burst of exultation might warm our hearts. The shout of "Glory!" might fire our spirits. This I know--I never feel more ready for true worship than when I am preaching in Wales--when the throughout whole sermon, the preacher is aided rather than interrupted by shouts of "Glory to God!" and "Bless His name!" Why, then, one's blood begins to glow and one's soul is stirred up! This is the true way of serving God with joy! "Rejoice in the Lord always. And again I say, Rejoice." "My spirit has rejoiced in God my Savior."

She sings sweetly, in the third place, because she sings confidently. She does not pause while she sings to questions herself, "Have I any right to sing?" but no, "My soul does magnify the Lord and my spirit has rejoiced in God my Savior. For He has regarded the low estate of His handmaiden." "IF" is a sad enemy to all Christian happiness--"but," "perhaps," "doubt," "surmise," "suspicion"--these are a race of highwaymen who waylay poor timid pilgrims and steal their spending money! Harps soon get out of tune and when the wind blows from the doubting quarter, the strings snap by the wholesale.

If the angels of Heaven could have a doubt, it would turn Heaven into Hell. "If you are the Son of God," was the dastardly weapon wielded by the old enemy against our Lord in the wilderness. Our great foe knows well what weapon is the most dangerous. Christian, put up the shield of faith whenever you see that poisoned dagger about to be used against you!

I fear that some of you foster your doubts and fears. You might as well hatch young vipers and foster the cockatrice. You think that it is a sign of Divine Grace to have doubts, whereas it is a sign of infirmity! It does not prove that you have no Grace when you doubt God's promise, but it does provc that you need more--for if you had more Grace, you would take God's Word as He gives it and it would be said of you as of Abraham, that, "he staggered not at the promise of God through unbelief, being fully persuaded that what He had promised He was able also to perform."

God help you to shake off your doubts! Oh, these are devilish things! Is that too hard a word? I wish I could find a harder! These are felons. These are rebels, who seek to rob Christ of His Glory. These are traitors who cast mire upon the escutcheon of my Lord. Oh, these are vile traitors--hang them on a gallows, high as Haman's--cast them to the earth and let them rot like carrion, or bury them with the burial of an ass. Abhorred of God are doubts--abhorred of men let them be! They are cruel enemies to your souls! They injure your usefulness, they despoil you in every way. Smite them with the sword of the Lord and of Gideon! By faith in the promise seek to drive out these Canaanites and possess the land. O you men of God, speak with confidence and sing with sacred joy!

There is something more than confidence in her song. She sings with great familiarity, "My soul does magnify the Lord and my spirit has rejoiced in God my Savior. For He that is mighty has done to me great things. And holy is His name." It is the song of one who draws very near to her

God in loving intimacy. I always have an idea, when I listen to the reading of the Liturgy, that it is a slave's worship. I do not find fault with its words or sentences, perhaps of all human compositions the Liturgical service of the Church of England is, with some exceptions, the noblest.

But it is only fit for slaves, or at the best for subjects. The whole service through one feels that there is a boundary set round about the mountain, just as at Sinai. Its Litany is the wail of a sinner and not the happy triumph of a saint! The service genders unto bondage and has nothing in it of the confident spirit of adoption. It views the Lord afar off, as One to be feared rather than loved and to be dreaded rather than delighted in. I have no doubt it suits those whose experience leads them to put the Ten Commandments near the communion table for they hereby evidence that their dealings with God are still on the terms of servants and not of sons.

For my own part I want a form of worship in which I may draw near to my God and come even to His feet, spreading my case before Him and ordering my cause with arguments--talking with Him as a friend talks with his friend, or a child with its father--otherwise the worship is of little worth to me. Our Episcopalian friends, when they come here, are naturally struck with our service as being irreverent because it is so much more familiar and bold than theirs. Let us carefully guard against really deserving such a criticism and then we need not fear it. A renewed soul yearns after that very communion which the formalist calls irreverent!

To talk with God as my Father--to deal with Him as with one whose promises are true to me and to whom I, a sinner washed in blood and clothed in the perfect righteousness of Christ may come with boldness, not standing afar off--I say this is a thing which the outer-court worshipper cannot understand. There are some of our hymns which speak of Christ with such familiarity that the cold critic says, "I do not like such expressions, I could not sing them." I quite agree with you, Sir Critic, that the language would not befit you, a stranger.

But a child may say a thousand things which a servant must not. I remember a minister altering one of our hymns--

"Let those refuse to sing Who never knew our God. But fa vorites of the hea venly King May speak their joys abroad."

He sung it--"But subjects of the heavenly King." Yes. And when he sang it, I thought, "That is right. You are singing what you feel--you know nothing of discriminating Grace and special manifestations and therefore you keep to your native level, "subjects of the heavenly King." But oh, my heart wants a worship in which I can feel and express the feeling that I am a favorite of the heavenly king and therefore can sing His special love, His manifested favor, His sweet relationships, His mysterious union with my soul!

You never get right till you ask the question, "Lord, how is it that You will manifest Yourself unto us and not unto the world?" There is a secret which is revealed to us and not to the outside world--an understanding which the sheep receive and not the goats. I appeal to any of you who during the week are in an official position--a judge, for instance. You have a seat on the bench and you wear no small dignity when you are there. When you get home there is a little fellow who has very little fear of Your Judgeship, but much love for your person! He climbs your knee. He kisses your cheek and says a thousand things to you which are meet and right enough as they come from him--but which you would not tolerate in court from any living man.

The parable needs no interpretation. When I read some of the prayers of Martin Luther they shock me, but I argue with myself thus--"It is true I cannot talk to God in the same way as Martin, but then perhaps Martin Luther felt and realized his adoption more than I do and therefore was not less humble because he was more bold. It may be that he used expressions which would be out of place in the mouth of any man who had not known the Lord as he had."

Oh my Friends, sing this day of our Lord Jesus as One near to us! Get close to Christ! Read His wounds! Thrust your hand into His side! Put your finger into the print of the nails and then your song shall win a sacred softness and melody not to be gained elsewhere. I must close by observing that while her song was all this, yet how very humble it was and how full of gratitude. The Papist calls her, "Mother of God," but she never whispers such a thing in her song. No, it is "God my Savior," just such words as the sinner who is speaking to you might use, and such expressions as you sinners who are hearing me can use, too.

She needs a Savior. She feels it. Her soul rejoices because there is a Savior for her. She does not talk as though she could commend herself to Him, but she hopes to stand accepted in the Beloved. Let us, then, take care that our familiarity has always blended with it the lowliest prostration of spirit when we remember that He is God over all, blessed forever and we are nothing but dust and ashes! He fills all things and we are less than nothing and vanity.

III. The last thing was to be SHALL SHE SING ALONE? Yes, she must, if the only music we can bring is that of carnal delights and worldly pleasures. There will be much music tomorrow which would not chime in with hers. There will be much mirth tomorrow and much laughter and I am afraid the most of it would not accord with Mary's song. It will not be, "My soul does magnify the Lord and my spirit has rejoiced in God my Savior."

We would not stop the play of the animal spirits in young or old. We would not abate one jot of your relish of the mercies of God, so long as you break not His command by wantonness, or drunkenness, or excess--but still, when you have had the most of this bodily exercise, it profits little--it is only the joy of the fleeting hour and not the happiness of the spirit which abides. And therefore Mary must sing alone, as far as you are concerned.

The joy of the table is too low for Mary. The joy of the feast and the family grovels when compared with hers, but shall she sing alone? Certainly not, if this day any of us by simple trust in Jesus can take Christ to be our own! Does the Spirit of God this day lead you to say, "I trust my soul on Jesus?" My dear Friend, then you have conceived Christ--after the mystical and best sense of that word--Christ Jesus is conceived in your soul! Do you understand Him as the Sin-Bearer, taking away transgression? Can you see Him bleeding as the Substitute for men?

Do you accept Him as such? Does your faith put all her dependence upon what He did, upon what He is, upon what He does? Then Christ is conceived in you and you may go your way with all the joy that Mary knew! And I was half ready to say, with something more--for the natural conception of the Savior's holy body was not one-tenth so meet a theme for congratulation as the spiritual conception of the holy Jesus within your heart when He shall be in you the Hope of Glory.

My dear Friend, if Christ is yours, there is no song on earth too high or too holy for you to sing! No, there is no song which thrills from angelic lips, no note which thrills Archangel's tongues in which you may not join! Even this day the holiest, the happiest, the most glorious of words and thoughts and emotions belong to you. Use them! God help you to enjoy them. And His be the praise, while yours is the comfort evermore. Amen.

www.ingramcontent.com/pod-product-compliance
Lightning Source LLC
LaVergne TN
LVHW010934100826
845153LV00001B/31

* 9 7 8 1 7 7 3 5 6 0 8 1 6 *